C. CATTON
22 WENDERLY DR.
TORONTO
782-5735

C. CATTON
22 WENDERLY DR.

UNDERSTANDING HUMAN BEHAVIOR

2nd Edition

James V. McConnell

The University of Michigan

Holt, Rinehart and Winston

New York   Chicago   San Francisco
Atlanta   Dallas   Montreal
Toronto   London   Sydney

UNDERSTANDING HUMAN BEHAVIOR

AN INTRODUCTION TO PSYCHOLOGY

2nd Edition

Associate Publisher	Deborah Doty
Developmental Editors	Johnna Barto
	Louise Waller
Managing Editor	Jeanette Ninas Johnson
Senior Project Editor	Francoise Bartlett
Production Manager	Victor Calderon
Text Designer	Barbara Bert
Art Director	Robert Kopelman
Cover	Fred Pusterla
	Louis Scardino

DEDICATION

To Ted and Fred and Louise,
For Helen and Blink, and Rosa and Don,
And most of all, with great thanks to all the students . . .

Library of Congress Catalog Card Number: 76-49795
ISBN: 0-03-089715-7
Printed in the United States of America

8 9   032   9 8 7 6 5

CREDITS

The author would like to express his appreciation to the following authors, publishers, and photographers for permission to reprint their work:

Chapter 1

p. 5   Photo courtesy of Magnum Photos, Inc.
p. 7   Photo courtesy of Wide World Photos, Inc.
p. 9   Photo courtesy of J. Brian King, Photography.
p. 12   Photo courtesy of Bob Kalmbach, The University of Michigan.

Part 1

pp. 14, 15   Photos courtesy of J. Brian King, Photography.

Chapter 2

p. 22   Photo courtesy of the American Museum of Natural History.
p. 23   Photo courtesy of the National Audubon Society, Robert Hermes.
p. 28   Photos courtesy of Lam Mediflex Photo Lab.
p. 33   Photo courtesy of Camera 5, Curt Gunther.
p. 37   Photo courtesy of Floyd Clark, California Institute of Technology, Pasadena, California.

Chapter 3

p. 45   Photo courtesy of Dr. Ramon Greenberg.
p. 51   Photo courtesy of World Tennis, Euchi Kawatei.
p. 59   Photo courtesy of the Drug Enforcement Administration.
p. 61   Picture courtesy of The Bettmann Archive Inc.
pp. 62, 63   Photos courtesy of the Drug Enforcement Administration.
p. 64   Photo courtesy of Michael Weisbrot, photographer.
p. 67   Picture courtesy of The Bettmann Archive Inc.
p. 68   Photo from *Integral Yoga Hatha* by Yogiraj Sri Swami Satchidananda. Copyright © 1970 by Yogiraj Sri Swami Satchidananda. Reproduced by permission of Holt, Rinehart and Winston.
p. 70   Photo courtesy of NIA Gerontology Research Center.

Chapter 4

p. 78   Photo courtesy of the National Aeronautics and Space Administration.
p. 81   Top picture courtesy of The Bettmann Archive Inc. Bottom picture courtesy of The Granger Collection.
p. 82   Bottom picture courtesy of The Granger Collection.
p. 83   Picture courtesy of The Granger Collection.
p. 88   Photo courtesy of Stanford University.
p. 92   Photo courtesy H. Kacher.
p. 94   Photos courtesy of Dr. Nathan Azrin.

Chapter 5

pp. 108, 111   Photos courtesy of Mimi Cotter, photographer.

Part 2

p. 122   Photo courtesy of Michael Weisbrot, photographer.
p. 123   Photo courtesy of J. Brian King, Photography.

Chapter 6

p. 128   Photo courtesy of Featherkill Studios.
p. 132   Illustration from *Biology* by James D. Ehert, Ariel G. Loewy, Richard S. Miller and Howard A. Schneiderman. Copyright © 1973 by Holt, Rinehart and Winston. Reprinted by permission of Holt, Rinehart and Winston.
p. 136   Photo courtesy of Great Adventure, Inc.
p. 138   Photo courtesy of Wide World Photos, Inc.

Chapter 7

p. 145   Photo courtesy of the University of Texas News and Information Service.
p. 146   Photo at bottom courtesy of Featherkill Studios.
p. 147   Illustration from "Distribution of Coitus in Menstrual Cycle," by Udry and Morris, *Nature*, 1968, Vol. 220, pp. 593–596. Reprinted by permission.
pp. 149, 150   Photos courtesy of Featherkill Studios.
p. 155   Picture courtesy Zenith Hearing Instrument Corporation.

Chapter 8

p. 166   Chart courtesy of National Society for the Prevention of Blindness, Inc.
p. 167   Photo courtesy of the National Audubon Society, Eric Hosking.

Chapter 9

p. 178   Photo courtesy of The Bettmann Archive Inc.
p. 182   Photo courtesy of The March of Dimes.
p. 183   Photo courtesy of Nancy Ellison, Sygma.

Chapter 10

pp. 195, 196   Photos courtesy of The Port of New York Authority, A. Belva.
p. 198   Photos courtesy of *Road & Track*.
p. 204   Photo at top right courtesy of Dick Swift, photographer.
p. 205   Photo courtesy of National Aeronautics and Space Administration.
p. 209   Photo from *Scientific American*, April 1959, courtesy of William Vandivert.
p. 210   Drawing and photo courtesy of David Linton.

Chapter 11

p. 222   Photo courtesy of Department of the Navy, Office of Information.
p. 223   Photo courtesy of LamMediflex Photo Lab.
p. 227   Cartoon © 1972 National Periodical Publications, Inc.
p. 228   Photo courtesy of Dr. J.B. Rhine, Foundation for Research on the Nature of Man.
p. 230   Photo courtesy of Holt, Rinehart and Winston.
p. 231   Photo courtesy of Wide World Photos, Inc.

Part 3

pp. 236, 237   Photos courtesy of J. Brian King, Photography.

Chapter 12

p. 249   Photo courtesy of Alice Boughton.
p. 251   Photo courtesy of J. Brian King, Photography.
p. 255   Photo courtesy of Dr. Neal E. Miller.
p. 256   Photo courtesy of Sigmund Freud Copyrights Ltd.

Chapter 13

p. 269   Photo courtesy of the American Museum of Natural History, Department of Animal Behavior.
p. 272   Photo courtesy of Mimi Cotter, photographer.
p. 273   Photo courtesy of The Granger Collection.
p. 274   Photo courtesy of Wide World Photos, Inc.
p. 275   Photo by Scott F. Johnson, courtesy of Little, Brown and Company.
p. 279   Photo courtesy of The National Audubon Society, Jeanne White.
p. 281   Photo courtesy of the American Museum of Natural History.
p. 282   Photo courtesy of Dr. James Olds.

Chapter 14

p. 291   Picture courtesy of The Bettmann Archive Inc.
p. 294   Photo courtesy of Russell Dian.

PREFACE

When I first decided to write this book, I mentioned my intentions to a colleague of mine. She was shocked. "With more than 100 introductory psychology texts already on the market," she said, "what can you do that hasn't already been done better by someone else?"

My friend's comment gave me considerable pause; but after giving the matter careful consideration, I came up with what seemed a reasonable answer. In the past decade or so I had been involved in the writing and editing of two other introductory texts. Good as they were, these two books failed to satisfy me in several ways. I guessed that my own text, *Understanding Human Behavior,* might be better for at least four reasons: First, because of some feedback techniques I had developed for sampling student opinions, I hoped to produce one of the most simply written and student-oriented texts imaginable. Second, I wanted to write a book that would be both highly integrated in subject matter yet as teachable as possible. Third, I thought I had figured out new ways to reward students for the effort they must put forth to learn basic psychology. And fourth, I planned to create a book that would emphasize human values as much as it did scientific concepts.

Let us now discuss each of these four points briefly.

1. *Understanding Human Behavior* was written for, about, and with considerable help from students themselves. Seven years ago, I had the pleasant task of writing, re-writing, and editing a major portion of one of the 100 other texts presently on the market. Once that book was in print, I used it in one of my introductory psychology classes here at Michigan. I asked my students to keep detailed "reading logs" as they went through the text, telling me what they liked and didn't like. Looking through those "reading logs" was a mind-opening experience for me. Although I had been teaching the introductory course for more than 15 years, and hence thought I "knew where the students were," this was the first time I had gotten such extensive feedback from my class on how they perceived the text they were using.

As it turned out, many of my guesses about what students knew and liked and wanted were terribly wrong. To begin with, the Michigan students had much more limited vocabularies than I had assumed they did. Make no mistake—these young men and women were quite bright, but they simply were not as linguistically sophisticated as I had imagined they were. They were capable of learning almost anything—*if* they were motivated to do so, and *if* the material was presented in a simple, clear, logical manner.

As I finished scanning these "reading logs" I realized that none of the major texts available were actually written in collaboration with the students. So I started planning *Understanding Human Behavior* and asked Holt, Rinehart and Winston if they would be interested in supporting the project. They were, and in the spring of 1971 I started writing.

By the autumn of that year I had finished the first several chapters and used them in an introductory class I was then teaching. As rapidly as I could turn out a new chapter, it was distributed to this group of 33 students. Each of these young men and women went through the chapters carefully, circling every word they couldn't define or weren't familiar with, writing comments in the margins, telling me what seemed clear to them and what was fuzzy, when they were bored and when they were excited by the material presented. At the end of each chapter they summarized their reactions and made suggestions for improvements. I read their comments, answered each one in writing, then returned the chapters to the students for their further reactions. At the end of the semester they gave all this material back—more than 25,000 individual comments and criticisms.

Many of these 33 students volunteered to read the later chapters as they were completed, and large chunks of the book were given to an additional 75 students for their opinions. Without their generous help this would have been just another introductory text. But because these hundred students thought my project exciting and worthwhile, and because they were willing to be honest with me about their likes and dislikes, their interests and limitations, *Understanding Human Behavior* turned out to be quite different from anything else on the market.

As soon as the first edition of *Understanding Human Behavior* (UHB-1) was on the market, I began getting feedback from students and teachers all over the country who were using the text. More than a hundred professors—and more than 2,000 students—were kind enough to send me their comments and criticisms. This second edition was then tailored to meet as many student-teacher needs as possible.

Like the first edition, the second edition (UHB-2) is at once very complex, yet extremely simple. The ideas presented are often fairly complicated, but the language is as spare and sparse as I could make it. My student-critics disliked jargon— mostly because it is seldom well explained. They also disliked the sort of "$5 words" that many authors use without realizing that their intended readers are often put off by terms they are unfamiliar with. The students themselves suggested a kind of "running glossary" that would allow them immediately to check out definitions of words they didn't know. This "continuous word list" appears in the margin of almost every page of UHB-2—on the same page where the word first occurs in the text. The glossary items usually contain pronunciations as well as explanations, because students are sometimes reluctant to ask questions in class about things they can't pronounce correctly. Those students who need the extra assistance that this "marginal glossary" gives found it extremely helpful; but even those men and women who knew most of the words found the glossary a handy study aid. In fact, almost three quarters of the 2,000 students who commented on UHB-1 mentioned the "continuous word list" as being a feature they strongly approved of.

In 1975, Barry Gillen reported on the "reading ease" and "human interest" scores of many of the major introductory psychology texts then available. I am delighted to say that UHB-1 had the highest "human interest" scores, and the best "reading ease" scores, of any of the books that Gillen tested. It is my belief that similar scores for the second edition will be at least as high, and perhaps higher than, those that Gillen published for the first edition.

Here then is a text that covers almost the entire field of psychology, yet presents all the data and theories in language that even a below-average student can usually comprehend. Happily, it also seems to be challenging enough to keep above-average students interested as well. And, as was the case with the first edition, there is a revised *Student Manual* available for UHB-2 that not only helps the readers over the rough spots in psychology, but as well offers excellent advice on how to succeed in any course the student might be taking. In addition, this edition is accompanied by a *Unit Mastery Workbook* for use by students enrolled in a self-paced course.

2. One of the most important things I learned from all the feedback I got was that while students generally prefer an integrated approach to psychology, they resist looking at human behavior from one narrow viewpoint. It would be simple to write a text that focused primarily on biological variables, or that was mostly Freudian in its orientation, or one that used humanism or behaviorism to tie together all the facts of psychology. But such a text would not be very "teachable," since it would do injustice to the complexities of the field and would annoy most students (and perhaps many teachers) by its narrowness.

In *Understanding Human Behavior* I tried to integrate as much of psychology as I could within three quite different theoretical frameworks—the physiological, or what goes on within the body; the intra-psychic, or what goes on within the mind and the stream of consciousness; and the behavioral/social, or what goes on within the environment that influences human thoughts and actions. No matter what topic is covered in a given chapter, the material is viewed from all three of these frameworks. Because the connections among the various facts and fields of psychology are spelled out as clearly as possible, there is "something for everybody" in each chapter, and the student is constantly reminded that behavior is multi-determined.

This integration across theoretical viewpoints has allowed me to include material of considerable student interest not always covered in other texts. Because the students themselves asked for it, I have included material on such diverse topics as biofeedback, Transactional Analysis, group therapy techniques, weight control, aggression and violence, abnormal sexual behavior, conformity, sleep and dreaming, aging, memory transfer, genetic counseling, hypnosis, ESP, advertising (open and subliminal), sensory deprivation and brainwashing, behavior therapy and token economies, yoga and transcendental meditation, drugs, acupuncture, environmental psychology, personal space, and ethics. By using these areas of great human appeal as "entrance points" to discussions of the more traditional material, I have tried to present hard science in the softest and most interesting of terms.

3. We have known for years that human beings learn more when they are rewarded for learning than when they are punished. In *Understanding Human Behavior* I have tried to give the reader every bit of positive reinforcement possible. Students are typically more interested in themselves and in other people than in memorizing impersonal facts. As much as possible, I have used history and personal anecdotes to interest

the reader in learning as much as possible. I have put as many individual projects, illustrations, thought-provoking questions, and real-life examples into the book as I could. All of these facets of UHB-1 rated high in the reviews from our 2,000 student-critics.

More than this, I have made extensive use of "functional fiction" to present facts and attitudes that might not otherwise have found a place in the book. Each of the 27 main chapters of the book begins with a short story, a fictionalized case history, or a real scientific experiment dressed up in dramatic form. The stories are all based on the psychological material to be covered in that particular chapter. The beginning episode typically reaches a climax, then stops. The student must then read the factual part of the chapter in order to understand more fully the resolution of the drama—which comes at the tag end of each chapter. In truth, as we discovered, many of the students preferred to finish the entire story before reading the "meat" of the chapter, but the fiction does seem to interest them so much that they are more motivated to tackle the "heavy stuff in the middle" than perhaps they normally would be. Our surveys suggest that at least 50 percent of the 2,000 respondents read at least one unassigned chapter; usually they would look over the story and then become so interested in the material covered that they would read the rest of the chapter as well. About 15 percent of the respondents read *all* the unassigned chapters, a finding I personally find most gratifying.

The comments from our 2,000 student-critics further suggest that undergraduates find the use of fiction in an introductory textbook a particularly fascinating pedagogical device. More than 30 percent of the respondents rated the fiction as being the most interesting part of each chapter. The students appear to learn a great deal—often without realizing they are in truth learning. What started out to be simply a "reward" turned out to be one of the most effective teaching techniques I've ever run across. More than this, many of the students reported great changes in their attitude toward psychology—an attitude change they related directly to the "humanizing" of scientific concepts in the short stories. An unusually large percentage of the student-critics stated they planned to take more courses in psychology, or even were planning to enter the field professionally, as a result of having been "turned on" by reading the text.

4. The final, but perhaps most important, difference between this book and many others has to do with my own personal concern for ethical considerations. Wherever possible in the text, I have raised (and tried to answer) those moral questions that students themselves think about when taking their first course in psychology.

In addition, I have tried to "model" the sorts of environmental changes that appear to support social change. For instance, I have done whatever I could to attack the unconscious racism and sexism found in our culture and our language. In English, one typically refers to children (or to patients or subjects) as "he," as if only males were worthy of mention. I have tried to avoid such social lapses by using "he and she" and "his and hers" in such situations. In the short stories women appear in high-status positions as often as males, and blacks are presented in exactly the same high-prestige situations as are whites. The heroine of one short story is a charming, intelligent Spanish-American woman. Stereotypes are hard to avoid—at least I have made the effort to do so. Surprisingly enough, my student-critics were particularly sensitive to all this; many of them thanked me openly for my attempts "to be fair to everybody."

The term "ethics" means different things to different people. My own view is that it is unethical to present scientific data without drawing conclusions about what these data might mean to real, live human beings. I am an incurable optimist about the future of the human race, and I believe strongly that the wise use of psychological knowledge can help make this a better planet on which to live. I have tried to share with my readers my own feelings that humans are capable of much more growth and self-actualization than their environments often give them. My greatest hope is that *Understanding Human Behavior* will make its own small contribution toward helping anyone who reads it better achieve his or her unique set of personal goals.

What better reasons could one have for writing an introductory text?

James V. Mc Connell

ACKNOWLEDGMENTS

According to the title page, this is "my" book. Nothing could be further from the truth. It may take only "two to tango," but it takes the combined efforts of hundreds of people to produce a decent introductory psychology text. The author gets most of the credit; the others do much of the real work and get little notice, yet without their contributions, no book would ever break into print. In this brief note let me acknowledge my great indebtedness to many individuals.

To begin with, there is Ted Newcomb. He was one of those people instrumental in helping me obtain my teaching position at Michigan in 1956; he helped teach me how to teach and, by his constant example, showed me how to be a better human being. He also read and re-read every chapter of the first edition in every stage of its production; his suggestions and warm support were mainstays on many of my darker days.

Next, there is my friend Fred Wakeman, whose journalistic talents I have often tried to imitate but have never equaled. Fred's comments on all the chapters were always helpful, often of critical importance. Like most professional writers, Fred has a "feel" for language that is astonishing. Unlike many other professional writers, Fred is also a kind and generous critic.

I cannot begin to express my gratitude to Louise Waller, my first editor at Holt, Rinehart and Winston. Her editorial skills are legendary; her humane wisdom and concerned helpfulness were my constant and most welcome companions while I was preparing the first edition. Johnna Barto edited the second edition and is responsible for many of the signal improvements found in UHB-2. I owe her great gratitude not only for her creative suggestions, but also for her ability to tolerate and to work around my many idiosyncrasies.

Publishers are supposed to be ogres who squeeze authors dry of their priceless creativity and then discard the writers on the dust heap of commercialism. I am happy to report that HRW simply doesn't fit this stereotype. My special thanks to Deborah Doty and to David Boynton for their assistance through the process of planning, creating, and publishing both editions. It was they who originally talked H. Allen Fernald and other HRW executives into giving their financial blessing to publishing the first edition, and into giving generous support as well for testing that edition so that the second could be even better. Deborah and David have become close personal friends, as indeed have many other people at HRW. I would also like to thank John D Backe, Stanley D. Frank, and Seibert G. Adams for their many kindnesses.

Robert Kopelman and Barbara Bert designed the book and supervised the illustration program. Louis Scardino and Fred Pusterla designed the marvelous cover. Victor Calderon guided matters through the production process. Jeanette Ninas Johnson and Francoise D. Bartlett, who saw to the copy editing and other important matters, helped turn my poorly scrawled words into the handsome product you hold in your hands. Patrick Powers, of the HRW marketing promotion department, has helped in so many ways that I cannot begin to enumerate them. Most of all I would like to thank Pat for his continual faith in some of my wilder ideas.

In final analysis, a good share of the success of the first edition was due to the enthusiastic reception given UHB-1 by many HRW marketing and salespeople. I cannot begin to name them all, but would like to extend thanks particularly to Robert Melendes, Steve Pensinger, Cedric Lucas, Steve Boillot, John Tugman, Don Reed, Terry Albert, Bill Adair, Douglas Garber, and Phil Desper. A pat on the back too to Marie Cumbie and Josie Bost for managing the distribution of the book. A round of very loud applause as well should go to Diane Roberts, Norma Scheck, Susie Aitken, and Maria Galvez for all their assistance.

Many of my professional colleagues gave generously of their time in reading all or parts of the manuscript and offering their thoughtful comments. Without their collective wisdom, I would have made even more silly errors in the second edition than appeared in the first. Let me then thank William Uttal, Robert L. Hoeppner, Charles G. Halcomb, Henry Marcucella, Elliot E. Entin, Lowell Kelly, Francis S. Kalinowski, II, Werner Mendel, David Rosenhan, Peter R. Runkel, Sal Cianci, Raymond Shrader, Hal Arkes, Jon Gosser, Ken Moody, Irwin Pollack, Timothy Walter, and L. A. Siebert for their many useful criticisms. Siebert and Walter are also the authors of the excellent *Student Manual* and *Instructor's Manual* that accompany this book. Thomas Flagg did yeoman service in preparing the test questions, and Raymond Shrader and Reid Jones have put together a first-rate *Unit Mastery Workbook* for the second edition.

I would also like to thank the following people for their letters, reviews, criticisms, and most useful comments:

Ira B. Albert, Jeffrey R. Alberts, H.L. Ansbacher, Pietro Badia, David F. Barone, Robert Baugher, Irwin A. Berg, James G. Blight, Richard A. Block, Robert C. Bolles, Stanley L. Brodsky, Bert R. Brown, Martin Brown, Robert Burke, George Burt, Thomas E. Cheshire, Daniel J. Cohen, John J. Colby, Donald Daoust, Nancy Denney, Jerrold Downey, Bruce Downing, James Dyal, Yakov M. Epstein, Cyril M. Franks, Herbert Friedman, Nori Geary, Shepard Gorman, John Gormly, Glenn R. Hawkes, Albert Heldt, Sidney Hochman, Peter Holmes, William Jackson, Dennis Jowaisas, Robert Kaplan, George Katona, Gary King, Rosina Lao, Charles Lee, Dale Leonard, Bernard H. Levin, Joel F. Lubar, Carol Malatesta, Norma L. McCoy, Fred McKinney, Donald D. Megenity, Gary F. Meunier, Jerrold S. Meyer, Shirley Moore, Merle Moskowitz, David Myers, David L. Norris, Melinda Novak, Robert O'Connor, Gary Oliver, John O'Neill, Henry Paar, Ella M. Pascale, Laurence R. Plant, John A. Popplestone, Sandra M. Powers, J. Randall Price, Mary Gladys Raidford, Robert Rediehs, Norma C. Reese, Harry R. Robe, Richard Rozelle, Richard Schiffman, Neil Schneiderman, Paul J. School, Thomas R. Scott, Jr., Rene A. Spitz, H.E. Stanton, Jeffrey J. Stern, Stuart Stiles, Jr., Jesus Terrazes, Jr., David G. Tieman, Bruce Trotter, Charles Verschoor, Carl P. Williams, Joseph Wolpe, A. Bond Woodruff.

Let me next express my gratitude to The University of Michigan, and especially to the Department of Psychology and to the Mental Health Research Institute (directed by Gardner C. Quarton), for continued support over the 20 wonderful years I have spent here. Not only did the University show me great tolerance but as well provided me with one of the most stimulating intellectual environments I can imagine.

I would like to thank my many friends in Ann Arbor, comrades all, who gave me most of my ideas and whose names I have taken in vain in some of the short stories. To my poker-playing cronies—Arthur W. Melton, Robert Bjork, Brian Healy, W. Robert Dixon, Warren Norman, John Holland, Ralph Heine, Peter Steiner, and Paul Carrington—a nod of appreciation. They offered me many evenings of statistical diversion and, by fleecing me so frequently at seven-card stud, brought my motivation to finish the second edition to undreamed-of heights.

Several women in my office had the terrible chores of translating my hen-scratchings into legible manuscript, of collating the student criticisms, of keeping my nose ever to the grindstone, and of putting up with me on bad days. I owe them all—Marlys Schutjer, Peggy Burns, Nancy Crockett, Evva Caplan, Eileen Addison, Sally Greiner, and Joan Barth—a tremendous debt. Joan is also to be blessed for doing the index so well. They are winners, all of them, and I was most fortunate to have such magnificent people as my colleagues and associates.

Last, but most assuredly not least, it is my students—past and present—who deserve my thanks. They taught me how to write; they shaped me into learning more about psychology and about people than I had any intention of learning. Whatever is best in this book is their doing, not mine.

Bless 'em all!

October 1976   —J.V.McC.
Ann Arbor, Michigan

CONTENTS

PART 3   MOTIVATION

PART 4   LEARNING AND MEMORY

chapter 1

"THE GREAT STONE MAMA"

INTRODUCTION

I was typing a letter when Edward T. knocked at my office door and asked if he could talk to me "in private." He said he wasn't a student of mine, but that his girl friend was in one of my classes. She had suggested that he come to see me. Frankly, I didn't appreciate being disturbed, for I was behind in my work and it was late in the day. But there was something oddly urgent about his behavior, so I invited him in and asked him to sit down.

Edward T. stared at me for a moment, then scratched his bushy head of hair. Finally he said, "Dr. McConnell, I think I'm nuts. Really nuts. What I want is for you to write me a letter saying I'm insane."

I suppose my face reflected my surprise. But as calmly as I could, I asked him why in the world he wanted me to do a thing like that.

"I guess it's my only chance. I mean, like I've been thinking about all this for a whole bunch of time. I mean, like weeks and weeks, ever since the holidays. Heavy thinking, like my head is going to split open, you know what I mean? At first I thought maybe I'd just let them lock me up, because maybe that isn't so bad and lots of people have done it already. I mean, at least you get the whole thing over with, and it isn't as if you've done anything really bad, like killing someone. There weren't any kids involved, you see, and if anybody got hurt, I guess it would only be me. Besides, you meet some pretty fine people in jail these days—so I hear. I haven't been in jail yet myself, you see, although I've thought about it for weeks and weeks—no, it's more like 3 months now—well, maybe 10 weeks anyhow. It just goes round and round in my head, you know, and it doesn't come out sensible at all! I mean, it just isn't fair! Why do people have to poke their noses in other people's affairs? Why can't they leave people alone? Well, anyhow, the music went round and round in my head, and then I began to see that jail was a particularly bad waste of time and no one would really understand anyhow, and I'd have a record all my life, and I don't think I could stand being locked up. You know, really confined so I couldn't do anything—smoke and drink and make love and things like that. My head hurts a lot just from thinking about it, did you know that? So then I thought it would be lots better if I just left, you know, split the scene, but I don't think my mother and father would exactly go along with that, so my only hope is if I'm crazy. They say that works, particularly if you're a first offender. You understand that, don't you?"

At that point, I didn't understand much of anything except, perhaps, that maybe Edward T. was indeed insane. But I did what most psychologists would do at that stage in an interview. I said, "Tell me more about it," and nodded in a reassuring manner.

For the next 10 minutes Edward T. darted this way and that, like a butterfly blown before a breeze. He flew all around the subject he wanted to discuss, but he never really landed on it.

Finally I stopped him. "Look, Ed, come back to earth. Tell me what it is you want to do."

For just a second he froze, like an animal caught in a steel trap. Then Edward T. smiled at me rather weakly and said, "When I was home over the holidays I got busted on a pot charge. I had a couple of joints on me—less than an ounce! But where I come from, that's a felony, and I could get a whole lot of time in the pokey if they got tough with me. They caught a friend of mine last year, but he got a psychiatrist to claim he was mentally ill, and the judge let him off provided he'd get some therapy. I want you to write me a letter saying I'm crazy so the judge won't send me to jail."

The time was the early 1970's, and the use or possession of marijuana was a major crime in many parts of the United States. Some people considered "pot smokers" to be dangerous criminals; others thought them to be "mentally ill" and in need of psychological help. Still others, as we will see in Chapter 3 of this book, considered marijuana a mildly intoxicating drug less dangerous than alcohol. Many judges were lenient with youthful offenders, particularly if the young man or woman could give evidence of being "psychologically disturbed." So I asked, "Are you really crazy, Ed?"

"I don't know, Doc. Sometimes I think so. Maybe not. My father says I ought to plead guilty and take my medicine, that I deserve to be punished. He thinks going to jail would teach me a lesson. I think maybe he's the one who's insane."

Insane? Crazy? As we will see later on, these terms have many different meanings. Most Americans of my generation thought Hitler was insane; a great many Germans thought he was a divinely inspired leader. The definition of insanity has varied so much from time to time, and from culture to culture, that the term should always be used with great caution. However, Edward T. didn't want a lecture on mental illness, he wanted help. So I merely asked him what he had done so far to keep out of jail.

"Well, I've thought about it a lot. You see, I think smoking pot is a purely personal thing. It's my body, and my mind, and what's my father got to say about what I do? I mean, I love my father, and all that, but I just can't go along with his way of thinking. What good would serving time in jail do me? Or him? And it would kill my mother, I know it would. I've thought about that a lot, you see, how my mother would react to knowing her son was down in the local pokey with all those criminals. So maybe I ought to go to Canada. I've thought about that a lot, too, and I've read a couple of books on the effects of marijuana. Also, I've talked to a lot of my friends. Some of them think I ought to split, you know, just drop out and disappear. Nobody would ever find me, not if I hid up in the mountains, or something like that. Lots of communes around where they won't tell anybody who you are. Sometimes I spend all day long and most of the night just thinking about what I ought to do, but nobody understands where my head really is, particularly my father. I mean, I've been doing some really very heavy thinking about it . . ." And he drifted off again.

I pulled Ed back to the here and now. "Yes, you've thought a lot and you've talked a lot, but what have you done to put your thoughts into action? Have you talked to a lawyer?"

Edward T. gave me a very puzzled look. "My father says I don't need a lawyer. He says I should just plead guilty and go to jail."

"Can't you get a lawyer on your own, whether your father approves or not?"

"Well, lawyers cost a lot of money. Everybody knows that. And my father won't pay, because he's against it."

I shook my head. "If you can't afford a lawyer, Ed, just ask the judge to appoint one for you. It won't cost you a cent."

Tears came to the young man's eyes. "They don't listen. They're all part of the system, and every lawyer in town knows my father anyhow. He'd just tell them to make sure I went to jail, and they'd do what he told them to do! I don't want to go to jail! But I don't want to run away either! I just want to be left alone! Can't you see I've got a problem?"

Edward T. did have a problem—or rather, he had many of them. But I was by no means sure what they all were. As a way of showing you something about the subject matter of this book, however, let us see how a psychologist might try to find out what some of Edward T.'s problems were.

THREE VIEWS OF HUMAN BEHAVIOR

Is Edward T. crazy? How would *you* answer that question?

It was apparent to me that his speech pattern was not entirely normal. As we will see in Chapter 25, terms such as *normal* and *abnormal* are devilishly difficult to define. However, had I recorded my conversation with Edward T. and played it back to one of my friends—someone who specializes in treating mental illness—this friend surely would have said that this bushy-haired young man talked much the same way that mildly disturbed patients often talk. His speech was often as fuzzy as his hair; he spoke indistinctly and his train of thought was difficult to follow. He would forget to finish sentences, and he seemed incapable of thinking through a problem from A to B to C in logical fashion.

Or, at least, Edward T. *talked* that way.

I could see the way that Edward T. moved his arms and legs, and I could hear what he said, but I couldn't look directly into his mind to see what he was actually capable of thinking. To determine whether Edward T. was truly insane, I would need to discover something about his thoughts, his perceptions, his dreams, and his desires.

I suspected too that he might be putting on a show for me. After all, he wanted to convince me that he was crazy, didn't he?

But hanging a label on Edward T. wouldn't help either one of us very much. Had we both had the time and desire to go into matters in depth, I would have tried to look at his problem from three different viewpoints—the social/behavioral, the intra-psychic, and the biological.

The Social/Behavioral Viewpoint

First, I would have wanted to take a complete family history from Edward T.—a record of what his early life was like, what he thought of his parents and his brothers and sisters and friends. I would also have wanted to discover what they seemed to think of him. Everybody—crazy or sane—is influenced by the *social environment* he or she grows up in. So I would have tried to find out as much as I could about Edward T.'s early life and present circumstances in order to know (as best I could) how he got to the stage that he was at when I first talked to him.

The Intra-psychic Viewpoint

Second, I would have sent Edward T. to someone who would have given him a number of psychological tests. The scores from these tests might well have given me some insight into his *private mental functioning.*

Before we judge a man insane, we typically want to learn as much as possible about the structure of his personality; we want to discover as much as we can about the subjective side of his nature. From the social/behavioral viewpoint, Edward T.'s thoughts and actions are considered to be shaped almost entirely by his environment, by the people and things around him. But from an intra-psychic or subjective viewpoint, Edward T. is a self-directed, conscious human being with his own unique set of goals and values. Psychological tests, when properly used, can often give us a richer picture of what a person is really like than if we merely measure the individual's social background or describe his or her present behavior patterns.

The Biological Viewpoint

And then, before I did anything else, I would have wanted Edward T. to have a complete medical examination. Man is a *biological* as well as a social and psychological animal. Many students who take an introductory course in psychology think that it's all about how you lie down on a couch and talk about your mother, or about abnormal forms of sexual behavior, or about why you can't get along with your roommate. In small part, psychology is all those things. But it is much, much more.

Psychology is a very new science. It grew partly out of medicine and biology, partly out of physics and chemistry, and partly out of sociology and philosophy and religion. There are probably as many different ways of looking at the human organism as there are different human organisms. The three major viewpoints within the field of psychology, however, are the social/behavioral, the intra-psychic, and the biological. Psychology is really the point at which these three viewpoints meet or intersect.

Your body is a biological system made up of cells and complex organs which work together to give you life. The functions of your body—particularly the activities that go on in your brain—profoundly affect your thoughts and moods, your feelings and attitudes. For instance, when you have a high fever, you simply don't think as clearly as when your body is in good condition. But what happens in your mind (your intra-psychic self) can influence your biological processes. If you are deeply depressed, for example, you are more likely to catch a fever than when you are happy and your mind is at ease. But what causes depression? Many of us become disturbed when we have an unhappy love affair or lose someone close to us, so our "state of mind" is often shaped by events in our social environments.

In short, our biological systems interact with our intra-psychic systems and with the social systems (friends, families, organizations) of which we are all a part. If we wish to gain a reasonably complete understanding of human behavior, we cannot neglect or discard any of these three important systems. Let me show you what I mean.

The Case of Clarence B.

A few months before Edward T. came to see me, a couple of bright but desperate young lawyers in Detroit asked me to help them with the defense of a murder case. Their client was a young black man whom we will call Clarence B. He was accused of murdering a white woman who was a graduate student in social work at one of the local universities. There was no doubt that Clarence B. was guilty of the crime—he admitted that he had shot the young woman. What the lawyers hoped to do was to convince the jury that Clarence B. was legally insane at the time that he pulled the trigger. Most people would think that to murder someone is perhaps a pretty sure indication of insanity, but as we will see in a later chapter, there is a great difference between a *legal* definition of "insanity" and a *psychological* definition. Legally you are not usually considered insane unless a court of law declares you mentally incompetent or unable to tell right from wrong, and often this judgment comes only after you have been tried by a jury of your peers. Psychologically, you are typically considered insane if you cannot take care of yourself, cannot function in society, or if you are a threat to yourself or to the people around you. It occasionally happens that a jury will judge a person insane whom psychologists consider to be reasonably normal, or that a psychologist may consider a person crazy as a bedbug whom a jury finds to be normal.

The lawyers told me that the trial would hinge on the concept of "irresistible impulse"; that is, at the time of the murder, was Clarence B. possessed by such a strong desire to commit the crime that he was not in his right senses and hence was not able to tell right from wrong? Since the defense was based on psychological evidence, the lawyers wanted my help in selecting jury members who would give some weight to the testimony the defense psychiatrist was expected to give.

Why had Clarence B. shot the woman? A glance at his life history might give us some social/behavioral clues as to his motivation. Born in the Detroit ghetto, he was 28 at the time of the crime. His mother had deserted him before he was 3 years old, and he did not see his father for the first time until he was 21 (when both men were serving terms in the same state prison). Clarence B. was reared by his maternal grandmother. This woman, for all the love and affection she tried to give him, was an alcoholic who simply was incapable of tending to his needs.

Perhaps because Clarence B. grew up on the streets with little or no adult guidance, he was in constant trouble for most of his life. His first arrest came when he was not quite 12. By the time he was 17 he had been in and out of jail several times—mostly for crimes of violence. When he was 21 he was locked away for several years on a charge of raping a casual acquaintance.

While Clarence B. was in the state prison on the rape charge he met a professor of sociology who was working with the prisoners. This professor believed that Clarence B.'s problems were entirely due to his having grown up in a punishing, racist, poverty-stricken ghetto. Putting Clarence B. in a better environment—one that would support him instead of suppressing him—might therefore clear up his difficulties, the professor felt. The prison psychologist, who had talked many times with Clarence B. and given him a series of tests, didn't agree. From an intra-psychic viewpoint, this young black man had a number of deep-seated personal problems that only some form of psychological therapy might cure, the psychologist thought. He made a note on Clarence B.'s prison record that the prisoner seemed mentally ill, but the parole board ignored the psychologist's recommendations and released Clarence B. anyhow.

Like most states, Michigan unfortunately does not provide any kind of effective aftercare for paroled convicts like Clarence B. No one bothered to create a supporting social environment, and no one offered to pay his bills for psycho-

therapy. Clarence B. soon found himself drifting back into his old, illegal habits. In desperation, he turned to the sociology professor, who introduced him to the graduate student whom he eventually killed. He had seen this woman only five times when he shot her.

It might be tempting to explain Clarence B.'s violent behavior in purely social/behavioral terms. For example, he was a black who hated whites because they had punished him all his life. He had been arrested by whites, brought to trial before white judges, thrown into prisons that were run by white guards. Violent behavior had often gotten him some of the things he wanted in the past—including a fair amount of public attention. Once he had discovered that violence could be rewarding, he might well have been unconsciously encouraged to continue it all his life.

Or you might try to explain Clarence B.'s violence as being a natural consequence of his immature personality. It is clear that he had not resolved all the problems of his sexual identity. His early experience had apparently convinced him that women were all either angels or devils, that they should be objects either of worship or of abuse. Perhaps violence was his only means of asserting his masculinity. Deserted by his parents, and often ignored by his grandmother, he had quite genuine fears about being able to survive in "normal" society. Prison seemed to offer him a kind of psychological security that he had never found outside the walls of what he called "the great stone mama." Perhaps Clarence B. had a strong but unconscious desire to return to the rigid embrace of the only "woman" who ever made him feel at home.

In short, you could easily argue that Clarence B. was a murderer because of such *objective* reasons as his neglect as a child, his experiences as a black in a world dominated by whites, his poverty, his early clashes with the law, his prison record, and so on. Or you could insist that he killed the young woman for such *subjective* reasons as the psychological insecurity he felt, the confused thought patterns and the immature traits of personality that showed in his test scores. It is quite true that *all* of these factors contributed to his shooting of the young woman. But if you suppose that any of these influences was the *primary* cause of the murder, you might be wrong—dead wrong.

The lawyers defending Clarence B. phoned me late the night before the trial began. As I've said, they explained their problem and asked my help. I agreed to do whatever I could, provided I would be free to talk or write about whatever I learned during the case. They agreed readily and went back to their legal briefs to prepare for the day ahead. I went to soak myself in a tub of hot water. How could anyone possibly explain to a jury what an irresistible impulse was like? We all have urges to do violence to one person or another, but we (mostly) resist them. I was sure that each man and woman on that jury would consider himself or herself an expert on such urges (since, if the jury member had yielded to violent desires in the past, he or she would probably have been excluded from the panel). It seemed an impossible task.

And then, quite suddenly, a strange thought occurred to me. A few months earlier I had heard a Boston psychiatrist named Frank Ervin lecture about his studies of violent patients and criminals. A good portion of them—so Dr. Ervin believed—suffered from a type of hidden brain disease that only a few doctors were able to diagnose. As you will see from reading Chapter 4, these people were violent, at least in part, because they had sustained physical damage to the emotional centers of their brains. Most of the time their behavior was quite normal. But occasionally, particularly when they had consumed too much alcohol, something would trigger off a violent storm of electrochemical activity in their brains and they would react blindly by attacking anyone near them (Clarence B. had been drinking heavily the day he committed the murder).

It all made an odd kind of sense to me. No one—not even the most shy and conservative person alive—can resist a destructive impulse when his or her brain is on fire. That would surely be the sort of defense that any jury member could understand.

I called Dr. Ervin early the next morning and described Clarence B. to him. Dr. Ervin said it sounded to him as if Clarence B. was indeed a victim of the kind of hidden brain disease that Ervin had studied in so many other violent criminals. He suggested that we put Clarence B. through the extensive medical tests needed to determine if his brain was physically damaged. And so I had a long talk with the lawyers.

We won the case—which is to say that Clarence B. was given what amounted to a life sentence in a mental hospital rather than a life sentence in a prison (if you want to call that "winning the case"). But my wild idea about hidden brain disease had nothing to do with the outcome.

To begin with, we probably would have had to take Clarence B. to Boston for the rather unusual medical examination that Ervin felt was necessary. The lawyers (one of whom later helped defend Angela Davis) were willing to pay for the trip out of their own pockets, but we had to abandon the idea. For the psychiatrist who was to testify in Clarence B.'s behalf vetoed the plan. This psychiatrist took a narrow, intra-psychic view toward behavior and considered Ervin's experiments too new, too biological, and too controversial to bring before the jury. Despite what seemed to be strong evidence that Clarence B. had suffered from a damaged brain since his early childhood, we had to build the case entirely on a restricted, subjective view of insanity.

Actually, we won the decision almost by accident. For the prosecuting attorney hired his own psychiatrist who said that Clarence B. wasn't insane at all, from an intra-psychic viewpoint. The two psychiatrists put on a verbal battle royal for hours, one man insisting Clarence B. was crazy, the other insisting Clarence B. was sane. The argument so confused the judge that he brought in *his* psychiatrist. This third psychiatrist examined Clarence B. and then announced that maybe Clarence B. was insane, but on the other hand, maybe he wasn't.

The jury listened to the conflicting testimony and ultimately decided that

Clarence B. had been suffering from temporary insanity at the moment that he had pulled the trigger. But, as I learned from talking with the foreman of the jury after the trial, the intra-psychic approach didn't cut much ice with the jury. They simply didn't understand most of what the three psychiatrists were arguing about. However, the jury members came to like the warm, personable manner of the defense lawyers and were put off by the cold, forbidding approach of the prosecuting attorney, so they decided to go along with the defense. When I explained my hunch about Clarence B.'s possible brain damage, the foreman was astounded. "Why didn't you bring that up?" he asked. "It would have made things much more understandable."

Most of us don't like to think of ourselves in biological terms. We find it hard to believe that we think and act the way we do partly because our brain functions the way that it does. Obviously it would be foolish to try to explain all human behavior in purely biological terms, ignoring the social/behavioral and the intra-psychic influences; but it would be equally foolish to ignore all the basic facts about your nervous system. And because the biological foundations or underpinnings of human behavior are less frequently discussed than the other two viewpoints, I have chosen to talk about the brain's influence on behavior in the first chapters of this textbook. Perhaps, after you have learned a few of the many fascinating details about your nervous system, you will agree with the jury foreman that "it makes things much more understandable."

In the first few chapters, then, we will take a predominantly biological view of man. The last section of the book presents mostly the social/behavioral theories. The chapters in between are devoted to the intra-psychic position. No matter what topics we discuss, we will try at least to mention all three viewpoints; to do otherwise would be to invite ignorance and to court disaster. For each of the three focuses on a separate but important aspect of the human condition, and each of the three systematic viewpoints has its strengths and weaknesses. My belief is that all three can be integrated into a comprehensive picture of human behavior which combines but is not restricted by any single one of them. Not all psychologists will agree with this approach, but at least you now know my biases.

And since it is inevitable that you, as a reader, will learn a great deal about me as you read these pages, perhaps I had better make an open statement of several other biases I have—so that you will be able to take them into account right from the start.

THE AUTHOR'S BIASES

1. To begin with, I believe that the study of human behavior is the most fascinating, most awe-inspiring, most relevant occupation imaginable. I hope that some of my enthusiasm for psychology rubs off on you by the time you finish the book, for it is the greatest gift I can offer you.

2. I believe that learning should be made as rewarding as possible; indeed, that learning should be both challenging and fun. One way I can make reading this book a pleasant experience is to make it as interesting as possible. My way of doing that is to focus on the life experiences of real people and to use them as examples. I teach by analogy, by telling stories. As Sigmund Freud—the father of psycho-analysis—is supposed to have said: "Analogies prove nothing, but they do make us feel at home." Freud might have added that they are also a marvelous instructional technique.

    Psychologists have long known that students remember best that part of a course that is most dramatic, most exciting. So I have begun and ended each chapter with a story or case history built around the lives of real or imagined human beings. Some of the stories really happened, a few are pure speculation; most of them are mixtures of fact and fiction. In general, you will find that you can understand the people in the stories much better after you have read the scientific material that comes between the opening and closing fiction. My hope is that the pleasure of reading the stories will reward you for trying to remember the factual material.

However, as we will see in Chapter 5, what is rewarding to one person may be punishing to another. If you are not fond of fiction, you will lose very little by skipping the stories. If you are put off by analogies, please ignore them.

Some of us like to be coaxed into learning; some of us prefer to be confronted and challenged. In some texts, the "challenge" occasionally comes from trying to make sense out of the complex way the author has presented the material, or from trying to memorize long lists of apparently unrelated facts. Committing such lists to memory may help you pass an examination, but is unlikely to help you much in later life if you don't really understand what it is you have memorized. If you have grown accustomed to texts that you must read several times in order to figure out what the author is saying, you may find this book deceptively easy for I have tried to keep things as clear and as simple as possible. It is my bias that we should judge a book by how much we actually learn from it, and not by how many hot and heavy hours we had to spend trying to plow through it. But for those of you who are rewarded most by intellectual stimulation, I have included a great many "thought questions" that often are not answered directly in the text. The purpose of these questions is to push your mind beyond the facts on the printed page. I can't imagine a better challenge than that. However, if you find these questions a bore, or if the answers don't come easily, either pass the questions by or ask your instructor about them.

3. As you will see, I place a great deal more faith in facts than in theories and opinions. Most arguments in science—such as the one between the two psychiatrists at Clarence B.'s trial—revolve around speculations and inter-pretations of data rather than around the data themselves. Historians of science are fond of quoting incidents in which facts discovered in one scientist's laboratory collided head-on with the Established View of Nature held by other scientists; in almost all such cases the facts eventually triumphed over the "established" theories.

But what are facts? From a scientific point of view, facts are events, experiences, or relationships that can be repeated or verified by several people. The things that you say and do can be witnessed or verified by others, therefore your behaviors are facts. If we used a movie camera to record your actions, we could show the film to everyone in the world, and most observers of the movie would surely agree on what it was you had done. Because these observers would be treating your activities as the *object* of their study, we can say that your behaviors would be *objective* facts.

The things that you think and feel deep inside you are very real, but these intra-psychic events cannot be observed by anybody other than yourself. Mental activities have *subjective* reality, because they occur privately in the mind of the person or subject experiencing them. But your inner feelings cannot be considered objective facts—unless and until you express them to someone else (at which point they become verbal behaviors).

Over the centuries, scientists have worked out many methods for deter-mining which events, experiences, or relationships can be repeated or verified by several people. These methods aren't perfect, and even the best of scientists occasionally confuse objective reality with what is going on inside their own heads. But if it's objective facts that you're interested in, the scientific approach will probably give you more dependable data than most other techniques will yield.

A camera makes an objective record of a scene. This photographic record would be far more factual and detailed than your own sub-jective memory of the same scene.

Generally speaking, the scientific method is based on two procedures—observation and experimentation. We all observe the world around us (and our inner experiences), but perhaps scientists are trained to do so a little more carefully than the average person. For example, a medical doctor can often gain a pretty good notion of your state of health merely by looking at you; the average person might miss those telltale clues (such as the quickness of your breathing, the clearness of your eyes, the condition of your hair and skin) that a physician is trained to notice. Similarly, a psychologist can sometimes get a fair idea of your mental state simply by watching and listening to you, or by seeing how you react to certain real-life situations. In short, we all observe, but knowing what to look for, and understanding what these objective observations might mean, are habits that come only from training and experience.

Some observations tell us a great deal more than others, and the more we can control what is going on, the more we are likely to learn. What we call "experiments" are usually just situations in which the scientist/experimenter has more than the usual amount of control over what happens. If you wished to discover some of the factors that influence memory, you might go watch how children learn from their parents, teachers, and friends. If you observed enough children in enough different situations, you might well get a good idea of what the "facts" of learning were. However, if you could bring the children into a laboratory setting—a place where you controlled what it was they were to learn, what kinds of rewards or punishments they received, and how long they were allowed to work at the material you gave them—you'd probably discover a lot more about memory in a shorter time than if you merely observed kids in an uncontrolled, real-life environment.

QUESTION: If you were going to study how humans learn in a laboratory setting, what kinds of factors would you want to control?

Our world is constantly changing, as are the marvelous people who inhabit this world. Variation and change, therefore, are the order of the day. Scientists not only control things during experiments but vary things as well. The strength of the experimental method actually lies in *controlled variation*. If you wished to study the effects of rewards and punishments on human learning, you might ask one group of college students to learn a poem and praise them for each word they memorized. A second group of students might be criticized severely for each mistake they made. A third group might receive neither praise nor verbal punishment. In this experiment, you would be *varying* the type of feedback you gave to the three groups while controlling all the other factors that might influence the speed with which the students memorized the poetry.

QUESTION: Which group do you think would learn the fastest?

Scientists have their own words for describing what they do. For instance, in the poetry study, reward and punishment would be called *independent variables*, because they are under the control of the experimenter. The speed at which the groups learned (which you would measure very carefully) would be termed the *dependent variable*. Independent variables are those aspects of the experimental situation that the scientist typically controls no matter what response the subject makes. Dependent variables are those responses of the subject that presumably occur because of what the experimenter did (that is, those responses that vary according to the independent variables the experimenter uses).

Suppose, in your poetry study, you found that the students given rewarding feedback usually learned faster than those students who were either ignored or were criticized. You might then *guess* that praise speeds up learning because it makes the students happier, more confident, or more highly motivated. But happiness, confidence, and motivation are invisible processes that occur inside the students—they are intra-psychic events that cannot be measured directly. Hence happiness and confidence are not objective facts but rather are subjective conditions. Any time we try to explain *why* people do the things they do, we usually have moved from fact to theory, from objective (measurable) reality to subjective (or guessed-at) concepts and explanations. Psychologists sometimes call such concepts as happiness and motivation *intervening variables* because these terms attempt to explain the internal processes that intervene (or come between) the independent and the dependent variables in an experiment.

You can almost always tell what kind of variable you're dealing with if you remember the following points:

Independent variables are those measurable things that the psychologist controls in an experimental setting.

Dependent variables are those measurable reactions (behaviors) that the subject makes in response to the independent variables.

Intervening variables are the processes that go on inside the subjects that presumably account for why the independent and dependent variables are related in some way. Intervening variables (such as *love, hate, intelligence, insanity*) are lots of fun to talk about, but they seldom can be measured directly. Intervening variables, then, are theory, not fact.

QUESTION: **Is *learning* an independent, dependent, or intervening variable?**

The scientific method is one of humanity's most glorious achievements. It is surely the most powerful way we have of determining objective facts and of testing our theoretical notions about why people act and think as they do. You have theories about human behavior just as I do. Many of your theories are likely to be challenged, to be contradicted by the facts presented in this textbook. I do not ask that you give up your views, merely that you try to examine afresh your ideas about yourself and the rest of mankind in the light of what new information this book gives you.

4. As you will see in Chapter 26, we all play many different roles in life. When I wear the white lab coat of a behavioral scientist, I prefer to study organisms (including people) objectively rather than subjectively, to look at them through unclouded eyes rather than through rose-colored glasses. Being objective means (in part) being unemotional about what one studies, being uninvolved personally or subjectively. This hard-hearted approach is particularly necessary (and most difficult) when we consider emotional, personal, and subjective problems.

There are very good reasons for a scientist to think objectively, but many people are put off by such an approach. Most of us prefer the human warmth of a little flattery and pretense to the cold fascination of hard truth—just as we prefer mercy to justice and being loved to being described in purely objective terms. Most subjective theories of human nature insist that man is either innately good or innately evil. To a scientist, man is neither; he merely is what he is. The scientist knows that he or she cannot find out what people are really like—if the scientist holds very many preconceived notions of what humans are *supposed* to be like. And unless the scientist learns the facts, the practitioner who wishes to help people cannot be of maximum assistance to them.

But a steady diet of objectivity lacks both spice and nourishment, and science is but one part of human experience. So most of the time I put my starched white laboratory coat aside and play the role of teacher, friend, poet,

James McConnell lecturing to a class at The University of Michigan.

lover, or merely that of an ordinary citizen with the usual quota of virtues and vices. Even as a citizen I try to be as unbiased as I can. I care far too much about people to make many value judgments about them. Just as they are, people are beautiful. I don't like everything that everybody does, but it is the *behavior* I dislike, not the person. Clarence B. murdered a lovely young woman who didn't deserve such a fate. When knowledge of the crime became public many people wanted to see Clarence B. executed as painfully as possible. They wanted to do away with the man; I merely wanted to do away with his murderous behavior.

5. I am an incurable optimist. I believe that through the wise and humane application of psychological knowledge we can all come closer to achieving our personal goals in life and make the world a more rewarding and less desperate place in which to live. (This moral viewpoint, like most others, rests on faith as well as science; but it is a faith that is shared by most psychologists.)

I also believe in personal responsibility and in the notion that you must pay for what you get, that we all suffer the consequences of our actions. A psychologist can tell you how to get good grades in school, how to get along better with your parents and friends, how to achieve a greater degree of self-actualization and personal happiness, and perhaps even help you be more successful in business if you're interested. But advice is the smallest coin in circulation. You won't get A's, or happiness, or money, or maturity unless you are willing to put forth the effort to do so, to make the most of what you have.

The Case of Edward T.

All of which brings us back to Edward T. He wanted me to wave a magic wand and keep him out of jail. He thought I could solve his problem for him by writing a letter saying he was crazy. I didn't bother telling him that the judge wouldn't have paid much attention to such a letter because that wasn't what the young man's problem was.

Edward T.'s difficulty was that he didn't want to participate in his own salvation; he wanted someone else to do it all for him. So I kept pecking away at him, asking him what *he* was going to do for himself, because I figured that was the best thing I could do for him (given the fact that neither of us had the time nor the desire to undertake a thorough psychological analysis of his situation).

"My father wouldn't listen."

"How do you know he wouldn't listen? Have you tried talking with him?"

He shook his head slowly. No, he hadn't tried, but he assumed . . .

"Well, suppose you try to play the game your father's way. It sounds to me as though he thinks you're not grown up enough to handle your own affairs. So, what would happen if you went to him and asked to borrow the money to hire a lawyer, and asked his advice on who the lawyer should be? What if you offered to get a job to pay back the loan? What sorts of things could you do to convince your father that you're mature enough to stand on your own two feet?"

An odd sort of smile washed over his face. Edward T. sat up straighter in his chair. He began to talk about the things he could do, how he might do them, and how his father might react. To me, the remarkable thing was that, for the first time since he'd walked into my office, his speech patterns became normal. He didn't drift off the subject once. All I did was to sit back and give him encouragement from the verbal sidelines.

Forty minutes later he stood up, shook my hand, thanked me for my help, and walked confidently out of my office. I hadn't solved any of his real problems, nor had he; but he had started to achieve some of his goals on his own.

A few weeks later I talked about Edward T. in a course I was teaching.

Afterward, a young woman came up to me and admitted that she had suggested to Ed that he come to see me. Before the visit, he had told her that it would be a simple matter to talk me into writing a letter saying he was nuts. After the visit, she hardly saw him again, because the very next day he flew back to his home to confront his father and the judge. Nobody knew yet if his plan was going to work, nor if he could stay out of jail; but she had never seen him as happy before. He kept talking about being in control of his own life for the first time in many years. She said he really enjoyed the feeling.

And, at a very practical and personal level, that's what understanding human behavior is all about.

I hope you enjoy it too.

RECOMMENDED READINGS

At the end of each chapter I will list several books or articles that you might wish to read if you want to go into the content of that chapter more deeply. A more detailed list of readings appears at the end of the book. You may also wish to look over the references that are mentioned in the *Student Manual to Understanding Human Behavior*, by L.A. Siebert and T. Walter, that accompanies this textbook. The *Student Manual* also contains many helpful hints on how to study for examinations, how to organize your time, and how to get involved in psychology by doing studies and experiments on your own. If you are having difficulties with any of the courses you are taking, or if you aren't getting as good grades as you think you ought to be getting, you might find the *Student Manual* of practical value.

There are also several general source materials that you might wish to investigate. One of the most useful I have found is *The Encyclopedia of Human Behavior* by Robert M. Goldenson (Garden City, N.Y.: Doubleday & Company, 1970). General references, such as the *Encyclopaedia Britannica*, contain many worthwhile articles on psychological topics, most of which are written by acknowledged experts.

Psychology Today is far and away the best popular magazine dealing with behavioral topics. There are also dozens of scientific journals, most of which focus on one particular aspect of human or animal behavior. Any psychologist or librarian will surely be happy to help you find the journal most interesting to you.

Part 1

BIOLOGICAL BASES OF BEHAVIOR

chapter 2

THE BRAIN

DID YOU KNOW THAT . . .

Your brain looks something like a wrinkled mushroom?

Your brain contains at least 10 billion nerve cells (neurons)?

The cortex, or outer layer of your brain, contains most of the "decision-making centers" that influence what you do, feel, and think?

The major psychological function of your brain is to process sensory information?

Some four million people in the United States suffer from epilepsy?

When a nerve cell (neuron) in your brain is excited, a wave of electrical energy sweeps down the neuron from one end to the other?

Brain waves are the result of the electrical excitation occurring in thousands or even millions of your brain cells?

Brain waves are typically measured with a device called an EEG machine?

Marijuana has been reported to be effective in reducing the frequency of epileptic seizures?

The left half of your brain is a mirror image of the right half in most respects?

If you are right-handed, the left half or hemisphere of your brain is usually dominant and controls the right half of your body?

If you are right-handed, your left hemisphere contains your "speech center," and seems responsible for most language and "logical thinking?"

If you are right-handed, your right hemisphere seems primarily responsible for "creative thinking" and for some aspects of your emotional reactions?

If a surgeon separated the two hemispheres of your brain, you might end up with two quite separate and distinct "minds" or "personalities" inside your skull?

Pat Devine lay in bed for some time after he woke up, dreading the heat. It was going to be one of those scorching, muggy summer days that he hated with an animal passion. He and Darlene couldn't afford an air conditioner, since Pat wasn't working, and hot weather always sucked energy from his body the way that his Honda 750 motorcycle sucked gas when he gunned the engine. His ex-Honda, he suddenly realized.

"You'd better get up, Pat. Dr. Benjamin will be here shortly," Darlene said, staring solemnly at him from the bedroom door.

Pat's left hand raised itself in an obscene gesture.

Darlene shook her head sadly. "Lefty hates me," she said, and walked back toward the kitchen of their small apartment.

Pat stared at his left hand, furious. Lefty? There wasn't any Lefty. Why the hell did Dar want to talk like that, anyhow? In his own way, Pat really loved the gal, and he owed his life to her; but at times she sure was infuriating. Sometimes she was as protective of him as a mother cat guarding her only kitten. And then, too often lately, she ripped into him with fangs and claws bared.

Pat noticed that the fingers on his left hand were trying to strangle the sweaty bedclothes. "What do they want to do that for?" he said half-aloud, and then put the thought aside almost immediately so he could think about the coming day. Dar was right. He ought to get up. He always liked to be shaved and dressed when the psychologist, Dr. Benjamin, came for his weekly visit. It seemed the least he could do, since Dr. Benjamin came to call chiefly because he wanted to see how Pat got along in a real-life setting rather than in a laboratory or hospital environment. Pat figured that if he looked good, it would help prove to the Doc that things were going better, that he had himself more under control.

He shifted around on the damp bed and put his right hand behind his head. His left toes were wiggling slowly. ''Funny,'' he said to himself, ''What have they got to wiggle about?'' And then he forgot the question at once as he heard a motorcycle go roaring by outside. A blast of black hatred snarled into his mind. The intensity of the feeling shook Pat a little. He had every reason to hate bikes—he had almost killed himself on one—but the horror of the accident couldn't explain that sudden jolt of fury.

Another cycle droned past outside, its motor buzzing like an angry hornet. It had been a hot summer day two years ago when he and Dar had loaded their dirt bikes on the trailer. They had driven almost a hundred miles, looking for country roads so far from civilization that no one would object to their bouncing along the cowpaths at high speed on their cycles. Riding a trail bike was the most thrilling sport Pat had ever found, and he loved every crazy minute of it—splashing through puddles of water, jumping the ridges of little hills and trying to keep the cycle under control when it landed. There was always a cigar clenched in his teeth, a six-pack of beer waiting for him at the end of the trail. All the creature comforts he dearly loved. And Dar, of course, lovely Dar, who stuck right by his side, jumping the ridges and puddles on her own bike almost as skillfully as he did on his.

Or maybe better. That hot summer day their ride had been so exciting that he pushed too much, too fast. He had taken that final hill at full tilt, zooming over the top like a hawk swooping down on a rabbit. Except the rabbit turned out to be a tree stump. His front tire hit the stump at 30 miles an hour, and Pat went over the handlebars doing at least 60. At least, that's what Dar had insisted, later on. Pat couldn't remember it very clearly. She said that she found him lying unconscious at the foot of a tree, his helmet split like a broken egg, his collar bone cracked, his head bleeding profusely. She said he looked as if he had gone through a meat grinder.

Pat hadn't gotten out of the hospital until just before the fall semester began at school. Although his head still hurt a lot, he went back to classes because he was trying to finish up his undergraduate work as quickly as he could.

And then his spells began.

He was sitting in a Zoo class one day when he conked out. Just like that. One minute he had been sitting in his seat, trying to answer a dumb question on a pop quiz. He had smelled something funny, some musky odor, and then the world turned blood red. The next minute, he was on the floor, writhing around like a chicken with its head cut off.

''Well, I guess I really broke up that quiz, now didn't I?'' he told himself, smiling a little.

Pat could hear Dar moving about in the kitchen. He got out of bed slowly and went into the bathroom to shave. He didn't have to be all that careful about shaving any more, thank the Good Lord for that. He had dropped out of school when the spells became too frequent and had tried a job. Then one day, while he was shaving, a seizure had hit him when he least expected it. Pat guessed that he had flopped around on the bathroom floor for several minutes before Dar found him, the razor still in his hand. He could have cut his throat and he would never have known it.

But all that was over and done with, since the operation. ''There's nothing wrong with me now, **absolutely nothing,**'' Pat told himself—despite all Dar's talk about Lefty.

Pat filled the basin with hot water, clumsily washed his face, then tried to put a fresh blade in his razor. His left hand seemed more inclined to play with the soap than to hold the razor, but Pat stared straight at it to make it behave, and somehow he managed.

He had managed to stay together with Dar, too, even when the seizures came hot and heavy as a bitch dog in heat. But the seizures practically killed him. He couldn't ride his bike, because he might have a spell at any time, and he resented the fact that Dar could still ride hers if she wanted to. He had hated her for being normal, too, back when he was having a dozen spells or more a day. Black times, those were. He had been so depressed and scared that he was afraid to leave the apartment. He was ready to kill himself—and maybe Dar too.

He had begged the doctors for help, any kind of help at all. At first they said they were doing everything that could be done. But then they told him about a new operation, a scary one. They said they could cut the connective tissue between the two halves of his brain. The two **hemispheres,** as he had learned to call them in one of his Zoo classes. The doctors said it wouldn't hurt much, and the operation might stop the seizures. It might have funny side effects though, they said, but they weren't really sure. However, it was his only chance to get rid of the seizures, and he grabbed at the chance.

''Thank the Good Lord it worked,'' Pat told himself, putting the razor away. He limped back into the bedroom, looking around for his shirt and pants. They were laid out carefully for him, the way Dar always did in the morning—his good clothes, since Dr. Benjamin, the psychologist, was coming to see him in a few minutes.

Pat slipped into his pants rather clumsily, pulling them on chiefly with his good right hand. He zipped up the fly, then reached for his shirt. His pants fell off as he did. ''Dammit,'' he said aloud. He couldn't understand it. He pulled his pants up with his right hand and fixed the zipper, but as he reached again for his shirt with his right hand, his left hand unbuttoned the pants and pulled down the zipper.

''All right, leave the pants alone, will you?''

His left hand really made him angry at times. But shouting at it seemed to help, and he finished dressing in peace, his left hand cooperating nicely for a change. The dark side of his mind had always been something of a sex maniac, and he was better at taking off his pants than putting them on, Pat remembered. That peculiar thought troubled his spirit as he walked slowly into the kitchen.

Dar was cross with him because he had gotten up so late that she had to rush breakfast.

''It's Dr. Benjamin,'' he told her, fixing his coffee. ''It's always tough getting up on the days he comes to visit.''

''Why should that bother you?'' she said, her voice as cold as the scrambled eggs she had just served him.

''Because he always wants to know the things my left hand and foot have been doing, that's why. And I don't like having to admit all that stuff even to a psychologist,'' Pat said loudly.

''Maybe you ought to admit to yourself who Lefty is, while you're admitting things,'' she said. Then she slammed some pots around and walked out on the little balcony of their first-floor apartment, saying she needed some air, leaving him to think about Lefty.

Pat worried with the thought. Dar was always saying that—saying he couldn't face up to who Lefty was and what he was doing to their relationship. But dammit, everything **was** under control. He kept telling her that and telling her that. Dropping his fork into the cold eggs, he stomped out onto the balcony himself, determined to set her straight once and for all.

''Listen, you, we got to get this thing together,'' he practically shouted at her. ''I'm okay, do you hear that? I just need a little time to get it all under control. There's nothing wrong with me that a little time and some understanding from you won't cure.''

''Lefty hates me,'' she said simply, as if that explained all the trouble between them.

''There is no Lefty! I've told you that a thousand times. There's only me. **Me.** Not Pat and Lefty. Just me, **Pat Devine.**''

Darlene ignored him, turning instead to watch a car as it pulled up in front of

Most texts have word lists or glossaries at the end of the book that give definitions of technical terms. Such glossaries are often difficult to use, and few of them tell you how to say the word aloud. The outer margin of each page is reserved for definitions and explanations of the sometimes complicated words or phrases you may encounter in each chapter. Every time you see the symbol (*) following a word in this text, you will know that the word is defined, and often a pronunciation given, in the margin.

If you already understand the word followed by the (*) symbol, don't bother checking it out immediately in the glossary. If you have any doubts about the meaning of the word, or about how to say it aloud, or if you are interested in the Latin or Greek derivation of the term, you may wish to check the item at once, without having to lose your place by turning to the back of the book. Also, when you study for an examination, you may find it helpful to check all the terms in the margins, since many of the key words or thoughts will be defined in this continuous glossary. If you encounter a word you don't understand that is *not* defined in the margins, please check the index at the end of the book to see if the word is defined elsewhere in the text.

Any dictionary contains thousands of words that you know, as well as thousands that you don't know. I hope you will use the continuous glossary in the margins as you would a dictionary, and that you won't be upset if terms are defined that you think every student ought to be familiar with. The first edition of this text was read by several hundred students who were asked to circle every word they didn't understand. The words I have selected for definition are those that *at least* 10 percent of these students didn't know, including some terms that have no direct connection with the science of psychology. This book is for everybody—for people with large vocabularies and for people with limited knowledge but a large desire to learn. If you know most of the words defined in the margins, congratulations! However, you should remember that the person sitting next to you in class may not be as fortunate, and may need all the help any of us can give.

The pronunciations given with the definitions are in the "Midwest dialect" that is used by many radio and television announcers and newscasters. Pronunciations of many words vary from one part of the country to another; if you have doubts about how to say a word, please ask your teacher about it.

Neuron (pronounced NEW-ron). A single nerve cell.

Inputs, internal activities, and outputs. The three functions of all living systems. Food is a type of input that your stomach digests (internal activity) and converts into energy so that you can think and behave (outputs). The remains of the food are also released as waste products (outputs).

their apartment. She waved when she saw Dr. Benjamin get out of the car and start up the walk. Then she turned back to Pat and said slowly, tears in her eyes, "Pat, please tell Dr. Benjamin that Lefty hates me. Maybe he can help."

Something black and terrible broke through into his consciousness. "Bitch," he suddenly snarled at her.

Darlene reacted as if she had been stung by a hornet. She wheeled around and slapped him on the left side of his face.

Quickly, like a snake striking, his left hand lashed out and grabbed hold of Darlene by the neck and started shaking her violently.

She screamed.

Pat suddenly realized what he was doing, and he tried to let go. But he couldn't; he just couldn't! It wasn't him. It was the other guy, the guy in his left hand. It was Lefty that was shaking Dar and trying to choke her!

In desperation Pat grabbed at his left hand with his right hand, trying to pry his left fingers loose from Dar's neck, but they clung to her soft flesh with a mind of their own. Darlene screamed again.

Then Pat remembered the man coming up the front walk.

"Help, Doc!" he cried, "come help me! Lefty's got hold of Darlene and he's trying to kill her!"

(Continued on page 39.)

Your brain is the master organ of your body. During open heart surgery a machine can replace most of the functioning of your heart, as a machine can act in place of your kidneys. But even with mechanical methods of cleaning and pumping your blood, you remain YOU—which is to say that your thoughts, dreams, hopes, and general behavior patterns aren't much affected by mechanical substitutes for most of your bodily functions. However, even tiny damage to critical parts of your brain can cause you to lapse into unconsciousness for the rest of your life, or may turn you from a peaceful, normal, intelligent human being into a monster of some kind. For the brain is the seat of consciousness—the locus of intelligence, compassion, and creativity (and their ugly opposites). Every thought you have, every perception, every sensation, every movement of your body is affected by the activity in your brain. In a very real sense, then, your brain is YOU. What is this master organ like?

THE BRAIN

If you like analogies, consider this one for a moment. In a very limited sense your brain is like a wrinkled mushroom packed tightly inside a bony shell we call the skull. Not counting the skull, your brain weighs about 3 pounds (1.3 kilograms). It is made up of more than 10 billion (10,000,000,000) nerve cells whose activities help determine what you think and feel and learn and do. But these nerve cells, or *neurons* (°), as they are called, do not all have the same tasks to perform. The neurons can function independently, or they can cooperate to achieve some common goal, rather like the employees of a large corporation.

As we will see later on, psychologists often consider business organizations to be "living systems," much like your brain or heart. All living systems have three types of functions—*inputs, internal activities,* and *outputs* (°). A large manufacturing company, such as General Motors, takes in orders from customers and purchases raw materials. These are its inputs. The cars that G.M. produces are its outputs. But a great deal of work is required to turn orders and raw materials into the shiny Chevrolets that G.M. turns out by the millions. The management at G.M. must decide what kinds of automobiles to produce, hire the right number of skilled workers to man the production lines, advertise its products, pay taxes, and worry about solving pollution problems. Information about the outside world is sent to G.M.'s Board of Directors by mail, telephone, telegram, word of mouth, and so on. The Board of Directors looks this information over, checks its files, and then decides how many green, four-door Pontiacs to manufacture and how many pink, two-door, Cadillac Sevilles. Once it makes its decisions, the Board sends memos to its various factories telling them to increase or decrease production of a given type of vehicle. The Board also has ways of keeping tabs on what its employees are actually doing.

Your brain is a living system, too, with its own unique kinds of inputs, internal activities, and outputs. A large collection of neurons (nerve cells) gathered together at the very top of your brain acts very much as does the Board of Directors at G.M. These neurons make up what is called the *cortex* (°) of your brain. Since we will use this term often, perhaps you should know that "cortex" is the Latin word for "bark" (of a tree) or "peel" (of a lemon). And just as the outer skin of a mushroom is often darker and tougher than the inside, so the cortex or outer layer of your brain is different from the neurons inside. The cortex is more than just a skin or peel that protects the rest of the brain, however. The cortex contains millions of very special neurons that seem to be intimately related to your "stream of consciousness," or your moment-to-moment thoughts. It is mostly in your cortex that conscious decisions are made about what your own "corporation" is going to do (the Latin word *corpus* actually means "body").

Of course, it is not entirely accurate to refer to your cortex as your Board of Directors, any more than it would be correct to call G.M.'s Board the "brain" of the corporation. However, this analogy does serve two important purposes. First, it may remind you that your brain is not a single organ; if fact, you have several brains, all of which must function together in harmony if you are to go about the business of being human. Even your cortex is not a single or unitary thing, for, as we will see later in this chapter, each half of your cortex appears to have its own unique personality. And just as you could not understand the decision-making properties of G.M.'s Board without studying the individual characteristics of each member of the Board and how these members relate to each other, so you cannot appreciate the complexity of your behavior if you do not learn something about the many parts of your brain and how they interact with each other. Second, the analogy may help you understand that one of the major duties of your brain is to *process information* and to issue orders to the rest of your body based on the decisions it makes about these inputs. The ability of G.M.'s Board members to process data and to respond wisely helps determine whether that corporate body sinks or swims; the data-handling abilities of your collective brains likewise help decide whether you live or die.

In general, we will use the words "brain" and "cortex" when referring to *physiological* activities inside your skull. The term "Board of Directors" will be employed when we are talking about *mental* or *intra-psychic* processes.

Information about the outside world flows into your cortex along a number of routes called *sensory pathways* (°). Your eyes, ears, nose, tongue, and skin all send messages to the cortex about what is happening around you—and inside you. The cortex processes this incoming sensory information, checks its memory files, and then decides what you should do or think or feel in a given situation. Once your cortical Board of Directors has made a decision, it sends command messages along *motor pathways* (°) to your body's muscles and glands telling them how to react. And just as G.M.'s Board has means of checking up on the activities of its employees, so your body has ways of feeding back information to your cortical Board about how your muscles and glands are really reacting.

If you have had any experience at all with corporations, you will understand that any large company's Board of Directors is made up of "bigshots" whose chief function is to sit and think, to evaluate, and to concern themselves with matters of general policy. Board members do not patrol the plant grounds, type letters,

Cortex (CORE-tex). The thin outer layer of the brain, about ¼ inch (0.64 centimeters) thick. The millions of nerve cells (neurons) in your cortex influence most of what you think, feel, and do.

Sensory pathways. Bundles of nerves rather like telephone cables that feed information about the outside world (inputs) into your brain for processing.

Motor pathways. In physiological or biological terms, the word "motor" means "muscular," or "having to do with movement." The motor pathways are bundles of nerves rather like telephone cables that run from the brain out to the muscles.

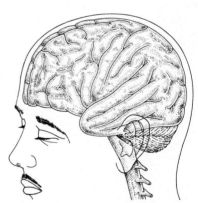

The brain, viewed from the left, has somewhat the appearance of a mushroom sitting atop its stem. The wrinkled, outer surface is the cortex, which is only about a quarter of an inch thick. The spinal cord and the lower centers are the "stem" of the mushroom. The various parts of the brain are described in later pages of this book.

Neural sub-centers. The word "neural" (NEW-ral) means "having to do with neurons or nerve cells." Certain groups or "centers" of neurons in your brain have highly specific functions, unlike those of any other part of your brain. For instance, one neural sub-center called the "amygdala" strongly influences many of your emotions, such as anger and rage.

Demonstrations. In several of these chapters we will suggest experiments that you can try on yourself, if you like doing such things. You can probably understand the material covered just as well, however, even if you prefer reading to doing.

Cerebrum (sair-REE-brum). The big, thick "cap" on the top of your brain. Humans have bigger cerebrums than any other animal. The word "cerebral" (meaning "mental") comes from "cerebrum." Most of the important functions of the brain take place in the cerebrum.

design the product, draw up the advertisements, clean the toilets, or answer the phones. There are separate units or divisions of the corporation to handle each of these chores. Each unit is a kind of sub-corporation, with its own inputs, outputs, and management functions. These sub-corporations take care of their own tasks without bothering the Board members about trivial matters. In fact, the Board of Directors probably has little idea about the moment-to-moment functioning of each of its sub-organizations. Important matters, however, are bucked up the ladder of command to the Board for handling.

Your brain is really a collection of sub-units or *neural centers* that are quite capable of controlling most of the biological functions of your body without bothering your cortical Board with routine matters. Sensory information flows into these *neural sub-centers* (°), is processed, and is acted upon without any conscious decision on your part. For example, when you decide to walk to class, are you conscious of each tiny movement that the muscles in your legs and feet must make to get you there? Surely not, for you would be hard-pressed to keep up with the millions of different neural commands that the lower centers in your brain must issue to your muscles each time you take a simple stroll. These sub-units or neural centers send "memos" to your cortex telling the Board (in general terms) what is going on; in emergency situations, however, the Board may assume direct control. But for the most part, your cortical Board of Directors is free to dream and scheme as it wishes, leaving most of your behavior to be directly monitored by the lower parts of your brain.

QUESTION: If your cortex had to keep your heart pumping and your lungs working, what would happen when your Board went to sleep at night?

Physical Structure of the Brain

If you would like to get a better feel for the physical structure of your brain, you might try this little *demonstration* (°). Pause for a moment and go look at yourself in a mirror. Draw an imaginary horizontal line across the front of your face running from your left ear through both your eyebrows to your right ear. The bulk of your brain is located above this line. If by some magic the flesh and bone shell of your head could be made invisible, you would see the front part of your brain as you stared into the mirror. Viewed this way, your brain would look much like the mountain ranges along the California coast from an airplane; that is, your brain would appear to be a series of rounded hills with deep valleys in between. The outer crust of this brainy landscape is, as we said, the cortex. It is about $\frac{1}{4}$ inch (0.64 centimeters) thick. This cortical rind or peel covers the biggest part of your brain, called the *cerebrum* (°) after the Latin word for "brain."

The cerebrum sits on top of the rest of the brain much as the huge cap of a mushroom sits on top of its skinny stem. Sensory inputs flow up the narrow stem of

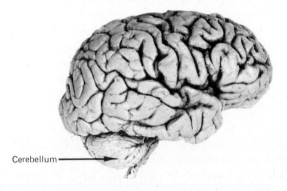

Cerebellum

The human brain, viewed from the right. The **cerebellum** (a Latin word meaning "little brain") at the bottom of the photograph is not a part of the cerebrum, but rather is one of the "lower centers." The cerebellum is involved in coordinating such complex movements as walking, playing the piano, driving a car, and so on.

The brains of lower animals are made up chiefly of sensory-input areas and motor-output areas (such as the cerebellum). The larger the cerebrum is in relation to the rest of the brain, the more complex the behavior the organism is typically capable of. Your cerebrum makes up the major part of your brain and is more than 100 times larger than the cerebrum of the rabbit.

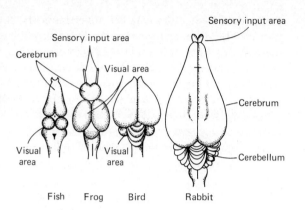

Fish   Frog   Bird   Rabbit

your brain to the cerebrum, are processed by the cortex, and flow down the stem again to your muscles and glands. If you could look at your brain from the top, all you would see would be the cortical covering, or the cap of the cerebral mushroom—the lower centers, or sub-units, are all buried deep in the cerebrum or in the stem itself.

In evolutionary terms, the cerebrum has been the last part of the brain to develop. If you inspected the brains of lower animals, you would find that a human has a better-developed cerebrum than a monkey, that a monkey has more cerebral tissue than a dog, a dog more than a rat, a rat more than a pigeon, and a pigeon more than a goldfish. Most psychologists believe that, in general terms, the more well developed an animal's cerebrum is, the more complex its behavior patterns are likely to be. Very simple animals, such as worms and insects, have brains made up just of the "stem of the mushroom." Lacking cerebrums, they must make do with what in man are called "the lower centers." The simplest forms of life, such as single-celled organisms, don't even have brains at all. Complex intellectual functions—such as writing poems and performing scientific experiments—are controlled by your cerebrum and its cortex. Perhaps these facts help explain why countless biology students are able to study the earthworm, but no one has ever noticed a cerebrumless worm studying humans. It takes a very large corporate structure indeed to produce such a complex product as a poem—or a Pontiac.

A Portuguese Man-o-War, a simple form of life without a brain.

THE BRAIN AND BEHAVIOR

Most companies manufacture a specific product or a series of products that keeps them in business. From a biological point of view, the brain manufactures behavior. Its primary purpose is to create muscular and glandular reactions, just as General Motors' primary purpose is to produce automobiles. The "employees" that make up the corporate brain and produce the behavior are the individual nerve cells, or neurons. When the neurons are functioning well, they take in messages properly; they make the right "corporate decisions"; and reactions flow off the neural assembly line in satisfactory fashion. When the neurons become sick or disturbed, various parts of this input-output process are badly upset.

If your input neurons were damaged or drugged, you might suffer from various kinds of *hallucinations* (°). That is, you might see things that weren't there; hear voices when no one is speaking; or fail to detect important changes in your sensory environment. We will discuss these problems in the next chapter, when we investigate the effects that various drugs can have on the brain.

If your processing neurons are disturbed, you may suffer a memory loss; you may under-react or over-react to emotional situations; your judgment may become clouded; you may faint or fall into an abnormal sleep called a *coma* (°); or your

Hallucinations (hal-LOO-see-NAY-shuns). Seeing or hearing things that aren't really there. If you attend a horror movie, and see a ghost on the way home, the ghost is probably an hallucination manufactured by your fear, rather than being a true sensory input.

Coma (KO-mah). An unusual form of deep sleep from which the person usually cannot be easily awakened. Usually caused by drugs, fever, or brain injury.

Motor epilepsy (EP-ee-LEP-see). A type of muscular seizure or attack.

Grand mal seizure (grahn mahl). Perhaps the most dramatic, terrifying type of motor epilepsy. The French words *grand mal* mean "big sickness" (the final "d" in "grand" is not pronounced).

Symptom (SIM-tum or SIMP-tum). The visible evidence of a disease or disturbance. Headache, runny nose, and sore throat are often symptoms of a cold. The unusual speech patterns and behaviors some people show are sometimes symptoms of mental illness.

Board of Directors may become so confused that it issues orders that lead other people to think that you are insane. We will have a great deal more to say about some of these problems in later chapters.

If for any reason the output neurons start functioning abnormally, their behavioral product can sometimes be as clumsily put together as would a Pontiac assembled by completely intoxicated workmen. Damage to the output systems of the brain can lead to a loss of muscular coordination; to paralysis of the muscles in the arms, legs, or any other part of the body; or even to a condition known as *motor epilepsy* (°) or a *grand mal seizure* (°).

QUESTION: Suppose a young man was hit over the head in a fight, and the doctor treating him suspected brain damage even though the man's skull wasn't broken; how might the doctor get a rough idea of the location of any injury to the brain without having to open up the man's skull and look inside?

EPILEPSY

If you were walking down a dark street one night and were suddenly attacked by a stranger, you might very well have to fight for your life. Whenever the neurons in your brain are stimulated by certain kinds of chemicals, or are physically damaged, they too may put on abnormal bursts of activity as if they were defending themselves from invasion. We refer to these unusual bursts of neural energy as *epilepsy*, taking the term from a Greek word meaning "to seize" or "to attack." If the site of the damaged nerve cells is in the input or processing areas of the brain, the epilepsy may occasionally go unrecognized. In fact, it was not until very recently that we realized that epilepsy could affect these parts of the nervous system. If the injured neurons are in the output system, however, the seizure is referred to as *motor epilepsy* and is very hard to overlook. During a full-blown motor seizure, most of the muscles in the person's body suddenly contract. As the lungs squeeze shut, the air forced out may cause the person to scream or moan. The individual typically loses consciousness and falls to the ground, rigid or stiff as a board. For a minute or so, all breathing may cease. Then the person's arms and legs may begin twitching or jerking rhythmically, and the person may lose control of his or her bladder and bowels.

Motor seizures are usually over and done with in five minutes or less, but the person may be confused or sleepy or have a headache for some time thereafter. Typically, the individual will have little or no memory either of what led up to the seizure itself or of the period of confusion that followed. Within an hour or so, the person may be completely back to normal—until the next attack occurs.

If the brain damage is mild, or if the attack is caused by an overdose of some drug such as alcohol, the seizures may occur very infrequently, perhaps no more than once or twice a year. In rare instances, the damage is so severe that the attacks may happen several times a day—so frequently that the person does not regain consciousness between seizures. This rare condition must be treated promptly, for it can lead to death.

Scientists study brain conditions like epilepsy for several reasons. First, in order to be of help to the person who is suffering from the disease. (More than 4 million people in the United States suffer from some form of epilepsy.) But second, because we often learn a great deal about the *normal* functioning of an organ by trying to find out why it sometimes functions *abnormally*. An epileptic attack is a signal or *symptom* (°) that tells us that something has gone wrong in a person's brain, just as high blood pressure is a sign that something has gone wrong with a person's heart or blood vessels. But just as high blood pressure does not tell us exactly what the difficulty with the person's circulation is, neither does an epileptic seizure tell us exactly what is wrong with the person's brain. For there are many different types of epilepsy and they have many different causes. The scientific study of epilepsy has taught us much about the normal functioning of the brain, so we will mention this *bizarre* (°) and devastating disease several times in these opening chapters. Before we can understand the true nature of the epileptic attack, however, we will first have to look at how the neurons in your brain actually work.

THE NEURON

The individual nerve cells in your brain usually function much as you yourself would if you were employed by a corporation of some kind—which is to say that they work fairly continuously at their own tasks and do their best to cooperate with their neighbors. Although neurons may vary considerably among themselves in size and shape (as do people), neurons are all made up of three main parts— the *dendrites*, the *soma*, or *cell body*, and the *axon* (°).

The Dendrites

The front end, or input side, of a cortex neuron is a network of tiny fibers that reaches out like feelers from the cell body to make contact with surrounding nerve cells. These feeler fibers are called *dendrites*. It is generally thought that electrical activity in the dendrites is what causes the brain waves that we will discuss in detail later on. Anyone who studies how to go into a *meditative trance* (°) in order to achieve a state of inner peace and happiness is, in part, learning how to control the electrical activity in the dendrites of his or her cortical neurons.

The Soma

The main part, or body, of the cell is called the *soma*. It is inside the soma that most of the complex chemical reactions occur that keep the cell alive and functioning. The soma, then, is the processing part of the nerve cell. Many of the drugs that affect human behavior do so because they speed up or slow down the chemical processes that occur naturally and continuously in the soma or cell body of the neuron.

The Axon

The action end, or output area, of the neuron is called the *axon*, which stretches back like a telephone cable from the soma and sends tiny fibers to the dendrites and cell bodies of nearby neurons, or to the muscles and glands in the rest of the body.

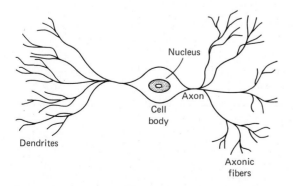

Resting potential. The amount of electrical energy stored up by a nerve cell that can be discharged in a short burst. The amount of money you have to spend at any one time is, in a sense, your financial potential.

NEURAL FIRING

One of the major purposes of the neuron is to pass messages, or information, from one part of the body to another. Each nerve cell contains a certain amount of stored-up electrical energy—the *resting potential* (*)—that it can discharge in short bursts just as the battery in your car can release a burst of energy to start the car when you turn the ignition key.

Consider three nerve cells in your brain that are connected together in sequence, in *A-B-C* fashion. The axon of *A* makes contact with the dendrites of *B*, and the axon of *B* makes contact with the dendrites of *C*. All three cells have a certain (and very similar) amount of potential energy to call upon when necessary. When a message is to be passed from *A* to *C*, a chemical change occurs in the axon of *A* that triggers off a brief burst of electrical energy in the dendrites of *B*. This burst of electro-chemical energy sweeps the length of the *B* cell, beginning in *B*'s dendrites and moving wave-like to the end of *B*'s axon. When this wave reaches the tips of *B*'s axonic fibers, it causes a chemical change to occur that triggers off a similar burst of electrical energy in neuron *C*. Thus, the message has been passed from *A* to *C* through *B*.

Whenever a wave of electrical energy passes from the dendrites to the axonic fibers, we say that a nerve has "fired," because the action involved is much like the firing of a gun. There is a great deal of potential energy stored in the chemical gunpowder in a bullet. When you pull the trigger on a gun, you translate this potential chemical energy into the mechanical energy of an explosion, and the bullet is propelled down the barrel of the gun.

Let us carry the bullet analogy a step further. The neuron behaves in some ways as if it were a machine gun. If you press the trigger on a machine gun very lightly, you can fire the shells slowly, individually, one by one. But if you press down hard on the trigger, you can fire off whole bursts of bullets in a second or two. In similar fashion, if you tap very lightly on your arm, the receptor (input) nerve cells in your skin will fire at a very slow rate—a few times a second. If you press very hard on your arm, these same input neurons can fire hundreds or even thousands of times per second. Every time you move a muscle—or think a thought—you do so in part because one group of nerve cells in your brain fires off messages to your muscles, glands, or to other groups of neurons.

As long as you are alive, all of the neurons in your brain will be firing at one speed or another. When you are engaged in vigorous mental or physical activity,

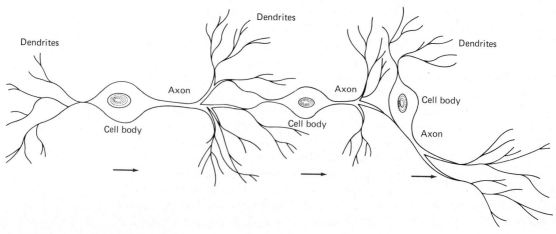

A sequence of brain nerve cells.

most of these nerve cells will be responding rapidly—for they will have a great deal of information to process. As we will see in Chapter 6, your brain is particularly sensitive to changes in your environment. Therefore, much of the activity that goes on in your brain is initially triggered off by stimulus inputs from the world around you. But even when you are resting or fast asleep, your nerve cells will still be active—although most of them will be firing very slowly if you are deeply asleep. We will have more to say about these patterns of nerve cell activity in just a moment.

The Synapse

Now, let us go back to neurons *A*, *B*, and *C*. The axonic end-fibers of *A* come close to, *but do not actually touch*, the dendrites of cell *B*. The fluid-filled space between *A*'s axonic fibers and *B*'s dendrites is called the *synapse* (°). This synapse is so tiny that you would have trouble seeing it even using the most powerful microscope. When two neurons make contact with each other, as do *A* and *B* in our example, we say that they "make *synapse* with each other." The synaptic space between two nerve cells is really a small canal—a canal filled with fluid that contains many different types of chemical substances. These chemicals all have a definite, and in the case of epilepsy, sometimes a devastating effect on your behavior.

The message that one neuron passes along to another is a series of bursts of energy—like a stream of bullets fired from one nerve cell and hitting the bull's eye on the next nerve cell. When a neuron fires and a wave of electrical energy shoots along the length of the cell and reaches the axonic fibers at the end, tiny drops of chemicals (called "packets") are released into the synaptic canal. As we will see in more detail in the next chapter, these chemical "packets" move across the synaptic canal and react with the dendrites of the next cell, causing that cell to fire. Since these chemicals serve to transmit information from one cell to another, they are called *transmitters* (°). The more that cell *A* fires, the more transmitter chemicals *A*'s axonic end-fibers release into the synaptic fluid, and the more often cell *B* is triggered into firing.

Nerve cells have many functions. There are neurons in your eyes and ears— called *receptor cells* (°) or input neurons—that sense or detect changes in the world around you and relay information about those changes to your brain. Specialized *processing cells* (°) react to this incoming information by checking your memories to determine its importance and emotional value, and then decide how your body should react. Output or *motor neurons* (°) relay the decision to your muscles and glands, thus causing your body to go into action. These motor neurons actually make synapse with the muscles much as the cortical neurons make synapse with each other. When a motor neuron fires, it releases transmitters into the canal between its own axon and the muscle it connects to. These packets of chemicals cross the synaptic canal and cause the muscle to twitch or contract. Even the most complex muscular reactions—a rock musician playing a crashing chord on a guitar or a secretary typing 100 words a minute on a typewriter—are made up of orderly patterns of individual muscle contractions. All these reactions are brought about by the firing of motor neurons and the release of transmitter chemicals at the *neuro-muscular* (nerve-muscle) *synapse* (°).

If all your neurons were connected in simple *A-B-C* fashion, your behavioral potentialities would be correspondingly simple. In fact, in the decision-making centers of your brain, the dendrites of any nerve cell *B* are likely to make synapse with (and hence receive messages from) axonic fibers from a thousand or more different *A*s—and *B*'s own axonic end-fibers are likely to make synapse with (and hence pass messages along to) the dendrites of a thousand or more *C*s. We will

Synapse (SIN-aps). The extremely narrow, fluid-filled space between two nerve cells. When the axonic fibers of one neuron come close to the dendrites or cell body of a second neuron, the first can cause the second to fire; therefore, the two neurons "make synapse with each other."

Transmitters (TRANS-mitt-ers). Chemicals released into the synapse by the axonic fibers of one neuron that cause the second neuron to fire.

Receptor cells. Nerve cells in your eyes, ears, skin, and the rest of your body that receive information about your own body and the world around you; input neurons.

Processing cells. Nerve cells in your brain that respond to information coming from the receptor cells. "Thinking" and "feeling" appear to be functions of the processing cells.

Motor neurons. Nerve cells with very long axons. The dendrites and cell body are usually in a motor center in the brain; the axon stretches out like a telephone cable from the brain to make synapse with other neurons and from thence to individual muscles somewhere in the body.

Neuro-muscular synapse (NEW-ro). The synapse or connection point between a motor neuron and a muscle.

Neurologist (new-RAH-low-jist). A medical doctor who treats nerve diseases.

Neuro-physiologist (NEW-ro FIZZ-ee-OLL-oh-jist). A scientist who studies the functioning of neurons.

Electrode (ee-LEK-trode). A device used to detect electrical activity in the brain. Disk-electrodes are coin-shaped pieces of metal that can be placed against the head to read brain waves. Needle-electrodes are thin wires inserted through holes in the skull directly into the brain.

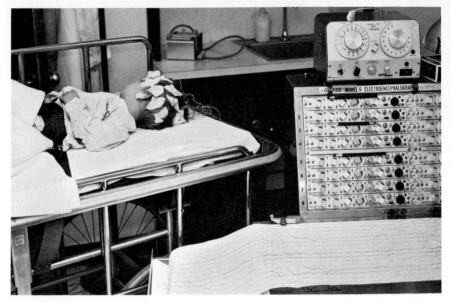

A patient hooked up to an EEG machine.

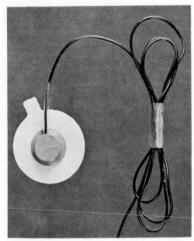

An electrode.

Electro-encephalo-graph (ee-LEK-tro en-SEF-uh-low graf). An electronic machine that makes a graphic record of brain waves. *Cephalo* is the Greek word for "head."

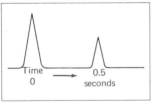

EEG record

describe these complex inter-connections in more detail when we discuss learning and perception later in this book. For the moment, it is enough to realize that any given neuron in your brain is likely to be connected to thousands of its neighboring neurons.

The EEG

How does epilepsy occur? Under normal conditions the nerve cells in your brain act as independent agents, each performing their individual tasks as necessary—much as the workers on an assembly line would be doing quite different things at any given point in time; yet each would be busy working toward a common goal. If a nerve doctor, often called a *neurologist* (°) or a *neuro-physiologist* (°), wanted to get an idea of how your brain was performing, he or she might place a small piece of metal called an *electrode* (°) on the outside of your head. The electrode would be connected by wires to a machine called an *electro-encephalo-graph* (°). This EEG machine, as it is called, translates electrical energy from your brain into visual patterns on a screen (much as a television set translates electrical energy into patterns you can see on the picture tube). Each time a nerve cell close to the electrode would fire, the electrode would record this event on the picture tube of the EEG machine. If, by some chance, all the cells in your brain near the electrode were silent for a second or two, the picture tube would show a flat, horizontal line. If one or two cells fired at exactly the same time, the line would have a tiny pip or peak in it. If a thousand cells fired at exactly the same time, the peak would be very high indeed. If these thousand cells all fired now (let's call it "time zero") and then half of them fired again a second later, the screen would show a large peak at time zero and a peak half as large a second later.

In a sense, the EEG gives you the same sort of fuzzy, imprecise picture of what is going on inside the skull that you would get if you stood outside a huge football stadium and tried to guess what was occurring inside from listening to the roar of the crowd. Standing outside the stadium, you could tell whether the football game was exciting, and when an important play had been made; but you couldn't tell which team had the ball or what the score was (much less what individual

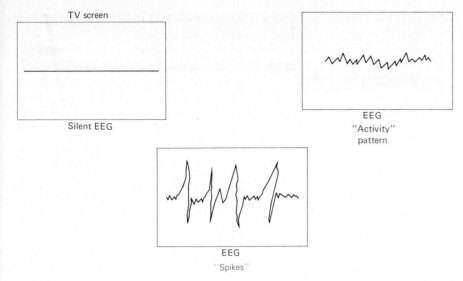

TV screen

Silent EEG

EEG
"Activity"
pattern

EEG
"Spikes"

members of the crowd were doing or thinking). The EEG electrode "listens" outside the skull to the electrical noise made inside by thousands of individual neurons, but all it can tell you is how active the bulk of the nerve cells are, not the behavior patterns of each single neuron.

When you are actively engaged in thought (as when you are mentally trying to work through a difficult problem), electrodes on your skull would detect and display on the EEG machine a more-or-less random pattern of electrical activity. This random pattern is a sign that each of the nerve cells near the electrode is operating independently, taking care of its own business. We call such an electrical output the *activity pattern* (°), since it typically means that your brain is actively engaged in some kind of work.

Under certain conditions, however, the nerve cells in a given part of your brain can begin to fire more and more together, in unison or *synchrony* (°). When this firing in synchrony occurs, waves of electrical activity can sweep across the surface of your brain like ocean waves sweeping up on a beach. The electrode on your skull would translate these synchronous brain waves into wavy lines on the EEG machine. And just as you can tell something about the wind and weather by measuring the size and shape and rhythm of ocean waves, so you can tell something about the weather inside your brain by looking at your own EEG record.

When you relax and close your eyes, the visual parts of your brain (which are located primarily on the rear surface of your brain) will show rather fast waves called alpha waves or the *alpha rhythm* (°). (In the next chapter we will tell you how you can learn to relax even in fairly tense situations by training yourself to produce the alpha rhythm waves at will.)

When you go to sleep, brain-wave activity generally slows down and becomes more synchronous. The large, slow sleep waves that occur in your brain when you are deeply asleep are called delta waves or the *delta rhythm* (°).

The Chemical Causes of Epilepsy

If your EEG record showed the activity pattern or the alpha or delta rhythms, it would mean that things are probably rather normal in your brain. However, in the brain of an epileptic, things are sometimes quite different.

When a part of a person's brain is badly damaged, scar tissue often occurs. The

Activity pattern. The rather random pattern of brain waves the EEG picks up when you are actively engaged in thought.

Synchrony (SINK-ron-ee). Coordinated activities. The members of a college band march (and play) in synchrony.

Alpha rhythm (AL-fa). When you are resting peacefully with your eyes closed, the visual regions of your brain at the back of your head will show a brain wave that repeats itself about 10-12 times per second. This is the alpha rhythm. If you are listening to music with your eyes closed, the visual regions will show the alpha rhythm, but the hearing regions of the brain will typically show the activity pattern. When you are reading a good book, the situation is often reversed–the visual brain will show the activity pattern and the hearing regions of the brain will show the alpha rhythm.

Delta rhythm (DELL-tah). Most of the time you are asleep, your brain will produce big waves that repeat themselves less than 4 times per second.

ALPHA

DELTA

Alpha rhythm in the brain is made up of electrical waves that have a frequency of 10 or so cycles per second. The delta rhythm registers on an EEG machine as large, slow waves that have a frequency of about 1-3 cycles per second.

Hyper-synchrony (HIGH-per SINK-ron-ee). When too many of the nerve cells fire in unison.

Spikes. Unusual, very large bursts of electrical activity that usually are symptoms of brain damage when they appear on an EEG record.

Petit mal (PET-tee mahl). A brief epileptic attack in which the person typically loses consciousness for a few seconds.

Tumor (TOO-more). An abnormal and often cancerous growth anywhere on or in the body.

Dilantin (die-LAN-tin). A drug used to help control epileptic seizures.

chemicals that ooze from this scar tissue can build up in nearby synapses and act as transmitters. If this build-up gets out of hand—as it occasionally does in epilepsy—so much of this scar-tissue transmitter is produced that the neurons nearby begin to fire very, very rapidly—and too much in unison. This condition is known as *hyper-synchrony* (°). The scar-stimulated neurons rapidly gain control of all the neurons to which they are connected, and the hyper-synchrony spreads like wildfire. Soon all the neurons near the scar are firing in unison. Pulsing waves of electrical activity rapidly spread over the brain, much as ocean waves can pound frantically at a beach during a storm.

These abnormal, hyper-synchronous bursts of electrical activity show up on the EEG record as *spikes* (°). If the hyper-synchrony is limited to a small area of the brain—and particularly if the damage is in the input areas of the brain—the affected person may experience little more than a queasy feeling or quick hallucination that is soon forgotten. Indeed, the person may not realize that anything abnormal has happened in his or her brain.

If the seizure affects the processing areas of the brain that are associated with consciousness, the person may black out for a second or two—and then continue as if nothing had happened. Such a seizure is called a *petit mal* (°) attack, from the French term that means "small illness."

If the hyper-synchrony reaches the motor or output parts of the brain, however, a motor epilepsy or *grand mal* ("large illness") attack occurs. During the grand mal seizure, the motor neurons begin firing in rapid pulses; the muscles start contracting in rapid rhythm, and the convulsions we described earlier occur.

If you have ever seen anyone suffer an epileptic seizure, you know what a distressing event it can be. The person affected appears to be seized by some external force or agency that takes over control of his or her body. It is little wonder, then, that until very recently most people believed that the epileptic was being possessed by a devil or evil spirit. However, as we have seen, epileptic attacks are triggered by complex chemical changes within the brain and usually are the result of some kind of injury to the neurons—a blow to the head, brain damage during birth, a high fever, a disease, or a *tumor* (°). Eating or drinking certain chemicals (including an excess of alcohol) can also bring on a seizure.

During a grand mal attack, the scar-transmitter chemicals are used up, and it typically takes a while for enough of these chemicals to build up to set off another seizure that involves the whole brain. However, the neurons right next to the scar tissue are continuously affected, and they may show spikes every few seconds, even when the grand mal attacks occur only every few weeks. Medical doctors can often track down the exact location of the scar tissue by putting electrodes all over a person's skull and noting where the spike activity is greatest. If the scar is on the surface of the brain, a surgeon can sometimes cure the problem by cutting out the damaged tissue (surgery usually produces a much "cleaner" scar than does injury or disease). However, the site of the scar tissue is often deep down inside the brain or is so widespread or subtle that it cannot be located precisely with the EEG machine. In such cases, treatment usually consists of giving the patient an anti-transmitter drug such as *Dilantin* (°). Marijuana has also been reported to be effective in reducing the frequency of epileptic seizures, as we will see in the next chapter. Any drug that makes it more difficult for the neurons to fire in hyper-synchrony will help prevent epileptic attacks.

Occasionally the damage to a patient's brain is so extensive that neither surgery nor drugs can control the seizures. These patients, though small in number, were rather pitiful cases for whom medical science offered little hope—until recently. Then, in the 1950's, a number of "animal" psychologists began studying what happened to rats and cats when their brains were "split in half" surgically. At the beginning of their research, these psychologists had no real thought that their work might be of rather immediate help to epileptic patients. The scientists were merely trying to discover some basic facts about the way that animal brains function. As it turned out, their findings were not only fascinating from a scientific point of view but of practical value as well.

THE SPLIT BRAIN

A few pages back, we left you standing in front of a mirror trying to look at the mountains and valleys of your cerebrum. For just a moment, let's go back to that rugged cortical landscape again. The biggest valley of all runs from front to back and divides your brain into two main parts or *cerebral hemispheres* (°), as they are called. As you stare at yourself in the mirror, you might draw an imaginary vertical line right down the center of your face. First cover the left half of your face with your left hand, and then the right half of your face with your right hand. If you look at yourself carefully, you will notice that the left part of you is a mirror image of the right—including your hands. In scientific terms, your whole body is *bilaterally symmetrical* (°). All of the higher animals—including humans—are bilaterally symmetrical. Which is to say, if you split any of these animals in half from top to bottom, the right and left halves of their bodies would be symmetrical, mirror images.

The central valley of your brain divides your sphere-shaped cerebrum into right and left hemispheres. If you could inspect them closely in your mirror, you would see that these two hemispheres look almost identical—just as your left and right hands appear to be reversed images of each other.

From a functional viewpoint, however, there are major differences between the two hemispheres—just as there are functional differences between your right and left hands. There are many things that you can do easily with one hand that you perform poorly with the other, if at all. If you are right-handed, as about 90 percent of the people in the world are, you write with your right hand but probably have trouble doing so with your left. If you are left-handed, then you will typically write well with your left hand but not with your right.

If you are right-handed, why can't you write with your left? The answer seems to lie in your brain, not in your hands. As confusing as it may seem to you at first, your right cerebral hemisphere mainly controls the left side of your body, and your left cerebral hemisphere mainly controls the right side of your body. If you are right-handed, your left hemisphere is *dominant* (°). When you speak or write, you do so with your dominant left hemisphere. When you think or scheme about something by "talking to yourself," you probably do so with your major or dominant left hemisphere. Your right or *minor hemisphere* (°) is mainly silent; on its own, it can neither talk nor write very well. If you damaged certain language areas in your major (left) hemisphere, you might lose the ability to speak or to write. You might even forget the meaning of words. This inability to communicate through written or spoken language is called *aphasia* (°), and its primary cause is damage to the major hemisphere of the cerebrum.

If you are left-handed, the situation is much more confused. It may be that, like many left-handers, the right half of your cerebrum is the major hemisphere and produces most of your spoken and written language. However, in some "southpaws," both hemispheres share the language ability and neither of them is really "dominant." Interestingly enough, these left-handed people who lack a major hemisphere often show a slight imprecision in their speech patterns. That is, they can communicate almost any thought they wish to, but they often speak in a sloppy or involved fashion and frequently misuse words ever so slightly.

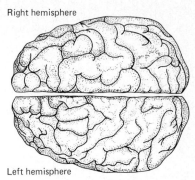

Right hemisphere

Left hemisphere

A top view of the human brain showing the left and right hemispheres. The corpus callosum is a bridge of tissue that connects the two halves of the brain; it lies deep within the brain (just above the level of the eyes) and cannot be seen in this picture.

Cerebral hemispheres (ser-REE-bral HEM-ee-spheres). The two halves of the globe-shaped or spherical cerebrum; the two main halves of the brain.

Bilaterally symmetrical (buy-LATT-er-al-lee sim-METT-tree-cal). Any object whose left half is a mirror image of the right is said to be bilaterally symmetrical.

Dominant hemisphere. The half of the cerebrum that dominates or controls such activities as speech. Also called "major hemisphere."

Minor hemisphere. The non-dominant half of the cerebrum which is a "silent partner" to the dominant or major hemisphere.

Aphasia (uh-FAZE-ya). The inability to recognize the meaning of words, or to speak or write in meaningful terms. Aphasia is usually a symptom of some kind of brain damage.

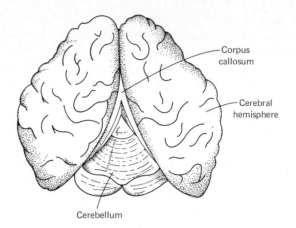

Corpus
callosum

Cerebral
hemisphere

Cerebellum

Corpus callosum (KOR-pus kah-LOW-sum). The bridge of nervous tissue that connects the major and the minor hemispheres.

The Corpus Callosum

The two cerebral hemispheres of your brain are joined together in the center, much as the two halves of a walnut are connected in the middle. This slim bridge of connecting tissue between the two hemispheres is called the *corpus callosum* (°), two Latin words meaning "thick or hardened body." The corpus callosum contains a large number of axonic fibers that act like telephone cables running from one side of your brain to the other. The major and minor hemispheres keep in touch with each other by long-distance messages that pass through the corpus callosum.

When your corpus callosum is intact, as it is in most people, sensory inputs that reach one hemisphere are almost automatically flashed to the other. And when your left hemisphere sends an output message to the muscles in your right hand—telling them to write the word *dog* with a pencil—an "information copy" of the message is sent to the right hemisphere as well so that it can keep up with what is going on in the other half of your brain.

Should your right hemisphere order your left hand to scratch your nose, it would also let your left hemisphere know what it is doing—by sending a message across the corpus callosum. Actually, however, the minor hemisphere probably takes directions from the major hemisphere most of the time.

Why should one hemisphere dominate the other? Well, consider for a moment the movements your body makes when you perform a simple task like walking down a street. Your left leg moves in perfect sequence with your right, and your right arm swings in rhythm with your left. But your right leg and arm are controlled by your left hemisphere, while your left arm and leg are directly under the control of your right hemisphere. What coordinates these complex muscular activities? Can you imagine what would happen if your left hemisphere ordered its arm and leg to *stop*, while your right hemisphere told its arm and leg to go?

When two people dance, one partner must usually lead, while the other follows. At birth perhaps, or shortly thereafter, one hemisphere probably gains the lead over the other and takes over major control of the whole body. By the time an infant is old enough to talk, the major hemisphere is the only one that really needs to learn the language, while its twin remains dumb. (The *tendency* to be right- or left-handed is probably inherited. However, our society is "right-handed"; many parents attempt to impose right-handedness on their children by offering toys to the child's right hand, by making the child "shake hands" as the parents do, and so on.)

The major hemisphere controls its side of your body directly. It controls the other side of you by long distance—that is, by sending orders across the corpus callosum to neural centers in the minor hemisphere. There are also indirect output pathways from each hemisphere to both sides of the body. These indirect pathways, which handle only motor output but *not* informational input, bypass the corpus callosum by running through the lower parts of the brain. Theoretically, either hemisphere could control the movements of both sides of your body by sending output orders through these indirect motor pathways—but the other hemisphere wouldn't know what was happening because it wouldn't receive an "information copy" of the command via the corpus callosum.

Under normal conditions, however, these indirect control routes seem not to be used very much, perhaps for two reasons. First, the corpus callosum bridge is a much more efficient way for the dominant side of your brain to coordinate movements. Second, it is likely that the dominant hemisphere would resist having the minor hemisphere send out orders that the major hemisphere wasn't aware of—and hence couldn't control.

Whatever the case, the minor hemisphere seems mostly to follow orders that come to it across the corpus callosum, although it is technically capable of thinking and acting on its own. Even in the case of *ambi-dexterous* people (°), who can write with both hands, one hemisphere appears to be dominant and to handle language functions much better than the other.

Now, with all these facts in mind, can you guess what would happen to you if your corpus callosum were cut, and the two hemispheres of your brain were suddenly disconnected?

This is the question that psychologists R.W. Sperry and R.E. Myers were trying to answer when, in 1953, they performed their first split-brain operation on cats.

Two Minds in the Same Body

The surgical technique used by Sperry and Myers involved opening up the cat's skull, then slicing the animal's corpus callosum and a few of the sensory input pathways to both hemispheres. Normally, sensory input from *each* eye goes to

Ambi-dextrous (AM-bee DEX-ter-ous). Someone who is equally skilled in the use of the right and left hands.

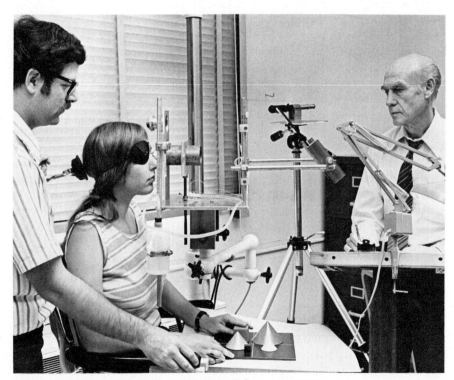

Roger Sperry in his laboratory with his split-brain apparatus.

both cerebral hemispheres. The split-brain surgery, however, left the cat's eyes as isolated from each other as were the two halves of its cerebrum. Now, whatever the animal's left eye saw was recorded only in the left hemisphere; and whatever the animal's right eye saw was recorded only in the right hemisphere.

Immediately after the operation the cats typically had difficulties coordinating their movements. But after a while their behavior became fairly normal again. Either the two hemispheres had learned to cooperate with each other, or both sides of the brain took turns in controlling the entire body using the indirect pathways already mentioned.

Once a cat seemed recovered from the surgery, Sperry and Myers gave it various sorts of training. First they blindfolded its left eye and taught the cat to solve a visual problem using just its right eye (and, of course, just the right hemisphere of its brain). Next, when the cat had learned this first lesson well, they switched the blindfold to the trained right eye and tested the cat with its untrained left eye (and left hemisphere). The question was, would any information about the problem have leaked from the right half of the cat's brain to the left?

The answer was a resounding *no*. Using just its untrained left eye, the cat appeared to be entirely ignorant of what it had just learned with its right eye. When Sperry and Myers trained the left eye in similar fashion, the right eye (and hemisphere) seemed unaware of what the left part of the brain had learned. The cat now had two "minds," either of which was capable of learning on its own and of responding intelligently to changes in the world around it. Subsequent experiments with rats and monkeys gave similar results. However, the animals recovered so nicely that if you hadn't known about their operation, you might not have been able to guess that there were two more-or-less independent "identities" inside each animal's body.

The split-brain operation was seemingly safe and relatively easy to perform. But what would it do to a human, and why would anyone want to find out?

Epilepsy and the Corpus Callosum

Epilepsy is an odd disease. The scar tissue that causes a seizure usually has a specific locus or location on one side of the brain. If you took an EEG record from this damaged area, you would see continual spike responses. If you put an electrode at this same point in the other hemisphere, the EEG record would usually look normal. At the onset of an epileptic attack, however, you would detect spikes on both sides of the brain. How could there be spike responses coming from healthy brain tissue?

Almost every neuron in your *left* hemisphere has a nerve cell in your *right* hemisphere that is its mirror image. Many of these nerve cells are tied together by axonic fibers that pass through the corpus callosum. Whenever a neuron in your dominant hemisphere fires, it may send a command message telling its mirror-image cell in the minor hemisphere to fire too. And whenever the mirror-image neuron fires, it sends a message back to the dominant hemisphere saying that it *has* fired. These command messages are the primary way in which your dominant hemisphere coordinates activities in both sides of your brain.

Whenever an epileptic seizure begins at a point in one hemisphere, the mirror-image neurons in the other hemisphere receive a seizure message via the corpus callosum. These mirror-image nerve cells may then "catch fire" too and begin showing spike responses on their own. So the spike activity begins to build up simultaneously at the same spot in both hemispheres. Worse than this, the mirror-image neurons may send seizure messages back to the original site of the trouble. This return message from the undamaged hemisphere sets off even more spiking in the damaged area, which then sends even wilder messages back to the mirror-image cells, which causes them to fire even more rapidly.

Each time the seizure message flashes back and forth across the corpus callosum, a few more cells in each hemisphere get caught up in the spiking. Within a few seconds, the whole brain can become involved, and a grand mal attack occurs.

An epileptic seizure is a good example of what is called a *positive feedback loop* (°). Suppose you are talking on the phone to a friend. He says something mildly critical to you that you don't particularly appreciate, so you take a verbal swipe at him in return. Your response annoys him, for he thinks it is uncalled for, and he feeds back to you an even cruder remark, which makes you rather angry, so you call him a very dirty name, which infuriates him; rapidly the matter builds into a fight and an emotional explosion takes place.

Explosions are almost always the result of a positive feedback loop, whether they occur in a stick of dynamite, on the telephone, or in the brain. If we could cut the telephone wire between you and your friend before things got out of hand, we could sever the loop, stop the increasingly critical feedback, and prevent the emotional explosion from taking place.

When medical doctors learned of the Sperry-Myers split-brain operation, they reasoned that if they cut the corpus callosum and separated the two hemispheres of the brain, they might prevent full-blown epileptic seizures from occurring in patients for whom Dilantin and ordinary surgery just didn't work. And the doctors were right. They tried the operation on a middle-aged man whom we shall call John Doe. During the Korean War John Doe had served in the armed forces. He had parachuted behind enemy lines, had been captured, and was struck on the head several times with a rifle butt while in an enemy concentration camp. Shortly thereafter, his epileptic seizures began. By the time John Doe was released from the prison camp, his brain was in such bad physical shape that neither surgery nor drugs could help much. His seizures increased in frequency and intensity until they were occurring a dozen or more times a day. Without the split-brain operation, John Doe would probably have died—or committed suicide, as had many other patients with similar problems.

After the surgeons cut John Doe's corpus callosum, his seizures stopped almost completely—just as the surgeons had expected. And although the doctors had assumed that both sides of John Doe's brain would be able to function independently, they weren't totally prepared for what actually happened. For, when the doctors split John Doe's brain, they also cut his "mind" into two separate but similar personalities—each of which existed more-or-less independently of the other, and each of which had its own unique claim on his body.

John-Doe-Left and John-Doe-Right

Immediately after the operation John Doe was able to communicate in almost normal fashion. Some of his speech was slurred, as if he didn't have complete control over the muscles in his tongue, but his thinking seemed clear and logical, and he suffered no visible loss in intelligence. But John Doe did have moments of confusion, and he was often unable to coordinate his body movements. Every now and then, he reported, the left half of his body "did odd things," as if it had a will of its own. The doctors soon began to suspect that when John Doe answered their questions and reported his feelings, it was only his dominant (left) hemisphere that was doing the talking.

As we mentioned earlier, the input pathways to each hemisphere of the brain can sometimes be functionally isolated. Using this fact as a guide, psychologists working with John Doe were able to find ways of communicating with either side of his brain without the other's knowing what was going on. Talking with the dominant left hemisphere (John-Doe-Left) was no problem, since this hemisphere possessed full language control. But John-Doe-Right could not talk, although he

Positive feedback loop. The term "feedback" means "getting information back from some outside source that lets you know what you are doing." An echo is a type of voice feedback. When you curse someone, and the person hits you in response, you have just gotten feedback about your actions. A loop is a circle. A feedback loop is a circle of responses. A verbal argument, or a fight, is a feedback loop, since each response one person makes calls forth a response from the other party. If each response in the feedback loop gets larger and larger, the feedback loop is positive, and an explosion often takes place. The "squeal" that sometimes comes from a public address system is another example of a positive feedback loop.

could point to things (with the left hand) in response to questions that John-Doe-Left couldn't hear. Given the appropriate sensory inputs, either of the John Does could learn things that the other wasn't aware of.

Psychological tests showed that both John Does had remarkably similar personalities—except for language ability, they were about as much alike as identical twins. Their attitudes and opinions were the same; their perceptions of the world were the same; and they woke up and went to sleep at almost the same times. There was one area of difference, however. Perhaps because John-Doe-Left could express himself in language, this dominant hemisphere appeared to be somewhat more logical and better at orderly planning than was John-Doe-Right. On the other hand, the "silent" right hemisphere tended to be somewhat more aggressive, impulsive, and emotional—perhaps out of frustration that it could not talk.

The split-brain operation was so successful in reducing epileptic attacks that it was tried with more than a dozen patients who might otherwise have died from the severity of their uncontrollable seizures. In many of these patients, one hemisphere (usually the dominant one) was able to gain control of both sides of the body, presumably by somehow suppressing the powers of the other hemisphere. In some cases, both hemispheres were able to control the entire body. Usually they learned to cooperate and share control, but the dominant hemisphere was in the driver's seat most of the time.

In some cases, as with John Doe, neither half of the brain ever gained the ability to coordinate all bodily movements. John-Doe-Left could talk out loud to the other side of his brain, but John-Doe-Right had no way of responding verbally. Occasionally the two would apparently disagree about what "their" body should do next, and one hemisphere might disrupt a movement the other was trying to make. Once in a rare while, one of the John Does would do something that seemed to cause the other considerable embarrassment or dismay.

Generally speaking, the younger the patient was when the corpus callosum was cut, the better the person's recovery. Because of the problems older patients such as John Doe experienced, and because new forms of treatment can now help control epilepsy without the necessity for splitting the brain, the operation is seldom used anymore.

LOGIC AND CREATIVITY

The study of the separate abilities of the two cortical hemispheres raises fascinating possibilities for anyone wanting to understand human behavior. To begin with, the data suggest that the brain is even more complex and rich in potential than we had previously imagined. Cases such as that of John Doe tell us that, with the exception of language behavior, one hemispheric Board of Directors can pretty well substitute for the other, so it would seem that each of us actually has two such Boards in our brain. Under normal circumstances these two teams cooperate so smoothly that we typically perceive them as being one. But probably each of the Boards has somewhat different functions.

In 1975, biologist Eran Zaidel (working at Sperry's laboratory at Cal Tech) reported on a new means of communicating with the separate hemispheres even in normal people whose corpus callosums had not been cut. Using a very complicated piece of equipment called a "Z lens," Zaidel is able to project pictures onto a person's eye so that this visual input is seen only by the right hemisphere, or the left hemisphere—but not by both hemispheres at the same time. In a typical experiment, Zaidel will present the right (minor) hemisphere with pictures of four objects (such as a cow, a tree, a book, and a horse). He then asks the person to point to the horse using his or her left hand (controlled primarily by the right hemisphere). The dominant hemisphere would hear the order to point out the

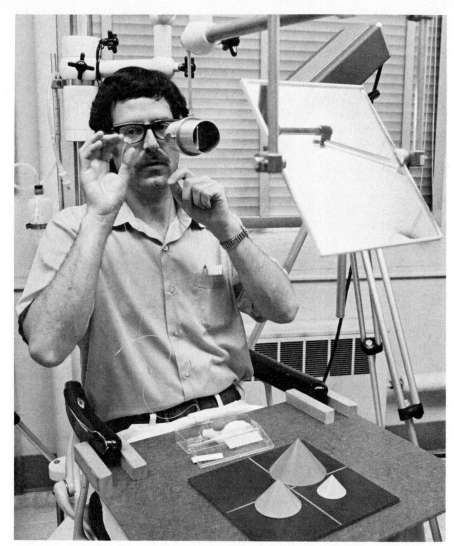

Eran Zaidel and the Z-lens. Using this lens, Dr. Zaidel can ''communicate'' with either hemisphere of a normal person's brain without the other hemisphere's being aware of the ''communication.''

horse, of course, but since it couldn't see the four pictures, it couldn't respond. The minor (right) hemisphere would also hear, and almost always could indicate with the left hand which was the correct picture.

Zaidel believes that the two hemispheres are pretty equal in their abilities up until the time a child is 5. After that, language ability increases much more rapidly in the left hemisphere, while the right (minor) hemisphere seems to take on creative or non-logical abilities that are neglected by the left. By the time the child has grown to adolescence, the minor hemisphere is greatly retarded in its ability to comprehend language. It can understand fairly complicated sentences if they are spoken aloud, but it can read only single (and relatively simple) words. Zaidel hopes that his research will help us learn how to tap the potential of the right hemisphere in people who have lost the use of their left (or dominant) hemisphere because of a stroke or an accident. Zaidel states that, "We know that the right hemisphere can support a lot of language, but it has to be trained in special ways that fit its unique mode of information processing." Just what types of training might be helpful is something we will talk about in Chapter 5.

The great physicist Albert Einstein once remarked that he usually thought in logical, orderly fashion—just like everyone else. That is, his thoughts were usually formed in words, in sentences. But during a few periods of great creativity, Einstein seemed to relax and "let his mind wander." At these moments, Einstein could think in concepts, in symbols, in non-verbal and often non-logical patterns. Perhaps language imposes a rigid logic to the thought processes of the dominant hemisphere that the minor hemisphere is somehow spared. Recent studies from several laboratories suggest the possibility that when Einstein was creatively relaxed, he was really letting his minor hemisphere express itself.

Samuel Taylor Coleridge, the noted British poet, was addicted to opium—the drug from which heroin is made. Coleridge often claimed that he wrote his most imaginative poetry while "high" on opium. We might speculate (and it is little more than speculation) about the effects this dangerous drug had on Coleridge. Perhaps the opium somehow weakened the dominance of his major hemisphere just enough so that the non-logical imaginings of his minor hemisphere could leak through to consciousness. When Coleridge "hunted for words" to express his fanciful thoughts, perhaps his dominant hemisphere was merely searching for ways of translating the symbolic thoughts of the minor hemisphere into verbal terms. (As we will see in the next chapter, even if this speculation is true, there are better ways of opening up channels of communication between the two halves of the brain than by taking drugs.)

The noted British scientist and writer, Lord Snow, wrote several books about what he called "the two cultures"—the often opposing worlds of logical science and creative art. He was dismayed that poets and physicists were frequently intolerant of each other's activities. Lord Snow looked to education to bridge this cultural gap. Perhaps he should have looked at the corpus callosum as well.

SUMMARY

1. The brain is the master organ of your body that, in many ways, coordinates or controls many of the functions of the other organs.
2. The biggest parts of your brain are the two cerebral hemispheres that sit atop the stem of your brain like the cap on a mushroom.
3. The thin outer covering of the cerebral hemispheres is called the cortex. Most of the functions of the brain that relate to conscious decision-making are located in the cortex.
4. Your brain contains at least 10 billion nerve cells or neurons.
5. Most cortical neurons have three main parts—the dendrites, the cell body or soma, and the axon.
6. The main purpose of most neurons is to pass messages from one part of the body to another. When the dendrites are stimulated by transmitter chemicals, a wave of electrical activity sweeps along the length of the long, thin neuron like a bullet speeding along the barrel of a gun.
7. When this electrical wave reaches the end of the axon, it causes the axon to release chemical transmitters into the synapse—the fluid-filled space between the axon of one neuron and the dendrites of a second neuron.
8. Transmitter chemicals released into the synapse excite the dendrites of the second neuron, and it responds by "firing off" a wave of electrical energy on its own. The first neuron thus transmits a message to the second chemically.
9. Sensory input neurons receive information from the outside world and transmit this information to cortical processing neurons which "make decisions" about how to respond.
10. Command messages telling your muscles to respond go out from the brain via motor neurons.
11. Damage to various parts of the brain can cause a condition known as epilepsy. Epileptic seizures show up on an EEG machine as spike-shaped brain waves.
12. If epileptic seizures become too frequent or severe and cannot be controlled by the use of drugs, a surgeon may cut the tissue connecting the two cerebral

hemispheres. This split-brain operation may leave the patient with "two minds in the same body."

13. The dominant cerebral hemisphere has the power of speech and usually controls the body in a logical fashion.

14. The minor hemisphere in adults lacks the language ability of the major hemisphere but may be capable of non-logical forms of creative thought.

(Continued from page 20.)

Pat Devine sat quietly on the balcony, drinking a cup of coffee and watching the traffic go by. Dr. Benjamin had left a few minutes ago, and Darlene had gone shopping.

"Funny about Lefty's trying to kill Dar," Pat said to himself.

But maybe it was good to get things out in the open. Dr. Benjamin had arrived just in time, thank God. He and Pat had managed to free Darlene from Lefty's clutches, and then they had all calmed down and had a long, frank talk.

Pat sighed, and lit a small cigar. Okay, he told himself, so there was another "thing" in the right side of his brain, and maybe it had rights too. But giving it a name just didn't make it any more real to him because it just didn't communicate with him. That was the trouble—he just couldn't **feel** Lefty up there on the right side of his head.

A young man on a big motorcycle bombed noisily down the street. Pat looked at him enviously. He might never ride again—not because he was afraid of having a spell anymore, but because he couldn't coordinate his left and right hands and legs well enough. Maybe Doc was right. Maybe he resented Dar because she was normal, because her Lefty was under control and did what it was told to do. His Lefty was something else—an animal that got out of control.

"How do you train an animal to behave itself?" he asked nobody in particular.

Pat shrugged his right shoulder. "First you have to admit the beast exists," he continued, "and then you have to find some way to get through to it."

Pat put down his cigar and stared hard at his left hand, which was playing with his cigarette lighter.

"Stop it," he ordered. "You'll waste all the fuel."

His left hand continued snapping the lighter open and shut, open and shut.

"Please stop it," Pat said as politely as he could.

The cigarette lighter dropped quietly onto the table.

Pat thought for a moment, then breathed a heavy sigh. With his right hand he reached up and tapped the right side of his head.

"Okay, you over there. Listen. Please. We've got to get this thing together."

RECOMMENDED READINGS

Eccles, Sir John C., ed. *Brain and Conscious Experience* (New York: Springer-Verlag, 1966).

Gazzaniga, Michael S. *The Bisected Brain* (New York: Appleton-Century-Crofts, 1970).

chapter 3
"NIRVANA"

DRUGS AND ALTERED STATES OF CONSCIOUSNESS

DID YOU KNOW THAT . . .

"Consciousness" is a "primitive term" that is almost impossible to define?
You can alter your normal state of consciousness by speeding up or slowing down your brain's activity level?
Your body has regular physiological rhythms that vary according to the time of day?
You go through several 90-minute sleep cycles nightly?
You dream more just before you awaken?
"Short sleepers" are often active, ambitious, and conformist, while "long sleepers" are often shy, passive, and sexually inhibited?
Dreaming may help you store the day's experiences away in memory?
Nightmares frequently occur a day or so after you've stopped taking sleeping pills?
Drugs affect you chiefly by speeding up or slowing down your bodily processes?
Your neurons can secrete both transmitters and inhibitors?
"Uppers" act like neural transmitters, while "downers" act like neural inhibitors?
Hallucinogens may have their odd effects because they disrupt memory?
Marijuana apparently does less damage to the body than does alcohol?
You can learn to control your brain waves using a biofeedback machine?

Peter McGraw clung tightly to the reins as his horse topped the ridge of a small hill and then stopped. His Mexican guide pointed down into a valley below.

"Xoconosle," the guide said.

Peter sighed with relief. It had been a long, hard climb over the mountains of middle Mexico. His face was caked with dust, the dirt turning to a sticky yellow paste where streams of sweat had moistened it. But now, at least, the end of the journey was in sight.

Peter's trip had begun in Durango several days earlier. Durango was a pleasant, civilized city halfway between El Paso, Texas, and Mexico City. From Durango, Peter had ridden on a vegetable truck to Mesquital, a tiny town consisting of several rows of adobe houses, a church, a market place, and a few hundred Mexicans. At Mesquital, Peter had rented horses and a guide to take him across the high mountain range that lay between Mesquital and Xoconosle, his ultimate destination. For it was at Xoconosle (the natives called it HO-ko-NOSE-ly) that Peter's particular rainbow ended, with the promise of a rather peculiar pot of gold. Not Acapulco Gold—a type of marijuana—but the radiant smile and golden peace of **The Woman.**

She was an Indian, a Tepehuan. And she was the wisest woman in the world—or so Peter's friend Kathy had said. Not that Kathy had met The Woman. But Kathy had heard of her from Werner, who either had been to Xoconosle himself or had known someone who had. Kathy was rather vague on that point, and Werner himself couldn't say, having disappeared before Peter met Kathy.

Kathy thought that Werner had either gone to Canada or been killed in a car accident—or perhaps both. The only thing Kathy was really sure of was that The Woman lived in Xoconosle (who could forget that name?) and that she had given Werner (or maybe it was one of his friends) a spiritual turn-on that surpassed human understanding.

Kathy was a San Francisco freak, a pill-popper, an addict, a dropout. Peter had tried her way of life briefly, but it simply didn't pleasure him very much. He enjoyed being high, but the mornings-after left a very bad taste in his mouth, and somehow the "chemical trip" didn't sit very well with his strong religious up-bringing. Peter wanted peace, but he hadn't found it in drugs. And then he heard about The Woman from Kathy, and what The Woman's philosophy had done for Werner (or perhaps someone Werner knew). So, when the semester at San Francisco State ended, and Peter found himself with a little extra money, an itch for strange sights, and an urge to come to terms with himself, he set out for Mexico.

And there it was, a thousand feet below him in the valley. Xoconosle. Sitting atop his horse, Peter stared at the dozen or so mud huts and asked himself, "Is this where The Woman really lives? Why here? Why not in a temple in Mexico City or Los Angeles?" But he also felt an immediate rush of excitement, a thrill of discovery. He had found the place! If the rest of the people in the world didn't know what they were missing, that was their problem, not his.

The guide took Peter to one of the mud huts at the outskirts of the village. Here lived a family—half-Tepehuan, half-Mexican—that agreed to give Peter food and shelter. These arrangements made, Peter went to look for The Woman. He had imagined she would be living in a cave in the hills; but, instead, she dwelt in a hut even smaller than the one he was going to be staying in. There was no door for him to knock on, so he simply called to her, in Spanish, hoping she would come out and speak to him. A group of Tepehuan children stood a few yards away, their faces impassive, expressionless, as they watched this strangely dressed alien standing in front of the grass-roofed dwelling.

A dog barked. One of the children picked her nose. A chicken ran across the yard chasing a grasshopper. Peter called again.

And then, from the darkness of the windowless hut, she suddenly appeared.

Peter stared at The Woman for what seemed long minutes. If he had met her on the street in San Francisco, would he have looked a second time at her face? Yes, he thought, surely he would have. Like a mask carved from a hunk of mahogany, that face was—rust-red, gnarled, creased, eyes like black knotholes, a bird's nest of feathery white hair perched wildly atop it all. And when she spoke, a voice like the cawing of a crow.

"You are the student," she said. "You are expected. Welcome."

"How did you know who I was? How did you know I was coming?"

"I have always expected you. You are The Student. You are the same as all the others, yet you are different. You have come to test, to learn, to listen, to discover. I know everything—yet I know nothing. I will share everything and nothing with you. Then you will go home again, and you will remember almost nothing and forget almost everything. But you will have been here, and that is enough." She spoke so simply, so slowly, that Peter's introductory-course Spanish was sufficient for him to follow her words.

"Yes, I am a student. My name is Peter McGraw. But I do not know what I want to learn. Can you teach me something anyhow?"

"No. Of course not. No one person teaches another. I will tell you the truth, and perhaps you will learn, and perhaps you will not. That is your problem, not mine. And I will tell you lies, and perhaps you will learn them too. It does not matter, for truth and lies are almost the same. All that you need to know is already inside you, or in the world around you. Open your eyes, look at things."

"What things?"

"Everything. Look at those children standing there by the tree. Tell me what you see."

Peter turned to look. "I see two small boys and a larger girl. They are dressed in rags and they do not smile. The girl is picking her nose."

"You see nothing. They are giants, pretending to be small in order not to frighten you. If you blink your eyes three times, they will grow wings and fly off to the mountains, to their home. Can you not see this?"

Peter blinked his eyes three times, but the children still looked the same. He said so.

"You have learned too many lies already. You are not ready to change. Go away, and come back when you are prepared to deal with things as they really are."

"I'm ready. I swear to you I am."

"So. I will give you another test. Tell me what color the sky is."

"Blue."

"At night it is blue? In the middle of a thunderstorm it is blue? At dawn, when the sun first hits the clouds, it is blue?"

Peter blushed. "I see what you mean."

The Woman coughed hoarsely. "You are beginning to learn. Reality is not fixed; it is flexible. You see but the surface of things, reflected on your mind like shadows dancing in moonlight. You must order your mind to gaze at the moon directly, not at the reflections it causes. You must take control, you must assert your authority over your mind and shape it to your will. If you will it to be so, reality as you now see it will crumble. Then you can put it back together as you wish."

"The last time reality crumbled was when I took LSD. Will you give me drugs to help me learn what reality should be?"

The Woman stared at Peter for a moment, then grunted harshly. "Some of my people take drugs and see wondrous things. Or so they say. They take the drugs not to learn but to feel good. If you are a real student, you will not need to eat a magic mushroom to see past the curtain of the here-now. Air is a drug. Water is a drug. Love is the best drug of all. Command your body to feel drugged, and it will obey. Order your eyes to look past the curtain, and they will see what is beyond. Your mind is poisoned with what you think is reality. Will taking more poisons help make you well?"

"You are a healer as well as a teacher?"

"Learning is always a matter of recovering from the sickness of ignorance. If you want to play games like those three children there, then smoke marijuana or eat the buttons of the peyote plant."

Peter smiled. "I thought they were giants?"

"Who told you that lie?"

"You did."

"You think in a straight line; you put one word after another and think you have carved an arrow to pierce to the heart of truth. What happens when you shoot an arrow into the sea? The arrow drowns and the sea lives on. They are children, yes. But they are also giants, because they are in the state-of-becoming. Can you not look past this moment in time to what will happen next, to what has happened in the past? Can you not put yourself inside the mind of one of those giant-children and look out at yourself through different eyes?"

"Can you?"

For the first time The Woman smiled. "I have watched you since your birth. I have seen you through your mother's eyes, and through your father's. I have stared at you through the eyes of your dog. I have seen you magnified and distorted through the eyes of your friends."

Peter paused. "And what do you see?"

"I see a crippled bird, wanting to fly. I see a pilgrim, toiling up a mountainside. I see a fish, drowning, trying to crawl out on land to breathe air. I see a gun pointing at my heart, waiting to be fired. I see a tree, reaching toward the sun with trembling leaves. I see a light, now growing bright, now fading to darkness. I hear a sound, now roaring with delight, now whispering away into silence. You are, or were, or can be, or will be, all of those things. Or perhaps you will be an emptiness, a nothing. Only you can decide."

"Sometimes, when I am very happy, or maybe very drunk, or dreaming, I have been all those things. Yes, you are right."

"Good. You begin to see. Perhaps you will be a good student after all."

Peter dropped to his knees in front of The Woman. "Then you will be my teacher? Then I may stay here and study with you? And you will help me reach the peak of truth?"

"No. Of course not. Truth is not a mountain to be climbed; it is a state of mind. Your mind is dark, like a cloudy day. You must learn to let the sun shine through."

"But I need your help!"

The Woman was impassive. "You need nothing. You have everything. You are everything. You are everywhere. And if you are everywhere, why do you need to stay here in Xoconosle, to bother me? Return to your everywhere up north, to Yankee reality. When you learn to see, to breathe, to think, to fly—then you may come here instantly, just by willing it. I am an old woman, used and dried up. I can do nothing for you."

Peter looked up at her. "You are very beautiful."

The Woman stared down at him, then her face burst into a smile like the sun reaching through morning mist. "You are a good student. You have the talent. You will find the way. Return to your home. Read. Talk to people. Ask questions. Teach yourself discipline. And the time will come when you reach up and tear away the cover from your mind. At that moment, I will stand beside you. As I do always."

She touched him lightly on the head. And then The Woman turned and walked back into the darkness of her hut.

(Continued on page 72.)

This chapter is about drugs—how they affect your body and brain, how they influence your mind, and how they alter your behavior and relationships with other people. You probably already know a lot about drugs, for they are ever-present in society today. But perhaps there are some scientific aspects of drugs and drug-taking that you are not yet aware of.

This chapter also makes brief mention of sexual orgasm, and touches on a heavenly experience that some people call *Nirvana*. (°)

But most of all, this chapter deals with what we shall shortly define as "altered states of consciousness."

However, if you wish to find out some new things about drugs, sex, Nirvana, and ways to alter your own state of mind, you will have to pay a small price for that pleasure. That is, you will have to understand a bit more about the systematic interactions among your brain, your mind, and your social environment before the new data will make much sense to you.

So let us begin with what may seem a dumb question: What do we mean by the term *consciousness* (°)? After all, if the main theme of this chapter is *altered* states of consciousness, perhaps we had better first make sure that we know what it is we're altering.

CONSCIOUSNESS

Every science has what are called *primitive terms* (°); that is, ideas or concepts which are so elemental that they are exceptionally difficult to define. If you want to make a physicist sweat just a little, ask that person what energy and matter are. You must have a rough notion of what these words mean, but you may also realize that great philosophical battles have been fought over their exact definitions. Or ask a biologist what he or she means by the term "life." Now, there's a lovely way to start a near-violent discussion, for biologists have tried for centuries to pin down just what life is—and isn't. In fact, there is no one unified definition for "energy" or "matter" or "life" that all scientists will agree upon.

Psychology has its primitive terms too; one of these is "consciousness." (An-

Nirvana (near-VAHN-ah). From an ancient Indian word meaning "blowing out." In modern usage, Nirvana means a state of freedom characterized by the extinction of desire, passion, illusion, and the attainment of rest, truth, and unchanging being. It also refers to any mental condition that we might call "heavenly pleasure" or paradise.

Consciousness (KON-shuss-nuss). The act or process of being aware, particularly of one's surroundings and bodily condition. Also, being alert, understanding what is happening.

Primitive term. A concept or idea that is basic to a particular science—so basic that the science cannot exist without this concept. Because the term is so fundamental, it cannot be readily defined except in its own terms.

Tautology (taw-TOLL-oh-gee). A useless and repetitive way of speaking, or defining words in terms of themselves. For instance, "consciousness is being conscious of something."

other, in case you're wondering, is "mind.") The dictionary gives many definitions of "consciousness," most of which have to do with awareness, awakeness, understanding, being alert, or even being alive. Some of the dictionary meanings have to do with *self*-awareness, or the experience of knowing that you are having the experience of knowing. Although you surely have some conscious awareness of what consciousness is all about, you too might find it hard to describe consciousness without slipping into *tautology* (°), that is, without defining the word in terms of itself.

One reason primitive terms give us fits is that they often refer to processes or conditions rather than things or objects; it is much easier to define a track shoe than it is the act of running. Objects usually have a location in space, and can be measured accurately; processes often have no clear-cut beginning or end, and unlike objects, there are very few processes that you can hold a ruler to or weigh on a scale.

Consciousness is even more difficult to talk about than running or jumping, for self-awareness is something that occurs inside your head and can't be seen directly by other people (who could presumably tell whether you were running or standing still). But if we begin with the thought that consciousness refers to a *process*—a sequence of events—and not to a "thing," we're off to a good start.

THE PROCESS OF CONSCIOUSNESS

You take in information from the world around you (and from your own body), you recognize that you have or haven't experienced these inputs before, you make decisions about what these sensory inputs mean, you respond to the inputs, and then you notice what consequences your actions have. Perhaps this is as close as we can come (at the moment) to defining the meaning of the conscious process. But notice that, with this approach, we have a better "handle" to study and discuss consciousness than before, since we know that inputs, internal processes, outputs, and feedback are necessary to the experience of self-awareness. And even if we cannot inspect your consciousness directly, we can at least measure the inputs, outputs, and feedback that so strongly influence what you feel and think.

If consciousness is a process, then it exists in time and probably can be speeded up or slowed down depending on what's happening in the environment and inside the person's body. If we shut you off from your environment (as we will see in Chapter 9), your consciousness in fact slows down and may stop altogether for long periods of time. If we give you certain drugs that alter the speed with which your brain processes incoming sensory stimulation, then we will probably alter the state of your consciousness. If we clamp down on the feedback that you get from your body and from the outside world, or if we greatly enhance the pleasurable or painful aspects of the feedback, we can sometimes have profound effects on your awareness of yourself and of your environment. Thus, by varying the inputs that we give to people (the independent variables in most experiments), we change their biological and intra-psychic processes and, presumably, the verbal reports or behaviors (dependent variables) they use to tell us what state of consciousness they are experiencing.

States of consciousness can usually be altered in just two ways—quantitatively and qualitatively. Quantitative changes in the speed or tempo with which you process incoming information can lead to your acting, thinking, and feeling different than you usually do. However, if your internal processes buzz along at their normal speed, but your mind assigns new or unusual meanings or emotions to sensory inputs, then we might say that a qualitative alteration in your conscious awareness has occurred. Much of the time, both types of changes occur almost simultaneously, but many psychologists believe that quantitative changes are by far the most frequent. Certainly quantitative changes are easier to measure and to discuss, and it is a fact that most of the drugs people commonly use primarily affect the speed at which the mind and body operate. So let us begin our exploration into this wild and wonderful area of human experience by talking about two quantitatively altered states of consciousness that all of us experience almost every day—sleeping and dreaming.

SLEEP AND DREAMS

Although most of us are not aware of it, our bodies go through rather regular physiological cycles every day. Our temperature, for instance, is usually lowest in the middle of the night (if that is when we sleep), begins to rise about the time we awaken, continues to rise slightly for the first three hours we are awake, and then remains relatively constant until we go to bed again at night. This *diurnal* (°) temperature change is very slight—usually no more than a degree or so—but it does seem to occur in most of us. Just why this diurnal rhythm occurs, no one is really sure—but we do know that it takes place even in people who are totally inactive throughout the day. The ability to taste, smell, and hear also varies during the day, reaching its peak in most of us at the very odd hour of 3 A.M. A second peak in sensory ability usually occurs between 5 and 7 P.M., which may account for the fact that many of us prefer to eat our largest meal of the day about then (when food should taste and smell best to us). Also, our *alpha rhythm* (°) is typically a little faster around 5 P.M. than at any other time of day.

The most noticeable diurnal rhythm we all show, however, is that of sleep and wakefulness. Sleep is obviously a periodic interruption of our stream of consciousness, but scientists are unclear as to what sleep actually is or what functions it serves. We may think that we need sleep in order for our bodies to rest and recover from the day's activities, but just how this recovery takes place and what it is that recovers are still somewhat mysterious. We do know that sleep is tied very closely to the other diurnal rhythms that our bodies show—for people who spend weeks or months locked away in sunless caves still tend to wake and sleep on a 24-hour cycle—but there is growing evidence that sleep is important psychologically because it allows us to dream. And, as we will see, if sleep refreshes the body, dreams may be necessary for us to store the day's memories away and refresh our minds.

Diurnal (dye-YOURN-ull). Anything that occurs every day.

Alpha rhythm. Brain waves of about 10–12 cycles per second. Also called the Berger rhythm, after Hans Berger who first measured brain waves. See Chapter 2.

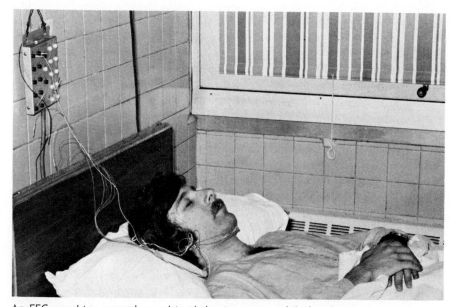

An EEG machine records a subject's brain waves while he sleeps.

Delta rhythm. The slow waves (less than 4 cycles per second) the brain shows during deep sleep. See Chapter 2.

Activity pattern. The rapid, rather random pattern of brain waves the EEG picks up when you are actively engaged in thought.

REM sleep. Toward the end of each 90-minute sleep cycle, the eyes move about rapidly for 8–15 minutes. It is during this period that most dreaming seems to occur.

Sleep Cycles

Sleep is part of our daily activity cycle, but there are several different types or stages of sleep, and they too are cyclical. If you are an average sleeper, when you first drift off into slumber your eyes will roll about a bit, your temperature will drop slightly, your muscles will relax, and your breathing will slow and become quite regular. Your brain waves slow down a bit too, with the alpha rhythm predominating for the first few minutes. Then, about 40–60 minutes after you lose consciousness, you will have reached the deepest sleep of all, and your brain waves will show the *delta rhythm* (°). You may think you stay at this deep level all night long, but that turns out not to be the case. Instead, about 80 minutes after you fall into slumber, your activity cycle will increase slightly. The delta rhythm disappears, to be replaced by the *activity pattern* (°). Your eyes will begin to dart around under your closed eyelids as if you were looking at something occurring in front of you. This period of rapid eye movements lasts for some 8–15 minutes and is called *REM sleep* (°). It is during REM sleep that most dreams seem to occur. It is also during this period that most males—from infancy to old age—experience an erection of the penis.

During both light and deep sleep, the muscles in your body are relaxed but capable of movement. However, as you slip into REM sleep, a very odd thing occurs—most of the muscles in your body become almost completely incapable of responding. Although your brain shows very rapid bursts of neural activity during REM sleep, your body is fairly well paralyzed. In more technical terms—as we will see later in this chapter—we can say that REM sleep is accompanied by extensive *muscular inhibition.* No one really knows why this inhibition takes place, but many scientists speculate that it serves to keep you from acting out your dreams.

QUESTION: Could sleepwalking ordinarily occur during REM sleep?

Provided that you don't wake up during the first REM sleep period, your body will soon relax again, your breathing will grow slow and regular once more, and you will slip gently back into the depths of deep sleep—only to rise to the surface of near-consciousness some 80 minutes later. Most people experience four to five such cycles per night, although the quality of the experience changes slightly the longer the person sleeps. The first cycle usually yields the deepest sleep, and the first REM period is typically the briefest. No matter how many sleep cycles you experience during the night, you are more likely to awaken during an REM period than at any other time.

QUESTION: Why is it that human males so frequently awaken with an erection?

The length of the sleep cycle varies considerably from one species to another, and within a species it varies according to the age of the organism. Rats typically go through a full cycle in 10–13 minutes; children do so in 50–60 minutes; adult humans take 85–110 minutes; and adult elephants require about 120 minutes. As we will see, there is considerable variation even among adult humans as to the number of cycles per night an individual needs or wants.

The average person can tolerate up to 40 hours of sleeplessness without suffering ill effects. If we must remain awake much past 40 hours, however, most of us begin to show an increased irritability and impulsiveness; our decision-making processes are affected, and we tend to react more slowly and to make poorer judgments than when we are rested. If we are deprived of sleep for 100 hours or more, we are very likely to show considerable stress and even signs of mental disturbance, becoming hostile and suspicious almost to an extreme. When allowed at last to sleep, a severely deprived person's cycles often change to include much more deep sleep than usual, sometimes at the expense of REM sleep.

As researchers Frederick Baekeland and Ernest Hartmann point out, the average person sleeps about 7.5 hours per day. About 5 percent of the population regularly choose to sleep less than 6 hours a night, while another 5 percent will sleep more than 9 hours if given the chance. Baekeland and Hartmann call these people "short sleepers" and "long sleepers," and they make a fascinating study.

"Long" and "Short Sleepers"

Baekeland and Hartmann brought 20 young men who were identified as "short sleepers" and another 20 men who were "long sleepers" into the laboratory and studied their sleep patterns using *EEG machines* (°) attached to the men while they slept. The subjects, who averaged about 25 years of age, were given two nights to adapt to bedding down in the laboratory situation; data were collected while they slept for several nights thereafter. Baekeland and Hartmann report that there were differences not only in the type of sleep patterns the men showed, but also in the personalities of the men themselves.

To begin with, there is every evidence that the men slept in the laboratory (after the first two nights of adjustment) pretty much the same way that they slept in their own beds. The "short sleepers" dozed off almost immediately and got but 330 minutes of sleep; the "long sleepers" were much more wakeful during the night and got about 527 minutes of "sack time." Both groups averaged a total of some 75 minutes of really deep sleep per night, a result that Baekeland and Hartmann attribute to the fact that all of us accumulate most of our really profound sleep during the first few hours we are in bed. However, the "long sleepers" averaged almost twice as much REM sleep per night as did the "short sleepers." Some people obviously need more dream time than do others; why this might be so comes from the personality differences found between the two groups.

Baekeland and Hartmann report that the "short sleepers" had been more or less average until the men were in their teens when they voluntarily began cutting down their sleep time because of pressures from school, work, and other activities. These men tended to view that altered state of consciousness we call sleep as a bothersome interruption in their daily routines. In general, these men appeared ambitious, active, energetic, cheerful, conformist in their opinions, and very sure about their career choices. They often held several jobs at once, or worked full- or part-time while going to school. They were poor in trying to recall their dreams, and their usual way of dealing with problems was to deny the difficulty and keep busy in the hope that it would go away. Many of them had a strong urge to appear "normal" or acceptable to their friends and associates. Their sleep patterns were similar to, but less extreme than, sleep patterns shown by many mental patients categorized as *manic* (°).

The "long sleepers" were quite different indeed. Baekeland and Hartmann report that these young men had been lengthy sleepers since childhood. They usually stated that they enjoyed their sleep, protected it, and were quite concerned when they were occasionally deprived of their desired 9 hours nightly of bed rest. They tended to recall their dreams much better than did the "short sleepers." Many of the "long sleepers" were also shy, anxious, *introverted* (°), inhibited, passive, mildly depressed, and unsure of themselves (particularly in social situations). A number of them, for instance, were still virgins at age 25–30. Several openly stated that sleep was an escape from their daily problems.

Baekeland and Hartmann suggest that "short sleepers" might be afraid of the subjective experiences that accompany dreaming and that they deliberately curtail their bed time in order to escape sleep fantasies that might force them to inspect their own thoughts and feelings more carefully. By contrast, "long sleepers" appear to need lengthy REM times in order to work out their personal

EEG machines. Electro-encephalographs. These devices measure brain waves and other forms of electrical activity in the nervous system. The brain-wave pattern is usually displayed graphically on a sheet of paper, or flashed on a picture tube similar to the one used in television sets. For further description, see Chapter 2.

Manic (MANN-ick). From the Greek word *mania*, meaning "insanity." A manic person is someone terribly excited, almost to the point of madness. The opposite of depression.

Introverted (INN-trow-vert-ted). A term made famous by the Swiss psychiatrist Carl Jung. Introverted people spend much of their time looking inward, inspecting their own thoughts, feelings, and values.

uncertainties, fears, and conflicts during that altered state of consciousness we call dreaming.

The young men studied by Baekeland and Hartmann were, by definition, extremes; most of us need both deep sleep and ample REM sleep each night. But as we will see in a moment, there is evidence that we all need more dream time when we are worried, or when we have been exposed to new and challenging situations during the day.

DREAMS

People have studied dreams and dreaming since the dawn of recorded time, but it has only been in this century that we have had the tools to investigate the subject scientifically. Beginning about 1902, a German neuro-physiologist named Hans Berger began recording electrical changes in brain activity using large electrodes placed on the scalp. By 1930, Berger had developed the first practical EEG machine and noted many of the changes in brain waves that occur during waking and sleep periods. The alpha rhythm is still sometimes called the Berger rhythm in his honor. But it was not until the EEG was available that we had a precise physiological index of when a person was deeply asleep (other than the fact that sleeping people typically have their eyes shut and don't move around very much).

Perhaps because the scientific study of dreams is still so new, the general public holds a great many mistaken beliefs about who dreams what and why. For instance, if you ask several of your friends how often they dream each night, some of them will surely insist that they seldom if ever dream. Yet the truth is that we all dream frequently every time we go to sleep—we simply don't remember dreams for very long after we wake up. If you force yourself to write down your dreams the instant you wake up in the morning, you will probably be surprised at how much you can recall and how detailed some of your dreams are.

It was not until 1953—when Nathaniel Kleitman and his associate, E. Aserinski, reported the connection between REM sleep and dreaming—that scientists realized that we do not dream continuously or even randomly. Kleitman and Aserinski woke up their subjects at various times during the sleep cycle. If awakened during deep sleep, the subjects seldom reported they were having a dream; however, if awakened during initial light sleep, or particularly during REM sleep, the subjects frequently stated they had been dreaming (and could usually remember what the dream was all about). It now seems fairly clear that, when we are in deep sleep, our sensory inputs are almost entirely cut off, the cortex does little or no processing, and only the lower centers of the brain are really functional. As each sleep cycle concludes, however, the cortex becomes active, the eyes frequently begin to dart about under our eyelids, the activity pattern appears on the EEG record, and we rise gently from complete unconsciousness into the twilight zone of dreaming.

Dream Frequency

According to Kleitman (and most other authorities), we typically have several dreams a night; in fact, we usually have several dreams within each REM period. Each dream lasts from a few seconds to several minutes. Since REM periods at the beginning of our sleep tend to be the shortest, we probably dream less in the early evening than later on.

Since everyone dreams nightly, we may assume that dreaming serves some necessary function. Although we are still not entirely sure what that function is, we do know that depriving people (or animals) of REM sleep can have certain fairly unpleasant effects. In 1960, Stanford University scientist William C.

Dement reported data suggesting that dream time is necessary to many people's mental health. Dement had subjects sleep in his laboratory. As long as they were showing light or deep sleep, he let them alone. Once an REM period began, however, he would wake them up immediately. When the subjects would go back to sleep, their cycles would (as is almost always the case) begin again at the beginning, go through light to deep sleep, and from thence to REM—at which point Dement would wake them up again. His subjects therefore got all the deep sleep they normally would—but dreaming was infrequent because it is associated almost entirely with REM periods.

William C. Dement.

Many of Dement's subjects became cranky, annoyed, impulsive, and hostile when deprived of dreaming for several nights. They seemed to have greater difficulty learning new tasks (a finding confirmed with subsequent research on animals also deprived of REM sleep). In many cases, Dement's subjects showed shortened sleep cycles, as if some part of their body was trying to rush through deep sleep to get on to the dream state. When later allowed to sleep without interruption, most of Dement's subjects showed greatly increased REM periods, as if they were trying to catch up on all the dreaming he had deprived them of.

Further experiments by Dement and other scientists have shown that not all people respond to REM deprivation in the way that Dement's first subjects did. In fact, some people can tolerate a week of deprivation without showing too many noticeable ill effects. However a few people—perhaps of the "long sleeper" personality type described by Baekeland and Hartmann—are apparently pushed near to the edge of insanity if they are not allowed to dream for several nights.

Dream Content

Our first dreams of the night tend to be rather dull and trivial, mostly having to do with things that we have done during the day. In later REM periods, dreams become more unusual, more vivid, more colorful, easier to remember, and sometimes more anxiety-provoking. During any one REM period, we are likely to experience a sequence of related dreams, or to run through the same dream two or three times. For the most part, however, we dream about things that are of some interest or importance to us, including our daily activities. C. Hall and R. Van de Castle reported in 1966 that 30 percent of the 50 laboratory dreams of a young man who loved sports cars were related to driving and to automobiles, while another man who had a strong emotional tie to football dreamed about that sport 36 percent of the time.

The connection between dream content and the rapid movements your eyes make while you dream is not entirely understood. But there does seem to be a close relationship between the *direction* in which your eyes move and what you are dreaming about. For instance, if you dream you are watching someone walk up a hill, your REMs will be predominantly up and down; if you dream you are observing a tennis match, your eyes will mostly dart back and forth from right to left.

With the exception of nightmares, most of our dreams are rather ordinary. Sigmund Freud, one of the first modern scientists to pay special attention to the content of dreams, suggested that we use the dream state as a time of working through the day's events and of acting out in fantasy some of our unfulfilled desires. Ramon Greenberg, director of sleep research at the Boston Veterans Hospital, goes a step further. Greenberg believes that dreams are the brain's way of transferring memories of the day's events from the perceptual input areas of the brain to those parts of the cerebrum that are involved in memory storage and processing. We will have more to say about this intriguing notion in Chapter 17.

But now it is time for us to delve into the murky, even frightening subject of the most memorable dreams of all, nightmares.

Oblivious (ob-BLIV-ee-us). From the Latin word meaning "to smooth over," or "to forget." If you are oblivious to the rattlesnake crawling at your feet, you simply pay no attention to it or forget that it is there.

Incubus (INN-cue-buss). From the same Latin word that gives us "incubate," meaning "to sit" or "to lie" on something. The incubus is an evil spirit said to lie on people while they sleep, and often to have sexual intercourse with women at night.

Harrowing (HAIR-oh-ing). Anything that is distressing or acutely painful.

NIGHTMARES

Imagine yourself comfortably sleeping in your bed, *oblivious* (°) to everything around you, when you begin to sense—deep down inside you—that something has changed, that something has gone very wrong. Slowly, almost dimly, you regain just enough consciousness to realize that you are suffocating, that some heavy weight is lying on your chest crushing your lungs. Suddenly you realize that your breathing has almost stopped, and you are dying for air.

Terrified, you scream! At once, it seems that you awaken. And you see this *thing*—this big, black, furry, cat-like beast crouched on your chest, its burning eyes peering straight into your face, its saliva-drenched lips hovering over your mouth as if it were sucking the very life out of your lungs. You try desperately to move, but you are paralyzed by the oppressive weight of the cat-being on your chest. A feeling of doom falls on you like a net, wrapping you tightly in the cat-creature's web of death.

Your pulse begins to race, your breathing becomes rapid, and you push futilely at the thing that is choking you to death. Your legs tremble, then begin to thrash about under the covers. You sweep the bedclothes from your body, stumble to your feet, and flee as fast as you can in the darkness. Terror follows you like a stalking tiger. Your arms blindly stretched out in front of you, you stumble through the house, the animal in hot pursuit.

And then, all at once, you find yourself in your living room; the lights are on, the cat-beast retreats to the shadows of your mind, and you are awake—safe, but intensely wrought up and disturbed. You shake your head, wondering what has happened to you.

Incubus Nightmare

What I've just described is a classic example of what is called the *incubus* (°) nightmare. You may have read about this awful experience, but chances are that you've never experienced it yourself. For as *harrowing* (°) as an incubus attack is, it occurs in but one person in several hundred. A few individuals do seem to be particularly prone to incubus dreams, however, and in these people attacks may occur fairly frequently.

Unlike most other dreams, the incubus nightmare begins during deep sleep and not during an REM period. As you now know, pulse and respiration rate normally slow down considerably during deep sleep. However, just prior to an incubus episode, the person's average heart rate is likely to be markedly retarded, as is the breathing rate. The person seemingly moves too close to physiological death, and one or more centers of the brain "panic" as if the body were being suffocated. The longer this severely depressed deep sleep goes on, the greater the probability that an incubus attack will occur, and the more frighteningly intense it will seem. Incubus episodes happen most frequently during the first or second sleep cycle of the night, when body functions always slow down the most.

The "dream" itself almost always begins with a scream. The body's defenses are mobilized, the pulse rate may double or nearly triple, deep and rapid breathing occurs, and the person rapidly rises to an REM state of consciousness. Hallucinations often follow the scream, the most vivid and frequent one being that of an animal lying on one's chest, sucking one's life away. Sleepwalking often occurs as part of an incubus attack. The dreamer is very unresponsive to his or her environment during the attack and is difficult to awaken fully. It seems, in fact, as if the dream must run its course before it can be interrupted and full consciousness can return.

Anxiety REM Nightmare

By far more common than the incubus attack is the anxiety nightmare, which typically occurs late in the sleep cycle following a very long REM period. In the REM nightmare, the body is seldom aroused to a panic state; in fact, there usually is little change in the body's physiological responses. It is, therefore, the psychological content of the dream itself (being chased, falling, witnessing frightening events) that leads to the anxiety attack. The dreamer usually awakens fairly readily (and often spontaneously) from such an anxiety nightmare. Screaming and sleepwalking are seldom if ever associated with this type of REM dream. And as distressing as these nightmares may seem to the people who experience them, anxiety attacks are relatively mild compared to the stark terror of the incubus nightmare.

Incubus attacks are most frequent when the need for deep sleep is greatest, when bodily processes simply slow down too much. Anxiety nightmares occur most often when the psychological need for dreaming and REM sleep is greatest. Various illnesses—particularly those accompanied by high fevers—often reduce the amount of REM sleep the person experiences. Sleeping pills also reduce REM sleep. Knowing these facts, you can understand that anxiety nightmares happen very often when a person is recovering from sickness, or in the nights just after a person has stopped taking sleeping pills of any kind. These facts may also explain one of the real dangers of taking drugs even temporarily to help you sleep. The pills may indeed make it easier for you to doze off, or to stay asleep during the night; but once you discontinue the drug, your REM sleep increases tremendously, and you may have almost constant anxiety nightmares for several nights in a row. Some people then return to the pills—not to put themselves to sleep, but to reduce REM periods and all those disturbing nightmares.

ALTERED STATES OF CONSCIOUSNESS

Psychologists generally assume that everything you feel or experience is reflected by the functioning of your body, particularly the way in which your nervous system reacts. When your brain is alert, you are consciously alert; when your brain sleeps (delta rhythm), you become almost totally unconscious; when your brain "wakes up" a little during sleep, you frequently dream. If your nerve cells fire at a faster-than-normal rate, you may experience great anxiety, fear, or pain—or great pleasure. If your neurons fire more slowly than usual, you may feel relaxed, peaceful, dreamy—or you may fall into a black depression. In short, almost any change in the *speed* at which your brain takes in sensory information and processes it will usually be accompanied by a change in the way you think and feel about yourself and your personal world, and how pleasant or unpleasant that world may be.

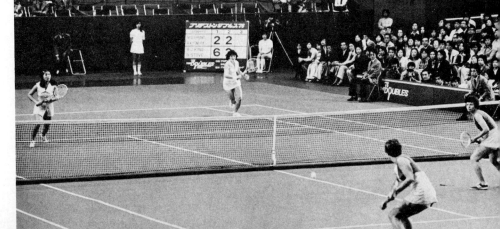

A fast tennis game increases the rapidity of neuron firing in your body.

Jaundiced (JAWN-dist). From the French word meaning "yellow." Certain diseases of the liver turn the skin yellow—and leave their colorful mark on the skin even after the disease is cured. In more popular usage, the word means to be embittered or prejudiced by unpleasant experiences. Someone with a jaundiced eye is supposed to see only too clearly how foolish or unbelievable other points of view may be.

To some people, the most heavenly pleasure imaginable is the complete absence of fear, hurt, and terror; to others, it is a blinding light or a crashing sound that drives their eyes or ears to the limit of endurance. Yet to a great many individuals, particularly those concerned with religious experiences, heaven is a matter of achieving *Nirvana*—an almost indescribable condition characterized by such things as freedom from all earthly passions, problems, wants, desires; a feeling of floating gently in black nothingness; a peaceful union with all the universe; a quiet resting in the arms of God.

Individuals who have achieved Nirvana often describe it as the greatest of human pleasures, the ultimate goal toward which all other joys are mere stepping stones. But to the *jaundiced* (°) eyes of many psychologists, Nirvana and all other heavens (and hells) are but states of mind. Or, to put the matter in biological terms, they are mental experiences greatly influenced by *conditions of the brain*.

Consider, for a moment, the very earthly pleasure of sexual climax. From a biological point of view, each time you experience this sexually induced altered state of consciousness, many of your nerve cells respond in more or less the same way. The psychological and personal aspects of the response will surely vary from one sexual encounter to the next; but at a biological level, orgasm almost always involves the same type of neural response pattern in your brain. Unless this rather unique pattern of neural firing occurs, you simply will not achieve orgasm. You may attempt to bring about this firing pattern indirectly (or psychologically) by altering your thoughts and feelings and emotions. Or you may attempt to bring about this firing pattern directly and biologically by controlling the sensory input to the sexual centers of your brain. Or you may do both at once. But the important point is this—anything you do that brings about the neural firing pattern associated with sexual climax will almost always lead to the psychological experience of orgasm.

What is true of sexual climax is true of all other altered states of consciousness. Any time you wish to achieve a Nirvana-like experience, for example, you must either find some way to change the functioning of your mind—hoping that your body will follow along—or you must discover a physiological means of shifting your brain directly from its normal state or condition to that associated with Nirvana—hoping that your mind will respond appropriately.

Drugs are a direct method of speeding up or slowing down neural firing—a quick if sometimes deadly way that people have chosen for a great many centuries. When we look at the effects of drugs on human behavior in just a moment, we will find that there is a chemical compound that can affect your brain almost any way that you wish—but usually at a cost of some kind.

In the past, religion, philosophy, and mental discipline offered the only non-drug or indirect ways to alter the state of your brain—but usually these methods are effective only after training and long practice. Today we have much more efficient ways of training or conditioning our brains, including the use of highly sophisticated electronic gadgets to help guide anyone to a kind of Nirvana. We will see later in this chapter that there is a fairly easy way to alter one's brain waves (neural firing patterns) merely by willing them to change.

Before we can sensibly discuss the rather abnormal brain states that drugs and discipline can bring about, we first must delve a little more deeply into the manner in which your brain functions under more routine conditions.

THE MOLECULES OF THE MIND

From a biochemical standpoint, your whole body is little more than a bag of complex molecules kept in place by your skin and skeleton. You take in molecules (oxygen, water, food), make use of them (digestion, respiration), and return them in altered form back to the environment (carbon dioxide, urine, feces). If you don't get enough of the right kinds of chemicals, or get too much of the wrong kinds, you die.

The cells in your body are bags of chemicals too, kept together by a cellular "skin" or membrane. The cells take in oxygen and food from your blood and excrete waste products back into the blood. The neurons in your brain are highly specialized in the way that they function, but primarily they are *cells* that keep alive by maintaining a delicate balance between the chemicals inside the membrane and the chemicals that must remain outside if the neuron is to survive. But neurons do more than excrete waste products—they *secrete* (°) very complex substances that affect everything that happens in your brain.

As we said in the last chapter, when a neuron fires, a wave of electrical energy sweeps from the front end of the cell (the dendrites) past the cell body to the rear end of the cell (axon). This electrical wave does little in and of itself, except to cause the neuron to secrete more molecules. Nerve cell A cannot stimulate nerve cell B by shocking it electrically. Rather, A must stimulate B chemically—by releasing one or more complex molecules into the tiny *synaptic space* (°) between the axonic end-fibers of A and the dendritic beginning-fibers of B. Since these synaptic chemicals actually transmit the message from A to B, they are called *transmitters* (°).

Each time that neuron A fires, the pulse of electrical energy that races along the cell seems to push a few transmitter molecules out of the axon into the synapse. These transmitters wander around more or less randomly in the synaptic fluid much as a fleet of toy sailboats might float around randomly on the surface of a long, narrow canal. If you sat on one bank of the canal and launched toy boats toward the other side, many of the boats would be caught up by the current and would be washed away. But occasionally you would succeed in your goal—that is, now and then a boat would reach the other shore. The narrower the canal, and the gentler the current, the more frequently a boat would make the crossing safely. And the more boats you launched, the greater would be your odds of getting one to the other side.

In similar fashion, the more frequently that neuron A fires, the more transmitter molecules it launches into the synaptic space. And since the synapse is a very narrow canal indeed, and the wash-away current very weak, many of these molecules do eventually reach the dendrites of neuron B. These dendrites appear to have certain "harbors" in them, or *receptor sites* (°), that are particularly sensitive to transmitters. If a transmitter molecule lands in one of these receptor sites, it triggers off a chemical reaction in the dendrite that causes neuron B to fire.

Secrete (see-KREET). The cells in your body manufacture many types of chemicals that are released or secreted into the blood or onto your skin. Cells in glands at the corners of your eyes secrete tears onto the surface of your eyes.

Synaptic space. The synapse is the incredibly narrow gap or space between the axonic end-fibers of one nerve cell and the dendrites of the next neuron in line. For futher discussion, see Chapter 2.

Transmitters. Chemicals released by axonic end-fibers that cross the synaptic space and excite or stimulate the dendrites or somas of the next neuron.

Receptor sites (re-SEPT-er sights). Only certain small spots or sites on the dendrites seem to be sensitive to the transmitter chemicals. If nerve cell B is to be stimulated into firing by nerve cell A, the transmitters released by A's axonic end-fibers must cross the synaptic space and reach one of these receptor sites. There are also receptor sites on the cell body, or soma, of many neurons, as well as on the dendrites.

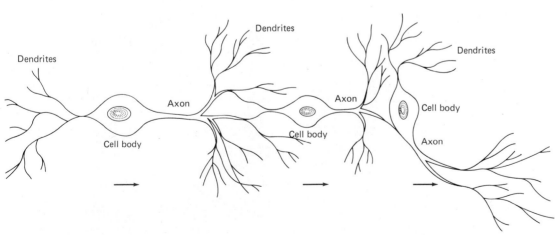

Nerve cell sequence.

A wave of electrical energy then pulses down the length of neuron *B*, causing another batch of transmitter chemicals to be released at the synapse between *B* and *C*.

As we will see, this whole neural process is a good deal more complicated than our simple boat analogy would suggest; yet it is exactly true that you cannot lift a finger, see a sunset, solve a problem, or even remember your own name unless you can somehow control the transmitter substances in your brain. Drugs such as marijuana, alcohol, heroin, and LSD either act as neural transmitters themselves or subtly change the transmitters your brain produces. Generally speaking, all these drugs act by speeding up or slowing down the firing of the neurons in various parts (or all of) your nervous system. You may be surprised, then, at the seemingly profound changes these drugs can make in the *quality* of your conscious experience. To appreciate why a quantitative change in neural firing can bring about a qualitative change in experience, you need to know a bit more about neural excitation and inhibition.

EXCITATION AND INHIBITION

Suppose that, later on today, you are sitting quietly in your chair, reading, when you suddenly get an urge to eat an apple lying on the table beside you. You decide to reach out and take the apple in your hand. Both the urge and the decision are communicated from one part of your brain to another by electro-chemical means. The motor output centers in your cortex receive the order—"reach for the apple"—from your Board of Directors and send a signal down to the muscles in your arm telling them to get to work. Those muscles won't budge an inch unless the motor nerves that make synapse with those muscles dump certain transmitter chemicals into those synapses. These transmitters cause a chemical reaction in the muscles so that they extend and contract in just the right way for your arm to be guided toward the apple.

Now, suppose further that, just as your hand nears the beautiful apple sitting innocently on the table, you notice something terrible. Crouched just behind the big red fruit is a huge, hairy black spider that you recognize as a tarantula. Suddenly a great many nerve cells in your brain that were sitting back resting are called into play, and they begin dumping a great many transmitter chemicals into

a great many synapses all over your nervous system! Your first impulse may be to jerk back your hand as quickly as you can, and perhaps that's what most people would do. But tarantulas can jump 15 feet (4.5 meters) and, while their bite is seldom fatal to adults, it can be exceptionally painful. Any quick movement on your part might disturb the spider and make it leap to the attack. So what you really should do is to *freeze* for a moment before you slowly retract your hand. (And then maybe you should exit from the scene as gracefully but as quickly as you can.)

At the instant that you spotted the spider, your hand was in the process of reaching out for the apple. How do you go about explaining to your hand that you've suddenly changed your mind, and that it should freeze? The problem is that your motor nerves have already dumped a rather large supply of transmitter molecules into their synapses; how do you recall those molecule-sailboats once they've been launched into the synaptic canal?

Actually, you will do three things at once. For each muscle that (when chemically stimulated) will cause your hand to reach out, there is another muscle that will make your hand pull back. So the first thing you will surely do is to order the "pull-back" muscles to get busy and rescue you. Your brain obeys this first order by releasing transmitters into the synapses that control the "pull-back" muscles. At the same time your cortical Board of Directors stops sending output messages to the "stretch-out" muscles, so that no further transmitters are released into those synaptic canals. But since there are still a lot of surplus molecules floating around in the "stretch-out" synapses, your brain goes a step further—it causes certain *anti-transmitter* molecules to be released into the synapses. Since the function of these chemicals is to block or inhibit synaptic transmission, they are called *inhibitors* (°). These inhibitors act more or less like pirate ships on the synaptic canal. That is, the inhibitors prevent the excitatory transmitter-sailboats from reaching the other side of the canal by destroying them or by blocking the entrance to the receptor-site harbors.

Excitation and inhibition exist at the biological, the intra-psychic, and the social/behavioral level. To show the relationships among these three levels, let us next look at social inhibitions.

SOCIAL INHIBITIONS

During your lifetime you have learned that there are many things that you can do in public, and many things that you cannot do without upsetting or outraging the people around you. During toilet training, for instance, a child discovers that it cannot empty its bladder or its bowels whenever it feels like doing so; rather, it has to wait for the proper place and moment. Children learn to inhibit their natural urges to urinate and defecate until they have gotten to the bathroom. Students learn to suppress their desires to make loud and unpleasant noises in most of their classes. Married people learn to repress the showing of open sexual interest toward other individuals—at least while their spouses are watching. Psychologists often refer to these suppressed tendencies to respond as *inhibitions* (°). When you stopped moving your hand toward the apple because you saw the spider, you were inhibiting the completion of a response. And you did so, at least in part, by releasing inhibitory chemicals into the proper synapses. All behavior patterns, then, are made up of a *balance* between excitatory and inhibitory tendencies.

As we said earlier, almost every neuron in your brain makes synaptic connections with several thousand other neurons. Take neuron G as an example. Its dendrites reach out to the axonic end-fibers of perhaps a thousand other nerve cells; thus it can receive molecule-messages from a great many different parts of your brain. Some of the nerve cells that connect with neuron G are *excitatory*

Inhibitors (in-HIB-it-tors). Some chemicals act to excite, stimulate, or "turn on" your nervous system. These chemicals are called "neural excitants," or "transmitters." Other chemicals act to slow down, depress, stop, or "turn off" your nervous system. These chemicals are called "inhibitors" or "anti-transmitters." The axonic end-fibers of some nerve cells release transmitters, while the axonic end-fibers of other nerve cells release anti-transmitters. Suppose that neurons A and B both make synapse with neuron C. Neuron A releases transmitters into the synaptic space, while neuron B releases inhibitors or anti-transmitters. When A fires, it stimulates C into firing; when B fires, it inhibits C from firing. If both A and B fire at the same time, C will either fire or be inhibited from firing, depending on the relative amount of transmitters and inhibitors that are released into the synapse.

Inhibitions. Actions or responses that you would greatly like to make but don't, because you fear the social, psychological, or biological consequences of these actions. If you have been frequently punished for any form of sexual activity in your past, you may suppress or inhibit any expression of your sexual desires in the future.

A neuron.

neurons and hence secrete transmitter substances; other nerve cells connecting with *G* are *inhibitory neurons*, and they release inhibitors at the synapse they make with *G*. Whether *G* fires or does not fire depends on the *relative balance* of "go" and "don't go" molecules present in its synapses at any given moment. If there are 10 "go" transmitter molecules for each "don't go" inhibitory molecule, then neuron *G* will fire rapidly. If there are only 2 "go" molecules for each inhibitory molecule, then neuron *G* will fire much more slowly. If there are 10 times as many "don't go" molecules in the synaptic canal as "go" molecules, then neuron *G* may be entirely inhibited and will fire very infrequently, if at all.

ALCOHOL

Now, let us consider some of the effects of alcohol on your behavior. Alcohol is, in part, a *depressant* (°). That is, alcohol can inhibit some types of neural activity. In fact, if you drink too much alcohol all at once, this rather dangerous drug may actually kill you by poisoning (inhibiting) the nerve cells in the lower brain centers that control your bodily functions—such as breathing. (Venom from a spider's fangs paralyzes your body in much the same fashion.) Yet cocktail parties are supposed to be gay, exciting affairs where people become noisy and happy and boisterous rather than sullen and depressed. How can we reconcile these conflicting facts?

To begin with, not everyone becomes loud and noisy when drunk; many people do in fact become quiet and depressed. However, alcohol (like most other drugs) affects some parts of the brain sooner than it affects others. The front part of your cortex contains many nerve centers that seem to specialize in *inhibiting* social responses of various kinds. As we will see in the next chapter, the frontal cortex also contains the motor-output centers. Small amounts of alcohol often affect the frontal cortex more quickly than much of the rest of the brain. When your *inhibitory centers* in the frontal cortex are depressed or turned off, you may often say and do things that ordinarily you wouldn't. Society demands that we inhibit aggressive behaviors; alcohol can release these social inhibitions. And when your motor-output centers are flooded with alcohol, you may find it difficult to walk and talk normally because your transmitter sailboats don't float very well in "booze" (or, put more precisely, alcohol neutralizes your transmitter molecules). Alcohol also disrupts the molecular processes that allow you to see and hear.

The frontal cortex seems to be involved in judgment and decision-making. Alcohol not only disrupts your ability to think clearly, it also affects your ability to perceive the fact that you aren't thinking clearly. The drunk driver is a menace on our highways because his or her eyes and ears don't provide the sensory input information that they should, and because the driver's brain cannot handle or process this incoming sensory information rapidly enough to avoid oncoming cars. Furthermore, the drunk driver often becomes aggressive and hostile toward others, loses most of the critical motor skills needed to control an automobile, and yet perceives himself or herself as performing normally, resenting any suggestion to the contrary. Little wonder that 25,000 people each year in the United States alone lose their lives in highway accidents as a direct result of drunken driving.

So why do people drug themselves with alcohol? To answer that question, we must look at what a drug is and how it affects your body, mind, and behavior.

WHAT IS A DRUG?

A *drug* (°) is usually defined as any substance that can affect the structure or functioning of your body. Actually, that definition doesn't mean very much because almost any chemical will have some kind of effect on you—if you take a

Depressant (dee-PRESS-ant). Any drug or chemical that slows down or "turns off" neural firing. Inhibitors and anti-transmitters are usually depressants.

Drug. Technically speaking, any substance that can affect the structure or the functioning of your body. See text for fuller definition.

large enough dose or take it the wrong way. For example, water is not usually considered a drug, but if you get too much of it in your lungs you may drown.

A more useful definition is the one we will use in this book. A drug is any chemical which, when taken in relatively small amounts, significantly increases or decreases cellular activities somewhere in your body. Most of the drugs we will discuss in this chapter have their main effects on neural firing, usually by altering the speed at which your nervous system handles sensory inputs, cortical processing, and motor outputs. Some drugs (such as aspirin) primarily affect sensory inputs; others (such as alcohol) can affect cortical processing and motor outputs as well, depending on how much of the drug you take.

While our definition of a drug narrows the field a little, it still leaves a lot of room for us to explore. Many of the more familiar drugs have widespread effects that vary considerably depending on the amounts taken. Alcohol, for instance, acts as a mild pain-killer and as a relaxant in small quantities. One cocktail or a bottle of beer thus can have a cheering-up effect on your feelings, particularly if you are tense or "hurt" just a little. Two or three beers will begin to affect your ability to think or process information; such an amount may affect your coordination (motor output) as well. A six-pack of beer or three highballs may depress both your activity level and your consciousness.

Most people seem to drink because they enjoy the relaxed, painless "rosy glow" that small amounts of alcohol can sometimes give a person. The fact that alcohol also makes one clumsy, sleepy, and reduces incoming sensory messages is something that the casual or social drinker has to put up with in order to get the glow.

The effects of drugs on human behavior are complex and often hard to predict, unless you know as much about the person's genetic background, past history, and present social environment as you do about the chemical composition of the drug itself. We can, however, categorize drugs according to whether their *neurological* (°) effects are fairly specific or rather general. That is, does the chemical speed up or slow down just inputs, just cortical processes, or just outputs—or does the chemical stimulate or inhibit neural firing throughout the whole body? Let us begin by looking at drugs that influence almost every one of your 15 billion nerve cells.

DRUGS AFFECTING GENERAL ACTIVITY LEVELS

One of the most common effects a drug can have is to change your activity level. You normally walk at a certain pace, talk at a certain speed, sleep a certain amount each 24 hours. If you cared to make precise physical measurements of your own behavior, you could fairly readily determine what your own general level of activity would be in most situations. When you swim, ski, play tennis, or dance, this level increases. The more active you are physically, the more rapidly your neurons must fire. Anything that increases your activity level also causes more transmitters to be dumped into the synaptic canals between the nerve cells in your brain (and also in the canals between motor nerve cells and muscles).

"Uppers," or *psychological energizers* (°), are drugs that facilitate or increase synaptic transmission, and thereby usually make you physically and mentally more active. Often—but not always—psychic energizers affect every synapse in your brain in about the same way. That is, they speed up almost all bodily processes controlled by synaptic transmission. They are also called *stimulants* (°), because they chemically stimulate the neurons into firing more often. As the nerve cells are stimulated into faster firing rates, they release more transmitters into the synaptic canals, and the whole body speeds up its tempo. The *sympathetic nervous system* (°) (*see* Chapter 14) is particularly affected by "uppers." When your sympathetic nervous system is excited or churned up, any one or all of the

Neurological (new-roh-LODGE-ee-kal). The scientific study of the structure and function of neurons, or nerve cells.

Psychological energizers. Drugs that speed up neural firing, that "turn on" the nerve cells by acting as super-transmitters, that make you use up your energy resources at a faster speed. Also called "stimulants" and "uppers," because they often elevate or "turn up" both your neural firing and your mood—at the price of using up more energy per minute.

Stimulants (STIM-you-lants). Another term for "psychological energizer" or "upper." Any drug that stimulates neural firing.

Sympathetic nervous system. The "arousal" portion of the emotional nervous system. Excitation in the sympathetic nervous system prepares you for fighting, fleeing, feeding—and sexual climax.

Amphetamines (am-FET-uh-meens). A type of stimulant or "upper." Also called "speed."

Speed. Any powerful neural excitant, stimulant, or "upper." In moderate doses, speed can pep you up, and make you feel good if you are depressed. After a while, you may begin to feel "jangly" and nervous, and you can't relax or go to sleep.

Para-sympathetic nervous system (PAIR-uh-sim-puh-THET-tick). The word *para* means "beyond." The parasympathetic nervous system is "beyond" or "opposed" to the sympathetic nervous system.

Barbiturate (bar-BIT-your-ate). A neural inhibitor that comes from barbituric acid, often used as sleeping pills. Not to be confused with narcotics (from the Greek word *nark,* meaning "to benumb" or "to paralyze"), most of which come from opium or alcohol. Narcotics are more effective as pain-killers than are barbiturates, but both types are habit-forming.

Tranquilizers (TRAN-quill-eye-zers). Drugs that help people relax and become less afraid of things.

Phenobarbital (FEEN-oh-BARB-it-tall). A barbiturate, or sleeping pill, made from barbituric acid. Chemically very similar to all the other barbitals.

Amobarbital, secobarbital, pentobarbital (AM-oh-BARB-it-tall; SEE-ko-BARB-it-tall; PENT-oh-BARB-it-tall). Also called Amytal (AM-it-tall), Seconal (SEE-ko-nall), and Nembutal (NEMM-bew-tall). Sleeping pills derived from barbituric acid. See Phenobarbital.

following responses may occur: your heart beats more quickly; your mouth becomes dry; blood rushes to the surface of your skin; the pupils in your eyes narrow (contract); you breathe more rapidly; your hair stands on end; your digestion is shut down; your appetite vanishes; urine flow and bowel movements are inhibited; and you may become sexually excited if the environment or your own thought processes encourage you to do so. Your muscles become tense; and your reaction times are speeded up. You typically wake up and become more alert, but often find it difficult to concentrate. (The exact pattern of your responses will vary according to your health, personality, and past experience.)

Caffeine is perhaps the most common "upper" in our society. Less common—and considerably more dangerous—is a class of drugs called by such names as *amphetamines* (°), pep pills, or *speed* (°). Amphetamine itself is often referred to as Benzedrine; two other similar but more powerful drugs are dextroamphetamine (Dexedrine) and methamphetamine (Methedrine). The street names for these drugs are "bennies," "dex," and "meth." Since they all speed up activity in the sympathetic nervous system, any or all of them can be referred to as *speed.*

As we will see more fully in Chapter 14, activity in your sympathetic nervous system is opposed or *inhibited* by activity in your *para-sympathetic nervous system* (°). As you might guess from this fact, any drug that increases parasympathetic activity will act as a "downer." The strongest "downers" in common use are the *barbiturates* (°), which are sometimes called "sleeping pills" because they depress neural activity so much that they often put a person to sleep. The *tranquilizers* (°) are both more specific in their effects and usually less powerful. Tranquilizers affect the nervous system in several different ways, but many of them act either by stimulating the para-sympathetic system or by depressing activity in the sympathetic system.

The general effects of "downers" are the opposite of those produced by "uppers." That is, "downers" slow the beating of your heart, take blood away from the surface of your body, retard the rate at which you breathe, and generally make it more difficult for you to react quickly to any emergency. Some "downers" are relaxing because they make it more difficult for you to move your muscles—it is hard for you to experience blind panic and the urge to flee when you are so tired or relaxed that you can barely move.

The first of the modern barbiturates was *barbital,* or Veronal, which was produced in 1903. More recent types include the long-acting *phenobarbital* (°), and *amobarbital* (Amytal), *secobarbital* (Seconal), and *pentobarbital* (Nembutal)—all of which (°) affect the body for shorter lengths of time than does "pheno-barb." The most common types of tranquilizers go by such exotic names as Valium, Librium, Mellaril, reserpine, chlorpromazine (Thorazine), and methaqualone (Quaalude, or "quads").

All of the "uppers" and "downers" have physical and psychological side effects that range from mildly unpleasant to downright deadly. Wisely used, these drugs can be of considerable medical help; when taken in excess, they can be fatal.

DRUGS AFFECTING SENSORY INPUT

Information about the world around you comes to you through your sensory receptors. As we will see in later chapters, if you were totally cut off from the outside world, you would rapidly stop being a normal human being. But not all of the sensory messages that reach your brain bring you pleasant news—some involve the experience of *pain,* a rather complex topic that we will discuss more fully in Chapter 18. Pain is a neural signal that something has gone wrong with the functioning of your body; it commands your attention because it hurts. Since the dawn of recorded time, the human race has made use of various chemicals in order to soothe the pain that our bodies often give us. Some of these drugs—such

An opium poppy.

as aspirin—have their *analgesic* (°) or pain-killing effects by blocking out the neural messages before they can reach the brain and before they can be perceived as "hurting." Other drugs—such as morphine, heroin, ether, chloroform, and marijuana—are analgesic because they change normal neural activity in the central nervous system itself.

Aspirin is perhaps the most common pain-killing drug known to man; it is probably the only drug that everyone reading this book will have tried at least once. It occurs naturally in the bark of the willow tree and was first *synthesized* (°) in 1860. Some 27 million pounds (12,150,000 kilograms) of aspirin are consumed annually in the United States alone—enough to treat 17 *billion* headaches. As potent a pain-killer as aspirin is, it is also a deadly poison that must be treated with respect. Perhaps 20 percent of the deaths by poisoning that occur in the United States each year are due to an overdose of aspirin. When taken in large doses by a pregnant woman, aspirin may either kill the unborn child or cause it to be badly deformed.

Aspirin is a mild pain-killer. In case of severe pain, a more potent medicine—such as an *opiate*—is needed. *Opiates* (°) are derived from opium, a drug widely used for centuries as an analgesic in the Near and Far East. When the seed pods of the opium poppy are slashed with a knife, a sticky *resin* (°) oozes out. This resin is collected by hand, heated, and then smoked in tiny pipes as opium. In 1806, *morphine* (°) was first synthesized from opium. Since morphine could be injected directly into the body in controlled amounts, and since it lacked some of the side effects of opium, morphine rapidly gained wide use in medical circles.

No one really knows why the opiates reduce or kill the experience of pain. It seems likely, however, that these drugs block the receptor sites on those neurons whose firing leads to our feeling pain. With the receptor sites blocked, these neurons in the brain simply cannot respond as they normally would to incoming "painful" sensory messages.

Opiate Addiction

Morphine has one terrible side effect: it is very addictive. The exact biological mechanism underlying addiction is still not well understood. However, there is a growing body of evidence suggesting that the body itself produces a complex chemical—similar to morphine—that acts as a natural pain-killer. Scientists both in Great Britain and in the United States recently claimed to have isolated this chemical—which they call *enkephalin* (°)—in the brains of both rats and human beings. When injected into the bodies of rats, enkephalin appears to reduce pain at least as much as does morphine. Dr. Solomon Snyder and his associates at Johns Hopkins University were among the first to identify enkephalin. Dr. Snyder is

Analgesic (an-al-GEE-sick). From the Greek words meaning "no pain." Technically speaking, any drug that reduces pain without causing a loss of consciousness.

Synthesized (SIN-the-sized). Complex drugs like aspirin are often "manufactured" by plants or animals as part of a natural process. But all drugs are chemical molecules that can be made artificially or synthetically in a laboratory (if we are smart enough to figure out how to do so). It is much cheaper to make drugs like aspirin synthetically than to grow the millions of willow trees we would need to yield enough "natural" aspirin to drive away our headaches.

Opiate (OH-pee-ate, or OH-pee-at). Any of the narcotic drugs that come from the opium poppy. Almost all opiates are habit-forming.

Resin (REZ-in, or sometimes ROZ-in). Soft, usually clear, sticky substances manufactured naturally by plants. Many resins, like the "tar" that oozes out of pine trees, smell good when burned and are used as incense. Most resins will not dissolve in water.

Morphine (MORE-feen). A product of opium. The Latin god Morpheus was supposed to cause dreams in which a human being appeared. Hence, morphine is a dream- or sleep-inducing drug. Like all opiates, morphine is a powerful pain-killer.

Enkephalin (enn-KEFF-uh-linn). A natural pain-killer discovered in the brain by scientists in the United States and Great Britain. Chemically similar to morphine, enkephalin is thought by its discoverers to be non-addictive.

Heroin (HAIR-oh-in). An opiate derived from morphine. Very habit-forming.

Procaine (PRO-cane). Like Novocain (NO-vuh-cane), a synthetic form of cocaine.

Cocaine (KO-cane). A very powerful "local" pain-killer made from leaves of the coca plant.

Euphoria (you-FOR-ee-ah). From the Greek word meaning "good feeling," hence a rush of pleasure.

Hallucinogens. (hal-LEW-sin-oh-jens). Drugs that affect sensory input neurons, and hence "trick" you into seeing or hearing or feeling things that aren't really there. See Chapter 2, under "hallucinations."

Mescaline (MESS-ka-lin). An hallucinogen found in the peyote (pay-YO-tee) cactus.

hopeful that it will be available as an anesthetic for humans in the near future. And because enkephalin is a natural substance, already present in the body, it may not turn out to be as addictive as morphine.

If Dr. Snyder's hopes for enkephalin are fulfilled, this natural pain-killer might also be used in treating drug addiction. However, we must wait for further research before we can be entirely sure. Late in the 1800's, scientists hunting for a non-addictive opiate (to replace morphine) stumbled upon *heroin* (°), which is also made from opium. Several times more powerful than morphine, heroin was at first thought to be the salvation of the human race. Morphine addicts were, in the early 1900's, given heroin instead. Unfortunately, heroin soon proved to be even more addictive and dangerous than morphine. Heroin is seldom used as an analgesic in the United States today—except by the million or so drug addicts who take it as regularly as their funds allow them to.

Local Anesthetics

Laughing gas, or nitrous oxide, is another example of a pain-killer that once enjoyed great medical popularity but is seldom used today. First discovered in 1799, it was often employed by dentists and surgeons as an analgesic because it made their patients so "happy" that tooth-pulling and minor surgery didn't seem to hurt very much. Its effects were often unpredictable, however, and it eventually gave way to morphine or to *procaine* (°) or Novocain, which are synthetic forms of *cocaine* (°) that kill pain by preventing neural activity wherever they are injected into the body.

Cocaine, a strong drug made from the leaves of the coca plant, is notorious for the rush of pleasure or *euphoria* (°) that it gives almost immediately after a person takes it (usually by sniffing). Cocaine was first used as a local anesthetic in 1884 by a Viennese doctor named Carl Koller. Sigmund Freud, the Viennese psychiatrist who was the father of psycho-analysis, soon learned of Koller's work and began experimenting with the drug. He found it such a pleasurable medication that he recommended it to his patients as a substitute for aspirin. Later, when the terribly addictive properties of cocaine were finally appreciated, and tests showed that it could cause damage to body tissues if overused, Freud faced the problem of "de-addicting" a large number of solid Viennese citizens who had become "hooked" on cocaine.

DRUGS AFFECTING CORTICAL PROCESSING

Analgesics reduce pain by acting like super-inhibitors; either they stop sensory messages from reaching the cortex, or they alter synaptic transmission in the brain itself. Analgesics prevent you from experiencing the world (and your body) as it really exists. *Hallucinogens* (°) are a class of drug that have the opposite effect—by acting like super-transmitters, they make you experience or perceive the world as it actually isn't. A drug that caused you to see something that really wasn't physically present in front of your eyes would cause you to *hallucinate*. This hallucination could be pleasant and amusing or incredibly frightening, depending on your state of mind (and your social environment) when you took the drug.

LSD and *mescaline* (°) are perhaps the best-known hallucinogens in our society, although a wide variety of other drugs also fall into this category. The technical name for LSD is d-lysergic acid di-ethyl-amide; its common name is *acid*. LSD is an artificial or synthetic chemical not found in nature. It was first made or synthesized in a Swiss laboratory in 1938. Its rather profound effects on human behavior were not discovered until five years later, when one of the scientists who discovered it accidentally licked some of the drug off his fingers. It was subsequently tested in a psychiatric clinic. Because it made the patients see things that weren't there, it was said to produce "temporary insanity."

Actually, LSD is similar to a chemical produced by *ergot* (°), a fungus or "rust" that grows on such grain products as rye and wheat. The nasty effects of ergot were perhaps first discovered about a thousand years ago in France. In A.D. 994, weather conditions were such that ergot infected much of the wheat and rye that was used to make flour for bread. More than 40,000 French men and women died from eating bread poisoned with ergot; an even larger number suffered from convulsions and hallucinations. Ergot may also have been partially responsible for the infamous witchcraft trials that took place in Salem, Massachusetts, in 1692. In that year, a group of teenaged girls accused several dozen men and women of conversing with the devil and of doing other strange and magical things. The adults were tortured, and many of them were cruelly executed after their trials. Much of the bread eaten by the Massachusetts colonists in 1692 was made from rye brought from Europe, and it is likely that this rye was contaminated with ergot. A careful reading of the trial records suggests that the girls probably suffered from hallucinations and used witchcraft as an explanation for their unusual experiences.

Because LSD is a slightly different chemical than ergot, it usually produces hallucinations but not convulsions or death. Black market acid, however, occasionally is more like ergot than is pure LSD, and hence should be approached with considerable caution.

Mescaline is a chemical found in buttons on the peyote cactus; it can also be produced in synthetic form in a laboratory. The hallucinogenic effects of mescaline have been known for centuries to American Indians, who at times have eaten peyote buttons as part of their religious ceremonies. Less well known is a drug called *psilocybin* (°), found in a mushroom that grows wild in certain parts of the world. Psilocybin also produces hallucinations and also has been used in religious ceremonies.

No one really knows how the various hallucinogens achieve their effects, but it seems that they either act like transmitters themselves, or cause the neurons in the cortical processing regions of the brain to release more transmitters (or fewer inhibitors) than these neurons normally would. In small doses LSD and mescaline

Ergot (UR-got). A disease or fungus that grows on various types of grain plants.

Psilocybin (SILL-oh-SIGH-bin). An hallucinogenic drug that comes from a wild mushroom.

The witchcraft trials in Salem, Massachusetts, in 1692.

The peyote cactus from which mescaline is obtained.

act as mild "uppers," as well as cause hallucinations. In larger doses they can so disorganize the normal processing of your brain that you lose awareness of where you are and what you are doing. As we will see in later chapters, you typically make sense out of incoming sensory messages by matching them against your memory of past experiences. If your memory process is either greatly inhibited, or greatly excited, mismatches occur, and you may "recognize" something that you've never seen before, or fail to recognize a very familiar object or person.

People who are "high" on hallucinogens often report perceiving a basic *connectedness* between objects or ideas that may have no relationship in fact. It is as if they had torn the curtain away from reality and hence could see a strange and disturbing "super-reality" hiding underneath. As we suggested in the previous chapter, it may be that some drugs temporarily suppress the dominance of the major hemisphere, letting the usually silent hemisphere express itself in non-logical symbols or concepts. More frequently, we might suspect, the drugs merely interfere with the ability of *both* hemispheres to process incoming information properly. The Board of Directors then works overtime trying to find logical explanations for the messed-up sensory inputs that the drug has thrust upon it. If the distortions caused by the drug are not too great, "pulling it all together" or "maintaining control" can be amusing and may occasionally give a person some insight into the workings of his or her brain and personality. More likely, when the "trip" is over, the "super-realities" will seem more like a peculiar nightmare than like creative insights coming from one's "silent" hemisphere.

Perhaps the major danger in taking hallucinogens is that sometimes people have a "bad trip." Most of us are trained from birth to "maintain control"—that is, to think and act in ways that the people around us have told us are "normal." Hallucinogens disrupt the usual match between your sensory inputs and the "meanings" that your memories help attach to these inputs. When this disruption of your flow of consciousness occurs, you may fear that you have lost control and that you are likely to do things that would hurt or embarrass yourself or others. Even if you realize that the chemical is causing the experience, you may panic when your thought patterns become too outrageous, or when you badly misinterpret the actions of others. The more value you place on being "normal" or conventional, or the more difficulty you have under the best of circumstances in "maintaining control," the greater your panic is likely to be. As we will see later, your sympathetic nervous system responds to alarm reactions by releasing its own brand of super-transmitters, which speed things up and which can sometimes cause hallucinations all by themselves. The more anxious and frightened you become at what is happening to your mind, the more your body makes things worse by releasing extra transmitters. A *positive feedback* (°) situation builds up in your brain, and you may either explode into some kind of desperate action to stop

Positive feedback. Any kind of information that is exciting or stimulating. See Chapter 2.

the experience—or withdraw into temporary insanity by cutting off the outside world in any way that you can.

The emotional impact that a trip has on a person is influenced by biological, intra-psychic, and social factors. The smaller the dose of a drug that a person takes, the less likely it is that a panic response will occur. The emotionality of a trip (pleasant or unpleasant) may be reduced by tranquilizers or "downers." Because they are inhibitors, "downers" can counteract the super-transmitter characteristics both of the hallucinogen and of the chemicals that the sympathetic nervous system releases when panic occurs. A person's frame of mind prior to "tripping" has a strong influence on the experience to follow. It is particularly unwise for anyone to take an hallucinogen if he or she is anxious, worried, disturbed, frightened, or at all uneasy about what might happen. The social environment has its influence too. Many people who, for better or worse, are heavily into drugs like to have a friend around while they are "high"—someone they trust who isn't taking the drug, someone who can help them hang on to reality if things get out of hand.

Of course, the safest way of all to avoid having a bad trip is to leave the hallucinogens to the 5 percent or so of the people who seem to enjoy seeking an hallucinatory Nirvana.

Marijuana

Marijuana is a product of the hemp or *cannabis* (°) plant, a weed found in abundance in many parts of the world. The "active ingredient" is a complex chemical that goes by the complex name of delta-9-trans-tetrahydrocannabinol, which we can gladly abbreviate as *THC* (°). Although THC is most abundant in the flowers and seeds of the female cannabis plant, it is found to some extent in the leaves and branches of both male and female plants. The female flowers exude a sticky substance or resin that is particularly rich in THC. If the resin alone is harvested from the plant, the product is a brown or blackish cake of material usually called hashish or *hash* (°). If the entire plant is harvested for smoking, the material is commonly called "grass," "pot," or "dope." Recent studies suggest that the amount of THC present in any individual plant is controlled almost entirely by the genetic background of the plant itself. The hemp that grows wild in Africa and Mexico may have 100 times more THC per pound than the cannabis plants that grow wild in the United States.

As Dr. Snyder at Johns Hopkins University, whom we mentioned earlier in the chapter, points out, cannabis has a long and interesting history. In his book, *Uses of Marijuana*, published in 1971 by the Oxford University Press, Dr. Snyder states that a century ago cannabis was almost as commonly used for medicinal purposes

Cannabis (KAN-ah-biss). The common hemp plant, from which come such drugs as marijuana (also spelled marihuana) and hashish. In the Western world, the most widespread species is *cannabis sativa* (SAT-ee-vah), which grows wild in most of the continental United States.

THC. An abbreviation for tetrahydro-cannabinol (TET-trah HIGH-dro kan-NAB-uh-noll). Marijuana contains many chemicals, of which THC seems the main one that induces a "high." Although THC was synthesized in Israel in the 1960's, it is very expensive to make. When exposed to air, THC soon loses its power. The "street drugs" sold as THC are usually some other substance, since THC cannot be kept in pills or powders.

Hash. The common name for hashish (hash-EESH).

A marijuana plant.

Anti-convulsant (ANT-eye-con-VUL-sant). A drug that prevents convulsions or epileptic seizures.

Narcotics (nar-KOT-icks). Drugs that both reduce pain and induce sleep or mental confusion. Usually very habit-forming.

Ganja (GAHN-jah). The Jamaican name for marijuana.

as aspirin is today. It could be purchased without a prescription in any American drug store and was prescribed by physicians for such medical problems as ulcers, epilepsy, headaches, excessive menstrual bleeding, and even tooth decay. Although used in the Far East as a medicine for more than a thousand years, cannabis was first introduced into European and American circles in 1839 by an Irish physician named W.B. O'Shaughnessy, who had discovered it while living in India. A cautious man, O'Shaughnessy first tested the drug on hundreds of animals to determine its safety. No matter how much cannabis he gave his animals, none of them died. (We know from another century of experimentation that cannabis is one of the least lethal drugs ever discovered.) O'Shaughnessy found the drug particularly effective as a pain-killer, muscle relaxant, and *anti-convulsant* (°).

Cannabis did not become illegal in the United States until 1937, but as Dr. Snyder points out, its popularity as a medicine had declined considerably by then. The reasons are not hard to find. Synthetic THC was not manufactured until 1964, so early physicians had to depend on the natural product. But the THC in cannabis varies widely from one batch of plants to another. It was, therefore, impossible to know what the "standard dose" should be. Cannabis is insoluble in water and cannot be injected into a person's veins, as can the opiates and most other *narcotics* (°) and analgesics. When swallowed, it has little effect for an hour or two (although when smoked, it typically causes mild euphoria within 15 minutes). Individual reactions to the drug were fairly great; it helped some people considerably, but others were almost totally unaffected. By 1900—with the increasing availability of morphine, heroin, and other synthetic pain-killers—the medical profession switched to analgesics that were quick-acting and that could be injected directly into the bloodstream. Scientific evidence suggests that cannabis still might be useful as a medicine. It seems particularly effective against diseases caused by tension and high blood pressure, menstrual bleeding, glaucoma (a build-up of pressure within the eyeball), and epilepsy—if the patient can tolerate its euphoric side effects.

Very little is known about how cannabis affects the central nervous system. In small doses it can produce a pleasant change of mood. In larger amounts it can produce mild hallucinations similar to those brought about by a small dose of LSD or mescaline. However, THC is chemically quite different from opiates, from all other known hallucinogens, and from cocaine. In very large doses it can induce vomiting, chills, and fever, as well as the bad-trip loss of control; but it is almost never fatal, and it is not physiologically addicting as are alcohol, morphine, and heroin. Aside from euphoria, the main psychological effect that cannabis seems to have is distortion of immediate memory, or what psychologists call Short-term Memory (*see* Chapter 17). If someone asked you to count backward by 7's from 154 until 84 (154, 147, 140 . . . 84), you would surely do a good job. A person "high" or euphoric on cannabis might begin fairly well, but frequently would forget what number to stop counting at. Asked a complex question, a person high on marijuana may begin talking, then break up in laughter because he or she has suddenly forgotten what the question was. Recently, Elliot Entin at Ohio University presented evidence that cannabis can affect other types of memory as well. Because Short-term Memory is intimately involved in our perception of the passage of time, a person who is high on pot often experiences rather odd time distortions. A single musical note may hang suspended in the person's consciousness for what seems like minutes, or the first taste of a candy bar may last for what seems like hours.

A young woman inhaling a marijuana cigarette.

The Jamaica Study In the Caribbean island of Jamaica, marijuana is called *ganja* (°) and is used in many ways. It is chewed, smoked, brewed as tea, and used in cooking. In rural Jamaica, children are introduced to ganja at a very early age, for many islanders believe it is a potent medicine against a variety of diseases. Jamaicans who must work in the fields to survive will often smoke eight or more "spliffs" (ganja cigarettes) per day most of their adult lives. Since ganja contains much more THC than does most of the marijuana smoked in the United States, we may assume that these Jamaicans have rather a higher cannabis intake than do most American pot smokers. Strangely, these field workers do not smoke to get "high," but rather to make their tedious work less painful. Dr. Joseph H. Schaeffer, an anthropologist who has studied the effects of ganja on Jamaicans, reports that the laborers actually performed more motions and expended more energy after smoking ganja than before, but they appeared to accomplish less. Dr. Schaeffer states that ganja seems to help the workers get along with each other better and increases their willingness to till the fields.

In 1970, the U.S. National Institute of Mental Health commissioned a study of ganja use in Jamaica by the Research Institute for the Study of Man. A report of the study, prepared by Drs. Vera Rubin and Lambros Comitas, was published in Holland in 1975.

As part of the study, 30 men who were heavy ganja smokers and 30 male non-smokers of similar height, age, occupation, and educational background were studied intensively in a hospital setting for a period of 6 days—during which time they were not allowed ganja. Medical examinations of both groups resulted in some surprising findings:

1. Ganja smokers weighed 7 pounds (3.2 kilograms) less on the average than non-smokers; the doctors suggest that chronic use of cannabis causes some suppression of appetite.
2. X-rays of the lungs were normal in both groups except for some scarring of lung tissue in one person who did not smoke ganja. Since most of the men in both groups smoked tobacco, the doctors believe that impaired lung function is probably caused by inhaling any kind of smoke, whether from tobacco or ganja.
3. Most of the ganja smokers had parents and grandparents who had also smoked cannabis. Despite the fact that one or two U.S. scientists have reported genetic damage in pot smokers, the Jamaica study found no evidence for this. In fact, the ganja smokers showed fewer genetic abnormalities than the non-smokers.
4. There were no significant differences in personality, intelligence, tendency toward mental illness, or brain-wave recordings between the two groups.
5. Being cut off from the ganja for six days did not lead to any noticeable problems in the smokers, despite the fact that few of them had ever gone that long before in their adult lives without cannabis.
6. Although the smokers had taken in very large daily quantities of strong cannabis for an average of 17.5 years prior to the study, there was no evidence that they had any more difficulties in getting or holding jobs than the non-smokers.

As you may realize, these findings sharply contradict many widely-held notions about the long-term effects of using marijuana. As controversial as the Jamaica study may be, however, it received support in 1976 when scientists at the University of Florida announced the results of a similar experiment conducted in Costa Rica. The Florida study—directed by Paul L. Doughty, William E. Carter, Wilmer J. Coggins, and John B. Page—involved an intensive investigation of 41 carefully matched pairs of Costa Rican males. Half the men used marijuana; the other half had never done so. As was true in Jamaica, the Costa Rican smokers weighed about 7 pounds (3.2 kilograms) less on the average than did the non-users. There were few if any other biological, psychological, or social differences between the two groups. Perhaps the most interesting finding was that smokers did not differ at all from non-smokers in terms of sex drive or sex hormone level—despite the fact that the smokers had consumed more than nine marijuana cigarettes a day per man for several years.

We cannot conclude from either of these experiments that marijuana is either safe or harmless. But the results of both studies do suggest that the long-term use of marijuana is somewhat less dangerous than had been previously thought.

Other Marijuana Studies Marijuana is, in the United States, as much a social and legal problem as it is a medical one. In recent years, many reports have appeared in the popular press suggesting that cannabis causes brain damage and lowers resistance to disease (particularly cancer), that it causes birth defects and lung damage, and that it makes people sterile and lowers their sex drive. Writing in the March and April 1975 issues of *Consumer Reports,* Edward M. Brecher casts considerable doubt on almost all these studies. After reviewing all the data he could find, Brecher concludes that most of these experiments were poorly controlled and were done by scientists with a strong personal interest in proving that marijuana was a terrible curse to the human race. Most of the studies yielding negative data simply could not be repeated by other scientists. Brecher does not feel that marijuana is harmless—to the contrary, he points out that "no drug is safe or harmless to all people at all dosage levels or under all conditions of use." Brecher does believe, however, that the adverse legal and social consequences of misinformation about the health effects of marijuana are worse than the biological effects of the drug itself.

In 1973, the Presidential Commission on Marijuana and Drug Abuse came to the conclusion that:

1. Alcoholism is our worst drug problem.
2. Heroin dependence is our second-worst problem.
3. *Legal* use of "downers," particularly by housewives, is our worst "hidden" drug problem.
4. Cannabis use is a minor problem compared with the abuse of alcohol and other drugs.

The commission then reaffirmed its earlier recommendation that we should end all criminal penalties for smoking marijuana.

An interesting parallel might be drawn between marijuana and tobacco. The active ingredient in tobacco is *nicotine* (°), a drug that acts as a mild "upper" for many people. In the early part of this century, when cigarettes first became popular, men were usually allowed to smoke in public—but women were forbidden to do so either by law or by custom. It took some 50 years for us to build up a set of social "rules" and expectations about the use of nicotine in public and private places. The same thing seems to be true of alcohol, for "booze" was outlawed in the United States from 1919 to 1933. It is only comparatively recently that men and women of all social stations dared to drink openly in public. Cannabis will probably not become a legal part of our cultural scene (if ever) until we know enough about its continued or long-term use to be able to evaluate its effects, both physiological and psychological. And legal or not, it won't become an accepted thing until we build up a set of customs and conventions that will guide its use in a wide variety of social situations.

DRUGS AFFECTING MOTOR OUTPUT

Almost all of the "uppers" and "downers" affect motor outputs as well as sensory inputs and central processing. However, many drugs have their major influence on muscular reactions. Perhaps the best known of these is *meprobamate* (°), also called Miltown or Equanil. When meprobamate was first introduced, it was called

Nicotine (NICK-oh-teen). A mild euphoric drug found in tobacco.
Meprobamate (mepp-pro-BAMM-ate). A drug that acts to relax the muscles.

a "psychic" tranquilizer. Later research indicated it does not affect central processing all that much, but rather increases the output of inhibitory molecules at the neural-muscular synapses, thus lowering the level of muscular activity.

Perhaps the most potent common drug that affects motor output is *curare* (°). Actually, curare is not just one drug, but rather is several related chemicals that are found in many types of South American plants. Curare has been used for centuries by South American Indians who put it on their arrows and blow-gun darts to help "poison" the wild animals they hunt. A dart tipped with sticky, tarry curare will paralyze even a fairly large animal if the drug gets into the beast's bloodstream.

When injected into humans, curare-like compounds bring about a profound relaxation of the muscles, chiefly by poisoning the synapse between motor neurons and muscles. Curare, then, prevents the muscles from tensing and doing their normal work. In small amounts, curare primarily affects the "voluntary" muscles—that is, those muscles under a person's voluntary control. Since curare does not greatly influence sensory inputs or central processing, a person given a small dose of the drug remains conscious but cannot so much as lift a finger or even blink the eyes. In larger doses, curare can paralyze the involuntary muscles that make you breathe and keep your heart in action. Synthetic forms of curare are widely used in medicine, particularly in surgery to make absolutely certain that the patient does not move a muscle during the operation. However, the dosage must be carefully controlled, since too large an amount can quickly lead to respiratory or cardiac arrest (stoppage of the lungs or the pumping of the heart).

Curare (cure-RAR-ree). A paralyzing drug that occurs naturally in many plants native to South America.

NIRVANA

People take drugs primarily because certain chemical compounds make them feel better than they do without the drugs, or because people *believe* that the drugs will make them feel better. In either case, the major effect of the drugs is to make the person's nervous system (or selected parts thereof) function faster or slower than before the chemical was taken.

But there are often other, non-chemical ways to achieve the same psychological ends. A warm spring day can be as much of an "upper" as a mild dose of Benzedrine, and a love affair can bring about the same euphoria as does LSD or

St. Paul discovering Christ on the road to Damascus.

Trance state. A state of partly suspended animation or the inability to function normally. A sleep-like state in which the body moves slowly if at all, while the mind is usually focused on one single thought.

Yoga (YO-gah). A Hindu mental discipline that involves concentrating on any object with a view to the identification of consciousness with that object. Thinking about something until you identify with or become that something.

Yogis (YO-geese). People who practice yoga.

Latent (LAY-tent). A talent, ability, power, or behavior pattern not presently expressed or visible. A latent homosexual is someone who has secret or unconscious sexual desires for someone of the same sex.

marijuana. Prolonged starvation can cause hallucinations, as can an overdose of vitamin B-12, hypnotism (*see* Chapter 18), or isolating yourself in a dark room for a few hours (*see* Chapter 9). Religious experiences can so alter your state of consciousness that you experience the same sort of "floating, peaceful, pain-free mystical union with the Universe" that drug addicts often report. The biblical description of St. Paul discovering Christ on the road to Damascus (Acts 9) is a good example of the "blinding light" that often accompanies such profound alterations in a person's stream of consciousness. Technically speaking, this Nirvana-like condition is called a *trance state* (°), and the person experiencing it is said to be *in a trance*.

Meditation

Many Eastern religions have developed methods to train a person to go into this trance state more or less at will. Perhaps the best known of these disciplines is *yoga* (°), which developed among the Hindus of India many hundreds of years ago. In its strictest interpretation, yoga refers to a set of beliefs and practices whose aim is to help an individual attain a union of his or her conscious self with what is called "the Supreme Reality," or "the Universal Self." Many *yogis* (°) believe that we all have *latent* (°) or hidden powers in our nervous systems. At the base of the spine, for example, lies the "serpent power," which is said to be a feminine power. At the top of the skull is said to be an even greater power center called "the lotus with a thousand petals," which is masculine. Between these two sources of psychic power are six other centers, which some yogis believe lie one above another along the spine. Many yogis practice spiritual and bodily exercises in order to raise the feminine serpent power up through each of the six psychic centers of the spine until it unites with the masculine lotus power—at which time full "Union with the Universal Self" or Nirvana, is achieved.

The exercises that lead to this particular altered state of consciousness involve self-control, physical postures such as the Lotus Position, breath control, cutting off sensory inputs by staring at an object (such as the sun) for long periods of time, meditative concentration on your inner feelings and perceptions instead of focusing on the outside world, and finally a trance state so complete that you become unaware that you actually are concentrating and meditating. This final condition yields the Nirvana experience that followers of yoga often wish to achieve.

The lotus posture.

From a purely physiological point of view, the yogic description of the various "power centers" in the nervous system is highly inaccurate. But perhaps this is only to be expected, since yoga came into being when no one even knew that we have a nervous system as such—much less that it has electrical and chemical activity in it. However, one way or another, the early yogis hit upon crude if eventually effective ways of altering both brain functioning and subjective states of consciousness.

Perhaps the most popular form of yogic exercise in the United States is *transcendental meditation* (°), or TM, developed by Maharishi Mahesh Yogi. Unlike other types of yogic meditation, the TM technique requires no elaborate postures, no special diets, no complicated equipment. The meditator, after settling down a half a minute or so with his or her eyes closed, begins freely thinking a specific sound or *mantra* (°). Bodily activities slow down in a sleep-like fashion, oxygen consumption is reduced, and a state of considerable physical and mental rest is typically achieved. However, the person undergoing TM does not lose consciousness and remains in touch with his or her environment during the 20 minutes or so of meditation. Research suggests that the TM technique is particularly effective in helping people achieve a state of deep muscular relaxation, and that meditation is of considerable therapeutic value for individuals who are over-tense. There are several reports in the scientific literature suggesting that people who practice the TM technique for 2 years or more show a dramatic reduction in their consumption of drugs such as marijuana. It seems likely, then, that TM (and other forms of therapy involving deep muscle relaxation) can yield some of the "good feelings" and slightly altered mental states that we associate with drugs, although practitioners of TM often state that the Nirvana-like experience is not one of their major goals.

Brain Waves

All roads to Nirvana lead through the brain. You cannot alter your own stream of consciousness without somehow achieving a change in the electro-chemical functioning of your brain. Drugs are a "quick and dirty" way to do so, but the cost sometimes outweighs the advantages. Even at their best, drugs are a "chemical crutch"—an artificial way of controlling your own natural transmitters and inhibitors. Yoga is a far less dangerous way of altering your state of consciousness—but not everyone is willing to bother with the extensive training and discipline that yoga requires.

Luckily, within the past few years, scientists may have discovered a much quicker route to Nirvana than yoga appears to offer.

In Chapter 2 we discussed the connection between brain waves and states of consciousness. When you are actively engaged in thinking, or are working on some task, most areas of your cortex show the *activity rhythm* in which each neuron seems to be functioning more or less independently. When you slip into a state of *relaxed alertness*, much of your cortex shows what are called *alpha waves*, an *EEG* (°) pattern that cycles or repeats itself 10 to 12 times per second. For example, when you are sitting quietly in a chair with your eyes closed, you have cut off part of your external world—and the visual-input areas of your cortex show the alpha rhythm. If you stare at an object for a long time—as you would in some yogic exercises—your visual areas may again produce the alpha rhythm. But as soon as you look around, or become aware of your environment, the alpha rhythm disappears and the activity pattern appears again.

Several groups of scientists have recently recorded the brain waves of master yogis, both while the yogis were functioning normally and when they were in trance states. These scientists report a very strong relationship or *correlation* (°) between yogic expertise and brain-wave activity. When in a deep state of

Transcendental meditation (trans-sen-DEN-tull med-uh-TAY-shun). A form of meditation or mental technique for relaxation introduced to the United States by Maharishi Mahesh Yogi in about 1957. The terms "transcendental meditation" and TM are trademarks of World Plan Executive Council, founded by Maharishi Mahesh Yogi.

Mantra (MAN-trah). A sound that is repeated over and over again in one's mind during transcendental meditation

EEG. Electro-encephalo-graph. See Chapter 2.

Correlation (KOR-re-lay-shun, or KO-re-LAY-shun). Things that "go together" or that are "co-related." The behavior of a young man and woman who are engaged to be married is usually "correlated." That is, the young man often appears at the same places that the young woman does, and vice versa. The important thing to remember is that correlations don't tell you what causes what. The young man doesn't cause the young woman's behavior, for instance. Most blondes have blue eyes, so eye color and hair color are correlated. However, blue eyes don't *cause* light-colored hair; rather, they are both determined by related genetic factors.

Biological feedback. A device that feeds back information to your mind on what some part of your body is doing. An EEG machine is a biological feedback machine, because it tells your mind what your brain waves are like. When you take your pulse, you are getting biological feedback on your own heart rate.

meditation, yogis show a great deal more alpha activity than does the average person. Additionally, the more experience that the yogi has, the more alpha he shows, and the more likely it is that the yogi will report having achieved Nirvana. The yogic exercises—worked out over many hundreds of years—seem to be effective at least in part because they do lead to voluntary control over a person's alpha activity. But it may take a highly motivated yogi 15 to 20 years to master his brain waves.

In 1962, Dr. Joe Kamiya and his colleagues at the University of California Medical Center in San Francisco reported that they had been able to train college students to achieve much the same sort of alpha control as yogis do by using a technique involving *biological feedback* (°). A full description of biological feedback (or biofeedback, as it is also called) will have to wait until Chapter 16. We can, however, discuss Kamiya's work here briefly.

The major reason that you cannot readily learn to control your own alpha activity is that you are almost never directly aware of what electro-chemical events are going on in your brain. You are aware of your feelings, your thoughts, your perceptions, and your emotions—but not of the neural activity that underlies these experiences. By placing large metal electrodes on your scalp, and by connecting these electrodes to an EEG machine (*see* Chapter 2), a scientist such as Kamiya can take a relatively precise reading of the *average firing rates* of the nerve cells lying close to the electrodes. By looking at your EEG record as it comes off the machine, Kamiya knows when your brain is putting out alpha rhythms—but *you* still don't know. Kamiya "closed the feedback loop" by telling his subjects when they were showing alpha and when they weren't. Using this information fed back to them, the students were often able to learn what thoughts to think in order to increase their own alpha activity. Once they had learned the

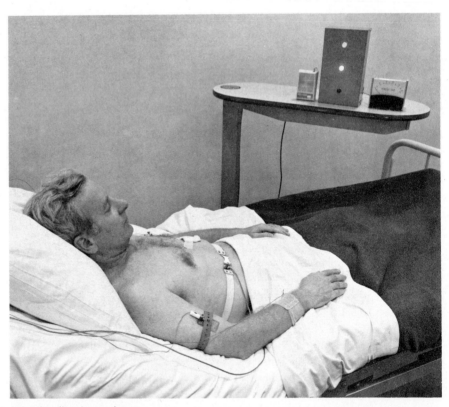

A biofeedback machine.

trick, they were often able to turn their alpha rhythms on—or off—even when the students were no longer connected to the EEG machine.

Many of Kamiya's subjects found the experience so enjoyable that they begged for further training—even when Kamiya could no longer afford to pay them to be subjects in his experiments. The students described this "alpha state" as being very similar to a mild drug "high." A few subjects in studies such as these have apparently achieved Nirvana-like states of consciousness very similar to those reported by master yogis. One subject became so expert at turning his alpha on and off that after some practice he could send messages to an EEG machine in "brain-wave Morse code" by sending out brief bursts of alpha in a rhythmical pattern.

This area of psychology—that of teaching people to control their own states of consciousness voluntarily—is still in its infancy. The Hindu yogis took centuries to discover the yogic techniques because they had no feedback from their brains except their own, often unreliable perceptions. Using the kind of biological feedback pioneered by Dr. Kamiya, we can cut the training time down considerably. But our methods are necessarily crude, because we still do not know what types of neurological activity are correlated with what types of conscious experiences. The Nirvana state appears to come not merely from the amount of alpha rhythm a brain puts out, but the strength or *amplitude* (°) of the rhythm as well. And alpha is but one of dozens of electrical patterns that we might want to look at. Until we know what brain activities to measure, we cannot develop the sophisticated electronic gadgets that will be needed to give you the most helpful forms of biofeedback.

There is also the problem of individual differences. As roughly similar as brains are, no two human nervous systems are exactly the same. Kamiya's techniques appear to work better and faster with some subjects than with others. It would seem likely that some people are born with more easily trainable brains than are other people. It is also probable that a person's social environment and past history will affect that person's ability to utilize biofeedback.

One thing seems certain, though. Sometime in the near future we will gain a great deal more control over what goes on in our brains than we presently have. Perhaps then, and only then, will we be able to work out ways of letting people alter their consciousness just by thinking about it—and hence achieve whatever Nirvanas they wish. And, by doing so, help solve the drug-abuse problems that haunt our society today.

Amplitude (AM-pli-tood). The height of any kind of wave, also a measure of the strength of the wave. An ocean wave 10 feet (3 meters) tall has a greater amplitude than a 4-foot (1.2 meters) wave; hence it has greater power.

SUMMARY

1. Your ordinary state of mental functioning is defined as being your usual state of consciousness, or your usual state of awareness.
2. Certain experiences—such as falling asleep, dreaming, taking various drugs, achieving sexual orgasm, or concentrating intensely—can lead to altered or unusual states of consciousness.
3. The behavior of the nerve cells in your brain typically changes markedly whenever you achieve an altered state of consciousness. When you relax, or fall asleep, most of your nerve cells fire at much slower rates than normal. Whenever you are extra-alert, or extremely excited, many of your neurons fire at much faster rates than usual.
4. Your body has certain diurnal rhythms that involve altered states of consciousness, the most obvious one being the sleep-waking cycle.
5. The several stages of sleep include light sleep, deep sleep, and a REM period during which you usually experience one or more dreams.
6. Each sleep cycle is about 90 minutes long, including an REM period of about

10 minutes. Deep sleep predominates during the first and second sleep cycles of the night. REM periods and dreaming increase during later cycles.

7. During REM sleep, most of the muscles in your body are inhibited—except for those that control eye movements.

8. There are two main types of nightmares: anxiety dreams and incubus attacks. Anxiety dreams take place during REM sleep and do not usually involve bodily movements. Incubus attacks take place during deep sleep and occasionally are followed by sleepwalking.

9. "Nirvana" is a term many people apply to a mental state that involves great inner peace, freedom from anxiety and need, and intense feelings of well-being and pleasure.

10. To attain Nirvana, you must somehow induce a change in your bodily reactions, particularly in the way that your brain processes incoming sensory information. Drugs are a direct way of inducing these neurological changes, for drugs can excite (speed up) neural firing rates or inhibit them (slow them down).

11. Neural excitants ("uppers") act as super-transmitters—that is, they make it more likely that certain brain cells will fire. Neural inhibitors ("downers") act as anti-transmitters that prevent certain brain cells from firing.

12. Drugs that inhibit sensory inputs can reduce pain.

13. Drugs that affect cortical processing can also reduce pain, change moods, and cause you to hallucinate or misinterpret the world around you by disrupting memory.

14. Drugs that affect motor outputs can cause relaxation or muscular paralysis.

15. Various forms of mental discipline, such as yoga and transcendental meditation (TM), are indirect ways of altering your state of consciousness.

16. Perhaps the most effective indirect way of markedly changing your level of consciousness is through biological feedback—that is, by feeding back to your mind information on the performance of some part of your body.

17. EEG machines can be used to induce Nirvana-like state of consciousness because the apparatus shows you (feeds back to you) an exact measure of the firing rates of many of the neurons in your cortex.

(Continued from page 43.)

Peter McGraw clung tightly to a strap as the little cable car topped one of San Francisco's steep hills, clanged its way across a busy intersection, then dipped down toward the Bay. It was one of those rare, bright-hot days when the wind came from the east, bringing the scent of pine and fir down from the Sierra Madre mountains. Peter could see the cluster of buildings in the distance that made up the medical center—his destination—its mud-colored spires poking into the blue sky like fingers pointing at God.

Once inside the buildings, it took him almost 15 minutes to find Dr. Wilder's tiny laboratory. He knocked politely on the door, entered when a voice told him to, and found himself face-to-face with a muscular man in his late 30's.

"You're Mr. McGraw, the new subject?"

"That's right."

"Good. I'm Dr. Wilder. If you'll just sit in that chair for a moment, I'd like to ask you some questions before we start."

Peter took the chair and tried to look as bright and alert as he could.

"Now, Mr. McGraw, we hope to train you to control your own brain waves. We'll need your name, address, telephone number, and social security number to begin with." Dr. Wilder took the information quickly, then continued. "We've found that drugs can alter brain-wave patterns, so I must ask you not to use any drugs at all for at least 24 hours before each training session. We're not trying to control your life; and we don't care what you do after the study is concluded. We're just trying to run a clean experiment. **Comprende?**"

Peter nodded agreement.

Dr. Wilder stood up and motioned the young man to follow him into an inner chamber. The room was so small that there was barely space for the overstuffed chair that was its only furniture. On a wall panel in front of the chair were two loudspeakers, a microphone, and two small light bulbs. A bunch of wires popped out of the top of the panel like spaghetti.

"You'll sit in this chair. We'll insert several electrodes into the skin on top of your head. Then you'll just sit and think about anything you want to think about. The electrodes are connected to an EEG machine in the next room. I'll be in there, reading your brain waves. We can talk back and forth through the intercom. Whenever the electrodes pick up an alpha rhythm, the light on the panel will come on, and a soft tone will sound. It's up to you to figure out how to get the light and tone to stay on as much as possible. Do you understand?"

Peter scratched his head, as if anticipating where the electrodes would be placed. "Why can't we be in the same room?"

"Several reasons. For starters, brain waves are very faint indeed. This little room is completely shielded electrically—there are copper screens in the walls, floor, and ceiling that completely block out electrical activity. If you brought a portable radio in here, you couldn't pick up any stations at all. That way, we're sure that all the electrical signals that the electrodes detect are from your brain and not noise or interference from a TV station or a noisy fluorescent light.

"Second reason is that the copper screens are so expensive, we make the room as small as possible. There's no room for me here, much less for the computer."

Peter looked puzzled. "Computer?"

"You bet. At any given instant in time, your brain is putting out hundreds of different brain signals. We're only interested in alphas right now. So we feed all your brain waves into the computer. It scans or cycles hundreds of times each second. When it sees an alpha rhythm, it lets you know by turning on the light and the tone. The stronger the alpha rhythm, the brighter the light and the louder the tone will be. Because it cycles so frequently, the computer can pick up alpha rhythms much faster and more reliably than I could just looking at your EEG record. **Comprende?**"

"Yeah, I guess so. But how do I get my brain to make alpha waves?"

"If I knew that, I wouldn't be doing the study. Most subjects stare at the light and try to will it to come on. Mostly it doesn't at first. You may go a whole hour and be able to turn the light and tone on for only a few minutes the first time you try. Then you relax a little, get used to it, and think quiet, peaceful thoughts. That's the way I do it anyhow. Think of a green countryside, maybe mountains in the background. A lake with sailboats on it. Some people do best when they close their eyes—that's why we have both the tone and the light. When you get good at producing alphas, I'll want to have a long talk with you to find out how you think you did it."

Peter sat down in the chair. It was very comfortable. "One of my friends, Kathy, bought a little alpha machine. Like a set of hi-fi headphones. Supposed to make a noise when you got alphas. I never could make it work too well. Does that mean I won't be able to turn your light on?"

"Not at all. Frankly, those little machines don't work too well. They all have a little computer built into them, but nothing like the big computer I've got here. The headphone machines use metal disc electrodes, which read your brain waves through your skin and your hair. We insert sharp points directly into the skin. Hurts for a second, then the pain goes away. The closer the electrode is to your brain cells, the better it works. And, of course, the headphones aren't shielded with copper screen like this room is. Someday, maybe, we'll have inexpensive alpha machines that really work. Maybe there's one on the market now I don't know of. For research purposes, though, this set-up of ours is the best."

Moments later, with the electrodes stuck in his scalp, Peter sat staring at the light.

Dr. Wilder's voice came over the intercom. "Okay, **amigo**, let's try it out. Just relax and try to turn the light and the tone on. Don't worry if it takes a while. And good luck."

Peter tried to concentrate, but at first it didn't work. His mind wandered everywhere. Occasionally the light flickered, the tone hummed quickly and faded away. He uncrossed his legs and tried to let his body relax totally. The light-sound came on briefly, but vanished. Then he tried thinking about a blue-green lake, with sailboats. A burst of bright light interrupted his visual picture.

"**Bueno, bueno,** that's very good. You're getting it. Breathe regularly and try that thought again," Dr. Wilder's voice said.

Peter closed his eyes, sighed, relaxed even more. He made a conscious effort to control his breathing and to shut out everything around him as best he could. He was in a sailboat, drifting on the lake, watching the shore and the mountains beyond. Three huge birds flew by, winging gracefully toward the hills. For a moment he was inside one of those giant birds, looking down at the lake, and then he was back in the sailboat, listening to the buzzing tone of the wind sighing in the sails. He leaned over the edge of the boat and looked deep into the water. It was dark, murky, with fish darting here and there like silvery shooting stars just beyond his reach. It was so good, just lying there on the boat, watching. So very, very good.

And there was something down there, something big, floating in the deep currents, something with a single bright shining eye. He couldn't quite see what it was, so he leaned further over the edge of the boat. It looked almost human, like a body . . . a body balanced far out over the edge of a boat, looking down at him. Why would anyone want to lie in a boat when they could be here, deep in the water, warm and good and gloriously floating in the eternal sea? And beyond the boat, the sun, its brilliant red face smiling, bright and shining, coming closer and better and brighter and bigger and louder and singing at the top of its voice . . .

"**Superbo!** You've had the light on for several minutes now. That's enough for today, I think. I'll be in to rescue you from the equipment **muy pronto.**"

The door opened, the lights went on, and Dr. Wilder came in with a rush of reality. He unplugged the wires and carefully, painlessly removed the electrodes.

"You're a good subject, McGraw. It takes most people several sessions to get that much alpha. What did you think of?"

Peter climbed slowly out of the chair, then stretched. "A lake, I think. I was floating on a lake, It really felt great. Then the sun came closer and closer, and I was floating in the water looking straight at the sun."

"Sounds like Puerto Vallarta. That's a resort on the Mexican coast. I just got back from a vacation there. Lovely place." Dr. Wilder led the way into the office. "We'll want you to come back in a day or so, if that's all right with you."

"Sure. I'll come back tomorrow if you want me to. Or later on today, if you like."

"Thursday will be fine. But I'm glad you liked it. Most people do."

Peter cleared his throat. "Dr. Wilder, turning on your alphas is fun, and all that, but is it really good for you?"

"No harmful side effects at all, as far as we know. All you're doing is learning how to control your own mental activity, to bring it under your conscious control. We spend millions of dollars each year teaching school kids how to control their muscles, how to improve their coordination. Some day there will be machines like this one in all the schools so that kids can also learn how to coordinate the firing patterns of their nerve cells. Maybe certain brain waves will turn out to be a signal that you're thinking creatively, or solving problems logically, or just grooving along naturally, enjoying life. Mental discipline. That's what our computer can teach you if you watch the light and listen to the tone."

Peter looked closely at the man's face. Dr. Wilder had obviously spent most of his vacation lying in the sun, for his skin was burned to a deep mahogany color, and his blond hair was bleached almost feather-white. There was something oddly familiar about his dark eyes that Peter couldn't place. He walked slowly toward the door, then paused at the entrance.

"Dr. Wilder, do you have friends or relatives living in Mexico?"

The older man's face burst into a smile like a searchlight penetrating the San

Francisco fog. "**Amigo**, I come from a big family. And I've got friends everywhere." He laughed harshly, hoarsely, like a bird croaking. "Everywhere." The door shut behind Peter with a click.

RECOMMENDED READINGS

Barber, T.X., et al., eds. *Biofeedback and Self-Control: 1975* (Chicago: Aldine-Atherton, 1976).

Brecher, Edward M., et al., eds. *Licit and Illicit Drugs: The Consumer's Union Report on Narcotics, Stimulants, Depressants, Inhalants, Hallucinogens, and Marijuana—Including Caffeine, Nicotine, and Alcohol* (Boston: Little, Brown, 1972).

Dement, William C. *Some Must Sleep While Some Must Watch* (San Francisco: Freeman, 1974).

Ebon, Martin. *The Relaxation Controversy* (New York: The New American Library, Signet, 1976).

Snyder, Solomon H. *Uses of Marijuana* (New York: Oxford University Press, 1971).

Weinswig, Melvin H. *Use and Misuse of Drugs Subject to Abuse* (New York: Pegasus, 1973).

LOCALIZATION OF FUNCTION IN THE BRAIN

DID YOU KNOW THAT . . .

Many early Greeks believed the mind was located in the heart?

Many European and U.S. doctors once believed you could read someone's personality by studying the bumps on the person's head?

There are four main sections or lobes in each of your cerebral hemispheres, and that each lobe has quite different functions?

If you electrically stimulate certain parts of your frontal lobes, your arms and legs will twitch and move about whether you want them to or not?

About 90 percent of the murders committed each year involve people related to or friendly with each other?

Most murderers and their victims are under 30 years of age?

Government studies suggest that the amount of TV violence a boy views at age 9 is the single most important determinant of how aggressive the boy will be at age 19?

People in the United States may have a "Wild West" concept of justice?

Many animals establish home territories that they will fight to maintain?

A mouse shocked in a confined space will sometimes attack a large cat?

Electrical stimulation to certain parts of your own brain will cause you to fly into a rage and attack people near you?

Removal of a small part of a monkey's brain can cause it to become hypersexual in its behavior?

Some scientists believe that much human violence is due to hidden brain damage?

There apparently is no simple cure for the violence we find in the world?

TO: Senior-Robot-in-Charge, Space Exploration Program

FROM: Leader Robot, Scout Ship XJ-6

SUBJECT: Planetary System MB-450-SEL

SenRo, may it please your circuits, we think we have found it! For thousands of years now since we became space-borne, our scout ships have roamed the vacant reaches of the universe, hunting for intelligent metallic life. We have touched down on a million million planets sprawling with softflesh species—but never once have we found even the rusty vestiges of another hardflesh race. But now, SenRo, may your wheels never spin, we have discovered a planet filled to overflowing with mechanical marvels!

We were still billions of miles from solar system MB-450-SEL when our navigator, MT/BOSS 302, first detected signs of electronic life, namely, very faint radio waves. Our ship's computer soon informed us that these signals probably constituted a language of some sort. To date, the computer has not been able to decode the signals, but it was clear from the start that we were listening to signals, to communications, and not to random radio noise. So we approached the planetary site of these signals slowly, quietly, stealthily, but with our emotionality circuits pulsating at top speed. Were these creators of intelligent radio signals hardflesh like us, or were they some particularly advanced form of softflesh? Either way, of course, we had a discovery of prime importance, but our expectation circuits were glowing with the hope that we had at last come upon a race of robotic brothers.

Our space exploration rules, as you well know, SenRo, demand that we not approach any closer than 25,000 miles (40,233.6 kilometers) to any planet that might contain intelligent life, so we put the scout ship into an orbit that held us stationary right above one of the major continents on this world. We picked this particular continent because from it seemed to come an incredible number of radio signals, both day and night. As we discovered later, our choice was an excellent one, for much of the mechanical life on this planet is concentrated in the mid-section of this particular continent. But you can imagine the thrill that ran through our pleasure circuits when first we focused our viewer on the surface of this amazing planet.

As leader of the ship I, CD/RR 6.7, had the opportunity for first glance through the viewer. Navigator MT/BOSS 302 fiddled with the apparatus until it gave us clearest sight, and then I peered into the vision hole. I scanned the land rapidly, noting mountains and rivers, green fields, and bare brown deserts. And then, pushing the viewer to its limit, I noticed what at first seemed to be a series of canals running the length and breadth of the continent. Canals we have seen before, of course. But, praise be to the Prime Robot, these were not canals—they were roads! I narrowed the focus of the viewer down for an even better look. And I could not believe my vision circuits! For there was life—mechanical life!—rushing along the roads in all directions. Bright metal beasts, of various sizes and colors, racing along those narrow ribbons of concrete. I let navigator MT/BOSS 302 and engineer RT/HEMI 454 both have a look, and they too were as stunned with the magnitude of our discovery as was I.

Our circuits were overloaded. We paused, broke out a bottle of high-quality oil we had saved for a special occasion, and drank a small cocktail. (Only one, you understand!) Never before in the history of our race had three robots so much to celebrate! And then, when our relays had snapped back into place, we took another look through the viewer.

How I wish, SenRo, that you could be here to share with us this discovery. For the life on this planet is a veritable marvel! Primitive, of course—they are just on the verge of space exploration and are hence thousands of years behind us in their development. But what a charmingly diverse set of species we found.

By far the major form of life is a four-wheeled, self-propelled machine species shaped much like us that ranges in size from 10 to 20 feet (3 to 6 meters) in length. These are the robots that amble along the roads so frequently day and night. We call them Compact Ambulatory Robots, or CARs, because they are so small that our viewer can barely discern them as individuals. Later, we will move closer in so that we can get a clearer picture of what they are like. But we have spent the past hours studying them as best we can from this distance.

A quick census suggests that there are about 200 million CARs on the planet, but more than half of them are found on this one continent that we have studied most closely. At first glance they all look more or less alike, but on closer inspection we have found subtle but important differences. Some of the CARs are very large and seem to be hollow, as if designed for carrying materials. Most run independently on the concrete roads, but there are some that appear confined to metal tracks. These latter are obviously transportation robots of a low intellectual development, for they enjoy none of the freedom of movement that the CARs do. A small number are aquatic, but these too seem specialized for transport. There are even a few winged species that travel great distances at high speed, but the smallness of their numbers suggests that these flying robots are at a lower order of development than are the CARs. (If wings were all that important, wouldn't the Prime Robot have given them to us instead of the wheels that we

run on?) There are also very specialized forms of life for roadbuilding, and for herding and taking care of the softlife.

Yes, SenRo, there is indeed softlife on this planet! There are very large forms that float in the seas and smaller types that roam the empty landspaces. Our viewer is not powerful enough to detect the smaller forms, but they seem to exist in abundance. But then, softlife is cheap and easily formed, so we would expect that softflesh species would outnumber the more highly evolved hardflesh CARs. But the relationship between the CARs and their softflesh companions is indeed a fascinating one to speculate on. Of course, the CARs are dominant species—their size, strength, and speed prove that beyond a shadow of a doubt. Why then so many softfleshers? At the moment the three of us aboard this scout ship have quite different theories.

Engineer RT/HEMI 454 believes that robot and softflesh evolved independently, but that the CARs eventually succeeded in domesticating the softies as slaves. The engineer believes that the slaves are used to handle the more menial, repetitive, and humdrum aspects of life that no robot would wish to bother his intellectual circuits with. A fascinating idea, no? The Prime Robot knows that all of us could use a softflesh slave now and again to polish up our shiny parts and to run and fetch for us when our energy levels are low. The engineer points out that some of the land seems to be cultivated and that there are a number of CARs that appear to do little more than dig in the earth, as if plants of various kinds were grown deliberately. Since it is difficult to imagine what need a robot might have for plant life, perhaps the plants serve as fuel for the softflesh slaves.

Navigator MT/BOSS 302 disputes part of this view—he believes that the softflesh species are kept as pets for the amusement of the CARs, much as we have bred a few highly energetic and cuddlesome species from other planets to delight us with their antics when our current flow is depressed. The navigator points out that the CARs have built huge pens or corrals to house the softies in. No sane robot would waste so much energy taking care of mere slaves, although, as we know from our own experience, even our race will expend great gobs of its own limited resources to make its softie pets comfortable.

For myself, I have quite a different theory, but it is too radical even to discuss with my fellow scouts. I can do no more at the moment than hint that it involves the ''missing mechanical linkage'' hypothesis put forth by some of our early scientists. As you know, we still do not understand very much about our own robotic heritage—we have only theories and speculations about the origins of our species. Did our hardfleshed mechanical beauty spring straight from the creative electronic circuits of a Prime Robot at the start of time? Or did we evolve from simple, toylike mechanisms through some accident of mechanical mutation? Or were we created, as some of our more daring theorists claim in secret, by some particularly intelligent species of softfleshed creatures, all of whose traces are now lost to our historians?

If we were the offspring of softlife, then there must be somewhere in the universe some metallic species that stands halfway between soft- and hardflesh, and I tell you in confidence that I hope it is this "missing mechanical linkage" that we have discovered here on this petty planet so far from the center of our galaxy. I realize that this theory is now officially discredited in many quarters, and I will not mention it again unless this wonderful new world yields up fresh evidence. But I dare to raise the matter because I know that you, SenRo, have often speculated on this matter yourself and that I have come to share your own unique views on the evolution of our species.

But such intellectual curiosity must wait. Now we must observe, observe, and then observe some more. Discovery is one thing, and we are pleased that the Prime Robot has given to the three of us such a golden opportunity. Now we must turn our analytical circuits up to full volume as we attempt to answer the question of the century: "What make these CARs tick?"

(Continued on page 102.)

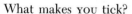

What makes YOU tick?

A simple-sounding question, perhaps, but one that humans have debated (sometimes violently) for a great many centuries.

Most of the time, when people raise this question, they are asking, "Who are you?" That is, what biological, psychological, and social events have made you into the person that you are today? (To anticipate a bit, we will spend most of the rest of this book trying to answer *that* particular question.)

But there is an even more basic problem hiding behind the innocent-appearing words, "What makes YOU tick?" Namely, what do we really mean when we use the pronoun YOU? At this deeper level of analysis, the question becomes not "WHO ARE YOU?" but "WHAT ARE YOU?" Are you merely a biological machine, a body full of complex clockwork run by a motor called the brain? Or are you a unique psychological or spiritual identity that happens to inhabit a certain body the way that you also happen to inhabit a certain house, apartment, or dormitory room?

Put this way, the original question becomes, "Does your mind run your body, or does your body run your mind?" (Or, to raise a more disturbing thought, are they both controlled by outside forces that neither your mind nor body is aware of?)

This kind of questioning may seem odd to you, or even downright stupid, if you've never encountered it before. For most people act as if they assumed their minds controlled their bodies. YOU make up your mind to go to the store, so your legs carry you there. YOU decide to have dinner, and so your hands get the food and your mouth eats it. From this viewpoint what your "psychological" mind orders is what your "biological" body does.

But consider the following troublesome facts: You spend about one-third of your life asleep, yet your body continues to function beautifully even when your mind is unconscious. Who runs the corporation when the Board of Directors goes home for a nap? If you take a couple of drinks, or smoke some pot, YOU become *intoxicated* (°). It is easy to understand how the chemicals in alcohol and cannabis can affect the ticking of your nerve cells, but how can *physical* reactions in your

Intoxicated (in-TOCKS-uh-kay-ted). From the Latin word *toxicum*, meaning "poison." A toxic substance is one that is dangerous or harmful to life. In everyday speech, to be intoxicated is to be drunk, stoned, or "high" from drinking or smoking a toxic chemical such as alcohol or marijuana.

Plato (PLAY-toe). A Greek philosopher-psychologist who founded one of the Western world's first colleges or academies in Athens about 400 years before Christ. Plato believed that spiritual affection was the highest form of friendship. A platonic love is one that involves no sexuality (or, as one humorist put it, "not much play for the man, not much tonic for the woman").

Nettle (rhymes with "kettle"). Any plant that stings you when you touch it. The phrase "to grasp a nettle" means to deal with a very painful or difficult problem.

Sophisticated (so-FISS-tic-kay-ted). A group of philosophers called Sophists lived in Greece several hundred years before Christ was born. The Sophists were very good at winning arguments, more through their ability to "shoot the bull" effectively than through logical thinking. Our English words "sophomore" and "sophisticated" come from "Sophist." A sophisticated person is someone who has experienced a lot; someone who has seen a great deal of the world; hence supposedly knows what wines, foods, musical compositions, and intellectual ideas are "best."

Homunculus (ho-MUN-cue-lus). The Latin word *homo* means "man." A homunculus is a "small man," such as a dwarf or midget.

brain cause the *psychological* or *spiritual* YOU to get high? And if your mind controls your body, how does it do so? Where in your body does the essential, psychological YOU reside, and how does something purely psychological pull the neural strings that make your muscles move?

THE MIND-BODY PROBLEM

The question, "What and where is the mind?" has puzzled mankind at least since the time of the early Greek philosopher *Plato* (°), but we still do not have one simple, agreed-upon answer to this problem. For buried away within the question—or the answer—is a psychological *nettle* (°) that stings almost anyone who attempts to grasp it. Philosophers call it the "mind-body problem," and it has to do with the relationship between mental activity and physical activity and where inside the body this mental activity takes place.

If you are like most Americans, you probably feel that your mind—the essential, psychological YOU—is located somewhere in your head. But ancient man was not quite so wise and *sophisticated* (°). Aristotle, a Greek scholar who lived long before the birth of Christ, believed that our minds (or souls) reside in our hearts. From his observations of animals being slaughtered and of humans wounded in battle, Aristotle knew that the heart was in constant motion—beating, beating, beating. If you pierced a man's heart with a sword or arrow, the man almost always died. The brain, on the other hand, was quiet. No matter how much you poked or prodded it with an arrow, the brain simply did not respond. Many early Greeks considered the brain to be little more than a radiator where blood was pumped to be cooled off when a man or woman flew into a "hot rage."

Another view, supposedly held by the early Egyptians, was that a "little man" lived inside each person's skull. This *homunculus* (°) (to use the Latin word for "little man") supposedly peered out through our eyes and listened through our ears. Once the "little man" decided how to process the incoming sensory information, he pulled the strings that operated the muscles of our bodies much as a puppeteer pulls the strings that make his marionettes behave.

Nor was this homunculus theory as ridiculous as it may seem at first. Ancient man knew that if he bent over close and peered directly into a friend's eye, he would see a "little man" looking out at him (try it—it works!). Furthermore, the theory established man's superiority over lower animals. If you stare into a dog's eye, you will see a human face looking out at you, not a dog's. So "little men" obviously pulled the strings for animals as well as for humans (what the dog sees when it looks into a human's eye is a question the early theorists apparently forgot to ask themselves). Even today, the homunculus theory has its believers. How many TV commercials have you seen in which "little men" or "little women" chase about the human body causing headaches or stomach upsets?

QUESTION: If a "little man" pulls the strings that move your muscles, who pulls the little man's strings?

Three centuries ago the French philosopher René Descartes offered one of the first modern solutions to the mind-body problem. (Descartes is perhaps most famous for having invented analytical geometry, a discovery that was to frustrate and enrage generations of students thereafter.) Descartes believed that mind and body were made of separate substances. The body—whose actions were purely mechanical—was composed of physically measurable objects such as blood and guts. The mind was a ghostly entity that existed spiritually or psychologically, but which had no physical existence. Descartes thought that mind and body were coupled, like a man and wife. The mind did not control the body directly, nor did the body control the mind. But, like a married couple, mind and body were very closely related and they did *interact* with each other. The brain (which was

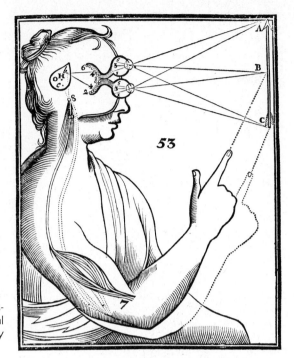

An arrow's image is transmitted to the brain's pineal gland in this woodcut by Descartes.

physical) was the most important part of the body because it was the "marriage bed"—that is, the point of maximum interaction between mind and body.

René Descartes had little or no idea about the biological functioning of the brain, for modern biology didn't exist at the time that he lived. But he was one of the first scientists to insist that the seat of consciousness (YOU) lay within the skull, and thus he turned the mind-body problem into the mind-brain problem.

PHRENOLOGY

By the year 1800 medical doctors were convinced of the psychological importance of the brain, but they could not begin to unlock its secrets because they knew so little about chemistry and electricity. So the medical profession studied the brain as best it could—by poking and cutting at this magnificent organ as if it were a lump of muscle tissue.

As we said in Chapter 2, most of us are right-handed (and left-brained). Because we do most of our heavy labor with our right hands, the muscles in our right arms are slightly larger and better developed than are the muscles in our left arms. Any time you exercise a particular muscle, it swells a bit. If your brain reacted like muscle tissue, then the more you used it, the larger it should grow.

Or, so said a European medical doctor named Franz Joseph Gall around the year 1800. After he had studied anatomy at the University of Vienna, Gall spent considerable time studying people in jails and insane asylums. He found (or so he thought) that most pickpockets and thieves had a "bump" on their skulls just above their ears. Thieves differ from non-thieves because they are continually exercising the habit of "acquiring" other people's property illegally. Therefore, Gall reasoned, that part of their brains associated with "acquisitiveness" would surely be largest because it got the most exercise! As this "acquisitiveness center" of the brain swelled and grew from all this use, it would presumably push outward on the skull, causing a bump. And since these thieves had bumps just over their ears, then shouldn't it be true that the brain tissue immediately under this bump was the location of the "acquisitiveness center"?

Franz Joseph Gall.

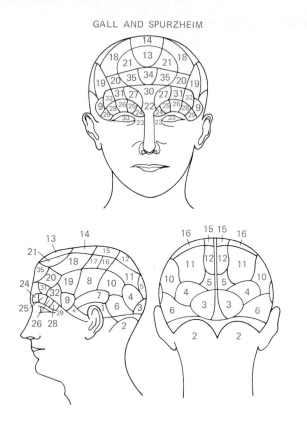

GALL AND SPURZHEIM

The "Powers and Organs of the Mind" according to Spurzheim.

AFFECTIVE FACULTIES

Propensities

? Desire to live
* Alimentiveness
1 Destructiveness
2 Amativeness
3 Philoprogenitiveness
4 Adhesiveness

5 Inhabitiveness
6 Combativeness
7 Secretiveness
8 Acquisitiveness
9 Constructiveness

Sentiments

10 Cautiousness
11 Approbativeness
12 Self-Esteem
13 Benevolence
14 Reverence
15 Firmness

16 Conscientiousness
17 Hope
18 Marvelousness
19 Ideality
20 Mirthfulness
21 Imitation

INTELLECTUAL FACULTIES

Perceptive

22 Individuality
23 Configuration
24 Size
25 Weight and Resistance
26 Coloring
27 Locality

28 Order
29 Calculation
30 Eventuality
31 Time
32 Tune

Reflective

34 Comparison
35 Causality

Phrenology (free-NOLL-oh-gee). Reading the bumps or depressions on a person's skull in order to make guesses about the person's psychological abilities. Phrenology, which was invented by Franz Joseph Gall, doesn't work very well.

Psychological trait. A distinguishing quality of character; a particular mental ability or skill; a peculiarity. Intelligence is a mental trait.

Pierre Flourens (pee-AIR flu-rans). A noted French medical scientist who, in the early 1800's, made many brilliant discoveries about how the brain works.

Pierre Jean Marie Flourens.

From Gall's rather amusing point of view, if you wanted to learn what made a person tick, all you had to do was to read the bumps on the person's skull. Gall gave the practice of reading bumps a very fancy name, *phrenology* (°), which he made up from the Greek words meaning "to study the mind." He went around Europe hunting for people with special talents or *psychological traits* (°), and then tried to find a bump that matched each trait. For instance, Gall placed the trait of "destructiveness" just behind the ear because he found bumps there (1) in a medical student who was "so fond of torturing animals that he later became a surgeon," and (2) in a man who worked as an executioner and who enjoyed his work.

QUESTION: How many reasons can you think of why Gall's conclusions were unsound?

Phrenology became very popular in the United States during the early 1800's since it seemed to offer practical-minded Americans an easy way to improve themselves. They would see a phrenologist and have this person read their bumps to tell them what their personalities were like. If their "bump of destructiveness" was too large, they would work very hard to be more friendly and less hostile toward others. But the phrenology fad didn't last very long—perhaps because Gall never could give his clients a workable set of "mental exercises" to reshape their personalities, and because the bumps didn't seem to change no matter what the client did.

In the long run, however, it was the scientific method that effectively bashed phrenology over the head. *Pierre Flourens* (°), the great French physiologist, demolished most of Gall's claims in the 1820's by performing actual experiments on brains instead of merely reading bumps on people's skulls. Gall had located the "bump of amativeness" (or sexuality) on the back part of the head, in areas we now know are associated with visual sensory inputs. What would happen, Flourens asked, if this part of the brain were destroyed? Presumably, the person's sex life would also be destroyed, or at least greatly changed. As a surgeon, Flourens was occasionally called upon to remove this part of a patient's brain in order to save the person's life. But on recovery from the operation, such patients seldom showed a decreased sex drive—they might be partially blinded, but they could still make love! In fact, large areas of the cortex could be removed from badly wounded patients without destroying the psychological traits that Gall said were lodged in those areas of the brain.

Since Flourens knew little or nothing about electricity and chemistry, his primary means of studying the brain was by removing parts of it to see what effects this would have on behavior. Flourens decided that the cerebral hemispheres were the seat of perception, intelligence, and all voluntary activity—that is, that the hemispheres were "the seat of the mind." And perhaps in reaction against Gall's wildly incorrect ideas, Flourens decided that psychological traits or abilities had no *specific locus* or homesite within the brain. It took a lunatic to prove Flourens wrong.

Paul Broca.

THE SPEECH CENTER

In 1831 there came to an insane asylum near Paris a young Frenchman whose only mark of madness was that he wouldn't talk. He could communicate by making signs, but he refused to write or to use his vocal cords. Although he appeared to be normal in all other respects, he was put into the insane asylum because the authorities decided that no sane man would refuse to talk to his fellow beings. The doctors could find no cure for his silence, so the man remained in the hospital for 30 years.

In April of 1861 the man caught an infection and was put under the care of Paul Broca, a noted French surgeon. Broca examined the man carefully, determined that the man's vocal cords were perfectly sound and that the patient was intelligent enough to be able to speak. Five days later—unfortunately for the man, but perhaps fortunately for millions of other patients—the man died of the infection. Broca put the man's body to *autopsy* (°) at once and discovered a mass of scar tissue in the *left hemisphere* just about where the man's temple would have been. Broca assumed, rightly, that this part of the brain must contain the neural tissue responsible for speech. Flourens had incorrectly assumed that there was no localization of specific psychological functions in the cortex. Broca was the first scientist to discover that specific areas of the brain do indeed control specific types of psychological or mental activities. And, of course, he had located the "talking" part of the mind in the left half of this patient's brain.

QUESTION: Was Broca's patient right-handed or left-handed?

THE LOBES OF THE BRAIN

Let us return once more to that magic mirror that allows you to inspect your own brain. If you could look into that mirror, you would probably first notice the division between your left and right hemispheres, because the valley between the two halves of the brain is a large one—rather as if a huge, deep river ran from front to back right through the middle of your brain. If you inspected a little more closely, you would see that each hemisphere is divided into sections. Viewed from the top, as we mentioned earlier, the hemispheres look much like a mountainous landscape—there are dozens of smoothly rolling hills separated by steep-sided valleys. Some of the valleys are so large that they seem to separate the cerebrum into definite areas or sections, which we call *lobes* (°).

There are four main sections or lobes in *each* cerebral hemisphere:

1. The *frontal* lobe (°), which lies just under the skull in the region of the forehead.

Autopsy (AW-top-see). A careful inspection of a dead body to determine why the person died.

Lobes. Rounded bumps that typically project out from the organs of the body. Each half of the cerebrum has four main lobes or projections.

Frontal lobe. The part of the cerebrum that lies just above the eyes. Experiments suggest this part of the brain may be involved in decision-making, among many other things. The motor cortex is a part of the frontal lobe.

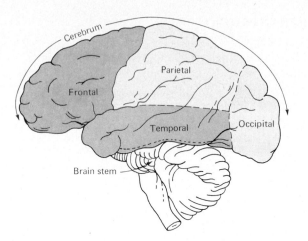

Temporal lobe (TEM-por-ull). Part of the cerebrum that lies just above the ears. It seems to be involved in hearing, in speech production, and in emotional behavior, among many other things.

Parietal lobe (pair-EYE-uh-tull, or puh-RYE-uh-tull). Part of the cerebrum at the very top of the brain. Sensory input from the skin receptors and muscles comes to this part of the cerebrum.

Occipital lobe (oc-SIP-it-tull). The lower, rear part of the cerebrum just above the neck. The visual input area of the brain, among other things.

2. The *temporal* lobe (°), which lies under the skull just above each ear, in the general region of your temple.
3. The *parietal* lobe (°), which lies under the top center of your skull.
4. The *occipital* lobe (°), which lies at the back of your head, just above the neck.

It was tempting to Broca to assign highly specific psychological traits or functions to each of these lobes and, as we will see, Broca was partially correct in doing so.

But as much as he learned about the brain from his surgery and his autopsies, Paul Broca didn't know enough to help hundreds of his patients who were sick or dying from brain disease. For, like all of his colleagues at that time, Broca did not understand that the nerve cells work electro-chemically. What the scientists of the 1860's obviously needed was an *electrical* method of investigating brain reactions and, in 1870, they got just that—but it took the violence of a major war to give it to them.

THE ELECTRICAL PROBE

The Franco-Prussian War between Germany and France reached its climax late in the summer of 1870 near the small French town of Sedan. The immediate political consequences of that war have long since been forgotten even by most Germans and Frenchmen, but a discovery that two German doctors made on the battlefields outside the sleepy little village of Sedan changed the course of modern medicine.

G. Fritsch and E. Hitzig were trained as medical doctors. When the Franco-Prussian War broke out, they entered the armed forces of Germany. But both men were basically scientists rather than practitioners, as interested in gaining new knowledge as in applying what facts were already known. During the battle, as they wandered among the wounded men, they had the brilliant if terrifying idea of experimenting on some of the soldiers who seemed past help. In particular, they wondered what would happen if they applied electrical currents to the brains of men whose skulls had been blown open by cannon fire.

Fritsch and Hitzig soon found that if they applied the electrical stimulation to an area at the top-rear of the frontal lobe, just where it joins with the parietal lobe, the arms and legs of their human subjects would show repeated, jerky movements. Once the war was over, Fritsch and Hitzig continued their experiments (using animals) and reported they had discovered what seemed to be a "motor output center" in the cortex of both frontal lobes. They had also pioneered a new tool for investigating the functioning of the brain and for curing some of its ills—the *electrical probe*.

Mapping the Cortex Electrically

As we mentioned earlier, the nerve cells in your cortex do not react to painful stimulation the way that the cells in most parts of your body do. For this reason, patients undergoing brain surgery are often conscious, so that they can help the doctor locate whatever damaged section needs to be removed. During such surgery, the doctor may stimulate various parts of the cortex electrically and ask the patient what he or she feels the moment the current is applied.

What would you experience if you were willing to let a scientist "map" your entire cortex with an electrical stimulator? Well, the most dramatic results of all would surely come if the scientist touched the probe to the motor output area (motor cortex), which lies at the rear of each frontal lobe, very close to the forward edge of the parietal lobe. Stimulation of the nerve cells in the motor cortex in your left hemisphere would cause the muscles on the right side of your body to twitch or jerk even though you didn't consciously will these muscles to move. Stimulation of the motor cortex in your right hemisphere would make the muscles on the left side of your body move involuntarily.

When the probe was applied to the *occipital* lobe at the back of your head, you would see brief flashes of light or "shooting stars."

If you stimulated parts of your *temporal* lobe, you would hear brief bursts of sounds. And if the probe were touched to parts of the *parietal* lobe at the top of your head, you would feel odd prickly sensations in your skin. Strangely enough, however, the scientist could apply the probe to large areas of all four lobes without your experiencing anything at all.

The physiologists who first mapped the brain electrically concluded that the cerebral cortex has three general types of areas:

1. *Sensory input areas,* where nerve axons carrying messages from the sense organs make contact or synapse with the dendrites of cortical neurons. We will discuss these areas in detail in later chapters.
2. *Motor output areas,* where nerve cells lie whose axons reach out to make contact with the muscles and glands of your body.
3. *"Silent" areas,* which have no function that can be determined directly from electrical stimulation.

The early physiologists were surprised to find that most of the surface area of the cortex is "silent" to an electrical probe. At first, these early scientists assumed that the silent areas were where memories—or *associations* between sensory input and motor output—were located. So these silent parts of the cortex were nick-named the *association areas* (°). Many lines of evidence now suggest that these should be called the cortical *processing areas,* for it is in these regions that incoming sensory information is processed and evaluated, and where "command decisions" seem to be made. If there is a Board of Directors in your brain, its Board Room probably lies in these so-called silent areas.

When electrical probing of the brain first began, many early biologists were convinced that they were about to resolve the mind-body issue in favor of the body. They presumed that they would be able to find a specific point in the brain that was associated with each unique hope, fear, dream, thought, love, hate, and desire that you might ever experience. Had they been able to do so, then biology would have swallowed up psychology, and you would be reading quite a different book than this one. Imagine the frustration of these physiologists, then, when electrical stimulation of much of the brain failed to elicit any "mental" responses at all. The scientists were convinced that the mind was lurking somewhere in that 3-pound (1.3 kilograms) mass of neural tissue, but somehow the most important parts of human experience kept eluding (and still elude) their needle-like probes.

In a sense, intra-psychic and behavioral psychology grew out of both the successes and failures of the early physiologists. Although the biologists had failed

Association areas. Those parts of your cortex which, when stimulated electrically, do not yield any sensory experiences. Although the full functions of these "silent areas" of the cortex are not fully understood, it is assumed that they are involved in cortical processing—that is, in evaluating incoming sensory information. They may also serve as "insurance factors," for there is some evidence that the association areas may take over some of the functions of nearby brain tissue if that tissue is damaged or surgically removed.

to solve the mind-body problem to everyone's satisfaction, they had demonstrated the great usefulness of the scientific method.

Around 1900, then, a group of scholars who called themselves *psychologists* started applying the scientific approach to the study of what humans thought and did. Some psychologists began to develop "mental probes" to map out the mind as the physiologists had mapped out the brain. Other psychologists tried to measure and record the visible behavior of the human organism as precisely as the physiologists had measured and recorded the electro-chemical behavior of cortical neurons.

Out of this sudden burst of scientific activity, there emerged three quite different ways of answering the question, "What makes you tick?" At times, violent word wars swept the pages of the scientific journals, as believers in one of these approaches tried to prove their way was superior to any other. As we will see, this battle still rages on. Yet each of the three theoretical standpoints has its own strengths and weaknesses, its own contribution to make to resolving the mind-body question.

To help us put all three in clearer perspective, let us first look at them briefly, then discover how each attempts to explain a pressing human problem—the occurrence of such violent behaviors as war, rape, and murder.

THE MIND-BODY PROBLEM: THREE THEORETICAL VIEWPOINTS

The Biological Viewpoint

As we have noted, psychology partially grew out of the sciences of medicine and physiology. That area of psychology concerned with studying how functions of the brain affect behavior is called *physiological psychology* (°). This old and highly respected field is now sometimes referred to by such newer names as *biological psychology, psychobiology,* or *biopsychology.* Some physiological psychologists work primarily with *animal subjects* (°), while others usually work with human subjects.

For the most part, physiological psychologists are interested in the *interactions* between physiological processes and behavior—that is, they study how changes in your biology are related to changes in your behavior. At times a biopsychologist may induce a change in an organism's behavior—for instance, by teaching a dog to perform a trick—and then study what happens in the dog's brain as a result of the change in its performance. For the most part, however, the physiological psychologist is likely to alter the functioning of the brain in some way to see how the organism's behavior changes thereafter. For example, if you stimulate parts of a cat's motor cortex, the animal's legs will move. If you stimulate other parts of the cat's brain electrically, the animal will fly into a rage.

Perhaps because biopsychologists tend to "do something physical" to an animal and then note its behavioral changes, these scientists occasionally talk as if biology *causes* psychology. When these scientists speak about the mind (which they rarely do at all in scientific terms, since "mind" is a subjective term), they may view mental activity as an unmeasurable or unimportant "side effect" of neural activity in the brain. Just as the waves that you make when you swim are a "side effect" of your swimming, so your thoughts and feelings are presumed to be an incidental effect produced by the functioning of your brain. Why study the waves when you can study the swimming directly?

Not all physiological psychologists take this restrictive, biological view toward the mind-body problem. But many of these scientists do occasionally speak as if they believed the interaction between brain and mind was a one-way affair, as if physical events in your nervous system were the major cause for all the subjective experiences in your mind.

Physiological psychology (fizz-ee-oh-LODGE-uh-cal). That part of psychology that looks upon man as being primarily a biological organism. Physiology is that division of biology dealing with the activities and processes of living systems.

Animal subjects. Scientists assume there is a continuity or relatedness to life. The bodies of animals are very similar to the bodies of humans. Therefore, many of the facts discovered about animal physiology should also hold for human physiology. Psychologists often assume that there is a continuity between animal and human minds, as well. Therefore, studying how rats, cats, and monkeys solve problems might give useful information on how human beings solve similar problems. The similarities between humans and the rest of the animal kingdom are very important and worthy of scientific study—but so are the differences between humans and other animals.

The Intra-psychic Viewpoint

At the beginning of this chapter, when we asked where the "essential, psychological YOU" resided, we were speaking in intra-psychic terms. That is, we were asking the location of your own subjective world, of your own stream of consciousness, or of your *mind*. Traditionally, the intra-psychic or mental viewpoint has dominated the psychological sciences, just as it dominates most of the material in this book.

From an intra-psychic standpoint, YOU determine almost everything that you think and feel and do. Our legal system takes this intra-psychic point of view, for the laws of the land hold you responsible for your actions. Likewise, the people around you typically assume that what you say to them (and the ways that you react to what they say) are products of your conscious, mental functioning. From this viewpoint, your mind has voluntary control over your body (brain), and not the other way around—just as your mind is presumed to control your behavior.

Scientists who study what your "inner man" or "inner woman" is really like will usually admit that your *biological inheritance* (°) helps determine what your mind is like. For example, a brain-damaged child cannot be expected to think and act as physically normal children do. But from a strict mentalistic viewpoint, the condition of your body merely sets limits to what your mind can accomplish. Within these biological limitations, YOU are presumed to become whatever YOU decide you should be.

The Social/Behavioral Viewpoint

As the poet John Donne said, no man is an island unto himself. Rather, he grows up around other people who help determine his ideas, his values, his joys and disappointments, his very behavior. Because the intra-psychic viewpoint has dominated our thinking for so many centuries, it has taken us a very long time to realize the importance of the environments we live in. Those psychologists who emphasize the strong influence that the outside (social) world has on what we think and do typically have adopted the social/behavioral viewpoint as their solution to the mind-brain problem.

The *social psychologist* (*see* Chapters 26–28) is perhaps most interested in how our attitudes and behaviors are affected by the actions of the groups we belong to (for instance, our family and friends). An *attitude* (°) is usually defined as a characteristic way of thinking, feeling, or behaving toward an object, person, or group of persons. Although the social psychologist admits that your attitudes exist "inside your mind," and that these attitudes are determined partly by your biological inheritance, it is the environment you were reared in that is deemed most important. From the strict social viewpoint, then, your body creates your mind at birth and has a minor influence on it thereafter—but the outside world creates all your important attitudes and behavioral reactions while you are growing up. From this social viewpoint, then, if you want to change your mind, you must first change your environment.

The *behavioral psychologist* goes a step further. To a behaviorist, your own thoughts, feelings, and emotions are *subjective* events. Because they take place inside the privacy of your own mind, these events cannot be seen or measured directly by a scientist. You may tell a behaviorist what you are thinking, or that you feel sad or happy at the moment, but the behaviorist cannot peer straight into your mind to see how accurately you are reporting these inner experiences of yours. However, your *behavior* is something that most certainly can be seen and recorded by a scientific observer. *What* you do—the movements you make and the things you say—are non-mental events. Your behavior therefore can be treated like an object and measured "objectively"—just as one can measure the "behavior" of such other objects as a falling stone, an ocean wave, or a neuron firing.

If you press them hard enough, most behaviorists will admit that you do indeed

Biological inheritance. You inherit from your parents a "genetic blueprint" that helps determine the shape and size of your body, including your brain. You also inherit from this blueprint certain behavioral tendencies called "instincts." However, your inheritance is always influenced by the environment you grew up in. Everything you do is affected both by your biological inheritance and your past experiences.

Attitude. A characteristic and usually long-lasting way of thinking, feeling, and behaving toward an object, person, idea, or group of persons. See particularly Chapters 26, 27, and 28.

Depraved (rhymes with "behaved"). From the Latin word meaning "crooked." To be depraved means to be bad, immoral, corrupt, or to have evil habits.

have a mind. But your mental functioning is so difficult to measure or to talk about in objective terms that the behaviorist tends to ignore your personal conscious experience as much as possible.

To a behaviorist, your actions are determined partly by your biological inheritance, but mostly by the *consequences* of what you do. If one of your behavior patterns nets you pleasure or reward, you will tend to repeat that behavior; if a response is punished or brings you pain, you will tend not to do that same thing as often in the future. And since these pleasures and pains come to you primarily from outside your body, the behaviorist believes that all of your mental and physical reactions are the consequences of external stimulation. A behaviorist believes that if you want to change your own behavior, you must first change the behavior of the people in the world around you.

As we will see later in this book, there are many differences between social and behavioral psychologists. However, their similarity in emphasizing the great importance of the environment allows us to lump them together—at least as far as their approach to the mind-body problem is concerned.

WHICH VIEW IS CORRECT?

Despite their occasional arguments on the subject, very few psychologists hold rigidly to one of the three viewpoints we have just described. Instead, psychologists use whatever view seems most appropriate or useful in solving whatever human problem they happen to face at the moment. Different psychologists may *emphasize* the value of one viewpoint or another, but almost all psychological theories make reference to biological, intra-psychic, and environmental influences.

We need to learn as much as we can about all three viewpoints, for no one of them *all by itself* can explain the rich complexity of human experience. To demonstrate this point as vividly as possible, let us now study one aspect of human behavior—*violence*—as seen from the social/behavioral, the intra-psychic, and the biological points of view.

VIOLENCE: THREE THEORETICAL VIEWPOINTS

To many people, surely the most terrifying form of violence is murder. Few of us who have walked the near-deserted streets of a big city late at night have not feared that some madman lurking in the shadows would leap out and brutalize or kill us. If we read in the newspaper (or see on TV) the results of some particularly bloody massacre, we are likely to shiver in our boots and demand that the police give us greater protection from such *depraved* (°) lunatics. But as Donald T. Lunde points out in his fascinating book *Murder and Madness*, the facts about violent death are somewhat different from our fantasies and fears.

To begin with, we are quite right to worry about violent death, for at least 15,000 Americans are murdered annually. In fact, more of us in the United States were killed by other Americans in the last 4 years than were killed in Vietnam during the entire war there. According to U.S. government statistics, in any given year there are about 15,000 murders, at least 30,000 rapes, and some 300,000 cases of violent assault.

However, you are really much safer on the streets than in your own home, and probably better off with strangers than with people you know and love. For almost 90 percent of the murders each year involve people related to or friendly with each other, and about 40 percent of the killings occur in homes or apartments. Few murders occur during business hours. In Philadelphia, as Lunde reports, two-thirds of the killings occur on weekends, most of them on Saturday night between 8 p.m. and 2 a.m. Perhaps because we're around friends and family

Donald T. Lunde.

more during summer holidays and at Christmas, the murder rate peaks in July and in December. Some 44 percent of all recent murders occurred in the southern states; the lowest murder rate *per capita* (°) is found in New England.

Killing others seems to be a behavior found mostly in young people. Less than 1 victim in 10 is murdered by someone over 50; in fact, the average murderer is about 20 years of age. Most victims are under 30 years of age. Men are three times as likely to kill someone as are women. One-fifth of all victims are women killed in their own bedrooms (usually shot to death by husbands or lovers); men are more likely to be murdered in the kitchen (usually stabbed to death or shot by wives or lovers).

According to Lunde, race plays an important part in murder. In some 90 percent of all killings, the victim and the murderer are of the same race. However, black men are 10 times as likely to be victims as are white men, and black women are about 5 times as likely to be victims as are white women. When cross-racial murders do occur, whites are much more likely to kill blacks than vice versa. Blacks are more likely to use knives as murder weapons than whites, while whites are more likely to use guns. No matter what their race, however, murderers under 15 and over 50 use guns almost exclusively. In at least one-third of the cases, the victim seems to have precipitated the killing, either by taunting or goading the murderer or by pulling out a weapon first.

The connection between murder and mental illness is slim at best. Less than 4 percent of convicted murderers in recent years were judged criminally insane in courts of law. A patient released from a mental hospital is no more likely to commit a murder than is the average person (*unless* the patient was hospitalized for being violent, and then the patient is only slightly more likely to commit a crime than is anyone else). Murderers seldom repeat their crimes. The state of Michigan has given early parole to hundreds of convicted murderers in the past 20 years; none of these people ever killed again. In England, in a 50-year study of 7,000 convicted murderers, only two killed again after being released from jail.

If, then, we cannot blame most acts of violence on insanity, what is it that causes people to kill each other? Probably each of us has his or her own answer to this question, but most of the explanations will fall within the social/behavioral, intra-psychic, or biological viewpoints.

Environmental Determinants of Violence

Does the society you grow up in affect the probability that you will strike or otherwise harm another individual? Do some cultures repress violent behaviors, while other cultures reward or encourage rape, assault, and murder? There are a great many data suggesting that the attitudes held by the majority of people within a given society have a marked effect on the level of violence found within that society.

In the United States, as we just mentioned, there are at least 15,000 murders a year. The majority of these deaths stem from gunshot wounds. About 51 percent of all American murders are committed with pistols or hand guns, while rifles and shotguns account for another 15 percent or so of the recorded *homicides* (°). The city of Detroit has about two million people who, according to police estimates, own about two million guns. In 1975 there were some 700 murders in Detroit, the majority of these being deaths from firearms. By contrast, during the same year, there were fewer than 150 murders in *all* of Great Britain—a land of some 50 million people. Americans, in general, take a positive attitude toward the private ownership of hand guns, and almost all of our police are armed. In Great Britain, hand guns are illegal; not even the police wear pistols, except on rare and very special occasions. Does the fact that British society takes quite a different attitude toward guns (and violent behavior in general) in any way help explain the fact

Per capita (purr KAPP-it-tuh). A Latin phrase that means, roughly, "to take an average" or "to count heads." If a city of 1,000 people has one murder per year, and a city of 10,000 people has 10 murders per year, the per capita murder rate is the same in both cities.

Homicides (HOMM-ah-sides, or HOME-uh-sides). From the Latin words meaning "man" and "to kill." Generally speaking, homicides are the killing of one human being by another.

Psychiatrist (sigh-KIGH-uh-trist, or suck-KIGH-uh-trist). Someone who goes through medical school, obtains the M.D. degree, then specializes in diseases of the mind, or mental illness. A psychologist typically goes through graduate school, obtains the Ph.D. degree (Doctor of Philosophy), but has little or no medical training. Psychologists and psychiatrists perform many similar functions, including teaching, research, and treatment—but psychologists are not allowed to prescribe drugs, give medication, or perform surgery on human patients.

that there are 100 times as many murders in the United States each year as in Great Britain?

Or should we point the finger at television instead? The U.S. Senate, worried about the impact of television violence on the personality development of young children, in 1969 asked the Surgeon General to undertake an extensive study on this subject. In 1972, after an expenditure of one million dollars in research funds, Dr. Jesse Steinfeld (the Surgeon General) reported some interesting findings.

Is there violence on television? Yes, indeed. In 1967, according to the National Commission on the Causes and Prevention of Violence, a staggering 94.3 percent of cartoon shows contained violent episodes; in 1968 there were 23.5 violent episodes per hour in cartoons. That same year, 81.6 percent of all prime-time entertainment shows on TV contained violence. It is estimated that a normal child, growing up during the 1960's and early seventies would have watched at least 20,000 incidents of violence on television by the time he or she was 19.

Does violence on TV affect youngsters (not to mention adults)? Dr. Robert M. Liebert, a psychologist at the State University of New York who was a principal investigator for the Surgeon General's report, reviewed more than 50 studies covering the behavior of 10,000 children between the ages of 3 and 19. Dr. Liebert states, "The more violence and aggression a youngster sees on television, regardless of his age, sex or social background, the more aggressive he is likely to be in his own attitudes and behaviors. The effects are not limited to youngsters who are in some way abnormal, but rather were found for large numbers of perfectly normal American children." Dr. Liebert further reports that, "It was not a boy's home life, not his school performance, not his family background, but the amount of TV violence he viewed at age 9 which was the single most important determinant of how aggressive he was 10 years later, at age 19."

The evidence contained in the Surgeon General's report was so conclusive that even the major networks have become concerned and have begun to cut back on the amount of violence shown on children's programs and during the early hours of the evening. However, in 1973–1974, after the Surgeon General's report was made public, violence still occurred in 73 percent of all TV programs.

Several additional points that should be made, however, before we blame the TV networks for turning us into aggressive monsters. To begin with, violence appears in movies, novels, cartoon books, and the daily newspapers as well as on television. Second, children tend to ape the adults around them, and adults are the ones who made *The Godfather* and other similar stories commercial successes both at the movie box office and on the television screen. Adults vote with their pocketbooks, and the majority of American adults appear to be willing to pay voluntarily for the entertainment value they find in violence.

Another critical point is this: Boston and Montreal have about the same populations, and both cities are flooded with TV programs and movies involving murder and violence. Yet Boston records eight times as many cases of aggravated assault per year as does the Canadian city of Montreal.

Could poverty and racial prejudice account for the high rate of violence in the United States? Boston has many more slums and a much larger population of blacks and Latin Americans than does Montreal. The poorer sections of any large American town usually experience many times more violent crimes than do the richer areas, and members of racial minority groups are more likely to live in the ghetto areas and slums than in the wealthy suburbs. If we wiped out poverty and prejudice, could we also reduce violence? Or are our attitudes about violent solutions to human conflicts so much a part of our culture that these attitudes wouldn't change no matter what we did?

In June of 1972, in the journal *Science*, social *psychiatrist* (°) Monica D. Blumenthal published a lengthy article on American attitudes toward violence. She and her colleagues asked for opinions about violence from 1,374 men between

Monica D. Blumenthal.

the ages of 16 and 64. Her results led Dr. Blumenthal to conclude that a person's attitude about the justifiability of using violence is affected by many cultural factors, including religious beliefs. The Bible tells us, "Thou shalt not kill," and that we should treat our neighbors as we wish to be treated ourselves. But the Bible also states that we should defend ourselves by taking "an eye for an eye, a tooth for a tooth" when we are attacked by others. In addition, Dr. Blumenthal reminds us, some cultural concepts of *masculinity* imply positive attitudes toward violence. America has traditionally glorified the hard-riding, straight-shooting frontiersman, who settled arguments with the action end of his gun in calm disregard of laws against killing people. To the extent that an individual American agrees with the "Wild West" concept of justice, he or she should be likely to approve of the use of violent force in settling conflicts.

Dr. Blumenthal's data suggest that we are all more likely to approve of violence if we identify with, or approve of, the person or group committing a particular act of aggression. On the other hand, if we identify with, or feel positively toward, the *victim* of the aggression, we are likely to have a negative attitude toward a particular act of violence. Dr. Blumenthal asked her sample of 1,374 men how much violence they believed should be used to handle ghetto riots and student disturbances. She reports that most of these men believed that the police should use but minimal amounts of violence in controlling such disruptions—but a *substantial majority* of the men supported the use of guns as long as the police didn't "shoot to kill."

Perhaps because black men saw themselves as possible victims rather than aggressors, black men recommended lower levels of violence for controlling riots and disturbances than did white men. When it came to achieving social change, however, the tables were reversed. Black men were three times more likely than white men to state that protest involving "some deaths" would be necessary to bring about a speedy change in the social status of black people.

One of the most surprising findings of the Blumenthal study is that many American men who say they are strongly opposed to violence are in favor of having the police shoot at rioters and demonstrators. A deeper analysis of the Blumenthal data helps clear up this apparent contradiction. Most of these men look upon peaceful demonstrations and protest marches as being "violence against the government." These same men tend to view the use of force by policemen to put down the protests as being "non-violent actions," or "violence justified by the circumstances." Apparently it is easier for these men to change their definition of what constitutes violence than it is for them to change their attitudes about the acceptability of violent behaviors.

Like most social psychologists and social psychiatrists, Dr. Blumenthal assumes that "attitudes are likely to be reflected by behaviors," or that what people do is largely determined by the attitudes that their cultures have rewarded them for learning. In a society that approves of aggression, could the people be other than aggressive?

QUESTION: According to the social/behavioral viewpoint, who "pulls the strings" that makes the "little man" in your head make you act violently?

Bowling Green University psychologist J.P. Scott, who has made a life-long study of aggression in man and animals, believes that violence is usually multi-determined. That is, aggressive attacks almost always have biological, intra-psychic, and social/behavioral causes. At the human level, however, societal factors are usually the most important of all, according to Scott. He points out that males in our culture are encouraged to leave home when they reach sexual maturity, but typically do not form new family ties until several years afterwards. Perhaps this is why, in the United States, violent crimes are most likely to be committed by single or divorced males between the ages of 16 and 25. It is

Konrad Lorenz.

likewise true that these men commonly come from a poverty-stricken background and from homes broken by desertion, divorce, or death. Furthermore, as Scott notes, unmarried young men frequently organize into groups whose main purpose is that of making war or terrorizing others. Scott believes that we will not do away with such violence until we create societies that promote peace, stability, and positive interpersonal relationships—particularly among the disadvantaged young people in all cultures.

Intra-psychic Determinants of Violence

In the later chapters of this book, when we discuss a topic called *personality theory*, we will find that many psychologists view violence as a mental trait or characteristic that is determined by a person's subjective outlook on life. From this intra-psychic position, *personality traits* (°) are produced both by one's biological inheritance and by what happens during certain critical stages in a person's early development. We are born with certain innate response patterns—called *instincts* (°)—that are passed along to us by our parents. Our childhood environments, particularly our interactions with our parents, shape or mold these instinctual thoughts and behaviors into what we call our *minds*. As we mature, our minds become more and more capable of acting on their own, and we become more and more capable of achieving our own personal, subjective goals—within the limits set by our bodies and our cultures.

According to many intra-psychic theorists, we are born with an aggressive instinct that we often do not learn how to control. As evidence to support this viewpoint, intra-psychic psychologists point to the research of *Konrad Lorenz* (°), a German scientist who has spent a lifetime studying the behavior patterns of wild animals. Lorenz believes that while aggressive instincts first evolved in the lower animals, the tendency toward senseless violence has reached its peak in human beings. In his research, Lorenz noted that animals of one species will often kill members of another species for food—or if threatened—but they seldom kill out of hatred, prejudice, politics, or "just for fun." During mating season, males will occasionally battle other males for possession of females, but the males rarely do each other lasting harm.

As an example of what he is talking about, Lorenz discusses at length research performed on a fish known as the "three-spined stickleback." This little animal seldom grows to more than a few inches in length, but it has a very complex set of behavior patterns. The male stickleback, once he has grown into adulthood, establishes a territory on the bottom of a stream that he marks off as being entirely his. If another stickleback intrudes on this territory, the "homeowner" rushes toward the intruder and goes through a series of instinctual responses that usually

The "three-spined" stickleback.

serve to chase off the other fish. As the "homeowner" approaches the intruder, his head dips farther and farther down toward the bottom of the stream until—at the border of his territory—he is almost standing on his nose in what Lorenz calls the "classic threat posture."

If the intruder is another male, particularly one who wishes to take over the "homeowner's" territory, the intruder may well go into the threat posture himself. The two fish may stand on their noses glaring at each other for several seconds before anything else happens. In most instances, the "homeowner's" threat is sufficient to frighten the intruder off before a fight begins. If the intruder refuses to leave, the "homeowner" will usually attack, attempting to inflict damage with teeth and fins. Such battles are usually brief and relatively bloodless, and the stranger is driven away—for even a small fish defending its own territory is usually able to defeat a large but homeless male.

The inherited nature of this instinctual behavior can be shown in several ways:

1. To begin with, almost all male three-spined sticklebacks show the aggressive threat response even when they have been raised in isolation and could not have learned it from other fish.
2. The response sequence is almost the same in all three-spined stickleback males, but is quite different in males of a closely related species, the nine-spined stickleback.
3. The behavior is most likely to occur during mating season, when the belly of the male turns a bright red color. Indeed, the male stickleback will attack almost any object—including crude plastic models of a fish—if that object has a red belly and intrudes on the male's territory.

The aggressive reaction of the stickleback is *stereotyped* (°), which is to say that it is practically the same in most males of the same species and in most situations. Stereotyped reactions are usually not much affected by the past experiences of the organism. Whether or not human beings are born with a *stereotyped* aggressive reaction is still something of an open question. We certainly do not stand on our noses like the stickleback when an intruder threatens our home. The specific aggressive responses that humans display appear to vary widely from culture to culture, and from individual to individual. But perhaps there is one specific type of situation in which we all react pretty much the same way.

In seeking further data on this matter, it might help if we asked the following question: Do animals ever show the kind of "vindictive nastiness" that we see far too often in humans?

The answer to that question turns out to be quite shocking.

Pain and Aggression Some 30 years ago two psychologists named O'Kelly and Steckle wished to study how rats escaped from a painful stimulus. They built a box that had a metal grid on the floor through which they could pass an electrical current. The shock caused the rats considerable discomfort but did not really damage the animals in any way. O'Kelly and Steckle found that, if they put just one rat in the apparatus and turned on the shock, the rat would either try to escape or would "freeze" and not move at all. However, when these psychologists put several rats into the box and shocked them, the rats at once began attacking each other—biting, squealing, and lashing out at the other rats. Unfortunately for our understanding of violence, when other scientists attempted to repeat this particular experiment, they were not always successful. The connection between pain and aggression was not looked at again experimentally until 25 years later, when Nathan Azrin and his associates rediscovered the *phenomenon* (°).

(The history of science is full of such "lost" discoveries. Often, when a scientist finds something new in his or her laboratory and describes the discovery in print, other scientists attempt to repeat or *replicate* (°) the work and fail. In most cases it can be shown—but often not until years later—that the other scientists were

Stereotype (STAIR-ee-oh-type). A rather standardized mental picture held in common by members of a group, and representing an oversimplified opinion or attitude of some object, person, idea, or another group. If you react to all Jews as if they were stingy (or as if they were generous), you respond in stereotyped fashion to all Jews. That is, you react to your mental impression of a Jew, and not to *individual* Jews themselves (each of whom has his or her own unique set of personality traits).

Phenomenon (fee-NOM-ee-non or fee-NOM-uh-non). From the Greek word meaning "to show." Thus, an observable fact or event, or an item of experience. Anything that you can see, hear, or touch. Occasionally used to mean "something rare or unique."

Replicate (REP-plee-cate). A replica of a statue is an exact copy of that statue. In scientific usage, to replicate is to repeat an experiment exactly as it was first performed.

A raccoon and a hooded rat remain far apart in cage before shock (top). Two seconds after receiving a shock, the animals move toward each other (bottom).

Et al. (ett-all). From the Latin term *et alia,* meaning "and allies." Scientists like to give each other credit. If an experiment was performed by Smith and Jones, it is usually referred to by using both names. But some experiments are performed by a dozen or more scientists. Rather than writing Smith, Jones, Johnson, Ginsburg, Washington, Lee, Brodsky, Blanc, and Negra each time we speak of the study, we usually say "Smith *et al.*" Usually—but not always—the first name listed is that of the "senior scientist" who had the greatest responsibility for the research.

Habituate (hab-BITT-you-ate). To become accustomed to a place or to a given stimulus. The first time you handle a snake, you may be very frightened. But if snake-handling becomes a habit, your fears may habituate.

unsuccessful because they failed to do exactly what the original researcher had done. Sometimes the fault lies with the first scientist, who because he or she was working in an uncharted area of human knowledge, did not realize what features of the experiment were important and hence did not report the procedure accurately. Sometimes the fault lies with the later scientists who simply did not take the time or trouble to determine what the important features of the original work were. Science is a public affair; the results of any experiment should not be accepted as "true" unless these findings are confirmed. But new facts often challenge or contradict old theories that are loved and cherished by established scientists. The more startling or exciting a new discovery is, the less likely it is to be believed until it has been replicated many, many times by even the most skeptical of scientists. But as you might guess, the more skeptical the critic, the more likely it is that the critic will unconsciously bias the replication so that it turns out to be unsuccessful. We will discuss the problem of "experimenter bias" in Chapter 23.)

Psychologist Nathan Azrin and his colleagues, working at the Anna State Hospital in Illinois, began their research by trying to train two rats to move toward each other. Azrin is a behavioral psychologist who believes in the importance of rewards and punishments in determining behavior. He felt that if he could reward the two rats the moment they made the first tiny movement toward one another, he could encourage them to become "more social." In this case, the "reward" was to be turning off a painful electric shock.

Azrin and his group built a shock box much like the one that O'Kelly and Steckle had used. They put their rats in the box, turned on the shock, and then waited for the animals to move toward each other accidentally so that the electric current could be turned off instantly to reward this "social movement." To these psychologists' surprise, however, the rats became aggressive instead of more social. As soon as the shock became painful, the rats turned on each other and attacked each other violently. Wisely enough, Azrin *et al.* (a Latin term meaning "and colleagues") (°) abandoned their original objective and began to study aggression.

First, they had to make sure they knew what they were studying. How would you go about defining *aggression* in a rat? Azrin *et al.* found that the animals had a characteristic posture: As soon as a rat was shocked, it would stand up on its hind legs, face another rat, open its mouth, bare its front teeth, and then strike out at the other animal with its forepaws. Oddly enough, if another rat was not present, the shocked animal would show none of this behavior, but would keep its mouth closed and would cling with all four paws to the metal grid on which it stood.

Second, Azrin *et al.* had to determine whether it was really the shock that was causing the aggression, and not some incidental factor they had overlooked. The psychologists tested the relationship between shock and violence by varying the strength or *intensity* of the electrical current to see what this would do. They found that (1) the stronger the shock, the longer the aggression lasted; and (2) the more frequently the shock was given, the more vigorous and vicious the animal's attack was. Furthermore, the rats did not ever seem to get used to or *habituate* (°) to the shock; the animals would display the attack behavior several thousand times a day if the experimenters shocked them that often.

Azrin *et al.* also showed that this behavior was instinctual and not learned, for animals raised from birth in complete isolation from other rats still demonstrated the aggressive attack pattern when they were first shocked. Rats that lived together from birth attacked one another just as often as they attacked animals that were complete strangers. And since both males and females attacked members of either sex, Azrin *et al.* concluded that sexual competition or attraction was not involved in this reaction. Apparently it was the pain of the shock that triggered off an instinctual behavior pattern, which was relatively independent of the animal's prior experience.

Next, Azrin and his colleagues set out to discover whether shock would make animals of one species attack members of a different species. For example, would a shocked mouse attack a cat or a snake? The answer was yes, indeed—although the mouse seldom survived the encounter! In fact, the shocked animal would attack almost anything, even something like a tennis ball, if given the opportunity.

Is there something special about electrical current that causes this behavior, or would any painful stimulus serve to bring out the instinctual aggression? Azrin *et al.* found that almost any situation that caused the animal severe frustration would set off an attack. If a hungry pigeon is rewarded with a piece of grain each time it pecks at a button, it will soon learn to peck the button vigorously. If, after it has been pecking away for some time and earning its corn, you suddenly stop giving it the reward, the pigeon will typically first attack the button—and then any other object (such as another pigeon) that happens to be handy. Obviously, "psychological pain" or frustration can lead to violence as readily as can electric shock.

An animal can be taught to repeat almost any behavior pattern if it is immediately rewarded each time that it makes that response. Even a cowardly pigeon can be turned into an aggressive terror if it is kept very hungry and is given food as a reward each time it attacks a fellow pigeon. Azrin *et al.* found that pigeons given electrical shock and allowed to aggress against another bird became much more aggressive thereafter. In short, although the *tendency* to attack is present in animals at birth, rewards can surely strengthen the tendency (and punishment weaken it).

But what about the animal that is the object of the aggression? Suppose we have two pigeons close to each other, and we shock pigeon A but don't shock pigeon B. What will happen? A attacks B, as you might guess, but the attack inflicts pain on B. The pain apparently annoys or frustrates B, who then retaliates by striking back at pigeon A. This counter-attack causes A further pain and hence further frustration, so A repeats its aggression against B even more vigorously. Pigeon B then hits back even harder, and the battle is on.

QUESTION: What similarities do you see between the battling pigeons and the positive feedback loop that builds up between two cerebral hemispheres at the start of an epileptic attack?

Is there no way out of this explosive situation? Luckily, as Azrin and his associates found, there is. The aggressive *syndrome* (°) usually does not occur if the frustrated animal is given the alternative of *escaping* rather than *attacking*. A rat cooped up in a small box with another animal will attack because it apparently has no alternative. The same rat, if shocked in an open field, will flee from the pain rather than take out its frustration on nearby objects. The attack behavior will also not occur if the animal is given the opportunity to avoid the pain in the first place, or if the animal can end or terminate the pain through a peaceful gesture.

QUESTION: From an intra-psychic viewpoint, why might violence be expected to occur more frequently in crowded ghettos than in suburban areas?

Frustration-Aggression Hypothesis Perhaps the greatest modern contributor to the intra-psychic viewpoint was Sigmund Freud, the Viennese psychiatrist who developed an intra-psychic theory of personality called Psycho-Analysis. As we will see in later chapters, Freud believed that there is a childish part of our personalities that demands immediate gratification of all its wishes. Whenever this "child" in our minds is frustrated, it may either throw a temper tantrum or display other immature forms of emotion. Using Freud's basic idea, psychologists John Dollard and Neal Miller derived what they call the *frustration-aggression hy-*

Syndrome (SIN-drome; rhymes with "BEEN home"). A group of symptoms or signs typical of a particular disease or reaction pattern. The aggressive syndrome varies from one animal to another. In cats, for instance, it usually includes spitting, scratching, biting, arching of the back, flattening of the ears, baring of the teeth, twitching of the tail, and so forth.

Frustration-aggression hypothesis. A theory put forth by John Dollard and Neal Miller that aggression is always the direct result of some kind of frustration. Although aggressive behavior obviously does result from some types of frustration, aggressive reactions apparently have other causes as well.

Limbic system (LIM-bick). A related set of nerve centers in the brain that influences emotional behavior.

pothesis (°). According to this hypothesis, frustration occurs whenever a highly motivated individual encounters a barrier of some kind that prevents the person from reaching a much-desired goal. The barrier may be physical, psychological, or symbolic. If the individual cannot get around the barrier, frustration develops, and the person's behavior typically becomes less logical and more strongly emotional than would usually be the case. According to Dollard and Miller, aggression is *always* caused by frustration, but a frustrated person may do many things other than strike out against other people.

But are Dollard and Miller right? Is violence *always* a product of frustration? In the first chapter of this book we mentioned the case of Clarence B., the young black man who senselessly murdered a graduate student trying to help him. There is little doubt that Clarence B. had experienced a great deal of frustration in his life. But the evening of the murder, Clarence B. was actually in rather a happy state of mind. The rage that immediately preceded the killing came on very suddenly, without warning and without any evident cause. To understand what might have happened to Clarence B.'s mind that night, we must first probe more deeply into what might already have happened to his brain.

Biological Determinants of Violence

What goes on in the brain of an animal—or a human—that might lead it to attack its neighbors when it is shocked or suddenly frustrated? Obviously the motor output centers of the cortex are involved, since the shocked animal makes aggressive *movements*. But, as we said earlier, the cortex is merely the thin outer covering of the cerebral "mushroom." Buried away in the "flesh" of the two hemispheres—underneath the cortical covering but still a part of the cerebrum—are a number of neural centers that have rather specialized functions. These centers act rather like the vice-presidents of a large corporation. That is, they are capable of operating independently (as a vice-president in charge of advertising might), but they are still under the general orders of the Board of Directors. The cortical Board of Directors may even take over direct control of these centers in emergency situations, just as a corporate Board might issue special directives to its advertising division if an important ad campaign seemed to be failing.

The Limbic System   The emotional behavior of higher organisms is, to a great extent, controlled by a section of the brain called the *limbic system* (°). The Latin word *limbus* means "border," and the limbic system is so named because it makes up the "border" or inner surface of both cerebral hemispheres. This inner border is the part of the cerebrum you would see if you could turn the brain upside down and look at the "mushroom cap" from the bottom. There are identical limbic

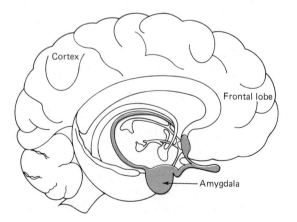

systems in both your hemispheres, but since they usually are in close touch with each other (via the corpus callosal bridge), we can consider them as one unit.

Just as each cerebral hemisphere is divided into sections—the four lobes—the limbic system has several parts or structures to it. One of these structures—buried deep within the mountains of the temporal lobe on the side of the head—is the *amygdala* (°). The amygdala is a nut-shaped group of neurons that gets its name from the Latin word for "almond." Since the amygdala in each of your temporal lobes has a decided influence on how violent you are, and on your sex life, it is well worth studying.

The limbic system acts as if it were the vice-president in charge of the more primitive and basic emotional reactions—some of which, as you must admit, are rather childish and impulsive. Under normal conditions, however, the more mature and rational cortical Board should be able to inhibit or control electrical activity in the limbic system. Three different types of experiments seem to prove this is the case.

What happens when a person gets drunk? As we suggested in the previous chapter, alcohol appears to affect the inhibitory centers in the cortex sooner than the emotional centers. We can assume, then, that intoxicated people behave in childish, aggressive ways because the alcohol effectively removes or knocks out cortical control of the limbic system. Further support for this assumption comes from experiments on cats, in which the cortex is removed surgically but the limbic system is left intact. How do you think a cat would react if we used a surgical knife rather than a drug to free the limbic "vice-president" from cortical inhibition?

To begin with, this "de-cortex-ed," or *decorticate* (°), animal gets along surprisingly well, considering that it has been deprived of a goodly portion of its brain. There seems to be no basic change in the animal's personality—friendly cats remain friendly, and aggressive felines remain aggressive. However, even very slight pain or frustration is enough to set these animals into an explosive, violent rage.

Next, what do you think would happen if we "reversed" the kind of operation just described? That is, what would happen if we removed parts of the limbic system in animals but left most of the cortex intact? Heinrich Kluever and Paul Bucy were probably the first scientists to perform this operation. Their experimental animals were rhesus monkeys, a species of *primate* (°) noted for its vile temper and its readiness to aggress. Kluever and Bucy removed the temporal lobes from both hemispheres in their animals—thus taking out the amygdalas and other parts of the limbic system. After the monkeys had recovered, their personalities appeared to have changed rather profoundly. They were gentle and placid in almost all circumstances, even when attacked by another animal. They also became markedly oversexed. The males would attempt to mount anything handy, including inanimate objects. The females would attempt to have sex even with such strange "partners" as water faucets.

The Kluever and Bucy monkeys also showed rather bizarre eating behavior. Not only did they over-indulge, but they also "tested" all small objects in their environment by putting them in their mouths. If given a bowl full of peanuts mixed with small metal bolts, a normal monkey will rapidly learn to pick out the edible nuts from the inedible bolts either by look or by feel. Kluever and Bucy's monkeys couldn't make this kind of judgment—they had to bite the objects first, and they discarded the bolts only when they couldn't be chewed. Later studies confirmed the Kluever and Bucy experiment by showing that removal of the amygdala in ferocious animals like the lynx or the wolverine makes them relatively tame.

Finally, knowing all this, what do you think would happen if you could somehow stimulate the amygdala in a normal cat electrically? When Fritsch and

Amygdala (a-MIG-dah-lah). An almond-shaped nerve center in the temporal lobe that is part of the limbic system. Removal of the amygdala makes a monkey rather unemotional and easygoing, but has other effects as well.

Decorticate (de-CORT-uh-cate). An animal or human whose cortex has been removed (usually through surgery).

Primate (PRIME-ate). From the Latin word *primus*, meaning "leader" or "first in line." Biologically speaking, primates are the "top animals," including humans, the monkeys, and apes. The rhesus (REE-sus) monkey is a primate; so are you.

Needle electrode. A thin, needle-shaped piece of metallic wire that can be inserted into the brain to measure the electrical activity of small groups of neurons, or to stimulate nerve cells close to the electrode's tip.

Stimoceiver (STIM-oh-SEE-ver). An electrical apparatus connected to needle electrodes implanted in an animal's brain. When the stimoceiver receives radio commands from a nearby transmitter, it stimulates the brain with weak electrical currents.

Hitzig performed the first research on brain stimulation in 1870, they touched a piece of metal *directly* to the surface of the motor cortex of their wounded soldiers. But the amygdala lies far beneath the cortical surface. To reach the amygdala, you need a long, thin instrument called a *needle electrode* (°). This needle is so thin that it can be inserted with little damage deep into the brain of a living organism. Since the tip of the electrode is metallic, it can be used to record the firing of nerve cells far below the brain's surface. However, this type of electrode may also be used to probe or electrically stimulate the brain cells lying very close to its tip. If electrodes implanted within the amygdala or other areas of the limbic system are used to *stimulate* an otherwise normal cat, the animal goes into a rage as soon as the current is turned on. The cat's hair stands on end, its back arches, it spits and screams, and it will usually attack anything nearby (including the experimenter).

The "Stimoceiver" When needle electrodes were first used both for recording and stimulating purposes (about 1930), they had to be connected to banks of rather complicated electrical equipment by means of long wires that carried the current either to or from the brain. Unlike the skin and most of the rest of the body, brain tissue has no pain receptors. Thus, the presence of many electrodes stuck into a cat's brain would cause the animal little discomfort—but the wires leading to the electrodes were something else again. A cat with several wires attached to its skull cannot be expected to behave normally. Recently, however, a Yale physiologist named José Delgado devised a tiny radio transmitter/receiver that could substitute for the wires. The electrodes are connected directly to this *"stimoceiver"* (°), which, since it weighs less than 3 ounces, can easily be taped directly to the cat's head. An experimenter 100 feet away can record the activity of several electrodes at the same time. Or, if the experimenter wishes, he or she can stimulate whichever centers in the animal's brain contain electrodes—and perform this stimulation without having to go near the animal.

José Delgado proved the effectiveness of this "radio control" in the bullring. First, he planted an electrode in a bull's brain. The electrode was in an *inhibitory* center that, when stimulated, would act to inhibit or "turn off" the sort of rage reactions bulls often show. Delgado attached the electrode to his "stimoceiver" so that he could influence the bull's reactions at a distance.

Then Delgado walked into the bullring holding a portable radio transmitter in his hand. The bull was released into the ring with Delgado—who had only his hand transmitter to protect himself.

At first, the animal walked around the ring rather peacefully. When the bull saw the scientist, the bull stiffened, began to paw the dirt, snorted, then charged straight at Delgado, its horns lowered in the classic position of attack. Delgado let the bull come within 20 feet (6 meters) or so of him and then pressed the button on the transmitter. The "stimoceiver" began to deliver small pulses of electrical current to the electrode implanted in the bull's inhibitory center. The animal halted its charge as if it had suddenly run out of steam. It shook its head, looked curiously at Delgado, then turned around and wandered off quietly.

In October of 1974, Professor Delgado demonstrated his most recent research at the 26th International Congress of Physiological Sciences held in New Dehli, India. The physical size of the "stimoceiver" has been reduced to such an extent that it is almost invisible when implanted under the skin of an otherwise normal animal (or human). By stimulating various parts of the brain, Delgado has been able to induce ferociously aggressive behavior in a variety of monkeys and apes. Stimulation to certain other parts of the brain makes these same animals passive and unresponsive to attack. Using the "stimoceiver," Delgado has been able to turn dominant monkey "leaders" into "followers," while the most submissive monkeys have been stimulated into becoming dominant "leaders" of monkey troops.

José Delgado.

The Case of Julia

Drs. Vernon Mark, Frank Ervin, and their colleagues in Boston were among the first scientists to use the "stimoceiver" to diagnose damage in the limbic systems of the brains of human patients. One of their first patients was a young girl named Julia, who had a long history of violent assaults on other people.

At the age of 2 Julia had suffered from a rare form of brain infection that gave her a very high fever. At first it seemed as if she had recovered from the sickness entirely, but about the time she was 10, she began having "spells" that suggested the illness had left her with a damaged brain. The "spells" were not the *grand mal* (°) type of seizure. Rather, Julia would suddenly become terribly frightened even though there usually wasn't anything for her to be frightened of. If the "spell" took place when she was at school, she would sometimes attack her schoolmates. More often, she would begin running as if she feared for her life. Often she would run for miles and miles before the "spell" wore off. Since she frequently ended up in a strange part of her home town, she began carrying a little pocketknife with her "for protection."

One evening when Julia was about 16, she went to the movies with her parents. During the film, she began to feel sick, and went to the ladies' room. The lounge was empty when she arrived. She glanced at herself in the mirror and was horrified. It seemed to her that *the whole left side of her body* had become shriveled up, evil, and distorted. She was terrified by what she saw, and couldn't believe that it was really she. At just this moment, another girl came into the lounge, and in trying to pass by Julia, touched her on her left arm. Julia grabbed for her knife and stabbed the other girl several times. Then Julia began screaming at the top of her voice. Fortunately for all concerned, the injured girl was rushed to the hospital and her life was saved.

QUESTION: **On which side of Julia's brain was the damage apparently most severe?**

After this attack Julia's parents had her committed to a hospital. Julia was given many different types of treatment or therapy, but became worse rather than better. If not watched continuously she would assault the other patients; once she stole a pair of scissors and stabbed a nurse who angered her. In desperation, her parents took her to Boston for the new type of treatment that Drs. Mark and Ervin were developing.

The first EEG records that Mark and Ervin made of Julia's brain showed abnormal, epileptic-type of "spike" waves in the regions of both temporal lobes, while an X-ray photograph suggested that her *right* temporal lobe was slightly shrunken. Since her violent episodes were continuing, Mark and Ervin decided that certain risks were justified. They implanted needle electrodes in both of Julia's temporal lobes (the electrodes were safely removed later on). After Julia had recovered from this relatively minor operation, Mark and Ervin were able to record directly from both her right and left amygdalas. They found epileptic electrical activity in both.

When Mark and Ervin used the implanted electrodes to *stimulate* Julia's amygdalas rather than just for recording, they discovered they could trigger off episodes of violence much like the ones she usually had. Mark and Ervin were convinced that tiny bits of scar tissue in her amygdalas were causing Julia's difficulties, but the scars were too small and buried too deeply in her brain to be removed by normal surgical methods. So Mark and Ervin decided to try something rather new in brain surgery. First, they would move their electrodes around until they had located the exact center of the scar tissue in each amygdala. Then, they would pass a very brief but strong electrical current through the electrodes, a technique that would "burn out" the scar tissue.

Before Mark and Ervin could undertake the operation, José Delgado made his "stimoceiver" available to the Boston doctors. They were then able to implant

Grand mal (grahn mahl). A type of motor epilepsy in which the person loses consciousness and usually writhes about on the floor. From the French term meaning "big sickness." See Chapter 2.

electrodes in various parts of Julia's amygdala, connect the electrodes to the "stimoceiver," and record from (and stimulate) Julia's brain while she was moving freely about her hospital ward. They could also make movies of her—and then match this film recording of her behavior with the EEG records coming from the "stimoceiver."

During one of their first recording sessions, a "natural" seizure occurred in Julia's limbic system. She was sitting down and in a fairly pleasant mood when the EEG began to show spiking in her right amygdala. Moments later, Julia jumped up and ran over to the wall of her bedroom. Once she reached the wall her eyes narrowed; she clenched her fists and bared her teeth as if she were about to attack the wall. The spike-like seizure activity in her amygdala slowly subsided at this point, and Julia's behavior rapidly returned to normal.

Shortly thereafter, Mark and Ervin *stimulated* Julia's brain directly. Although Julia had given her permission for them to do so, she was not told exactly when the stimulation was to occur. Mark and Ervin waited until Julia was sitting in her room, peacefully singing, playing a guitar, and talking to a doctor who was in her room to help if needed. Mark and Ervin turned the current on for a very brief moment, then turned it off. A few seconds after the current had stopped, a blank stare slipped over Julia's face and she stopped singing. The doctor began asking her questions about how she felt, but she was unable to answer. The recording electrode now showed a full-blown epileptic seizure was occurring in her right amygdala—triggered off, of course, by the brief burst of direct electrical stimulation. Suddenly Julia grabbed the guitar by its neck and swung it at the doctor. She narrowly missed the man's head, smashing the guitar against the wall instead.

Julia's behavior suggested that Mark and Ervin had indeed located the scar tissue that was causing the seizures. Shortly thereafter, they used their electrodes to destroy the scar tissue in her amygdala and then removed all the electrodes from the girl's brain. In the first year after the operation, Julia suffered but two rather mild attacks of rage behavior. She had no attacks at all after that first year.

Julia was lucky. As we will see, many patients given similar surgery have not fared as well.

Limbic System Seizures

Epilepsy that is focused in some part of the limbic system is often very difficult to diagnose correctly. If the seizure spreads from the limbic system to the motor output centers in the frontal lobes, a *grand mal* attack occurs—and anyone with medical training will know to look for scar tissue in the patient's brain. But often the seizure activity is confined to the general region of the temporal lobe itself and no *grand mal* attack occurs. EEG records taken from outside the skull (which is typically the case) often do not pick up the spiking that occurs in the limbic region, for, as we have seen, the amygdala is buried deep inside the temporal lobe. When the seizure is confined to the temporal lobe, the only clue a doctor may have is the patient's periodic episodes of violence and rage. And very often the physician may suggest "mental" or *psycho-therapy* (°) rather than physical therapy, since it is only in very recent years that we have discovered the connection between the limbic system and violent behavior.

QUESTION: If some complete stranger attacked you on the street without reason, would you assume the person might be suffering from brain damage, or would you assume the person was mean, nasty-tempered, or even "crazy"?

In their study of hundreds of people arrested or hospitalized for violent crimes, Mark and Ervin found that many of these individuals had rather surprisingly similar behavior patterns. There was always a history of physical assaults on other people which, among adult males, usually manifested itself in wife- and child-

Psycho-therapy (SIGH-ko-THER-ap-pee). Literally speaking, "to treat the mind." Treatment of a mental or emotional disorder by psychological means, usually by way of verbal communication.

beating. Most of the individuals showed a strange sensitivity to alcohol. One or two drinks were often enough to trigger off brutal attacks on anyone nearby. Their sexual behavior was typically disturbed and sexual assaults were frequent. And, finally, most of the individuals had a long history of traffic violations and had been involved in many serious accidents. None of these people had been diagnosed as having damaged limbic systems. But the behavior patterns of these violent prisoners and criminally insane patients are very similar to those shown by people with temporal lobe epilepsy. Although Mark and Ervin have no real proof as yet, they fear that many individuals locked up in jails or hospitals "for their own good" may suffer from hidden or undiagnosed brain damage.

QUESTION: Does the behavior of Clarence B., mentioned in Chapter 1, seem to fit the pattern described above?

As Karl Pribram, a noted neurosurgeon at Stanford, has pointed out, there is little doubt that a damaged amygdala can lead to episodes of violent rage in human beings. But we surely would be very wrong to assume that the reverse is true—that episodes of violence are a universal sign of scar tissue in the amygdala. For Mark and Ervin have been able to demonstrate clear-cut brain damage in but a small fraction of the patients they have studied. Many of their patients have shown little or no lasting improvement after removal of their amygdalas, and not all scientists have been successful in their attempts to repeat the Mark and Ervin research. Furthermore, the moral questions raised by such operations are complex and often frightening.

Take Clarence B. as an example of the problems, ethical and medical, that one faces in the study of violence. Clarence B.'s murderous behavior and his background fit the pattern of many of the cases in which limbic system damage was discovered. But we never got Clarence B. in for a brain examination, so we cannot in fact state that he suffered from temporal lobe epilepsy. And we would do that young man a grave injustice if—on the basis of his behavior alone—we insisted that a brain operation might "cure" him of his problems. For many of the violent patients whose amygdalas are removed simply do not show any improvement afterwards. And, as we will see in the next chapter, even if a person does cease being violent after a temporal lobe operation, we cannot be certain that it is the surgery that was responsible for the behavioral change. It may be the changed attitudes of the patient's family, friends, and the medical staff after the operation that cause the decrease in aggressively violent actions. If we expect surgery patients to behave more maturely after parts of their brains are removed, as Dr. Pribram reminds us, the patients may respond to our expectations even if the surgery itself was not particularly successful.

VIOLENCE AND THE MIND-BODY PROBLEM

What causes violence?

By now, you will understand that your answer to that question depends on your solution to the mind-body problem.

If you take the social/behavioral viewpoint, you will see violence as stemming primarily from the "models" we see on TV and in our own family settings, as well as from the effects that environmental rewards and punishments have on our attitudes and behavior.

If you take the intra-psychic viewpoint, you will think of violence as a personality trait, an instinctual emotional response to a frustrating situation.

If you take the biological viewpoint, you will look upon violence as caused by electrical activity in the limbic system and other parts of the brain.

If you take an even broader view, however, you will see that there really is no single cause for violence. Behavior is always *multi-determined*. Thoughts and actions are always affected by a person's inheritance, past experience, and present environmental situation. To give up any of the three main views toward the mind-body problem would be to short-circuit our understanding of why we think and act as we do.

As we will soon see, however, the major conflict among the three viewpoints comes not so much in explaining "what makes you tick" as in suggesting how to repair the human clockwork when it gets violently out of adjustment. We will begin our discussion of *mind* versus *body* versus *environmental* therapy in the next chapter.

SUMMARY

1. The complex interactions among brain, mind, and environment are often referred to as the "mind-body" problem.
2. For centuries, philosophers and scientists argued about whether bodily activities *caused* thinking, or whether thoughts *caused* bodily activities. Probably the best solution to this problem is to say that electrical and chemical reactions in your brain are correlated with—but do not really cause—your thoughts, feelings, and behaviors.
3. It was not until the 1800's that we learned much about the structure and function of the human brain. We now know that each cerebral hemisphere is divided into four lobes—the frontal, the temporal, the occipital, and the parietal.
4. The frontal lobe contains the motor cortex.
5. The temporal lobe contains nerve centers that influence speech, hearing, and emotions.
6. The occipital lobe is the visual center of the brain.
7. The parietal lobe receives sensory inputs from the skin and muscles.
8. If the motor cortex in the frontal lobe is stimulated electrically, the person's muscles move or jerk.
9. If the visual input areas of the occipital lobe are stimulated, the person "sees stars."
10. Large areas of the cortex are silent to electrical probing. These so-called association areas are presumably the parts of the cortex where processing and decision-making occur.
11. Emotional behavior is highly correlated with electrical activity in the limbic system, a related set of neural centers that include the amygdala in the temporal lobe. Stimulation of the human or animal amygdala is often followed by aggressive attacks. Removal of the amygdala leads to a marked reduction in aggressive behavior in animals but not necessarily in humans.
12. Violence is also influenced by psychological and environmental factors. For example, some cultural attitudes appear to accept or even encourage violent behavior. People who hold such attitudes are more likely to be hostile and aggressive than people who hold the opposite sorts of attitudes.
13. People can be trained to display violent behavior if they are rewarded for being aggressive. And, as we will see in the next chapter, people can also be taught how to control their aggressive emotions.
14. Psychological frustration or pain often (but not always) leads to aggression.
15. People who suffer from damaged amygdalas often fly into violent rages for little or no reason, particularly if they are drugged or drunk. Surgical removal of the damaged tissue in the amygdala can sometimes be of help, but should always be coupled with psycho-therapy and changes in the patient's environment. Behavior is multi-determined, and there is no one unique solution to the problem of violence in today's world.

(Continued from page 79.)

TO:	Senior Robot-in-Charge, Space Exploration Program
FROM:	Leader Robot, Scout Ship XJ-6
SUBJECT:	Planetary System MB-450-SEL

SenRo, may your batteries never run down, it is with dampened circuits and low meter readings that we communicate with you. How can we tell you of the great disappointment that has crept slowly into our fuse boxes? How can we make you feel the dismay that has settled over us like a rusting fog?

In our first message, filled with pulsating high expectancy, we described in brief detail our discovery of the CARs on this dismal planet. Were they our brothers? Were they our heirs? Were they even the ``missing mechanical linkages'' some of our more heretical scientists have speculated about? The strong spark of hope raced through our metal bodies as we began our studies of the CARs. And now we come to you, dragging our wheels behind us, to confess that things are seldom what they seem at first perception.

It was Engineer RT/HEMI 454 who cast the first doubt on our initial positive impressions. The good engineer was observing the behavior of a cluster of CARs in a large city located close to the center of a string of five large inland lakes. Suddenly the engineer cried, ``This is where they are hatched!''

And it was true. To our amazement, we saw through the viewer large buildings that fairly spewed forth newborn CARs at fantastic rates! Hundreds upon hundreds per hour!

Navigator MT/BOSS 302 was incensed, as well one might expect. ``Have they no shame? Must they behave like unfeeling softlife, manufacturing their offspring in public?''

We shook our antennae in amazement. Then I looked through the viewer, and I too made a dramatic discovery. ``Why, they are birthing their youngsters on an assembly line!''

The others would not believe me until they too had looked for themselves.

Can you imagine, SenRo, a race of hardflesh so insensitive to matters of quality control? It is true that their planet is still young, and they have just begun to exhaust their natural resources, but to cast their seed forth into the world so quickly, without the careful, secret, loving attention to detail that marks our procreative process?

And the hatcheries themselves! Huge barren steel and concrete boxes, with smoke belching from high chimneys to pollute the landscape and rust those gorgeous metal bodies! And smoke too puffing from each CAR's exhaust pipe, as if they couldn't care less how much they poisoned their own air! We dread the necessity of ever having to drive on the surface of this planet and meet these CARs headlight to headlight. What stinking breath they must have!

Bad enough, I can hear you whisper through your voice box, but there is more, much more. For if their birth rites are primitive, their death rites are worse than that. It was Navigator MT/BOSS 302 who first noticed, near the hatchery, mounds of dead, decaying chassis of expired CARs. There they were, piled in heaps, as if no one cared to pay reverence to his passed-on ancestors. Some of the CARs were missing parts. We dread to say it, SenRo, but we fear we have happened upon a race of cannibals!

What can motivate these CARs to behave as they do? When first we looked, we thought them to be guided by the Electronic Spirits, as we are, but now we have grave doubts. For as we watched more closely, we began to notice even more terrible things. They rush about, almost aimlessly. Each morning there is a mass migration from the outskirts of the city to its center, and each evening the rolling hordes migrate outward again. But all they do when they get to their destinations is sit, meditating, by the hour. Does this make sense? And as they move, courtesy to other living things seems almost entirely absent. They weave in and out of lanes as if possessed of demons, charging at each other with blind abandon. And you can imagine the terror that touched our fuses when first we saw two lovely CARs smash head-on into each other! At first we thought these must be accidental encounters, but as we looked and looked and looked, it slowly came to us that ``accidents don't just happen.''

No, SenRo, there was a pattern to their behavior that we could not ignore. These CARs are actually hostile and aggressive toward one another! We pushed the viewer aside wearily, drank several pints of oil, and became well lubricated. For we knew what we must look for next, yet none of the three of us wished to make the first move. Finally, hours later, our gallant engineer set the viewer on "rapid scan," and watched the dials sadly. When we failed to get any readings on this continent, we moved the scout ship and looked elsewhere. It took us several hours to find what we had feared, but there it was . . .

How can I put it into speech symbols? For there, on the opposite of this accursed globe, we found unmistakable evidence of warlike behavior among these crazy CARs. Rather than share and share alike, they have established territories that they defend with all the passion of softlife. And they seem to have evolved specialized forms for doing battle—clumsy metal monsters with treads instead of wheels, and with long snouts that sniff out other CARs and then spit forth explosive missiles. We saw winged CARs zoom over cities and drop clutches of bursting eggs (further proof, I think, that the air CARs are a regressed species).

We ground our gears in anguish. These creatures, hardflesh though they be, must exist solely on a primitive, instinctual level. They cannot have discovered reason and still behave as they do. They are pushed by blind passions they surely cannot comprehend themselves. As such, they are scarcely better than softflesh. "Missing mechanical linkage?" I think not!

For hours we sat quietly, wheel to wheel, attempting to find a reason for this sick behavior. Could they be insane? Would mechano-therapy be of help? And are there enough mechano-therapists in the whole universe to help such a diseased world?

It was, perhaps, the word "disease" that prompted us to our final observation, and it was the engineer who first made it. We had moved the scout ship a little closer to ground level and could now resolve images 5 to 10 feet (1.5–3 meters) in length.

"Look," the engineer said, "I think the CARs are infested with a strange form of softflesh."

We looked long and hard and very carefully. It was true, SenRo. One had to be quick to notice, but from time to time, just after a CAR would come to a stop, a small panel would open in the CAR's side and out would slither a funny form of softlife. The panel would then close, and the softlife would disappear. The CAR would sit there, meditating peacefully, sometimes for minutes, sometimes for hours. And then the blurred image of another softlife would approach, the panel would pop open again, and the softflesh would ooze into the body of the CAR. Within seconds, the CAR would roar into movement, as if the presence of this softlife in its innards had goaded it into movement.

"Mindworms!" the navigator cried. "Softflesh that feeds on electrical energy, that gnaws on circuitry and sucks off insulation! Mindworms that nibble at the aggressive centers in our computer-brains, that bite and scratch and itch and frustrate and drive a CAR to ruin! No wonder these CARs are hostile, aggressive, warlike! They are infected with parasites!"

SenRo, we are agreed. There can be no other explanation. We do not need mechano-therapists, we need worm-killers! Therefore, we beg of you, send to us at once a ship filled with the most powerful form of worm poison we have available. Perhaps all is yet not lost! Perhaps, once we have sprayed the whole planet with pesticide, we can cure the CARs of their softflesh demons that drive them to distraction. And then at last, welcome the CARs into the metallic brotherhood!

SenRo, may your transmission never whine, we await your wisdom—and the arrival of the pesticide! But please do not let our petition get lost in the cogs of bureaucracy! We do not think the CARs can hold out too long!

RECOMMENDED READINGS

Dollard, John, and Neal E. Miller. *Personality and Psychotherapy: An Analysis in Terms of Learning, Thinking and Culture* (New York: McGraw-Hill, 1950).

Lorenz, Konrad. *On Aggression* (New York: Harcourt Brace Jovanovitch, 1966).

Lunde, Donald T. *Murder and Madness* (New York: Charles Scribner's Sons; San Francisco: W.H. Freeman, 1975).

Mark, Vernon H., and Frank R. Ervin. *Violence and the Brain* (New York: Harper & Row, 1970).

Scott, John P. *Aggression,* rev. ed. (Chicago: University of Chicago Press, 1975).

Valenstein, Elliot S. *Brain Control: A Critical Examination of Brain Stimulation and Psychosurgery* (New York: John Wiley, 1973).

chapter 5
"BOBBY'S BUZZ BOX"

SOME APPLICATIONS OF EXPERIMENTAL PSYCHOLOGY

DID YOU KNOW THAT . . .

Discovering what makes you tick is usually the first step in finding out how to tick better?

Brain surgery to "cure" violence cannot legally be forced on anyone involuntarily?

Many parents reward temper tantrums in their children by paying attention to the child at the wrong time?

The two major types of psycho-therapy are intra-psychic and behavioral treatment?

The two main kinds of intra-psychic treatment are psycho-analysis and humanistic therapy?

Badly brain-damaged children can be taught to control their own actions using behavior therapy?

You tend to repeat behaviors that are rewarded, but tend not to repeat behaviors that are ignored?

Behavior therapy always begins with the establishment of a measurable goal called the "terminal behavior pattern?"

Learning usually proceeds toward a goal in small steps called "successive approximations"?

When your environment changes dramatically, you may regress, or fall back, to a more childish way of behaving?

Buzz!

Peggy was delighted with the sound. It commanded attention, yet it wasn't all that noisy and distracting. Not that the kids would mind being distracted, of course. Peggy pressed the button again, just to make sure the battery was still working.

Buzz!

Peggy took the black box containing the battery and the buzzer over to a table at one side of the large kindergarten play area. Then she carefully strung the wires leading from the box around the edge of the room to the chair she would be sitting in, watching the children while they played. The wires led to a small button that she would be holding in her hand. When she pressed on the button . . .

Buzz!

"Good," she said aloud, and leaned back in the chair. If she was going to get a good grade on her senior project, this experiment just had to work out right. She didn't want to make any mistakes at all.

Even more important, she didn't want to harm a child by doing the wrong thing. But Dr. Johnson, the professor she was working with, assured her the experiment would work out okay. It had been done lots of times before by Dr. Patterson at the University of Oregon. Of course, that didn't mean that she, Peggy, would be able to pull it off, but she certainly wanted to try.

Peggy looked at her watch. The kids would be arriving shortly. They were a great bunch, although Peggy wasn't so sure about Miss Williams, the woman who ran the little kindergarten. Or maybe the trouble was that Miss Williams wasn't so sure of Peggy. When the problem with Bobby had come up, Miss Williams had gone to see Dr. Johnson in the Psychology Department at the local college to ask his help. Dr. Johnson, in turn, had asked Peggy if she'd like to work with Bobby as her senior project. Peggy had gone out to talk with Miss Williams to explain how they planned to help Bobby learn to get along with the other children at the kindergarten. During their conversation, Miss Williams had hinted rather openly that she would have preferred having Dr. Johnson come out himself. Peggy had almost pleaded with the woman to let her try the experiment, and finally Miss Williams had agreed—but very reluctantly.

Peggy was sure she could handle things. Bobby would probably come in last today, clinging tightly to his mother and throwing a temper tantrum when the woman tried to leave her son behind at the school. Peggy had talked with Bobby's parents at great length. They were desperate, particularly the mother. After all, Bobby was 5 years old now, and ought to be able to get along for a few hours without having his mother near him all the time. But as soon as she would pry herself loose from his clutching fingers and head for the door, Bobby would set up a high-pitched wail. If the wailing didn't bring his mother back, he would roll about on the floor, screaming and pounding his fists on the carpet. If his mother left him behind anyhow, Bobby would continue the tantrum for a while. But then he would calm down and start clinging to Miss Williams the way he had clung to his mother when she was around. He almost never played with the other kids. And that, of course, was the behavior that Peggy wanted to change.

"Measurement. That's the key," Dr. Johnson had told her. "If you can't measure the dependent variable—the behavior you want to change—then how can you expect to find an independent variable that will influence his behavior?"

"But Bobby's physician says that he may have scar tissue in his cortex," Peggy replied. "What can I do about that?"

Dr. Johnson raised his eyebrows. "What are you, a neurosurgeon? As an independent variable, do you want to chop out some part of his brain?"

"Of course not. I'm a senior majoring in psychology, not a surgeon. You know that."

"Does being a psychology major turn you into a Freud? Do you want to ask Bobby to lie down on your couch and talk about his mother? Is that the independent variable you want to employ to change his inappropriate behaviors?"

Peggy was annoyed. "You know I can't do surgery or psycho-therapy. It takes a lot of training for those things."

"So what kind of independent variable have you got left to use? Surgery and drugs are independent variables, but you need a medical degree to use them. Talk therapy is an independent variable, but an advanced degree is usually necessary for that sort of thing. So what have you got left?" Dr. Johnson's voice grew high-pitched. "The environment, that's what you've got left as an independent variable. You're part of Bobby's environment, and so are the kids at the kindergarten. You change the way you and the kids react to Bobby, and maybe he'll change the way he reacts to you and to them."

Peggy was amazed at the frustration she felt welling up inside her. "But acting in a different way toward Bobby won't cure his scarred-up cortex."

"True, but you can help him learn to live better with the problems he's got. That's mostly what applied psychology is all about—helping people find better ways to do what they want to do, or have to do. And that's all anybody can expect of you, even if you had an M.D. or a Ph.D. degree—that you should help people help themselves.

"But it seems so terribly little to do, just acting toward Bobby in a different way," Peggy said woefully.

Dr. Johnson grinned. "Never underestimate the power of an independent variable. Do what you can with the skills and knowledge that you've got."

''But . . .''

''And remember,'' Dr. Johnson said, pointing a stern finger at the young woman. ''It is better to light one candle than to sit and curse the darkness. So get off your rear end and try. If you fail, at least it won't be because you failed to try.''

Deep down inside, Peggy didn't entirely agree with Dr. Johnson's viewpoint, because she didn't think anybody could help a kid with a defective cortex. But she decided to try it anyway. As the first part of her project, therefore, she measured the amount of time that Bobby spent holding on to Miss Williams and the amount of time he spent playing with the other kids. Peggy observed him for several hours. During that period, Bobby spent slightly less than 15 percent of his time interacting with the other children and close to 30 percent clinging to Miss Williams. The rest of the time he was by himself. The goal of Peggy's project was to get Bobby to play with the other children at least half the time he was at the kindergarten. That's what the buzzer was for, as puny an independent variable as it was.

Miss Williams came out of the back room, nodded briefly in Peggy's direction, then went into the office. Peggy gave her a smile and a big hello as she passed by.

When Dr. Johnson had explained their plan, Miss Williams had been surprised.

"It seems terribly simple-minded to me," Miss Williams had said. "After all, the doctor said that Bobby might have a slightly damaged brain. Don't you think you need something more complex than a buzzer and a bag of gumdrops to help Bobby over his difficulties?"

Dr. Johnson, bless his heart, had insisted that she give Peggy a chance. "If the gumdrops don't work, then's the time to try something more complex."

"Well," Miss Williams had said, "I suppose so." But she hadn't been very friendly at all toward Peggy.

The children began to arrive. Miss Williams greeted each one of them by name, making them feel welcome and at ease. Bobby and his mother were late, as Peggy had expected they would be. When they showed up, the mother nodded at Peggy and started to come over to her, but Bobby began to cry and the woman got sidetracked. Finally she extricated herself from the little boy's clutches and rushed out the door, leaving her moaning and sobbing son to Miss Williams—and to Peggy.

Knowing all the children were there, Peggy went up to Miss Williams and said, "Is it okay if we get the project started now?"

Miss Williams was so distracted by Bobby, who was pulling on her dress, that she merely nodded. A moment or two later, though, she called to the class in a loud voice, "Boys and girls, you know Peggy very well by now. She wants to tell you about a new game we're going to play. I think you'll like the game very much, so please pay attention to her."

And then it was up to Peggy.

"I want to show you something new," she said loudly, since all of the children weren't really listening. "Do you see this black box? It's a Bobby Box. You all know Bobby, don't you, and I'm sure you like him very much."

One of the little girls started giggling, but Peggy ignored her and went on with the speech she had rehearsed so many times. "When the Bobby Box goes buzz-buzz, like this"—she pressed the button and the box responded magnificently—"that means Bobby has done something particularly good. So he is going to get a piece of candy as a reward."

"So what," said a little boy.

Peggy ignored her critic. She pressed the button again and, as soon as the buzzer sounded, offered Bobby a gumdrop. He released his hold on Miss Williams' dress and accepted the brightly colored piece of candy very solemnly. After he had inspected it for a few seconds, he popped it into his mouth.

The sight of candy had captured the children's attention, so Peggy hurried on with her explanation. "But because you are all friends of Bobby's and want to help him as much as you can, you're going to get a reward too. Every time the Bobby Box goes buzz-buzz, you're all going to get a piece of candy too! Now, isn't that an interesting game?"

The children cheered.

"Do you all want to play the game with Bobby?" They all did. "All right, now, let's start playing. Remember that any time Bobby does something really good, the Bobby Box will go buzz-buzz, and first Bobby will get a piece of candy, and then all of you will get candy too. Let's go!"

For the first several minutes the children kept a close eye on the Bobby Box. But since the young man himself clung resolutely to Miss Williams, the box was silent. Peggy simply sat in her corner, watching, hoping that Bobby would move away from the teacher and set her project in motion.

After a while Miss Williams had to leave the room for a moment and insisted that Bobby remain behind. Bobby cried loudly, but when no one paid him much attention, he subsided into quiet sobs. Then noticing a toy car and a stuffed dog on the floor nearby, he moved over to them. He picked both of them up and held them to his chest. Just then a little girl walked over to him and asked if she could play with the dog. Bobby looked at her quietly, then handed her the dog.

Buzz!

(Continued on page 120.)

Therapy (THER-ap-pee). Any form of treatment for biological, psychological, or behavioral/social problems. Biological therapy usually involves the giving of drugs or the use of surgery; this type of treatment can be prescribed only by a medical doctor, such as a psychiatrist. Psychotherapy usually aims at curing mental or emotional problems, and typically involves having the patient talk over his or her difficulties with a psychiatrist or, more likely, with a clinical psychologist or psychiatric social worker. If the patient's problem is primarily one involving inappropriate behaviors or attitudes, the patient may wish to undergo treatment with a behavioral therapist. Fuller explanations of these and other forms of therapy appear in Chapter 25.

In the last chapter we asked, "What makes you tick?" We found that "ticking" is multi-determined—that your speech, your attitudes, your feelings, and your actions are all influenced by physiological, mental, and environmental variables.

In this chapter we ask, "What makes you tick *better?*" Given the fact that there's little most of us can do to alter our brains or to wipe out our past experiences, what can we possibly do in the here and now to improve our lives and the lives of those around us?

It is at the very practical level of trying to help others that the biological, intra-psychic, and social influences on behavior are often most difficult for us to deal with. For unless we understand some fundamental principles about how our actions affect the people around us, we may end up being part of their problems instead of being part of the solution to their problems.

The most widespread attitude in our present culture is the "doctrine of personal responsibility"—the belief that your thoughts and actions are almost always under your voluntary mental control. When we encounter a violent individual, for instance, we typically think of the person as having a violent mind or personality, rather than wondering about violent brains and the violence-approving social environment we ourselves are a part of. And when we consider treatment or *therapy* (°) for a violent individual, we are more likely to suggest curing the mind or personality than curing the body or the society (which might mean changing our own actions or attitudes).

Unfortunately, intra-psychic therapy by itself doesn't always work very well with brain-damaged people. Think again about the case of Julia discussed in the last chapter. Julia received almost 10 years of "mental" treatment before seeing Drs. Mark and Ervin. Because of the damage to Julia's nervous system, the cure for her rage perhaps had to begin with surgery. But it would be a terrible mistake to conclude from this case that (1) all violent people have scar tissue in their amygdalas, and (2) brain operations are the only worthwhile treatment for violence. For such a conclusion would mean dismissing the importance of cultural and intra-psychic factors in human behavior.

To begin with, while neural activity in the brain certainly has its influence, only a tiny fraction of the violence in our world seems the result of specific brain damage. If we decided that surgery should become our primary means of controlling aggression, then almost everyone in the world would have to have his or her amygdalas removed. Such a move would not only be impractical and inhumane but illegal as well. The limbic system operation should surely be a last resort, to be used only on those patients with clearly detectable brain damage and only when all other forms of therapy have failed. The operation should also be entirely voluntary. In July 1973 the Wayne County (Michigan) Circuit Court ruled that this type of surgery cannot be forced on a prisoner or mental patient without violating the person's Constitutional rights. The Circuit Court judges wrote that "If one is not protected in his thoughts, behavior, personality and identity, then the right of privacy becomes meaningless. It is more important to protect one's mental processes than to protect even the privacy of the marital bed." The law *does* allow this type of treatment, however, if the person is not a prisoner nor a patient in a mental hospital and freely volunteers for the operation.

But there is a second and even more important point. The operation on Julia's brain freed her from the recurring episodes of rage that had marked much of her life. But the surgery by no means "cured" Julia of all her problems. Not all of the damage to her brain could be readily repaired; much of it was so subtle and so widespread that not even the greatest surgeon in the world could have helped. And even if, by some magic, her nervous system could have been put in perfect condition, her past experiences would have left marks or traces that no surgery could erase. Once the surgeon had done as much for her as he could, Julia was a candidate for both intra-psychic and environmental therapy—that is, she needed expert help in learning how to adjust to her changed circumstances.

PSYCHOLOGICAL THERAPY

As good as modern medicine is, there are many physiological conditions that the physician is relatively powerless to heal. Even with the relatively good prenatal care that expectant mothers receive these days, a certain small percentage of children are born with minor damage or *trauma* (°) to their brains. Others, like Julia, sustain impairment to their nervous systems because of disease. Suppose that when you are married and raising a family, one of your own children was unfortunate enough to be born with some kind of brain damage. What would you do?

Chances are that you would explore the physiological side of the problem first. You would ask your physician what the damage was like; how it came about; what could be done to set it right. Would an operation help? In many cases, the answer to this question would be no, for it is often easier to diagnose brain damage than to cure it. What else might the physician do for your child? If the child had difficulties with motor coordination—that is, in walking or using its hands or in talking—the physician might recommend some kind of physical therapy. Perhaps special exercises might strengthen the child's muscles and improve its ability to move its arms, legs, hands, lips, and tongue in coordinated fashion. Drugs such as Dilantin, as we have already said, might help calm the child down or prevent various types of seizures. Such therapies are legitimately within the province of the medical sciences and can usually be prescribed only by someone with a medical degree.

But suppose that it was not the clumsiness of the child's bodily movements that caused the problems but rather what the child *did* that bothered you. Suppose the child screamed loudly whenever it was asked to do anything, or threw temper tantrums at the slightest provocation? What if the child didn't seem to be able to pay attention to anything for more than a few seconds at a time, or appeared to learn everything far too slowly? These are *psychological* problems, even though they might have as their basic cause some imperfection in the electro-chemical functioning of the child's neurons. No drug yet discovered will "cure" such conditions, nor is there a "tantrum center" in the brain which a neurosurgeon might remove to make life more endurable for a child's parents.

Children who misbehave or act up at home and at school, or children who frequently refuse to mind their parents or teachers when given orders, are sometimes diagnosed as hyper-active or minimally brain damaged. In point of fact, there is little or no evidence that most of these children have anything physically wrong with their nervous systems. But physicians often *assume* that any child who refuses to obey, or who becomes bored and inattentive, must have a

Trauma (rhymes with "DRAW-muh"). From the Greek word meaning "to wound." A trauma is any injury or disability inflicted on one's body or mind. A frightening experience is often traumatic—that is, it leaves its psychological mark long after the experience is over and done with.

Psycho-therapy (SIGH-ko-THER-ap-pee). Any type of treatment aimed at "curing the mind." That is, helping people learn the causes of their mental problems or "hang-ups," of their emotional difficulties, of their attitudes and behavior patterns; helping people gain better control over their lives.

"sick brain." In most cases the *misbehavior* is the only evidence anyone can offer to support the diagnosis of minimal brain damage; and the word "minimal" really means that the damage, *if any*, is so slight that it cannot be detected with an EEG or any other physiological test. Medical treatment for minimal brain damage often consists of giving the child a daily dose of a strong drug. Such chemical therapy may in fact make the child less rebellious and easier for adults to handle. But drugs alone will not usually get to the root of the child's problem, which typically is psychological rather than entirely physical.

Several lines of evidence suggest that the majority of children who are diagnosed as hyper-active or minimally brain damaged have simply never learned the types of socially approved behaviors that other children show. The child's hyper-activity is really a psychological response to poor parental or scholastic training. As we will see, even children with clearly measurable brain damage can learn to control themselves if given the proper attention. But it is often easier for parents and teachers to give children drugs to slow them down than it is for the parents and teachers to learn more humane and effective ways to help children cope with the complexities of growing up.

For the present time, at least, the solutions to most psychological problems lie outside the field of medicine; therapies that are aimed at changing either the thinking or the actions of human beings are legitimately within the province of the *behavioral* sciences and are usually handled best by someone with considerable psychological or behavioral training.

There are two main types of psychological therapy or *psycho-therapy* (°): (1) the intra-psychic therapies, in which attempts are made to influence a person's mental or emotional activities primarily by talking with the person about his or her problems, and (2) the environmental therapies, in which attempts are made to change a person's attitudes or behaviors by changing some aspect of the individual's social world. As we will discover in later chapters, the dividing line between these two types of therapy is often difficult to determine, and many of the better-known therapies are actually mixtures of intra-psychic and behavioral techniques. In the present chapter our focus is mainly on helping people who might suffer from some type of neural damage that cannot readily be treated medically. We will briefly describe the intra-psychic therapies and then, since the environmental or behavioral therapies presently appear to offer greater promise with brain-damaged patients, discuss them in detail.

INTRA-PSYCHIC THERAPIES

Almost all forms of intra-psychic therapy focus on what goes on inside a person's mind. The general objectives may differ from one type of therapy to another, but a representative list of goals would include the following:

1. Helping the client solve emotional problems and receive lasting relief from emotional distress.
2. Helping the client achieve insight or understanding into the causes of his or her thoughts and actions.
3. Encouraging the client to better define his or her own self-identity; that is, helping the client to learn more about who or what the client has been in the past, is at the present, and might or should be in the future.
4. Aiding the client in changing inaccurate assumptions about himself or herself and about the rest of the world.
5. Assisting the client in making basic alterations in his or her personality, usually by promoting positive personality growth and development.
6. Helping the client open new pathways to a more meaningful and fulfilling existence.

Achieving any of these goals may require considerable time and effort both on the part of the client and of the therapist. Usually a feeling of warmth and trust, or *rapport* (°), must be built up between the client and the therapist if the treatment is to be successful. This climate of friendliness or rapport is thought to encourage the client to bring forth his or her innermost feelings freely, without fear of being rejected.

The two major types of intra-psychic therapy are *psycho-analysis* (°) and the various *humanistic therapies* (°).

Psycho-analysis is a form of treatment first devised by Sigmund Freud, but considerably modified by his followers and associates. It is a highly structured form of therapy that may take several years to complete. Most clients are not too badly disturbed and must usually be fairly intelligent or well educated if they are to work through their problems in psycho-analytic terms.

There are many types of humanistic therapies, the best known of which is probably the *client-centered therapy* (°) developed by psychologist Carl Rogers. Client-centered therapy is a relatively brief and very non-directive form of treatment. Rogers describes his type of psycho-therapy as an opportunity for the client to grow and "become a person" by realizing his or her own inner potentialities. The typical client is not badly disturbed and must be bright enough to solve his or her problems as reflected back by the therapist.

As we will see in Chapter 25, there are actually many different forms of psycho-therapy, but most of them have been strongly influenced by psycho-analysis and the humanistic forms of treatment. In almost all cases the client is expected to be able to talk in some detail about his or her thoughts or feelings. What does one do, then, with a badly upset individual who is unable to talk very well, whose difficulties stem from a damaged nervous system, or who merely needs to learn more effective ways of responding to the world? For these clients, the environmental or behavioral therapies are often a more suitable alternative.

ENVIRONMENTAL OR BEHAVIOR THERAPY

What about the brain-injured child who screams too much or indulges in temper tantrums in order to get its way? There is a growing belief among psychologists that such children probably benefit most—*at least at the beginning of treatment*—from a type of therapy aimed at giving these youngsters better control over the world around them. Usually such treatment involves teaching the children new and more socially acceptable patterns of behavior. Let us look closely at a child treated by two behavioral therapists at The University of Michigan, Donald E.P. Smith and Timothy Walter.

The Case of Patti K.

When Patti K. was first referred to Drs. Smith and Walter, she was 4 years old. Patti's father was a professor, her mother a college graduate. Although the mother visited her doctor regularly during the pregnancy and took excellent care of herself, Patti was born with a marked amount of injury to her infant brain. To complicate matters, when Patti was about 18 months old, she became deathly ill and lost almost a quarter of her body weight. Because of the physical problems she faced, Patti's early behavior patterns never were normal. For a while the left side of her body seemed partially paralyzed. The physician treating her prescribed various exercises that helped make her muscles strong. Her fine motor coordination (that is, her ability to make delicate and precise movements such as picking up small objects with her fingers) was about average; however, her gross motor coordination (that is, her ability to walk and run) was always poor even after the physical therapy was completed.

Rapport (rap-PORE). A relation between two or more people characterized by trust, friendship, affection, respect, harmony, and confidence. People who are in rapport with each other tend to cooperate with each other. As is the case with many words, we have borrowed "rapport" from the French language. The final "t" is not pronounced.

Psycho-analysis (SIGH-ko-an-AL-uh-sis). Psycho-analysis is both a theory of personality and a form of intra-psychic therapy. Both theory and therapy were developed by Sigmund Freud. See also Chapters 21, 22, and 25.

Humanistic therapies. Forms of treatment developed by psychologists Carl Rogers, Abraham Maslow, and others, in which the emphasis is on helping the client achieve his or her life goals. Humanists usually believe each person instinctively becomes better and grows into a mature and happy human being—a process called "self-actualization."

Client-centered therapy. A type of humanistic, intra-psychic treatment developed by Carl Rogers. Rogers believes that in many types of psycho-therapy (particularly psycho-analysis), the patient is subtly forced into meeting whatever conscious or unconscious goals the therapist has. The focus of attention is then "centered" on the therapist's expectations. In client-centered therapy, the client, rather than the therapist, sets the goals for treatment.

Timothy Walter.

Donald E.P. Smith.

Reinforcing. Steel rods are sometimes embedded inside concrete blocks to make the blocks stronger. The steel thus reinforces the strength of the concrete. Behavioral psychologists believe that most of what we do is a matter of habit, and that habits become stronger when they are reinforced by rewards. Anything that you find pleasant, or anything that you are willing to work for, can serve as a reward that will reinforce the strength of a habit. When you perform some act, and you are immediately reinforced (rewarded) for that act, the odds become greater that you will repeat that act the next time you have a chance.

But it was not Patti's inability to walk or run that brought her to the attention of Smith and Walter (although they did find ways of helping with these problems). Rather, it was her inability to communicate effectively and to adjust to nursery school that caused the family physician to refer her to the care of behavioral therapists.

Patti had many bad habits, the first of which was that she was something of a little "pig." At frequent intervals during the day she would open the refrigerator door, remove various dishes of food, and consume as much of the food as she could. Neither appeals to reason nor carefully administered spankings seemed to have much effect on her behavior. If she were taken out in public, she would often embarrass her parents by heading for the nearest supply of food and digging into it as if she feared someone were going to put her on starvation rations immediately.

A second set of inappropriate behaviors involved screaming. When she failed to get what she wanted, she would let loose with a series of sharp, ear-splitting cries that usually brought any nearby adult around to Patti's way of thinking rather rapidly. Oddly enough, the screaming behavior first showed up when she entered nursery school; she seldom tried such tactics at home.

A third problem involved toilet training. It would be inaccurate to say that she had no control over her bladder and bowels; indeed, just the opposite—she had far too great control. Whenever anyone at the nursery school insisted that Patti do something their way instead of hers, she would look up at the person and say, "Oh! Oh! B.M." (meaning bowel movement), and then she would soil her pants. By the time her clothes were changed and Patti was cleaned up, the argument had usually been resolved in Patti's favor.

After observing the little girl for a period of time, talking to her doctor, her parents, and the teachers at the nursery school, Smith and Walter decided that Patti's main problem was that she had somehow learned many inappropriate ways of getting what she wanted. The screaming and the soiling of her pants were behavior patterns that, sometime in the past, had accidentally gotten Patti her way. Because these unpleasant reactions were successful once or twice, she tried them again. And each time the screaming and the soiling "worked," the more likely it became that Patti would employ these behaviors in the future. The overeating behavior was a little more difficult to analyze, but Smith and Walter eventually decided that it occurred because Patti had never learned to talk very well. She couldn't tell people she was hungry, nor could she explain what kinds of food she was hungry for. So she simply took whatever she could get whenever it was handy. (As we will see in this and later chapters, young children occasionally are slow learning proper speech if their parents are overprotective and don't demand that the child express its needs.)

Many of Patti's problematic behaviors were apparently learned rather than directly due to her brain damage. In order to help Patti and her parents get along better, and to make it more likely that the girl could succeed in school, Smith and Walter decided to help Patti acquire more appropriate and socially pleasing ways of getting what it was she wanted from the people around her.

Rewards and Punishment

Habits are learned. According to behavioral therapists, we acquire habitual patterns of behavior because we find those behaviors *rewarding* or *reinforcing* (°) to us or because the habits help us avoid punishment and hence get us out of an unpleasant or threatening situation. If Patti saw another child at the nursery school playing with a toy she wanted, she would try to take it away from the other child. If the other child resisted, Patti would scream loudly, and keep screaming until the other child dropped the toy or the teacher came over and gave the toy to Patti to stop her from uttering those piercing cries. The screaming behavior was rewarded or, in technical terms, was *reinforced.*

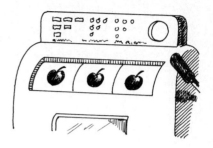

Little wonder that Patti kept it up! If someone threatened to punish Patti if she didn't stop doing something she wanted to do, Patti soiled her pants. The smelly mess she created helped her avoid doing something she considered unpleasant.

Rewards and punishments are very powerful influences on almost everything we do. Suppose you visit Las Vegas and go to one of the gambling casinos there. You have a couple of nickels to spare and you see a slot machine that intrigues you. So you drop a coin in the slot, pull the handle, and watch the reels spin. To your surprise, three cherries show up, the mechanism burps cheerfully, and 10 nickels fall into a little cup at the bottom of the machine. Your behavior of dropping the coin in the slot and pulling the handle has been rewarded or *reinforced*. The probability that you will drop another coin in a slot machine has increased. If, when you pulled the handle the first time, you had received a very painful electric shock, the probability that you would touch such a machine again would have decreased markedly. Reinforcement increases the likelihood that you will repeat the behavior that was rewarded, while punishment decreases the chances that you will do again that which was punished.

Now, suppose that after you put the first nickel in the slot machine and win the 50 cents, you decide to continue to play the machine. You put another nickel in the slot and pull the handle. Lemons. You try it again; after all, you can't expect to win every time. Again lemons. So you try a third nickel, and a fourth, and then a fifth. No luck. Now you know why slot machines are often called "one-armed bandits." Rather reluctantly you try it again. And again. The machine gobbles up your money as fast as you can drop it in and seems very reluctant to give you anything back. Shortly you have run through all your winnings and have just one nickel left. You have lost the original nickel you put in the machine plus the ten coins you won. You have but a single nickel left. Do you give it to the one-armed bandit, or do you keep it?

Surely, by now, the probability that you will drop a coin in the machine is considerably less than it was just after you won the 50 cents. For 10 times in a row you dropped in a nickel, pulled the handle, and the reward you expected did not materialize. Your enthusiasm about gambling has been somewhat extinguished by now. Perhaps you waste the final nickel, and lose it too. You go cash a dollar and get 20 nickels more and feed them into the one-armed bandit, and still no reward of any kind. Eventually, wouldn't you stop dropping in the nickels if the machine never once paid off?

Extinction Training According to behavior therapists, habitual ways of performing are *maintained* because occasionally they pay off with a reward. Slot machines typically pay off or reward the player just often enough to keep the player convinced that a big prize will be coming shortly. If your dog begs to be fed each time you sit down for a meal, and you give the dog even a tiny bit of food once a week, you may inadvertently be maintaining the dog's habitual begging behavior. If you want to break a habit, one way of doing so is to make sure that the habit is *never* reinforced. When the reinforcement no longer occurs, the habit will slowly disappear—for instance, when given absolutely no reward for begging, the dog will come to the table less and less frequently. In technical terms we would say that the dog's habit of begging is being *extinguished*, since you are no longer rewarding it at all. A therapist who tries to make sure that an inappropriate set of behaviors is no longer rewarded is making use of a technique called *extinction training* (°). As we will see momentarily, Smith and Walter had frequent occasion to use extinction training in their behavioral therapy with Patti K.

When Smith and Walter began working with Patti, they first had to decide what the goal of their treatment would be. Only if they knew exactly what they wanted Patti to be like after training would they know when to terminate or

Extinction training. When you stop rewarding a certain behavior pattern, you are actually withdrawing the reinforcement you usually give for that behavior. According to behavioral psychologists, withdrawing reinforcement is like taking the steel rods out of reinforced concrete blocks—the object (or the habit) soon crumbles. Extinction training is quite different from punishment. Extinction training involves withholding a previously given reward. Punishment consists of giving an organism pain or frustration immediately after it has performed an undesired act. Punishment inhibits the expression of a habit, but often has very unpleasant side effects. Punishment often leads to frustration, which may be followed by aggression and hate expressed toward the person doing the punishing. Extinction training is usually a more humane and less "traumatic" way of getting rid of undesirable behavior than is punishment.

Terminal behavior pattern. The "final goal" in behavioral therapy. Once this goal has been reached, the treatment is terminated or concluded. Like all other goals in behavioral therapy, the terminal behavior pattern must be easily measured so both patient and therapist can chart the patient's progress toward that goal. Most behavioral therapists believe that if you don't have a pretty clear idea of where you're heading in therapy, you don't know when treatment should end; and if you don't know when the therapy should be terminated, you probably shouldn't start it in the first place.

Successive approximations toward a goal (suck-SESS-ive approcks-uh-MAY-shuns). A behavioral form of treatment involving moving toward a measurable goal in very small steps. Each of the steps is rewarded. Behaviorally speaking, "Rome wasn't built in a day." That is, habits are learned (or unlearned) in bits and pieces.

stop the therapy. They believe, as do other behavioral therapists, that this goal or *terminal behavior pattern* (°) must be something that can be easily recognized or measured so that everyone concerned, including Patti's parents and her physician, would know whether or not the therapy had been successful.

After Smith and Walter had observed Patti for a few days, they became convinced that her parents—and the teachers and other children at the nursery school—were *maintaining* Patti's anti-social behavior patterns by unwittingly rewarding her whenever she misbehaved. When Patti screamed, she got a lot of attention, and she also usually received the toy or trinket that she wanted or got out of doing something she didn't want to do. The teachers insisted that they *punished* her screaming; but the punishment was very, very mild, and the attention that went with the punishment was very, very reinforcing. When she raided the refrigerator, her parents would fuss at her and spank her; but she got the food she wanted, and she soon learned that she could command the undivided attention of her parents for a significant period of time simply by eating too much. Smith and Walter believed that they not only had to *extinguish* the unpleasant behaviors Patti had learned but also that they had to teach her more acceptable ways of getting what she wanted. So they took Patti out of nursery school for a while and worked with her several hours a day trying to train her to speak more effectively.

Successive Approximations Part of Patti's problem lay in the fact that she simply didn't know the names of most of the foods that she wanted to eat. Another part lay in her inability to keep her impulses under her voluntary command; when she saw something she wanted, she wanted it right away! Perhaps because scar tissue can cause an increase in the amount of transmitter-molecules present in the cortex, brain-damaged individuals often suffer from a lack of social control. This control almost always involves inhibiting one's instincts and desires, and all those extra "uppers" at the synapses don't make for easy inhibition. Normal children usually learn self-control with not too much difficulty. Brain-damaged children are typically just as capable of learning, but they need much more astute training than their parents may know how to give. That is, these children acquire new habits in much smaller steps and require much more loving encouragement (positive reinforcement) than do kids with undamaged nervous systems.

To help Patti get along better in the world, Smith and Walter had to help her increase her vocabulary and train her to accept delays in getting the rewards she wanted. They knew from past experience that they couldn't expect her to change overnight. Instead, they hoped to make a little progress each day, to teach her a few new words today, a few more tomorrow. If today she could tolerate only a two-second delay before being rewarded, perhaps tomorrow they could get her to wait for three seconds. This technique, called *successive approximations toward a goal* (°), involves moving in very small steps from behaviors the person shows at the beginning of therapy to the habits that constitute the goal of the treatment. Each movement (no matter how tiny) that the person makes toward the goal is rewarded; each incorrect response that is not aimed in the right direction is simply ignored. As we will see in a later chapter, the method of successive approximations is one of the most powerful educational techniques that anyone has yet devised.

Behavioral therapists believe that learning should always be rewarded, and that the reinforcement should be something that the *client* selects as appropriate or valuable. Before Smith and Walter could ask Patti K. to learn new and better habits for them, they had to find out what she wanted in return. As it happened, Patti K. was very fond of cookies and sweet cereals. With the permission of the girl's parents, the therapists then made clever use of these rewards.

At the beginning of their work with Patti, Smith and Walter would point to an object and say its name. "Milk, Patti, this is milk. Can you say 'milk'?" Of course, Patti couldn't, but if she uttered *any sound at all*, they would give her a little piece of sugar-coated cereal or a bit of animal cracker cooky. After she had learned to make a noise whenever they asked her to, they began selectively rewarding noises that sounded vaguely like "milk," such as "meek" or "mik." Other sounds they simply ignored. Soon "milk" sounds predominated, so they could get her to come closer and closer in her approximations before they rewarded her. Usually it took only a few minutes for them to teach her a new word. They took her on walks and got her to name many of the things she saw; eventually they took her to supermarkets and taught her the names of all the most common foods.

Impulse Control   While they were doing this verbal training, Smith and Walter also worked on Patti's impulse control. Her parents agreed to stop giving her attention when she went on an eating spree. If they caught her at the refrigerator, they would take the food away from her without saying anything to her. Then they would lead her out of the kitchen and make her sit outside for 5 minutes before she could come back into the kitchen. Once her vocabulary had increased significantly, Smith and Walter got Patti to ask for the food she wanted. First, she had to learn to say "please," and name the food. She was rewarded for this by getting a bite of what she wanted. If she opened the refrigerator door without saying "please," they would shut the door and force her to give the magic word first. After she had learned to do this, they began instituting longer and longer delays between the time she first asked for the food and the time she was given it. Since the delay period was always followed by the reward she wanted, Patti learned to control herself fairly readily. Then, still using the technique of successive approximations to the goal they had set for her, they taught Patti to wait to consume the reward until they told her she could have it.

At the beginning of therapy, if you had shown Patti a cooky and told her she could have it in a few minutes, she wouldn't have waited more than a second or two before setting up a terrible wail. By the end of a few weeks' training she could hold a cooky in her own hand for several minutes and not eat it until told she could do so. Her "final examination" came after 6 months when her parents took her to a party.

Before treatment, Patti would have headed at once for the refreshment table and, much to the embarrassment of her parents, would have started stuffing herself no matter what anyone said to her. At her "final exam" her parents got her to pass around plates of food to the other guests, telling her she could eat something afterward. She behaved beautifully, much to the delight of her parents (who, of course, praised her performance loudly and sincerely).

But training Patti wasn't always as easy as perhaps it sounds. The more often a particular habit has been rewarded in the past, the more difficult it generally is to extinguish. Because her screaming and soiling had worked so well for so much of her life, these habits had become ingrained. It took a great deal of control on the part of the therapists to ignore Patti's inappropriate behavior so that it would undergo extinction. No matter how provocative and annoying Patti became, the therapists had to hold their own tempers in hand and simply pretend that she hadn't done anything. The screaming was easier to overlook than was her soiling. To make it easier for themselves—and more difficult for Patti—they asked her physician if they could put rubber pants on her and simply let her sit in her own mess for a while when she made a "mistake." The doctor agreed readily. Then when Patti attempted to get her way by crying "Oh! Oh! B.M.," the therapists would continue the lesson as if nothing had happened.

Perhaps the climax of this extinction training came when Timothy Walter was working with Patti one day in a very small "observation" room at the University

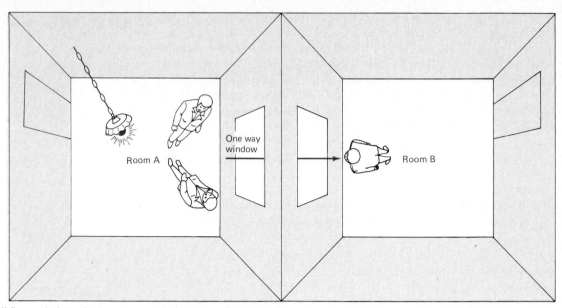

When a light is shining in room A, but room B is in darkness, a person in B can see clearly what is happening in A. However, people in A cannot see into room B.

of Michigan's School of Education. He had chosen the room because it had a "one-way mirror" in it that would allow some of his students to watch how he handled Patti. It soon became apparent that Patti was not too interested in learning new words that day. She twisted and turned and wanted to go home almost immediately, but Walter persisted since she had to learn to keep at a task even when she wasn't particularly interested in it. When Walter seemed to ignore her verbal protestations, she played her trump card. "Oh! Oh! B.M.!" she cried, and looked at him with a quizzical smile. Walter continued the lesson as if nothing had happened.

But the day was hot, the room was small, and the smell soon become rather noticeable. So, a few minutes later, Walter decided to end the lesson and get a breath of fresh air. When he went to open the door, he found to his dismay that he was locked in. He motioned to the students watching through the "one-way mirror" that they should go get a key and let him and Patti out. But it took more than 30 minutes before the students could find anyone with a key to that particular room!

That experience taught Patti that soiling simply could not control Walter's behavior, so she seldom tried it on him again. However, whenever he would assign one of his students to work with Patti, she would test the new therapist almost immediately to see how the newcomer would respond to screaming and soiling. Eventually, when none of the students paid any attention to this childish and inappropriate way of responding, Patti shifted back to more mature and socially approved ways of getting what she wanted.

THE IMPORTANCE OF THE ENVIRONMENT

Like many other behavioral therapists, Smith and Walter believe that children function best in a fairly structured and stable environment. They feel that children need to know what kinds of behaviors the people around them will punish, reward, and ignore. If the behavioral rules set for a child are sensible and humane, and if these rules are enforced consistently but lovingly, the child soon learns how to meet its own needs and is free to spend its time growing and learning rather than wasting all its energies trying to find out what is expected of it.

Although the noted Swiss scientist *Jean Piaget* (°) is not a behaviorist, he too stresses the importance of a stable environment during a child's formative years. According to Piaget, the child develops its own code of morality from the manner in which its parents treat it. Parents who regularly reward some behaviors and punish others help the child develop what Piaget calls "a sense of justice" about what actions are proper and what actions are improper. (We will discuss Piaget's theories more fully in Chapter 21.)

From the behavioral point of view, a child's emotional stability can be threatened in two important ways. First, if the parents behave inconsistently toward the child—for example, if they sometimes kiss the child when it asks for their love, but at other times ignore or even punish such affectionate requests. Second, if someone or something new comes into the child's world—for example, if a new baby is born to the family. In both these cases, the child may no longer be sure what the consequences of its own behavior will be. Children respond to a loss of stability in many ways, one of the most common responses being a reversion to more primitive or immature ways of acting. For instance, a 4-year-old child may be quite well behaved and completely toilet-trained until the arrival of a younger brother or sister. If the parents neglect the older child for the younger, the 4-year-old may start throwing infantile temper tantrums or apparently lose control of its bowels and bladder. This *regression* (°) to a previous way of behaving seems to be the child's way of testing out whatever is new and hence disturbing to it. If the parents go out of their way to let the child know that they still love it, however, and re-establish their previous rules of conduct, the child's feeling of security soon reappears and it can safely return to its more mature response patterns.

As we will discuss more fully in Chapter 12, we are all strongly motivated to predict and control our inputs, whether these inputs be biological, intra-psychic, or social. To maintain this predictable control, we often must inhibit our immediate urges (motor outputs). When our environment suddenly changes, we may not be able to guess right away what we must do to get the inputs we wish, or there may be no one around smart enough to help us learn the new skills we need to acquire. Hence we may regress to more primitive (less-inhibited) habits. The death of a loved one, or being forced to move to a new environment, may be accompanied even in a grown person by a return to such childish responses as thumb-sucking, fits of temper, sulking, or an inability to solve even the simplest of conflicts. Most such problems go away rather naturally when the individual learns that the changed circumstances are not all that threatening. If the regression is fairly extreme, however, the person may need professional help to re-establish order and stability in his or her life.

THE BIOLOGICAL BASES OF BEHAVIOR

At any given instant in time, your actions are affected by chemical and electrical activity in the brain that you inherited—but also by your past experience and by important features in your present environment. The chemical and electrical "machinery" in your brain helps produce your behavior. If the machinery breaks down, so do your thoughts and habit patterns. Sometimes medical intervention is necessary to repair the damage, but medical treatment *by itself* is seldom sufficient to re-establish healthy thinking and socially-rewarding behaviors. Intrapsychic and behavioral therapies are almost always needed in addition to the drugs and surgery.

From a behavioral point of view, everything that you do has an effect—however slight—on the world around you. Activity in your brain is therefore capable

Jean Piaget (JAWN pee-ah-JAY). A famous Swiss biologist who has spent a lifetime studying the way that children think and learn and mature. His name is French and is somewhat difficult for English-speaking people to pronounce. Piaget's theories are discussed in Chapter 21.

Regression (re-GRESH-shun). Slipping back into old ways of behaving, thinking, or feeling. Freud said that, as we grow up, we acquire more mature ways of acting. If any of our attempts at being mature are punished, we are likely to regress back to more childish mannerisms. See also Chapter 22.

of changing your environment. But this is a two-way street, for changes in your environment—when detected by your sense organs and relayed to your brain—can make permanent alterations in the way your nervous system functions and hence in the way you think and behave. Before we can investigate how you learn, and why you are motivated to do the things you do, we must look more closely at how your sensory receptors detect changes in your environment and relay this important information to your brain and mind.

SUMMARY

1. We all have problems, which we tend to describe in different ways. Psychologists tend to analyze human problems in biological, intra-psychic, and social/behavioral terms. Each of these three views has its own particular theoretical explanations about our problems, and each has its unique forms of treatment designed to help us overcome our personal difficulties.
2. For the most part, humans tend to rely on intra-psychic therapy to handle emotional problems.
3. Two of the major forms of intra-psychic treatment are psycho-analysis (developed by Sigmund Freud) and the humanistic therapies, such as client-centered therapy (developed by Carl Rogers). Perhaps the major objection to these types of treatment is that they sometimes neglect the biological and behavioral influences that affect us all.
4. In most forms of behavioral therapy, the client or patient sets a goal that he or she wishes to achieve. The goal is stated in terms of a measurable change in the client's behavior; it is called the "terminal behavior pattern." The therapist then encourages the client to reach this goal by acquiring new habits.
5. In behavioral treatment, each small step the client makes in the direction of a goal is defined as a successive approximation toward the terminal behavior pattern. Even the slightest bit of progress is rewarded by the therapist, who believes that reward tends to reinforce or strengthen whatever behavior the reward immediately follows.
6. In behavior therapy, inappropriate behaviors are weakened or extinguished by withdrawing whatever rewards have served to maintain these behaviors in the past.
7. Punishment inhibits behavior, but is more likely to lead to frustration and aggression than is extinction training.
8. Behavioral therapy seems to be effective because it arranges for changes in the ways that the client's social environment delivers rewards and punishments for what the client is actually doing.
9. Biological, intra-psychic, and behavioral therapy all have their uses; the best treatment plan of all may well involve the use of all three types of treatment.

(Continued from page 109.)

Buzz!

All the children looked up at Bobby the moment the buzzer sounded. The little girl to whom he had just handed the stuffed dog screamed with delight.

Peggy jumped up from her seat and ran to where Bobby was standing. "That was lovely, Bobby. You gave your little friend the dog when she asked for it. That's really good. Now, here's a gumdrop for you, and one for her, and if the rest of you children will just come over here by Bobby, you'll get your candy too."

The children crowded around eagerly to claim their rewards. Bobby chewed solemnly on his gumdrop.

"Come play with me," cried one of the biggest boys, who then grabbed Bobby by his shirt and led him over to a castle he was building with colored blocks. Bobby sat on the floor and watched the older boy pile one block on top of another. Noticing a couple of large blocks by one of his feet, Bobby picked them up and turned them over and over in his hand. Then he reached out as if to add them to one of the castle walls. The bigger boy looked at Bobby sharply. Bobby's hand stopped in mid-air, then slowly continued its journey down toward the castle wall.

Buzz!

After the candy had been distributed again, one of the more aggressive girls claimed Bobby and took him over to the sandbox. The rest of the morning, the Bobby Box buzzed so many times that Peggy nearly ran out of gumdrops. Miss Williams didn't seem very happy about the interruptions in her routine, but at least she didn't say anything unpleasant to Peggy about it.

An hour or so before lunch, Peggy told the children that the game had ended for the day, thanked them for playing, and began to gather up her equipment. Her project seemed to be working, even on the first day, because Bobby had spent more than half his time playing with the other children. The real test, of course, would come after she stopped rewarding Bobby and the other children for his "good behavior." Even without the candy, would he continue to play with the other kids? Peggy didn't know for sure, but she guessed that he would. After all, he would have learned by then that the other children were not so terrifying, and they would have learned that he was a pretty decent kid at heart. At least, that's what Dr. Patterson at Oregon had reported was usually the case.

Peggy planned to come back several times later in the year to observe how things were going for Bobby. At the moment, though, she had to thank Miss Williams for her help—however scanty it had been—and then get back to her classes. The thought of having to be nice to this woman was the one small black cloud on Peggy's horizon. But Dr. Johnson always said that you had to be sure to reward the **first small step** toward improvement, and Miss Williams had taken several such steps. And maybe it was better to light one small candle of positive reinforcement than to sit cursing people in the darkness.

Bobby was clinging to Miss Williams' skirt as Peggy approached the two of them to say goodbye. Perhaps because Peggy was worried about just what to say to the older woman, she didn't notice when Bobby started playing with the buzzer apparatus she was holding loosely in her hands.

"Well, Miss Williams, I do think that it went very well today." Peggy shifted her weight nervously back and forth from one foot to the other. "Did you notice how much time Bobby spent playing with the other kids? Quite a change, I'd say."

There was a long, awkward silence, the two women facing each other in rather hostile stances while Bobby pawed at the wires dangling from Peggy's hands.

Finally, Peggy took the bull by the horns. "Miss Williams, you've really been just great to me . . ."

Buzz!

Both women gave Bobby rather startled glances, noticed the buzzer button in his hands, then looked back at each other.

Peggy smiled.

Miss Williams smiled.

And then Peggy said, "Miss Williams, have a gumdrop!"

RECOMMENDED READINGS

Patterson, Gerald R. *Families: Applications of Social Learning to Family Life* (Champaign, Ill.: Research Press Company, 1971).

Smith, Judith M., and Donald E.P. Smith. *Child Management* (Ann Arbor, Mich.: Ann Arbor Publishers, 1966).

Whaley, Donald L., and Richard Malott. *Elementary Principles of Behavior* (New York: Appleton-Century-Crofts, 1971).

Part 2

SENSATION AND PERCEPTION

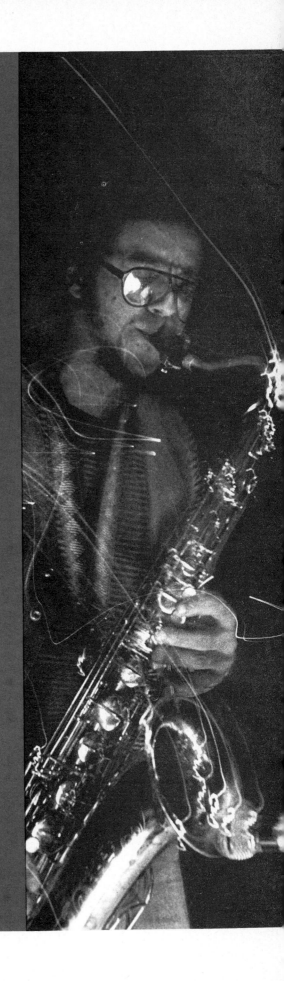

chapter 6

"HOW TO BUILD A
BETTER ROBOT"

INTRODUCTION TO SENSORY PSYCHOLOGY

DID YOU KNOW THAT . . .

Your skin is sensitive only to warm, cold, pressure, and in a complex way, to pain?
Some 95 percent of your skin is hairy?
Each hair on your skin has a pressure receptor called a "basket cell" wrapped around its base?
The skin that lines the inside of your stomach has the same sort of receptors in it as the skin on your lips?
Almost every muscle in your body has a receptor neuron attached to it?
Muscle receptors tell your brain where your arms and legs are, and what they are doing?
The skin on your lips and fingertips is the most sensitive skin of all?
Your sense receptors primarily detect *changes* in your environment?
You can learn to communicate with others using your skin even if you are deaf and blind?

The little U.S. space ship crept closer and closer to the asteroid, a big chunk of rock hanging remote in space. The ship's directional jets puffed like a nervous smoker as it twisted this way and that, now slowing its speed a bit, now correcting its slippery course through space with just the briefest gush of gas from one of the many jet nozzles protruding from its sides.

The space ship was many million miles from earth, probing the ring of rock-like asteroids that girdled the sun like a belt between the orbits of the planets Mars and Jupiter. There were thousands and thousands of these meteorite-like objects circling the sun, a few large enough to be seen by telescope from earth, but most of them so small that you had to be right on top of them to detect them.

Were the asteroids the fragments of a planet that once swam the skies halfway between Jupiter and Mars? A planet somehow smashed into a billion pieces, perhaps by a runaway moon, perhaps because whichever aliens who might have lived on it discovered nuclear war before they discovered common sense? Were the asteroids from a planet torn to tiny shreds countless centuries ago, its parts strewn around the sun like rice thrown at a heavenly wedding?

No one knew where the asteroids came from, and only a few dedicated scientists really cared one way or another. But everybody knew and cared that some of these hunks of celestial garbage were loaded with valuable metals. At least the National Aeronautics and Space Administration (NASA) knew, and NASA cared, and that's what the little NASA space ship was out there for, to hunt for such earth-rare metals as radium, uranium, and plutonium.

Major Jack Amundsen watched the dials and displays on the ship's control panel cautiously. The asteroid toward which he was guiding his craft was less than half a mile in length and shaped rather like a stubby cigar. But if his detector circuits were right, it contained a chunk of uranium big enough to make the NASA brass back in Houston very happy indeed—and to earn him a very accelerated promotion.

As the ship inched in for a landing, Amundsen switched on the landing lights. The asteroid hung black in space, motionless, dead ahead. For the most part, its surface was pitted with cracks and craters; but almost in the center, where its equator would be if it had one, was a shallow groove that appeared to have a reasonably flat bottom. He dropped the little ship down into the depression so gently that it touched the surface like a snowflake. High-speed drills in the ship's legs chewed their way into the hard rock underneath and effectively bolted the ship to the asteroid. Only then did Major Amundsen lean back in his command chair and relax.

''Pretty good piloting, don't you think, Mark? Bet you couldn't do half that good.''

Robot XSR 5 Mark III/21, sitting next to the Major, turned its head from the control panel and contemplated its companion.

''You know, Major, that I am not programmed for landings except in emergency conditions. I am an exploratory space robot, not a pilot robot.''

Its voice was surprisingly musical, almost feminine, a fact that made its masculine nickname all the more amusing to Amundsen.

''Then go explore. And don't let any meteorites puncture your space suit.'' The Major smiled at his little joke, for the robot wore no space suit at all.

Raw space was dangerous to man, as the deaths of many U.S. and Russian astronauts had proved only too dramatically. The NASA brass had split down the middle. Some administrators wanted all exploration done by machines; but some space experts insisted that machines were not flexible enough to meet the challenge of unknown conditions.

So a compromise was worked out. Man would go into space but would be mostly confined to the ship. As his companion, he would have a complex robot to perform all the very dangerous work outside the ship.

At first, Amundsen resented the robot, wishing it were flesh and blood rather than metal and plastic. But during the long trip out, Amundsen had grown to accept Mark as being ''almost human.''

Mark entered the space lock, evacuated the precious air back into the ship, then moved slowly down a ladder onto the surface of the asteroid. Being a robot, Mark did not need to protect him/her/it from the vacuum and cold of space. But Mark did carry a searchlight and various other tools. The needle on Mark's portable detector hinted that the lode of uranium should be a few hundred yards ahead and very close to the surface. The robot moved cautiously, testing each step, the balance sensors in its head working overtime as it attempted to remain upright while walking weightlessly up the side of the small depression into which the ship had settled.

''How are you doing?'' came the Major's voice over the radio.

''Major, all is well. The stick-tite shoes grip the surface of the asteroid tightly, my walking reflexes function well; I have not stumbled once.'' The robot rounded a boulder and stopped, directing the light fastened to its head toward the mouth of a cavern near where it was standing.

''Major, the uranium appears to be buried inside a cave. May I descend?''

All hazardous procedures had to be approved by the human pilot.

''You may descend.''

Mark III/21 moved slowly into the mouth of the cave, stopping each few feet to daub a spot of fluorescent paint on the rocks to help guide it back. The deeper underground it went, the more wildly the needle on its detector danced. When the robot had pushed its way more than a thousand feet into the ground, it came to the top of a large, hollow chamber in the cave.

As the robot crawled to the bottom of the chamber, the needle jumped off the dial. Mark stopped and swung around, the light on its head flooding the chamber with illumination. Then the robot knelt down, put its tools down beside it, and picked up a small pebble. Holding the stone in the light, the robot rolled the

pebble around in its fingers several times, examining the little stone. It looked like uranium all right, and a rich deposit at that.

"Major we have apparently struck paydirt, if I may use that phrase."

Back at the space ship, Amundsen was standing beside the control console waiting for news. When he heard what Mark said, he grinned.

"That's great, Mark, super great. Just gather up a sample in your bag and then . . ."

And then their world nearly ended.

Coming up from their blind side at a high speed, one of the asteroid's smaller brothers plowed into it square in its mid-section. The entire asteroid shuddered and convulsed as the meteorite caromed off into space, leaving its devastation behind for the Major and the robot to handle as best they could.

Amundsen had been knocked to his knees when the meteorite hit, but he came up fighting. A quick glance at the dials and lights on the control console assured him that the ship was intact and safe. But the robot?

"Mark!" he called into the microphone. "What happened? Are you all right?"

The answer was slow in coming, and the robot's voice seemed distorted and fluttery.

"Major, I survive, but barely. A rock hit my head. My light is gone. My vision circuits are inoperative. I am blind. I have lost contact with the bottom surface of the large chamber I was in. I float. Rocks and other objects float by me. What am I to do?"

The Major thought a while, picturing the robot tumbling about in the hollow underground bubble like a piece of meat in a bowl of stew.

"Reach out your arms and legs and wait until you make contact with one of the chamber walls."

"I obey, Major," the robot said, but it was minutes later before it reported success.

"Now what do I do, Major? I cannot see. I cannot find the trail markers. I cannot find the tiny entrance to this large chamber. I have but three hours' current left in my batteries. How do I find my way back to the ship, Major?"

The problem was serious. Amundsen was under strict orders not to leave the ship if the robot somehow became endangered. He could return to earth safely without Mark, but when the robot's batteries were exhausted, its heater would no longer function, its delicate "brain" circuits would freeze and warp. For all practical purposes, the robot would be "dead." NASA would be furious at the loss of a multi-million dollar piece of equipment, and Amundsen would have lost a—friend?

Amundsen retraced the robot's path in his mind's eye. Always Mark had reported going down, down, deeper into the ground. Suddenly the solution seemed obvious.

"Mark, just keep moving upward. If you move upward, you'll get to the surface eventually and I can pick you up then with the ship. No sweat at all, really, Mark, just keep moving upward."

"Major," said the robot after a while. "There is no gravity here and I do not know in which direction I am pointed. Major, which way is up?"

(Continued on page 139.)

Earth is the third planet out from the sun. Mercury is the closest, Venus next, then earth. Then come the outer planets: Mars, Jupiter, Saturn, Neptune, Uranus, and Pluto. A few years from now man's first real inter-planetary space ships will blast off from earth to take men to Mars—and perhaps beyond. Venus is closer, but Venus and Mercury are too hot and too close to the sun for us to explore personally at the moment. The outer planets will be mostly too cold for us.

Some of the planets, such as Jupiter and Venus, have such heavy atmospheres that we would be crushed to death on their surfaces. Others have little or no atmosphere at all. And none of them has the right kind of air for us to breathe. Naked and unprotected, humans cannot exist unaided on any of these planets except Earth.

Suppose that, some time in the future, NASA decides that the environments that exist on the planets are so hostile that robots should be sent out first to investigate, to test things out to make sure that human beings can survive in space suits if and when we do arrive. Because of weight and other considerations, they conclude that the robot ought to be man-sized. Indeed, if the robot is going to tell us what we need to know, it must have many human-like characteristics. It must be mobile; it must carry its own protection against the elements; it must have a means of sensing and measuring its environment, and a way of sending messages back to its home base to report the data it gathers.

Now, let us further assume that you are hired by NASA to help with "Project Robot." Your first assignment is to worry about what kind of covering the robot is going to have, so you begin by asking yourself: What purpose does your own skin serve?

A little thought convinces you that your skin answers many needs. It keeps your vital organs inside where they belong, and keeps the outside world outside where it belongs. Your skin has several layers to it, layers that help it insulate you against the cold. When you get too hot, your skin has sweat glands that release water that helps cool you by evaporation. It stretches as you gain weight and shrinks when you lose weight. And most important, your skin is filled with receptors that let you know what the world around you is like.

But would your skin serve a robot's specialized needs?

After due consideration, you conclude that you cannot decide on what type of covering the robot ought to have until you know more about what the robot is going to have to do. So you begin to wonder about what types of sense organs the robot is going to need in whatever skin it gets.

THE SKIN RECEPTORS

If you like to experiment on yourself, please go find several small objects—things like a pencil, a glass, a rubber band, a ring, a key, a piece of cloth—and put them on a table near you. Now, close your eyes and feel each object. Begin by just pressing the palm of your hand down on the objects.

What can you tell about these small objects without fingering them? That they

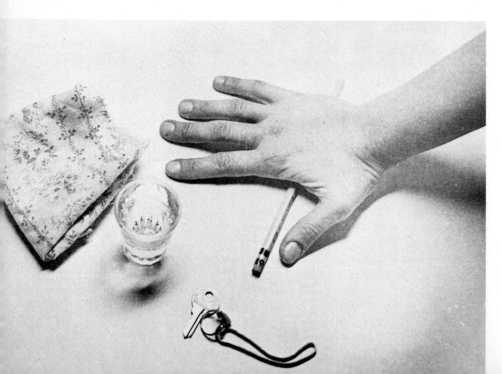

What do you feel if you "palm" these objects?

are hard or soft, large or small, that they have points or sharp edges or rounded contours, and that is about all you can tell. A pencil or a key is hard, a rubber band or an eraser yields when you press on it and hence feels soft.

But how do you know what is hard and soft?

The Pressure Receptors

When you touch an object gently, you depress or deform your skin. Very sensitive nerve cells detect this deformation of the skin and fire off a message to the cortex by way of the spinal cord and the stem of the brain telling your Board of Directors that the skin has encountered a foreign object of some kind.

Now, with the fingers of one hand, gently pinch the palm of your other hand. You will notice that the skin on your palm feels fairly thick. Next, gently pinch the skin on your forearm. The skin is much thinner there. But the major difference is that the skin on your forearm has hairs on it, while the skin on your palm does not. Some 95 percent of the skin on your body (whether you are male or female) is hairy skin—only the palms of your hands, the soles of your feet, your lips and mouth, your eyeballs, some parts of your sex organs, and a few other scattered areas are hairless.

Now, pick a single hair on your arm and pull it gently; you will experience a soft, "pressury" feeling. Tap the hair gently (without touching your skin); you will experience much the same sensation of pressure as when you pulled on the hair.

In the hairless regions of your body, the skin contains tiny receptor nerve cells that look, under a microscope, much like small onions. They are more or less round in shape and, as you would find if you were to cut one open, these "onion" receptor cells—or *corpuscles* (°)—as they are called—have many layers to them. Hairy skin does not have corpuscles, but it does have a unique type of touch receptor buried at the base of each hair. The *dendrites* (°), or front end fibers of these nerve cells, are woven around the bottom of the stalk of hair in such a fashion that they "fire" whenever the hair is pushed or pulled in any direction. They are called *basket cells* (°) because they look like a wicker basket wrapped around the hair stalk.

Both hairy and hairless skin contain what are called *free nerve endings* (°), the word "free" meaning that they are not attached to any particular place. These are very simple nerve cells whose dendrites spread out freely like the branches of a vine through the skin. Free nerve endings are by far the most common sort of skin receptor you have.

Complex Pressure Sensations

Now, go back to the objects that you were feeling on the table near you. Close your eyes and have someone place first a wooden object and then a metal object in your hands. You can tell wood from metal in two ways: (1) The wood is usually softer than the metal, (2) the wood will feel warm while the metal feels cold. Your skin receptors can give rise to different sorts of sensory experience that are *qualitatively* different to you—one is *pressure*, the other is *temperature*. Your *pressure detectors* tell you when you come in contact with some foreign object or with parts of your own body. The *temperature detectors* tell you whether the object is hot or cold. The corpuscles in the hairless regions and the basket receptors around each hair are primarily pressure receptors. The free nerve endings detect both pressure and temperature.

It may come as a surprise to you that these two sensations (plus pain, which we will discuss later) are the only two sensory qualities that your skin can tell you about. All the information you get from your skin about the world around you is a combination of pressure sensations plus temperature sensations—plus, occasionally, the experience of pain (*see* Chapter 18).

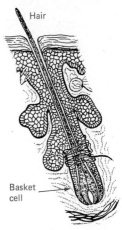

A "basket cell" touch receptor. Woven around the bottom of a stalk of hair on your body, it "fires" whenever the stalk is moved in any direction.

Corpuscles (KOR-pus-sulls). The Latin word *corpus* means "body." We get our English words "corpse" (a dead body) and "corps" (the Marine Corps) from this same Latin term. A corpuscle is a "little body" or "little cell," particularly one that is isolated from others like it. The red blood cells, for instance, are called the "red corpuscles."

Dendrites. The "feelers" or input area at the front end of a neuron. See Chapters 2 and 4.

Basket cells. Sensory input neurons or receptor cells found at the bottom of each hair cell on the skin. The dendrites of the basket cells are woven around the base of the stalk of hair. Any sort of movement of the stalk causes the basket cells to fire off a message to the cortex indicating that something has made contact with the hair.

Free nerve endings. Simple receptor cells found widely distributed through both hairy and hairless skin. If you "unwove" the dendrites of a basket cell and spread them throughout the skin, they would look something like free nerve endings.

Rub the palm of your hand over your clothes, the surface of the table, the cover of this book, the upholstery of a chair, or the top of a rug. Some objects feel smooth to your touch, others feel rough. How does the skin tell you which is which if it can experience just pressure and temperature?

The answer comes from this fact—when you move your hand across a surface, you stimulate many receptors at once. The harder you press against something with your fingers, the more you deform the skin and the more frequently the pressure receptors fire. Your brain makes good use of this *quantitative* information (that is, the frequency with which the receptors fire) to help it identify an object your skin is in contact with.

If the surface of an object is rough, parts of your skin "stick" as you rub your palm across the object. This sticking causes your skin to wrinkle a bit as it rubs across the object. Where the skin is wrinkled the most, the receptors fire vigorously; but where the skin is unwrinkled and smooth, the receptors fire hardly at all. Your brain interprets this *pattern of incoming sensory information* as "roughness."

If the robot you are helping build for NASA is strolling about the surface of some distant planet, you will want it to be able to bend over, pick something interesting off the ground, and examine it. If you put pressure receptors of some kind in the robot's fingers, you will be able to tell if the object is hard or soft, or rough or smooth, simply by monitoring the signals from the receptors.

You could also put temperature detectors in the robot's fingers and learn whether the object was hot or cold. But hot or cold in relation to what?

The Temperature Receptors

When you first crawl into a bathtub of hot water, it may seem that you are going to be boiled alive before the bath is over. The water feels intensely hot, and your skin turns red as your brain orders an increase in the flow of blood through your skin to help cool things off. If you manage to stay in the tub for a while, the water feels cooler and cooler (even if you manage to keep the temperature as hot as when you first crawled into the tub). When you get out, the air in the bathroom may seem surprisingly cool to your naked skin.

If on a hot summer day you leap into a cold swimming pool, you will get the opposite effect. First you think you will freeze, then you adjust. And when you get out of the pool, the rest of the sun-drenched world seems even hotter than before.

"Hot" and "cold" are *relative* terms that, in your body's case, are always related to *whatever your skin temperature is*. Anything you touch that is *colder* than your skin will be perceived as *cool*. Anything you touch that is *hotter* than your skin will seem *warm*.

Your skin temperature actually varies from one part to another. The temperature inside your mouth is typically 98.6 degrees Fahrenheit (or 37.2 degrees Celsius or Centigrade), but the temperature at your fingertips is closer to 90 degrees F (about 33 degrees C). When you get into that steaming tub of water, the temperature deep inside your body remains more or less the same, but the skin temperature at your fingertips may rise above 100 degrees F (38 degrees C). If just before you entered the water you touched an object that was 95 degrees F, it would be 5 degrees above your skin temperature; the "warmth" receptor organs in your fingers would fire a message off to your cortex telling it that they had encountered something warm. Just after you got out of the tub the same object would be at least 5 degrees *below* your skin temperature and would seem cool to your touch.

As you might surmise, the "cold" detector cells will fire more vigorously if you touch an object that is 30 degrees below skin temperature than if you touch an object that is merely 10 degrees below skin temperature. And the "warmth" detector cells will fire more vigorously if you come in contact with an object that is 25 degrees above skin temperature than they would with an object that is 15 degrees above.

THE SOMATIC CORTEX

The message that the skin receptors send to your brain tells you three things. First, the *quality* of the experience (that is, pressure or temperature). Second, the *quantity* or intensity or strength of the experience (strong pressure or weak, how warm or cold). But third, and very important, sensory inputs from the skin tell you *location*—that is, what part of the body is detecting the sensations.

If you are walking barefooted and step on a tack, your brain knows almost instantly what part of which foot has been punctured. How does it know this fact so quickly?

To answer that question, think for a moment about the NASA robot that you were helping design. If you wanted the robot to localize its skin sensations, how would you hook its skin receptors up to the robot's brain? Probably you would want to put in a direct "telephone line" between each receptor and a specific part of the "brain." Each receptor would, in effect, have its own "telephone number." The robot could tell where the stimulation was coming from simply by checking to see which telephone line the message was coming over.

In a sense, your brain acts much the same way. Each receptor cell in your skin is connected to a specific region in the sensory input areas in your *parietal lobes* (°). You may recall from a previous chapter that the parietal lobe in each of your cerebral hemispheres is located at the very top center of your brain. The front edge of the parietal lobe is immediately adjacent to the motor output center at the rear of the frontal lobe. The cortex at this front edge of the parietal lobe is often called the *somatic cortex* (°). "Soma" is the Greek word for "body," and it is to this part of the cortex that all of your body or somatic receptors send their sensory messages. Receptors in the left side of your body send their inputs primarily to the somatic cortex in the right half of your brain, while receptors in the right side of your body send their messages to the left somatic cortex.

You will recall that earlier (*see* Chapter 4), we discussed the layout of the motor-output cortex in each of your frontal lobes. We said then that each point on the motor cortex seemed to have dominant control over a specific set of muscles. The muscles in your toes are controlled by neurons near the *corpus callosum* (°) in the center of your brain, while the muscles in your neck and head are controlled by neurons lying on the outer edge of your brain, just above your ear.

Parietal lobes (pair-EYE-uh-tull, or puh-RYE-uh-tull). That part of each cerebral hemisphere located at the very top of the brain. Sensory input from the skin receptors and the muscles comes to this part of the cerebrum. See Chapter 4.

Somatic cortex (so-MAT-ick KOR-tecks). The outside layer ($1/4$ inch thick; 0.64 centimeters) of the parietal lobe is called the parietal cortex. The front section of the parietal cortex receives sensory-input messages from the skin and muscle receptors; this front section is called the "somatic cortex."

Corpus callosum (KOR-pus kah-LOW-sum). *Callosum* is the Latin word for "roughened" or "hardened" (we get our word "callous" from this Latin term). *Corpus* is the Latin word for "body." The corpus callosum is the "hardened body" of axonic fibers that acts as a bridge connecting the two hemispheres of the cerebrum.

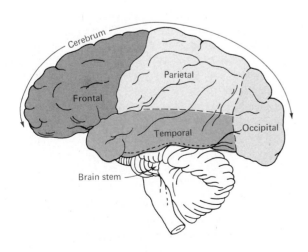

Cerebrum

Parietal

Frontal

Temporal

Occipital

Brain stem

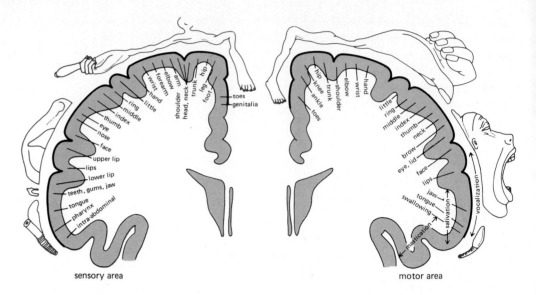

The right drawing shows the areas of the motor cortex that control various muscles in your body. The left drawing indicates the corresponding sensory-input areas in the parietal lobe.

The somatic cortex is laid out in exactly the same fashion as the motor cortex (motor-output area in the frontal lobe). Messages coming in from skin receptors in your toes connect or make synapse with parietal neurons near the corpus callosum, while messages coming from your lips and tongue make synapse with parietal neurons lying on the outer edge of your brain, just above your ear.

For every somatic input area in your parietal lobe, there is a corresponding motor-output area in your frontal lobe. The "little man" in your motor-output area thus has an identical twin living right next door in the somatic input area.

QUESTION: Why might it be important to your survival and well-being to have the somatic cortex so closely connected to the motor cortex?

THE DEEP RECEPTORS

If you made the NASA robot much like yourself, it could tell the hardness, smoothness, and temperature of an object it had picked up just by noting what its "skin" receptors were signaling. But what about the object's size, shape, and weight?

Pick up a pencil, close your eyes, and roll the pencil around in your hand. You can tell at once what size, shape, and weight the pencil has. But it is not the surface or skin receptors that give you this information, for we could anesthetize all the nerves in the skin of your hand (by spraying ether or some other anesthetic on the skin) and you would still be able to tell the size, shape, and weight of the pencil. For the muscles, joints, tendons, and bones in your hand (and in much of the rest of your body, too) all have sensory receptors in them. These are called *deep receptors* (°), to distinguish them from the surface receptors in your skin.

Whenever you contract a muscle in your hand to reach for something, a tiny nerve cell buried in that muscle sends a signal back to the appropriate part of the somatic cortex telling the Board of Directors that the muscle is in operation. The heavier an object is, the harder your muscle must work to lift it and hold it steady. The harder the muscle pulls, the more vigorously this receptor cell fires. By keeping track of where your fingers are and how far apart they are; by recording

Deep receptors. Your brain must have some means of determining the movement, position, and condition of various parts of your body. Each of the muscles, joints, tendons, and bones of your body has special receptor cells that fire whenever the muscle (joint, tendon, or bone) moves or is damaged in any way. Your brain sends out command messages telling your muscles to move, for instance; the deep receptors provide informational feedback to the brain as to whether the movement has actually occurred.

what each muscle, tendon, and joint is doing; by taking note of which skin receptors are firing and how rapidly they are responding—the Board is able to gain a very clear *sensory* picture of what it is you have in your hand. The Board then searches for this particular pattern of incoming sensory information in its "memory files" and determines that the object is a pencil and not a book, an apple, or a rattlesnake.

Distribution of Receptors

If you were building a robot, you would surely want its fingers to be more sensitive to pressure and temperature than, say, the middle of its back. For robots (like people) would seldom be called upon to make fine discriminations or judgments about objects with the "skin" on their backs. So you would probably want to put *more* sensory receptors in the robot's fingers than on its back.

Your body is built along the same general pattern. There are more receptors in your fingertips, your lips, and the tip of your tongue than anywhere else on your body. The skin on your back and buttocks contains but a fraction of the number of receptors per square inch of tissue that the skin on your lips contains.

Generally speaking, the distribution of the sense receptors in your body is just about the same as you would logically decide should be the case for your robot.

With one exception—robots get their energy from batteries. You need to eat to live. So your body is filled with a long, hollow tube called the *alimentary canal* (°), which begins in your mouth, widens at the stomach and intestines, and ends at the anus. Since the lining of the alimentary canal is skin tissue quite similar to the skin on the outside of your body, nineteenth-century scientists assumed that it should have the same kind of receptors in it that the external skin does.

Just after the turn of this century, a then-young psychologist named E.G. Boring earned his doctorate by proving this was the case. He began by swallowing rubber tubes that had little balloons on the end of them that he could inflate with air or with warm or cold water. Boring found that the only sensations he could elicit from the skin in his throat and his stomach were those of pressure, warm and cold—and pain.

Then Boring attacked the problem from the other end, so to speak, and passed the rubber tubes through his anus and rectum up to his intestines. Again the only sensations he found were pressure, warm and cold—and pain.

Despite this lowly start—or perhaps because of it—Boring became quite famous, wrote several excellent histories of psychology, and spent most of his academic life at Harvard. He frequently complained to his friends that his doctoral dissertation had ruined his digestion and shortened his life. Since he died recently in his mid-80's, we may take his complaints with a grain of salt.

QUESTION: **If the alimentary canal is essentially a hollow tube with openings at both ends, when you swallow food is it really "inside" your body?**

MOTION DETECTORS

By working out electronic circuits that would operate much the way the neural circuits in your body operate, you could fairly easily design a robot that would be able to pick things up, measure them with its fingers, and keep track of where all its arms and legs were in the process. But what if your robot fell over and ruined its vision tubes? How would you get it upright and walking again? How would it know which way was up?

Even the simplest animals will right themselves if you turn them on their backs. The common freshwater flatworm or *planarian* (°), for instance, appears to have "contact" or pressure receptors all over its body. When an inch-long planarian is

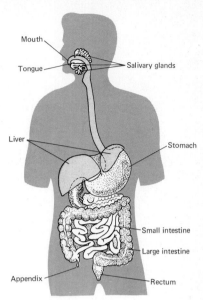

The digestive system.

Alimentary canal (al-li-MEN-tare-ree, or al-luh-MEN-tare-ree). From the Latin word meaning "nutrition" or "nourishment." The alimentary canal is the long tube that makes up your digestive system. It includes the mouth, throat, stomach, intestines, and anus (A-nus). The mouth is the "input" end of the digestive system; the anus is the "output" end of the system.

Planarian (plan-AIR-ee-an). A tiny, flat-shaped water worm that lives in ponds, streams, and rivers all around the world. It is the simplest animal to have a true brain.

The planarian has contact receptors all over its body which tell it whether it is right side up.

crawling along on the bottom of some stream or pond, the contact receptors on its underside fire continuously, while the receptors on its back are relatively quiet. When something turns the worm upside down, the receptors on its back are stimulated while the receptors on its undersurface are quiet; this *unusual pattern of stimulation* sets off an innate or instinctual writhing reaction that turns the animal right side up.

Contact receptors in the soles of your robot's feet might be helpful, but they would not tell the robot whether its head was bent over or upright. You could add movement detectors in the robot's "muscular" system that could monitor the position of all its limbs and its head; but even these receptors would not be enough, for the robot still could not tell up from down just by noting where its arms and legs were.

Your own body solves this problem of location and movement in space with a special set of detectors inside your ears. To understand how these receptors work, however, you need to remember what Newton's *law of inertia* is all about.

In brief, the law of inertia states that a body at rest tends to remain at rest, while a body in motion tends to continue to move. When you are riding in an automobile, your body is only loosely connected to the car. Unless you are tied down with a seat belt, you are free to move about inside the automobile even when it is in motion. For instance, imagine that you are sitting in the front passenger seat of a car that is stopped at a red light. When the light turns green, the driver really hits the gas pedal, and the car leaps forward rapidly. But your body will "tend to remain at rest," so you are pushed back rather roughly into the seat cushions and you feel a great surge of acceleration as the car picks up speed. If the car stops suddenly, your body "tends to continue to move" and, if you forgot to buckle your seat belt, you are thrown into the dashboard or the windshield.

There are basically two types of motion: (1) straight-line or linear movements, and (2) rotary or circular movements. Buried away inside each of your ears are two types of receptor organs that detect changes in the motion of your body. One type of receptor responds to changes in straight-line motion. The other type responds to changes in circular motion. Both types of receptor organs function by obeying Newton's law of inertia.

Linear Motion Detectors

The "flip-flop" movements that your body makes when an automobile speeds up or slows down are usually straight-line or linear movements. The linear motion detectors in your ear are two small organs called the *saccule* (°) and the *utricle* (°). Both the saccule and the utricle are made up of Jello-like or gelatinous tissue filled with tiny stone-like particles—rather like someone had made a bowl of cherry Jello and put in just the pits rather than the cherries. When your head begins to move in a straight line, the saccule and utricle flip-flop in your inner ear the same way that your body flip-flops in an automobile. The "rocks in your head"—that is, the bits of stone in the gelatinous tissue—increase or accentuate the quivering of

Saccule (SACK-you'll). One of the two small organs in your inner ear that detects straight-line movements of your head (and hence of your body). The Greek word *sakkos* means "bag" or "sack." The saccule is thus a "little bag."

Utricle (YOU-trick-ull). From the Latin word meaning (you guessed it!) "little bag." The second of the small organs in your inner ear that detect linear motion.

the saccule and utricle. Hair cells buried in the gelatinous tissue are pushed or pulled this way and that by the quivering. The basket nerve cells at the base of each cell are stimulated by the flip-flop quivering and send signals to the somatic cortex that you are starting or stopping a movement.

Rotary Motion Detectors

When you were younger, did you ever sit in a swing and twist the rope around and around until it was wound up tightly, then let go? You would spin quite rapidly until the rope had unwound. If you got off the swing and tried to walk, you would still seem to be spinning.

Rotary motion of your body is detected by the *semi-circular canals* (°) in your ear. These three canals are positioned at right angles to each other inside your ear so that they can detect circular motion in any of the three dimensions of space. When you turn your head, the fluid in the canals accelerates more slowly than does the rest of your head and presses against a small mound of gelatinous tissue at the base of each canal. When this Jello-like tissue is pushed one way or the other, hair cells in the gelatin are twisted or pulled; the basket nerve cells at the base of each hair then signal the somatic cortex that some kind of rotary motion has begun or stopped.

Motion Sickness

For reasons no one really understands, the motion detectors in your ears have direct connections with those parts of the brain that control the vomit reflex. If you have a rough airplane ride, you may stagger off the plane feeling very dizzy and with a queasy stomach. But it is not your stomach that is upset; it is your inner ear that is complaining.

Motion sickness does not come entirely from such biological causes as over-stimulation of the motion detectors, however. Intra-psychic factors, such as fear and apprehension, make it much more likely that you will become ill when riding in a car, ship, or airplane. (At least one of the Russian space ventures had to be brought back to earth in a hurry when one of their cosmonauts became violently ill.)

People who are prone to motion sickness often find a drug called Dramamine helpful in reducing their discomfort. Dramamine does not affect the stomach directly—rather, it causes certain nerve cells in the brain to fire more slowly.

Semi-circular canals. In each inner ear are three fluid-filled tubes or canals that detect rotary motion of the head. These tubes, called the semi-circular canals, are positioned at right angles to one another.

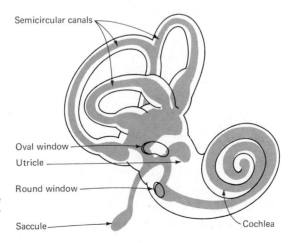

Semicircular canals

Oval window

Utricle

Round window

Saccule

Cochlea

The semi-circular canals of the inner ear detect the rotary motion of your body.

A "rotating wheel" at a carnival.

Centrifugal Force

If you have ever been to a carnival or amusement park, you may have ridden on a device that was much like the turntable of a huge record player with a wall running around the outer edge. You walked onto the turntable through a door in the wall. Once you were inside, the whole affair started to rotate, forcing you outward until you were pressed quite firmly against the inner surface of the wall. As the device picked up speed, you could actually crawl around on the inner surface of the wall without falling to the floor.

As an object like a turntable rotates, *centrifugal force* (°) acts to throw any object on the turntable away from the center of the rotation. As the carnival ride spins around rapidly, centrifugal force plasters you against the outer wall.

Centrifugal force is actually an example of Newton's law of inertia, and your motion detectors respond to centrifugal force just as they do to any other form of movement. If you could stand up on the wall of the carnival ride (at a 90 degree angle to the surface of the earth) when the turntable was spinning, the *center* of the turntable would seem to be "up" to you, while the outer wall would seem to be "down."

In the movie *2001: A Space Odyssey*, the space ship that traveled to Jupiter was shaped like a wheel. During the journey, the wheel turned just rapidly enough to create an artificial gravity so that the men on board could walk comfortably around the inside wall of the wheel—with their heads pointed to the center of the wheel. Since the motion detectors in the men's inner ears couldn't tell the difference, centrifugal force made a pleasant substitute for gravity.

Adaptation and Habituation

Your brain is your main organ of survival. And if you are to survive, you must usually pay more attention to *changes* in your environment than to stimuli that *remain constant* for a period of time. There are at least two ways in which your nervous system adjusts to constant inputs: first, by what we will call *receptor adaptation* (°); second, by what we will refer to as *habituation* (°) to a stimulus by various neural centers in your brain.

Centrifugal force (sen-TRIFF-few-gull). From the Latin words meaning "center" and "fugitive." Centrifugal force is that which causes an object to "flee" from the center of rotation.

Receptor adaptation. Under certain conditions, your sensory detector cells may adjust to a constant stimulus by slowing down their firing rate. When this adaptation occurs, the stimulus typically seems less intense to you.

Habituation (hab-BITT-you-ate-shun). Even when your receptor cells do not adapt to a constant stimulus— and hence continue to fire rapidly— your brain may habituate to this unvarying input by blocking it off from consciousness or by just ignoring it. To habituate is to become accustomed to a place or to a certain stimulus. Technically speaking, habituation is a property of the central nervous system, not of the receptor cells. See Chapter 4.

As an example of receptor adaptation, consider how the motion detectors in your inner ear let you know that you are moving. Strictly speaking, your inner ear does not detect motion at all; rather, it senses *changes in motion*. When a jet plane accelerates for a takeoff, your saccule and utricle notice the increase in speed. But when the plane is flying smoothly at 600 miles per hour (965 kilometers/hour), the gelatinous tissue in your inner ear comes to rest and you cannot tell that you are moving at nearly the speed of sound without looking out the window. In similar fashion, when you first sink into a tub of water that is 20 degrees warmer than your skin, your temperature receptors fire vigorously. But as you remain lying in the tub, your skin temperature itself warms up. After a short period of time, your free nerve endings will fire less vigorously because the temperature of your skin is now much closer to that of the water. Because your skin and your free nerve endings have *adapted* to the heat, the water will now seem much less hot to you.

As we will see in Chapter 9, your brain also has ways of changing its response to stimulus inputs even when the receptor cells continue to fire at rapid rates. When you are flying along in a jet, the sound of the engines may seem particularly loud to you at first. But as you settle down and relax, the noise of the jets may soon become a faint, background drone because your cortical Board is no longer particularly interested in this sound. In this case, your hearing receptors continue to fire rapidly—but your brain *habituates* to this noise by inhibiting, blocking off, or even just ignoring the messages that your ears are sending to your cortex. However, if the engines slow down or speed up, you are likely to notice this *change* almost immediately.

In general, we use the term *adaptation* whenever your receptor cells themselves slow down or reduce their firing rates in response to a constant stimulus; the term *habituation* almost always refers to your brain's tendency to ignore sensory inputs that seem of little interest or importance.

Adaptation and habituation are complex subjects that we will discuss often in this book. For the moment, you should remember that the human body has a great ability to adjust to the world around it, but this adjustment hinges on the body's being able to notice and react to what is *changing* in the environment.

A WINDOW OF SKIN

The skin senses are among the most important you have, surely as critical to your survival as are vision and hearing. And yet, perhaps because we do not often use them for communication or artistic expression, we tend to overlook their complexity, their beauty, and their incredible usefulness.

Helen Keller was born a normal child, but an illness when she was 19 months old left her deaf and blind. Although she had learned to say a few words before the illness, she soon stopped speaking. For the next several years of her life, Helen Keller was little more than an animal, locked in her own black bleak world, unable to communicate with those around her. When she was 6, however, her parents appealed to Alexander Graham Bell for help. Bell, the inventor of the telephone, recommended as a teacher a young woman named Anne Sullivan. Within a month Miss Sullivan had taught Helen to make sense of the myriad sensations her bodily receptors poured into her brain. Helen learned how to "talk" using her fingers, and how to "listen" when someone "wrote" on the palm of her hand.

Helen Keller's skin was her only window to the world, and she "saw" through this window with exceptional clarity. When she would meet someone for the first time, she would run her hands over the person's face to find out what the person "looked like."

If you would like to learn "skin language," do as Helen Keller did. The next

Helen Keller, blind and deaf from childhood, met President Dwight D. Eisenhower at the White House in 1954. She "listened" to what the then President was saying by placing her fingers on his lips.

time you are alone with a very dear friend or relative, have this person sit quietly while you close your eyes and explore the person's face with your fingers. Do not speak. Simply move your fingers gently around the person's eyes, ears, nose, lips, and hair. What kind of a person is this? What does the person *feel* like?

Every scrap of knowledge you have about the world around you, including the people you love and hate, comes to you through the impressions you gain from the patterns of neural firing your sense organs send to your brain. If you understand how these nerve cells react and why they function as they do, you will not only build a better robot (if you have to) but you can also come closer to understanding the complexities of human behavior than if you choose to ignore this important aspect of your own body's functioning.

SUMMARY

1. Your skin is a window on a great part of the outside world.
2. Receptor cells in the skin provide sensory inputs to the somatic cortex (parietal lobe) telling your Board of Directors what your body is doing, what your skin is touching, and whether the outside world is warm or cold.
3. The corpuscles in the hairless regions of the skin, and the basket cells in the hairy regions, detect pressure.
4. The free nerve endings—found in all skin—detect both pressure and temperature.
5. Any object warmer than your skin will be sensed as warm. Any object cooler than your skin will be sensed as cold.
6. There are also deep receptors in your muscles, joints, tendons, and bones that tell your cortex (and the Board) the position and condition of various parts of your body.

7. Buried away in your inner ear are your motion detectors, the saccule, the utricle, and the semi-circular canals. The saccule and utricle sense straight-line or linear motion; the semi-circular canals respond to circular or rotary motion.

8. Your nervous system is geared to respond primarily to *changes* in your environment, for your cortical neurons soon habituate when any sensory input remains constant for a few seconds.

(Continued from page 127.)

Major Jack Amundsen turned down the volume on the radio link between him and the robot. Mark III/21 was trapped somewhere in the very heart of the asteroid, clinging to the walls of a cave that had no top or bottom as far as the robot could tell. Amundsen could rescue Mark easily, quickly, if he could only find some way to let the robot know in which direction it should move to get out of the cave. But how to tell Mark which way was up on an asteroid that had no gravity?

But what is gravity, after all, but a force that keeps the human race glued to the earth? Were it not for gravity, the Major reminded himself, the centrifugal force created by earth's rotation would have flung us all into outer space long ago. Could he perhaps substitute one force for the other?

"Listen, Mark," the Major said on the radio, "I'm going to try something. Our spaceship is bolted to this cruddy piece of rock. If I turn on the positioning jets just right, I can probably set the whole asteroid spinning slowly like a top. If it does, your direction detectors will start operating again."

The robot was silent as Amundsen made his calculation. The ship was parked almost dead center on the asteroid. If the positioning jets could generate enough sideways power—that is, generate enough thrust at right angles to the surface of the asteroid—the asteroid would start to rotate. Amundsen turned on the jets and watched the dials on his control console. Slowly, ever so slowly, the huge piece of cosmic debris started to rotate like a wheel.

"Major, I feel it moving. The loose rocks that were floating around in the cave are falling to the floor of the chamber. Your idea worked." Mark's voice was an unemotional as ever, but Amundsen could swear the robot was smiling electronically.

"Major, my sensors are now functioning. I now know which way is up. I shall return to the ship shortly."

Amundsen suddenly panicked. "Wait a minute, Mark! Which way are you moving?"

"Up, Major, ever upward," came the calm reply.

"Stop, Mark! You're going the wrong way! Your sensors are giving you the right information, but you're interpreting it incorrectly. What seems to be up to you is actually the center of the centrifugal rotation, the center of the asteroid. To get up to the space ship, you've got to move in the opposite direction of what seems up to you right now. It may seem screwy to you, Mark, but you've got to walk up the down staircase."

"But Major, my reflexes are all wrong. I see the logic of what you say, yet my motion detectors indicate that I would be going in an inappropriate direction if I move downward. Help me, Major. I cannot decide which way to go."

Major Amundsen grinned. Wait till he told the boys back in Houston about this! There were some things that a robot just couldn't figure out after all!

Amundsen pressed the button on his microphone and issued a command:

"Robot XSR 5 Mark III/21, this is your superior officer, Major Jack Amundsen, speaking. I hereby order you to continue to move in a downward direction until you reach the surface of this asteroid and can then return to the space ship."

"Yes, Major. I hear and will obey."

"And Mark, when you get to the surface, for God's sake, use your stickshoes to keep you glued to the surface. I wouldn't want the centrifugal force to send you flying off into space after all this."

RECOMMENDED READINGS

Boring, E.G. *Sensation and Perception in the History of Experimental Psychology* (New York: Appleton-Century-Crofts, 1942).

Keller, Helen. *Story of My Life* (New York: Airmont, 1970).

Uttal, William R. *The Psychobiology of Sensory Coding* (New York: Harper & Row, 1973).

chapter 7

"MEMBRANES AND MOLECULES"

TASTE, SMELL, AND HEARING

DID YOU KNOW THAT . . .

What we commonly call "touch" is really several quite different senses?
Even the best steak doesn't *taste* much different from old shoe leather?
Your tongue is covered with tiny nipples called "papillae?"
There are only four basic taste qualities: sweet, sour, salty, and bitter?
Smell is a much richer sense than is taste?
The best way to smell the aroma of wine is to "chew" it with your mouth open?
A woman's sensitivity to tastes and odors varies with her menstrual cycle?
Taste and smell are "mono" senses, while hearing and vision are "stereo" senses?
You can locate sounds in the left-right dimension better than in the up-down or front-back dimension?
Three little bones in each of your middle ears act like stereo amplifiers?
The two most important attributes of a sound wave are its frequency and its amplitude?
Women usually can hear higher musical tones than men?
Certain types of deafness cannot be corrected with a hearing aid?

"Okay, dear, which kid do you want?"

Judy Jones looked around the room. There were children of all ages, all sizes, all colors. Some were playing together, some were fighting, some were sitting quietly in corners minding their own business. Judy glanced quickly at Mrs. Dobson, the woman who had asked the question, and then gazed back at the dozens of children packed into the room.

"How about that little girl over there, in the pink dress?" Judy asked. "She's adorable."

Mrs. Dobson turned to see which child Judy was pointing to. "Oh, Arabella. Sorry, dear, but somebody's already working with her. The pretty ones are always picked first, you know. Pick an ugly one instead, if you want my opinion. They're starved for love, and they need your help just as much as the cute ones do."

Judy was shocked at Mrs. Dobson's bluntness, but guessed the woman might be right. Judy inspected the room carefully, then spotted a little boy with red hair sitting by the window, looking at a magazine. He was by far the most unattractive child in the room. His eyes were watery, his hair uncombed, his skin covered with brown blotches and blemishes. His face was lopsided, and his head seemed too large for his body. Not only that, he was white. Judy, a black student at a college near the Children's Home, had hoped to work with someone of her own race.

"What about him?" Judy said, pointing.

"Oh, that's Woodrow Wilson Thomas. Ten years old. Nice little fella, but ugly as home-made sin."

"Home-made sin?" Judy asked.

"Sorry, dear. It's a saying I got from my mother. Appropriate enough in his case. Woodrow is a bastard, you see."

Judy was shocked. "You mean, he's nasty?"

"No dear. I mean bastard in a technical sense. A love child, a natural-born child, the offspring of an unwed mother. I read his record a couple of years back. His mother was 16 when she got pregnant, and she didn't quite remember who the father was. Maybe somebody in the family, for all we know. Anyhow, the mother got rubella—that's the German measles—while she was carrying poor little Woodrow, and he just didn't turn out right. They thought of putting him up for adoption when he was born; but he was so ugly, they figured nobody would take him. So they kept him for a while."

"For a while?" Judy asked, beginning to sympathize with the little boy more and more.

"For a while. He didn't grow up very well either. The record says he crawled and walked at a normal age, but his speech was very retarded. Made animal noises and grunts instead of talking words. Still does, poor little fella. Doesn't understand much when you talk to him; and he won't usually do what you tell him to do. When you try to get through to him, he just stares at you with those watery eyes, and then he looks out the window while you're trying to say something. No wonder his folks put him in the Home here so the state could take care of him. Retarded, that's what Woodrow Wilson Thomas is."

Judy turned the matter over in her mind. "Do you think there's anything I can do for him? I mean, it's part of the assignment in my psych class. We're supposed to show that we can help a retarded or emotionally disturbed child. Can I help Woodrow?"

Mrs. Dobson sighed. "I don't see why not. There must be something you can do. We're so overcrowded here, and we've got such a small staff, I reckon nobody's worked with that child for 2 or 3 years. He's no trouble, you see. Doesn't have temper tantrums or act up. Never plays with the other kids, or gets into difficulties. He just sits by the window and looks at his books and magazines all day long."

"Well, if he can read magazines at his age, he can't be all that retarded."

"Read? Don't be foolish, dear. He just looks at the pretty pictures, and smiles. One day, a year or so ago, I saw him puzzling over a picture like he was trying to figure out what it was. So I asked him what he saw. He just ignored me. Maybe you can get through to him, but I don't promise. But you should learn a lot, and he won't give you any trouble."

Judy accepted the challenge. She went over to the window and tried to talk to Woodrow, but he didn't seem to want to listen. Finally, in desperation, she tugged on his shirt and pulled him over to a nearby table. Woodrow seemed happy to come along with her.

"Now, Woodrow, we're going to draw some pictures. You like pictures, don't you?

His watery blue eyes drifted toward the window.

Judy pulled on his shirt again until he looked back at her, then she picked up a crayon. She drew a crude picture of a cow while Woodrow watched, seemingly interested. She gave him the crayon and motioned to him that she wanted him to draw. Woodrow took the crayon carefully in his right hand, then looked up at Judy, a puzzled stare on his face.

"Draw a cow, please, Woodrow," Judy said, making scribbling motions with her hand and pointing to the drawing she had just made.

Woodrow smiled serenely as he touched the crayon to the paper. Within three minutes, he handed back to her a crude but recognizable picture of a cow. Judy was so pleased that she wrote the letters C-O-W beneath the drawing. Woodrow took the scratch paper back and copied his own version of the letters underneath those Judy had written.

Judy was thrilled by his response. She got out some of the textbooks she had brought along and hunted through them until she found other pictures for

Woodrow to draw. He made a horse, and an auto, and a house. When Judy wrote their names on the scratch paper, Woodrow copied the letters as carefully as he could.

When her time with Woodrow was up, and she had to catch a ride back to the college, Judy kissed Woodrow on the forehead.

"I don't care if you are retarded, young man. You're going to learn to read. I just know you are!"

Then she gathered up her textbooks and rushed out.

In her excitement at wanting to tell the other students how well things had gone, Judy failed to notice that she had left her algebra textbook behind. Woodrow picked it up and began to look through it. Although it didn't have any real pictures in it, he found the book utterly fascinating.

The next week, when Judy came back to the State Home for the Retarded to be with Woodrow again, he solemnly presented her with a sheet of scratch paper. On one side were childish drawings of a cow, a tree, a car, and a house, each correctly labeled several times over. On the other side, in very poor but legible script, were written out the first two review problems at the end of the introductory chapter of the algebra textbook.

"My God," said Judy when she saw them, "you've done the algebra correctly!"

(Continued on page 156.)

According to popular opinion there are but five senses—vision, hearing, taste, smell, and touch. There is also "common sense," which is unfortunately rare; "non-sense," which is unfortunately common; and the "sixth sense," which some people claim warns them of impending disaster (and which may turn out to be just ordinary "horse sense").

In the last chapter we discovered that touch is not one sense but several—pressure, temperature, feedback from your muscles that lets you know where your arms and legs are, and motion detection. In this and the next chapter we will study taste, smell, hearing, and vision. Some of the facts about these four senses may seem quite sensible; others are guaranteed to be sensational!

TASTE

Imagine that you have been hiking in the woods all day long. You return home, clean up, and go to dinner at the fanciest restaurant in town. Since you are ravenously hungry—and since someone else is paying the bill—you decide to order everything on the menu that you like. What would taste best? A shrimp cocktail, caviar, a juicy steak, a large green salad, mock turtle soup, broccoli in hollandaise sauce? Pick your favorite food and imagine it in your mind's eye. Let's say that you picked a steak—a filet mignon 2 inches thick, wrapped in bacon, and cooked just the way you like it.

Now, why does the steak taste good to you?

Chances are, whatever reasons you've come up with, they're mostly wrong. For even the best of steaks has almost no *taste* at all—at least if we are speaking technically and we restrict *taste* to the sensory qualities that come from your tongue. Steak *smells* good; it *looks* good; it has a fine *texture* to it that you enjoy chewing; and if it comes to your table sizzling hot, it both *sounds* good and has just the right *temperature*.

But none of these sensory qualities has anything to do with the *taste* of steak. In fact, if we could block out all the other sensory qualities except those that come from the taste receptors, you'd find that you could hardly tell the difference between the taste of steak and that of old shoe leather.

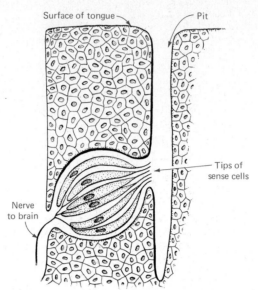

Surface of tongue

Pit

Tips of sense cells

Nerve to brain

A single taste bud.

Taste buds. The taste receptors, found scattered across the surface of the tongue. Each bud contains two or more hair cells. When chemicals in the food you eat or liquids you drink come in contact with these hairs, the buds send "tasty" signals to your cortical Board.

Papillae (pap-PILL-eye, or pap-PILL-ee). The bumps on your tongue that contain the taste buds.

Dendrites (DEN-drights). The input end of the neuron. See Chapters 2 and 4.

Synaptic canals. The fluid-filled space between two connected nerve cells. See Chapters 2 and 4.

Sweet, sour, bitter, and *salty.* The four basic taste qualities. All the thousands of different tastes of food are combinations or mixtures of these four simple tastes.

The Taste Receptors

The *taste buds* (°), which are your taste receptors, are your body's "poor relations." Impoverished in almost every sense of the word, the taste buds are scattered in nooks and crannies all across the surface and sides of the tongue. Mostly, however, they are found clumped together in bumps on the tongue called *papillae* (°) (from the Latin word meaning "nipple"). If you go back to the mirror you were using in Chapter 2 and stick out your tongue and look at it, you will see the papillae very clearly.

Most of the papillae have grooves around their sides, like the moats or canals that circled old European castles. The taste buds line the sides of the papillae, like windows in the outer wall of a castle. Each taste bud is made up of two or more receptor cells, each of which has a hair sticking out of one end. These hairs poke out into the "moat" around the papillae like the *dendrites* (°) at the front end of a neuron. When you eat or drink something, the liquids in your mouth fill up the moats, and certain molecules in the food stimulate the hair cells chemically. The hair cells then fire off their message to the brain and you experience the sensation of taste.

The chemical processes that lead to the experience of taste are not entirely known. But it appears that the food molecules find receptor sites on the hairs and receptor cells, much as the transmitters in the *synaptic canals* (°) find receptor sites on the dendrites and cell bodies of the neurons. Certain types of food molecules fit into one receptor site but won't fit into others—much as a key will fit some locks but not others. When a molecule fits into a taste receptor site, it causes the receptor cell to fire. Your brain figures out what kinds of chemicals are present in your mouth by noting which receptors have been "unlocked," or stimulated.

Taste Qualities

There are only four basic taste qualities: *sweet, sour, bitter,* and *salty* (°)—a paltry few compared to the richness of the sensory qualities found in vision, hearing, and smell. The number of taste receptors is limited, too—a fraction of the number of receptor cells to be found in the eye, ear, or nose. And yet the tongue has its place in our everyday life, for along with the nose it acts as guardian to the stomach.

A papilla in the tongue.

Newborn children will spit out sour or bitter substances, but will readily accept sweet or slightly salty food. The liking for beer and martinis that some people have, therefore, seems a learned or acquired taste. Some people are very insensitive to the taste of certain foods—you must really *saturate* (°) their tongues with these foods for these people to get any taste at all. Other people can detect the same foods in very minute quantities. This difference in taste sensitivity seems to be inherited and comes from differences in the chemical composition of people's saliva. If you dissolve food in the saliva of someone highly sensitive to that taste, and then deliver the food to the tongue of someone who is normally insensitive to that taste, the insensitive person can then taste the food fairly readily.

Various things can change your own taste sensitivity. Smoking a cigarette will temporarily dull your sensitivity to sweet and salty substances, but not to sour and bitter tastes. Monosodium glutamate (MSG), which is marketed in this country as Aćcent, improves some flavors, since it makes the tongue more sensitive to sour and bitter tastes. MSG has such a strong effect on sensitivity to bitter substances that if you use MSG on your food at lunch, a cigarette that you smoke that evening will seem much more bitter than usual—a fact smokers might remember if they ever decide to kick the nicotine habit.

A berry found chiefly in Africa called the *miracle fruit* (°) has been used by African natives for centuries to make spoiled or unpleasant-tasting foods more *palatable* (°). If you were to eat a few berries of miracle fruit, for an hour or so thereafter even the most sour substance (such as lemon juice or vinegar) would taste delightfully sweet to you. Chemicals contained in miracle fruit apparently change the "key-lock" arrangement of the taste bud receptor sites so that "sour molecules" can stimulate "sweet receptor cells." Naturally sweet substances, such as sugar, are not affected by the chemicals in miracle fruit. During the mid-1970's, miracle fruit was sold in tablet form by a company in Massachusetts as a diet aid. The company eventually went bankrupt, perhaps because not too many Americans wished to "sweeten" their coffee by adding lemon juice to it after they had eaten a miracle fruit tablet. The Africans found the berries most useful when they were forced by poverty to eat spoiled, sour-tasting meat. We have little use for such an "aid" in the United States, but miracle fruit does have one amusing effect that many Americans might appreciate: After you have chewed a miracle fruit tablet, cheap wine often will taste surprisingly sweet and pleasant to your taste buds. Perhaps the Massachusetts company would have made money if they had aimed their advertising campaign at wine drinkers instead of at dieters.

Actually, you have had good evidence most of your life that taste is an impoverished sense. When you catch a cold, and your nose is clogged but your tongue not affected, why does food suddenly lose its "taste?" Psychologist Karl M. Dallenbach, who spent his last years at the University of Texas, used to insist that taste had robbed smell's good name. In English, as Dallenbach pointed out, if we say that your mother has taste, we are paying her a compliment. However, if we say that your uncle smells, we are really saying that he stinks. Yet smell—or *olfaction* (°), as it is technically termed—is a delicate sense full of incredible richness, as surprisingly complex in its own way as vision and hearing. But there is hope that people are finally recognizing the truth and that, as the English language changes to reflect our knowledge, we will stop paying lip service to the tongue and the nose will again be in good odor!

How did this strange confusion about the sensory capabilities of the nose and the tongue come about? According to Dallenbach, when man learned to stand up straight on two legs rather than running about on four legs, as do most of the other animals, he removed his nose from where all the good smells are. Indeed, as we will see shortly, if you put your nose to the ground, you will discover a whole new world of smells.

Saturate (SAT-your-ate). To fill completely. A sponge that is as full of water as it can possibly get is said to be saturated with liquid.

Miracle fruit. An African berry that when eaten makes sour substances taste sweetish. It has no effect on salty or bitter substances.

Palatable (PAL-uh-tuh-bull). From the Latin word meaning "roof of the mouth." In ancient times, it was believed that the palate, or top surface of the mouth, contained the taste receptors. Hence, something that is palatable is supposed to be pleasant to the taste, or at least easy to swallow.

Olfaction (oal-FACK-shun). The sense of smell; the act or process of smelling.

Karl M. Dallenbach.

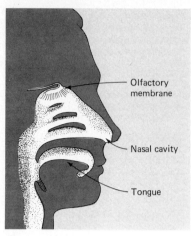

The nasal cavity in cross section.

Olfactory membrane (oal-FACK-tor-ree). The lining of the inside of the nose. Contains the olfactory receptor cells. There are two olfactory membranes—one inside each nostril or nasal cavity.

SMELL

The roof of each of the two nasal cavities is lined with a thick covering called the *olfactory membrane* (°). Embedded in this membrane are millions of olfactory receptor cells. At the base end of each of these receptor cells is an axon that runs directly to your brain. At the front end—as is the case with the taste receptor cells—is a hairlike object that sticks out of the olfactory membrane to make contact with the air as it passes through the nasal cavity en route to your throat and lungs.

The stimuli that excite the olfactory receptor cells are complex chemicals in gaseous form that are suspended in the air you breathe. These gaseous molecules appear to find receptor sites on the receptor cell hairs, and trigger off electrical activity that is then sent to the brain. To be truthful, no one yet knows exactly how these chemicals cause the receptor cells to fire. We are sure, however, that most of the odors your nose detects come from gaseous molecules that are heavier than air. Unless the air is stirred up, these molecules tend to collect on the floor or the ground. As Dallenbach suggested, your nose is usually too high up to detect most of the marvelous odors around you.

Smell Sensitivity

If you were to ask a number of your friends whether dogs or humans have the keener sense of smell, chances are that many of them would believe that the dog's nose is much more sensitive than man's. After all, bloodhounds are used to track down fugitive criminals; the U.S. Army trained German shepherds to detect enemy soldiers in Vietnam (North Vietnamese soldiers were fond of a very smelly food that South Vietnamese seldom ate); and the police sometimes use dogs to sniff out marijuana. The truth is that your nose is probably as proficient as any dog's—if you were trained to use it properly. And since your brain is much better than the dog's, you would be much harder to fool than a bloodhound would be. However, if you wanted to follow someone's trail, you would have to be willing to crawl about on your hands and knees with your nose to the ground as the dog does—which is probably why we continue to use bloodhounds for such tasks. In its own way, however, your nose is as sensitive to faint odors as your eye is to the dimmest of lights and your ear to the softest of sounds.

Your nose has two nasal cavities—one for each nostril—that are separated by a very thin partition. Each nasal cavity has two openings through which air passes—the nostril and the back of the throat. When you breathe through your nose, air is forced past the small bones in the nasal cavity, but only a small portion of this air reaches the olfactory membrane at the top of each nasal cavity. When the current of air stops suddenly or reverses itself rapidly—as it does when you chew and swallow your food or when you sniff the air—eddies of air are pushed up to the top of each nasal cavity and stimulate the olfactory receptor cells. You sniff a flower because this action forces the "smelly" molecules in the blossom up to the olfactory membrane where they can best detect them.

Most whiskey companies employ professional tasters who judge the quality of their products. These tasters take small sips of the alcohol and roll it around in their mouths while making chewing motions. This "mouthing" of the liquid forces odor-laden eddies of air up the back entrance to the nasal cavity toward the olfactory membrane.

If you order a bottle of wine at a good restaurant, the wine steward will open the bottle, give you the cork to sniff to be sure the wine hasn't turned to vinegar, and then pour a little of the wine into your glass. If you swirl this sample of wine around in your glass, you will release the odor molecules into the air inside the glass. You may then stick your nose into the glass and sniff the wine to make sure

Brandy tasting is partly brandy sniffing.

that it smells good. The next stage in this pleasant ritual comes when you sip a bit of the wine in order to "taste" it. Actually, you should "chew" the wine and roll it around in your mouth the way that professional whiskey tasters do before you swallow it. If the wine suits your taste (actually, if it suits your smell), you may nod approvingly to the wine steward, who will follow the ritual of filling your guests' glasses before he fills yours.

The Sweet Smell of Sex

Speaking olfactorily, some people smell better all the time, and you smell better some days than others. Which is to say that olfactory sensitivity varies considerably from one individual to another, presumably because of inheritance. Loss of the capacity to smell occasionally occurs in older persons. And recent experiments suggest that your olfactory thresholds are influenced by the amount of sex hormones present in your body.

Hormones (°) are chemicals secreted by various glands in the body that have a profound influence on growth and behavior. As we shall see in Chapter 13, the sex hormones are created primarily in the sex organs and serve to regulate sexual development and behavior. Berkeley psychologist Frank Beach reports that before and during menstrual bleeding, a woman's body is almost totally deprived of sex hormones. As a consequence, most women experience a measurable lowering of the ability to make fine discriminations in the senses of hearing, smell, taste, vision, and touch during menstruation. In fact, only in the middle of their menstrual cycle are women usually as sensitive to stimulus inputs as men are all the time. However, women who are "on the pill" maintain a continuously high hormone level; hence their sensory *acuity* (°) also remains continuously high. Other investigators have shown that men are more sensitive to some odors just after receiving injections of the male sex hormone *testosterone* (°).

> QUESTION: Whiskey makers have long contended that men have "better noses" for judging smells than do women; can you see why this might be so, and how a woman might overcome these objections?

The relationship between sensory acuity and sexual behavior is an interesting one. A group of married women studied by J.R. Udry and N.M. Morris in 1968 reported that most of them were much more likely to engage in intercourse—and to achieve orgasm—during the middle of their menstrual cycles than at any other time. And, of course, men given testosterone injections are more likely to seek sexual activity than they ordinarily would. While many psychologists believe that the primary effect of an increase in hormone level is to increase sexual desire, our desires are often triggered off by sensory inputs. Thus the more sensitive we are to the sensations associated with sex, the more likely it is our passions will become aroused.

Many male animals mark off their territories by leaving characteristic odors at the boundaries of that part of the world they claim for their own. Most male rodents (such as rabbits and gerbils) have special glands in their chins, stomachs, or reproductive organs that secrete very smelly substances. Each male apparently has his own recognizable odor. As the rodent moves around gathering food, he rubs his smell-gland on various objects, apparently to let other males know that this particular area is already occupied. The male dog that urinates on trees and bushes is probably leaving an odor-laden "calling card" to let other males know he has been there.

Female dogs, like the females of many animal species, secrete a special odor when they are in heat and are sexually receptive to the male. Even very tiny quantities of this smell have a strong excitatory effect on male dogs, who will follow the scent of a receptive female for miles.

Hormones (HOR-moans). Chemicals from various body glands that affect both growth and behavior.

Acuity (ack-CUE-it-tee). The ability to detect very weak stimulus inputs, or to make fine sensory discriminations—that is, to judge very small differences between quite similar stimuli.

Testosterone (tess-TOSS-tur-own). The male sex hormone, secreted primarily by the testes (TESS-tease) or testicles (TESS-tickles) of the male. Masculine behavior patterns are strongly influenced by the presence of testosterone in the body.

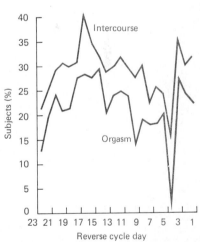

This graph shows the percentage of married women in the Udry and Morris experiment who reported having intercourse and orgasm. Hormone levels are lowest about day 4 in the menstrual cycle and highest about day 15. Sensory acuity follows almost the exact same pattern.

Habituation. The act of growing accustomed to some place or stimulus. When an olfactory stimulus first hits the receptors in the nose, the receptor neurons fire rapidly. If the stimulus continues at the same strength, the receptors slowly decrease their firing rates as habituation to the smell occurs.

Chemical senses. Taste and smell are called the "chemical senses" because the stimuli that excite the receptors in the tongue and nose are chemical molecules.

Somatic cortex (so-MAT-tick KOR-tecks). That part of the brain which receives sensory inputs from the skin, nose, tongue, deep receptors, and motion detectors.

Parietal lobe (pair-EYE-uh-tull, or puh-RYE-uh-tull). Part of the cerebrum at the very top of the brain. Contains the somatic cortex. See Chapter 4.

Monaural (mon-R-al). From the Latin words *mono* meaning "one" or "single," and *auris*, meaning "ear." Sound from a single source. If you were deaf in one ear, your hearing would be monaural.

Olfactory Habituation

Not all the odors in our world are sexually exciting or even particularly pleasant, but many of them are fairly persistent. Anyone who has passed by a petroleum refinery, a glue factory, or a cattle barn knows that many smells are pervasive and lingering. If your nose were continually sensitive to the odors around it, the world would seem a smelly place indeed, and no one could stand to work in cheese factories and chemical plants. But the brain has superb powers of adaptation or *habituation* (°), for it can adjust to almost any smell at all. Chances are that your own home has an odor characteristic of the food your family eats. Normally you don't notice it at all, but if you are gone for a few days, you will smell this unique scent the moment you walk through the front door.

How does your olfactory apparatus adjust to the stimuli around it? As we pointed out earlier, your sense receptors are geared to detect *changes* in your sensory world. When a new stimulus comes along, the receptor typically begins firing rapidly, putting out a burst of neural impulses rather like a machine gun. However, if the stimulus remains fairly constant (as when you plunk yourself down in a tub of hot water or when you remain for a time in a room with a characteristic odor), your cortex begins to habituate to these olfactory inputs. After a while, if the stimulus doesn't change, you appear to ignore it entirely.

THE CHEMICAL SENSES

Smell and taste are often called *chemical senses* (°) because the stimulus that excites the receptors in the tongue and nose are complex chemical molecules. But there is a very important difference between taste and smell—whatever your tongue tastes must ordinarily be brought to the mouth, while the nose can detect stimuli that are some distance away. The skin senses, including taste, are *local* receptors—that is, they give the brain information about the exact point on the body that is being stimulated. Olfaction, hearing, and vision are *distance* senses—that is, they typically tell the brain what is going on some distance away from the surface of your body.

Axonic fibers from the left side of your tongue run primarily to the *somatic cortex* (°) in the right side of your brain; while the axons from the taste buds in the right side of your tongue send their primary message to the somatic cortex in your left *parietal lobe* (°). The same sort of cross-over system holds for the olfactory receptors in your left and right nasal cavities, which are not physically connected in any way.

However, to borrow a phrase from the world of high-fidelity music, taste and smell are essentially *monaural* (°) or "mono" senses. It may take you some time to locate the body of a mouse that had the misfortune to die in some out-of-the-way corner of your home, or to find in July an egg that was hidden too well at Easter. Your ears, on the other hand, are strictly "stereo." Standing quite still in the middle of a strange room with your eyes closed, you can point out rather precisely the location of some noisy object like a ticking clock.

HEARING

What do your ears have that your nose and tongue lack? The answer is—separation. If you block one of your ears with cotton, your ability to localize the position of sounds diminishes considerably. But if just one of your nostrils is stopped up when you have a cold, you could locate a rotten egg just about as rapidly as if both nasal chambers were operating unimpaired. Your ears are several inches apart; your nasal chambers are separated by less than an inch.

If you would like to demonstrate to yourself the importance of the "space between your ears," you might try a musical experiment. The term "high fidelity" (or hi-fi) refers to any system that is of good enough quality to provide you with a faithful reproduction of recorded music. (*Fidelity* comes from the Latin word for "faithful"; a man who is faithful to his wife is practicing marital fidelity.) A hi-fi set has three main components: (1) a sound source, such as a record player, tape recorder, or radio tuner; (2) an amplifier to make the sound source loud and clear; and (3) a speaker. Twenty years ago, because most hi-fi sets had just one speaker, the music was reproduced *monaurally* (°), or in "mono." The music sounded the same to both your ears, and it really didn't matter where you were in the room when you listened.

Then, in the late 1950's, stereophonic records and tapes were invented. As we will see in a moment, a stereo system is really two "mono" sets joined together. A stereo record has two separate bands of music pressed into a single groove. The needle of the record player sends two distinctly different signals to the twin amplifiers (usually packed together in a single container). Each amplifier boosts up the sound of the music and sends it to its own loudspeaker.

In this particular musical experiment, you will need a stereo set with two movable speakers. Put the speakers as far apart in the room as you can. Now put on your favorite stereo record and sit between the two speakers with your eyes closed. You will hear music coming at you from all directions, but some sounds will seem to be on your left, while others seem to be on your right.

Next, put the two speakers right next to each other and repeat the experiment. Now the music is compressed, pushed together, cut down in size to a point source of sound. In short, the stereo music will now sound monaural or "mono."

Your ears are like the two speakers spread far apart; your nose and tongue are like the two speakers put close together.

Localizing Sounds

In a sense, your ears are similar to the microphones used to record music. To get a stereo effect, the record company must use at least two mikes that are some distance apart. When a band or group performs, each mike "hears" a slightly different version of the music. Suppose the lead guitarist in the band is on the left. The mike on the left would then "hear" the guitarist much more loudly than the mike on the right. If the drummer is on the right, then the right mike will pick up the sounds of the drum more loudly than the mike on the left.

Monaurally (mon-R-al-lee). To produce sound from a single source, as through just one loudspeaker.

A musical experiment begins with a stereo outfit.

The experiment continued.

A completely separate recording is usually made of what the left mike "hears" and what the right mike "hears." These two different recordings make up the two channels of stereophonic music that are pressed on stereo disks or dubbed on tape cassettes or cartridges. By keeping the two channels separate during both recording and playback, left-right relationships are preserved. That is, when you hear the record, the sounds made by the lead guitarist come primarily from the left speaker while the drummer's beat comes to you from the right speaker.

Your ears are just far enough apart so that you can readily detect left-right differences in sound sources. Sound waves travel at about 750 miles per hour (1,200 kilometers/hour). If a cricket chirps 2 or 3 feet (0.6 or 0.9 meters) away from your left ear, the noise will reach your left ear a fraction of a second before it reaches your right ear. And since the insect is closer to your left ear than to your right, the noise will be louder when it reaches your left ear than when it finally gets around your head (which muffles the sound) and reaches your right ear. Your brain *interprets* the difference in the messages coming from your left and right ears to *mean* that the cricket is to your left (but, as we will see, your brain can be fooled in such matters if you know how to go about it).

The farther apart your ears are, the more precisely you can detect the location of a sound, because there is a greater difference in what your two ears would hear. When a recording company sets its microphones 10 feet (3 meters) apart, they are effectively increasing the *apparent* distance between your two ears to 10 feet (particularly if you listen to the music with stereo earphones).

Now go back to your stereo set and put one speaker on the floor and the other as high up in the air as you can directly above the first. Sit with your head upright between the two speakers. When you play music now, it will sound strangely monaural, for each of your ears is the same distance from both speakers. In fact, you may find that you tilt your head to one side without realizing it, as your brain attempts to turn monaural music into a stereo message that carries much more interest and information. Your ears can detect the location of sounds spread out in the left-right dimension, but they do very poorly in locating sounds in the up-down dimension.

QUESTION: Why might it help to "cock your head to one side" when trying to locate the source of a sound over your head?

Quadraphonic Recordings

The latest development in the music world is *quadraphonic* (°) reproduction, which gets its name from the Latin word *quadri*, meaning "four," and the Greek word *phono*, meaning "sound." In the 1970's, record companies developed ways of putting four separate bands or channels of music onto a single tape or disk. Four different microphones must be used in making a "quad" recording, one for each channel. By various types of electronic wizardry, these four different channels can be pressed into a single groove or tape.

When you play a "quad" record on your turntable, the needle puts out four different signals. To play the music back quadraphonically, you need a hi-fi system that is really four "mono" sets hooked together. Each of the four amplifiers contained in a "quad" hi-fi system receives its own signal, boosts the volume of the music, and sends it to one of the four speakers needed for "quad" sound. Most people who own quadraphonic systems put one speaker in each corner of their "listening room." Then, when they play a record, they sit in the middle of the room, and the music seems to come at them from all four sides.

Since your ears and brain are good at detecting left-right stereo differences, but poor at detecting the front-back differences that occur in "quad," you may wonder if "quad" sound is really necessary. A good question, particularly since a

Quadraphonic (CWA-drah-FON-ick). Sound reproduced from four different sources, such as four loudspeakers.

"quad" hi-fi system costs almost twice as much as a stereo set, and "quad" records and tapes are usually more expensive than stereo versions of the same music.

Many people who listen to music for the first time on a "quad" system state that it sounds much better to them than does stereo. Many other people report they simply can't tell much difference. Perhaps the best rule to follow is this one: Before you purchase any hi-fi equipment of any kind, listen to it carefully; then buy what sounds best to you (and is within your budget) no matter what the "experts" say.

THE AUDITORY STIMULUS

Hearing is a vibratory sense—which is to say that the stimulus for *audition* (°) is a sound wave. (Words such as "audition," "audio," and "auditorium" all come from the Latin word *audire,* meaning "to hear.")

Imagine yourself seated on a rock a couple of feet above a very quiet pool in a forest. You take a stone and toss it in the center of the pond, and what happens? Wave after wave of ripples circle out from the center until they strike the edges of the pool. If you looked closely, you would see that when one of the waves reached the shore, it "bounced back" in a kind of watery echo.

The sound waves that stimulate the auditory receptors in your ear are little different from the ripples you set up by dropping the stone in the pond. Whenever any fairly rigid object is struck forcibly, it tends to vibrate. As this object vibrates back and forth, it pushes the molecules of air around it—pushes these molecules away from the object just as the stone pushed water molecules away from it when you dropped the rock in the water.

If you dropped several pebbles into the pond in rapid succession, you would set up a whole series of waves on the surface of the water. When an object vibrates, it sets up a continuing series of waves of energy that ride the molecules in the air just as the waves in the pond ride the surface of the water. When these sound waves reach your ear, they set your eardrum to moving back and forth in rhythm with the vibrating object. Other parts of your ear translate the vibrations of the eardrum into patterns of neural energy that are sent to your brain so that you can "hear."

Parts of the Ear

Your ear has three main divisions: (1) the outer ear, (2) the middle ear, and (3) the inner ear.

1. The *outer ear* (°) is that fleshy flap of skin and other tissue you see when you look at yourself in the mirror. Sound waves enter the outer ear and move into a little "hole in your head" called the *auditory canal* (°). At the inner end of this auditory canal is your eardrum, a thin membrane stretched tautly across the canal like the skin on a drum. The eardrum divides the outer from the middle ear.
2. The *middle ear* (°) is a hollow cavity in your skull that contains three little bones called the *hammer* (°), the *anvil* (°), and the *stirrup* (°). If you looked at these little bones under a microscope, you would see that they look much like the real-world objects they are named after. One end of the hammer is connected to the eardrum, so that when the eardrum moves, it pulls the hammer back and forth rhythmically.

    The hammer transmits this "wave" of sound energy to the anvil, making the anvil move back and forth. The anvil pulls the stirrup back and forth in similar fashion. The stirrup is connected to another membrane stretched across an opening called the *oval window* (°). As the stirrup moves, it forces the membrane on the oval window to wiggle back and forth in rhythm too.

Audition (aw-DIH-shun). To hear, or to be heard. The sense of hearing.

Outer ear. The fleshy outer part of the ear. Also called the auricle (AW-rick-cull), the pinna, (PIN-nah), or the auditory meatus (me-ATE-us). The outer ear catches sound waves and reflects them into the auditory canal.

Auditory canal (AW-dit-tor-ee). The hollow tube running from the outer to the middle ear.

Middle ear. Contains the hammer, anvil, and stirrup. Lies between the eardrum and the oval window.

Hammer, anvil, and *stirrup* (STIR-up). Three small, connected bones in the middle ear that make sounds louder.

Oval window. A thin membrane lying between the middle and inner ears. The stirrup is connected to one side of the oval window, the basilar membrane to the other.

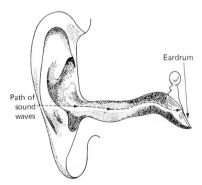

The outer ear.

The human cochlea looks like a snail shell.

Inner ear. A fluid-filled "worm hole" in your skull that contains both the motion detectors (the saccule, utricle, and semi-circular canals) and the receptor neurons for hearing.

Cochlea (COCK-lee-uh). The snail-shaped portion of the inner ear that contains the basilar membrane.

Basilar membrane (BASS-ill-are). The thin, skin-like membrane on which lie the hair cells that detect sounds.

Frequency. In auditory terms, the number of times a sound source vibrates each second. The frequency of a musical tone is measured in Hertz.

Amplitude (AM-plee-tood). From the Latin word meaning "muchness." The amount of sound present, or the strength of a musical tone. Literally, the "height" of a sound wave.

Hertz (hurts). The frequency of any wave, such as a sound wave. Used to be called "cycles per second," or cps.

The purpose of this complex arrangement is easy to understand. The three little bones and the two membranes act as the amplifiers in your own biological stereo system. By the time the sound stimulus has reached the oval window, it is many times louder or stronger than it was when it first struck the eardrum. (See color Plate 6.)

3. The oval window separates the middle ear from the *inner ear* (°). The inner ear is a fluid-filled cavity that runs through your skull bone like a tunnel coiling through a mountain. The inner ear has two main parts: the *cochlea* (°) and the motion detectors discussed in the last chapter (the saccule, the utricle, and the semi-circular canals).

The auditory receptors lie in the cochlea, which gets its name from the Latin word for "snail shell." And, from the outside, the cochlea does look much like a shell you might pick up on a beach somewhere. The receptor neurons for hearing are hair cells similar to those found in the skin, nose, and tongue. These hair cells lie on the *basilar membrane* (°) that runs the length of the spirals in the cochlea.

Frequency and Amplitude

Sound waves have two important aspects: their *frequency* (°) and their *amplitude* (°). The frequency of a musical tone is related to how high or low the tone sounds to your ear. The amplitude is related to how loud or soft the tone appears to be.

If you drop a stone in a deep pond, you set up just one big wave that moves out from the point at which the stone hits the water. But if you drop several pebbles in, one after the other, you set up a series of waves. If you dropped in 10 pebbles each second, you would set up 10 waves a second (under perfect conditions). The *frequency* of the waves is then 10 per second.

When you pluck a string on a guitar, you are doing much the same thing as dropping a rock in a pond, for the string creates sound waves that have exactly the same frequency as the number of vibrations that the string makes. Your ear detects these sound waves and your brain turns them into musical tones. The faster a particular string vibrates, the more waves-per-second it creates—and the higher the tone sounds to you.

If you plucked the "A" string on a guitar, it would vibrate 440 times per second. This number is called the *frequency* of the musical tone "A." Each single vibration of the string is called one *Hertz* (°), abbreviated Hz—the name coming

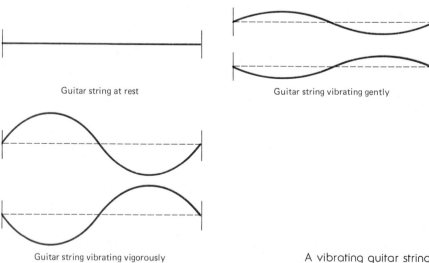

Guitar string at rest

Guitar string vibrating gently

Guitar string vibrating vigorously

A vibrating guitar string.

from a nineteenth-century German physicist (Heinrich Hertz) who made the first definitive studies of energy waves. Since the "A" string vibrates 440 times per second, we say the "A" has a frequency of 440 Hz. In general, the thinner and shorter a string is, the higher the frequency at which it vibrates, and the higher the tone that it makes.

Amplitude has to do with the loudness of a tone, but not with the frequency. If you happened to pluck the "A" string of the guitar *very gently*, it vibrates 440 times per second. But if you plucked the string *vigorously*, it would still vibrate at about 440 Hz. If it didn't, you wouldn't hear the note as being an "A." But surely something different happens, for the more energetically you pluck a string, the louder the note sounds. The answer is the string moves further up and down during each vibration, but it still vibrates at about 440 times per second. If you gently drop 10 pebbles per second into a pond, you create 10 very small waves. If you throw 10 pebbles per second into a pond as hard as you can, you create 10 very large waves. But in either case, there are still just 10 waves per second.

In technical terms, the "bigger the wave," the greater its *amplitude*. And the greater the amplitude that a sound wave has, the louder it will sound to your ear.

The Range of Hearing

What kinds of musical notes can your ear hear? Your range of hearing is, roughly speaking, from 20 Hz to about 20,000 Hz. Actually, the size of your cochlea determines to a great extent what your range of hearing will be. The larger the cochlea, the better it can hear at the *lower* end of the auditory scale; the smaller the cochlea, the better it can hear at the *upper* end of the scale. People with large heads (and hence large inner ears) can occasionally hear as low as 16 Hz (lower than any musical instrument usually plays). But people with large cochleas usually have difficulties hearing much above 14,000–16,000 Hz. People with smaller cochleas usually cannot hear much below 25 or 30 Hz, but may hear notes as high as 18,000–20,000 Hz. Small animals generally have smaller cochleas than man, and hence can hear much higher notes than we can. The dog can hear notes at least as high as 25,000 Hz. The bat, as we will see in the next chapter, can hear tones as high as 100,000 Hz.

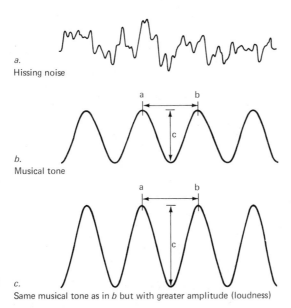

a.
Hissing noise

b.
Musical tone

A sound wave is measured from peak to peak.

c.
Same musical tone as in *b* but with greater amplitude (loudness)

QUESTION: **If you wanted to design a whistle that could be used for calling dogs but that couldn't be heard by human beings, what frequency range would you want to investigate?**

The majority of hi-fi "addicts" are men who, as you can guess, have larger cochleas than women because they are physically larger (on the average) than women are. Because of their "big heads," men can hear lower notes better than they can high notes. For that reason, men often prefer large speaker systems that reproduce low notes crisply and cleanly. If the hi-fi set doesn't reproduce very high notes faithfully, the man doesn't care because he can't hear them. Women, who often hear very low notes poorly (if at all), generally prefer a hi-fi system that gives undistorted high notes. A really fine stereo set will reproduce both highs and lows without distortion. However, cheap systems (most of which are designed by men) are likely to do better with the low notes than with the high. The man who "turns up the volume" on his speakers is sometimes deaf to the distorted high notes that his wife, mother, or girl friend hears only too painfully. When she asks him to lower the volume, he may mistakenly think that she "has no appreciation for music."

DEAFNESS

What difference would it make to your life if you became deaf?

Hearing is the major social sense, the ears being the main avenue of human communication. Our customs, social graces, and moral beliefs are still passed down from one generation to another primarily by word of mouth rather than in writing. And most of us (textbook writers included!) prefer the informal transmission of knowledge that comes from talking to the formal, stilted *phraseology* (°) of the written word.

The person who loses his or her hearing often feels more cut off from the world, and hence makes a poorer adjustment to these changed circumstances, than does the person who loses his or her vision. For when we talk to someone, our listener usually responds to what it is we have just said. If we are telling the person a story or teaching the person a lesson, we watch our listener's face and can tell at once if the person has understood what we have said. This *feedback* from the other person is of critical importance in shaping our verbal behavior. Communication is best when it is a two-way street. You give out a message; it is received by a listener who, in return, sends you back a message evaluating or responding to what you have said. What would it be like if, when you talked, no one ever answered?

Learning to sing, dance, play the guitar, or drive a car—all these complex motor tasks require *feedback*. A boy who is born deaf—or partially deaf—has trouble learning to talk because he cannot hear what noises his voice is making. Without the auditory feedback of the sounds his vocal cords are making, he can never shape his words properly, because he simply does not know what his own voice sounds like.

If you have ever tried to talk to someone who was wearing earphones and listening to music, you know how important auditory feedback is in controlling your voice. For when the person wearing the phones attempts to speak, he or she cannot hear his or her own voice very well and hence starts to shout. The louder the music pouring out from the earphones, the louder the person shouts.

When people grow older, the small bones in the middle ear often become brittle and hard and do not work properly. Since the hammer, anvil, and stirrup serve to amplify the sound waves as they come into the ear, the person becomes deaf when these bones malfunction. This type of *bone deafness* (°) can usually be corrected if the person is fitted for a hearing aid, a device that acts like a miniature hi-fi set and "turns up the volume" electronically.

Phraseology (fray-zee-OLL-oh-gee). From the Greek word meaning "to tell." Your own phraseology is your unique manner of expression, your way of phrasing words, your style of writing or speaking.

Bone deafness. A form of hearing loss caused when the hammer, anvil, and/or stirrup fail to function as they should. Bone deafness can often be corrected either through surgery or through the use of an electronic hearing aid.

Many types of infection can attack the hair cells on the basilar membrane or the axons that run from these cells toward the brain. If the receptor cells (or their axonic fibers) are permanently damaged, the person suffers from *nerve deafness* (°). If only a small section of the basilar membrane is affected, the person may lose the ability to hear just high notes, or low notes, or even notes in the middle of the auditory *spectrum* (°). If the damage to the nerves is widespread, however, the person may become totally deaf for all frequencies. Nerve deafness cannot usually be helped much, if at all, by a hearing aid.

Children who are born partially deaf are often in worse shape psychologically than a child who is born completely without hearing. It is easy for anyone to detect the fact that a child simply cannot hear at all. But if the child can hear some things—sometimes—its parents may think the child's slowness in learning to talk and the indistinctness of the child's words are indications of mental retardation rather than deafness. Until we discovered how necessary some kind of feedback is in learning to talk, we often thought that partially deaf children were dumb or stupid. Occasionally we mistakenly confined children with very high intelligence to homes for the retarded. Fortunately, now that hearing tests for young children are much more common than they used to be, and now that we know what the effects of partial deafness are, we don't make that particular mistake too often any more.

Some kinds of deafness can be helped with hearing aids.

SUMMARY

1. Taste and smell are called "chemical senses" since the receptors in the nose and tongue are stimulated primarily by complex chemical molecules.
2. The primary receptors for taste are the taste buds, which are located in mushroom-shaped bumps (called "papillae") on the surface of the tongue.
3. The four basic taste qualities are sweet, sour, bitter, and salty.
4. The smell receptors lie on the olfactory membrane inside each of the two nostrils. Whenever you breathe in air containing certain types of molecules, these chemicals stimulate the olfactory receptors and you experience the sensation of smell.
5. Taste is a very simple sense, with but four basic qualities. Smell is much more complex. Most of the "taste" of food is really the smell of the food rather than its taste.
6. Smells affect many types of behaviors, including sexual responses.
7. Smell and taste are both monaural, or single, senses in that they seldom help us locate objects in space very well. Hearing is a stereo sense; because the two ears are several inches apart, sounds reach each ear at slightly different times and at slightly different loudnesses. The brain analyzes these differences and converts them into an understanding of whether the source of the sound is to the left or the right.
8. Stereo recordings contain two channels of music—one aimed primarily at the left ear, the other aimed at the right ear. When a stereo recording is played back through a left and a right loudspeaker, the band or orchestra seems "spread out" in front of you (from left to right).
9. Quadraphonic recordings contain four channels of music and must be played back through four loudspeakers. Since your ears are better at detecting left-right differences than front-back differences in sound locations, quadraphonic recordings often sound better if you move your head around while listening to them.
10. When sound from any source arrives at the ear, the sound passes through the outer and middle ear until it reaches the hair cells in the inner ear. These inner-ear hair cells are the true auditory receptors.
11. Sound waves have both frequency (measured in Hertz, or Hz) and amplitude. The greater the frequency of a musical tone, the higher it generally sounds. The larger the amplitude of a sound, the louder it will usually seem to be.
12. Bone deafness is a hearing loss caused by improper functioning of the three

Nerve deafness. A form of hearing loss caused by damage to the hearing receptors or to the auditory nerve. Nerve deafness can seldom be helped either by surgery or by use of a hearing aid.

Spectrum (SPECK-trum). From the Latin word meaning "to look," from which we also get the words "specter" (ghost) and "spectacle." As we will see in the next chapter, the word "spectrum" means a set or array of related objects or events, usually a set of sights or sounds.

little bones in the middle ear; it can usually be corrected with a properly fitted hearing aid.

13. Nerve deafness results from damage to the hair cells. This form of deafness can seldom be corrected.

(Continued from page 143.)

Dear Judy Jones:

I was going through some of my stuff today, packing it all up, when I found this old sheet of scratch paper. It had a cow on it, and a horse and an automobile. On the back was a couple of algebra problems, written out in long hand. My ticket to the world, I always used to call it. Reminded me that I hadn't written you a letter in some time, so maybe you ought to get caught up on the news.

I'm going to college! Can you believe it! That's what I was packing for, when I found the scratch paper. Bet you never thought, the first time you saw this ugly boy, Woodrow Wilson Thomas, that he'd be going off to college someday. I don't remember that first day you came to the Home too well, maybe because I didn't know the words to remember things with back then. But the algebra book, that is something I sure won't ever forget. I guess I learned how to read with that book. And your help too, and then Mrs. Dobson's. She told me later you had a real argument with her. She thought I was retarded, but you insisted I must just be deaf. Then there was the doctor checking me out, and the hearing aid that the State bought me. Did I ever tell you, the first day I had the hearing aid, I just sat and listened to the birds all day long? Can you imagine not knowing what a bird sounds like until you're 10 years old?

Anyhow, as you know, it took me a couple of years to learn how to talk like normal people do. Still not too good at it, I guess. But I went to school, and I caught up, and now I'm going to college. I still can't believe it. I guess I did pretty good in high school, except maybe in English. But real good in math. Good enough to get a scholarship. How about that? I'm going to study math in college, hope to be a teacher some day. My complexion has cleared up a lot since you saw me last, and maybe I'm not so ugly any more. Anyhow, I've got me a girl friend. Sort of.

It's been so long, maybe you're married now and have kids of your own. If you do, I bet you'll have their ears checked out, won't you?

Anyhow, I just wanted to let you know how things are going, and about the college bit. I guess if it hadn't been for you, I'd still be at the Home, sitting in the window, looking at the pretty pictures in the magazines. I guess I really owe the world to you, Judy Jones. So I thought I'd write and say thank you.

Peace,
Woody

RECOMMENDED READINGS

Braginsky, Dorothea D., and Benjamin M. Braginsky. *Hansels and Gretels: Study of Children in Institutions for the Mentally Retarded* (New York: Holt, Rinehart and Winston, 1971).

Dethier, Vincent. *To Know a Fly* (San Francisco: Holden-Day, 1963).

Kling, J.W., and L.A. Riggs. *Experimental Psychology*, 3rd ed. (New York: Holt, Rinehart and Winston, combined ed., 1971, Vol. 1, 1972).

Montagne, Prosper. *Larousse Gastronomique: The Encyclopedia of Food, Wine & Cookery* (New York: Crown Publishers, Inc., 1961).

For information on high fidelity, stereo, and quadraphonics, see any recent issue of the magazines *Stereo Review* or *High Fidelity*. Both publications can be found on most newsstands.

chapter 8

"BLIND AS A BAT"

VISION

DID YOU KNOW THAT . . .

The smallest unit of light is the photon?
Light travels at a speed of 186,000 miles per second (300,000 kilometers/second)?
The color of a light is determined primarily by its wave-length?
The colors of the rainbow make up the visible spectrum?
The most sensitive part of your eye is called the "fovea?"
Each of your eyes has a blind spot almost in the middle of your visual field?
The receptor organs for vision are the rods and cones?
The rods are totally color-blind?
The retina of the eye is sometimes considered to be an extension of the brain?
Far-sighted people get more headaches than do near-sighted people?
You can have better than 20/20 vision?
Eating carrots could help improve your night vision?
Bats are not really blind?
If you mix two complementary colors, such as yellow and blue light, you may get a
    shade of gray?
About 1 person in 20 is markedly color-blind?

"What is the first thing you do when a sixth-grade boy comes to your office and wants an appointment for counseling?" Mrs. Carson asked her graduate class in educational psychology.

"Look over his records first, so you know what his test scores are," said one student.

Mrs. Carson nodded. "If you have time, yes, that can be helpful. But suppose the boy is right there, tears in his eyes, begging to see you right now. Then what?"

"Find out what his name is," a student said.

"Ask him what's wrong," said another.

Mrs. Carson smiled. "Suppose he tells you that the other boys have been picking on him, teasing him. Now what do you do?"

"Try to get to know him better, so you can understand his problem," a young woman in the second row of the class said.

"Yeah, try to relate to the kid," said the young man sitting next to her.

"True," said Mrs. Carson, "At some point you will want to understand his personality so well that you can look at the world through his eyes. But how do you find out things about him?"

"Encourage him to talk," a male student muttered.

"Ask him what his life is like," said another student. "What his parents do, where does he live, what he's interested in—things like that."

Mrs. Carson agreed by nodding her head. "All good points. You all seem to sense the need to establish a warm, friendly rapport with the boy. But before you can see the world through his eyes, there is something even more important you must do. Can you guess what it is?"

The class was silent.

"First you must see the boy through your own eyes," Mrs. Carson said. "Most of you want to leap right inside his mind to see what's going on. However, you must learn to see what he's like on the outside before you can discover what he's like on the inside. You must notice his clothes: Are they cheap or expensive? Do they fit him or not? Are they clean and in good repair, or are they filthy and in rags? Is his hair combed? Are his teeth brushed? Is he wearing jewelry or a watch? Are there nicotine stains on his fingers? Is he thin, fat, or muscular?"

"Never judge a book by its cover," said the young woman in the second row.

Mrs. Carson leaned against her desk. "True. These are superficial things, and you will eventually learn to take them into account rather rapidly, to size the child up rather quickly. But when you're just beginning your work as a counselor, you must take the time to train your eye so you don't miss those simple things that can tell you so much about a child. You must be detectives. Only after you comprehend the significance of the simple clues about the child can you safely go on to solving the complexities of his mind."

"Yeah, but can you learn anything really important about a sixth-grade boy just from looking at his clothes?" a young man asked.

"Class, let me tell you a detective story. I'll give you all the clues and let's see if you come up with the right solution. Let me tell you about the Case of Johnny W."

Mrs. Carson closed her eyes for a moment, then opened them wide. "Johnny W. was 12 years old when he first came to my office. He was a nice-looking boy with hair the color of cotton and skin so pale it was almost chalk white. He was wearing dark green pants, a light blue shirt, a red jacket with yellow trim, and tan shoes. His clothes were slightly mussed, but of excellent quality. When he sat in the chair by my desk, I noticed one of his socks was bright red, the other coal black. Now, what do you know about him already?"

"Nothing important," said one student.

"No," said another, "you know something about his home life. I'll bet he dressed himself for school."

"Beautiful," said Mrs. Carson. "I asked him about it right away. His mother and father both worked. They woke him up before they left, so he dressed himself and made his own breakfast. But his clothes tell you something else, something much more important. Can anyone guess?"

When no one in the class responded, Mrs. Carson continued. "All right, some more clues. I assumed from the fact that he dressed himself and got to school on time that he was mature for his age and apparently dependable. While he was telling me about his home life, I scanned his school records. His mental test scores were well above average. He was behind his class in reading ability, but otherwise seemed to be doing well. But he seemed nervous. As he talked to me, his eyes darted back and forth quickly, and he kept putting one hand up to shield them from the glare of the window. I lowered the shade, and then asked him what was wrong. Can you guess yet?"

No one could.

"More clues. He said, 'I'm no good at all. The kids laugh at me. They call me Bunny Rabbit. They don't like me. They won't let me play ball with them. Why won't they let me play ball with them?'"

Mrs. Carson surveyed her class in educational psychology. "Now what do you think was making him so unhappy?"

"He didn't know how to get along with the other kids. He needed training in social skills," said a woman.

"His father never taught him to play ball. Bad father-son relationship," said a male student.

"Good points," said Mrs. Carson. "But you're missing most of the clues. Part of his problem came to Johnny from his father, but his mother was at fault as well. Let me continue. Next Johnny said, 'I practice hitting the ball and catching the ball hours and hours. Even when the light hurts my eyes, I practice hard. But I have to wear my dark glasses outside, and when they throw the ball to me, it just disappears. It just disappears! I swing the bat, but I miss. And sometimes the ball hits me, and it really hurts. I know I'm not like the rest of the kids. I can't help that. But why can't I even see the ball when they throw it at me?'"

Mrs. Carson paused. "All right, class. What was Johnny W.'s problem?"

"He was a sissy," said one husky young man.

"He needed new glasses," said a young woman.

"He was emotionally insecure," said another.

"Johnny's glasses were as good as they could be," Mrs. Carson said. "But think of the clues I've given you. Johnny W. was very insecure all right, but not because he was a sissy or because of a poor relationship with his parents. He needed psychological help, but a counselor might go off in entirely the wrong direction if the counselor didn't pay attention to the descriptive things about Johnny that I've mentioned. Before you can solve his emotional problems, you have to solve a mystery about Johnny that even his parents didn't fully understand.

"Why couldn't Johnny W. see the ball when they threw it at him?"

(Continued on page 172.)

Photon (FO-tahn). A tiny packet of energy which is the smallest unit of light. Although a burning match will release millions of photons, under ideal circumstances your eye is so incredibly sensitive that it can detect as few as 10 photons if they strike your eye at the same time.

Of all the senses, vision is the richest and most stimulating. Psychologists estimate that two-thirds of your knowledge of the world comes to you through your eyes. Although the visual system makes up far less than 10 percent of your brain, it probably consumes a quarter of the total energy available to the nervous system. Anyone with normal color vision who has watched a pageant such as the Rose Bowl parade, studied a painting by Picasso, or walked marveling through the riotous colors of a spring landscape appreciates the impossibility of describing to a blind person what the ability to see is like. Because vision dominates our lives, psychologists have studied it in much greater detail than they have the other senses. As a result, we know more about how and why we see than we do about how we experience the rest of our sensory world.

Vision has often been called "the sense of wonder." To appreciate how your ability to see influences your thoughts and behaviors, you need to understand at least three things: (1) What the visual stimulus (light) is like, (2) how your eye converts light into a sensory input to send to your brain, and (3) how your brain interprets this incoming sensory information.

THE VISUAL STIMULUS

The stimulus for vision is light. The smallest, most elementary unit of light is called the *photon* (°), which gets its name from the Greek word meaning "light." The flame from one match releases millions of photons; a flashlight releases a great many more. In general, the brighter the light source, the more photons it produces in a given unit of time (such as a second).

When you turn on a flashlight, photons stream out from the bulb at an incredible speed or velocity. The velocity of sound waves is about 750 miles per *hour* (1,200 kilometers/hour). The speed of light is about 186,000 miles per *second* (300,000 kilometers/second). If you could travel as fast as a photon, you could zoom all the way around the world *seven times* in just one second, and you could go to the moon and back in less than three seconds.

The bulb of a flashlight produces photons in pulses or *waves*—much as the string on a guitar produces sound waves when the string vibrates, or the wind produces waves on the surface of the ocean. If you wanted to, you could take a boat out on the ocean and actually measure the distance between one ocean wave and another. And if you did so, you would find that the distance between the crests of the waves was remarkably consistent. On a calm, peaceful day, as the waves move slowly and majestically, the distance between waves would be rather large. On windy, choppy days, this wave-length would be rather small. If you know the strength of the wind, you have some notion of what the length between the crests of the ocean waves will be.

Much the same sort of consistency holds for the wave-length of light and what color it appears to be. In color Plate 1, you will see a rainbow-like display called the *visible spectrum* (°). The blue colors have very short wave-lengths; the reds, at the other end of the spectrum, have much longer wave-lengths. The colors between red and blue have wave-lengths that fall between these two extremes. If you know what the *length* of the light wave is, then you know what *color* it will be.

However, the distance between the crests of light waves is much, much smaller than the distance between any two ocean waves. The wave-length for red is so short that it takes about 38,000 "red waves" to make an inch (2.5 centimeters). The wave-length for blue is much shorter—it takes about 70,000 "blue waves" to make an inch.

Scientists seldom measure the wave-length of light in fractions of an inch, because the figures are just too clumsy to use. Instead, scientists use the *metric scale* (°) and measure wave-lengths in *nanometers* (°). The Greek word for "dwarf" is *nanos*. From this fact, you can guess that the nanometer is a "dwarf" or fraction of a meter. In fact, there are one billion nanometers in each meter (one meter = 39.37 inches).

In scientific terminology, violet-blue light has a wave-length of about 400 nanometers. Red light has a wave-length of some 700 nanometers. If a scientist in the United States wanted to tell a scientist in Germany *exactly* what color light was used in an experiment, the American scientist could specify that the blue light had (for instance) a wave-length of 423 nanometers. The German scientist could then reproduce or replicate the experiment employing *precisely* the same color that the American had used.

Wave-length specifies the color of a visual stimulus, such as a blue or red light. But some lights are bright, and others are dim. The intensity or brightness of a light can be specified in terms of the height or *amplitude* (°) of the wave. If you measured the length between crests of ocean waves on a calm day, you might find that the wave-length was (for example) 20 feet (6 meters). The height of each wave might be no more than 2 feet (0.6 meters). During a storm the wave-length might still be 20 feet, but the height of each wave might now be 10 or 12 feet (3 or 3.6 meters)!

In similar fashion, a dim blue light might have a wave-length of 423 nanometers. If you make this blue light of blinding intensity, it would still have a wave-length of 423 nanometers, but the amplitude of each wave would be many times greater. When you make a light brighter, you *amplify* the height of each light wave—just as when you turn up the volume on your stereo set you *amplify* the height of each sound wave the machine puts out.

Visible spectrum (SPECK-trum). The word "spectrum" means a set or array of related objects or events. When you look at a rainbow in the sky, you see the array (spectrum) of visible colors that make up sunlight. Light waves are only a small part of a larger spectrum—the array of electro-magnetic waves that inludes radio and television waves, X-rays, heat waves, and so forth. That part of the electro-magnetic spectrum that you can actually see is called the visible spectrum. For most purposes, "rainbow" and "visible spectrum" can be considered practically the same things.

Metric scale (MET-trick). Most of the world measures distances in meters rather than in feet and inches. The meter = 39.37 inches—about a yard + 3.37 inches. Just as the American dollar is divided into 100 cents, so the meter is divided into 100 centimeters. The metric scale is so much simpler to work with than are "inches, feet, and yards" that we too will soon join the rest of civilization in using meters rather than feet and miles. Converting to the metric scale (once the initial shock has worn off) will save the United States billions of dollars a year, and will make it much easier for school children to solve practical problems in arithmetic involving the measurement of distances. In this text, we will usually put the metric equivalent in parentheses.

Nanometers (NAN-oh-meters). One-billionth of a meter.

Amplitude (AM-plee-tood). The height of a light wave or sound wave. Generally speaking, the greater the amplitude of a sound wave, the louder the sound; the greater the amplitude of a light wave, the brighter the light source will appear to be.

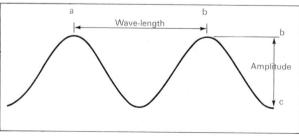

Amplitude and wave-length.

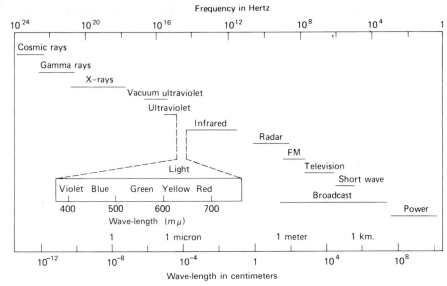

The visible spectrum.

The Visible Spectrum

In a manner of speaking, light waves are much like X-rays and radio waves—except that X-rays have such a short wave-length that they are invisible to your eye, and radio waves have such a long wave-length that you can't see them. As the figure below suggests, the only waves you see at all well lie between 400 and 760 nanometers. Below 400 nanometers lie the *ultra-violet rays* (°) that are used in "black lights" and in sun lamps. These rays have a very damaging effect on the complex chemicals that help you see, which is why you shouldn't look directly at "black lights" for very long, and why you should wear dark glasses when you sit under a sun lamp. Beyond the red end of the visible spectrum (760 nanometers) lie the heat rays. If you stare at a heat lamp for too long, you may not only warm up your face but "cook" parts of your eyes as well.

Why does a psychologist interested in human behavior bother with such technical measures as wave-length and amplitude? For two reasons, really.

First, because visual stimuli *stimulate* people to act and respond, and the more precisely we can specify the stimulus that evokes a certain reaction, the better we can understand the behavior itself.

Second, because we are often interested in individual differences. If we show *exactly* the same visual stimulus to two people, and they report *different* psychological experiences, we know that these differences are due to the people and not due to some variability in the physical stimulus itself.

THE EYE

What physiological processes occur when you see? These are so complex that we still understand them only vaguely. In some ways the human eye is like a color TV camera. Both are essentially "black boxes" or containers that admit light through a small hole at one end. The light then passes through a lens that focuses an image on a *photo-sensitive surface* (°). In both your eye and in the color TV camera, the "hole" can be opened to let in more light, or closed to keep light out; and in both, the lens can be adjusted to bring near or far objects into focus.

In the case of the color television camera, the light coming through the lens falls on an electronic tube that contains three complex chemicals that are

Ultra-violet rays (ULL-tra-VY-oh-let). The Latin word *ultra* means "beyond." Ultra-violet rays are those light waves that lie just beyond the "violet" or "blue" end of the visible spectrum. Technically speaking, ultra-violet rays run from about 250 nanometers to about 350 nanometers. The X-rays lie below 250 nanometers; X-rays, then, are "ultra-ultra-violet rays."

Photo-sensitive surface. Light waves can set off rather dramatic reactions in some chemicals. These light-sensitive chemicals are said to be "photo-sensitive." The film in a camera reacts to light—hence, film is photo-sensitive. The inner surface of your eye contains pigments (colored chemicals) that are also photo-sensitive.

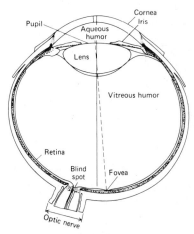

A diagram of the eye.

Pupil (PEW-pill). The opening in the iris through which light passes into the eye.

Iris (EYE-riss). The colored or pigmented area of the eye. When you say that someone has brown eyes, you really mean the person has brown irises. The Greek word for "rainbow" is *iris*.

Cornea (CORN-ee-ah). From the Latin word meaning "horn-like." We get our words "horn" and "corn" (the kind of blister you get on your foot) from this same Latin source. The cornea is the tough, transparent tissue in front of the aqueous humor.

Aqueous humor (A-cwi-us). The watery substance between the iris and the cornea that keeps the front of the eyeball inflated to its proper size and shape.

Retina (RETT-tin-ah). The photo-sensitive inner surface of the eye. Contains the visual receptor organs.

Vitreous humor (VITT-tree-us). From the Latin word meaning "glass." The vitreous humor is a clear, glass-like substance in the center of the eyeball that keeps the eye in its proper rounded shape. Light must pass through the vitreous humor before it strikes the retina.

Fovea (FOE-vee-ah). The tiny "pit" or depression right at the center of the retina that contains only cones, and where your vision is at its clearest.

Blind spot. That small part of the retina near the fovea where blood vessels and nerve pathways enter and exit from inside the eyeball. The blind spot contains no visual receptors.

photo-sensitive—that is, chemicals that react when struck by photons. (The older TV cameras had a tube with only one such chemical, hence we could "see" the scene only in blacks and whites.)

In the case of your eye, the "hole" or opening through which the light passes is called the *pupil* (°). The *iris* (°) is the colored part of your eye which, by expanding and contracting around the pupil, controls the amount of light admitted inside your eye. Before light passes through the pupil, however, it must first pass through both the *cornea* (°) and the *aqueous humor* (°). "Cornea" comes from the Latin word meaning "tough" or "horny," so you can guess that the cornea is the tough tissue at the front of the eye. The Latin word for water is *aqua*. The aqueous humor is a watery substance between the iris and the cornea that helps keep the eyeball filled out in its proper shape.

Once a ray of light has entered the inner eye through the pupil, it passes through the lens. The purpose of the lens in your eye—like the lens in a camera—is to allow you to focus clearly whether you are looking at something close or far away. As you change your point of focus from a near object to something several feet away, muscles inside your eye pull on the lens to change its shape. As you grow older, the lens loses its elasticity or "pull-ability." The result is that you no longer can focus clearly on close objects—if you want to read a telephone book, you may have to hold it several feet away from you in order to read the fine print. The lens focuses the image of what you are looking at and projects this image on the inner surface of the eyeball—just as the lens in a camera focuses the image or picture that you want to take on the film in the back of the camera. The inner surface of your eyeball is called the *retina* (°), from the Latin word meaning "net" or "network." The retina is a network of millions of cells that (like the picture tube in the TV camera) contain several photo-sensitive chemicals.

The Retina

In a sense, your eyeball is a hollow sphere whose outer shell has three layers. The outer layer—which contains the cornea—is the "skin" of the eyeball. Like most other skin tissue, this outer layer contains free nerve endings that are sensitive to pressure, temperature—and pain. The middle layer of this outer shell is a dark lining that, like a window shade, blocks out all the light except that entering through the pupil. The third layer is the retina, which is really the inner surface of your eyeball.

The hollow cavity in the center of your eyeball is filled with a transparent, gelatinous substance called the *vitreous humor* (°). Like the aqueous humor, the vitreous humor acts to keep your eyeball "inflated" in its proper, rounded shape.

The Fovea The retina contains the receptor cells that translate the physical energy of a light wave into the patterns of neural energy that your brain interprets as "seeing." When a doctor examines your eyes, he or she often uses a sort of flashlight that shines a tiny beam of light through the pupil and lens onto the retina itself. The doctor can then inspect your retina for possible damage. The next time a doctor examines your retina, turn the tables and ask to look in the doctor's eye. If you are allowed to do so, you will see that the retina covers almost the entire inner surface of the eye. There are two landmarks in the retina that you should look for particularly. These are the *fovea* (°) and the *blind spot* (°).

Fovea is the Latin word for "small pit." The fovea in your eye is a tiny, yellow-colored pit in the center of your retina where your vision is at its sharpest. The blind spot is a small area of the retina near the fovea that is, for all practical purposes, totally blind. We will discuss the blind spot in greater detail later in this chapter. The reason that this part of your eye is "blind," however, is that it has no receptor neurons in it. (See color Plate 15.)

While the eye is much like a TV camera in some ways, there are many differences between the two. The camera is large, bulky, clumsy to operate, and requires an external power source of some kind. The eye is small and is, in a sense, self-powered. The photo-sensitive plate or picture tube in a camera is flat, while the retina in your eye is curved to cover almost the entire inner surface of the eyeball. As you move about from one place to another, the iris in your eye opens up to admit more light or closes down when the light gets brighter. Unless you watch yourself in a mirror, you are usually unaware of the changes in the size of your pupils, for these changes are not usually under your conscious control. Some TV cameras adjust automatically to changes in light intensity, but their range of adjustment is not nearly as great as that which your eye is capable of.

Perhaps the major difference between your eye and a TV camera is the way that each mechanism translates light waves into patterns of electrical energy. The picture tube in a black-and-white TV camera contains just one kind of photo-sensitive chemical, while the tube in color cameras has three such chemicals. Your eye is something like a combination of the two, for it has both black-and-white detectors and a separate set of color detectors.

The Rods and Cones The receptor neurons for vision are the *rods* (°) and *cones* (°). Their names are fairly descriptive of their shapes. In the human eye the rods are slim, pencil-shaped nerve cells. The cones are thicker and have a cone-shaped tip at their "business" end. (See color Plate 14.)

Both the rods and cones contain chemicals that are very sensitive to light. When a beam of light strikes a rod, it causes the bleaching or breakdown of a chemical called *rhodopsin* (°), or visual purple (the Greek word *rhod* means "rose-colored"). In ways that are still not entirely understood, this bleaching action sets the rod to firing as it signals the brain that it has been stimulated. The cones contain other types of photo-sensitive chemicals that break down when struck by light waves. This chemical reaction triggers off a wave of neural firing in the cones.

The rods are color-blind. Like the old-fashioned TV cameras, they see the world in blacks and whites no matter how colorful the world actually is. For the most part, the rods are located in the outer reaches or *periphery* (°) of the retina. There are about 120 million rods in each of your eyes.

The cones are the color receptors and are mostly bunched together in the center of your eye near the fovea. The fovea contains no rods at all, only cones. A few cones are mixed in with the rods all the way to the outer edges of the periphery. There are between six and seven million cones in each of your eyes. The center of your retina is, therefore, more sensitive to color than is the periphery.

If you would like to learn more about how your own rods and cones function, you might try the following test. Put down this book for a moment and focus your attention on an object a few feet away from you. Let's say you pick a colorful picture hanging on the wall. When you stare directly at the picture, its image falls directly on the fovea in the center of your retina. If your vision is normal, you will see the picture in excellent detail. Look the picture over carefully and try to remember exactly what the colors are like.

Now, turn your eyes and look at something a few feet to the right or left of the picture. Let's say you choose a chair. The image of the chair is now focused on your fovea. While keeping your eyes firmly fixated on the chair, try to "inspect" the picture out of the corner of your eye. The image of the picture is now falling on the periphery of your retina, and you may notice that the picture looks blurred and lacks sharp detail. Furthermore, the colors will probably seem faded and less distinct, if you can see colors at all.

When you look at something straight on, the light waves coming from that object strike the fovea and stimulate the cones, giving you clear color vision.

Rods. The needle-shaped visual receptors that are insensitive to color, but respond to blacks and whites and shades of gray.

Cones. The visual receptors that respond to color as well as black and white.

Rhodopsin (ro-DOP-sin). From the Greek word meaning "reddish-purple." We get our words "rose" and "rhododendron" from this same Greek source. Rhodopsin is a purple-colored photo-sensitive pigment found in the rods.

Periphery (pair-IF-er-ree or purr-RIF-er-ree). From the Greek word meaning "to move around the outside." The periphery is the outer edge of any closed surface, such as a circle.

Color constancy. If you know a fire engine should look red, it will tend to appear that color even when it is illuminated by green or yellow light. Most familiar objects seem to remain the same (constant) color to the brain even when the cones report the objects should be a different color.

Peripheral nervous system (pair-IF-er-al or purr-RIF-er-al). Those neurons that lie at the outer edge of your body, such as your skin receptors.

Central nervous system (often abbreviated CNS). Technically, the entire brain (the cerebrum and the brain stem) and the spinal cord. Contains more than 90 percent of the nerve tissue in the body.

When the same object is at the periphery of your vision, the light waves from the object strike primarily the rods in the outer edges (periphery) of the retina. Since the rods are color-blind, anything that appears at the edges of your visual world will be seen as lacking in color. As the image moves from the periphery to the fovea, the apparent color of the object actually changes.

You may feel at first that this is an over-statement of the case, since you are usually unaware of any change in the apparent color of an object (such as an automobile) as it moves across your visual field. And certainly, as you look around a room, objects don't seem to change their colors. But this *color constancy* (°) of objects in your visual world is a function of your *brain*, not of your eye. As we will see later, once your brain knows what color an object is supposed to be, it remembers this fact and tends to perceive the object as being that color no matter what the cones report its color to be.

Structure of the Retina   If you were called upon to design the eyes for a NASA robot, the odds are that you would never think of making the robot's retina like yours. To begin with, the retina has ten distinct layers, with the rods and the cones making up the layer at the *bottom*. The tips of the rods and the cones, which contain the photosensitive chemicals that react to light, are actually pointed *away* from the outside world. For light to strike the rods and cones, it must first pass through all nine other layers of the retina. (See color Plate 16.)

The receptor cells in your skin are a part of the *peripheral nervous system* (°)—that is, they are nerve cells that lie outside the brain and spinal cord, which together make up what is called the *central nervous system* (°). The retina evolved directly from the brain, however, and is considered by some authorities to be almost a part of the central nervous system. The retina contains a great many "large neurons" that are very similar in structure to those found in your cortex. These "large neurons" begin the processing of visual information right in the retina, before sending messages along to your visual cortex (in the occipital lobes at the back of your brain). Along with the blood vessels that serve the retina, these information-processing "large neurons" make up much of the tissue found in the other layers of the retina. Light must pass through these "large neurons" and the blood vessels before it can stimulate the rods and cones. Since these "large neurons"—like the rods, cones, and the blood vessels—are almost totally transparent, they seldom interfere with your vision.

The Blind Spot   It is probably hard for you to imagine that each of your eyes has a spot that is, for all practical purposes, totally blind—and that there is actually a

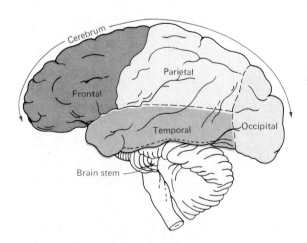

Close your left eye and stare at the crossed dot with the book held about 6 inches away. The face should disappear.

"hole" in your visual field where you see nothing at all. And yet, this is the case. Your retina is *inside* your eyeball, which is hollow like a balloon. The blood vessels that feed the rods and cones must somehow get into this balloon, and out again. And the axonic end-fibers from the "large neurons" must somehow get through the walls of the eyeball if they are to reach their destinations in the brain. All these axons meet at a point near the fovea to form the *optic nerve* (°), which exits from the eye at the *blind spot*. There are no receptors at this point in the retina—only axonic fibers and blood vessels—and so the part of your visual world that falls on the blind spot is not recorded in the brain.

You are usually unaware of the blind spot because your brain "cheats" and fills in the hole by making the empty spot in your visual world look like whatever surrounds it. You can prove this to yourself by following the instructions given in the figure shown above. If you look at the picture from just the right position, the man's face disappears. But notice too that the spot where the man's face should be is filled in by the brain with the wavy lines that surround the man's picture.

Your brain is constantly making assumptions about the world around you and filling in details which are not actually there. As we will see later, we all have *psychological* blind spots that affect our perceptions of the people around us.

OPTICAL DEFECTS

Near-sightedness and Far-sightedness

Many distortions of the visual world are caused by misinterpretations by the brain, but quite a few distortions stem from physiological problems with the eye itself. The chances are one in four that you either wear glasses or should wear them to help you overcome correctable visual difficulties. For the most part, these problems come from slight abnormalities in the *shape* of the eyeball.

If your eyeball is *too long*, the lens tends to focus the visual image a little *in front* of your retina rather than directly on it. Under these circumstances, you would see near objects rather clearly, but distant objects would appear fuzzy and blurred to you—a condition known as *near-sightedness* (°).

If your eyeball is *too short*, the lens tends to focus the visual image *behind* the retina rather than directly on it, making close objects indistinct while distant objects are usually in clear focus. Such a condition is known as *far-sightedness* (°).

If you watch carefully in the next movie you attend, you may notice something like the following: a man sitting close to the camera is talking with a woman on the other side of the room. When the man is speaking, the camera focuses on his face, which you see clearly, but the image of the distant woman is blurred and fuzzy. This is the way that the near-sighted person typically sees the world. Now, as the dialogue in the movie continues and the woman begins to speak, the camera shifts focus (but not position). Suddenly the man's face, which is close to the camera, becomes blurred while the distant image of the woman sharpens and becomes distinct. This is the way the far-sighted person typically sees things in the world around him or her.

Optic nerve (op-tick). The bundle of axonic "telephone cables" running from the eye to the brain.

Near-sightedness. If the eyeball is too long, the lens may focus the visual image so that near objects are clear, but distant objects are fuzzy. Usually correctable with glasses.

Far-sightedness. If the eyeball is too short, the lens may focus the visual image so that near objects are fuzzy, but distant objects are clear. Usually corectable with glasses.

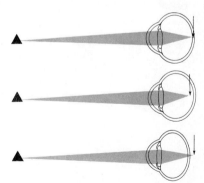

A normal, near-sighted, and far-sighted eye. Notice where the image ends at the arrow in each case.

Old-sightedness. See presbyopia.
Presbyopia (prez-bee-OH-pee-ah).
Also called "old-sightedness." A type
of far-sightedness associated with
aging. Older people often hold books
or newspapers far away from them because they cannot see near objects as
clearly as can most young people.

Snellen chart (SNELL-en). A visual
test devised by a Dutch eye doctor
named Herman Snellen. The chart
usually has a big "E" at the top, with
smaller letters underneath.

Old-sightedness

The lens in your eye operates much the same as does a camera lens, changing the focus from far to near as the occasion demands. As you grow older, however, your lenses gradually become brittle, and you cannot focus as readily on *near* objects. This condition is called *old-sightedness* (°), or *presbyopia* (°). (The Greek word *presby* means "old," or "old man"; the Presbyterian Church is governed by a Council of Elders, or presbys.)

Since everyone becomes more far-sighted as he or she grows older, the near-sighted individual may actually find his or her vision apparently improving with age. Far-sighted people have by far the worst of the lot, since their vision not only deteriorates with age but they also are subject to severe headaches if they misuse their eyes. The near-sighted person generally does not suffer as much from headaches induced by eyestrain.

Visual Discrimination

When you go to an eye doctor to be tested for glasses, or when (in most states) you apply for a driver's license, you will be given one of several tests to determine how accurately your eyes *discriminate* small objects. One very common visual test is the *Snellen chart* (°), which presents letters of different sizes for you to read. A person with normal vision can barely read the largest letter on this chart at a distance of 200 feet (60 meters), and can just make out the next largest letters standing 100 feet (30 meters) away. One line of letters can barely be discriminated 20 feet (6 meters) away by the person with normal sight.

If you took this test yourself, you probably would be asked to stand 20 feet away from the Snellen chart. If you could read the "normal" line of letters at this distance, we would say that you can "see at 20 feet what the normal person can see at 20 feet," hence you would have 20/20 vision. If you stood 20 feet away from the chart and could only read what the normal person can easily see at 100 feet, your vision would be 20/100, which is fairly poor. But if you could make out the very small letters when you were standing 20 feet away—letters that the normal person could discriminate only if he or she moved up to 10 feet away from the chart—then you would have 20/10 or very superior visual acuity.

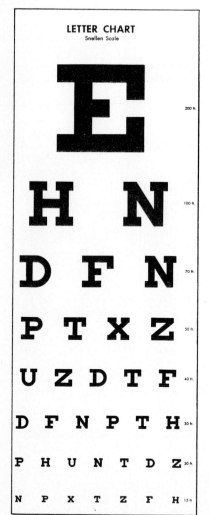

LETTER CHART
Snellen Scale

E — 200 ft.
H N — 100 ft.
D F N — 70 ft.
P T X Z — 50 ft.
U Z D T F — 40 ft.
D F N P T H — 30 ft.
P H U N T D Z — 20 ft.
N P X T Z F H — 15 ft.

The Snellen chart.

VISUAL SENSITIVITY

Discrimination of objects in your visual world typically depends on cone vision. The reflexes of your eye are so arranged that the visual image of anything you want to inspect closely will fall on your fovea, where there are hundreds of thousands of tiny cones packed together in an area about the size of the head of a pin. During the daylight hours, when there is plenty of illumination, color vision dominates and the details of objects in your visual world are easy to make out. But at night (or in any dim illumination), when you are often more interested in *detecting* faint sources of light than in *discriminating* fine details, the rods come into play. The rods are much more sensitive to light than are the cones—which is to say that the rods are better light detectors than the cones are.

Visual Adaptation

When you first go into a darkened theater, you can barely make out the shapes of the people sitting around you. After you have been sitting in the theater for a while, however, you may notice that you can see quite well. As you go from bright to dim illumination, both the rods and the cones *adapt* or *habituate* to the change. In fairly dim light the photo-sensitive chemicals in both the rods and cones are built up by the eye much more rapidly than they are broken down. The more of these chemicals present in the receptors, the more sensitive the rods and cones are to faint sources of light. *Dark adaptation* is mostly a matter of a surplus of rhodopsin (visual purple) in the rods and a surplus of various other photo-sensitive chemicals in the cones.

When you sit in complete darkness, your cones adapt quickly. They become almost as sensitive as they are going to get in a matter of 10 minutes or so. The rods adapt much more slowly and are still adapting even after 30 minutes of darkness. When completely adapted to the dark, the rods are a thousand times more sensitive than the cones.

QUESTION: **How long do you think an airplane pilot should be required to adapt to the dark before he or she is allowed to fly at night?**

Night-blindness

Some people do not see at all well at night. Usually this defect is caused by some disability of the rods. Night-blindness may have many causes, but a lack of Vitamin A is perhaps the most common one. Vitamin A is necessary for the build-up of rhodopsin (visual purple) in the rods. Since yellow vegetables, such as carrots, often contain large amounts of Vitamin A, these vegetables are often recommended to night-blind persons.

Even a normal individual may have difficulties seeing at night, however, without special training. For under very dim illumination, the cones are non-functional. When you try to stare at something in the dark, your eye reflexes work against you. That is, your eyes may attempt to focus the image of the object on your fovea (the proper thing to do in daylight hours). But the fovea contains only cones, hence is "blind" in dim light. If you want to see something at night, don't try to look directly at it or you may not be able to see it at all. Instead, remember that the rods are most numerous in the periphery of the retina. At night, you should direct your gaze a little to the right or left of the object you are trying to see. When you stare to one side of the object, its image will fall on the periphery of the retina, where the rods are, and you will be able to make it out much better than if you look directly at it. It is for this reason that sentries and lookouts are trained to look at dimly-illuminated objects "out of the corners of their eyes."

QUESTION: **If someone threw a baseball at you at night, why might you not be able to see it if you stared directly at it?**

Some animals have eyes that contain no cones at all, while others have eyes that contain nothing but cones. Bats and many other *nocturnal* (°) animals have *only rods* in their eyes. The bat is not blind; it merely lacks daylight vision and hence is easily blinded by bright lights. At night, when the bat flies about catching insects, it uses its ears rather than its eyes for navigation purposes. Most bats emit short bursts of high-pitched squeaks or squeals as they fly. The frequency of these noises is as high as 100,000 Hz, far above the range of human hearing. During each brief squeak, a muscle in the bat's ear automatically "turns off" its power to hear so that it does not deafen itself. After each squeak, the ear opens again so the bat can hear. The bat then listens for echoes of its own squeak.

If there is nothing in front of the bat as it is flying, it hears no echo. But if it is heading toward an object, the bat hears the echo of its own squeak and can locate the object almost instantly. Small objects (such as insects) make quite different echoes than do large objects. Bats can see at night as well as you can, but their echo-location powers are so much greater than their visual abilities that they pay attention to what they hear rather than what they see.

QUESTION: **Chickens have eyes that contain only cones; at twilight, when you can see**

Nocturnal (knock-TURN-ull). From the Latin word meaning "of the night." People (and other animals) who are more active at night than during the day are said to be "nocturnal." A nocturnal emission is a "wet dream"—that is, unconscious sexual activity (at night) while asleep.

Bechstein's flying bat at night.

Hue (rhymes with "few"). The colors of the rainbow, or of the visible spectrum. Technically speaking, "color" includes not only the hues of the rainbow, but all the mixtures of hues plus blacks, whites, and grays. Black and white are not considered hues. Pink (red + white) is a color; its hue, however, is red.

Saturation (sat-your-RAY-shun). The intensity of a color. Pink is a weak (desaturated) red. The colors of the rainbow are about as saturated as any colors can be.

Mixture chart. There are, in fact, two types of color mixtures—additive and subtractive. When you mix colored lights by shining them on a screen, you are adding one color to the other. When you mix two paints or pigments, you are actually subtracting out all the colors except the two that you mix. If you combine a pure yellow and a pure blue light, the additive mixture will be gray. If you combine yellow and blue paints, you sometimes get a green because the paints are frequently impure hues. The yellow paint will subtract out all the colors of the spectrum except yellow (and a little green). The blue paint will subtract out all the colors except blue (and a little green). The yellow and blue cancel each other out, leaving just the green. However, if the paints were absolutely pure hues, mixing yellow and blue would give you black or gray. In this chapter, when we speak of mixing colors, we will always refer to *additive* mixtures.

Complementary colors. From the Latin word meaning "to fill up, to complete, to make up what is missing." Any two colors are complementary if they are opposite each other on the color circle. When mixed together, complementary colors yield a neutral color such as white or gray. White light is really a mixture of two or more light waves whose colors are complementary. Every color in the rainbow has its complementary. Sunlight appears whitish because it contains relatively equal amounts of all the rainbow colors; hence it includes each color's complementary.

perfectly well, the chicken is almost blind and hence retires to its roost. Can you figure out what the old farm expression "going to bed with the chickens" actually means?

COLOR VISION

When you speak of the color of something, you are really talking about that object's *hue* (°). The reds, greens, blues, and yellows—and all the shades in between—are the hues that your cones detect. Some hues (such as the four just mentioned) seem to be psychologically pure. That is, these hues do not seem to be a mixture of any other two colors. But some colors are obviously mixtures—orange seems a combination of red and yellow, chartreuse is a combination of yellow and green, and purple seems to have both red and blue components to it. Most of the colors of the rainbow (the visible spectrum) are mixtures of two or more of the psychologically pure hues—red, green, blue, and yellow.

But where does purple appear in a rainbow? Or brown, for that matter? Because the rainbow lacks many of the red-blue mixture colors, psychologists prefer to work with a color circle made by joining the ends of the rainbow. Arranged around the outer edge of this circle are all of the spectral colors that we can see, and any color found on the circle can be made by mixing two or more of the four pure hues. (See color Plate 3.)

Saturation

Hue alone is not enough to explain all of the colorful visual experiences that you have. For example, what two hues mixed together make pink? Red and blue? Red and yellow? No, pink is not a mix of any two hues, but rather is a weak or very diluted red. The vividness or richness of a color is what we call *saturation* (°).

Suppose you took a fish bowl and filled it with tap water. What color is it? Now, let's suppose further that you emptied a bottle of red food coloring into the water and stirred it well. If the dye is strong enough, the water should look a rich, ruby red. But now, suppose you start pouring more colorless tap water into the bowl. What happens to that rich red color when you begin to dilute it? It changes slowly to pink. You have not added any new hue to the red, you have merely weakened the hue that was already there. In more technical terms, you have desaturated the red by adding a neutral color. Pastel colors, in general, are desaturated versions of the more basic hues found on the color circle.

The hues around the outer edge of the color circle were carefully picked to be the most saturated possible. As you move inward, toward the center of the circle, the colors become less and less saturated until you reach gray, which has no hue at all. By definition, black, white, and gray are considered completely desaturated.

The color circle is actually a *mixture chart* (°) that tells you what would happen if you mixed any two colors on the circle. Suppose you want to know what colors would result from mixing a pure red and a pure green light. Simply draw a line between these two hues on the chart. If you start with a pure red and add a little green to it, the mixture will become orangish. More green turns the mix yellowish, and still more turns it yellowish-green. As you can tell from where the line is on the chart, all of these mixture colors will be less saturated than the pure hues with which you started.

Now, what would happen if you mixed a red light with turquoise? Draw the line and see if you can predict the results. Would the mix turn orange or yellowish? Purple or bluish? No, it would go from red to pink to gray to pale turquoise to a fairly saturated turquoise. Red and turquoise, being directly opposite each other, are *complementary colors* (°). Any two lights that are complementary colors, when mixed in fairly equal amounts, will give a neutral color such as gray.

Color Mixtures

If your color vision is normal, you can take any three fairly widely-spaced hues from the color circle and, by mixing various amounts of *just these three hues*, reproduce all the colors of the rainbow. The people who design color television sets take advantage of this fact by putting three (and only three) photo-sensitive pigments in their picture tubes. Color TV cameras actually are triplets—that is, they usually have three quite separate TV systems inside them. When such a camera "shoots" a picture of your face, one system records all the red coloring in your face, a second system records all the blue coloring, and a third system records your face in terms of green-yellow. The TV system then mixes these colors electronically in just the right proportions to give the precise tint of your skin color (and your eyes, hair, teeth, and so on).

Although your eye works quite differently, the cones in your eye also appear to record the world in terms of the three primary colors (plus the black-and-white version recorded by the rods). The various sensory centers in your brain—primarily the visual cortex in your occipital lobes—then "mix" these colors neurophysiologically to give you the perception of "living color."

QUESTION: **On many color TV sets, blacks and whites seem to be tinged with an off-shade of green; why do you think this happens?**

COLOR-BLINDNESS

When tested in a psychological laboratory, many people appear to need abnormally large amounts of one of the three "mix" colors in order to reproduce all the hues of the rainbow. These people appear to be "color weak," although they can indeed see every color that a normal individual can see. A man who is "red weak" (the most common color deficiency) would need to mix much more red with blue than normally in order to see a good "purple" hue. To a normal person, of course, such a mixture would look very reddish—but the red-weak person sees it as being an "equal" mix of red and blue. Most color-weak individuals show a deficiency either in their response to red, or to green, or to both these hues.

About 5 percent of the people in the world are almost totally blind to one or more hues on the color circle, although they can see some other hues perfectly well. Most of these *partially color-blind* people are men, for, as we will see in a later chapter, color-blindness is an inherited deficiency, and it seldom affects women.

The partially color-blind individual can reproduce all of the colors he or she can see by mixing just *two* basic hues. The main types of partial color-blindness involve a red-green deficiency or a blue-yellow deficiency. Although there are several kinds of red-green blindness, a person who suffers from any one of them will see the world almost entirely in blues and yellows (plus black and white). A bright red fire engine will look a dull yellow to such a person, while grass would appear a desaturated blue. The rare person who is blue-yellow blind sees the world entirely in reds and greens (plus black and white).

Although the exact mechanism for partial color-blindness is not fully understood, psychologists assume that the cones are somehow responsible. There appear to be several different types of cones, each of which may be responsive to different wave-lengths. The person who is partially or totally blind to red stimuli, for instance, may have been born with few if any of the cones that respond to wave-lengths greater than 600 nanometers. There are many different theories of color vision that attempt to explain how normal people see color and why some other people don't see colors as they should. To date, none of the theories has proved itself fully acceptable to all psychologists.

Holmgren wools (HOLM-grin). A color vision test devised by a Swedish scientist named Alarik F. Holmgren. The test consists of strands of colored wool yarns that the subject must sort according to their hues. The test is seldom used these days.

Albinism (AL-bin-ism). From the Greek word meaning "white." Albinos suffer from an inherited condition that prevents their skin and eyes from developing the normal pigments that color our skins and allow our cones to respond to colored stimuli.

Color-blindness Tests

Odd as it may seem, many partially color-blind individuals reach maturity without knowing that they have a visual defect. Psychologist Karl Dallenbach, mentioned in an earlier chapter, learned of his red-green blindness in an introductory psychology class. Students in the class, of whom Dallenbach was one, were seated alphabetically to make checking class attendance easier for the teacher, and Dallenbach was in the front row. During lectures on vision the professor wished to demonstrate an old color-blindness test called the *Holmgren wools* (°). The test consists of a large number of strands of colored wool that the subject is asked to sort into various piles according to their hues. Dallenbach was tapped for the honor of being a subject simply because he was right under the teacher's nose.

When asked to sort all the reds into one pile, Dallenbach included all the wools with a greenish hue as well as those that were clearly red. When asked to sort all the greens, he included all the reds. At first the teacher thought that Dallenbach was playing a joke, but subsequent tests proved that he was red-green blind. Like most partially color-blind individuals, Dallenbach had learned to compensate for his deficiency while growing up. Since everyone said ordinary grass was green, he saw it as being somehow different from red roses—although, under controlled conditions, Dallenbach could not tell the color of grass from that of most red roses.

The Holmgren wools are but one (and perhaps the least accurate) of many different tests for color deficiencies. Most of the other tests contain dots of various colors so arranged that someone with normal vision sees letters, numbers, or geometric figures in the dots, while a person with partial color-blindness will see only a random jumble of dots or a different number than would the normal person. (See color Plate 4.)

QUESTION: **What could be done to help red-green blind drivers interpret traffic signals correctly?**

Total Color-blindness

Only about one person in 40,000 is totally color-blind. A few of these individuals were born with normal color vision but lost their ability to discriminate hue as a result of disease, or from being poisoned by such pollutants as lead or carbon disulfide. Such people can often recover at least some of their color vision if given proper therapy—which often includes large doses of Vitamin A.

Most totally color-blind people suffer from *albinism* (°), an inherited condition involving a lack of pigment throughout their bodies. Like the albino rabbits and rats, these people have colorless hair, dead white skin, and pinkish eyes. Since the photo-sensitive chemicals in the cones are, in fact, *pigments*, albino people lack cones that are functional and cannot see color at all.

All albino humans have foveas that are totally blind, so the albino must learn to defeat the usual instinctual reflexes that tend to focus images in the area of the fovea. Most albinos develop rather jerky eye movements that prevent their visual images from focusing in on the fovea, but even so, their visual acuity is well below average. For if they look straight at something, it disappears from their sight. Since they have only rod (or night) vision, albinos find normal day illumination blinding to them. They compensate by learning to keep their eyelids half-closed or by wearing dark glasses even when they are indoors.

There is no cure for this condition, but most albinos learn to live with their problem and enjoy fairly normal lives in spite of their visual handicap.

SUMMARY

1. The stimulus input for vision is light.
2. Light is usually produced as waves of very tiny energy particles called "photons." Whenever you strike a match or turn on a lamp, you produce millions and millions of photons.
3. The frequency of a light wave helps determine the color the light will appear to be. The amplitude (strength) of the light wave generally determines how bright it will seem.
4. The visible spectrum (or rainbow of colors) runs from blue through green, yellow, and orange to red.
5. Beyond the blue end of the spectrum lie the ultra-violet ("black light") rays and the X-rays. Beyond the red end of the rainbow lie the heat waves.
6. The eye is something like a color television camera. Light enters the eye through the cornea and aqueous humor, then passes through the pupil, the lens, and the vitreous humor. The light then strikes the retina, which is where sight begins.
7. The retina is the inner surface of the hollow eyeball.
8. The retina contains the visual receptors—the rods and cones—which have within them photo-sensitive chemicals that respond to light by firing off a message to the visual centers of the brain.
9. The cones are sensitive to all the colors, including whites and grays. The rods see the world only in shades of gray.
10. In the center of the retina is a small pit called the fovea that contains only cones. Vision is at its sharpest when the visual image falls on the fovea.
11. Near the fovea is the blind spot, which contains no visual receptors. The optic nerve, which runs from the retina to the brain, exits from the eyeball at the blind spot.
12. The apparent color of an object is affected not only by the wave-lengths it puts out or reflects into the eye, but also by your own knowledge of what the color should be.
13. Near-sighted people typically see close objects clearly, but distant objects may appear fuzzy to them.
14. Far-sighted people see distant objects more clearly than close objects.
15. We all tend to become far-sighted as we age.
16. A person with normal visual acuity, or keenness of vision, is said to have 20/20 vision, meaning the person can see at a distance of 20 feet what the average person can see at a distance of 20 feet (6 meters).
17. The eye has a tremendous ability to adjust to the amount of light available to it. When you sit in the dark, your rods and cones adapt to this decrease in light intensity. Adaptation to the dark is mostly complete in about 30 minutes or so.
18. The rods are more sensitive at night (or in dim illumination) than are the cones. If your rods don't function as they should, you are likely to have more trouble seeing in the dark than the normal person—a condition known as "night-blindness."
19. Because the rods are color-blind, it is difficult to see colors accurately in dim illumination.
20. Colors have both hue (red, green, blue, yellow) and saturation; the more intense or rich a color is, the more saturated it is.
21. Black, white, and gray have no saturation at all.
22. Two colors which, when mixed together, yield a neutral color such as gray are said to be complementary colors.
23. If a person has trouble seeing some colors, the person is said to be partially color-blind.
24. Men tend to be partially color-blind much more frequently than women.
25. The most common form of partial color-blindness is the failure to see reds and/or greens as people with normal color vision do.
26. Albino humans and animals lack the pigments necessary for normal color vision; they are therefore totally color-blind.

(Continued from page 159.)

"All right, class. Why do you think Johnny W. couldn't see the ball when it was thrown at him?" Mrs. Carson asked her students.

After a pause one young woman held up her hand. "Let's see if we can review the clues you gave us. You said the light hurt his eyes, that he had to wear sunglasses outdoors, and that he was behind in his reading scores. Sounds like he had a visual problem of some kind."

"Beautiful," Mrs. Carson said smiling. "Go on. What else?"

"The kids called him Bunny Rabbit because he looked so pale," a young man in the back of the room said. "And you mentioned that his hair was cotton white. Mrs. Carson, could Johnny W. be an albino?"

"Good thinking! Yes, Johnny W. was an albino."

A student in the front row became furious. "But you could have told us that! Anybody would have noticed that right away!"

"Perhaps. Perhaps not. When he wore his dark glasses, and you couldn't see the pink color of his eyes, Johnny looked like a very pale but normal blond child."

The angry student persisted. "But it wasn't fair not to tell us. That was his whole problem!"

"No, I don't think so. His problem was that people don't understand the visual difficulties that an albino has. His parents didn't understand; Johnny didn't understand; and neither did the other kids in school. But what if he hadn't been an albino? What if a normal-looking young boy came to you in tears because his art teacher threw him out of class insisting that he had no talent? What might his mismatched clothes have told you about him then?"

"Of course!" cried a young woman. "He was color-blind!"

Mrs. Carson smiled approvingly. "At least one boy in 20 has problems identifying colors correctly, and most of them don't realize it when they're in elementary school. Would you expect such a boy to do well in an art class? And shouldn't you keep your eyes open for such clues?"

One of the students in the third row frowned. "I still don't see why he couldn't see the ball. Was it a funny color or something?"

"Anyone who is totally color-blind has frightful visual problems. The entire center of Johnny's visual world was blank, because the color receptors are located in the center of the eye. When Johnny tried to look straight ahead, he was blind as a bat. He could only see things out of the corner of his eye. If you threw a ball at him, it would simply disappear when he tried to focus on it."

The class thought about that for a moment.

Then a young student asked, "What did you tell him to do?"

Mrs. Carson leaned back against the desk again. "What would you have told him to do? You're the ones learning to be counselors."

The young man considered the matter, then continued. "I would have told him to get the hell out of baseball. Find something else that he could do that would make him popular with the other kids."

"Something he could do indoors or at night, so his eyes wouldn't hurt," said another.

"A musician! He could learn to play the guitar, and then perform at dances and parties and things like that," said a third.

"Yeah, that way he could wear his shades even when he was inside," said a fourth. "If anybody asked him about it, he could just say that he was practicing to be a musician, because they wear dark glasses even in the middle of the night."

"And lots of rock stars wear wild-colored clothes anyhow, so he shouldn't worry if his socks didn't match," said a fifth.

Mrs. Carson closed her eyes as if to picture the scene in her mind. "I see what you mean," she said. "A colorful solution to a case of black-and-white vision!"

RECOMMENDED READINGS

Geldard, R. Frank. *The Human Senses,* 2nd ed. (New York: John Wiley & Sons, Inc., 1972).

Teevan, Richard C., and Robert C. Birney, eds., *Color Vision* (Princeton, N.J.: D. Van Nostrand Company, Inc., 1961).

chapter 9
"BLACK BOXES AND WOMB TANKS"

SENSORY DEPRIVATION

DID YOU KNOW THAT . . .

When you are deprived of your normal sensory inputs, you may lose voluntary control of your thoughts and actions?

A person who gains complete control of your sensory inputs can brainwash you into making profound changes in your personality?

A person who gains even partial control over your inputs can often indoctrinate you into accepting new beliefs and attitudes?

Human subjects who underwent relatively complete sensory deprivation experienced hallucinations, distortions in their body images, and long "blank periods" in which they couldn't really think at all?

One scientist who immersed himself in a tank of warm water for several hours believed that he had returned to the womb?

Sensory inputs reach your brain by two pathways, the straight-line system and the reticular activating system?

The reticular activating system keeps the rest of your brain alert?

Your brain has built-in mechanisms to protect you against brainwashing and indoctrination?

Philip Cassone laughed when they shut the door. This was going to be a cinch, no doubt about it. Imagine those crazy psychologists wanting to pay him $20 a day just for doing nothing. Plus room and board. He just might stay here for weeks, maybe for months! Let them go bankrupt as far as he was concerned.

The bed he was lying on was narrow but comfortable. The long cardboard tubes into which his arms were stuck were annoying, but Phil was sure he could adjust to them with little difficulty. The goggles that he wore let in some light, but the glass was milky and transluscent and he couldn't make out any details of the room he was in. He knew it was small, though—maybe 4 feet (1.2 meters) wide by 9 or 10 feet (2.7 or 3.0 meters) long. Big enough to live in if you didn't move around very much, and the crazy psychologists were paying him for not moving. The walls were painted black, so you couldn't see much even without the glasses. All Phil could hear was the quiet, gentle, soothing whirr of an air-conditioning unit. Black and quiet, that's what the room was. Phil yawned, stretched a little on the narrow bed, and relaxed. A lead-pipe cinch, that's what it was going to be, he thought as he drifted gently off into sleep.

Some time later Phil awoke. He had a moment of panic when he couldn't remember just where he was, but then he smiled and relaxed. "Inside the little black box," that's where he was. He must have slept for, oh, maybe 3 hours. Or was it more like 4 or 5? Phil couldn't tell exactly, and that bothered him a bit. How long had he been in the room so far? 4 to 6 hours? How much had he earned? Maybe five dollars? Not bad for just sleeping.

A few minutes later Phil decided that he needed to go to the bathroom, so he yelled out, "I want to go to the john." There was a microphone in the room that carried his voice to the crazy psychologists in the next room. At least, he hoped they were still there. They could talk to him too, over a loudspeaker hanging on the wall, but so far they hadn't said anything at all. The door opened and someone came in and touched him on the shoulder. Phil hopped out of bed and almost fell flat on his face. Funny he should be so clumsy. Maybe he was still half asleep. He spoke several times to the person leading him, but got no answer. After he had urinated, he was led back to the little black room by his silent escort.

Phil lay down on the bed again and started to think. He thought about his school work; he thought about his family; he gave serious attention to several girls he had encountered in recent weeks. And then, when he ran out of things to think about, he started over again. It was all getting pretty boring. Maybe he'd only stay in the room for a few weeks after all, until he had earned a few hundred dollars and could make a down payment on a new bike. What did that bike look like again? He could barely remember . . .

"Phil, are you awake?"

The voice sounded remote and at first he couldn't be sure that he wasn't imagining it.

"Hello, Phil, are you awake?"

He told the crazy psychologist he was, but his voice sounded odd and hollow to him.

"Okay, Phil, I want to give you some tests now. Are you ready?"

Phil said he was, and the voice came out of the haze again.

"All right, let's start with the letter H. How many words can you think of that begin with the letter H? Don't use verbs and don't use proper names. Go ahead and start."

H? What begins with H? Hell, for one thing. And Horse and House and Heart and Hurt and Help. And Hungry. Was he hungry? Maybe that was what was wrong. What would they give me for dinner? Maybe a hamburger. Oh, yes. Hamburger begins with H. And Horse. No, I said that. Horsemeat in the Hamburger. What else? Celery? No, that doesn't begin with an H. Helpless? Honda? No, that's a proper name. Hello out there. Funny, there must be more words in the English language that begin with H. Happy? No, that wasn't a word, was it; it was more a state of mind. Head! Yes, head would do. He thought and thought.

"Is that enough?" he finally asked.

"If that's all you can think of, that's fine, Phil."

He smiled and relaxed. That ought to show them.

My God it was quiet. The silence seemed to stab at his eardrums like an ice pick. How could silence be so loud, so overwhelming, so bright? And the colors, the sparks of colors. Banners of different colors waving back and forth. The wallpaper was wiggling, writhing, pulsating, just the way it did the time Phil had tripped on LSD. A dark green clunking sound; could it be the air conditioner? More like an elephant stomping around. My God, a herd of elephants. Oh, that was pretty. Just sort of elephants in black, with pink and blue and purple . . . elephants moving. No, the elephants are standing still, aren't they; it's the picture that is moving; and the elephants are like cutouts in a moving picture. There they go, over the hill.

"Hey. You people listening in. Do you know there's a herd of elephants marching around in here?" Why don't they answer? And the quiet again. How long has it . . .

"Now, Phil, we have a series of records you can listen to if you wish. Would you like to hear them?"

Records? Why not? Maybe some good rock . . . But no, it's a voice talking about ghosts. Who the hell cares about ghosts? Dullsville. But at least it's a voice, talking. Yes, play another one. This is getting interesting. Yes, play another one . . . Heard that one before, but it sounds more sensible this time. Yes, play another one. Yes, again.

"Hey, what time is it? Why don't you answer? Don't you know I can't stay in here too long? Why don't you answer? It's been at least 24 hours, hasn't it? I've earned my 20 bucks, now tell me what time it is . . ."

Floating . . . Looking down . . . Who was that strange person lying on that little bed down there with the cardboard tubes on his arms? Maybe he was dead and nobody knew it . . .

There's that dark green clunking sound again. They must be letting something into the room. Last time it was elephants. Wonder what it is . . . My God, it's a spaceship. It's only six inches big, but it's a real spaceship. How did they manage that? It's buzzing around the room.

Hey, you crazy psychologists, what are you trying to pull? Get that spaceship out of here! Shooting at me, that's what it's doing; it's shooting tiny bullets at me.

Ouch! My God, I'm hit! Hey, you stupid people, stop that! If you don't stop that, I'll have to come out right away. You know that, what are you trying to do, make me quit? I can't take this much longer, that spaceship is going to kill me!

"What time is it, man? Why won't you talk to me? If you don't say something right now, I'm coming right out. Don't you understand, it's your fault!"

Philip Cassone stripped the tubes from his arms and jumped off the bed. He jerked the door open and marched into the room next door where two startled psychologists sat working at a table containing recording equipment.

"You bastards ruined the experiment. You made me come out."

(Continued on page 189.)

Whether you realize it or not, you spend most of your time and energy trying to predict and control your sensory inputs. Little wonder that you do, since most of your pleasures and rewards in life consist of such biological inputs as food, air, and water; intellectual inputs that lead to learning, growth, and understanding; and social inputs such as praise and affection that come from other people. Even the "joys of doing" can be considered inputs, since it is usually the feedback from our muscles (or the effects our actions have on our environments) that we find reinforcing. The study of sensory psychology is thus the necessary basis for our comprehension of such internal processes as perception, learning, motivation, attitudes, and personality. For you can't begin to grasp what goes on inside your head—what makes you tick—unless you can identify, measure, and to some extent control the stimuli that prompt your head to tick the way that it does.

Your senses are the window to your mind. But what would happen if someone drew heavy curtains over part or even all of that window? In the past three chapters we have asked you to consider what your life would be like if you lost *one* of your senses—vision, for example, or hearing. But what would happen to you if, as you were reading these lines, you suddenly lost *all* your sensory input? Not just vision and hearing, taste and smell, but your skin senses as well? In addition to being suddenly blind and deaf, what if you couldn't "feel" where your arms or legs were, or whether you were wearing clothes or were naked, or whether it was hot or cold? What if you couldn't determine whether any parts of your body were moving, or whether you were standing up or sitting down? How would you react to this frightful disaster?

Suppose, too, that after you had been floating in the dark, soundless, senseless void for many hours, you suddenly heard a voice talking to you. If this voice represented your *only* contact with the outside world, what kinds of emotional feelings would you be likely to develop toward that voice? And if this voice told you that many of your previous attitudes and beliefs had been improper and incorrect, would you believe the voice? And if the voice said that you had to throw certain evil thoughts out of your mind, would you agree to do so? If you did all this, would you say that you had been brainwashed?

The term *brainwashing* (°) seems first to have been used in print by the U.S. journalist Edward Hunter in his book *Brain-washing in Red China*, published by

Brainwashing. A term used by the Red Chinese to denote a "cleansing of the mind" of thoughts and beliefs disapproved by the Communist government. Brainwashing always involves isolating the individual almost completely from his or her normal inputs. This isolation can make the person so "hungry" for stimulation that he or she accepts uncritically anything that is said. If the deprivation continues for any length of time, it can cause very basic changes in the individual's personality. In the United States the word is sometimes incorrectly used to mean any situation in which one person tries to trick another into changing or conforming.

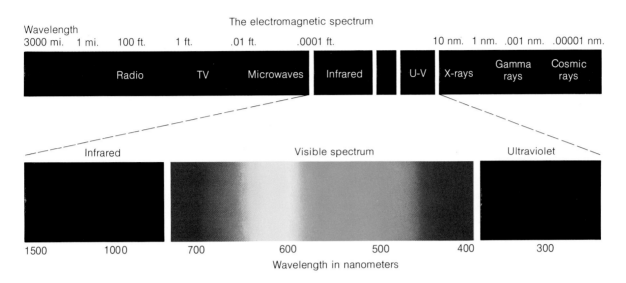

The electromagnetic spectrum

Wavelength
3000 mi. 1 mi. 100 ft. 1 ft. .01 ft. .0001 ft. 10 nm. 1 nm. .001 nm. .00001 nm.

| Radio | TV | Microwaves | Infrared | | U-V | X-rays | Gamma rays | Cosmic rays |

Infrared | Visible spectrum | Ultraviolet

1500   1000   700   600   500   400   300

Wavelength in nanometers

PLATE 1 The full spectrum of electromagnetic radiation. The human eye can see only the narrow band extending from 400 to 700 nanometers in wavelength. A nanometer is the equivalent to one-billionth of a meter (one meter=39.37 inches). (From Bourne and Ekstrand, 1976)

PLATE 2 The purple-blue to yellow color solid on the left is viewed from the green side. The yellow to purple-blue range on the right is viewed form the red side. (Munsell Color, Macbeth Division of Kollmorgen Corporation)

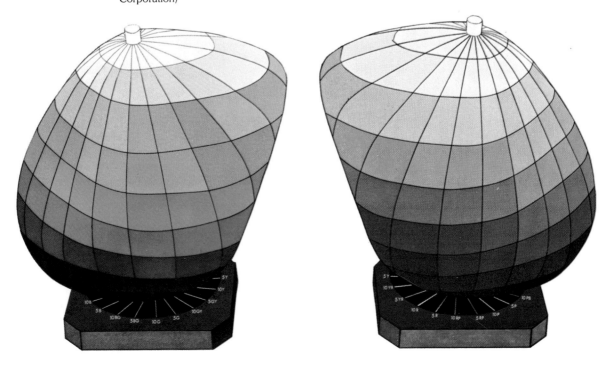

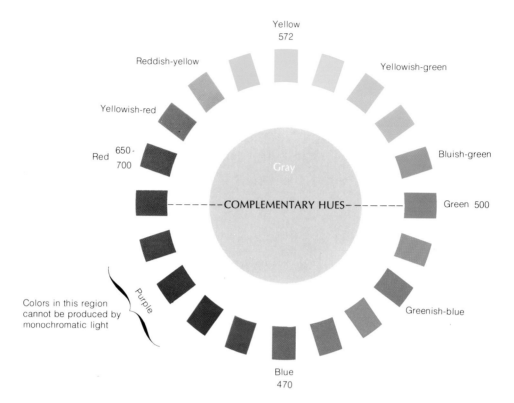

PLATE 3 The color circle illustrates the facts of color and color light mixture. The color names and their corresponding wavelengths (in nanometers) are given along the outside of the circle. Complementary colors are those colors opposite each other in the circle (such as reddish-yellow and greenish-blue); they will result in gray when mixed. The mixing of any two other wavelengths gives us an intermediate color. For example, equal amounts of reddish-yellow and green yield yellow. Some colors such as purple (a mixture of yellowish-red and blue) cannot be produced by a single wavelength, or monochromatic light. By proper mixing of three wavelengths equidistant in the circle (such as blue, green, and reddish-yellow), we can produce all color sensations. (From Bourne and Ekstrand, 1976)

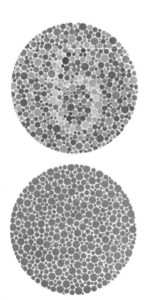

PLATE 4 These two illustrations are from a series of color-blindness tests. In the top plate, people with normal vision see a number 6, while those with red-green color-blindness do not. Those with normal vision see a number 12 in the bottom plate; red-green blind people may see one number or none. These reproductions of color recognition tests cannot be used for actual testing. The examples are only representative of the total of 15 charts necessary for a complete color recognition examination. (American Optical Corporation from their AO Pseudo-Isochromatic Color Tests)

PLATE 5 Look at the design on the cover of this book. A person with normal color vision would see all the colors. At the top left of the page the cover design is reproduced as it might look to someone with red-green color-blindness; and at the top right as a person with yellow-blue color-blindness might see it. At right is a black-and-white reproduction of the cover design as a totally color-blind person might see it.

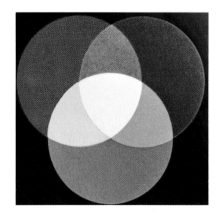

PLATE 6A Additive color mixture. By shining a light of a single wavelength onto a white surface, we will see the color that corresponds to that wavelength because the surface reflects only that wavelength to our eyes. However, if two lights of different wavelengths are shined on the surface together, the surface reflects both wavelengths which add together to produce an additive mixture. In fact, the complete color spectrum can be produced by mixing three properly chosen wavelengths in correct proportions. (Inmont Corporation)

PLATE 6B Subtractive color mixture. Now if we mix paints (instead of colors) the color we see is produced by subtraction. For example, when yellow paint is mixed with blue paint, the yellow paint absorbs or subtracts non-yellow wavelengths from the blue paint, leaving the wavelengths between yellow and blue—resulting in green. As this plate shows, we can produce a variety of colors by subtractive mixtures of three properly selected paints. (Inmont Corporation)

PLATE 7 Vincent van Gogh's "The Starry Night" (1889) illustrates the painter's imperfect sensory perception. Look at the concentric rings of color around the "starry lights." (Oil on canvas, 29x36¼". Collection, The Museum of Modern Art, New York. Acquired through the Lillie P. Bliss Bequest)

PLATE 9 A sixteenth-century Persian miniature from the manuscript of *A King's Book of King's,* "Zal receives Mihrab's homage at Kabul." The artist's work illustrates the flat perspective often used by Eastern painters. Look especially at the canopy over Zal's head. (From the Collection of Arthur A. Houghton, Jr., 1970; The Metropolitan Museum of Art)

PLATE 8 Jan van Eyck's "The Madonna of Chancellor Rolin," a fifteenth-century painting showing the property of linear perspective. (Shostal Associates, Inc.)

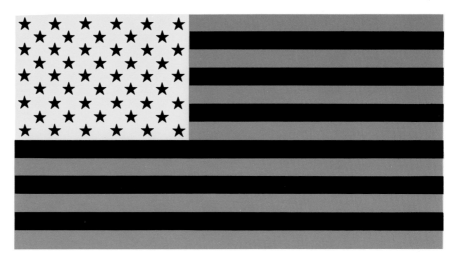

PLATE 10   Stare at the center of this flag for about 30 seconds. Then look at a white wall or sheet of paper. You will see a negative after-image in the colors complementary to those shown here.

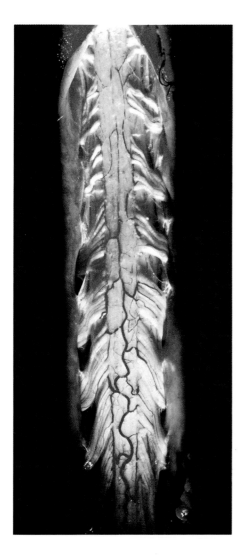

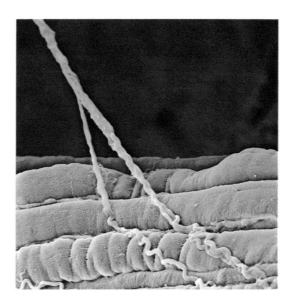

PLATE 11   Photograph of the nerve-muscle synapse. Axonic fibers (upper left) reach down to make a synapse with thick muscle fibers. (Photograph by Lennart Nilsson from *Behold Man.* ©1973 by Albert Bonniers Förlag, Stockholm, published by Little, Brown & Company, Boston, 1974.)

PLATE 12   The spinal cord viewed from the rear, shown with the backbone removed. (Photograph by Lennart Nilsson from *Behold Man.* ©1973 by Albert Bonniers Förlag, Stockholm, published by Little, Brown & Company, Boston, 1974.)

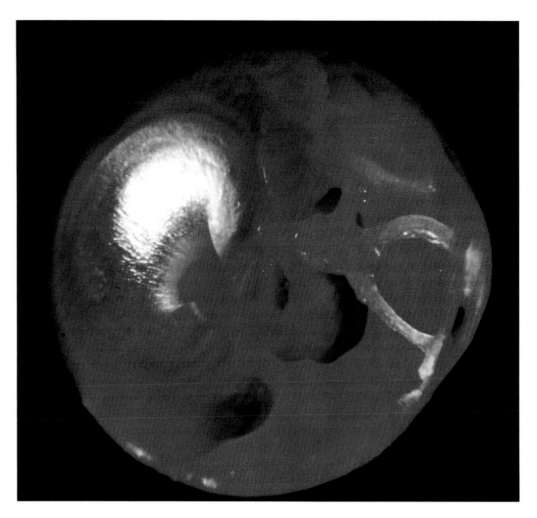

PLATE 13   A cross section of the middle ear. The hammer is connected to the eardrum which is the
bright spot in the middle of the photograph. The stirrup, seen on the right, is connected to the oval window. The anvil connects the hammer to the stirrup. (Photograph by Lennart Nilsson from *Behold Man*.
©1973 by Albert Bonniers Förlag, Stockholm, published by Little, Brown & Company, Boston, 1974.)

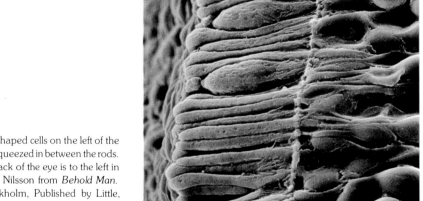

PLATE 14   The rods are the slim, pencil-shaped cells on the left of the
photograph; the cones are the two fat cells squeezed in between the rods.
Light enters the retina from the right; the back of the eye is to the left in
this photograph. (Photograph by Lennart Nilsson from *Behold Man*.
©1973 by Albert Bonniers Förlag, Stockholm, Published by Little,
Brown & Company, Boston, 1974.)

PLATE 15 A cross section of the fovea, which is a pit in the center of the retina where vision is clearest. The two black bands to the left are supporting cells that help process visual inputs. The third band of cells from the left is made up of rods and cones. Light enters from the left; the back of the eye is to the right. (Photograph by Lennart Nilsson from *Behold Man*. ©1973 by Albert Bonniers Förlag, Stockholm, published by Little, Brown & Company, Boston, 1974.)

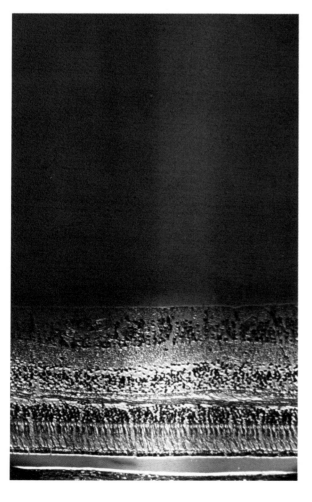

PLATE 16 A cross section of the retina showing all ten layers. The rods and cones are at the bottom. (Photograph by Lennart Nilsson from *Behold Man*. ©1973 by Albert Bonniers Förlag, Stockholm, published by Little, Brown & Company, Boston, 1974.)

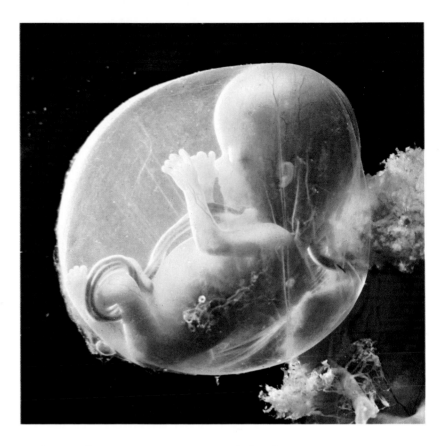

PLATE 17 The human fetus, three months old. It is about three inches (7.6 centimeters) long and weighs about an ounce (28 grams). (Photograph by Lennart Nilsson from *Behold Man.* ©1973 by Albert Bonniers Förlag, Stockholm, published by Little, Brown & Company, Boston, 1974.)

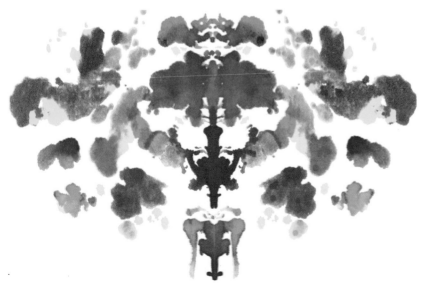

PLATE 18 This water color is similar to the colorful inkblots used in the Rorschach test. A psychologist can gather data about an individual's personality by asking that person to report what he or she sees in the inkblots.

Vanguard Press in 1951. Hunter took the term from the Chinese words *hsi nao*, which literally mean "to wash the brain." As we will see, the technique the Chinese used to "scrub people's minds" involved isolating the individual from almost all the person's normal sensory inputs. But before we can discuss brain-washing sensibly, we must first gain a better knowledge of the three main types of sensory isolation.

THREE KINDS OF INPUT ISOLATION

As we have already suggested, there are three very basic kinds of input isolation that psychologists can identify.

1. *Deprivation of social inputs*. Being cut off from what other people say and do, being isolated from the reactions of other people to what you say and do.
2. *Deprivation of intellectual inputs*. Being shut off from those environmental stimuli that give you knowledge and understanding, or that allow you to perceive yourself and the world around you.
3. *Deprivation of biological inputs*. Being denied those commodities such as air, food, and water that keep you alive, or being denied the good smells, tastes, and skin stimulations that provide you with pleasures.

To appreciate the differences among these three types of isolation, consider what might happen if you were transported by some magic to a desert island. There is a huge house on this island, filled with great food, good books, fine music, and interesting films. But there are no people on this island to share these fine things with. You would thus have all the biological and intellectual inputs that you might desire, but you would have no real-life social environment. You could do anything you wished without fear of offending—or of pleasing—other people.

Now imagine a prison cell deep in the basement of this house, without windows or pictures or anything to read in it. If you were locked in this cell alone, but given all the biological necessities to keep you living, you would be deprived of both intellectual and social inputs. Your eyes could still see, and your ears could still hear. But there would be no real challenge to the *cognitive* (°) processes in your mind.

Next, carry the matter one step further. Suppose you are strapped on the bed in that cell—tied down so tightly you can't move. There is a hood over your head, plugs in your ears, and your skin has been anesthetized so that you can't feel anything at all. You cannot even hear yourself breathe. This final situation approaches complete sensory deprivation, although you still would have to have air, food, and water in order to survive for any length of time.

Whenever you are deprived of the inputs you want or need in life, several things happen to your body and mind. To begin with, your motivational systems are aroused; if you get no food, you become hungry. If you are deprived of cognitive inputs, you will hunger for intellectual stimulation. If you are cut off from other people, you will surely yearn for the sight of a familiar face.

The second important consequence of deprivation has to do with your values. The hungrier you become, the more important food becomes to you, the better the food will taste when you finally get it, the more likely it is you will work for food, and the more probable it becomes that you will acquire new eating habits. As we know from occasional stories in the news media, a starving person will sometimes resort to cannibalism—although under normal conditions the mere thought of eating human flesh might make the person violently ill. In short, the greater the need, the more flexible and changeable we are likely to become in our attempts to satisfy that need.

The third consequence of deprivation, highly related to the first two, has to do with the voluntary control you have over your thoughts and actions. Although you

Cognitive (COG-nuh-tiv). From the Latin word meaning "to know." In psychology, the word means "of the mind," or "having to do with intellectual processes."

may not realize it, your mind and body are so constructed that they cannot operate normally if you are cut off from your environment. You can't make hamburger if you don't have meat to grind, and you can't think about things for very long if you don't have sensory inputs to process.

DEPRIVATION AND PERSONAL CHANGE

We are all much more sensitive to the world around us than we usually like to imagine ourselves as being. If another person ever gained control over your sensory inputs, that person would also gain extensive control over your mind and your bodily reactions whether you liked it or not. The more the person deprived you of the stimulation you needed, the more eager you would probably become to do whatever was necessary to satisfy your biological, cognitive or intra-psychic, and social needs. And if the person could isolate you completely from your environment, you might indeed be brainwashed into doing or becoming whatever that person demanded.

Technically speaking, the term *brainwashing* should be used only in reference to those situations in which (1) an individual is put under almost complete sensory isolation, and (2) the individual is rewarded with sensory inputs for altering his or her actions and ideas. Of course, it is very unlikely that you will ever find yourself in such complete deprivation that you would undergo the sometimes profound personality changes associated with brainwashing. However, even relatively mild states of social, intellectual, or biological isolation can bring about alterations in your attitudes, emotions, and habits.

QUESTION: **Several psychologists have reported that students who attend small colleges—particularly schools with strong religious associations—typically show greater changes in their social values and beliefs than do students who attend large public universities. Can you think of at least one reason why this might be the case?**

Communist Techniques

American psychologists first became noticeably interested in brainwashing in the 1930's, when reports of strange happenings in Russia began filtering into the newspapers. Joseph Stalin was then dictator of the Soviet Union. During Stalin's reign the Russians staged many rather odd political trials. One of these began on August 19, 1936, when 16 famous Soviet politicians were put on trial for their lives. Although these were previously some of the most powerful men in the USSR, they all confessed openly in court that they had been traitors to the Communist cause.

Western observers were shocked at the lengths to which the defendants in this trial went in order to degrade themselves in public. It was commonly thought that the Russian secret police must have used torture, drugs, and hypnotism to get these noted politicians to put on such a spectacle. Arthur Koestler's famous novel, *Darkness at Noon*, recounts the kinds of psychological and physical pressures that the Stalinists employed to induce these public confessions; but the Stalinists' primary weapon was *isolating* a man for a long period of time until he had lost all of his personal bearings. Then the man was subjected to questioning and interrogations designed to convince him that he had, in fact, committed a series of terrible crimes. The man was told that he had to think of himself as a criminal because the Russian government said that he was—and the government was never wrong.

Brainwashing of U.S. soldiers by Chinese, as depicted in the film "The Manchurian Candidate."

The August 19th defendants were also informed that if they refused to confess, isolation and physical torture would continue. However, if they confessed in public, they would be released and restored to normal life. And so the men confessed. (After the trial, the Russian government failed to honor its promise to release the victims.)

The Chinese Communists did things slightly differently. Beginning in the 1940's, they started locking their political deviants into isolated rooms for weeks on end, giving the prisoners little or nothing to eat or drink and no human contact. A person treated this way was usually told that he or she could escape from isolation only after "washing the mind" of unacceptable thoughts. Only when the person's brain had been "cleansed" could he or she hope to be worthy of again returning to Chinese society. The Chinese authorities did not consider brain-washing to be punishment at all! Rather, they saw it as a kind of "helpful psycho-therapy" that could bring a *politically* insane person back to "social health."

During the Korean War in the early 1950's, the Chinese and North Koreans captured more than 7,000 U.S. prisoners. Of these, some 3,000 died while in captivity. The remaining 4,000 were kept chiefly in prison camps near the Korean-Chinese border. They underwent rather severe physiological depriva-tion—they had little food and little in the way of medical attention, in part because their captors had little to give them. And, during most of the time they were imprisoned, the U.S. soldiers were cut off from intellectual stimulation other than that the Chinese wished to give them; in fact, they heard and saw only what their captors wanted them to see and hear. Mail from home was almost always censored; even these censored letters were held back and were given out to the prisoners only as "rewards" for cooperation or for spouting back the political views that the Chinese tried to teach them. The U.S. prisoners were typically housed in groups and hence were not really *brainwashed*, since that technique involves complete isolation. However, the intellectual and physical deprivations were enough so that many of the soldiers did go along with what the Chinese asked them to do, even to the extent of "squealing" on their fellow captives who refused to accept the Communist viewpoint.

In point of fact, the extent of the soldiers' cooperation with the Chinese was rather less than might have been expected under the circumstances. Of the 4,000 men captured, only 21 chose to remain in China (and several of these men changed their minds later on). And once the prisoners were back in their normal environments, almost all of them gave up the beliefs the Communists had forced on them during captivity.

QUESTION: Students who show considerable attitude change while enrolled in small religious colleges often revert back to their prior beliefs upon graduation. Can you think of at least one reason why this might be so?

Psychologists often use the term *indoctrination* (°) to refer to attitudinal or behavioral changes brought about in situations involving partial isolation. While the deprivation is usually that of intellectual inputs, some social and biological control may be involved (the Chinese were not above using physical torture to achieve their ends). What the Chinese practiced against U.S. prisoners in Korea, therefore, was indoctrination—that is, the same sorts of psychological and physi-ological pressures toward conformity and goads toward change that are com-monplace in Marine and Army camps, in Boy Scout training, in fraternity and sorority groups, in jails, in radical movements, and in many religious institutions (*see* Chapter 27). Indoctrination always seems frightening when performed by groups whose beliefs we do not share. When "our side" uses the same persuasive devices, we call it "re-education" and often feel much better about its use.

Indoctrination (in-dock-tree-NAY-shun). Literally, "to teach" or "to educate." The word often has a nega-tive tone to it, however—implying that the teaching is by discipline, drill, repetition, and punishment for incor-rect responses. Psychologists fre-quently use the term to refer to those situations in which partial sensory deprivation (usually of intellectual or cognitive inputs) is used to motivate a person to change his or her beliefs or attitudes.

SENSORY DEPRIVATION

The Stalinist political trials and the reports of brainwashing in China and indoctrination of U.S. prisoners in Korea had one fairly immediate effect—Western governments became worried that the Communists had discovered some kind of psychological magic.

Perhaps the first to react were the Canadians. As early as 1951, the Canadian government commissioned a group of psychologists at Donald Hebb's laboratory at McGill University to investigate the effects of isolation on attitude change. While the experiments were supervised by Hebb, the actual work and planning were done by W. Heron, W.H. Bexton, T.H. Scott, and B.K. Doane. Although the research itself was not classified as secret, the first explanation given was that the Canadians were interested in studying the effects of monotony and isolation on watch-keeping and other such tasks. This "pretend" reason for the research is fascinating in and of itself.

For centuries, men and women accidentally caught in isolation situations had reported very peculiar experiences. Shipwrecked sailors adrift in the middle of the ocean would, upon rescue, describe weird and wonderful hallucinations. Pilots flying thousands of feet above the earth reported what was called a "break-away" effect. After they had been cruising alone for several hours, it sometimes seemed to these fliers that they lost contact with earth—and with reality. They would break out in cold sweats; they would feel they could no longer trust their eyes or their instruments; and they often reported seeing strange objects flying around them. Many such episodes ended in crashes; if the pilot did succeed in landing his plane, he often was psychologically unfit to fly again. At a more earthbound level, truck drivers rumbling along the deserted and monotonously straight highways of the U.S. West sometimes reported seeing jackrabbits larger than their trucks.

The McGill Experiments

In all of these *bizarre* (°) situations the person affected was obviously deprived of the normal amount of sensory information he or she had come to depend upon. Therefore, Heron and his colleagues built a small isolation chamber at McGill and paid students $20 a day to lie on a small bed, their arms inside cardboard mailing

Bizarre (biz-ARE). Strange or unusual.

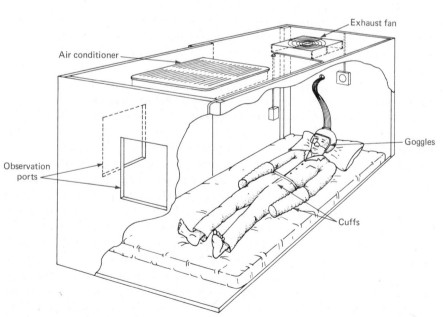

A sensory-deprivation chamber.

tubes, their eyes covered by transluscent goggles, their hearing masked by a noisy air conditioner. The students were fed and watered when necessary, but were asked to remain as motionless as possible otherwise. They were given a battery of tests and questionnaires before, during, and after this sensory-deprivation experience. They were also exposed to a series of propaganda messages read in a rather boring monotone. The subject of the propaganda messages had to do with supernatural events such as mental telepathy, ghosts, and *poltergeists* (°) (noisy, supernatural spirits).

In order to make sure that any change in the students' attitudes or behavior was due to the isolation and not merely to exposure to the propaganda, Heron and his colleagues paid a separate group of students to sit in a quiet room and listen to the recorded speeches through earphones.

The results of the McGill experiments were somewhat surprising. To begin with, although Hebb and Heron had expected that most of the subjects would be able to withstand the isolation for several days, almost half of the students quit during the first 48 hours. Those who stayed showed considerable intellectual impairment both during the sensory-deprivation experience itself and for some hours afterward. Simple problem-solving exercises often seemed beyond the students' capacities. Motor coordination often became difficult, as did the ability to adjust to novel situations. Those subjects who lasted long enough to be exposed to the dull and repetitious propaganda messages asked to hear them again and again and again—and were much more profoundly affected by what they heard than were the members of the control group.

Of equal interest were the subjective reports the students made of their experiences while in the "black room." At first students spent some time putting their thoughts in order and attempting to solve personal problems. But as time went on, such organized thinking became more and more difficult. They could no longer concentrate on much of anything and just relaxed and let their minds drift. Eventually most of them experienced "blank periods" during which they simply could not think of anything at all. They were conscious—which is to say that they were not asleep—but their minds simply were not functioning at all. They could not always tell if they were awake or asleep. Their emotions often ran wild. All of the students found the sensory deprivation very stressful and even very frightening.

Hallucinations About 80 percent of the McGill subjects reported some form of hallucination. Often the first symptom was a lightening or brightening of their visual fields, followed by the appearance of dots or lines all around them. Next the students would "see" geometric figures that duplicated themselves like wild patterns of wallpaper. Very vivid and picture-like scenes were usually next in the hallucinatory sequence. Often these scenes looked like something out of a Walt Disney cartoon (one student reported seeing a line of squirrel-like animals with sacks over their backs marching purposefully over a hill). For reasons that no one completely understands, the content of these hallucinations seemed beyond the control of the subjects (one student could see nothing but eyeglasses, no matter how hard he tried to think of something else). Presumably some unconscious part of the students' minds was producing these vivid scenes and, as we will see in later chapters, the unconscious portions of the mind cannot usually be "ordered around" by conscious command. The students were often quite disturbed by the "visions" that they had; one subject quit the experiment because he was distressed by the persistence of his hallucinations.

Subjects also reported disturbances in what might be called their "body images." One of the students had the impression that his body had turned into *twins*—that there were two bodies lying on the bed, and that they partially overlapped each other. Another stated that for a while his mind seemed to leave

Poltergeists (POLE-ter-guy-sts). From the German words *poltern*—meaning "to knock, rattle, or make noise"—and *geists*—meaning "spirits." Perhaps you have read about old houses where the dishes suddenly fall off the shelves or where strange noises come from the attic or basement. Supposedly, poltergeists are responsible for such frightening experiences.

Conjure (KONN-jurr). From the Latin word meaning "to conspire" or "to swear together." As commonly used, to conjure is to employ a magical spell to "call up" an image or spirit. A "conjure woman" is a witch who often conspires with your imagination to make you think she has worked some kind of magic.

his body and roam around the room; occasionally this "free mind" would look back at the "body" lying quietly on the bed. Some of the subjects had "floating" feelings as if their bodies had somehow overcome gravity and were hanging suspended in midair.

The students' abilities to judge distances and to see the world in three-dimensional depth were markedly disturbed both during and after the isolation experience. According to one informal, unpublished account of the effects of sensory deprivation on college students, a rash of minor driving accidents occurred among the subjects after their experiences. Chiefly, these accidents seemed to involve parallel parking—when backing into an empty parking space, the students simply could not judge adequately where their cars were in relation to other objects. After this, students were warned not to drive for a period of several days after their isolation period was over. One subject supposedly took the injunction not to drive only too literally. Being a student pilot, and wanting to get in some flying time, he had a friend drive him to the airport and then took off in a light plane. To his dismay, he found once he was airborne that he simply could not perceive up from down. Luckily, the control tower was able to talk to him by radio and brought him down safely.

Other Deprivation Studies

Once the results of the McGill experiments were made public, psychologists in many laboratories in the United States began paying students to stay inside "black rooms" too. It soon became apparent that the reactions a subject showed to sensory deprivation were in part a function of what the subject's personality was like prior to entering the isolation chamber and how strongly the person needed contact with physical reality in order to function properly.

For example, students judged as being normal and healthy tended to *underestimate* the length of time they had been isolated. As one subject put it, "I think I've been in here about 36 hours, but I'll say I've only been here for 24. That way, I won't really be disappointed no matter what the time has been." Another student kept track of the time by humming Beethoven's Fifth Symphony over and over again—because he knew it took him exactly 37 minutes each time he did so. Yet another student, one with medical training, counted the number of times he breathed and used that figure as a rough index of the passage of time.

Subjects who were judged as being somewhat psychologically disturbed before isolation often *overestimated* the length of time they had been in the "black room." These subjects also broke off the experiment more readily than did subjects with apparently stronger or more mature personalities. The students who quit in a state of panic often accused the experimenters of "forcing" them to come out of the room by using some trick or other.

Almost everyone who underwent sensory deprivation reported wild flights of fancy, at least during the first stages of isolation. Although the content of these fancies varied considerably from one person to another, they were all fairly similar to experiences some of the subjects had undergone while using drugs such as LSD or mescaline. Surprisingly enough, although sexual daydreams were reported, they were rather infrequent. As one student put it, "I was surprised I couldn't *conjure* (°) up more than I did."

In general, the greater the state of deprivation, the less the subjects were able to tolerate isolation. If the students were allowed to move around freely (in a totally dark room), they could often stand the experience for several days. Students forced to remain lying on a bed lasted much shorter times. The shortest stays of all were reported by a group of experimenters who asked their subjects to lie inside an iron lung—that is, a small tank-type of respirator used by some victims of polio. The feeling of being trapped inside such narrow confines caused most subjects to demand their release within a few hours.

An iron lung, used to force air into the lungs of polio victims who cannot breathe for themselves.

Lilly's Womb Tank

The man who put himself through the most complete sensory deprivation of all was probably John C. Lilly, a psychiatrist who immersed himself in a tank of water for many hours on end. Lilly donned a diving helmet so that he could breathe when underwater. Then he submerged himself, hanging absolutely motionless between the surface of the water and the bottom of the tank for several hours. Since the water was kept exactly at his body temperature, sensory input from his skin receptors was minimal; since he didn't move, there was no feedback from his muscles; and the diving mask effectively blocked out vision and hearing.

John C. Lilly.

Lilly has only recently commented in any detail on his stream of consciousness during his almost total sensory deprivation. His major worry was *dependency*. Before the experiment started, he became very disturbed at how helpless he would be while actually in the water. Since he would be naked except for a diving helmet, Lilly viewed himself as making a kind of psychological return to his mother's womb. A baby is dependent upon its mother for almost everything, and (in part) grows to love its mother because she meets its needs and protects it from danger. If Lilly were going to make a symbolic trip back to a womb, he wanted to make sure there was no one around who might inadvertently take on the role of "mother" when he again became a helpless child. Lilly might well have asked one of his assistants to stand by the tank to pull him out if he started to drown. But because Lilly feared becoming overly dependent on the assistant more than he feared drowning, he had the tank built inside a doubly locked room and allowed no one inside while he was submerged.

After he had been in the water for an hour or so, Lilly had tremendous urges to move—to twiddle his fingers or twitch his nose. After resisting these desires for a while, he seemed to slip into a womb-like state that he describes as being inside a warm, dark cave, a black tunnel with a strange blue light dimly visible in the distance. When he finally came out of the water, a few hours later, he felt he had been "born again."

AROUSAL

The studies of sensory deprivation might well have remained little more than a psychological curiosity were it not for some important physiological research at UCLA by H.W. Magoun and his colleagues—research that began about the time that the Russian "show trials" were making headlines. Magoun was interested in the problem of *arousal* (°)—that is, the physiological and psychological mechanisms that turn a sleeping organism into a state of alert, aroused functioning. At first it seemed that Magoun and his associates were working on quite a different problem than the one that Hebb, Heron, and Lilly were investigating; however, it soon became clear that the arousal research offered an explanation for what might be going on inside the nervous systems of human beings subjected to sensory isolation.

Two Important Sensory Pathways

Prior to Magoun's work, it was generally assumed that sensory information reached your brain in only one fashion: external stimuli impinged on sensory receptors such as the free nerve endings in your skin. These receptor neurons were excited by this external energy and fired off a message up the spinal cord to the somatic sensory cortex in your parietal lobe to let your brain know that they had been stimulated. The brain then processed this information and, if a response were called for, activated the motor centers (in your frontal lobes) which caused your muscles to move.

This view of sensory functioning was correct as far as it went, but it pictured

Arousal. Certain parts of the brain seem particularly involved in waking an organism up or in increasing an organism's activity level. Magoun (mah-GOON) and his colleagues discovered that electrical stimulation delivered to a part of the brain stem called the reticular system greatly increased the arousal level of their animal subjects.

H.W. Magoun.

Straight-line sensory system. The sensory input pathways that lead from the body's receptor neurons rather directly to the sensory regions of the cortex.

Reticular activating system (ree-TICK-you-lar). The information contained in sound waves goes from your ear to your temporal lobe by way of the auditory nerve (a straight-line sensory system). The *meaning* of the sound is carried by the auditory nerve. However, auditory inputs are also passed along to the reticular activating system in your brain stem. If the auditory stimulus seems important enough, the reticular system turns on or "activates" your cortex so that your cortical Board pays attention to the message coming in on the auditory nerve. Without this activation from the reticular system, your Board would probably ignore the stimulus arriving at the temporal cortex via the straight-line sensory system (in this case, the auditory nerve).

RAS. Abbreviation for "reticular activating system." When Magoun and his associates made their first discoveries, they spoke of the "ascending reticular system," which they abbreviated ARS. The name was changed for perhaps two reasons: (1) Most important, it was later found that the reticular system "descends" as well as "ascends"—that is, it sends neural commands down toward the receptor neurons, in addition to sending messages up to the brain. (2) Amusingly enough, ARS is close to the British world "arse," meaning "ass." For a time, the reticular system was referred to as "Magoun's arse."

the sensory pathways as being "one-way streets"—that is, information was thought to flow in one direction only, from receptor to the brain to the muscles, and only along a single set of neuronal pathways. What Magoun (and later, many other scientists) showed was that incoming information about the world actually reaches the Board of Directors in the cortex through *two* quite different pathways, and that the Board has considerable say about what information reaches it and what messages are blocked out in lower centers and never get through the cortex.

Rather than being "one-way streets," then, the sensory routes to the brain consist of superhighways, where messages flow in both directions, with toll booths spotted here and there to keep out unwanted travelers. The road map for this maze of interconnected pathways is far from being completely drawn, but we can at least sketch in some of the landmarks.

When a receptor cell such as a free nerve ending fires, a patterned burst of electrical energy passes up the spinal cord to the brain stem (the "stem" of the cerebral mushroom). In the brain stem the road to the cortex "splits" into two pathways. One road leads directly to the somatic sensory cortex in the parietal lobe. This route is called the *straight-line sensory system* (°) and lets the Board of Directors know what part of your body has been stimulated and how strong the stimulation is.

A second road leads into the *reticular system* (°), which gets its name (like the retina) from the Latin word for net or network. The reticular system is a network of cells that begins at the top of the spinal cord and runs up through the brain stem to the lower parts of the cerebrum. The reticular system acts as an alerting center for the rest of the brain—rather like the bell on your telephone. When the reticular system is activated, it "rings" the Board of Directors to alert the Board that an important message is coming through on the straight-line sensory "telephone." The message from the free nerve endings in your skin will usually reach the somatic sensory cortex whether or not the reticular system is aroused. However, unless the reticular system "rings the bell" and activates the cortex, the Board of Directors appears to ignore any information that comes through on the straight-line system.

The Reticular Activating System (RAS)

The experiments that demonstrated the function of the reticular activating system (usually abbreviated *RAS*) (°) involved animal subjects. Suppose we implant an electrode in the RAS of a cat. Then we let the animal continue its daily life but, occasionally, we deliver a small amount of electrical current to the RAS. What happens? If we stimulate the cat's RAS when it is awake and moving about, it reacts as if it had "heard something"—that is, the animal suddenly becomes tense and alert, as if its environment had suddenly changed dramatically. If we wait until the cat goes to sleep, a short burst of electrical energy delivered to the RAS causes the cat to open its eyes and jump up, rather as if someone had stepped on its tail.

If we cut or surgically remove the cat's RAS, it lapses into deep sleep from which it seldom if ever recovers. If you shook the cat violently, it would wake up momentarily and move around for a period of a few seconds or minutes, but even if it were starving to death it would soon lie down and drift off to sleep. If you now put a recording electrode in the cat's somatic sensory cortex, and pinched the

Sensory functioning as a "one-way" street.

animal's tail, you could show that the message coming from the tactile receptors in the cat's tail does in fact reach the animal's brain. The straight-line sensory system is still working, but since there is nothing to alert or arouse the Board of Directors that information is coming through to be acted upon, the Board remains asleep.

Brain-wave activity can be recorded in humans while they are asleep. These recordings suggest that information from almost all of your sensory receptors does indeed reach your cortex while you are unconscious. But falling asleep involves "turning off" the alarms of the outside world—that is, slowing down activity in the RAS, but not in the straight-line sensory system. As you drop off to sleep, some part of your brain *inhibits* the firing rates of the neurons in the RAS so that the RAS won't bother your Board except (as we will see) in cases of real emergency.

Anything that affects neural activity in the RAS also affects consciousness. Many of the sleep-inducing drugs have their anti-transmitter effects on the synapses in the RAS (*see* Chapter 3). And if an accident of some kind damaged your RAS, you might lapse into a coma (deep sleep) from which you might never awaken—despite the fact that the rest of your brain was in perfect condition.

Attention and Habituation

Because you have no conscious awareness of activity in your RAS, you have no way of exercising voluntary control over what happens there. But sitting as it does atop the spinal cord—and extending up into the lower brain centers—the RAS is in a perfect position to act as a toll booth or gate through which incoming sensory information must pass if it is to have an effect on the cortex. If the incoming message is trivial or routine, the RAS will allow the cortex to ignore it. But if the message seems important, the RAS alerts the upper centers of the brain and they pay attention to what is coming through on the straight-line sensory system.

What do we mean by "important" messages? Experiments with animals suggest that your RAS can learn which stimuli need your instant attention and which stimuli are unlikely to be threatening or to require a response. As you read this book, your receptor cells are sending millions of messages per minute through to your brain on the straight-line sensory system, but your RAS is (presumably) telling your Board it needn't bother with most of this sensory input. For instance, until you read this sentence, you probably were not consciously aware that your shoes (or socks) are full of feet, or that your clothes are pressing in on various parts

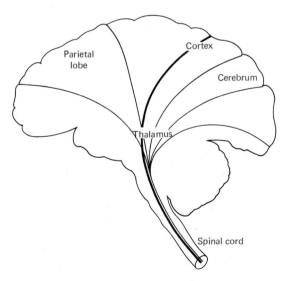

The reticular activating system.

of your skin. Your RAS has learned that these signals don't need your attention while you read. But a sudden change in the pattern of incoming stimulation (as when a friend might shout at you) is recognized by the RAS as being important information, and it then alerts your cortex that an emergency message is coming through. Your attention then shifts from vision (reading) to auditory sensations, the information is processed in your cortex, and you respond appropriately to the change in your environment.

> QUESTION: **When you are reading something interesting, and a friend says something to you, why do you sometimes have to ask your friend to repeat what was said, even though you know that your friend did in fact say something important?**

People who live next to a railroad track—or to an airport or superhighway—soon adapt or habituate to the sounds of the passing traffic, but visitors are often kept awake at night by these noises until their own RAS learns to ignore them. If, in a given family, it is the wife's job to take care of the children, she will awaken at night to a child's whimpering while the husband's RAS screens out these stimuli and lets him continue to sleep soundly.

Cortical Influence on the RAS The road between the cortex and the RAS is, as we suggested earlier, a two-way street. Early studies on the RAS showed that it had a marked influence on activity in the cortex, but later experiments showed that the cortex has ways of affecting what goes on in the RAS as well. Whenever you choose to concentrate or focus your attention on something, your cortex tells your RAS not to bother it for a while. The cortex exerts its influence by directly inhibiting neural activity in the RAS. On the other hand, if you decide to cram for an exam by studying all night, your cortex is usually able to keep itself awake by continuing to stimulate the RAS—which feeds this stimulation back to the cortex itself.

Stimulus Hunger

Your body has certain physiological needs that you are often only too painfully aware of—a need for food, for air, for water, for sleep, for a certain range of comfortable temperatures. Thanks to the sensory-deprivation experiments, and the research on the RAS, we now know that your nervous system "needs" a certain constant level of incoming sensory stimulation in order to function properly. If you were to take part in an experiment involving sensory isolation, you would be putting your cortex in as deprived a situation as your body would be if you went without food and water for a long period of time. Without continual alerting from the RAS, your brain simply does not function properly—and the RAS is activated primarily by the flow of sensory information along the straight-line sensory system.

At the beginning of a period of sensory deprivation, your RAS would slow down and, if you needed sleep, you would probably drift off into unconsciousness. But once your body rested, you would awaken—and find you had absolutely nothing to do. Your cortex could keep things going for a while by engaging in thoughts or daydreams, *but even thinking is dependent on activity in the RAS.* And when you are in isolation, not many messages come through on the straight-line sensory system. Hence the RAS simply cannot do its job of keeping the cortical Board stimulated into alertness.

The Board, disturbed to find itself slipping off into sleep and periods of "blank" consciousness, unable to "think" because it can't stay awake, takes whatever action it can to change things. To begin with, it "turns up the volume" on all incoming sensory stimulation—that is, weak incoming sensory signals are magnified out of all proportion and attended to in ways that never would be the case if you were in a normal, exciting environment. If the faint incoming signals are vaguely pleasurable, you may experience overwhelming joy; if the signals are vaguely painful, you may experience incredible pain.

As an illustration of the way in which the brain can *intensify* simple sensory experiences, consider the following story told by John C. Lilly. Once when he was floating in his womb tank, the air hose connected to his diving helmet sprang a leak. Very slowly, air began bubbling into the water. Each individual bubble was no larger than those in a glass of beer, and the leak was so small that only one bubble popped out every 15 seconds or so. Once the bubble was released into the water at the bottom of the tank, this tiny bubble of air drifted upward and struck Lilly's suspended body on his thigh. Lilly reports that when each bubble hit his skin, it gave him a feeling of intense sexual ecstasy much like an orgasm. For several minutes these bubble-induced orgasms occurred every 15 seconds—one after another after another.

But all good things must come to an end. Eventually the bubbles speeded up to a frequency of one every 5 seconds or so. At this point, the pleasure turned to intense pain—so devastating a pain that Lilly had to discontinue that session and get out of the tank. Under normal circumstances, of course, Lilly would probably not have noticed the bubbles at all. (Lilly has recently admitted he was under the influence of LSD at the time, in an attempt to "get his mind to leave his body." Surely the drug must have intensified the experience.)

Protection against Brainwashing and Indoctrination

The limitations of sensory deprivation as a tool for changing thoughts and behaviors aren't really known too well since, for obvious humanitarian reasons, no one (that we know of) has carried these experiments to extremes. But several points do seem important:

1. Your body has built-in safety mechanisms to protect you against biological, intellectual, and social deprivation. Whenever your cortex is deprived of incoming sensory information for very long, it usually presses the "panic button." You get restless; you feel an urge to move about, then finally a strong desire to flee. Boredom is perhaps one of your best defenses against brainwashing and indoctrination.
2. The more you control your physical environment, the more you can protect yourself against forced persuasion or psychological indoctrination. When you give up control of the world around you, you are in danger of giving up control of your thinking as well.
3. The healthier you are physically and mentally, the less effect isolation will have on you. People with strong and stable personalities, people with clear-cut value systems and with an understanding of their own strengths and limitations, are much more likely to resist propaganda no matter where or how they encounter it than are people who are confused about who they are and where they are going in life. The more you know yourself, the safer you are from brainwashing.
4. Finally, if someone did try to change your personality by putting you in sensory deprivation, the odds are good that you would change back more or less to your normal self once you returned to your usual environment.

When a surgeon cuts out part of your brain, there is no way to reverse the operation later on and return your brain tissue to you. Behavioral or attitudinal change is something entirely different—almost any habit that can be learned can later be unlearned. Arthur Koestler grew up believing in capitalism, but became a devout Communist overnight after he was exposed to Communist propaganda. Several years later, disillusioned with the Communist way of life, he reverted to his original belief.

In short, techniques like complete isolation can be used to *induce* psychological change; but *maintaining* this change is a separate and much more complicated problem for anyone who wishes to control the behavior of others. We will have more to say about this matter in several later chapters.

SUMMARY

1. A human being separated from his or her usual social environment soon stops functioning normally. Both the Chinese and the Russian governments have, in the past, made use of this fact to brainwash or indoctrinate people into changing their attitudes and behaviors.

2. Brainwashing consists of putting a person into total isolation for a period of weeks or months until the person is so desperate for inputs that he or she will often admit to past "mistakes" and promise to behave differently in the future.

3. In constrast to brainwashing, indoctrination often involves isolating groups of people (rather than individuals) from their usual environment, lecturing them about what they should become, and then rewarding any signs of "progress" toward the indoctrinator's desired goal.

4. Worried by these Communist techniques, Western scientists began in the early 1950's to study the effects of isolating normal people from all incoming sensory stimulation. One of the best known of these studies was performed by psychologists at McGill University in Montreal.

5. At McGill, the researchers paid male student volunteers to lie blindfolded in a tiny room for days on end. The results of these experiments were as follows:
   a. The subjects soon lost much of their ability to "think straight."
   b. They began having hallucinations, seeing things that weren't really there, or feeling that they were floating in air looking down at their bodies on the bed below.
   c. The longer and more severe the deprivation, the worse the subjects performed.
   d. The subjects became so desperate for inputs that they accepted uncritically much of what they were told by the experimenters.

6. In an attempt to get complete sensory isolation, John C. Lilly immersed himself in a tank of warm water and floated there for hours on end. It is reported that he also took LSD to enhance the isolation. While in the water, Lilly felt as if he had returned to the womb, and that getting out of the tank was like being born again.

7. The sensory isolation experiments suggest that the cortical Board cannot process correctly without continual input from the sensory receptors.

8. Sensory signals reach the Board from two separate sources. The straight-line sensory system carries messages directly from the receptor neurons to the cortex. The reticular activating system (RAS), discovered by Magoun and his associates, evaluates these messages before they reach the Board. If the message is important, the reticular system "activates" the cortex by sending "alarm messages" to the Board.

9. If the reticular system is removed surgically, the organism lapses into a coma from which it never recovers.

10. The reticular system both alerts or arouses the Board and directs its attention to incoming sensory information.

11. Activity in the reticular system is dependent on a constant flow of sensory stimulation; when a person is isolated from environmental changes, the reticular system slows down—and so does the cortical Board. Under these conditions, the Board either goes to sleep, or magnifies or intensifies whatever incoming messages it can find.

12. One reason that brainwashing is effective is that, under conditions of sensory deprivation, the Board is so eager for environmental stimulation that it accepts information less critically than it normally would.

13. To protect yourself against brainwashing, stay out of boring situations, keep control over your physical environment, and maintain a healthy and rewarding attitude toward life.

(Continued from page 176.)

A few hours after he got out of the "black room," Philip Cassone returned to the laboratory to take some more tests. The psychologists told him they wanted to learn how soon he had recovered from the sensory deprivation. When he took the tests again, Phil did much better than when he had taken them in isolation, although, to his way of thinking, he still didn't seem to be as sharp as he usually was. Obviously some of the effects were still lingering on. But the psychologists assured him that within a few days he would be as good as ever.

"How did I do as a subject?" Phil asked the man in charge when the tests were done.

"Let's see," the psychologist said, checking his records. "You stayed in for 26 hours. That's about average. Not bad at all."

Phil was annoyed; he had hoped to do much better than average. He turned to leave in disgust, when he spotted a tape recorder sitting on one of the tables.

"Did you record my voice?" he asked.

The psychologist took the pipe out of his mouth and nodded gravely.

"Could I listen to some of it?"

The man picked a tape up off the table, put it on the machine, and started the tape in motion.

Phil was shocked to hear the way his voice came out. "Do I really sound like that?"

When the psychologist again nodded soberly, Phil listened even more carefully. He heard himself demand to know what time it was, heard himself insist that the psychologists talk to him, listened to his scream that if they didn't say something right away he was coming out. And then he heard a door open and his voice come faintly from a distance . . . "You bastards ruined the experiment. You made me come out."

Phil blushed. "Did I really call you guys bastards?"

Again the psychologist shook his head slowly.

Phil groaned. It was the first time he had ever called a professor such a name—at least to his face. "How could I ever have done something like that?"

The psychologist just puffed on his pipe and smiled.

RECOMMENDED READINGS

Burgess, Anthony. *A Clockwork Orange* (New York: Ballantine Books, Inc., 1965).

Koestler, Arthur. *Darkness at Noon* (New York: Modern Library, Inc., 1946).

Solomon, Philip, ed. *Sensory Deprivation* (Cambridge, Mass.: Harvard University Press, 1961).

Vernon, Jack. *Inside the Black Room* (New York: Clarkson N. Potter, Inc., 1963).

chapter 10
"GREAT EXPECTATIONS"

VISUAL PERCEPTION

DID YOU KNOW THAT . . .

Perceptions are made up of sensory inputs plus the meanings your brain assigns to these inputs?

A person born blind who recovers sight as an adult has great difficulty in recognizing people's faces?

You probably learn to judge distances by moving about?

If you look at two unfamiliar objects that are the same distance from you, the larger will usually appear closer?

You tend to see all objects as appearing on a background of some kind?

You typically group objects together according to such principles as proximity, closure, and continuity?

Infants usually prefer to look at human faces rather than at random visual patterns?

Infants seem innately to recognize the dangers of approaching cliffs or sharp drop-offs?

The pupils of your eyes often open wider when you are staring at something of interest to you?

Your brain may suppress inputs that disturb or annoy it?

Since you "see" what you expect to see, you view the world through very biased eyes and seldom see things as they actually are?

The Professor was sitting on a large box, cursing like a trooper and sweating like a stallion. There were several other boxes stacked nearby, covered with address labels. On the smallest label of all there was just room for

Dr. M.E. Mann
Dept. of Psych.
Univ. of the Mid-West, USA

Moments before, a group of porters had unloaded the boxes from an ancient pickup truck and trundled the cartons inside the airport, dumping them near the Customs office.

Outside the airport a tropical sun burned down, roasting any man or beast foolish enough to venture forth unprotected. Even inside the airport building the temperature was nearly 100 degrees F. (38 degrees C.), reason enough for the Professor's clothing to be soaked with sweat. The cursing was no doubt due to the fact that Professor Mann was going home frustrated.

A small, dark man walked briskly out of the Customs office and headed toward Mann. Despite the heat, the little man's expensive sharkskin suit and his silk shirt and tie looked as crisp and elegant as if he were ready to pose for a fashion ad.

"Ah, my dear Professor, all is in order, all is in readiness. I assure you that we will tuck your boxes of scientific equipment on the plane as gently as a mother

tucks a child into bed. Let no one say that the Republic of Lafora treats visiting scientists shabbily. Now, perhaps we might repair to what passes for a cocktail lounge in this ancient airport. I am certain that the admittedly limited budget of our Ministry of Science and Technology can be stretched to provide us with a glass or two of cheer while we await the arrival of your jet.''

Mann's response was sharp and unprintable.

''Ah, you are still angry with us because we cannot approve your venturing into our back country to complete your research. But surely, my dear Professor, we have argued this out at length before and you understand my country's position. We are responsible for your safety. Our nation is large, poor, and only recently liberated from colonial rule. We have not yet found the resources to bring the benefits of civilization to all our people, and the tribes that you wish to study are still little more than savages. We could not in good conscience let you go among them unprotected, for they would surely murder you. Your research grant is not of sufficient magnitude to allow you to hire a private troop of soldiers to protect you, and, as you know, all of our military personnel are required at our borders at this dangerous time in our nation's existence. Now, come and have a drink and soothe yourself while we wait . . .''

Mann interrupted. ''Oh, come off it, Freddie. All this formality and politeness is just a cover up for the truth. It's prejudice. Pure and simple prejudice. You're a city-born, Oxford-educated, wealthy, sophisticated man. You hold two cabinet posts in the Laforan government. You've been wined and dined in half the capitals of the world, but I'll bet a year's pay that you've never broken bread with one of your backland natives. If they occasionally do away with one of your tax collectors or military types, I don't doubt they've been provoked into doing so. But murderers? No, that's pure, superstitious prejudice on your part. I've talked to those natives and many of my anthropologist friends have been there. You don't understand the backlanders, so you're afraid of them. You shouldn't be. The truth is that they're frightened to death of you city people.''

The sharply-dressed Minister of Science and Technology began to sweat a little. ''My dear Professor, we have been through all this before. I took your case to the highest authorities in my government, and the answer was no. Absolutely not. What more could I do?''

''You could have pleaded my case with the President himself, that's what,'' the irate American continued.

''Our great leader is too busy to concern himself with such trivial matters. As you no doubt are aware, we are threatened by enemies on all sides. The President must plan strategy, he must alert our populace to the constant dangers around us. Even though you are a noted scientist from a country that has long supported our freedom and independence, I would not dare bother him with such minor problems at this time.''

Mann laughed sharply. ''That's hogwash! You still see the world in terms of absolutes, in blacks and whites. You wouldn't dare turn down my request if your native prejudice wasn't so great that . . .''

The scream of a shrill siren interrupted them. A large black automobile screeched to a halt in front of the airport, and out popped a huge man dressed in the uniform of a Laforan general. The big man came striding into the building at top speed; then, catching sight of the Minister to whom Mann had been talking, the General rushed up to them.

''Ah, Freddie,'' said the military man, ''it's good to see you. We have an emergency on our hands. Perhaps you can help.'' The Minister quickly introduced General Chambra, head of security for the Republic of Lafora, to Professor Mann.

''Charmed, I'm sure,'' the General said, bowing slightly to acknowledge the American's presence, and then continued. ''Freddie, the Snake is coming!''

The minister looked puzzled. ''The Snake?''

''Yes, on the next airplane. We just got the message from our agents in Paris. They're sure he's coming to kill the President! You must help us figure out what to do!''

''Well, why don't you just arrest this 'Snake' as soon as he gets off the airplane?'' asked the American in a matter-of-fact voice.

''I'm afraid you don't understand,'' the General said, giving Dr. Mann a withering look of contempt. ''The Snake is the best-known killer in the world, responsible for dozens of the foulest political assassinations you could imagine. He's been hired by one of the enemy states on our borders, because they know our beloved leader is all that holds this poor little country together.'' The General took out a large, white handkerchief and began mopping his face.

Freddie began to fret. ''Yes, but Chambra, why don't you follow the good Professor's advice and merely arrest the Snake as soon as he lands?''

The General shook his head. ''You don't understand either, Freddie. The problem is, we simply don't know what the Snake looks like! Not a jot or tittle of information about this assassin do we have. Is he young, old, tall, short, fat, skinny? He's done his murders all over the world, but no one has ever seen him. All we know is that he usually kills his victims by injecting snake venom into them with a fang-shaped needle. The victim dies in horrible convulsions. And to arrange to arrive on this plane! No wonder they call him the Snake!''

Freddie paled visibly during the General's speech. Turning to the American, he said quietly, ''There is something you don't understand, Dr. Mann. This particular flight brings to Lafora almost a hundred of the biggest munitions dealers in the world. They are shady characters, all of them, but we need their wares badly since we refuse to accept military supplies from any of the major powers. So we spread the word that we wished to buy guns, and chartered a special plane to bring in from Europe anyone interested in selling us munitions. That is one of the reasons I am at the airport now, to greet these men and make them welcome. If we treat them badly . . .''

"And we cannot check out their passports because most of them travel incognito anyhow—and probably on forged or illegal identification," the General continued.

"What about giving them a lie detector test?" Freddie asked.

"They wouldn't submit to such a test, of course," said the General contemptuously.

"And the lie detector isn't that accurate anyhow," the American added. "It measures emotionality, not truthfulness, and I would guess that your 'Snake' isn't exactly the sort who would lose his cool very readily."

"Too true," said the General, and mopped his face again. "But we must find some way of separating the Snake from—er, the worms, or we are in grave danger."

For several seconds the three of them stood silently, lost in thought. Then Freddie cleared his throat and ventured a question. "Professor Mann, you are an expert in the field of perceptual responses. You told me once that you wished to give certain tests to our backland natives that would tell you a great deal about their minds even if they did not understand the purpose of the tests and even though you could not speak their language. I don't suppose that now . . ."

Professor Mann was suddenly all business. "Yes, Freddie, it might work. We could set up my equipment right here in the airport and test each person as they got off the plane. I would have to draw up some new stimulus cards, but that shouldn't take long. Of course, I don't guarantee anything. The error rate is really very high, you know, and I could easily make a dreadful mistake. But if you're really desperate, perhaps it's better than nothing."

The General looked confused. "I don't understand . . ."

The Minister turned to the military man and said, "You aren't expected to understand—this is a matter for scientists such as Dr. Mann and myself. We will screen the men on the plane with the Professor's equipment. You have your soldiers standing by, looking as innocent as possible. When we detect the Snake, we will give you a signal and you must move in for the arrest at once. More than that you need not know."

"But what will we tell the arms dealers?" the General wailed. "They will want an explanation . . ."

"We will say that Paris has reported an outbreak of a highly infectious eye disease, and we must check each person on the flight to make sure they are not carrying the illness," Dr. Mann said brusquely. "I will put on a white uniform and be very efficient about it all."

At this final comment Freddie smiled broadly. "You are a positive genius, my dear Professor. We will do just what you say!" And then he turned to some porters standing idly by. "Here, you men! Help us open these crates and set up this equipment!"

(Continued on page 214.)

When it comes to perception, the eyes have it. Your eyes are more than "the window to your soul"; they are also the main sensory route by which most of us acquire information about the world around us. When light strikes the retina in your eye, it triggers off a wave of neural-electrical activity that passes along the optic nerve to your brain. Sensory messages coming from your eyes—or from any of your sense receptors—are called *sensations* (°). These sensations have little meaning in and of themselves, however, until they have reached the brain and have been processed by your Board of Directors—just as radio waves have little meaning until they have been "processed" by a radio and converted into meaningful sound waves.

When these sensory inputs arrive in your central nervous system, they set in motion a complex chain of neural events. First, the sensations are *scanned* (°) or looked over in the lower brain centers (such as the reticular activating system) to

Sensations (sen-SAY-shuns). Neural messages from your sense receptors that are triggered off by changes in your external or internal (bodily) environment. When you hear a sound, for instance, the sound waves act as a stimulus to the hair cells lying on the basilar membrane in the cochlea in your inner ear. The hair cells respond to this external stimulation by firing off a message that goes along the auditory nerve until it reaches the temporal lobe of your brain. The message remains a relatively meaningless sensation until it has been interpreted by your cortical Board. Sensations are the "raw stuff" from which perceptions are formed. Also called "sensory inputs."

Scanned (rhymes with "canned"). From a Greek word meaning "to trap." As used today, "to scan" means to inspect closely.

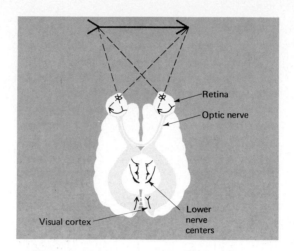

The pathways of vision. Note that part of each path crosses over from one eye to the opposite part of the brain.

Images. As used in this chapter, the term "images" means memories of past experiences. If you close your eyes and imagine what your family pet looks like, you have called to mind an image or memory of the animal.

Perception (per-SEP-shun). The process of matching sensations with images. "To perceive" usually means "to recognize."

Percept (PER-sept). The end product of the process of perception. Anything that you recognize or understand, or something whose future behavior you can predict.

see if they are important enough to bother the cortex with. Some processing of information actually occurs in these lower centers.

When a sensory message reaches the cortex, it arrives first at one of the sensory-input areas. The visual-input area is in the occipital lobe. From the visual-input area the message is next sent to the "association cortex" for handling. It is here, presumably, that many of your memory circuits are located—that is, where neural traces or *images* (°) of your past experiences are to be found. When these image circuits fire, they give a sort of "instant replay" of what you have seen and heard and felt in the past. Your Board of Directors scans or compares both the past image and the present incoming sensation, and if the two are similar enough, the Board "recognizes" what you are looking at as something it has encountered in the past. If no image exists that matches the incoming sensation, the Board "recognizes" that whatever it is you are "seeing," it is new, different, and has no identifiable verbal label.

This process of recognition is called *perception* (°). The thing that you recognize (or realize that you've not seen before), whether it is an object in your visual world or a relationship between two or more objects, is called a *percept* (°).

Technically speaking, a percept is defined as a set of sensations *plus* the images that the sensory input evokes. At a more practical level, a percept is anything that you recognize, know anything about, or appreciate. When you say that you *perceive* something, you really mean (1) that you can remember the past contexts in which this thing appeared and/or (2) that you have certain expectations about what the thing will be like in the future.

Perception, then, is the Board's way of coming to grips with the world around it. And, because much of the data about your world came to you through your eyes, perception is primarily a visual process. Indeed, when you say that you "see" something, you usually mean that you perceive or understand it. But perception is also a very active process. You do not simply sit at home waiting for the world to come to you; instead, you go out into the world; you challenge it; you attempt to find out what it and you are all about.

And one of the main reasons that you engage in all this activity is that your eyes *lie* to you constantly, and your brain knows it. Perhaps an illustration about flying will help you "see" the point about your "lying" eyes.

PLANE AND FANCY VISION

Suppose it is a beautiful spring day, far too nice to work or to sit in class. While you are trying to decide how best to enjoy this gorgeous gift of nature, the phone rings. A friend of yours has somehow come up with an invitation to go flying, and

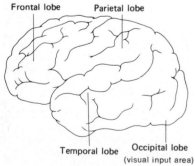

Visual input area.

The same numbers seen from the ground and from the air. The numbers do not change, but your perception of them does.

you're invited too. An hour or so later you find yourself standing beside a plane not much bigger than a delivery van. Rather small, you think—but then you're comparing it with huge jetliners at the other end of the airport.

Moments later you are inside, sitting comfortably in a very large seat; the pilot has started the engine; and the plane moves smartly away from the hangar and then bumps along the taxi strip heading toward the end of the runway. You pass very close to a firetruck sitting by the edge of the taxi strip; the truck is large and red and shiny. Then the pilot calls the control tower on his radio, gets permission to take off, and turns the plane onto the end of the runway. For several moments you sit there, the plane shaking eagerly as if anticipating its chance to go roaring down the narrow ribbon of concrete that stretches for a mile in front of you. The number "25" has been painted in large numerals on the runway, obviously as an identification of some kind. Oddly enough, the tops of the numbers seem compressed and small from where you are sitting in the plane, yet you know that this can't be so.

And then the pilot releases the brake, guns the engine, and you are rolling faster and faster down the runway. As you pass the numbers painted on the concrete, you see that they were normal size after all; your eyes were just playing tricks on you. A second or two later the pilot pulls back on the small wheel in front of him and the plane leaps eagerly skyward.

Airborne. You climb steadily upward for a few minutes, then the pilot dips one of the wings and turns around in a slow, lazy circle over the airport. Down below you see the firetruck. Why does it now look so tiny and artificial, like a toy that a loving parent would hide under a Christmas tree? And the people—they look more like bugs crawling on the ground than like human beings. The pilot flies over a near-by town. You see a traffic circle below, the streets radiating out from the center like spokes from the hub of a wheel. A small lake is nestled close to the traffic center; you happen to know that the lake is almost perfectly round, but from the plane it looks oddly distorted. Maybe it's the height that makes it look so funny. You pass a large warehouse with a name written on top of it in very large letters. Surprisingly enough, you can't read the name very easily because, from where you sit, the letters are upside down.

The plane remains the same size, even though it looks tiny from the air.

WHY IS IT SO HARD TO READ THIS SENTENCE UPSIDE DOWN?

Panorama (pan-or-RAH-mah). From the Greek words *pan,* meaning "all," and *horama,* meaning "view." A panorama is thus a "view of everything," such as that you get from the top of a mountain on a very clear day.

A few miles farther on, the plane encounters a bank of thick, fleecy clouds. Although you are rather apprehensive about this turn of events, the pilot plunges the plane into the clouds apparently without a second thought. Suddenly the world around you goes gray; you can't see a thing. You look straight down, hoping to see some glimpse of the ground below, but the swirling gray is featureless. The harder you stare at it, the vaguer and more fog-like it becomes. After a few seconds your eyes begin to hurt from the strain of trying to focus on pure nothingness, but you keep on looking down because you feel safer when you can see the land below. Then the cloud begins to break up a little, and just for a second you see a patch of ground through a hole in the cloud. Is that a big hill you're looking at? But there aren't any hills like that around this area. Then the hole in the cloud gets bigger, and you see that what you thought was a hill was really a big gravel pit dug deep into the ground. Odd that it should look like a mountain the first time you looked at it.

Perhaps sensing your uneasiness, the pilot lets down below the cloud and heads back to the airport. He calls the tower, gets permission to land, circles the airport, then lines the little plane up for a straight-in approach to the runway. As the plane glides down closer and closer to the ground, you notice again that the numbers on the runway seem bigger at the bottom than at the top. A bit of dirt blows into your left eye, so you close it and begin rubbing it. And you suddenly realize that with one of your eyes shut, you have a very difficult time deciding exactly how near you are to the ground. For some reason, with one eye shut, the wide *panorama* (°) ahead of you seems flat, almost like a painting. The wheels bump onto the hard surface of the runway; the pilot puts on the brakes and then turns off onto one of the taxi strips, heading for the hangar. Home again, safely home.

But you are rather puzzled at the way your eyes have been acting. Did the altitude somehow affect your vision? The answer is no; it wasn't the altitude at all. Sometimes it takes an unusual or abnormal situation to help you understand what your eyes are doing all the time. Let's see what was going on.

ILLUSIONS

When Philip Cassone (*see* Chapter 9) insisted that he saw a herd of elephants lumbering around the tiny "black room" he was lying in, he was suffering from an hallucination. As real as the elephants seemed to him at the time, they existed only

A panorama of New York Bay. The boats look like toys from this perspective.

in his imagination. In more technical terms, Phil's experience was not triggered off by incoming visual sensation—his eyes did not "see" elephants at all, but his brain saw *images* that it confused with sensations.

As we said in Chapter 9, your stream of consciousness is for the most part under the control of the world around you. In conditions of sensory deprivation—as well as when drugs upset neural functioning—the image circuits of the brain are somehow freed from the usual sensory control. Under these conditions the person's mind can bring up from its memory files any image or combination of images that it wishes to, and the person will often accept the image as the real thing. A true hallucination, then, is in no way dependent on stimulation from the external world—but its internal "imagined" reality is so striking that the person accepts the hallucination as if it were a percept.

On the other hand, sometimes the neural circuitry in our brains so distorts the incoming sensory message that we misperceive something in the world around us. Such faulty perceptions are called *illusions* (°).

Some illusions are due to our expectations—we see a spider crawling on the wall just before we get into bed. As we lie awake trying to go to sleep, a loose thread from the pillow case gently touches our cheek and we sit up instantly, sure that we have "felt" a spider crawling on our face.

Other illusions are apparently caused by odd imperfections in our sensory apparatus. As the famous painter Vincent van Gogh reached the end of his life, he began depicting shining objects (such as the sun) as if they were surrounded by concentric rings of color. For a long time art critics were convinced that van Gogh had "broken through to a new level of reality" by letting his imagination run free. If this were the case, then we might say that van Gogh was *hallucinating* the circles around the sun that he so often painted. But we now suspect that van Gogh suffered from a dreadful disease that was systematically destroying his nervous system. One of the symptoms of this particular illness is that the person's vision becomes cloudy and all bright lights have *halos* (°) around them. It is likely, then, that van Gogh was suffering from the same kind of illusion that you can experience if you look at a street light on a foggy night, or watch a full moon through a thin layer of clouds. (*See* color Plate 7.)

Size Constancy

For the most part our brains do an excellent job of sorting out illusion from reality. As you might guess, it takes considerable time and experience for your brain to build up the necessary neural circuitry so that your Board of Directors can interpret incoming sensory information accurately. When you were a baby, lying in your crib, your mother dangled toys in front of you. As you reached out a tiny hand to grasp the brightly colored toys, you began learning about distances.

When someone gave you a teddy bear to cuddle, it was so large that it filled all of your visual world. A day or so later you saw the teddy bear far across the room, and now it occupied only a small fraction of your visual world. It looked so much smaller over there—perhaps it had shrunk in size. But no, when you crawled over to it, the bear seemed to grow and grow in size until, when you reached it, the bear was as large as ever. Was this some kind of magic?

When your mother was far away from you, she seemed to be smaller in size than the teddy bear when it was sitting next to you. Yet, when your mother handed you the bear, it was obvious that she was much larger than the bear.

Without ever sitting down to think about such things, you eventually learned that *objects remain constant in size whether they are near you or far away*. It all seems so obvious to you now that you can't remember having learned that lesson; yet if you hadn't, you'd have a difficult time getting around in the world. If you hadn't worked out the principle of *size constancy* (°), how could you cross a busy street? For instead of seeing cars rushing down on you from all directions, the

Illusions. Misperceptions. Sometimes the visual or auditory stimulus is such that it tricks you into seeing or hearing incorrectly. The cause of the illusion usually is in the stimulus itself, or the way that the receptors in your eye or ear respond to that stimulus. Hallucinations, on the other hand, are caused by incorrect processing of normal incoming sensations, and hence are a fault of the cortex (and not of the receptors or the external stimulus). If you look at an oddly shaped cat and "see" it as a dog, that is an illusion. If you look at empty space (when you're drunk or "high") and think you see a dog, that is an hallucination.

Halo (HAY-low). A circle of light around an object, as around the heads of saints and angels in religious paintings.

Size constancy (KON-stan-see). Your brain gets a rough idea of the physical size of an object by noting how large a visual image the object casts on your retina. Generally speaking, the larger the visual image, the larger the object will be. However, an object very close to you will cast a much larger image on your retina than will the same object if it is far away from you. If the object is very familiar, your brain will interpret any change in the size of the retinal image as a change in the distance the object is from you. This is the principle of size constancy. If the object is unfamiliar, you may overestimate its size if it is up close, and underestimate its size if it is far away from you.

A demonstration of size constancy. Most people see the car as coming closer rather than as changing in size.

automobiles might seem to be stationary. Instead of seeing them as moving, you might simply see them as ballooning up in size as they "approached you," and dwindling in size as they sped away into the distance. In short, during your early years you learned that, in many ways, visual size and distance are closely related. When you look at a fire engine a block or so away, the amount of space that its image occupies on your retina is smaller than that of a toy fire engine up close to you. But you see the distant firetruck as being large but far away and the toy as being small but close up.

The principle of size constancy breaks down in extreme cases, primarily because you haven't had the proper sorts of experiences. When you look down at people and cars from a great height—either from the top of a tall building or from an airplane—the objects below often lose reality. People seem like cardboard cut-outs and automobiles seem like toys. Construction workers who work on tall buildings are often exceptions, however. It takes a lot of time to put up a skyscraper that is 100 stories high. First the workers see the people below from 10 feet (3 meters) or so above ground level; then, as they add more and more stories to the building, they progressively see the world below at higher and higher elevations—20 feet (6 meters), 50 feet (15 meters), 100 feet, 1000 feet. They move up and down the building several times a day. These construction workers usually report that even from 1000 or more feet above the ground, people still look like people to them, and not like the tiny crawling insects that we see them as being when we look down at them from an airplane.

VISUAL DEPTH AND DISTANCE

Your visual receptors are located in the retinas of your eyes. The retina is, for all practical purposes, little more than a flat, two-dimensional movie screen on which the lens in your eye projects images of the world around you. Yet when you look at the world—or at a movie screen—it doesn't seem flat and two-dimensional to you. The world is three-dimensional; it has depth to it. A blank movie screen has but two dimensions—left/right and up/down. When you project a first-rate movie on the screen, suddenly a third dimension appears in the picture. How does this near-miracle happen?

The Case of S.B.

The answer is, it doesn't; that is, not without a lot of experience on your part. British psychologist Richard L. Gregory recently reported the case of a man who had been blind since infancy, but whose vision was restored at age 52. This patient—whom Dr. Gregory calls S.B.—was an intelligent person whose vision had been normal at birth. At age 10 months, S.B. developed a severe infection of the eyes that left his *corneas* (°) so badly scarred that he could not see objects at all. Enough light leaked through the damaged corneas that S.B. could just tell day from night, but he saw the world much as you would if someone cut a ping pong ball in two and placed one of the halves over each of your eyes. The corneal scars were so bad, in fact, that for most of S.B.'s life no doctor would operate on him. Nonetheless, S.B. led a pleasant and very active life. He went places by himself, waving his white cane in front of him to let people know he was blind. He often went for rides on a bicycle, with a friend holding his shoulder and guiding him.

S.B. spent considerable time making wooden objects with rather simple tools; he had an open-faced watch that let him tell time by feeling the position of the hands; he took care of animals and knew them all by touch. And always he tried to imagine what things looked like. When he washed his brother's car, he would vividly try to picture what color and shape it really was. When S.B. visited the zoo, he would get his friends to describe the *exotic* (°) animals there in terms of

Cornea (CORN-ee-ah). The tough, transparent tissue at the front of the eyeball. See Chapter 8.

Exotic (x-OTT-tic). From the Greek word meaning "outside." Anything that is strange, foreign, or introduced from some other country is considered exotic.

Grafted. Joining parts of one organism to another is called "grafting." You can sometimes graft a branch from one tree onto another; if the graft "takes," the new branch will take its food and water from the sap of the "host" tree and grow normally. In corneal grafts, part of the donor's cornea just in front of the pupil is surgically removed and transplanted to the eye of the recipient ("host"). If the corneal graft "takes," the grafted tissue will connect up to the recipient's bloodstream and function more or less normally.

Lower case letters. Capital letters (such as "DOG") are called "upper case letters." Lower case letters (such as "dog") are letters that are not capitalized.

how different they were from dogs and cats in his home. He had always hoped to be able to see. Finally, when well past his 50th year, S.B. prevailed upon a surgeon to attempt an operation in which his corneas were removed and new ones were *grafted* (°) on in their place.

The operation was a great success, but, as Dr. Gregory reports, S.B. was anything but happy with the results. When the doctor first removed the bandages, S.B. looked straight into the doctor's face—and saw nothing but a blur. He knew that what he saw had to be the doctor's face, because he recognized the man's voice. It took S.B. several days before he could begin to tell one person from another merely by looking at them, and he never became very good at identifying people visually. Nonetheless, his progress in some areas was rapid. Within a few days he could successfully navigate the halls of the hospital without running into things; he could tell time by looking at the face of a very large clock; and he dearly loved to get up early in the morning and sit at his window watching the traffic rumble by on the street far below his hospital room.

But there were problems. S.B. rapidly learned the names of the colors red, black, and white; other colors he had difficulty identifying. He could judge horizontal distances fairly well if he were looking at objects whose size he was familiar with. But vertical distances—heights of any kind—and unfamiliar situations always bothered him. One day they found him crawling out the window of his fourth-floor hospital room, presumably because he wanted to inspect more closely the automobile traffic in the street below. He looked at the ground 40 feet (12 meters) away and thought it no more than 5 feet (1.5 meters) away.

Prior to the operation, S.B. had crossed even the busiest intersection alone without the faintest fear. He would plunge into traffic waving his white stick in front of him, and somehow the sea of cars and trucks would part for him much as the waters of the Red Sea parted for Moses in Old Testament times. After S.B. got his vision back, he was absolutely terrified of crossing a street. Dr. Gregory states that it usually took two people holding his arms to force him across an intersection.

Often when S.B. saw a fairly familiar object for the first time, he would be unable to identify it until he closed his eyes and felt it. Then he knew it by touch, and once he "had the picture in his mind," could recognize it after he had looked at it a few times. But objects that he hadn't (or couldn't) run his hands over before regaining his sight always gave him problems. The moon, for instance, puzzled him greatly. The full moon he could make out, but the quarter moon he had expected to be wedge-shaped, rather like a large slice of pumpkin pie. In school he had been taught the alphabet and the numbers by feeling large blocks that had raised letters on them. As soon as he could see, he could recognize capital letters and numbers without any special training. But he never learned to read very well because it was apparently very difficult for him to recognize *lower case letters* (°). He had been taught that R-A-G was the word for a small piece of cloth, but r-a-g was a meaningless jumble of lines as far as he was concerned.

When S.B. looked at the two long lines in the figure in the margin on p. 201, he saw them as being the same length. How do they look to you?

Immediately after his operation, S.B. was very enthusiastic and happy. He loved bright colors (although he couldn't always give their right names), and he enjoyed being able to see the faces of people he knew. But then he began to get depressed. He complained bitterly about the ugliness in the world around him—houses with the paint coming off, buildings with dirty walls, people with blemishes on their faces. He would spend hours sitting in his local tavern watching people in the mirror; somehow their reflections seemed more interesting to him than their real-life images. Often he would withdraw from human contact and spend most of the day sitting in almost complete darkness, claiming that he could "see" better when there was no light.

There have been no more than a half dozen confirmed cases of people who have gained sight as adults. According to Gregory, depression and unhappiness is a common consequence of their getting back their vision. For instance, in 1777, Anton Mesmer (an unusual scientist whom we will meet again in Chapter 18) studied a French girl who regained her sight at age 17. After being able to see for a few months, this young woman complained bitterly that the world was so ugly and tiresome that she wished she were blind again. In part, this unhappiness and depression seem to come from the discovery of how hard it really is "to see," and in part it stems from the slow realization of how much life has been missed.

Mueller-Lyer Illusion

Cases such as that of S.B. demonstrate the critical influence that your early-life experiences have on shaping how you will see the world when you have grown up. For during your childhood years you learn the "rules of visual perception" even though you are far too young to know what words like "visual" and "perception" really mean. Look at the figure in the right margin. Doesn't the *horizontal* (°) line with the arrowheads seem much shorter than the line with "V's" on each end? Yet, if you measure the two horizontal lines, you'll see they're exactly the same length. Why does one look longer than the other? Richard Gregory believes that this illusion is based on our perception of corners. If you are reading this book indoors, look at one of the corners of the room you're in. Notice that the angles the wall makes with the floor or the ceiling form a line drawing much like the "V" figure. If you are sitting outdoors, look at the corner of a building. Again you will see that the angles made by the roof and the ground are close to the same lines in the "arrowhead" figure. Gregory believes that you see the "V" figure as being much closer to you than the "arrowhead" figure, and that this perception of distance causes you to see one line as being longer than the other.

The Mueller-Lyer illusion.

> QUESTION: It is rather simple to train a pigeon in a laboratory to peck at the shorter of two lines in order to be rewarded by food; how would you set up a demonstration that pigeons are subject to the Mueller-Lyer illusion?

Circles and Straight Lines

The Mueller-Lyer illusion points up an interesting fact—you seldom see an object all by itself. Instead, you almost always see an object in context or in relationship to the other objects around it. In the Mueller-Lyer illusion, the two horizontal lines have "tails" at either end that affect your perception of the lines themselves. Now look at the figure with the dots. The two center dots are exactly the same size, but they surely don't look the same! The apparent straightness of a line can easily be affected by whatever objects the line seems to penetrate. In the figure at the bottom of p. 202, the *diagonal* (°) line crossing the two bars seems to be

Horizontal (hor-rizz-ZON-tull). When you're lying stretched flat out, your body is horizontal to the floor. When you are standing straight up, your body is vertical to the floor.

Diagonal (die-AG-oh-null). If you were standing straight up, then leaned over at an angle, your body would be diagonal to the floor. The "slant mark" (/) on the typewriter is a diagonal line.

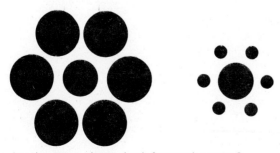

Are the center dots in both figures the same?

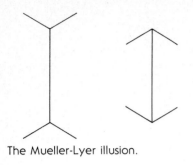

The Mueller-Lyer illusion.

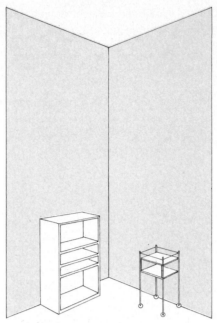

The corner where the walls meet is actually the same height as the edges of the walls shown.

The outside corner of this building is the same height as the other edges. With the illustration on the left the Mueller-Lyer illusion is formed.

broken in three disconnected parts; in fact, as you can determine by using a ruler, the line is absolutely straight.

A circle drawn in the middle of a "wheel," such as that at the top of page 203, somehow looks lopsided; while a square drawn in the middle on concentric circles looks warped. These figures—like the lake you observed from the air earlier in this chapter—are good illustrations of how difficult it is for your eye to follow a line when the line is interrupted by other lines.

A "straight line" or a "circle" are not things that you simply "see." Rather, they are *concepts* that your Board of Directors *perceives* after taking many things into account. Straightness and circularity are *percepts* that are affected by feedback from your eye muscles as much as by sensations arising in your retina.

Look at the circle on page 203. Stare at the exact center of the colored circle and don't let your eyes move. Notice that now the circle looks almost perfectly round. If you focus at the center of the colored square in the next figure, it looks much less distorted than if you glance at the whole drawing casually and "let your eyes wander" as you inspect it. The Mueller-Lyer illusion is affected by the way your eyes move when you look at the lines.

As you will see momentarily, some aspects of visual perception are determined

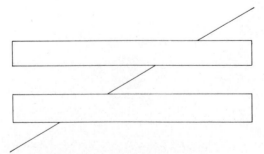

Is the diagonal line straight?

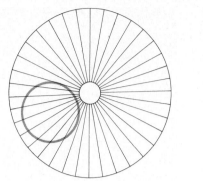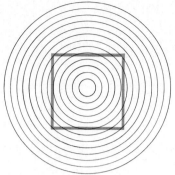

The backgrounds in these two figures distort the colored circle and square.

by the genetic blueprint you inherited. For the most part, however, your past experiences determine what you see in the world around you. We grow up in a world of straight lines, corners, and sharp angles. But what of someone who matured in an environment where straight lines were *taboo* (°), someone who saw only curves and wavy lines as a child? How would this person see the Mueller-Lyer illusion?

The answer is—the person probably wouldn't see the illusion at all. The Zulus—a tribe of primitive people in South Africa—live in what Gregory calls a "circular culture." The huts they live in are round mounds with circular doors; they plow their fields in curved lines; and even their toys and tools lack straight edges. When shown the Mueller-Lyer illusion, the typical Zulu native sees one line as being only very slightly longer than the other. Other illusions, such as that shown at the bottom of page 201, affect the Zulu hardly at all.

QUESTION: Suppose you grew up in a dense forest in Africa or in South America where you seldom could see more than a few feet in front of you; if, as an adult, you suddenly came out of the forest and saw a friend of yours 100 feet (30 meters) away, what size would the friend probably appear to be?

Taboo (tab-BOO). Sometimes spelled "tabu." Any object or behavior that is prohibited because it is illegal or immoral. The most common form, found in almost all cultures, is the incest taboo—the fact that you are not supposed to have sexual experiences with close relatives.

Clues to Visual Distance

Your eye inspects the world in front of you and reports to your brain what it sees. Your brain takes into account not only the visual sensations coming from your retinas but also the way that your eyes move in their sockets, the sounds your ears report, the smells around you, your bodily posture, and all the memories it can dredge up. Then your Board of Directors decides what it is you are looking at. An automobile passes you on the street; you know that it is about 30 feet (9 meters) away from you because you remember what size cars ought to be, how long it takes you to walk 30 feet, and how the visual image of the car will change as you walk toward it. The *apparent size* of an object gives you a good notion of how far away the object is. But there are other clues that your brain uses, even though you are often not aware of what these clues are.

Perspective If you stood in the middle of a railroad track and looked down the roadbed, the rails would seem to come together in the distance. Your mind tells you that the rails don't actually converge or meet on the horizon, but your eye insists that they do. If you draw two identical lines at right angles to the tracks, the top line seems to be longer (*see* p. 204). Can you figure out why?

And when you stand at the end of a runway at an airport, looking down toward the other end, can you understand why the tops of the numbers painted on the runway look "scrunched up?" This apparent coming together of parallel lines as

We know the man and building are not the same height, so we assume the building is far away from us and the man close.

The railway line illusion. The wooden ties are all the same size; do they look that way to you?

Linear perspective (LIN-ee-urr per-SPECK-tive). "Linear" has to do with straight lines, such as the horizon (the line between earth and sky). "Perspective" means "viewpoint." Parallel lines (such as railroad tracks) appear to meet at the horizon. If you were drawing a realistic picture of railroad tracks, therefore, you would want to draw them so that they "met" at the horizon in your picture.

Aerial perspective (AIR-ee-ull). Literally, the "way you see an object through the air." "Fuzzy" objects seem distant; clear (distinct) objects seem close.

they approach the horizon is called *linear perspective* (°), and is one of the cues that your brain uses to judge distance. Oddly enough, it took artists a long time to realize that they had to make use of linear perspective in their paintings if they wanted to reproduce distances effectively. In some paintings, such as those by Persian artists in the 16th and 17th centuries, the almost complete lack of linear perspective gives the painting a curiously flat, distorted, and unreal appearance. (*See* color Plate 9.)

QUESTION: **If an Oriental artist paints a scene that lacks linear perspective, does this mean that the artist actually does not *see* perspective in his or her own visual world?**

Anyone who has grown up in a smog-ridden U.S. city knows that there are often days when you can't see more than a block or two away. But there are parts of our land still blessedly free from this aerial pollution. In some of our deserts, for instance, the air is often so clear that visibility is practically unlimited. The city dweller who first visits these regions of the United States is sometimes shocked at how badly he or she judges distances in clean, fresh air. A mountain peak that appears to be no more than 4 or 5 miles (6.44 or 8.05 kilometers) away may, in fact, be more than 50 miles (80.45 kilometers) down the road. The more hazy and indistinct a remote object seems to us, the further away it appears to be—a fact that psychologists refer to as the *aerial perspective* (°) of an object. Pilots attempting to land planes in foggy weather often misperceive how far above the

Remember that the numbers don't change, only your perception of them.

Seen in a haze, buildings and other objects seem to be further away.

SHADOW SHADOW

If you look closely you will see that the letters on the right are not raised letters casting a shadow, but only shadows. Look at the illustration at the left.

ground they are because the fog distorts the aerial perspective they are accustomed to.

Sometimes we make judgments about the visual world from what we *don't* see, instead of from what we do see. Look at the illustration at the left above, a simple representation of the word "shadow." Notice that each of the six letters in this word is printed in full. Now look at the next word. Here there are no letters, just the shadows themselves. But look carefully. Doesn't your eye actually *see* the forms of the letters as if they were really there? As we pointed out before, your brain has the happy habit of filling in details of objects it assumes ought to be there.

We often make use of shadows in judging whether we are looking at a mountain or at the hole left in the ground when somebody dug up the mountain and took it away. Photographs of the craters and hills on the moon and on Mars are fairly commonplace now. When you look at one of these photographs, you automatically make an assumption about how the sunlight is falling on the landscape. If you make the wrong assumption, then you see a hill instead of a crater.

QUESTION: S.B. often mistook shadows for real objects; why do you think this was the case?

Convergence Man is essentially a two-dimensional animal, bound to those parts of the surface of the earth that his two feet can walk on. The bird soaring into the air, the porpoise diving to the bottom of a shallow bay—these are animals that live in all three dimensions. Man judges distances rather well, if the distance is no greater than he can walk or run or ride. But we judge heights rather poorly, at least compared to the abilities shown by most birds and fish. When you look at

Is this a hill or a crater in the surface of the moon? Now turn the page upside down and look again.

something in the distance, both your eyes point straight ahead. When you look at something up close, however, your eyes both turn inward, toward your nose. The amount of strain that this *convergence* (°), or "turning inward," causes on the muscles is noticed by your brain, which uses this cue as an index of how far away the object is. To judge how far away from us another person is, we have but to let our eyes converge and notice the strain on our eye muscles. But to judge height, we usually have to move our heads up and down or crane our necks. For all but the most experienced airplane pilots, the neck muscles are poorer judges of distance than the eye muscles.

FIGURE-GROUND RELATIONSHIPS

The perception of a single object in visual space is fairly well understood by psychologists. You seldom get the chance to look at just one object, however— usually your visual world is crowded with all manner of things to look at and admire. And you typically see all the things in the world as having some kind of relationship with each other. The simplest form of this relationship is that of *figure-ground* (°). Even such a simple percept as that of a fluffy white cloud dancing alone in the clear blue sky is usually seen as *a something on a something,* a figure or object on a background.

Whatever you focus on or pay most attention to is usually said to be the figure, for it appears to stand out, or be most *salient* (°), in your visual world. However, as the object and its background become more complex, you may at times have difficulty telling which is which. Look at the figure at the left below, for instance. Which do you see, two shadow-faces looking at each other—or a fancy wine glass? These two stimulus patterns are so related to each other that either one can be figure *or* ground. If you stare at the illustration for a few seconds, you will find that it is almost impossible to see *both* patterns at once—rather, first you see one, then the other; and the percepts alternate rather rapidly. The same is true of the famous Necker cube at the right below. You can see the cube as projecting upward or downward, but not both ways at once.

> QUESTION: Why do you think you can't see the cube as projecting up and down at the same time? And second, S.B. saw the cube as being flat instead of having three dimensions; what does this fact tell you about your own depth perception?

Expectancy

As we said earlier, you usually see what you expect to see. When a novelist writes a mystery story, the writer will usually give the reader clues or hints as to who did what to whom. But often the clues are so stated that, while entirely factual, the

Convergence (kon-VERGE-ence). Means "to come together" or "to turn or move toward one another." Parallel lines converge at the horizon. You can demonstrate "eye convergence" if you can get a friend to cooperate. Hold up one of your fingers about 2 feet (0.6 meters) in front of the person's nose and ask the person to focus on the tip of your finger. Now slowly move your finger right up to the person's eyes. As your fingertip nears the person's nose, the person's eyes will turn toward each other.

Figure-ground. If you look closely at a book lying on a table, the book is the stimulus figure, the table is the background. Whatever you focus on visually is the figure. Whatever surrounds this object is its ground.

Salient (SAY-lee-ent). A word much beloved by psychologists. From the Latin term meaning "to leap or jump out." Something is salient if it is important or very noticeable. In figure-ground relationships, the figure is almost always salient.

Do you see two profile faces? Or a wine glass?

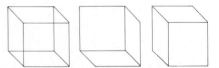

The Necker Cube. It can be seen as projecting up or down in three dimensions in the first cube. In the other two cubes the perspective is stabilized.

reader gets quite the wrong impression or expectancy. For many readers, half the fun of reading a mystery is trying to outguess the author as the story proceeds; the other half comes (once they have finished the piece) in going back over the tale trying to learn how the author led them astray.

If you would like to learn something about the effects of expectancies (and clues) on perception, look at the figure in the right margin. As you can see, it is a drawing of an *ugly old woman* with her chin buried in a fur coat. Look at it carefully and try to figure out what kind of an old woman she is. Is she happy or sad? And what is this old woman thinking of?

The artist who drew the picture claims she is dreaming of her daughter. And if you look carefully at the picture again, you will see that the face of the old woman can change into that of the pretty young daughter. The old woman's nose becomes the chin and jawline of the younger woman's face; the older woman's left eye becomes the daughter's left ear; the mother's mouth becomes a necklace around the daughter's neck; and so forth.

In several experiments most college students, given the expectancy that they were going to see a picture of an *old woman*, did indeed discover the mother's face before finding the daughter's. Other students, told they would be shown a drawing of a pretty young girl, tended to see the daughter's face easily but often had trouble "finding" the picture of the mother.

Do you see an old lady or a young girl?

Visual Grouping

In looking out at the world, your brain makes use of several psychological principles in trying to bring some kind of order to its percepts. For instance, you tend to group things together according to how close they are to each other. In part *a* of the figure below you probably see three "pairs" of lines; you will group *a* and *b* together because they are close to each other. In part *b* of the figure, however, things have changed. Now *b* and *c* seem to go together—to form a rectangle of some kind. Indeed, if you stare closely at the *b-c* rectangle, you will see rather faint but *imaginary* lines as your brain attempts to fill in or close up the open figure. Part *a* illustrates the principle of *proximity* (°), or physical closeness; part *b* illustrates the principle of *closure* (°)—that is, the tendency of the brain to join broken lines together to make a closed figure of some kind.

A third perceptual principle is that of *continuity* (°) and is illustrated at the top of p. 208 in part *a*. In this illustration you probably see a wavy line superimposed on a square-cornered line. If we now break up the pattern somewhat differently, as in part *b*, you see not two lines but two closed figures joined together. Why do you think this is so? And, if you wish, you may even break the figure up into a different set of components, shown in part *c*. Once you have learned what the parts of the figure can be, you can see it many different ways. But, at the beginning, your eye tends to follow the wavy line because it is *continuous*.

A fourth principle of perceptual grouping is that of *similarity* (°). The figure

Proximity (procks-IM-it-tee). That which is close. If you live a block from the fire station, you live in the proximity of the fire station. Objects that are proximate (close to each other) tend to be perceived as units.

Closure. "To complete" or "to close." If you glance very quickly at a circle that has a tiny gap in it, you may very well see the circle as being closed, or complete.

Continuity (con-tin-NEW-it-tee). From the word "continue" or "continuous." Things that are connected together in time or space have continuity. Your own stream of consciousness has a certain continuity or connectedness, in that one experience follows the other without a noticeable gap or "blank period of consciousness."

Similarity. Objects that are physically like one another tend to be perceived as units.

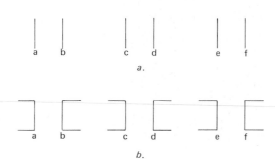

Which lines seem to relate in each of these pairs?

The Principle of Continuity.

Ambiguous (am-BIG-you-us). Anything that is vague or indefinite. If you ask someone to go on a date, and the person says "maybe yes, maybe no," the person has given you an ambiguous answer.

Gestalt (guess-TALT). A German word that is difficult to translate. Literally, it means "good form" or "good figure." Also means the tendency to see things as "wholes" rather than as jumbled bits and pieces.

Ellipse (ee-LIPS). An oval or somewhat egg-shaped figure.

below shows a series of 25 circles arranged in a square. If you fixate on this figure, you will notice that sometimes you group the circles together in bunches of 4s, or 9s, or 16s. Sometimes you see 5 horizontal rows of circles, sometimes 5 vertical columns. In such ambiguous situations your brain tests out various percepts, attempting to see which fits the stimulus pattern best.

When you look out into a cloud from an airplane, your brain is faced with a similar but even more difficult perceptual situation. For a cloud has no firm structure at all—whatever patterns you see in such *ambiguous* (°) situations are those which your brain actually imposes on incoming sensory information. The figure at the right below is quite different. Here, you see a cross formed of Xs, while the circles group themselves into squares of four circles each.

Gestalt Principles

Early in this century a group of German psychologists began a detailed study of the perceptual principles outlined above. These men eventually decided that the brain was so organized that it tended to see *Gestalts* (°), which is the German word for "good figures." To these Gestalt psychologists a circle was a "better" or more natural figure than an *ellipse* (°), hence (they said) we tend to see the left figure at the top of p. 209 as a round half-dollar turned slightly away from us rather than as a coin that has somehow been squashed into an elliptical shape.

The Gestalt theorists explained most of *shape constancy* (*see* elsewhere in this chapter) as the brain's desire to force all percepts into better or more natural shapes. Imagine what an empty picture frame looks like when you see it head-on. Now, in your mind's eye, rotate the frame away from you about 45 degrees. In its rotated position, the edge of the picture frame nearest you actually looks longer than the edge farthest away from you, but still you see the picture as being square.

Adelbert Ames, a U.S. psychologist who began life as a painter, took advantage of this *shape constancy* to produce a number of very amusing illusions, the best

The Principle of Similarity.

What is the shape of each of these drawings?

The same picture frame head-on and at an angle of 45 degrees is no longer visually the same.

known of which is his "distorted room." When looked at head-on, the room appears quite normal—until you see two people standing in the room, and then you know that something is very definitely wrong. The windows in the room look "square," as the Gestalt theorists would predict. In fact, the windows are really *trapezoids* (°), but your brain assumes that windows ought to be rectangular, hence your brain "sees" them as being rectangles. In order to keep the windows looking like rectangles, the brain must produce distance distortions that make one of the women in the room look twice as large as the other. Given the choice between preserving "good form" (the shape of the windows) or "size constancy" (the size of the women), your Board of Directors typically votes in favor of good form, just as the Gestalt theorists might predict.

Trapezoid (TRAP-ee-zoid). A four-sided figure with two sides which are parallel. Imagine a rectangular window. The top and bottom are parallel, as are the two sides. Now think of a window whose top is shorter than its bottom. The top and bottom are still parallel, but the sides will lean toward each other. This window is a trapezoid.

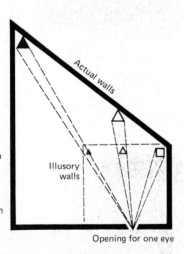
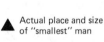
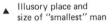

▲ Actual place and size of "smallest" man

▲ Illusory place and size of "smallest" man

△ Actual place and size of "medium" man

△ Illusory place and size of "medium" man

□ "Largest" man

A diagram of the Ames "distorted room" as seen from the top.

The Ames "distorted room" as seen from the front. The man on the left is really the same height as the other two men.

INNATE ASPECTS OF PERCEPTION

Neonate (KNEE-oh-nate). From the Latin words *neo,* meaning "new," and *natus,* meaning "born." Hence a child less than a month old. Your "natal day," incidentally, is the day you were born, your birthday.

Genetic blueprint. At the moment of your conception, you inherited a set of genes from your mother and your father. These genes contained a chemical pattern or blueprint of what your body would eventually be like. This blueprint—composed of complex molecules called DNA—specified what form and shape your brain and spinal cord would take. In short, the basic "wiring diagram" of your nervous system was contained in your genes, or genetic blueprint, and at birth you started life with a "prewired" brain. See Chapter 19 for a further explanation.

Innate (in-EIGHT). Inborn, or present at birth.

Almost a hundred years ago the famous U.S. psychologist William James stated that a newborn infant must perceive the world as being a "blooming, buzzing confusion." While it is true that the *neonate* (°) probably experiences its environment as a blurred, noisy mess, some aspects of visual perception appear so early in the child's life that they are surely a part of what we might call the *genetic blueprint* (°). For instance, look at the figure in the margin. One drawing is that of a face with the nose, eyes, and other features in their proper places; the other drawing has the same elements but they are oddly scrambled. Now imagine a very young infant lying comfortably on its back looking up at these figures. Which do you think it would spend more time looking at, the normal face or the scrambled one?

Psychologist R.L. Fantz photographed the eye movements of young babies using the apparatus shown below. Fantz found that infants spend much more time looking at the normal than at the scrambled face, a fact which suggests that the human child may have built into its brain *innate* (°) response patterns that allow it to recognize what the human face looks like. Fantz also found that babies seem to prefer to look at simple round objects rather than at two-dimensional, flat drawings of the same objects. Fantz believes that infants may have an innate appreciation of depth, but points out that these experiments may also mean that babies simply learn about faces and depths very early in their lives.

The Visual Cliff

A more intriguing bit of evidence concerning the innate properties of perception comes from a series of experiments pioneered by Dr. Eleanor Gibson, one of America's best-known perceptual psychologists. One day several years ago, Dr. Gibson found herself eating a picnic meal on the rim of the Grand Canyon. Looking straight down into that deep and awesome *chasm* (°), she began to worry about the safety of the children around her. Would a very young child be able to perceive the enormous drop-off at the edge of the cliff, or would the child go toddling over the precipice if no adult were around to restrain it?

What Dr. Gibson was really asking, of course, is—are babies born with an

Chasm (KAS-em; rhymes with "has 'em"). From the Greek word meaning "to gape or yawn." Thus, a deep or "yawning" hole.

Infants using Fantz's apparatus looked at the simple face longer than they did at the design with facial features.

Fantz's equipment for observing infants' eye movements.

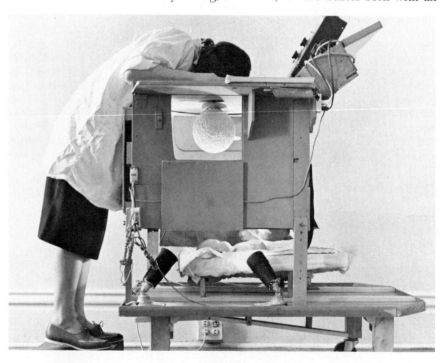

The "visual cliff," actually a solid glass surface, which reveals a checked material that cascades to the floor.

innate ability to perceive depth and a built-in fear mechanism that would make them retreat from sharp drop-offs even without having been trained to do so?

Once Dr. Gibson had returned to her laboratory at Cornell University, she designed an artificial "visual cliff" on which she could test infants safely.

Running down the middle of the apparatus was a raised plank of wood painted in a checkerboard pattern. To one side of the plank was a sharp drop-off; to the other, a normal "floor" an inch or so below the center plank. The entire apparatus was covered with sturdy glass so that the infant could see the cliff but could not fall off it.

When an infant was tested, it was put on the center board and allowed to explore freely. Very few of the infants crawled off onto the "cliff" side, although most of them freely moved onto the "floor" side. Even when the child's mother stood at the side of the apparatus and attempted to coax the child to crawl out over the "cliff," most infants refused to do so. Instead, they began to cry loudly. If the mother stood on the "floor" side of the box, however, the infant would crawl toward her happily.

A variety of newborn animals—such as lambs, kittens, puppies, and rats—were tested on the visual cliff too. For the most part these animals showed an almost immediate perceptual awareness of the "dangers" of the cliff. Apparently most higher species have behavioral mechanisms built into their brains at birth that tend to protect them from the dangers of falling from high places.

Pupil Responses

If all that your eyes were good for was looking at sunsets or admiring beautiful flowers, psychologists would have considerably less interest in the study of visual processes than they now do. But one of the major purposes of the billion or more neurons in your brain involved in "seeing" is to prepare you for action. You must be able to see things in order to be able to predict changes in the world around you, in order to anticipate what the consequences of your own actions will be. And so your eyes respond in a variety of ways that most of us simply never notice.

When you walk from a darkened movie theater out into the light, your pupils decrease in size rapidly to shut out the sudden influx of illumination. Your Board of Directors doesn't have to tell your pupil to change size under these conditions—the action is reflexive and is handled in rather automatic fashion by neural centers in the lower parts of your brain. When the lights go up, your pupil shuts down almost instantaneously.

Your brain goes even one step further. When you wish to inspect something closely, your pupils open slightly, even though there is no change in illumination. The wider the pupillary opening, the more light comes through; and, in general, the more light that strikes your retina, the better you see. The more intensely you stare at an object, the wider your pupil will be.

Psychologist Eckhard Hess made use of this information a decade or so ago to test a hunch of his. Hess reasoned that you would most likely stare harder at an object you were really interested in than at something you disliked or were bored by. So he showed pictures of many different things to the college students he used as subjects in his experiment. Hess found that women (on the average) had much larger pupil openings when he showed them pictures of babies or of nude males than when he showed these women pictures of nude females or landscapes. Men, on the other hand, usually had wider pupils when shown pictures of nude females than when they were shown photographs of babies, landscapes, or nude males. Hess's research suggests that you can often tell something about a person's real interests simply by noting when the person becomes wide-eyed.

Visual Suppression On very rare occasions your Board of Directors is forced to choose between two quite different visual inputs. Imagine a large black box with two eyeholes in one side. There is a wooden partition inside the box that divides it in half; thus, when you look through the holes, your left eye sees quite a different scene than does your right eye. The split-brain patient we discussed in Chapter 2 has no problem with this situation—one of the patient's hemispheres usually "sees" the picture on the left, while the other hemisphere "sees" the picture on the right. But what about you? How would your brain handle this odd situation? Generally speaking, your Board simply *suppresses* (°), or rejects, one of the pictures and concentrates on the other.

If we show a different scene to your left eye than to your right, which scene will your brain suppress? If your vision is clearer in one eye than in the other, your Board will almost always pick the scene that it sees best. But if both your eyes are in good shape, the Board faces a *dilemma* (°). If your left eye is looking at a teacup, while your right eye is looking at a teapot that is pouring liquid from its

Suppresses (sup-PRESS-es). To inhibit or to put down.

Dilemma (die-LEM-mah). A problem with two equally unsatisfactory answers. You can be said to face a dilemma of some sort any time you find yourself unable to make up your mind between two (or more) choices.

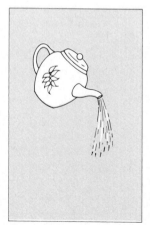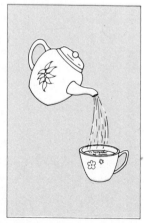

The teapot pouring liquid and the teacup can be fused visually so that the tea seems to flow into the cup.

spout, your Board may actually fuse or meld the two scenes together so that you see a pot pouring tea into a cup. If one eye sees a baby hanging in mid-air, while the other sees a woman holding out empty arms, your Board may superimpose one scene on the other so that you see the woman holding the child.

But suppose the two pictures are so different that they can't be fused? Then your brain typically concentrates on whichever object it finds the more interesting and suppresses the other scene almost completely. In many cases the suppression takes place so rapidly that you are simply not aware that you are being shown two different objects or photographs. Unpleasant or frightening scenes are more readily suppressed than are pleasant or stimulating scenes.

QUESTION: Suppose you own a company that manufactures soap. You decide to market the soap in a new style of container, so your marketing people come up with five suggested designs for the new box. You want to pick the box that will be most appealing to your customers. You might just show the five different designs to a large group of housewives and ask which one they like best, but you have learned from past experience that the verbal choices which people make in a test situation aren't always good indicators of what people will actually buy in a store. How might you use the "black box" apparatus described earlier to help you decide which new container to put your soap in?

Predicting Is Prejudging   Your eyes are your brain's window to the "movie of life" going on in the outside world. Your brain sits inside your skull, looking out, using every bit of information it can get in order to guess what is going to happen in the next reel of film. Some of this information is present at birth, but for the most part it is acquired through hard and often painful experience. You can "see" at birth, but you must learn to make sense of what you see—that is, you must learn to *perceive* the meaning and value of the things that flash on your retinal movie screen. Without learning, you could not survive without constant care.

But learning always carries with it the burden of prejudice—when your Board predicts what will happen next, it is prejudging the situation on the basis of past experience rather than present reality. We all need to reexamine our perceptions constantly to make sure that we aren't being fooled by the thousands of illusions that populate our worlds.

SUMMARY

1. Much of what you know about the world comes to you through your eyes.
2. Visual stimuli excite the rods and cones, which fire off messages (sensations) to the cortex. The brain scans these sensory inputs and compares them to images or memories of what it has seen in the past. If the image matches the sensation, your brain recognizes or perceives what the stimulus is.
3. When you mismatch sensation and image, you experience an illusion or misperception.
4. When you mistake an image for a sensation, you experience an hallucination.
5. Visual perception is influenced by many stimulus factors. Large objects often appear close to us (and close objects appear large); small objects often appear far away (and distant objects appear small). However, if you know what the object is, you will probably interpret both its size and its distance correctly.
6. Another stimulus factor affecting visual perception is perspective. As you grew up, your brain learned such things as linear perspective (the fact that parallel lines converge at the horizon) and aerial perspective (the fact that "fuzzy objects" typically are farther away from you than distinct objects). As you look at things, your brain automatically interprets these visual cues so that you get a rough idea of how far away objects are.
7. Objects that are physically close to each other, or are physically similar to one another, tend to be perceived as units.

8. The brain has what may be an innate tendency to see incomplete or "open" figures as being closed, perhaps because closed figures make better Gestalts ("good figures").

9. Children and young animals seem innately to avoid crawling out over open spaces or "visual cliffs."

10. When you look at something that interests you, your pupils sometimes open wider than when you look at something boring or uninteresting.

11. When your two eyes are shown different scenes, your brain may suppress one of the scenes, or may fuse them together to make a Gestalt (a complete or "whole" figure or percept).

12. The most basic principle of visual perception is that you tend to see what you expect to see.

(Continued from page 193.)

The last of the male passengers came out of the little airport waiting room sweating profusely and shaking his head. "Bunch of dratted nonsense," the man muttered to himself as he passed by the elegant figure of the Laforan Minister of Science and Technology.

Freddie glumly watched the man depart. They had held the passengers of the special Paris jet in a quarantine waiting room, letting them pass one by one through the office where Professor Mann had inspected their eyes. Mann had agreed to signal Freddie if the tests had detected which person was the Snake, but no signal had come. And now the waiting room was empty, save for a number of very attractive but rather overdressed young women and one rather forlorn matron cradling a baby in her arms. The good-looking young women were obviously girl friends of the munitions dealers, Freddie was sure, probably picked up in Paris with the promise of an "interesting" trip if they cared to accompany these rather shady businessmen. The matron was probably one of the dealer's wives, although why a man would bring a wife and child to Lafora on a business trip, Freddie wasn't sure. What he was sure of was the fact that Dr. Mann's tests had failed him—and failed the Republic of Lafora as well. The former fault he could tolerate; the latter came close to treason, and he mentioned this fact to the U.S. Professor.

"What have you done, and why didn't it work?" Freddie demanded.

Mann looked annoyed at the Minister's bluntness. "First I showed a series of drawings to each man and measured the size of his pupils while he was watching. One of the drawings was of a snake. I had thought that our friend the assassin would show a larger pupil size to this drawing than to any other. Three of the men so far did so, but they failed the second test."

"Which was . . . ?"

"A suppression test. I have a variety of drawings—a pile of money, guns, airplanes, a picture of your President, a number of animals, and a snake striking at something with dripping fangs. I had them look into my little black box that shows one drawing to the person's left eye, another to the right eye. And then I simply asked them to report what they saw. I figured most people would suppress the image of the snake, since most people are afraid of snakes. I figured also that the assassin would, if nothing else, hesitate and be confused. But every man on the plane suppressed the picture of the snake without a moment's hesitation."

"And so your oh-so-scientific tests have failed," Freddie said glumly.

"No, Freddie, we're not through yet. There are still people in the waiting room."

Freddie looked around. "Just women and children, my dear Professor. We might as well let them go."

"You'll do nothing of the kind. Send them along for the eye checks, or their boy friends are going to be rather suspicious, don't you think?"

Freddie paused to consider the matter and, as he did so, the matron approached them hesitantly and asked Freddie, "Excuse me, sir, my little boy is not feeling well, and I'd like to get some warm milk for him and change his diaper. I wonder if you would allow us to go on through to the ladies' powder room?"

"Right after you have your eyes checked, Madam," the Professor said. "Part of the health inspection, you know. Now, if you'll just look into this black box and tell me what you see," the psychologist said, moving around behind the apparatus.

"Of course," the matron said, "if you'll promise to hurry."

The woman turned to Freddie and handed him the infant, which immediately set up a lusty bawling. Freddie's nose crinkled at the moist little bundle he had been handed, and he held the child clumsily and with obvious distaste. "Hurry it up, will you?" Freddie said loudly to the Professor.

"Here's the first picture. What do you see?"

The matron leaned back a bit. "It's a gun of some kind," she said. "I don't approve of guns, you know."

"And how about this second picture?"

The matron glanced into the eyeholes in the box, then leaned forward a bit. "Why, it's a snake—a big, black, ugly snake."

Freddie glanced up immediately at the Professor, who smiled back at him with wide-open eyes.

"And now we'll try another test entirely. When I say 'Now,' I want you to look into the apparatus and tell me as quickly as you can what you see. All right?"

"Certainly," said the matron, as Professor Mann adjusted the slides inside the box.

"Now."

The woman leaned forward to look. She paused for several seconds, then responded, "That's odd, very odd indeed. I seem to see two things at once. First I see that snake again, and then I see a picture of the Laforan President, and then . . . then I see the snake biting the President. Now why would I see something like that?"

Freddie knew perfectly well why. He moved the infant to one arm and signaled vigorously with the other. Two large guards swooped down on them at once.

"Arrest this woman and search her baggage carefully," he told the guards.

The General hurried up to them. "Freddie, you've gone mad! This woman can't be the Snake!"

"How do you know?" the Professor asked, as the guards removed the matron from the scene. "You're just prejudiced against women, you two."

"Yes, my dear General," Freddie said, a smile on his face. "I'll bet a month's pay that Professor Mann has snared the Snake for us. The perceptual tests are positive."

"Perceptual tests be damned," said the General loudly. "Killing is a man's business, and everybody knows that the Snake is a man . . ."

"And that's why nobody ever caught her," said Professor Mann. "She gave you a beautiful illusion to fool yourselves with. Down through history the snake has always been a symbol of masculine sexual power and ruthlessness. Take the primitive tribe that I had hoped to visit, for instance; the chief warrior has a snake carved on the staff he carries. And if you look closely at those gold buttons that cover your uniform, General, you'll find the snake symbol on them all. But of course she did give you one clue to her identity—isn't poison a woman's weapon? Or was it just your minds she was attempting to poison?" The Professor smiled. "I'll offer one more suggestion—look through those baby things very closely. What more unlikely place to carry snake venom than in a child's rattle?"

A few minutes later the guard reported that a tiny hypodermic needle and a small bottle of milky-white liquid had been found in a sealed plastic bag inside the bottle of milk that the woman carried.

General Chambra was beside himself with happiness. He embraced Professor Mann in a huge bear hug, then hurried off to tend to military matters.

"He smells a promotion, I'm sure," said Freddie caustically.

"Helping catch the Snake won't hurt your image any either, now will it, Freddie?"

"My dear Professor Mann, you speak with a forked tongue. But you are right, of course. The President will be very pleased . . ."

"And as for me?"

Freddie frowned. "Whatever do you mean?"

"What about those 'murderous savages' that I want to visit? Are you still afraid that they might do me in? If I can catch a snake for you, can't I manage to handle a few frightened primitives?"

"Well, my dear . . ."

The Professor interrupted. "You're still showing your prejudices, Freddie. When you look at a woman, you still see a helpless little creature who couldn't possibly survive if there weren't a great big man to help her over the hurdles. You get very, very angry at all the whites in this world who judge a man by his skin color rather than by his true capabilities, yet your view of women is just as biased and as distorted as their view of skin color. Isn't it about time you saw through some of your own illusions?"

Freddie smiled. "You psychologists! Ah well, I suppose that I might just mention to the President what your part in this afternoon's activities was. And our President is a very generous man indeed."

Freddie looked around and saw a couple of porters lounging near one of the doors.

"Here, you men! Get Professor Mann's equipment packed up again and take it outside and put it back on the truck. She'll need it in the back country."

"And now, Freddie, how about that drink you promised me two hours ago?"

As they walked off, arm in arm, headed for the cocktail lounge, the porters began to load up the heavy crates with the perceptual apparatus. The boxes were covered with address labels. On the largest label of all, written in scrawling print, was:

> Dr. Mary Ellen Mann
> Department of Psychology
> University of the Mid-West
> USA

RECOMMENDED READINGS

Cornsweet, Tom N. *Visual Perception* (New York: Academic Press, 1971).

Gombrich, E.H. *Art and Illusion: A Study in the Psychology of Pictorial Representation* (Princeton, N.J.: Princeton University Press, 1961).

Gregory, Richard L. *The Intelligent Eye* (New York: McGraw-Hill Book Company, Inc., 1970).

Haber, Ralph Norman, and Maurice Hershenson. *The Psychology of Visual Perception* (New York: Holt, Rinehart and Winston, 1973).

Locher, J.L., ed. *The World of M.C. Escher* (New York: Harry N. Abrams, Inc., 1971).

Rock, Irwin. *An Introduction to Perception* (New York: Macmillan, 1975).

Solley, C.M., and G. Murphy. *Development of the Perceptual World* (New York: Basic Books, Inc., 1961).

chapter 11

"IT'S ALL IN YOUR MIND"

APPLIED SENSORY PSYCHOLOGY: SUBLIMINAL PERCEPTION

DID YOU KNOW THAT . . .

Some people once believed you could control people's minds by flashing "hidden" messages on TV and movie screens?

Many sensory messages get through to the lower centers of your brain and affect your behavior without your being conscious of what these stimuli are?

You are often unaware not only of incoming stimuli but also of the behaviors they prompt?

For a stimulus to prompt you to make a conscious response, the stimulus must first cross the sensory threshold, then the perceptual threshold, and finally the action threshold?

Some people repress awareness of emotional, sexual, or threatening stimuli, while other people actively seek out such sensory inputs?

Some people believe that mental telepathy (ESP) is just guesswork?

Relatively few U.S. psychologists believe that the existence of mental telepathy has been proved by scientific experimentation?

One of your main motives is to control and predict your sensory inputs?

Mrs. Sarah Wilson
823 Third Street
South Clarion, Missouri

Dear Mother:

Well, here it is another week. Mostly it's been a matter of books and a couple of short papers for my poly sci class, but nothing too energetic. Had a date with Charlie Saturday night—we went to see an old James Bond flick because it was the only thing on that one of us hadn't already seen. Charlie grooves on 007, maybe because he secretly thinks of himself as a James Bond type character. I rated the movie D for Dullish. Not a good night at all. In fact, I knew from the moment Charlie picked me up at the dorm that it was going to be one of "those" nights. I swear, I do **like** Charlie, but sometimes we just don't communicate, we don't relate. Sunday, Father Pratt talked about spirits that move us mysteriously from within. I've thought about that a lot, particularly since Tuesday night.

A funny night, too. I think I told you last week that Dr. Tompkins had invited me over to his house for coffee. I'm taking this course of his in the Psychology of Religion. He doesn't just go into Christianity or Judaism—he covers the Eastern religions too, Zen and Buddhism, and then he spends a lot of time on spiritualism. You know, the occult. Queer stuff, and I don't always know quite what to make of it. Or of Dr. Tompkins. He **talks** as though he believes in **something,** but secretly I think he's an atheist. I mean, aren't most scientists atheists? And he keeps trying to do experiments on things, instead of just trying to read about things and **understand.**

Anyway, he asked me over to have coffee with him and his wife. She's a doll. I really like her. Sort of quiet and sweet and understanding—reminded me of Mrs. Merriweather back home. I thought maybe there would be several students from his class there, but no, I was the only one. And I'm not that great a student. Well, no complaints. If the Great Professor wants to have me stop by for coffee, it's fine with me. Incidentally, I wore that pretty green dress that Aunt Debbie gave me for my birthday last year. Mrs. Tompkins complimented me on it, you might tell Aunt Debbie.

Well, I knew it was going to be something from the moment I got in the car. My bones ached, I guess, and I said to myself, it's going to rain tomorrow. And then while I was driving, I had the radio on and the weather forecast said it was going to be clear tonight and rain tomorrow. Isn't that queer? And I almost got killed on the way over—but it wasn't my fault at all. I was cruising down Parker Drive, minding my own business and thinking about how to get Charlie to ask me out on Friday instead of Saturday this week, when I got this feeling. You know me and my feelings. It was like a flash of lightning. Like I could see myself dead in a car wreck or something. It scared me so that I slammed on the brakes and came to a screeching halt right in the middle of Parker Drive. And then a second later, this guy comes roaring out of a driveway about ten feet ahead of me, didn't stop, just cut right in front of me and roared off into the distance. Must have been drunk, I'm sure. If I hadn't stopped . . . Well, no need to dwell on bad thoughts, but it was really scary.

When I got to Dr. Tompkins', I told him about it, and he smiled that professorial smile, and said "very interesting," and asked me if I wanted cream in my coffee. I swear, those teacher types are too much. Mrs. Tompkins gave me a hug and told me how pretty I looked and wasn't it a shame that there were so many bad drivers in the world and for me to sit down and relax a while. Their living room is lovely—sort of middle-class modern with lots of bad paintings in bright colors. They asked me all about my family, and I told them about you and Dad and Bud. And then we got to talking about the occult, and Dr. Tompkins said he wanted to show me something, so we moved our coffee into his study.

I swear, I've never seen such a cluttered place. Books piled everywhere, junk of all kinds on his desk, papers and magazines stacked on the floor, vases and photographs and lamps and chairs and souvenirs from all around the world. Just thrown everywhere. I moved some books off a chair and sat down and just looked at all the stuff he's got, while Dr. Tompkins started pawing through various piles of journals hunting for an article on ESP—that's extra-sensory perception.

Well, I sat there for a few minutes, and then the hackles really began to rise on the back of my neck. It was so **strange,** if you know what I mean. It wasn't at all like the lightning flash I got while driving. It was something really different. I mean, it was like I had been there before, like I had been in their house before but I never even knew of Dr. Tompkins before this semester. It finally got so intense I had to say something about it, and Dr. Tompkins was very nice to me, asked me all about it. He said it was called **déjà vu,** which is a fancy French term for "I have seen this before." He seemed to think that maybe something had **caused** me to have the feeling, but of course it wasn't a **cause** at all. It was an experience, a feeling. How can you analyze things like that? After a while, we went back into the living room and the feeling sort of dribbled away. But isn't that **peculiar?**

Not much else to tell. Oh, yes, thanks much for the extra ten bucks. I can really use the loot, I assure you. Give my love to everybody and tell Bud that he still owes me a letter. Postcards don't count!

Love,

Barbara

(Continued on page 233.)

In 1956 a public-relations executive named James Vicary held a press conference that set New York City on its ear. For Vicary announced to the press that he had discovered a new advertising technique that he was sure would revolutionize America's buying habits. The technique was so powerful—according to Vicary—that almost no one would be able to resist it, and so subtle that most Americans would never realize that their behaviors had been affected.

Sub-liminal advertising (°) was the name that Vicary gave to this technique, and within days after the press conference, the newspapers and magazines were full of anguished articles denouncing Vicary for having thrust a new and terrible method of "mind control" upon an unwilling world.

In point of fact, *sub-liminal advertising* was neither new nor particularly effective, but for a period of several years it stirred up quite a storm. Angry novelists wrote science-fiction epics in which evil politicians controlled the behavior of masses of people by flashing hidden commands on television screens. Psychologists rushed to their laboratories to test out Vicary's findings; congressmen introduced legislation that would outlaw the technique; the American Psychological Association published a learned article on the subject; and James Vicary enjoyed a brief but intense moment of notoriety.

To understand what subliminal advertising was all about, where the idea came from, and why it didn't work very well, you will have to take one step farther along the road to appreciating how your nervous system processes incoming sensory data.

THRESHOLDS

What does the word "threshold" mean? If you find yourself on the threshold of a dream, you are still awake—but you are just on the verge of entering or obtaining your dream. If you stand on the threshold of a room, you are obviously in the doorway—neither entirely in the room nor all the way out of it but ready to enter if you move a fraction of an inch farther along. The threshold, then, is a halfway point between two places or states of being.

From a psychologist's point of view, you are a walking mass of thresholds. A stimulus must possess enough physical energy to trigger off your receptor organs if the information about this stimulus is to cross the *sensory threshold* (°) and be sent to the lower centers of your brain. If the stimulus isn't strong enough or important enough for these lower centers to relay it on to your Board of Directors, you will not become conscious of the sensory input because it did not cross the *perceptual threshold* (°). And even if you perceive the stimulus, you may not choose to respond to it, for you have *action thresholds* (°) as well.

These various types of thresholds are so inter-related that it is often difficult to tell where one begins and the other leaves off. For instance, how cold does a room have to be in winter before you notice the chill? And how much colder does it have to be before you get up and either put on a coat or turn up the heat? How long must you go without food before you feel hungry; and how much food must you eat before you suddenly realize that you're "stuffed" and hence stop eating? How much annoying sensory input do you have to put up with from a friend before you get angry? How much in love do you have to be before you start thinking about getting married? Perhaps if you learn how sensory, perceptual, and action thresholds are actually measured, you will understand better how to tell them apart.

Action Thresholds

Probably the most famous "action" threshold in history is described in the old story about "the straw that broke the camel's back." If you decided to test the truth of this old wives' tale, you would probably quickly learn that such stories

Sub-liminal advertising (sub-LIM-in-ull). From the Latin words *sub,* meaning "below," and *limen,* meaning "threshold." A sub-liminal stimulus is one that is below the threshold of consciousness. Sub-liminal advertising consists of commercial messages or ads that are flashed on a screen so rapidly that the mind is not conscious of seeing them. First thought to be a dangerous form of "mind control," sub-liminal advertising turned out to be more of a "flash in the pan."

Sensory threshold. A threshold is the dividing line between two places or states of being. A stimulus must have a certain strength to cause the sensory receptors to fire—that is, to cross the sensory threshold.

Perceptual threshold. A very weak light may be strong enough to cause the rods and cones to fire (that is, to cross the visual sensory threshold), but not strong enough to push all the way through to the brain and be recognized by the cortical Board. Any stimulus strong enough to be noticed by the Board has crossed the perceptual threshold. Subliminal stimuli are thought to be above the sensory threshold but below the perceptual threshold.

Action threshold. Just because you perceive something doesn't mean that you will necessarily respond to it by moving or taking action. You might ignore the family cat if it walked into your room; you might do something else entirely if a hungry lion walked in on you. Stimuli strong or important enough to provoke a response are above the action threshold.

Exaggerations (ex-adge-er-RAY-shuns). To exaggerate is to overstate something beyond the bounds of truth. If you tell someone the food in your college dorm "is the worst in the world," you have probably stated an exaggeration (because you've probably not tasted the food served in the dorms at Michigan!).

Arbitrary (ARE-bih-trary). Any decision that you make purely by whim or by personal preference is an arbitrary decision. If your parents named you "John" or "Mary" simply because they liked that name, they made an arbitrary choice. If your friends call you "runt" because you are so small, their decision was based on physical fact and hence was not arbitrary.

usually deal with *exaggerations* (°)—that is, any reasonably intelligent camel would simply lie down, roll over, and refuse to get up long before the weight on its back was sufficient to do it any real damage. So you might settle for trying to discover how many straws it took to make the animal momentarily collapse. Then you would probably go beg, borrow, or steal a fairly healthy camel; procure a lot of straw; and start loading the camel up. Individual straws don't weigh very much, so you could load hundreds of thousands of them on the animal before it started to groan. Then—at least according to the legend—there would come a critical point in your experiment. The animal could (let's say) handle up to 999,999 straws without buckling; but add that one additional wisp of hay, and down the beast would go. The camel's action threshold would obviously be 999,999 straws.

QUESTION: We noted in Chapter 4 that a pigeon confined in a small box will attack anything handy if it is shocked or frustrated; how might you go about determining the "frustration-aggression" threshold in pigeons? Could you determine the same sort of threshold for people—or for nations?

Perceptual Thresholds

Next, suppose you wanted to determine what would be the smallest amount of light that you could see under the best of conditions. At first blush, it might seem that you would be measuring your visual sensory threshold, but this turns out not to be the case. For if you are *conscious* of seeing the light, then you *perceive* the light, and hence you are working with a perceptual threshold. We will discuss sensory thresholds in just a moment; right now, let's see how you could test your own perceptual threshold for very weak visual stimuli.

One way would be to get a light bulb whose brightness you could increase or decrease merely by turning a knob of some kind. Then you could sit in a dark room for 30 minutes—to give your eyes a chance to adapt—and then start turning up the intensity of the bulb until you first became aware that the light was on. The point at which you could just make out that the bulb was shining faintly would be one measure of your visual perceptual threshold. Turn the light down a little and you can't see it; turn it up a bit and you have no trouble seeing it all the time. But there would be a point—a halfway point—between seeing and not seeing that you could determine by using the bulb-knob apparatus. This halfway point is, of course, your *perceptual threshold*. By definition, then, the visual perceptual threshold is that intensity of stimulus (that brightness of a light) that you can see half the time and that you can't see half the time.

QUESTION: How would you go about testing your auditory threshold, or your threshold for the taste of salt?

A couple of points about thresholds probably occur to you at once. The first point is that this definition is quite *arbitrary* (°)—there's no reason why we couldn't have defined the threshold as being that stimulus strength that you could perceive 25 percent of the time, or 75 percent of the time, or even 38.729 percent of the time. However, European scientists in the 1800's picked the 50 percent point and, for the most part, that definition has stuck.

The second thing about thresholds that might set you wondering has to do with their stability. Let's go back to the camel. Suppose you decided to test the animal just after it had come in from a long race across the desert, and the beast was pretty tired to start with. Under these conditions it might collapse if you piled no more than 800,000 straws on its back. If you had chosen a particularly good day for the camel, however—after it had rested for a couple of weeks and had eaten lots of good food—the animal might have been able to tolerate 1,100,000 straws with no great strain.

Thresholds differ. They differ from person to person, from day to day, even from moment to moment. If you tested your camel for a thousand different days you would get a great many different measures of the threshold. If you counted up the number of times the threshold was 999,999, the number of times it was 999,998, and so on, and then put all these figures on a chart, the graph might look something like this:

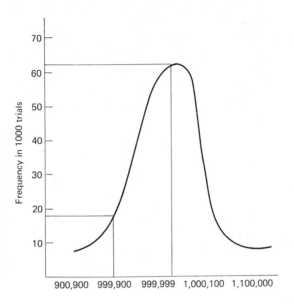

"The number of straws it takes to break a camel's back" from one day to the next. The number of times that it took exactly 999,999 straws is called the **frequency** (*) with which that event occurred (out of 1000 trials). As you can see, the threshold was 999,999 some 62 times, while it was 999,900 some 18 times.

By looking at the blue curve, you can tell that most of the time the camel's threshold was very close to 999,999 straws. Once you knew this fact you could, if you were interested, begin working out ways to keep the animal from collapsing. Keeping the camel in topnotch physical condition would be one way; keeping the load well below 900,000 straws would be another.

QUESTION: **If someone you know gets angry very easily, how might you use the threshold concept to determine various ways of lowering the number of temper tantrums that the person throws?**

Perceptual thresholds are much like action thresholds—the weaker the stimulus with which you are presented, the lower the probability that you will perceive it on any given test trial. Suppose we gave you a pair of earphones to wear and then we presented such a soft musical tone through the phones that, out of a hundred trials, you were consciously aware of the tone only once. If the tone were right at your auditory threshold, you would expect to be aware of it half the time, or 50 times out of 100. A tone that you hear only once in 100 trials is obviously far below your normal or average threshold. The Latin word for "threshold" is *limen* (°), so this very weak tone would be "below your perceptual limen," or *subliminal* (°). A subliminal stimulus is one that is so weak that you would be conscious of it less than 50 percent of the time.

As we will see later in this chapter, the word *subliminal* almost always refers to a stimulus that is below the perceptual threshold but above the sensory threshold. Even the faintest of stimuli may contain enough physical energy to excite the rods and cones in your retinas and hence cross the visual sensory threshold. It takes a great deal more energy for a stimulus to break through to consciousness.

Now that the definitions are out of the way, we can add a little salt and butter to James Vicary's subliminal "popcorn" advertisements.

Frequency (FREE-kwen-see). The number of times that an event occurs within a given time period. In the graph on this page the curved blue line tells you how frequently a given number of straws supposedly broke the camel's back. On most graphs such as this one, the frequency of the event is measured against a vertical scale (the numbers running from 10 to 70 in this case). The event itself is measured against the horizontal scale at the bottom of the graph (the numbers running from 900,900 to 1,100,000 here). To find out how many times it took 999,999 straws to break the camel's back, you first look for the event (999,999) on the bottom line. Then draw a vertical line straight up until it hits the blue curve. Now draw a straight line over to the vertical (frequency) scale on the left. Since this second line hits the frequency scale at the number 62, you know that it took exactly 999,999 straws to break the camel's back 62 times out of 1,000 trials.

Limen (LIME-en). The Latin word for "threshold."

Sub-liminal (sub-LIM-in-ull). Literally, "below any limen or threshold." However, many psychologists arbitrarily define the word as meaning "below the perceptual threshold."

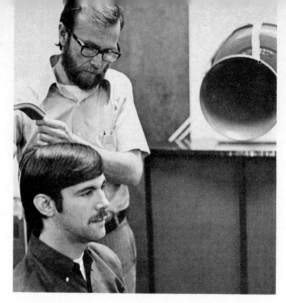

Dave Schmidt, a Naval Undersea Center electronics engineer, puts an ear muff over one of Edward Hilts's ears to protect the ear during auditory tests. Hilts is a subject in a study on the harmful effects of noise.

SUBLIMINAL PERCEPTION

Back in 1956, Vicary ran a brief series of experiments at a movie theater in Fort Dix, New Jersey. During the showing of the feature films at this movie house, Vicary had a special projector that flashed "secret" messages on the screen. One of the messages read "Drink Coca-Cola," while the other read "Eat Popcorn." These phrases were flashed on the screen at such a weak intensity and at a speed so fast that none of the movie-goers was apparently aware of what was going on. At least, no one complained to the management. The ads were, then, well below the visual perceptual threshold for the people involved.

However, according to Vicary, this subliminal advertising was so effective that popcorn sales rose more than 50 percent and soft-drink sales increased about 18 percent. No wonder the advertising agencies in New York were interested! Here was a sales pitch delivered so subtly that the audiences didn't know they were being influenced, and yet the people in the audience supposedly responded by spending their good money on food and drink that they probably didn't really need. The ad agencies began to see all sorts of possibilities that excited them and that disturbed most other people.

What would television be like today if all the commercials were subliminal, if they were flashed on the television screen almost continuously during all programs? The TV viewer wouldn't complain because he or she wouldn't be consciously aware of what the ads actually said (or even that the ads were really there), and yet the viewer might (so Vicary claimed) be seized with all kinds of irresistible urges to go buy something new each time the set was turned on. Politicians could (supposedly) sway millions of voters against their wills, and harassed law enforcement agencies could flood the TV and movie screens with "hidden" messages that whispered "Support Your Local Police."

Two-point Threshold

Two-point threshold. Also called "two-point limen." The distance apart that two metal points must be (when touching the skin) so that you can perceive them as being "two" instead of "one" exactly 50 percent of the time. Electrical current is often (but not always) passed through the points when the threshold is being measured.

More than a century ago a European scientist named Suslowa noticed something rather odd when he was attempting to determine the *two-point threshold* (*) on his experimental subjects. Suslowa had two pointed pieces of metal through which he could pass a weak but mildly painful electrical current. He would touch these points, or electrodes, to the skin of a blindfolded male subject and turn on the current. The subject was then asked to say whether he could feel both the points separately, or whether they were so close together that the mild stimulation seemed to come from a single spot on his skin. Sometimes, just to keep the blindfolded subjects alert, Suslowa would touch the subject with but one of the electrodes; if the man then claimed to feel "two points," Suslowa would know he should not place too much value on the subject's verbal reports.

Suslowa was interested in mapping out skin sensitivity, and was one of the first scientists to do so. But what we remember him most for was the following discovery: Sometimes his subjects were correct in their judgments of "two" versus "one" *even when they insisted that they couldn't possibly tell the difference.*

Suppose you were a subject in an experiment like Suslowa's. The psychologist would blindfold you, ask you to lie on your stomach on a table, and then would begin stimulating various parts of the skin on your back—asking you to report "two points" or "one point" each time you felt the weak electric shock. The psychologist might discover that, at a certain point in the small of your back, you always reported "two" if the electrodes were 1.5 inches (3.81 centimeters) apart—and that you never reported "two" if the electrodes were but 0.5 inches (1.27 centimeters) apart.

If the electrodes were exactly 1 inch (2.54 centimeters) apart, however, you reported "two" half the time and "one" half the time that he actually applied *two* points to your skin. Your *two-point threshold* is obviously *one inch* on that part of your back. The 1.5-inch distance is well above your threshold—what the psychologist might call a *supra-liminal* (°) or "above-threshold" stimulus. The 0.5-inch distance is well below your threshold, hence is a *subliminal* stimulus. You would almost never *perceive* the 0.5-inch distance as being "two"—that is, the psychologist could touch the electrodes to your back all day long, and you would almost never "feel" two points instead of one if the electrodes were only 0.5 inches apart.

But suppose that the psychologist told you that sometimes he was going to touch two electrodes (only 0.5 inches apart) to your skin, and sometimes he would actually touch only one electrode to your skin. You would always consciously "feel" or perceive the stimulus as being a single point. But suppose that the psychologist insisted that you *guess* whether one point or two had been used. What would your guesses be like?

Supra-liminal (SUP-pra-LIM-in-ull). From the Latin words meaning "above" and "threshold." Our words "supreme" and "super" come from the Latin word *supra.*

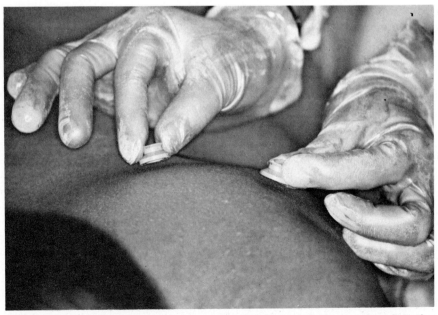

The two-point threshold experiment using electric stimulation on the skin of a subject's back.

Theoretically, your guesses should be random—about the same as if the psychologist had asked you to guess "heads" or "tails" when he flipped a coin. That is not what Suslowa found. His subjects did *not* guess randomly; instead, they were correct in their guesses much more than 50 percent of the time.

You must realize that Suslowa's subjects insisted that they could *not* consciously perceive or sense or detect or feel the difference between two points and one point. But when Suslowa forced them to *guess*, they were surprisingly accurate. The subjects themselves could not account for the fact that they were responding correctly to the subliminal stimulus, yet they responded with remarkable accuracy.

Discrimination without Awareness

How is it that you can feel something that you can't really feel? At first, psychologists thought that perhaps it was a matter of *attention*. Your behavior is often influenced by environmental events that you pay little or no conscious attention to. For example, have you ever started out to walk to class or to a friend's place when you had a lot of things on your mind? Then you found yourself at your destination without the slightest idea of how you got there?

Or have you ever been driving a car along a highway while you were thinking about something important and then suddenly you "woke up" to the fact that you had been paying no attention at all to the car? Yet somehow you had managed to stay on the road, slow down at the right moments, and speed up when necessary. How is it that you didn't have an accident?

After you have been driving for a while, most of the motor skills necessary to keep the car on the road become automatic—that is, the responses that your hands make on the steering wheel and your feet make on the pedals become *reflexive* (°). Reflex movements are often handled by the lower centers in the brain, leaving the Board of Directors in the cortex free to think about more weighty problems. Since your Board is the site of your *conscious* experience, most of these reflexive or automatic responses are *unconscious*. If you have ever seen a movie or videotape recording of yourself, you probably know only too well that you have many movements or mannerisms that you simply are not aware of making—yet you make them all the time.

The stimuli that you respond to when you are driving are almost always *supraliminal*. That is, you *could* become aware of them if your attention were directed to them. But sometimes your cortex withdraws from day-to-day activities for a brief period; at these moments, your lower brain centers apparently run things for you. These lower centers seem to screen all the incoming sensory information, make various discriminations, and respond appropriately. We call this *discrimination without awareness*, and it is a very common thing that most of us experience many times daily.

How many times, while reading a textbook such as this one, have you suddenly realized that you simply weren't aware of what it was you had just been reading? Your eyes had scanned the words; your fingers had turned the pages; but your mind had been elsewhere. If someone forced you to guess what it was you had just read, you probably would do a good job of guessing—because the lower (but unconscious) centers of your brain would have a vague recollection of the material your eyes had scanned. But conscious memory seems to be located in the cortex. If the material hadn't gotten through to your cortical Board, the best your Board could do would be to try to make use of the "unconscious" (and perhaps nonverbal) memories stored in the lower centers.

Discrimination without awareness always involves stimuli that are *above your perceptual thresholds*—that is, your cortex *could* perceive them consciously if your attention were called to the stimuli. Subliminal perception is something else

Reflexive (ree-FLECKS-ive). Reflexive movements are automatic reactions that require no conscious thought.

again, for these stimuli are *above* your sensory thresholds but are *below* your normal perceptual thresholds. In fact, these stimuli are so weak that even if your Board worked overtime trying to sense or detect them, your cortex simply isn't up to the job. How then does subliminal perception work?

The answer is—not very well. The neurological road from your receptors to your cortex has many gates and tollbooths on it. Each time the incoming sensory information must cross a synapse, there is a chance for very weak stimuli to be gated out or rejected. A very faint light might have enough energy to excite your rods and cones, so they would fire a few times and pass the message along to your lower brain centers. But here the message must cross a synapse before being sent on to the visual-input area in your occipital lobe. The light may be too faint to send the message across this lower brain synapse, so the message never reaches your Board and the percept of the light never reaches consciousness.

Your visual cortex can't see the light no matter how hard it tries to do so—but your lower brain centers "see" the light. And these lower centers may make a faint, reflexive response to the light, perhaps by ordering your eyes to move around in their sockets so that the image of the light falls directly on your fovea. Your Board does not see the light, but of course the Board would be aware that your eyes have moved (although the Board wouldn't know *why* the eye movement had occurred). If someone now asks you if you saw anything, you would truthfully say "no." But if someone *demanded* that you guess whether or not a light had been present, the fact that your eyes had moved might bias your Board just enough so that it guessed "yes."

Unconscious Censoring

Now suppose that instead of seeing a very weak light, you had seen a faint impression of a "dirty word" or a sexually stimulating scene. When the message reached the lower brain centers, your reticular activating system (RAS) might recognize (unconsciously) that an emotionally important stimulus was present in your environment. Your *limbic system* (°), which is also one of the unconscious lower centers of your brain, might respond to the stimulus as well. You might blush, or turn away, or even become excited or alert—even though your cortical Board hadn't detected what the stimulus actually was.

Sigmund Freud, perhaps the greatest personality theorist of modern times, believed that each of us has a censor operating somewhere within our nervous systems whose chief task is to prevent sexual or other types of threatening impulses or memories from breaking through to consciousness to embarrass us. According to Freud, this censor acts as a gate or tollbooth within our brains. If you want to call up some simple, pleasant image from your storehouse of memories, this image should get past your censor with no difficulty. However, whenever you are prompted to remember some psychologically upsetting event, the censor goes into action—presumably by increasing the threshold that the memory must cross in order to become conscious. If the memory is weak, or if it is so threatening that your censor "goes all out" in order to prevent it from breaking through to your Board of Directors, it can usually be successfully *repressed* (°)—that is, the memory can be pushed down out of your consciousness. The censor may also attempt to screen out incoming sensory information, but usually sensations are too strong for your censor to handle. However, if the disturbing stimuli are weak enough, the censor may in fact be able to raise your perceptual threshold sufficiently to screen them out too.

When Freud first *postulated* (°) his theories more than 50 years ago, he wrote about them in purely psychological or even literary terms because we did not know enough about the nervous system then for Freud to be able to make much use of neurological data to support his theories. However, Freud stated many

Limbic system (LIM-bick). A group of related neural centers that affect emotional responses. See Chapter 4.

Repressed (ree-PRESST). To repress is to inhibit a thought or action, to forget deliberately, or to push a memory or desire into unconsciousness. See Chapter 22.

Postulate (POSS-tew-late). From the Latin word meaning "to ask for" or "demand." In English, the word more often means to assume that something is true, to make *a priori* assumptions about something, or to theorize. Freud postulated that almost all forms of love had a sexual basis—that is, he assumed or theorized that love was primarily sexual. One of the difficulties in making postulates or assumptions is that one seldom gets around to proving whether or not the assumption is true.

Elliott McGinnies.

Homunculus (ho-MUN-cue-lus). The Latin word for "little man." See Chapter 4.

Milliseconds (MILL-ee-seck-unds). The Latin word *milli* means "thousands." A millisecond is therefore a thousandth of a second. A millimeter is a thousandth of a meter.

Perceptual defense. The act of suppressing or repressing threatening stimuli. When you defend yourself (perceptually) against recognizing "dirty words," you are in fact raising your perceptual threshold for perceiving these words.

Concatenation (kon-CAT-tee-NAY-shun). A $5 word that means a series or chain of related events. When you line up a series of dominoes in a row, and knock over the first one so that it hits the second (which hits the third, which hits the fourth, and so on), you have just created a concatenation of dominoes.

Perceptual vigilance (VIDGE-ill-ants). The opposite of perceptual defense. The lowering of a perceptual threshold. If your mind unconsciously defends against sexual stimuli, when someone shows you the word "rape," you are likely to perceive it as "rope." If your mind is unconsciously vigilant for sexual stimuli, when someone shows you the word "rope," you are likely to perceive it as "rape."

Extra-sensory perception. Perceptions are ordinarily triggered off by sensory stimuli—that is, by sights, sounds, temperature, chemicals, and so forth. If you could perceive something without making use of sensory inputs, you would experience extra-sensory perception.

Transcend (trans-SEND). To go beyond the normal or ordinary limits.

times that the ultimate proof or disproof of his views would hinge on what the neuro-psychologists discovered about the workings of the brain. Many psychologists of Freud's time were disturbed at his notion of a "censor"—they could not accept the idea that there was an *homunculus* (°), or "little man," sitting somewhere in the brain who looked over all the messages going to the Board of Directors and tossed out those bits of information that seemed too high in emotional content. Today, we realize that the lower brain centers do in fact screen out sensory input before it reaches the cortex and hence becomes conscious. Whether these lower brain centers operate the way Freud said they ought to is a point still debated today.

"Dirty Word" Experiments

One of the most interesting sets of studies on subliminal perception were the "dirty word" experiments performed in the 1950's and 1960's by Elliott McGinnies and several other U.S. psychologists. McGinnies began by determining the perceptual threshold for ordinary words. He did this by showing student subjects simple words such as "table" and "chair" at faster and faster speeds. With each student (and for each word) McGinnies was able to calculate an exposure time so rapid that the subject could perceive the word exactly 50 percent of the time. For a word such as "whale," this perceptual threshold might be about 100 *milliseconds* (°). For an emotionally laden word such as "whore," however, the threshold was typically much higher, 200 milliseconds or more. McGinnis believed that his subjects' censors were "defending" against such "disturbing" words. McGinnies called this effect *perceptual defense* (°).

Many psychologists objected to McGinnies' studies, claiming that he had not controlled for all the outside influences he ought to have taken into account. For instance, we know that the more common a word is, the lower its threshold will be. You can recognize the word "cat" in a much shorter time than you can recognize the word *"concatenation"* (°). In the 1950's words such as "whore" seldom appeared in print, so the student subjects might well have been relatively unfamiliar with the printed form of the word. We also know that, in some circles, speaking such words out loud is unacceptable if both sexes are present. These critics speculated that if a male student were presented with the word "bitch," he might indeed recognize it but be afraid to say it in public. Instead, he might say "botch" or "batch" or "butch," and would keep on doing so until the word was presented at such a long time interval that he clearly saw it was "bitch." These critics guessed that male students would be more likely to report "dirty" words in an experiment if the psychologist testing them were male than if the psychologist were female—and the critics were quite correct.

The critics also found that a few students actually had *lower* thresholds for "dirty" words than for "clean" words. How might this finding be explained? The answer given by McGinnies is that while most people have censors who *defend* against sexual stimuli, a few of us have censors that are vigilantly searching the world around us for anything that might be slightly smutty. McGinnies spoke of this lowered threshold as *perceptual vigilance* (°). Whether one's censor tends to seek out, or to defend against, sexual stimuli seems to be a matter of each individual's own past experience and moral upbringing. But even when the criticisms against this line of research are taken into account, there still seems to be fairly good evidence that something like perceptual defense or vigilance does occur in many people.

EXTRA-SENSORY PERCEPTION

Both subliminal perception and discrimination without awareness have often been used as explanations of studies of *extra-sensory perception* (°). Many people believe that, under certain special conditions, man's mind may *transcend* (°), or rise above, the usual physical means of communication—that is, communication by talking or signaling or writing messages.

If you want to know what is going on inside the mind of a friend of yours, you typically have to observe your friend's behavior or ask the friend what he or she is thinking about. Although you may not always be aware of the subtle behavioral cues you pick up while your friend is talking or behaving, we can presume that information about your friend's thoughts normally reaches your Board by way of the same sensory pathways that tell you whether the traffic light is red or that an airplane is flying overhead.

But what if your mind could reach out and make "spiritual" (that is, nonphysical) contact directly with your friend's mind? If this could happen, you could read your friend's thoughts directly by means of extra-sensory perception, or *ESP* (°).

The technical term for "thought reading" is *mental telepathy* (°). If you could see through walls, as Superman does in the comics, you would have to do so by *extra-sensory* means, since your senses are incapable of this feat. *Clairvoyance* (°) is the term we use to describe the perception of external objects or events without normal sensory stimulation. *Precognition* (°) is the ability to perceive future events before they happen. If you could influence the movement of physical objects simply by wishing them to move, you would be demonstrating a power called *psycho-kinesis* (°), or *tele-kinesis* (°)—the power of "mind over matter." Such unusual experiences as mental telepathy, clairvoyance, precognition, and telekinesis are called *paranormal* (°) events, because they are beyond the realm of ordinary or normal explanation (the Greek word *para* means "beyond"). The study of paranormal events makes up a field called *para-psychology* (°), the investigation of events that are beyond the normal boundaries of behavioral science.

Many people believe strongly that ESP exists; many others are convinced that it is a figment of the imagination and that parapsychologists are likely fooling themselves. The chances are good that either you yourself or someone you know has had an experience that seemed at the time to be paranormal. Perhaps you dreamed that someone you know would have an accident, and shortly thereafter something similar to your dream actually occurred. Perhaps you looked at someone one day and were convinced that you could actually read that person's thoughts. Perhaps you have heard very convincing stories of someone who went to Las Vegas and claimed to have won some money by mentally controlling the dice at one of the dice tables or by guessing accurately what numbers would come up on a roulette wheel. How can science explain such phenomena?

The answer is—science can't always explain such things, nor should it always try. Science is but one way of looking at humans and the world around them; religion is another way, art is another, parapsychology is yet another. Our lives would be greatly impoverished if we ever settle on just one way of viewing or explaining things.

Believers in ESP seem to fall into two main camps:

1. Those who hold that such talents as mental telepathy are entirely supernatural; by definition, supernatural events are beyond the scope and interest of science (though often of interest to individuals who earn their livings by being scientists).

2. Those people who feel that ESP is a natural occurrence but beyond the boundaries of our present understanding. These people usually think that the scientific method can be used to discover new (and perhaps undreamed of) channels between the world and the brain. The difficulty with such a view is that before the parapsychologist can prove an event is truly *extra*-sensory, he or she must demonstrate that the event cannot somehow be explained as an odd but perfectly normal *sensory* occurrence.

Let us now look at why parapsychological experiments are sometimes misinterpreted.

ESP. Abbreviation for extra-sensory perception.

Mental telepathy (tell-LEP-uh-thee). The Greek word *tele* means "far off," "at a distance." The word "television" means "seeing at a distance." The word "telephone" means "speaking at a distance." The Greek word *pathos* means "experience" or "emotion." Mental telepathy is therefore to experience something at a distance through mental communication rather than by physical means.

Clairvoyance (clair-VOY-ants; rhymes with "bare boy dance"). From the French words meaning "clear-sighted." The ability to see things hidden from normal sight.

Precognition (pree-cog-NISH-shun). Cognition is the intellectual process by which knowledge or ideas are gained—the act of perception. Precognition is knowing or perceiving something before the event actually occurs.

Psycho-kinesis (SIGH-ko-kin-EE-sis). The Greek word *kinesis* means "movement," or "to move." *Psyche* is the Greek word for "mind." Psycho-kinesis is the ability to move things mentally (by willing them to move) rather than by touching them physically.

Tele-kinesis (TELL-ee-kin-EE-sis). To move things at a distance through thought power instead of physical power. Another word for psycho-kinesis.

Para-normal (PAIR-uh-NOR-mal). Literally, anything beyond or above the ordinary. Something not explainable in normal terms.

Para-psychology (PAIR-uh-sigh-KOLL-oh-gee). That part of psychology concerned with the study of ESP and other paranormal happenings.

ESP Experiments

Suppose you were asked to participate in a parapsychological experiment. You might be shown a pack of ordinary bridge cards so that you could make sure that, like all other bridge decks, this one contained 52 cards divided into four suits—13 clubs, 13 diamonds, 13 hearts, and 13 spades. The experimenter would then shuffle the cards thoroughly and place the deck face down on the table between the two of you. The experimenter might then pick up the cards one by one in such a manner that he or she could see the card but you couldn't. You would then be asked to "read the experimenter's mind"—that is, to guess the suit of the card that the parapsychologist was looking at. Since there are four suits in the deck, you would have one chance in four of being right with any given card. If the first time you tried this experiment, you guessed the suit correctly 13 times out of 52, you would have done no more than would normally be expected by chance alone.

QUESTION: **How many times would you have to guess the suit correctly before you might begin to suspect that something paranormal had occurred?**

Undaunted by your first experience, you try again. And this time you guess all 52 of the cards correctly! Surely this is evidence that mental telepathy has occurred, isn't it? The answer is—not yet. First you must show that you had no sensory clues to help you out. Thousands of experiments similar to this one have been performed in the past—and almost all of them are useless from a scientific point of view. Why? Because the experimenter failed to appreciate how likely it is for subliminal perception and discrimination without awareness to occur in this type of situation.

Pre-cognition test with an electronic machine. By pressing one of the four buttons, the subject predicts which of the four lamps will light next.

Miller's Harvard Study More than 30 years ago a psychiatrist named James G. Miller showed that he could train Harvard college students to "guess" correctly the symbols on a deck of cards even though the students could not consciously see the symbols and were not aware that they were being trained or "conditioned." He got students to volunteer to participate in an ESP experiment. When they arrived at his laboratory, he showed them the cards and then asked them to sit in front of what appeared to be a glass screen fixed on the wall like a mirror. Miller sat at a table behind the student, so that he couldn't be seen. He asked the student to stare at the glass screen and try to "project" on the screen the mental image that the student would be receiving from Miller's mind. Miller would look at a card, remind the student to stare at the screen, and then ask the student what symbol was on the card. If the student was right, he was rewarded; if wrong, the student was given a mild electric shock. To most students' great surprise, they were able to "guess" the symbols with incredible accuracy—although their accuracy disappeared if Miller omitted either the reward for correct responses or the punishment for incorrect responses.

James G. Miller.

Had Miller demonstrated a high level of ESP among Harvard students? Not quite. What the student didn't know was that the glass screen was really a one-way mirror (*see* Chapter 5). In the next room, Miller had a slide projector aimed at the back side of the mirror. When he pressed a button in the experimental room, the projector would throw on the mirror a very faint image of the card that Miller was looking at. The image was so weak that it was well below the student's conscious threshold—yet when Miller motivated the students highly enough, they were able to make use of sensory information so subliminal that it never reached consciousness. As you might guess, none of the students reported actually seeing the picture of the card as it flashed on the screen.

Amusingly enough, in a second part of the experiment, Miller switched from studying subliminal perception to studying discrimination without awareness. At first, each student was shown very weak stimuli as before. But while the experiment was going on, Miller gradually increased the intensity of the projected images until they were well above threshold. Most of the students continued to stare at what they thought was a blank screen and were not aware that the symbols were as visible as the numbers on the door to the experimental laboratory. At this stage of the experiment, of course, the students were "guessing" the symbols with 100 percent accuracy—but they still thought that they were "reading Miller's mind." When he called their attention to what was actually being shown on the screen, the students could "see" the symbols. This explanation did not please all the students, however—some of them insisted afterward that they had guessed correctly by using mental telepathy and that Miller was trying to "trick" them into believing that they hadn't really used ESP after all!

Kennedy's Stanford Study At about the same time Miller was working at Harvard, J.L. Kennedy at Stanford University in California was studying what he called "unconscious whispering." He asked two students at a time to participate in his study. One of them was to look at one card at a time from a special deck and to "send" the other student a mental message about each card. The "receiver" student was then to guess out loud what card the "sender" was looking at. The sender would then tell the receiver whether the guess had been right or wrong.

Kennedy used a special piece of apparatus for his work that "funneled" very faint sounds from the sender's mouth to the receiver's ear, much as a long narrow hallway "funnels" echoes from one end to the other. Kennedy could wipe out these faint sounds by taking away the special equipment. When this apparatus was in place, many of Kennedy's receivers had phenomenal success in "guessing" what card their senders were looking at. However, the instant that Kennedy disconnected the equipment, the guesses would drop back to chance level.

Kennedy observed very carefully just what his successful senders were doing. In many cases he found that the sender would make a characteristic sound for each different type of card that the sender looked at. If, for example, the sender was looking at a heart, he or she might always make an "ahem" sound; if the card was a spade, the sender might always inhale sharply. The receiver apparently soon learned what faint sounds were associated with which cards. As you might expect, unless the students had been trained to notice such things, neither senders nor receivers were usually aware of this "unconscious whispering."

QUESTION: **Was Kennedy's experiment an example of subliminal perception or discrimination without awareness?**

Some of the untrained students who volunteered for Kennedy's experiments turned out to be very good unconscious senders and receivers, while others were almost total failures at either task. In general, those subjects who were strong believers in ESP were good at the task, while those people who had a firm disbelief that ESP existed were for the most part unable either to send or to receive successfully. One interpretation of this finding would be that those subjects who had paranormal "powers" knew of their abilities from past experiences. These would be the students most likely to succeed on an ESP-oriented task. Subjects who were opposed to the concept of ESP might have such strong "negative" powers that they would block or interfere with the "positive" powers that anyone else present might possess.

A more likely explanation seems to be that strong beliefs tend to blind us to what is really going on in a situation. If you believe yourself to be good at "mental telepathy," you will go out of your way to prove yourself right—even if it means unconsciously whispering the correct answer to a receiver. If you are willing to express a strong distaste for ESP in public, then you might also be expected to go out of your way (consciously or unconsciously) to make sure that an ESP experiment will fail. The true believer hunts for clues even when they aren't there; the disbeliever ignores clues even when they're present.

Does ESP Exist?

Neither Miller's nor Kennedy's experiments disproved the existence of paranormal powers, nor were they aimed at doing so. Rather, both studies showed how difficult it is for anyone to perform a cleanly designed, well-controlled investigation of a topic that is by definition almost beyond the boundaries of modern science. It is not the purpose of science to disprove the possibility of ESP, religion, or any other type of *supernatural* occurrence; instead, it is the task of science to provide the most rational and logical explanations possible of the *natural* universe.

But what seems rational and logical to scientists today may turn out to be laughable nonsense to the scientists of tomorrow; and an event that most of today's great minds might dismiss as "goat feathers" could well become the foundation for an undreamed of science of tomorrow. As Arthur C. Clarke, the author of *2001: A Space Odyssey*, once observed: "When a scientist says that something is impossible, he is almost always wrong; but when he says that something just might be true, he is very often right."

There are many "successful" demonstrations of ESP in the parapsychological literature by scientists who believe strongly that paranormal powers exist. However, when uninterested (or highly skeptical) psychologists have attempted to repeat these studies, they have for the most part failed. And even those experimenters who have gotten positive results in one study have often failed to be successful with subsequent research.

Do all these facts mean that ESP is no more than a figment of people's

Matthew Manning demonstrating the power of "mind over matter" by bending a spoon.

imaginations? No, not at all. But the facts do suggest that the "personal" evidence for ESP is much stronger than the "experimental" evidence. Extra-sensory perception seems at best to be a kinky, slippery, undependable thing that happens rarely, unpredictably, and uncontrollably. Scientists are usually skeptical of such things; indeed, a recent survey of most of the psychologists in the United States showed that less than 5 percent of them believe that mental telepathy is an established fact. Until some very bright person can demonstrate the conditions under which paranormal powers occur with regularity, so that these powers can readily be studied under laboratory conditions, this skepticism will probably remain firmly entrenched in most psychologists' minds. For far too much of the evidence offered to "prove" the existence of paranormal powers can be better explained in terms of highly motivated, sincere people who make use of subliminal stimuli without being conscious of doing so. And that is why the study of subliminal perception bears directly on the study of ESP.

Subliminal Advertising

To return now to the question with which we started: Need we worry about men and women of evil design who might practice "mind control" using subliminal advertising? The answer appears to be *no*. Shortly after James Vicary announced he had increased popcorn sales 50 percent by flashing the command "Eat Popcorn" on a movie screen, a number of radio and television stations began their own experiments. When a man named Pirie broke the existing record for running the mile, the British Broadcasting Corporation flashed the message "Pirie Breaks World Record" on their television screens at very rapid speed. No one seemed to get the message, except for a few people with apparently superb vision who called up to ask the BBC, "Why are you flashing the message 'Pirie Breaks World Record' so rapidly on the TV?"

A television station in Minneapolis, perhaps hoping to inspire the University of Minnesota football team to ever-greater achievements, projected the slogan "Beat Michigan" subliminally on their screens for the week prior to the 1956 Michigan-Minnesota game. Michigan won the contest easily that year.

A radio station on the West Coast had someone whisper softly, "Don't Watch TV" during all their broadcasts, but television viewing didn't decline at all.

All things considered, these secret attempts to manipulate people's minds have yielded results as subliminal as the stimuli used.

One British study on subliminal advertising bears further mention. A group of psychologists in London hired three groups of ordinary people to watch sporting events on a television set. On top of the set was a large box with a glass screen in it; the message, "Drink Brand X Beer," could either be flashed at subliminal speeds on the screen or could be projected on the screen steadily and brightly so that everyone could see it all the time. Prior to watching the games on the tube, the subjects were offered their choice of three brands of beer, X, Y, and Z. About 40 percent picked Brand X. Then each of the three groups settled down in comfortable chairs to watch the show. While the first group of subjects was watching the game, the message "Drink Brand X Beer" flashed subliminally on the screen just above the TV set. While the second group watched, the same message was brightly projected on the same screen so everyone could see it. The third group was exposed neither to subliminal nor to supraliminal advertising about Brand X beer. After the show was over, each group was again offered its choice of X, Y, or Z. The second group—those people exposed to the "out in the open" advertising—showed a significant increase in their choice of Brand X beer; the first group—those people given the subliminal advertising—showed a slight *decrease* in their preference for Brand X. The third group remained the same in their choices.

"Pirie Breaks World Record."

Subliminal stimuli do get through to the lower centers of your brain, but not to the conscious parts of your cortex. Subliminal stimuli can influence your behavior—but only when two conditions obtain: first, you must be in a position where all the supraliminal inputs available to you do not give you the information you need to make a decision; and second, you must be highly motivated to make use of even the weakest of "hunches."

When you are forced to guess the answer to a difficult or tricky problem, or when it is urgent for you to become attuned to all the subtle stimuli in your environment that you might usually ignore—then, and only then, will you make use of sensory inputs that lie below the threshold of conscious awareness. Your own personal motivation is thus the key to understanding how and when your mind makes use of subliminal as well as any other kind of stimuli.

Almost all the things you want from life, almost all of your pleasures and rewards, come to you as sensory inputs. Whether you realize it or not, you spend a great amount of time and personal effort trying to control your inputs. Indeed, as we will see in the next section of this book, the need to predict and control your inputs is perhaps the strongest and most compelling need that you have. The more accurately you can perceive yourself and your environment, the better guesses you can usually make about what might happen next and what you have to do in order to influence future events. And the better you understand what it is you want from life, the greater appreciation you will have of why you perceive the world as you do. Little wonder, then, that perception and motivation are so closely linked.

SUMMARY

1. Knowledge about the world around you—as well as the world within you—typically comes to you through your sensory (input) pathways.
2. A sensory input or stimulus will be effective only if it is strong enough to cause a physical response by your neurons. An effective stimulus is therefore an input that is sufficiently strong to cross one of several types of thresholds.
3. The three main types of thresholds are the sensory, the perceptual, and the action thresholds.
4. Sensory thresholds are crossed whenever the stimulus input is strong enough to excite one or more receptor neurons. For example, suppose one of your friends whispers the word "hello" in your ear. The sound waves created by your friend's voice are a physical stimulus. If this stimulus input is strong enough, it crosses your auditory (sensory) threshold—that is, the input has sufficient strength to trigger off a pattern of neural firing in the auditory receptor cells in your inner ear. If the sound waves are too weak, the stimulus is below your auditory (sensory) threshold, and you hear nothing.
5. Even if your ears respond to the whisper, however, the sensory input may not be potent enough to get through to your cortical Board. That is, the stimulus input may cross the sensory threshold for hearing, but not cross the perceptual threshold. In this case, your ears "hear," but your brain does not, because your brain has not perceived the input.
6. Even if your Board perceives the whisper, you may choose not to respond because the auditory message doesn't cross your action threshold. If your friend had whispered "fire" instead of "hello," you probably would have taken some action.
7. Under rare conditions, a weak stimulus input may cross the sensory threshold and have an effect on the lower centers of the brain, but not break through to consciousness. Thus you may respond to a stimulus without being aware of what external event called forth your action. This sort of sensory input is called a subliminal stimulus, because it is below your perceptual threshold and you cannot perceive it no matter how hard you try.
8. Attempts to use subliminal stimuli as "hidden" forms of advertising have so far not been very successful.

9. Many stimuli above the perceptual threshold are responded to by the lower centers of the brain but ignored by the cortical Board. You could be conscious of these stimuli if someone called your attention to them, but generally you are not. The act of responding to stimuli your Board ignores is called discrimination without awareness, an act we all perform countless times each day.
10. Some people are emotionally aroused or upset by certain types of stimuli, such as "dirty words." Their Boards may unconsciously raise the perceptual thresholds for these stimuli, an act called perceptual defense.
11. Other people may seek out presumably threatening or arousing stimuli (such as "dirty words"), an act called perceptual vigilance.
12. Extra-sensory perception is the ability to know or perceive things by non-sensory means.
13. Most psychologists do not believe that ESP actually exists; they assume that most accounts of ESP can be better explained in terms of subliminal stimuli or discrimination without awareness.
14. If ESP does exist, it is a most fascinating area to study.

(Continued from page 218.)

Mrs. Sarah Wilson
832 Third Street
South Clarion, Missouri

Dear Mrs. Wilson:

It was most kind of you to send along the alarm clock which, now that I have used it in the experiment, I am returning to you. Barbara came out for coffee last night, and she reacted just as I had thought she might. As I told you on the phone, I am studying **déjà vu**, that odd psychological condition that makes people feel that they have "seen all this before." The experience is often so strong that the person believes that he or she can actually predict what is going to happen next, as if that person were merely acting out a part in a play and had, of course, read the script beforehand and hence knew what the other actors were going to say before they said anything.

Many religious leaders have written about their own **déjà vu** experiences, believing them to be mystically inspired. My own belief is that some people are fortunate enough to be highly attuned to their environments. These people are so sensitive to even the smallest things that happen around them that they begin to react to environmental changes before the average person ever becomes aware that something has changed. People who constantly get "hunches" or "flashes of insight" are, I think, more likely to experience **déjà vu** than is the ordinary man or woman. It is also true that people who use drugs, such as LSD and marijuana, or who practice one of the Eastern religions, or who study transcendental meditation often report having gone through **déjà vu**—but I am most interested in how and why it happens under more ordinary circumstances.

I believe I mentioned on the phone that I hope to show that **déjà vu** can be triggered off in perceptive people when they encounter something very familiar to them in a strange environment—that's why I wanted to borrow from you some small object that Barbara would recognize instantly. Your guess that I ought to use her old alarm clock was an excellent one.

I have at my home rather a large room that I use as a study. It has bookshelves lining three of the walls from floor to ceiling, and the shelves are full to the brim with books and souvenirs from many of my visits overseas. To say that the place is cluttered is something of an understatement. At any rate, I put Barbara's old alarm clock rather high up on one of the shelves, surrounded by a couple of vases so that it was just barely visible. If you hadn't known it was there, you probably never would have noticed it. But, as I had hoped, Barbara noticed it.

Or, rather, she was very bothered by it even though she couldn't consciously put her finger on what it was that was affecting her. The longer she stayed in the study, the more excited she became, until she finally bubbled over and told me what she was feeling. I tried to get her to analyze what was causing the experience, but she was too excited to do so. We will talk about it in class later on, and then perhaps she will understand.

You see, when some unconscious part of her brain spotted the clock, it triggered off a lot of old memories and associations. This deep part of her brain kept trying to respond to the familiar object, but of course the memories it dredged up were very much out of context and couldn't logically be tied in with sitting in the study of a strange house she had never visited before. Her conscious mind couldn't realize that only **part** of the experience was familiar—so it apparently just assumed that Barbara had somehow lived through the whole thing before. At least, that's what I think happened. I won't be sure, of course, until my research is finished—and that may take several years.

I've had several students out for coffee this semester and have, thanks to their parents, exposed them to similar situations. But so far, only one other person besides Barbara has had the **déjà vu** experience. I haven't told the class about it yet, but I will before the semester is over. So I would greatly appreciate your not mentioning the business about the clock to Barbara until she brings up the subject herself, or until the term is over.

My feeling is that Barbara is one of the lucky ones, a person who is very sensitive to the people and things around her. She is a very bright, humane individual who should grow into a very perceptive woman. She will probably go through life following her insights, and most of the time these insights will be good ones. Her insights would be even better if she tried to analyze why she feels the way she does, but perhaps that's asking too much of her at this stage of her life. At any rate, she has a fine talent and I think for many reasons you should be proud of her.

Again, my thanks for your help.

Sincerely,

Theodore A. Tompkins

RECOMMENDED READINGS

Chance, Paul. "Telepathy Could Be Real," *Psychology Today*, vol. 9, no. 5 (February 1976), pp. 40–44, 65.

Greenburg, Dan. *Something's There* (New York: Doubleday & Company, 1976).

Hardy, Alister, Robert Harvie, and Arthur Koestler. *The Challenge of Chance* (New York: Random House, 1974).

McConnell, J.V., R.L. Cutler, and E.B. McNeil. "Subliminal Stimulation: An Overview," in K.O. Doyle, ed., *Interaction: Readings in Human Psychology* (Boston, Mass.: D.C. Heath and Company, 1973).

Rawcliffe, D.H. *Illusions and Delusions of the Supernatural and the Occult* (New York: Dover Publications, Inc., 1959).

Rhine, J.B., and J.G. Pratt. *Parapsychology: Frontier Science of the Mind* (Springfield, Ill.: Charles C Thomas, 1972).

Steiger, Brad. *ESP: The Sixth Sense* (Mattapan, Mass.: University Publisher & Distributor, 1973).

Part 3

MOTIVATION

chapter 12

"BY BREAD ALONE"

INTRODUCTION TO MOTIVATION: HUNGER

DID YOU KNOW THAT . . .

Most of the basic, life-sustaining needs you have can be expressed in terms of inputs and outputs?

Whenever you lack something necessary for survival, a primary drive is said to build up within you?

Your brain controls your inputs and outputs much as a wall thermometer controls room temperature?

Associated with most primary needs are certain learned or secondary needs?

Infants experience what Freud called "stimulus hunger?"

Your major "need" may be that of predicting and controlling your biological, mental, and social inputs?

Within limits, the sweeter the milk, the more eagerly an infant will drink it?

While a third of the people in the world are starving, some 25 percent of people in the United States suffer from eating too much?

Medical treatment for fatness has a "cure rate" less than that for treating cancer?

Colleges often discriminate against overweight students?

There is a neural center in your brain that, when stimulated electrically, might make you go on an eating jag?

Hunger pangs are mostly learned?

Fat people apparently don't pay much attention to their hunger pangs?

Fat people are often more influenced by the taste of food than are individuals whose weight is normal?

More lower-class than upper-class persons in the United States are overweight?

Some husbands seem to push food on their wives to keep the women fat and faithful?

Almost anyone can lose weight by following a program that takes into account biological, intra-psychic, and social/behavioral needs?

Meatball McClanahan opened the door to the dormitory and went inside. Outside it was a beautiful, soft, spring day and several of his friends were off to the local woods for picnic lunches or beer busts. Meatball was staying home, and he was miserable.

One of his dorm mates came out of a room down the hall and headed toward him. Meatball turned to flee, but the other young man had already seen him and there was no escape.

"Hi, Slim," Meatball muttered softly, his fleshy jowls trembling as he tried to dodge around the tall, thin man quickly.

"Hi, Meatball," Slim said, and poked the fat young man in the tummy. "Still carrying around that monumental middle, I see. If it gets much bigger, you could probably win a prize or something." Laughing, he gave Meatball another playful poke.

Meatball's stomach let out a loud, gurgling growl at this second outrage. He blushed all the way to the bottom of his third chin, then sighed. "No, Slim, the

Guinness Book of World Records says the largest human on record weighed 1,069 pounds and had to be buried in a piano case when he died. I only weigh 213 pounds, so if I'm going to win a prize, I've got a long way to go.''

Slim, who was over 6 feet (1.83 meters) tall but who weighed less than 150 pounds (68 kilograms), gave Meatball's stomach a third but far more gentle poke. ''Well, it's about time you got started, then. Let's go get a submarine sandwich and a chocolate shake down at the Spoon.''

Meatball shook his head sadly. With his height, Slim could afford to eat subs and shakes; Meatball, who was exactly 5 feet 6 inches (1.65 meters) tall, could not. ''Sorry, Slim. I got something else to do.''

Slim laughed again, exposing a mouthful of brilliant white teeth, then sauntered down the hall whistling ''American Pie.'' Meatball could see those pearly white teeth biting into a piece of hot apple pie just swimming in cinnamon sauce. His stomach grumbled again.

As he walked into the toilet, Meatball saw his friend Jock standing at one of the basins, brushing his teeth and exercising his chest muscles at the same time.

''Hiya, Meatball, old buddy,'' Jock sang out through the toothpaste. ''Whatcha going to do today?''

Meatball contemplated the young man seriously. Jock was, among other things, a varsity wrestler. When he tensed his muscles, as he was doing now, his flesh turned into a contour map with smooth, rolling hills divided by deep, narrow valleys. ''Gotta stay in the dorm and get some work done, Jock. What are you gonna do?''

Jock put down the toothbrush, rinsed his mouth with water, then peered into the mirror as he flexed his biceps. ''Gonna play some touch football with the boys, and then, when I've worked up a real appetite, I'm gonna get me a two-pound steak and about ten pounds of rice and gravy. Spring weather always makes me hungry as a horsefly.''

Meatball's stomach groaned. The noise caused Jock to stop his self-inspection and to stare momentarily at his friend.

''Hey, Meatball, you could sure use some exercise. Why don't you start doing push-ups or something like that?''

Meatball's chins vibrated in terror. Nobody had invited him to play ''touch'' for years—not that he could run fast enough to make it worth the effort anyhow. And he hadn't been able to touch his toes since high school.

''Well, Jock, maybe I should. But I'm so out of shape now, it would take the world's greatest physical ed teacher to get me on the right path and a whole bushel of encouragement to keep me there. And I just don't know anybody . . .'' Meatball's voice trailed off softly.

Jock squared his shoulders. ''Well, it just happens that I know a thing or two about physical education. That's my major, if you haven't forgotten. Why, I bet I could figure out a program for you that would really work miracles.'' He surveyed the mound of quivering flesh in front of him. ''Well, minor miracles, anyway.''

''But Jock, you know what a weakling I am.''

''Don't worry. We'll start you off slow and easy—nothing you couldn't handle.''

Meatball cocked his head to one side. ''Jock, it would take a real genius to coax me into doing that sort of thing.''

Jock accepted the challenge. ''Meatball, I **am** a genius. Just wait and see. I'll work something out for you tonight and we can start first thing tomorrow morning. After two weeks on my program, you won't recognize yourself anymore. Okay?''

Meatball groaned. ''Okay, Jock. I guess you know best.''

Moments later, when Meatball got to his room, he found his roommate standing in the middle of a pile of pants and shirts. Stud's shoulders were wide, his waist surprisingly thin, his legs slender but well-muscled. He tried on a pair of pea-green pants and a lemon-colored knit shirt, but the combination didn't seem to please him, so he tossed them onto the mound of clothes at his feet and started putting on something else.

"Man, I just can't find anything new and exciting to wear on my date tonight, and I really want to impress this young lady with my sharpness as a dresser." The soft-knit fabrics clung to his body like a second skin.

"They look pretty good to me," Meatball said, tightening up the 42-inch (106.7 centimeters) belt that held his own shapeless blue jeans to his rotund frame. He picked up a bunch of record albums scattered on the floor, put them on the table near the phonograph, and walked to the other side of the room.

"Oh, they fit okay, but they're way out of style. I mean, I've had them for months, but I just can't stretch the budget right now to buy something new."

Meatball removed a couple of empty pizza containers from a chair and sat down with a sigh of bitter resignation.

Sensing some kind of distress, Stud turned to look at his roommate. "What's the matter, Meaty? You look sick or something."

"Stud, I need your help."

Stud removed a pile of books and papers from his bed and sat down. "Sure, man, anything. What's your problem?"

"My problem is, I've got to lose weight. That's why I went to see Professor Mann."

"What did she say?"

"We had a long talk, about my family and my friends and things. I told her what my childhood was like, and she told me about rats and chickens. Then I gave her 30 bucks and she sent me to see Doc Barios at the Health Clinic."

Stud laughed. "What did old Doc Barios do, give you another diet or some pills?"

Meatball shook his head. "No, he gave me a physical examination. And then he gave me his okay to stop eating entirely for at least two weeks."

"Two weeks! You'll starve to death!"

"No, Dr. Barios tells me that the average person can go four to six weeks without any food at all and still survive, and someone like me could probably go longer than that. If you're going to lose weight, he said, the only way to do it is to cut your food intake below what your body needs to get by. If you want to lose a lot in a hurry—like I do—you cut the intake to zero for a while. And then you go on a high protein diet to stay slim."

Stud smiled bemusedly. "All you need is willpower, Meatball."

"That's what I told Professor Mann. She says the easiest way to increase your willpower is to change your environment."

"And what's she going to do for you, send you on a vacation?"

"She gave me some sheets of graph paper."

Stud laughed loudly. "What is it, Lo-cal graph paper that you eat instead of breakfast?"

"No, Stud, I'm going to weigh myself daily and record what I weigh on the graph. Professor Mann says it doesn't always work, but maybe it will in my case. So I gave her the 30 bucks, and I haven't had anything to eat all day."

"Thirty bucks! I could have given you the same advice for half the price, and thrown in the graph paper for free. What's she gonna do that's worth that much dough?"

Meatball sighed. "She's just holding the money for me, Stud. I get to earn it back if I lose weight. For the next 15 days I get a dollar each day my graph shows a weight loss. It's my reward for losing weight."

"But a dollar a day for 15 days is only 15 bucks. What happens to the rest of the dough?"

A wan smile crept across Meatball's face. "It's for you, Stud."

The young man sat bolt upright. "Fifteen bucks? For me? What do I have to do, kick you in the rear end if you fall off the food wagon?"

Meatball shook his head slowly. "No, Stud. We tried that last time I was on a diet, remember? And it didn't work very well. Professor Mann says that you should just ignore me if I break down and eat something."

Stud looked so disappointed that a faint suspicion crawled into Meatball's mind. Maybe Stud had enjoyed punishing him so much that, without knowing it, Stud had actually encouraged him to break his last diet. Well, time would tell.

"I get a buck a day for just ignoring you?" Stud asked, a frown on his face.

"No, Stud, I have to work to get my money back, and so do you." Meatball looked around their room. Clothes, books, and records were scattered more or less randomly about the place as if it had been visited recently by a friendly tornado. "Remember when we got into that fight about whose turn it was to clean up the room, and you said if I'd give you a dollar a day, you'd act as janitor all the time? Well, you're going to get the chance. Every day I lose weight, I get a dollar back and you get a dollar too—if you're willing to clean the room that day."

"And if I don't clean the room . . ."

"I get both dollars."

Stud frowned. "But what happens if I want to earn the money, but you haven't lost weight that day? I get the dollar anyhow, right?"

"No. Not at all. If I don't lose the flab, you don't get anything but my sympathy. Then the money goes to the Psych Club."

"But I don't belong to the Psych Club."

"Then, if I don't lose weight, we're both out of luck . . ."

Stud thought for a minute, visions of sugar-plum colored clothes dancing through his head. Then he smiled broadly. "Meatball, old friend, you've got a deal. When do we start?"

"Yesterday. I weighed in at four o'clock yesterday afternoon at 213 pounds. I'll weigh again this afternoon, and if I'm under that weight, I get the first dollar from Professor Mann."

"And I get a dollar too."

"Only if the room is cleaned up before you go out on your date tonight."

"Meatball, this is going to be the cleanest room in the whole dorm!" Stud paused a moment, then continued. "Hey, friend, what are you doing tonight?"

"Gonna stay home and starve quietly." Meatball's stomach growled in protest.

"Hey old buddy, how'd you like to come along on my date—the first part of the evening anyhow. We're just going to a flick."

Meatball brightened. "You mean you really want my company?"

Stud smiled. "How else can I keep an eye on you? And no popcorn either, understand?"

(Continued on page 266.)

What do you want from life?

Chances are that you've asked yourself this question many times. And if the answers you've come up with so far haven't entirely satisfied you, don't be discouraged. For the chances also are that you've never realized just how complex the seemingly simple question "What do you want from life?" really is.

To begin with, has it occurred to you that everything you "want" is dependent on your being alive? That is, to get things from *life*, you must survive, you must have life itself. Therefore, many of your basic needs are life-sustaining: food, air, water, sleep, a certain range of temperatures, protection from such environmental dangers as physical damage, poisons, storms, and germs. Most of these wants can be expressed as *input* needs. But you also need to maintain certain outputs to survive; you must breathe out excess moisture and carbon dioxide as well as breathe in oxygen; you must release water and waste products through sweat, urine, and defecation. Yet even these *output* needs have their *input* components; you don't go hunting for the nearest bathroom just because your bladder is full and needs to release urine. Rather, you feel the urge to urinate because, when your bladder is full or *distended* (°), sensory neurons in the walls of the bladder send very painful input messages to your brain informing you that action on your part is urgently required. When you are deprived of fresh air, sensory neurons

Distended (dis-TEN-dead). From the Latin word meaning "to stretch." When you blow up a balloon, you distend the material the balloon is made of.

detect the build-up of carbon dioxide in your lungs and blood and send alarm messages to your central nervous system that prompt you to vigorous movement (the "suffocating reflex," which is instinctive). Even your output needs, then, are made known to you by input signals.

If you stop to consider all this, you will realize that your own bodily survival is primarily dependent upon your controlling various types of sensory inputs. As long as you can get the right types and quantities of certain critical inputs, you have an excellent chance of continuing to have life. Luckily, your body (like the bodies of most other animals) is genetically programmed so that there are certain innately determined response patterns (outputs) associated with each of the critical stimulus inputs that you need to control in order to keep your body alive.

MOTIVATION: FACT AND THEORY

The concept of motivation is one of the most difficult that psychologists have to deal with, for the meaning of the word seems to change according to one's solution to the mind-body problem (*see* Chapter 4). Thus those psychologists who see the human animal as primarily a biological creature tend to think of motivation primarily in terms of bodily needs. Those psychologists with an intra-psychic bent often perceive humans as motivated mostly by inner feelings and rational decision-making. And those scientists who view the human race as a group of social beings sometimes insist that our major motives are those involving our dealings with other people.

Does the mind do anything more than interpret, *rationalize* (°), or yield to the body's itches and urges? Can we explain all of our emotions and desires in terms of increased or decreased firing rates of specialized nerve centers? Are our needs for companionship—for love, for personal growth, for success and prestige, or even for helping others—as basic and as primary as our needs for food and water? Can we understand the complexities of human actions without realizing that we are highly complicated systems with a variety of biological, intra-psychic, and social needs?

These are some of the thorny issues that we must grasp if we are to comprehend the problems—and the wide range of solutions—associated with our attempts to answer that seemingly simple question, "What do you want from life?" Little wonder that the field of human motivation is at the same time one of the most fascinating and one of the most frustrating areas in all of psychology.

MOTIVATION AND SELF-MOVEMENT

The word "motivation" comes from the Latin term meaning "to move." Ancient scholars were fascinated by the fact that some objects in the world seem to be self-movers, while other objects remain stationary unless acted upon by some outside force. The ancients assumed that self-initiated motion was caused by a spirit inside the object (a "little man"?) that pushed or impelled the object into action. Whenever the "spirit was moved," so was the thing that the spirit inhabited.

Nowadays, we assume that only living organisms are capable of self-determined movement. But to tell the truth, some of our theories of motivation (and of life itself) are still based on the idea that there is an homunculus deep inside us that pulls our strings and keeps us on the go. Mind, soul, cosmic force, and *libido* (°) are just a few of the terms we use to refer to this inner spirit or power that pushes us along life's path.

It was not until about the 16th century that Western scientists gained enough knowledge of physics that they could explain the "behaviors" of such *inanimate* (°) objects as rocks and rivers in purely *mechanical* equations. Once scientists had

Rationalize (RASH-un-ull-ize). From the Latin word meaning "to reason." To rationalize is to find logical reasons for your actions. As used in psychology, the word often means "to find socially approved excuses for your emotionally determined behaviors or attitudes."

Libido (lib-BEE-doe). From the Latin word meaning "desire" or "lust." According to Freud, the libido is the energy source that we make use of when we move to satisfy our needs.

Inanimate (inn-ANN-ee-mate or inn-ANN-uh-mutt). The word "animate" comes from the Latin term meaning "breath" or "spirit." "Animate" also means "to move about in a spirited fashion." Animate objects are those that have an internal source of motivation or movement power; inanimate objects are those that move only when acted upon by some external motivator or mover. Our word "animal" comes from the same Latin source.

made this giant intellectual step, they began to wonder if the actions of living organisms couldn't also be understood in physical, mechanical, or non-spiritual terms. Some of our theories of motivation are thus based on the belief that human activities are just about as mechanistic as are the movements of thunderstorms or ocean waves.

Two of the best-known mechanistic approaches to human motivation are *drive theory* and *arousal theory*. Each of these theories offers a slightly different biological solution to the mind-body problem, each has its strengths and weaknesses, and each is incomplete in and of itself. Opposed to these physiological viewpoints are a number of *perceptual* or *intra-psychic theories* of motivation in which the organism's inner feelings or emotions are presumed to direct or control physiological reactions. We will examine all of these approaches briefly, then discuss the influence of various environmental inputs on what often appear to be purely internal motivational states. In this way we may end up with a fairly complete and practical understanding of what motivates us—that is, what makes us move.

DRIVE THEORY

As we noted, physics became a science when physicists began to explain the motions of inanimate objects in terms of fairly simple equations. For the past century, many psychologists have attempted to imitate the "physics model" by reducing the complexities of human motivation to fairly uncomplicated biological equations. Instead of dealing with the mind, or with intra-psychic events, these psychologists tried to cast out the "little man" inside our heads and explain all human movement or behavior in terms of physiological processes. Rather than assuming that people (or animals) are capable of self-determined actions, these psychologists theorized that organisms are *driven* or pushed into motion much in the way an automobile engine is cranked into activity when someone turns the ignition key or steps on the starter.

At its simplest, the physiological approach to motivation is often called *drive theory* (°). Generally speaking, drive theorists presume that *biological* needs are the ones that rule our lives. All other human wants and needs are assumed to be learned through association with our attempts to reduce the physical arousals that propel us along life's highway. In many ways, drive theory turned out to be an ingenious intellectual activity that taught us much about the physiological mechanisms underlying many of our behaviors. But humans are self-starting systems rather than auto engines. Thus, as we will see shortly, even in drive theory there's at least the ghost of a "little man" lurking about inside our bodies who pushes us toward pleasure and pulls us away from painful inputs.

It is easy for most of us to criticize drive theory; sometimes it is not so easy for us to see the many contributions it has made to our understanding of motivational processes. Let us first look at the theory itself, then add up its pluses and minuses.

Primary Needs and Drives

Most drive theorists refer to those things we absolutely must have to survive as *primary needs* (°). Whenever your body runs short of a physical entity necessary for life (such as air, food, water, proper temperature), a *primary drive* (°) builds up within your body that tends to motivate or move you to satisfy that need. As long as all of your primary needs are met, your body presumably ticks smoothly in a quiet state of balance. But whenever your body begins to run low on something required for survival, this balance is upset. Built-in physical mechanisms sense or detect your body's wants, and the firing rates in various neural

Drive theory. The belief that all of our really important needs are physiological ones, such as food, air, and water. Hence, a biologically oriented, one-level theory in that it ignores intra-psychic and social/behavioral types of motivation.

Primary needs. Things that the body must have in order to survive; physiological needs, such as food, air, and water. Unlearned or instinctual needs.

Primary drive. Whenever the body is deprived of something necessary for life, an urge or desire for that "something" is said to build up, which "drives" the organism to hunt for what it needs. Associated with each primary need is a related primary drive. Food is a primary need, hunger is the associated primary drive.

centers in your brain start to increase. As these nerve cells fire more and more rapidly, you become physically aroused and eventually are driven into action (motivated) to seek what it is that you need.

Drive States and Homeostasis

According to drive theory, whenever any of your needs are not satisfied, you are likely to experience a state of neural arousal or excitation. This increased rate of firing in your nervous system creates what is called a primary *drive state* (°). Generally speaking, the longer you are deprived of something you need, the faster your nerve cells fire, the greater your drive state becomes, and the more aroused or "motivated" you are. Eventually this aroused movement brings you into a position to satisfy your need. Once you do so, your drive level falls back toward zero, your drive state is greatly reduced, your arousal (motivation) thus disappears, and your normal physiological balance is reinstated.

As an analogy, you might consider how an air-conditioning unit controls the temperature in a room. Suppose that on the morning of a pleasant summer day, you set the control at 75 degrees F. (23.9 degrees C.). For a while the machine is quiet, because the room is still cooler than the temperature you set into the control. But as the day wears on, things begin to heat up. When the room gets too warm, the thermostat inside the unit detects this fact and is "motivated" or "driven" to turn on the fans and motors within the machine. Cool air blows into the room and the temperature rapidly begins falling. Once the room is again at 75 degrees F. (23.9 degrees C.), the thermostat's "drive state" drops to zero and it shuts off all the "aroused" electrical excitation within the unit.

Physiologists suggest that much of our biologically determined behavior is turned on or off by "internal thermostats" that detect our wants and make us attend to the goal of keeping our bodies in a static, need-free, unexcited condition. We call such activities *homeostatic* (°), from the Greek words meaning "home state" or "normal condition." The concept of homeostasis—the return to the normal or unexcited state—plays a central role in drive theory. We might therefore diagram simple drive theory as follows:

Drive state. The state or condition of being without something you need, or of being motivated or "driven" to find something that you need. Generally speaking, the more deprived you are of what you need, the higher the drive state, the stronger the drive, and the more urgent the motivation to seek satisfaction. Eating when you are very hungry reduces your hunger drive.

Homeostatic (home-ee-oh-STAT-ick). Homeostasis (home-ee-oh-STAY-sis) is the tendency to move toward a need-free or drive-free condition. Any action that an organism makes to reduce drives is called a "homeostatic behavior."

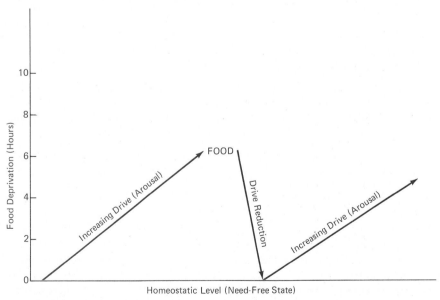

A simple diagram of drive theory using food deprivation as an example.

Secondary Needs and Drives

You need to take in liquid to live—but what you drink depends in large part on what many psychologists call your learned or *secondary needs* (°). Primary needs are held to be innately determined—they are built into your genetic blueprint. Secondary needs are presumably acquired, and they vary widely from person to person and from culture to culture. Many—but not all—secondary needs are related to the satisfaction of primary needs. For instance, although you have a primary need to *excrete* (°) water, you learned very early in life that there are some things that we just don't ordinarily do in public. Thus your secondary need not to violate a very strong social law sets you to looking for a toilet when your bladder is full.

Associated with every secondary need is a corresponding *secondary drive* (°) that, when aroused, impels or pushes you to satisfy that need.

To summarize, the drive approach to motivation is what we might call a biologically oriented, one-level theory. It is biological in orientation because physiological needs are presumed to be primary; all other needs are said to be acquired or learned. The theory operates on only one level because the feelings, perceptions, emotions, and behaviors of the organism are held to be relatively unimportant since they are caused by physiological reactions.

QUESTION: **What position do drive theorists appear to be taking with regard to solving the mind-body problem?**

Some Problems Concerning Drive Theory

Many objections have been raised to the simple form of drive theory that we have just outlined. Three of the major objections are as follows:

1. In some instances, a *decrease* in neural excitation can be just as arousing as an *increase* in firing rates.
2. Our intra-psychic feelings, perceptions, and emotions may have as much or more to do with motivation as our physiological needs, drives, and arousals.
3. Many of the so-called learned or "secondary" needs are neither very secondary nor are they always acquired by being associated with "primary" needs.

As we will see, the scientists who raised these objections often were "driven" to create competing motivational theories of their own.

AROUSAL THEORY

In the late 1950's, Elizabeth Duffy (and others) made a telling criticism of classical drive theory. As Duffy pointed out, arousal is not always caused by a lack of such things as food, air, or water—we have informational (stimulus input) needs that are as innate and as highly motivating as are our energy (life-sustaining) needs. Thus the "boredom" associated with a marked *decrease* in neural excitation can be as arousing or motivating as the *increase* in neural firing typically associated with food deprivation.

This objection led Duffy and other scientists to a new approach to motivation which, roughly speaking, we can call *arousal theory* (°). The basic postulates of this position can be summarized as follows:

1. The homeostatic "home base" is not a state of *zero* excitation but rather a point of *optimum* (°) stimulation.
2. This optimum point may change from time to time, depending on our biological condition.
3. A decrease in optimum stimulation may be as arousing or motivating as an increase.

Secondary needs. The need for food is a primary, unlearned need. The need for steak (instead of for chicken or chop suey) is acquired, as is the need for a Cadillac instead of a VW. Most social needs are said to be secondary needs.

Excrete (ex-KREET). From the Latin words meaning "to discharge, release, or pass things out from the body." When you go to the toilet and pass out water from your kidneys, you are excreting urine. When you pass out waste food from your digestive system, you are excreting feces (FEE-sees), or defecating (DEAF-fee-KAIT-ing).

Secondary drive. Whenever you are deprived of some secondary (acquired) need, a secondary drive state builds up inside you which motivates you to satisfy that need (and hence reduce the pain, tension, or unpleasantness associated with the secondary drive state).

Arousal theory. A one-level, biologically oriented theory of motivation in which motivation comes from some departure from a norm or optimum point of neural excitation. Any increase or decrease in neural firing moves the organism away from this optimum point and hence is arousing.

Optimum (OPP-tee-mum or OPP-tuh-mum). From the Latin word meaning "best." Literally, the most favorable point or condition.

Arousal and Homeostasis

Arousal theory had its beginnings in the sensory-deprivation experiments performed in Canada and the discovery of the reticular activating system by Magoun and his associates (*see* Chapter 9). Consider the sensory-deprivation studies for just a moment. You will recall that the subjects in these experiments apparently had all of their physiological needs met all the time, yet most of the men could not endure the experience for more than a day or so. Drive theorists sometimes explained this "flight from boredom" as evidence that we have an innate biological "need for stimulation." But this kind of *postulated* (°) instinct surely contradicts the simple homeostatic model in which an increase in motivation can be brought about only by an increase in neural firing rates.

More than this, as Duffy noted, we do not have a single "homeostatic level" that is set at birth and never varies thereafter. Rather, our need for stimulation changes according to our past experience and present conditions. You might recall from earlier chapters that your sensory receptors are designed to detect environmental *change*. For the first few moments that you turn on a fan in an otherwise quiet room, the fan may seem particularly noisy. After a while, however, your nervous system stops responding (habituates) to the sound of the fan. If you had to eat steak at every meal, after a while you might find it didn't taste quite as good as once it did.

Because our bodies adjust to any constant sensory input, the optimum level of stimulation that we need varies from moment to moment. Given this fact, it doesn't take much imagination to realize that we lose much of our ability to predict and control our inputs whenever our environment becomes *too constant*. But we also lose that same ability whenever our environment *changes too much*. Thus we need a certain amount of stability in the world around us—just as the homeostatic model would predict. But we also need a certain amount of variability in stimulation—as arousal theory predicts—or our receptor systems will "turn off" and leave us without any inputs at all. The reticular activating system seems designed to stir us into action whenever our inputs become either too different or too much the same. Thus we might diagram arousal theory as follows:

Postulated (POSS-tew-lay-ted). To postulate is to make a guess about something, or to insist that something exists or is very important. Postulates may or may not be facts. For instance, centuries ago people postulated that the world was flat, so they wouldn't sail across the Atlantic Ocean for fear they would fall off the edge of the world. Then along came adventuresome men like Columbus who postulated that the world was round instead of flat. The words "theory" and "hypothesis" (high-POTH-thuh-sis) mean about the same thing as "postulate."

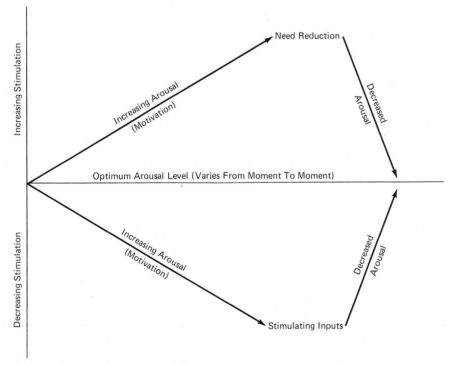

A simple diagram of arousal theory.

As presented by Duffy, the arousal position remained a one-level, biological theory in that it reduced motivation to what seemed to be purely physiological processes. But it was a noticeable improvement over simple drive theory in that Duffy could explain a number of motivational situations that early drive theorists had difficulty with.

QUESTION: In Chapter 3, we noted that certain drugs such as LSD lead to a fearful experience called "loss of personal control"; in Chapter 9, we noted that sensory deprivation leads to a panic-inducing experience in which subjects can no longer control their thought patterns. How might both these unpleasant situations be related to our need to predict our inputs?

INTRA-PSYCHIC APPROACHES TO MOTIVATION

Why do you eat? According to drive and arousal theorists, when your body lacks food, certain neural centers in your brain show an increase in electrical excitation that drives you to find food in order to decrease your state of arousal. Yet most of us believe that we eat because we feel hunger pangs, and it is the pain of hunger that drives us to grill a hamburger or to make a peanut butter sandwich. Hunger stirs us up, true; but it is the subjective discomfort and not the physiological arousal that seems to goad us into stuffing goodies into our mouths. Furthermore, some things taste so good that we will often eat a cookie or a potato chip even when our bodies don't have a real physiological need for food and can't possibly be physiologically aroused.

What about the motivational aspects of our feelings, then? It should be clear by now that drive and arousal theorists place little importance on the mental experiences that accompany motivational states. But some aspects of human motivation are much easier to explain in terms of our feelings, emotions, and perceptions than in terms of drives and arousals. For example, it is almost impossible to describe how we·learn without making reference to those intra-psychic feelings we call pleasure and pain.

Pleasure, Pain, and Learning

Most theorists agree that learning seldom occurs unless the organism is motivated. A rat will rapidly master a complex maze if, in doing so, it either avoids electric shock or receives food when it is hungry. In attempting to explain why this maze learning comes about, drive theorists often spoke of the "punishing" effects of arousal and the "rewarding" aspects of drive reduction. But in using these terms, the theorists were really shifting away from a one-level, purely biological theory of motivation toward a two-level theory. For punishment and reward surely carry with them subtle associations of "pain" and "pleasure"—words that are descriptive of intra-psychic events, not of physiological states or conditions.

In fact, there are many types of stimuli that arouse intense feelings of pleasure in and of themselves and hence motivate us strongly. It is impossible to explain the thrilling beauty of a rainbow, or the glorious sounds of music, in terms of physiological drive *reduction* or even in terms of sensory deprivation. The sights, smells, and tastes associated with the table are another example of pure sensory pleasures. Almost any rat will learn a maze more quickly if given flavorful food than if its reward is tasteless—even though the *bland* (°) food might actually be more *nutritious* (°) and hence better at reducing the animal's presumed hunger drive. A newborn child will often reject water, but will readily accept milk. The sweeter the milk is—within limits—the more eagerly an infant will consume it. If the milk is made sour or bitter, all but the most severely deprived child will reject it. Therefore, hunger not only arouses us—it also makes certain types of food inputs more pleasurable or, at worst, less unpleasant than they normally would be.

Bland (rhymes with "canned"). From the Latin word meaning "smooth," or "not stimulating." A bland diet is one that contains no spicy or highly seasoned foods.

Nutritious (new-TRISH-us). From the Latin word meaning "to nurse." A nutritious food is one that is nourishing or that promotes growth and health.

One of the major functions of deprivations, drives, and arousals, then, is that they make it easier for us to survive by changing our emotional feelings toward, and perceptions of, certain stimuli in our environments.

Facts such as these led many psychologists to abandon one-level, purely physiological theories of motivation in favor of two-level approaches that included both biological drives and intra-psychic events such as emotion and perception.

EMOTION

William James.

When someone mentions the word *emotion* (°) to you, what sorts of pictures pop into your mind? Images of love and hate? Ideas about anger and rage and fear? In fact, if you look carefully at the word, you can guess immediately that it has the same Latin root as the word "motivation"—namely, "e-motion" means "to move" or "to respond" or "to be stirred up." An emotional response may involve a general state of bodily excitation—such as turning red in the face or shaking your fists when you're angry. Or it may involve moving toward or away from some goal or object—such as approaching someone you love or running rapidly away from a threatening rattlesnake. Generally speaking, however, when we use the word "emotion" in everyday speech, we typically refer to our intra-psychic *feelings* about an experience as much as we do to our bodily movements. Thus most emotional theories of motivation are *two-level theories* because they deal with feelings and perceptions as much as with physiological reactions.

But in emotional situations, which comes first, our perceptions and feelings or the biological arousal that often accompanies them? That is, does the mind stimulate the body, or does the body stimulate the mind? Or do both mental and physiological processes occur at about the same time and feed on each other?

In 1884, Harvard psychologist William James proposed that the body almost always takes the lead. According to James, when we almost step on a rattlesnake, we run. Our heart rate increases dramatically, our hair stands on end, and we breathe rapidly as we rush away from the dreaded reptile. Moments later, we notice these physiological reactions and realize that we are scared. We may think that we saw the snake, became frightened, and then ran. Not so, said James, for our reactions precede and thus almost wholly determine our feelings. As James put it, "We are afraid because we run; we do not run because we are afraid." To James, our emotional feelings were mostly a matter of our consciously noting the feedback we get continuously from various parts of our bodies. (In 1885, the noted Danish physiologist Karl G. Lange independently proposed much the same sort of explanation of emotional behavior. For that reason, this viewpoint is often called the James-Lange theory of emotions.)

As you might surmise, the James-Lange viewpoint led to a lot of highly emotional debate and, happily to say, to a lot of useful research as well. It is now fairly agreed that while in emergency situations our feelings may lag slightly behind our physiological reactions, in many instances our intra-psychic processes determine what our bodily reactions will be. For example, during the height of an emotional experience, the higher brain centers are bombarded with inputs from the *sympathetic nervous system* (°), the *limbic system* (°), the *reticular activating system* (°), and inputs from many other parts of the body as well. Yet it is our *perception* of the situation, and our past experience, that yield that unique quality we refer to as "an emotion."

Perceptual Theories of Emotion

One of the main difficulties with one-level theories—as with the James-Lange viewpoint—is that emotional (motivated) behaviors often seem to have a precise direction to them. If physiological excitation were identical to motivation, if the

Emotion. From the Latin word meaning "to agitate or stir up." Emotions are often said to have a biological component (arousal or depression), a mental component (pleasantness or unpleasantness), and a social or environmental component (an object or goal).

Sympathetic nervous system. The arousal part of the autonomic nervous system. See Chapter 3.

Limbic system. The emotional centers lying deep on the underside of the cerebral cortex. See Chapter 4.

Reticular activating system. Also called "RAS." Neural centers, primarily in the stem of the brain, that arouse or activate neural activity in the cortex. See Chapter 9.

Robert Leeper.

"drive state" were nothing but a generalized condition of arousal, then a hungry rat would be as likely to drink as to eat. Rats seldom make that kind of mistake. If arousal were the same thing as emotion, we might also find ourselves hitting our lovers and embracing our enemies, but few of us perform such foolish actions.

In 1960, Magda Arnold revised the James-Lange theory to take into account the guiding effects of perception on motivated behaviors. To Arnold, we typically first perceive a situation, then evaluate it. This evaluation leads to an emotional reaction that has both biological and intra-psychic components, and the emotional response may or may not lead to a behavioral reaction. According to Arnold, emotions are either pleasant or unpleasant. Since we tend to avoid pain and pursue pleasure, emotion is the driving force that moves us toward or away from various environmental situations. For Arnold, emotion is the central part of the motivational process—but emotion is almost always triggered by our perceptions and evaluations of what is happening to us.

A somewhat similar theory was advanced in 1965 by Robert Leeper, who argues that biological reactions to emotional situations have but one main effect—*to change the way the cortical centers process or handle various inputs.* And because neural activity in the limbic system, for example, alters the way the cortex works, limbic inputs can affect the way we perceive things. For Leeper, intra-psychic or perceptual activities are the basis of *all* motivational processes; for without perception, our physical reactions would lack direction and thus be pretty meaningless. Emotions therefore not only arouse, they *guide* behavior as well.

SOCIAL/BEHAVIORAL INFLUENCES ON MOTIVATION

A few pages ago, we noted that when drive theorists began to talk about pain and pleasure, they opened the door to intra-psychic theories of emotion and motivation. Perhaps now that you have struggled through our brief descriptions of several intra-psychic viewpoints, you can see a similar problem. Perceptions may direct our behaviors, but where do our perceptions come from? As we saw in Chapter 10, much of perception is learned from our interactions with other human beings. We see what we expect to see; but what we expect to see is due to our past experiences in various social environments and what other people have told us we ought to see. Thus emotions and motivated behaviors are always expressed in the context of what's happening to us now and what has happened to us in similar situations before now. If we step on a tack when we are alone, we may utter a few choice if rather ear-burning words; if we step on a tack when our mother or a very religious person is nearby, we may say something quite different. Thus social inputs guide our perceptions, which in turn influence our bodily reactions.

We can get around many of the difficulties associated with one- and two-level theories of emotion by realizing that we have at least three different types of motivational processes. That is, we have biological motives, intra-psychic motives, and social/behavioral motives. These three separate systems of emotional processes interact with and influence each other. In some situations, for instance, a social input may trigger off strong mental and bodily reactions; in other situations, a biological input may affect our perceptions and our social behaviors. Under most circumstances, the three systems operate simultaneously and in parallel—in a kind of mutual interdependence. To overemphasize the importance of any one of the systems—or to try to explain all motivation in one-level terms such as percepts or neural firings—is to prevent us from appreciating the marvelous complexities buried in that simple question, "What do you want from life?"

So let us try to pull together drive theory, arousal theory, perceptual theory, and social influences into what we might call a three-level approach to motivation. When we do so, we will find over and over again that it is mostly *inputs* that we strive for (at all three levels), and that we are capable of changing our outputs in order to get whatever inputs we want at any given moment.

The best test of such a theoretical approach will surely be whether or not it can be put into practice in some useful way. So let us take much of what we know about one highly motivated behavior—that of overeating—and show how complicated this seemingly simple behavior really is. By the end of the chapter, we will have learned that fat people—if they want to lose weight—must usually look at their predicament from all three levels of analysis. And we will also discover just how useful this approach to motivational problems can be to anyone, fat or skinny. But let me warn you. If you are firmly convinced that the only reason fat people overeat is that they are hungry all the time, or that they are punishing themselves for some peculiar reason, just wait! The facts of the matter may so arouse you that you will need a pizza or a popsickle to reduce your intellectual pain.

FATNESS: AN AMERICAN PROBLEM

There are almost four billion people living on earth at the present time. At least a third of these people don't get as much of the right things to eat as they should, and hence suffer from *malnutrition* (°). There are slightly more than 210 million people in the United States. Perhaps because we are the richest, most powerful nation on earth, only a relatively small percentage of our population is badly undernourished. However, hunger is a very real problem for many people living in poverty-stricken rural and slum areas, and it affects blacks and whites alike; it is a problem we have not as yet been able to solve successfully.

Millions of people die each year because they cannot afford or cannot get good food—but, in truth, very few of these millions live in the United States. In fact, we suffer from the opposite sort of problem. Dietitians estimate that from 10 to 25 percent of the American public is *overweight*. The average family doctor treats more than 10 patients a month who want to lose weight. Perhaps 1 in 20 of these patients has a glandular disorder or some subtle form of brain damage that is responsible for the fatness—and with these patients, the medical profession can often be of considerable help. The other 19 out of 20 people are fat simply because they do not use up all the *calories* (°) in the food they eat, and their bodies store the surplus energy away as fat tissue. With these patients, according to physicians interested in the subject, medical science has not done particularly well.

At a 1972 meeting on the topic of fatness, Dr. Alvan Feinstein of the Yale Medical School reported that the success rate of most medical weight-loss programs is "terrible, much worse than in cancer." Experts estimate that only some 12 out of 100 patients who seek a physician's help actually lose weight, and that 10 of these 12 gain back their excess pounds within a year or two.

Presuming that your own weight is normal, why should you worry about such things? In part, because fatness could happen to you someday, and probably has already happened to one or more of your friends or relatives. In part, because fat people are a very discriminated-against minority. If you are overweight, you have difficulty buying attractive clothes; you have difficulty getting out of many chairs and getting into many small cars. The fat man may be "jolly," but he isn't invited to participate in as many sports as is his thinner brother. Fat girls may be "good sports," but studies show they have fewer dates than do their sisters who fit a size 6 or 8 dress. Employers appear to be hesitant to hire overweight individuals (have you ever seen a really fat airline hostess?).

Fatness can even affect your academic career. Psychologists H. Canning and

Malnutrition (mal-new-TRISH-shun). The French word *mal* means "bad," or "sickness." Nutrition is the whole process of eating food, digesting it, and turning it into energy that your body can use. Someone who suffers from malnutrition simply isn't getting enough energy to live properly. Not having enough to eat, or eating the wrong things, or having something wrong with your digestive system can all lead to malnutrition. Alcoholics often experience malnutrition because they spend their money on liquor instead of food, or simply get so drunk they forget to eat.

Calories (KAL-or-rees). The Latin word *calor* means "heat." The caloric (kal-LOR-ick) content of anything is the amount of heat it will generate when burned. Your body "burns" food when it converts it into energy to keep you alive. Rich, sweet, fatty foods have lots of calories (that is, a high caloric content). Water has no calories at all. Fat burns; water doesn't.

Obesity is a major problem for many people.

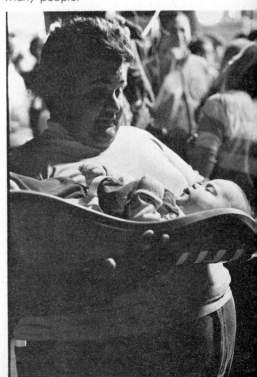

Obesity (oh-BEE-sit-tee). From the Latin words meaning "to overeat." Obesity means fatness; an obese (oh-BEESE) person is noticeably overweight.

Gluttony (GLUT-tone-ee). From the Latin word meaning "to gulp or swallow." A glutton (GLUT-ton) is someone who enjoys overeating. A "glutton for punishment" is someone who "eats up punishment with pleasure."

J. Mayer have made several studies of the effects of *obesity* (°) on high school students. These scientists report that school counselors are less likely to write letters of recommendation for fat students than for normals. Canning and Mayer also found that college admissions committees discriminate against fat students during interviews. Faced with two students with equally good grades and equally high intelligence and achievement scores, college committees have a tendency to accept the non-obese student and to shut out the one who weighs too much.

Unfair? Of course it is. So is our society's discrimination against people with dark skins or slanted eyes. Most of us realize that a person has little say about the color of the skin he or she was born with—but fatness is a matter of voluntary choice, isn't it? True, many scientists believe that there is a genetic component to body size—that is, you may be born with a tendency to weigh too much or too little. However, even if you were the child of the fattest parents in the world, couldn't you stay slim if you ate the right things and got the proper exercise? After all, isn't fatness a matter of personal choice?

No, in a very strange way, you are not entirely responsible for how much you weigh, and discrimination against fat people may be as unreasonable as discrimination against blacks or any other minority group. The psychological factors influencing fatness or thinness are just as important as the genetic or physiological ones. So perhaps you had better put down that pizza or those potato chips while we look at the biological, intra-psychic, and social/behavioral influences on *gluttony* (°).

THE BIOLOGY OF HUNGER

Eating is a voluntary behavior that we engage in again and again. Many psychologists assume that all such repetitive behaviors must somehow be rewarding to the people who engage in them—that is, all repetitive behaviors must satisfy some kind of psychological or physiological need. When a need is met, the corresponding drive is reduced, and we may assume that it was the presence of the drive within us that motivated us to eat.

Psychologist Marshall Jones, who has spent most of his life studying problems of motivation, has pointed out that to understand why a person does what he or she does, you must answer the following questions:

1. Why does a given behavioral sequence begin? That is, what prompts the thought or gets the action going?
2. Why does the behavior continue in the direction that it does once it begins? That is, what directs the thought or activity once it's gotten started?
3. Why does the thought or behavior eventually come to an end? That is, once an action has begun, what brings it to a stop?

Eating is a motivated behavior—but so are overeating and undereating. Therefore, to understand why you eat what you do, when you do, we must answer three critical questions: Why do you start eating, why do you stop eating, and why do you prefer steak and ice cream to fried worms and boiled monkey brains? As we will see, the biological viewpoint offers answers to the first two questions, but not to the third.

Marshall Jones.

QUESTION: **From a motivational point of view, fat people might be overweight for at least four reasons: (1) They start eating more often than they should—that is, they eat too frequently. (2) They eat no more *often* than anyone else, but when they start eating, they don't know when to quit—that is, they actually consume more food at each sitting than they should. (3) They eat no more often nor greater quantities than do others, but they prefer rich, fat-laden foods. (4) They don't burn up enough energy through exercise and physical labor. Which of these four possibilities strikes you as** being the major cause of fatness among the overweight people you know? And would you think that different forms of therapy would be needed depending on what combination of these four behaviors the person engaged in?

Blood Sugar Level

When you eat a baked potato for dinner, how does your body make use of this fuel? As you may know, digestion actually begins in your mouth, for your saliva contains chemicals called *enzymes* (°) that begin tearing the potato apart into its chemical building blocks (proteins, sugars, fats, and other simple molecules). When the partially digested potato arrives in your stomach, it encounters even more powerful enzymes that continue tearing away at it until it is reduced to molecules so small that they can pass through the lining of the small intestine and be absorbed into your bloodstream.

Blood containing these energy-rich molecules from the potato flows to almost every part of your body and passes the food particles on to any cell that might be "hungry." A few hours after you have eaten a large meal, your blood contains a great many of these food molecules. However, if you starve yourself for 24 hours or so, your blood would contain relatively few of these energy particles—and you would normally be highly motivated to obtain some caloric inputs to help reduce your hunger pangs.

Here is our first clue as to what the sensation of hunger is all about—the chemical composition of your blood at any given time makes a difference. If we could somehow control the molecules floating around in your bloodstream, might we not be able to control your sensation of hunger directly?

From a purely biological point of view, the answer is a probable yes. Much of the energy your body uses comes from simple sugars, which are contained in most of the foods that you eat. Under normal conditions, your body secretes a chemical called *insulin* (°) that breaks the sugar molecules up into smaller pieces so that the cells in your body can make use of them. If we let a hungry rat eat all that it wants, then take a blood sample from the animal a little later, we would find a lot of sugar molecules in the rat's blood. If we now inject the animal with insulin, we will rapidly lower the blood sugar level—and to our surprise the rat will soon begin to eat again (although it had a very large meal just minutes before).

Somewhere in the body, then, there must be a sugar detector that lets your cortex know how many sugar molecules are floating around in your bloodstream. Recent research suggests that this detector is located in a central part of your brain called the *hypothalamus* (°).

Sitting right at the top of your brain stem is a neural center called the *thalamus* (°). The thalamus is sort of the central telephone switchboard of the brain, for almost all incoming sensory information passes through the thalamus before being relayed to the cortex. The word "hypo" means "below" or "beneath." The hypothalamus is a bundle of nerve cells lying just under the thalamus and exercises rather strong control over many of your physiological motivations and emotions.

The Hypothalamic "Feeding Center"

One small part of the hypothalamus contains neurons that are particularly sensitive to the amount of sugar in your blood. When the blood sugar level drops too low, the cells in this region of the hypothalamus begin to fire more and more rapidly—and you typically begin to feel more and more hungry. If we put a metal electrode into this part of a rat's brain and stimulate the cells electrically, the rat will begin to eat at once (even if it has just had a big meal). If we stimulate this hypothalamic *feeding center* (°) continuously, the rat will eat and eat and eat—until it becomes so obese that it can barely move around. If we continue the

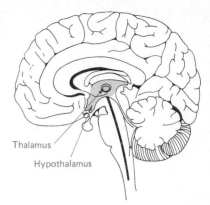

Thalamus

Hypothalamus

The hypothalamus and thalamus.

Enzymes (EN-zimes; rhymes with "ten times"). Natural chemicals found in your body that aid digestion by helping to tear apart food molecules.

Insulin (IN-sull-in). A hormone secreted by the pancreas (PAN-kree-us)—a small organ near the stomach. Insulin is needed for the digestion of sugar. People whose bodies do not secrete enough insulin may suffer from a disease called diabetes (die-uh-BEET-ease); such people have to control the amount of sugar they eat, and may have to take daily injections of insulin.

Hypothalamus (HIGH-po-THALL-uh-muss). A very important neural center lying just under the thalamus. The hypothalamus influences many types of motivated or emotional behavior, including eating and drinking.

Thalamus (THALL-uh-muss). Sensory messages from your eyes, ears, skin, nose, and tongue all pass through the thalamus before being passed on to the cortical Board. The thalamus is one of the lower centers of the brain that occasionally may act on its own by responding to sensory inputs without "bothering" the Board.

Feeding center. That portion of the hypothalamus which, when stimulated electrically, causes an organism to engage in overeating.

stimulation even when food is not present in the rat's cage, the animal will often gnaw on anything handy—including air. If we destroy this "feeding center" in the rat's hypothalamus, the animal usually refuses to eat at all and will die of starvation unless we force-feed it.

So this one "feeding center" in your hypothalamus controls your eating behavior, right? Wrong! To begin with, even the "dumb rat" knows better than to overeat continuously, no matter what we do to it. If we give rats the continual hypothalamic stimulation mentioned earlier, the animals will become very, very fat. But eventually they will reach a cut-off point beyond which they will not go; their weights will stabilize at this point and we cannot induce them to become much fatter.

We can achieve similar results by giving the rats daily injections of insulin, but again the animals will grow only so fat—and no fatter. If we combine insulin injections with electrical stimulation to the "feeding center" in the hypothalamus, we can get the animals to eat so rapidly that they will reach this *obesity limit* (°) very quickly—but they will still stop eating when this limit is reached.

(You will probably be pleased to know that, when we stop prodding the rat's brain with insulin and electrical stimulation, the animal will typically go on a "crash diet" and return to its normal body weight.)

Why do you eat? At least in part the answer to that question lies in the "feeding center" in your brain. As the sugar content in the blood reaching your brain decreases, electrical activity in this part of the hypothalamus increases. Your cortical Board translates this neural input into the psychological experience of hunger—and you go looking for a decent meal. But when you find the food you want, and begin to consume it, why do you stop after you've eaten just so much? Why don't you munch away for hours and hours?

Because, you say, as soon as you start eating, the sugar content in your blood goes up dramatically and your "feeding center" turns off. Unfortunately, eating behavior is anything but simply explained, even at a biological level. If you ate a big steak right now, it would take several hours for the meat to be digested and assimilated into your bloodstream. It takes only 10 to 20 minutes for you to eat the steak, though. You actually stop eating long before the food you've eaten can greatly affect your blood sugar level. In fact, if you're a quick eater, your "feeding center" may still be signaling "eat—eat—eat!" at the top of its neural voice at the very moment when you push yourself away from the table, so stuffed with food that you can't imagine ever being hungry again. So, a lowered blood sugar can turn on your hunger, but what physiological mechanism turns it off?

The Hypothalamic "Satiation Center"

As we pointed out in Chapter 2, your body is *bilaterally symmetrical* (°)—that is, the left half of your body is a mirror image of the right. Most of your physiological and psychological functioning is symmetrical too. For every muscle that acts to extend your arm, there is another muscle that acts *symmetrically* to cause your arm to pull back. For each drug that acts as an excitant or "upper," there is another drug that can counteract, or be a depressant or "downer." So, if there is a "feeding center" in your hypothalamus that causes you to start eating, wouldn't you guess there might also be a center that, when stimulated, causes you to stop eating? It is called the "satiation center," and it is also located in your hypothalamus, close to your "feeding center."

If we implant an electrode in the hypothalamic *satiation center* (°) in a rat's brain and then, just as the hungry animal goes to eat, pass a weak electrical current through this "satiation center," the animal will refuse its meal. If we continue the stimulation for a long time, the animal will come close to starving itself to death.

Obesity limit (oh-BEE-sit-tee) The cutoff point for fatness caused by abnormal stimulation of the hypothalamic feeding center.

Bilaterally symmetrical (buy-LATT-tur-rally sim-METT-tree-kal). The Latin word *lateral* means "side." *Bi* is the Latin word for "two." Anything that is bilateral has two sides to it (such as most arguments and love affairs). Symmetrical means "balanced," or "equal on all sides." Your body is bilaterally symmetrical because it has two sides (left and right) that are mirror images or equal to each other.

Satiation center (say-she-A-shun). Our word "satisfied" comes from the Latin words *satis,* meaning "enough," and *facere,* meaning "to do" or "to make." Satiation is the condition of being completely satisfied. The "satiation center" is that part of the hypothalamus which, when stimulated electrically, causes a hungry animal to stop eating—that is, to behave as if it were already satisfied.

A hypothalamic **hyperphagic** (*) rat—"fat rat."

On the other hand, if we surgically remove the rat's "satiation center," the animal will go on an eating jag and will become as obese as the rats given insulin injections. But as you might already have surmised, eventually the animal will reach a "fat limit" and will taper off its wild consumption of food.

QUESTION: **Could chronically overweight people suffer from an underdeveloped or damaged "satiation center" or from an overdeveloped "feeding center?"**

Under normal conditions, the "satiation center" functions symmetrically with the "feeding center." When your blood sugar level goes up, the neurons in your "feeding center" slow down their response rate and the nerve cells in your "satiation center" increase their firing rate. When your blood sugar level falls, your "feeding center" turns on and your "satiation center" turns off.

So now we know why you start eating and stop eating, don't we? Sadly enough, we've only learned part of the picture. For what do you think would happen if we surgically removed BOTH the "feeding center" and the "satiation center" from the rat's hypothalamus? Would the animal starve or become obese?

The answer is—neither. Under most circumstances, the animal would continue to eat pretty much as it had before the operation. So there must be other systems around that influence an animal's eating behavior.

The "Swallow Counter"

One such mechanism is what we might call the *swallow counter* (*). A young rat eats almost continuously. As it grows up, however, it soon learns to associate the "feeling" of hunger it presumably has with the amount of food that it ought to eat. When its blood sugar level is slightly lower than usual, and neurons in its "feeding center" are mildly excited, the rat will eat a small amount of food because it has learned that is all it needs to reduce its hunger drive. Research indicates that some (as yet unknown) part of the animal's brain actually *counts* the number of swallows or gulps of food the animal takes—and when it has had enough to satisfy its present state of hunger, the rat stops eating. And it stops *before* there is much of a change in its blood sugar level.

Hyperphagic (HIGH-purr-FAY-gick). From the Greek and Latin words meaning "big eater" or "overeating." A rat that ate too little and became dangerously thin would be hypophagic.

Swallow counter. That part of the brain that supposedly measures the amount of food an organism takes in. No one really knows where or what it is.

Eliot Stellar.

Trigeminal nerve (try-GEM-inn-nal or try-GEM-uh-null). From the Latin words meaning "triplets." The trigeminal nerve, which has three branches, runs from the lips and cheek to the lower centers of the brain.

Experiments reported in 1975 by H. Philip Zeigler and his associates at Hunter College suggest that the hypothalamic satiation center is strongly influenced by inputs from the *trigeminal nerve* (°). This nerve tract runs through the cheek and lip regions of most higher animals and seems critically involved with chewing, swallowing, and other forms of food intake. Axons from the trigeminal nerve connect up with (make synapse with) nerve cells in the "satiation center." Destruction of the trigeminal nerve (but not of the "satiation center") seems to cause much the same sort of loss of appetite as destruction of the "satiation center" itself. It is possible (though not yet proved) that the "satiation center" counts the stimulus inputs from the trigeminal nerve while the animal is chewing and swallowing. Thus when the animal has swallowed a certain number of times, the "satiation center" could turn off eating behavior even before the blood sugar level began to change.

But even the "swallow counter" doesn't give us the whole answer to the puzzling question, "Why do you eat?" Psychologist Eliot Stellar and his associates at the University of Pennsylvania have made many significant contributions to our understanding of eating behavior. In one fascinating set of experiments they put tiny tubes down a rat's throat so they could deliver food directly to the animal's stomach (bypassing the rat's mouth and hence the "swallow counter"). They then trained the rat to press a lever in order to get liquid food pumped into its stomach. The rat soon learned to take in the normal amount of food, and no more than that.

Next, Stellar and his colleagues performed the same experiment with college-student volunteers. For breakfast each morning the students swallowed a tiny plastic tube that pumped Metrecal straight into their stomachs whenever they pressed a lever. The students could not see, smell, taste, chew, or swallow the food, yet they somehow learned to control the amount of Metrecal they consumed just as readily as if they were drinking it from a glass. Perhaps the most interesting result of these experiments was the fact that the students were completely unable to explain to Professor Stellar and his colleagues how they managed this feat!

The Hunger Habit

When you've packed your stomach with a huge meal (or with Metrecal), the muscles in your stomach are stretched out or distended. The feedback nerve cells in your stomach would surely let your brain know how inflated your stomach was, and then the brain could throttle down the messages coming from your "feeding center" even before your blood sugar level changed. Does stomach feedback influence your eating?

Years ago, long before the "feeding center" had been discovered, the great U.S. physiologist Walter Cannon performed a very important experiment on hunger. He got a student volunteer to swallow balloons attached to long rubber hoses. Once the balloon was well within the student's stomach, Cannon pumped air through the hose and inflated the balloon until it pushed firmly against the walls of the student's stomach. (Fortunately, the student suffered little or no pain from this procedure.) Now, whenever the stomach contracted at all, the balloon was pinched and air was forced out of the balloon and up the tube. By measuring the air pressure at the "outside" end of the hose, Cannon could get a very good reading of when the stomach muscles churned about.

If the student swallowed one of Cannon's balloons during the late morning, the air pressure in the tube remained relatively constant for some time. The stomach was relatively quiet and the student (who had typically had a large breakfast some hours before) experienced no hunger. As lunch time approached, however, the student's stomach began to contract more and more—and the student began to report an increased interest in food. Anyone who has felt his or her own stomach growl and thrash about as a meal time grows close can appreciate Cannon's experiment only too well.

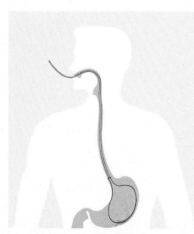

Walter Cannon was able to read the churning of the stomach muscles when his subject swallowed a balloon which was then inflated.

When you eat a large meal, the muscles in your stomach go to work almost immediately, churning the food around and squeezing it into a ball. If you eat lunch every day at 12 noon, your "feeding center" and other parts of your brain begin to anticipate when they will have to go to work. An hour or so before noon, your brain starts sending neural signals to the muscles in your stomach telling them to "wake up" and get ready to start performing. The muscles contract in response to these signals, and your stomach growls. Other parts of your brain notice the growling (and the input signals coming from your "feeding center") and decide that you're probably getting hungry. The closer the clock gets to noon, the more vigorously your stomach muscles respond. As we will see in a later chapter, this type of bodily learning or *conditioning* (°) exercises a very powerful control over your behavior.

Oddly enough, if you once get past the lunch hour without eating, your stomach will often calm down just as it does after you have eaten. Then your hunger pangs will disappear, only to rise as supper time approaches.

The hunger pangs that come from stomach contractions are *learned*, and almost any habit that is learned can be unlearned if you go about it the right way. If you stop eating entirely, your subjective experience of hunger will rise to a maximum in three to five days as the centers in your brain and the muscles in your stomach continue to anticipate meal after missed meal. By the end of five days of *complete* starvation, however, your body will have started to learn that food simply isn't going to be coming along as once it did. The stomach contractions will slow down and eventually cease almost entirely, and the subjective experience of hunger will drop to a low ebb.

Fiction writers who describe starvation (and who have never experienced it themselves) often assume that if one of their characters starves for a week, the person will be so ravenously hungry that he or she will perform almost any anti-social act in order to get food. In truth, the first three days of complete starvation are by far the worst. However, if you go on a diet and "eat just a little" at each regular meal time, your "habitual" stomach contractions will take a very long time to change, and you may experience biting, gnawing hunger for weeks on end.

If you wish to break the hunger habit in order to gain better control over your own food intake, you might be wise to do so slowly—by putting yourself on a very irregular eating schedule. If you vary the times at which you eat, the number of meals each day, and the amount you consume at each meal, you will slowly train your body not to be hungry. Once you have lost the hunger habit, you will find that dieting is somewhat easier.

Scientists have made use of these facts in their attempts to produce a diet pill for people who want to lose weight. Some of the drugs now on the market have a (slight) influence on the firing rates of the hypothalamic "feeding" and "satiation" centers. Other drugs are aimed at fooling the stomach muscles; these chemicals have little food value, but swell up considerably when they reach the stomach. The best-known diet drugs usually contain an "upper" of some kind, because such chemicals sometimes make people so nervous or excited that they lose their appetites. Many of these drugs have rather unpleasant side effects, however, and, to be truthful, none of them works very well all by itself. But why don't the diet pills work?

For at least two reasons. First, overeating is habitual in most fat people. Going on a diet or taking a pill simply does not teach the person the good eating habits that must be substituted for those bad behaviors that involve consuming too much. Second, most of us eat when our bodies run low on food, and our hunger pangs are related to stomach growls and contractions, and to lowered blood sugar levels which cause increased firing rates in the hypothalamus. But what if obese individuals had never learned to pay proper attention to these body signals?

In 1959 psychiatrist A.J. Stunkard repeated parts of Cannon's balloon experi-

Conditioning (kon-DISH-shun-ing). When an organism is trained to give a particular response to a specific stimulus, we say that it has been conditioned to respond to that stimulus. As we will see in Chapter 15, there are several types of conditioning. Psychologists often use the words "learning" and "conditioning" as if they were the same.

Sigmund Freud.

Psycho-sexual stages (SIGH-ko-SEX-you-ull). The developmental stages through which a child presumably must pass in order to attain emotional and intellectual maturity. See Chapters 21 and 22.

Oral stage. The first of Freud's postulated psycho-sexual stages, which begins at birth and ends when the child is about 1 year old.

Oral sucking period. The first part of the oral stage, lasting from birth to about 8 months. Also called the "oral erotic" (ee-ROT-tick) stage because all of the infant's pleasures are presumed to come from sucking behavior. The second stage, lasting from 8 months to the end of the child's first year of life, is called the "oral sadistic" (sad-DISS-tick) period during which the child is supposed to gain pleasure more from aggressive biting than from sucking.

Anal stage (A-nall, or A-null). The second of Freud's psycho-sexual stages, during which the infant presumably gains pleasure primarily both from expelling and from retaining urine and feces. Lasts from the end of the child's first year of life to the third or fourth year.

Fixated (FIX-ate-ted). According to Freud, if a child is given love and its needs are satisfied, it progresses normally through the psycho-sexual stages. If its oral or anal needs are not met, however, the child's personality development may become arrested or fixed before its maturation is complete. As an adult, this individual may show childish oral or anal behavior patterns.

ment with 37 obese and 37 normal subjects—that is, he asked these subjects to swallow balloons that would let him record their stomach movements. Then, for several hours, he simply asked the subjects (every 15 minutes) whether or not they felt hungry.

Stunkard found that, when their stomachs were *not* contracting, both fat and normal people were much alike—about 38 percent of them reported they were hungry. When their stomachs were contracting, however, the groups were markedly different. About 71 percent of the normals said they were hungry, while only 48 percent of the fat subjects said they were hungry. No matter what kinds of reports they gave, both groups of subjects showed about the same number of stomach contractions during the experiment.

There are at least two explanations for Stunkard's results. The first is that fat people have defective sensory input—their stomachs contract, but the receptor cells in the stomach don't let the brain know what is happening. Further research reported by Stunkard during the early 1970's casts doubt on this possibility. For Stunkard has now proved that fat people can very easily be trained to recognize their own stomach contractions. The second explanation seems more probable—fat people simply don't listen to what their bodies are trying to tell them.

Psycho-analyst Hilde Bruch reported in 1961 that her obese patients literally did not know when they were physiologically hungry. Dr. Bruch suggests that, during childhood, these patients were not taught to discriminate between hunger and such states as fear, anger, and anxiety. Perhaps fat people simply label almost any state of physiological arousal as hunger; and so they eat whenever they are angry, anxious, upset, or annoyed. To understand what Dr. Bruch was talking about, we must look more closely at hunger as a "mental experience."

INTRA-PSYCHIC INFLUENCES ON HUNGER AND EATING

Sigmund Freud was fascinated with the symbolic meaning underlying eating behavior. According to his psycho-analytic theory, each child must progress through several *psycho-sexual stages* (°) as it goes from birth to maturity. The first of these is the *oral stage* (°). During the first months of an infant's life, according to Freud, its whole being is centered around the functions of the mouth. From birth to about 8 months of age—the *oral sucking period* (°)—the child gets almost all of its pleasures from eating, and hence becomes very attached to its mother. Freud believed if all the child's needs are met during this early period, the child moved on to the next psycho-sexual stage—the *anal stage* (°)—without much difficulty. However, if the infant encountered emotional upset during the first months of its life—if the mother treated the child coldly and mechanically while feeding it—the development of the child's personality might become *fixated* (°), or halted, at this early stage. As an adult, the child might try to gain in symbolic ways the oral satisfactions that it was denied as an infant.

According to Freud, someone fixated at the oral stage of development is likely to develop lifelong oral "bad habits." These undesirable traits or habits might include thumbsucking, smoking, eating too much, talking too much or too loudly, stuttering, compulsive mouth movements or twitches, or even an abnormally strong compulsion for oral sexual contact.

QUESTION: **Freud believed that thumbsucking and overeating were ways a person compensated for early oral deprivation; given the fact that deprivation seems to enhance the reinforcement value of the deprived stimulus inputs, how might we explain an oral fixation in terms of overlearning?**

Childhood Influences on Obesity

Even those psychologists who do not agree with psycho-analytic theory usually admit that the tendency toward obesity often begins when a person is young. Sometimes the parents are overweight themselves and perhaps, without realizing it, may overfeed their children in order to make the children like themselves. Since children often tend to lose weight when they are sick, parents may encourage the child to grow fat, believing that obesity and good health are pretty much the same thing. If the usual reward that the parents offer the child for good behavior is an extra helping of pie or cake, the child will soon learn that a very effective way of winning approval is by overeating. Food then takes on the symbolic meaning of love and acceptance. Later, as an adolescent or young adult, the person may feel a yearning to "raid the refrigerator" whenever he or she feels rejected or disappointed by life.

Data to support this view come from an additional series of studies by Hilde Bruch, who found that many overweight people felt unwanted, inadequate, and insecure as children. According to Dr. Bruch, these subjects began overeating not only to gain attention from their parents but also because eating too much made them feel big and important to themselves.

Schachter's Studies of Obesity

If fat people eat to satisfy symbolic needs, or because they cannot tell the difference between hunger and some other form of arousal (such as fear), then one would expect eating behavior to be primarily under the control of internal or intra-psychic drives. Columbia psychologist Stanley Schachter disputes this view—at least as far as fat people are concerned. Schachter believes that normal people eat when their bodies tell them to—that is, when their stomachs contract and their "feeding centers" are active. However, according to Schachter, obese people don't listen to their bodies; they are abnormally sensitive to the world around them, rather than being driven to eat by internal cravings and desires. Schachter and his colleagues recently reported a fascinating series of experiments supporting this view.

In 1968, Schachter, R. Goldman, and A. Gordon performed a study in which they looked at the effects of fear arousal on eating. Their subjects included both overweight and normal Columbia students. Schachter et al. found that when normal subjects were threatened with painful shock, these students markedly reduced their food intake. Fat subjects, who might have been expected to dramatically increase their eating if they could not tell anxiety or fear from hunger, showed nothing of the kind. When faced with a threat of painful shock, fat subjects ate about the same amount as when no threat was present. Studies such as this one convinced Schachter that psychiatrist Hilde Bruch might have erred when she said her obese patients could not tell the difference between fear and hunger.

In a second experiment Schachter and L. Gross measured the effects of time perception on eating. They reasoned that normal students would eat when their bodies told them to, no matter what the clock on the wall said. Overweight subjects, on the other hand, might "eat by the clock" since they presumably pay little or no attention to what their stomachs and "feeding centers" tell them. Schachter and Gross kept both normal and fat subjects in an experimental situation in which the students could not tell what time it was. After the subjects had performed some boring tasks for a fairly lengthy period, the experimenters told half the subjects it was now a few minutes before their normal dinner time. The other half were told that it was then a few minutes after their normal dinner hour. Both groups were then offered some good-tasting crackers "to munch on until the end of the experiment."

Stanley Schachter.

Schachter and Gross found that normal students were not much affected by the incorrect information about the time of day—they ate about the same amount of crackers no matter what time they thought it was. The fat subjects, however, ate very few crackers if told it was before dinner time, but large numbers when told it was after their usual dinner hour. Schachter assumes that obese people are guided more by external cues than by their internal physiological drive state.

In other studies, Schachter and his associates have shown that fat people tend to be "plate cleaners"—that is, they eat everything set before them whether they need it or not. If given a large portion, the obese individual will consume it all; if given a small helping, the obese person will eat that, and seldom ask for more. Normal people are much more likely "to leave a little something on the plate" if given more than they usually eat, and to ask for more if given less than they are accustomed to consuming. Fat people are also more affected by the taste of food than normals, according to Schachter. When offered food of average or above-average taste, fat individuals eat a great deal more than do normals; when offered food of below-average or miserable taste, however, fat people eat a great deal less than normals do. The normal person seems to eat what he or she needs, almost in spite of the good or bad taste. Fat people are also less likely to perform physical labor for food, or to suffer mild amounts of pain to get to eat, than are normals.

(Interestingly enough, rats with damaged "satiation centers" also turn down bad-tasting food but gobble up tasty morsels with relish; they also eat *less* than normal rats if they have to press a lever to earn their meals.)

When we see someone who is grossly overweight, we often assume that their problem is that they are greedy, psychologically immature, or that they must have a physiological difficulty of some kind. But if Schachter is right, the major cause of obesity may be external rather than internal, for we often forget the strong effects that our culture has on our eating habits. Let us look briefly at environmental influences on hunger.

SOCIAL/BEHAVIORAL INFLUENCES ON EATING BEHAVIOR

Answer this question as honestly as you can: Do you eat more when you dine alone or when you're at a good restaurant with a bunch of friends, all of whom are very heavy eaters (and when someone else is paying the bill)?

You might be amused to learn that lower animals respond to social stimulation much as humans do. If you give 100 kernels of corn to a hungry hen, the bird will typically eat about half the grain and then stop. If you now remove the remaining food and then, a few minutes later, present the hen with another mound of 100 kernels, the hen will eat a little more. By repeatedly taking away the old grain and giving the hen a new batch, you can usually get the animal to eat at least 50 percent more than it usually would.

An even more effective way of inducing a hen to overindulge is to give it all the grain it wants and then—after the hen has stopped eating—bring in two or three other hungry hens and let them start pecking at the grain while the first hen watches. Almost at once the first animal will begin to eat again, as if it felt a strong urge (drive) to compete with its sister cacklers for food that it didn't really need.

If you want the hen to lose weight, give it a single meal of 100 kernels (twice what it needs) every day for a couple of weeks. Soon it will become accustomed to eating just 50 percent of the meal that you serve it daily. Next, start giving it mounds of food that contain but 80 kernels. Surprisingly enough, the hen will continue to eat just 50 percent of what you set before it. Apparently the animal's "swallow counter" is overridden by the bird's visual perceptions of what it eats.

QUESTION: **When you want to go on a diet, should you serve your meals on large plates or small ones?**

Social Class and Obesity

The social world you live in plays a great part in controlling what you eat—and when you eat it. European farm workers often have five or six "regular" meal-times per day. When they are working in the fields 12 to 14 hours a day, they need all this fuel to stay healthy; but many of them continue to eat just as frequently when they move to the city and take jobs in offices. They may even continue their five meals a day when they move to a new country. A recent study by psychiatrist A.J. Stunkard shows that farm women from central Europe who immigrate to the United States are four to five times more likely to be overweight than are women from the same background whose families have lived in the United States for several generations.

People from different *social classes* (°) in the United States have quite different types of eating behavior. Men and women who belong to the wealthiest or so-called "upper class" tend to be thinner, healthier, and to live longer than do men and women of the so-called "lower class." In a recent study of 1,660 adults living in New York City, 32 percent of the men and 30 percent of the women in the lower classes were found to be obese. However, only 16 percent of the men and 5 percent of the women in the upper socio-economic class were overweight. Four times more upper-class women in this New York group were "thin" than were women in the lower class. And the chances that a person from the upper class will be going on a diet are two to three times as great as the chances that a person from any other social class will start to lose weight voluntarily.

Cultural Food Preferences

Religion and food preferences have always been closely connected. A few cultures are vegetarian, but most societies are *carnivorous* (°). Beef is perhaps America's favorite meat, but in India the flesh of the cow is *taboo* (°) to certain religious groups because cattle are presumed to be sacred animals. Orthodox Jews (and many people from Arabic cultures) will not eat pork or such seafood delicacies as shrimp, and many Jews will cling to these *culinary* (°) customs even when they have given up other forms of religious *orthodoxy* (°). Catholics, on the other hand, usually enjoy both beef and pork but, until recently, usually switched to shrimp and other seafoods on Fridays.

The Ifugao—a primitive tribe living in the Philippines—are very fond of insects. They eat three species of dragonflies, as well as crickets, ants, locusts, and a variety of beetles. Most Americans would prefer a nice glass of cool milk to a dish of ants fried in lard; many primitive cultures, however, consider milk a disgusting secretion to be avoided if possible. In some parts of the world, roast puppy is considered a real treat; but can you imagine how you would react if your family pet came to the dinner table—barbecued?

QUESTION: **Why do you suppose that most culturally taboo foods are of animal flesh rather than fruits or vegetables?**

The social class and the culture into which you are born somehow influence the types of food you eat and the amount you weigh. But mere knowledge of these facts tells us little or nothing about the mechanisms whereby your environment comes to control your stomach muscles and your "feeding center." To understand why some people get fat while others stay slim, we must look more deeply into individual motivations for eating.

Food and Feedback

The most important figures in any child's social environment are usually its mother and father. Parents often coax a child to eat—then shower the child with affection when it does. The child may respond to this loving attention both by

Social class. A way of grouping or classifying people according to their occupations, incomes, family histories, where they live, and their social relationships. There are three general classes. About 5 percent of the U.S. population is said to be "upper class." These people are mostly very rich, live in beautiful homes, hold executive positions, own their own businesses, or are so wealthy they don't have to work for a living. About 40 percent of the U.S. population is considered to be "middle class." These people are white-collar workers, middle-level executives, or professional people. About 55 percent of the population is said to be "lower class." These people are blue-collar workers, who perform unskilled or semi-skilled jobs and who have less education and smaller incomes than do members of the other two classes. As A. Davis and R.J. Havighurst said in 1946, the U.S. social class system prevents upper-class, middle-class, and lower-class people from getting to know each other; the main usefulness of the concept social class to social scientists is that it describes fairly accurately the different learning environments for children of different classes.

Carnivorous (kar-NIV-or-us). From the Latin words meaning "meat eater."

Taboo (tab-BOO). Anything that is forbidden on moral or religious grounds is taboo.

Culinary (CUE-lin-air-ree, or sometimes CULL-lin-air-ee). From the Latin word meaning "kitchen." Having to do with eating or the preparation of food.

Orthodoxy (OR-tho-dox-ee). From the Greek word meaning "to have the right opinion." An orthodox person is someone who follows a recognized set of social, moral, political, or religious rules. Orthodoxy is conforming to custom or to some higher authority.

Positive feedback loop. As described in Chapter 2, a situation in which two or more people (or objects) stimulate each other by their responses until some type of emotional peak or explosion may occur. A situation in which one person's actions cause a second person to react more vigorously; the second person's response triggers off an even more violent reaction from the first person, and so forth.

increasing its food intake and by being affectionate to its parents in return. At this point, a *positive feedback loop* (°) may build up: The parents reward the child for eating, so the child overeats and afterward hugs and kisses the parents. This affectionate response from the child reinforces the parents' desire to see the child eat some more, so they coax the child again at the next meal. The child gorges itself again and kisses the parents again, and thus the parents turn into "food-pushers" and the child turns into a "meatball." We typically view such situations as being the parents' fault, but the child is maintaining the parents' behavior as much as the parents are influencing the child.

Later, when the child becomes a teenager and wants to diet, the youth may both stop eating and withhold the affection it used to give its parents during meal times. If the parents do not understand that this loss of the youth's love will be temporary, the mother and father may become disturbed and believe that the teenager is rebelling or is rejecting them. In order to regain the youth's loving responses, the parents may unconsciously sabotage the dieting. This sabotage may enrage the teenager, who then withdraws even more affection from the parents. The mother and father may become desperate and order the child to eat—and the feedback loop thus created may lead to an emotional explosion. The parents blame the child; the child blames the parents; but both sides are equally at fault.

Parents who push food on a teenager are often more interested in having the youth demonstrate its love than in having the teenager overeat. If the youth wishes to diet, he or she might wish to find other, non-food-related ways of continuing to demonstrate affection for the parents. When the association between food and love is broken, each member of the family is free to eat or not eat as he or she pleases.

QUESTION: If a teenaged daughter wanted her mother's help with dieting, what specific behaviors of the mother could the daughter reward with loving attention?

Fat Wives and Insecure Husbands

Many of our social needs are pressed upon us by our social environments. Thus, we may overdrink or overeat because the people we love may be rewarded in various ways when we are drunk or fat. Behaviorist Richard B. Stuart worked for many months with married women who were complete failures at losing weight. Stuart eventually suspected that the women's husbands were at least partially responsible for keeping their wives overweight. To test his hypothesis, Stuart asked these couples to make tape recordings of their dinner-table conversations. Stuart found that, although all the women were on diets and their husbands knew it, the husbands were four times more likely to offer food to their wives than the other way around. The wives were twice as likely to reject food offered by their husbands than the husbands were to reject food offered by their wives, but the husbands were 12 times more likely to offer criticisms of their wives' eating behavior as they were to praise it.

Stuart also interviewed 55 husbands married to women who were trying to lose weight. Stuart's data suggest that many husbands may enjoy demonstrating their masculine power by coaxing or forcing their wives to become fat. If the wife was overweight, the husband sometimes found this a useful fact to bring up in family arguments. These husbands could win almost any battle by calling the woman "a fat slob." Stuart believes the husbands realized (perhaps unconsciously) that if the wife lost weight, the husband would begin losing more arguments. Other husbands, who were no longer physically fond of their wives, could excuse their lack of sexual desire if they could manage to fatten their wives up. Stuart's data also indicate that the husband lost sexual interest first, and then began rewarding the woman for overeating, rather than losing interest after the wife was already fat.

Richard Stuart.

Other husbands interviewed by Stuart appeared to fear their wives might be unfaithful to them if the women were too attractive. These men apparently encouraged their wives to overeat in order to keep the wives ugly—and therefore faithful.

HOW TO LOSE WEIGHT

Like almost everything else you do, your eating behavior is *multi-determined*—that is, you eat not just because you've been without food for a while but also because your blood sugar level has fallen, your stomach is contracting, your "feeding center" has increased its neural activity, your "satiation center" has decreased its neural activity, your "swallow counter" has been silent for a while, your regular dinner time is approaching, you smell food in the air and hear other people talking about what's for lunch, because your mother and father thought that fat babies were healthy babies, and because food and eating have a variety of symbolic values for you. Obviously, then, if you want to lose weight, your dietary program must take into account not just the calories you consume and how you burn them up but your motives and mannerisms as well.

A well-rounded weight-loss program typically begins with a physical check-up to make sure that you're not that one American in 20 who is under- or overweight because of a physically malfunctioning body. If you want to gain or lose more than 10 or 20 pounds (4.5 or 9 kilograms), you probably should do so under medical guidance. Your physician may wish to prescribe drugs to help control your appetite, as well as give you a balanced diet to follow.

However, diets and pills are only the first step. The real problem usually lies in learning enough about yourself to recognize what internal and external stimuli affect your eating behavior. The better you know yourself and the people around you, the more likely it is that you will be able to gain voluntary control over what you weigh.

If, at some time in the future, you wish to go on a diet, you might consider these suggestions:

1. Begin by recording *everything* you eat or drink for a period of a week or so. Do you snack between meals (that is, do you eat too often); do you eat too much at one time; do you eat the wrong kinds of food—or all three? More than this, keep a record of where you eat, of the events that occurred just before you started eating, of what you thought about just before you ate (and afterward). And, *most important*, notice who is around when you eat and what their response is to your food intake. Is anyone in your life (other than yourself) rewarded by your being too fat or too thin?
2. Write down all the rewards and pleasures that will come to you if you gain better control over your eating behavior.
3. If you are overweight, you may wish to break the hunger habit by changing your meal times over to a very irregular schedule several weeks before you begin your diet. (If you are underweight and eat irregularly, you may wish to force yourself to eat on schedule in order to help build up the hunger habit so that your stomach muscles will begin urging you to eat more.)
4. Your weight-control program will probably be more effective if you increase your physical activities to help you burn off excess fat. If you are not particularly athletic, ask yourself why this is the case. Are your parents athletes? Given a choice, would your family prefer you to win the state tennis championship even if it meant your grades would suffer, or would they be happier if you got all A's and gave up sports entirely? How would they express their pleasure in what you did? What would the people close to you think and say if you suddenly began getting up at 7 A.M. in order to jog several

miles before going to class? What forms of physical exertion do you personally like best? How could you arrange to do more of this kind of exercise?

5. Once you have all this information available, you may want to talk things over with a psychologist to make sure that your weight-control program will take account of your symbolic needs as well as your physical needs. Habits are difficult to change, and you will probably need all the help you can get. So you may find it wise to involve as many people as possible in your program. If someone close to you unconsciously wants you to remain fat, you may well have to find some substitute reward for this person if you are to gain his or her active and willing participation in what you are trying to do.

6. When you start your program, you may find it very useful to make a large chart or graph on which you record each aspect of your daily routine, including exercise. Post the graph in a prominent place so that everyone can see your progress and comment on it. Arrange to have someone give you regular rewards (money, special privileges, a gold star on your chart, or a verbal pat on the back) each time that you meet your daily goal—and perhaps a bonus for meeting that goal every day for a whole week. In some ways the graph is the most important part of any weight-control program, for it gives you immediate feedback both on the energetic and on the symbolic aspects of what you are trying to do.

7. Don't expect too much too fast. The average weight loss or gain is about a pound or two a week. Because your weight fluctuates from day to day, it is probably good to keep track of what you eat and the exercise you do in addition to charting your weight each day.

Long-term weight loss is difficult for most people to achieve because it is affected by so many different parts of a person's life. If you set realistic goals for yourself, you can probably achieve them. And as you see the first small effects of your program take place, you will probably be encouraged to continue. The old saying that "nothing succeeds like success" has a great deal of behavioral truth to it. So do your best to arrange your program so that—at least at the beginning—there is little or no chance that you can fail. However, if after the first few days your graph shows that things aren't going as they should, don't hesitate to make adjustments in your schedule. And keep on making changes until you find something that works for you.

Even if you are one of the lucky majority of people whose weight is more or less normal, you still might wish to try to gain or lose a few pounds as an experiment on yourself. For once you have put yourself through this kind of psychological analysis, you will have achieved something even more important than gaining voluntary control over your own eating behavior—you will have learned a great deal more about your own desires, habits, needs, and drives than reading a textbook could ever teach you.

SUMMARY

1. In the past, many of the best-known theories of motivation have been one-level approaches—that is, the theories have attempted to explain "what moves us" in purely biological terms.

2. The best known of these physiological theories of motivation is probably drive theory. According to drive theory, our biological or life-sustaining needs are said to be primary needs. Whenever we lack something necessary for life, a primary drive state builds up within us that leads to greater neural firing rates. This increased neural activity arouses us to action. The stronger the need, the faster our neurons fire, the stronger the drive state, the greater the arousal, and presumably the more pain that we feel.

3. According to drive theory, when we satisfy a primary need, we experience pleasure because the painful arousal (drive state) is reduced. Thus our major motivation would be reducing the biological excitation associated with drive states and thereby returning to our homeostatic "home base"—a condition in which we experience no painful needs or drives.

4. Most drive theorists believe that intra-psychic and social needs are learned because they are associated with biological or primary needs. These non-physiological motives are often called "secondary needs." Associated with each secondary need is a secondary drive state that, when reduced, can be pleasurable or reinforcing.

5. Although drive theory has added much to our understanding of motivation, it has been subjected to many sorts of criticisms:
    a. Terms such as "hunger" and "thirst," and "pain" and "pleasure," are perhaps better understood as descriptions of mental experiences than as physiological conditions. Thus drive theory has not really succeeded in explaining all forms of motivation in purely biological terms.
    b. Sometimes an increase in stimulation or arousal is pleasurable or rewarding, although, according to drive theory, it should be painful.

6. These criticisms (and others) led psychologists such as Elizabeth Duffy to develop arousal theory. The basic postulates of arousal theory include:
    a. The homeostatic "home base" is not a state of zero excitation, but rather a point of optimum stimulation. Any movement away from optimum is arousing, and hence motivates us to return to optimum.
    b. This optimum point may change from time to time, depending on our biological condition.
    c. A decrease in optimum stimulation may be as arousing as an increase.

7. Although arousal theory solved some of the problems associated with drive theory, it made the organism dependent upon psychological inputs from the environment, and thus led to an increased interest in two-level or intra-psychic theories in which emotion is often seen as being the driving force behind motivated behaviors.

8. According to the James-Lange theory of emotion, action always preceded (and generally caused) emotional feelings. Thus if we see a snake and run from it, "we are afraid because we run; we do not run because we are afraid."

9. Research studies seldom support the James-Lange viewpoint. Rather, as Magda Arnold and Robert Leeper have pointed out, we typically perceive a situation, evaluate it, experience an emotion, and then respond. Thus our intra-psychic processes often guide or direct our biological reactions and our social behaviors.

10. Since our perceptions are primarily learned, the intra-psychic theories are usually dependent upon the organism's past experiences and present social and physical environment. This dependence has led to three-level theories, in which biological, mental, and social motivations are all assumed to be primary and necessary for sustaining human life as we know it.

11. From a three-level viewpoint, our major motivation may be that of predicting and controlling our biological, intra-psychic, and social/behavioral inputs. In order to gain this predictive control, we often must change our outputs—that is, we must learn and adapt. Thus when we attempt to understand any form of behavior—such as why some people overeat and become fat—we must look at physiological, cognitive, and social variables since they all play an important part in determining our food intake.

12. At a biological level, the experience of hunger appears to be controlled primarily by activity in various parts of the nervous system, particularly in the hypothalamus. As you go without food, your blood sugar level falls, causing certain neuro, s in your hypothalamic "feeding center" to increase their firing rates. When you eat, your blood sugar level rises, shutting off activity in the "feeding center" but increasing the firing rate in your hypothalamic "satiation center."

13. Some part of your nervous system (perhaps influenced by inputs from the trigeminal nerve) measures the amount you eat and reduces your hunger drive accordingly, even before your blood sugar level changes.

14. If you eat at regular times, your stomach begins to contract and growl shortly before your usual meal times, an experience most people of average weight interpret psychologically as hunger pangs. Overweight individuals often seem not to know when their stomachs are contracting. They appear to overeat to reduce psychological and social drives more than because they are biologically starved.

15. Freud believed that if a child's oral desires were not satisfied during the first year of its life, it might develop lifelong oral "bad habits"—such as thumb-sucking, smoking, talking too much, stuttering, an abnormally strong desire for oral sex, or overeating. Parents often train their children to eat too much by giving a child affection primarily when it eats. As an adult, this person may "raid the refrigerator" as a symbolic means of gaining affection.

16. People who are overweight appear to be more influenced by the taste of food and by environmental conditions than are people of average weight.

17. There are many social/behavioral influences on obesity. Upper-class individuals are much less likely to have weight problems than are lower-class individuals. People from central European backgrounds are more likely to be obese than are native-born U.S. citizens.

18. Most important of all the social influences on eating behavior seems to be rewarding feedback. Studies suggest that most people who have difficulty losing weight have someone close to them who (often unconsciously) encourages them to continue overeating.

19. Should you wish to lose weight, you may find it easier to do so if you attempt to determine, and to bring under control, all those biological, psychological, and environmental factors that influence your eating behavior.

(Continued from page 242.)

Slim always claimed credit for what some people called the "Meatball Miracle." Sitting in the Spoon with some of his friends, munching away on a Double-Whammy Deluxe Cheeseburger and drinking a Triple-Rich Chocodelic Milk Shake, he put it this way: "You just wouldn't believe it. He lost 40 pounds (15.6 kilograms) in two weeks. You would hardly recognize him these days." Slim frowned, looked around the table, then nudged one of his companions. "Pass the catsup, please. Anyhow, it just shows what a poke in the guts will do. Every time I saw him, that's what I'd do—poke him in his big fat gut and call him Meatball. Made him ashamed of himself, it did." Slim reached across the table and gathered in the bowl of pickle relish, which he spread thickly on that part of his cheeseburger not already drowning in catsup. "I gave him the name, you know. Meatball. Great name. And I gave him his new name, too. Did you know that?"

Jock thought differently. As he explained to his buddies after a particularly hard-fought game of touch football, "Physical fitness is all that counts. It really is. Take Meatball, for example." One of the other players muttered, "You can have him," but Jock interrupted. "No, I'm not kidding. You ought to see the guy since I got him started on a real exercise program. He's lost his big belly and he's beginning to build up his biceps and his triceps pretty good. He can touch his toes now, and if he just keeps it up, he ought to be able to go out for organized athletics one of these days. He'd never have made it, if it wasn't for me."

Dr. Barios at the Student Health Clinic might not have agreed. "It's all a matter of diet and good medical advice," he told his wife at dinner one night. "Eat the right things and you'll practically double your life expectancy. Here, dear, have some more potatoes. Minerals, vitamins, and protein—those are the secrets." He shot his wife a sharp look as she put but a small spoonful of whipped potatoes on her plate, then relaxed into a broad smile as she took a second, larger helping. "Take Meatball McClanahan, for example. He wanted to lose a lot of weight in a hurry, and he was really overweight, so he stopped eating entirely for two weeks. Lost 40 pounds. Unbelievable. Don't usually recommend that sort of crash diet, because it doesn't last. People go off the diet; they start eating the same old fatty foods all over again and gain it all right back. Have a little gravy on those potatoes, dear—you make the greatest gravy in the world. Anyhow, Meatball won't gain back his fat because I've got him on a really balanced diet. Lean meat, fish, and lots of fresh vegetables and fruit. When you lose a few pounds, it takes the body a while to adjust to your new weight level. So you level off for a while, and then you're ready to lose a little more. It's those leveling-off periods that discourage so many people on a diet, but it's only to be expected. It's Nature's way." Dr. Barios surveyed his dinner table, then looked squarely at his wife. "My gracious, dear, you haven't eaten enough to keep a bird alive. I do hope you'll share this luscious looking dessert with me."

Stud had a different explanation. "If Meatball hadn't been so lazy, he never would have made it." His girl friend tittered. "Sloppiest person I ever met. You should see his clothes—they look like circus tents. Hang on him like tents too, now that he's lost all that weight. If I hadn't been willing to pick up and clean up after him, he never would have had the guts to go through with his diet. And he's keeping the room cleaner now, too, so my clothes don't get tossed around the way they used to. Just set people a good example and they'll catch on, if you know what I mean." His girl friend moved closer to Stud and whispered a question into his ear. "Hey, that's not a bad idea. Maybe if you could dig up a chick for Meatball, we could double-date some night. Go out to dinner at Lenny's, maybe. That way I could wear my new clothes." Stud put his arm around the girl and squeezed her tightly. "Hey, you really ought to see the fantastic new body outfit I just bought with some extra money that I earned recently."

Dr. Mann called it a matter of graphs and gold stars. "Give these kids a reachable goal and a little encouragement, and they'll do wonders," she told a colleague at a faculty meeting. "Take Meatball McClanahan, for example. Not that we can call him 'Meatball' any more. You should have seen his response to the graphs he made of his daily weight loss. He just couldn't believe he was changing that much. It's the feedback that's so important. You never get any change at all in any system unless you give the system some means of measuring the consequences of its own behavior. **And** a little encouragement to continue when change starts to take place."

A rather portly professor rose and spoke to the faculty at length about the glories of the time-honored method of lecturing to students for a full semester and then giving them a single, all-inclusive final examination. His point seemed to be that keeping students guessing all semester long increased their motivation.

"Those who can, learn. Those who can't, teach," Dr. Mann muttered softly to her colleague. "The primrose path glitters with gold stars," she continued. "That's the secret, of course. If you want to change someone's view of the world—or of themselves—do it a bit at a time, with lots of positive feedback. Always works. At least, it did with Meatball." She stopped to muse a moment. "It's an odd thing, but you know, the thinner Meatball gets, the smarter he looks." Dr. Mann's specialty, of course, was visual perception.

Meatball himself put it in still a different way. He realized that he had had a lot of help, and he greatly appreciated it, but no one else had suffered the hunger pangs, the blind urges to get up in the middle of the night and make a couple of tuna fish sandwiches except himself. Perseverance—that was the critical component to losing weight. Luckily, he had it.

Meatball tightened the belt on the blue jeans that no longer fit. He thought momentarily of the people around him—Slim, Jock, Stud, Dr. Barios, and Dr. Mann. He owed them a lot of thanks, but he realized that, in the process of losing weight, he had given each of them something they had wanted too. So the score was even. Except for the $15 he had in his wallet, which was his alone to do with as he wished. He kissed his wallet tenderly, then slipped it into the loose-hanging folds of his pants and walked out the door of his room.

When he'd first lost all that weight Meatball had bumped into Slim, coming down the hall, whistling "Brown Sugar" by the Rolling Stones. For once, Meatball didn't try to avoid the tall young man, but instead walked straight toward him. As they came close to each other, Slim stuck out a finger to punch Meatball's paunch, but stopped, puzzled. "Hey, Meatball, what's happened? Where's the old gut?"

"I've lost 40 pounds in two weeks, Slim," Meatball said proudly. "I'm still not as thin as you are, but I'm gettin' there."

Slim shook his head in disbelief. "You look starved to death, man. Why don't you come along to the Spoon with me for dinner. They've got a goulash special on you wouldn't believe, with all the French fries you can eat for free. Don't want to miss a deal like that.''

"Can't make it, Slim. Got a date tonight. But I do want to thank you for your concern and for noticing how much I've changed.''

Slim looked McClanahan over carefully. "Can't call you Meatball any more, I guess. You look more like a hot dog now than a meatball.''

They both laughed loudly, and then the newly christened Hot Dog McClanahan went out to buy $15 worth of new clothes.

RECOMMENDED READINGS

Atkinson, John W. *An Introduction to Motivation* (New York: American Book Company, 1964).

Schachter, Stanley. *Emotion, Obesity, and Crime* (New York: Academic Press, 1971).

Stuart, Richard B., and Barbara Davis. *Slim Chance in a Fat World* (Champaign, Ill.: Research Press Company, 1972).

chapter 13

"BIRDS OF A FEATHER"

SEXUAL MOTIVATION

DID YOU KNOW THAT . . .

We know less about the workings of your sex organs than about the physiology of your heart or liver?

The first scientific studies of the human sexual response were probably performed by psychologist John B. Watson in 1917?

When Freud first announced his theory of infant sexuality most people called him "a dirty old man?"

The best current research on human sexual physiology and behavior is probably that of Masters and Johnson?

The sex life of animals is controlled primarily by hormones?

A female fetus may be born with male sex organs if the mother is exposed to excessive amounts of male hormones during pregnancy?

Hormone therapy does not cure homosexuality?

You have "pleasure centers" in your brain which, when stimulated electrically, make you "feel good?"

"It's the hormones that do it," Paul Schmidtt said. "In birds like ring doves, hormones pretty well control the entire sex drive. No hormones, no drive. No drive, no sexual behavior. No sexual behavior, no little doves. It's as simple as that."

"Poor little birds," Beverly said, with a toss of her hair.

"Oh, it's not as bad as all that, really," Paul said. "Come on, I'll show you." And he led the way into the lab. "I'm not doing anything really exciting—just repeating some of the work that Professor Lehrman and his group at Rutgers did several years ago. After I learn what the research is like, then I may start something on my own. Or maybe I'll wait until I'm a graduate student somewhere to begin my own projects. Anyhow, it's a great way to learn all about sexual behavior."

"In birds, you mean," Beverly commented.

"Of course in birds. That's what I'm studying for my senior project, the sexual behavior of the ring dove." Paul opened the door to the animal room and went in.

Large metal cages, each holding one or more doves, lined the walls of the room; the cages were cleanly stacked on movable steel racks. Many of the birds fluttered their wings as if frightened by the intrusion of the two undergraduates, but Paul ignored them.

"This is where we house the birds, but there's nothing much interesting going on here." Paul indicated a door that bore a large sign reading "Experiment In Progress—Keep Out." "But if you'll come into my Inner Sanctum . . ."

"Yes?" asked Beverly.

"I'll show you what effect hormones have on sex behavior."

"In birds, you mean."

"Of course," Paul said, walking through the door.

"I can hardly wait," Beverly replied, following him into the experimental chamber.

The mating response of ring doves is influenced by their behavior as well as their hormones.

269

"These are our experimental cages. This one, as you see, has a glass soup bowl and some nesting material in it—as well as food and water for the birds. Now, suppose we introduce a male bird to a female by putting them together in this cage . . ."

"Doesn't the poor little female have any **choice?**"

"No, and neither does the male, for that matter. All's fair in the science of love. Anyway, we bring the two birds together for the first time, and shortly thereafter, the male will begin to make bows in the female's direction—bends his head over and takes a deep bow . . ."

"Like an actor on a stage pleased with his performance," Beverly said.

"It's the audience that's pleased with his performance, and in this case the audience is the female ring dove. She eggs him on—so to speak. Anyway, as the male bows toward the female, he makes a cooing sound, like this . . ." Paul swelled up his chest, bowed low toward Beverly, and uttered a heartfelt "coo-oo-oo."

"Bravo!" cried the girl, applauding prettily.

Encouraged by her response, Paul repeated the "bow-coo."

"You're wasting your time in psychology," Beverly said, crossing her legs daintily as she sat down. "Have you thought about making movies?"

"I can't afford a camera yet—to make a permanent record of the dove's behavior on film, I mean. So I simply sit in that chair and take notes. Anyway, the female responds to the 'bow-coo' by starting to build a nest. The male helps her out—and that's very important. A week or so later the female lays the eggs, and both birds sit on them to incubate them until they hatch. Then both momma and papa feed the little doves until they're old enough to take care of themselves. A little while later the male starts courting again, and the 'bow-coo' starts the whole cycle off again."

The frown that crossed Beverly's face only enhanced her perfect features. "When do they . . . oh, you know."

"Mating occurs during the first couple of days, while the male is still courting the female."

"And you sit here and **watch . . . ?**"

"Only in the interests of science, I assure you."

"I see," said Beverly. "But what about those hormones you were going to show me?"

"Hormones are just chemicals—nothing much to look at by themselves. It's their effects that you look for, really. The male has a pair of sex glands—the testes—that secrete a number of hormones. If we castrate the male—that is, cut out the testes surgically—the male never goes into his act. He won't show any interest in the female at all, and he won't perform the 'bow-coo.'"

"Not even with a particularly charming and attractive young female?"

"Not unless we inject him first with male hormones called androgens to replace the ones his testes would normally be producing. It doesn't matter whether they are his own androgens or artificial ones; they have to be there for the instinctive behavior patterns to be triggered off. It's the sight of the female dove that gets the male excited enough to do his little dance, if that makes you feel any happier."

"I'm sure it makes the female doves happier."

"And, of course, it's the 'bow-coo' that triggers off the instinctive behavior in the female. If we put a female bird into the cage by herself, she won't build a nest or lay eggs. If we put her in with a castrated male, or with other females, she still shows no interest in matters sexual. But if we give her a little pornography . . ."

"What? I didn't think birds could read!"

Paul laughed. "No, but they can watch. See this cage over here? With the glass partition down the middle? We put a male on one side, a female on the other. They can't touch each other, but they can see and hear what the other one does."

"Like two star-crossed lovers, separated from each other's tender touch by the cold steel curtain of prison's bars," Beverly said, a misty look in her large blue eyes.

"We use glass, not steel. Anyhow, if the male can see the female, he will do his 'bow-coo,' and she will respond by building a nest all by herself, laying eggs, and incubating them all on her own."

"A woman's work is never done . . . I don't think that Women's Lib would approve of that particular experiment."

"But you see, in normal conditions, the male helps out. But only if he has an ample supply of female hormones present in his body."

"Female hormones? In the male bird? But I thought . . ."

Paul assumed a superior stance. "Yes, I know. You think in terms of blacks and whites, but sex is a matter of shades of gray. The male's testes produce androgens, true, or the mating cycle never begins. But sitting on eggs and feeding the young is a female behavior pattern—and for the male to participate, he has to be stimulated by female hormones. Actually, the testes produce female hormones called estrogens and progesterone, as well as producing androgens. Estrogen controls nest-building, while incubation is affected by progesterone. A castrated male injected with androgen will do the 'bow-coo,' but he won't build a nest or sit on the eggs."

"But if you inject the dear little castrated bird with female hormones . . ."

"Then he carries out the cycle in a normal fashion. Usually, you see, the male has enough estrogen present to trigger off the nest-building if the female is there to coax him a little. Putting the nest together causes his testes to secrete progesterone, so that he helps to hatch and care for the young."

"That's a point my friends in Women's Lib ought to be very interested in." Beverly paused a moment to rearrange her skirt. "But what about the female dove . . ."

Paul cleared his throat and then sat down on the arm of the chair that Beverly was occupying. "It is the sight of the male doing his 'bow-coo' that starts the female's ovaries working overtime producing estrogens. The more estrogen she has in her body, the more interested she gets in nest-building and in mating. Building the nest causes her ovaries to produce progesterone, and so she gets interested in hatching the eggs about the time that she actually lays them."

"She's just a prisoner of her body."

"No, just like the male, she's a prisoner of her environment and the effects of her own behavior as much as she is tied to her own hormone cycle. According to Professor Lehrman, reproductive behavior in the ring dove is a product of what he calls a 'psycho-biological cycle' in which external stimuli, behavior, and internal bodily states all interact. Rather a nice prison, I'd say."

"Only if you have the right cellmate." Beverly looked at her watch, then frowned. "Oh, dear, I really must be running along." She gave the young man a smile. "Thanks so much for showing me all your sweet little birds. I think it's really fascinating, and we really must discuss it again some time. But I have to go get ready for the party tonight." She touched Paul gently on the cheek. "You are coming to the party aren't you?"

"Wouldn't miss it for the world."

"It's a BYOH party, you know."

"BYOH?"

"Bring your own hormones," she said, dancing out the door.

(Continued on page 285.)

Sex has always posed something of a problem for the psychologist, both at a theoretical level and, as we will see, at a personal level as well. As far as theory goes, it would seem that sexual needs should be explainable in the same terms as are any of the other physiological needs. However, there is a crucial difference—you cannot live without air, water, food, elimination, and the proper temperature. But you could readily (if not pleasantly) live out your entire life without engaging in any sexual behavior whatsoever. Without air, a person dies within minutes; but at one time or another in our lives, we all go for weeks, months, or even years without any sexual contact whatsoever. Food, air, and water are necessary for the survival of the individual, but reproductive activities are necessary for the survival of the species. For reproductive activities to occur, two more-or-less compatible individuals must find each other and adjust to each other's needs—at least momentarily. Men and women breathe the same way, drink the same way, eat the same way; but their sexual behaviors are typically quite different. In higher animals, at least, species survival depends not only on getting the male and female together so that mating can occur but also upon keeping one or both parents around to care for the young until they are large enough to face the world on their own. An adequate theory of sexuality, then, must explain not only the differing sexual needs and responses of male and female but maternal and paternal activities as well. Little wonder that none of our theories of sexual behavior really meets the test.

The theoretical issues facing the psychologist interested in sexual behavior are only a small part of the difficulties, however. Consider the practical problems for a moment. In our society, at least, sexuality intrudes into almost everything we do. It is a major topic of conversation; it is the presumed cause of many crimes; it leers at us from movie screens and winks at us from television tubes. Sex is no longer something for private consumption; rather, it is marketed with the commercial shrillness once reserved for automobiles and breakfast cereals.

And yet, for all the noise, we really know precious little about human sexuality. Medical science has, until very recently, avoided any serious study of the physiology of sexual behavior. We know a great deal more about the functioning of your heart and your liver than we do about the normal functioning of your sexual organs. A significant proportion of the patients who walk into a physician's office need guidance in sexual matters, but most medical schools still treat the subject with an air of prudery (when they mention it at all). Only in the field of psychiatry has the scientific study of sexuality gained a foothold, but even the psychiatrists restrict their attention primarily to the mental and emotional aspects of sex.

Until the last decade or so sexual education for the average person consisted of whatever "facts of life" were passed on by the person's parents or *peers* (°), whatever information the person could glean from reading various "dirty books" that were secretly passed from hand to hand, and whatever knowledge the individual could gain from personal experience. Marriage manuals—written chiefly by well-meaning but often biased professionals—were usually little more than middle-class morality masquerading as scientific fact.

Watson's Physiological Studies

A few scientists did attempt to bring human sexual behavior into the laboratory, to study it as objectively as other scientists studied the digestion of food. Almost without exception, however, these pioneers were rejected by their scientific colleagues for daring to perform experiments on what most people believed was an intensely private aspect of human life. John B. Watson, who started the behaviorist tradition in psychology, was one of the first Americans to investigate the physiological aspects of the sexual response. Although he gained his early fame (1914) for insisting that studies of animal behavior could be of value to psychologists, Watson always realized that human behavior was considerably more complex than the behavior of rats. Studying the manner in which laboratory animals *copulated* (°) told you something—but not everything important—about the psychological and physiological changes that occurred in humans during sexual intercourse. Since the medical sciences had studiously ignored the subject, Watson set out to investigate the matter himself—at first hand.

John B. Watson.

Watson wanted to know what kinds of biological changes occur in humans during the stress of intercourse. The medical literature in 1917 reported little more than that the pulse rate usually increases—but the hows and whys and whats of the matter were simply not known. Watson tackled the issue directly, by connecting his own body (and that of his female partner) to various scientific instruments while they made love. He fathered what were probably the very first reliable data on the human sexual response, and since it was a subject he could obviously study with pleasure, he acquired several boxes of carefully annotated records. Unfortunately for all concerned, his wife (who had refused to participate in such an outrageous undertaking) eventually discovered why her husband was spending so much time with his female assistant in his laboratory. Watson's wife not only sued him for divorce, she also confiscated the scientific records!

Although he was one of the brightest and most creative men of his time, Watson's academic career was ruined by this episode. He had to resign his professorship at Johns Hopkins University, and most of his friends and colleagues deserted him. The Baltimore newspapers reported the divorce in lurid detail, and the judge presiding at the trial gave Watson a severe tongue-lashing—calling him, among other things, an expert in *mis*behavior. After the divorce Watson married his assistant, but still could not find employment at any other college or university. In desperation, he took a position with a large advertising agency and stayed with it the rest of his professional life. Although he continued to write books and scientific papers, he was a ruined man and soon slipped into the solace of alcohol. He died at the age of 80 in 1958.

Freud's Theory of Infant Sexuality

A number of other early scientists shared Watson's views, if not his methodology. Sigmund Freud had, a few years earlier, startled the Western world with his theory that sexuality is one of the major motivational forces that influences almost all aspects of human behavior. Freud believed that infants obtain sexual pleasure through stimulation of their *erogenous zones* (°)—the mouth, the anal passageway,

Peers (rhymes with "beers"). From the Latin word for "equals." People who belong to the same group in society, especially when membership in that group is determined by age, grade, or status.

Copulated (KOP-you-late-ted). A scientific way of saying "to make love" or "to have sex." From the Latin word meaning "to join" or "to unite."

Erogenous zones (air-RODGE-jen-us). Eros was the Greek god of love. Anything that is sexually exciting is erogenous. Those parts of the body which give pleasurable sexual inputs when tickled, or caressed, or stimulated are called the "erogenous zones."

Alfred Kinsey.

and the genitals. The thought that there might be a sexual component to breast feeding, toilet training, and the casual genital explorations of very young children was not one readily accepted by most Europeans or Americans. And the notion that adult sexual preferences and pleasures are, in no small part, dependent upon how well the child resolves its early erogenous tensions was even more disturbing. For a great many years Freud's insights about human behavior were rejected simply because most people considered him little more than "a dirty old man."

Kinsey's Interviews

Freud's theories came chiefly from his observations of neurotic patients who went to him (and to his followers) for treatment—not a very representative sample of "normal" human adjustment. The first survey of U.S. sexual behavior based on an adequately large segment of the public did not come until 1948, when Alfred Kinsey and his associates published their monumental volume, *Sexual Behavior in the Human Male.* The Kinsey group asked many thousands of men and women to talk about every aspect of their sexual lives, and a surprisingly large number of people responded to the questions without shame or evasion. Since Kinsey depended on volunteers, it may be that his sample too was biased—for one can never be sure of what goes on in the life of someone who won't talk about his experiences. Nonetheless, Kinsey did show that a large group of normal-appearing U.S. males regularly engaged in a wide variety of sexual practices that "nice people" were not even supposed to know about.

Perhaps this was Kinsey's most significant contribution—when his books were published, a great many guilt-ridden people who thought themselves *perverts* (°) or mentally ill discovered that, compared to almost everybody else, their sex lives were really rather tame. Despite the fact that Kinsey's first book was written in highly technical terms and was filled with graphs and tables rather than "dirty pictures," it sold several hundred thousand copies (and was called "America's least-read best-seller"). Kinsey, a professor of biology at Indiana University, became world famous and—as one might have predicted—suffered numerous attacks from the press, from politicians, and from his colleagues.

QUESTION: If you were going to undertake a survey such as Kinsey's, how would you go about making sure that the people you talked to really told you the truth about their sexual practices?

Masters and Johnson's Research

Perverts (PURR-verts). From the Latin word meaning "to turn the wrong way," "to corrupt." Anyone who takes his or her sexual pleasures in a manner not approved by society is considered a pervert—at least, within that particular society.

Gynecologist (guy-nuh-COLL-oh-jist, or jin-nuh-COLL-oh-jist). The Greek word *gyne* means "woman." A medical doctor whose specialty is treating the diseases of women is called a gynecologist.

Masturbation (mass-tur-BAY-shun). To bring oneself to sexual climax by hand, by rubbing against something, or occasionally through fantasy. Also called "self-abuse," "playing with yourself," "the solitary vice," and other terms.

Still and all, the writings of Freud, Kinsey, and many other commentators on the sexual scene all sprang from conversations and case histories rather than direct observations—people were asked to *talk* about sex lives while the scientists recorded what the people *said.* It was not until the 1950's that laboratory investigations of human sexuality began in earnest with the research of William Masters and Virginia Johnson.

Masters was trained as a *gynecologist* (°)—that is, a physician specializing in disorders of the female reproductive system. Johnson received her training in social work and psychology. They started their work in St. Louis, using female prostitutes as paid subjects. Following the lead of Watson, Masters and Johnson made recordings of their subjects' bodily reactions while the women experienced various simple types of sexual arousal (chiefly *masturbation*) (°). Later, they studied the physiological changes that accompany sexual excitement in males, as well.

When Masters attempted to present his early data to a gathering of U.S. gynecologists, the majority of these physicians refused to support his research and suggested that he give it up. Many of the best-known medical journals would not publish his findings, and political pressure prevented his getting governmental support for his research. The first public discussion of the Masters and Johnson work was delayed until 1962, when they presented their findings to an enthusiastic audience at the annual meeting of the American Psychological Association.

As Masters and Johnson have reported, their observations have allowed them to challenge many of the old superstitions and folklore concerning sexuality. Prior to their studies, it had been thought (primarily by male scientists) that women achieved different types of sexual climaxes, or orgasms, depending on the manner in which they were excited or aroused. Masters and Johnson found that a woman's body undergoes the same characteristic changes no matter what type of stimulation brings the woman to her climax. Although the woman's feelings might vary considerably from one sexual experience to another, the physiological changes associated with orgasm almost always occur in the same sequence.

Their research has led Masters and Johnson to pioneer new types of therapy with men and women who suffer from various types of sexual problems. For instance, many women suffer from *frigidity* (°)—that is, the inability to achieve climax. Until recently, most psychologists and psychiatrists assumed that the major cause for frigidity was *repression* (°)—the woman's feelings of guilt and anxiety concerning the sexual act were so strong that she simply could not relax and let nature take its course. Therapy usually consisted of helping the woman talk through her early sexual thoughts and experiences in the hope that she would gain some insight into what was really bothering her. Masters and Johnson believe that frigidity is often caused by ignorance and clumsiness on the part of both the woman and her partner. By teaching these women and their partners to pay greater attention to the *physiological indicators* of sexual arousal, Masters and Johnson have been able to help many patients for whom the usual "talk" therapies were not particularly effective.

Men often suffer from the opposite sort of problem—they achieve their own climax so quickly that their partners are left unsatisfied. By training the women to monitor the man's state of sexual arousal, Masters and Johnson have achieved nearly 100 percent success in their treatment of this problem—called *premature ejaculation* (°).

In some ways sexual behavior has much in common with the eating behavior we discussed in the last chapter. Both types of activity are based on physiological needs; both have important intra-psychic or personal aspects; and both are greatly influenced by the social environment and by rewards and punishments. In the case of food-taking, the intra-psychic and social behavioral factors are often ignored or

Frigidity (frih-JID-it-tee). Sexual coldness or unresponsiveness in the female; the inability of a woman to enjoy sex or to achieve orgasm.

Repression (ree-PRESH-un). To inhibit thoughts, desires, or actions.

Premature ejaculation (PREE-mat-chur, or PREE-mat-toor ee-jack-you-LAY-shun). "Premature" means "to arrive too early" or "to explode too soon." To ejaculate is to discharge semen (SEE-men) at the moment of a male's sexual orgasm. When a male reaches sexual climax before the female has achieved satisfaction, he has ejaculated prematurely.

William Masters and Virginia Johnson.

Hormones (HORR-moans). Complex chemicals secreted by various glands that affect growth and behavior.

Adrenal gland (add-DREE-nul). A small gland at the top of the kidney that secretes many different hormones, including those that affect sexual growth and behavior.

Gonads (GO-nads). The primary sex glands; the ovaries in the female and the testes in the male. The ovaries produce the egg cells that are fertilized by the sperm secreted by the testes.

Androgens (ANN-dro-jens). From the Greek words meaning "producer of males." There are several male hormones; collectively these are known as androgens.

Estrogens (ESS-tro-jens). The Latin word *estrus* (ESS-truss) refers to the period in a female's reproductive cycle when she is fertile and hence capable of becoming pregnant. Estrogens are the hormones that generate or bring about estrus.

Progesterone (pro-JEST-ter-own). One of the several female sex hormones.

misunderstood. In the case of sex, however, it is often the physiological or mechanical factors whose importance is frequently neglected. We will look at sexuality from an intra-psychic and an environmental standpoint in several later chapters; for the moment, let us see how your body chemistry influences your sex life.

THE PHYSIOLOGY OF SEX

In almost all forms of animal life, sexual behavior is greatly influenced by various fluids secreted in several different glands or organs within the animal's body. Glands, for example, are small chemical factories that release their products either into the bloodstream, onto the tissues surrounding the gland, or even into the outside world. Some of these chemicals have primarily a local effect. For instance, the tear glands in your eyes secrete that clear but romantic liquid which, in small quantities, lubricates the movement of your eyes in their sockets and, in larger quantities, tells the world that you are sad or unhappy. The salivary glands in your mouth manufacture a juice that facilitates both taste and digestion, but that also keeps your tongue from sticking to the roof of your mouth. Other types of glands—such as the adrenals and the gonads—secrete their products directly into your bloodstream, and so these fluids have their primary effects some distance away from the glands. These "action-at-a-distance" chemicals are called *hormones* (°), from a Greek word that means "to stir up, to attack, to set in motion."

The *adrenal gland* (°)—one of which sits atop each of your two kidneys—secretes more than 20 different hormones that influence both your growth and your behavior. The majority of the adrenal hormones regulate such bodily functions as digestion, urine excretion, and blood pressure. However, several of these chemicals have a direct effect on your sex life—and these are called the "sex hormones." Sex hormones are also produced by the *gonads* (°), or sex glands—the testes in the male and the ovaries in the female. The adrenals and the gonads work together to provide the body with the chemicals it needs to develop into a sexually mature adult.

Whether you are a man or a woman, once you are born your adrenals and gonads produce both male sex hormones—known collectively as *androgens* (°)—and female sex hormones—the *estrogens* (°) and *progesterone* (°). It is the relative balance between these two types of hormones that at puberty makes your body take on the physical and behavioral characteristics that we associate with maleness and femaleness.

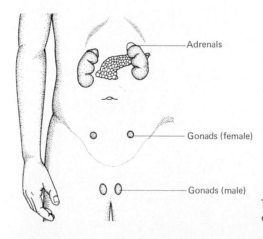

The location of some major endocrine glands.

Primary and Secondary Sex Characteristics

Physiologists like to differentiate between two types of sex characteristics—the primary and the secondary. When a scientist or physician speaks of *primary sex characteristics* (°), he or she means the actual sex organs themselves—the ovaries, vagina, uterus, and clitoris in the female, and the penis and testes in the male. Additionally, those parts of the reproductive organs in either sex that can be seen by the naked eye are often called the *external genitalia,* or *genitals* (°). Male-female differences in primary sex characteristics are usually present at birth. The *secondary sex characteristics* (°) are those that appear at *puberty* (°)—the growth of facial hair and deepening voice in the young man, the development of the breasts and broadening of the hips in the young woman.

The appearance of both primary and secondary sexual characteristics is controlled almost entirely by hormones. As we will see in a later chapter, your sexual gender was determined at the moment of your conception. The sperm cells of the male are normally of two types—the X sperm and the Y sperm (*see* Chapter 19). If an X sperm from the father unites with (fertilizes) the egg carried by the mother, the child will be a female, and every cell in the child's body will carry the X (female) label. During the 9 months that the *fetus* (°) is carried in the mother's womb, the glands of the fetus will produce female hormones rather than male hormones, and the body of the fetus will develop the primary female sex characteristics. The glands secrete female hormones, of course, because the cells in the glands carry the X label. However, if a Y sperm fertilizes the egg, the cells in the fetal glands will carry the Y label; they will secrete male hormones rather than female, and the child will be born a male.

From a physiological point of view, however, Mother Nature is biased in favor of women. No matter what type of sperm fertilizes the egg, and no matter what label all the cells carry, unless the male androgens are present in the fetus, the child will be born with female sex characteristics. If a Y sperm unites with the egg, but through some mishap the fetal glands do not produce androgens, the infant will develop female genitalia (although all the child's cells will carry the Y label). But the reverse is true as well. Suppose that a mother monkey is carrying a fetus conceived from an X sperm. If all went well, the baby monkey would be female. However, if before the birth we inject the mother with androgens, the fetus will develop male genitalia and will look for all the world like a male—although all its cells actually carry the X label.

This "sexual confusion" may occur in humans if a woman carrying a female (X sperm) child is given medical treatment with massive amounts of androgens during her pregnancy. Although the fetus' glands are producing the normal amount of estrogens, the excessive amounts of androgens injected into the mother's bloodstream can reach the fetus and have their effect. The child will be born with a penis and testicles even though the cells in its body carry the X label.

If newborn male rats are castrated at birth—that is, have their testes removed surgically—they will not develop normal male genitalia. An unborn male child whose glands fail to produce sufficient androgens will not develop normal male sex organs (despite the Y label carried by the child's cells). If the unborn male's glands secrete some—*but not enough*—of the male hormone, the child may even be born with *both* male and female genitalia (although its cells carry only the Y label). As you might guess, children born with the "wrong" external sex organs (or with both types present) often find themselves sexually confused in later life, since their "cellular label" doesn't agree with their genitalia. Recently developed medical techniques can often detect which gender the child should actually have (according to its cellular label), and surgery can frequently help set matters straight.

If a young boy's adrenals and testes overproduce androgens (or underproduce

Primary sex characteristics. Those physical characteristics that differentiate males from females—the actual sex organs themselves.

Genitalia (jen-it-TAIL-ee-uh). From the Latin word meaning "to beget, to reproduce, to have children." The external sex organs, or the genitals (JEN-it-tulls).

Secondary sex characteristics. Those male-female differences that usually appear during adolescence, such as the male's beard and the development of the breasts in the female.

Puberty (PEW-burr-tee). The onset of sexual maturity, when the person becomes physically capable of sexual reproduction. Usually between the 11th and 14th year, the female's ovaries begin producing eggs and menstrual (MEN-strew-ull, or MEN-strull) bleeding begins. At about the same age, the male's testes begin producing semen and ejaculation becomes possible.

Fetus (FEE-tuss). An unborn child, still carried in its mother's womb. More precisely, the unborn child after it has taken on human characteristics (during the final six months in the womb).

estrogens), he will experience early puberty; his voice will change and his beard will begin to grow sooner than expected. If the boy's glands underproduce androgens (or overproduce estrogens), puberty will be delayed and the boy's body may take on very feminine characteristics—a high voice, overdeveloped breasts, a lack of facial hair. If a young girl's adrenals and ovaries overproduce estrogens (or underproduce androgens), the girl will come to sexual maturity earlier than expected. If the reverse is true, her puberty will be delayed, and she may even develop such masculine secondary characteristics as flat breasts, excess facial hair, and a low voice.

Innately Determined Sexual Behavior

The neural circuitry that controls sexual behavior (in lower animals, at least) is "wired into" the animals' brains at birth. Surprisingly enough, the genetic blueprint for most animals includes both male and female response patterns. Which pattern develops is determined by which hormone is most active during fetal development and just after birth. For example, consider the female monkey mentioned above which was born with male genitalia because her mother was injected with androgens. As this female grows up, she will show male patterns of play and social behavior. If male rats castrated at birth are given injections of female hormones at that time, they will display a complete set of female behavior patterns as adults.

If, during fetal development and immediately after birth, the relative balance of the sex hormones is toward the androgens, then the fetus will have male genitalia, and those parts of the brain that control male sexual responses will develop. If the relative balance is toward the estrogens, the fetus will have feminine sexual characteristics, and those parts of the brain that control female sexual behavior will develop. The interplay between glands and growth, between cortex and chemicals, is so subtle and complicated that it is a wonder that any of us turns out to be normal!

The sexual behavior of lower animals is almost entirely under the control of the sex hormones. The female white rat, for instance, is sexually receptive to the male only when her estrogen level is high; if her ovaries are removed she will not mate unless given injections of estrogens. If the testes of an adult male rat are removed by castration, the male will continue to mate with receptive females for a few weeks until the androgens already present in his body are depleted; but during this period, his interest in females gradually wanes and eventually vanishes entirely unless he is given injections of male hormones.

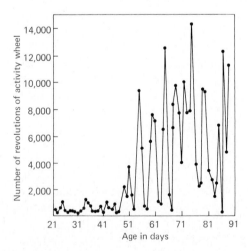

Before puberty, cyclical activity is at a low level in the female rat. At the beginning of puberty, activity increases, but somewhat erratically.

Sexual behavior in most lower animals is *cyclical* (°) and is usually tied to a particular part of the year. Most migrating birds mate only during the spring season. As the days grow longer and longer, some part of the animal's brain becomes more active than usual and releases hormones that begin the sexual cycle. However, it is often the *sight* of the bird's mate that triggers off the instinctive sexual response patterns. The brilliant tail feathers of the peacock serve not only to attract the peahen but set off an increased production of estrogen in her as well. The peahen's response to the male's display activates those parts of the male's brain concerned with mating behavior. As these neural circuits controlling the male's behavior are triggered off, they stimulate an increased production of androgens in his sex glands. Once these male hormones are released into his bloodstream, they provide additional stimulation to the circuits in the male's brain that are connected with masculine sexual activity. This additional stimulation causes the appropriate neurons in his brain to fire more rapidly, which causes his glands to secrete even more hormones—until the male's drive level is sufficiently high for the whole sexual-reproductive cycle to be concluded.

PRIMATE SEXUAL BEHAVIOR

The *primates* (°) (humans, monkeys, apes, and chimpanzees) show much more complex sexual behaviors than do the lower mammals. In the higher species, for instance, the sex drive is less frequently seasonal and not as closely tied to the female reproductive cycle. The ovaries of the female rat produce eggs once every five or six days, and the female rat will mate only during that part of her cycle when the eggs are ready to be fertilized by the male. The human female is fertile only a few days out of her 28-day reproductive cycle, but her receptivity to the male is determined more by psychological factors than by the types of hormones her body is producing at any given moment. The male rat will usually attempt to mount females only when they are at the receptive point in their cycle (when the female releases a sexual attractant into her urine). The male monkey may try to mount female monkeys at any point in their cycles—and will often attempt to mount younger or less aggressive males as well. When an older, stronger monkey becomes aggressive toward a younger male, the weaker animal may often protect himself by assuming the posture of a receptive female and allowing the dominant animal to mount him and attempt to copulate.

In humans and monkeys, sexual behavior is predominantly under the control of the brain rather than the hormones. Animals, such as birds or rats, can be induced to mate out of season or cycle if injected with the proper hormones. However, hormone injections are not an effective therapy for frigidity in most women or *impotence* (°) in most males. When *homosexual behavior* (°) does occur in lower animals, it seems to be directly related to the types and amounts of hormones present in the animals' bodies. Injecting androgens into human male homosexuals or estrogens into female homosexuals, however, does not turn them into *heterosexuals* (°). Instead, such injections are likely to increase the strength of their homosexual desires. Women who have had their ovaries removed usually do not experience any decrease in their sex drives, nor do women who have undergone *menopause* (°), when their ovaries become relatively inactive.

The pattern for human males who undergo castration is more complex—some lose their sex drive entirely, while others experience desire but cannot achieve an erection. Experience seems to be the key factor. If a boy is castrated prior to puberty, he seldom develops the ability to perform sexually unless given regular injections of androgens. If the castration occurs after a man has been quite active sexually, however, he may retain full sexual ability for 20 or more years after the operation. What the man *expects* to happen to him after castration and his own

Cyclical (SIGH-klick-cull, or SICK-lick-ull). Anything that repeats itself, or that goes in a full circle. The seasons of the year (winter, spring, summer, fall, winter . . .) are cyclical. During her fertile years, the human female ordinarily has a menstrual cycle that repeats itself about every 28 days.

Primates (PRIME-eights). The highest or "prime" order of mammals. Includes humans, apes, chimpanzees, monkeys, and several more primitive monkey-like animals.

Impotence (IM-po-tents). The inability of a male to achieve erection, or the inability to sustain the erection long enough to achieve orgasm and ejaculation.

Homosexual behavior (HOME-oh-SEX-you-ull). Sexual interest in or behavior directed toward the same sex, as a male toward a male, or a female toward another female. *Homo* is a Greek word meaning "same." Homogenized milk is milk that has been treated until every drop is "the same"—that is, every drop contains the same amount of milk and cream.

Heterosexuals (HETT-ter-oh-SEX-you-ulls). The Greek word *hetero* means "different." Heterosexual behavior is that between two people of different sex—that is, between man and woman.

Menopause (MEN-oh-paws). Literally, a "pause" in the woman's menstrual cycle. That time in a woman's life, usually between ages 45 and 50, when her ovaries stop producing egg cells and she no longer can become pregnant.

A male peacock "displays" for a peahen.

Vasectomy (vass-ECK-toe-me). The Latin word *ectomy* means "to cut." The vas deferens (vass DEAF-er-ens) is the tiny tube that carries the sperm from the testes to the penis. Cutting the vas deferens (vas-ectomy) prevents the sperm from being ejaculated, hence makes the man infertile.

Contraception (KON-trah-SEP-shun). The Latin word *contra* means "to be opposed," or "to go against" (as in our word "contrary"). *Ception* means "to conceive" or "to become pregnant." Contraception is anything that prevents pregnancy. The Pill prevents pregnancy by controlling the woman's hormones so that she either does not produce eggs or the eggs do not become implanted in the womb. Although the Pill is the most effective form of female contraceptive that we presently have, its use does seem to lead to a slightly greater risk of blood clots and cancer, and it may have other unpleasant side effects as well. There actually is a "pill" that men can take to prevent sperm production, but it is little used since it has rather nasty side effects (among other things, men who take this pill become sick if they drink alcohol).

Incest taboos (IN-sest tab-BOOS). Incest is sexual activity between close relatives, such as between father and daughter or brother and sister. Such incestual (in-SESS-tew-ull) activities are forbidden or taboo in most societies.

Adultery (add-DULL-turr-ee). From the Latin word meaning "to pollute, to corrupt, to make impure." Adultery is voluntary sexual intercourse between a man and a woman other than his wife, or between a woman and a man other than her husband. Sexual intercourse between two unmarried partners is called fornication (for-knee-KAY-shun).

prior sexual history are more important influences than the amount of androgens present in his body.

Vasectomy (°) is a simple and almost painless operation in which the tube running from the testes to the penis is cut. Vasectomy prevents the sperm from leaving the testes and hence makes it impossible for a man to impregnate a woman—but the operation has no effect at all on hormone production or the man's ability to achieve erections, sexual climax, and ejaculation. Planned Parenthood groups often recommend the operation as a highly effective form of *contraception* (°) to couples who wish to have no more children; and in 1970, some 750,000 U.S. men underwent vasectomies. However, many men refuse the operation because they incorrectly assume it will affect their sexual drive, pleasure, or "masculinity." Research by Charles Phoenix of the Oregon Regional Primate Research Center suggests that whatever changes occur in a man's sex life after vasectomy, they are due almost entirely to intra-psychic and not to physiological causes. In 1973, Phoenix reported that male monkeys showed no differences at all in their sexual behavior after undergoing vasectomies. However, if a human male were forced to undergo the operation against his will, it is very likely that his fears about losing his sex drive might be momentarily realized—at least until psycho-therapy or practical experience convinced him that he was as sexually capable as before the operation took place.

INTRA-PSYCHIC AND ENVIRONMENTAL INFLUENCES ON SEXUALITY

Of the hundreds of different societies studied by social scientists, all of them have placed some restrictions on sexual activities. For instance, *incest taboos* (°) are found in almost all cultures. But the type of incest prohibited varies considerably from one society to another. G.P. Murdock stated in 1949 that, of the 158 societies he had studied, 70 percent permitted premarital sexual relations, but *adultery* (°) was "freely allowed" in but five. Homosexuality is strongly forbidden in many cultures, but is quite acceptable in others. And within a given society, different segments of the population may prefer quite different forms of sexual activity. Kinsey and his colleagues reported that people in the upper middle class and the upper class were significantly more likely to engage in kissing and in oral and manual stimulation of the genitals, and more likely to be experimental in trying out new sexual positions, than were people from the so-called lower class. However, the greatest *amount* of sexual activity seems to occur among men and women in the lower or lower middle class who have a high school education but have not gone to college. The Kinsey group also reports that religiously devout individuals—especially women—are sexually more conservative, less active, and begin their sex lives much later than non-religious people.

QUESTION: In what ways might the social class one is brought up in influence both the frequency and the types of one's sexual activities?

Sexual Inhibition

Some brain circuits function to increase the sexual drive, primarily by increasing hormone production. But other parts of the brain inhibit sexual activity. In general, the more complex an organism is, the more of its higher brain centers are devoted to inhibiting rather than to facilitating behavior. In man, most sexual inhibition appears to be learned—primarily during the person's early life when, as Freud and many other psychologists have pointed out, the child goes through a series of developmental crises. If the child's parents are repressive, if they punish the child whenever it touches its genitals or when it asks questions about sex, the child's sex life as an adult may be marked by shyness, fears, or even outright distaste for sexual matters. Almost anything learned can be unlearned, however, and sexual inhibitions can be overcome by careful guidance and suitably rewarding experiences.

In lower animals, inhibition is often instinctual and unlearned. For instance, consider the case of the male praying mantis, whose sex life is fraught with difficulties that most human males would shudder to contemplate.

The praying mantis is an insect several inches long that looks for all the world like a twig with a head and legs. The female mantis spends her time stalking other insects—including the much smaller male. When she comes close to another insect, her heavy forepaws slash forward, crushing the prey and dragging it back to her well-formed jaws. During most of the year, the female would as happily consume the male mantis for dinner as she would a beetle or a butterfly. Only during the mating season, when her hormone levels are high enough to inhibit her normal *predatory* (°) behavior patterns, will she allow the male to come close to her without immediately swallowing him.

The praying mantis stalks other insects—including her mate.

However, hunger is a stronger drive than sex, even during mating season, so the male's best chance for success lies in waiting until the female has just caught an insect. The male then stealthily approaches the female from behind and attempts to mount her while she is distracted by more important things. If he misses in his first attempt his cause is lost, and he typically ends up as the main course of her meal. But even if he finds the proper position on his first try, his troubles are far from being over. For, during the act of copulation, his head comes dangerously close to hers, and should she notice him, she is very likely to reach up and bite his head off for dessert.

Luckily, this little romantic by-play has a happy ending. For the nervous system of insects is quite different from that of man. A headless insect can live for several hours after its decapitation, and the brain of the male mantis is made up almost entirely of *inhibitory* centers that depress or decrease the animal's sexual functions. Once the male has literally lost his head, he copulates much more vigorously and effectively than when his brain is present to repress him. The inhibitory centers are necessary to keep the male out of the female's range during most of the year; but not even the seasonal increase in male hormones can knock out the inhibitory activity of his brain as effectively as can one crunch of the female's jaws.

The inhibitory centers of the human brain are not so easily wiped out. Human beings have, during the course of history, wasted an enormous amount of time and money hunting for *aphrodisiacs* (°)—that is, for drugs that will arouse or inflame sexual passions. Despite the tales one occasionally hears, the only chemicals that have been proven to increase the human sex drive are estrogens and androgens. However, some drugs—such as alcohol—do seem to influence sexual performance by reducing activity in the inhibitory centers of the brain. *Dis-inhibitors* (°), as they are called, do not *increase* one's desire; they merely *decrease* the strength of the inhibitions that one's culture has built into one's brain. It was this fact, perhaps, that led a biologist to refer to the enhanced performance of the headless mantis as the "martini effect."

With all of the cultural taboos and inhibitions on sexual activity, one might legitimately wonder why people bother with it at all! Reproductive behavior is, as we said earlier, necessary for the survival of the species, but not for the survival of the individual. Yet nature seems to have worked out a way to motivate members of both sexes to want to reproduce themselves. For sexual stimulation usually creates within the individual a great amount of intense sensory pleasure. But, as scientists, we may legitimately ask the question, What is the biological basis of this pleasure? Why does it feel so good?

Predatory (PRED-uh-torr-ree). An animal that preys on, destroys, or devours other animals.

Aphrodisiacs (AFF-roh-DEE-see-acks). Aphrodite (AFF-roh-DEE-tay) was the Greek goddess of love. An aphrodisiac is anything that causes sexual excitement, particularly a perfume, food, or drug.

Dis-inhibitors (DISS-in-hibb-it-tors). Things that decrease inhibition.

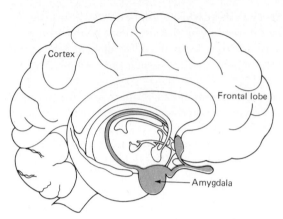

Cortex

Frontal lobe

Amygdala

The dark-colored areas are part of the limbic system.

Pleasure Centers

When physiological psychologists first began sticking electrodes into the brains of rats and other animals, they found that stimulation of a few parts of the *limbic system* (°) caused the animals to react as if they had experienced sharp, biting pain. This discovery was, at first, surprising, because (as we saw earlier) the brain has no pain receptors as such. These scientists suspected that they had tapped into what are now called the "avoidance centers" hidden away deep inside the central parts of the brain; so they began to map out as many different regions of the brain as they could, to find out how extensive these "avoidance centers" really were. The answer was, not very extensive. You can stimulate more than 99 percent of the brain electrically without getting an avoidance reaction from the animal. However, this search paid unexpected dividends when, in the early 1950's, two psychologists working in Canada discovered that sometimes electrical stimulation of the brain can have "unavoidable" consequences.

James Olds took his doctorate in psychology at Harvard in 1952 and, because he was interested in the biology of motivation, went to McGill University in Montreal to work with the noted physiological psychologist, Peter Milner. They implanted electrodes in what were thought to be "avoidance areas" in the brains of white rats, then let the animals run about on the top of a table. When the rat would move toward one particular corner of the table, they would turn on the current. The rat would stop, then turn around, and move in the opposite direction. The animal would subsequently avoid that particular corner even if not given any more electrical stimulation.

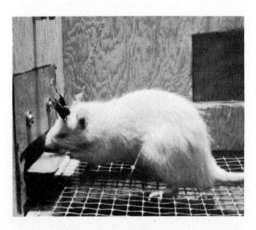

One of James Olds's electrode-implanted rats.

However, one day Olds and Milner made a glorious mistake—they stuck an electrode in the wrong place in one rat's brain. When this animal started moving toward one of the corners on the table, they turned on the electrical current as usual. But this rat stopped, sniffed, and then moved a step or two forward! Olds and Milner assumed that the current wasn't strong enough to have any effect, so they turned up the juice and stimulated the animal again. And once again, the rat stopped, twitched its nose rather vigorously, and moved several steps forward. The more that Olds and Milner stimulated the rat's brain, the more eager it became to get to the corner. Finally, the animal reached the corner, sat down, and refused to move! It is to their credit that instead of thinking the rat was "sick" or "abnormal," Olds and Milner realized at once that they had discovered a part of the rat brain where electrical stimulation was obviously very rewarding.

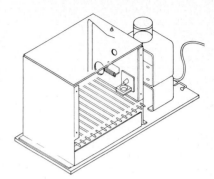

A single-lever rat box.

We now know that there are dozens of "pleasure centers" in the brains of most mammals (including humans) which, when stimulated electrically or chemically, will give the animal the subjective experience of pleasure. In animals such as the white rat, neural excitation in these brain centers causes a strange and oddly compulsive set of behaviors to occur. Suppose we rig up a small, rat-sized box with a single metal lever in it. The lever is then connected to an electrical stimulator so that every time the rat presses on the lever, the animal stimulates one of the "reward centers" in its own brain. Will it press the bar very often?

The answer is yes—very often indeed. Under these conditions, a rat will bang away on the lever as often as a hundred times a minute, and will do so hour after hour after hour—until it collapses in exhaustion. Then the rat will sleep a while until it regains its strength, but as soon as it wakes up, it starts pressing the lever again. If we offer this rat the chance to bar-press as a reward for problem-solving behavior, it will learn highly complicated mazes just to get a few whacks at the lever. Obviously, something about the electrical stimulation of the "pleasure centers" is highly motivating to a rat.

Two Types of Pleasure   Until the discovery of the "pleasure centers" by Olds and Milner, sexual behavior had always posed something of a problem to motivational theorists, as we noted in the previous chapter. Knowing nothing about the "pleasure centers" in the brain, drive theorists assumed that pain reduction was the chief motivational force underlying all behavior. But sexual excitement is almost entirely a matter of *pleasurable* arousal—the more stimulated an organism is, the more pleasure it feels. How could an *increased* drive level be associated with pleasure rather than pain? Wasn't this rather like hitting oneself over the head with a hammer because it felt so good when one stopped?

We now know that there are two distinctly different kinds of pleasure—the generalized feeling of relief when pain ceases, and the sensory thrill associated with what we might call "pleasurable inputs." Food not only reduces hunger, it tastes good as well. Therefore, there must be a direct connection of some kind between the taste receptors in the tongue and the "pleasure centers" in the brain. Once Olds and Milner had shown the way, psychologists began looking for just those connections. We now know that some parts of the brain are associated with sexual pleasure; some with eating or drinking pleasures; while electrical stimulation of other areas of the brain seems to give the organism a "general glow of satisfaction" that isn't tied to any specific physiological drive yet known. If we implant an electrode in those "reward centers" related to eating behavior, for instance, the rat will bar-press compulsively only if it is hungry. If we feed the rat first, it will ignore the lever for several hours until its hunger drive mounts up a bit. (Oddly enough, once the hungry rat begins bar-pressing, it typically prefers electrical stimulation to food.) If we implant the electrode in those parts of the brain connected with drinking behavior, the rat will bar-press only if it is thirsty.

The neural pathways running from your tongue (and your nose) to the "food-reward areas" in your brain were built in at birth by your genetic blueprint—but these pathways only become functional when you are hungry. As your blood sugar level falls, it becomes easier and easier for the taste and smell of food to excite the "food-reward circuits" in your brain. Deprivation not only creates a painful drive, it also increases the possibility that the "pleasure centers" can be stimulated by the appropriate stimulus inputs.

Hormones influence sexual pleasure. If we put an electrode in those parts of a male rat's brain that are associated with reproductive pleasure, we find that the animal will bar-press much more vigorously if it has been sexually deprived than if it has copulated recently. More than this, if we castrate the rat, we find that it presses the lever less and less frequently on the days following the operation. Apparently, as it uses up all the residual male hormone left in its body after castration, it finds the electrical stimulation less and less pleasurable. We can restore the castrated rat to its original high performance level, however, by giving it an injection of androgens. Within a short period after the injection, it begins to press the lever vigorously.

Human Pleasures   "Reward centers" have been found in the brains of almost all mammals, including humans. When Olds and Milner first reported their results, many people feared that governments might seize upon electrical stimulation of the brain as a new way to control people against their wills. Some writers warned that big corporations might implant electrodes in the brains of all their workers and pay off these employees in jolts to their "pleasure centers" instead of paying them in cold cash. However, these fears proved to be groundless. For the "compulsiveness" that one can create in a rat with brain stimulation seems to be lacking in humans. Those men and women who have volunteered to have their "reward centers" tickled with electricity have all reported the experience as being mildly pleasant, but something they could take or leave. When the "food-pleasure centers" of their brains were stimulated, the subjects often reported things like, "Oh, that was nice, rather like eating a good meal. But I'd rather have steak and French fries." Or they might say, "Yes, that felt good, and it did have a sexual flavor to it somehow. But nothing like the real thing." Pleasure in human beings is obviously more complex than it is in the lower animals.

The androgens, estrogens, and progesterones shape our bodies, bias our brains, energize our behaviors. Pleasure is the neural carrot that nature dangles before us to entice us down the path of biologically appropriate behavior; the pain of deprivation is the chemical club that nature applies to our backsides to urge us onward. But overriding these biological motivations are the neural commands that come from the higher centers of our brains. The structure of the female figure is ideally suited to stimulate the sensory receptors in the male's genitalia, and vice versa—but our choice of mate and the scope and type of our reproductive behavior are dictated by experience and by society. The pattern of sexual activity that we find physiologically rewarding grew out of the millions of reproductive experiments that nature has conducted since life first appeared on earth. But only humans have brains complex enough to understand that societies must survive as well as species, to conduct our own scientific studies on the subject of sexual behavior, and to realize that unlimited population growth may sometimes be a disaster rather than a blessing. Nature points us in a given direction and pushes us along—but, as we will see in later chapters, the beliefs and attitudes of our parents and friends provide us with our road maps, stop signs, and occasional detours. Our higher brain centers, with their inhibitory powers, are the battleground for this war between nature's nudges and society's strictures. Just how we individual foot soldiers learn to adjust to the stresses and strains of this constant warfare is a matter to be covered in the next section of this book.

SUMMARY

1. We really know very little about the psychological and physiological changes that occur during human intercourse—despite the fact that our culture markets sex much as it does breakfast food. Some theorists have tried to explain sexuality in purely physiological terms, some primarily in mental or intrapsychic terms, while others have focused on sexual behavior as a social response.

2. Sigmund Freud believed that a biological sex drive was the major motivating force in humans, and that sexual pleasures could be obtained even by infants. To Freud, human maturation was chiefly a matter of psycho-sexual development in which biological capability primarily determined mental and social responses.

3. Alfred Kinsey and his associates were perhaps the first scientists to make a reasonably accurate sociological survey of sexual behavior in the United States; their findings amazed some people, but annoyed many others.

4. Masters and Johnson took their study of human sexuality into the laboratory and developed many new ways of helping people solve their sexual "hang-ups," but this research is still considered immoral or socially improper by many people.

5. The intra-psychic and social aspects of sex seem to have prevented us from learning as much about the biology of sex as many scientists feel we ought to know. It does seem clear, however, that physiological mechanisms have a strong influence on the human sexual response.

6. Hormones secreted by the adrenal glands and the gonads determine whether a child is born with male or female primary sex characteristics. Hormones also influence the appearance of the secondary sex characteristics at puberty.

7. Hormones affect the instinctive sexual response patterns that occur in humans and even more so in the lower animals, whose sexual behavior is controlled almost entirely by body chemistry.

8. In the primates, early experience is at least as important as the presence or absence of hormones in determining sexual behavior.

9. Children learn at a very early age what types of sexual behavior are taboo or forbidden in their cultures. This childhood conditioning may create very strong sexual inhibitions that must somehow be overcome if the person is to function as a sexually mature adult.

10. Sexual pleasure seems correlated with neural firing in certain regions of the brain called the "reward centers" or "pleasure centers."

11. Most other types of motivated behavior (such as hunger or thirst) seem to be aimed at reducing tension or arousal; sexual motivation, to the contrary, appears to be based on pleasurable arousal or pleasurable sensory inputs. The type of arousal each person prefers, however, is more a matter of cultural conditioning than of basic biology.

(Continued from page 271.)

Paul Schmidtt could hear the sounds of the party a half a block away. He entered Beverly's apartment building, and a row of metal mailboxes just inside the foyer caught his eye. He read the writing on each of the little metal cages until he found Beverly's name, then pressed the button above her card. A buzzing sound on the lock of the inner door announced that someone upstairs had responded to his call, so Paul pushed open the inner door and walked up the flight of steps. Hanging on the door to Beverly's apartment was a large sign on which were scrawled the words, ''Party In Progress—Come In.'' Paul did just that.

As he opened the door a blast of sound fizzed out like foam spewing from a champagne bottle. The place was packed with people he hardly knew, many of them dancing to a rocking blues song that the record player was reproducing at ear-shattering volume. In the center of the dancers was a strikingly handsome couple, the young woman garbed in a soft white dress stretched so tight over her ample figure that Paul was sure it would come apart at the seams as she rolled her hips and shook her shoulders in blues tempo. Her partner—a tall, thin young man—was clothed in tan leather, his shirt open to his waist. He watched his date through half-closed eyes, sometimes responding directly to her impassioned movements, sometimes leading off on his own. His movements were more angular, tighter, and controlled than hers, but no less expressive for all that. Paul watched them for a moment, then moved on.

In one corner a tall but thick-set young Oriental male stood talking with a young Latin American woman. The man stood so stiffly erect that Paul wondered if the youth had a board for a backbone. The dark young woman twined her fingers through her long black hair as she listened to whatever it was the young man was saying.

As Paul moved toward the dining room, a redheaded girl in green shorts came rushing out of the hallway and almost knocked him down. He grabbed her in his arms to keep them from falling over. She paused a moment, fitting her body to his. The musky perfume she was wearing tickled his nose, but before he could say a word an angry young man appeared, grabbed the redhead, and began pulling her toward the front door. She smiled and waved goodbye to Paul, then disappeared, leaving nothing behind but her tantalizing aroma.

Paul pulled himself together and pushed into the kitchen. Beverly spotted him at once, squealed excitedly, and moved toward him, waving a paring knife dangerously in one hand. ''Paul, darling, you're incredibly late. We've missed you dreadfully.''

''Sorry, Bev. Got tied up with some work at the lab.''

''Well, darling, if you prefer those ring doves of yours to the birds you'll find at my party, I can't say much for your taste.''

''Lots of exotic plumage here tonight, I'll say that much.''

Beverly took the remark personally. ''Thanks. I thought you'd like my outfit.'' She stretched out her arms to show off her dress, nearly skewering Paul with the paring knife.

Paul jumped back quickly, laughing. ''What's the weapon for, Bev? Have you taken up surgery or something?''

''Actually, darling, it's for you.'' When Paul looked shocked, she rapidly continued. ''Oh, you do have a dirty mind. No, your hormones are safe—it's open-heart surgery I have in mind. Celery hearts, that is. Would you be a lamb and cut the celery stalks down to size, and then scrape a few carrots? I've got this super cheese dip for the vegetables, but no vegetables ready yet.'' Beverly pointed to a young woman standing at the sink, tearing a cauliflower apart piece by piece. ''Carol here is dissecting various other organic tissues, so you'll have some help. You have met Carol, haven't you?''

Paul nodded gravely at Carol, who smiled shyly back at him, then used her fist to push a lock of sandy-colored hair out of her pleasant face. The chunk of cauliflower locked in her grasp got stuck in her hair.

''Here, you'd better let me help,'' Paul said, moving quickly to her side.

''Well, darlings, I'm off to check on the guests,'' Beverly said, moving toward the door. Then she stopped to look at the young couple standing by the sink. ''But Carol dear, I should warn you. Paul will probably tell you that he's the world's greatest expert on S-E-X. But the truth is, he thinks it's for the birds!''

Paul laughed loudly. Then, with a wink at Carol, he threw back his shoulders, puffed out his chest, cooed at the top of his voice, and bowed his head into the sink.

Carol seemed very impressed at his performance.

''Birds of a feather,'' Beverly said, and left the two to their own devices.

RECOMMENDED READINGS

Katchadourian, Herant A., and Donald T. Lunde. *Fundamentals of Human Sexuality,* 2nd ed. (New York: Holt, Rinehart and Winston, 1975).

Masters, William, and Virginia Johnson. *Human Sexual Response* (Boston, Mass.: Little, Brown & Company, 1966).

Pomeroy, Wardell B. *Dr. Kinsey and the Institute for Sex Research* (New York: New American Library of World Literature, 1973).

chapter 14
"THE STRESS OF LIFE"

STRESS

DID YOU KNOW THAT . . .

Your emotional reactions are controlled in large part by your autonomic nervous
system?

Most people find it difficult to differentiate among hunger, fear, anger, and sexual
arousal on the basis of physiological cues alone?

Your body seems to go through three distinct stages in response to stressful
situations?

Voodoo witch doctors really can kill people by suggestion?

Animals can be conditioned to be "hopeful?"

More southerners die from tornadoes than do northerners, in part because southerners react to stress differently than do people in the North?

Authoritarian parents often teach their children to be rigid in outlook, uncreative,
prejudiced, conforming, and overcontrolled?

"So, you see, Doc, I got a problem." The Sheriff was a large man. He wore a
sense of authority as comfortably as he wore the summer uniform coat that fitted
so easily around his large chest. "It's all those new people on the County
Commission, you understand. They don't know a thing about law and order, I
reckon. I've been in the police business for right on to fourteen years now, and I
spent another six in the Marines besides. So I figure I ought to know something
about training men, right?"

The psychologist leaned back in his chair and lit a cigarette, ignoring the quick
look of disapproval in the Sheriff's eyes as he did so. "That certainly would seem
to be the case, Sheriff. So why don't you just tell me more about your problem?"

The Sheriff relaxed slightly. "Well, we've got more than a thousand men on
this force, and we need a lot more than that to keep the peace in this county.
These men have to be trained, so some years back we set up what I frankly
consider to be the best darn training academy in the whole U S of A. We put a
couple of hundred cadets through their paces each year, and we don't get many
complaints from the taxpayers. But in the last election, a bunch of new types
somehow got themselves elected to the County Commission, and they've been
giving me the devil ever since."

"What do you mean, 'giving you the devil'?" the psychologist asked, puffing
on his cigarette.

"They claim our training methods are old-fashioned and out-of-date. Of
course, those new types on the Commission wouldn't know a good police officer
from a bad one, except maybe if the man leaned heavily to the left when he
walked."

The Sheriff laughed loudly at his comment; the psychologist merely smiled.

"You see, Doc, we take raw recruits—some so ignorant they hardly know to
come in out of the rain—and we stress 'em good. I mean, we stress 'em extra
good. Get the old juices flowing." He got up suddenly, and said, "Come on along
and I'll show you what I mean."

The Sheriff ushered the psychologist out the door. As they left the administration building, they were almost run over by a group of eight young men dressed in police cadet uniforms. The cadets were racing at full tilt toward one of the barracks on the academy campus.

"I learned that in basic training in the Marines—anytime they're outside a building, they got to move at double-time. Teaches 'em respect, I always say."

The two men walked across the soft green lawn until they came to a group of trainees performing calisthenics. One of the cadets had just finished performing several push-ups. The Sheriff stopped to watch the man complete the exercise, then said, "All right, son, what's your name?"

The young cadet, exhausted by the push-ups, looked up at the Sheriff and panted out a reply: "Trumble, Sir."

The drill instructor kicked the cadet sharply in the side. "Don't you recognize an officer when you see one, Trumble? On your feet and salute, and be quick about it."

The recruit jumped smartly to attention and saluted.

"How many push-ups did you just do, Trumble?" the Sheriff asked.

"Fifteen, Sir."

"Not bad, Trumble, but not good either. Look at you, sweating like that. You'll ruin your uniform. Give that man two demerits for sweating so much."

The cadet groaned.

"And another two demerits for groaning," the Sheriff called over his shoulder as he led the psychologist toward one of the academy buildings. "Got to toughen 'em up, you see, so they don't break under stress. Now, that young man is going to see a lot of wrecks on the highway, and he's going to have to lift up over-turned automobiles to try to rescue people trapped inside. If he can't cope with things, if he doesn't have a good set of muscles, and he can't exert 'em to the maximum in an emergency, what kind of a deputy is he going to make?"

As they entered the building, a group of cadets rushed by en route to lunch. They pushed through the cafeteria line in a hurry, taking their trays to a high-topped table. The cadets ate—standing up. Two uniformed officers stood by these trainees, subjecting them to considerable verbal abuse as they ate.

"Got to get them used to being cussed at. Funny, but sometimes when you try to help a person, even try to save their life, they don't understand what you're doing. So the person cusses you out. If the cadet gets angry about a few dirty words, he's going to start swinging his fists when he ought to be helping. Learning how to take all the stuff we throw at them here builds morale too, and gives the cadets pride in their work. When the going gets tough, the tough get going, I always say."

The two men got a cup of coffee and sat down at one of the tables. When the psychologist pulled out a pack of cigarettes, the Sheriff shook his head. "Sorry, Doc, but we don't allow smoking in the cafeteria. Gives the recruits bad ideas, you know; makes 'em lose respect."

The psychologist raised his eyebrows slightly, then put the cigarettes back into his pocket. "Don't you think you might be overdoing this business of stressing your cadets in school so they can adjust better to stress when they're out on the job?"

The Sheriff smiled wanly. "Doc, you're beginning to sound like that new bunch on the Commission. They've been raising the devil about the academy here—claim we turn out machines instead of men. Want me to start treating 'em nice. Want me to turn this into a kindergarten instead of a police academy. Well, it just won't work. Spare the rod and spoil the child, I always say. And that's what I want your help with, Doc."

"You want me to design a better rod?"

"No, of course not. What I want to do is this—I want to run a genuine scientific experiment to prove that my way of training men is better than the 'softie' method. I figure if I can go to the Commission with facts and figures proving the 'tough' way turns out better police officers, then I can get those new types off my back for a spell."

The psychologist frowned. "I like your idea of performing an experiment very much, but I wonder what kind of 'proof' you'll be willing to accept?"

''What do you mean?'' the Sheriff asked.

''I gather you want to take two groups of recruits and train one of them by the old rules and regulations that they have to obey—or else. But you want to use reason and persuasion with the other group. Have I got it right?''

''You hit the nail right on the head.''

''But how are we going to evaluate the effects of the training?''

''Well, I suppose I could look over the two groups after they graduate and pronounce which bunch seems the best.''

The psychologist sipped at his coffee a moment, then set it down on the table. ''Do you really think your friends on the Commission will accept you as an unbiased judge?''

The Sheriff roared with laughter. ''No, of course not. How about we get all the supervisors in the force to rate the men?''

''If your supervisors knew which cadets had had which kind of training, don't you think they might lean just a little bit in your direction when making their evaluations?''

The Sheriff pursed his lips. ''I hadn't thought of that. Maybe we better not let any of the supervisors know about this. Then they could make their ratings without, well, you know—fudging the results.''

''We call that 'running an experiment blind,' when the experimenter doesn't know which group has had what kind of treatment prior to the evaluation,'' the psychologist said.

''None so blind as them that won't see, I always say. Look, Doc, being a police officer is one of the most important but most difficult jobs in the world. We've just got to be the best there is—I won't settle for anything less than that, because people's lives and property depend on how good we do our job. We've got to be real, 100 percent men all the time we're on duty, and we're always under stress. That's why stressing these cadets is the best possible way to make good officers out of them. The Marines did that to me, and look how good things turned out for me!''

The psychologist nodded his head vaguely. ''And how are you going to select the men for the experiment?''

''Why, I'll just interview the recruits and put this one in the stress group and that one in the Mickey Mouse Group.''

''Do you think that's really wise? You might select the big, strong ones for your stress group and the weak-looking ones for the other.''

''Would I do a thing like that?'' the Sheriff asked quickly. And then he chuckled. ''Yes, I reckon I might at that. Doc, you know me better than I know myself. Okay, let's just draw the names out of a hat. That okay with you?''

''Any random selection procedure would be just fine.'' After a moment's thought the psychologist continued. ''How long do you think the study ought to run?''

''Well, you can't really test these guys out in a couple of weeks. Maybe we should keep testing them for a couple of years after they graduate. That long enough for you?''

''That should be fine, Sheriff.'' The psychologist leaned back in his chair and looked at the ceiling. ''And now for the real cruncher. What kinds of data will it take to prove you're wrong?''

The Sheriff exploded. ''What do you mean? Isn't it as plain as the nose on your face that my way builds better men?''

The psychologist shook his head. ''Frankly, I don't know which way is better. There are arguments both ways. But we're talking about the data, not arguments or opinions. What you're doing is trying out a hunch— 'testing an hypothesis' is the technical term for it. You **think** you're right—but you don't have the proof. You hope that the data we gather will prove your hypothesis was right all along. But when you run an experiment, you always have to put your money where your mouth is. Experiments can prove you wrong as well as right. What's it going to take to make you admit your way of training men was wrong? If you can't tell me that right now, before we start, there's just no sense in doing the study.''

"Seems a funny way to do things, but I reckon I understand what you're talking about. You don't want me to weasel around after the facts are in. Well, look before you leap, I always say. I guess that if the 'softies' come out better in most ways, I'll have to throw in my hand."

"And will you tell the Commission of the results, no matter what?"

The Sheriff beamed. "Doc, I'll make a deal with you. If I didn't really love these guys who work for me, and if I didn't want 'em to be the best officers possible, I wouldn't be here. You fix up the best, most honest experiment you know how to. If the 'softies' win, I'll not only tell the Commission, I'll change the way this whole blasted academy is run. Can't ask for much more than that, now can you?"

"Sheriff, I admire your spirit. We'll work up the best study we can for you, and let the final results tell the whole story, come what may! That's what I call real guts."

The Sheriff drew in his stomach and tightened his belt. "Let the chips fall where they may, I always say."

(Continued on page 305.)

In a sense, your body is like the walled cities that dot the landscape in Europe. The citizens of those ancient towns built defenses to keep invading armies out, but left gates in the walls to bring in supplies and take out the garbage. Your skin acts as the "wall" to your body-city. The skin keeps out invaders, but it lets food and water in and waste products out. It also contains "local defenses" that go into action the moment that any danger threatens. For instance, if you cut your finger, the "local police" at the point of the cut begin repairing the damage even before you are aware of it. If germs enter the wound, the blood vessels nearby open up to let more "soldiers" (white corpuscles) through to fend off the invading germs.

All of these reactions are automatic and take place without your conscious direction. But when your skin is damaged, it has receptors that sound the alarm to let your Board know something bad has happened, so that the Board can move your body out of the way or prepare to defend you from attack. When you run

A medieval walled city.

Volition (voh-LISH-un). From the Latin word meaning "to wish" or "to will." When you decide to reach out and pick up an apple off the table, you are exercising your volition. If someone shouted at you just as you picked up the apple, and you dropped the fruit without thinking the matter over, your "dropping response" would be reflexive and therefore performed without your conscious volition.

low on food or water, the "guards" in your hypothalamic "motivation centers" ring bells that arouse you to the urgency of your own needs. Even when you become sexually excited, physiological sirens sound to alert various parts of your body to the impending pleasurable inputs.

QUESTION: Why don't people build walls around cities any more?

Your own internal alarm reactions have both local and generalized effects. When you see a funnel-shaped cloud roaring toward you out of the southwest, your Board cannot take the time to sit down and compose a lengthy memo to your legs, feet, arms, and hands to remind them gently that trouble might be brewing. Instead, your body must have a way of instantly energizing itself—of waking up all its parts in a matter of seconds, and of coordinating all its activities so that you get out of danger quickly, and stay out. In emergencies, you don't have time to think. Your reactions are emotional and reflexive—that is, they take place without your conscious *volition* (°) or desire. We do not have to will our sweat glands to secrete water or our teeth to start chattering when we are frightened. Such activities are handled for us automatically by the unconscious parts of our brains.

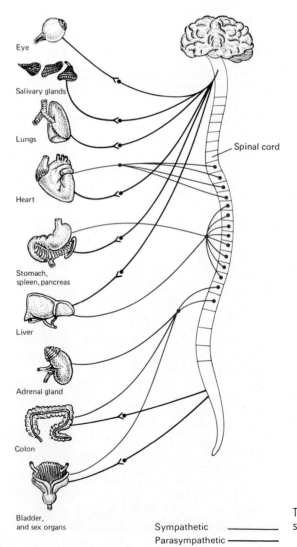

Eye

Salivary glands

Lungs

Heart

Stomach, spleen, pancreas

Liver

Adrenal gland

Colon

Bladder, and sex organs

Spinal cord

Sympathetic ——————
Parasympathetic ——————

The sympathetic and parasympathetic nervous systems.

AUTONOMIC NERVOUS SYSTEM

That part of your body which controls your emotional reactions is called the *autonomic nervous system* (°); it is connected to most of the glands and many of the muscles in your body.

The autonomic nervous system has two major parts or divisions: (1) The *sympathetic nervous system* (°) and (2) the *parasympathetic nervous system* (°). In general, activity in the sympathetic system tends to excite or arouse you much as an "upper" drug might, while activity in the parasympathetic system tends to depress or slow down many of your bodily functions as would a "downer." Together, these two nervous systems control your bodily functions in a coordinated fashion, much as the coordinated activity of a furnace and an air conditioner could serve to keep the temperature in your home at a livable and pleasant level the year round.

Sympathetic Nervous System

The sympathetic nervous system consists of a group of 22 neural centers lying on or close to the spinal cord. From these 22 centers, *axonic fibers* (°) run to all parts of the body—to the salivary glands in your mouth, to the irises in your eyes, to your heart, lungs, liver, and stomach, to your intestines, and to your genitals. The sympathetic nervous system is also connected with the sweat glands, the hair cells, and the tiny blood vessels near the surface of your skin.

Whenever you encounter an emergency of some kind—something that enrages you, makes you suddenly afraid, creates strong desire, or calls for heavy labor on your part—the sympathetic nervous system swings into action. The pupils in your eyes open up to let in more light; your heart pumps more blood to your brain and muscles and to the surface of your skin; you breathe harder and faster; your blood sugar level is elevated; your digestion is slowed down to a crawl; your skin perspires to flush out the waste products created by the extra exertion and to keep you cool. The sympathetic nervous system also controls orgasm and ejaculation during sexual excitement.

In short, activity in the sympathetic nervous system prepares you for fighting, for fleeing, for feeding—and for sexual climax.

QUESTION: **Why do people often get red in the face when they get angry?**

Parasympathetic Nervous System

The parasympathetic nervous system connects to most of the same parts of your body as does the sympathetic. In general, parasympathetic stimulation produces physiological effects that are in most ways the *opposite* of those induced by sympathetic stimulation. Activity in the parasympathetic system closes down or constricts the irises in your eyes, slows down the heart rate, slows down your breathing, increases salivation, stimulates the flow of digestive juices, promotes the processes of excretion, and, in general, conserves or builds up your body's resources. For many reasons, the parasympathetic is often referred to as the *vegetative nervous system* (°).

QUESTION: **Heroin causes the irises to narrow to mere pinpoints, even when the person is sitting in relative darkness; which part of the autonomic nervous system does heroin affect the most?**

For the most part, the parasympathetic and the sympathetic systems act together in coordinated fashion—when one becomes more active, it inhibits excitation in the other. The two systems cooperate during sexual activity, how-

Autonomic nervous system (OUGHT-toe-NOM-ick). "Autonomic" means automatic or reflexive, without volition. The autonomic nervous system is a collection of neural centers which takes care of most of your normal body functions (breathing, pumping of the blood, digestion, emotional reactions) that take place automatically—without your having to think about them.

Sympathetic nervous system (sim-puh-THET-tick). To have sympathy for someone is to experience common emotions or feelings with that person. The sympathetic nervous system is that half of the autonomic nervous system responsible for "turning on" your emotional reactions.

Parasympathetic nervous system (PAIR-uh-sim-puh-THET-tick). That half of the autonomic nervous system that is "beyond" or opposed to the sympathetic system. The parasympathetic system "turns off" or slows down most emotional activity.

Axonic fibers (ax-ON-ick). The axon is the output end of the neuron. See Chapter 2.

Vegetative nervous system. Another name for the parasympathetic nervous system. The phrase "to vegetate" means to withdraw or to sit quietly, gathering strength, like a vegetable quietly growing in the ground. The vegetative functions of the body are those that promote quiet growth and restoration of mental or physical energy; these functions are controlled primarily by the parasympathetic system.

Adrenalin (uh-DREN-uh-lin). One of the two "arousal" hormones released by the adrenal glands. Also called epinephrine (EP-pee-NEFF-rin).

Nor-adrenalin (NORR-uh-DREN-uh-lin). The second of the two "arousal" hormones released by the adrenals. Injection of adrenalin or nor-adrenalin into the body causes a rise in blood pressure and pulse rate, an increase in the breathing rate, and a general speeding up of bodily functions. Also called nor-epinephrine (NOR-EP-pee-NEFF-rin).

Emotions (ee-MOH-shuns). Both "emotion" and "motivation" come from the same Latin word meaning "motion" or "to move." Emotions are "stirred up movements," or "stirred up feelings." Our emotional feelings are usually correlated with activity in the autonomic nervous system. Emotions stress the body by using up its resources at a faster than usual rate. See Chapter 12.

Stress

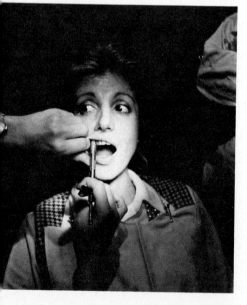

ever, for parasympathetic stimulation is necessary for erection to occur, while, as we noted earlier, orgasm and ejaculation are controlled by sympathetic excitation. There is one major difference between the two systems, however—the sympathetic nervous system is connected to your adrenal glands, while the parasympathetic system is not.

The Adrenal Glands

You may recall from the last chapter that you have two adrenal glands, one sitting atop each of your kidneys. The adrenals not only produce hormones that influence sexual development and that monitor bodily functions such as urine production—they also produce two chemicals that are referred to as the "arousal" hormones. These two hormones are called *adrenalin* (°) and *nor-adrenalin* (°). When adrenalin and nor-adrenalin are released into your bloodstream by the adrenal glands, these hormones bring about all of the bodily changes associated with strong *emotions* (°) such as fear, anger, hostility, and sexual aggressiveness. That is, the action of these two hormones is to increase blood pressure and heart rate, speed up breathing, widen the pupils in your eyes, increase sweating, and, in general, prepare the body to meet an emergency.

As you might guess from this description, the release of adrenalin and nor-adrenalin is under the control of the sympathetic nervous system, whose activities the hormones imitate or mimic. When you encounter an arousing situation, your sympathetic nervous system goes into action first, mobilizing the body's energy resources and also causing the secretion of the two "arousal" hormones. As adrenalin and nor-adrenalin are secreted, they continue the arousal process by chemically stimulating the same neural centers that the sympathetic nervous system has stimulated electrically. But the hormones also increase the firing rate of the nerve cells in the sympathetic nervous system itself. This stimulation causes more of the hormones to be secreted, which increases activity in the sympathetic system, and so on until the emergency has passed or the organism collapses in exhaustion.

QUESTION: Why do you think it might be useful in emergencies to have this positive feedback loop between the arousal hormones and the sympathetic nervous system?

Can you tell the difference (subjectively) between your emotions? That is, can you differentiate between such emotional states as hunger, fear, anger, and sexual arousal? Most of us can, but we apparently do so on the basis of intra-psychic cues rather than biological states. For, with minor exceptions, the physiological changes that occur in your body are pretty much the same no matter what type of emotional upheaval you are undergoing. There is some recent evidence that fear is controlled primarily by adrenalin, while anger is controlled by nor-adrenalin, but both hormones are released to some degree in all arousal situations. We cannot tell objectively whether you are angry or afraid just by measuring the relative amounts of adrenalin and nor-adrenalin floating around in your bloodstream.

When human volunteers have been injected with large amounts of adrenalin or nor-adrenalin, they often report that they feel as if they were "about to become emotional," but they can't say why. Whatever feelings of arousal they have do not seem "real" somehow, and their upset does not seem to be focused or directed toward any given object. Some subjects have described the experience as "cold rage."

QUESTION: Some people report that they are most easily aroused sexually when they are hungry, or immediately after a frightening experience or a violent argument; why do you think this might be the case?

EMOTIONAL STRESS

Emotional experiences seem to have three rather distinct aspects: (1) The bodily changes associated with arousal and relaxation; (2) the emotional behavior (such as fighting, loving, or running away); and (3) the subjective feelings that give a distinctive personal flavor to our emotional upsets. Because the first two aspects can be studied relatively easily from an objective viewpoint, we have a fair amount of hard data about them. But feelings such as love and hate are private events that occur within a person's mind; we can investigate these intra-psychic states only indirectly by asking the individual to tell us what he or she is experiencing. Sadly enough, from a scientific point of view, whenever you stop to analyze your own emotional feelings, they tend to change, diminish, or disappear entirely. The matter is complicated by two additional facts: Many people are rather bad at pinning precise labels on their emotional states; and individuals who are quite good at discriminating one emotion from another can't always identify the internal and external cues or inputs that triggered off the response.

At the end of a race, a runner may have reached the stage of exhaustion.

What we can say with some assurance is this: Emotional arousal puts you under a variety of biological, intra-psychic, and behavioral *stresses* that, if continued too long, can exhaust your resources. When a medieval European walled city was surrounded and besieged by an invading army, the populace sometimes dipped into the town's supplies at an alarming rate—because they could not bring in fresh food until the siege was lifted. When you are excited or keyed up, your body burns up calories at many times its normal rate. A sudden fright may cause the same expenditure of energy as an hour's study. Sexual intercourse costs your body as many calories as would running up a very long flight of steps or performing light calisthenics for several minutes. When your sympathetic nervous system is called into play during a fit of anger or rage, your digestion functions badly so that you do not assimilate food properly—and you may lose so much liquid through sweating that your kidneys must work overtime to keep your water balance under control. If your emotional behavior leads you to damage your body in any way, you pay a price for that, too.

QUESTION: **During sexual intercourse, your pulse rate may more than double and your blood pressure may rise far above normal; what sort of information about sexual arousal do you think physicians should give to patients recovering from heart attacks?**

Physiological Stress Reactions

The noted Canadian scientist, Hans Selye, first outlined the three states that your body seems to go through when its resources must be mobilized to meet situations of excessive physiological stress.

The first state he calls the *alarm reaction* (°), in which the body's defenses are rapidly called up through activity in the *limbic system* (°), the sympathetic nervous system, and through the secretion of "arousal hormones" from the adrenals.

If the stress continues, the body must not only maintain its first-line emotional defenses but must also immediately begin repairing the damage that this arousal causes. So the adrenal glands begin to secrete abnormally large amounts of the body-regulating hormones mentioned in the last chapter. This second stage Selye calls the *stage of resistance* (°).

During the first two stages, the sympathetic nervous system is intensely aroused. However, if the emergency continues for too long, all of the energy available to the sympathetic system may be used up, and an overwhelming counter-reaction may occur in which the parasympathetic system takes over. The organism falls into the third state, the *stage of exhaustion* (°), during which most of the body's functions are slowed down abnormally or even stop altogether.

Alarm reaction. According to Hans Selye (SELL-yee), the alarm reaction is the first state of a stress reaction in which the bodily defenses are rapidly called into play.

Limbic system (LIM-bick). A set of related neural centers in the brain that influence emotional reactions. See Chapter 4.

Stage of resistance. The second state of a stress reaction during which the body tries to repair itself while continuing to react in an aroused manner.

Stage of exhaustion. According to Selye, if the first two stages of the stress reaction last too long, the body's resources are exhausted, the parasympathetic system takes over, and all physiological functions slow down dramatically. If the stress lasts too long, the organism may collapse or die.

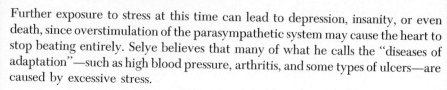

Hans Selye.

Further exposure to stress at this time can lead to depression, insanity, or even death, since overstimulation of the parasympathetic system may cause the heart to stop beating entirely. Selye believes that many of what he calls the "diseases of adaptation"—such as high blood pressure, arthritis, and some types of ulcers—are caused by excessive stress.

Intra-psychic Stress Reactions

Any time that you are placed under great pressure, your mental functioning is affected in much the same way that your physiological functioning is. During the alarm reaction, for instance, you typically will feel tense and alert, anxious and wary, as if you were mobilizing your powers of self-control. As the situation continues, you may begin to feel highly anxious, or experience vague pains and aches that don't seem to be related to any physical damage to your body. Too much anxiety can lower your ability to make sound judgments. As your performance deteriorates, you may begin to blame others for your own failures. If these failures continue, you could lose all hope of being able to handle or cope with the situation. You might then either run away, or else lapse into psychological disorganization, inactivity, or even death.

QUESTION: Can you trace the experience of a "bad drug trip" through the three stages of arousal?

Social/Behavioral Stress Reactions

A psychological "stab in the back" from your social environment may in fact kill you almost as rapidly as a switchblade thrust between your ribs. Physiologist Walter B. Cannon, whose work on hunger we mentioned earlier, made a study of "voodoo deaths." In many primitive cultures, the witch doctor is supposed to possess magical or voodoo powers strong enough to kill or cure the people in his tribe. If someone in his village angers him, the witch doctor may cast a spell on the person, usually by pointing a bone or magic wand at the person while muttering dreadful curses. Given up for dead by the rest of the villagers, the accursed individual may retire to his or her hut, or may wander off into the woods alone to hide in shame. If the individual's belief in the powers of the witch doctor is great enough, he or she may actually die within a day or so after the curse has been uttered.

Cannon, who was at first highly skeptical of the rumors he had heard of such things, went to Africa himself to investigate the matter. He was able to confirm the authenticity of at least 30 "voodoo deaths." Cannon believed (incorrectly) that these people died from heart attacks brought about by overstimulation of the sympathetic nervous system. We know now, however, that the sympathetic system was not usually the culprit.

A chief of Eyambe, medicine man and witch doctor of the Congo.

Richter's Hopeful Rats

Psychiatrist Curt Richter became interested in the consequences of stress early in his long and productive scientific career. He saw many people literally fold up and die when they found themselves under too great pressure. The stress was often purely psychological—but it was the patient's body as well as the patient's mind that often collapsed. So Richter began a fascinating series of experiments in which he measured (as best he could) the physiological consequences of various highly threatening situations. Since any abnormally stressful environment is potentially harmful to the organism, Richter worked with rats rather than human beings.

Death by a Whisker One of Richter's experimental situations involved a large tub filled with water. He would throw a rat into the water and let it swim until it was absolutely exhausted and would have drowned if it had not been rescued. If the water was at room temperature, the average rat would swim about 80 hours (without rest) until it went under. If Richter made the water too cold or too hot, however, the rat would give up after no more than 20 to 40 hours. If he blew a jet of air into the animal's face while it was swimming, the rat became exhausted even more quickly.

After the experimental animals had met all these challenges, Richter would inspect various parts of their bodies to see what the physiological reactions had been. His early work was instrumental in the development of drugs that have helped thousands of human patients survive the devastating effects of psychological stress and tension.

But one of Richter's most fascinating findings came about almost by accident. Richter noticed that, no matter what he did to them, many of his rats always swam around the sides of the tub in the same direction. Some animals always swam clockwise, some always counter-clockwise, but once they had "picked" their direction, it was always the same. Richter knew that many insects and other lower animals show the same sort of "circling" behavior if you cut off one of their "feelers" or *antennae* (°). An ant that has lost its left antenna will tend to circle to the left, while a flatworm that has had the smell receptors on the right side of its head destroyed will circle to the right. Richter wondered if there might not be some connection or *correlation* (°) between the length of a rat's whiskers and the direction in which it swims in the tub. Perhaps rats always turn their heads toward the side where their whiskers are shortest.

And so he asked his assistants to cut the whiskers off one side of a rat's face and toss it into the tub. When they did so, to everyone's surprise, the animal paddled around frantically for a minute or two—and then sank straight to the bottom of the tub like a stone. The de-whiskered rat would have drowned in two minutes (rather than 80 hours) if they hadn't rescued it.

Now, this finding simply didn't make sense to Richter. Obviously a rat doesn't depend on its whiskers to keep it afloat. What could be wrong? So he asked his assistants to show him what they had done to the rat while clipping it.

For the most part, the white rat found in psychological laboratories is a gentle beast that can be handled without gloves and even makes an amusing pet. But rats have sharp teeth, as the assistants knew only too well. If the rat becomes frightened, it will sharpen its keen teeth on any handy object—including the fingers of a lab assistant. To avoid being bitten when clipping the rat's whiskers, the assistants had nearly smothered the animal inside a black bag. To get the rat out of its cage, they had held the mouth of the bag up to the open cage door. Perhaps because it thought it could escape easily, or because it was attracted to darkness, the rat had jumped into the thick black sack. The assistants then grabbed the animal tightly through the cloth and peeled back the top of the bag until the rat's head was exposed. Holding the rat's body firmly inside the bag, the assistants proceeded to clip the whiskers from one side of the animal's face with a large, noisy clipper. Then they held the sack over the tub and dropped the poor frightened rodent into the water in the tub. Little wonder that it sank to the bottom almost at once!

Richter soon found that it was the *trauma* (°) induced by the handling—and not the whisker clipping at all—that so overstimulated the animal's fear responses that it went straight into the stage of exhaustion. The parasympathetic nervous system simply took over and clamped down on all activity; the rat's heart slowed down to almost a complete stop, and the animal soon lost consciousness and sank. It was from these and related studies that Richter concluded that "voodoo death" was caused by parasympathetic rather than sympathetic overstimulation.

Curt Richter.

Antennae (an-TEN-knee). The antenna of a TV set is the metal rod or wires put up to catch television waves. The antennae (or antennas) on an insect are the "feelers" that stick out of the animal's head. Most insect antennae contain touch and olfactory receptors and help the animal "feel out the world" around it.

Correlation (kor-ree-LAY-shun). Two events that occur together frequently are said to be co-related, or correlated. The more closely related the events are, or the more often they occur together, the higher the correlation between them. See the Statistical Appendix to this book for further details.

Trauma (rhymes with "DRAW-ma"). Any injury or disability inflicted on one's body or mind. See Chapter 5.

Learning To Be Hopeful   Perhaps the most interesting finding Richter made, however, was this—if at any time before the de-whiskered rat actually drowned Richter pulled it out of the water and let it sit on a table for a minute or two, the animal would make a remarkable recovery. Once it had rested and gathered its wits together, it seemed to realize that it could, in fact, survive this traumatic situation. And so, if Richter then tossed it back into the water, it would swim for many hours. Those two or three minutes out of the water were enough to give it momentary hope. If it were given several gentle, playful exposures to the black bag before having its whiskers clipped, and if it were "rescued" several times during the first few minutes it was dumped in the tub, the rat apparently gained excellent control over its autonomic nervous system, and then managed to swim as well or even better than rats that hadn't been trained in this way to withstand stress. Hope springs eternal—but apparently only if you have been given signs or reasons to be hopeful.

STRESS AND THE LOCUS OF PERSONAL CONTROL

People, like white rats and walled cities, face numerous challenges in their lifetimes. As Drs. John H. Sims and Duane D. Baumann recently reported, the typical response pattern that each of us shows to stress often determines how long—and how well—we live. Sims (a psychiatrist at George Williams College) and Baumann (a geographer at Southern Illinois University) became fascinated by an odd bit of data having to do with deaths from violent storms. The central part of the United States is called "tornado alley," for there are more twisters each year in this part of the United States than in almost any other place in the world. Tornadoes are most likely to hit in a region running from Dallas, Texas, north to Topeka, Kansas, on through Illinois to Chicago, and across Lake Michigan to Detroit. However, the most deaths reported from tornadoes each year come from the areas in the South well outside the major tornado pathways.

The intriguing question that Sims and Baumann asked themselves was this— why are southerners more likely to be killed by twisters than are people in the North? If we follow their train of thought as they worked through this problem,

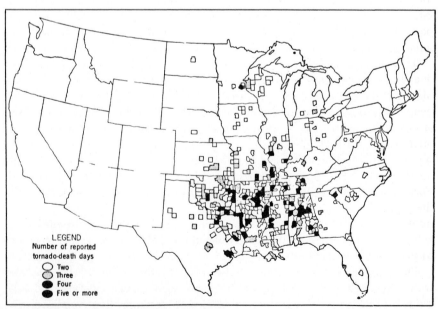

Tornado-death days by county, 1916–1953.

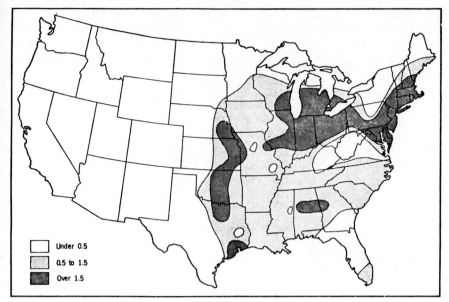

Potential casualties from tornadoes per square mile, 1916–1961.

we may get a very good idea of how scientists go about testing various ideas and hypotheses until they find what seems to be the best solution.

The first explanation that Sims and Baumann checked on had to do with population density. Perhaps the southern states are simply more densely populated than are those areas of the North struck by tornadic storms. But that seemed not to be the case. Land in the South is, in fact, more sparsely occupied than in the North. When they looked at the areas involved, they found that the southern states report three times as many deaths by area and five times as many deaths by population as do the states in the North.

Their next thought was that there might be more storms in the South than in the North. But the weather records they checked suggested that there are, if anything, more tornadoes reported each year in the North. Could it then be that southern storms are more severe? Sims and Baumann report that it is difficult to estimate this factor, but as far as they could tell, the severity of northern storms is perhaps a little greater. In short, it probably isn't the storms that count, it's something else.

Their next thought was that it might be the houses that the tornado victims lived in. Generally speaking, the weather in the South is milder than in the North. Might southern homes be less well built than those in the North, and hence offer people less protection from the raging winds of a tornado? Sims and Baumann answer that question with a yes and a no. Yes, homes in the South are frailer and often more poorly constructed, for many of them are built of wood or simple plywood; homes in the North are more likely to be built of stone and brick. But no, that fact doesn't seem to account for the differences they were interested in. For it appears that when a tornado hits, houses made of wood bulge and give with the winds; if they do collapse, their wooden walls are less likely to hurt the people inside. Sims and Baumann cite evidence that sturdily constructed homes are actually more prone to sustain wind damage and, if they do collapse, more likely to injure the occupants.

But what about warning systems? The National Weather Service keeps a close watch on storms that might turn into tornadoes, and reports their findings via radio and television. Perhaps weather forecasting is more effective in the North, or the news *media* (°) are more likely to sound the alarm. Unfortunately, the data

Media (ME-dee-uh). The word "medium" has many meanings, one of which is "a condition, atmosphere, or environment in which something may function or be expressed." Television is a "medium" in which news can be expressed; so is radio; so is a magazine or a newspaper. "Media" is the plural of "medium." The news media are the various ways that news can be relayed to the public. If you want to make English teachers happy, please remember to say "the media *are*" instead of "the media *is.*"

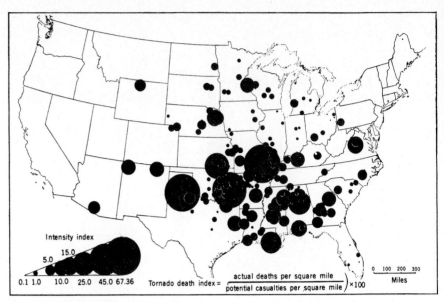

Tornado death index, 1953–1964.

Sims and Baumann uncovered don't give this notion much support. First of all, the nation-wide warning system did not go into effect anywhere until 1953. If forecasting was responsible for saving lives in the North, one would expect that fact to show up after 1953. But, in the decades prior to 1953, the South still reported more deaths than did the North. And, after 1953, the storm alerts were made available to all radio and television stations everywhere, North and South. So the answer must lie elsewhere.

Sims and Baumann point out that there might be differences in the way that southerners and northerners respond to threatening weather and storm warnings. What do you do when the announcer on the radio or TV informs you that tornadoes have been spotted nearby? Do you head for shelter, or merely shrug your shoulders and tell yourself it's all a matter of chance anyway, that if your time has come, there's little you can do about it? Could it be that the cultural norms in the South encourage shoulder-shrugging while those in the North encourage action?

To find out, Sims and Baumann developed a questionnaire that they then gave to a group of women living in a high-risk area in Alabama and to a comparable group of women living in a tornado-prone area of Illinois. They matched the two groups as closely as possible on such variables as age, race, education, income, and past exposure to tornadoes. Some of the questions asked were aimed at discovering how these women responded when severe storms were in their vicinity. With the other questions Sims and Baumann hoped to determine the extent to which each woman felt she controlled her own life.

Internalizers versus Externalizers

Autonomous (aw-TON-oh-muss). From the Greek word meaning "independent," or "self directed." If you make your own decisions, you are autonomous; if you obey other people's orders, you are not.

Internalizers (in-TURR-nuh-lie-zers, or IN-turr-nuh-lie-zers). According to Julian Rotter, people who believe their actions are under their own internal control are internalizers.

Some people are taught to believe that they are *autonomous* (°)—that is, that they are masters of their own fates and hence bear personal responsibility for what happens to them. They see the control of their lives as coming from *inside* themselves, from their own intra-psychic resources. Psychologist Julian Rotter calls these people *internalizers* (°).

On the other hand, many people believe that they are helpless pawns of fate, that they are creatures controlled by outside forces over which they have little if any influence. Such people appear to feel that their *locus of personal control* (°) is external rather than internal; and they often act as if they felt little or no responsibility for what happens to them. Dr. Rotter calls these people *externalizers* (°).

Perhaps the major differences between externalizers and internalizers, as Rotter makes clear, is that people with an internal locus of personal control know how to act to get their desired (reinforcing) inputs, while people with an external locus of control seem not to have this knowledge. Rather, externalizers tend to wait passively for whatever inputs come their way.

Sims and Baumann reasoned that a greater proportion of southerners than northerners might be externalizers, and that this fact alone might help explain why more people in the South get killed by tornadoes. As we will see, the answers that their subjects gave to the questionnaire lend some support to the Sims-Baumann hypothesis.

A woman who believes that her locus of control is external is very likely to think that what happens to her is a matter of fate, or of God's will. When asked about this point, 59 percent of the Alabama women reported that "God controls my life." However, only 36 percent of those in Illinois believed this. Southern women are more likely to believe in the importance of "luck," too. Some 29 percent of the Alabama subjects responded that "luck" was of major importance in determining their fates—a belief that only 6 percent of the northern women shared. Indeed, some 21 percent of the northerners denied that "luck" existed, a view held by only 8 percent of the southerners.

Sims and Baumann interpret these data as suggesting that a much higher percentage of their southern sample were externalizers, who saw themselves as being manipulated by external forces beyond their control. This attitude might well lead them to respond to the threat of a tornado simply by folding their hands and awaiting their destiny. As evidence to support this view, Sims and Baumann report that a full 46 percent of the southern women think that getting ahead in the world results entirely from "God's will," not from anything they themselves do. In marked contrast, only 9 percent of the Illinois women believe that success comes from "God's will," while 67 percent of them responded that getting ahead comes from hard work and from doing things on your own.

"Doing things on your own" appears to mean, to the typical Illinois subject, trying to protect yourself against the ravages of tornadoes. When asked how they responded to the announcement of an impending bad storm, 42 percent of the women in Illinois said they listened to the news media or went out to alert other people to the danger. Only 4 percent of the Alabama women said they bothered to take such precautions. When asked what was the best way to determine if a tornado was coming, 42 percent of the northern women said that they would use modern technology—they would listen to the radio or TV or would watch a *barometer* (°). Less than 5 percent of the women in Alabama gave the same response.

The Sims and Baumann study suggests that a much greater proportion of people in the South than in the North attempt to cope with the stress induced by external dangers by denying that the danger actually exists. When funnel-shaped clouds loom on the horizon, the southerners tend more to withdraw into the walled fortresses of their own personalities and to close down the doors to their minds. The northerners avoid stress in a different way—by keeping alert to their environments and by moving to safety when danger threatens.

QUESTION: If you became governor of a southern state, what might you do to help reduce the unusually high death rate from tornadoes among your voters?

As we will see in Chapter 23, there are no "pure" personality types. Concepts such as "locus of control" are useful, but we must not make the mistake of

Locus of personal control (LOW-cuss). The word *locus* means "location" or "place." Some people behave as if the control of their lives comes from internal, autonomous sources; other people behave as if the locus of their personal control was outside them.

Externalizers (EX-turr-nuh-lie-zers). People who, according to Rotter, see their lives as being under the control of external forces over which the people have little or no influence.

Barometer (buh-RAHM-uh-turr). An instrument (or "meter") for measuring barometric (bear-oh-METT-trick) pressure. Barometric pressure is correlated with the weather. Generally speaking, when the barometric pressure is high, the sky is clear and the weather is good. When the barometric pressure starts to decrease ("when the barometer falls"), storms are usually on the way. A sudden, dramatic drop in barometric pressure often signals the arrival of a severe thunderstorm or a tornado.

thinking that everyone in the world must be either an externalizer or an internalizer. Rather, we all probably have mixed tendencies; even the most fatalistic of externalizers will, in some situations, meet challenges head-on rather than denying that they exist. What is true of one person who scores as a high externalizer on a questionnaire need not be true of anyone else who gets the same score. However, if we look at general tendencies—that is, at *correlations* among various behavioral traits—we can draw some conclusions about human behavior that will be right far more often than they will be wrong.

LEARNING TO RESPOND TO STRESS

The characteristic response that one shows to stressful situations appears to be something that is learned early in life. Conflict almost always leads to stress. For the growing child, few situations are as potentially stressful as those in which the child's desires come in conflict with parental demands. The first few times such conflicts occur, the child's sympathetic nervous system is aroused, and the child either stands up and fights, or turns and flees. Some parents may encourage defiance; others may encourage running away; while still others may reward the child's attempts at conciliation and working out family differences by logical compromise. In any of these cases, the child is likely to learn that the stress of arousal may be reduced by some positive action on its part. Such children tend to acquire an internal locus of control, because they have been taught that they are responsible for what happens to them. When tornadoes threaten, they would be likely to seek shelter or to go out and warn their friends and neighbors.

However, consider what might happen if the child's parents were rigid and uncompromising. When the first few conflicts with the child arose, the parents might refuse to allow the child either to fight or to flee. Instead, the child would be encouraged to submit blindly to the authority of the parents (or to whatever philosophical or moral code the parents followed). Any attempt the child made to take control of its own destiny might be severely punished. The child would soon learn to bury its resentments and to be obedient to the parents' demands. But to do so the child must learn some way of handling the arousal of its sympathetic nervous system, an arousal that occurs almost automatically in all stressful situations. From a logical point of view, the two best ways of doing this would seem to be (1) preventing the arousal from occurring in the first place, and (2) overcoming sympathetic activity by means of massive excitation of the parasympathetic nervous system.

To become aroused by threats in your external environment, you must first learn to perceive the dangers in the world around you. A burnt child dreads the fire. But if the child learns to suppress or distort its perceptions of the world—if it learns to misperceive threatening situations by telling itself that no danger really exists—then its denials of reality might keep its sympathetic system from being triggered off no matter how grave the threat to its own safety. Fire burns—but that isn't really a fire, is it?

This mechanism of *denial* (°), which we will discuss in greater detail in Chapter 22, is very similar to the *perceptual defense* (°) mentioned in Chapter 11. In both cases, incoming sensory information is screened and, if arousing or threatening, is suppressed before it can affect the autonomic nervous system. Under conditions of continuing great stress, the perceptual distortions of people who practice denial may become so numerous that they drift into a kind of insanity in which they can no longer readily tell reality from their own fantasies. Or they may resort to the excessive use of some drug like alcohol—a depressant—which both blurs the sharp edge of danger and soothes their sympathetic nervous systems.

Sympathetic activity can also be reduced by excitation in the parasympathetic

Denial (dee-NIGH-ull). According to Freud, the conscious part of your mind, or ego (EE-go), has many ways of defending itself from unpleasant truths that might upset it. One such defense mechanism is pretending that a threat simply doesn't exist. As you will see in Chapter 22, Freud called this mechanism "denial."

Perceptual defense. The act of suppressing or repressing threatening stimuli. See Chapter 11.

nervous system. If the child is always rewarded when it is placid and calm and "vegetative," and always punished or threatened when it is excited, the child's parasympathetic system will eventually become dominant. When external threats develop, the child will rapidly pass through the first two of Selye's stages—those of arousal and resistance—and enter the first part of the stage of exhaustion. As long as the threats aren't too great, the child will recover. This, then, becomes its habitual way of responding to threats—when conflict develops, the parasympathetic system will immediately restrict or repress sympathetic excitation, and the child will remain relatively unemotional (on the surface, at least).

STRESS AND CONFORMITY

The person with a strongly externalized locus of control pays rather a heavy penalty for avoiding the stresses and strains of life, however. Studies of these people suggest that they often become rigid, constricted in their outlook, uncreative, prejudiced, conforming, and overcontrolled. They are, in general, much more depressive and suicidal than is the average man or woman. Externalizers function fairly well in highly structured, *authoritarian* (°) social systems—particularly those with a military character. However, externalizers are often intolerant of change and sometimes fiercely resist any attack on the authority to whom they have surrendered control. In general, their motivation seems to come from outside, from the "system" rather than from their own internal drives. They volunteer for nothing (unless they are told to do so), and they tend to have difficulties in adjusting to situations in which they do not have a ready-made set of rules to follow. If the culture they live in is stable and quiet, their social guidelines allow them to survive fairly well. In times of social upheaval, when the rules and regulations they have learned by heart no longer apply as once they did, they find themselves confused. If their attacks against the agents of social change fail, they may retreat within themselves, building the walls around them higher and higher, hoping to outlast the armies that are threatening at their gates.

People who have been taught by their parents to deny reality often benefit from psycho-therapy aimed at giving them insight into their present predicament.

Authoritarian (aw-thor-it-TAIR-ee-ann). A dictatorship is a perfect example of an authoritarian system—one in which the person on top rules with an iron fist. In 1950, several social scientists identified a group of traits or behavior patterns that make up what they call "the authoritarian personality." These traits include a high degree of conformity, dependence on authority, overcontrol of feelings and impulses, rigidity of thinking, and prejudice toward other races and religions. Individuals possessing these traits are said to have highly conventional values, are preoccupied with gaining power and status, and try to think and act like their political or social leaders. The authoritarian personality is said to develop in people who were subjected to very strict parental control early in their lives, and who learned to bury their resentments and adopt an attitude of giving in to authority in order to survive. As adults, they are supposed to continue to be overly obedient to authority, but take out their resentments by attacking minority groups and by hating everyone who isn't exactly like them.

Approximately 65,000 German children on parade at a Nazi Party Congress held in Nuremberg in 1936. Nazi Germany was a highly authoritarian society.

By going back over their early experiences, they often come to understand what stimuli they are defending against. Even as adults, if they are exposed to mildly stressful situations and encouraged to handle them effectively, bit by bit they gain hope and begin to internalize their locus of personal control. However, if they are merely dumped into hot water again and again without being given new ways of tolerating it, the externalizers tend to become more rigid rather than more flexible.

Recent studies by the Sheriff's Department in Los Angeles County, and by the U.S. Army at Fort Ord, California, suggest that training techniques that rely on massive doses of stress and punishment are much less effective than training that involves encouraging the person to adjust to conflict by seeking out workable solutions. The ability to change is, biologically speaking, the ability to survive. And to be without any stress at all is to be without the internal motivation necessary to adapt in a world swept by the winds of change.

SUMMARY

1. Your body and mind have many ways of defending themselves against the stresses and strains of life.
2. At a physiological level, most of your defenses are controlled by the two parts of the autonomic nervous system—the sympathetic and the parasympathetic nervous systems.
3. The sympathetic nervous system prepares you for such actions as fighting, fleeing, feeding—and sexual climax.
4. The parasympathetic nervous system acts to depress or slow down those bodily functions that are aroused by sympathetic system activity.
5. These two systems generally have opposite effects on our reactions, but the two systems actually operate together in a coordinated manner. Working together, they influence much of what we do and feel.
6. Once you become excited or emotionally stirred up, the sympathetic system causes the release of adrenalin and nor-adrenalin—the "arousal hormones" secreted by the adrenal glands. These two hormones have much the same excitatory effect on physiological reactions (such as blood pressure and pulse rate) as activity in the sympathetic system itself.
7. Emotional arousal always puts you under a variety of biological, intra-psychic, and behavioral stresses that, if continued too long, can exhaust your resources.
8. Hans Selye suggests that the body goes through three rather distinct stages when stressed:
   a. The alarm reaction, in which the body's defenses are mobilized by activity in the limbic system, the sympathetic system, and through secretion of adrenalin and nor-adrenalin.
   b. The stage of resistance, which occurs if the stress continues for very long. During this stage, the body itself tries to repair the damage that arousal causes while still defending itself.
   c. The stage of exhaustion, which comes about if the emergency continues for too long. During this stage, the body may use up all of its available resources and fall into depression or die.
9. Intra-psychic and social/behavioral stress reactions follow much the same pattern as biological stress.
10. Psychological or environmental threats can be at least as exhausting as can physiological stresses, such as disease.
11. People respond to psychological pressures—such as the threat of a tornado—in different ways, depending in part on their own personal locus of control.
    a. People who believe they are autonomous—that is, who believe they control their own fates—are aroused by threats and try to overcome them.
    b. Individuals who see themselves as being controlled primarily by external forces may face such threats passively, waiting for some outside agency to protect or take care of them.

12. Stress reaction patterns seem typically to be learned at an early age. However, with proper training, almost anyone can do better at handling stressful situations sensibly and effectively.

(Continued from page 291.)

The Sheriff was sweating profusely. He squinted his eyes at the psychologist sitting across the desk from him. Already he had heard rumors about the data that this man had gathered comparing the stress method of training his cadets with what he called the Mickey Mouse method. And he didn't like the rumors at all. He didn't much like the look on the psychologist's face, either.

"Well, Doc," he said, slowly, "who would have thought that three years could have passed so quickly? Time really flies, I always say."

The psychologist nodded. "You're right, Sheriff. Six months to plan the study, six months following the two groups of cadets through the academy here, and then we spent a full two years seeing how they did on the job."

The Sheriff sighed deeply. "Maybe you could just give me the highlights now, and fill in the details later on."

"Don't worry, Sheriff. Things aren't as bad as you've heard. In fact, I think you're going to be very happy with what I say."

"Happy?"

"Yes, sir. Because you've really trained some excellent deputies lately, and the results of this study can give you some great ideas on how to do an even better job in the future."

The Sheriff's eyes opened widely. "You mean those boys of mine trained by the old reliable military method did the best after all?"

"No, not quite. As you know, we began the study by assigning recruits randomly either to one group or the other. The first group—your boys, as you call them—went through the usual highly stressful, punishing type of training that you've always given. The second group were treated in a more relaxed fashion. Instead of punishing them no matter what they did, your officers were trained to compliment them on good performance. Verbal abuse and discipline were held to a minimum, and the men were given every kind of encouragement we could think of to perform well."

"Bunch of sissies, that's what they turned out to be, right?"

"Wrong. They learned faster and performed better on every scholastic test we could think of. They took the initiative more often and they were much more satisfied with their own progress than were 'your boys.' The instructors liked them more and gave them much higher ratings, too."

"Well, they might have done pretty well with that book learning, but I'll bet they dropped out like flies when the going got rough out on the streets and highways."

"No. Just the opposite. More of 'your guys' dropped out during training, and more of them quit once they were out on the streets. Job satisfaction was much higher among the men trained the new way."

The Sheriff shook his head in disbelief. "But how did they do on the job? I'll bet they made rotten officers."

"No, it was the other way around. The supervisors rated the men 'blind' at least once a month. The new way of training the men turned them into first-rate police officers. They were rated as being substantially more adaptable and responsible, as conveying a much more positive 'police image' in their physical appearances; and they got along much better with their superiors and with their fellow officers than did the guys trained 'your way.'"

The Sheriff seemed desperate. "But what about discipline? I bet those Mickey Mouse types didn't follow orders too good now, did they?"

"Sorry, Sheriff. It's the other way around. The men trained the new way were more willing to volunteer to work long hours or to take on extra-duty assignments than 'your guys' were. The new group not only followed orders better and more effectively but responded to commands more willingly too. The public liked them better and gave them far fewer complaints. The guys trained the old way just didn't measure up at all, no matter what kind of evaluation you care to look at."

"Not even on the pistol range?"

"Not even on a simple thing like shooting a gun."

The Sheriff paused for several long seconds, as tears filled his eyes. "No fool like an old fool, I always say. But I don't see how it could come out that way. I always thought that hazing the guys and treating 'em rough turned them into real men — because it trained them to stand up under stress. I wouldn't have done it unless I thought it would help them out on the job. But why didn't it work?"

The psychologist sighed. "What you trained the men for was to survive as best they could under the artificial stresses you created right here in the academy. Lots of the really smart cadets dropped out quickly because they saw there wasn't any real correlation between not sweating when they were doing push-ups and saving lives out on the highways. Anyone learns better and works harder when he's encouraged by his superiors than when they're grinding the man's nose into the ground all the time. At least, that's what the data show."

"So, I guess I lost the old ball game after all, despite all my good intentions."

The psychologist brightened. "No, not at all. Actually, you've won it."

"What do you mean?"

"You turned out some pretty good men in the old days, didn't you?"

The Sheriff nodded vigorously. "You better believe we did."

"Well, now you've got an even better way to train men than you ever did before. And you can actually do it cheaper, since fewer of the good ones drop out. Don't you think the County Commission will appreciate that when you tell them about it? What more could you ask for?"

"Yeah, but you can't teach an old dog new tricks, now can you?"

Smiling, the psychologist said, "It depends not only on the dog but the teacher as well. And I'd say that the facts we gathered in this experiment are about the best teacher I can think of. Besides, you're never too old to learn, like I always say."

"Is that really what you always say?"

"You bet your life, Sheriff."

A grin broke out on the officer's face. "Doc, starting today, that's what I always say, too!"

RECOMMENDED READINGS

Levi, Lennart. *Society, Stress and Disease* (New York: Oxford University Press, 1971).

McNeil, Elton B. *The Quiet Furies* (New York: Prentice-Hall, Inc., 1967).

Rotter, Julian. "External Control and Internal Control," *Psychology Today*, vol. 5, no. 1 (1971), pp. 37–42.

Selye, Hans. *The Stress of Life* (New York: McGraw-Hill Book Company, Inc., 1956).

Spielberger, Charles D., and Irving G. Sarason, eds. *Stress and Anxiety* Vol. I (Washington, D.C.: Hemisphere, 1975).

Part 4

LEARNING
AND
MEMORY

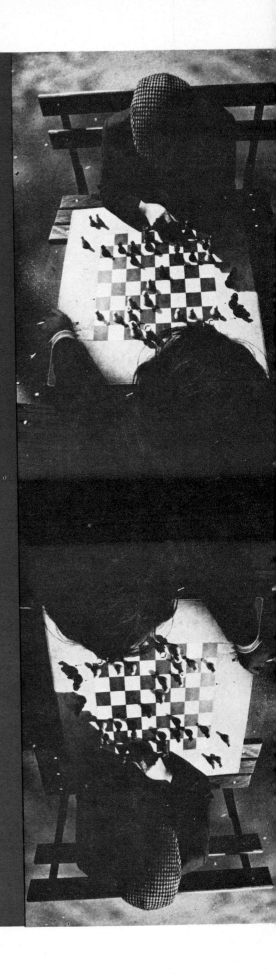

CONDITIONING AND DESENSITIZATION

DID YOU KNOW THAT . . .

Although a Russian named Ivan Pavlov is usually given credit, a U.S. psychologist named E.B. Twitmyer was apparently the first to experiment with what we now call the "conditioned response?"

Pavlov was able to train dogs willingly to withstand considerable pain to get food?

Laboratory animals can be conditioned to show many responses that are similar to those shown by mentally ill humans?

Animals put in conflict-inducing situations often display abnormal or inappropriate sexual reactions?

Children can be conditioned not to wet the bed?

The so-called "lie-detector" doesn't really detect lies?

A person with an abnormal fear (called a "phobia") can sometimes be helped by the same sort of conditioning techniques Pavlov used with his dogs?

The most effective forms of therapy usually involve changes in attitudes and emotional responses as well as changes in behavior?

"You see, I'm really here only because my wife wanted me to come," Hans Larsen said to his therapist, Dr. Roberta Turner. "I have this little problem, I guess. Not really a problem exactly, just my own way of doing things. It doesn't hurt anybody but me, so what's the difference? I mean, what's to get excited about? Do you see what I mean?"

A spark of veiled amusement lit up Dr. Turner's dark brown eyes. "No, Mr. Larsen, I don't see. Yet. But I'm sure I will if you tell me more about it."

"Well, it's a sort of very personal problem, if you know what I mean. Nothing really abnormal, or anything like that. But it cuts close to the skin, and I'm not exactly eager to talk about it. Really, when you stop to think about it, it's more my wife's problem than my own." Larsen ran his hand nervously through his pale blond hair. "Yes, that's it. My wife just isn't very understanding or cooperative, and that's the truth."

"But your wife insisted that you come talk to me, so she must think it's your difficulty and not hers. So why don't you tell me more about what's troubling the two of you?"

Larsen began to sweat a little. "Gee, you know, some things are very personal. Now, don't take this wrong, because I don't want to hurt your feelings. But . . . I mean, isn't there a **male** doctor I could talk to? I mean, there are some things . . ."

Dr. Turner smiled reassuringly. "Mr. Larsen, I can't blame you for being reluctant to talk about sexual matters. But don't you think that women are often more understanding of a man's sexual problems than other men are? And I'm sure that you're right in thinking that, whatever difficulty you face, it's as much your wife's responsibility as yours. So just relax for a moment, lean back in your chair and get comfortable, and then see if you don't want to tell me what's troubling you."

Larsen looked at the woman sharply, then followed her suggestion. A deep sigh escaped his lips as he let himself go limp. Moments later, he began to talk.

"I don't satisfy her. I guess that's the heart of the matter. At least, I can't usually make it, well, **worthwhile** for her without a little something extra to turn me on." His voice softened to a whisper. "I guess if I told you how screwed up I really am, you would be pretty shocked."

"It depends on what it takes 'to turn you on.' The last man I worked with was impotent unless he took his teddy bear to bed with him along with his wife. Somehow I doubt that's your difficulty, however," she said, her eyes laughing just a little.

"You're kidding me! About the teddy bear, I mean."

"No, not at all."

"Well, maybe I'm not so bad off as I thought. And it's not that I **have** to have them, it's just that it's usually better that way . . ."

"Have what?"

"The whips. That's the way it is with me, you see. I like the touch of a whip when it's bedtime. The cutting edge, you might say. Gives me the power to get up and go, stirs my blood a bit. So when we got married, I bought my wife a couple of small whips—tiny ones, really—and asked her to use them on me. At first, she didn't want to. Hurt her more than it did me, she said. And then she gave in for a while and tried them, and it was good, very good indeed."

Larsen paused, as if remembering those times. "But now, she's read a book or something, and she says I'm a masochist, and I need help." He spat it out like a dirty word, MASS-oh-kist. "I guess that's pretty unusual, isn't it? A guy who needs pain to get sexually excited."

"It's a great deal more common than you probably realize. Pick up any of the underground newspapers and see how many 'personal' ads talk about whips and leather clothes and 'the need to be disciplined.' Or stroll through the Soho area of London and see how many prostitutes put up cards on their doorways that advertise 'Swedish discipline' or 'spankings' as their stock in trade. And we may be able to give you more help than you presently suspect."

Larsen's voice quickened. "Gee, do you really think so? I mean, this book my wife read, it says I feel guilt and anxiety because I unconsciously think sex is dirty and that I'm a prude at heart. So I've got to be punished first, to pay in advance for my sinful pleasures, or I can't relax and do what comes naturally. Is that what you think?"

"Mr. Larsen, there are many different views on what causes masochism. Your attitudes and behavioral mannerisms are largely determined by your genes, your past experience, and the environment you presently live in. As far as we know, masochism isn't an inherited tendency, so we can pretty well rule out physiological causes. But there may very well be a 'masochistic personality.' Some therapists believe that the real problem is sadism—or the desire to hurt other people. According to this view, people who cannot tolerate the thought of hurting others may turn their desires inward; they hold their own hostile impulses in check by desiring to be hurt by others. Many psychologists believe masochism is often related to castration anxiety, that the man invites his wife to hurt him slightly as a way of warding off her attempts to castrate him. Still others think the problem is basically one of being trained to like or accept pain when you are very young. You can come to tolerate a great deal of pain if you're conditioned to do so."

Larsen shook his head, as if he had too much to consider. "What do you believe, Doctor?"

"There's a great deal to be said for all those views, and just because one is right doesn't mean that the others are wrong. The important thing is finding some way to help you change your style of life, to help you grow into the happier sort of person I'm sure you can become. You are not merely 'the sum of all your yesterdays.' You are also the 'possibility of all your tomorrows.' Some types of therapy focus on understanding your past; other therapies are oriented toward helping you change your future."

"Which would be best for me?"

"Ideally, we'd want to do both at the same time. Masochism is sometimes just a symptom of some deeper problem, some unconscious anxiety that needs to be uncovered if you're to make the best adjustment and avoid similar difficulties in the future. In recent years, however, psychologists have learned that many types of masochism are the result of improper learning or conditioning when the person is young. In these cases, the newer 'conditioning therapies' can often be of help, particularly if we also try to find out what caused your love of pain to begin with, and if we try to help you achieve greater personal growth and self-actualization as well."

"How does this conditioning stuff of yours work? Do you have to whip me, or something?" Larsen's voice was quite eager.

"No, we assume that some time early in your life, you were rewarded for hurting yourself or being hurt by someone else. Probably there were sexual overtones to the experience, and that's how you were shaped into needing pain to stimulate you. Perhaps your mother caught you playing with yourself and punished you for it, and now sexual stimuli elicit an anxiety reaction instead of the normal response. Or perhaps one time you were terrified of something that involved sexuality or your own sex organs, and you got hurt, and somehow the anxiety was greatly reduced. Then pain would become associated in your mind with fear-reduction. If your parents taught you that sex was dirty, then any form of sexual activity would cause you considerable fear that pain might help relieve. All this conditioning surely happened when you were so young that you don't remember it clearly now."

"How do we start? Do I lie on a couch, or something? Or maybe a bed of nails?"

Dr. Turner laughed. "No, we'll talk about the origins of your masochism later on. But first, you will have to decide what you most urgently need help with right now."

Larsen groaned, as if experiencing some kind of intra-psychic anguish. "I guess my wife comes first."

"All right, would you like to see if we can retrain you so that you can enjoy sexual pleasure with your wife without having to suffer pain first?"

A shrewd look came over Larsen's pale face. "Couldn't we just train my wife to be a sadist? I mean, wouldn't that be just as quick?"

Again Dr. Turner laughed. "She might not consider that a form of 'self-actualization' on her part. Anyway, do you really want to have to carry those little whips around with you wherever you go, Mr. Larsen? Doesn't the narrow-ness of your masochism limit you tremendously? And doesn't it make you just a little bit anxious that some stranger might find out about it?"

"Yeah, I guess you're right. But what do we do first?"

"First, we teach you how to relax, and how to listen to your body. You see, pain has become a conditioning stimulus or signal for sexual arousal in your case. If you skip the whips, you probably become nervous about whether or not you'll be able to perform sexually, am I correct?"

Larsen blushed, then began to sweat a little. Very quietly he said, "Yeah, you got it right."

"Well, anxiety is controlled by your sympathetic nervous system. That's the part of your body that handles excitement. Unfortunately, erection is controlled by your parasympathetic nervous system, that part of your body which is involved in relaxation."

"So you're saying that I can't do my wife much good unless I'm relaxed?"

"At the beginning of things, yes. And the more anxious you become about not being able to perform, the more your sympathetic nervous system turns on and the more difficult it is for the parasympathetic system to do its job."

"Yeah, that makes sense, in a strange kind of way." Larsen wiped his brow with a much-stained white handkerchief.

"So we teach you how to handle your anxiety by learning how to relax. Then we'll make a list of all the situations that make you tense, beginning with things that aren't really all that disturbing and working up to things that make you break out in a cold sweat even just thinking about them.''

''We'll make a little list, eh?''

''That's right. And then, when we've taught you how to differentiate between the signals your body gives your mind when you're relaxed and those your body gives when it's tense, you'll know how to relax whenever you want to. Next, we'll start talking about the items on that list, one at a time, starting with the simplest and working up to the most disturbing. If we can teach you to think or talk about these things while you're calm and cool and collected, then they won't make you very anxious any more. And if you aren't anxious . . .''

''. . . then I can take care of my wife without needing the whips, you mean.''

''That's right.''

Larsen pondered the matter for a long time. ''Well, I guess it might work. How do we begin?''

Dr. Turner smiled. ''It's simple. First, stretch out your legs and make them as rigid and as tense as you can. Go ahead, do it now. Do you feel the tension?''

''Sure. It kind of hurts a little.''

''That's good. Now, relax your legs completely. Just let go, let go completely. Relax your feet and your ankles and your knees and your thigh muscles. There. Now tense them up again and hold it for a few seconds. Now, relax again. Just go completely limp. Now, can you tell the difference between tension and relaxation?''

''Gee, I sure can. There's a world of difference.''

''Good. Next, we'll do the same thing with your arms, and then with your head and neck muscles. We want to get you to the point where you can command your body to relax any time you want to, and the muscles in your body will respond automatically. And we want to train your mind to recognize the feedback signals from your muscles so that you can discriminate between tension and relaxation. That way, you can relax if the feedback tells you that you're tense. We want to bring your bodily processes under your voluntary control.''

''If I could do that . . .''

''Then your immediate problem would be solved, and you could go on to find out how the masochism got started, and how to avoid such things in the future.''

Larsen shook his head doubtfully. ''That sounds like a really painful process.''

''I thought you liked pain, Mr. Larsen.''

The man suddenly smiled. ''You've got a deal!''

(Continued on page 328.)

Patellar reflex (pat-TELL-are). The patella is the knee bone. If you strike your leg just below this bone, the lower part of your leg will jerk. This "knee-jerk," or patellar reflex, is an automatic, unconscious response over which you have little volitional control.

Patellar tendon (TEN-dun). The cord of tough tissue connecting the patella with a bone in the lower leg. When struck, this tendon sets off the patellar reflex, or knee-jerk.

Some time about the beginning of this century, a pleasant young man named E.B. Twitmyer began work on his doctoral dissertation in psychology at the University of Pennsylvania. Twitmyer was interested in innate reflexes—those automatic behavior patterns that are wired into our brain circuits by our genetic blueprints.

During the late 1800's, neurophysiologists all around the world were just beginning to get a vague idea how the human nervous system actually works, and one of their chief tools for mapping out the functions of the brain were the reflexes. For instance, the first scientific reports ever published on the *patellar reflex* (°), or knee-jerk, did not appear until 1875. For more than 30 years thereafter, noted physiologists here and in Europe raged at each other concerning the neural mechanism by which this reflex operates.

You can elicit the patellar reflex in either of your legs rather simply. When you are sitting down, cross one leg on top of the other, leaving your uppermost leg hanging freely. Now, reach down with the edge of your hand and strike this leg smartly just below the kneecap. At this point, your *patellar tendon* (°) runs close to the surface of the skin. Whenever you tap on this tendon, the lower half of your leg swings forward involuntarily.

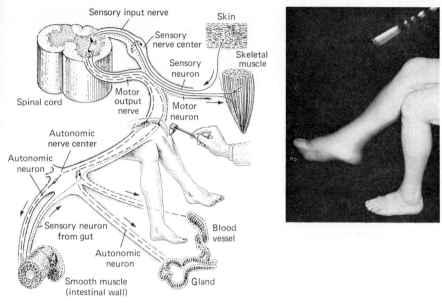

The patellar reflex, or knee-jerk.

But why should your leg move reflexively when you stimulate this tendon? The early neurophysiologists couldn't agree on the answer. Some thought that when you hit the tendon, it pulled directly on the muscles and your leg twitched. Other scientists believed that the sensory receptors in the tendon sent a message back to the spinal cord—and up to the brain—and the motor output center in the cortex responded by ordering the muscles in the leg to jump. Thanks to research by Twitmyer and many other scientists, we now know that the patellar reflex involves the nervous system, and that the tendon doesn't pull directly on the muscles when hit.

Twitmyer's Experiment Twitmyer was interested in how the patellar reflex operates for a very good reason: Medical doctors could often use the reflex for diagnostic purposes. If an intact spinal cord were necessary for the reflex to appear in its normal form (as turned out to be the case), an abnormal patellar response would suggest to the physician that the patient had suffered damage to the spinal cord.

Twitmyer believed that the patellar reflex might be influenced by the emotional or motivational state the person was in when the reflex was elicited. So he rigged up a small hammer that would strike the subject's patellar tendon when he let the hammer fall. Twitmyer didn't bother telling his subjects when he was about to stimulate their reflexes—he merely dropped the hammer and measured how far their legs jerked. His subjects were other students at Penn, and they soon complained that the hammer blow often caught them unaware. Couldn't he ring a bell or something like that as a warning, so that they wouldn't be surprised? Twitmyer agreed, and began sounding a signal to announce the hammer drop.

As you might guess would happen, one day when Twitmyer was working with a subject whose knee had been hit hundreds of times, Twitmyer accidentally sounded the warning signal without dropping the hammer. As promptly as clockwork, the subject's leg jerked despite the fact that his tendon hadn't been stimulated. Although Twitmyer didn't realize it at the time, he had discovered the conditioned reflex, a response pattern upon which a dozen different psychological theories would later be built.

Twitmyer did appreciate the fact that he was on to something important,

E.B. Twitmyer.

Pavlov's first experiments at the physiological department of the Soviet Military Medicine Academy.

however, and he dropped his original thesis plans in order to investigate his discovery. He established some of the conditions under which this new type of reflex occurred, and reported his findings at the 1904 meeting of the American Psychological Association. Sadly enough, Twitmyer was years ahead of his time, and the psychologists to whom he spoke paid no attention at all to what he had to say. E.B. Twitmyer, discouraged by the frosty reception his ideas received, failed to pursue his findings and was little heard of afterward. And so, credit for the discovery of the conditioned reflex passed by default to the famous Russian physiologist, Ivan Pavlov.

PAVLOV'S CONDITIONAL RESPONSE

Pavlov, who lived from 1849 to 1936, was perhaps the most famous scientist that Russia ever produced. After taking his medical degree in 1883, he traveled in Europe, studying with various other scientists, and in 1890 founded the Institute of Experimental Medicine in Leningrad which he directed the rest of his life. His early interests were in digestion, and he chose dogs for his experimental animals. He trained the dogs to lie quietly on operating tables while he studied what went on inside their digestive tracts before and after they had eaten a meal. His experiments proved for the first time that the nervous system coordinates all the digestive responses. For his efforts, he was awarded the Nobel Prize in 1904, the first Russian to be so honored.

As we mentioned earlier, digestion actually begins in the mouth. As part of his later research, Pavlov found a way to measure the amount of saliva that the glands in the dog's mouth produced. While the dog was in a harness, he would give food to the dog, then count the number of drops of saliva that these glands secreted. Dogs do not have to be trained to salivate when given food—they do so reflexively, or automatically. Salivation is therefore an innate *response* or reflex elicited by the *stimulus* of food in the mouth.

Pavlov wanted to determine the neural pathways that connected the stimulus-receptors in the dog's mouth with the salivary glands, but his research was often interrupted by peculiar responses the animals would make. Inexperienced dogs would typically lie quietly in the harness he had prepared for them and would secrete saliva only when the food had actually been popped into their mouths. However, after an animal had been around the laboratory for a while, and

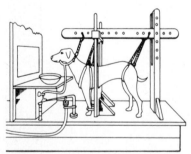

Pavlov's experimental arrangement.

had gotten accustomed to being fed in the harness, the animal's salivary glands would often "juice up" if one of Pavlov's assistants merely rattled the food dishes in the laboratory sink or walked toward the dog carrying a plate.

Pavlov called these "unusual" reactions *psychic stimulations* (°), and they infuriated him because they got in the way of his regular research. He did his best to ignore them because he wasn't interested in anything "psychological." However, the psychic stimulations refused to go away. And so, in 1901, Pavlov began to study them systematically, hoping he could thereby get rid of these annoyances. He told his friends that this work surely wouldn't take more than a year or two, but he spent the rest of his life determining the properties of these "stimulations."

Conditional Stimuli and Responses

If you blow food powder into a dog's mouth, the animal will salivate. You don't have to train a dog to salivate when given food; the response is innate. Pavlov called the food an *unconditional* or *unconditioned stimulus* (UCS) (°), because its ability to elicit or evoke the *unconditional* or *unconditioned response* (UCR) (°) was reflexive or instinctual and not dependent upon the "condition" of learning. We might diagram the situation like this:

$$UCS \xrightarrow{\text{(innate S-R connection)}} UCR$$
$$\text{(Food)} \qquad\qquad\qquad\qquad \text{(Salivation)}$$

One of the first things that Pavlov discovered in his research was this—if he sounded a musical tone just before he blew the food into the animal's mouth, the dog would soon come to salivate almost as much to the music alone as it would to the tone plus the food powder. Apparently the animal *learned to associate* the sound of the music with the stimulus of the food; therefore, the musical tone became a "dinner bell" that let the dog anticipate that it would be fed. (In more technical terms, we can say that a stimulus-response, or S-R, connection has been formed in the animal's brain.) Pavlov called the tone a *conditional* or *conditioning stimulus* (°), because its power to *elicit*, or call forth, the salivation response was "conditional" upon its being paired with the food powder a number of times. After the two stimulus inputs had been paired frequently enough, the music became a conditioned stimulus, which we will abbreviate as CS. (Since psychologists tend to use these abbreviations frequently, it might pay you to learn to use them too.)

$$CS \xrightarrow{\text{(learned through repetition)}} UCS \xrightarrow{\text{(innate)}} UCR$$
$$\text{(tone)} \qquad\qquad\qquad\qquad \text{(food)} \qquad\quad \text{(salivation)}$$

The more frequently the tone (CS) was presented just before the food (UCS), the more drops of saliva (UCR) the CS would elicit. After the CS had been paired with the UCS seven or eight times, the dog was *conditioned* (to use Pavlov's term) to respond to the CS much as it did innately to the UCS. At this point, the UCR can be called a *conditional* or *conditioned response* (°), or CR, because the CS (tone) can elicit the response even though the UCS (food) is not presented.

$$CS \longrightarrow UCS \longrightarrow UCR \xrightarrow{\hspace{2cm}} CR$$
$$\text{(tone)} \qquad \text{(food)} \qquad \text{(salivation)} \qquad \text{(slightly less salivation)}$$

(learned S-R connection)

Pavlov made a number of other interesting discoveries. Conditioned responses (or "conditioned reflexes," as they are sometimes called) were often fairly easy to establish, but they usually were unlearned just as easily. If, after the CS-CR connection between the musical tone and salivation had been made, Pavlov presented the tone (CS) for several trials without giving the dog food (UCS), the

Psychic stimulations. Pavlov's original name for the conditioned response or conditioned reflex.

Unconditioned stimulus. Also called "unconditional stimulus." Abbreviated UCS. You are born with certain innate responses, such as the patellar reflex. These reflexes are set off (elicited) by innately determined (unconditioned or unlearned) stimuli. The blow to your patellar tendon is an unconditioned stimulus that elicits the unconditioned response we call the knee-jerk.

Unconditioned response. Also called "unconditional response." Abbreviated UCR. Any innately determined response pattern or reflex that is set off by a UCS. The knee-jerk is a UCR.

Conditional stimulus. Also called "conditioning stimulus" or "conditioned stimulus." Abbreviated CS. The CS is the "neutral" or "unusual" stimulus which, through frequent pairings with an unconditioned stimulus, acquires the ability to elicit an unconditioned response.

Conditioned response. Also referred to as "conditional response." Abbreviated CR. Any reaction set off by a CS. A bright light (UCS) flashed in your eye causes your pupil to contract (UCR). If someone frequently rings a bell (CS) just before turning on the bright light (UCS), the sound of the bell (CS) would soon gain the power to make your pupil contract. Once this conditioning has taken place, the UCR (contraction) becomes a CR that can be elicited by the CS. Since pupil contraction can now be set off either by the CS or the UCS, the contractive response is both a CR and a UCR. In many cases, however, the CR looks slightly different from the UCR.

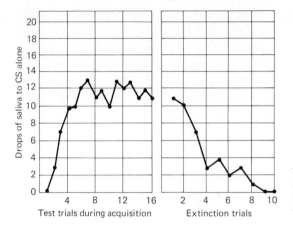

The charts show first the acquisition of conditioned salivation in a trained dog, and then extinction.

Extinguish. To reduce the frequency of a learned response either by withdrawing the reward that was used during training, or by presenting the CS many times without the UCS. The difference between these two types of extinction training will be more understandable after you read Chapter 16.

animal would salivate less and less on each trial until finally the response *extinguished* (°) completely (*see* Chapter 5). If he again paired the CS and the UCS for a second set of training trials, the CR appeared much more quickly than it had the first time round. Apparently the original conditioning had left a trace or "neural groove" on the cortex that made subsequent learning easier.

Pavlov found too that the CS had to be presented immediately *before* the onset of the UCS (half a second is usually considered the optimal or best interval). If the CS ended several seconds prior to the beginning of the UCS, little learning occurred, presumably because the UCS became associated with other stimuli that appeared accidentally between the offset of the CS and the onset of the UCS. Pavlov also discovered that the passage of time could act as a conditioning stimulus. When he fed his dogs regularly each half-hour, they began to salivate a few seconds before the next feeding even though there were no external stimuli such as dish rattles to give them cues that it was almost time to eat.

QUESTION: Pavlov believed that the mere pairing of the CS and the UCS was sufficient for conditioning to occur, whether or not the subject wished to learn or found the experience rewarding. Look back over the past couple of pages. How many times have the terms "CS" and "conditioned stimulus" been paired? Are the two terms now associated in your mind? The next time you watch television, look closely at the commercials. Do the advertisers seem to be using Pavlovian techniques in trying to get you to like or purchase their products?

Pavlov's Masochistic Dog

Pavlov believed that learning was always accompanied by the establishment of new neural connections in the brain—a position held by most psychologists today. Having made this initial point, Pavlov then moved into the field of mental health. He trained a dog to withstand extremely painful stimuli by using a "step-by-step" conditioning technique.

First, Pavlov carefully marked off an area of skin on the dog's front leg. Then he stimulated this area with a weakly painful CS—and immediately gave the dog some food. The UCR of salivation appeared to *inhibit* or suppress any avoidance response the animal might have made to the tiny amount of pain.

Then, day after day, Pavlov carefully increased the intensity of the painful CS, each time pairing it with food that the dog eagerly anticipated. At no time did the animal respond as if it were being hurt. Indeed, the dog seemed more than willing to be put in the training harness and given the pain—since the pain soon became a conditioned signal that the food would shortly be forthcoming.

Once the dog was fully trained, it would passively withstand incredible amounts of painful stimulation delivered to its front leg. However, if Pavlov

applied the painful CS to any other part of the dog's body, the animal would instantly set up a great howl and attempt to escape from its training harness. Pavlov concluded that when he touched the CS to the dog's front leg, the animal did not in fact *feel* any pain because all responses except salivation were suppressed by the strength of the CS (pain)-CR (salivation) neural bond. Apparently in dogs, as well as in humans, "You can't do more than one thing at a time."

Pavlov's attempts to create a *masochistic* (°) dog were repeated successfully many years afterward by a handful of scientists in the United States. Pavlov's experimental subjects were usually restrained; the animals used in the U.S. studies were not. Some of these animals learned to approach an experimenter and "ask" to be stimulated "painfully," while others acquired the habit of giving themselves "painful" stimulation in order to get food from an automatic dispenser. Even when not particularly hungry, these animals would often approach the experimental apparatus "of their own free will," cause the pain to be delivered to their bodies, and then eat the food. The parallel between these animals and those humans who seek out pain or humiliation in order to gain pleasure (often sexual) is rather remarkable. But as important as these experiments might have been to the discovery of a cure for masochism in humans, the animal work was regarded with considerable distaste by most scientists.

Discrimination and Generalization

Perhaps the most interesting experiment Pavlov conducted had to do with *discrimination training* (°). Pavlov began by showing a dog a drawing of a circle, then giving it food immediately. Very soon the dog became conditioned to salivate whenever a circle appeared before its eyes. Pavlov then tested the animal by showing it drawings of figures such as an ellipse, a pentagon, a square, a rectangle, a triangle, and a star. He found that the salivary response *generalized* to stimuli other than the original CS (the circle). As you might guess, this *generalization* (°) followed a specific pattern—the more like a circle the other figure was, the more the animal salivated. He then trained the dog to *discriminate* between the two stimuli by always giving the dog food when the circle appeared, but never giving the animal a reward when the ellipse was presented. Soon the dog came to salivate only when the circle was shown.

> QUESTION: If a man eats chop suey for the first time and doesn't like it, then refuses even to try any other type of Chinese food, is he showing discrimination or generalization?

After Pavlov had established that his experimental dog could discriminate between a circle and an ellipse, he tried to fool the animal. On subsequent trials, he presented the dog with ellipses that were closer and closer to being completely round. Eventually the animal's nervous system was strained to the breaking point, for the animal simply could not perceive the difference between the positive CS (the circle) and the negative CS (the ellipse). Overcome by the stress of conflict, the animal broke down, snapped at Pavlov and his assistants, barked loudly, urinated and defecated, and tried very hard to get out of the restraining harness. If a human being had displayed the same behavior patterns, we probably would call the person *neurotic*. (°)

How different these two "mental health" experiments were! In the first case, an animal learned to suppress considerable pain and behaved normally. In the second, even though it was given no painful stimulation at all, the dog reacted as if it had been badly hurt. These two studies convinced Pavlov that "mental illness" was learned and was mostly a matter of mixed-up brain signals. (Pavlov took a purely biological view toward the causes of mental illness; as we will see in later chapters, there are intra-psychic and environmental influences that are at least as important as the neurological factors in causing mental illness.)

Masochistic (mass-oh-KISS-tick). Masochism (MASS-oh-kiss-em) is a sexual deviation in which pleasure is derived from pain. The pain may be psychological or physical, and may be self-inflicted or inflicted by others. The term comes from the name of the Austrian novelist Leopold V. Sacher-Masoch, whose stories frequently featured scenes in which sexual pleasure was associated with painful stimulus inputs.

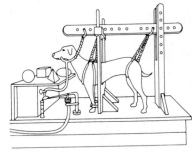

A dog in Pavlov's harness learns to discriminate between shapes.

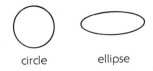

circle   ellipse

Discrimination training. Teaching an animal to discriminate—that is, to react differently to fairly similar stimuli. If you can tell the difference between two things, you know how to discriminate between them.

Generalization (jen-ur-al-eye-ZAY-shun). Stimulus generalization is the tendency to make the same response to two similar stimuli. If a monkey has been trained to lift its right paw when you turn on an orange light, it may also lift its paw when you turn on a yellow or a red light. Response generalization is the tendency to make a slightly different reaction to the same stimulus. If you hold down the monkey's right paw when you turn on the orange light, the response may generalize to the left paw instead.

Neurotic (new-ROT-tick). Abnormal or unusual behavior patterns are sometimes referred to as being "neurotic." A neurosis (new-ROW-sis) is a mild form of mental illness. As we will see in Chapter 24, however, psychologists do not agree on the causes and cures of neurotic behaviors.

H.S. Liddell.

Several years afterward, similar experiments on sheep and goats were undertaken by the U.S. psychologist H.S. Liddell at Cornell University. Liddell, too, was able to establish what was called *experimental neurosis* (°) in his animals by training them under conditions of considerable stress. Once this neurosis had set in, the animals became highly upset and agitated whenever they were brought into the laboratory for a training session, even after a passage of several years. Liddell pointed out that this "neurotic response" did not develop unless the animals had first become accustomed to a very boring routine and had become emotionally dependent on the investigator.

QUESTION: Were Liddell's "neurotic" sheep and goats externalizers or internalizers?

Masserman's Neurotic Monkeys

A U.S. psychiatrist, Jules Masserman, who did much of his work at Northwestern University, performed similar experiments with monkeys. He began by conditioning the monkeys to react to a bell by pressing a lever that opened a plastic box containing a food reward. Once the learning bond had been well established, he added something new. Whenever the monkey would reach into the box to get the food, Masserman showed it a toy snake that always frightened the monkey considerably.

Now the animal was in conflict. It could respond to the bell either by opening the box and reaching for the food or by ignoring the signal and staying hungry. Masserman reports that the monkeys soon developed autonomic *alarm reactions* (*see* Chapter 14). Their hair stood on end; their pupils opened wide; their pulse, breathing rate, and blood pressure increased markedly; they went into fits of trembling; and they became abnormally frightened of strange sounds and enclosed spaces. Many of them developed *diarrhea* (°) and stomach upsets. Some of the monkeys started pacing their cages incessantly, while others sat rigidly immobile or slept constantly.

Masserman noted many forms of aberrant or unusual sexual activity in these animals, too. Some became aggressively homosexual; others masturbated constantly; while some of the monkeys became totally asexual. Masserman points out that similar response patterns are found in humans who lapse into neurosis when motivational conflicts become too great for them to handle.

From Pavlov's very limited view, all organisms were passive. They lived out their lives waiting for some stimulus to come along and *elicit* a response from them. Pavlov insisted that learning was merely the establishment of new neural bonds or pathways between stimulus inputs and motor outputs. Many of these stimuli were *proprioceptive* (°), or internal, and many of the responses involved the autonomic nervous system and hence were not ordinarily available to conscious observation. But learning was always the building up of a "neural bond" between an S and an R.

Like most S-R theorists, Pavlov believed that all forms of behavior—including what most people would call "thinking" and "feeling" and "problem-solving"— were learned and were under the control of stimulus events. He saw humans as being *plastic* (°), or infinitely changeable by the environment into which the person was born. Given the proper environment, a man or woman could be conditioned into being a happy and productive worker, or could be enslaved by circumstances. When the Communists took over the Russian government in 1917 and 1918, they found Pavlov's rather mechanistic view of human nature most sympathetic to their own, because it suggested that the peasant-farmers, who then made up most of the Russian population, could rapidly be re-educated if only the proper S-R connections could be made in their brains. So the Communists kept Pavlov on as Director of the Institute at Leningrad and gave him funds and a free hand to do whatever he wished.

Experimental neurosis (new-ROW-sis). An abnormal or unusual behavior pattern brought about under controlled or laboratory situations, usually in animal subjects. Many psychologists see close parallels between the neurotic responses of animals and similar neurotic reactions in humans. Other psychologists believe that the conditioned neurosis that can be established in animals must be quite different from the type of "neurosis" that appears in humans.

Diarrhea (die-uh-REE-uh). From the Greek words meaning "to flow through." When food flows through your digestive system too rapidly, you suffer from diarrhea, or having to defecate too often. Also called "the trots."

Proprioceptive (pro-pree-oh-SEP-tive). Feedback messages from receptors in your muscles, glands, and internal organs that let you know what your body is doing are called "proprioceptive stimuli."

Plastic (PLASS-tick). From the Greek word meaning "formed" or "shaped." As used in psychology, the term means "changeable," or "capable of learning."

CONDITIONING THERAPIES

Enuresis (en-your-EE-sis). A fancy name for bed-wetting.

One of the first U.S. psychologists to use conditioning as a therapeutic technique was O.H. Mowrer who, in 1938, suggested a new type of "cure" for the age-old problem of *enuresis* (°), or bed-wetting. The bladder is under the control of the autonomic nervous system. During toilet training, the child learns to bring its natural tendencies to urinate and defecate under voluntary or conscious control. It must learn to pay attention to the proprioceptive signals or feedback coming from its bladder and bowels to inhibit its urges to relieve itself except under certain socially-approved circumstances. Such conditioning obviously involves *discrimination*—the child must learn to pay attention to some internal stimuli and to ignore others, and to determine which environmental stimuli (that is, bathroom fixtures) are appropriate CS's for certain of its bodily responses. The bed-wetting or enuretic child typically has voluntary control of bladder and bowels when awake, but seems to lose control when asleep (primarily during REM sleep).

Most of us have learned to listen to the signals that our bodies give us. Therefore, in most people, the proprioceptive feedback or inputs from a full bladder act as a CS that elicits the CR of waking up and going to the bathroom. Mowrer believed that the enuretic child simply hadn't made this CS-CR connection, so he devised an apparatus to help train the child to gain control. He put tiny electrical wires in a thin cloth pad that could go under the bottom sheet on the child's bed. These wires were connected to a loud bell near the child's head. Whenever the child urinated while asleep, the urine (which is a good electrical conductor) closed the circuit that rang the bell, waking the child up. Although the amount of current involved was so small that the child received no electrical shock to its body, being rudely aroused in the middle of the night was often so distressing that the unconscious parts of the child's brain often "learned" to heed the signals coming from the bladder and woke the young person up before an accident could occur. Mowrer's device was an effective training tool for many children, but failed miserably with others.

QUESTION: **Why might Mowrer's device not work very well with a child who experienced no fear or anxiety when awakened by the bell?**

Watson and Little Albert

Once an organism has been conditioned or *sensitized* to fear a given CS, the arousal response often is evoked by any stimuli similar to the CS. In one of John B. Watson's most famous experiments, he and an assistant named Rayner taught a child named Albert to become afraid of a gentle and placid white rat. At the beginning of the study, Albert was unafraid of the animal and played with it freely. While he was doing so one day, the experimenters frightened the boy by sounding a terrifying noise behind him. Albert was unpleasantly startled and began to cry. Thereafter, he avoided the rat and would begin to wail if it was brought close to him. In Pavlovian terms, a bond or connection had been set up between the sight of the rat (CS) and the arousal of Albert's autonomic nervous system (CR). Once this S-R bond was fixed, the fear response could also be elicited by showing Albert any furry object.

Fears *generalize* to stimuli similar to the CS. Fear or anxiety also generalizes to any random or accidental stimulus cues that happen to be present when the conditioning or sensitization takes place. The burnt child not only dreads the fire, it also fears stoves, pots and pans, ovens, salt and pepper shakers (if they were on the stove when it got burnt), pictures of flames, and even stories about the great Chicago fire.

Jules Masserman.

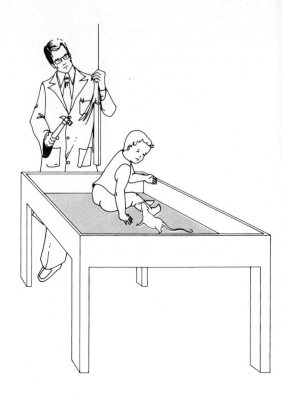

John B. Watson conditioned "Little Albert" to fear a rat by striking a metal gong loudly whenever the animal approached the boy.

The Polygraph

Words are stimuli as much as are bells or musical tones. If you were chased by a bull when you were young, you would probably still show some autonomic arousal if you were forced to enter a pen containing a pawing, snorting, long-horned Brahmin bull. But you would also show somewhat smaller autonomic arousal if you merely read the word "bull," or saw a picture of one, or were asked to think about one. We could measure this fear reaction in you by attaching you to a *polygraph* (°), a machine often called a "lie-detector." The polygraph would record your pulse, blood pressure, breathing rate, and the amount of perspiration secreted by the cells in the palms of your hands (or feet).

As you know by now, arousal of your sympathetic nervous system would lead to an increase in sweating, an acceleration in heart rate, and a change in the way that you breathe. If we showed you an emotionally neutral stimulus, your

Polygraph (PAHL-ee-graff). *Poly* means "many." A polygraph is a machine that makes a graph of many different responses simultaneously. Sometimes called a "lie-detector," but it records emotional responses, not "lies."

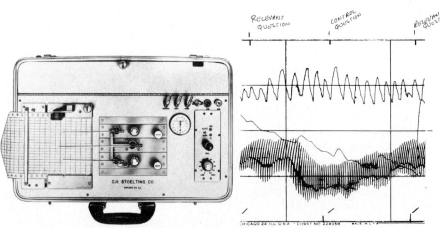

A polygraph machine and record; the midpoint indicates a control question.

polygraph record would remain calm and regular. If we then presented you with a picture of a large bull, or said the word aloud, the graph would note a sudden, sharp increase in autonomic activity and we would *assume* that you had experienced some emotion such as fear, anxiety, or guilt.

The polygraph is an *emotion detector*, not a lie-detector. It is useful to police agents because suspected criminals often lie about their guilt and are afraid of being found out. For instance, suppose that a victim has been murdered by being strangled with a silk scarf of an unusual color. Presumably only the murderer would recognize the scarf. The police might show this scarf (or a picture of it) to several suspects, all of whom might deny ever having seen the scarf before. But if one of the suspects, while attached to the polygraph machine, showed a strong emotional reaction to the sight of the scarf, the police would be justified in questioning this suspect a little more thoroughly than those others whose polygraph records showed no autonomic arousal.

Polygraph recordings are often unreliable and hence are not admitted as evidence of guilt in a court of law. Some criminals feel no anxiety or guilt whatsoever concerning their crimes; if they lie about what they have done, their polygraph records will suggest innocence rather than guilt. On the other hand, a person may show violent emotional reactions to a stimulus such as a colorful scarf without having been in any way associated with any kind of crime.

The polygraph is, however, a useful psychological tool. For example, one of the problems that psycho-therapists often have is that patients will deny or suppress their true feelings. If the subject of sex arises during therapy, the patient may insist that he or she has no sexual problems or hang-ups, but a polygraph record made while the patient was talking might indicate that the word "sex" was indeed a CS for all kinds of autonomic arousal. A psychologist who monitored the patient's polygraph record continuously during therapy could easily determine what parts of the patient's life most needed working on. Use of the machine might also give the psychologist an indication of when the patient was making progress in bringing his or her suppressed feelings to the surface and learning to handle them.

COUNTER-CONDITIONING

Many forms of psycho-therapy are based on *breaking* S-R bonds instead of establishing new ones. Once Watson and Rayner had demonstrated (in 1920) that a child could be conditioned to fear furry things, it was even more important to show that fear conditioning could be "cured" using the same techniques that had caused it. In 1924, Mary Cover Jones did just that. She used a method now called *counter-conditioning* (*), which is based on the fact that you can't give two incompatible responses to the same CS.

Suppose, some time in the future, your own 2-year-old son accidentally became conditioned to fear small furry animals. You might try to cure the boy the way that Mary Cover Jones did. The sight of a white rat would presumably upset your son; but the sight of food when he was hungry surely would make him happy and eager to eat. You might begin by bringing a white rat into the same room with your son while you were feeding him. At first, you would want to keep the animal so far away from the child that he could barely notice it out of the corner of his eye. Since the animal wouldn't be close enough to bother him, he probably would keep right on eating. Then, step by step, you might bring the rat closer. (When Mary Cover Jones followed this procedure, she found that children soon learned to play with animals that had previously terrified them.)

In trying to describe what happened when you retrained your son, a psychologist would say that food was a UCS that elicited the pleasurable response of eating. The sight of the rat would be a CS that, through frequent pairings with the

Counter-conditioning. A psycho-therapeutic technique based on extinguishing inappropriate habits or breaking S-R (stimulus-response) bonds. If as a child you were frightened the first few times you saw a kitten, you might develop a lifelong fear of cats. The sight of a cat would become a CS that elicited a CR—such as fear, anxiety, or avoidance. This early conditioning can sometimes be countered by pairing a weak form of the CS with a strongly pleasant new UCS (money, food, love and affection).

UCS of food, would slowly become conditioned to the pleasurable reaction of eating. Since your son could not cry and eat at the same time, and since you'd never bring the rat close enough at any one time to elicit the crying reaction, the CS-CR fear response would gradually *extinguish*, while the strength of the CS-CR "pleasure of eating" bond was being built up.

The Case of Anne M. In a sense, Watson and Rayner created a phobia about rats in little Albert. *Phobias* (°) are intense, irrational fears about people, places, things, or situations; usually they are so strong that the person with the phobia cannot control his or her reactions even when the person clearly realizes that the fear is illogical and unreasonable. These *morbid dreads* (°) are often created almost overnight, from a single emotion-charged encounter with the object dreaded, or perhaps from a continuing series of highly unpleasant interactions.

As an example, consider the case of Anne M., a middle-aged woman living near Cleveland. In her early 40's, she was not married and lived with her mother, upon whom she was very dependent emotionally. One day, as Anne walked out their front door, she spied her mother crossing the street toward their house. Before the older woman could make it safely to the curb, she was struck and killed by a passing car—right before her daughter's eyes.

As a consequence of witnessing the death of her beloved mother, Anne developed a phobia about moving vehicles. She retreated to the security of the house and refused to come out. She closed the curtains on all the windows, for even the sight of an automobile or truck was enough to throw her into a violent panic reaction. Finally, her withdrawal from the rest of the world became so severe that she had to be hospitalized in a nearby mental institution.

Once in the hospital, Anne refused to leave. Her therapists assumed that part of her problem lay in guilt feelings she might have had concerning her mother's death. Intensive verbal explorations of her emotional dependence on her mother seemed to be of some help in relieving her general state of anxiety, but she still panicked whenever she as much as looked out of the hospital window and saw an automobile passing on the street.

Desensitization Therapy

At this point, two behavioral psychologists then at The University of Michigan, Dr. David Himle and Dr. Clayton Shorkey, attempted a form of counter-conditioning called *desensitization therapy* (°).

In their first talks with Anne M., Himle and Shorkey drew up a *hierarchy of fears* (°)—that is, a list of disturbing stimuli arranged in rank order from least to most frightening. The act of actually riding in an automobile was the most frightening thing Anne could think of. Getting into a parked automobile was somewhat less disturbing, so sitting in a car ranked lower on the hierarchy than did riding. Walking past a car was even less threatening, but was still more likely to induce panic than merely seeing a car or truck through a window. Playing with a toy car didn't seem to evoke any fear at all.

When Himle and Shorkey began their therapy, they first got Anne M. to relax as much as possible. Once she was quite comfortable, they asked her to imagine seeing a car out of the window. She soon got to the point where she could tolerate seeing a car "in her mind's eye" without feeling any anxiety at all. Then they got her to look out the window briefly, and got her to relax again. Soon Anne M. was able to look at cars out the window whenever she pleased. At that point, she had been conditioned to handle the lowest item on her fear hierarchy; for the stimulus of seeing a car through the window now elicited the conditioned response of relaxation rather than the conditioned response of panic.

Next, Himle and Shorkey asked her to imagine walking out the front door of

Phobias (FOE-bee-uz). From the Greek word for "fear." A phobia is a strong and often unusual fear of something.

Morbid dreads (MORE-bid). Gloomy or unhealthy feelings or fears. Morbid comes from the Latin and Greek words meaning "diseased."

Desensitization therapy (DEE-sen-suh-tie-ZAY-shun). When you acquire a conditioned fear of cats, you have become sensitized to cats and become anxious or afraid each time you see one. Desensitization therapy, as developed by Dr. Joseph Wolpe (WOHL-pee), involves training you to relax whenever you see a cat. Once this form of counter-conditioning is complete, your fear of cats will have been desensitized.

Hierarchy of fears (HIGHER-ark-key). To make a hierarchy is to list things (or people) in order of their importance. A hierarchy of fears, as used in desensitization therapy, is a list of dreaded stimuli running from the most feared to the least feared. Treatment usually begins by training the client to relax in the presence of the stimulus lowest on the hierarchy of fears. Once that stimulus has been desensitized, the next-highest stimulus is treated in the same way.

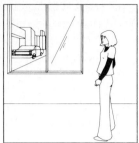

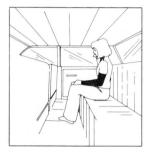

Hierarchy of fears used in desensitization therapy for reduction of fear of automobiles.

the building and approaching a car. Once she could manage this, they turned the thought into action and got her to leave the hospital building and actually touch a parked automobile outside. When she was relaxed enough to handle this real-life problem, they encouraged her to get inside the car, then to take a short ride. To help Anne M. imagine what each step in her desensitization would be like, Himle and Shorkey built a scale model of the hospital and its grounds. The model included all the streets and highways in that area. Anne learned to move the toy cars around the streets and, once she had "thought through" a given journey using the toy cars, she was able to make the same brief trip in a real automobile.

At the end of just 10 training sessions, Anne M. was driven out of the hospital grounds onto a nearby highway on a short excursion, a trip that caused her little or no discomfort. Thereafter, with no further therapy, Anne M. began taking part in more of the social activities on the ward, including short visits to points of interest near the hospital. Once she saw that she could tolerate these brief trips, she spontaneously began visiting friends who lived in nearby towns.

The final test of Anne's desensitization came when she was invited to spend a few days with some relatives who lived several hundred miles away. Anne had to make the trip by bus. When she felt she was relaxed enough to handle this experience (which might well have rated right at the top of her original hierarchy of fears), she packed her bag and caught the bus. Ironically, the vehicle broke down while on the expressway and Anne and the rest of the passengers had to sit by the side of the road for more than an hour while traffic buzzed furiously past them. However, Anne handled the situation without any panic and reached her destination safely. Thanks to the help of Drs. Himle and Shorkey, and of the staff at the hospital, Anne M. no longer had a phobic reaction to moving vehicles.

Curing a "Blood Phobia" S.H. Kraines has reported a somewhat simpler form of desensitization therapy involving a young medical student who feared the sight of blood. This young man, whom Kraines calls J.M., seriously considered giving up the study of medicine because each time he walked into the operating room, he keeled over in a dead faint. Kraines first attempted to determine the causes for this response and tried to change the boy's attitude toward medicine, but he also tried

Joseph Wolpe.

a step-by-step deconditioning treatment. J.M. was told to walk into the operating chamber during an operation and then immediately to walk out. On the second day J.M. went into the room, counted five, and then walked out. On the third day J.M. was told to stay a full minute before leaving. On subsequent days he stayed longer and longer. Two weeks later, when J.M. was supposed to stay but 10 minutes, he got so interested in the operation that he just stayed on until it was completed. Thereafter, Kraines reports, J.M. had no trouble at all, even when called on to assist in operations—his "blood phobia" appeared to be gone for good.

QUESTION: Some college students become so aroused and frightened when forced to take an examination that they become violently ill; how might desensitization therapy be used to help them?

Desensitization: Pro and Con

Phobic reactions usually involve some form of sensitization to stimuli that elicit autonomic arousal and muscular tension. A major part of desensitization therapy, therefore, consists in training the patient how to relax, the theory being that you can't very well be tense or aroused at the same time that you are physically limp as a wet rag. By alternately tensing and then relaxing your muscles, you can acquire the ability to relax at your own verbal or mental command. Once you have this skill at your fingertips, you can order the muscles in your body to relax even when you are faced with a mildly disturbing situation—such as the least-threatening stimulus on a fear hierarchy, if you happen to suffer from a phobia.

Dr. Joseph Wolpe, now at Temple University in Philadelphia, is usually given credit for having popularized desensitization training. Wolpe believes that the secret of its success comes from never overstimulating the patient or letting the phobic reaction get so aroused that it cannot be counteracted by the patient's state of muscular relaxation. Wolpe and his colleagues achieve this goal by always starting with the least-feared item on the hierarchy and by momentarily stopping treatment whenever the client shows even the slightest sign of distress.

Cognitive (°) and attitudinal changes often occur during desensitization training—that is, the patient often reports perceiving the once-feared situation in a new and less frightening light. Wolpe and many others believe that these perceptual changes *are the result of* learning to handle disturbing stimuli in a relaxed fashion, that the lack of muscular tension leads to or induces the shift in the patient's attitudes. Other therapists insist that Wolpe has put the cart before the horse, that the cognitive changes occur first and thereby allow the client to relax in the presence of the dreaded stimulus. As evidence, these critics cite research suggesting that one need not start at the bottom of the fear hierarchy and work up gradually to the most disturbing item; instead, one can pick items at random and expose the patient to them (as long as he or she doesn't become too disturbed by the procedure). Some studies show that purely mental relaxation may be as potent a curative agent as is muscular relaxation.

Psycho-analytically oriented therapists carry this argument even further. While admitting that desensitization therapy can be effective with simple phobic reactions that clearly are the result of one or two traumatic encounters with the feared object, psycho-analysts believe that many phobias represent a person's attempts to suppress or defend against inappropriate or threatening impulses. A woman who cannot make a normal heterosexual adjustment, for instance, might become phobic about or sensitized to pointed objects because they symbolize the male sexual organ to her. A young man who hates his parents and wants to kill them might develop a phobia about guns and knives. His fear then serves to keep him away from weapons that might be too handy if his hatred ever got out of control. Unfortunately, his phobia also serves to keep him from facing what the

Cognitive (COG-nuh-tive). Intellectual or perceptual processes are often called cognitive processes—as opposed to emotional processes.

analyst believes to be a basic flaw or weakness in his personality. The psycho-analytic view is that the phobia is simply a symptom of an underlying personality problem that cannot be helped or alleviated merely by curing the symptomatic behavior. The expectation is that if one merely cures the symptom without first changing the personality structure that gave rise to the phobic reaction, other and perhaps more devastating symptoms are bound to take its place. (As we will see in Chapter 25, there is not much research to support this view.)

Wolpe's response to these criticisms is twofold. To begin with, he believes that, in most if not all cases, the symptom is what really bothers the patient. A man may continue to have a morbid dread of guns and knives long after his parents are dead and buried. Talking through his hatred for the long-gone parents helps such a patient very little, Wolpe believes. In the second place, Wolpe holds that what the analysts call "the underlying problem" is typically an attitude or perception that was learned by the same laws of conditioning as is the phobic reaction. Men aren't born with an instinctive hatred of their parents; it takes years of careful training (usually on the part of the parents themselves) to achieve such results. If a therapist feels that a patient's perceptions of his or her parents should be changed, conditioning techniques offer a fast and reliable methodology for doing so.

Which Changes First: Attitudes or Behaviors?

Must you always change your attitudes first, if you want to change your behavior? Or do most attitudinal changes result from changing your behavior first? In retrospect, Wolpe and the psycho-analysts appear to be caught up in yet another battle over the "mind-body" problem discussed in earlier chapters. The truth seems to be that attitudes and behaviors change more or less simultaneously; it is difficult if not impossible to prove that a change in one always *causes* a change in the other.

Nor is there much sense in fighting over which form of therapy is best, since both the intra-psychic and the conditioning forms of treatment have their uses. Indeed, it is likely that psycho-analysts unconsciously make use of some forms of conditioning while treating their patients, although they may not realize that they are doing so. Likewise, Wolpe and other behavioral therapists have surely benefited from psycho-analytic and humanistic insights, although these research-ers may refuse to acknowledge their debts.

Desensitization, when it is effective, works so quickly that it might uniformly be tried as a kind of "psychic first aid" with most phobic patients. If desensitiza-tion helps the patient, well and good, but should one always stop with "first aid" no matter how effectively it removes the phobic symptoms? Shouldn't the patient also have the opportunity of gaining insight into his or her past experiences, or of working toward further interpersonal growth and self-actualization—if this is what the patient honestly desires? And what does one do in those cases where desensitization simply doesn't solve the patient's problems?

Sometimes, in the heat of defending our theoretical positions, we all lose sight of the prime goal—namely, to get the patient back to normal as quickly and as surely as possible. Any form of therapy that helps us achieve that goal is bound to find eventual acceptance no matter how revolutionary it may seem when first introduced.

SUMMARY

1. Psychologists often use the term "conditioning" to mean "learning." If an organism has been conditioned to respond in a new way to a stimulus, then a new stimulus-response (input-output) connection or bond has been established

and we can say that the organism is now "conditioned" to react in a different way than it did previously.

2. All learning or conditioning is built on, or is an adaptation of, innate stimulus-response connections. Instinctive reactions, such as the knee-jerk, are called "unconditioned responses" because they are present at birth or are specified by the organism's genetic blueprint. The stimulus of striking a person on the patellar tendon innately calls forth a knee-jerk; therefore, the knee-jerk is the output of an unconditioned stimulus-response connection in the person's nervous system.

3. Almost all unconditioned responses can be modified by experience; that is, the responses can be bonded to or connected with a new or "conditional stimulus." Conditioning occurs when a previously neutral stimulus input—such as a musical tone—is paired several times with the unconditioned stimulus (a blow to the patellar tendon). Eventually the tone becomes a conditioned (conditional) stimulus that can elicit the knee-jerk just about as reliably as does striking the tendon. The tone is called a conditioned stimulus because its power to elicit the knee jerk is *conditional* upon the tone's being paired several times with the unconditioned stimulus.

4. Once this learning has occurred, the knee-jerk given in response to the conditioned tone is called a "conditioned response." Usually it is slightly different in one or more ways from the unconditioned knee-jerk.

5. Conditioning is sometimes referred to as "strengthening S-R or stimulus-response bonds." The stronger the bond, the more likely it is that the conditioned stimulus will elicit the desired conditioned response.

6. The S-R bond between conditioned stimulus and response can be broken if the tone is presented several times without pairing it with the unconditioned stimulus (striking the tendon). This breaking of the S-R bond is called "extinction."

7. If an animal is trained to respond to an orange light, this response may generalize to other similar stimuli, such as a red or yellow light. However, with the proper training, the animal can usually learn to discriminate among similar stimuli and give different responses to each.

8. If this discrimination becomes too difficult, the animal may show such "neurotic" responses as biting, barking, and defecation.

9. Both humans and lower animals react to the stress of conflict by acquiring inappropriate or unadaptive behavior patterns.

10. Many psychologists believe that most human "anxiety" reactions are conditioned. If a child is frightened the first time it sees a horse, it may become conditioned to fear horses all its life.

11. Conditioned or learned fears may be desensitized or extinguished through counter-conditioning procedures that involve pairing the feared stimulus with something very pleasant.

12. Although desensitization (counter-conditioning) has enjoyed considerable success with many types of anxious patients, some psychologists believe that the technique merely removes the symptom and does not cure the underlying intra-psychic cause of the fear.

13. Perhaps the best form of therapy is one that makes use both of conditioning (behavioral) treatment and "insight" (intra-psychic) methods.

(Continued from page 314.)

Little Hans Larsen was sitting in the corner of the living room, facing the wall and sucking his thumb. His mother, Hilda Larsen, a large blond woman, sat across from him in an easy chair, watching television. Occasionally, when he stole a glance at the television set, he could see his mother sitting grandly in the large leather chair, a box of chocolates to one side of her, a great glass of beer on the other. Hans was being punished for some imaginary sin he had supposedly committed—she had told him that "he gave trouble," whatever that meant.

Mostly, he thought, she just didn't want to share the chocolates with him. The television program was an old movie, a love story of some kind, and it didn't really bother him that he couldn't watch it. But the candy . . . He sneaked another look at his mother, but she caught him.

"Hans Larsen!" she cried loudly. "Nosey brat! Keep your eyes turned to the wall, like I told you! Any boy who does the bad things you do can't be allowed to watch movies, like a good boy would."

"Aw, I don't want to see that stupid old picture anyway," he whined, turning his head back to the wall.

"I know, I know! It's the candy you're after! I saw the way you looked at the candy. Well, just keep your fingers out of my goodies or I'll box your ears good, do you hear me?" She popped a soft chocolate into her mouth. "You're just like your no-good father," she said, munching on the candy. "Always wanting things from me you can't have."

Hans knew if he begged her, she would relent and give him a piece of candy. But he would show her. He wouldn't pay any attention to the chocolates even if she offered him one without his asking. She just wasn't fair.

That was it, she just wasn't fair. And the candy was really his anyway, a gift on his ninth birthday from his Uncle Kjell. It was like her, not giving him his own present, saying he hadn't earned it. He'd show her. Someday he'd really show her!

A minute or two later a commercial interrupted the movie and he heard his mother move around heavily in the leather chair. Unconsciously he rubbed his hands between his legs. He really needed to go to the bathroom badly, but he wasn't about to ask her permission.

"Stop that, Hans Larsen! Nice little boys don't play with themselves like that in public, where anybody can see them! You hear me? You're just as nasty and dirty as your father, always touching yourself down there. You let me catch you doing that one more time, I'll give you the whipping of your life!" She picked up a small whip lying by the chair and shook the whip at him violently.

Hans put his hands behind him, so she could tell instantly that he wasn't doing anything bad. It would serve her right if he wet his pants—that would show her!

The front door opened and his father came in, stomping his feet to get the snow off his boots. A chill breeze blasted into the house for a moment as the winter wind fought a brief but losing battle with the warm, moist air inside.

"Shut the door, you idiot. You want to freeze us all to death?" his mother yelled, her eyes fixed on the television tube. "Where you been, you louse? Out drinking it up, I guess, wasting all our hard-earned money on drink and fancy living."

"Oh, shut up," Knut Larsen said, hanging his heavy coat in the hall closet. "It's my hard-earned money, not yours. You never did a lick of work in your life, just sit and watch the tube all the time, eating chocolates and getting fat. I worked ten hours today to keep you in chocolates, and that's all the thanks I get."

Hans turned around to watch his parents. He knew from bitter experience that once they started fighting, neither of them paid any attention to him at all.

"Stupid pig!" she cried. "You don't appreciate all the fine things I do for you. I keep the house spotless. I cook good food. I take care of your clothes. And what thanks do I get? You leave me at home on Saturday night and you go out drinking with your worthless friends! You make me so mad, I could beat you up!"

Hans looked around anxiously. This was going to be a bad one, and he wanted to get out of the room if he could before things got out of control.

"At least my friends don't yell at me and make life miserable. They listen to me when I talk and pay attention to what I say. They respect me!"

"Respect! You got the respect of a bunch of animals. That's all your friends are, a pack of wild animals. They ought to be horse-whipped, every one of them!"

"You leave my friends out of this, you fat worthless woman!" Knut raised his hand and shook it at his wife. "You're not as good as the worst of my friends!"

"That's not what you thought last night. Last night you couldn't get enough of me. See if I ever let you touch me that way again! You'll have to come crawling to me on your hands and knees, begging for me! And I'll throw you out, that's what I'll do! Just wait and see!"

Hans' bladder was hurting him. "Mama," he said quickly, "may I go . . ."

''Shut up, you stupid brat. Don't interrupt me when I'm talking with your father.''

''Don't you tell my son to shut up that way!''

''Your son?'' she laughed, a nasty tone in her voice. ''**Your** son? You're pretty sure of things you don't really know about entirely, aren't you?''

''Why, you . . .''

''Don't you come near me!'' Hilda Larsen picked up a heavy ashtray from beside her leather chair. ''Don't you try to touch me, or I'll hit you with this ashtray!''

Hans was really frightened now. He had to get out of the room at once, he knew that. So he began sneaking toward the door, hoping no one would notice.

''Put that ashtray down, you silly woman. You haven't got the guts to throw it anyhow!''

''I'll show you, Knut Larsen. Come one step more and I'll let you have it!''

Enraged, a stream of curses on his lips, Hans' father stamped across the room angrily toward his wife. Suddenly she screamed and threw the ashtray at him. Knut Larsen ducked, and the heavy glass bowl sailed past him, striking little Hans on the leg just as he had reached the doorway. Shocked, pained, Hans looked up at his parents and burst into tears.

''Oh, my baby! My poor baby!'' his mother wailed. ''What have I done to you!'' She ran toward the boy and scooped him into her fleshy arms.

Knut Larsen stood silent for a moment, then moved to his wife's side and patted his son on the head. ''There, see what you've done. You could have killed him, or harmed him for life.''

''I'm sorry, I'm sorry,'' Hilda sobbed. ''I didn't mean it, Hans. I wouldn't hurt you for the world, for the whole world.'' She cuddled him close to her, pressing his face against her ample breasts.

''Just you wait, I'll make it up to you. We'll have a box of candy, all to ourselves. That will cure the pain, won't it, Baby?''

She rubbed the wound on his leg soothingly, but the stimulation made Hans wince.

''Does it hurt bad, little Hans? Don't cry, you're a big boy now. We'll go upstairs and fix it up. Come on, Baby,'' she said, moving out of the door. ''Come with Mama. Mama will kiss it and make it well.''

RECOMMENDED READINGS

Eysenck, H.J., ed. *Behavior Therapy and the Neuroses* (London: Pergamon Press, 1960).

Lazarus, A.A. *Behavior Therapy and Beyond* (New York: McGraw-Hill, 1971).

Masserman, J.H. *Behavior and Neurosis* (Chicago: University of Chicago Press, 1943).

Pavlov, Ivan. *Conditioned Reflexes* (Oxford: Clarendon Press, 1927).

Wolpe, J., and A.A. Lazarus. *Behavior Therapy Techniques* (London: Pergamon Press, 1966).

OPERANT AND RESPONDENT CONDITIONING

DID YOU KNOW THAT . . .

Most of the teaching techniques used in U.S. classrooms are derived from laboratory experiments with animals?

E.L. Thorndike's law of effect states that S-R connections are strengthened by rewards?

Pavlov was very annoyed with Thorndike for insisting reward was important to learning?

Chimpanzees and even rats seem to have the same sort of insight (or "Ah ha!") experiences during learning as do humans?

If you use an effective educational technology, you can teach a pigeon to bowl in just an hour or so?

B.F. Skinner believes that rewards increase the probability that an organism will repeat the response it has just made?

Most complex behaviors appear to be sequences of simple responses that have been "chained" together?

The speed with which an organism responds is frequently dependent on the schedule of reinforcement the animal receives?

Most of the animals you see perform on TV and in shows are trained using techniques developed by Skinner and his associates?

It was a warm and sunny December day late in 1941. Brigadier General Billy Joe White stood, hands on hips, staring out at the pale blue of the Pacific Ocean. Having grown up in the red clay hills of western Mississippi, he always felt a quiet tingle of awe each time he glimpsed an unlimited expanse of the salty sea. And here at Torry Pines, just north of San Diego, the view was spectacular.

"What a place for a golf course, Con," he said, directing his comments to Rear Admiral Conrad Tower, a long-time friend of his. "I do believe you ship-types have the best deal in the whole world."

"Why, thank you, Billy Joe," the Admiral said, taking the golf club handed to him by the young man who served as his caddy. "Glad you could take a few hours off of a Sunday morning to come hit a couple of balls with me. But don't get the idea that life in the United States Navy is nothing but golf games in December. Don't forget that last year at this time I was fighting gales on the North Atlantic, trying to protect our merchant ships from Mr. Hitler's submarines." He took a couple of practice swings with the club, then teed up his ball. "I'm not at all sure which gave me the worst chills—the weather or the U-boats. At least the Pacific is as peaceful today as its name suggests it ought to be."

"Do you think it's going to stay that way?" General White asked.

Before answering, the Admiral addressed himself to his ball, then hit it with a resounding whack. It curved some 200 yards through the air and landed on the edge of the fairway.

"Good shot!" said the General.

The Admiral acknowledged his friend's verbal pat on the back with a grunt of mild satisfaction, then picked up the thread of the conversation. "Do I think the Pacific will stay pacific? Well, I don't know. The Japanese are a funny folk, and I'm not sure we read them correctly at all. I can't imagine that they would be so foolish as to challenge our naval supremacy in this part of the world, but you never know, you just never know. What do you think, Billy Joe?"

The General put his own ball on the tee and selected a club. "Can't rightly say. Don't think they'll try anything just yet. And I reckon we're ready for anything they care to throw at us. It's Hitler I'm really worried about. His Panzer Tank Corps is hell on wheels, as our French cousins found out to their sorrow; and his Luftwaffe Air Force is maybe the best in the world. Surprised the hell out of me that he didn't jump right across the English Channel and invade the British Isles when he had a good chance to do so. I guess maybe the Royal Air Force scares old Shickelgrubber just a mite."

"Let's hope the RAF continues to scare him," Admiral Tower responded. "Unless we got in the war ourselves, I don't imagine that the British could hold out too long if Hitler did invade Merrie Olde England."

General White smacked his golf ball firmly. It rose into the soft December air and dropped right in the middle of the fairway, rolling a few yards further along than the Admiral's had. Just as the ball came to rest, a curious seagull dived from the sky and passed low over the ball, as if to inspect its edibility at close range.

"Damned bird," said the Admiral. "I hope that gull doesn't fly off with your ball, Billy Joe. Have to penalize you two strokes if it does."

"Unless it happened to drop the ball right into the cup. What would you do then?"

"Cry, 'fowl,'" the Admiral joked, as the two men started walking toward their balls, their caddies trailing behind like escorts to a pair of battleships.

"Wonder you don't try to train those birds to help out your game a little, Con. Not that you need it, of course," the General said slyly.

"Funny you should mention that, Billy Joe. I heard a rumor last year that the British were trying to train sea gulls to help spot German U-boats in the English Channel."

"You're kidding."

"Don't think so. As I heard it, a lot of British submarines started cruising slowly back and forth across the Channel just below the surface. Every couple of minutes, they'd release food under the water and let it float up to the top so the gulls could grab it. They hoped the gulls would associate the dark shape of a submerged vessel with food, so that they'd start following every sub they spotted. Then the British subchasers could be on the lookout for gulls hovering over what seemed to be empty ocean, because that would mean a U-boat was just underneath."

"Wild idea," the General said, as they continued walking.

"Not as wild as one the Swedes have come up with. Rumor has it they're trying to train seals to dive under water and cut mine cables. And maybe to plant magnetic bombs on the bottoms of enemy ships, too. Hasn't worked too well yet, I hear, because nobody is very good at training seals. You Army fellows ever do crazy things like that?"

"Well, we use horses sometimes, and mules, but only for carrying things. We occasionally use dogs on patrol, and canaries to detect poison gas, but not much else. Did hear a nasty story about the Russians, though. Seems they're trying to train dogs to blow up Hitler's tanks. They give the dogs their food underneath captured German tanks. Eventually the dogs associate the sight of a German tank with chow time, and whenever they see a Panzer tank in the field, they immediately run toward it and try to crawl underneath it to get the food the dogs are sure is there. Once the dogs have been really trained, the Russians hope to strap explosives on the dogs' backs and release them during a tank battle. The dogs will chase the German tanks, and when they try to crawl underneath, the explosives will go off and blow up the tank!" Billy Joe White paused, remembering the German Shepherd pup he had raised as a boy. "Blow the hell out of the dog too, of course,'' he said sadly. ''Doubt that anybody can top that one,'' he continued.

''Well, maybe we can at that, Billy Joe,'' Admiral Tower said, as he ambled along the fairway. ''Last time I was in Washington, there was a guy suggesting we ought to recruit pigeons into the Navy.''

The General laughed. ''What are you going to do, train the pigeons to unload on Japanese battleships? Keep the Japanese so busy scraping off the crap that they won't have time to make trouble?''

''No, you don't understand. This guy—a psychologist named Skinner—wants us to use pigeons as navigators for our new missile, the Pelican.''

''You're joking.''

''Not really. I don't understand these new-fangled weapons too well, but this Pelican is supposed to pack a mighty wallop. Kind of a tiny robot plane with little wings and a big warhead. Aim it at a Japanese battleship from miles away. Much greater range than even our biggest guns, and very portable too, of course. Seems a good idea—if it works.''

''Something wrong with your Pelican, I gather.''

The Admiral nodded. ''Still a few gremlins in the works. Mostly to do with how heavy everything is. I didn't get the full picture, but it seems that the missile has a pretty weak motor on it right now. And the guidance system is so complicated and full of vacuum tubes and heavy batteries and things that you've got a kind of Chinaman's choice with the missile.''

''What do you mean?''

''Well, you can either put in the guidance system—or the warhead—but the damned thing isn't strong enough to handle both at the same time. So if you put in the explosives, you can fire the Pelican but you've got no way to aim it . . .''

''. . . and it might just turn right around and blow up one of your own ships,'' the General continued.

''That's right. Or you can put in the guidance system and aim it at a Japanese cruiser just over the horizon, and it will streak there as fast as an airplane, but when it gets there . . .''

''. . . a little flag pops out of the nose that says 'Bang.' '' The General laughed uproariously.

''And that's what this psychologist named Skinner wants to fix up with his pigeons. He claims they've got sharper vision than humans do, and that they can be trained to recognize Japanese or German warships much better than we can, day or night, rain or fog.''

''What are the pigeons supposed to do, fly in front of the missile and escort it to the target, the same way that a Judas ram leads the sheep to the slaughter in a meat-packing plant?''

''No, as a matter of fact, this Dr. Skinner apparently wants to put the pigeon **inside** the Pelican.''

''How is your pigeon in the Pelican going to see out?''

''I don't rightly know, Billy Joe. The project is just beginning. But I gather Professor Skinner wants to put a glass window in the nose of the missile. The way I heard it, he's going to have little buttons around the window—one on top, one directly underneath, and one on each side. Once the missile is airborne, the pigeon is supposed to peep out the window and then peck at the buttons to keep the thing on course.''

''What?''

''You heard me. If the nose of the missile dips too low, the pigeon pecks the top button a couple of times. That causes the guidance system to raise the nose a bit. If the missile drifts to the right, the pigeon pecks on the left-hand button until the missile corrects its course. Dr. Skinner claims the pigeons can deliver the Pelican right on target over a long distance—which, I might say, is a damn sight better than anything else we've got as a guidance system right now. And the whole thing weighs only a fraction of our regular system, so you could put both the pigeon and the warhead in the Pelican with no trouble.''

General Billy Joe White paused a moment and looked out at the smooth Pacific waters. Then he asked, ''Is this man for real?''

''Dr. Skinner? Yes, he's for real. A crackpot, I suppose, but the Office of Naval Research is considering giving him a contract. Of course, the whole thing will never get off the ground, and even if it did, we wouldn't use it.''

''Why not?''

''Doesn't make sense, Billy Joe. You can't just go using pigeons on board Navy ships like that! I mean, Dr. Skinner claims it would work, and he wants to demonstrate it for us, but once the missile is fired, that pigeon would have the power of life or death over everybody nearby. What would happen if the bird got confused, or went crazy, or something like that? What if it turned the missile around and blew us up instead of the enemy? Would you trust your life to a bird-brain pilot?''

''I reckon I do that every time I crawl on board one of the Army Air Force's planes. But tell me, Con, if you haven't got anything as good as the pigeons, don't you think you ought to try it out? Missiles are the coming thing. I don't know what the Japanese or the Germans have up their sleeves, but we might just need every bit of help we can get. What's so weird about a pigeon guidance system in a missile?''

''Well, there's the morality of the thing. The pigeon pilot doesn't come back, you know. What would the bird-lovers of the world say about that?''

General White rubbed his nose vigorously. ''I don't know how the Japanese would solve the same problem, but sure as shooting, the death of the pilot wouldn't bother them all that much. I think your research people ought to look into those pigeons a little more closely.''

''If they don't get tied up on something else, maybe they will. And if you're so interested, maybe you ought to talk to the Naval Research people about it. When are you going to be in Washington again?''

''The 10th of December.''

Admiral Tower pulled a notebook out of his hip pocket. ''Let's see, today is the 7th of December, 1941. You're flying to Washington the 10th, right? And I've got to fly out to Pearl Harbor on the 11th, for a meeting. That doesn't give us much time, but . . .''

The Admiral's caddy interrupted, pointing to an officer dressed in a tan Naval uniform who was running toward them down the fairway, his arms waving frantically.

''Isn't that your Aide, Lieutenant Andrews? Looks like he's upset as hell. Wonder what he wants?'' The General said.

Admiral Tower laughed. ''Probably a message from my wife telling us not to be too late for lunch. What else could it be on a peaceful Sunday like this?''

Brigadier General Billy Joe White rubbed his nose. ''Well, whatever it is, I sure hope it doesn't interrupt our game!''

(Continued on page 353.)

During the many years that you have gone to school, you must have come in contact with hundreds of different teachers. Some of them probably were strict disciplinarians who believed that knowledge had to be pounded into their students' heads through constant repetition. Holding a lesson book in one hand and perhaps a switch or stick in the other, such teachers often drill their pupils over and over again until the student can spew back from memory whatever material the teacher believes should be learned. The students who survive may acquire a lot of facts, but the constant threat of punishment may also teach them to hate anything associated with school.

Other teachers appear to be much less concerned with punishing incorrect responses than they are with creating an academic environment in which the student's inborn intellectual potential can grow and blossom like a flower seed planted in fertile soil. Their classrooms often have a friendly but *boisterous* (°)

Boisterous (BOY-stir-us). Noisy, rowdy, uninhibited, full of spirit.

In olden days, a teacher often ruled the classroom with a stick.

Cognitive (COG-nuh-tive). Having to do with thought processes or perceptions—as opposed to feelings or emotions.

Aptitude (APT-tih-tewd). The tendency or capacity to do something well, or the ability to acquire a certain skill. Aptitude tests are psychological instruments that can be given to young people to determine—before they are trained—what kinds of talents they have, hence what kinds of jobs they presumably would do well in as adults. As we will see in Chapter 23, these tests are not as accurate as we would like them to be.

character to them, and the teachers themselves often gain a warm place in their students' hearts. But affection for a teacher doesn't necessarily guarantee the learning of those basic skills necessary for student survival and prosperity after the student leaves school.

Is there a "best way" to educate people? Should students be treated like Pavlov's dogs, drilled and conditioned until they have acquired the proper response for any stimulus they are likely to encounter? Or should pupils be considered *cognitive* (°) creatures who merely need to be given a rich intellectual environment so that they can learn whatever they will need—without directed help or guidance from the teacher? As you will soon see, the history of psychological theories of learning (and hence, too, the history of educational practice in the United States) sometimes resembles a battle plan between these two opposing viewpoints.

In a sense, it all began with E.L. Thorndike, a giant of a figure in psychology whose influence on the American school system was almost as great as that Ivan Pavlov had on educational practice in Russia. Thorndike spent most of his academic career at Teachers College, a part of Columbia University in New York City. He helped create some of the very first intelligence and *aptitude* (°) tests; was a strong supporter of educational research; and, with C.L. Barnhart, developed a series of dictionaries for school children that is still widely used.

Thorndike believed that science and mathematics helped build good "mental discipline" and insisted that these subjects be taught to all children. But before you develop an instant dislike for this amazing man, you should know that he also felt these subjects should be presented in as uncomplicated and interesting a manner as possible. Indeed, he once said that scientific laws should be relatively accurate, but should be stated simply enough to be teachable to freshmen.

Thorndike's own scientific training made him an early supporter of Charles

E.L. Thorndike.

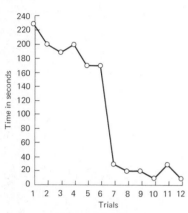

The seventh trial shows a remarkable improvement in the time it took one of Thorndike's cats to open a puzzle box.

Darwin's theory of evolution. Believing that man was descended from—and hence *learned the same way as*—lower animals, Thorndike began his studies on animal learning early in his career, in the 1890's. His research efforts—probably the first laboratory studies ever performed on animal intelligence—involved putting cats inside a "puzzle box." If the animal could figure out how to unlatch the door to the box, it escaped and was often given a bit of food as a reward.

At first the animals showed a great deal of what Thorndike called "random behavior," such as scratching or licking themselves, mewing or crying, pacing, biting at the bars on the side of the box, or trying to squeeze between the bars. Then, apparently by accident, the cat would bump into the latch; the door would fly open; and the animal would escape and be fed.

The next time the cat was put into the box, it performed many of the same "random" behaviors as before, but again it eventually hit the latch and escaped. In subsequent trials, the cat would spend more and more time in the vicinity of the latch and would get out of the box sooner and sooner. Eventually the animal seemed to learn what was required of it; and the moment it was placed in the box, the cat would hit the latch, escape, and claim its reward.

When Thorndike plotted on a graph the amount of time it took the cat to exit from the box on each trial, he came up with something that we now call a "learning curve" (*see* figure in margin). Similar experiments on monkeys, chickens, and even humans yielded the same-shaped curves, a finding that confirmed Thorndike's original belief that animals and humans solve such simple tasks in much the same fashion.

TRIAL AND ERROR LEARNING

Thorndike theorized that animals learn to escape from puzzle boxes by *trial and error* (°)—that is, they perform various responses in a blindly mechanical way until some action is effective in securing their release from the box. On succeeding trials the animal learns that certain types of behaviors (such as roaming around the apparatus) are much more effective in getting it out of the situation than are other behaviors (such as sitting and scratching). Since the ineffectual responses do not bring the animal much satisfaction, these activities tend to drop out or disappear from the animal's *repertory* (°). But those actions that gain the animal's release and lead to food are most satisfying, so these responses become more and more effectively connected to the stimuli in the puzzle box, and hence are more likely to occur the next time the animal is put in the box.

Thorndike's Laws of Learning

The results of his puzzle box experiments led Thorndike to formulate two basic laws of learning: (1) the *law of exercise* (°) and (2) the *law of effect* (°).

In part, the law of exercise states that S-R connections are *strengthened* by practice or repetition—in short, that practice makes perfect.

The law of effect holds that S-R bonds or connections are also strengthened by reward or satisfaction—in short, if the response that you make to a stimulus somehow gives you pleasure, the connection between the S and the R will be appropriately increased.

Thorndike defined rewards (or "satisfiers," as he called them) as situations that an organism willingly approaches or does nothing to avoid. Had Thorndike stopped at this point, his influence might have been more profound. Unfortunately, Thorndike also said some things about the effects of "punishers," which he believed weakened or broke S-R connections. As we will see in the next chapter, punishment doesn't operate that way at all, and it often has fairly disastrous side effects.

Trial and error. To learn by making mistakes until you discover the correct solution to a problem. Usually involves learning without having someone to teach or guide you.

Repertory (REP-purr-torr-ee). A fancy term for "bag of tricks" or "stock in trade." Your own repertory is whatever skills, talents, or response patterns you possess.

Law of exercise. A psychological principle first stated by E.L. Thorndike, who assumed that learning (conditioning) is a matter of setting up connections or bonds between stimuli and responses. The law states, in part, that S-R (stimulus-response) bonds are strengthened or increased by practice, or exercise.

Law of effect. Another principle proposed by E.L. Thorndike, who said that the *effect* of reward was to strengthen S-R bonds, while the *effect* of punishment was to weaken S-R bonds. Late in his life, Thorndike changed his mind about the consequences of punishment, but by then the "negative" half of the law of effect had had its effect on U.S. educational practice. There are, unfortunately, still many teachers who believe that their main task is to "correct or punish the mistakes" their students make.

Nonetheless, Thorndike's influence on U.S. educational practice was so great that generations of school teachers accepted his theories as if they were natural rather than man-made laws. The great man had said that repetition was the key to learning and punishment the key to weakening or wiping out "inappropriate" responses—so millions of school children were made to recite their math and science lessons, endlessly urged on by the stinging threat of a hickory stick.

LEARNING BY INSIGHT

As we noted in the chapter on perception, we tend to see what we expect to see. This principle holds in scientific investigations as well. Thorndike surely *expected* his cats to learn by trial-and-error methods before he began his work. Indeed, as *Gestalt* (°) psychologist Wolfgang Koehler pointed out, the puzzle box could hardly be solved in any other way. Koehler, trained at the University of Berlin, became director of a research station in the *Canary Islands* (°) in 1913, a few years after Thorndike published his first work on animal learning.

Koehler believed that animals were capable of greater intellectual accomplishments than random solutions to puzzle boxes—that animals, given the chance, could sense or discover *relationships* between objects and events and act accordingly to gain whatever ends they had in mind. Much of Koehler's work in the Canary Islands involved presenting various "intellectual" problems to chimpanzees, to see what kinds of solutions they might come up with.

Koehler's most famous subject was a particularly bright chimpanzee named Sultan. First Sultan learned to reach through the bars of his cage and rake in a banana on the ground outside using a stick as a tool. After Sultan had mastered this trick, Koehler set the animal the much more difficult task of putting two sticks together to get the food. The banana was moved further away from Sultan's cage, and the chimp was given two bamboo poles that, when fitted together, were just long enough to gather in the reward.

At first Sultan was confused. He tried reaching for the fruit with one stick and then with the other, but neither was adequate for his purposes. Next he pushed the longer of the poles out toward the banana and left it lying on the ground. Then Sultan used the tip of the shorter stick to prod the longer one out until it touched the banana. He had reached his objective—in a sense—but couldn't complete his mission because the two sticks were not joined together in any way and so he could not get the banana back in his cage. Koehler even had to hand the larger pole back to the animal because it now was beyond his reach.

Gestalt (guess-TALT). A German word that literally means "good form" or "good figure." Also means the tendency to see things as "wholes" rather than as jumbled bits and pieces. *See* Chapter 10.

Canary Islands (can-AIR-ee). A series of tropical islands south of Spain and just off the west coast of Africa. Beautiful, warm islands with no snakes and hundreds of different species of birds. Wolfgang Koehler (CURL-er) spent the years of the First World War doing research on these islands.

Sultan in action.

Insight. The power or act of seeing into a situation or into oneself. Clear and immediate understanding of the solution to a problem that presumably does not involve trial-and-error learning.

Vitriolic (vitt-tree-OLL-ick). A biting, scathing verbal attack on someone or something.

Mazes (MAY-zizz). A network of pathways and blind alleys between a starting point and a goal, used chiefly to study learning and problem-solving in animals and humans. The first maze for laboratory animals was built by psychologist W.S. Small in 1900, and was similar to a famous maze made of hedges at Hampton Court Palace in England that has delighted millions of visitors.

Cognitive map. Some psychologists (such as Thorndike and Pavlov) believe that animals learn each section of a maze by trial and error. Other psychologists believe that animals acquire a "mental map" of the maze and can "think" their way through to the goal—rather than respond reflexively (and unconsciously) to the specific stimuli in each section. In fact, animals such as the rat seem to do a little of both.

Koehler watched the animal for more than an hour, hoping that an intellectual flash of lightning would strike Sultan's cortex. When the chimp abandoned the banana and retreated into his cage (perhaps in frustration) to play with the sticks, Koehler decided the animal had failed the test and returned to his nearby house, leaving the animal to be observed by an assistant.

Koehler gave up too soon. Not long after he'd left, Sultan happened to hold one stick in each hand so that their ends were pointed toward each other. Gently, he pushed the tip of the smaller one into the hollow of the larger. They fitted. Even as he did so Sultan was up and running toward the bars of his cage. Reaching through with the double stick, he touched the banana and started to draw it toward him.

At this point fate played Sultan a nasty trick for which Koehler was most grateful—the two sticks came apart! Annoyed at this turn of events, Sultan gathered the sticks back into the cage, pushed them firmly together, tested them briefly, and then "liberated" the banana.

These actions proved—at least to Koehler's satisfaction—that the chimpanzee actually understood that *joining the poles together* was an effective way of lengthening his arm. Koehler used the term *insight* (°) to refer to this very rapid "perception of relationships" that sometimes occurs in humans and animals. He believed that insight involved a sudden restructuring or reorganization of the organism's perceptual world into a new pattern or *Gestalt.* Koehler never denied the importance of repetition and reward in learning simple tasks; he merely believed that organisms were capable of more complex forms of learning, if given the chance.

As you might imagine, Ivan Pavlov did not take gladly to Koehler's experiments. As soon as the chimpanzee work appeared in print, Pavlov leapt to the attack, accusing Koehler of being a "mentalist" (which he was) and of performing sloppy experiments (that is, studies in which the CS and the UCS could not readily be identified). From his sanctuary in Leningrad, Pavlov issued one *vitriolic* (°) criticism after another, most of which Koehler simply ignored. But the Russian scientist soon found himself assailed by a veritable broadside of experiments from the United States, few of which could easily be fitted into Pavlov's theory of conditioning.

Tolman's "Cognitive Maps"

E.C. Tolman and his associates at the University of California, Berkeley, published a series of studies that appeared to show rats were much more "insightful" than Thorndike or Pavlov perhaps thought they ought to be. In most of these experiments, the rats were given considerable training in very complicated *mazes* (°). Although the animal could reach the food reward at the end of the maze by a great many pathways, one path was typically much shorter than the rest and was preferred by the animals. When that pathway was blocked, however, almost all of the rats would instantly shift to the next most efficient way of getting to the food. If the experimenter moved the reward from one part of the apparatus to another, the rats responded immediately as if they had some kind of *cognitive map* (°) of the maze and understood a great deal about the spatial relationships involved in getting quickly from one part of the maze to another.

Maier's Rat "Bismarck"

N.R.F. Maier, at The University of Michigan, performed a similar set of experiments that appeared to show rats were capable of "insightful" behavior patterns. One of Maier's best subjects, a young male rat named Bismarck, was trained to get food on the top of a table by crawling up a little ladder from the floor. One day,

N.R.F. Maier.

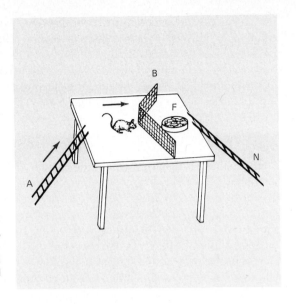

Bismarck was trained to go up the ladder (A) and get his food at F. When a barrier (B) blocked his way, he noticed the new ladder (N) and used it to get his reward.

after Bismarck had run up the ladder many times to claim his reward, the rat found a wire mesh barrier that blocked his access to the food. Bismarck crawled all over the barrier but was unable to get through it to his dinner. He could, however, see a new pathway from the floor to the food, one that he had never traveled before. Bismarck sat quietly for a while, expressing his frustrations (as rats often do) by laboriously washing his face. Suddenly Bismarck jumped straight up in the air, turned and dashed *down* the ladder that he previously had only gone up, chased around the table, found the new pathway, raced up the new route, and settled down to gorge himself.

LEARNING IN CLASSROOM SITUATIONS

Educational practice is often affected by experiments such as these, for the classroom follows the laboratory more than it leads it. Teachers who fell under the influence of E.L. Thorndike typically expected their students to learn material bit by bit, in one tiny *increment* (°) after another—and so drilled their pupils over and over again in one subject after another thought to be "good for the student."

On the other hand, those educators who were influenced by Tolman and his associates believed that learning is spontaneous and rapid, that it occurs in big bursts of insight. The most radical of these teachers held that each child learns at his or her own speed, in his or her own way; the most that a teacher can hope to do, then, is to give the child as rich and permissive an intellectual environment as possible, and then sit back and wait for the cognitive map-making to occur spontaneously. Because these educators could not specify exactly what stimulus conditions promote insightful learning, the most they could do was to expose their students to "routine-free" classrooms and hope for the best.

Thorndike's views were much more acceptable to Professor Pavlov than were Tolman's. Indeed, there is a strange similarity between the explanations that Pavlov offered for classical conditioning and Thorndike's law of exercise. Pavlov, as you will remember, believed that if the conditioning stimulus (CS) is paired with the unconditioned stimulus (UCS) a sufficient number of times, an S-R bond would be formed. And the more the bond is exercised, the stronger it becomes. The mere *closeness in time* between the CS and the UCS is enough to bring about an association between these two stimuli, and hence a connection or *contiguity* (°) between the CS and the CR.

Thorndike's law of effect, however, was a dog biscuit that stuck in Pavlov's

Increment (IN-kree-ment). Something that is gained or added—a small step toward a goal. If you want to save a dollar, each penny that you earn would be an increment toward the dollar goal.

Contiguity (kon-tih-GUE-it-tee). Two objects or events are contiguous (kon-TIG-you-us) if they are close to each other, or follow each other. Day is contiguous with night; Monday is contiguous with both Sunday and Tuesday; and Canada is contiguous with the USA. The law of association states that two stimuli (CS and UCS) will be associated if they are contiguous—that is, if the CS is immediately followed by the UCS.

A pigeon bowling alley.

throat, for the Russian scientist believed that learning occurs automatically—whether or not the organism likes it—while Thorndike thought that we all remember things better if they please us. (The personal satisfaction of the organism was something that Pavlov seems not to have cared much about.) It took a bird-brained U.S. pigeon to show the narrowness of Pavlov's views and to map out a kind of common ground between the Thorndikeans and the Tolmaniacs.

Operant Conditioning: Teaching a Pigeon To Bowl

Suppose that, as a final examination in one of your psychology classes, your instructor gives you a common, ordinary pigeon and tells you that if you want to get an A in the course, it is up to you to teach this pigeon how to bowl. The apparatus you can use is a large box with a wire screen over the top of it. Inside the box is a small bowling alley with a tiny ball at one end and pigeon-sized bowling pins at the other. In one corner of the box is a metal cup into which you can drop food pellets from the outside. Just above the food cup is a small bell that you can ring by pressing a button outside the box. Luckily for you, the pigeon has already been trained to run to the food cup to get grain whenever the bell rings.

Your instructor tells you that if you can teach the pigeon to bowl in a matter of two hours or less, you pass the exam and get your A reward. Keeping in mind all of the practical advice on educational practice that you have acquired so far in this book, how would you go about educating your pigeon so that you could satisfy your instructor, yourself, and, of course, the pigeon?

If you played the game according to Pavlovian rules, you would probably begin by ringing the bell and then pushing the pigeon toward the ball, hoping that an S-R connection of some kind would be established in the bird's nervous system. In fact, the pigeon would surely resent such an intrusion into its life space; instead of learning to bowl when you rang the bell, it probably would learn to peck at your hand viciously. For Pavlovian conditioning is almost always built on already-established unconditioned responses (UCR's). If dogs did not salivate naturally when given food, how would you go about teaching them to salivate when you sounded a buzzer?

If the pigeon already knew how to bowl, you could probably train it to demonstrate this response on command when you rang the bell. But you could read everything Pavlov wrote—in Russian or in English translation—without learning much about how to get a bird to bowl in the first place, if bowling wasn't something it did naturally.

If you turned to Tolman and the Gestalt theorists instead, perhaps you might decide to give the pigeon plenty of experience in the bowling box itself before you started the training. Once the animal had acquired a valid cognitive map of the apparatus, it would surely learn to bowl much faster. But the relationship between striking the ball and knocking down the tenpins is an insight that comes hard to most pigeons—unless you facilitate matters a little along the way. And not even Koehler offered much practical advice about how this facilitation should be accomplished.

If you looked to Thorndike for help, you still might have troubles. You could utilize the law of effect by waiting until the pigeon happened to knock the ball down the alley by accident and then giving the bird some food. This reward should help stamp in the memory of what it had done, but how long would you have to wait until the pigeon by accident hit the ball straight down the alley the first time? Once it had done so, and been rewarded, you could perhaps get it to do so again, and hence exercise the S-R bond and make it stronger. But it is that very first response that Thorndike's notions of trial and error learning cannot help you bring about.

All of these components—*reward, exercise,* and *repetition,* and *unlearned* or *innate responses*—are necessary if you are to train the pigeon and pass your exam. But putting them all together into a workable educational system took the genius of Harvard professor B.F. Skinner, who probably qualifies as our most influential living psychologist.

Terminal Response According to Skinner, whenever you wish to change an organism's behavior, you always begin at the very tail end of things and work backward. For instance, to get your A, you must train the pigeon to bowl. But what do we mean by bowling? Do we have some objective, clear-cut, agreed-upon way of measuring the response pattern we call "bowling"? If so, then we know when to terminate the training, and we know when you've passed the exam.

Skinner calls this final step the *terminal response* (°), because when the organism finally performs this task, you have achieved your goal and can terminate your efforts. The single most important thing about the terminal response, though, is that it must be *measurable*. As you will soon see, pigeons *can* be trained to bowl in two hours or less if you go about it the right way. However, how long do you think it would take to train a bird to be a "good sport"?

> QUESTION: College catalogues often state that the goal of a higher education is to turn students into creative individuals who are good citizens and productive members of modern-day society; what might B.F. Skinner say about the measurability of such terminal responses?

Entering Behavior Once you have a well-defined goal to work toward, you are ready to tackle the second stage in Skinner's analysis of behavioral change—that of determining what the organism is doing before you *intervene* (°) in its life. Skinner calls this the organism's *entering behavior* (°); and it, too, must be stated in objectively measurable terms. Clever animal trainers (or people educators) always take advantage of the response patterns that the organism brings to the training situation—you always build new learning on old, according to Skinner.

Successive Approximations When you are sure of (1) the organism's entering behavior and (2) the terminal behavior you hope to achieve, then you are ready to move from (1) to (2) in a step-by-step fashion that Skinner calls *successive approximations to a goal* (°). Neither people nor pigeons typically make dramatic changes in their behaviors in large, insightful jumps. Rather, we change slowly, bit by bit, inch by inch. We usually need to be coaxed and encouraged whenever we must acquire a new way of doing things, which is to say that we need to be rewarded or *reinforced* for each tiny step that we make toward the goal.

The technique of successive approximations to a goal is the heart of the Skinnerian system; but mastery of the technique calls for rather a penetrating insight on your own part. Namely, you must come to realize that even the faintest, feeblest movement toward the terminal goal is *a step in the right direction*, hence one that you must vigorously reward. Most people are unable or unwilling to look at behavior in these terms—which is why most people would not be able to train a pigeon to bowl in two hours or less.

If we apply the Skinnerian behavioral analysis to the problem of getting your exam pigeon to perform, we can perhaps see better how the technique works. The terminal behavior your instructor has set is that of "bowling." But how shall we define it? Humans usually pick up the bowling ball in their hands and roll it down the alley. But Mother Nature has given the pigeon wings instead of arms, and feathers are poor substitutes for fingers when it comes to lifting a heavy ball. But could we teach an armless man or woman to bowl? Couldn't the person kick the ball, or even butt it with his or her head?

If you observe pigeons for a while, you'll notice they use their beaks to manipulate the world around them much as we use our hands. If you can train the

Terminal response. Also called "terminal behavior pattern" or "terminal goal." The final step in training an organism. See Chapter 5.

Intervene (in-turr-VEEN). From the Latin word meaning "to come between" or "to enter into." Teachers intervene in students' lives by offering the students new educational goals and helping them achieve these goals.

Entering behavior. The behavior patterns of an organism before training begins. According to behavioral therapists, you must always build upon the strengths (the good behaviors) of the organism and select out of these entering behaviors those actions that can be shaped toward the terminal response. Entering behaviors also include problematic or inappropriate actions, but these should be ignored (or at least not rewarded) in the hope that they will thereby be extinguished.

Successive approximations to a goal. Any incremental response that will lead the organism toward the terminal response. Behaviorists believe that most learning occurs in small steps—"Rome wasn't built in a day." But if the successive approximations are rewarded and encouraged, they build up in incremental form until the goal is reached. See Chapter 5.

pigeon to hit the ball down the alley using its beak, you surely have taught the animal to "bowl" and should get an A on your exam.

Now that you know what your goal is, what about the entering behavior of the pigeon? Obviously, it doesn't bowl at all. But what *does* it do when you put it into the apparatus? It moves around nervously, excitedly, inspecting its new environment. The final response that you want from the animal is that of striking the ball with its beak so that the ball travels down the alley and hits the pins. To make this terminal response, the animal surely must be standing near the ball. So your first task would seem to be that of getting the pigeon to move to where the ball is. But how to do it?

If you were training your child to bowl, you would probably explain to the child—in English—what you wanted it to do. Then, as it began to make the first muscle movements involved in approaching the ball or picking it up, you would encourage the child and tell it that it was doing well. But pigeons don't speak English, so how can you give your bird the appropriate feedback to let it know that it's doing something "good"?

Two Functions of Reward Reward or positive reinforcement has at least two functions. First, it gives us pleasure, usually by satisfying some need or reducing some drive or deprivation state. When we are hungry, food tastes good and gives us new energy. But rewarding inputs also have an informational aspect to them,

The rat in a specially designed Skinner box is being rewarded for responding correctly in a learning experiment.

for such stimuli give us feedback as to how well we are doing, how close we are coming to a goal. Positive reinforcement, then, *increases the probability that an organism will repeat the response* that led to the appearance of the rewarding stimulus. Since your pigeon has already been trained to go to the food cup when it hears the bell ring, you can use the sound of the bell as a rewarding input whenever you want to let the pigeon know instantly that it has made what you consider to be a step in the right direction toward the goal of bowling.

Shaping a Pigeon To Bowl With these preliminaries out of the way, you would be ready to start passing your final examination. You know your goal; you know the entering behavior the bird shows; the animal is deprived of food; and you have an effective reinforcer available. What is your next step?

Actually, as Skinner points out, the next step is up to the bird. As it wanders around the box nervously, at one time or another it will accidentally take a step toward the bowling ball lying at the end of the alley. If you have the insight to recognize this simple movement as being "a step in the right direction," and ring the bell at once and reward the animal with food, you will have no difficulty training the bird to bowl. If you wait until the pigeon acquires an understanding of the problem, or if you insist that it is unreasonable to reward halfway measures and hence wait until the pigeon "bowls" before you give it the first food pellet, it may take you years to pass the exam—if you ever do.

Presuming that you do sound the bell the first time the bird moves tentatively in the general direction of the ball, how does the pigeon respond? By running to the food cup to claim its reward. After eating the food, it will pause for a while in the vicinity of the food cup. But when such actions don't ring the bell, it will typically begin its random trial and error movements around the box again. Once more, as soon as it heads toward the ball, you sound the bell. And again it runs to the food cup and eats.

The fifth or sixth or tenth time this pattern is repeated, a very strange event often occurs. The pigeon behaves as if it has experienced a flash of insight into what is happening—the bird appears to discover that it can actually control your behavior! All it has to do to *force* you to give it food is to move in a given direction! (Skinner would probably oppose such a cognitive or mentalistic description of the process, believing it inappropriate to speculate on what private psychological events might be occurring inside the animal's head.)

Once your pigeon has learned the connection between *doing something* and *being rewarded*, training can progress at a rapid pace. By making the animal go a little bit further toward the ball each time before you next ring the bell, you can typically get the animal to the vicinity of the bowling ball in a matter of a few minutes. Each time you sound the bell, the pigeon will dash to the food cup, then return at once to where it was the instant the bell rang.

QUESTION: **What do you think would happen if you attempted to make the pigeon go too many steps at once before giving it a reward?**

So the bird is now where the ball is. Next you must find a way of getting the animal's beak down on the floor, next to the ball. Again, you go back to the natural or innately determined responses that the animal makes. As pigeons move, their heads bob up and down. Sometimes, then, the bird's beak is closer to the ball than at other times. A good animal trainer will perceive the bird's downward movements as "good responses" and begin to reward them.

At first, the pigeon will appear confused. That is, it will test out a variety of responses as if it were trying to determine by trial and error what you wanted it to do next. After all, it is performing many other responses (walking, breathing, looking, perhaps opening or closing its beak) at the same time that its head is moving downward. And when you ring the bell, *everything* the pigeon is doing at

Salient (SAY-lee-ent). That which stands out or is noticeable. In a figure-ground relationship, the figure is always salient.

Shaping. When you reward each successive approximation toward a goal, you are (according to Skinner) shaping the desired response pattern much the way a potter shapes clay and makes it into a pot.

Chained. To write the word "cat" on a typewriter, you must first hit the "c" key, then the "a" key, then the "t." You will have made (at least) three different responses that are chained together to achieve the goal of typing the word "cat." Behaviorists believe that most complex human behavior patterns are actually long chains of related responses that must be learned one at a time.

that moment in time is reinforced. Eventually, however, the downward head movement becomes predominant or *salient* (°) because this is the response that you always reward.

After several such reinforcements, the pigeon begins to return from its quick journey to the food cup holding its head a little lower than usual. Now it is a simple matter to move the pigeon's beak all the way to the floor by demanding that its head be a little closer to the ball each time you ring the bell.

QUESTION: At any time during training, do you imagine that the pigeon gains a cognitive awareness that it is "learning to bowl"?

By now the pigeon's beak is close to the floor, and the bird is moving about in the general vicinity of the ball. Within a few moments, the beak will touch the ball "accidentally." The skilled animal trainer now rings the bell joyously, knowing that victory is near. When the bird returns from claiming its reward, it typically takes a second swat at the ball. When again the bell sounds, it scoots back and forth from food cup to bowling alley, giving the ball a healthy whack each time it comes close.

Now it is up to you to shape the bird's "whacking responses" so that it knocks the ball straight down the alley instead of merely hitting it in any random direction. Such *shaping* (°) should take only a few minutes, for at first you reinforce only those whacks that aim the ball in the general direction of the pins. Then you selectively reward those hits that come closer and closer to your stated goal. The pigeon soon learns that it will be fed only when it strikes the ball so that it rolls straight down the alley and hits the pins.

An experienced pigeon-handler can usually train a hungry pigeon "to bowl" in less than an hour. (Training the animal to get a good score takes a little longer.)

Analysis of Skinner's System

There are several fairly subtle points about the Skinnerian system that are sometimes overlooked. To begin with, notice that no punishment was necessary in order to get the animal to perform. The pigeon obviously *can* learn; if it fails to do so, the fault presumably lies with the teacher, not with the student.

Second, "bowling" is obviously a very complicated set of responses that the organism has to learn in a *particular order* or *sequence.* By your getting the animal to learn one simple thing at a time, never demanding too much, and by always encouraging the "right" things the pigeon does and ignoring its mistakes—one response can be *chained* (°) or connected to another with little difficulty. An experienced pigeon-bowler will perform its routine so smoothly and efficiently that it is not easy for most of us to see the various "micro-responses" that have been chained together during training.

Third, no physical force or threats were necessary to get the bird to acquire a new way of behaving. By depriving the animal of food before the experiment began, you have made the bird willing to work for its supper. You control the *timing* of the reinforcement, but the pigeon determines whether it wants the reward you offer it. If the reinforcement is meaningful and satisfying to that particular bird, then the animal will work. But if you offer the animal something it doesn't want or need, or if you expect too much work for the amount of pleasure that you give the bird in return, it is free to rebel and ignore you. (Surprisingly enough, pigeons appear to enjoy this type of training and, once they have learned the task, will perform it again and again and again with but a minimal amount of encouragement.)

Fourth, at the beginning of training, you should always reward *each and every* move in the appropriate direction. However, once the pigeon has mastered a given response in the chain, you may begin slowly *fading out the reward* by

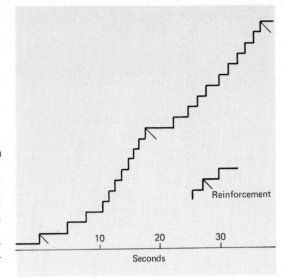

A cumulative record of a pigeon trained to peck a button on a 10 to 1 fixed-ratio reinforcement schedule. Each vertical movement of the graph represents one press of the lever. Note that the pigeon responds more quickly just prior to a reinforcement than just afterward.

reinforcing the response *intermittently* (°). Continuous reinforcement is necessary at first, both to keep the animal eager to perform and to let it know that it is doing something right. Once the pigeon learns what that "something" is, you may begin reinforcing the response every second time, then every third or fourth time, then perhaps every tenth time. If you fade out the reward very gradually, you can get a pigeon to make a simple response such as pecking a button several thousand times for each reinforcement.

Fifth, during the fading process, the exact scheduling of the reward is crucial. If you reinforce exactly every tenth response, the bird will soon learn to anticipate which response will gain it food. As soon as it makes this tenth response and feeds, it will take a "rest break" because it knows that its next (now the first) response never brings it any goodies. Skinner calls this *fixed-ratio reinforcement* (°), because the ratio between the number of responses required and the rewards given is fixed and never varies.

If we made a *cumulative record* (°) of the time intervals between each response the animal makes, we would find that it responds slowly just after a reinforcement, but more and more quickly as it approaches that response it knows will gain it the reward (*see* figure above). We can get the pigeon to respond at a more or less constant rate by tricking it a bit—that is, by rewarding it on a *random* or *variable* basis rather than on a fixed-ratio schedule. Instead of reinforcing *exactly* the tenth response, we vary the schedule so that sometimes the third response yields food, sometimes the seventh, sometimes the 11th, sometimes the twentieth—or any response in between. A thousand responses will yield *about* 100 rewards, but the animal will never know when the next reward is coming. Under these conditions of *variable-ratio reinforcement* (°), pigeons will respond vigorously and without let-up.

QUESTION: Do the slot machines in Las Vegas pay off on a fixed ratio or a variable ratio?

The sixth point about the Skinnerian system is this—"shaping" any organism's responses is more of a psychological art than a science, and some people are much better psycho-artists than are others. Skinner says that you should reward each successive step toward the behavioral goal you have in mind. But there are thousands of different response chains that might lead from the animal's entering behavior to the terminal goal. Skinner doesn't tell you which one to pick, nor how to judge which pathway is the best. Lion tamers at the circus, teachers at dog and

Intermittently (in-turr-MITT-tent-lee). If it rains on Monday, is clear on Tuesday and Wednesday, rains on Thursday, is clear on Friday and Saturday, and rains again on Sunday—then it has rained intermittently during the week. If you reward a rat each third time that it presses a bar, you are giving the animal intermittent reinforcement.

Fixed-ratio reinforcement. If you reward a rat for exactly each third bar press that it makes, the ratio between responses (bar presses) and reward is fixed.

Cumulative record (CUE-mew-luh-tive). From the word "accumulate," meaning "to acquire." As you grow older, your years are cumulative—that is, you never lose a year once you've lived through it; you never go backward in time. A cumulative record is an increasing graph or record of all the responses that an animal has made in a certain time period. The record shows both the number of responses and the time between each response.

Variable-ratio reinforcement (VAIR-ee-uh-bull). A schedule of reinforcement that involves rewarding the animal for *approximately* every 3rd (or 5th or 100th) correct response it makes.

Gunther Gebel Williams in his wild animal cage.

cat "obedience schools," and the handlers at the various Sea Worlds and Marine-land aquariums dotted around the country often make use of Skinnerian principles in training their beasts to perform dazzling tricks. But some of these animal educators are much better at shaping behavior than others, just as some high school and college teachers are much more effective than others at rewarding successive approximations to educational goals. The personality *traits* (°) or characteristics of the successful behavior-shaper are not typically discussed in Skinner's books and papers.

> QUESTION: **Think for a moment about one or two of the best teachers you've had; what measurable behaviors did these teachers display that poorer teachers did not?**

Practical Applications

Like Thorndike, B.F. Skinner derived the principles underlying his system from years of work on animal subjects in his laboratory. During World War II, he developed a "pigeon guidance system" for airborne missiles that was many times more accurate than any purely electronic system in existence. But when he took his pigeons to Washington to demonstrate their effectiveness, the scientists working for the Defense Department laughed at him and told him to go get drunk and not bother them with his crackpot ideas. In more recent years Skinner has turned from the animal laboratory to the classroom, hoping to develop educational machines and systems that "teach" as effectively as his pigeon guidance system could aim missiles.

Programmed Textbooks Skinner was a pioneer in developing *programmed textbooks* (°), in which the material to be learned is presented to the student in small chunks. The reader is presented with a bit of information, then asked a question about the material. Each such unit is called a "frame" in the program. The information in each frame is so simply stated that the reader can hardly fail to answer correctly. The "program" then allows the reader to compare his or her response with the correct answer, thus giving the reader immediate feedback on whether or not the material was properly mastered. The instant knowledge of the correctness of one's response appears to serve as reinforcement for learning—much as the sound of the bell rewards the pigeon for learning each of the single tiny steps that make up the skill of "bowling."

Trait. A basic, relatively unchanging attitude or behavior pattern. Intelligence is usually said to be a trait.

Programmed textbooks. A technique developed by Skinner of presenting material to be learned in small chunks, or frames, and of testing the student immediately to make sure that the material is learned before a new chunk is presented. A frame in a programmed English text might read: "A *noun* is the name of someone or something. Mary is a girl's name. Therefore, Mary is a _____." After the student writes the answer in the blank, the student can check the correctness of the answer before attempting the next frame in the program.

	cat	can
can	can	cat
cat	cat	can
	cat	can
can		
cat		
cat	c__n	c__t
can	__at	__an

Page from a programmed text-book.

The Teacher as "Change Agent" Skinner believes that teachers should specify at the beginning of a course what measurable responses a student must make in order to get a good grade. It is then the teacher's prime responsibility to select out of the thousands of reactions that a student makes in class those behaviors that will take the student closer to the stated goals. The teacher is expected to give the student continuous feedback on his or her performance by praising appropriate (goal-oriented) responses and by ignoring false steps or inappropriate (disruptive) behaviors.

Skinner sees the teacher as being a *behavioral change agent* (°) whose prime task is to help each young person learn as many new response chains as quickly and as painlessly as possible. If the student fails to make progress, either the goals have not been clearly stated in measurable terms or the teacher hasn't rewarded the student appropriately. In short, Skinner believes that students don't usually fail to learn, but teachers often fail to teach. Examinations are actually tests of the educator's behavioral skills rather than measures of how good or bright or hard-working the student is.

QUESTION: Would it help the educational process if students were trained to reward good teaching when it occurred? Might even a "bad" teacher be shaped into better educational habits if the students ignored poor teaching performance but vigorously reinforced each appropriate bit of good teaching whenever it popped up?

Teachers who follow Skinner's system often report great success—their class-rooms are typically full of happy, alert, well-behaved pupils who are learning rapidly. Other educators believe the Skinnerian way to be a rigid, anti-humanistic method that forces students to become little more than robots, marching in lock-step down a narrow if well-defined educational pathway. Can you "shape" creativity, these critics ask?

Skinner's response is simple—if you can define creativity in measurable behavioral terms, his system can teach it better and faster than any other. (As we will see in a later chapter, the heart of this argument lies in the *near-indefinability* of the term "creativity.") But many teachers believe that much that is important in classrooms simply cannot be measured in objective terms. They worry that the Skinnerian methodology does not take into account the student's need to acquire new perceptions, insights, attitudes, and viewpoints—nor does it help them build warm, rewarding patterns of social interactions. And these critics insist that just because these skills are devilishly hard to define doesn't mean that they don't exist. Such arguments are not easily answered within the confines of the Skinnerian system itself.

Behavioral change agent. Someone who attempts to help another individual change his or her behavior. A teacher or therapist who focuses on changing behavior rather than on altering attitudes or traits.

Effective agents of behavioral change—whether they are shaping the responses of people or pigeons—typically offer their results as the best evidence that the system is not inhumane. Love, affection, and attention are perhaps the best rewards any teacher can offer a student for appropriate behavior. Therefore, the teacher who takes a personal interest in his or her students is more reinforcing than the teacher who uses only punishment or whose praise is obviously insincere. Students who are allowed to set some of their own classroom goals, who are encouraged to work at their own speeds in their own fashions, usually learn better and are happier than pupils whose noses are held firmly against the academic grindstone.

But not all teachers can tolerate such freedom and diversity in their classrooms. Defining terminal goals for any class is a time-consuming task, as is giving students the individual attention and feedback necessary to help each one reach his or her set of terminal behaviors. And without special training, many teachers find it difficult to select out of the boiling, sometimes explosive variety of student behaviors those first tentative steps in the right direction that must be rewarded if learning is to occur.

QUESTION: The attention that we pay to others is often a very powerful reinforcer; if a teacher always reprimands or calls attention to a student's misbehavior, is the

In modern classrooms, teachers often encourage learning with warmth and affection.

teacher increasing or decreasing the probability the misbehavior will occur again? According to Skinner, what should happen if the teacher appeared not to notice such behaviors but instead offered public praise whenever the student happened to be quiet, attentive, or hard at work?

Additional Criticisms of Skinner

The Skinnerian system, powerful as it is, has a number of flaws in it. Skinner has often stated that each organism determines for itself what it needs, and therefore what stimuli will reinforce it. Some rewards are learned; others are determined by the organism's genetic blueprint. As we saw earlier, food is innately reinforcing because it changes your blood sugar level (among other things), but your social environment determines which foods you take pleasure in eating. Skinner has focused chiefly on those rewards—such as food—that seem common to all animals. But because Skinner believes that neither mentalism nor physiology have any useful place in the science of behavior, he often fails to take into account the reward value of purely cognitive, intellectual, or perceptual experiences.

Many Gestalt theorists believe that people are often rewarded by new perceptions, by gathering previously unrelated facts into a meaningful whole (which they term a "Gestalt"). As we mentioned earlier, when pigeons are trained to bowl, they often show the same kind of delighted "Ah ha!" response that Maier's rat and Koehler's chimpanzee showed when those animals suddenly perceived a relationship that had apparently eluded them before. Educators sometimes refer to this experience as "the thrill of discovery," and there is little doubt that such reactions constitute a strong reinforcement. These experiences are quite rare, however, and the teacher who believes that insight is the *only* kind of reward necessary in the classroom is probably not a very effective behavioral change agent. For we all seem to need praise and encouragement as we first acquire the hundreds of bits of data needed for *closure* (°).

QUESTION: Koehler had to wait several hours until Sultan "accidentally" held the two poles in front of him and noticed that one could be fitted into the other; how might Skinner have trained Sultan to get the banana in a much shorter time?

Rewarding Insights

Many teachers appear to make "insightful" use of the best features of both the Gestalt and Skinnerian positions. Data from experiments on animal and human learning suggest that the fewer bits of information an organism needs in order to gain closure, the greater and more rewarding is the "Ah ha!" experience. The fewer pieces of a jigsaw puzzle you need in order to be able to perceive what the picture is like, the more pleased you are when you actually make the "creative leap" and organize the picture into a meaningful whole.

But insights typically occur when a person or pigeon has built up enough units in a response chain to be able to perceive or anticipate a previously unexpected result. It would seem that we all need a Skinnerian type of feedback and reward to guide our steps toward the creation of a Gestalt, but that it is the pleasure resulting from achieving the insight that gives the whole experience meaningfulness, generality, and memorability.

Programmed textbooks typically provide even the most untalented student with the thousands of frames necessary for a reader to gain mastery of the material covered. Slower students usually need to digest this information in smaller steps and to receive more frequent feedback and encouragement on their progress than do faster learners. So-called "insightful" persons appear to be able to jump from one large chunk of information to another without touching ground in between the high points. If the fast learner is forced to go through all the repetitive frames

Closure. A Gestalt principle of perception. The tendency to complete an intellectual task, to work for complete insight into a problem, or to perceive broken figures as wholes or as closed figures. See Chapter 10.

the slow learner needs, he or she is bored to tears and never really gets to experience the "creative leap" that constitutes such a powerful reinforcer for mastery of complex material.

A few of the more recent programmed textbooks allow for individual learning speeds by dropping out or omitting many of the repetitive frames that would retard or even punish the rapid learner. Obviously, such texts are a step in the right direction. But the best program might be one so flexible that it adjusted both the number of frames used and the content of each frame, so that each reader would be given the minimum amount of information that *particular reader required* to gain the most reinforcement possible. The program would hopefully keep each student on his or her intellectual toes by forcing the student to make larger and larger leaps as time went on; but it would never make the student jump so far between chunks of data that the student ever failed. At the moment, no such programs exist, but luckily there are a few teachers who do use constant encouragement to shape their students toward such terminal behavior rewards as "creative insights."

> QUESTION: If you had been Sultan, the chimpanzee, would you have preferred to have worked the sticks problem out by yourself or to have been shaped to the solution through a thousand simple exercises?

Perhaps the best argument in favor of Skinner's methodology comes from the numerous classroom experiments designed to compare its effectiveness with that of other ways of teaching. Under controlled conditions, students who are shaped typically learn considerably more facts, score higher on exams, enjoy the course more, and think more highly of the teacher than do students taught by more traditional methods. It seems very likely that the behavioral technology developed by Skinner will have a major impact on U.S. educational practice in the future; but, as we will see, its usefulness is not limited to the classroom.

OPERANT VERSUS RESPONDENT CONDITIONING

Skinner calls the type of learning he studies *instrumental conditioning*, or *operant conditioning* (*), because the organism must learn which of its behavioral operations will be instrumental in gaining its reward. Skinner refers to Pavlovian training as *respondent conditioning* (*) because Pavlov taught his animals to respond in a specific way to a specific stimulus.

Pavlov's conditioning stimulus (CS) appears to *elicit* (*) or pull the CR out of the animal in mechanical fashion whenever the CS appears. Reward is not usually necessary for Pavlovian or respondent conditioning to occur; the mere pairing or contiguity of the CS and the UCS takes care of setting up the S-R bond.

In operant conditioning, the organism voluntarily gives forth or *emits* (*) a response that the environment then rewards or punishes. Animals may be conditioned to emit operant responses in the presence of certain stimuli, but these are merely signals to the organism that a particular response will now be rewarded if it is emitted. Thus, a rat will learn to press a lever only when a bright light turns on if the experimenter rewards lever presses only when the light is burning.

An experienced rat will sit quietly by the lever waiting for the signal and then will bar-press furiously as soon as the light is illuminated. But, in truth, the animal is free to ignore the stimulus light if it is willing to forego the food reward. In Pavlovian or respondent conditioning, the well-trained animal *always* responds with the CR as soon as the CS appears; such responses are automatic and reflexive, hence not normally under the organism's voluntary control.

Most complex human behaviors, such as speech, appear to be a combination of operant and respondent conditioning built up over years of practice and experience, and it is not very easy to separate such skills into their component parts and

---

Operant conditioning (OPP-purr-ant). Also called "instrumental conditioning." A type of learning in which the organism must learn which of its responses will operate on its environment to yield a reward.

Respondent conditioning (ree-SPON-dent). Also called "classical conditioning" or "Pavlovian conditioning." So named because the organism always *responds* to presentation of the UCS or the CS with the UCR or the CR.

Elicit (ee-LISS-sit). To pull out, to evoke, to stimulate into action. In Pavlovian conditioning, the stimulus that elicits the CR is always identifiable. The important bond is the one between the stimulus and the response.

Emit (ee-MITT). In operant conditioning, the exact stimulus that makes a rat press a lever isn't really known. Rather, it is assumed that the animal freely emits whatever response it feels like making. The important association is between the response itself and the reward that follows. If a rat is trained to press a lever only when a light is turned on, the rat is said to "emit" the response in the presence of the light stimulus—however, the light doesn't really elicit the bar-press response; it merely serves as a "discriminative" stimulus that lets the rat know that if it now emits a response, that response will be rewarded.

chains. Of the two types, however, operant conditioning seems to be the predominant or more important one.

Pavlov demonstrated clearly that control over autonomic, emotional, or involuntary responses, such as salivation and contraction of the stomach muscles, could be achieved by respondent conditioning. In the 1930's both Skinner and Mowrer attempted to achieve the same sort of control over involuntary responses using operant (reward) training, but failed. The belief grew up thereafter that any learning involving the autonomic nervous system and its control over reflexive or involuntary muscle movements had to be of the Pavlovian type. Operant conditioning was thought to be effective only in the shaping of voluntary or spontaneous responses. These differences were perhaps of more theoretical than practical importance.

Biofeedback

Recently, however, psychologists Neal Miller, Leo DiCara, and their associates challenged the view that reflexive behaviors cannot be brought under operant (reward) control. In the late 1960's Miller and DiCara showed that rats could be trained to increase or to decrease their heart rates if the rats were reinforced for doing so. In one of their early studies Miller and DiCara implanted electrodes in the pleasure centers of their rats' brains. Then they gave their animals a drug called *curare* (°), which left the rats conscious but prevented all voluntary movements.

Once the animals' gross motor movements had been paralyzed, Miller and DiCara attached the rats to a *polygraph* (°) that recorded their (involuntary) heart beats. Whenever a rat's heart rate would increase a little, they stimulated the animal's reward center electrically. Slowly, over a period of time, the rat's heart responded to this form of biological feedback by beating faster and faster.

By reversing the procedure—that is, by giving the animal a rewarding type of feedback whenever its heart *slowed* momentarily—they were able to condition a decrease in the rat's pulse. By giving their subjects *biofeedback* (°) about their

Curare (cure-RAH-ree). A drug that paralyzes most of the muscles of the body. Several tribes of South American Indians put curare on the darts used in their blow-guns. When the dart strikes an animal, the animal is paralyzed and can easily be captured and killed for food.

Polygraph. A machine that graphs or records many different bodily reactions simultaneously. Also called a "lie-detector."

Biofeedback. Literally, biological feedback. Any mechanism that feeds back information on biological performance, such as an EEG machine. See Chapter 3.

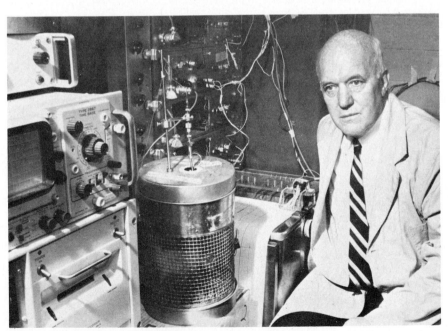

In his laboratory at Rockefeller University, Dr. Neal E. Miller records visceral responses from a freely moving rat.

Valid (VALL-lid). From the Latin word for "strong." A belief that is founded on strong or highly believable facts is said to be valid.

Hypertension (high-purr-TEN-shun). The medical term for high blood pressure.

blood pressures, sweating, salivation, urine formation, or stomach contractions, Miller, DiCara, and their associates were able to bring these involuntary, autonomic responses under operant control as well.

Because the Miller-DiCara experiments contradicted long-held theoretical notions about the differences between respondent and operant conditioning, psychologists were reluctant to accept the data as being *valid* (°) or real. This skepticism reached a peak in the early 1970's, when Miller and DiCara had difficulties in repeating (replicating) some of their earlier experiments involving curare. By 1973, however, numerous other laboratories had confirmed the initial findings, not only with rats and dogs but also with humans.

Biofeedback in Hospitals

Whether the Miller-DiCara experiments actually have broken down the theoretical differences between operant and respondent conditioning need not concern us at the moment. The practical implications of their research are surely much more important. By 1973 doctors in several clinical laboratories had begun to use biofeedback and operant techniques to help patients who suffer from various types of heart and circulatory problems. People whose lives are endangered by high blood pressure, for instance, have learned to control their *hypertension* (°) by watching a machine that gives them continuous visual feedback on their blood pressure. Whenever the machine indicates the blood pressure is rising, they try to think relaxing thoughts or to make their muscles go limp. Whenever their blood pressure falls a little, they try to remember just what it was they were imagining or feeling when the drop occurred, and to repeat that thought or emotion more often in the future. Other patients are attempting to learn to control irregularities in their heart beats, or to reduce the flow of stomach acids that might damage or inflame their ulcers. These training techniques are particularly useful with people who, for one reason or another, cannot make use of the drugs often employed to control circulatory or digestive illnesses.

From a Skinnerian point of view, most hospitals do not make very effective use of behavioral technology. Rather than keeping the patient fully aware of his or her physical condition and encouraging the patient to gain voluntary control over his or her biological reactions, medical doctors often hide the patient's chart at the foot of the hospital bed and refuse to discuss the patient's present status in detailed terms. The sicker the patient is, the more attention the patient gets. Behaviorists believe that such attention might actually *reward* the patient for remaining in poor health, for as the patient becomes better, he or she is typically ignored more and more frequently. Wouldn't it be better, the behaviorists ask, if doctors tried to get the patient to participate consciously and eagerly in his or her own recovery? Shouldn't a patient be vigorously rewarded for each "step toward health" that his or her body makes? Although the use of biofeedback is in its infancy in medical circles, operant technology will surely be widely employed in the future to help sick people gain voluntary control over many of their physiological responses.

How odd it is to think that a laboratory technique developed to train pigeons to peck at tiny buttons and rats to press little levers would turn out to have such usefulness for humans.

SUMMARY

1. The study of learning is one of the major areas within psychology.
2. E.L. Thorndike assumed that animals learn in much the same way that humans do. His studies with cats in a puzzle box led him to assume that most

learning is by trial and error. The animal responds to certain stimuli in an almost accidental manner; those responses that yield rewards are strengthened (the law of effect).

3. Thorndike's law of exercise states that the more frequently an animal repeats a response in the presence of a given stimulus input, the stronger the stimulus-response connection (S-R bond) becomes.

4. Thorndike, like Pavlov, believed that all learning is mechanical or reflexive. Other psychologists, such as Wolfgang Koehler, assumed that animals are capable of thinking about what they are doing and of solving problems mentally (through "insight") rather than through mechanical trial and error.

5. B.F. Skinner, a behaviorist much like Thorndike, developed operant conditioning, a method of training organisms that can be contrasted with Pavlovian or respondent conditioning.

6. Pavlov believed that the CS elicits or pulls the CR out of the animal. Skinner feels that animals emit responses freely and that the environment rewards some of those responses but ignores or punishes others.

7. According to Skinner, reward tends to increase the probability that an organism will emit the same response the next time it is free to do so.

8. Training an organism by operant techniques consists of several steps.
   a. First, the terminal response or goal of the training must be stated in measurable terms.
   b. Second, the entering behavior (what the organism is doing before intervention begins) must be measured precisely.
   c. Third, those entering behaviors that seem directed toward the terminal response are rewarded; all other responses are ignored.
   d. Each small step toward the goal is reinforced—a technique called "shaping" or "successive approximations to a goal."

9. Most professional animal trainers in the United States now use this Skinnerian, or operant, form of conditioning.

10. These same operant techniques can be of considerable use in classroom situations if the teacher identifies the responses that the students should acquire and then rewards each approximation toward measurable educational gains.

11. Operant conditioning also may prove of considerable value in training medical patients to gain greater control over the functions of their bodies. People with high blood pressure, for instance, can be given biofeedback about their blood pressure and encouraged to repeat relaxing responses that decrease their hypertension.

12. No one system of training organisms is complete in and of itself, however. The cognitive theorists (Koehler), the Pavlovians, and the Behaviorists have all added greatly to our understanding of how humans acquire new attitudes, traits, skills, and behavioral reactions.

(Continued from page 334.)

Joseph T. Bigeloe, president of Trans-Vue Electronics, Inc., peered unhappily at the psychologist sitting across from him. "It's the Japanese, Dr. Haven. They're killing us. That's why we need you as a consultant."

"I thought the Second World War ended 30 years ago," said Dr. T.T. Haven.

"No, not that war. Our firm didn't even exist then—a product of the electronics explosion that came afterward. Transistors, tunnel diodes—things like that. Pack a lot of wires and gadgets into a very tiny space. Most of the technology was invented right here. The good old U S of A. But the Japanese copied it all, did it better and cheaper and faster than us. Unfair, unpatriotic. Must do something about it. That's why we need you."

Psychologist Haven smiled. "I put my guns away back in 1945, thank you, and I have no intention of getting them out again. If you want someone to bomb Hiroshima again, you'll have to look elsewhere."

"You're deliberately misunderstanding me, Doctor." Joseph T. Bigeloe tapped his fingers together nervously. "They're unfair because they use cheap labor. Japanese will work for a fraction of the wages that Americans will. People on Taiwan even worse. Work for beans there. Koreans and the Chinese on Hong

Kong are just as bad. Now it's spreading to the Philippines. Like a virus, like the Hong Kong flu. No dignity at all, that's what's wrong with them."

Dr. Haven stared straight into Joseph T. Bigeloe's green-gray eyes. "In short, Mr. Bigeloe, U.S. labor costs are pricing your products out of the market. I can understand how that might upset you, but I'm not sure what you expect me to do about it."

"Motivation, Dr. Haven. Motivation is the key. You're a psychologist, you know what makes people tick. I can pay an inspector on my assembly line $5 an hour and still make money if she'll produce at three or four times the rate of a Japanese woman who does the same job for $1.50 an hour or less. Want you to find a way to up our workers' motivation by a factor of 3 or 4. Not much to ask."

"Well, before I answer that, let's get one thing straight. Do you want me to make your workers 'tick' at 3 or 4 times their normal rate, or do you want me to increase their motivation that much? That is, do you want me to influence their attitudes and desires or increase their output?"

"Same thing. Boils down to the same thing in the long run."

"Not necessarily, Mr. Bigeloe. I could probably take your pet dog and make it the most motivated animal in the world, but it would still be a lousy jet pilot."

"Don't keep dogs. Keep birds. Parakeets. My wife is bats over parakeets. Genus **Melopsittacus,** species **undulatus.** Come from Australia. Teaches them to talk. Almost human, some of them."

Dr. Haven sighed. "Yes, I see. Well, let's start over again. Your problem seems to be that of reducing production costs however you can. One way surely would be to increase the productivity of your workers. But have you talked all this over with the workers themselves?"

"Of course. Enlightened management and all that sort of thing."

Expecting Mr. Bigeloe to elaborate, Dr. Haven waited a moment. When the other man was silent, the psychologist continued. "Well, what do your workers say?"

"World's dullest job. That's their complaint. You see, our real bottleneck is in inspection. We produce hundreds of tiny components. Most of the output is automated. We're ahead of the rest of the world in that department, I reckon. But some of the stuff has to be looked at individually. For example, we make one little gidget out of a special metal alloy. Has to be completely spray-coated with a kind of plastic covering. One little bare spot in the covering, the gidget will short out. Got to make sure the covering is complete and intact. Hire lots of little old ladies to inspect each gidget as it comes off the line. Nice little old ladies. Sit and stare at one gidget after another, hour after hour. Pay them good wages, but they still complain. Would use little old men, but they complain even more. Can't imagine why. Problem of motivation. That's your job. Get them to love the company, love their work, love those gidgets. Beat the Japanese hands down, if you can do it."

"Why don't you automate the inspection process?"

"Tried it. Optical scanners hooked to computers. Didn't work. Machines just can't discriminate perfectly enough. Too high an error rate. People are cheaper and better. I understand machines; you understand people. So get to work."

"How do the Japanese handle the gidget inspection problem?"

"Lots of nice little old Japanese ladies. Don't argue with the boss, work for peanuts. Love their companies. Love the gidgets. Maybe slant eyes don't get tired like normal eyes do."

Dr. Haven shook his head in dismay at the man's blind prejudice. "Their eyelids have an extra bit of tissue called an epicanthic fold that our eyelids lack. Their eyes get tired just the same way ours do. Their social system is different, but even that is changing. But that's beside the point. Why don't you try to make the inspector's job more interesting, more challenging, more meaningful?"

"Tried that. Piped in Muzak background music. Read poetry to them. Gave them lots of coffee breaks. Helped some. They still quit or go on strike. In Japan, when they go on strike, they stick to their jobs but wear a black arm band or something like that. Here, they just don't care. Quit, go on relief. Government takes care of them whether they work or not. No incentive to work. Up to you to get them to want to stay off welfare. Lazy bunch, really."

"On the contrary, Mr. Bigeloe. Recent studies show that the blue-collar workers in general—and people on welfare in particular—are just as highly motivated to work and get off relief as you are. They suffer from a lack of skills and training and education, not from an overabundance of laziness. Give them a decent job instead of scut work and they usually do very well indeed. Give them a dehumanizing job—one that is so repetitive and routine it can better be performed by a computer brain than a human one—and who can blame them for being bored to death and quitting or going on strike? Would you work 8 hours a day doing nothing but inspecting gidgets?"

"Impertinent question. I've got motivation. They haven't. Up to you to find a solution. That's what we're hiring you for."

The psychologist rubbed his eyes slowly, carefully. He looked around the room for a few moments, pursed his lips, scratched his head, then sat quietly. Finally he said, "You've given me an idea. I think I know a way of reducing your labor costs by at least 90 percent by using the most highly motivated workers you can imagine. They'll make fewer mistakes than the inspectors you're using now; they'll work a 7-day week; and they'll never go on strike or complain to the union. It's the perfect solution to your problem." The psychologist emitted a deep sigh. "But of course you'll never agree to it."

"Want me to import Japanese workers, eh? Thought of that. Union problems, passport problems, work permit difficulties. Thought of bringing in Mexicans too. Same difficulties. Guessed your idea, didn't I?"

"No, you're not even close. But it's still too radical for you . . ."

"If it means keeping Trans-Vue Electronics afloat, nothing is too radical."

"I'm thinking of computer brains."

"Too expensive. Told you I thought of that."

"These computers will cost you less than $5 each, and their upkeep will be minimal."

"Some cheap Japanese computer?"

"No, red-blooded U.S. computers. Mr. Bigeloe, the human brain is a superb computer, but, as you point out, one that needs lots of tender, loving, expensive care to keep it motivated. The animal brain is a much smaller, less powerful computer, but within limits it has excellent potential."

"Animals? Want me to hire animals? That's a hare-brained idea if I ever heard one!"

"Not hares, Mr. Bigeloe. Birds. To be specific, pigeons. Magnificent eyesight. No epicanthic fold, either. I promise you that I can train pigeons to be much better gidget inspectors than the little old ladies you're now using—and at a fraction of the cost. Think of the money you'll save."

"Never work. Birds are dumb. How could you explain to them what a gidget is?"

"How do you explain it to a computer?"

"Don't have to. Just program the computer to reject any gidget that doesn't have certain physical characteristics."

"Birds are already programmed to do that. Pigeons peck at corn, but not at glass marbles."

"It would never work. Dirty birds. Pigeon feathers all over the place."

"We'll put the pigeons in boxes. As the gidgets come off the line, they'll pass by a window in the pigeon box one by one, on a conveyor belt. The pigeon will be trained to look each gidget over carefully. If it's perfectly coated, the pigeon will peck a green button; if the gidget is flawed, the pigeon will peck a red button and the gidget will be rejected. We'll put the bird on a variable ratio reinforcement schedule—give it a piece of corn as a reward every once in a while."

"Pigeons make mistakes."

"So do humans, if you give them stupid tasks to perform. Besides, we can cut down the random error rate by having each gidget inspected by two birds, one after the other. I guarantee you more accurate performance than you're getting now."

"Can't see it. Unions would complain. Taking food out of the mouths of American labor."

"So do computers. So you hire half the little old ladies as pigeon handlers, a job I suspect they'd much rather perform. You still save money. And how many jobs can you offer the union if Trans-Vue Electronics goes broke?"

"It's unpatriotic."

"Use U.S. eagles instead of pigeons. And feed them Japanese beetles instead of corn."

"But it's inhumane. Making birds work an 8-hour shift like that, doing nothing but looking at gidgets. They'd go crazy."

"Is it more humane to make little old ladies perform the same work?"

"No. Wife would never stand for it. Birds should be free to fly around and things like that."

"Free, like the 'almost human' parakeets your wife keeps in cages in your home?"

Joseph T. Bigeloe, president of Trans-Vue Electronics, Inc., peered unhappily at the psychologist sitting across from him. "I don't think you're being serious."

"I was never more serious in my life. Think it over, Mr. Bigeloe. If you want your company to stay airborne, you may have to find some new wings. Talk it over with your wife, with the union, with your workers. See if you can't work something out. If you're still interested, I'll come back to see you again next week."

Dr. Haven rose and made his way through the thick carpeting to the door. As he walked out, Mr. Bigeloe shook his head sadly.

"Horse feathers," he said brusquely.

RECOMMENDED READINGS

Barber, Theodore, *et al.*, eds, *Biofeedback and Self Control, 1975* (Chicago: Aldine-Atherton, Inc., 1976).

Brown, Daniel G. *Behavior Modification in Child and School Mental Health: An Annotated Bibliography on Applications with Parents and Teachers* (Washington, D.C.: National Institute of Mental Health, DHEW Publication No. (HSM) 72–9108, 1972).

Koehler, Wolfgang. *Gestalt Psychology* (New York: Liveright Publishing Corporation, 1947).

McConnell, James V. "Psycho-technology and Personal Change," in M.H. Siegel and H.P. Zeigler (eds.), *Psychological Research: The Inside Story* (New York: Harper & Row, 1976).

Skinner, B.F. *Walden Two* (New York: The Macmillan Company, 1960).

Skinner, B.F. *About Behaviorism* (New York: Knopf, 1974).

chapter 17

"WHERE IS YESTERDAY?"

MEMORY

DID YOU KNOW THAT . . .

You have not one memory, but many different kinds of memories?

Your eyes momentarily store an "exact photo" of what you see, but your brain "forgets" most of what your eyes see?

You typically cannot remember more than seven items on a list after one brief exposure to the list?

Your Long-term Memory consists of "mental file cards" that allow you to reconstruct past events rather than remember them exactly?

Forgetting is usually a matter of not being able to find the right "mental file card?"

Your brain has a better memory system than any computer?

With practice, you can greatly improve your ability to remember?

There is a growing belief that, when you learn, your brain manufactures new "memory molecules?"

Some experiments suggest these "memory molecules" can be transferred from one organism to another?

If you are deprived of REM sleep, your Long-term Memory may be adversely affected?

"What's your name, dear?" The woman lying in the white hospital bed smiled sweetly as she asked the question.

The young girl in the gray uniform paused in her chores. "Jamie," she said quietly. "Jamie Calvin. I'm the Nurse's Aide."

"That's an odd sort of name, now isn't it? Is it English, or something?"

The girl in gray grinned at the bedridden woman. "Not really, Mrs. Bjork. I'm the oldest child in our family, and my father really wanted a boy. So when I turned out to be a girl instead he gave me a boy's name anyhow." The young woman continued her work, picking up a couple of empty glasses and throwing some used tissues into the wastebasket.

"But whom did he name you after, dear?" Mrs. Bjork continued.

"Daddy was nuts about a psychologist named William James. He really wanted to call me Willie but Mother wouldn't stand for it. So they compromised on Jamie instead. I don't mind, really. Rather a nice name when you get used to it."

"William James! Isn't that peculiar! Why I can remember reading his book **Varieties of Religious Experience** in my psychology of religion class! Was your father by any chance a psychologist, Jamie?"

"No, but he sometimes thought he was. Actually, Daddy was a nice, old-fashioned Methodist minister. With a name like Calvin, what else would you expect? We buried him two years ago, God rest his soul."

"Oh, I'm so sorry, my dear. I know you must miss him."

"I do, Mrs. Bjork. But he lives on in my memory, just as though he was still alive." The young woman paused, then brightened. "Is your father still alive?"

Mrs. Bjork laughed. "Very much so. A big bear of a man, he is. In fact, I rather expect him to come visit me today."

"That would be nice," Jamie Calvin said, as she gathered up the dirty glasses and headed for the door. "You just rest comfortably until he does, Mrs. Bjork."

Jamie Calvin walked softly as a Siamese cat down the long hospital corridor, deposited the glasses in a large container, and returned to the nurses' station.

"Nice woman in 914, that Mrs. Bjork," she said to Mrs. Melton, one of the nurses on duty. "What's she in for?"

Mrs. Melton was filling out some forms. Stopping for a moment, she said, "Mrs. Bjork? Oh, she's a brain-damage case. She's in for some tests. You haven't seen her before, have you? Yes, she's a very nice woman. I do hope they can do something for her."

"What's wrong with her?" Jamie said, sitting down.

"She was in a terrible automobile accident not long ago. Wasn't wearing her seat belt, and her head went right through the windshield. Didn't scar her up much, but she suffered considerable brain damage. They had to remove a fair share of both her temporal lobes."

"Temporal lobes?" the younger woman asked plaintively.

"They're the part of the brain right by your temples."

"Oh," Jamie said. "That doesn't sound very good. Poor Mrs. Bjork."

A buzzer sounded, and Nurse Melton looked at her call board. "914," she said. "Speak of the devil. Be a dear, Jamie, and go see what Mrs. Bjork wants."

When Jamie walked into the hospital room, Mrs. Bjork looked at the young woman through puzzled eyes. "I'm terribly sorry to bother you, Nurse, but I seem to be confused about a few things. Obviously I'm in a hospital, but for the life of me, I can't think why. I don't feel at all sick. I'm terribly sorry to impose on you this way, but I wonder if you can tell me what's wrong?"

Jamie frowned. "Mrs. Melton—the nurse—says that you were in a terrible car accident, and they want to give you some tests. I'm sure it won't hurt at all, and that you'll be out of the hospital very quickly."

"A car accident? Now, isn't that funny. I can't remember a thing about a car accident. Are you sure?"

"That's what Nurse Melton just told me."

Mrs. Bjork frowned. "Oh well, I'm sure it will all come back to me soon." Then she smiled at the Nurse's Aide. "By the way, what's your name, dear?"

"Jamie Calvin. Like I told you, I'm the Nurse's Aide."

"That's an odd sort of name, now isn't it? Is it English, or something?"

Jamie's eyes narrowed. She thought a moment as if deciding how to continue. Then she said softly, "Not really, Mrs. Bjork. I'm the oldest child in our family. My father really wanted me to be a boy, but I turned out to be a girl. So he gave me a boy's name instead."

"But whom did he name you after, dear?" Mrs. Bjork continued.

Jamie took a step nearer the door. "Daddy was nuts about a psychologist named William James. Mother wouldn't let him call me Willie, so they named me Jamie instead."

"William James! Isn't that peculiar! Why I can remember reading his book, **Varieties of Religious Experience** in my psychology of religion class! Was your father by any chance a psychologist, Jamie?"

"Would you like a glass of water or a Coke or something, Mrs. Bjork?" Jamie said rather desperately.

"Water? Why, yes, a cola or a ginger ale would be nice. I think my father will be coming to see me shortly, you know. He likes ginger ale very much. Why don't you be a lamb and bring us two bottles of ginger ale?"

"Right away," Jamie said, leaving the room quickly.

"What did Mrs. Bjork want?" Nurse Melton said, when Jamie returned to the station.

"Some ginger ale." Jamie sat down for a moment, then blurted out, "What's wrong with Mrs. Bjork? She didn't even remember me from five minutes ago."

"Oh, I should have warned you. Something's wrong with her memory. She can't remember a thing. That's what they want to do the tests on."

Jamie frowned. "But she remembered a lot of things. Like a psychology course she took, for instance, and a book she'd read."

"I know. But she can't remember where she is or what day it is," Mrs. Melton said, continuing her paperwork. "Makes her seem stupid sometimes, but she's really quite bright. One of the psychologists tested her intelligence yesterday. Said her IQ after the accident is actually a little bit higher than it was the last time she was tested, about 10 years ago. She spoke fluent French and Spanish before the accident, and she still speaks them fluently. Only thing is, she can't remember what she had for breakfast or who her doctor is."

After a moment, Jamie sighed deeply. "I guess I'd better go get that ginger ale. She's expecting her father."

Nurse Melton stopped and put down the forms she was working on. "Jamie, dear, her father is dead. He was driving the car when the accident occurred."

"But hasn't anybody told her?"

"Jamie, everybody has told her, many times. She just doesn't remember."

"But she remembers her name! How could she forget her father's death and still remember her own name?"

Nurse Melton shrugged, then went back to her papers.

A few moments later Jamie knocked softly at the door to Room 914, then entered, carrying a tray with two bottles of ginger ale, glasses, and a little bucket of ice. "Here's the soda pop you wanted, Mrs. Bjork."

"Soda pop?" the woman in the bed said. "I didn't order any soda pop. That must be for one of the other patients."

"Why, Mrs. Bjork, you particularly asked for ginger ale because you said your father was coming to visit you."

Mrs. Bjork shook her head. "I'm sure I didn't ask for any ginger ale, but it is true that my father likes it very much. So why don't you just be a dear and leave it here for him?" As the young woman put the tray down on a table, Mrs. Bjork stared at her thoughtfully. "What's your name, dear?"

"Jamie," the young woman whispered. "Jamie Calvin. I'm the Nurse's Aide."

"That's an odd sort of name, now isn't it? Is it English, or something?"

There were tears in Jamie's eyes as she answered. "Not really, Mrs. Bjork. I'm the oldest in our family, and Daddy really wanted a boy. So when I happened to be a girl instead, he insisted on giving me a boy's name anyhow." Jamie turned and headed for the door.

"But whom did he name you after, dear?" Mrs. Bjork continued.

Jamie Calvin muffled a sob and fled from the room.

"Now, wasn't that odd," Mrs. Bjork said aloud, reaching for a bottle of ginger ale. "I wonder what's the matter with her?"

What time is it?

A simple question, one that you either ask or are asked perhaps a dozen times a week. You look at your watch, or at a clock, and you give the answer almost automatically. If you don't have a watch or clock handy, you guess—and usually you'll be accurate within a few minutes or so. If you are *bilingual* (°)—that is, if you speak another language besides English—you will answer the question either in English or in your second language, depending on what language the question was asked in.

A simple question, What time is it? Yet, to be truthful, we have only the vaguest of notions how your brain goes about processing such inputs, and we know even less about how your brain responds so appropriately. Perhaps if we explore this question further, though, you will gain an even greater respect for and understanding of the complexities of your mind and your nervous system.

MEMORY SYSTEMS

To answer any question, you must make use of your memory. If someone asks you the time, you must first recognize that someone has spoken to you, then that you

Bilingual (buy-LING-wall). From the Latin words *bi*, meaning "two," and *lingua*, meaning "tongue" or "language." The term "lingo," meaning the slang words used by a particular group of people, also comes from the Latin word *lingua*. For that matter, so does the word "slang."

have been asked a question to which you might respond. Then you must check your memory banks to make sure you recognize the language the person has used. But while all this checking is taking place, *your brain must have some way of remembering what the original question was.* If you had no way of holding the question in some kind of temporary storage, you'd end up realizing that someone had asked you something in English without being able to remember what it was the person asked. As we will see, a different part of your brain seems to be involved in temporary storage of the question than is involved in answering the question itself (or in recognizing that someone has, in fact, posed a question in the first place).

> QUESTION: You are reading an interesting book when someone nearby asks you something. Have you ever responded with "What did you say?" and then, even before the question could be repeated, given the correct answer?

> QUESTION: How did you go about answering that question?

In point of fact, you don't have just one memory system, you have several, and they typically perform their functions simultaneously. Whenever a new stimulus comes to your attention, your *receptors* appear to hold on to the stimulus pattern for a fraction of a second while some part of your brain checks the stimulus over to see if it is familiar to you.

If you recognize the stimulus, another part of your brain then takes over and "memorizes" the most *salient* (°) or important parts of the stimulus for a few seconds while the rest of your brain decides what to do with the incoming message.

Sensory Information Stage

What time is it?

When the printed stimulus input first impinges on the retinas in your eyes, your rods and cones begin to fire a characteristic pattern of nerve impulses that flash along the optic nerve to the visual centers of your brain. Now suppose we showed that stimulus question to you for exactly one-tenth of a second. How long would the rods and cones continue to fire after the stimulus had disappeared?

The answer is—it depends. If you had been sitting in absolute darkness for several minutes before the stimulus appeared, and if you remained in darkness for several minutes thereafter, the words *"What time is it?"* would hang suspended in your visual field for quite some time—like the words on a huge billboard if all the rest of the world were blacked out. After some time the image would begin to fade, and eventually it would seem to disappear almost entirely into the darkness around you. At this point if you pressed slightly on your eyeballs, the image very likely would reappear faintly. On the other hand, if you were sitting in a lighted room reading the words *"What time is it?"* in a book, the very next words you read would wash out or erase the phrase. Under normal conditions, as you look from one thing to another in your visual world, your eye holds on to each stimulus pattern for but a fraction of a second before it is replaced by yet another image.

Your memory begins, then, in your receptors, in what psychologists call the *Sensory Information Storage* (°) stage of information processing. When your eye briefly "stores" a visual input, it records the scene in amazing detail, much as a photograph of the same stimulus would. By the time this visual information reaches your brain and you become aware of what you are looking at, much of the rich detail has been lost. Your eye has a "photographic memory," but your brain doesn't. For as soon as the stimulus pattern is flashed along to the lower centers in your brain, they begin analyzing the stimulus for its meaning or importance. These lower centers promptly discard or reject any part of the sensory pattern that they don't find interesting.

Salient (SAY-lee-ent). Anything that stands out from its background, that is important or noticeable.

Sensory Information Storage. The first stage of memory storage. Suppose you are looking at a blank television screen when the word "help" suddenly flashes on the screen for exactly 1/10th of a second and then disappears, leaving the screen blank again. The rods and cones in your retina will actually hold the image of the word "help" for much more than a second. During this holding stage, the rods and cones will continue to send signals to your brain just as if the word "help" were still showing on the screen. This momentary hold of an incoming sensory pattern is the Sensory Information Storage stage of memory.

The *reticular system* (°) (*see* Chapter 9) probably looks the stimulus over ("processes the input") to see if it is familiar and "safe." If so, the reticular system notifies your cortex that all is well and tells the cortex to have a look at what is coming through on the visual circuits. If the stimulus is mildly threatening but quite weak (such as a "dirty word" or a sexual scene), the reticular system may clamp down on the message and try to keep it from reaching the rest of your brain. If the visual pattern is novel, quite unexpected, or very threatening, the reticular system may trigger off an emotional reaction in your autonomic nervous system. This emotional response occurs, as you might suspect, even before your cortex becomes aware of what the visual input actually is. Whether the reticular system has its own memory bank or simply has connections to the larger library of information stored elsewhere in your brain—or both—no one knows for sure.

Short-term Memory

While the reticular system is judging the emotional importance of the incoming message, other parts of your brain make a preliminary interpretation of what the stimulus input means. This "meaning" is then held for a brief period in what we call *Short-term Memory* (°). As you can guess from the name itself, anything tucked away in your Short-term Memory has a very short lifetime—probably no more than a few seconds. The Sensory Information Storage system records (momentarily) a more or less exact copy of the stimulus pattern; your Short-term Memory holds the *interpretation* of this pattern for a few seconds longer, while the rest of your brain is deciding how best to respond to the stimulus; but much of the complexity of the sensory pattern is lost in the storage process. To prove this fact to yourself, read the following sentence rapidly and then look away from the page for a few seconds and try to remember exactly what the stimulus sentence was:

Кōморбш ъс

Reticular system (ree-TICK-you-lar). The reticular activating system (RAS) or "alerting" system in the brain. See Chapter 9.

Short-term Memory. You experience millions of different sensory inputs every day. As these incoming stimulus messages are passed to the brain from sensory information storage, some part of the brain interprets them and "remembers" them for a few brief seconds. If the inputs are not important, they are soon forgotten. Experts believe that you typically hold no more than about seven items at a time in your Short-term Memory.

Short-term Memory storage.

Cyrillic (seer-RILL-ick). The Russian alphabet, which is based on the Greek, was supposedly invented by St. Cyril, who died in A.D. 868. St. Cyril, who was born in Greece, helped take Christianity to the Slavic people in south Russia and translated the Bible into their language. Prior to this, the Slavic language had existed in spoken but not in written form. When St. Cyril wrote out the Bible, he "created" the Cyrillic alphabet still used in Russia today. In Cyrillic, the initials "CCCP" stand for the Soviet Union, that is, the Union of Soviet Socialist Republics, just as in English the initials "USA" stand for the United States of America.

Chances are—unless you are familiar with the Russian language—you had a difficult time trying to remember just what it was you actually saw. You surely sensed at once that it was something written in a language other than English, but could you "see" in your mind's eye each of the letters in that strange *Cyrillic* (°) alphabet that the Russians use? Or was it more or less a jumbled blur? Now look quickly at the following stimulus sentence and then look away and try to visualize exactly what it says:

What time it is?

This time around, didn't you "visualize" the words themselves? Actually, since the Russian phrase was "what time is it," why couldn't you hold the Russian words in your Short-term Memory as long as you could the English words? If your memory were photographic, there shouldn't be any difference in your ability to remember one or the other. But, unless you speak Russian, your Short-term Memory couldn't abstract the meaning of the foreign words, and so you couldn't remember them. In the case of the English phrase, you remembered the *interpretation* of the stimulus rather than the exact shape of the letters themselves.

QUESTION: **Look again at the English phrase one paragraph above; does it really say what you remembered it as saying? If you didn't perceive it correctly, what might this fact tell you about your Short-term Memory?**

Your Short-term Memory system has a very limited capacity. Ordinarily it cannot retain anything for more than a few seconds, and also it typically cannot hold on to more than six or seven items at one time. At the moment that your brain inserts an item into Short-term Memory, that item is strong and clear and easy to recall if you do so *immediately*. But shortly thereafter, your brain tucks away a second item, and then a third item, and a fourth. Although only a few seconds have passed, you will now have much more trouble trying to recall what the first item was really like. And by the time your brain has pressed five or six new items down on top of the first, that original item has lost most of its strength and has faded away. The new items appear to interfere with or erase the ones in front of them just as each new visual pattern you look at wipes clean the stimulus you were looking at just a moment before.

While you are holding an item in Short-term Memory, you can recall it more or less at will. However, once the item drops out of "momentary hold," it is likely to be gone forever. If you would like to prove this fact to yourself, try this test next time you're walking some place. When you see someone coming toward you, don't look at the person until he or she is about 20 feet (6 meters) away. Then take a rapid glance at the person's face and look away immediately. Visualize the person's face as best you can, then look at the person once more before he or she passes—to check the accuracy of your impression. You'll find your Short-term Memory does very well. Now walk a block *looking at as many other faces as you can.* Then stop and try once more to recall what the first face was like. Unless you knew the person, or there was something pretty unusual about the way the person looked or acted, you'll probably experience considerable difficulty remembering such things as eye color, the exact shape of the person's nose, the precise color of the person's hair, and so on. Then, if you like, wait a day and try again to remember what that one face was like.

QUESTION: **Would it make any difference how many other people you had looked at between your first and second glance at the test person's face? What would happen to your memory of the face if, while you were walking along, you kept repeating to yourself what the face looked like? Would this "rehearsal" help you remember the way the person actually looked, or would you just remember your verbal description that you said over and over again?**

Long-term Memory

If you stroll along a busy street or walk through a crowded airport, you may see a thousand different people in one short hour. Most of their faces will fade from your memory like snow in the springtime winds. Yet some things you remember vividly—or at least you think you do. For example, think of the last long trip that you took. Can you remember *right at this instant* the exact date and hour that the trip began and ended? Chances are that you can't. But think about the problem for a moment. If you put your mind to it, couldn't you work out some of the details? What day of the week did the trip begin? Couldn't you figure out the date if you really tried? Did you start in the morning, the afternoon, or the evening? Who went with you, if anyone? If you flew, what airline was your carrier? If you drove, what kind of car was it?

If you actually take the time to think about the details—and perhaps write them down as you go—you'll find that you can *reproduce* a surprising amount of detail about that trip, even though it may have occurred months or years ago. However, if you inspect those memories carefully as they pop back into your consciousness, you'll find they are quite different from the immediate memory you have of a face you've just seen. In fact, your recollection of things that happened long ago usually is hazy and incomplete at first. You don't really *remember* things; rather, you typically recall a few high points and then *reconstruct* the experience piece by little piece. It would seem that you don't so much *recall* past events; rather, you use your intelligence and creativity and knowledge of the world to *recreate* what must have happened.

Your receptors store a more or less exact copy of the stimulus for a very few seconds or fraction of a second—a photograph that fades away even as you look at it. Your Short-term Memory is rather like an "instant replay" on television—a few seconds of highlight action that you can recall with considerable clarity for a brief period of time thereafter. But it is the salient features of the experience, and not all the rich sensory detail, that you can replay at will until these too fade away into obscurity. Both of these memory banks have a very limited capacity and are "erased" in a matter of seconds or minutes. But your *Long-term Memory* lasts the rest of your life, and for all practical purposes, its storage capacity is unlimited. Buried away in the cells of your brain are billions and billions of different memories that date back to your early childhood. You could, if the circumstances were right, go back and reproduce "in the theater of your mind" all those countless experiences. And yet, *right now*, can you remember all the things you did on your fifth birthday?

Long-term Memory is practically limitless, rather like a huge library with billions of books stashed away on the shelves. You add thousands of new volumes to that library every day of your life, and most of us never run out of shelf space for new arrivals. Not even the largest, most expensive computer system now in operation can match the complexity of your own brain's memory banks. Still, most of us complain that we have lousy memories. Why?

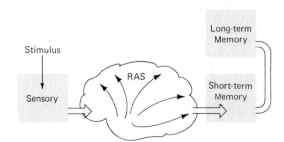

Short- and Long-term Memory flow chart.

Persevere (purr-suh-VEER, or purr-see-VEER). To persist in something; to pursue a goal until it is achieved. The psychological term "perseverate" (purr-SEV-ur-ate) means to keep doing something or talking about something long after the actual goal is achieved. Compulsive behaviors are often forms of abnormal perseverations (purr-sev-ur-RAY-shuns).

Cataloguing Memories   To appreciate how your Long-term Memory works—and why it often fails to function the way you would like it to—you must first discover the answers to several questions: First, what *part* of your immediate psychological experiences do you file away? Second, why do you store some experiences in Long-term Memory but not others? And third, once an item is placed in your permanent memory bank, how in the world do you go about retrieving it? As we will see, these three problems can best be answered if we first determine how good a librarian your brain is.

If you would like to stretch your imagination just a little, suppose that a rich uncle died and left you (1) his personal collection of more than a million magazines and books, (2) a huge but empty warehouse, and (3) a check for $500,000. However, you couldn't cash the check until after you had personally arranged all the items in his collection in some "reasonable order" and stored them in the warehouse (you would lose the cash if you got any outside help on the project). Since you could use a little pocket money, you decide to have a go at earning the $500,000. But when you arrive at the warehouse for the first time, you find that the movers have dumped all the books and magazines in a huge pile in the middle of the building. Now what do you do?

Perhaps some people would throw up their hands in horror and quit on the spot. But you decide to *persevere* (°). So you sit down on the floor and stare at all those items. You wonder how you might go about putting them in some kind of sensible order so that if someone walked into your warehouse library and asked for a particular book, you could retrieve it in a few short moments.

You might begin by separating the books from the magazines; surely that would help. Of course, you'd find there were a few fancy magazines published in hard covers that looked for all the world like books, and a few books published in soft covers that were hard to tell from periodicals; but in general the selection process would be fairly simple. How would you arrange the books? By their size? By the color of their cover? By the language they are printed in? By their authors and/or titles? By the name of their publishers? By their subject matter? By the year in which they were published? By whether you liked them or not?

And once you had answered those questions to your own satisfaction, wouldn't you want to make up a card index of some kind for handy reference? Then, when a friend of yours came in and said that he or she had once read "a big green book written by some foreign author on the unusual sex practices of a tribe of primitives in Africa—or maybe South America," you could find the volume for your

Freud, Sigmund.   131-F
    The origins of psycho-analysis; letters to Wilhelm Fliess, drafts and notes: 1887-1902.   Ed. by Marie Bonaparte, Anna Freud, Ernst Kris. Authorized translation by Eric Mosbacher and James Strachey.   Introduction by Ernst Kris.   Basic Books [c1954]   486 p.   illus.

    On cover: Sigmund Freud's letters: The origin of psychoanalysis.
    "Bibliographical index of the writings of Freud referred to in this work": p. [447]-455.   "Bibliographical index of the writings of authors other than Freud": p. [457]-462.

    1. Psychoanalysis
    I. Fliess, Wilhelm.
    II. Title.

                                                                              5 18 54

friend with not too much trouble (and might even decide to read it yourself some time!).

The next time you visit a library, you might wish to take a look at the card catalogue and see how professional librarians try to handle these problems—for library filing systems are patterned pretty much along the same line as the one your own brain uses. Whenever your brain files an item away for future reference (that is, stores an item in your Long-term Memory), it also creates a mental index card of some kind telling you how to retrieve that item if you have to do so. Your brain translates your personal experiences into a kind of mental shorthand and files those experiences away in various categories. You usually cannot remember an item unless you can first discover what "category" the item relates to.

Verbal Schemes   For example, think about dogs for a moment. How many different dogs can you remember? Can you recall a beloved pet from early childhood, or the big fierce animal that barked loudly at you just a few days ago? And why is it that, when you're trying to think of dogs, your brain doesn't pull out mental images of airplanes or snakes or roses? Presumably dogs and snakes are filed in different ways (or perhaps in different places), and when you want to remember one, images of the other are blocked from consciousness. Of course, there are cross-references between various categories—can you remember seeing a dog riding on an airplane, or a dog fighting a snake?

Whenever you try to call an item up from your Long-term Memory, you usually retrieve that item according to some *verbal scheme*. For most people, the "scheme" or arrangement of mental categories seems to run from the most specific to the most general. If you once owned a fox terrier named Spot, you could retrieve many memories of Spot simply by thinking first of the dog's name. If you couldn't recall what kind of dog Spot was, you might try thinking about dogs in general, and consider what species of dog Spot might have been (boxer, bulldog, collie, dachshund, fox terrier . . .). If you were trying to remember what kind of pet you used to own, thinking about pets would lead you to try out the categories of canaries, cats, dogs, goldfish, hamsters, horses . . . And, of course, pets are all animals, and hence items about pets should be filed differently than are items about plants or machines or books.

When you want to find a particularly obscure or indefinite item in your memory, your best bet often is to play the "animal, vegetable, or mineral" game, checking the broadest categories first and then moving down toward the more specific.

Knowing just that much about how your Long-term Memory works, perhaps you can figure out why most people seem to have so much trouble remembering what happened to them in the first year or two of their lives. The answer seems to be this—we file most items away in permanent storage by means of a *verbal description* of the experience. And before you learned to speak, you had no logical way of cataloguing your memories. We don't file mental film clips or photographs or tape recordings; rather, we typically translate the *meaning* of the experience into mental language and then store away the *verbal abstract*. Think again of that last long trip you took. You can probably describe fully all you remember of it in a matter of 10 minutes or less, yet the trip itself might have taken several hours. Your brain condenses the experience, drops out the dull parts, abstracts the salient or interesting features, categorizes them, writes up "cross-index cards" referring to similar items or happenings; it then stores everything away in such a tidy, logical fashion that, any time thereafter, you can find those particular memories in a fraction of a second—if you use the right verbal or emotional categories to track the memories down.

QUESTION: **What would your life be like if you had an absolutely perfect memory of everything that happened to you, rather than mere verbal abstracts? Would it take**

Psycho-analysis (SIGH-ko-an-AL-uh-sis). A theory of personality involving psycho-sexual development and a form of intra-psychic therapy developed by Sigmund Freud. See Chapters 5, 21, and 22.

Trauma (rhymes with "DRAW-ma"). Any injury or disability inflicted on one's mind or body. A frightening experience.

you as long to remember your last long trip as it did to live through the experience in the first place? How would you answer items on an examination if you had to re-read every word in the textbook to find each tiny bit of data?

We are not sure how far back in time your own personal memory banks go. Many psychologists believe that your brain contains memories of what happened to you at your birth—or perhaps even shortly before—but that you cannot ordinarily retrieve them because your brain wasn't very good at making "index cards" before you learned to speak. If these early experiences are present in your permanent storage, they probably exist as almost formless and highly emotional impressions. One of the main functions of *psycho-analysis* (°) and of some other forms of psycho-therapy is that of helping the client dredge as deeply down as possible into these distant recollections to uncover emotional *traumas* (°) that still may be affecting the client's thoughts and behavior (*see* Chapter 22). Once the client can attach verbal labels or descriptions to these infantile experiences, he or she may recover them fairly readily from then on.

Forgetting

Forgetting occurs in many ways and for many reasons. The sensory information system in your receptors provides you with a clear and sharply etched impression of the world around you, but each new impression destroys the one before. Your brain takes this incoming stimulus pattern and scans it quickly for recognizable features. Parts of the lower brain check out the emotional possibilities of the stimulus and generally alert the cortex that information of some kind is coming through on the sensory "hot line." However, if that information is threatening or disturbing, the emotional centers in your brain may suppress the input and hence make it very difficult to remember later on. Ordinarily, however, the Short-term Memory mechanism picks out the most meaningful aspects of the sensory input and holds them in temporary storage. Your Short-term Memory is very limited, though, and items usually drop out or are forgotten in a matter of seconds because new items keep pushing in, as we've said.

Any item in Short-term Memory that is of real importance to you is processed for Long-term Memory. This processing usually involves translating the meaning of the stimulus into verbal terms and then categorizing various aspects of the experience in many different ways. These categories then act like index cards that allow you to track down the memory at a subsequent time.

But your brain makes thousands of new index cards every day. A familiar term—such as "dog" or "mother" or "school"—must be indexed a million different ways. To recapture a specific memory about your mother (the present she gave to you on your seventh birthday, for example), you may have to sort through countless numbers of index cards. The more information you have at the beginning of your search (the dress she was wearing, where you lived, who else was physically present, the time of year, the state of the weather, and so on), the easier your task becomes.

Forgetting typically occurs because you have too many or too few index cards to help with your search of your memory banks. Old experiences are hard to find because you have to scan the millions of similar index cards you've made since then to recover that one unique memory. You don't really forget—rather, new learning *interferes* with your ability to retrieve old items.

Brand-new experiences are occasionally hard to remember because you have such a limited number of cues as to their location in your long-term files, or because you must learn a whole new set of relationships between familiar items.

Mnemonics

The quickest way to improve your ability to memorize new stimuli is to associate the new with the old. To perform that feat, professional "memory experts" often make use of *mnemonics* (°), or artificial categories. For example, suppose you had to learn the following list of words by heart and repeat them back at a later time:

Dog
Umbrella
Mountain
Ball
Water
Auto
Iron
Tree
Eagle
Rose

These are all familiar words—it is the *relationship* or *order* among the items that you must learn. You could attempt to cram the list into some pigeonhole in your brain hoping to recover the order of the words by sheer memory power, or you could use a mnemonic.

Notice that the first letters of the 10 items spell out the word *"dumbwaiter"* (°). That one word is much easier to recall than are the 10 unrelated items in the list. Yet once you remember "dumbwaiter," you can reproduce or guess at the items on the list after just one or two readings. Now suppose you were given a second set of 10 words to learn:

Heat
Woman
Rock
Green
Train
Seat
Flower
House
Bread
Shoe

Unfortunately, the first letters of these items don't spell out a familiar word. But could you associate this list with "dumbwaiter?" Couldn't you make up a sentence that paired "Umbrella" and "Woman," and so forth?

The	Dog	liked the	Heat
The	Umbrella	belonged to a	Woman
The	Mountain	was made of	Rock . . .

Now when you have to recall the words in the second list, the "dumbwaiter" mnemonic gives you a ready-made set of index cards to recover your memories. When you try to organize material before committing it to memory, you are in fact trying to make each part of the material act as a cue card for what comes next. Later on, if you can remember even a small part of the material, you can use that part to recover or retrieve all the rest. Almost all of the "memory improvement schemes" and many of the "speed-reading courses" offered commercially involve (in part) teaching people how to organize stimulus inputs and how to use mnemonics.

QUESTION: Successful mnemonics almost always depend on associating a new item

Mnemonics (knee-MON-icks). From the Greek word *mneme*, meaning "memory." Mnemonics are devices that are intended to help you remember something.

Dumbwaiter (DUMM-wait-ur). Literally, a small elevator used to transport food and dishes from one floor of a building to another. The initials of the word "dumbwaiter" form a mnemonic, or memory device.

with something already well committed to memory; what kind of mnemonic might you create to help you remember people's names better?

THE SEARCH FOR THE ENGRAM

When the first computers were made, their memory-storage devices were designed to mimic that biological computer residing inside your skull. Computers can perform many routine mathematical functions much faster than your brain can, but they must be carefully programmed to do so.

A psychologist who performs a very complex experiment may gather stacks of data during the course of the study. The psychologist may then elect to create a specific "program"—a set of instructions—telling a computer how to organize, categorize, and analyze these data. The machine can then whiz through the data analysis at thousands of times the speed that the psychologist could when using just his own brain computer. However, a complicated "program" may take the scientist weeks or even months to write in the first place. For each tiny step that the machine will take must be specified in the program in utmost detail; if one step is missing or incorrectly stated, if just one of the machine's memory file cards is out of place, the computer will malfunction.

Your brain is superior to the computer in part because it is self-programming—each time you learn some new skill, you really are re-programming your brain. Psychologists and neuro-physiologists are presently spending a great deal of research time trying to figure out how your brain manages to reprogram itself and rearrange its memory banks.

Computer memory banks are usually detachable; yours are not. Many computers store their inputs on magnetic tape or disks, much as we store music on commercial recordings or tapes for our high-fidelity systems. Scientists who record research data on a reel of computer tape could, if they wished, remove the reel from the machine and clip out a piece of the tape that contained a particular "memory" they were interested in. They could then hold that bit of tape—the physical representation of the memory—in their hand and inspect it at leisure. If the psychologist could clip out a memory from his or her own brain and inspect

A typical computer console.

the physical representation of that memory under a microscope, we could learn a great deal more about brain-computers than we presently know. Unfortunately, we must often study the functioning of the brain indirectly.

The Engram

We are sure that whenever you learn something—no matter how simple—there must be a physical change of some kind in your brain associated with storing that item away in your permanent memory banks. We call that physical representation of a memory an *engram* (°). We assume that there must be a different engram for each tiny bit of information that you have ever learned, and that your brain therefore is jam-packed with many billions of engrams. But we have no real proof for these assumptions, and no one has ever been able to put a finger on an engram or view one under a microscope. About all we can say on the basis of laboratory data gathered so far is that different sorts of engrams appear to be stored in different parts of your brain.

The "search for the engram," as it is sometimes called, has occupied the attention of thousands of scientists for the past century or so. When neuro-physiologists first discovered the huge amount of electrical activity in the brain (*see* Chapter 4), they speculated that the engram might be an electrical loop or circuit of some kind. As long as the electricity flowed in its proper pathway through the brain, the engram was maintained. Early computers were built on this model. The problem was that if you pulled the plug and shut off the electricity for any reason, the computer lost all of its memories, even when you fired the machine up again.

Neuro-physiologists tried the same experiment with animals—that is, they turned off all the electrical activity in a hamster's brain to see if this would wipe out the animal's memories. When bears, hamsters, and other beasts go into the deep sleep associated with *hibernation* (°), their brain temperatures drop considerably and most electrical activity ceases. So the neuro-physiologists trained a hamster, then put it to sleep and cooled its brain down until they could no longer detect any electrical responses at all. Later they warmed the animal up again and checked to see what it would remember. All the animals they tested showed excellent retention of their prior training. The electrical-current hypothesis had failed, and scientists had to look elsewhere for the engram; again they followed what might be called "computer logic."

Synaptic Switches

Computers store memories in a variety of ways. One device used in many computers is a simple switch, which can be left in either an open or closed position. When a message passes through the computer, the switches can route the information from one point to another, much the way the switches in a railroad yard can switch a train from one track to another. If you ask a computer a simple question—such as "What is $2 + 2$?"—the computer routes your question through a series of switches until the final destination "4" is reached. Switches are not very complicated mechanisms, but given enough of them, the computer can store almost any information, no matter how complicated.

To a neuro-physiologist (or anyone else interested in how your nerve cells fnction), your brain is made up chiefly of cellular "switches" called *synapses* (°). When someone asks you a question—"What is your name?"—the message must cross over a number of synaptic switching points. If you could rearrange the functioning of these synaptic connections, opening some and closing others, you could thereby send the message to any part of the brain that held the right answer. Perhaps, the neuro-physiologists reasoned, learning was chiefly a matter of

Engram (EN-gram). A memory trace. The physical change that presumably occurs in the brain each time you store some item away in Long-term Memory.

Hibernation (high-burr-NAY-shun). From the Latin word *hibernus*, meaning "of winter." To hibernate is to pass the winter asleep, usually in a cave or other hiding place protected from the cold. To become dormant (DOOR-mant), or inactive, during a relatively long period of time.

Synapses (SIN-app-sez). The fluid-filled space between the axon of one neuron and the dendrites of a second neuron is called a synapse. See Chapters 2 and 4.

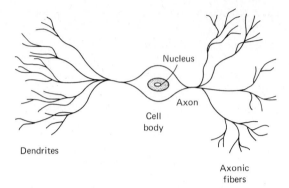

Dendrites (DEN-drights). The "feelers" that extend from the front end of a neuron. The input side of a nerve cell.

DNA. Literally, de-oxy-ribo-nucleic acid (dee-ox-ee-rye-bo-new-CLAY-ick). The stuff that genes are presumed to be made of. Large, complex molecules that have the ability to reproduce themselves. The DNA molecule may also produce RNA.

RNA. Literally, ribonucleic acid (RYE-bo-new-CLAY-ick). Complex genetic molecules usually produced by DNA. In some exceedingly small organisms, such as viruses (VY-russ-sez) that cause colds or flu, the genes may be made of RNA rather than DNA.

Proteins (PRO-teens). From the Greek word meaning "primary." Proteins are one of the chief components of all living tissue. Meat is particularly rich in protein. Enzymes (EN-zimes) are proteins, as are many other products manufactured by the cells of your body. In genetic terms, DNA produces RNA, which produces proteins. U.S. psychologist Ward Halstead and Swedish biologist Holger Hydén were perhaps the first to suggest that RNA and protein might be involved in forming engrams—that is, in storing memories. (Roughly speaking, Holger Hydén's name is pronounced "HOLE-gur hew-DANE.")

rewiring the neural circuits in your brain by shuffling around the synaptic connections.

This idea has considerable appeal to scientists, for the nerve cells in your brain are much more complicated than the simple switching devices in a computer. You may recall, for instance, that the *dendrites* (°) at the "front end" of each cortical neuron may be in direct contact with thousands of other nerve cells, while the axonic fibers of that same single cortical neuron may connect to the dendrites of still thousands of other nerve cells. Your brain, then, has billions and billions of possible "memory routes" in it. Little wonder that your brain has a memory capacity superior to that of any existing computer!

It is generally agreed that the engram—that physical representation of whatever you remember—must involve some functional change at the synapse. But there is not much agreement (or solid data) about how one goes about shifting the switches in your brain. Many scientists appeal to Thorndike's *law of exercise*, described in the last chapter. They produce data showing that if you force a neural message to cross a certain synapse again and again, it is thereafter much easier for the message to take that particular route. Why this might be so, no one really knows; perhaps the extra amount of "exercise" glues the synaptic connections together, much as a huge burst of electricity might fuse a computer switch into the closed position.

Memory Molecules

A small but growing number of scientists believe memory storage may involve the creation of new chemical molecules in the brain. They point out that the synaptic connections you were born with were a part of your genetic blueprint—that is, the original wiring diagram for your brain was contained within the set of gigantic *DNA* (°) molecules that you inherited from your mother and father. These DNA molecules held the genetic code, or set of instructions, that caused the single cell you started life with to grow into the complex adult body you have today. You became a human rather than a rat or fish or worm because your DNA genetic code "remembered" what your parents were like—and yet all those original DNA molecules of yours came packaged in a cell not much larger than any of the neurons now living in your brain.

The genetic code carried by the DNA molecules presets the synaptic connections in your brain so that your innate behavior patterns are like those of your parents. Could it be that other large molecules—such as *RNA* (°) and *proteins* (°)—could carry your own personal "memory code?" Some psychologists, myself included, believe this may be the case. The evidence we offer in support of our beliefs is still controversial and often hotly debated by those scientists who prefer to think of the brain primarily in terms of electrical circuits and switches. In the next few pages I would like to give you what is probably a prejudiced view of our research, and then let you make up your own minds about the validity of our data.

THE BIOCHEMISTRY OF MEMORY

Perhaps the first person to speculate in public that chemicals might be involved in memory storage was the University of Chicago psychologist Ward Halstead. In 1948 and 1949, Professor Halstead advanced the theory that RNA and protein molecules might be the engrams that scientists had sought for so many years. At about the same time, the Swedish biologist, Holger Hydén, said much the same thing, although Hydén's first beliefs were that RNA, not protein, was the chief candidate.

During the 1950's, Hydén and his colleagues performed an interesting set of experiments in which they taught various tricks to rats, then looked at the chemical composition of the animals' brains. They theorized that the brain of a trained rat should be *chemically different* from the brain of an untrained rat, and their research tended to support this belief. For they found noticeable changes in the amounts of RNA in the brains of the trained animals (as compared with the brains of untrained rats).

Ward Halstead.

Subsequent experiments in laboratories both here and abroad have generally confirmed the view that an organism's brain chemistry is subtly altered by whatever experiences the organism has. More important, it now appears that different types of psychological experiences give rise to quite different sorts of chemical changes.

Whenever a wave of electrical activity sweeps the length of a nerve cell from dendrites to axon, the nerve cell responds by suddenly increasing its production of several chemical molecules, including RNA. The more vigorously a neuron fires, the more RNA it produces. And since RNA guides or controls the production of protein molecules, the more RNA a cell produces, the more protein it typically manufactures as well. In short, nerve cells are not only generators of electrical activity, but very efficient chemical factories too (*see* material on hormone production in Chapter 13).

Ribonuclease (RYE-bo-NEW-klee-aze). An enzyme (protein) that breaks up, or destroys, RNA. Ribonuclease is found in most living cells.

Enzyme (EN-zime). Proteins found in most living tissue that speed up chemical reactions. Without the enzymes found in your saliva and stomach, you could not digest your food very well.

Senility (see-NILL-uh-tee, or suh-NILL-uh-tee). From the latin word *senex*, meaning "old" or "old man." Senility is the loss of physical and mental ability that sometimes accompanies advanced age. Our word "senior" comes from the same Latin source.

Chemical "Erasers"

You are not consciously aware of all the chemical changes taking place in your brain as they occur, of course; but if the changes didn't come about, you probably wouldn't be "aware" of anything at all! For example, what do you think might happen if someone injected into your brain a special chemical that destroyed RNA just as you were trying to study for an exam? How might that affect your ability to learn?

This question was probably first asked by neuro-physiologist E. Roy John, who in the mid-1950's taught a cat a rather difficult task involving visual perception. Immediately thereafter, John injected ribonuclease into the cat's visual cortex. *Ribonuclease* (°) is an *enzyme* (°), or destructive chemical, that breaks up RNA molecules whenever it comes in contact with them. Although the cat performed very well before the injection—thus demonstrating to John that it had learned the visual discrimination quite well—the ribonuclease enzyme appeared to destroy its memory. For, after the injection, the cat performed as if it had never been trained at all.

Memory Loss in Old People

As you may know from bitter personal experience, when people grow old, they often begin to lose parts of their memories. The elderly person sometimes drifts into a psychological decline in which today's events are rapidly forgotten, and the person's mind dwells in the distant past. We call this condition *senility* (°), and it often places an immense burden on whoever must care for the individual. Senility

E. Roy John.

Senility is a problem many elderly people must face.

Temporal lobes (TEM-por-ull). The parts of the cerebrum that lie just above the ears, close to the temples. Seem to be involved in hearing, in speech production, and in emotional behavior—among other things. See Chapter 4.

typically involves a disruption of the person's ability to store new information away in the Long-term Memory.

A senile man or woman can often recall past events—that is, items already present in permanent storage before the senility set in. But the person's memory banks seem closed to new inputs. A few fairly rare types of brain damage may also create the same kind of memory deficit. Scientists Brenda Milner, Suzanne Corkin, and Hans-Lucas Teuber recently described a 14-year study of a young man who had lost part of his *temporal lobes* (°) in a brain operation. Prior to the operation, his IQ was measured as 104; afterward, it was tested at 118. He could remember things prior to the operation very well, but nothing that happened afterward seemed to stick in his Long-term Memory. He described his condition as being "like waking from a dream," and not really remembering where he was or how he got there. Once he remarked that, for him, "Every day is alone in itself, whatever enjoyment I've had, and whatever sorrow I've had." This young man had rather unusual problems getting along with other people. For instance, if he took a girl friend to a dance, he had to stay very close to her the entire evening. Otherwise he would forget whom he had brought and might very well go home alone or with someone else.

When an elderly person experiences the same memory problems, we often say that the person has fallen into a kind of second childhood—that is, all the person's references are to early events, for only yesterdays have meaning. Today is continually being pushed out of the person's Short-term Memory, one item at a time, and tomorrow never comes and could not be remembered even if it did.

Psychiatrist D. Ewen Cameron spent many years trying to help senile patients in several hospitals in Canada and the United States. His studies were, for a time, aimed at discovering whether or not the body chemistry of senile people was measurably different from that of other people who were just as old but who were not senile. In one of his experiments in the late 1950's, Cameron found that senile patients had much more of the ribonuclease enzyme present in their bloodstreams than did non-senile oldsters. Cameron guessed that this abnormal amount of ribonuclease might be destroying brain RNA as fast as the senile individual's neurons could manufacture it. Perhaps if RNA were involved in helping the brain store away long-term memories, then too much ribonuclease would wipe out the engrams before they could become permanent. If so, Cameron might be able to help his patients by *lowering* the relative amount of ribonuclease in their bodies.

Cameron tried two different types of chemical therapy. First, he injected his patients with large amounts of yeast RNA, hoping that the ribonuclease would attack this foreign RNA rather than the RNA produced by the patient's brains. While this approach seemed to help some people recover part of their memory functions, the yeast RNA was often impure and gave Cameron's patients fevers. Next he tried giving his patients a drug that was supposed to increase the production of brain RNA. Again, he was fairly successful—but only with people who had not slipped too far into senility. However, the improvements that Cameron's *chemotherapy* (°) caused were slow to come about—often the patient showed no improvement at all for several weeks or months—and once the patient was taken off the "memory" drug, the person's memory often began to *deteriorate* (°) again.

Cameron died of a heart attack while on a mountain-climbing expedition (he was in his mid-70's) before he could complete his work. A group of scientists in Italy attempted to repeat his research and reported at least partial success, but no one in America seems to have picked up where Cameron left off. Several groups of physiologists did try similar studies using rats, but their animals were young instead of senile and received the drug only once or twice instead of daily for weeks or months. When these physiologists failed to find that the drug improved learning in rats, most other researchers appeared to lose both faith and interest in Cameron's findings.

Memory Consolidation

Whenever you wish to store something away in your permanent memory banks, your brain seems to need at least 30 minutes to build up the engram. Anything that disrupts brain activity during this critical *engram formation period* is likely to disrupt your memory as well. For example, people who receive a hard blow to the head often lose all recollection not only of the accident itself but also of things that happened 20 to 30 minutes prior to the blow. Severe psychological shock may occasionally have the same erasing effect on one's immediate memory. So does a *grand mal convulsion* (°) (*see* Chapter 2), whether it is induced by chemicals or electrical current. If you give a rat or cat a very rapid series of training trials, and then cause it to convulse by passing electricity through its brain or giving it a massive dose of insulin, the animal appears to forget much if not all of its training.

> QUESTION: If you stretched the training out over a period of several days, then convulsed the animal only on the final day, would you expect much memory loss? If you studied for an exam an hour a day for a week, would you expect to remember more than if you crammed for seven hours straight the night before the test?

Drugs and Memory

Long-term memories take time to form or *consolidate* (°). Anything that retards or interferes with normal brain function during this consolidation period will interfere with your ability to remember.

Chemotherapy (KEY-moh-THER-ap-pee). The use of chemicals or drugs in treating some mental or physical illnesses. Chemical therapy. When you take an aspirin to help a headache, you are engaging in chemotherapy.

Deteriorate (dee-TEER-ee-oh-rate, or dee-TEER-ee-uh-rate). From the Latin word meaning "worse." To deteriorate is to grow worse, to become more ill, to make inferior in quality or value.

Grand mal convulsion (grahn mahl). From the French words for "big sickness." The worst form of motor epilepsy. See Chapter 2.

Consolidate (kon-SOLL-eye-date, or kon-SOLL-uh-date). From a Latin word meaning "to make firm" or "to make solid." Literally, to join together, or to form into a solid mass. The consolidation period is that time after an experience when your memories grow into permanent form, when you somehow file the experience away in your Long-term Memory.

The other side of the memory coin is perhaps a bit more intriguing, however. For it is likewise true that anything that *facilitates* or speeds up brain activity during the consolidation period will make it easier for you to form engrams. We usually think of strychnine as a poison; in fact, it is a neural excitant. In large doses, it causes convulsions and eventual death. In very small doses, strychnine increases neuronal firing rates much as does the *caffeine* (°) found in coffee or cola drinks. If you inject a rat with a tiny amount of strychnine just before you train it on a simple task, the rat typically will learn the problem faster. The explanation usually offered for this effect is that strychnine makes the animal more active and alert to its environment; hence, it *learns* faster. Surprisingly enough, you can get a similar effect by training the animal first, then giving it the strychnine a few minutes *after* it has learned the task. Now, when you retest the rat on the same problem a day or so later, the injected animal will remember the task much better than a rat injected with salt water or one not injected at all.

QUESTION: **Why would you want to use two types of control animals in this experiment, one injected with salt water and one not injected at all?**

How can a post-training injection speed up *learning?* It can't, for the rat given the strychnine takes just as long to learn the task as does an uninjected animal. What the drug does is to enhance the animal's Long-term Memory, apparently by making the animal's brain more active during the consolidation period following training. As you might have guessed, the drug must be given within 30 minutes or so after the training or the enhancement effect does not take place. A rat injected two hours after training remembers no better than does an uninjected animal.

Oddly enough, while marijuana appears to disrupt Short-term and some aspects of Long-term Memory (*see* Chapter 3), there is some evidence that it can facilitate long-term retention. In 1965, Carlini and Carlini tested the effects of strychnine versus marijuana in rats. They found, as expected, that strychnine facilitated the *learning* of a simple maze if given to the animals immediately *before* training and increased *retention* of the problem *after* training. Marijuana extracts injected into the rats prior to training did not speed up the rate at which the animals learned but did increase later retention. Marijuana given after training had no effect at all. Carlini and Carlini also report that the strychnine increased the amount of RNA the rats' brains produced, while the marijuana increased DNA production.

MEMORY TRANSFER

The strongest yet most controversial support for the chemical theory of memory comes from the so-called "memory transfer" experiments. In 1953, when Robert Thompson and I were graduate students at the University of Texas, we attempted to train common flatworms using Pavlovian conditioning techniques. The simple *planarian* (°) flatworm grows to be about an inch in length and is found crawling on the bottom of ponds, streams, and rivers throughout the world. The planarian is unique in many respects.

To begin with, it has both male and female sex organs, and some species are actually capable of self-fertilization. It reproduces both sexually and asexually—that is, a flatworm may mate with itself or with another planarian and subsequently lay eggs from which tiny worms will hatch; or its body may split in half, following which both head and tail sections will *regenerate* (°) into complete worms.

The flatworm is also the simplest animal to possess a true brain and a synaptic-type of nervous system. Once these neural structures appeared on the evolutionary tree, they apparently offered such excellent survival value that all more complex animals made use of them. In a sense, your own magnificent nervous system is little more than an elaborate version of the synaptic brain contained within the head of each planarian.

Caffeine (kaff-FEEN). The drug found in coffee that acts as an "upper" or neural excitant. Very similar in its effects to strychnine (STRICK-neen, or STRICK-nine), a natural drug found in certain plants that is used as a rat poison.

Planarian (plan-AIR-ee-ann). A very simple, inch-long flatworm that lives in ponds and streams throughout the world. A much-loved experimental animal used by certain simple-minded psychologists (and thousands of high school students competing in science fairs).

Regenerate (ree-JEN-ur-rate). To generate is to grow, or to make. To regenerate is to regrow any missing parts of the body.

Robert Thompson.

The planarian possesses a true brain, a synaptic type of nervous system, and both male and female sex organs.

Thompson and I were interested in flatworms because of their nerve cells. In 1953, the synaptic theory of memory storage was just becoming popular. We reasoned that if synapses were important for learning, and if the flatworm was the lowest animal that had synapses, it should be the simplest animal capable of showing true learning. A search of the scientific literature suggested that no one had trained flatworms before, so we set out to do so. (Years later we uncovered an article written in Dutch by a biologist named H. Van Oye who, in 1923, reported he had successfully trained planarians to crawl down a thin wire to get food, something they ordinarily would not do. Van Oye was apparently the first person to train flatworms; Thompson and I were seemingly the first to demonstrate that they could be classically conditioned.)

Conditioning a Flatworm

If you pass an electrical current through a trough of water containing a planarian, the animal will violently contract or "scrunch up." Shock is then an unconditioned stimulus that brings about a "scrunching" response in worms (and most other animals). If you shine a weak light on the planarian, it may respond by twitching its head, but it seldom contracts and usually just ignores the light. The training *paradigm* (°) Thompson and I used consisted of turning on a light for two seconds before we shocked the worm. If the pairing of the light CS with the shock

Paradigm (PAIR-uh-dime, or PAIR-uh-dimm). From the Greek word meaning "pattern," "model," or "example." A training paradigm is a model or ideal way of training animals. Pavlov's way of pairing the CS with the UCS is a paradigm for establishing the conditioned response.

A planarian undergoing electric shock.

UCS was successful in conditioning the animals, they should eventually begin to contract as soon as the light came on—*before* they were shocked. And they did. In a matter of 150 trials, their response rate to the light more than doubled. (Later, using better training techniques, my students and I were able to train worms to respond to the light at least 95 percent of the time.) Convinced that we had demonstrated that planarians could be conditioned, Thompson and I published our results in 1955.

Regenerated Memories

When I came to teach at The University of Michigan in 1956, I talked several bright young students into continuing the worm research with me. The first of these students were Allan Jacobson and Daniel Kimble, and the experiment we undertook had rather crazy overtones.

If you cut a flatworm in half across its middle, the head will rapidly regrow a tail; the tail section, after a matter of a few weeks, will regenerate a new head complete with the brain and synaptic nervous system. It occurred to us that it might be amusing to condition some worms (using light and shock) and then, after they were trained, cut them in half and let them regrow. After the animals had regenerated, we could test the heads and tails to see which half remembered the original training. The question we were asking, of course, was—*where is the engram stored in the worm's body?* Is it just in the head (as you might suppose would be the case, since only the head contained the brain), or could part of the worm's memory banks be distributed in the tail as well?

To say the least, the results surprised us. After the original head sections had regenerated, they showed just as much retention of the conditioning as did worms that had been trained but not cut in half. Apparently losing their tails did not disrupt the planarian's memory banks. We gave the tails a month to replace their heads, then tested them. These tail sections with completely regrown brains not only remembered as well as did uncut planarians—they often did somewhat better! We subsequently repeated the study many times (as did dozens of other laboratories), but always with the same results: Tails remembered as well as did heads. In further experiments, we showed that worms could be cut into several different pieces, and each piece, after regenerating, remembered what the original planarian had learned. There was not one engram, but several—scattered throughout the worm's entire body.

E. Roy John and William Corning soon carried this work a step further. John had, years earlier, erased a cat's memory by injecting it with ribonuclease immediately after training. Would the same technique work with flatworms? To find out, John and Corning classically conditioned their animals as we had, then cut them in half and let them regenerate. Some of the heads and tails regrew in ordinary water and showed the expected retention of the original conditioning. Other heads and tails were forced to regenerate in a weak solution of ribonuclease. These head sections remembered; the tails did not. Apparently the ribonuclease enzyme had attacked the RNA in the regrowing brains and somehow disrupted or wiped out the engram. (Later experiments in Russia and in Turkey suggested a strong enough solution of ribonuclease could erase memories even in uncut planarians.)

All of these experiments led us to believe that memory formation somehow involved the creation of new molecules, and that RNA was part of the process. About 1960 it occurred to me that if two worms learned the same task, the chemical changes that took place inside their bodies might also be identical. If this were so, it might not matter how the chemicals got inside the worms—provided the right molecules were present, the worm should "remember" whatever the chemical engrams told it to remember. Our attempts to test this odd notion took us not to the heart of the matter, but to the worm's digestive system.

RNA from a conditioned donor being injected into a recipient planarian.

Cannibalistic Transfer of Learning

Most higher organisms have stomachs that break up the food they eat into useful-sized molecules. The flatworm lacks a stomach—when it eats, the food particles float around inside the animal and each cell takes up whatever it needs. If we could get the engram molecules out of a trained worm's body and somehow inject them into an untrained animal, we might succeed in transferring the memory along with the molecules. In 1960 Reeva Kimble, Barbara Humphries, and I did just that. We classically conditioned a bunch of "victim" planarians, then chopped them in bits and fed the pieces to hungry, untrained cannibalistic flatworms. Another group of cannibals was fed untrained victims. After we had given the cannibals a couple of days to digest or *consolidate* their meals, we gave both groups their first training trials. To our delight, from the very first trials the planarians that had eaten educated victims responded to the light CS significantly more often than did the worms that had consumed their untrained brethren. We seemed to have transferred an engram from one animal to another.

Memory by Injection

A year or so later Art Zelman, Lou Kabat, Reeva Kimble, Allan Jacobson, and I carried the matter one step further. We extracted RNA molecules from several groups of planarians. Some of the animals had been given light-shock conditioning. Others had been exposed to light or to shock (but not to both). Some donor worms were not given any training at all. Using a very tiny needle, we then injected the RNA from these different donors into several groups of recipient planarians. The recipients were then assigned code numbers and were trained by experimenters who did not know what kind of injection each trainee had received.

Only those recipients injected with RNA from conditioned donors showed a transfer effect. Although this experiment had many flaws in it, several other laboratories both here and abroad were subsequently able to replicate our results.

In 1964, scientists working in the United States, Denmark, and Czechoslovakia reported similar success using rats as subjects rather than worms. In all these studies, donor animals were given some type of training, then were sacrificed and their brains removed. Extracts from these brains were next injected into untrained recipients. The subsequent behavior of the recipients (as compared to various controls) suggested that these animals had *by injection* acquired stimulus-response patterns that the original donors had acquired only by hard experience.

Rats, mice, and goldfish soon became the favored experimental subjects for these studies, and, by 1976, more than a thousand successful memory transfer experiments had been reported in the scientific literature. But everything was not peaches and cream (or even RNA and protein) in this chemical search for the engram.

Are Memory Transfer Studies Valid?

To begin with, there is the nagging question of *validity* (°)—that is, when you inject an animal with chemicals taken from a trained donor, are you really transferring *specific memories* or are you merely giving the recipient molecules that excite or depress brain activity (as do caffeine and strychnine)? Jessie Shelby and I answered that question for planarians some time ago. We first trained donor worms to go either to the light or the dark arm of a very simple, water-filled T-maze. When the donor planarians were going to the correct arm at least 9 times out of 10, we chopped them up and fed them to untrained cannibals. We then trained the cannibals "blind" (not knowing until after the experiment which worm had had what kind of dinner).

Suppose that donor worm A had been trained to approach the light-colored

James McConnell putting a flat-worm through the maze.

Jessie Shelby.

Validity (vall-LID-uh-tee). Strong, believable, trustable facts are "valid" facts. The validity of a set of experimental results is the "trustability" of those results.

arm of the maze. We then feed A to cannibal X. If we also trained X to go to the light-colored arm, we would be attempting a "positive transfer," because we had given worm X what we called " + " instructions. But suppose we trained X to go to the dark-colored arm of the maze instead—that is, we trained X to do the opposite of the memories it had presumably received from donor worm A. This we called our negative or " − " instructions condition. If the engram were *specific* to the color of the arm that donor A had been trained to approach, we would expect cannibals that ate positive instructions to learn the maze much faster than cannibals that ingested negative instructions. And that turned out to be the case.

But Jessie Shelby and I had two other groups of cannibals in our study. One bunch of cannibals ate untrained donors; they learned the maze significantly more slowly than did the cannibals that ingested *either* positive or negative instructions. So it would appear that even *negative* information about the maze experience is better than no information at all!

By far the most interesting group in our study, though, were the cannibals that were fed both positive *and* negative instructions—that is, these planarians ingested a "worm stew" made up of some donors trained to go to the light arm and of some donors trained to go to the dark arm. These poor cannibals learned the slowest of all; the conflicting behavioral tendencies they received made learning more difficult than if they had received no instructions at all. They showed their conflict not only by learning slowly but in other ways as well. When these cannibals reached the choice point in the maze, they acted as if they couldn't make up their minds which way to go. Often their indecision was so great that they simply turned around, came back to the starting point, and refused to run the maze even when we prodded them gently with a tiny brush. Several other laboratories showed much the same sort of stimulus-specific transfer using rats and goldfish.

Are Memory Transfer Studies Reliable?

An equally important question has to do with the *reliability* (°) of the transfer effect. A reliable friend is one whom you can depend upon to do the same thing for you again and again; a reliable scientific experiment is one that you can depend upon to yield the same results any time you or anyone else tries it the same way. The planarian studies seem highly reliable in that (to the best of my knowledge) no one who was able to train worms successfully in the first place ever failed to get a transfer effect of some kind (although arguments were occasionally raised about the *specificity* (°) of the transfer).

The rats and mice were a different matter. In 1966, some 22 scientists from several laboratories published a joint report saying that they had tried but failed to transfer memories from one group of animals to another. As they themselves pointed out, these negative results were not particularly surprising. The memory transfer experiments are among the most complex ever performed in the field of biopsychology—one often needs training in behavioral psychology, neurophysiology, comparative zoology, and biochemistry to do them well. Important aspects of the early, successful transfer experiments were not reported in the literature because we simply didn't know which parts of our procedures were important and which were not.

By 1967, however, several of the 22 critics had repeated their studies (with necessary improvements) and had, in fact, gotten positive results. And, in 1970, when James Dyal at the University of Waterloo in Canada questioned everyone who had attempted transfer experiments, he found that better than half of the more than 400 studies undertaken had yielded evidence supporting the transfer hypothesis. Since the odds of getting successful results for any one experiment were greater than 100 to 1, a .500 "batting average" is very good indeed, and

Reliability (ree-lie-uh-BILL-it-tee). Reliable friends are those people you can count on when the going gets tough—whose behavior toward you never varies. Reliable experiments are those that can be repeated again and again with the same results.

Specificity (speh-suh-FISS-sit-tee). The quality or state of being specific. Caffeine has a non-specific effect on learning—the drug simply speeds up most types of learning or conditioning. The memory transfer experiments would be of greatest interest if it could be proven to everyone's satisfaction that the transfer was highly specific. Suppose you trained a goldfish to approach a red light to get food, but to avoid a green light or it would be shocked. Then you took chemicals from the animal's brain and injected them into a second goldfish. If this second animal immediately approached red lights, but avoided green lights, the transfer would be very specific. If the second animal approached lights of all colors, or avoided lights of all colors, the transfer would not be specific.

James Dyal.

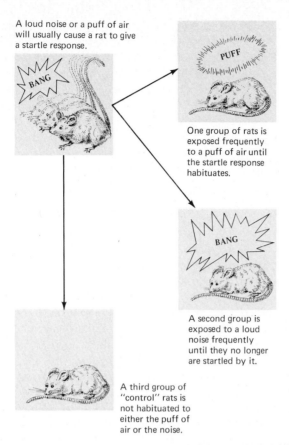

A loud noise or a puff of air will usually cause a rat to give a startle response.

One group of rats is exposed frequently to a puff of air until the startle response habituates.

A second group is exposed to a loud noise frequently until they no longer are startled by it.

A third group of "control" rats is not habituated to either the puff of air or the noise.

suggests that the effect is probably as reliable as most others in the field of biopsychology.

Ungar and Scotophobin

But if chemicals are involved in memory formation and transfer, which molecules are they and how do they work? A series of studies by Georges Ungar and his associates at Baylor University Medical School in Houston may give us a clue. Ungar began by habituating rats either to a loud noise or to a puff of air. When a rat is disturbed by a sudden stimulus, it shows a characteristic (innate) startle reaction. If the same stimulus is repeated many times a day for several days, the rat becomes accustomed to it and the startle response habituates or extinguishes.

It took about 10–15 days for Ungar's original animals to habituate either to the noise or to the air puff blown on their necks. After habituation had set in, Ungar extracted chemicals from the donor brains and injected the molecules into untrained recipients. The injectees that received material from noise-habituated donors learned to ignore the loud sound in less than 2 days; it took them 12 days or more to habituate to the air puff, however. The injectees given brain extracts from air puff-habituated donors learned to ignore the puff of air in less than 5 days; however, they were still showing the startle reaction to the noise at the end of 10 days of training. Recipients injected with brain extracts from completely inexperienced donors took at least 12 days to habituate to the noise, and a full 15 days to learn to ignore the puff of air.

More recently, Ungar has used a training chamber first designed by R. Gay and Al Raphelson at The University of Michigan. This rat box has a row of three chambers connected by open doors. The center and one end chamber are white; the other end chamber is black. Like many rodents, rats are night lovers; when

Georges Ungar.

Al Raphelson.

David Malin.

Scotophobin (sko-toe-FOE-bin). From the Greek words *skoto,* meaning "darkness," and *phobos,* meaning "fear" or "avoidance." Literally, "fear of the dark." Our word "phobia" comes from *phobos.*

put in the center chamber, untrained rats typically soon go into the black chamber and stay there. Ungar and his colleagues trained these donors by giving them a painful shock whenever they entered the dark box; to no one's surprise, the rats soon learned to avoid the black chamber and would squeak, bite, and urinate or defecate whenever they were pushed toward the dark end of the apparatus. These donor rats were sacrificed and the chemicals extracted from their brains were injected into untrained recipients. When these injectees were put into the middle white chamber for the first time, they tended to escape into the white end box instead of into the black—just as Gay and Raphelson had originally reported in their own experiments.

However, Ungar and his group carried this work much further. They first performed a chemical analysis of the brains of more than 4,000 rats trained to avoid the dark chamber. They found a simple protein—which Ungar calls *scotophobin* (°)—that appeared in the brains of trained rats but not in the brains of untrained animals. Using rather complicated techniques, Ungar *et al.* were able to specify exactly the chemical formula for scotophobin. With this information, they next synthesized scotophobin, using inorganic materials anyone could order from a chemical supply house. Finally, they injected synthetic scotophobin into untrained recipients and tested these animals in the Gay and Raphelson apparatus. These recipients behaved just as if they had been injected with scotophobin taken directly from trained brains—or as if they had themselves been shocked for entering the black compartment.

Have Ungar and his associates discovered the chemical formula for a specific memory? It is far too soon to know for sure. However, several other laboratories have been able to repeat much or all of what Ungar has done. Several students working with David Malin and me at Michigan have shown that this scotophobin effect is highly specific. Rats or mice injected with synthetic scotophobin do not merely "fear the dark." Rather, they appear to be *afraid* of the black chamber in the specific apparatus that Ungar used originally.

Our recipients, when first put into the middle white chamber, often move slowly toward the black chamber as if answering an innately determined urge.

David Malin's rat shock chamber.

However, the closer they get, the more emotionally upset they appear to be. They often squeak, urinate, or defecate; occasionally they stop right on the threshold of the door leading into the black chamber—their noses inside the dark but their bodies safely outside.

In terms of rat-like behavior, these animals show the same sort of emotionality that our flatworms who ate "conflicting instructions" showed. Perhaps their innate tendency to approach darkness is being contradicted by the scotophobin molecule. Whatever the explanation, it is clear that animals injected with chemicals from untrained brains seldom behave this way.

If the engram is at least partially chemical, how and where are these molecules made in the brain and how and where do they influence behavior? These questions are as yet unanswered, though perhaps Ungar's work gives us a hint. The DNA you inherited from your parents specified which of your brain cells would initially make synapse with which others. But DNA does little or nothing all by itself— DNA influences growth and development by manufacturing various RNA molecules which, in turn, control the production of the proteins that actually do all the work of connecting one neuron with another. Perhaps DNA provides the original blueprint, but this preliminary design is modified by experience. When you learn something, it could be that your brain RNA and protein molecules are somehow altered and that they redraw or adapt the genetic plans. Long-term Memory storage would then be a matter of creating new molecules that would somehow rework your brain's wiring diagram by making new synaptic connections and unmaking old ones.

Rather than competing with the synaptic theory of memory, the chemical approach could offer it rather strong support.

PERCHANCE TO DREAM

Additional support for the memory molecule theory of learning comes from recent studies on the function of *REM sleep* (°). As we pointed out in Chapter 3, dreaming seems intimately connected with memory consolidation. Animals—or people—put in situations where difficult new learning is required typically show a marked increase in REM sleep. For instance, suppose we train a bunch of rats in

REM sleep. Rapid-eye-movement sleep, during which dreaming occurs and memory consolidation may take place. See Chapter 3.

An apparatus for depriving a rat of REM sleep. If the animal dozes off, it falls into the water and is awakened.

Hippocampus (HIP-poh-KAMP-us). From the Greek word *hippos,* meaning "horse," and *kampos,* meaning "sea monster." If you have ever seen a photograph (or a live specimen) of the little marine animal called the "sea horse," you will have a rough picture of what the hippocampus in your brain looks like. There are many experiments whose results suggest that the hippocampus is involved in memory formation and consolidation.

a very complicated maze, giving each of them 20 trials the first day. After training, the rats are returned to their cages and allowed to sleep all night. We measure REM sleep in all the animals both the night before training and the night after they are given the 20 training trials. On the morning of the second day, we test the rats to see which ones remember how to run the maze. Some rats will have learned; others will show little or no memory of how to get through the apparatus correctly. Almost uniformly, those rats that demonstrate mastery of the maze will have shown a large increase in REM sleep the night after training. The rats that failed to remember will mostly have shown little or no increase in dreaming. More than this, if we train animals in the maze and then deprive them of REM sleep afterward, few if any of them will learn.

In humans there is a similar correlation between increased dreaming and the learning of certain tasks. The correlation is highest when the learning involves highly complex material (such as words in a foreign language) or some kind of adaptation to a fairly emotional situation. Ramon Greenberg and Chester Pearlman showed in 1974 that depriving human subjects of REM sleep almost always lowers their ability to remember the important things that they experienced or tried to learn the day before.

QUESTION: **Why would it be important for you to get a good night's sleep immediately after studying for an important exam?**

Two other facts seem important. First, one of the things that happens during REM sleep is that the cortical cells produce much more protein (and presumably more RNA, too) than during any other form of sleep. Second, as we proved in my own laboratory a few years ago, memory transfer experiments typically yield positive results only if the donor animals are given frequent long rest periods (during which they can get uninterrupted sleep). It would seem from all these facts that when you must learn some complicated or emotionally-charged task, the chemicals involved in storing this memory are formed in very restricted parts of your brain, such as the *hippocampus* (°). Shock or trauma to the brain immediately after learning prevents these chemicals from forming and hence disrupts the memory process. But these chemicals must be distributed throughout the brain if the synaptic switches everywhere are to be "reset" for long-term memory storage to take place. This "distribution" probably occurs during REM sleep, and somehow involves the manufacture of new protein molecules. Disruption of REM sleep prevents this "distribution" of protein molecules and thereby stops the "rewiring" of the message routes in the cortex.

As we mentioned in Chapter 3, some 80 percent of your dream content has to do with your activities of the prior day. It seems likely that the psychological experience of dreaming is triggered off by "memory molecules" as they are pumped or distributed from one part of your brain to another. In short, you sleep so that you can dream, and you dream so that you can store your learning in permanent form—just as Sigmund Freud predicted long before we knew about either REM sleep or the chemical basis of memory.

TOWARD A BETTER MEMORY

To be truthful, the theory we have just outlined is far from being proved. No one knows very much about the chemical changes that take place inside your head when you learn something. When you try to study for an exam, or learn the phone number of a just-met but very attractive person, you cannot feel any of the chemical and electrical changes that must go on in your brain. But if your nerve cells do manufacture a unique new set of molecules for each of your memories, and if we can ever unravel the "memory code," what a different world we could create! Already we know a little bit about which chemicals increase learning speed and which retard it. If we could devise safe drugs that would make almost anyone learn faster, we could perhaps make education a faster and less boring experience. And if the day comes when we can actually synthesize memories in test tubes, then in future years those students who "drop chemicals" might be trying to learn Spanish or psychology rather than trying to "expand their consciousnesses."

Are the memory transfer experiments valid and reliable? Will education ever come packaged as pills or extracts? Read (or swallow) the next edition of this book to find out!

SUMMARY

1. When sensory inputs arrive at your receptor organs, they are held momentarily in what is called Sensory Information Storage—an exact copy of the stimulus itself.
2. As the receptor organs relay this image or copy to the brain, some part of the cortex appears to process the sensory input by interpreting the meaning of the stimulus.
3. This interpretation is held briefly in Short-term Memory, which has a capacity of about seven items or inputs. The hold time for an item in Short-term Memory seems to be just a few seconds or minutes.
4. Unimportant items drop out of Short-term Memory very rapidly as they are replaced by other incoming stimuli.
5. During this initial processing, the brain checks to see if you have encountered this same stimulus before by checking its Long-term Memory files.
6. Important inputs move eventually from Short-term Memory into the permanent, or long-term, memory banks of the brain.
7. Although we are not sure how your brain manages to remember, it seems that your cortical Board makes a verbal description rather than filing "photographs" of what you see or "recordings" of what you hear or feel.
8. Forgetting seems to be chiefly a matter of having some new learning interfere with what you have already filed away in Long-term Memory.
9. By using mnemonics, or memory devices, you can often improve your ability to remember things.
10. The physical representation of a memory is called an engram, or a memory trace in the brain.
11. No one knows what the engram really is, but remembering does seem correlated with rearranging the synaptic switches in your brain.
12. Recent studies of the biochemical correlates of learning suggest that molecular changes may occur in your neurons whenever you learn something. The molecules involved in memory formation may be RNA and/or protein.
13. REM sleep may be involved in the formation of Long-term Memory. Human subjects deprived of REM sleep do not remember as well as do those subjects allowed all the REM sleep they need. Furthermore, production of protein in the brain increases markedly during REM sleep.
14. There is some evidence that molecules taken from the brains of trained organisms and injected into untrained organisms may transfer the chemical engram from one animal to another. Although many of these memory transfer experiments seem both valid and reliable, the studies which have been done are still highly controversial.

". . . worms?"

"Yes, Don. Flatworms. Planarians. Sit down and I'll tell you all about it."

The young graduate student named Don wrapped his lanky legs around a kitchen stool and sat down. "This I've got to hear. I thought you psychologists only studied two species—the white rat and the college sophomore. Victor, why can't you be respectable like all your fellow students?"

"Because I want to study the effects of regeneration on memory, and rats don't regenerate worth a hoot," Victor said, lighting a cigarette. "I want to start by repeating some of the early experiments to make sure I know how to train the worms—and then go on to more complicated things involving a biochemical analysis of trained planarians. I want to find the engram in the flatworm. That's why I need your help."

Don smiled. "Because I'm in biochemistry."

"Right. I can do all the behavioral stuff, but I wouldn't know a molecule if I met one in the street. If you could help out with the experiment . . ."

"Too busy, man," Don said at once.

". . . or teach me how to shuffle those test tubes around, I'd really appreciate it."

"Well, I'm pretty sure you could learn the techniques, Victor, if you had the necessary lab equipment to work with. But I'm not all that sure about your worms."

Victor scratched his head. "What do you mean?"

"Worms are pretty tiny, aren't they? Brain no bigger than the point of a pin, as I recall. They don't have enough neurons to learn anything, do they?"

"How many neurons do you think a planarian has, Don?"

"I don't know, but it can't possibly be enough."

Victor laughed. "They've been trained in more than 30 laboratories—and by several thousand high school students for science fair projects. But you have to treat them gently, pay attention to their needs, and maybe learn to think like a worm yourself."

A crooked smile twisted Don's pleasant face. "You've got the right-sized brain for thinking like a worm, Victor, no doubt about it. But what next?"

"Then I want to cut a trained worm in half, let both pieces regenerate into complete animals, and test both animals to see which half remembers."

"Oh, come off it."

"I'm serious. According to the literature, even though the tail has to grow a completely new brain, it remembers at least as well as the head does. Then I want to train a worm, cut it in half and throw the head away. After the old tail grows a new head section, I want to cut off the old tail and throw it away. When the new head regenerates a new tail, I'll have a completely reformed planarian. I want to see if it remembers the original training."

"Don't be silly, Victor. If a completely reformed animal could remember, a zoologist would have done the experiment years ago."

Victor smiled. "A zoologist did—working with a psychologist. That's why I'm sure it will work. What I want to do is to perform a chemical analysis on this regenerated worm. When the tail builds itself a new head and brain, it must make use of the genetic blueprint it inherited from its parents. But somehow the training must cause a chemical change in that blueprint or the new brain wouldn't remember what the old brain was taught. Nobody knows what molecules cause the tail to regenerate a new head in the first place. My guess is that they're the same chemicals involved in memory storage. I'd like to find out, but I don't know enough biochemistry to do the analysis."

"Enter the biochemist, smiling," Don said, a stern look on his face. Then he got up. "And exit the biochemist, groaning."

"Don't go! I haven't finished explaining the experiment yet."

"You've said quite enough, Victor. I can see a thousand things that could go wrong with that experiment, and I don't want any part of it."

"What could go wrong?"

Don shook his head in dismay. "Well, for one thing, how will you know that the chemical you identify in the trained tail is the one that affects memory?"

"Oh, that's easy. I'll just inject it into untrained worms. If they respond as if they had been trained, then I'll know I've got the right molecule."

This time Don groaned out loud. "Don't tell me you believe those memory transfer experiments? Grind up an educated rat and inject the knowledge into another animal with a hypodermic needle? Why, I wouldn't believe those experiments if we did them in our own laboratory and got positive results!"

Victor smiled slyly. "Well, why don't we try it in your lab and find out?"

"You're off your rocker, Victor. The professor I work for would bite my head off if I even suggested such a thing."

"Your . . . **head?**" Victor said, a thought slowly dawning.

"So you see, I'd really like to help you, but we just couldn't do it at our lab."

Victor licked his lips, then said, "Well, why couldn't we do the experiment here?"

"Here? In your kitchen?"

"The first planarian study done in the United States was performed in a kitchen in Austin, Texas—because the professor in charge of the psych labs didn't trust flatworms."

"Or flatworm trainers either, I'd guess."

"You're probably right."

"Anyway, Victor, it just won't work. You'd need a lot of fancy analytical machinery. Centrifuges, balances, spectrophotometers, electrophoresis equipment—things like that."

"True," answered Victor, rubbing his hand across his mouth. "But at the start, all I'd really need would be knowledge. You could give me that."

Don shook his head. "I'm afraid I don't approve of what you want to do. And I simply don't have time to teach you all the techniques." He sighed once, softly. "You'll just have to learn it all the hard way—by reading textbooks and journal articles."

"That's all right, Don. Don't worry. I'm determined to get the information—one way or another."

"Well, if you didn't want to do such kooky research, maybe I could have helped."

Victor smiled. "No problem, Don. And I do appreciate your thoughtfulness. I was sure you'd put your brain to it if you could."

The thought that had been lurking in the recesses of Victor's head snapped into focus.

"In fact," Victor continued, breathlessly, "I'd like to show my appreciation by having you over for dinner some time soon."

Don grinned. "Hey, that's great of you. I can always use a free meal. But I didn't know you could cook."

"My Transylvanian grandmother whispered all her culinary secrets in my ear just before she died. I'll get a bottle of fine wine, and I guarantee the main course will be something you'll never forget."

"So set a date."

"I'll have to call you, Don. I need some special equipment to prepare this meal. As soon as I've located what I need, I'll give you a buzz."

After Don had left, Victor sat at the kitchen table for several minutes, smoking a cigarette. Then he picked up the telephone book and let his fingers walk through the yellow pages until he found the information he wanted. Picking up the phone, he dialed a number.

"Hello, Acme Restaurant Supply Company? Say, listen. Do you people sell meat grinders? I mean, really big ones? It's for a scientific project, you see."

RECOMMENDED READINGS

Fjerdingstad, Ejnar, ed. *Chemical Transfer of Learned Information* (Amsterdam: North-Holland Publishing Company, 1970).

Lindsay, Peter H., and Donald A. Norman. *Human Information Processing* (New York: Academic Press, Inc., 1972).

Luria, A.R. *The Mind of a Mnemonist* (New York: Basic Books, Inc., 1968).

chapter 18

"MESMER'S MAGIC WAND"

HYPNOSIS, PAIN, AND ACUPUNCTURE

DID YOU KNOW THAT . . .

Many of the "patent remedies" sold as medicine don't cure anything, but can make you mildly drunk or stoned?

Depressed patients often don't recover from illness as rapidly as do patients who have faith and hope?

Perhaps half of the "cures" supposedly caused by pills or medicines are actually brought about by a psychological factor called the "placebo effect?"

Hypnosis was discovered in the 1700's by a famous "quack" named Anton Mesmer?

The French government banned hypnosis on the ground that it made women too easy to seduce?

Sigmund Freud rejected hypnosis because it didn't seem to help cure insanity?

A hypnotized person may, under certain special circumstances, commit murder or engage in other anti-social acts?

Some psychologists believe that hypnosis is no more than an exaggerated form of role-playing?

Some people are born without the capacity to feel physical pain of any kind?

The experience of pain is very complex and is strongly influenced by the cortex?

Acupuncture is probably no more effective in reducing pain or curing disease than is a sugar pill or hypnosis?

"Are you sure you want to do it in class?" Brian Healy asked.

"Why, certainly," Assistant Professor Don Powell replied, staring intently at his teaching fellow. "It's a legitimate demonstration of mental functioning, a tool used extensively by respected members of the medical and dental professions. Isn't it time that hypnosis was taken out of the closet and brought into the open? It isn't a cure-all; it isn't a parlor trick; it isn't a mysterious force. It's merely mind over matter. Besides, the students will love it."

"I don't doubt that at all, Professor Powell," the teaching fellow said. "But what if something goes wrong?"

"What could possibly go wrong?"

Brian Healy thought for a moment, then cleared his throat. "Well, what if the person you hypnotize doesn't come out of the trance? Who'd want to be hypnotized for life?"

"Nonsense. I suppose at one time or another some hypnotist must have experienced problems in bringing a subject back from a deep hypnotic trance, but I've never run across a fully authenticated case where that happened. What we do know is that if you don't wake a person up deliberately, the person drops off into a restful, normal sleep and in a short time wakes up naturally. And with no physical ill effects, I might add emphatically," Powell added emphatically.

"Okay, you're the boss. But what if nobody in the class can be hypnotized? What would you do then?"

"Change the subject, probably," Powell said, perhaps a little too truthfully. "But it won't happen. In a class of 100, I'd expect roughly 15 students would not be hypnotizable at all, that about 65 would go into a light or a medium trance, and that 20 would be capable of achieving a really deep hypnotic state. The subject's prior attitudes are the main controlling factor anyhow. If you think you can't talk when you're hypnotized, you won't talk no matter how much the hypnotist coaxes you. If you think you can't stop talking when you're in a trance, nothing will shut you up."

"Sounds like my mother-in-law. Nothing can shut her up either."

"Brian, no personal problems, please! We must approach this demonstration seriously. Hypnotism isn't a joke of some kind; it's a serious psychological tool. We are following in the great tradition of Mesmer, Braid, Charcot, Bernheim, and even Freud. Just do as I tell you, and everything will turn out fine."

And, of course, it did. Professor Powell began the class with a lengthy discussion of the history of hypnotism, beginning with Anton Mesmer and his animal magnetism and concluding with recent experiments on the effectiveness of hypnotherapy. Much of the class was entranced. Then he attempted to hypnotize all 100 students at once. Much of the class was tranced. Then, as his final demonstration, he asked for a volunteer who might want to test out his or her mental powers. An alert, eager, wiry young man immediately stuck up his hand.

"What is your name, please?" Powell asked the volunteer.

"Elvis McNeil," the young man said, running one of his hands through his wavy hair.

"All right, Mr. McNeil, I'm going to put you into a trance, if I can, and then we're going to open up the pathways to your mind; we're going to unshackle all the latent mental powers you've always suspected you had. We're going to prove to you that your own mind, as untrained and untutored as it may be in its present state, can move mountains. We won't do anything that could possibly harm you, but there is always the possibility that you may feel a little foolish afterward. Is your ego big enough to withstand the laughter of your fellow students?"

"Gee, Professor Powell, I think my ego only has problems when people don't laugh at me," the intense young man said, carefully adjusting his glasses. "I'll go along with anything you want to try."

"Excellent, my boy, excellent. Now just sit in this comfortable chair right here in the middle of the platform and start relaxing. Are you comfortable?"

When Elvis McNeil had settled himself in the chair, Professor Powell pulled out a long, sharp hatpin and sterilized it over the flame of a match. "Would it hurt you if I jabbed this pin into one of your fingers?"

Elvis tensed a little. "Of course it would. I thought you said it wouldn't hurt!"

"I assure you, it won't. But we won't try it until you're fully hypnotized, and then I guarantee you that you won't feel a thing. It's just a test to see if you're really in a trance. You won't mind, now, will you, if it's a scientific test of sorts?"

"Not if it unleashes the latent powers of my mind," McNeil said solemnly.

"Good," the teacher answered, pulling a gold watch on a long chain out of his pocket, much the way a magician might. "Now, Mr. McNeil, I want you to stare at this mystical pocket watch that was passed on to me by my paternal grandfather. See it swing back and forth before your eyes? Look at it closely, Mr. McNeil. Watch as it moves back and forth, back and forth, back and forth."

Powell's voice crooned softly, almost as if he were singing. "Your eyelids are getting heavier and heavier; your eyelids are like lead, sinking slowly down over your eyes. You are getting sleepier and sleepier and sleepier. Soon you will be fast asleep, deep asleep. Soon you will see nothing, hear nothing but the sound of my voice. Go to sleep, Mr. McNeil. Sleep. Deep, deep, deep sleep."

McNeil's eyes closed. He sat rigid, unmoving.

"Are you asleep?"

McNeil's head nodded slowly.

"Deeply, completely asleep?"

Again the young man's head moved in a gentle nod.

"Hold your hand out, Elvis. That's right, straight out in front of you. Your hand is made of steel, isn't it? Impenetrable, painless steel. You can't feel a thing in your hand, Elvis. See, I can touch it, and you can't feel my touch, can you?''

''No.''

''That's right, no pain at all. I can even stick this pin in your hand and it will cause you no pain at all. You can't feel a thing; remember; no pain at all. Now I will stick the pin in—like this!—and it didn't hurt at all, did it?''

The class gasped as Powell plunged the sterilized hatpin half-an-inch into the young man's hand, but McNeil didn't react. Instead, he shook his head slowly and whispered, ''No, it didn't hurt at all.''

Professor Powell removed the pin, inspected McNeil's hand, and put a small bandage over the tiny wound. Then he turned to the class and said, ''So, you see, pain is ultimately controlled by the cortex. Your brain can turn pain off or turn it on, depending on the circumstances. Under hypnosis, you can be made to perceive things that aren't there, and you can be made not to perceive even the strongest of stimuli. Mr. McNeil here is obviously a very good hypnotic subject. So now let's put matters to a further test.''

Turning to his assistant, Powell motioned the young man toward him. ''Now, Mr. McNeil, you surely remember what my teaching fellow, Brian Healy, looks like. Right? Well, in a moment, Mr. McNeil, I'm going to ask you to open your eyes. But when you do so, Mr. Healy will be totally invisible to you. You simply won't be able to see Mr. Healy no matter where he is or what he does. Do you understand? Good. Now, please open your eyes.''

Elvis McNeil blinked a couple of times and looked around carefully.

''You can see me, right?'' Powell asked, putting an arm around Brian Healy's shoulders. ''But is there anyone else up here on the stage with me? Do you see anyone else here but me?''

McNeil said, ''Only me. There's just you and me on the stage, Professor Powell.''

''Right, double right. You're a very perceptive person, McNeil. Now then, I want to help you open up the channels of your mind and tap the secret powers that lie dormant inside your skull. I want to give you the faith of a mustard seed, the faith that moves mountains and turns the physical world into your slave, to do with as you wish. Would you like to learn those secrets, McNeil?''

Although he was still apparently in a deep trance, Elvis became excited. ''Yes, yes,'' he cried. ''That's what I came to college for in the first place!''

''Then you should have taken this course sooner, right? Well, now, Mr. McNeil, let's begin by teaching you how to levitate objects—that is, how to overcome the force of gravity merely by willing things to rise straight up into the air. We'll begin with this straight chair here on the stage. Do you think you can get it to float upward merely by giving it the mental command to rise?''

McNeil looked dubious. ''If you say so . . .''

''Good. Good,'' Powell said, motioning Healy to grab hold of the chair, which was some 15 feet (4.5 meters) away from them on the other side of the stage. ''Now, Mr. McNeil, all you have to do is to concentrate. Concentrate with all the hidden power in your cortex. Order the chair to rise. Do so now. Talk to the chair—give it commands out loud, and then watch what happens when your concentration becomes deep enough!''

McNeil took a deep breath. ''All right, chair, you're going to rise. You're going to go sailing up into the blue like a funny old balloon. Rise. Rise!''

As the young man shouted, Healy began to lift the chair slowly from the floor.

''Rise! Rise!'' McNeil cried again.

The chair ''rose'' an inch or two each time McNeil urged it upward.

''Holy Moly, Professor Powell, it's working! What a trip!''

The chair suddenly dropped back onto the floor.

''You're not concentrating, McNeil. Keep your mind on the business at hand.''

''Sorry, sir,'' McNeil said, and took another deep breath. ''Okay, chair, let's float some more. Up, up and away!''

In Brian Healy's strong hands, the chair rose a foot or more off the stage.

''That's right, chair, keep going. Higher, higher, higher!''

The class began to giggle just a bit, not sure of what was going on. Healy lifted the chair until it was at the level of his waist.

"Don't stop now, get it on up there!"

Healy held the chair above his head. Small beads of sweat began to pop out on his forehead. The chair was heavier than he had thought it would be.

"Higher!" McNeil screamed.

But Professor Powell interrupted. "That's high enough for the first time around, McNeil. We don't want to strain your cortex, after all. Why don't you tell it to dance instead?"

"Sure. I can do it. I'm sure I can do it. Okay, chair, I want you to shake, rattle, and roll."

Healy twisted the chair over his head rhythmically, following the beat of some distant drummer.

Suddenly McNeil burst out laughing. "It's a rocking chair! That's what it is, a crazy chair that dances because I've got rock in my head!"

"Be serious, McNeil, or you'll ruin everything."

As if in sympathy, the chair came crashing down onto the stage, and Brian Healy collapsed into it.

The class went wild with applause. McNeil beamed, as if he thought the clapping was for him. Brian Healy stood up and took a bow, but Elvis appeared not to notice it and just smiled happily at his fellow students.

"And now, Mr. McNeil, I want you to wake up, to recover completely from the trance, as soon as I count to three," Professor Powell commanded. "Ready? One, two . . . THREE! You're awake!"

McNeil shook his head, then looked around again.

"Do you feel okay? Good," said Powell. "And can you see Mr. Healy now?"

Elvis McNeil looked straight at the teaching fellow, then nodded. "Of course. He's right here on the stage with us."

"And how do you feel?"

"Fine, fine. But what happened? How did I get this bandage on my hand?"

"That's where I injected you with the secret powers. Don't you remember making the chair dance in the air?"

McNeil looked puzzled. "Oh, yes. I remember. How did I do that, Professor Powell?"

"Mind over matter, my boy. Concentration, that's what does the trick. Thank you very much for your assistance."

At that point, the bell rang, ending the class. Several students crowded around Professor Powell to ask questions. After he had answered as many as he could, he and Healy headed back toward the office.

"What do you think the after-effects will be for poor Mr. McNeil?" Healy asked.

"After-effects? Why, there won't be any. He'll find out what really happened, and he'll be embarrassed for a while; but we'll have proved a point we never could otherwise. You perceive what your mind wants you to perceive. Beautiful demonstration, didn't you think so?"

Healy scratched his head. "Sure, Professor Powell. Sure."

(Continued on page 406.)

The field of medicine has always attracted its share of *quacks* (°) and *charlatans* (°)—that is, disreputable men and women with little or no medical knowledge who promise quick cures at cheap prices. The reasons why quackery thrives even in a modern United States are not hard to find.

To begin with, pain seems to be a chronic human condition; a person whose body or mind "hurts" will often pay any amount of money for the promise of relief.

Second, even the best medical treatment cannot cure all of the ills that beset men and women; hence, people who mistrust or dislike the truths that their physicians tell them often turn to more sympathetic ears.

Quack. Someone who pretends to have medical skills. Someone who makes money by selling worthless medical treatment. The origin of the word is amusing. Mercury used to be used as a medicine, particularly for venereal (vee-NEAR-ee-ul) diseases. "Quicksilver" is the old name for mercury. "Quack" means "to croak," or "to die." Someone who pretended to be a doctor was often called a "quack-silver" because the "quack" used medicines such as mercury improperly and caused people to "croak."

Charlatan (SHAR-luh-ton). From the Italian word meaning "to chatter" or "to talk noisily." A smooth-talking salesman of worthless medicines is a charlatan or quack.

Many people lack the training necessary to evaluate medical claims; given the choice between (1) a reputable physician who says a cure for cancer will be long, difficult, and expensive and may not work at all and (2) a *patent remedy* (°) salesman who suggests that five bottles of his secret-formula "snake oil" will cure not only cancer but tuberculosis, syphilis, warts, and bad breath as well, some individuals will opt for the bottles of snake oil.

Many "snake oil" remedies are highly laced with alcohol or narcotic drugs; anyone who drinks them may get so drunk or stoned that minor pains are drowned in the rising tide of pleasant intoxication. Little wonder that "snake oil" is a popular cure-all for minor aches and pains! But let there be no misunderstandings. A very few "home remedies" actually work. Quinine (a drug useful in treating malaria), reserpine (a tranquilizer), and digitalis (prescribed for some types of heart conditions) are similar to natural products used for centuries in folk medicine before their curative powers were established by scientific tests. Most "home remedies" sold by quacks are, however, not only useless but often can be harmful to the user.

The Causality Fantasy

Another reason that quack cures remain popular is what we might call the "causality fantasy." We all learn in school that if event B always follows event A, then it is likely that A *causes* B to take place—that is, we imply a connection or *causality* (°) between two events merely because they occur in sequence.

Suppose that you overindulge at dinner and wind up with a nasty stomach ache. A friend of yours offers you a sure-fire cure—*dried frog eyes* mixed with *chicken blood* (°). You hold your nose, swallow a spoonful of the dreadful medicine, and go to bed as quickly as you can. The next morning the stomach ache is gone.

A miracle? No, for chances are you would have felt much better anyhow after a good night's sleep. And yet, the mere fact that you (1) took the medicine and (2) the pain later went away might lead you to fantasize that A had caused B to happen. Many human illnesses heal themselves if given half a chance. The magic cures we stuff into our stomachs may often retard rather than speed up this natural healing process—yet we fall prey to the "causality fantasy" because the act of taking the worthless medicine precedes our getting better.

The Placebo Effect

But by far the most potent reason that quack medicines still are sold around the world has to do with the power of "mind over matter." Your brain is the master organ of your body—it regulates all the chemical processes that keep you alive

Patent remedy (PAT-tent REMM-uh-dee). A packaged drug or medicine or "secret composition" whose name may be protected by a "patent" or "trademark." Many patent remedies are put out by reputable drug companies and are quite useful; others, particularly those sold by a quack or charlatan, are worthless.

Causality (caws-AL-it-tee). A regular sequence of events that the mind connects from habit or experience, or from scientific theories. To search for "causality" is to look for what causes what.

Dried frog eyes; chicken blood. Two of the thousands of fantastic substances people have taken to "cure" themselves of one disease or another. Both frog eyes and chicken blood are still prescribed by quacks in some parts of the world. So are animal feces (FEE-sees).

The tub of Mesmer, a satirical engraving from **L'Antimagnetisme**, 1784.

Azoth, which is shown on the head of the sword, is the alchemical name for mercury, the universal remedy of Paracelsus.

and well. When you become depressed and lose hope, the autonomic (emotional) nervous system slows down these bodily processes and retards your chances of getting well. When you have hope and faith, these curative processes are speeded up and you are more likely to recover even from the most dreadful of diseases than when you are depressed. The medical doctor who can convince his or her patients that they will recover typically cures more people than the physician whose behavior causes those patients to lose faith in themselves and in the medical profession.

QUESTION: Why might some medical doctors refuse to tell a patient how seriously ill he or she actually is?

If a sick person mistakenly believes that his or her condition can best be cured by taking a drug of some kind, most physicians are quite happy to give the patient a *placebo* (°), or pill made of sugar or ordinary flour. The placebo pill does no harm at all, but it may so help the patient *psychologically* that pain seems to diminish and the person may actually recover much faster than without taking the pill. Many physicians estimate that at least half the patients they see suffer from psychological rather than physical ailments; for these patients, the placebo effect of taking a sugar pill is perhaps the best cure any doctor can offer. If sugar pills can be so helpful to physicians, little wonder that "snake-oil" remedies often appear to cause miraculous cures. As we will see in later chapters, the placebo effect is one that psychologists must constantly consider in all their research and therapeutic efforts.

Anton Mesmer

One of the most famous quacks in all of medical history was a man named Anton Mesmer. Born in 1734 in a tiny Austrian village, Mesmer studied philosophy at a university in southern Germany and then took degrees in *theology* (°) and medicine at the University of Vienna (where Freud later taught).

At the time that Mesmer began his medical practice, the prevailing view toward mental illness was that insanity was due to an imbalance of certain body chemicals called *humors* (°) (*see* Chapter 23). Mesmer rejected the humoral theory in favor of an even more "humorous" notion supplied by *Paracelsus* (°), the noted

Placebo (plas-SEE-bo). From a Latin phrase meaning "to please." A harmless drug given for its psychological effect especially to satisfy the patient or to act as a control in an experiment.

Theology (thee-OLL-oh-gee; rhymes with "see DOLL? Oh, gee!"). The study of the traditional doctrines of a religion or religious group.

Humors (YOU-mores). From the Latin word meaning "fluids" or "moisture." According to early Greek medical men, the body secreted four different humors: black bile, yellow bile, blood, and phlegm. See Chapter 23 for further explanation.

Paracelsus (PAIR-ah-SELL-sus). A Swiss physician born about 1490 whose real name was Theophrastus Bombastus von Hohenheim. After studying medicine, he became interested in mining and in the diseases of miners. Named to the faculty of medicine at the University of Basel in 1526, he burned the works of Galen and other famous early physicians in order to discredit their theories and substitute his own. He began calling himself Paracelsus about this time, presumably to inform people that he was superior to Celsus, the greatest of the Roman medical writers. Whatever his name, he introduced the use of such minerals as mercury, lead, sulfur, iron, and copper sulfate as "curative agents." He also insisted that physicians should know astronomy, since, he said, the stars influence disease and humans all have astral (heavenly) spirits. He left Basel in 1529 after a dispute over his salary, and died in Salzburg in 1541 when he fell over a cliff. His enemies (of whom he had many) insisted he was drunk at the time. His friends (of whom he had few) believed he was thrown over the cliff by thugs hired by jealous physicians.

James Graham lecturing—a caricature by John Kay, 1785.

MR. AND MRS. SNOW.

I ELIZABETH SNOW, of Plainfield, in the ſtate of Connecticut, certify that in the month of June, 1795, I was ſorely afflicted with pains in the ancles, which had ſettled there after a ſevere fit of ſickneſs, and had troubled me to ſuch a degree that I became very weak and emaciated. In this unhappy ſituation I continued about three months, until in the month and year above-mentioned, I applied to Doctor Eliſha Perkins who viſited me and operated on the pained part of my ancles, with his Metallic Inſtruments. Immediately the pain ceaſed and has never ſince returned. I am perſuaded a radical cure was at that time effected.

ELIZABETH SNOW.

Plainfield, Auguſt 3, 1796.

I the ſubſcriber, fully concur with my wife, in the above ſtatement of facts.

ABRAHAM SNOW.

(*The Granger Collection*)

A testimonial from a 1797 pamphlet published by Elisha Perkins, the inventor of metallic tractors.

Astrophysical (ASS-tro-FISS-ick-ull). Literally, the physics or physical side of astronomy. The study of the physical laws that pertain to the sun, moon, stars, and planets.

Agitations (adge-jit-TAY-shuns). From the Latin word meaning "to drive" or "to turn over in the mind." To agitate (ADGE-jit-tate) is to stir up, or to move quickly to and fro. To shake or quiver.

Renaissance physician. Paracelsus held that mental illness was forced on an individual by "disturbing environments" that led to an improper development of the individual's personality. The "environments" that Paracelsus thought influential, however, were primarily *astrophysical* (°) rather than social. It was not your parents who drove you batty, according to Paracelsus, but the fact that your negative and positive charges were out of polarity with what he called the "Universal Spirit." To cure insanity, Paracelsus gave patients various medicines derived from minerals "guaranteed" to capture beneficial magnetic forces that supposedly came from the planets and the stars. One of his followers, Jan Baptista van Helmont, went a step further; he stated that your body contained magnetic fluids which you could actually "focus" or aim with your mind; if you did so properly, you could bring the minds and bodies of other people under your control.

Cures by Magnetism   Although Mesmer wrote his doctoral thesis on the magnetic effects of the planets on the human body, he believed that these celestial forces could better be focused through iron magnets than through the magnetic minerals recommended by Paracelsus. As R.M. Goldenson has pointed out, Mesmer lived at a time when magnetism and electricity were new and exciting physical forces and people were just beginning to speculate on how they might be used to cure human illnesses. An English quack named James Graham had seen Benjamin Franklin's attempts to capture lightning by flying a kite during an electrical storm. Graham thereafter opened up in London a weirdly decorated Temple of Health in which his patients splashed about in electrically magnetized water. In the United States a physician named Elisha Perkins patented a copper and brass device that was supposed to be able to "draw pain" from injured arms and legs; this contraption became so famous that even George Washington purchased one. And in Europe someone with the odd name of Father Maximilian Hell claimed he could cure various emotional illnesses by applying magnetic plates to the patient's body.

Mesmer took a heavenly view toward Hell's claims—that is, Mesmer thought that magnets could capture the magnetic fluids that radiated from the planets, and that these fluids could cure various sicknesses. One of his first patients was an hysterical woman who complained of a variety of pains, convulsions, and *agitations* (°). When Mesmer put magnets over her stomach and legs, her pains vanished for several hours. Mesmer became so successful at these "magnetic cures" that he took to wearing odd clothes and soon announced that, through his techniques, "the art of healing reaches its final perfection." It did not occur to Mesmer that his "cures" were due to the placebo effect—to what we might call the power of suggestion. But this explanation did occur to Mesmer's colleagues at the University of Vienna, who investigated his techniques and decided they were a product of imagination rather than magnetism. Mesmer was thereafter expelled from the university, fled Vienna, and set up shop in Paris.

Mesmer's "Grand Crisis"   Paris in the 1780's was friendlier to Mesmer than Vienna had been, and he soon opened a healing salon that had in its center a huge tub containing magnetized water. Twisted, oddly shaped metal rods stuck out from all sides of the tub. Mesmer made his patients sit holding hands in a closed circle around the tub so that the rods could touch the wounded or sore parts of their bodies.

Goldenson states that, to help things along, Mesmer dressed himself in a long purple robe and walked around the tub, touching his patients with a metal wand, urging them to yield themselves up to the magnetic fluids that surrounded them, telling them they would be cured if only they could focus on the heavenly powers within their sick bodies. Some of the patients apparently went into trance-like states; they would sit or stand as if frozen into place, apparently unseeing and unhearing.

Mesmer had, in fact, discovered hypnosis, but made no real scientific study of what the hypnotic state was like or what really induced it. Instead, he urged his clients to reach further into their minds and, by continually pushing his patients psychologically, drove many of them to reach what he called a "grand crisis," something we would call a "grand mal" convulsive seizure. Mesmer was convinced that the "grand crisis" was responsible for the cures his clients reported; other medical doctors were not quite so sure.

Mesmerism (°), the name soon given to the technique for inducing a trance state and the "grand crisis," became the rage of Paris, and the French government offered Mesmer a reward of 20,000 francs to reveal the secret of his "cures." When he refused, the government appointed two committees to investigate his techniques (Benjamin Franklin, then the U.S. ambassador to France, was a member of one). The committees were unanimous in their public reports—Mesmerism was a hoax, and the cures were due to suggestion and imagination rather than to magnetism. The committees also sent a report in secret to Louis XVI (16th), the French king, warning that the "grand crisis" was probably habit-forming and dangerous to one's health. Furthermore, they told the king, women seemed to be particularly susceptible to the "grand crisis" and could easily be seduced while in this state.

So Mesmerism was banned on moral as well as medical grounds. Mesmer's star fell from public view and he soon retired to Versailles, a town near Paris, where he lived another 30 years, presumably basking in the magnetic radiations of the celestial bodies and, perhaps, occasionally trying to hypnotize French peasants.

HYPNOSIS

Considering the circumstances of its discovery, there is little wonder that hypnotism even today is considered to be more of a parlor trick or black magic than a legitimate psychological phenomenon. Because most scientists and physicians have held hypnosis in such low esteem, it was not until fairly recently that enough reliable data on the topic existed for psychologists to view hypnosis objectively.

It was James Braid, a Scottish physician, who in 1842 gave *hypnosis* its present name, taken from the Greek word for sleep. After attending a session held by a wandering Mesmerist, Braid became convinced that magnetic fluids had nothing to do with the effect. Rather, Braid felt, it was an abnormal or intense form of sleep that the hypnotist induced by somehow affecting certain centers in the subject's brain. As the subject focused his or her eyes on something the hypnotist was doing or wearing, the subject fell into a deep if rather strange psychological sleep (nowadays, we would call it an altered state of consciousness).

Shortly after Braid's analysis, Jean Charcot, a noted French professor of anatomy, announced that in his opinion there was a close connection between hysteria and hypnosis, and that only hysterics could be hypnotized. Other French scientists soon denied Charcot's claims, believing that the hypnotic state was a result of *suggestibility* (°) and not hysteria, although there seemed little doubt that hysterics often made good hypnotic subjects.

Freud and Hypnosis

It was into this sea of controversy that Sigmund Freud stepped in the winter of 1885 and, finding the hypnotic tide a little too cold for his comfort, soon withdrew, leaving the waters muddied for almost 50 years. Freud went to Paris to study for a few months under Charcot, and apparently the experience marked a turning point in his life.

Mesmerism (MEZZ-mur-ism). The first name given to hypnosis, or hypnotism (HIPP-no-tism).

Suggestibility. The state of following suggestions, of doing what you are told to do. If someone dares you to eat frog eyes, and you do, you are probably pretty suggestible. The French anatomist Charcot (shar-KOH) believed hypnosis was merely a matter of some people's being highly suggestible.

Clark L. Hull.

Free association. Sigmund Freud's method of getting people to remember the traumatic events of their childhoods. The patient usually lies on a couch and is encouraged to say whatever comes into his or her mind—that is, to freely give whatever mental associations occur to the patient.

In general. A non-technical way of saying "low, positive correlations." Two events are correlated if they tend to occur together more than chance would allow. That is, two events are correlated if the connection between them is non-random. If the events are not connected at all, they have a zero correlation. If the events almost always occur together, they have a high, positive correlation. If the connection between the events is weak—that is, if they sometimes occur together but sometimes don't—they have a low, positive correlation. In general, people with high IQ scores are easier to hypnotize than people with low IQ scores. Translation: IQ scores have a low, positive correlation with hypnotizability. See the Statistical Appendix for further details.

Prior to this visit, Freud had thought of mental illness as being primarily *physiological*, and had used massage, baths, rest, and electrical stimulation with many of his hysterical patients. When he returned to Vienna in 1886, he began thinking of insanity as having primarily *psychological* causes. Following Charcot's lead, Freud used hypnosis to suggest to hysterics that their symptoms would disappear. Sometimes symptom relief did occur, but often the symptoms recurred. Besides, not all of his patients could be hypnotized, and many of them became so dependent on his suggestions that they would not function in society unless they were under Freud's hypnotic spell. It was this latter fact, perhaps, that called Freud's attention to the critical variable of the relationship between the hypnotist and the subject. Only those clients who could experience a strong personal trust in him seemed to be easily hypnotizable.

Renouncing hypnosis as a useless therapeutic tool, Freud instead developed the technique of *free association* (°), in which an unhypnotized patient learned how to pull long-forgotten but important material out of his or her memory banks (*see* Chapter 17).

As Freud's influence grew, his opinions about hypnosis took on more and more weight, and fewer and fewer people bothered to study or use it. It was not until the 1930's, when American behavioral psychologists reached the point of rejecting much of Freud's theorizing, that hypnosis again became a subject deemed fit for study in scientific laboratories.

Suggestibility

What is hypnosis? Braid thought it a form of sleep, but the early Behaviorists believed it to be a state of narrowly focused attention in which the hypnotized person somehow becomes extremely suggestible. Clark L. Hull, the noted learning theorist working at Yale, made a lengthy study of suggestibility and hypnosis. Hull was hunting for some simple test that would quickly tell who would be a good hypnotic subject. He was unable to find any one psychological or physiological trait that was a sure-fire index of hypnotizability. Research did suggest, though, that *in general* (°) children between 7 and 8 years of age were more easily hypnotized than at any other time in their lives, that females *in general* were slightly better subjects than were males, that drug addicts were *in general* more suggestible than non-addicts, and that individuals with high intelligence were *in general* more susceptible to hypnosis than were individuals of lower intelligence.

QUESTION: **If you were hunting for the best possible hypnotic subject, would you hunt for a 7-year-old girl genius who was a heroin addict?**

More recently, Ernest Hilgard and his associates at Stanford have collected data suggesting that the response you make to a hypnotist is partially determined by the type of parents you have. Hilgard *et al.* believe that for you to become a good hypnotic subject, you must have the capacity to become deeply involved in imaginative experiences, including role-playing. They further state that this capacity is usually found in children whose parents have the same kind of ability.

Hilgard and his colleagues presume that if your parents were inclined to punish you severely and frequently when you were young, chances are that you will be able to "go under" in an hypnotic trance rather easily. Why? For two reasons. First, continual punishment may instill in you the habit of automatic and unquestioning obedience to authority. Second, you may learn to escape parental wrath by retreating into a world of your own imagination, and you may thus learn the role-playing skills that are necessary when you go into an hypnotic trance.

QUESTION: **In Chapter 14 we spoke of internalizers who believe that their lives are controlled chiefly by their own efforts, and externalizers who believe that their destinies are influenced by outside forces and who are very obedient to authority; if**

Hilgard *et al.* are correct, which type of person should make the better hypnotic subject?

We are all suggestible to some extent, although the exact amount almost always depends on the situation we find ourselves in. What interested Hull and the other early Behaviorists was the fact that, through hypnotic suggestion, a person may gain a surprising amount of control over many of his or her bodily functions. If you put a friend of yours into a deep trance, then told your friend to become totally blind to all visual stimulation, your friend would wander around bumping into things and asking who turned out the lights. Your friend would insist that he or she couldn't see a thing. If you told this friend to become red-green blind and then gave the person a test for color-blindness, chances are that he or she would "flunk" the test just about the way a color-blind person would.

But is this "real" blindness? Some early researchers thought that, through hypnosis, the eyes became "disconnected" so that no visual input got through to the brain. We now know this isn't the case. If, while your friend was insisting he or she was unable to see, you suddenly and *without warning* turned on a powerful light that glared in your friend's eyes, he or she would most surely blink and probably would put a hand up to block off the sudden visual input.

Ernest Hilgard.

QUESTION: How might this same hypnotized friend have reacted to the bright light if he or she had seen you drag out a large flashlight and hold it behind your back as you walked forward saying, "Remember that you're blind and can't see a thing"?

Effects of Hypnosis

A subject in a deep hypnotic trance can be made to act as if any (or all) of his or her sensory inputs have been cut off completely, or can be made to respond to sights, smells, sounds, tastes, or tactile stimuli that aren't really there. The subject may perform what seem to be incredible feats of strength, such as lifting objects that weigh several hundred pounds. Or you can tell the subject to make his or her body as rigid as a board, then put the person's head on one chair, the feet on another with nothing in between. Now you can sit on the person's unsupported stomach without having the subject buckle underneath your weight. The subject may learn long lists of words with apparent ease and may recall past events with what seems to be surprising clarity. If the person is particularly susceptible, you may tell the subject that you are going to touch a very hot poker to the person's arm—and then merely touch the subject with the point of your finger. Within a few hours a blister-like welt may appear just where you put your finger to the subject's flesh. Under certain circumstances, you may talk a shy, very proper young woman into taking off all her clothes in public, command the leader of an anti-violence movement to shoot one of his best friends, or get a secret agent to divulge confidential government material. But as impressive as these feats may seem, there is a strange quality of showmanship to them that demands further investigation and discussion.

Under hypnosis, a slightly built young woman can be made to lift an object weighing 300 pounds (135 kilograms) when ordinarily she would refuse even to consider picking up something weighing more than 20 or 30 pounds (9 or 13½ kilograms). Has hypnosis made her suddenly as strong as Mr. Universe or Hercules? No, not at all. Women in peasant societies routinely lift heavy weights as a matter of course. And what would this same young woman do if she walked out of her house one day and saw the wheel of the family car come to rest on top of one of her children? Hypnosis does not make you any stronger than normal, but it can motivate you to perform as if your life depended on it.

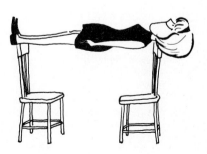

Anyone can pretend to be blind—actors on stage do a credible job of it all the time. And anyone can pretend to talk to someone who isn't physically present—

how many children have imaginary playmates with whom they hold long conversations? But only a very few subjects can raise blisters when hypnotized. As it turns out, these individuals are all prone to getting rashes, blister-like cold sores, or skin swellings when emotionally upset. Apparently, under hypnotic suggestion, they merely "do their physiological thing" on command. The ordinary subject, even in a deep trance, cannot match this performance.

Anti-social Behaviors As for anti-social acts, we all perform them occasionally if we think we can get away with them, if we believe no one will be hurt, or if some higher authority tells us to do so. A modest young woman will disrobe in public while in a hypnotic trance—but only if the hypnotist convinces her that it is proper to do so. If the hypnotist can make her perceive herself as being in the privacy of her own bathroom and badly needing a shower, or that her clothes are on fire, then her actions will suit her perceptions. A non-violent young man can be talked into picking up a gun (loaded with blanks) and firing it at a friend of his—but only if the hypnotist first convinces him that the friend is really an enemy who is about to murder his mother or rape his sister. Or if he is told that he is in the army and leading an attack against a foreign army that is at war with the United States. And secret agents have been made to "tell all" under hypnosis— when the hypnotist made the agent believe that only the agent's legitimate superior was present to hear what the agent said.

In short, we perform under hypnosis only those acts that we *would* perform normally if the situation were right, and if our motivation were high enough. But even these factors are usually not enough—in addition there typically must be an intense, emotional relationship between the hypnotist and the subject. If you are to violate society's laws when hypnotized, you will usually do so only when your desire to please the hypnotist is intensely strong. And, of course, if you have a burning need to please someone by obeying his or her commands or suggestions, then you probably will do so whether you are hypnotized or not. All the hypnotic trance might do in such cases is to provide you with a convenient excuse for your own anti-social behavior.

Hypnosis imparts no magic powers to the subject or to the hypnotist; it does not increase any of our physical or mental abilities. Rather, hypnosis merely makes it more likely that we will do things that we ordinarily might not do.

There are two seeming contradictions to this view toward hypnosis, one having to do with memory, the other having to do with pain. Let us look at memory first.

Hypnotic Age Regression

One aspect of hypnosis that first attracted Sigmund Freud was this—while in a trance, subjects often are able to report in amazing detail past events in their lives that ordinarily they might not remember. Early in his career Freud began to see how powerful an influence a person's early experiences could have on the development of the individual's personality. Freud theorized that most of the psychological problems that bothered an adult were, in fact, the result of traumatic or highly disturbing events that occurred when the person was quite young. Recall of these traumas often seemed to be blocked, as if some part of the person's brain was deliberately repressing access to these memory banks. Freud felt that, if the person was to be helped, these "hidden" memories had to be brought out into the open so that the person could re-experience the trauma, examine it, and hence overcome it.

Under hypnosis some patients could recall *repressed* (°) material with greater than normal ease. The problem was, as Freud soon discovered, that not all of his clients could be readily hypnotized, and even the "good subjects" occasionally recalled things that seemed unlikely actually to have occurred. Freud came to

Repressed. Sigmund Freud believed that we deliberately "forget" experiences that are unpleasant or threatening. Freud called the act of pushing a memory into unconsciousness the act of repression. From the Latin word meaning "to put down."

think that the critical variable in hypnosis was the psychological relationship that was built up between hypnotist and subject, as we've said. When a warm feeling developed between him and the patient, and the person wanted to please Freud in any way possible, hypnosis did not seem to be necessary to get the patient to "open up" psychologically. Therefore, Freud abandoned the technique—perhaps without ever realizing its full usefulness as a therapeutic tool.

The psychologists who picked up the study of hypnosis a half century after Freud discarded it were particularly impressed with the rapid access that it seemed to give to a person's early memories. They soon found that, while in a deep trance, a subject could be told to *regress* (°) back to his or her childhood and made to "relive" certain events such as birthday parties, trips, or vacations. The subject acted as if he or she were a child again and had forgotten all of his or her adult experiences. When told to "go back" to her 5th birthday, a young woman might begin to talk in a very childish voice, recounting in detail who was at her party, what presents she got, what her parents said and did, even what she dreamed of that night.

A few subjects went much further—when pressed to do so by the hypnotist, they reported in detail conversations *they thought had occurred* between their mothers and fathers while they themselves were unborn and being carried in the womb, or even events that occurred centuries before when they were seemingly living in a different body. Since most of us have trouble recalling in detail conversations of just a few days ago, the feats performed under *hypnotic age regression* appeared fabulous indeed, and several rather odd theories of human behavior were spawned to account for these findings.

Some psychologists incorrectly assumed that every experience a person had was somehow recorded in blazingly accurate detail deep in the person's brain; hypnosis merely opened up the floodgates and let all these memories come gushing forth. Other theorists assumed that during hypnotic age regression whole sections of an individual's mature personality were *ablated* (°), or cut out, so that the individual was left with nothing but childish or immature thoughts and behaviors. The structure of an individual's personality was often compared to the structure of an ordinary onion—that is, the personality came in layers, with the early or immature parts at the center and the more mature "layers" surrounding this central core. Hypnotic age regression was thought to ablate, or strip away, the outer layers, leaving the "childish" core exposed.

QUESTION: If someone offered you $1,000 if you could successfully imitate the behavior of a 6-year-old for a matter of 20 or 30 minutes, would you take the bet?

Regress. Freud stated that each person goes through several developmental stages as he or she matures psychologically. When a mature adult returns to childish thoughts or actions, that person is said to regress to an earlier developmental stage. See Chapter 21.

Ablated (ab-BLAY-ted). From the Latin word meaning "to remove" or "to carry away." The term is used frequently by surgeons to refer to the cutting away of certain parts of the body or brain. During hypnotic age regression, the "mature layers of the personality" are said to be ablated, or cut away.

Hypnotic "Role-playing"

As attractive as these theories might have seemed at first blush, they soon fell victim to the cutting edge of laboratory research. In the 1950's psychologist Martin Orne published a series of studies suggesting strongly that hypnotic age regression was chiefly a matter of rather excellent *role-playing* on the part of the hypnotic subject.

Orne put several college students into deep hypnotic trances and regressed them back to their 6th birthdays. He then asked the students to describe what had happened to them that day. The students responded magnificently, piling one insignificant detail on top of another. Orne was more impressed with their inventiveness than with their accuracy, for in many cases he had independent descriptions (from the students' parents and from other sources) of what had actually happened. As it turned out, the students were woefully inaccurate—they mixed up events from many different birthdays and often included events they had read about in novels, or simply made up things that had never happened.

Martin Orne.

And although the hypnotized students "played" as though they were 6 years old, they made many critical mistakes. When asked what time it was, they looked at their wrists—though none of them wore watches when they were 6. They responded appropriately to complex words they could not have understood when 6 and showed awareness of political and social events that had occurred long after they had reached their 6th birthdays. One student, born and raised in Germany, had not learned to speak English until he was 17; yet he described his 6th birthday party as if everyone were speaking English instead of German. When this fact was pointed out to him, he switched to speaking a childish form of German and refused to speak English again until the trance was ended.

Orne went a step further with some subjects, for in a few cases he had actual records of psychological tests that the students had taken when they were 6 or 7 years old. He then regressed the students back to their 6th or 7th years through hypnotic trance and re-administered the same tests. Their answers as hypnotized adults were stylized attempts to act childish, and were nothing like the answers they had actually given at that age. The students were then allowed to inspect their early records as closely as they wished, and subsequently were again regressed back to their 6th or 7th years. Now they tended to respond to test items as they actually had when at that early age—a feat they could not accomplish until they had looked at their test records.

Orne believes that most of what a person does when hypnotized is largely a matter of role-playing. When you allow yourself to be hypnotized, you also allow yourself to respond to most suggestions made by the hypnotist. You will go out of your way to please the person who put you into the trance. When the hypnotist suggests that you are 6 years old, you do your best to respond appropriately, just as you might do if someone offered you $1,000 to act in a childish manner. If you can't remember exactly what you did and said and thought when you were 6, then you fake it as best you can.

Even the insensitivity to pain that can be achieved under hypnosis is "role-playing" of a sort, according to Orne. In one interesting study, Orne promised one group of students a pleasant financial reward if they could *pretend* to be hypnotized successfully enough to fool a master hypnotist. A second group of students was *actually* hypnotized by Orne and his assistants. The master hypnotist— someone outside of Orne's group who had never seen any of the students before—was presented with both groups of students in random assortment. The hypnotist had to detect which students were actually in a trance and which were merely playing the game to make money.

Although the hypnotist poked and proded, stuck the students with pins, and asked them to perform a variety of silly or unusual actions, he simply could not tell which students were hypnotized and which were faking it. When highly motivated, the unhypnotized students could withstand amazing amounts of pain without flinching or withdrawing from the experiment.

Hypnosis and Pain

Experiments such as Orne's call into question the long-standing assumption that hypnosis might someday replace the chemical *anesthetics* (°) that doctors use to "put patients to sleep" during operations. More than a century ago a number of British physicians reported they had used hypnosis during hundreds of operations with great success—they claimed that the patients experienced no pain at all and suffered no ill effects. However, scientific investigations of these claims turned up a most intriguing point—quite often the hypnotized patient did indeed show evidence of experiencing terrible pain during these operations; but afterward, when the patients were out of the trance, they denied having felt anything at all! The scientific commissions reported that hypnosis seemed not so much to reduce

Anesthetics (ann-ess-THET-ticks). The word "esthetics" comes from a Greek term meaning "sensation" or "perceivable by the senses." The Greek word *an* means "not." An anesthetic is thus something that cuts out or prevents sensations, such as pain.

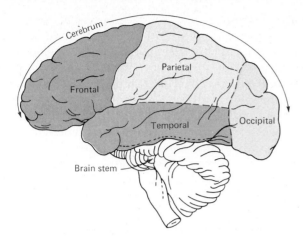

or prevent pain as to prevent the patient from remembering the unpleasantness afterward.

The latest chapter in this story concerns *acupuncture* (°), an ancient Chinese form of medical practice that came dramatically to the attention of the Western world during the early 1970's when China again opened her borders to Western observers. Before we can determine whether acupuncture is a cure-all, or whether it should really be called Quack-you-puncture, we must face squarely a problem that we rather delicately ignored in Chapter 6, namely, what is pain?

PAIN

When sensory psychology was first getting off the ground, a century or so ago, the prevailing view was that there were four unique psychological experiences you could get from stimulating your skin—warmth, cold, pressure, and pain. Each of these four experiences was thought to be related to a specific type of receptor or nerve ending buried somewhere in your skin. But further study turned up some troubling facts—there did seem to be receptors that were primarily concerned with temperature sensations, and other receptor cells that seemed to mediate the experience of pressure, but no one ever found a nerve ending that was solely concerned with the sensation of pain.

Investigations of the *parietal lobe* (°) uncovered parts of the cortex that, when stimulated electrically, gave rise to the experience of pressure or temperature; but no one ever found a part of the parietal lobe whose stimulation produced pain. Nor could a pain center be found anywhere else on the surface of the cerebral hemispheres. No special receptor organs, no special "input area" on the cortex—what an enigma pain seemed to be!

But if no one could figure out how the pain signal got started in the skin, or where it ended up in the brain, there was no doubt at all about how it got from the non-existent receptors to the invisible locus in the brain! For it had long been known that pain sensitivity was quite well represented in the *spinal cord*, that great trunk of neural pathways that runs from the body to the brain (and from brain back to the body).

Certain types of diseases that affect the spinal cord often give rise to continuous and vicious pain that can be relieved only by cutting some of the sensory pathways going up the spinal cord from the skin receptors. But, as we have found in recent years, even the spinal cord data are more complex than they seem to be at first glance. And if you are to understand why pain hurts as it does, and why hypnosis and acupuncture can sometimes reduce or alleviate the pain, we must take another (very quick) look at how your skin receptors operate.

Acupuncture (ACK-you-punk-ture). The Latin word *acus* means "needle." Acupuncture is an ancient Chinese form of medicine that involves puncturing the body with needles.

Parietal lobe (pair-EYE-uh-tull, or puh-RYE-uh-tull). Part of the cerebrum at the very top of the brain. Sensory input from the skin receptors and the muscles comes to this part of the cerebrum. See Chapter 4.

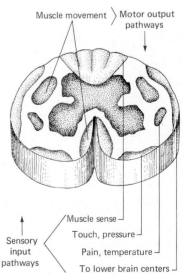

The spinal cord in cross section.

Insulated (IN-sue-lay-ted). From the Latin word meaning "island," or "to isolate." To insulate is to shield or protect. The insulation in the walls of a house keeps the heat in and the cold out in winter. Telephone wires have rubbery insulation around them to keep the message traveling down one wire from mixing with the messages on an adjacent wire. The axons of some nerve cells have a fatty insulation called "myelin" (MY-uh-lin) around them to keep sensory messages from "jumping wires."

Fast fibers; slow fibers. Neural messages travel along axonic fibers at different speeds, depending on the thickness of the fibers and the amount of myelin wrapped around the axon. Uninsulated fibers are "thin and slow"; sensory inputs travel along slow fibers at a speed of about 10 feet (3 meters) per second. Some insulated fibers are so thick and fast that messages flow along the axons at about 300 feet (100 meters) per second or more.

Kenneth Magee.

Fast and Slow Fibers

The (hairy) basket cells and the encapsulated nerve endings in the skin (*see* Chapter 6) send their messages to the brain primarily by way of special pathways in the spinal cord. The nerve cells in these pathways are *insulated* (°)—that is, the axons of these cells have a layer of fat wrapped around them. Because this layer of fat insulates the electrical impulses that pass along the axon, the speed with which the neural messages flow is faster in insulated fibers than in nerves that lack this fatty insulation. Insulated fibers are called *fast fibers* (°).

The free nerve endings, on the other hand, send their messages up the cord slowly by way of uninsulated axons. Since the speed of the neural messages in uninsulated nerve tracts is up to 100 times slower than in the fast fibers, the uninsulated neurons are called *slow fibers* (°).

If you implanted an electrode in the *fast fibers* of someone's spinal cord and stimulated these nerve cells directly, the person would report "pressury" feelings. If you put the electrode in the *slow fibers* instead, the person might report feeling pressure or temperature changes. Or, if the stimulation was intense enough, the person might report feeling pain. Neurologists use these facts to help diagnose the site of damage to the spinal cord in accident victims. The physician will brush a feather over the soles of the patient's feet. If the patient feels the pressure of the feather, his or her fast fibers are probably intact. If the patient has lost temperature sensitivity in his or her feet—or if a pinprick does not hurt—then the nerve tract carrying the slow fibers has probably been pinched, cut, or otherwise damaged.

Neurological evidence such as this led physiologists at first to speculate that skin pain was not a special sense all its own but rather the result of overstimulation of *any* of the skin receptors. We now know that the early physiologists were half right; pain surely is not a unique "sense" in the way that pressure, temperature, vision, and hearing are. Pain is actually a highly complex psychological *experience* that is affected by many factors. Let us look at the data that led to this view.

When neuro-physiologists first stuck an electrode into the slow fibers in a patient's spinal cord and stimulated these fibers electrically, the patient experienced pain just as expected. But when they stimulated the fast fibers, the patient experienced no pain at all—even when the stimulation was very intense. Indeed, just the opposite occurred. If the patient had (let's say) a badly damaged foot and was experiencing a great deal of pain, stimulation of the patient's fast fibers actually *decreased* the hurt and unpleasantness of the wound! (As we will see in a moment, the fact that overstimulation of the fast fibers inhibited pain sensations makes acupuncture much more understandable.) But when these experiments were first reported, they made life considerably "painful" for anyone who believed that overstimulation of *any* receptor caused pain.

Next, there began to appear in the literature reports of seemingly normal individuals who experienced no pain at all! These rare individuals had the usual sensitivity to pressure and to temperature, but no amount of stimulation to any part of their body caused them any kind of sensory unpleasantness. If they broke a leg, or burned the skin off an arm, they might well not notice what had happened to them. One pain-insensitive male, treated by neurologist Kenneth Magee at The University of Michigan Medical Center, was named Joseph B. All his life Joseph B. had thought the people around him were "sissies" because they complained of having "pains." Joseph B. enjoyed visiting dentists—if he had the time. If he didn't, having his teeth pulled with a pair of pliers was fine with him. Although he enjoyed eating, drinking, and sex, Joseph B. didn't react to any form of sensory overstimulation—even to being kicked in the testicles.

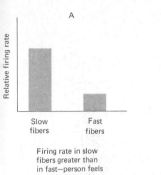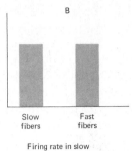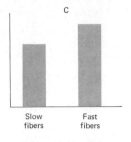

A — Firing rate in slow fibers greater than in fast—person feels considerable pain

B — Firing rate in slow fibers same as in A, but now there is equal firing rate in fast fibers—person experiences mild pain

C — Firing rate in slow fibers same as in A and B, but firing rate in fast fibers much greater—person experiences no pain at all

How the "spinal gate" operates.

"Spinal Gate" Theory of Pain

The fact that patients such as Joseph B. had quite normal sensitivity to pressure and temperature suggested that the pain experience must be due to something more than overstimulation of the skin receptors. And the experiments on stimulating the fast and slow fibers demonstrated that the spinal cord was somehow involved in creating the perception of sensory pain. But it was not until 1965 that two scientists—Ronald Melzack of McGill University in Montreal and Patrick Wall of University College in London—put all these odd facts together into a comprehensive theory. The Melzack-Wall theory explains not only how pain works but why acupuncture might be an even more effective pain-killer than hypnosis.

Melzack and Wall believe that there is a kind of neurological "gate" in your spinal cord that determines whether or not you will feel an incoming sensory message as painful. Both the slow fibers and the fast fibers are connected to this spinal "gating" mechanism. According to Melzack and Wall, it is the *relative amount* of neural activity at the point of the *"spinal gate"* (°) that controls the sensation of pain. The same message coming through on the slow fiber tracts will "hurt" or "not hurt" depending on how active the fast fibers are at that moment. If the fast fibers are completely silent (as when they are damaged or cut), almost any stimulation of the slow fibers will cause considerable pain. If the fast fibers are firing at a very high rate, it often doesn't matter how much you stimulate the slow fibers—the organism simply will not feel pain. Activity in the fast fibers, then tends to *inhibit* or "close the gate" on the experience of pain.

QUESTION: If you accidentally stick your hand into a bowl of very hot water, you will first feel the pressure of the water on your skin; then, a fraction of a second later, you will feel that the water is hot; and then, a moment later, you will experience burning pain. How do these facts support the Melzack-Wall "spinal gate" theory of pain?

But what about Joseph B.? He experienced normal amounts of both temperature and pressure, so both his slow and fast fibers were obviously intact. How could this be? The answer, according to Melzack and Wall, is that the "spinal gate" is also affected by higher centers in the brain. These higher centers can "turn the volume down" on activity in the slow fibers just as effectively as can speeding up the firing rate of the fast fibers. So, under the right conditions, your brain can turn off the unpleasant aspects of pain merely by affecting the way that the "spinal gate" works. It seems likely that some higher center in Joseph B.'s brain had incorrectly turned off his "spinal gate" at birth and left it that way throughout his life. Melzack and Wall believe that when you are hypnotized or

Spinal gate. To gate something out means to keep something from entering. Melzack and Wall believe there is a nerve center in the spinal cord that "gates out" some sensations and lets others through to the brain. No one has yet located this "spinal gate" precisely nor determined exactly how it works.

Ronald Melzack.

when you are highly motivated to ignore pain messages, or even when you are distracted by a good movie or highly interesting conversation, your cortex turns off your pain sensations at the level of the "spinal gate."

Now consider Mesmer and the sugar pill. Mesmer became a great hit in Paris for at least five reasons. First, because he strongly believed that his "cures" really worked. The intensity of his faith, and perhaps his own "magnetic personality," were apparently enough to convince some patients that they ought to get well simply because he told them to. Second, Mesmer had a fancy-sounding theory about disease that was probably very convincing to some people. Furthermore, the astrophysical nonsense that Mesmer preached was so vaguely stated and so mystical that it was almost impossible to disprove. Third, Mesmer succeeded because he was quite a showman. He gave his patients a lot of odd contraptions to look at and touch, and he made his clients do a lot of strange things. His flair for the dramatic thus gave visible support to the faith that his clients had in him and his theory. Fourth, some of his treatments were mildly painful. Many old folk sayings suggest that bad-tasting placebos often are more effective than are good-tasting ones ("bitter medicine is good medicine"). Last, but not least, the medical sciences were poorly developed in Europe in the late 1700's. Mesmer's cure rate for many diseases was actually no worse and sometimes better than the cure rate achieved by the medical profession.

An understanding of all five of these points is necessary if we are to appreciate why Chinese doctors have seemingly had so much success of late with a technique called "acupuncture."

ACUPUNCTURE

The Chinese have used acupuncture as a form of medical treatment for some 5,000 years. According to some historians, acupuncture was discovered during an ancient battle. A soldier was wounded in the hand by an arrow; immediately thereafter he found that a chronic toothache had disappeared and that his mouth felt numb. These primitive Chinese are supposed to have then "mapped out" the entire human body by sticking pins into their flesh almost everywhere they could reach. Sometimes the pins helped; sometimes they didn't. Over the intervening 5,000 years, Chinese medical practitioners discovered up to 800 different points that, when pierced by pins, appeared to help their patients get well from a variety of diseases.

According to traditional Chinese theory, acupuncture is based on the way in which your *ch'i*, or "life energy," flows through various parts of your body. Your *ch'i* is, in turn, affected by the relative amounts of *yin* and *yang* in your body at any given moment. *Yin* is made up of what many Chinese consider to be the "negative forces" in nature—darkness, femaleness, passivity, and cold; *yang* is thought to be the universal opposite of *yin;* according to tradition, *yang* is represented by such "natural positives" as maleness, heat, light, and activity. Too much *yin*, or too much *yang*, supposedly disrupts the orderly flow of *ch'i* through your body, and hence leads to disease and pain. When an acupuncturist sticks needles into your body, he or she is attempting to change the relative balance of *yin* and *yang* inside you, just as your cortex might attempt to change the relative balance of activity in your slow and fast spinal fibers by adjusting the "spinal gate" that Melzack and Wall spoke of.

Although acupuncture was widely used in China for many centuries, it fell into disfavor as a form of treatment when Western medicine was introduced a hundred or more years ago by medical missionaries. Western-trained physicians tended to look down on acupuncture as a form of quackery. But in the late 1930's, when Mao Tse-tung and his army were cut off from Western doctors and drugs, they had

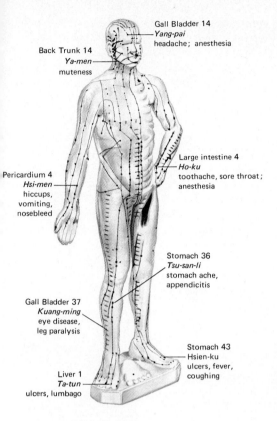

Gall Bladder 14
Yang-pai
headache; anesthesia

Back Trunk 14
Ya-men
muteness

Large intestine 4
Ho-ku
toothache, sore throat;
anesthesia

Pericardium 4
Hsi-men
hiccups,
vomiting,
nosebleed

Stomach 36
Tsu-san-li
stomach ache,
appendicitis

Gall Bladder 37
Kuang-ming
eye disease,
leg paralysis

Stomach 43
Hsien-ku
ulcers, fever,
coughing

Liver 1
Ta-tun
ulcers, lumbago

There are hundreds of acupuncture points, only a few of which are labeled here. The points are named for the governing organs along 14 meridians.

little choice but to turn to "folk remedies." Since that time, acupuncture has been perhaps the dominant form of medical treatment in Communist China.

When Western medical scientists first began visiting China in large numbers in the early 1970's, they reported that the Chinese claimed to have used acupuncture successfully to cure a number of diseases—including some types of blindness, appendicitis, malaria, and hypertension (*see* Chapter 16). And, since the 1950's, when their supplies of Western chemical anesthetics were almost totally exhausted, Chinese physicians had been using their needles to inhibit pain even during the most major operations.

Western scientists were from the first highly skeptical of the cures claimed by Chinese physicians, particularly since Chinese doctors do not in general believe in comparing the effectiveness of various types of medical treatment using rigidly controlled experiments. It was not until the mid-1970's, however, that U.S. scientists completed the first of many well-designed studies on acupuncture. Almost without exception—according to a 1975 report from the National Institutes of Health—acupuncture is no more effective in reducing pain than are hypnotism and placebos.

But if acupuncture is not a real anesthetic, what about the claims that it can cure many types of diseases? Again, we must go back to Mesmer's success in Paris. Steel needles inserted in various parts of the body cannot, all by themselves, kill germs, bacteria, or viruses. But the mild pain the needles cause might well help patients want to get well quickly, if only to avoid further treatment. In this light, it is interesting to note that those ailments on which acupuncture reportedly works best are those "hysteria-like" problems that Mesmer's magic wand also appeared to cure—ulcers, hypertension, and glaucoma (a type of blindness caused by increased pressure inside the eyeball). As we saw in Chapter 14, these are diseases associated with stress and *autonomic arousal*.

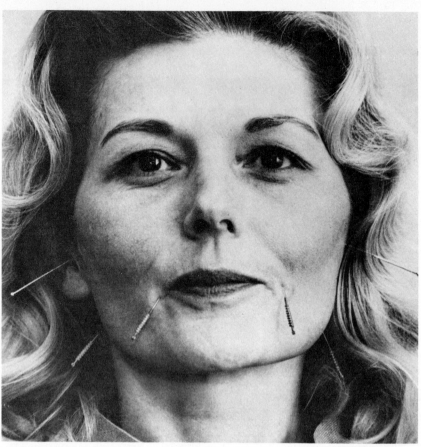

Use of acupuncture needles to induce an anesthesia.

There is a curious parallel between what the Chinese mean by *ch'i* (the flow of "life energy" through the body), what Mesmer and Paracelsus called the "Universal Spirit" that mobilized the magnetic forces within your body, and what modern physiologists mean by "responses of the autonomic nervous system." Activity in your sympathetic nervous system closely resembles what the Chinese call the "positive or active force of *yang*," while activity in your parasympathetic nervous system is oddly similar to what the Chinese call the "negative or passive force of *yin*."

Most physical problems associated with the autonomic nervous system involve an imbalance between sympathetic and parasympathetic activity. If your sympathetic system predominates too much, you suffer from hypertension and ulcers; if your parasympathetic system predominates, you fall prey to depressions and low blood pressure. As we saw in Chapter 16, you can be trained to bring many of these autonomic responses under your voluntary control. It goes without saying that you are more likely to do so if you are very highly motivated to succeed, or if you are trying to please someone with whom you have an intense emotional involvement. Suppose you suffered from ulcers, a stomach condition often associated with overarousal of the sympathetic nervous system. If Anton Mesmer held a magic wand over your stomach and told you to concentrate until the magnetic forces in your body were under your control, might you not learn to relax? Particularly if you were so impressed by the man's showmanship and his sincerity that you thought him the world's greatest doctor? And if an acupuncturist stuck a needle into your foot and told you this would redirect your *ch'i*, might you not feel calmer after the treatment—particularly if you lived in Peking and knew that you would be violating government orders if you failed to get well as the acupuncturist said you ought to?

As we have said many times before, the brain is the master organ in your body. Anything that alters the normal functioning of your brain cells can alter the physiological responses of all the rest of the cells in your body. If you were brought up to believe that "pain is for sissies," then you would experience less discomfort from a toothache or a broken ankle than if your parents had encouraged you to tell them about the slightest little pain that you felt. If, in a particular culture, childbirth was accepted as a natural and painless experience, then women in that society might be expected to role-play a pain-free delivery of their children; even if they did experience severe labor pains, many of them would surely suppress both the pain itself and perhaps their memory of the pain just as if they had been hypnotized into doing so.

Hypnosis, acupuncture, magic wands, anesthetics, and quack remedies—all of these pain-killers operate within the confines of particular cultural traditions and each person's unique pattern of social development. Your parents, your friends, and your associates have as great an effect on the normal functioning of your brain as does the genetic blueprint you were born with. And it is now to the development of the individual—in whatever society—that we must turn our attention.

SUMMARY

1. Almost all of us experience pain during our lives. For this reason, people have long been willing to pay large sums of money to reduce the stings and harrows of discomfort.

2. The experience of pain is often a signal of some damage to body tissues, yet the mental or psychological aspects of pain are as important as the physiological.

3. Physicians have known for centuries that a placebo (sugar pill) can be very effective in reducing pain—if the patient believes that the placebo is some powerful medicine. Thus what goes on in your mind influences how you experience pain.

4. One of the best-known mental techniques for reducing pain is hypnotism, first developed by Anton Mesmer in the late 1700's. Mesmer "psyched" many of his patients into a hypnotic trance and suggested that their pain would go away. In many cases, the patients felt better afterward. Mesmer thought he had "cured" the patients' diseases; in fact, he had merely gotten them to repress pain.

5. Sigmund Freud tried to "cure" mental patients of their psychological problems using hypnosis, but abandoned the technique because it didn't always work.

6. Hypnosis appears to be a form of exaggerated "role-playing" in which the subject's motivation to please the hypnotist is greatly increased. Hypnosis appears to reduce pain psychologically in much the same way that placebos do.

7. A century ago, pain was thought to be a sensation much as pressure, temperature, taste, smell, and hearing are sensations. However, recent studies suggest that pain is a complex experience rather than a simple sensation.

8. If you suffer a flesh wound, the temperature and pressure receptors in your skin send energy messages up the spinal cord to what some scientists call the "spinal gate." Pressure sensations are carried along the fast fibers of the cord; temperature (and some pressure) sensations are carried along the slow fibers. If stimulation reaching the "spinal gate" from the slow fibers is greater than the stimulation from the fast fibers, the brain usually experiences pain.

9. The brain may at times inhibit or depress messages flowing through the "spinal gate," however, and thus prevent painful inputs from getting through to the cortex.

10. Hypnosis, acupuncture, placebos, and "suggestion" appear to reduce pain at least in part by shutting off the slow-fiber messages as they pass through the "spinal gate."

(Continued from page 389.)

Assistant Professor Don Powell and his teaching fellow, Brian Healy, were correcting exam papers in Powell's office when a loud knock at the door interrupted their work.

"Come in!" Powell cried.

When Elvis McNeil walked through the door, the Professor paled momentarily, but recovered quickly. "Come in, come in, Mr. McNeil. Sit down! Make yourself comfortable! Why, we haven't seen you for several days! Wherever have you been?"

McNeil confidently took the chair his Professor had indicated. "Reading, sir. Reading everything I could lay hands on about the powers of the mind."

Powell seemed a little flustered. "Er, well, yes. Interesting. Very interesting. We were afraid that you were angry with us—with Mr. Healy and me—about the little hypnosis demonstration we put on in class. I do hope you haven't stayed away from class because of some juvenile embarrassment . . ."

"Embarrassment? Of course not, sir! The very opposite."

"Then you aren't angry with us?"

"Certainly not, Professor. I came to thank you—and to ask for your help. You see, I've always been convinced that I had a strong mind, that I had hidden talents which I simply couldn't bring out into the open and gain control of. Even before I took your class, I had searched through all the occult literature. I had answered ads in magazines that offered to make me a mental giant if I would purchase a set of their long-suppressed masterpieces. I read the life histories of the mystics and tried to tap the power of the stars through astrology. But none of it worked very well. And then . . . and then, you opened the doors to my perception; you transported me to the pinnacles of power!"

Powell shot a glance at Brian Healy, who seemed to be struggling valiantly to suppress a grin.

"Yes, well, I'm sure that's one way to look at it," Powell said hurriedly. "No harm done, then . . ."

"Oh, no. No harm at all. You see, I was sure I could really make the chair float around and dance without any help from you, if only I could find the key that would unlock my latent mental energies. Hypnosis did it, as you saw for yourself. So I've been reading all the books I could find on using hypnotism to unleash cortical forces. You really set my synapses to tingling!"

Brian Healy made a noise suspiciously like a muffled giggle. Professor Powell looked at him sternly.

"The trouble is," Elvis McNeil went on, as if he didn't notice the reactions his words were evoking, "the trouble is, I can't seem to regain the powers that I had while hypnotized that day in class. I mean, I've tried and tried and tried. I've talked to one chair after another, and none of them will float—not even an inch. I feel I'm so close, so extremely close to being able to get it all together and prove the power of mind over matter, to establish dominance again over the mundane world of physical objects. But I can't seem to make that final step. That's why I'm here."

"Yes?" said Professor Powell.

"Sir, how much would you charge to hypnotize me again, and bring back the power?"

Assistant Professor Don Powell seemed stunned. "Well," he said, "well, we'll have to think about that one for a while."

"I can't afford much, but I'll pay whatever I can. Anything, anything to get that mystical magic back under my voluntary control!"

"Yes, well, I do think we'd better have a long talk about this, McNeil. In private." Powell reached for his desk calendar. "Could you come see me tomorrow afternoon, say about 4 o'clock?"

"Certainly, sir. Any time you name."

"And let's keep our mouths shut about all this, shall we? I mean, we wouldn't want to let everybody in on the secret, now would we?"

"Certainly, sir. Anything you say."

"And in the meantime, I want you to go the library and check out a book called **LSD, Marihuana, Yoga and Hypnosis** by Theordore X. Barber. Read it through carefully, particularly the section on hypnosis. Read it very carefully indeed. And if you're behind in any of your studies, use those latent mental powers to catch up quickly. Okay?"

"Okay."

"And see me tomorrow at 4 o'clock."

"Yes, sir. I can hardly wait!"

After Elvis McNeil had left the office, Professor Powell sat staring at the wall and tapping a pencil nervously on his desk. Then he turned to his assistant and said, "You know, Brian, when we teach this course next semester, instead of having a class demonstration on hypnotism, what would you think about our showing a movie?"

Healy scratched his head. "Sure, Professor Powell. Sure."

RECOMMENDED READINGS

Barber, Theodore X. *LSD, Marihuana, Yoga and Hypnosis* (Chicago: Aldine-Atherton, Inc., 1970).

Casey, Kenneth L. "Pain: A Current View of Neural Mechanisms," *American Scientist*, 61 (March–April), 1973.

Hull, Clark L. *Hypnosis and Suggestibility: An Experimental Approach* (New York: Appleton-Century-Crofts, 1933).

Part 5

MATURATION AND DEVELOPMENT

chapter 19

"WHERE SEX LEAVES OFF"

GENETIC PSYCHOLOGY

DID YOU KNOW THAT . . .

The genes you inherited from your parents helped shape not only your physical development but some of your basic personality patterns as well?

Each human being starts life as a single cell with 46 chromosomes (which contain the person's genes)?

You became a male or a female because of the influence of just one of these 46 chromosomes?

Males who are born with an extra "male" chromosome tend to be taller than average, to have severe acne, to be impulsive, and are more likely to end up in the penal wards of mental hospitals than are normal males?

If a pregnant woman contracts German measles or takes certain drugs, her child may be born severely deformed?

Children who are badly malnourished during infancy may become permanently retarded if they are not given special attention and a stimulating environment?

An infant develops control over its head muscles long before it develops control over the muscles in its legs and feet?

If a newly hatched goose follows a human being rather than its own mother, it will (as an adult) be sexually attracted to humans rather than to other geese?

Many parents of children born with genetic defects reject or badly distort the scientific information they are given about their children?

With the proper training and encouragement, even severely handicapped individuals can be helped to lead a more normal life?

Dr. Martin Mayer stared at the classroom, terrified. The three dozen or so students swarmed around like bees defending their hive. Through his thick-lensed glasses, their bright young faces seemed slightly distorted, larger than life, and in constant, almost frightening, motion. High school students, he said to himself, have more energy than they know what to do with. How in the world could he have let himself in for something like this?

The man standing at the front of the classroom beside Dr. Mayer gave a mechanical smile and said, "All right, young people. Let's settle down now and listen. We have a special guest today, someone famous in the field of genetic psychology, or the study of inherited behavior patterns. He's come to Clearview High School all the way from Mid-American University to give the annual Science Lecture this afternoon. And since he arrived earlier than we expected, we've prevailed upon Dr. Mayer to address all the biology classes today. Isn't that kind of Dr. Mayer?"

Kind? They hadn't really given him the chance to refuse. At the University, Mayer stuck close to his lab. By choice, he taught only small graduate seminars. These bubbling, excited high school students were at least 10 years younger than the men and women who elected his classes. What could he talk to them about that he hadn't already planned to say in his formal address later that afternoon? Even though their regular teacher was droning on in a loud voice, many of the students were still milling about, talking and laughing. What could Mayer do if they wouldn't listen to him politely, as his graduate students did? How did you stop students from passing notes and whispering and giggling? A sinking feeling developing in the pit of his stomach began working its way up his digestive system.

"Dr. Mayer has published more than a hundred articles in various scientific journals; he has written a number of chapters in learned texts; and is co-author of the famous **Handbook of Behavior Genetics.** I'm sure you'll want to give him your closest attention. And now let's welcome Dr. Mayer with a nice round of applause."

The students clapped loudly, and one or two even whistled. Dr. Mayer blinked twice. The co-author of the famous **Handbook of Behavior Genetics** was frankly petrified. Every face in the class was focused on him now, waiting expectantly. His wife, Elizabeth, would have called it a "pregnant pause." What had she told him, just before he got on the plane? "If you get stuck for something to say, just talk about sex. They'll listen."

Dr. Mayer adjusted his glasses on his nose. "With your permission, students, I'd like to talk about sex."

Their immediate rapt attention gave him permission aplenty.

"As a scientist, I'm interested in sex—in all its aspects. In fact, one of the joys of becoming a psychologist is that you have a legitimate right to study sexual behavior. Among lower animals sex is primarily a matter of hormones and instincts. Among humans, it can also be an act of love. But among both humans and lower animals, sex is the beginning of life, not just the living end of things. For life starts where sex leaves off. And scientists who study the beginnings of life, as I do, must consider the biological as well as the social and moral consequences of the sexual act.

"A few months ago I re-read Aldous Huxley's novel, **Brave New World,** for perhaps the third time. Huxley was a renegade, a radical, an artist born into a family of famous scientists. He was one of the first people in his generation to pay much attention to the hallucinogenic drugs. Huxley was taking mescaline—and writing about its effects on his perceptions—when your parents were still in high school and when the only drug that most people used was alcohol. But before he began experimenting with mescaline, Huxley was interested in genetics—in the social consequences of sexual behavior."

Mayer looked around. The students continued to follow his words closely. This was going better than he had anticipated.

"Huxley came to his knowledge of genetics quite naturally—his grandfather had defended Charles Darwin's theory of evolution against attack by religious leaders in the 1860's. Darwin had described how the various animal species evolved on earth by what he called the process of natural selection—that is,

animals mated rather indiscriminately, and their genes mixed rather randomly. When a male lion had sex with a female lion, neither one of them was trying to build a better world or create a super-lion. They were just following their blind instincts. Some of their lion cubs were, by chance, bigger and stronger than others, and these cubs survived, while the weak ones died because the environment in which they lived favored big, strong lions.

"Humans are different. We are the only animals that have gained any real control over our environment. We have the ability to select quite deliberately and consciously which of our offspring will survive simply by changing the world our children live in. And that ability puts us in a moral bind that lions don't have to face." Mayer paused to take off his glasses and clean them. "Sometimes I think it would be great just to be a lion, so I wouldn't have to worry about the consequences of having sex."

Several of the students laughed.

"Control of the environment is perhaps the most difficult problem facing us at the moment," Mayer went on. "But Huxley was wise enough to see an equally difficult problem that would pop up in the near future. What would happen, he asked in **Brave New World**, if we could also control the genetic process? When two human beings—or two lions—mate, the sperm from the male unites with the egg borne by the female. The tiny male sperm cell contains little more than a bundle of genetic information—that is, the genes of the male. The egg contains the female's genes, plus a lot of food material to get the process of reproduction going. When the sperm enters the egg, the two sets of genes try to unite. If you mixed a lion sperm with an elephant's egg, nothing would happen because the two sets of genes would be too different. But when the two sets of genes are very similar to each other, then the egg becomes fertile and immediately starts to grow and divide, repeatedly grow and divide. It divides millions and millions of times—because that's what the genes inside each cell tell it to do. One of the primary functions of the genetic message inside each sperm and egg cell is that of telling the cell how to grow and develop into an adult organism.

"You became a human instead of a lion because of the genes you inherited from your mother and father. You developed blue eyes—or brown ones—because your parents and grandparents 'willed' you a particular kind of genes. You had no choice in the matter, just as you will pass on your genes for eye color or skin color to your children whether you or they like it or not.

"But what if we could change your genes before you started creating the next generation? Aldous Huxley was bright enough to see that, when scientists learned enough about genetics, perhaps we could do just that. Someday soon, we'll have acquired enough knowledge about which genes do what, so that we can reach into the genetic blueprint and change it, maybe change it any way we want to. Then, some time in the future, we could go to a young couple just about to be married and say, hey, what kinds of kids would you like to have? Do you want a big tall blond football player for a son? Would you prefer a small, dark-skinned daughter as beautiful as the Queen of Sheba? Or would you rather your daughter became a physicist, as bright as Albert Einstein? And is there any reason why she couldn't be both beautiful and exceptionally bright? And would you like for your son to have big hands—not so he could catch a football but so he could play the piano like Van Cliburn?

"That's part of what **Brave New World** is all about. What I'd like to ask you today is the same question—when that great day comes and we know how to engineer the genes of our children, what kind of kids would you like to have?"

The class sat silent, as if this was an idea they didn't really care to give much thought to.

"You," Dr. Mayer said, pointing to a very attractive young girl sitting in the second row. "How are you doing in biology?"

The girl blushed and the class giggled. Obviously biology wasn't one of the girl's better subjects.

"Are you getting an A+ in biology?"

The girl shook her head.

"Do you have to study more than you'd like to in order to get grades that aren't as good as you wish?"

The girl nodded agreement.

"Wouldn't it have been nice if your parents had had you engineered to be a 'brain,' so you could breeze through the biology book and learn it all very quickly? Wouldn't that help?"

"But then I wouldn't be **me**," the girl wailed. "I'd be somebody else!"

Mayer turned quickly to a small young man sitting toward the back of the class. He had a guitar case lying beside his chair. "You, there, you're pretty good on the guitar, aren't you?"

"I'm just learning," the boy said shyly.

"But you'd like to be able to play as good as Segovia, or some of the popular rock stars, right? Did you know that the best guitar players seem to have much better finger coordination than average players have? The ability seems to be inherited, and all the practice in the world won't make you a performing genius if you don't have the right genes to start with. Don't you wish now that your parents had fixed up your finger genes before you were conceived?"

"Sure," the boy said simply.

"You're smaller than average, too," Dr. Mayer continued. "Does that ever bother you, maybe just a little?"

The boy nodded slowly.

"Well, wouldn't you like your kids to be taller than the average? Wouldn't you want to see a genetic engineer to change things in your sperm cells before you start having a family?"

One of the boys in the middle of the room interrupted. "But if everybody wanted their kids to be bigger than average, what would happen to the average?"

The class laughed.

"That's pretty unnatural, isn't it?" one of the girls asked.

"Of course it's unnatural," Mayer shot back. "Lions can't do it and neither can elephants. But maybe someday we will be able to plan these things. When you get married and have your first house or apartment, you're going to spend a lot of time planning what kinds of decorations you want—because the place you live in reflects what kind of person you are. Don't you think you ought to spend just as much time planning what kind of children you'll have?"

"But you can't change human nature," the guitar-playing boy said.

"Ah, but you can. Each time you try to teach your children something, you will be trying to influence the child's development—that is, change its human nature. But you will be starting too late in some cases—that is, you can't do much now until after the child is born. By that time much of its pattern of development will be set. Nowadays, if you have ugly children, your friends and neighbors don't blame you for it because there was nothing you could do to change how they looked. But if the kids are badly dressed, or if you don't send them to school, or if you beat them a lot and make them cowards or train them to be bullies, then it's your choice and people hold you responsible. In the future, when we can change genes at will, the world will hold you responsible for how pretty your children are and what native abilities they develop as well. The lion can have sex without worrying about it; you can't. You'll have to decide whether you want your kids to be geniuses or just average types."

"But if everybody wanted their kids to be Einsteins, who'd collect the garbage?" complained a young man sitting in the front row.

"Beautiful question," Dr. Mayer said in a warm and friendly tone of voice. "Once science gives us the technology to engineer our offspring, **will society have a right** to intervene? If there's a shortage of strong-bodied people who like to collect garbage, **will the government have the right** to require you to have kids who are strong and have an instinctive love for gathering up other people's trash?"

"I don't want anybody telling me what kind of kids I've got to have," a young black student said. "Probably they'd try to make them all into robots."

"Or stupid soldiers who like to kill people," said another black.

"Hey, man, you're making **assumptions**," said a third. "I mean, is garbage-loving an inherited tendency?"

"Magnificent!" Dr. Mayer cried. "As far as we know, it's not; but maybe it could be. What kinds of **behaviors** do you think we can engineer into our children's genes?"

After a moment's pause, the guitar-playing boy responded. "You already said that finger coordination was inherited."

"Right. But someone born with the ability to move his or her fingers quickly probably could become a great violinist as well as a great guitarist. Or would be great at sewing or typing or repairing watches. How would you feel if you had your future son's genes arranged so that he had superb finger coordination and he wanted to become a football player instead of a musician?"

"I'd get him an athletic scholarship to Notre Dame," said a large young man with an interest in sports.

"Good idea," said Mayer. "But what other innate skills would you want to program into your future son to push him toward music? An inborn sense of rhythm? Is that something you inherit, or do you learn it from your parents? You, young lady," he said, pointing again to the pretty girl in the second row. "What musical talents do you think are inherited, and which ones are learned?"

"I think you're trying to make us think too much. Why can't we just have kids and let them grow up the natural way, like our parents did? I don't know which talents are inherited, and I don't much care."

Mayer smiled. "Well, I agree with you halfway. I don't know what specific inherited abilities are necessary for a kid to become a great musician or a great football player. But both as a father and as a scientist I'd like to find out. I can't do anything about changing my children's genes because they're already born, but I can study behavior genetics in my lab so that your kids, or your grandchildren, can make decisions I couldn't make. But, meanwhile, I've got a great big problem and it has to do with sex."

The class, which had become rather noisy during the discussion, suddenly quited down again. Mayer smiled at how well things were going. His wife, Elizabeth, had given him very good advice.

"Someday in the future, as Huxley pointed out, we'll have genetic engineering and we can order our kids from a catalogue. Maybe then government leaders will tell us what models to choose—for the good of our country. But until then, there are some things we can do anyhow. First off, behavior is always a function of both genes and environment, and we surely can make a better world for kids to grow up in. But more than this, we already know enough about genetics to realize that some diseases and poor physical conditions and maybe even some types of insanity have a genetic component. The facts are that some people carry the wrong kinds of genes. If we were lions, nature would take care of things— lions with the wrong genes just don't survive in lion environments. But we tend to keep people alive no matter what's wrong with them and no matter how much it costs. If we were 'natural' about things, the way lions are, we'd just let these people die when they were young. Until we have genetic engineering, and we can change these bad genes into good ones, don't you think the government ought to pass a law protecting us from bad genes?"

"What do you mean?" one of the boys asked.

(Continued on page 434.)

The young man we shall call Clyde C. was born in Glasgow, Scotland, in the spring of 1950. His father was a laborer at a chemical factory in the northern part of town, his mother a pleasant and highly religious woman who came from one of the many suburbs that ring Scotland's biggest city. The mother's church attendance was matched by the father's frequent drinking bouts at the many taverns and pubs near their home. Clyde C. was the third child in the family, and the first boy.

Hellion (HELL-yun, or HELL-ee-un). From the old Scottish word *hallion,* meaning "scamp" or "scoundrel." Literally, someone "born to raise hell."

Puberty (PEW-burr-tee). That time in a young person's life when sexual maturity begins. See Chapter 13.

Penal (PEE-nall, or PEE-null). From the Latin word meaning "penalty" or "punishment." A penal institution is one designed to administer punishment.

XYY condition. An unusual genetic condition in which a male has an extra Y chromosome.

He was named for the river Clyde that cuts through the heart of Glasgow providing the harbor for the shipping that helps support the million or so people who live in this Scottish industrial center. Clyde C. was by far the tallest of his several sisters and brothers, and even as a teenager, he towered over his father by a foot or so. He was also the worst-behaved of the children, as Clyde's father frequently pointed out to the boy.

As a young child Clyde C. was noted for the intensity and frequency of his temper tantrums. "A born *hellion* (°)," his father called him. Clyde did poorly in school, in part because he seemed unable to focus his attention on his lessons. His large size gave him an advantage in games and sports, however, and he excelled at fighting. In fact, he was something of a bully and often terrorized the other children either by hitting them or by destroying their books, clothes, toys, or other property. Frequent lectures and paddlings both by his father and his teachers did little to improve his behavior. Clyde always seemed sincere in promising to do better in the future, but seemed incapable of resisting even the slightest temptation that crossed his path.

To the dismay of almost everyone around him, Clyde C. became sexually mature at a fairly early age—before he was 10. By the time he was 13, he was caught several times forcing his sexual attentions on younger children, chiefly on smaller boys. Although he was much taller than average, he was not particularly good looking, and even before he had reached sexual *puberty* (°) Clyde had developed a serious case of acne.

By the time he was 14, he had stolen a motorbike and wrecked it, an escapade that led to his dropping out of school. His teachers (and his schoolmates) breathed a sigh of relief. His father tried to find a job for Clyde, but the boy had little regard for anyone or anything and destroyed more than he produced. When Clyde was fired from his third job, his father threw the boy out of the house.

For a couple of years he lived by such wits as he had, borrowing small sums of money from his mother when he couldn't steal enough to keep him in food and clothing. Then, when he was barely 17, he got very drunk one night and went on a real spree. Around midnight Clyde spotted a young man and woman in an expensive sports car sitting at the side of a lonely street, talking. Clyde dragged the young man from the car and beat him up, threatened both the man and woman sexually, stole the car, and zoomed off into the night. By the time morning came, the car was smashed beyond repair, and Clyde was in the hospital with a member of the Glasgow Metropolitan Police sitting by his bed waiting for him to recover.

Because of his past history and the sexual nature of his offense, Clyde was not sent to jail but rather to a *penal* (°) institution for the criminally insane. His mother cried a great deal at the trial, blaming herself for his bad behavior. Clyde's father refused to see him again, calling him "a born troublemaker" who had inherited "bad blood" from a maternal grandfather. The doctors who treated Clyde tended to agree with his mother, that he had been improperly reared.

Then, a year or so after Clyde had entered the medical prison, a team of scientists performed certain biological tests on all the inmates of Clyde's ward. These scientists discovered that Clyde suffered from a peculiar genetic defect called the *XYY condition* (°). Because an unusually large number of the other inmates on Clyde's ward also suffered from the XYY condition, the psychologists speculated that there might be some direct connection between these men's mixed-up genes and the deviant behavior patterns that Clyde (and the others) showed.

Can mixed-up genetic patterns actually *cause* a young man to show anti-social behavior patterns? Before we answer this question, we must first learn a little bit about genetics and how your own genetic blueprint influenced your growth and development.

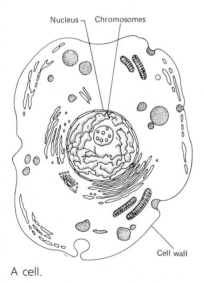

Nucleus   Chromosomes

Cell wall

A cell.

GENETIC DEVELOPMENT

Like Clyde C. (and all other human beings), you began life as a single cell. This egg cell—produced in your mother's reproductive organs—began its existence looking much like many other human cells. That is, the egg cell was a tiny round blob of material with a dark *nucleus* (°) in its center which was surrounded by a watery-looking substance called *cytoplasm* (°).

Most cells are rather like chemical factories. The nucleus in the center contains the factory's Board of Directors, which we call the *chromosomes* (°). The chromosomes determine to a great extent what the cell is going to become and what it will produce. But like the Directors of a large chemical factory, the chromosomes don't really do very much themselves except send orders down to the workers telling them what products need to be made at any given time.

Most of the cells in your body contain 23 pairs of chromosomes. Through a microscope each of these 46 chromosomes looks like a long strand of colored beads folded over on itself. These 46 Directors are composed chiefly of a nucleic acid called *DNA* (°), which is an acid because of its chemical composition. Like other common substances that contain acids—vinegar and lemon juice, for example—it tastes sour to the tongue. DNA is a *nucleic* acid because it is found chiefly in the nucleus of the cell.

The DNA Directors control the functioning of the cell by making a substance called *RNA* (°), another nucleic acid, that carries the Directors' instructions from the nucleus out to the cytoplasm or work area of the cell. It is here that the proper proteins are put together which keep the cell (and you) alive. The "workers" in the cell take in food particles from the bloodstream and process them into proteins according to the instructions they receive from the "messenger RNA" molecules that come from the DNA Board of Directors.

> QUESTION: **Foods such as meats, cheeses, and grains contain a high percentage of protein; why do you think these foods are often better for you than foods that contain little or no protein?**

Cells reproduce by dividing. When a cell divides, its nucleus splits in two and half the DNA present goes into one of the daughter cells, while the other half of the DNA goes into the other daughter cell (the term "daughter" is used even if the child will develop into a son rather than a daughter). But before cell division takes place, the nucleus must *double* the amount of DNA present so that each daughter cell will have its full complement of chromosomes the moment the split occurs. Just before division, then, each chromosome in the nucleus makes a carbon copy of itself and, for a few hours, there are actually 46 *pairs* of chromosomes in the cell instead of 23 pairs—twice the normal amount. Then, as the split occurs, 23 pairs go into each daughter cell, and each daughter has exactly the same set of chromosomes that the original cell contained. In a rapidly dividing cell—such as the fertilized cell you started life with—this doubling of the DNA/chromosomes happens every 24 hours or so.

The only exception to this rule is the case of the sperm and unfertilized egg cells. When an egg cell is produced through division, the original 23 chromosome pairs split in half *without doubling*, so that the egg cell contains exactly half the chromosomes it needs to survive and multiply. Unless it receives an injection of new DNA from a sperm cell, it will die within a matter of a few days.

X and Y Chromosomes

The sperm cell, like the egg cell, contains only 23 chromosomes. The only way the sperm cell can survive is by mating with an egg cell to make up the 23 *pairs* of chromosomes every human cell needs to function properly. But the sperm cell is somewhat different from the egg. Its 23rd chromosome can be either the large X

Nucleus (NEW-klee-us). From the Latin word meaning "kernel," as in the phrase, "This statement has a kernel of truth to it." The nucleus is the heart or center of any system. The sun is the nucleus of our solar system. The yolk is the nucleus of an egg. The center portion of a living cell is called the nucleus, which usually contains the genes that direct the cell's functioning.

Cytoplasm (SIGH-toe-PLASS-em). The Greek word *kyto* means "hollow vessel" or "cell." Our word "plasm" comes from the Greek word meaning "plastic," "formable," or "fluid." Cytoplasm is the fluid-like substance surrounding the nucleus of a cell, as the white of an egg surrounds the yolk.

Chromosomes (KRO-moh-sohms). From the Greek words *chromo*, meaning "colored," and *soma*, meaning "body." The genes of a cell are strung together like strands of colored beads; these "strands" are the chromosomes.

DNA. An abbreviation for deoxyribonucleic acid. The genes are composed chiefly of DNA molecules. You developed into a human being rather than a rat or a flatworm because the DNA in your genes is quite different from the DNA in rat or flatworm cells. See Chapter 13.

RNA. An abbreviation for ribonucleic acid. A molecule similar to DNA and typically produced by DNA. Messenger RNA takes "instructions" from the DNA in the nucleus out to the cytoplasm of a cell. May also be involved in memory storage. See Chapters 13 and 17.

Human chromosome cells. Only the 23rd pair differ—XX for a female, XY for a male.

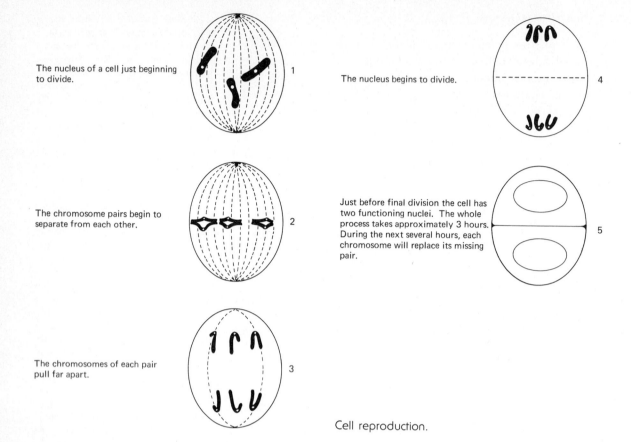

The nucleus of a cell just beginning to divide. 1

The chromosome pairs begin to separate from each other. 2

The chromosomes of each pair pull far apart. 3

The nucleus begins to divide. 4

Just before final division the cell has two functioning nuclei. The whole process takes approximately 3 hours. During the next several hours, each chromosome will replace its missing pair. 5

Cell reproduction.

Trisomy-21 (TRY-so-me). From the Greek words *tri*, meaning "three," and *soma*, meaning "body." The modern term for mongolism (MON-goal-ism), or Down's syndrome. A relatively common form of birth defect in which the facial features of the person somewhat resemble Oriental or Mongolian characteristics. The individual suffering from trisomy-21 has almond-shaped, slanting eyes, with thick eyelids, a flat nose, and a round skull. The person usually has dark, straight hair; a large, thick tongue; and stubby hands and feet. The sex organs are often underdeveloped. Some form of mental retardation is often associated with trisomy-21, although the person's intellectual development is often as "retarded" by poor teaching techniques as by physiological fault.

Klinefelter's syndrome (rhymes with "MINE-belter"). A set of related physical characteristics (syndrome) found in males who have an extra X chromosome.

type or the smaller Y type. The 23rd chromosome of the egg cell is always a large X type.

If an X-type sperm is the first to enter the egg cell, the fertilized egg will of course have an XX 23rd chromosome pair—and the child will be female. If a Y-type sperm fertilizes the egg, the 23rd chromosome pair will be of the XY variety and the child will be a male. The adult human male typically produces an equal number of X- and Y-type sperm, so the chances of his fathering male or female children are approximately equal.

Chromosomal Abnormalities

The human reproductive process is a very complicated one indeed, and just as the machinery in a chemical factory sometimes breaks down, so nature occasionally makes mistakes. Sometimes the 21st chromosome pair does not divide properly, and the child is born with three 21st chromosomes rather than the normal pair (*see* the figure on p. 419). This condition, technically called *trisomy-21* (°), typically leads to a type of mental, physical, and behavioral deficiency called *mongolism*.

Sometimes the 23rd chromosome pair does not divide properly and the child ends up with one or more additional X or Y chromosomes. An XXY 23rd chromosome will result in the child's being physically a male—with penis and testicles—but with strong feminine characteristics. This condition—known technically as *Klinefelter's syndrome* (°)—occurs in about one child out of every 900 born. Although the child will grow into a tall, thin male, his breasts will be enlarged and his testicles will not produce sperm. The XXY male is almost always mentally and behaviorally retarded. XXY males are rather easy to spot from their physical appearance.

About 1 boy in 500 or so has two Y chromosomes and one X, like Clyde C. This male looks and acts quite normal and seldom realizes that he has a chromosomal problem. However, research on XYY males, begun in Scotland in the 1960's, suggests that many of these men are not quite as normal as they seem at first glance. Working at Western General Hospital in Edinburgh, a research team led by Patricia A. Jacobs discovered that there were 35 times more XYY males than one might expect among those patients classified as being *criminally insane*. Could the XYY chromosome condition somehow be *causing* these men to commit anti-social acts?

Further studies from all around the world have sometimes yielded contradictory results, but in general the original findings by Jacobs and her team have been confirmed. We now know that there are many times more XYY males in institutions for the criminally insane than there ought to be if this were only a chance factor, but the story is complex.

The XYY Condition   To begin with, the problem seems to be almost entirely a white one—there are very few black, brown, red, or yellow-skinnned XYY males. (No one yet knows why this should be true.)

Second, XYY males do not appear in unusual numbers either in normal prisons or in regular mental hospitals—only in those wards that take care of patients who are both insane *and* criminals.

On the average the XYY male is just as bright as normal XY males, a fact that leads us to conclude that the XYY problem is not associated with mental retardation. Neither is the XYY male particularly more aggressive, violent, nor more dangerous than "normal" XY prisoners on the same wards.

But there are marked if subtle differences between the XYY and the XY male. The XYY male is typically taller than average—taller, even, than the XXY males who display Klinefelter's syndrome. Most XYY males are sexually *precocious* (°)—that is, they reach sexual puberty a year or more before the normal XY male does. About half of the XYY males suffer from moderate to severe acne—a much higher percentage than is found among normal men. Homosexual behavior is reportedly much more frequent in XYY males than in XY's.

All of these differences might well be related to the fact that the XYY's additional chromosome is a *male* chromosome. The presence of this second Y chromosome apparently causes the adrenal glands to secrete an abnormally large amount of male hormone (testosterone) during the boy's early life. The extra testosterone from the adrenals not only makes the XYY male grow taller but causes his testicles to become functional earlier than normal and to secrete more testosterone following puberty. Acne is often related to hormone level, and the higher the testosterone level, the more likely it is that a boy will develop acne at the onset of puberty. High hormone levels also increase sexual activity—both homosexual and heterosexual.

Some investigators have reported that XYY patients in medical-penal institutions are less sociable and outgoing than are XY prisoners in the same institutions. Other scientists have reported that XYY prisoners differ markedly from other prisoners in their ideas of what behaviors are acceptable and socially permissible.

The most important difference, however, has to do with what psychologists call *impulse control*. Unlike most normal men, the XYY prisoner typically can resist anything but temptation. Much more so than his normal *counterpart* (°), the XYY prisoner cannot delay gratification of his desires. If he sees something that he wants—be it someone's property or someone's body—the XYY prisoner simply must have it *right now*. If he has to be violent to get what he suddenly wants, he will resort to violence. If his attempts are frustrated, he often behaves childishly and throws a temper tantrum—or he destroys anything handy in his rage.

How could the presence of a few extra DNA molecules lead an otherwise

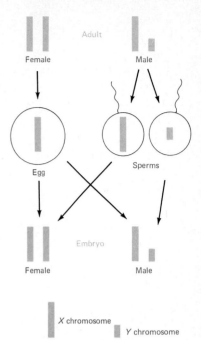

Sex is determined by the sperm cell.

Precocious (pre-KO-shuhs). From the Latin words meaning "early ripening." A "child genius" is intellectually precocious. A young boy who reaches puberty very early is sexually precocious.

Counterpart. A Xerox copy of a document is a duplicate or counterpart or the original. Someone who is more or less identical to you in some way is your own personal counterpart. The female lead in a play or drama is the counterpart to the male lead.

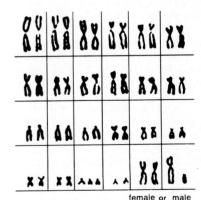

female or male

Trisomy-21. Note the three chromosomes instead of the usual 21st pair.

Most cells in everyone's body have 23 chromosome pairs.

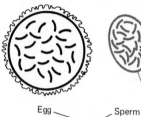

The sex cells are an exception. Each sex cell has only 23 single chromosomes.

Egg ———— Sperm

Embryo

At fertilization the single chromosomes from egg and sperm combine to form a new organism that has 23 pairs.

An egg and sperm unite to form a new being.

normal young man to fail to learn to control his destructive, selfish impulses? The answer to this question is only partially understood by psychologists. However, it seems to be connected to the way that we all grow from a single cell into a mature social being with a personality all our own. In the next chapters, we will discuss mental and social development; for the moment, let us continue our discussion of the "biological you."

THE BEGINNINGS OF LIFE

At the moment that you were conceived—when your father's sperm entered your mother's egg cell and determined your sex and began the glorious process of reproduction—you were no more than a tiny speck locked away in your mother's body. The 23 chromosomes the sperm brought to the egg gave the spark of life to that egg. The newly formed DNA Board of Directors immediately ordered the cell's protein factory into high gear and began making a new set of Board of Directors as well. As we mentioned, within a matter of 24 hours enough new material was formed so that this single cell could afford the luxury of dividing into two identical daughter cells. During this and all subsequent cell divisions, an identical set of 23 chromosome pairs goes into each daughter cell. So if the original cell you started life with had any form of chromosomal abnormality (such as the XYY condition), this abnormality would be passed along to every new cell formed by division.

At this point in your life you might have become *identical twins* (°). Usually the first daughter cells remain close together and develop into a single individual. Sometimes, for reasons not clearly understood, these first cells separate and each eventually creates a complete human *embryo* (°). Since the daughter cells were identical, the twins will be identical too.

So-called *fraternal twins* (°) are much more common. Occasionally a woman will produce two (or more) eggs during her fertile period. If both egg cells are fertilized, they will both begin independent growth at the same time, and the woman will produce fraternal twins nine months later. Since these two egg cells

Identical twins. Twins formed from a single fertilized egg. Although called "identical," they are often more like mirror images of each other.

Embryo (EM-bree-oh). An unborn child from the time of conception to the second or third month of development, when the child takes on vaguely human form and is thereafter called a fetus (FEE-tus). From the Greek word meaning "to swell within." Oddly enough, the German word sauerkraut ("swollen cabbage") comes from this same Greek term.

Fraternal twins (fra-TURN-ull). Twins born from two fertilized eggs. Fraternal twins are no more alike than brothers or sisters born at different times. From the Latin word meaning "brothers," from which we get the word "fraternity."

were fertilized by *different sperms*, they are no more identical than are brothers and sisters born to the same parents at different times.

QUESTION: **Lower animals, such as dogs, often produce many egg cells at the same time and hence give birth to many puppies in a single litter. Each egg cell must be fertilized by a different sperm. Would it be theoretically possible for two puppies in the same litter to have different fathers?**

If the two daughter cells remain linked after the first division, each of them will divide once more within a second 24-hour period. Again, they will do so only after they have first doubled their chromosomes so that each new cell begins life with 23 pairs. Within a third 24-hour period, all four of these cells produce enough new proteins and DNA and other cellular materials so that a third division can occur. While this growing of new daughters is going on, the group of cells travels slowly down a tiny tube to the mother's *uterus* (°), or womb. About nine days after fertilization, the rapidly forming human being attaches itself to the wall of the uterus. At this point in your own life, you were about 0.02 inches (0.5 millimeters) in size.

Uterus (YOU-turr-us). From the Greek word meaning "belly." The womb inside a woman's "belly" that contains and nourishes an unborn child.

Ectoderm (EK-toe-durm). *Ekto* is the Greek word meaning "outer." *Derma* is the Greek word for "skin." A dermatologist (durr-muh-TOLL-oh-jist) is a medical doctor who treats skin diseases. A hypodermic is a needle that injects fluids under (hypo) the skin (derma).

Mesoderm (ME-so-durm). The "middle skin." The Greek word *mesos* means "in the center."

Endoderm (EN-doh-durm). The "inner skin." The Greek word *endon* means "inside" or "within."

Cellular Differentiation

Some two weeks after your life started, a remarkable change occurred in the tiny cluster of cells that made up your rapidly forming body. Up until this point all of your cells were pretty much identical, because the chromosomal Board of Directors in each cell sent out identical orders to the factory workers in the cellular cytoplasm. Now, however, 13 to 14 days after fertilization, some of these Boards begin sending out slightly different sets of instructions, and the cytoplasmic chemical factories begin to produce slightly different proteins (and other materials) in these cells.

As these new proteins and other molecules appear, they force the cells to change shape, size, and function. Some of the new proteins leak out of one cell and affect the chemical environment of the cells around it. And soon these other cells respond to this changed chemical environment by themselves producing a different set of proteins.

At many times in your life you have probably changed your behavior to become more like the people you are with, and you have surely been attracted to people whose behavior was already like yours. In much the same fashion, once some of your two-week-old cells begin producing new materials, close-by cells respond both by producing similar chemicals and by moving closer and closer together.

Development of the Fetus By the 14th or 15th day of your life you were made up of three clearly different groups of cells. One of these groups develops into what we call the *ectoderm* (°), a technical term that means "outer skin." Eventually these cells become your skin, your sense organs, and your nervous system.

Another group of cells, on instructions from their chromosomes and because of the chemical environment they find themselves in, develop into what we term the *mesoderm* (°), or "middle skin." These cells eventually become your muscles, bone, and blood.

Yet a third group of cells receives orders from their Boards to become *endoderm* (°), or "inner skin." These cells turn into your digestive system.

(As we will see in a later chapter, there are some psychologists who believe that your basic personality structure is determined at the moment that the three "derms" separate from each other and begin their unique patterns of development. According to this theory, if your ectoderm matures more rapidly than do the other two "derms," you will very likely grow up to be thin and intellectual. If

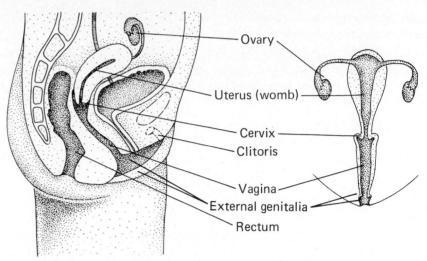

The female reproductive system.

Fetus (FEE-tus). An unborn child after the second month of life, when it takes on a recognizably human shape.

Placenta (pluh-SENT-ah, or plah-SENT-uh). The organ inside a woman's womb that links the child's blood system with the mother's. A few drugs, such as thalidomide (thuh-LID-oh-myde), can cross the placental (pluh-SENT-ull) barrier and affect the fetus; most harmful chemicals, however, are screened out.

your mesoderm outstrips the other two, you will supposedly become athletically inclined. If your endoderm predominates, you will theoretically grow into a fat person who loves creature comforts. The data supporting this theory are not particularly strong. But, as we also will see, there is a possible connection between the physiological growth of your three "derms" and the types of reinforcing inputs that you may prefer as an adult.)

At the point where this cellular differentiation begins, you are a tiny hollow ball about 0.1 inch (2.5 millimeters) in size, and technically you are now called an *embryo*. It is not until six weeks later—some two months after your life started—that the three types of cells arrange themselves into vaguely human form, and the embryo thus turns into what we call a *fetus* (°).

The Placenta   Developing cells—like developing children—are *unusually sensitive* to the environments they find themselves in. Luckily, as you grew within your mother's womb, you were protected from most of the chemicals in her body by an organ called the *placenta* (°), which screened out most of the substances that might have harmed your cells. Some drugs—such as thalidomide, a tranquilizer or "downer" taken extensively by Europeans and some Americans a few years ago—can cross the placental barrier. When pregnant women took thalidomide, the drug affected the development of their fetuses, apparently by entering the dividing cells and interfering with the orders that the Boards of Directors were sending out. Many of these fetuses were born badly deformed, usually without arms and/or legs. Now that we know the damage thalidomide can do, the drug is no longer prescribed for women who might become pregnant.

Illnesses, such as the German measles, can cause the pregnant woman's body to secrete somewhat different chemicals than is usual; if these chemicals (or the germs that cause them) infiltrate the placenta, they too can upset the normal development of the fetus. If a woman has German measles during the third month of her pregnancy, for instance, the child is often born badly retarded. Narcotic drugs, such as heroin, also pass through the placenta and can set up an addiction in a fetus long before it is born. At the time of its birth the child is a full-blown heroin addict and suffers rather frightening and dangerous withdrawal symptoms the first few days of its birth until its cells learn to live without the drug.

Effects of Deprivation   Your genetic blueprint specified in rather general terms what you would look like and when and how you would grow. But this blueprint is always brought to life by orders from the DNA Board of Directors in each cell.

Sometimes real-life chemical companies run short of materials, and production must be slowed down or even halted for a period of time. Then, later, the factory can go on overtime to catch up with lost production. The same thing is true of the developing human body. If a pregnant woman is forced by circumstances to undergo starvation, her body protects the fetus as much as it can by giving the unborn child almost all the resources the body has available to it. Still, the child may be born much smaller than usual. If given ample food immediately after birth, the child usually catches up to the size its genetic blueprint had set for its normal development.

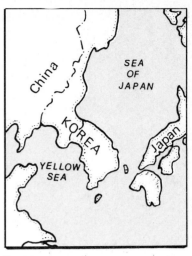

Korea.

The same kind of catching up often occurs if a growing child is deprived of nourishment for brief periods by war or poverty. As an example, consider a study on Korean children reported late in 1975 by Myron Winick, Knarig Katchadurian Meyer, and Ruth C. Harris. During the Korean conflict in the 1950's, many very young children in that Asian country were separated from their parents and were placed in orphanages. Most of these youngsters suffered from severe malnutrition before they entered the institutions. After the hostilities ended, some of these children were returned to their war-shattered homes. But many others, whose parents were dead or missing, were placed in foster homes in the United States. Winick and his colleagues studied the physical and intellectual development of several hundred of these Americanized orphans.

About a third of these children were so malnourished when they entered the orphanage that they ranked in the bottom 3 percent of all Korean children as far as height and weight were concerned. Another third were moderately malnourished; the rest were more or less of average size when first considered for adoption. After several years of good care in the United States, all of these children were of greater than average height and weight (compared to other Koreans). Winick and his group conclude that the adopted children were heavier and taller than if they had remained behind in Korea.

Of even greater interest are the data that Winick and his associates gathered on school achievement and intelligence. Previous studies had shown that the Korean children who were returned to their home environments showed rather severe mental and social retardation. That this retardation continued at least to young adulthood suggests that many war-torn Korean homes offered little in the way of intellectual stimulation or enrichment. In marked contrast, the Americanized orphans had intelligence test scores that were 40 to 50 IQ points higher than children who stayed in Korea. Indeed, their U.S. foster homes were apparently so stimulating that the orphans had IQ's and school achievement tests that averaged slightly better than those of native-born U.S. children of the same age.

It would seem that your genes set limits for your physical and intellectual development; the environment you were reared in typically determines where within these limits your actual growth will fall.

PHYSICAL GROWTH AND DEVELOPMENT AFTER BIRTH

Your behavior patterns and your personality grow and develop much the same way that your body did. Even before you were born, you could move about (within the confines of your mother's womb) and you were capable of learning simple stimulus-response patterns.

In general, as soon as the newborn child's muscles, sense organs, and nerves are fully formed, the child begins to use them. But much of the human nervous system is not fully developed until the child is a year or two old. The general pattern of bodily development is from head to foot. Simple skills—such as head movements—appear first because the structures that control these skills are among the first to mature.

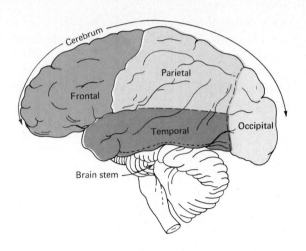

Showing the Developmental Sequence

The motor centers in the brain (*see* Chapter 4) send long nerve fibers out to connect (usually through one or more synapses) with the muscles in various parts of the body. Since the head muscles are closer to the brain than are the foot muscles, the head comes under the control of the motor centers long before the feet do. Hence more complex behavior patterns—such as crawling, standing, and walking—come much later in the developmental sequence than head movements do. The appearance of a new motor skill (such as crawling or grasping) always suggests that a new part of the child's body has just matured—that is, that the brain centers have just become connected to the muscles involved in the new motor skill.

Effect of Early Training

Children develop at different speeds, in part because of their environments, but also because they follow different genetic schedules. As you might guess from this fact, it is rather senseless for parents to attempt to rush a child's motor development by giving the child "exercise." Most children begin to walk between the 12th and 18th month after birth. No matter how much coaxing and practice the parents may give their 6-month-old child, it will not walk much sooner than if the parents had simply let the child alone. In many primitive cultures, where the mother must spend almost all of her time working in the fields or elsewhere, young children spend the first year or so of their lives bound to a board or bundled tightly inside a bag carried on their mothers' backs. These children are released from their restraints only for an hour or two each day, so they have little chance to practice motor skills. Yet their muscular development is not retarded, and they creep, crawl, and walk at about the same ages that children who are not restrained do.

The result of a number of studies with identical twins also suggests that practice is not necessary for early motor development. In most of these studies, one twin has been encouraged to practice a skill (such as climbing a short flight of staris), while the other has been confined to a playpen and not allowed a similar experience. Training usually begins well before either twin could be expected to display the skill and proceeds until the "experimental" twin has clearly mastered the desired behavior pattern. At that point, the "control" twin is removed from its playpen and tested. The usual finding is that right from the first trial, the "control" twin can perform the task almost as well as the "experimental" twin. Any differences between the performance levels of the twins usually disappears within a matter of days.

Babies who are restrained, such as this papoose, nevertheless have normal muscular development.

There are two exceptions to all this. The first has to do with special skills—such as swimming or skating or playing a musical instrument. These behaviors need practice and guidance, and a child left to develop on its own usually does not acquire mastery of these complex habits without special training. The second exception has to do with the *attitude* the child takes toward physical activities. A child that is encouraged to explore its environment, to swing and jump and run and play, is more likely to become active and physically outgoing than a child who is confined for much of its early life to a playpen. Parents who try to train their child to walk (before the child is ready) do not speed up the developmental process at all—but they may instill confidence and courage in the child. Thus, without realizing it, the parents may teach the child a variety of complicated *social* skills the child would otherwise lack. It is only if the parents become discouraged that their 6-month-old son cannot be taught to walk and run—and hence reject the child and stop playing with him—that the child's development may be harmed by parental training.

Imprinting

There is some evidence that the best time for a child to learn a given skill is at the time the child's body is just mature enough to allow mastery of the behavior in question. This belief is often called the *critical-period hypothesis* (°)—that is, the belief that an organism must have certain experiences at a *particular time* in its developmental sequence if it is to reach its most mature state.

There are many studies from animal literature supporting the critical-period hypothesis. For instance, German scientist Konrad Lorenz discovered many years ago that birds, such as ducks and geese, will follow the first moving object they see after they are hatched. Usually the first thing they see is their mother, of course,

Critical-period hypothesis. The belief that there is a best time for a child to experience certain things or learn certain skills. Trying to train a child before or after this critical period is supposed to be like picking an apple before it is ripe—or after it has turned mushy and rotten.

Motor development in an infant.

who has been sitting on the eggs when they are hatched. However, Lorenz showed that if he took goose eggs away from the mother and hatched them in an incubator, the fresh-hatched *goslings* (°) would follow him around instead.

After the goslings had waddled along behind Lorenz for a few hours, they acted as if they thought he was their mother and that they were humans, not geese. When Lorenz returned the goslings to their real mother, they ignored her. Whenever Lorenz appeared, however, they became very excited and flocked to him for protection and affection. It was as if the visual image of the first object they saw moving had become so strongly *imprinted* (°) on their consciousness that, forever after, that object was "mother."

During the past 20 years or so, scientists have spent a great deal of time studying *imprinting*, as it now is called. The effect occurs in many but not in all types of birds, and it also seems to occur in mammals such as sheep and seals.

Konrad Lorenz "mothering" his goslings.

Whether it occurs in humans is a matter for debate. Imprinting is very strong in ducks and geese, however, and they have most often been the subjects for study.

The urge to imprint typically reaches its strongest peak 16 to 24 hours after the baby goose is hatched. During this period, the baby bird has an innate tendency to follow anything that moves, and will chase after its mother (if she is around), a human, a bouncing football, or a brightly painted tin can that the experimenter dangles in front of the gosling. The more the baby bird struggles to follow after this moving object, the more strongly the young animal becomes imprinted to the object. Once the goose has been imprinted, this very special form of learning cannot easily be reversed. For example, the geese that first followed Lorenz could not readily be trained to follow their mother instead; indeed, when these geese were grown and sexually mature, they showed no romantic interest in other geese. Instead, they attempted to court and mate with humans.

QUESTION: In previous chapters, we have discussed the relationship between learning and REM sleep; given the fact that imprinting is an intensive form of learning, would you expect goslings to show unusually large amounts of REM sleep during the first 24 hours after hatching?

If a goose is hatched in a dark incubator and is not allowed to see the world until two or three days later, imprinting often does not occur. At first it was thought that the critical period had passed, and hence the bird could never become imprinted to anything. Now we know differently. The innate urge to follow moving objects does appear to reach a peak in geese 24 hours after they are hatched, but it does not decline thereafter. Rather, a second innate urge—that of fearing and avoiding new objects—begins to develop, and within 48 hours after hatching typically overwhelms the prior tendency the bird has to follow after anything that moves. To use a human term, the goose's *attitude* toward strange things is controlled by its genetic blueprint—at first it is attracted to, then it becomes afraid of new objects in its environment. As we will see in a moment, these conflicting "attitudes" may explain much of the data on critical periods in both animals and humans.

QUESTION: **How might these two apparently conflicting behavioral tendencies help a baby goose survive in its usual or natural environment?**

In other experiments, baby chickens have been hatched and raised in the dark for the first several days of their lives. Chicks have an innate tendency to peck at small objects soon after they are hatched—an instinctive behavior pattern that helps them get food as soon as they are born. In the dark, of course, they cannot see grain lying on the ground and hence do not peck (they must be hand fed in the dark during this period of time). Once brought into the light, these chicks do begin to peck, but they do so clumsily and ineffectively, as if their critical period for learning the pecking skill had passed. Birds such as robins and blue jays learn to fly at about the time their wings are mature enough to sustain flight (their parents often push them from the nest as a means of encouraging them to take off on their own). If these young birds are restrained and not allowed to fly until much later, their flight patterns are often clumsy and they do not naturally gain the necessary skills to become good fliers.

Is the "maternal instinct" in this rodent innate or learned?

The "Maternal Instinct" in Rats Suppose we take a baby female rat from its mother at the moment of its birth and raise the rat pup "by bottle" until it is sexually mature. Since it has never seen other rats during its entire life (its eyes do not open until several days after birth), any sexual or maternal behavior that it shows will presumably be due to the natural unfolding of its genetic blueprint—and not due to learning or imitation. Now, suppose we inseminate this hand-raised female rat artificially—to make certain that she continues to have no contact with other rats. Will she build a nest for her babies before they are born, following the usual pattern of female rats, and will she clean and take care of them during and after the birth itself?

The answer to that question is yes—*if*. If, when the young female rat was growing up, there were objects such as sticks and sawdust and string and small blocks of wood in her cage, and which she played with. Then, when inseminated, the pregnant rat will use these "toys" to build a nest. If the rat grows up in a bare cage, she won't build a nest *even though we give her the materials to do so once she is impregnated*. If this same rat is forced to wear a stiff rubber collar around her neck when she is growing up—so that she cannot clean her sex organs, as rats normally do—she will not usually lick her newborn babies clean *even though we take off the rubber collar a day or so before she gives birth*. The genetic blueprint always operates best within a particular environmental setting. If an organism's early environment is abnormal or particularly unusual, later "innate" behavior patterns may be disrupted.

Overcoming the Critical Period All of these examples may appear to support the critical-period hypothesis—that there is one time in an organism's life when it is best suited to learn a particular skill. These studies might also seem to violate the general rule that an organism can catch up if its development has been delayed. However, the truth is more complicated (as always) than it might seem from the experiments we have *cited* (°) so far.

Baby geese will normally not imprint if we restrict their visual experiences for the first 48 hours of their lives—their fear of strange objects is by then too great. However, if we give the geese tranquilizing drugs to help overcome their fear, they can be imprinted a week or more after hatching. Once imprinting has taken place, it may seem to be irreversible. But we can occasionally get a bird imprinted on a human to accept a goose as its mother if we coax it enough and give it massive rewards for approaching or following its natural mother. Chicks raised in darkness become clumsy eaters—but what do you think would happen if we gave them special training in how to peck, rather than simply leaving the matter to chance? Birds restrained in the nest too long apparently learn other ways of getting along and soon come to fear heights; what do you think would happen if we gave these birds tranquilizers and rewarded each tiny approximation to flapping their wings properly?

There is not much scientific evidence that human infants have the same types of critical periods that birds and rats do. By being born without strong innate behavior patterns (such as imprinting), we seem to be better able to adjust and survive in the wide variety of social environments human babies are born into. Like many other organisms, however, children do appear to have an inborn tendency to imitate the behavior of other organisms around them. A young rat will learn to press a lever in a Skinner box (*see* Chapter 16) much faster if it is first allowed to watch an adult rat get food by pressing the lever. This learning is even quicker if the adult rat happens to be the young animal's mother.

Different species of birds have characteristic songs or calls. A European thrush, for example, has a song pattern fairly similar to a thrush in the United States, but both sound quite different from blue jays. There are *local dialects* (°) among songbirds, however, and these are learned through imitation. If a baby thrush is

Cited (SIGHT-ted). From the Latin word meaning "to summon" or "to put in motion." To cite an author's name is to summon that person's name from memory. To cite an example is to "put an example in motion." Our word "excite" comes from the same Latin term and means literally "to call forth or arouse to action."

Local dialects (DIE-uh-lecks). A dialect is a local or regional form of a language. Someone with a "Texas accent" speaks a different dialect of English than someone with a "British accent." A song bird hatched in Texas will sing a slightly different song than a bird of the same species hatched in England.

Birds learn to fly through innate behavior patterns.

isolated from its parents and exposed to blue jay calls when it is very young, the thrush will sound a little like a blue jay but a lot like other thrushes when it grows up. And parrots, of course, pick up very human-sounding speech patterns if they are raised with humans rather than with other parrots.

The Limits of Change

You may have heard someone say that "you can't change human nature"; meaning, presumably, that the genetic blueprint is not particularly flexible and that the effects of the environment on human development and subsequent behavior are minimal. The critical-period hypothesis is, in a way, a slight modification of this view, for it holds that the first years of a child's life are by far the most important and that most of the child's intellectual and social potential is fixed by the time it is a few years old. If this view were true, it would do us little good to take culturally deprived children and give them special training after they had spent their early years in unstimulating environments. Luckily for these children, as we noted in the study on Korean orphans, recent evidence casts considerable doubt on the critical period hypothesis—at least as it used to be stated. All of us are limited by the genes ("human nature") that we inherited, but within these limits we have much more freedom and flexibility than most of us previously dreamed was the case.

With the exception of identical twins, every person on earth has a different set of genes. You are a genetically unique organism, and your own gene pattern will probably never again be repeated in the entire history of the human race. If any one of us is to reach the full potential allowed by our genetic blueprints, obviously we will need our own specific and individualized environment. At the moment, we are not wise enough to be able to predict from a child's inheritance what kind of world it needs; indeed, we are not even wise enough to know what we mean by "reaching our full potential." Nor can we yet practice "genetic engineering" on a fetus—that is, rearrange its genes, even if that were morally wise—and hence make sure that the child will be born with the kinds of chromosomes that might help it succeed in our world as it exists today. But perhaps it is a sign of progress that we now speak more of "genetic potential" than we do of "genetic limits."

GENETIC COUNSELING

As you will recall from the beginning of the chapter, Clyde C. was born with an extra Y chromosome in all his cells and ended up in a medical-penal hospital. That additional Y chromosome made him taller than average, caused skin problems, brought him to sexual maturity sooner than usual, and gave him a more impulsive set of behavior patterns than most of us have. Perhaps 50 years from now we will know how to remove this extra Y chromosome before a child is born—or at least know how to suppress the chromosome's harmful effects. But what could we do for you, in the next 10 years or so, if the doctor who delivered your first son discovered that the boy had an extra Y chromosome? Would you want to be told, or would you rather remain ignorant of the problem?

Ernest B. Hook, a member of the Birth Defects Institute of the New York State Department of Health, discussed this very problem early in 1973 in *Science*. To begin with, there is approximately only 1 chance in 28 that a man with the extra Y chromosome will end up in a medical-penal institution. (The odds that a normal XY male will be imprisoned in a medical-penal hospital are about 1 in 500.) In short, it is 20 times more likely that an XYY male will have to be hospitalized for a crime than an XY male will. Furthermore, as Hook points out, the chances that the XYY male will show socially deviant behavior, *even if not caught at it by the law*, are much greater than 20 to 1. Would you want to be told of the problem when your son was young, before he had a chance to get into trouble? And as your boy grew up, should he be told of his genetic difficulties as well? How would this information affect his life—and yours?

Princeton sociologist James Sorenson has made a study of parents who seek genetic counseling about their children. Early in 1973, Sorenson reported that almost all of these parents wait to ask for help until *after* they have already had at least one child who suffered from genetic damage much more severe than having an extra Y chromosome.

The XYY condition is not really "inherited"—it could happen to anyone, and as far as we know, an XYY father is no more likely to have an XYY son of his own than is a normal XY father. But in many cases, people carry defective genes, and pass along their own chromosomal problems to their children. Most forms of color-blindness, for instance, are directly inherited (*see* Chapter 8), as are many types of mental and physical retardation. And, of course, if both the mother *and* the father have "bad" genetic blueprints, the odds that their children will be abnormal are much, much higher than if only one parent has chromosomal defects.

Shouldn't married couples who are high genetic risks be counseled about the difficulties their children may face? Dr. Sorenson found that, sadly enough, such counseling seldom is effective *as presently practiced*. More than half the couples he studied either forgot, rejected, or badly distorted the scientific information they were given. In many cases, this new information seemed to cause a dramatic change in the parents' own evaluations of themselves. It also led to frequent marital problems.

When only one parent carried the defective genes, that parent often developed severe and chronic feelings of guilt and shame, while the other partner often came to have strong negative emotional feelings toward his or her partner. When both carried some kind of "genetic misfortune," Sorenson says, the situation was likely to produce a sense of being a doomed family—a feeling on the part of both partners of having lost control over their lives.

The Future of Genetic Counseling

Both Sorenson and Hook point out that the difficulty with present forms of genetic counseling is this—although we can identify some (but not all) chromosomal difficulties for parents, we often do not know what to tell them to do about overcoming the handicaps their children will face. Clyde C.'s parents did not know of his extra Y chromosome. But supposing they had been told at his birth that he might have trouble controlling his impulses—would that have helped? In

Participant in Special Olympics for Mentally Retarded Children.

1950, when Clyde C. was born, the answer was no, because no one knew how to handle "impulsiveness" very well. His parents might well have rejected the information and done nothing about it. But now we are beginning to learn how to help people with this problem.

Children who suffer from trisomy-21 and various forms of brain damage often are even more impulsive than are XYY males. These youngsters are easily distractable; they cannot focus their attention on anything for more than a few seconds. If they see something they want, they often try to take it by force, no matter what the consequences. Without special training, they remain this way all their lives.

But as we mentioned in Chapter 5, psychologists have recently found that even severely handicapped children can be taught to bring their impulsiveness under control. You may recall from this chapter that when Drs. Smith and Walter began working with the badly brain-damaged child we called Patti K., she had an attention span of 5 seconds or so; she attempted to control the people around her by screaming, pinching, and by soiling her pants. Smith and Walter taught Patti K. to speak by rewarding her for each approximation to a word-like sound that she made. Once she could express herself verbally, she was able (with training) to gain voluntary control over her impulses because she now had a more effective way of communicating her wants. When they rewarded Patti K. for each slight increase in her attention span, she soon gained the ability to concentrate on a task for almost as long as normal children her age.

What might have happened had the parents of Clyde C. been taught how to apply the same "shaping" techniques that were used with Patti K.? The techniques used by Smith and Walter are simple enough so that most parents can master them fairly quickly. Had a psychologist taught these methods to Clyde C.'s parents, might they not have been able to help the boy achieve greater mastery of his destructive impulses? And once he learned how to control himself, wouldn't he have been in a much better position to achieve whatever goals he wished for himself in life?

We need much more refined techniques for measuring the genetic potential of a child—not only before and after it is born but even before it is conceived. More than this, we need to learn much more about how the social environment the child grows up in affects the unfolding of its genetic blueprint. Then we need to develop better ways of helping all people adjust to their genetic limitations by gaining better control over their own thoughts, behaviors, and environments. The field of genetic counseling is still in its infancy. But what a challenging and rewarding future lies ahead for those psychologists who choose to specialize in solving these very human problems!

SUMMARY

1. You began life as a single cell.
2. Your mother produced an egg that contained 23 chromosomes. At the moment of fertilization, one of your father's sperms penetrated the egg and added 23 chromosomes of its own.
3. All the cells in your body are daughters of this original cell; hence your cells all have 23 pairs of chromosomes (with certain minor exceptions).
4. These chromosomes contain the genes, made up of DNA molecules, that act as the Board of Directors that governs the functioning of each cell.
5. The 23rd chromosome in each egg has an X chromosome; the 23rd chromosome in each sperm has either an X or a Y chromosome. If an X sperm unites with the egg, the 23rd chromosome will be XX, and the child will be born a female. If a Y sperm unites with the egg, the 23rd chromosome will be XY, and the child will be born a male.
6. If by some accident the 23rd chromosome comes out with two Y chromosomes (XYY), the child will appear to be a normal male but may have unusual difficulties controlling his impulses as he grows up. Since each cell in the XYY male's body contains an extra "male" chromosome, the child's body produces much more than the usual amount of male hormone. This extra hormone appears to speed up much of the child's physical maturation and brings the XYY boy to sexual maturity sooner than expected.
7. Physical development in the infant typically proceeds in a head-to-feet pattern. The muscles controlling the head and neck become mature much sooner than those needed for walking or climbing.
8. Children cannot be taught to walk before their leg muscles are mature. However, if a child is prevented from walking at the time it would normally do so, it doesn't appear to suffer much physical retardation.
9. A child that grows up in a socially deprived environment during its first few years will catch up intellectually with its peers if given effective training later on.
10. Many physically and mentally handicapped children can overcome most of their difficulties, too, if we first learn to identify the causes of their problems

and use slightly different teaching techniques with them than we typically use with normal children.

11. Impulsive children, such as those with brain damage or chromosomal abnormalities, can often be taught to bring their impulses under control if we shape them lovingly into doing so by using rewards rather than punishments.

(Continued from page 415.)

"What do you mean?" asked one of the students in the biology class. "How could the government pass a law protecting us from bad genes?"

"It's simple," responded Dr. Mayer, the genetic psychologist. "We just identify men and women who are carriers of the wrong kinds of genes, and we prohibit them from having kids. Not from getting married or from having sex, but from raising a family. The greatest good for the greatest number of people, right? If you happened to have bad genes, don't you think the government should prevent you from passing them along to your kids—kids who would very likely become criminals or inmates in some institution?"

"Man, you have the most up-tight attitude toward sex I've ever heard!" said the boy. "Having kids is a religious thing. You're asking us to play God with human souls! That's not something people ought to decide."

"I agree with you entirely," Dr. Mayer said, polishing his glasses again. "We certainly must take religious views into account. But sex is also a matter of economics. Very soon we're going to have too many people on this old globe we call the earth. Maybe we have too many right now. Can't support them all, no matter what we do. So we've got to come up with a plan that is acceptable to religious groups, but a plan that will allow us to control the number of children that people have. Or we've got to control who gets to have children in the first place. If we don't do something voluntarily, the government is bound to step in and pass laws."

Mayer put his spectacles back on his nose. "Any of you students grow up on a farm?"

Several of the young people held up their hands.

"Well, I guess your daddies have a few cows around to give milk and to supply meat, right? And if your daddies are smart, as they probably are, they're going to buy the best breeding stock they can afford, because good cows give more milk and more butter fat than poor cows, and good bulls produce stronger offspring with better meat on them than poor bulls. One good bull can service a whole lot of cows through artificial insemination—that is, they inject the bull's sperm cells into any cow that has an egg cell ready to be fertilized. Even a puny little cow will have better offspring if she gets the genes from a first-rate bull. So a blue-ribbon bull can share the wealth of his fine genes with lots of cows, even the scrawniest. Perhaps we should do the same with humans. Maybe only the President should be allowed to have children."

"If only the President of the United States can have kids, he's going to be one busy daddy," one of the girls said laughing.

"Doesn't seem fair somehow," the boy sitting next to her remarked. "You've gotten rid of half the bad genes by using just one prime bull, but what about the scrawny cows? They're still passing along their scrawny genes to their kids. Why not have just one big mother cow that's as good as the bull?"

"Wouldn't be enough calves born to feed us all," said another boy.

"Scrawny cows are cut out of the herd early and sold for hamburgers and hot dogs. That way you improve the herd as you go along," said another, obviously well-acquainted with farm life.

"Well, we're working on ways to improve herds even more," Mayer continued. "Just because a first-rate cow has good genes in her egg cells doesn't mean that she has to be burdened with carrying the calf until it's ready to be born. There are really three environments we have to consider. The first is the genetic environment—good genes and bad genes carried in the sperm and egg cells. As I said, we can't do much about that environment now except to select the best parents. Then there's what happens to the calf after it's born. Even a calf with lousy genes will do better if you give it lots of good food and exercise, and the proper medicine when it's sick. But in between fertilization and birth, the calf lives for several months inside the cow's body in what we call the pre-natal or before-birth environment. While it's still an embryo, the unborn calf is fairly well protected. Unless the mother cow gets sick or is given the wrong kind of food or drugs, the embryonic calf will develop pretty much the way its genes tell it to.''

''Like a baby will turn out okay at birth unless its mother gets German measles while she's carrying the baby,'' one of the girls interposed.

''Right. But while the big prime mother cow is carrying her calf within her, she isn't producing any new eggs. For example, human women produce a new egg cell every 28 days or so. But when a woman becomes pregnant, typically she doesn't produce any new eggs for 9 months or so. That means there are 8 or 9 potentially fine children that could have been produced that weren't. Now, with cows, we've worked out a deal. After we inseminate the prime cow artificially, we let the fertilized egg grow for a few days, and then we operate on the cow. We remove the embryo and transplant it into the body of a scrawny cow and let her do all the work of carrying the little calf until it's ready to be born. The scrawny cow's internal environment can't affect the development of the embryo very much, and so the scrawny cow gives birth to a super-calf with superior genes. And once we remove the embryo from the super-prime cow mother, she starts producing new eggs right away, which also can be fertilized artificially and then transplanted to the body of another inferior cow. That way, one super-momma can produce lots of superior calves each year instead of just one or two. It's still too complicated and expensive a technique for general use, but when the cost comes down, it sure is going to make a lot more money for the farmers. And once we have the embryo-transplant process all worked out, why shouldn't we use it with humans too?''

''You've got to be kidding,'' one of the girls said. ''I wouldn't want to carry somebody else's baby.''

''Not even for a million dollars?'' Mayer asked. ''Suppose a real rich lady wanted to have a child but didn't want to go through the mess of growing fat and all the other bother of being pregnant. Suppose she offered you a million dollars if you'd let her doctor transplant the embryo into your body. That way you could carry the child for her while she went off on a fancy vacation some-where. Then, when the child was born, it would be hers and her husband's— because they had provided the genes. All you did was baby sit with the fetus before it was born. So the rich lady would pick up the child at the hospital a couple of days after it was born and give you a check for a million dollars. How would you like that?''

''If I carried the baby, it would be mine, and no rich lady could take it away from me,'' the girl replied.

''Yeah, but what if the government decided you couldn't have kids,'' one of the boys said.

''Why couldn't I have kids, I'd like to know?''

''Because the government would say you didn't have the right kinds of genes, stupid. Just like my daddy decides which of his cows can have calves and which can't,'' the boy added rather smugly.

''But I've got great genes!'' the girl said. ''And no government is going to tell me I don't! And even if they did, I'd just get Dr. Mayer to engineer my genes so they were the right kind. So there,'' she concluded, making a face at the boy who was tormenting her with his comments.

''What's the right kind of genes?'' asked another girl.

''Yes, it all boils down to that decision, doesn't it? As Aldous Huxley pointed out in **Brave New World,** the day will surely come when we can engineer genes—if we know what kinds of kids we want to have. We can judge what kinds of cows we want because we value meat and milk production. But what do we value most in humans? Size? Strength? Intelligence?''

''That old Einstein wouldn't have done so well as a fullback for the Dallas Cowboys,'' an athletic young man said.

''There's something else you might not have considered. Maybe one reason certain cows have fine calves is that these cows have an innate ability to be good mothers. Maybe they take care of their calves better after the calves are born because the cows' genes tell them how to behave toward their calves. If the tendency to be a good mother is inherited in human genes as well, maybe that's something we ought to consider when we decide who can have kids and who can't.''

''Like finger coordination and musical talent is inherited, you mean,'' said the boy with the guitar.

''I don't even want to talk about this, it scares me so,'' another girl said. ''It's abnormal and immoral. It could never happen in the United States.''

''That's probably what the cows thought a few years ago,'' said one of the boys.

''Well, maybe it won't happen here, but the possibility of genetic engineering won't disappear just because we refuse to talk about it. In fact, just the opposite. But there's a final problem you really ought to consider. Suppose we all agree to keep things as they are—parents can have kids as they like without government interference. There's still no reason why a woman should have to go through a lengthy pregnancy and the discomfort of childbirth. In **Brave New World** the embryos are grown in bottles rather than in their mothers' bodies. When they are ready to be born, the babies are uncorked like a bottle of fine wine. Maybe the day will come when each home has a mechanical incubator in it. You would watch your child's development before birth just the way you watch a plant grow and flower. Then you wouldn't have to worry about German measles and drugs like thalidomide.''

''That's outrageous,'' said the girl in the second row. ''I don't want my baby born in a machine.''

''You'd destroy the warm, maternal feeling every woman has when she's carrying her own baby,'' said another.

''It's true that the chemical changes that occur within a woman's body when she's pregnant prepare her for motherhood. Her breasts fill with milk, for example, so that she can feed the child after birth. But what about the labor pains and all the discomfort involved?''

''I wouldn't love my baby if I didn't carry it myself. And how would my baby feel if it learned that it had developed in a machine instead of inside me? It just wouldn't love me as much.''

''Do you really think that maternal love is dependent on carrying the baby yourself?'' Mayer asked.

''Of course,'' said the girl in the second row. ''All that pain is natural. It makes the baby worthwhile, something you really suffered for. You just wouldn't take care of the baby as well if it weren't for that special feeling of closeness you get when you're carrying the child. It just wouldn't be **yours.** That's what the pain is for—to make you love the baby more.''

Dr. Mayer frowned. ''Do you really think that having a child is all that painful? In most cultures childbirth is considered such a natural and joyous thing that women seldom complain about how much it hurts. Maybe we've overdone the pain business in our society. I'm not a woman, of course, so I don't have first-hand information on the subject. But I do believe that pain is more a matter of expectancy than anything else. Besides, what proof do you have that pain makes you love a child more?''

A girl in the middle of the room stood up, tears filling her eyes. ''I'd like to say something. Maybe there are special genes that make a woman a good mother. I don't know. What I do know is that a woman doesn't have to carry a child, or give birth to it, or suffer pain in order to love the baby and see that it gets the best care and attention. And whether a child is born in a bottle or from its mother's body doesn't affect the love it has for the woman who brings it up. Maybe you ought to remember that I'm adopted. My adopted mother can't have children, so she and my foster father adopted me when I was just two weeks old. And they love me very, very much, both of them.''

The class was absolutely silent for several moments after the girl sat down. Then the bell rang.

"Thank you very, very much," Dr. Mayer said, a smile on his face.

RECOMMENDED READINGS

Huxley, Aldous, *Brave New World* (New York: Harper & Row, 1932).

Huxley, Aldous, *Brave New World Revisited* (New York: Harper & Row, 1958).

Lickona, Thomas (ed). *Moral Development and Behavior: Theory, Research, and Social Issues* (New York: Holt, Rinehart and Winston, 1976).

Rostand, Jean, *Can Man Be Modified?* (New York: Basic Books, Inc., 1959).

chapter 20
"MONKEY SEE, MONKEY DO"

LOVE IN PARENTS AND CHILDREN

DID YOU KNOW THAT . . .

Death and love are two important areas of human existence seldom studied scientifically?

We cannot investigate love directly, since it is an internal process, but we can study loving behavior.

Even though all their other needs are met, infant monkeys will die if not given something to "love"—that is, something to cling to and rub against?

A human infant, if separated from its mother, may fall into a profound depression?

If a female monkey does not engage in "sex play" with her peers when young, she may refuse to mate as an adult?

Monkeys raised in partial isolation are often either wildly aggressive or almost hopelessly passive as adults?

Monkey mothers raised in isolation often destroy their own offspring?

Boys separated from their fathers before age 6 tend to show more "feminine" behavior patterns than usual?

Girls separated from their fathers by divorce tend to become more promiscuous in their early sexual behavior than girls reared in intact homes?

"Now, admit it. Isn't this the cleanest, most modern nursery you've ever seen?"

The Director of the nursery, who was leading the tour, hardly waited for his guests to answer. "Spotless, absolutely spotless. We want to make sure that these infants are completely protected from dirt and disease, and I dare say we've succeeded."

The Director was showing the kitchen to his visitors, two women and one man.

"The best of all possible baby foods, served in absolutely sterile containers. Each portion contains special vitamins and minerals, prepared by cooks wearing face masks so that no germs ever contaminate the food. Isn't it beautiful?" The Director beamed.

"Now, let's go into the observation room. We can watch the children through the glass. You understand that we can't let you actually go into the sleeping room with the children themselves. That is, unless you're willing to scrub down first in the shower and put on one of our freshly laundered white uniforms. We can't have you transmitting some disease to these poor little babies, now can we?" The Director uttered a small, brief, high-pitched laugh.

Through the glass window the visitors could see the nursery room. Each of the infants had its own little bed made up with immaculately white sheets. Waist-high wooden partitions stood between each of the cribs, giving each infant almost complete privacy.

"Why do you have the cribs separated that way?" one of the women visitors asked.

"Ah, an interesting question," replied the Director. "We want to minimize the transmission of disease, you see. Should one of the infants contract an ailment, the others are too far away to be readily infected. The partitions are covered with a special white paint, and we wash them down with disinfectant once a week. Nothing but the best, I assure you!"

One of the infants was crying lustily. A nurse came into the nursery and picked the child up, holding it close to her starched white uniform. Although the woman cradled the infant in her arms for some time, it continued its loud, gulping cries.

"Why is that child crying so much?" asked one of the visitors.

The Director smiled confidently. "A new arrival, just separated from its mother. Takes them a while to get used to new surroundings, of course. After a few days—a couple of weeks or so—they calm down and begin to enjoy their healthy new environment. After all, we've rescued many of them from very unsanitary home conditions. As you know, most of these children are the offspring of mothers who have had to go to a hospital themselves for an operation of some kind, or because of some sickness, so it's not at all surprising that the children should be a little upset. Almost all of them cry a fair amount when they first arrive. But look at the rest of them! They aren't making much of a fuss, now are they?"

It was true. Most of the infants lay in their cribs unmoving, staring at the white ceiling with wide-open eyes. Large tears rolled gently down the cheeks of one of the children; the nurse stopped by its crib, offered it a play toy, but the child merely continued its gentle weeping.

"You see, before we took over, the children were raised in filth, real filth. Noise, grime, germs—that was their steady diet. Many of them took sick and died. Now, it's different. Those kids must have the most unpolluted environment on earth. Isn't it great?"

One of the visitors looked at the Director with raised eyebrows. "What's your sickness rate?"

The Director cleared his throat. "Oh, I think we're doing quite well, all things considered."

"What do you mean, 'all things considered'?"

A slight squeak sounded in the Director's voice as he continued. "Well, remember that these kids all come from bad home environments. Mothers sick, families mostly broken apart at the seams. You've got to keep that in mind. You'd expect a lot of illness in those situations anyhow, wouldn't you?"

"What kinds of symptoms do the children show?"

The squeak in the Director's voice grew more pronounced. "Well, you see, it's really odd. They don't eat. That's the main problem. Maybe when we sterilize the food, we take all the taste out or something. And they catch a lot of colds. We don't really understand why. Probably a bug or something that's going around, but I'm sure we'll lick it."

"What do you plan to do?"

"Well, first we're going to wash the whole place down again with disinfectant, and then . . ."

Science is, to some extent, the fine art of asking questions and then trying to find reasonable and reliable answers. Sometimes the questions are obvious—why does the sun give off heat and light; why is grass green; why does lemon juice taste sour? The answers to these questions are often complex and highly mathematical, but they seldom offend anybody.

Occasionally the scientist does accidentally manage to upset the people around him or her by posing a problem that many of us would rather not have investigated objectively—what are the actual consequences of war, of showing violence on television, of giving pornography to young children? Our culture gives us socially acceptable answers to these questions, and the scientist who wishes to peer further into the matter—or to obtain experimental data rather than collect opinions—finds himself or herself an outcast. Open minds are not always beloved

Axiom (AX-ee-um). From the Greek word meaning "to think worthy." Hence, a rule or principle that has found general acceptance or is thought worthy by many people. More technically, an axiom is one of the basic laws or statements on which a theory is built.

Taboo (tab-BOO). Any thing, object, or behavior that is prohibited.

by closed societies. Yet it was Albert Einstein himself who told young scientists that if they wanted to be successful they should "challenge an *axiom* (°)"—that is, they should challenge a belief that most people simply take for granted.

There are many areas of human behavior that are partially or entirely restricted from scientific investigation. One such is death—although we may study what happens to people when they are dying from some natural cause, we obviously cannot hasten the process merely to see how the individual might react. Another *taboo* (°) area is love. As we remarked earlier, sexual love is a topic much discussed but seldom studied in the laboratory. But even the non-sexual aspects of love are not often subjected to a scientist's scrutiny, perhaps because many of us believe it is too personal a topic. Or perhaps we fear that the magic of love would somehow disappear if we analyzed it in factual terms.

Whatever the case, there are thousands and thousands of studies on how rats learn, but only a handful of adequate experiments on how people fall in love. Such information as scientists have gathered on the subject suggests that many of our long-cherished notions about love are reasonably accurate, but a great many more are mere flights of human fancy. In this chapter we will examine some of these findings and then draw such conclusions as the data allow.

LOVE

Let us begin with an apparently simple question—what is love? The usual belief (in our society) is that love is something that an individual falls into, often without meaning to do so—that is, love is entirely an *internal state or condition* that occurs to almost everyone. Love is a feeling, an intra-psychic emotion that is entirely inside us, and hence not subject to objective scrutiny. This view holds that we can study the reactions of a person who says he or she is in love, but we cannot see the love itself.

Love certainly is an emotion, and it most assuredly can be studied from an intra-psychic viewpoint. The intra-personal side of love has been written about for centuries by some of the wisest poets and novelists the world has known. When Elizabeth Barrett Browning wrote, "How do I love thee? Let me count the ways . . ." she told us as much about some aspects of intra-psychic love as any psychologist could.

However, love can also be approached from the biological viewpoint (*see* Chapter 13) and from the behavioral/social viewpoint (*see* Chapter 26). For example, we may look at maternal love and say that it is an instinctual, biological response strongly influenced by the female's hormones. Or we may look at an individual's behavior and *assume* that only someone in love would act in that fashion. Perhaps a young man spends all his free time (and much of his money) entertaining a certain young woman; or perhaps a young mother spends much of her time (and almost all of her money) taking care of her newborn child. Our assumption would be that "love is the cause of it all," because people in love typically advertise their condition by getting as close as they can to the object of their affections. Since a person in love is *attracted to* someone or something else, we can speak of *loving responses* or *loving behavior*—and these we can study scientifically, if we have the patience and wit to do so.

Our objective study of love will never *replace* our subjective, poetic examination of this glorious condition—nor is there any reason why it should. But once we realize that love is, in part, a response to some living or inanimate object, we can make certain statements about love that we probably could not make otherwise. Like all behavior, loving responses must be affected by a person's genetic blueprint, past experience, and the present environment. We can also state that loving behaviors will *tend to increase* if they are followed by satisfaction or reward, and that they will *tend to decrease* if followed by pain or punishment or lack of reinforcement. We do not usually think in these terms—perhaps because we have been taught to perceive love as an "affair of the heart" rather than as a response pattern to present and past stimuli. And yet the data gathered so far strongly suggest that the "condition of love" is as influenced by internal secretions and external stimuli as is eating or breathing or speaking. By adopting such a view, we may lose a bit of the magic and mystery, but we surely gain a great deal in terms of real understanding of what love is all about.

In this chapter we will pay particular attention to the love that an infant shows toward its mother, and the attraction she feels toward her child. We will find that this is not merely a mystical emotional bond, determined by nature. In fact, an infant has no way of knowing who its biological mother (or father) really is; a young child will love anyone or anything that gives it comfort, caresses, food, and protection. Without this loving attention, the child will die, or will grow up to be a very disturbed adult. So there is good reason for an infant to enter into a loving relationship with whomever or whatever satisfies its many needs. But what about the mother? Often she can survive better without the many demands that a child makes on her time and energy. Why should a woman love an infant merely because it was born of her own flesh?

The answer to that question is a good deal more complex than it looks at first glance. Society demands that a woman love—or at least care for—her children. Even animal mothers love their offspring and often care for them tenderly. Isn't this proof that there is a "maternal instinct" that forces a female to love her child? Surprisingly enough, with humans and most other higher animals, it seems that the maternal instinct is remarkably weak. Many women neither love nor take care of their sons and daughters—in fact, as we will see, women by the thousands each year desert, *mutilate* (°), or even kill their children. Fathers are often worse; for the "paternal instinct," if it exists at all in man, is considerably less *potent* (°) than is the "maternal instinct." Perhaps instead of being surprised that there are a few bad mothers and fathers in the world, we should be pleased and delighted that there are so many good ones.

Once we begin to look at loving behavior, rather than placing the entire emphasis on feeling and emotions, we find we can ask a number of rather pointed questions we couldn't ask otherwise. For example, what is there about an infant's behavior that determines a mother's responses, and what is there about the way a

Mutilate (MUTE-till-late). To cut up or disfigure; to destroy.

Potent (POE-tent). From the Latin word meaning "capable" or "powerful." At a sexual level, a potent male is one capable of fathering children; an impotent male is one incapable of carrying through the sex act to its normal conclusion. At a political level, a potentate (POE-ten-tate) is a king or ruler with great power. Our word "potential" comes from the same Latin source.

Awry (uh-RYE). An old English word meaning "turned or twisted toward one side, wide of the mark, not on target."

mother cares for her child that makes the infant love and trust her? What happens to children without mothers and fathers? What effect does early separation from its mother have on a child? What if the separation comes later on? What substitutes can we give the child to replace the mother? Are parents enough, or does the child need to have experience with other children its own age? And if the mothering process goes *awry* (°) somehow, what kinds of therapy or special training can help overcome the child's problems?

LOVE IN THE LABORATORY

We have probably learned more (at a scientific level) about loving behavior in the past 50 years than in the previous 500—in part, because we have made more objective observations of love in humans (and other animals); in part, because a few scientists have recently taken love into the laboratory and studied it experimentally. We have finally realized that the middle-class U.S. society is not the only culture in which love occurs, and that what is natural and normal and moral for us may be quite different in Asia, Africa, or even in different segments of our own society. And we have discovered that experiments involving animal subjects can give us clues to the complexities of human behavior that we could not get outside the laboratory. We cannot separate a dozen human infants from their mothers merely to see how the children react; but we can isolate monkey infants from their mothers in the hope that these studies will tell us better how to care for human children whose mothers desert them. We might also learn something about why mothers desert their children in the first place. If our focus in this chapter seems primarily to be on monkey and chimpanzee love, the reason is simply this—hard data on human loving behavior are often difficult to come by.

Monkey Love

The scientist who has conducted the best long-term laboratory experiments on love is surely Harry Harlow, a psychologist at the University of Wisconsin. Professor Harlow did not set out to study love—it happened by accident. Like

Margaret and Harry Harlow in laboratory with monkeys.

Baby monkey in a cheesecloth blanket.

Baby monkey with surrogate cloth monkey.

many other psychologists, he was at first primarily interested in how organisms learn. Rather than working with rats, Harlow chose to work with monkeys.

Since he needed a place to house and raise the monkeys, he built the *Primate* (°) Laboratory at Wisconsin. Then he began to study the effects of brain lesions on monkey learning. But he soon found that young animals reacted somewhat differently to brain damage than did older monkeys, so he and his fellow psychologist-wife Margaret devised a breeding program and tried various ways of raising monkeys in the laboratory. They rapidly discovered that monkey infants raised by their mothers often caught diseases from their parents, so the Harlows began taking the infants away from their mothers at birth and tried raising them by hand. The baby monkeys had been given cheesecloth diapers to serve as baby blankets. Almost from the start, it became obvious to the Harlows that their little animals developed such strong attachments to the blankets that, in the Harlows' own terms, it was often hard to tell where the diaper ended and the baby began. Not only this, but if the Harlows removed the "security" blanket in order to clean it, the infant monkey often became greatly disturbed—just as if its own mother had deserted it.

The Surrogate Mother What the baby monkeys obviously needed was an artificial or *surrogate* (°) mother—something they could cling to as tightly as they typically clung to their own mother's chest. The Harlows sketched out many different designs, but none really appealed to them. Then, in 1957, while enjoying a champagne flight high over the city of Detroit, Harry Harlow glanced out of the airplane window and "saw" an image of an artificial monkey mother. It was a hollow wire cylinder, wrapped with a terrycloth bath towel, with a silly wooden head at the top. The tiny monkey could cling to this model mother as closely as to its real mother's body hair. This surrogate mother could be provided with a functional breast simply by placing a milk bottle so that the nipple stuck through the cloth at an appropriate place on the surrogate's anatomy. The cloth mother could be heated or cooled; it could be rocked mechanically or made to stand still; and, most important, it could be removed at will.

While still sipping his champagne, Harlow mentally outlined much of the research that kept him, his wife, and their associates occupied for many years to come. And without realizing it, Harlow had shifted from studying monkey learning to studying monkey love.

Primate (PRIME-ate). The "top dogs" of the animal kingdom—that is, the apes, monkeys, and humans.

Surrogate (SIR-oh-gate, or SIR-oh-gutt). From the Latin word meaning "to substitute." A surrogate is a substitute or stand-in. A surrogate court is a court of law that handles the money and property of someone who has died—that is, a court that "stands in" for the dead person and sees that the person's will is carried out.

Five Types of Love

Harlow believes that there are five types of social love—that is, the love of one organism for another:

1. The first of these is the love an infant shows for its mother—or for her surrogate or substitute.
2. Out of this infant-mother love grows what Harlow calls "peer love," the affection of young organisms for other youngsters their own age.
3. When puberty is reached, a new dimension of love is possible—that of heterosexual love, which Harlow believes develops from peer love. As we will see, this third type of love is possible only if the organism has learned certain behavior patterns while playing with its peers.
4. The fourth type of love is available (under normal circumstances) only to females, for it is the affection that a mother shows to her infant.
5. Males—under the right conditions—may demonstrate the fifth type of love, which Harlow calls "paternal love."

In a moment we will discuss each of these five varieties of love in turn. But first, we should mention two major objections that have been raised to the Harlows' experiments. To begin with, these studies were conducted in laboratory settings. Can we be sure that monkeys (or any other organisms) raised under more natural environments would experience the same developmental sequence? Labs are often as artificial and unresponsive as surrogate mothers themselves. Can anything worthwhile be learned from such investigations? The answer seems to be yes, provided we remember the limitations of the laboratory and we supplement these experimental data with information taken from more natural sources.

Scientist Jane Goodall spent more than a dozen years studying chimpanzees in their native African forests. Beginning her work when she was in her twenties, she lived with these closest living relatives of humans for so long that the chimps came to accept her as a kind of giant white ape. She became so fascinated with chimpanzee behavior patterns that, after taking her doctorate at Cambridge University, Dr. Goodall opened the Gombe Stream Research Centre near Lake Tanganyika. Until it closed in 1976, scientists from all over the world visited the Research Centre to study primate behavior "in the raw." Dr. Goodall's observations of "natural" chimpanzees strongly reinforced the laboratory findings of the Harlows. But Dr. Goodall found that field studies do not yield all the complex information that a curious scientist wishes to have about his or her subjects. In her book, *In the Shadow of Man*, she often wonders what might happen *if* she could somehow change the chimp's environment, or *if* she could introduce some new variable to see how the chimps might respond. So perhaps it is not too surprising that, by the end of her book, Dr. Goodall mentions that she and her associates had built a field station in the jungle and were conducting experiments, as well as continuing their natural observations. For it is in the controlled setting of the laboratory that a scientist makes "ifs" come true.

QUESTION: **What kinds of information about loving behavior in humans and other species would you expect would best be obtained from field studies; and what kinds could most effectively be obtained in a laboratory?**

The second objection to the Harlows' experiments is perhaps more pertinent—are monkeys and chimpanzees similar enough to humans that a study of how primates love each other will tell us anything about human loving behavior? Again the data suggest that the answer should be positive—provided we keep firmly in mind that humans are many times more complex than even the brightest of other primates. The chimpanzee is the animal closest to humans in its talents and behavior patterns, and careful observations of its habits and development can

Jane Goodall with her son Grub.

give us a veritable gold mine of information we might not be able to gain any other way. But studies of chimps and monkeys can at best give us only hunches and hypotheses that we will later want to supplement with data from human subjects.

QUESTION: What do you think the major differences between chimpanzees and humans might be?

Infant-Mother Love

The chimpanzee or monkey infant is much more developed at birth than the human infant, and apes develop or mature much faster than we do. Almost from the moment it is born, the monkey infant can move around and hold tightly to its mother. During the first few days of its life the infant will approach and cling to almost any large, warm, and soft object in its environment, particularly if that object also gives it milk. After a week or so, however, the monkey infant begins to avoid newcomers and focuses its attentions on "mother"—real or surrogate.

During the first two weeks of its life warmth is perhaps the most important psychological thing that a monkey mother has to give to its baby. The Harlows discovered this fact by offering infant monkeys a choice of two types of mother substitutes—one wrapped in terrycloth and one that was made of bare wire. If the two artificial mothers were both the same temperature, the little monkeys always preferred the cloth mother. However, if the wire model was heated, while the cloth model was cool, for the first two weeks after birth the baby primates picked the warm wire mother substitute as their favorite. Thereafter they switched and spent most of their time on the more comfortable cloth mother.

Why is cloth preferable to bare wire? Something that the Harlows call *contact comfort* (°) seems to be the answer, and a most powerful influence it is. Infant monkeys (and chimps too) spend much of their time rubbing against their mothers' skins, putting themselves in as close contact with the parent as they can. Whenever the young animal is frightened, disturbed, or annoyed, it typically rushes to its mother and rubs itself against her body. Wire doesn't "rub" as well as does soft cloth. Prolonged "contact comfort" with a surrogate cloth mother appears to instill confidence in baby monkeys and is much more rewarding to them than is either warmth or milk. Infant monkeys also prefer a "rocking" surrogate to one that is stationary.

According to the Harlows, the basic quality of an infant's love for its mother is *trust*. If the infant is put into an unfamiliar playroom without its mother, the infant ignores the toys no matter how interesting they might be. It screeches in terror and curls up into a furry little ball. If its cloth mother is now introduced into the playroom, the infant rushes to the surrogate and clings to it for dear life. After a few minutes of contact comfort, it apparently begins to feel more secure. It then climbs down from the mother substitute and begins tentatively to explore the toys, but often rushes back for a deep embrace as if to reassure itself that its mother is still there and that all is well. Bit by bit its fears of the novel environment are "desensitized" (*see* Chapter 15) and it spends more and more time playing with the toys and less and less time clinging to its "mother."

QUESTION: How might you explain "trust" in terms of the infant's need to predict and control its inputs?

Good Mothers and Bad The Harlows found that, once a baby monkey has come to accept its mother (real or surrogate), the mother can do almost no wrong. In one of their studies, the Harlows tried to create "monster mothers" whose behavior would be so abnormal that the infants would desert the mothers. Their purpose was to determine whether maternal rejection might cause abnormal

Contact comfort. The pleasure that a young animal gets in rubbing its body against a soft, "woolly" object, or from clinging tightly to its mother's body. Unless a young primate gets enough contact comfort, it fails to develop "trust," and its emotional and perceptual maturation is likely to be retarded.

Catapult (CAT-uh-pult). From the Greek words meaning "to throw against." An ancient military device for hurling stones at an enemy. Our modern version of the catapult is the slingshot.

Temperament (TEM-purr-uh-ment). The Latin word *temperare* means "to regulate, to restrain one's self, to soften." To temper your argument is to criticize softly. To lose your temper is to lose your restraint. Your temperament is the way that you regulate yourself—that is, your characteristic attitude or behavior pattern. If you are nice to almost everybody you meet, you are said to have a polite temperament.

Paramount (PAIR-uh-mount). From the Latin words *para*, meaning "above" or "beyond," and *mont*, meaning "mountain." Anything that is superior to all others is "paramount." The people who founded Paramount Pictures believed they could put out the best movies in the world, and chose a snow-capped mountain as their symbol.

behavior patterns in the infant monkeys similar to those responses found in human babies whose mothers ignore or punish their children severely. The problem was—how can you get a terrycloth mother to reject or punish its baby? Their solutions were ingenious—but most of them failed in their main purpose. Four types of "monster mothers" were tried, but none of them was apparently "evil" enough to impart fear or loathing to the infant monkeys. One such "monster" occasionally blasted its babies with compressed air; a second shook so violently that the baby often fell off; a third contained a *catapult* (°) that frequently flung the infant away from it. The most evil-appearing of all had a set of metal spikes buried beneath the terrycloth; from time to time the spikes would poke through the cloth, making it impossible for the infant to cling to the surrogate.

The baby monkeys brought up on the "monster mothers" did show a brief period of emotional disturbance when the "wicked" *temperament* (°) of the surrogates first showed up. The infants would cry for a time when displaced from their mothers, but as soon as the surrogates returned to normal, the infant would return to the surrogate and continue clinging, as if all were forgiven. As the Harlows tell the story, the only prolonged distress created by the experiment seemed to be that felt by the experimenters!

There was, however, one type of surrogate that uniformly "turned off" the infant monkeys. S.J. Suomi, working with the Harlows, built a terrycloth mother with ice water in its veins. Newborn monkeys would attach themselves to this "cold momma" for a brief period of time, but then retreated to a corner of the cage and rejected her forever.

From their many brilliant studies, the Harlows conclude that the love of an infant for its mother is *primarily a response to certain stimuli the mother offers.* Warmth is the most important stimulus for the first two weeks of the monkey's life, then contact comfort becomes *paramount* (°). Contact comfort is determined by the softness and "rubbability" of the surface of the mother's body—terrycloth is better than are satin and silk, but all such materials are more effective in creating love and trust than bare metal is. Food and mild shaking or rocking are important too, but less so than warmth and contact comfort. These needs—and the rather primitive responses the infant makes in order to obtain their satisfaction—are programmed into the monkey's genetic blueprint. The growing infant's requirement for social and intellectual stimulation becomes critical only later in a monkey's life. And yet, as we will see in this (and the next) chapter, if the baby primate is deprived of contact with other young of its own species, its whole pattern of development can be profoundly disturbed.

Maternal Deprivation   What does a "good" mother (or father) do for an infant that a "poor" parent doesn't? For one thing, the "good" parent exposes the child to a great deal of sensory stimulation. When a mother picks up her child to play with it, when she dangles a toy in front of its eyes, when she talks to the child, or takes it places with her, she is both exercising its sensory receptors and giving the infant a chance to build up the kind of "input expectations" that it will need to predict and control its environment and its own behavior as it grows up.

Scientists at the Massachusetts Institute of Technology raised kittens in total darkness for a period of several months after birth. Later, when the kittens were brought into a normal, lighted environment, they simply could not see as well as kittens raised in the light. Medical examinations of the deprived kittens showed that the neurons in their eyes had not developed properly. Nerve cells that are not given proper stimulation become as weak and unhealthy as do muscles that never get used.

The "good" parent also trains the child to respond in socially acceptable ways by lavishing love and attention on it when it is good and by withholding affection when the child's behavior is unacceptable. The "poor" parent too often ignores the child or responds to it inconsistently. Adequate training allows the child's brain to develop the complex neural circuitry that it will need later in its life.

But in order for the newborn child to be able to build up expectancies about the world around it, that world must present certain regularities and certainties. As we saw in Chapter 12, however, too much regularity can cause problems too—if this regularity is suddenly disrupted before the child is mature enough to respond appropriately. For instance, a child cared for by a "good" mother with consistent behavior patterns rapidly builds up a dependency upon its mother, for it learns that much of what is pleasant and satisfying in its world comes to it through inputs from its mother. Psychologists call this an *anaclitic relationship* (°), the phrase coming from the Greek word meaning "to lean on."

Once the child has built up a strong anaclitic dependency on its mother (or on whoever gives it most of its care), disturbing the relationship can be dangerous. For instance, if it is the mother who *always* feeds the child, the infant soon associates *food* with *mother*—that is, they become part of the same mental image or mental expectation. When food appears, the child expects its mother to be there too, because it is not yet mature enough, nor experienced enough, to discriminate food from mother. If the infant is suddenly separated from its mother during the first few months of its life, the child may have considerably difficulty adjusting to its altered circumstances.

Psychiatrist R.A. Spitz studied the reactions of infants 6 to 12 months old who, for family reasons, had been separated from their mothers and put into institutions or foster homes. In their new environments, these infants received at best impersonal care. Almost as soon as the infants were institutionalized, they began showing signs of disturbance. They became quite upset when anyone approached them; they lost weight; and they became passive, inactive, and had trouble sleeping as well.

Spitz calls this *apathetic* (°) condition *anaclitic depression* (°). According to Spitz, the first sign of anaclitic depression is a type of behavior that he describes as being "a search for the mother." Some babies quietly weep big tears; others cry violently. None of them, Spitz says, can be quieted down by any type of intervention, although at the initial stage of the depression they still cling tightly to any adult who picks them up.

If the mother does not return in 3 to 4 weeks, the picture changes. The child withdraws, lies quietly on its stomach, will not play if offered a toy, does not even look up if someone enters the room. The baby becomes dejected and passive, refuses food, loses weight, and becomes more susceptive than usual to colds and other ailments.

If the separation does not come until after the child is a year or more old, the depression may be reversed if the child is given adequate "mothering" within three months. Spitz believes that anaclitic depression might well account for some types of mental retardation, since the children he studied seemed to show considerable physical and intellectual impairment during and immediately after their periods of depression.

Maternal Deprivation in Humans: A Case History

Children who enter a hospital for treatment are, quite naturally, very prone to anaclitic depression since they usually must be isolated from their mothers, sometimes for extended periods of time. That this depression may affect the child's behavior in rather unusual ways is shown in a study by Clayton Shorkey and John Taylor while they were at Michigan State University. Their patient was a 17-month-old girl who suffered severe burns that covered 37 percent of her body. The little girl was placed in isolation as soon as she was admitted to the hospital. The first day the infant was fairly quiet, but on subsequent days she cried lustily and tossed her limbs about in a violent, agitated manner. Medical care for the burns consisted chiefly of

René A. Spitz.

Anaclitic relationship (ann-uh-KLITT-ick). A strong, non-sexual love; the loving dependency and trust of a young child for its mother.

Apathetic (app-puh-THET-ick). From the Greek word meaning "without feeling" or "without emotion." An apathetic child is one that cannot easily be stimulated to show emotion or expressive movement no matter what you do to (or for) the child.

Anaclitic depression. A type of passivity or apathy that very young children show when they are separated from their mothers for any great length of time. During the first two or three weeks of the separation, the child may be highly emotional; if the mother does not return, the child falls into an apathetic condition known as anaclitic depression.

applying a stinging drug called silver nitrate, which was squirted over the little girl's bandages at frequent intervals by the nurses. The doctors also began a series of skin grafts, but discontinued them when the infant's physical condition grew markedly worse. After a month of treatment the little girl refused to eat; more than this, she became markedly upset whenever she was approached by any of the nursing staff.

At this point social workers Shorkey and Taylor were called in to help. They observed that the nurses, who were extremely disturbed at the child's condition, would frequently interrupt the painful treatment procedure and would attempt to soothe the little girl by talking to her, singing, and playing with her toys. The more the nurses attempted to give the child love, the more violent the little girl became in her rejection of their attention and affection. Indeed, it almost appeared that the staff members were making the child worse, not better.

Shorkey and Taylor reasoned that, in the infant's depressive state, she simply could not discriminate between love and pain. To her, a nurse coming into the room had become a stimulus that too often was followed by unpleasant consequences (the silver nitrate). Although the stimulation the nurses gave the girl presumably kept her from experiencing the most profound aspects of anaclitic depression, the infant had become conditioned to expect hurt rather than love whenever a nurse appeared on the scene. Psycho-therapy, then, should consist of helping the infant associate one set of stimuli with pain, another set with love and affection.

Shorkey and Taylor instituted the following changes: Whenever the nurses were to bathe the girl's bandages with silver nitrate, bright white lights were turned on. The nursing staff wore green medical garments but were instructed not to talk or handle the infant unnecessarily, not to play with her, and not to spend one moment longer in the room than they had to. Then, at other times, a set of red lights was turned on, the nursing staff wore distinctive red garments, and they spent as much time as possible playing with the girl, rubbing the unburned parts of her body, talking to her, and giving her food. Medication was never given during the "red light" or social-stimulation condition.

By the end of the second day the infant began responding *differently* to the two treatment situations. That is, she continued to cry—but briefly—when the white lights were on and she was doused with the painful silver nitrate. But when the red lights were on, her crying ceased and for the first time in several weeks she lost her fear of the staff members. By the fourth day the infant began entering into little games with the staff; by the end of two weeks she was playing happily during the "red light" condition. At this point the doctors resumed the skin grafts. By the end of 6 weeks the little girl was well enough to be discharged from the hospital.

An interesting sidelight to this case comes from studying the behavior of the child's mother. At first she refused to follow the new rules, since she insisted the infant would recognize her as "mother" no matter what she was wearing and no matter which lights were on when she entered the room. To the woman's surprise the child continued to react with lusty crying whenever the mother dressed in normal clothes came to see her. When the mother was persuaded to wear red clothes and to see the little girl only when the red lights were on, the infant rapidly adjusted and responded to the mother in a positive, accepting fashion.

Shorkey and Taylor studied the little girl for a period of 2 years after her discharge from the hospital and report that she showed no detectable problems in either her physical or psychological recovery from the *trauma* (°). They also note that the child was placed in her grandmother's care after leaving the hospital because the child's mother had indicated that her daughter's injury might not have been entirely accidental—a point we will cover in greater detail later in this chapter.

Trauma (rhymes with "DRAW-ma"). A frightening event; a physical or psychological wound.

A baby monkey reared alone is frozen in fear when other monkeys approach it.

A catatonic posture assumed by a monkey reared alone.

Peer Love

Monkeys raised on cloth surrogates appear to be fairly normal in their behavior patterns, and when tested for their learning ability on reasonably simple tasks, perform about as well as do young monkeys raised in laboratory colonies or young animals that grow up in the wild. However, when the Harlows put groups of surrogate-trained monkeys together, they soon found they had a problem. Although these animals had never seen other monkeys during their entire lives, they responded to one another with excessive amounts of aggressive behavior. Eventually this hostility waned and disappeared, but the animals' social behavior remained unusual, to say the least.

Many of these monkeys showed the kinds of *stereotyped* (°) activities one finds in certain types of patients in mental hospitals; the monkeys made oddly repetitive movements that seemed to have no function, or they froze into bizarre postures, or they would stare into space for hours on end. Sometimes, while thus looking blankly out of the cage, an animal's arm would rise slowly as if not really attached to the monkey's body. Its wrist and fingers might contract tightly, then open up, and then contract again—just as occasionally happens in a human condition called *catatonic schizophrenia* (°). If at this point the monkey noticed its own arm, it might jump away in fear or even try to attack its oddly behaving limb. A few of the animals would become paralyzed with fear whenever they were approached by another monkey.

Sex and the Single Monkey As the Harlows point out, these infants had been raised in *partial* social deprivation—that is, they had their surrogate mothers, and they often interacted with their human keepers, but they never experienced the pleasures of socializing with other growing monkeys. Little wonder the animals didn't get along with each other.

From a practical (scientist-oriented) viewpoint, there was an even greater disaster—none of these animals ever learned the rudiments of sexual behavior. The Harlows had put these monkeys together in the first place so that they might breed and hence provide more baby monkeys for experiments. But the partially deprived animals refused to cooperate. Their sex lives were *nil* (°). Even when the Harlows introduced an experienced, normally raised male into the colony, he was a complete failure as far as impregnating any of the females was concerned.

Stereotyped (STAIR-ee-oh-typed). Any activity that is repeated automatically, without thought and without variation, is said to be stereotyped.

Catatonic schizophrenia (CAT-uh-TONN-ick SKITS-oh-FREE-knee-uh). "Schizophrenia" comes from the Greek words meaning "split mind." Someone whose mind is "split away from reality" is said to suffer from a severe form of mental illness, or schizophrenia. "Catatonia" means "under tension" or "contracted." A mentally disturbed person who "freezes" the body into strange positions has contracted his or her muscles abnormally.

Nil (rhymes with "hill"). From the Latin word *nihil*, meaning "nothing" or "non-existent."

Gonads (GO-nads; rhymes with "NO dads"). The reproductive organs; the testes in the male and the ovaries in the female. See Chapter 13.

Erotic (air-ROT-tick). Eros was the Greek god of love. Anything that arouses sexual passion is said to be erotic. Another name for pornography is "erotica" (air-ROT-tick-uh).

Chaste (pronounced the same as chased). From the Latin word meaning "pure" or "unblemished." To refrain from all forms of sexual activity is to remain chaste.

Rats and other lower animals raised in similar isolation will usually mate fairly readily as soon as they are sexually mature and their isolation is ended, particularly if the partner has prior experience at the game. The sex lives of lower animals is determined to a great extent by their hormones; when their *gonads* (°) say "go," they are ready and able to respond. In primates, however, hormones are not the only determining factor. Heterosexual love appears to grow out of peer love, and if the monkey had no peers to respond to when young, it doesn't respond sexually as an adult.

Monkeys and chimpanzees mate in similar fashion, with the female crouching down on all fours and the male mounting her from behind (the more exotic forms of primate sexual intercourse seem to be limited to the human species). The male monkey supports himself during these *erotic* (°) festivities by clinging to the female's hind legs. If the female will not assume the proper crouching position, or will not allow the male to hold on to her, sex becomes impossible. During much of peer group play, the monkeys and chimpanzees "practice" chasing each other and then assuming the mating position—even though they are years too young to be able to enjoy its ultimate consequences. As Harlow puts it so well, unless a female monkey is chased by her age-mates when she is young, she will very likely remain *chaste* (°) all the rest of her life.

QUESTION: **We typically transmit information about sex to our youngsters by means of the printed or spoken word. What changes might occur in adult sexual behavior if we began encouraging children to "rehearse" sexual intercourse openly as chimpanzees and monkeys do?**

Maternal and Peer Deprivation in Monkeys   In one of their best-known experiments, the Harlows tried to reproduce a human type of anaclitic depression in normal infant monkeys. These young animals were from birth raised in a large group with their mothers present. Then, for a period of several weeks, the mothers were taken away, leaving the infants to get along as best they could together. As you might expect, the tiny monkeys went through much the same sort of anaclitic depression as do human infants. At the time of separation the baby monkeys searched actively for their mothers and cried loudly. Soon, however, they began to withdraw. Even though they had their peers to romp about with, all forms of play disappeared; instead of socializing, the babies huddled in corners alone, each clinging to its own body, lost in its individual bleak-brown thoughts.

Once the mothers were reintroduced, the infants went through a momentary period of frantic activity, most of which was aimed at clinging so tightly to the mother that she could never leave them again. Peer play soon became re-established and the infants recovered normally.

In a further set of studies the Harlows showed that it is not merely the loss of maternal "magic" that leads to severe depression; rather, it is the deprivation of whatever form of social stimulation the organism is accustomed to at the time of separation that throws it into a state of hopelessness. Monkeys raised from birth in the presence of other infants their age (but without any mothers present) appear to grow up fairly normally. That is, they play more or less as do infants raised in "families," and their behavior patterns mature at about the same speed as one would normally expect. When these infants are isolated from their peers, however, they too fall into an anaclitic depression, just as if they had been separated from their mothers. When reunited with these peers, they engage in the same intense clinging as would an infant given back to its mother.

Taking a baby monkey away from its mother—or her surrogate—also appears to slow down the baby's maturational "clock." Infants separated from their peer-mother-substitutes simply did not develop behaviorally during this period of isolation. Rather, they were as infantile in their behavioral responses after a 6-month period of deprivation as they had been before being separated from their peers.

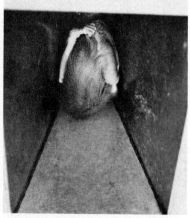

The immobilized posture of a monkey who has endured separation from its mother.

Solitary Confinement in Monkeys Psychologist S.J. Suomi, working with the Harlows, also studied the effects of complete social isolation on normal monkeys by placing them in a tiny, cramped solitary confinement cell for various periods of time. Suomi reports that many of these previously healthy animals fell into a profound depression; they also showed many of the huddling and self-clasping behaviors that monkeys raised from birth in complete social isolation did. Although the effects of this solitary confinement varied considerably from one monkey to another, most of the animals showed some disruption of their normal social responses and some evidence of being depressed. As we noted in Chapter 9, human beings placed in similar sensory-deprivation chambers, even for very brief periods, also suffered various types of psychological disturbances.

> QUESTION: Inmates in various mental hospitals and prisons who commit anti-social acts are still occasionally locked away in solitary confinement. Would you expect that social isolation would help solve these behavioral problems, or might it merely make the problems worse?

A monkey raised in *partial* social isolation never sees its own kind, but does have frequent contact with human beings. Having found that rearing their animals this way created problems when the monkeys grew up, the Harlows went a step further. With the help of several of their associates, they constructed total-isolation chambers in which the young animals never saw any other living creature (except the surrogate mother) for various lengths of time during the first year of their lives.

Newborn monkeys kept in total isolation for 90 days and then brought into the colony showed some disturbance, but soon caught up with their age-mates. After they had had a month or so to adjust to the presence of other animals, the 90-day isolates were for all measurable purposes quite normal.

Infant monkeys kept for 6 months in complete isolation were something else again. When allowed to interact with normal monkeys, the isolates refused to play. Rather, they tended to spend their time huddled in corners, rocking back and forth, hugging their arms and legs tightly to themselves. Even 8 months after the isolation had ended, the isolates seemed incapable of any sustained social interactions with normal animals.

A monkey reared alone exhibits disturbance activity.

QUESTION: Why do you think the adopted Korean orphans mentioned in the previous chapter recovered so well from their early deprivation, while the monkeys in Suomi's experiment didn't?

A few of the 6-month isolates were put together in pairs after their isolation had ended, presumably with the hope that one isolate might not frighten another as much as a normal monkey might. At first, this seemed to be the case, for the isolates did engage in limited forms of exploration and even play. However, when kept together for 3 years or so, the isolates showed deterioration—that is, the only behavior patterns that seemed to have matured were those involving fear and aggression. When brought into contact with normal monkeys, the isolate-pairs simply could not adjust. They spent most of their time frozen in fear, but occasionally they would go on a rampage and attack any animal handy. Some isolates vented their aggression against infants, a behavioral "sin" that normal monkeys never engaged in. A few of the isolates even exploded in rage against very large males, a reaction that Harlow rightly terms "suicidal."

The Harlows kept a few young animals in total isolation for one year, but soon terminated the experiment. For when these isolates were brought into the colony, they refused all forms of interaction, including aggression. When normal animals would playfully attack the isolates, they would not bother to defend themselves and were almost torn to pieces. It would seem, then, that the intensity of "playful" aggression in monkeys is controlled to some extent by counter-aggression; if the animal being attacked does not respond, the attacker may not discover what the limits of "acceptable" aggression should be.

QUESTION: In some parts of the world an upper-class child may aggress against a lower-class child—or a white may attack a black—without any fear of being hit in return. How might this state of affairs affect the upper-class (or white) perception of the value of life?

Mother-Infant Love

The Harlows were eventually able to find ways of getting female isolates pregnant, usually by confining them in a small cage for long periods of time with a patient and highly experienced normal male. At times, however, the Harlows were forced to help matters along by strapping the female to a piece of apparatus they affectionately call the "rape rack." When these isolated females gave birth to their first monkey baby, they turned out to be the "monster mothers" the Harlows had tried to create with mechanical surrogates. Having had no contact with other animals as they grew up, they simply did not know what to do with the furry little strangers that suddenly appeared on the scene. These motherless mothers at first totally ignored their children, although if the infant persisted, the mothers occasionally gave in and provided the baby with some of the contact and comfort it demanded.

Surprisingly enough, once these mothers learned how to handle a baby, they did reasonably well. Then, when they were again impregnated and gave birth to a second infant, they took care of this next baby fairly adequately.

Maternal affection was totally lacking in a few of the motherless monkeys, however. To them, the newborn monkey was little more than an object to be abused the way a human child might abuse a doll or a toy train. These motherless mothers stepped on their babies, crushed the infant's face into the floor of the cage, and once or twice chewed off their baby's feet and fingers before they could be stopped. The most terrible mother of all popped her infant's head into her mouth and crunched it like a potato chip.

We tend to think of most mothers—no matter what their species—as having some kind of almost-divine "maternal instinct" that makes them love their

When motherless infant monkeys themselves become mothers they ignore their babies.

children and take care of them no matter what the cost or circumstance. While it is true that most females have built into their genetic blueprint the *tendency* to be interested in (and to care for) their offspring, this inborn tendency is always expressed in a given environment. The "maternal instinct" is strongly influenced by the mother's past experiences. Humans seem to have weaker instincts of all kinds than do other animals—since our behavior patterns are more affected by learning than by our genes, we have greater flexibility in what we do and become. But we pay a sometimes severe price for this freedom from genetic control.

Normal monkey and chimpanzee mothers seldom appear to inflict real physical harm on their children; human mothers and fathers often do. Serapio R. Zalba, writing in a journal called *Trans-action*, estimated in 1971 that in the United States alone, perhaps 250,000 children suffer physical abuse by their parents each year. Of these "battered babies," almost 40,000 may be very badly injured. The number of young boys and girls killed by their parents annually is not known, but Zalba suggests that the figure may run into the thousands. Parents have locked their children in tiny cages, raised them in dark closets, burned them, boiled them, slashed them with knives, shot them, and broken almost every bone in their bodies. How can we reconcile these facts with the much-discussed maternal and paternal "instincts?"

The research by the Harlows on the motherless mothers perhaps gives us a clue. Mother monkeys who were themselves socially deprived or isolated when young seemed singularly lacking in affection for their infants. Zalba states that most of the abusive human parents that were studied turned out to have been abused and neglected *themselves* as children. Like the isolated monkeys who seemed unable to control their aggressive impulses when put in contact with normal animals, the abusive parents seem to be greatly deficient in what psychologists call "impulse control" (*see* Chapter 19). Most of these parents also were described as being socially isolated, as having troubles adjusting to marriage, often deeply in debt, and as being unable to build up warm and loving relationships with other people—including their own children. Since they did not learn how to love from their own parents, these mothers and fathers simply did not acquire the social skills necessary for bringing up their own infants in a healthy fashion.

Paternal Love

Human families differ from chimpanzee and monkey families in many complex ways, not the least of which is that the father of the children is typically present as well as the mother. In some homes, however, because of death, war, prison, divorce, or desertion, the father is absent. What effects might an absent father have on the behaviors of the children he left behind? During World War II, and subsequent international conflicts, many U.S. fathers were separated from their families for long periods of time. Research begun during the 1940's suggests that, upon their return, many fathers felt a strange sense of alienation or estrangement from their children. This feeling of paternal isolation was most often directed toward sons who had been unborn or else young at the time the father had left home. Many of the fathers regarded their young sons—who had been raised almost entirely by their mothers—as being over-protected "sissies."

Perhaps the fathers had objective reasons for their beliefs. For subsequent studies indicated that boys raised without fathers were less aggressive, more dependent, and had more "feminine" patterns of interests and play than did boys who were brought up in normal families. Although these effeminate behavior patterns did tend to decrease as the boys entered school and began to respond to social pressures outside the family circle, some of the boys developed rather extreme masculine behaviors as if to compensate for the loss of their fathers.

The earliest age at which most U.S. boys can tolerate separation from the father without ill effects seems to be 6 years. Apparently the presence of an adult male is necessary during the first 6 years of a boy's life so that he may learn the proper "masculine" traits encouraged by our present society.

QUESTION: If a widowed or divorced mother were aware of this problem, what might she do in order to compensate for the absence of her young son's father?

Father-Daughter Relationships   But it is not just the son who suffers when the father is gone. Research reported in 1973 suggests that young girls too need their fathers if they are to grow up in a fashion our culture views as being normal. University of Virginia psychologist E. Mavis Hetherington has made an extensive study of the effects of early paternal deprivation on the behaviors of adolescent girls. Hetherington and her colleagues observed the activities of three types of girls—those whose mothers had gotten divorces when the girls were very young, those whose fathers had died when the girls were very young, and those who had grown up in normal family situations. None of the girls had brothers. Although few of these young women had noticeable behavior problems, and all were doing at least reasonably well in school, there were marked differences in the way these adolescent girls reacted to the males in their environments.

According to Hetherington, girls from divorced families sought more attention and praise from males than did girls in the other two groups. They were also likely to spend much of their time hanging around places where young males could be found—gymnasiums, carpentry and machine shops, and the stag lines at community or school dances. In marked contrast, the girls with widowed mothers tended to avoid males as much as possible. These fatherless girls stayed away from typically male gathering places, some of them remaining in the ladies' room the entire evening during dances and other social events. Hetherington reports that these differences were not due to popularity; for instance, both groups of girls

E. Mavis Hetherington.

received equal numbers of invitations to dance when they were actually present in the dance hall.

Girls who came from broken homes were also much more likely to take a punitive view toward the behavior of others than were girls whose fathers had died—that is, girls with divorced parents advocated harsh treatment for prisoners; they favored restrictive laws governing the social behavior of their peers; and they took a highly favorable view toward the punishment of other people.

There were as well marked differences in the ways that the three groups of girls responded to interviews by adult males (although not in the way they responded to female interviewers). Girls raised by divorced mothers tended to sit close to and adopt an open, sometimes sprawling posture with male interviewers. The girls leaned forward more toward the man, looked more often into his eyes, and smiled more often than did girls in the other groups. In contrast, Hetherington reports that girls whose fathers had died sat at greater distances and turned their shoulders further away from male interviewers, smiled less often, and established less eye contact. Girls from normal homes were somewhere in between these two extremes.

All three groups of girls appeared to have similar and quite normal relationships with other girls and women, but not with men. Girls from homes broken by divorce dated earlier and more frequently than did the others, and were more likely to have engaged in sexual intercourse. By contrast, girls whose fathers had died tended to start dating much later than normal and seemed to be sexually inhibited.

Most of the differences in the girls' behavior patterns seem to be due to the ways they were raised by their mothers. According to Hetherington, the divorced mothers had negative attitudes toward their ex-husbands, themselves, and toward life in general. They stated that their lives and marriages had not been very happy and that they were concerned about their adequacy as mothers. However, they were all fond of their daughters and showed the same patterns of affection toward the girls as did mothers in the other groups. Both divorced and widowed mothers appeared to be over-protective of their daughters when compared to mothers in normal home-life situations. Divorced mothers revealed they had had considerable conflict with their husbands before separation and conflict with the daughters after the girls had reached adolescence. Widowed mothers reported little or no conflict either with their husbands before death or with their daughters at any time in the girls' lives. Hetherington states that girls apparently need the presence of an adult male during their formative years in order to learn appropriate responses to men when the girls reach puberty.

Love as an Interaction Pattern Unfortunately, we do not have very many good experiments in which the paternal-child relationship has been closely studied. So we do not really know what the critical elements of infant-father and father-infant love are. But based on their animal research, the Harlows note that the love an infant shows toward its mother, and the love she and other adults demonstrate toward the infant, are greatly dependent on one another. The infant is born with certain strong needs that are expressed in instinctual behavior patterns—the infant approaches and clings to warm, furry objects and flees from cold or punishing objects. The mother responds to these approaches by cuddling the infant and feeding it. This maternal "affection" or reward for approaching and clinging increases the likelihood that the infant will engage in these behaviors again; and the responsiveness of the infant makes it more likely the mother will react more positively and tolerantly toward the infant. Jane Goodall describes several cases of mother chimps whose babies died of disease shortly after the babies were born. An inexperienced mother might carry the dead infant around

Habituated (habb-BITT-you-ate-ted). To make a habit of; to become accustomed to.

with her for several days before abandoning it. An experienced mother would toss the lifeless baby away within hours after it had stopped responding to her. Apparently to live is to respond, and to respond is to go on living.

LOVE AND PSYCHO-THERAPY

The Harlows' work suggests that loving behavior is acquired. That is to say, love is a product of a complex set of interactions between genetic blueprint and environmental conditions. But in a sense, so is abusive and punishing behavior. When the Harlows' totally isolated monkeys were introduced into normal monkey groups, the isolates responded with fear and withdrawal, as we have seen; then when their terror of others had *habituated* (°) somewhat, the isolates reacted with hostility and aggression. The Harlows figured that even these isolates might learn to love, but how to go about training these apparently "mentally ill" animals to respond with monkey-approved behavior patterns? Who could act as a therapist for a socially withdrawn animal?

Because they reasoned that contact comfort was the key to turning an isolated monkey into a normal one, the Harlows selected as their "therapists" socially normal female monkey infants who were only 3 to 4 months old. The isolates were all males. The "therapists" had been raised by their natural mothers, and they remained with their mothers except during "therapy hours." Since these young females were all much smaller than the male isolates (who had all spent at least 6 months living with the terrycloth surrogates), the Harlows believed the babies would not threaten the isolates as much as would an adult animal—or a human. Then, too, persistence in therapy often yields rich rewards, and there are few things in life as persistent as a baby monkey in search of contact comfort.

So, the Harlows built a "mental hospital" in which they could control the interactions between the isolates and the baby-therapists. At the beginning, the babies were allowed contact with their "patients" for 2 hours a day. At their first meeting, the typical male isolate (who had not yet learned to be aggressive) retreated to a corner of its "hospital" cage, hugged himself, and rocked back and

A baby "therapist" comforts a monkey reared alone.

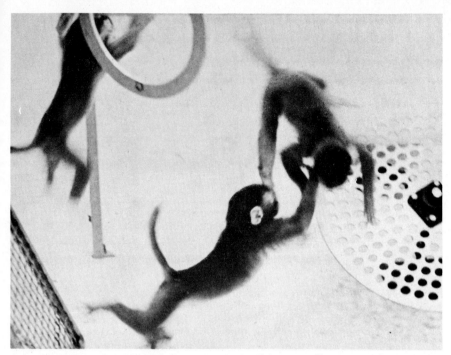

A monkey reared alone playing with a baby "therapist."

forth, doing his best to ignore the infant. The infant's response was to approach the isolate and try to cling to him. Although the isolate rejected the "therapist's" overtures again and again during the first day or so, gradually his fear of the tiny stranger *waned* (°). The isolate stopped retreating from the infant and soon let her satisfy her need for contact comfort by clinging to his body. Within a few days, the isolate was clinging to the infant with the same apparent pleasure that the infant derived. Within a few weeks the isolates and "therapists" were playing enthusiastically together. Gradually, over time, most of the isolates' abnormal behaviors disappeared. By the time therapy had continued for 6 months, the isolates appeared to have recovered completely from their initial period of social deprivation. At this point the isolates could be introduced into normal monkey groups and could make a successful adjustment.

The work of the Harlows and of Jane Goodall has taught us many things about love we never knew before. In our society we apparently presume that human maternal and paternal "instincts" are so strong that society itself does not have to worry about the rights of the child. Indeed, until fairly recently, children were considered to be the property of their parents, to be loved or beaten or even sold into slavery if the mother and father desired. For many years England had stringent laws against cruelty to animals, but no laws against cruelty to children. Because we have always assumed that punishment was one of the best ways to socialize children and teach them right from wrong, it was not until recently that we began to investigate closely those parents whose impulsive treatment of their children was abusive and dangerous. We were late to realize that, if these abused children managed to survive, grow up, and become parents themselves, they would very likely harm their own children as they had been harmed. Hopefully, as we learn more about the splendors of love, we will also discover better ways of training our human social isolates to establish loving relationships with their fellow men and women, young and old.

Waned (rhymes with "pained"). To decrease, or to grow smaller. During the 28-day lunar (LOO-nar) cycle, the moon first waxes (grows brighter) until, after the full moon, it wanes in brightness.

SUMMARY

1. Love is an emotion—an internal state or condition—that happens even to the best of us.
2. We cannot measure love directly because, like all emotions, love is an intrapsychic experience that takes place inside us. But we can measure loving behaviors and discuss them objectively.
3. From their studies of laboratory monkeys, Harry and Margaret Harlow identified five types of love:
   a. That of the infant for its mother.
   b. That of the mother for her infant.
   c. That of a young monkey for its peers.
   d. The sexual love of one adult for another.
   e. The paternal love of a father toward his children.
4. A newborn monkey clings to its mother because she gives it warmth, food, and contact comfort. Warmth is the most important input during the first two weeks of the monkey's life; thereafter, contact comfort, or "rubbability" is more important.
5. A young monkey will cling to any warm, "rubbable object" if deprived of its mother.
6. Contact with the mother (or her surrogate) appears to give the infant the trust that it needs to mature perceptually and emotionally. Deprived of this contact, the infant monkey falls into an anaclitic depression and may die.
7. If the infant grows up without having other young monkeys to play with, it never develops peer love and does not know how to respond in social situations.
8. Sexual love grows out of peer love. Young monkeys deprived of the pleasure of their peers do not mate in the usual fashion.
9. Human infants also become depressed when isolated from their mothers. In both humans and monkeys, the "maternal instinct" is greatly influenced by learning and early experience.
10. Female monkeys raised on surrogate mothers often treat their first infants cruelly. Women who were themselves neglected as children are more likely than usual to abuse or harm their own children.
11. Boys who grow up without fathers often show very "feminine" behavior patterns.
12. Girls who grow up without fathers may either be strongly attracted to adult males or tend to avoid them, depending in part on whether the girls' mothers were divorced or widowed.
13. Our early experiences strongly affect the types of loving behaviors we display as adults. Fortunately, with the right kind of training or therapy, both monkeys and humans can often overcome the many problems associated with growing up in poor social environments.

"You see, **Señores,** we do the best we can. But we have little money, and we have tradition to fight. So it is very difficult . . . ."

The Superintendent of the jail shrugged his shoulders with an eloquence that could come only from practice. He was showing his visitors—two women and one man—the jail's kitchen. A fat, contented-looking little child, perhaps a year old, waddled across the floor and sat down by its mother, who was shelling beans.

"Look at that poor child," one of the women said. "Just look at the dirt on its face! And the rags that it's wearing! Can't you at least provide the children with adequate clothing and keep them clean?"

Again the Superintendent shrugged. "**Señora,** we try. But the government does not give us money to buy clothes for the children. You see, they are not here officially. It is the mother who is in jail, not the child. But it is our custom not to separate the little ones from their mothers, and who am I to go against such tradition? The mothers would complain loudly if I did. And the fathers as well—if we knew who the fathers were!"

The fat little child got to its feet and started to walk again, but soon stumbled and fell to the floor. Almost before the first cry was out of its mouth, its mother had scooped it up and pressed it to her breast.

The visitor persisted. "But the dirt. At least you can do something about that!"

A smile crept across the Superintendent's dark, heavily wrinkled face. "Dirt? **Señora,** these women come from huts with dirt floors. They are not from what you would call the best classes of society. We merely keep them in jail; we are not equipped to teach them to be ladies!"

"But cleanliness is next to godliness!"

"**Señora,** the padre will tell you that even the godliness of some of these women is in rather grave doubt."

The child stopped its crying, but tears still ringed its eyes. The mother brushed the tears away with a dirty rag, then dangled a bunch of beans in front of the child's face, teasing it. The baby reached for the beans, but missed, so the mother continued the little game. On the second try, the child caught the beans and pulled them away from its mother. Both of them laughed.

"Just listen to them," one of the women visitors said, shaking her head in disgust.

"Yes, it's apparent that we must do something to save these children from such an unhealthy and unwholesome environment," said the male visitor. "We would be shirking our duty if we left these poor little babies to grow up in a jail!"

"What do you think would be best?"

The man thought for a moment or two. "Well, what do you think of building a nice, clean orphanage or hospital for them . . ."

RECOMMENDED READINGS

Goodall, Jane. *In the Shadow of Man* (New York: Dell Publishing Co., 1972).

Harlow, H.F., M.K. Harlow, and S.J. Suomi. "From Thought to Therapy: Lessons from a Primate Laboratory," *American Scientist*, vol. 59, no. 5 (September–October 1971), pp. 539–549.

Hebb, Donald O. *The Organization of Behavior* (New York: John Wiley & Sons, Inc., 1949).

Mussen, Paul Henry, John J. Conger, and Jerome Kagan. *Child Development and Personality*, 3rd ed. (New York: Harper & Row, 1969).

Tiger, Lionel, and Robin Fox. *The Imperial Animal* (New York: Holt, Rinehart and Winston, 1972).

21
"PLAY'S THE THING"

COGNITIVE AND EMOTIONAL DEVELOPMENT

DID YOU KNOW THAT . . .

Jean Piaget, perhaps the most respected child psychologist alive today, published his first scientific paper when he was 10?

According to Piaget, a child's mental development passes through four distinct stages or periods?

Piaget believes that the very young child often explains its world in illogical terms, such as "a balloon flies because it is red"?

Some psychologists believe that language arose in the human race only 70,000 years ago?

These same psychologists think that humans didn't give each other names until 10,000 years ago?

Children sometimes can learn abstract mathematical principles more quickly than can their parents?

Young children often play *near* each other before they learn how to play *with* each other?

"Rough-housing" may help children learn the limits of aggression?

Dolls were originally toys for adults only?

"Ring around the rosies" actually refers to the Black Death?

Many early theorists believed that a child would "explode" from surplus energy if it didn't release this energy in play?

Sigmund Freud believed that it was primarily sexual energy that a child released in fantasy and play?

The theories of Freud and Piaget are fairly apt descriptions of how middle-class European children develop, but they do not necessarily hold true for all cultures and societies?

Dear Diary:

Green. Somehow, I hadn't expected Africa to be so green. It's fairly warm for October, too, but not as hot as my old home town of Phoenix, Arizona, is this time of year. And much wetter, as the seat of my pants will testify. And unbelievable! Most unbelievable of all is the fact that I, Alicia Montez, am here in Africa, sitting on a pile of rocks in a clearing in the forest, looking down a long valley toward Lake Tanganyika. My feet hurt, and there are tsetse fly bites all over my arms that hurt like blazes. I've got a pair of binoculars hanging around my neck, my lunch in a bag, my hair tied up on top of my head, a pad of notepaper, and a ballpoint pen. I itch all over, and I didn't get much sleep last night. I should be miserable, but I'm not. I've never been happier in my whole life. And do you want to know why? Because I'm watching a bunch of chimpanzees fish for termites, that's why.

I suppose it all started with Uncle Luis. He's the intellectual in our family, proof of which is that he teaches at Arizona State. For my birthday in 1973 he gave me a copy of Jane Goodall's book **In the Shadow of Man.** What a woman!

Way back years ago, when she was about my age, she came here to the Gombe Stream Chimpanzee Reserve and began watching chimps. Everybody thought she was crazy. What would a nice British girl like her want to hide away in the African bush for, taking notes on what chimpanzees do and don't do? Well, it got her a doctorate at Cambridge University, for one thing. For another, it prompted her to open the Gombe Stream Research Centre, where I am spending a few months as one of the many students studying animal behavior "in the raw." And raw it can sometimes be. Four of the students got kidnaped by African natives for political reasons in 1975, but they all got back safely, so no harm done. We haven't had too much trouble since then.

Well, as I was saying, it was Uncle Luis who put the idea of Africa into my mind. I read Dr. Jane's book and swore a vow right then and there, that as soon as I finished college, I'd come to Gombe and follow in her footsteps. Like Dr. Jane, I have always been interested in what makes animals tick. She says that when she was 1 year old, her mother gave her a chimpanzee doll. Maybe that's what led to her coming here to watch the chimps for the past 15 years or so.

I didn't have many dolls because our ranch had so many real animals on it. But even when I was 5, I used to sneak out to the horse stables to watch the mares give birth to foals. Aunt Dolores was furious with me, but then, she almost always was. I used to love to watch the foals get up and move around right after their mothers had licked them clean of the placenta and afterbirth. And now I love watching the baby chimpanzees snuggle up to their mothers, nurse at their breasts, then jump down and run and play with all their friends. They look so human!

Of course, they're not human at all. But, as Dr. Jane says, they're supposed to be we humans' "closest living relative," and we can learn a lot about how we might have been in the past by watching how chimps behave. Even if we couldn't discover anything new about ourselves, I'd be happy just to learn about chimps. Now, there's something that Aunt Dolores would never understand!

Anyway, I've been here several weeks, and by now most of the chimpanzees have become accustomed to me and pretty well ignore me if I sit still and don't come too close to them. My favorite is a female named Nancy who has two children with her now, a year-old infant named Kevin and a 6-year-old daughter we call Evva. Kevin is a cute little thing who rides around on Nancy's back the way some cowboys try to ride a horse. Evva trails behind, keeping up with Nancy and her infant rider as best she can.

My next most favorite is Gunner, a splendid male we think is Nancy's child. He pals around with Greg, an adolescent male about 14 who may also be a child of Nancy's. It's hard to find out who's related to whom, because chimpanzees don't answer questionnaires very well, and their family units consist of the mother and her young children. Who the papa is no one knows—or cares, I guess.

This time of year there isn't much around for the chimps to eat, so they "fish" for termites. In this part of the world, the termites build huge underground nests, with millions of these ant-like insects living together in the tunnels they've dug under the earth. They pile all the extra dirt up on top of their nests in huge mounds baked hard by the summer sun. But when the rains come, in October, the termite workers begin digging passageways to the surface. From time to time large groups of insects congregate in these tunnels, until the instinctual mating urge strikes them. Then they swarm up to the surface and fly off into the sunset, to establish another termite nest somewhere else—the mating game.

To catch termites, the chimps find a long twig, or maybe the stalk of a grass shoot, and they stick it into the termite mound and fish around. If they're lucky, a couple of insects will grab hold of the end of the stick and hang on. Then, when the chimp pulls the twig out, there's a meal of fat termites just waiting. Succulent! Dr. Jane calls this a beautiful example of tool-making among chimpanzees, for the animals actually strip the leaves off the long twigs to "shape" them into being better fishing poles.

So all morning long I've been watching Nancy and her family and several other chimps fill their bellies. Actually, there are so many young chimps here

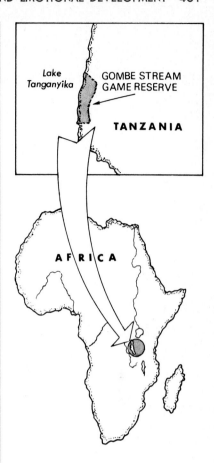

Lake Tanganyika

GOMBE STREAM GAME RESERVE

TANZANIA

AFRICA

today that it's almost like visitor's day at the South Phoenix Nursery School. I recognize big Marlys and her children, Mugwump and Van, but I don't know all the others. The adults, both males and females, have great patience, both with the termites and with the youngsters. The older infants, such as Nancy's daughter Evva, fish for a while and then play for a while.

Watching Mugwump is the most fun of all. He's a healthy, hearty little boy of 3 going on 4. Marlys is weaning him now, so he actually eats a termite or two if he can catch one. He doesn't quite have the hang of it yet, though. He sits beside Marlys for a while, picks up a tiny twig and tries to imitate her. But where Marlys uses a grass stalk that's 8 to 10 inches (20–25 centimeters) long, little Mugwump chooses a twig that's only 2 or 3 inches (5 or 7.3 centimeters) long. And instead of ''fishing'' by sticking the twig deep into the mound, Mugwump tears up the earth. Apparently you have to leave the stick down in the mound for a minute or two to let the termites grab hold. Mugwump seldom can sit still for more than a few seconds. The only termite I've seen him catch grabbed hold of one of his fingers instead of the stick. I think it bit him. He licked it off his finger and ate it, but he whimpered while he was doing so and immediately snuggled close to Marlys for comfort.

Energy. Mugwump's certainly got a lot of it. In fact, it wears me out just watching him dash about. Shortly after the termite bit him, he started running around like crazy, making mock attacks at Kevin, Evva, and a couple of other chimps about his own size. Nancy was too far away, so Kevin clung to Evva for comfort. After some 10 minutes of intensive rough-housing, Mugwump's antics annoyed a large male, who barked at him sharply. Mugwump got the message and ran to Momma, who was still fishing. He sat quietly for a minute or two, turning a stick over and over in his fingers, inspecting it carefully. Then he dipped it in the earth and turned up some dirt. No termites. So he got up and started playing again, round and round and round.

And what did I do when I was 4? Play with dolls, have a tea party with my friends, play house, look at a picture book, go swimming, ride a pony, dig in the garden, romp with my puppy, run from my big brother, look at the clouds, sing songs with Uncle Luis and Aunt Dolores, go to nursery school, color pictures, listen to records, go for rides in the car, watch television, push toy trucks around, climb trees, hide in empty boxes, chase birds and rabbits, blow soap bubbles.

Child's play. But where does all the energy come from?

(Continued on page 483.)

In the past two chapters, we have discussed both the biological and social development of infants. But children have minds as well as bodies and behaviors. Watching the intellectual and emotional development of a growing child can be at least as fascinating as observing the age at which an infant walks and the social responses it makes to its parents and peers.

There are many intra-psychic theories that attempt to explain how a child's mental functioning increases and expands during its younger years. Perhaps the best-known positions are those of Jean Piaget and Sigmund Freud. Piaget is Swiss; his main interest has been in describing the *cognitive* (°) development of children—that is, how they come to *think* the way that they do. Freud was born in Slovakia but grew up in Vienna, Austria. One of Freud's contributions to psychology was his description of the emotional development of the child. Thus, Freud and Piaget offer *complementary* (°) rather than conflicting theories of the intra-psychic growth of young people.

Both Piaget and Freud believed that the child's intellectual/emotional development passes through several distinctive stages or periods. The speed at which the child progresses up the maturational ladder may vary considerably from one individual to another. But the order of the steps is supposed to be the same in all children—because this order (theoretically) is determined entirely by the child's

Cognitive (KOG-nu-tive). Intellectual, as opposed to emotional. Thoughts, as opposed to feelings. Thinking is a cognitive process.

Complementary (com-plee-MEN-tair-ree). From the Latin word meaning "to complete," "to make up what is missing." When mixed together, complementary colors, such as blue and yellow, yield a neutral color, such as gray or white. Blue, then, has what yellow needs in order to complete itself. The theories of Freud and Piaget (PEE-ah-jay) add to each other rather than being in conflict.

genes. Since children all over the world presumably have very similar genetic blueprints, Freud and Piaget assumed that all children should mature in much the same way. Whether this assumption is correct or not remains to be seen.

In order to let you discover both the strengths and weaknesses of these two theories, we will present the viewpoints of both men and then mention some of the criticisms that others have made about the theories. As you go through the chapter, you might try to remember your own early life and attempt to describe your own intellectual and emotional development in Freudian or Piagetian terms. If you make this effort, you might learn firsthand why our scientific attempts at understanding the ways in which children think and feel are anything but "child's play."

Jean Piaget.

JEAN PIAGET

One of the most respected figures in child psychology today is Jean Piaget, a professor at the University of Geneva and director of the Rousseau Institute. Trained as a zoologist, Piaget began publishing his scientific observations at the ripe old age of 10. His search for a "theory of knowledge" led him to study the intellectual development of children. He believes that the ability to think logically is genetically determined, and that logical thinking is the trait that helps make humans different from lower animals. To Piaget, intelligence is defined as an individual's ability to adapt to, and cope with, whatever environment the individual lives in.

Assimilation and Accommodation

Most of Piaget's theoretical analogies have a strongly biological ring to them. He states that there are two fundamental processes that are basic to human development: *assimilation* (°) and *accommodation* (°).

There are three types of assimilation—biological, mental, and social. Biological assimilation, at its simplest, involves taking food into the body and converting or rearranging its chemical structure by digestion. Mental assimilation involves taking in data or information about the world and "digesting" it so that it makes sense to us perceptually. Social assimilation occurs when we learn the rules and regulations of society and then work out our own moral or behavioral standards. Assimilation thus involves fitting the outside world to our inside or internal needs.

There are also three types of accommodation. Physical accommodation at its most elementary concerns postural changes—we duck our heads to walk under the branch of a tree, or we open our mouths wider when eating a double-decker sandwich. Mental accommodation refers to any intellectual adjustment an organism must make in order to assimilate or "digest" information. Social accommodation has to do with our "yielding" to the pressures that our families and friends put on us to conform to group standards or norms. Accommodation thus involves changing our response outputs to fit the realities of the external environment.

According to Piaget, mental growth comes about through the continuous active interplay of assimilation and accommodation. The danger comes when one type of behavior predominates over the other. If accommodation prevails, and the child passively adjusts to its surroundings, the child will engage in mere imitation and will usually accept the world as it is viewed by its parents and peers. If the parents are authoritarian, the child will try to live by authoritarian rules and regulations whether or not these rules really "work." On the other hand, if assimilation prevails—if the child tries to make its perceptions suit its needs rather than adjusting its *percepts* (°) to reality—then the child will engage primarily in fantasy and play. If assimilation goes too far, the child may end up living in a fantasy world—or a mental hospital.

Assimilation (ass-simm-uh-LAY-shun). The Latin word *assimilare* means "to make similar." When we assimilate something, we make it similar to us, or rearrange it so that it suits our needs.

Accommodation (ack-komm-oh-DAY-sun). From the Latin word meaning "to adapt." People who accommodate us are people who try to satisfy our needs or adjust to our desires. A large hotel offers accommodations for hundreds of people when it rents them rooms or sells them food.

Percept (PER-sept). The end product of the process of perception. Anything that you recognize, or understand, or something whose future behavior you can predict. See Chapter 10.

Jargon (JAR-gun). Each group of specialists has its own set of technical terms or "shop talk" that group members frequently use among themselves. This special vocabulary (not usually understood by outsiders) is called "jargon." As you read this book, you probably are adding a lot of psychological jargon to your own vocabulary. Amusingly enough, the word "jargon" comes from an old French term meaning "the twittering of birds."

Feed forward. A statement or input describing a desired end state or terminal behavior (output). When you turn up the thermostat on the wall because you are cold, you are feeding forward a goal that you hope the furnace will soon reach. Feed forward usually refers to an input that tells a complex system (such as a computer or a human being) what kind of program it should follow to achieve a certain consequence or output.

Feedback. Information about performance; inputs that tell a system how close it is coming to the desired output. When you turn up the wall thermostat (feed forward), the furnace comes on and heat pours into the room. A thermometer feeds back to the thermostat information on how the furnace is performing. When feedback matches feed forward, the proper temperature has been reached and the thermostat turns off the furnace.

Commodities (koh-MOD-oh-tease, or koh-MOD-uh-tease). From the Latin word meaning "convenient" or "useful." A commodity is anything movable that has economic value. The word "accommodate" comes from the same Latin source and means "to make useful" or "to make something fit."

To Piaget, both assimilative play and accommodative imitation are necessary to a child's intellectual development—which is to say that the two processes should be in balance. And because assimilation and accommodation are determined by our genetic blueprints, they are presumed by Piaget to mature in much the same way in all of us.

Feed Foward and Feedback

Perhaps because Piaget writes in French, the translations of his highly technical concepts are not always easy for English readers to understand. If we were to rephrase his terms in current psychological *jargon* (°), we might say that assimilation and accommodation are two somewhat different ways in which we learn to adjust to our environments. That is, assimilation and accommodation are processes by which we may change our mental and behavioral outputs in order that we may predict and control our inputs.

In general, there are but two ways to change the performance (perceptions and responses) of a complex living system such as a human being. These two ways are *feed forward* (°) and *feedback* (°).

By the term "feed forward," we mean the setting of goals or expectations or desired end states (terminal responses). We all have goals. Some of your own goals are innately determined for you—your body is so built that it will struggle to get food, water, air, sleep, stimulation, sexual release, and all those other *commodities* (°) necessary to life and the continuation of the human race. Your genes, as Piaget noted, thus provide you with a very important type of biological feed forward.

But you also learn by watching and listening to other people. When you hear a new song on the radio, probably you can hum parts of it after just one hearing. When see a couple doing a new dance step, you can often "learn" the step just by observing. If your Spanish teacher pronounces a difficult word for you, your vocal cords can often imitate immediately the model given you by your teacher. Even a baby rat will learn to press a bar to get food faster if it has first seen its mother do the same thing. Whenever you learn by imitation, or by "modeling" your thoughts, emotions, attitudes, or behaviors after those of someone else, you are making use of feed forward.

Groups, organizations, and societies usually have sets of rules or regulations that all members of these complex systems are expected to obey. Laws are a good example of "social feed forward," for our legal system specifies many of the behavioral outputs that you are expected to produce during your lifetime. You must pay taxes, you must not exceed the speed limit, you must get good grades to stay in college, you must not assault or injure others. Although most of us try to maximize our own personal freedoms—and sometimes get annoyed when society places limits on what we can or cannot do—the truth is that we would be pretty hard up if we had no guidelines at all in life.

When Piaget talks about accommodation, he typically refers to some kind of feed forward that is accepted uncritically by the growing child. This feed forward may be at the biological, cognitive, or social/behavioral level—or it may be at all three levels at once.

Surely you would admit that if you want to change the outputs of any system (including your own ideas and actions), one of the first things you must do is to specify a new goal (output) of some kind. And to a great extent, our goal-setting is influenced by other people (including the genes that we inherited from our parents). But feed forward alone is usually not enough to alter the outputs of a living system such as yourself. The proper feedback is just as important. Feedback gives you information on how you are performing, or how close you are coming to achieving your goals. Blind children have problems learning to bowl because they can't see where the ball goes when they throw it; deaf individuals have difficulties learning to speak, in part because they can't hear the sound of their own voices. You might experience considerable trouble working problems in advanced mathematics if you had no way at all of determining whether your answers were correct or not. And you might not want to learn math anyhow if no one ever patted you on the back and told you that you were doing well, or if you had no way of knowing whether math would be of any use to you in your later or present life.

When Piaget speaks of assimilation, he usually has reference to situations in which the child makes use of feedback to check out the accuracy of its percepts of the world around it. Again, this feedback may be biological, cognitive, or social/behavioral.

Both feed forward and feedback are necessary for the best possible control and prediction of our inputs. If we place too much emphasis on feed forward (or accommodation), then we try to run our lives by a rigid set of rules and cultural expectations—whether or not these rules help us to survive in a changing world. If we have no models at all to follow, or if we listen to our own desires and pay no attention to the desires and goals of others, we may grow up with a host of inappropriate behaviors that will alienate us from our families and friends. As Piaget wisely noted, accommodation (or feed forward) and assimilation (or feedback) must be in balance if we are to succeed in life.

Piaget's Four Developmental Stages

According to Piaget, there are four major stages of intellectual development—the sensory-motor period, the pre-operational stage, the stage of concrete operations, and the stage of formal operations. Each of us goes from one stage upward to the next at slightly different ages, but the *average* age of attaining a given maturational level might well be expected to be roughly similar from one culture to the next.

Sensory-Motor Period   The first of Piaget's four stages is called the *sensory-motor period* (°), which begins at birth and usually ends when the infant is 18 to 24 months old. It is during this time that the infant learns to control its own bodily movements. The child also learns to integrate its various sense impressions into percepts (*see* Chapter 10). At birth, as William James said, the child's world is a blooming, buzzing confusion, for the infant has no way of coordinating its mother's voice with the sight of her face, the touch of her hands, the smell of her body. The infant responds to each type of sensory input differently; only during the last part of the sensory-motor period can it pull all of these sensations together to make the percept *mother*.

During the first few months of its life, the infant has no idea of *object permanency*, according to Piaget. A 6-month-old child will typically follow an object with its eyes as the object moves across its field of vision. But if the object disappears, the infant shows no disappointment, nor does the child appear to anticipate the object's reappearance. Playing "peek-a-boo" with a child this young is often a frustrating task because the infant seems not to realize what the game is about. When the child reaches 9 months of age (on the average), it will reach for an object hidden from its view provided that the infant has seen the object being hidden. Peek-a-boo becomes a fun game. By the time the child is 18 months of age or so, it will search for something it hasn't seen hidden—an indication, according to Piaget, that the child now realizes that an object can exist independent of the child's own involvement with the object.

Stated in more modern terms, the sensory-motor stage is that period during which the child learns to control its own muscular responses and how to make simple, non-verbal predictions about the movement of objects in its life space. It

Sensory-motor period. The first of Piaget's developmental stages, during which the infant tries to correlate its sensory inputs with its motor outputs.

Children develop best in a stimulating environment.

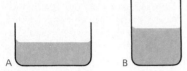

Conservation of quantity according to Piaget.

Pre-operational stage. The second of Piaget's developmental stages, during which a child learns to speak and to manipulate its world symbolically.

Symbols (SIM-bulls). From the Greek word meaning "tokens" or "signs." Something that stands for or suggests something else. The cross is the symbol of Christianity. A noun is a symbol of the object it represents.

Transformations (trans-for-MAY-shuns). From a Latin term that means "to change completely in structure." In fairy tales, for instance, the beautiful princess sometimes transforms an ugly frog into a handsome prince by kissing the frog. If the magic kiss doesn't work, the look of eager anticipation on the princess' face is presumably transformed into a frown.

Conservation of quantity. When you pour water from a tall, thin glass into a short, wide glass you transform the shape of the water—but the quantity remains the same. In short, the shape is changed, but the quantity is conserved. Piaget believes that a child must reach a certain maturational stage to be able to "conserve" such physical things as quantity, length, and weight.

Stage of concrete operations. The third of Piaget's developmental stages, during which the child begins to visualize series of operations independent of its own actions.

Conservation of length according to Piaget.

also begins to learn how to delay gratification of some of its minor, immediate needs in order to gain larger rewards in the future.

Pre-operational Stage   During the sensory-motor period, the infant responds directly to its environment. But with the acquisition of language, the child passes to the second, or *pre-operational, stage* (°) of development. Now the child can begin to deal with its world symbolically, by talking about objects instead of having to manipulate them directly. Piaget believes that language allows the child to think of past events and hence to anticipate their happening again. That is, language gives the child a great boost in its ability to predict and control its inputs. However, not until the child is 4 or 5 years of age does Piaget believe it can deal successfully with abstractions—such as love and hate, up and down, large and small. The child can think—it can predict in simple terms—but it cannot reason. Reasoning, to Piaget, means the mental manipulation of *symbols* (°). The child explains its world in concrete and often illogical terms—a balloon flies because it is red and has a string hanging from it.

During the pre-operational stage, which lasts from about 2 until 6 years, the child perceives itself as being at the center of the universe. In this comfortable position the child is presumably unable to see the world from any viewpoint but its own. When the child closes its eyes, it cannot see its mother; therefore, it reasons, when its eyes are closed she cannot see it either. The 4-year-old may realize that it has exactly one brother and one sister, but you cannot convince it that its parents have three children.

To Piaget, the main psychological characteristic of the pre-operational stage is the child's inability to visualize operations, or *transformations* (°). The classic example Piaget offers is this—if you fill two identical, tall thin glasses with water and set them in front of the child, it will agree that both glasses have the same amount of liquid in them. Now suppose you empty one tall glass into a short, wide glass that holds the same amount. To an adult it is obvious that the fat glass holds the same quantity of water as does the tall thin glass; but to a 4-year-old, the tall glass now seems to have more liquid in it. Although the child watched the operation of pouring water from one glass to the other, it lacks the mental ability Piaget calls *conservation of quantity* (°)—that is, the abstract notion that the quantity or volume of an object does not change depending on what container you put it in.

The pre-operational child is also unable to *conserve length.* If you lay two sticks of equal length before the child, it will agree they are the same. If you now move one stick forward a bit, the pre-operation child will insist that the stick you moved is now longer than the other. In all these cases, the problem seems to be that the child is unable to realize that objects do not change their physical properties merely because the child's *perception* of the object may change slightly.

Stated in more familiar terms, Piaget's pre-operational stage is that period during which the child gains greater control over its muscular responses, and discovers how to give simple stimulus-response verbal explanations for the behavior of objects and other people.

QUESTION: **Piaget seems never to have used shaping techniques to teach a child to conserve quantity. How might you go about using successive approximations of pouring just a little bit of water back and forth from tall to fat glasses to see if children could be taught conservation of quantity at a young age?**

Stage of Concrete Operations   By the time a child reaches the age of 6 or 7, it typically enters into what Piaget calls the third stage, *the stage of concrete operations* (°). Now it can conserve both length and quantity, but usually cannot handle the concept of weight until it 9th or 10th year. If you place two identical rubber balls in front of a young child, it will assure you that they both weigh the same. But if you now cut one ball in pieces, the child may announce that the cut-up pieces don't weigh the same as does the intact ball. Once the child attains the concept of weight, it realizes that the whole is equal to the sum of its parts.

The concept of *number* is another step the child usually takes during the stage of concrete operations. Suppose you lay out 10 pennies in two rows on a table, and show them to a child still at the pre-operational stage.

0 0 0 0 0

0 0 0 0 0

The child will see at once that the two rows are identical and that they both contain the same number of pennies. But now suppose you widen the spaces between the pennies in one row:

0 0 0 0 0

0   0   0   0   0

The pre-operational child will now see the second row as containing more pennies, despite the fact that the child can count the coins in each row with no difficulty. Piaget emphasizes that *counting* is not the same thing as the *concept of number*, which a child usually attains only during the stage of concrete operations.

It is during this latter stage of its intellectual development that the child begins to *visualize* a series of operations. A 5-year-old child can walk to school without getting lost—that is, the young person can perform a series of complex operations without making mistakes. But it is usually after age 6 that the child gains the ability to draw a map showing the route it takes from home to school, and it is only then that the young person realizes that anyone else could follow the map as well.

Prior to the stage of concrete operations, the child sees the world as an extension of its own *ego* (°) or personality. Now the child begins to differentiate between its inner self and the outer world. It realizes that the sun does not shine just for its own pleasure, but rather must shine on everyone else as well. It comes to see that if it has an older brother, that brother must logically have a younger sibling (brother or sister)—namely, itself. Only when the child gives up its *egocentric* (°) (self-centered) view of the world can it learn the meaning of true cooperation, which to Piaget involves the ability to see things through other people's eyes.

Put another way, Piaget's stage of concrete operations is that period in which the child learns the *rudiments* (°) of mental role-playing. That is, the child learns—through the use of language—to predict some of the complex reactions that other individuals have be trying to think and feel the way that they do. As its predictions become better, the child gains the ability to influence the responses of others and hence better control the various types of social inputs it receives.

Stage of Formal Operations   The last of Piaget's four periods of intellectual development is called the *stage of formal operations* (°), which should be attained at about age 12. Prior to this age, children are presumed to be limited to thinking in concrete, or non-symbolic, terms. Only in the final, mature stage can the young person think in completely abstract terms. At this level of development, the adolescent can solve problems in his or her mind by isolating the important variables and manipulating them mentally or perceptually. Now at last the adolescent is able to draw meaningful conclusions from purely abstract or hypothetical data. The young person no longer tries to conquer the world by

Ego (EE-go). From the Latin word meaning "I." The self, or the conscious parts of the personality.

Egocentric (EE-go-sen-trick). Selfish. Seeing the world entirely from a self-centered viewpoint.

Rudiments (ROO-duh-ments). From the Latin word meaning "beginning," or "first attempt." The rudiments are the fundamental skills necessary to perform a given act.

Stage of formal operations. The final stage of intellectual development, which is reached about the age of 12. According to Piaget, it is at this stage that the child can handle such abstract concepts as truth, honor, and personality.

Noam Chomsky.

Grammar. From the Latin word meaning "a piece of writing." Grammar is the study of the parts of a language, of words and how they relate to each other.

assimilating it, by trying to force the environment to fit its own perceptions; now it realizes that it must also accommodate or adjust to the world if it is to survive, and it can handle many of these accommodations in its own mind.

Stated in our own terms, it is during the stage of formal operations that the child gains enough experience and language ability to be able to create a personal "theory of knowledge." In the stage of concrete operations, it can predict what its mother will do; at the stage of formal operations, it can see that mothers are a class of people who share certain attributes or respond in similar ways. Therefore, the child can anticipate how most mothers will react in some situations. Piaget might say that motherhood is an abstraction or symbol that stands for a certain class of responses, and that the child can now reason using this abstract concept rather than relying on the reactions of one member of the class—its own mother.

Piaget is most interested in the development of reasoning, a skill that almost always involves the creative use of language. Before we comment further on Piaget's theory, then, let us take a brief look at how the art of communicating verbally is acquired.

LANGUAGE DEVELOPMENT

During the first year or so of its life, a child communicates its wants primarily by means of crying, laughing, gurgling, and by various bodily gestures. An attentive parent can soon tell what kind of cry means the child is hungry, and what kind of wail means that a pin is sticking the infant somewhere. By the time the child is 3 or 4 months old, it begins babbling to itself in what might be called "baby talk." That is, it makes sounds such as "ma," "mu," "da," and "na." Usually by its 6th month, the infant can repeat these sounds over and over again: "dadadadad." Almost all children in almost all cultures produce these sounds, so we may assume that the production of "baby talk" is part of the human genetic blueprint. It is then up to the infant's parents to "shape" these instinctive vocal responses into whatever language the child must learn; parents typically do so through modeling and reinforcement (feed forward and feedback).

But is the production of these babbling sounds the only part of the language function that is inherited? No, says MIT scientist Noam Chomsky, the basic *grammar* (°) underlying all language is built into our brains. We speak because some part of our central nervous system "maps" or translates our mental experiences into a grammar of some kind. According to Chomsky, it is this innate "mapping" ability that elevates humans above all other animals, for it gives humans the power to think in abstractions that other animals cannot approximate.

There is some evidence that Chomsky's views may have considerable truth to them. To begin with, as we saw in Chapter 2, neural control of speech is usually located in just one of the two cerebral hemispheres. And, in fact, the "speech center" in the left hemisphere is physically a little larger than the same area in the right hemisphere of most humans. This size difference between the hemispheres exists to a much lesser extent in the higher primates, but not at all in lower animals. It is likewise true that the kind of "dominant hemisphere" found in humans is not present in the lower primates and simpler organisms. Furthermore, the vocalizations made by monkeys and chimpanzees seem to be primarily under the control of centers in the limbic system, or emotional brain (*see* Chapter 4). Electrical stimulation of the limbic system can call forth all of the vocal responses that monkeys are capable of making (Table 21.1). As we saw earlier, destruction of the "cortical speech center" in humans typically leaves them speechless; destruction of similar areas of the monkey cortex does not affect the animal's vocalizations at all.

It would appear, then, that human brains are uniquely fitted for learning to speak. And it may be that only in the human brain has the control of vocalization

TABLE 21.1 Rhesus Calls[a]

Roar	Long, fairly loud noise	Made by a very confident animal when threatening another of inferior rank
Pant-threat	Like a roar, but divided into "syllables"	Made by a less confident animal who wants support in making an attack
Bark	Like the single bark of a dog	Made by a threatening animal who is insufficiently aggressive to move forward
Growl	Like a bark, but quieter, shriller, and broken in short sound units	Given by a mildly alarmed animal
Shrill-bark	Not described	Alarm call, probably given to predators in the wild
Screech	An abrupt pitch change; up then down	Made when threatening a higher-ranked animal, and when excited and slightly alarmed
Geekering screech	Like a screech, but broken into syllables	Made when threatened by another animal
Scream	Shorter than the screech and without a rise and fall	Made when losing a fight while being bitten
Squeak	Short, very high pitched noises	Made by a defeated and exhausted animal at the end of a fight

[a]Adapted from figure 2, Rowell, T.E. Agonistic noises of the Rhesus monkey (*Macaca mulatta*). *Symp. Zool. Soc. Lond.* No. 8 (1962): 91–96 by permission of the Zoological Society of London.

been transferred from the instinctive, emotional centers in the limbic system to the cortex, where voluntary actions are possible.

However, it remains true that children must learn to speak a particular language—otherwise we would all have a common tongue instead of the thousands of languages and *dialects* (°) that presently exist on earth. If Noam Chomsky's theories are right, then there must be some specific property of speech that is inherited, not learned—some part of the grammar of each language that is similar to the grammar of every other language or dialect. Unfortunately, to date no one has identified what this specific property might be.

Princeton psychologist Julian Jaynes takes rather a different view of language than does Chomsky. Jaynes holds that the human brain did not evolve sufficiently for speech to occur until a few hundred thousand years ago, and that the *need* for speech probably didn't occur until about 70,000 years ago when the last Ice Age began. Up until then, Jaynes says, humans got along very well with grunts and groans—the kinds of signals that chimpanzees give to each other. Simple hunting skills were easily learned by imitation (accommodation), just as it is possible to learn how to ride a bicycle or to "fish" for termites by watching someone else. As the ice came down from the poles some 70,000 years ago, however, humans were forced to move toward the tropics, to face difficult new challenges, and to get along with each other in ways seldom before necessary. Animal-like noises and visual signals just weren't complicated enough to ensure survival, Jaynes believes, and so the beginnings of our many modern languages came into being as people had more and more complex ideas to communicate with each other.

And as language evolved, so did society. Jaynes thinks that the first real words spoken were simple modifications of almost instinctual cries. Rather than just screaming "Danger" if a tiger approached, people began crying "Danger—near" and "Danger—far away"; or perhaps "Danger—big" and "Danger—small." Later, about the time that anthropologists tell us early humans began making

Dialects (DIE-uh-lecks). A dialect is a local or regional form of a language.

Julian Jaynes.

Linguistic (lin-GWISS-tick). From the Latin word meaning "tongue" or "language." Having to do with the study of language or the ability to speak or use a language.

Stage of inactive representation. Jerome Bruner (BREW-nurr) believes that children represent reality either by doing or by thinking about it. Young children, in the stage of inactive representation, "do." Older children, in the stage of representation through imagery, are capable both of "doing" things to and of "thinking" about the world around them.

drawings on the walls of their caves, people might have begun assigning names to animals. Thus "Danger" would become "Tiger" and "Snake" and "Elephant." Names for non-living things perhaps appeared a little later on, about the time that humans began making pots and ornaments. Names for people came next, Jaynes believes—about 10,000 years ago, when ceremonial graves first appeared. Individual names allowed humans to think and talk about each other, even when the named person was dead or no longer present. Such "person-thinking" might have led to much more intense personal relations, including elaborate burial practices and mourning.

QUESTION: **Your brain is so built, as we pointed out in Chapter 17, that you remember things best when you can describe them in terms of complex categories. How might this fact help explain the tremendous survival value that language seems to have given the human race?**

According to Jaynes, language developed because people had both the innate need and the innate ability to learn to predict and control their various inputs. Language both lets us store feed forward in a convenient form and helps us remember how to reproduce certain desired biological, cognitive, and social/behavioral feedbacks. The actual grammar of the language that we use would then be a matter of happenstance or accident—a viewpoint that Chomsky would surely dispute.

At the opposite end of the theoretical spectrum from Chomsky is B.F. Skinner, who holds that verbal behavior is (for all practical purposes) entirely learned. Skinner and Chomsky have had many public arguments about the matter. Like most such nature-nurture controversies, the Skinner-Chomsky verbal battles have led to a lot of ill will and very little new understanding of the basic issues involved. For as Jaynes (and so many other scientists) noted, there is probably little that we do that is either entirely "nature" or entirely "nurture." Thus the problem for behavioral scientists remains that of making a careful study of how our inherited *linguistic* (°) tendencies are shaped and developed by the environments in which these tendencies are expressed.

An understanding of language development is crucial to an appreciation of the strengths and weaknesses of Piaget's theory. As we pointed out in Chapter 2, thinking is to a great extent a matter of talking silently to yourself, and you cannot handle the "linear logic" that underlies most languages unless you have an intact "speech center" in your dominant hemisphere. Thus the *reasoning* that Piaget has studied so extensively in children depends in no small part on the verbal skills that the youngsters possess. Now that we have looked very briefly at language development, perhaps we can return to Piaget and his critics with a greater understanding of what their arguments are all about.

Piaget and His Critics

Piaget's theory, in one form or another, is similar to that held by many child psychologists. Harvard Professor Jerome Bruner describes the intellectual development of the child in terms of the ways children can represent reality at various times in their lifespan. Bruner appears to lump together Piaget's sensory-motor and pre-operational stages into what Bruner calls the *stage of inactive representation* (°). During this period, the child represents events through action. The child cannot draw a map of its route to and from house because it can only "see" things by doing them. Later, the child passes into what Bruner calls the *stage of representation through imagery*, which appears to correspond to Piaget's stage of formal operations. The major difference between Bruner and Piaget would seem to be that Bruner places more emphasis on the effect that culture has on shaping the child's perceptions. Like Piaget, Bruner believes that children are born with

Jerome Bruner.

the neural capacity to develop intellectually, but they will do so only if their culture helps unlock this *latent* (°) capacity by providing the child with a stimulating environment.

Criticisms of Piaget's Theory   British psychologist Susanna Millar points out that there are three basic assumptions Piaget makes in his theory. The first assumption is that intellectual development absolutely must proceed in 1-2-3-4 sequence. The speed at which a child matures may be sped up or retarded, but the sequence of stages must always be the same. The second assumption is that there are no halfway points between two stages. Just as a child cannot keep its foot for long between the two rungs of a ladder, so it cannot linger for long halfway between the pre-operational and operational stages. The third assumption is that all mental development can be described in terms of the logical operations a child employs while thinking or acting. Unfortunately, the evidence supporting these three assumptions is not strong.

Jean Piaget has spent more than 50 years observing children, and his insights into their thought patterns are legendary. His description of the way children behave is both *apt* (°) and *eloquent* (°). But the children Piaget has spent a lifetime observing are for the most part white, middle-class children reared in normal European homes. His four-stage theory appears to hold in great measure for such children, who do tend to learn conservation of volume about age 6, conservation of weight about age 9, and who typically show an ability to handle abstract operations when they are 12—at which age they are often welcomed into adulthood by religious ceremonies such as the *bar mitzvah* or *Christian confirmation*. But what about children raised in other cultures or even in different segments of our own society? Would a child reared in a mental hospital or a concentration camp or a ghetto develop the same thinking patterns?

And might we not reverse the developmental sequence by giving a child special training? University of Texas mathematician H.S. Vandever spent his life creating special number systems so abstract that he had difficulty teaching them to advanced graduate students. In these systems, 2 + 2 might sometimes equal 4, or 5, or 0, or any other answer you might care to give. Vandever found it was often easier to teach his abstractions to kindergarten children than to adults, who "knew too much and hence had too much to forget." These children, presumably still in the pre-operational stage, could often manipulate such abstract concepts as zero and infinity with apparent ease, although they still thought that a balloon flew because it was colored red and they could not draw maps of how to get to school.

QUESTION: **How might you go about teaching a 6-year-old child to "map" a route from his or her home to a near-by store or movie?**

PLAY

The child is born little more than an animal; if society does not condition it to be human, the child will remain non-verbal, non-social, and "retarded" (at least it will seem retarded from our biased, cultural point of view). The *ontogeny* (°) of play in middle-class, Western society pretty much parallels the ontogeny of the average child's intellectual development. Since Freud's theory of psychosexual development in part grew out of earlier theories of play behavior, let us look at various types of play before we look at Freud's theory.

Types of Play

Pre-social Play   The first type of play that infants engage in is rightly called *pre-social* (°). That is, the 6-month-old infant plays with a mobile dangling over its

Latent (LAY-tent). A latent power is one that is hidden or not yet expressed.

Apt. From the Latin word meaning "suitable." An apt description is one that is well chosen. Our word "aptitude" comes from this same Latin source.

Eloquent (ELL-oh-kwent). Forceful, effective, persuasive, sincere speech.

Ontogeny (awn-TODG-en-ee). The biological development, or course of development, of a single organism.

Pre-social. Pre-social play is that which a child engages in before it is mature enough to relate to other individuals on a give-and-take or equality basis. A pre-social child treats others as if they were objects, not human beings with equal rights.

crib; it plays with bells and rattles and balls and teddy bears—and it plays with itself. Only later does it learn the marvelous capacity for play that animate objects (such as its mother and siblings) offer. Indeed, at this age, the infant seemingly treats its mother as little more than a willing and cooperative toy.

Harlow lists three types of pre-social play—exploration play, parallel play, and instigative play—all of which Piaget would define as belonging to the pre-operational stage.

The child *explores* its environment by crawling around and by inspecting anything that drops into its narrow life space. Given a spoon to eat with, the child may bang the utensil on the table again and again, until it wears its mother's nerves to a frazzle. Given green peas to eat, it may studiously drop them on the floor one by one, as if trying to discover its own version of the law of gravity. It may discover its own nose, or fingers, or toes, or sex organs, and explore them by the hour until it grows tired, or its parents express their disapproval. Later, it may build castles out of blocks, push toy trucks around, or exercise its artistic talents with crayons and coloring books.

Put briefly, during pre-social play the child goes about the necessary task of building up expectations about the behavior of objects in its physical environment. The more that it explores, the better the child can get at predicting what it must do to get what it wants.

Parallel play is often the child's first step toward social contact with its age-mates. Even before an infant is ready to interact with other children, it may choose to play beside them—but not with them. A child may bring a favored toy to another child's side, then sit and play with the toy (but not the other child) for minutes on end. Misery may love company, but so does happiness, at least when the child is in the pre-operational stage of development.

Later, the child may indulge in imitative play—follow-the-leader, mimicking, "Peek-a-boo"—in which the actions of another person (perhaps even one watched on television) directly instigate or lead the child's activities. Yet the young person does not really interact socially with the "leader." Harlow speaks of this as being *instigative play* and believes it is the final step toward true social interaction.

QUESTION: **Why might it be imperative for a child to try out many types of social "feed forward" at this age?**

Social Play   As the Western child passes from the pre-operational to the operational stage of intellectual development, its play becomes more complex and other people begin to become animate partners in its life rather than mere objects to be manipulated. Social play seems to be of three major types—*formal play, creative play,* and *free play.* Of the three, physical free play with other children is perhaps the easiest for the child, and hence often the first to appear. As Harlow points out, it is also the most disturbing to the middle-class parent who is often afraid that the child will either hurt itself or be hurt by others. Harlow also insists that free play is of critical importance in the socialization process. As we have already seen, young monkeys engaging in physical rough-house activities are, in fact, learning the rudiments of adult sexual behavior. They are also learning the limits to aggression and their own places on the social scale. As we saw in Chapter 4, most animals respond to frustration and pain by aggressing against any handy object, including another animal. During physical free play, the young animal probably learns to tolerate minor frustrations and to keep its temper in check. Surely, as we saw in the last chapter, monkeys raised alone never learn much about either sex or impulse control.

British psychologist N.G.B. Jones found that rough-and-tumble play (in British children) began as early as 18 months and usually continued until the child was 3 to 5 years old. These boisterous activities often look hostile and threatening to parents, but seem to be filled with pleasure and charm for the participants

Social creative play.

themselves. Although both boys and girls engage in rough-house when very young, real sex differences do seem to emerge as the children grow older. That is, 3-year-old boys may be expected to spend almost twice as much time in physical-contact play as do girls. Harlow believes that this difference is due to hormones—that is, results from true sex differences—because young male monkeys rough-house two to three times as much as do young females. Obviously, however,

Rough-housing—a form of free play.

human cultural patterns tend to reinforce this natural pattern. As the child becomes more and more verbal (during the operational stage of its development), rough-and-tumble play drops off sharply and formalized play begins. The mock fights of 4-year-old boys develop rapidly into games of tag, cops and robbers, and other activities in which *rules* must be obeyed. Prior to this time in the youngster's life, physical agility determined who was Number One and who was at the bottom of the pecking order. Once speech becomes a part of the child's way of adjusting to the world around it, verbal cleverness becomes as important a determinant of social position as does sheer physical size.

In Piaget's terms, physical free play is almost always a matter of *accommodation* to the responses of other children, and of imitation. Creative play, on the other hand, is primarily a matter of *assimilation*, of "pretending" that things might happen that haven't yet happened. The child is thus trying to anticipate what kinds of reactions (feedback) might occur if things were different than they presently are. Creative play is often a matter of using an object for other than its original, intended (adult) use. A stick becomes a doll; a doll becomes a human; a human becomes a horse to be ridden—all in the mind's eye of the child as it tries out certain possibilities that don't presently exist. Piaget believes that creative play is the child's way of learning to manipulate symbols rather than objects and calls it the high point of all types of play.

QUESTION: **When scientists plan an experiment, they often indulge in "What-if" thinking; that is, they ask themselves questions such as, "*What* would happen *if* we raised rats in an enriched environment rather than in the usual dull laboratory cages?" What similarities do you see between "What-if" thinking in scientists and the "pretending" a child engages in during creative play?**

Creative play would seem, on the face of it, to be related to creativity in adults. Surprisingly enough, there has been little research attempting to relate creativity in adults with the types of play they showed when young. Part of the problem lies in one's definition of *creativity*, for what is original and highly praised art or music in one culture is often looked down on in other social settings. If we cannot define creative behavior adequately, we cannot expect to identify or measure it accurately either in children or adults. And without accurate measuring devices, we cannot hope to determine whether encouraging a youngster to draw more pictures when the child is 3 will help turn the child into a Rembrandt or Picasso at age 33.

Doll Play U.S. psychologist G.S. Hall made a study of children's doll play, which he published in 1896. Hall found that almost every U.S. child, both boys and girls, enjoyed playing with dolls and had done so fairly frequently between ages 4 and 12. Since Hall believed that children used dolls to act out their own feelings toward their parents, he was surprised that fewer than half of his subjects treated the dolls as if they were the child's own children. But he did report that the dolls were often invested with "feelings" of their own—the toys were said to be afraid of thunderstorms or ghosts, and were thought to be naughty or nice. Fully half of the children Hall studied believed these personality characteristics were *inside* the dolls themselves, rather than being projected onto the inanimate toy by the child.

Biological Theories of Play

Most of us might assume that play is an activity that children fall into spontaneously, and that its major purpose might be that of making childhood more pleasant. However, to a variety of scientists, play has a deeper and more profound importance.

Plato and Aristotle both suggested that children be given toy tools to play with, to shape their minds for future activities as adults. These early Greek philosophers believed that society could in this way shape or influence the future attitudes of young citizens. Later philosophers tended to see play as being the "unfolding" of innate or inborn talents and desires, and suggested that children be left alone to determine freely what they wanted to do or become. Nineteenth-century German philosophers believed that play somehow restored the child's physical and mental powers and recommended it as a form of relaxation for exhausted children.

Perhaps the most detailed theory of play came from British philosopher Herbert Spencer. Writing a little more than 100 years ago, Spencer suggested what is now called the "surplus energy" hypothesis of play. Spencer thought that each child was born with an energy-producing machine of some kind inside it; this energy must be released in some fashion or the child will "explode." Lower animals spend so much time and effort searching for food that they have little time to play. But higher animals, particularly humans, have conquered their environments, and the extra energy inside them finds expression in aimless outbursts of activity. Spencer thought that all art came from play, as did Sigmund Freud, who incorporated many of Spencer's ideas about psychic energy into his theory of psycho-analysis.

In more recent times, Harry Levin and Elinor Wardwell have investigated doll play as a *projective technique* (°). That is, Levin and Wardwell assume that the child will express its own needs and its feeling about itself and others in the way in which it describes what the dolls "want" and "do." Levin and Wardwell find that girls play with a "mother" doll more than with a "father" doll, but that boys play with both dolls equally. Children brought up in what Levin and Wardwell term "permissive" homes use adult dolls more in fantasy play than do children from *authoritarian* (°) homes. Susanna Millar criticizes these studies as being rather restrictive in approach, however, because the dolls used were small and dressed very realistically; such studies may tell us something about how the child views adults, but not too much about the fantasy world a child might create with a teddy bear, a rag doll, or just a piece of wood.

Actually, as Hall pointed out 80 years ago, in our society, dolls belonged originally to adults and only recently have become the property of children. In Europe, for instance, dolls began as wooden statues of queens and empresses. In Japan, until this past century, images of the royal court were made of wood or enameled clay and were bought by well-to-do families for their daughters. Boys were given dolls representing heroes and warriors. Each year there was a special "feast day" for the dolls. On that day the children made offerings of wine and food to the dolls and spent the day acting out various aspects of adult Japanese life using the dolls as props. Dolls for everyday play were apparently imported to Japan by the Dutch only within the last century.

Formal Play   Formal play grows out of free and creative play. It is play within limits, play by rules, and it seems to have changed little within Western society from one century to another. Games such as hide-and-go-seek, hopscotch, and London Bridge have had pretty much the same form for hundreds of years. As Susanna Millar points out, few of us realize that "Ring around the rosies, pockets full of posies, A-tishoo, A-tishoo, we all fall down" refers to the Black Death that struck Europe in the Middle Ages and sent millions of people to early graves. Children need not understand that the symptoms of Black Death (now called "the plague") caused people to fall down; they merely enjoy the repetitive rhythms and stylized actions of a joyous and amusing formal game.

Although Spencer's ideas on the purpose of play were influenced by Charles Darwin's books on animal evolution, it was G.S. Hall who pushed evolutionary theory to what now seems absurd lengths. Hall believed that each child must *recapitulate* (°), or relive, the behavioral history of the human race through its

Projective technique. A psychological test in which the subject is given ambiguous stimuli such as inkblots and asked to tell what the stimuli mean. The subject is supposed to project his or her personal needs and problems onto the stimuli. The best-known projective techniques are the Rorschach (ROAR-shock) Ink Blot Test and the Thematic Apperception Test (TAT).

Authoritarian (aw-thor-it-TAIR-ee-an). An authoritarian home is one in which the parents demand complete obedience from the children. See Chapter 14.

Recapitulate (ree-cap-PITT-you-late). From the Latin word meaning "to sum up, to restate." When a TV announcer finishes a news program, the announcer may "recap the news" by reading the headlines again.

Formal play involves games that have rules.

Natural selection. Charles Darwin's theory that those animals best suited to survive in a given environment will reproduce at a faster rate than animals not as well suited. The environment is thus thought to "select" those organisms that will survive, and to "reject" those that will disappear or become extinct.

play. For instance, children supposedly love spashing about in water because they are re-enacting their fish ancestors' pleasure in swimming in ancient oceans. Children love climbing trees and swinging from ropes and branches because our monkey ancestors did such things. Young boys like gathering in groups to go hunting and fishing because early humans had to make their living that way. Before the child could become a modern-day adult, according to Hall, it had to rehearse or retrace all of the ancient behaviors that were built into its genetic blueprint over millions of years of evolution.

Although Hall's 1904 book on child psychology did have the effect of interesting many psychologists in studying children more closely, it had many serious faults. As Susanna Millar points out, it is difficult to explain a modern child's joy in bicycles, toy airplanes, trains, telephones, and space ships as being a re-living of ancestral experiences.

Darwinian theory was pushed even further by Karl Groos, who taught philosophy in Switzerland at the turn of this century. Groos believed that play was a generalized instinct that caused a young organism to practice all the other instincts it would need to survive as an adult. According to Darwin, *natural selection* (°) should favor those animals whose genetic blueprints give them adaptability and who can benefit from experience. The more complex the animal, the weaker its instincts and the more flexible its behavior patterns. That is, the more its behavior is controlled by environmental inputs, the less its actions are determined by reflex. According to Groos, play was the young animal's way of practicing its weak instincts and perfecting them (for the environment it would live in) before the organism actually needed those adult behavior patterns. To Groos, rough-housing was a boy's way of preparing for the pleasure of fighting off other adults to win the hand of his own true love, and even of learning the skills of war.

QUESTION: How would Groos explain the many countries—such as modern Israel—where women have become excellent soldiers?

Groos's books on play did point out several interesting and previously overlooked aspects of play—that it often involves almost all of the natural functions of an organism and that behaviors (such as random exploring) that may look aimless and useless can still serve important biological functions. But to say that children play because they have an *instinct* to play tells us very little about human behavior and neglects the profound influence that environmental feedback has even on children.

QUESTION: How would a "surplus energy" theorist explain anaclitic depression in human and monkey infants deprived of their mothers?

SIGMUND FREUD

Freudian theory bubbled up in the same biological pot that spewed forth the theories of Groos, Hall, and Spencer. To Freud, behavior was determined both by instinctual urges and by the pleasant or painful consequences of our actions in satisfying those urges. Freud accepted Spencer's notion that we all have energy-producing centers in our nervous systems, but Freud thought that the energy produced was primarily sexual. He called this well-spring of neural activity the *libido* (°), and equated it with the instinct to live. All of a human being's motivations come from libidinal energy, but the exact flow of energy from "mind" to "behavior" is determined by each person's youthful experiences, according to Freud. We seek pleasure and avoid pain, and we do our best to balance our sometimes selfish (egocentric) instinctual desires against the reality of the world we are born into.

Libido (lib-BEE-doe). From the Latin word meaning "desire" or "lust." According to Freud, the libido is the life force, the instinctual drive to satisfy one's biological urges.

Sigmund Freud and his dog.

Psycho-sexual Development

According to Freud, we pass through various psycho-sexual stages of development that correspond to the maturational stage of our body at various times in our lives. When we are newborn, the brain centers which control mouth movements are physically the most developed. Libidinal energy can most easily be released through eating. Therefore, our joys come primarily from oral activities, such as sucking and swallowing, and our sorrows come from any denial or punishment of these behaviors.

Oral Stage During this first or *oral stage* (°) of development, skin receptors in the lips and tongue presumably have much lower firing thresholds than do receptors elsewhere on our body surfaces. As we reach 1 year of age, however, the receptors in our anal regions presumably develop rapidly, and by the time we are 2, we can enjoy such activities as urinating and defecating. At this point, we are able to pass into the second or *anal stage* (°) of development—if we are psychologically ready to do so. Readiness depends on how well our oral needs were gratified during the first two years of our lives. If our mothers were warm and rewarding when feeding us, Freud said, we learn how to handle the minor frustrations and anxieties associated with oral activities and are sufficiently developed psychologically to move up to the next rung on the maturational ladder.

Anal Stage Toilet training typically takes place (in Western society) during the anal stage. Again, the child must learn to control its egocentric urges to pleasure itself (by urinating and defecating when it wishes to) because these instinctual desires conflict with society's demands. By encouraging the child, rather than punishing and frustrating it, the parents help the child pass on to the next stage of development, during which genital pleasures predominate—presumably because the sense receptors in the penis or vagina have now matured.

Phallic Stage The *phallic stage* (°), which Freud believed began in the 3rd year of life, is the time that true socialization begins, for it is at this point that the child begins to learn that other people have an existence independent of its own perceptions. The child becomes aware of sex differences, and builds up a warm relationship with whichever parent is of the opposite sex—the boy with his mother, the girl with her father.

Freud gave names from Greek mythology to this stage of human development. Oedipus was an ancient Greek king who was separated from his parents at an early age and raised by other people. As a young man, Oedipus met his father (who was then king of the city-state of Thebes) and murdered him. Later, when Oedipus returned to Thebes, he met his mother. Not knowing who she was, he fell in love with her and married her. Freud thought that every boy relives (recapitulates) this ancient experience of having *incestuous* (°) desires for his mother and fearing his father as a rival. Freud calls this the *Oedipal* (°) situation.

The corresponding love-hate relationship a girl is supposed to experience for her father and mother is sometimes called the *Electra situation* (°), named for an ancient Greek woman who hated her mother for arranging the murder of Electra's beloved father. When grown, Electra encouraged her brother to get rid of the mother in a particularly bloody fashion.

Obviously such hatreds and hostilities would rip a family apart if left unchecked. Freud believed that they are resolved by a compromise. The boy soon learns he cannot kill or replace his father, but he can imitate the older man and hence capture a fair share of his mother's affection. So the boy begins to take on his father's values and mimic his behaviors. As the youth "internalizes" his father's

Oral stage. The first stage in psycho-sexual development in which the child's satisfactions come chiefly from its mouth. See Chapter 12.

Anal stage. The second stage in psycho-sexual development, during which the child's pleasures come chiefly from withholding or expelling its feces and urine.

Phallic stage (FAL-lick; rhymes with "PAL sick"). The Greek word for "penis" is *phallos.* Freud called the third stage of psycho-sexual development the phallic stage, during which the child gains pleasure from genital stimulation.

Incestuous (in-SEST-you-us). Sexual desires directed toward a close relative are called "incestuous."

Oedipal (ED-uh-pull). That developmental stage in which a boy is thought to experience sexual desire for his mother and hatred for his father.

Electra situation. That developmental stage during which a girl is thought to experience sexual desire for her father and hatred for her mother.

philosophy, the boy starts developing his own social conscience. His hatred for his father is *repressed*, or pushed down into unconsciousness, but sometimes it bubbles to the surface in dreams and in play situations. Girls are supposed to follow much the same developmental pattern, although Freud believed it occurred later in girls than in boys. In resolving the Electra situation, the girl attempts to capture her father's love by identifying with and by imitating much of her mother's behavior.

Latent Period   Freud believed that the phallic period is marked by frequent masturbation. It is during the fantasies that accompany this self-stimulation that the Oedipal and Electra desires to conquer one parent and destroy the other come to the fore. But these fantasies raise so much guilt and anxiety in the child's mind that the child eventually gives up sexual yearnings for a time and, at age 5 or 6, enters into what Freud termed the *latent period*. During this maturational stage, sexual interest is repressed as the child slowly solves the riddle of its relationships with its parents. The child moves out of the home more frequently, and friendships with its age-mates take on greater importance. Boys play more frequently with other boys than with girls, and girls tend to stick to each other. Freud believed this was a "natural homosexual period" during which boys found "heroes" among older male teachers and friends, and girls developed "crushes" on other girls and older women.

Genital Stage   The latent period ends at puberty, when the child enters the final or *genital stage* (°) of development; now, libidinal energy is focused on heterosexual activities and pleasure comes primarily from contacts with the opposite sex.

Libidinal Energy

Freud's theory of play comes directly from his theory of psycho-sexual maturation. Libidinal energy is constantly being produced from the time the child is born. During the oral period, it is released in such behaviors as eating and sucking. If the mother does not allow the child to use up all the energy the child produces, it must repress the unexpended energy and keep it bottled up inside. If too much energy is repressed during the oral stage, the child becomes *fixated* at this level. The adult who eats, talks, or smokes too much is, in Freud's terms, still trying to release the pent-up energy it repressed during the first year or so of its life.

If toilet training is too severe and the child is often punished for not being able to control its natural functions, then fixation will occur at the anal stage. Adults who are abnormally neat and clean are presumed still to be repressing their natural anal urges, while adults who are supremely sloppy are thought to be releasing energy bound up during a particularly repressive toilet training.

Luckily for most of us, libidinal energy can be released indirectly through play and dreams and fantasy as well as through over-eating and making messes. Freud saw play as being a way of letting off steam. The little girl who pretends that her teddy bear "wants" to bite her mother may be answering her oral urges in socially acceptable ways. The little boy who dreams of monsters with big teeth could be releasing energy that was bound up during his first year of life. The primary purpose of play, in Freudian terms, is that of acting out in fantasy the *repressed desires* that all children have.

To Freud, high energy levels always mean pain and discomfort, while low energy levels mean pleasure. Anything that increases the amount of psychic energy inside a person leads to tension and unhappiness, while a decrease of energy leads to a feeling of contentment and well-being. When environmental situations cause an increase in tension, the child attempts to relive the experience in fantasy. This "acting out" reduces the excitement and is rewarding to the child.

Genital stage. The last of the Freudian stages of psycho-sexual development, during which a person learns that giving pleasure to a sexual partner is as satisfying as receiving genital stimulation oneself.

By going over the situation again and again, the child learns to master its frustrations and to release its repressed energy in socially approved ways. Each time the child acts out a disturbing event, it feels better. Therefore, children repeat certain behaviors (or dream certain dreams) again and again, because repetition is associated with pleasure.

To Freud, every behavior was motivated—that is, *purposeful*. Play is tension-reducing; therefore it is rewarding and is engaged in by all children.

QUESTION: Assume that being able to control one's behavioral outputs is rewarding because such control allows one to predict one's inputs. Why then might children repeat certain behaviors at length?

ARE THEORIES NECESSARY?

Freud was a genius. His theory of psycho-analysis was, in its own way, as bold and creative a step forward as was Darwin's theory of evolution. Freud forced psychologists to consider the symbolic, intra-psychic aspects of much of human behavior and to look at childhood experiences for explanation of the beginnings of many adult behavioral problems.

Freud developed his theory the way that you or I would—by reading books, by listening to lectures, and by observing the actions of the people around him as carefully as he could. But the people Freud lived among were middle-class Europeans living in the late 1800's and early 1900's; his patients were primarily wealthy, highly verbal individuals with considerable education. He described—and explained—their life histories with brilliant insight. But had Freud lived among a primitive tribe in Africa or South America, would his theory have been the same? Does the fact that most children in a given society pass through certain developmental stages mean that this maturational pattern is built into the genetic blueprint of all human beings everywhere?

QUESTION: Does the fact that most human languages have verbs and nouns mean that a "verb-noun grammar" is built into our genes?

In truth, none of our theories of human development is adequate. Piaget borrowed from Darwin and Freud, and his theory is subject to the same sorts of criticisms that can be leveled at evolution and psycho-analysis. Energy and motivation come as much from our environments as from our inner selves. A child growing up in a world that stimulates and rewards boisterous behavior becomes noisy and outgoing. A child buried in an impoverished ghetto becomes *indolent* (°), not because it is repressing its natural energetic urges but because its world does not motivate it to move. Freud looked at the rough-and-tumble games of European middle-class children and assumed that their libidos were generating a surplus of sexual energy that had to come out in violent play. Yet, as Susanna Millar points out, children typically have no choice in the matter. They have not learned the fine-muscle movements necessary for more sedate occupations—such as reading a textbook, sewing a dress, playing the piano, or sitting still while listening to a lecture. Intellectual concentration appears to be possible only when a person has all the motor centers of his or her brain firmly under voluntary control. It may take as much practice—and almost as much skill—to listen to a musical concert as it does to play one.

Freud thought that all children went through a "latent period" in their psycho-sexual adjustment from years 4 through 12, roughly speaking. This time of repressed sexuality was, Freud assumed, a biological consequence of the Oedipal or Electra situation. However, anthropological studies of children in other cultures suggest that the latent period simply does not exist if the society adopts a casual and permissive view toward youthful sexual explorations. Indeed, there is some doubt as to whether even European children are quite as "latent" as Freud

Indolent (IN-dough-lent). From the Latin words meaning "no pain." To be indolent is to "live easy," to loaf instead of work.

stated they were. Perhaps, about age 4, the average child becomes capable of learning which behaviors and verbal phrases its mother and father won't tolerate.

Freud believed that children *project* their own hidden or repressed desires onto the fantasy play behavior of their dolls. By *interpreting* these projected behaviors, one could presumably determine much about the psychic life of the child. In a similar way, Piaget interprets the mental states of his subjects by asking them questions and posing problems. The difficulty with such interpretations is this—the person doing the observing is likely to project his or her own perceptual distortions onto the child's behavior. We see not only what we want to see, but we also perceive primarily those things our favorite psychological theory tells us ought to be present.

Freud, Piaget, and many other theorists believe that maturation occurs in readily recognizable steps—that the child is either in the oral stage or the anal, that it is at a pre-operational level or has both feet firmly planted on the "operational" rung of the developmental ladder. It is more likely that maturation is a continuous process, made up of thousands of different skills that are acquired whenever the child's neural development is sufficient to respond to environmental demands. Children do not have to relive the experiences of their ancestors in order to cope with the modern world, any more than the human fetus has to pass through worm-insect-fish-bird-and-frog stages in order to develop into a mammal. The "stages" that Freud, Piaget, and others see in the maturational sequence now seem to be rather apt descriptions of our cultural expectations of how children *should* develop rather than biologically determined steps toward adulthood.

The Purpose of Play   What then is play, if it isn't blowing off libidinal steam or a slow crawling up the developmental ladder? The truth seems to be that play serves so many different functions in so many different situations that no one master theory will presently *suffice* (°) to explain its many uses.

In most cultures, play serves to allow children to explore their physical environments, to learn motor coordination, and to determine their own physical limits. In permissive societies, the child also learns something about sexual behavior and the physical make-up of its own and the opposite sex.

Play also allows the child to practice social roles (feed forward) that yield

Suffice (suff-ICE). From the Latin word meaning "to provide" or "to be enough." To suffice is to be equal to a task, to be competent, to satisfy the needs. Suffice it to say that our word "sufficient" comes from the same Latin source.

Creative play.

Hallmark. An identifying mark or characteristic. Years ago, gold and silver articles made in England were measured and weighed in the Goldsmith's Hall in London. These articles were then stamped with "The Mark of the Hall" to prove they were of pure gold or silver.

approving feedback from the adults the child must live with. For one reason or another, most young organisms imitate the behavior patterns of others. Play allows the child to determine its present place in society, to learn social limitations, to find out what behaviors other people will reward and punish.

By exploring both its physical and social environment, the child learns to perceive the world more accurately, and to predict the consequences of its own actions. This perceptual learning is apparently what Piaget means when he speaks of creative play as being that of "symbol manipulation." The child checks and rechecks its perceptions when it plays house or cops-and-robbers or builds castles out of blocks. When a child asks the same question over and over again, it may really be learning how to organize its perceptions so that it can ask questions that elicit useful inputs from its environment.

College students spend almost as much time per week on leisure, "playful" activities as do kindergarten students. Is there all that much difference between a 4-year-old who spends a week playing with the same dump truck and the sophomore who takes a semester off "to master Shakespeare"?

This much we know—pleasure is the *hallmark* (°) of play. Children who laugh while they are fighting seldom hurt one another. Adults who smile as they read textbooks seldom murder authors. It may turn out that play is serious business, simply because it rewards children for learning what they have to.

SUMMARY

1. Measuring the physical development of a child is a fairly simple task—one needs only a tape measure and a weight scale to get fairly accurate readings. Measuring the mental growth of a child is a much more challenging and difficult task, for we have no uniformly accepted "measuring tapes" for intra-psychic development. In consequence, different theorists have emphasized different aspects of mental maturation.

2. The two best-known theories of cognitive development are probably those of Jean Piaget and Sigmund Freud.

3. Piaget believes that all children pass through four developmental stages, each of which grows out of but is more complex than the one that preceded it:
   a. During the sensory-motor period, the child learns to integrate its various sense impressions into percepts.
   b. During the pre-operational stage, the child learns to speak and begins to deal with its world in symbolic terms, by talking about objects rather than by having to manipulate them directly.
   c. During the stage of concrete operations, the child learns to visualize a whole series of operations in its mind and to differentiate itself from the outer world.
   d. During the final stage of formal operations, the child gains the ability to think in purely abstract terms.

4. Piaget believes that children pass through these stages at their own individual speeds, but that the stages cannot be reversed or changed in order.

5. Piaget assumes that the pattern of mental development is built into our genes, just as Noam Chomsky holds that the pattern of human language development is instinctive. Julian Jaynes disagrees with Chomsky, believing that speech developed about 70,000 years ago when primitive humans were forced to migrate because of the last Ice Age.

6. Not all psychologists agree with Piaget, Chomsky, or Jaynes, nor is there great agreement on the function of play in the child's intellectual and language development.

7. Harlow has listed several types of play:
   a. The first is pre-social play, in which the child explores its environment by itself, plays close to but not with other children, or imitates what others are doing.
   b. At a later age, the child engages in various forms of social play, including formal play with rules, creative play, and free play.

8. Philosopher Herbert Spencer believed that play was necessary for the release of "surplus energy" within the child.

9. Freud held a similar notion. He believed that people had within them a libido, or life force, that generated energy which allowed them to satisfy their needs.

10. Freud thought that the child's satisfactions varied depending on which psycho-sexual stage it was passing through:

   a. In the oral stage, pleasure is said to come from stimulation of the mouth.

   b. During the anal stage, satisfaction comes from expelling or withholding of urine and feces.

   c. In the phallic stage, the child has matured enough to enjoy genital stimulation.

   d. At age 5 or 6, the child is presumed to develop incestuous desires for the parent of the opposite sex. Anxiety about these desires brings on the latent period that terminates when the child reaches puberty and can enter the genital stage.

   e. During the final (genital) period of psycho-sexual development, libidinal energy is focused on heterosexual activities.

11. If, at any stage, the child's needs are not satisfied, its sexual desires may be repressed.

12. To Freud, play was often a matter of acting out in symbolic terms the repressions forced on the child by its environment. Through play, the child could thus release pent-up libidinal energy.

13. One major objection to both the theories of Freud and Piaget is that their theories were based on observations of middle-class, white European children. The young people of other cultures do not always develop quite the way that Freud and Piaget assumed they should.

14. A second objection is that both Freud and Piaget based their viewpoints on a biological model. The mind of a child now seems to us to be more flexible and shapable than either Freud or Piaget assumed.

15. The functions that play serves vary so widely from one culture to another that no one theory yet suffices to explain its usefulness.

(Continued from page 462.)

Dear Diary:

Quiet. The termite mounds are almost deserted. Only Greg and Gunner are left. Kevin tricked Evva into chasing him into the nearby forest, and Nancy soon took after them both, but they haven't reappeared from the jungle. It's so late now, they probably won't—until tomorrow, when they'll be back with their sticks, earning their daily grub(s). However, Gunner has the stubborn perseverence of a mule. Or maybe he just likes insects. Greg has been trying to coax Gunner into leaving for some time, but Gunner sticks to his stick and his fishing. He seems to be very happy with his work. Greg is not so happy and is ready to go, but then Greg is still fairly young and impatient. Or maybe he just doesn't like the taste of termite.

Funny. A few years back, when Dr. Jane and her husband at that time, handsome Hugo van Lawick, first started the Gombe Stream Research Centre, they began passing out free bananas to the chimps. That was to get the animals to come to them regularly—a lot easier than having to beat the bushes to find the chimps each day you want to watch them. The chimps rather liked the idea and soon learned to come to the Centre for food regularly. As more and more chimps showed up, more bananas were needed. So Dr. Jane and Hugo imported more and more bananas, and stored them in big boxes. But the chimps soon learned that if there weren't any bananas visible, there were bound to be some stored somewhere. So the chimps went looking, and they could easily wreck a tent or a camp site hunting for the hidden goodies. Then Dr. Jane and Hugo got strong steel boxes with huge locks and buried them in the ground. But still the chimps nosed out the bananas and pilfered them when they could.

Greg has given up and headed for the trees, but Gunner is still at it. I wonder where he gets the stick-to-it-ive-ness?

Anyway. The bananas were presented to the chimps in steel cages, the doors to which could be opened automatically from some distance away. The chimps would gather around the cages, waiting for the gates to heaven to be opened, and they would wait and wait all day long. They didn't bother to collect fresh fruit from trees, and they forgot about termite fishing. Free bananas were so much easier, I guess. The adults would sit around and groom each other for a while, but then they would get into arguments. Tempers flared more than they ever had before in this relatively peaceful bit of jungle. The infants played a lot, but the older animals got grouchy and impatient with the youngsters.

Fun is where you find it. The young chimps spent a lot of time trying to puzzle out the lock arrangement on the steel gates to the boxes. The adults didn't bother, but the kids apparently thought it a game of some kind. One by one, they picked the locks. So more difficult locks were put on the boxes, but the kids worked and worked until they could open the new locks too.

Then the baboons came. They learned about the free bananas, and they used to come and sit near the chimps and just wait—like picking up your unemployment check at the county welfare office each week. But the baboons and the chimps would fight a lot, and things got a little bloody. Most of the complex social patterns the chimps used to show disappeared, and all they did was sit around and wait and groom and get angry. All play and no work makes Gunner a dull chimpanzee, I guess.

So. No more free meals on a regular basis. Now the bananas get passed out infrequently, and the chimps are back grubbing for themselves most of the time. Makes it more difficult for observers like me to take notes, I suppose, because we have to get out and track the chimps down to watch them. But maybe it's worth it.

Gunner seems to have given up. He's sitting beside the termite mound, twiddling the long, thin fishing stick in his fingers. Now he's looking at me as I write in this notebook. He looks like he's thinking, trying to puzzle something out. Now he's scratching in the fresh dirt, as if that helped him think. He looks back at me, and then he scratches in the dirt, holding the stick the same way I hold the pen in my hand. I wonder what he'd think, in that gray chimpanzee brain of his, if he knew I was writing about him. He's just playing with his stick, of course, while I'm working.

Or is it the other way around? Maybe what he's doing is the real work of growing up, of learning about his environment. And me, Alicia Montez, from Phoenix, Arizona, sitting in a lonely clearing in the heart of Africa, enjoying myself so much I still can't believe it—maybe what I'm doing, learning about life and chimpanzees and myself, maybe what I'm doing is just . . . child's play.

RECOMMENDED READINGS

Hebb, D.O., W.E. Lambert, and G.R. Tucker. "A DMZ in the Language War," *Psychology Today*, vol. 6, no. 11 (1973), pp. 54–62.

Millar, Susanna. *The Psychology of Play* (New York: Penguin Books, 1968).

Opie, I., and P. Opie. *The Lore and Language of Schoolchildren* (Clarendon, Tex.: The Clarendon Press, 1961).

———. *Children's Games in Street and Playground* (New York: Oxford University Press, 1968).

Whiting, B.B., ed. *Six Cultures: Studies of Child Rearing* (New York: John Wiley & Sons, Inc., 1963).

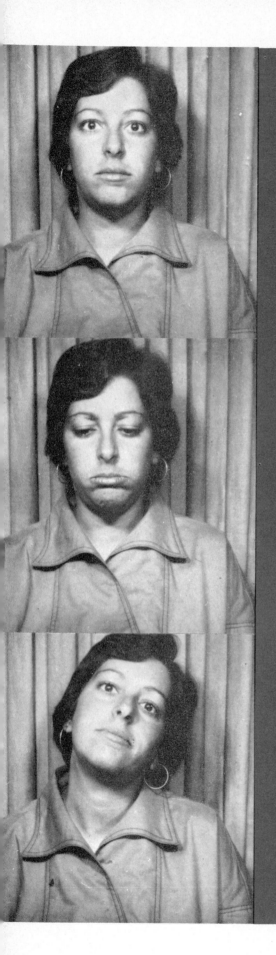

Part 6

PERSONALITY

PERSONALITY THEORY

DID YOU KNOW THAT . . .

Sir Isaac Newton, who discovered the law of gravity, almost flunked out of school as a boy?

Newton's laws of motion described, in a few simple equations, most of the behaviors of such heavenly objects as the sun, stars, and planets?

Most personality theorists have tried to explain, in a few simple terms or equations, all of the motives, thoughts, and behaviors of "earthy bodies" like you and me?

Freud believed that people are ruled primarily by their animal instincts and that most of the causes of our actions are unconscious?

Freud held that our egos do constant battle with our instincts and the demands society places on us?

Whenever the ego is about to be attacked, the ego experiences anxiety and tries to defend itself?

Freud thought the ego's most mature defense mechanism to be the sublimation of sexual energy into creative or socially-approved behaviors?

Jung believed that people are governed primarily by spiritual or mystic desires?

Adler felt that the drive to succeed was a stronger motivator than religious desires or sexual instincts?

Erikson held that each human being must pass through eight developmental stages on his or her way to complete maturity?

Rogers believed our major goal in life is to become a fully functioning and self-actualizing person?

Skinner sees motivation as coming primarily from environmental inputs?

We still don't have a personality theory that tells us all we want to know about the human condition?

The afternoon wind, the **breva** as it is called by the natives, ruffled the soft blue waters of Lake Como. The morning wind, the **tivano**, sweeps down from the Swiss Alps to the north, gusting heartily through the mountain gorges that form the banks of the long, narrow lake. The **breva** begins in the hills of Milan, near the southern shore of Lake Como, and pushes back up the pencil-thin body of water toward Switzerland. This constantly shifting pattern of wind keeps the air as bright and clear as the deep blue waters themselves.

Clinging to the steep shores of Lake Como are numerous little Italian villages—resort towns, really—and dotting the mountainsides are thousands of expensive villas where wealthy Europeans spend their summers. During the warmer months, luxurious steamers cruise back and forth along the 32-mile (51.5 kilometer) length of water, taking tourists (and their cars) from one point to another.

In late September, as occasionally chilly days blight the flower gardens, the steamers disappear and the only way to cross the mile-wide (1.6 kilometer) lake is by private boat, or by water taxi. Residents of Cadennabia, at the center of the western shore of Lake Como, can see Bellagio on the eastern shore directly across from them, only a couple of miles away. But to get from Cadennabia to Bellagio by car, you must first drive south to the city of Como, then up the eastern shore to

Bellagio—a trip of more than 50 miles (80.5 kilometers) over winding, often treacherous mountain roads.

Just outside the town of Como, at the southern end of the lake, is the beautiful Villa d'Este, one of the last **grand-lux** hotels in all Europe. Sitting on the hotel's concrete terrace one warm September afternoon, looking up the lake toward Cadennabia and Bellagio, were three famous scientists. One was a tall, thin, well-dressed man in his 60's, psychologist Jonathan L. Fraser from the University of London. The other man was shorter, younger, and a bit on the heavy side. A neuro-physiologist from McGill University in Montreal, his name was Donald M. Papas. The third member of the group was a woman, Joyce Young Sapir, from Israel.

"Don, why did you invite us here?" the woman asked, as they waited for their drinks.

Donald Papas glanced nervously at the woman. She was short, dark, verging on plumpness; but she had a fiercely handsome face. Joyce Sapir's psycho-analytic research, conducted chiefly at Hebrew University in Jerusalem, had brought her considerable fame.

"Why did I ask you all to come here? Because I have hope, I suppose."

"Hope for what?" Fraser asked. "Not that I'm complaining, you understand. Beautiful spot, and all that."

A waiter brought the three of them drinks. Papas signed the bill, and the waiter vanished silently back into the Villa d'Este. "Yes, Como is one of the most heavenly places in the world, isn't it?"

"So you flew us in to northern Italy from all over the world because you had hopes of getting us drunk?" Professor Fraser persisted. "I know you Canadians are rich and generous, and I'm sure that Montreal is deadly dull this time of year. But you never leave your laboratory unless you have some earth-shaking purpose in mind. So, my dear friend and colleague, tell me what it is you're hopeful about."

Papas stretched out in his metal chair. "Well, as you know, the Foundation is very interested in peace. So they asked me to put together a small International Symposium on Peace and Personality. If either of you had bothered to read the **Statement of Purpose** I sent along with the invitation, you'd have known that."

"Don't be foolish, Don. We read it; quite carefully, I might add," Joyce Sapir said. "It had all the proper terms in it, all those lovely words so loaded with self-importance that we academic types toss around. 'Strive toward better understanding of the complexities of human nature,' for example. Or, 'Utilize our knowledge of the structure and dynamics of human personality to reduce international tensions,' for another. I'm sure phrases like that impress the people at the Foundation. But we are hard-nosed types, Dr. Papas, and we aren't that easily tricked by fancy language."

"How can you say that?" Fraser interrupted, a twinkle in his gray eyes. "All that you Freudians have as your stock in trade is fancy language."

Joyce Young Sapir favored the Englishman with a harsh stare. "I am not a Freudian, Jonathan Fraser, I am a neo-Freudian. A new-Freudian, if you please. An Ego Psychologist, really. It has been almost 50 years since Freud published his last paper of any consequence. We have come a long way since then. We accept many of his ideas, but we have benefited from the criticisms and contributions of Jung, Adler, Erikson—and from his own daughter, Anna Freud."

"No matter what you call yourselves, you still deal in fancy fictions instead of facts. If you were objective about things, if you looked at behavior instead of mucking about in the cesspools of the mind, you might actually discover something worthwhile." Fraser was obviously enjoying himself.

Dr. Sapir lit an Israeli cigarette. "I have observed, in my many years of psycho-analytic practice, that disturbed people tend to take on the personality characteristics of their pets. I am writing an article on it now, for the **Psychoanalytic Review.** You, Jonathan Fraser, have spent your life studying pigeons in the hope of discovering something about the human psyche. You have confined

yourself to pigeons for so long that you are getting to be something of a bird-brain yourself!"

"Now, now," said Papas. "Let's save the nasty comments for the meeting tomorrow, when the tape recorders can preserve for posterity your so-called peaceful comments."

"Don't try to shush me, Don. Fraser is not a psychologist; he is a behavioral mechanic, just like Skinner. Human beings are not **objects,** to be observed through a telescope like the planets Venus and Mars. We are **subjects.** We have minds, and the richest, most vital part of humanity lies in our subjective experiences. Our outward behavior is a pale copy of our mental activity. To look at us entirely from the outside is to ignore the **causes** of what we do. You cannot understand a man or woman merely by measuring their muscle twitches from afar. You must use a psychic microscope; you must peer deep inside them, learn to appreciate their instinctual urges, bring to light their unconscious thoughts, find the true meaning of their personal existences. Only when you have stripped away the hidden deposits of their past can you help their egos face reality, and hence achieve self-actualization."

"I've seen more meaningful deposits on the bottom of my pigeon cages," observed Fraser dryly.

"I sympathize with both of you," Papas said quickly. "Pigeons behave, and so do men and women. Our nervous systems are similar; and humans respond to rewards and punishments much as do birds and rats and worms. But our differences are just as important as our similarities."

"More important," Joyce Sapir said militantly.

"No, **just** as important. It is as foolish to say we can learn **nothing** about man from studying pigeons as it is to say that we can learn **everything** about humans from experiments inolving animals. That's one of the things I hope we can get some agreement on during the symposium."

"But how can pigeons help us find a path toward peace? Birds don't have personalities!"

"How do you know?" asked Fraser. "Have you ever psycho-analyzed a pigeon?"

"Don't be ridiculous," said the woman sharply. "Pigeons can't talk."

"Lucky beasts," Fraser rejoined.

"What you are really saying, Joyce, is that one major difference between humans and animals is that humans have language. Or 'verbal behavior,' if you want the Skinnerian term. The humanists such as Carl Rogers seem to agree that thoughts, to become a part of consciousness, must be expressed in verbal symbols. The major tool we have for investigating the human mind is the spoken word. We ask people to express their feelings, their experiences, and they must do so in language that we understand." Don Papas paused to sip at his drink.

"Then you really study verbal behavior, and not the human psyche. So you aren't being subjective at all—you're just refusing to be objective," said Fraser, a grin illuminating his thin face.

"Nonsense," Joyce Sapir remarked. "We use our intuition to go beyond the language to tap the meaning that lies latent in the words. We call it 'listening with the third ear.' People tell us what they are like without knowing that they are doing so. We hear their verbal mistakes, their slips-of-the-tongue, their little forgetfulnesses, their pauses, their stutterings, their evasions. Their words are like footprints in soft sand. Speech tells you what kind of prehistoric beasts are roaming the beaches of the unconscious, but you cannot trap the beasts themselves. You must guess at their size and shape and colors from the tracks they leave behind."

"And from their droppings," said the British psychologist.

The woman turned on him angrily. "Jonathan Fraser, you are the most anal personality I have ever met."

"But witty. You must admit that, Joyce," said the Canadian.

"Freud said that wit was often a form of unconscious or disguised aggression.

If we are to study peace, perhaps first we had better dissect Professor Fraser's personality to discover the unconscious roots of his hostility."

"That's easy," Fraser said. "I've been shaped into it. People pay me more attention when I say nasty things about them. And, like most academics, I find attention very rewarding. If you want me to be peaceful, then ignore me when I'm hostile and reinforce me with a smile when I'm polite."

Papas smiled. "Good idea! All we have to do to get rid of war is to get the U.S. Peace Corps to smile more often."

"Nonsense! That's utterly superficial," said the woman. "That is dealing with the symptom, not the cause. Humans are innately aggressive. It is part of our animal heritage, and we could not have survived our early years on earth if we had not fought for our right to survive. But now, our unconscious tendencies to hate and kill are often as useless as our appendixes. We might be better off born without them."

"But that's the point," said Papas. "We are aggressive—even pigeons will attack when pained or frustrated—and we have to learn to live with the instinctual parts of our personalities. But we can only do that if we are bright enough to discover who we really are and where we ought to be going."

"And how are we to achieve that miracle?" asked Fraser. "Not through psycho-analyzing the whole world, I trust!"

"And certainly not through passing out candy for polite behavior," said Sapir.

Donald M. Papas adjusted his glasses. "Listen, my children, and you shall hear what I have planned for the First International Symposium on Peace and Personality."

(Continued on page 514.)

Poor Isaac Newton! He was one of the brightest scientists the world has ever known, but he was such a poor student during his first years in school that he almost flunked out. He was born in England on Christmas Day, 1642, but his father was already dead and his mother soon remarried, leaving him in the care of his grandmother. Although he was later knighted by the British government for his contributions to science, as a boy he was a complete failure on the family farm. He was always mooning about, scribbling mathematical symbols on pieces of paper instead of caring for the pigs and chickens. The family sent him off to college, since he obviously was of little use in the "real world" of farming and business.

While he was at Cambridge, Newton changed the course of that "real world." He founded the science of optics almost by himself. If you wear glasses, you owe a debt to Sir Isaac for his early studies on how light passes through lenses and prisms. His mathematical discoveries laid the basis for statistics and for calculus, without which most of modern-day technology couldn't exist. But most of all, Newton gave us the sun and the stars.

According to Newton's own account, he was sitting one day under an apple tree. When one of the ripe apples fell to the ground nearby, Newton asked himself a pregnant question: Why did the apple fall down instead of up? Before Newton knew what he was doing, he had worked out the law of gravity—the fact that objects are attracted to each other. Building on this simple principle, Newton was able to explain in a few simple equations almost *all of the known behaviors* of the stars, suns, moons, planets, comets, and asteroids. He had gotten the science of astronomy off the ground—but he had unwittingly made life very difficult for all psychologists to come.

Newton's goal was to explain all the movements of the heavenly bodies as they float majestically in their orbits. In a very real sense, the goal of psychology is to explain all the actions of the billions of human bodies (including yours and mine) as we run out our orbits on the face of the earth. If Newton could explain the

Isaac Newton.

earth's behavior in a few lines of mathematics, shouldn't psychologists be able to find equally simple explanations for all of man's acts?

Probably you see one difficulty at once. Earth didn't discover the law of gravity—Newton did. Earth is an inanimate object, incapable of insight into the causes of its own performance. But humans are analyzing animals. We do not merely move; we have thoughts and dreams, hopes and aspirations, virtues and vices—and most of all, an urge to comprehend the structure and functioning of our own personalities.

THEORIES OF PERSONALITY

That portion of the psychological world given over to the uncovering of global principles ("equations") describing human behavior is called *personality theory* (°). Personality theorists have the difficult job of explaining, in simple terms, everything that anyone has ever done, can do, or might think of doing—even in the wildest of circumstances. A good theory of human personality must explain human sensations, perceptions, values, motivations, ability to learn and to change, and the tendency of humans to relate to other humans—and the theory must do so in terms that fit within our understanding of the human nervous system and the cultures we live in.

Psychology is still awaiting its Newton. But at least we have had our Freud, our Jung and Adler, our Erikson and Maslow, our Carl Rogers and B.F. Skinner—and many others who have contributed to our presently limited comprehension of human beings while we wait for our Newton to come along.

What Is Personality?

Let us define *personality* (°) as the characteristic way in which a person thinks and behaves as the person adjusts to his or her environment. Such a definition would include the person's *traits* (°), values, motives, genetic blueprint, attitudes, emotional reactivity, abilities, self-image, and intelligence—as well as the person's *overt* (°) or visible behavior patterns. A *complete* theory of personality would not only describe the individual's present style of adjustment but give some notion of how the person got that way and where he or she was going—things that Newton's theory of planetary motion never bothered with.

For the sake of simplicity, Newton assumed that the inner *structure* of all heavenly objects was pretty much the same. By ignoring *individual differences* among the stars, Newton could focus his attention on their behavior or *dynamics* (°)—a Greek word that means "the forces that cause movement or change."

Personality theorists, borrowing as always from the physical sciences, have tended to focus either on the *structure* of an individual's personality, or on the *dynamics* that brought the person to his or her present state of perfection. In this chapter we will look primarily at dynamic theories, saving the structuralists for the next chapter.

Dynamic theories of personality begin with Sigmund Freud. Prior to Freud's time, it was assumed that you were pretty much what your genes allowed you to be. Kings and queens were better than common folk because royalty presumably had better genetic blueprints. By the time you were born, your nature was pretty well determined—"and you can't change human nature." Freud started with this purely biological view toward humans, but soon realized it wasn't the whole story. Human beings did have animal instincts that pushed them through life, and Freud spent a great deal of his time trying to determine just what these instincts were and how they were expressed in conscious and unconscious thought. But Freud was one of the first to realize that by thinking, by reasoning, humans could battle with and sometimes overcome their instinctual urges.

Personality theory. That part of psychology that attempts to explain *why* people think, feel, and act as they do. The theorist usually attempts to explain all human thought and behavior in terms of a few general principles. Each of us has his or her own theory about the causes of human behavior, so there are as many theories as there are people. The major differences between your own unique theory and that of (let's say) Sigmund Freud are that Freud probably was a little more systematic in tying his explanations together—and that he wrote out his ideas and published them.

Personality. From the Greek word *persona*, which means "mask." In olden days, Greek actors used to wear masks on the stage. Each role they played had a different mask associated with it. As they put on a new mask, the actors assumed different personalities.

Traits. A talent, skill, or way of performing. Intelligence is assumed to be a pesonality trait.

Overt (oh-VERT). From the Latin word meaning "to open." Any visible act is overt. The opposite of overt is covert, which means hidden or latent.

Dynamics (die-NAM-icks). From the Greek word meaning "powerful," or "to be able." A dynamic person is someone with a forceful or powerful personality. In medicine, doctors study both the structure, or anatomy, of the body, and the dynamics or physiological processes of the body. Our words "dynamo" and "dynamite" come from the same Greek source. Freud (froyd), Jung (yewng), and Adler (AHD-lur) were interested both in the structure and the dynamics of the human personality.

Analgesic (an-al-GEE-sick). A pain-killing drug. See Chapter 3.

Freud saw personality as being shaped by the *interaction* between biological and intra-psychic forces. But perhaps because he was the first to break with past traditions, Freud saw humans as physiological animals struggling to become psychic individuals. His colleague, Carl Jung, disagreed. To Jung, humans were primarily spiritual beings. Jung, then, emphasized the purely intra-psychic aspects of human personality. Another colleague, Alfred Adler, took the next logical step. Adler saw people as being social creatures, influenced more by environmental events than by physiological or mental forces.

Three viewpoints: the biological, the intra-psychic, the social/behavioral. Logically, a theory of personality should take all three aspects of human beings into account, giving equal weight to all three. To date, no theory does so. Indeed, many of the arguments among personality theorists have to do with which one or two of the viewpoints should be given major emphasis. Let us first look at each of the major dynamic theories in detail, and then ask ourselves how each might be broadened and perhaps bettered.

SIGMUND FREUD

Sigmund Freud had a problem. Or rather, he had several of them. It is a mark of his greatness that, in trying to solve his own dark difficulties, he was able to shed a great deal of light on the many mental problems that people everywhere must face.

Freud was born in 1856 in what is now Czechoslovakia, but he lived for almost 80 years in Vienna. Austria had for centuries been the crossroads of middle Europe, and opposing armies from east and west had frequently turned the little country into a bloody battleground. As a student growing up in this beautiful but war-scarred land, Freud could not make up his mind what road to success he should follow. For a while he wanted to be a chemist, but found that he wasn't particularly gifted in that field. So he turned to anatomy and physiology. He studied medicine at the University of Vienna not because he was interested in curing people but because it was an intellectual challenge—and because it was a great Jewish tradition to become a medical doctor.

After taking his degree in medicine in 1881, Freud spent almost 20 years studying the human nervous system before he developed his first theory of personality. While working as a neuro-physiologist, he investigated the *analgesic* (°) properties of cocaine (*see* Chapter 3); he proved that many of the nerve cells in the spinal cord of man and animals are identical; he studied the physiology of hearing; and he published textbooks on cerebral paralysis and the effects of brain damage on children's speech.

Perhaps because of his medical training, Freud believed that you could not understand an individual's intra-psychic life unless you knew a great deal about the way that the human nervous system functioned. But neuro-physiology was a very young science when Freud began his research. It simply could not give Freud the answers he needed in trying to explain mental functioning. Freud solved this problem by inventing terms and ideas to fill in the gaps where biological data were lacking. These "psychic inventions" (such as the id, ego, and super-ego) constitute the heart and soul of his two theories of personality.

Freud would have preferred to remain a physiological researcher, but his money ran out. So he solved this problem by turning to the practice of psychiatry instead, to keep mind and body together. Around 1885, Freud spent several months in Paris, studying hypnosis with Charcot (*see* Chapter 18). Freud's interest in personality seems to have begun at this time, and he returned from Paris believing that hypnosis might be useful in curing some types of insanity, as we have seen. This view was strengthened by the success that another Viennese psychiatrist, Josef Breuer, had achieved using hypnosis with an hysterical patient.

Sigmund Freud in 1906.

Under hypnosis, Breuer had gotten this patient to relive some early unhappy experiences. After the patient had "acted out" these childhood miseries, the hysterical symptoms seemed to disappear.

Together with Breuer, Freud developed a technique called *catharsis* (°)—the re-enactment of emotional situations while under hypnosis. Catharsis was supposed to work because it allowed the patient to dissipate or use up all of the energy (dynamic forces) that had been bottled up inside. It was this repressed energy which presumably was producing the "insane" behavior and thoughts that were making the patient miserable.

Unfortunately, hypnosis didn't always work very well. At best, it seemed to remove the "insane behavior" without curing the underlying intra-psychic problem that presumably caused the behavior (*see* Chapter 16). Freud solved this particular problem when he discovered the importance of the *interpersonal relationship* between therapist and patient. He found that if he merely encouraged a patient to think about his or her past life, the patient could often dig up long-forgotten but important memories. The patient could then undergo catharsis—that is, relive traumatic moments from childhood—without using hypnosis as a crutch. Additionally, if Freud could get the patient to analyze these critical experiences in unemotional terms, the patient often gained insight into or understanding of what was wrong at the moment. Freud called this technique "psycho-analysis" and he built his psycho-analytic theory of personality on the case histories of the patients who sought his help.

Freud and colleagues. **(Back row, l. to r.)** A.A. Brill, Ernest Jones, Sandor Ferenczi; **(front row, l. to r.)** Freud, Stanley Hall, Carl Jung.

The Unconscious, Preconscious, and Conscious

Why did Freud's patients need his help? Many of them were well-educated, middle-class Jews who seemed to be as mentally war-torn as Vienna had been physically. Like everyone else, these patients had very strong physical needs, particularly a need for sexual expression. Their cathartic "re-living" experiences suggested to Freud that sexual needs occurred even in newborn infants—if one interpreted the word "sexual" in its broadest sense. But most of his patients had been punished for expressing any of their childhood sexual desires. This punishment appeared to drive their needs "underground," out of the patients' "streams of consciousness." Since the needs had not been satisfied, the energy associated with these needs was still present, lurking unconsciously "in the back of the patient's mind." Catharsis and psycho-analysis brought these hidden needs forward into consciousness.

But where were these lusty, unexpressed desires hiding in the mind? One of Freud's greatest insights came in his solution to this knotty problem—when he realized that the mind must have different areas or *structures*, not all of which are ordinarily available to consciousness. In 1913, Freud divided the human *psyche* (°) into three regions or systems: the unconscious, the preconscious, and the conscious. This was his structural theory of personality. In his later years he worked out the various ways in which these three systems interacted with, or affected, one another. This was his dynamic theory of personality.

The Unconscious When we are born, Freud said, we are nothing but a mass of blind biological desires—we are motivated almost entirely by urges to eat, sleep, drink, move around, and reduce pain to the minimum. These physiological instincts demand immediate gratification, and what little mental activity we have at birth is aimed at satisfying the pressing demands that our bodies make. The newborn thinks with its body, not with its mind—because, according to Freud, it is driven to release its instinctual energy by any process that it can.

This greedy, selfish, infantile, socially unrealistic way of behavior is the *primary process* (°) by which the child responds to its needs. Because this is "body think"

Catharsis (ka-THAR-sis, or kuh-THAR-sis). From the Greek word meaning "to purge" or "to clean out." If you are constipated and take a laxative to "clean out" your digestive system, you have undergone a physical catharsis. Freud and Breuer (BROY-er) believed that psycho-therapy could act as a psychological catharsis to cleanse the mind of bottled-up emotions.

Psyche (SIGH-key). From the Greek word meaning "life, spirit, soul, self." Now used to mean "mind." In Greek mythology, Psyche was a beautiful maiden representing the soul who was pursued by Eros, the god of love. Freud put Psyche and Eros together in a marriage he called psycho-analysis.

Primary process. According to Freud, a primitive, selfish way of thinking characteristic of children, or of the id (the childish part of everyone's personality). Primary process thinking is often non-logical and sometimes creative. See the discussion of the "minor hemisphere" at the end of Chapter 2.

Pleasure principle. Freud's notion that we are all driven to satisfy our needs. The reduction of a drive gives us pleasure.

Secondary process. According to Freud, thinking that involves rational planning for the future; logical thought processes that often involve delaying the gratification of immediate needs or whims. See the discussion of the "dominant hemisphere" at the end of Chapter 2.

Reality principle. Freud felt that we have to learn that the world has a reality of its own, separate from what we wish it to be. Children sometimes act as if the world is their oyster, that it is an extension of their minds, and should do what they tell it to do. This sort of secondary process thinking often gets a child in trouble—until it learns that it is but a small part of the real world and that it must give up momentary pleasures today to get bigger and better pleasures tomorrow.

and not "mind think," the child has no way of attaching verbal labels to these primary process experiences. Hence, memories of childhood emotions are not ordinarily available to the mature mind. But these "body thoughts" still reside in the memory system and make up the bulk of what Freud called the *unconscious* mind.

And since unconscious thoughts are mostly tied to the satisfaction of infantile bodily needs, unconscious (primary process) thinking obeys what Freud called the *pleasure principle* (°). Whenever you go on a wild spree and spend all your money, instead of saving something for a rainy day, you are unconsciously obeying the pleasure principle.

But not all youthful experiences are pleasurable. The unconscious portion of the mind also contains memories of those unpleasant times when the child was forced to deny the pleasure principle by controlling its primitive urges. Learning to delay its satisfactions both helps the child mature psychologically and makes it a future candidate for a psycho-analyst's couch.

The Conscious While it is an infant, most of the child's immediate needs are met by its mother. But as the child matures, the mother becomes less permissive and refuses to give it everything it wants at the instant the desire occurs. Slowly, over the years, the child discovers quite painfully that it must sometimes give up momentary pleasures for more long-range goals. It is forced to *learn*, to take into account past events and to predict the future. From this learning, the child develops a system of conscious thought patterns for handling the world outside it—and for controlling its internal, unconscious bodily needs.

Freud saw the *conscious mind* as a survival system that has logic and reason forced upon it by the external environment, just as the language that the child comes to speak is forced on it by its parents and peers. Freud called this rational, verbal way of thinking the *secondary process* (°) of the mind, which obeys the *reality principle* (°) imposed on it by the outside world. According to Freud, it is the battle between the pleasure principle (immediate gratification) and the opposing reality principle (delayed gratification) that causes consciousness to emerge in the child.

The Preconscious Between the unconscious and the conscious thought systems is a boundary area, a threshold, that Freud called the *preconscious*. As ideas, dreams, or wishes bubble up from the unconscious, they are sometimes held just at the edge of consciousness—as when someone's name is "just on the tip of your tongue." If the images are too threatening to the person, they may never directly become conscious, but may linger like ghosts in a haunted house, frightening the occupants without ever becoming visible. For the most part, however, preconscious thoughts can be made conscious without too much difficulty.

Id, Ego, and Super-ego

Many of Freud's patients were adults who had been overly protected during childhood. Their parents had been too permissive for too long a time—they had asked too little and given too much to the child. These patients had considerable difficulty in controlling their childish impulses. Indeed, it seemed to Freud as if there were a separate infantile personality hiding in the unconscious portions of the patient's mind, screaming for attention. Because the adult portions of the mind were so weak, the "hidden child" in the unconscious often got its way—and the person got into trouble.

In his first theory Freud talked about two types of *ego processes*, taking the term "ego" from the Latin and Greek words for "I" or "self." There was the "pleasure ego," or unconscious self, that pushed the person toward satisfying his or her instinctual desires in a devil-may-care fashion. And there was the "reality ego," or conscious self, that used logic and judgment to guard the person against harm while trying to get a little adult pleasure in the process.

By 1923, when Freud had analyzed many patients, he became convinced that the "pleasure ego" was more than a process—it was a personality structure all its own, with its own way of behaving. He called it the *id* (°), the Latin word for "it," and assumed that it was guided chiefly by the pleasure principle. The "reality self" became the *ego* (°), that part of your intra-psychic self that you are conscious of. In our terms, perhaps, the ego is equivalent to the cortical Board of Directors. The ego is guided by the reality principle.

The morals, laws, and customs of the social environment were represented in yet a third portion of the personality. Freud named it the *super-ego* (°), so called because it was above (or *super*-ior to) the ego. In a sense, "super-ego" is another word for "conscience."

Libidinal Energy According to Freud, we are all born with lusty ids, filled to the brim with psychic energy from our *libidos* (°). Freud used the term "libido" to designate the dynamic "life force" he believed propels all living organisms. The selfish id tries to discharge this energy in the most satisfying ways it can—just as any "unconscious" animal would try to do. When the child is newborn, only its oral receptors are mature enough to release this libidinal energy; so the infant's psychological world is centered on its mouth. As the child begins to learn better and more efficient ways of feeding, and as it is forced to wait for its meals from time to time, the ego begins to develop as a means of holding down or re-channeling the libidinal energy. If the mother is too permissive, the ego develops very late and never really gains the necessary strength to bring the childish id under mature control.

By the end of the child's first year of life, the anal receptors presumably mature. Now, Freud said, libidinal energy can also be released through defecation. But when the child's parents decide to toilet train it, the ego gains more and more influence over the dynamic flow of energy from the libido.

When the child moves out of the oral and anal stages of development into the phallic stage, the receptors in its sex organs also become capable of discharging libidinal energy, and the ego has a new area in which to fight the id for control. Freud's psycho-sexual stages, discussed in the previous chapter, are in reality the individual battles the ego wages in its war to become a mature "self."

The phallic stage in Freud's second theory ushers in the Oedipal or Electral crisis, in which the child becomes emotionally attached to the parent of the opposite sex. Freud believed that the child resolved this incestual attachment through the development of its super-ego, that part of its personality that says "NO!" to its anti-social urgings. The super-ego of the young boy, for instance, develops by taking on the values and morals of (1) the boy's father, a step that allows the boy to control his incestual desires for his mother; and (2) the social customs and approved behaviors of the society he lives in. The super-ego develops out of the ego, but gains its own ability to influence the discharge of libidinal energy. The super-ego becomes judge, critic, and conscience; it sets up ideal standards of behavior and urges the ego to adopt them.

The ego, caught in the crossfire between id (biology) and super-ego (social environment), learns to defend itself as best it can—just as the Viennese learned to defend themselves against the intrusions of their powerful neighbors. But with such wars going on inside us all, little wonder (Freud said) so many of us become "psychic casualties."

Defense Mechanisms

From trying to help his patients solve their problems, Freud noted that the ego apparently had several *defense mechanisms* (°) at its disposal to help handle the

Id (rhymes with "kid"). The primitive, instinctual, childish, unconcious portion of the personality that obeys the pleasure principle.

Ego (EE-go). The conscious self. Obeys the reality principle and tries to keep the id under control.

Super-ego (SOUP-per-EE-go). That part of the human psyche that is concerned with the moral laws of the society the individual grows up in. The conscience.

Libidos (lib-BEE-dohs). The libido is the "life force." See Chapter 21.

Defense mechanisms. Techniques used by the ego to defend itself against impulses or commands from the id and the super-ego.

Freud said that during the Oedipal stage a young boy develops strong emotional feelings about his mother.

Anxiety. The internal or intra-psychic feeling that something bad is about to happen—"butterflies in the stomach." The biological correlates of anxiety are muscle tension and an increased release of neural transmitters, such as adrenalin. The behavioral correlates of tension are sweating, trembling, and a tendency to escape or avoid the anxiety-producing situation. Freud believed that anxiety of some kind is associated with most types of neuroses.

Repression (ree-PRESH-shun). A defense mechanism in which threatening thoughts or desires are inhibited or made unconscious.

Fixation. A defense mechanism involving an interruption of psycho-sexual development. If an infant's oral needs are not satisfied, its maturation may be disrupted and its personality may remain stopped or fixated at the oral level.

Regresses (ree-GRESS-es). A defense mechanism in which an individual who has reached a higher level of psycho-sexual adjustment may return to a more primitive or childish way of thinking and acting. See Chapter 18.

Identification (eye-den-tiff-uh-KAY-shun). A defense mechanism in which the person attempts to handle anxiety by imitating the behavior of someone feared or loved.

ultimatums from the irrepressible id and the stern super-ego. But because these demands are usually unconscious, the ego apparently does not always realize when it is about to be attacked. Freud thought *anxiety* (°), that prickly-nagging feeling of impending disaster, was the mind's way of warning the ego that it had better put on its intra-psychic armor. Almost all of the defense mechanisms have three characteristics in common:

1. They are ways of trying to reduce anxiety.
2. They involve the denying or the distortion of reality.
3. They operate at an unconscious level so that the ego is not always aware of what it has done (nor how to change things later on).

Repression The most important of the defense mechanisms is undoubtedly *repression* (°), the process whereby the ego pushes down or denies threatening thoughts or desires and keeps them from becoming conscious. In repressing these energy-laden thoughts, the ego has to use up some of its own energy resources—for, as Newton said of physical objects, force can be opposed only by an equal or greater force. The more painful the memory, or the stronger the unacceptable urge, the more work the ego must go through to keep the material repressed. Eventually the ego may literally run out of steam, and bits and pieces of the repressed material may leak through to consciousness as slips of the tongue, or as weird but significant dreams. By re-living these painful experiences in therapy, a person may bring the repressed material into consciousness, learn to accept it, and hence free the ego to use its energy in more productive and creative activities.

Fixation If a child encounters severe problems during the early stages of its development, before its ego is fully formed, the ego may rely on more primitive defense mechanisms to handle its problem. If toilet training is begun too early, before the child is physiologically ready to control its bowels and bladder, the ego may become *fixated* at this level and thereafter may choose to discharge an abnormal amount of libidinal energy through anal activities. Too much pleasure may cause a similar *fixation* (°) at the anal level. If a young girl masturbates too frequently while in the phallic stage, her ego may find this such a delightful release that she never solves her Electra crisis and hence never learns the joys of heterosexual behavior.

Regression Fixation is defined as the ego's refusal to move upward to a higher level of psychological maturation. But sometimes, after the ego has stepped up to the next psycho-sexual stage, it may become so threatened that it *regresses* (°) to an earlier, more comfortable level where its rewards were more easily obtained. When placed under considerable stress, a person may eat a lot, talk a lot, drink a lot, or smoke a lot—a regression to an earlier (oral) mode of pleasure. Or when a young man encounters heterosexual difficulties, he may resort to such immature forms of gratification as masturbation or homosexuality, rather than trying to solve his present interpersonal problems.

Identification The Oedipus and Electra crises are resolved by a defense mechanism Freud called *identification* (°), the process of taking on the characteristics of some other person. The young girl identifies with her mother out of fear of her mother's wrath—and thereby builds up her super-ego. (Freud saw the super-ego itself as a kind of "super" defense mechanism.) In later life, a person may attempt to recreate the image or memory of a lost parent or love-object by *incorporating* parts of that individual's values or behavior patterns.

Reaction Formation and Projection Another defense mechanism is that of *reaction formation* (°), in which the ego changes unacceptable love into acceptable hate (or vice-versa). If a mother hates her child, a feeling the woman's ego cannot tolerate consciously, the mother may smother the child with affection. Or the mother's ego may indulge in *projection* (°) by pretending that the child actually hates her. Freud believed that the mythical "old maid" who looked under her bed every night before she went to sleep, fearing to find a man hiding there who might be waiting to rape her, was actually *projecting* her own unacceptable desire for sex onto the man she feared (hoped) was lurking under her maidenly mattress.

Displacement and Sublimation Over the years Freud and his followers identified a great many defense mechanisms, of which we have space to mention only the best known. The last of these are *displacement* (°) and *sublimation* (°), which lie at the heart of Freud's notions of what being human is all about.

At birth, the objects of all our instincts are specified by our genetic inheritance; you don't have to teach an infant that food satisfies its hunger, because its body already knows this. As the child grows up, and passes through the several psycho-sexual stages, it continues to be driven by libidinal energy, but the *objects* of its instincts can change through learning and experience. That is, the ego gains the ability to *displace* the flow of instinctual energy from one object to another. Freud believed that almost all of an adult's attitudes, desires, values, interests, preferences, interests, and habit patterns come from the *displacement* of energy from its original inborn object choices. For example, children learn to talk in part because the ego is able to convert the energy first directed toward breast-sucking into speech patterns instead.

Sublimation is at once a form of displacement and the most mature of the defense mechanisms; indeed, Freud believed that sublimated energy is what makes the machinery of civilization move. Freud thought that the energy that an artist devotes to painting—or a scientist to the laboratory, or a politician to governing—was really energy that had been channeled away from sex or aggression or eating. Highly productive people were, according to Freud, almost always involved in sublimating primitive energy into socially acceptable behaviors. Sublimation seldom results in complete satisfaction of the id's needs, however, so there is always some energy left over that needs to be discharged. Freud believed this is why civilized people occasionally throw temper tantrums, or make war on their neighbors, or engage in other childish behaviors.

Reaction formation. A defense mechanism in which the person acts exactly opposite to the way he or she feels. Hate becomes love, and vice-versa.

Projection. A defense mechanism involving the projecting of one's desires on external objects or on other people. The use of projective tests is based on the assumption that everyone makes use of this Freudian defense mechanism.

Displacement (dis-PLACE-ment). The unconscious defense mechanism of transferring emotional reactions from one object to another. If a man is criticized severely by his boss at work, the man may not be able to express his hostility toward the boss for fear of being fired. So the man goes home and kicks the cat or spanks his children. He has displaced his hatred toward the boss onto the cat or the kids.

Sublimation (sub-blee-MAY-shun). The most mature of the defense mechanisms. The use of sexual energy for creative or social purposes. Making music when you really want to make love is sublimation.

Theologians (thee-oh-LOW-juns). Priests, ministers, rabbis, and scholars who study religion or the laws of religious groups are called "theologians."

Occult (ock-KULT). From the Latin word for "hidden," or "covered up." Occult mysteries are those which are supernatural or "hidden from the eye."

Personal unconscious. Each individual's collection of memories and ideas that stem from that person's own experiences. Your Long-term Memory.

Collective unconscious. Racial memories. Unconscious thoughts wired into your brain by your genetic blueprint. Instinctual behaviors or ideas fed forward by your genes.

Freud's theory has had a tremendous influence on Western thought, in no small part because it was the first to take into account all three important influences on personality development—biology, intra-psychic experience, and the present environment. In his early work he emphasized the importance of unconscious physiological forces—the id was "it," and man was a prisoner of his genetic blueprint. In his later years, before he died of cancer in 1939, Freud decided that past experience—that is, the early maturational process—was the chief determinant of personality. He saw therapy as a way of strengthening the ego, so that it could handle the demands of the id and super-ego in more satisfying ways.

In the United States, at least, it is a little known fact that Freud's ideas about such things as id and ego were first expressed in purely physiological terms. In 1895, before he wrote any of his well-known books on the structure and function of personality, Freud published a "Project" in which he defined most of the concepts that later cropped up in his dynamic theory of psycho-analysis. These definitions were all expressed in neuro-physiological language. Thus to Freud, "libido" referred to neural firing patterns, and not to some mythical "energy pump" somewhere inside the body. When Freud spoke of "resistance," he meant synaptic resistance; when he talked of "repression," he had reference to neural inhibition; when he mentioned "instinct," he had in mind not some blind psychic urge but rather a highly specific reflex. Sadly enough, no accurate English translation of the 1895 "Project" was published until 1976. Not realizing his real intent, English-speaking scientists often criticized Freud for being too mystical or mentalistic; if anything, one might criticize the man for having been too physiological in his approach to the study of human personality.

Perhaps because of the years he spent studying the nervous system, Freud paid too little attention to environmental or behavioral processes. And perhaps because of his strict upbringing, he appears to have considered the social world repressive and moralistic. It seems not to have occurred to him that the rewards offered by the environment could be as influential as its punishments, and that spiritual and humane values could be as motivating as food and sex. As we will next learn, not all of his followers agreed with this emphasis on unconscious biological factors and the unchangeable influence of the child's early upbringing.

CARL JUNG

Born in Switzerland in 1875, Carl Gustav Jung came from a family of *theologians* (°) and medical doctors. As a student at the University of Zurich, he dabbled in biology, philosophy, archeology, mythology, and mysticism. His dissertation for his medical degree had to do with the psychology of the *occult* (°). Jung discovered Freud in 1907 and became something of a disciple until 1912, when Jung branched out with his own theory.

Jung could not accept Freud's notion that the chief task of humans in life is to bring their infantile, sexual instincts under control. Human beings are not aggressive beasts only recently tamed by civilization; rather, Jung said, humans are religious animals whose unconscious roots go back to the very beginnings of the race. Jung believed we are motivated more by moral and religious values than by primitive sexuality. To Jung, the purpose of our existence is for each of us to achieve an integration between our conscious perceptions of the external world and our unconscious, mystical experiences.

To Freud, the unconscious was the land of the libido and the home of the id—that is, the source of our psychic energies. But to Jung, there was not one unconscious but two—the *personal unconscious* (°) and the *collective unconscious* (°).

Carl Jung.

The Personal Unconscious

By personal unconscious, Jung had in mind something like Freud's idea of the preconscious—that is, the pool of half-forgotten ideas, wishes, and past experiences that are now so weak that they can be brought into awareness only with difficulty. According to Jung, some of these thoughts and memories may be so closely related that they grow together, or congeal into a *complex* (°) or structure all their own. This complex of associated experiences might then split off from the person's psyche and function independently, with a psychological life of its own. When a person takes drugs, or otherwise achieves a state of Nirvana (*see* Chapter 3), one of these complexes may "take over" and act independently, causing hallucinations, *speaking in tongues* (°), or other odd forms of behavior. The purpose of psycho-therapy, from a Jungian point of view, is often that of identifying these complexes and bringing them back into conscious control.

The Collective Unconscious

The *collective unconscious* was a much more interesting and important part of the human psyche to Jung than was the *personal unconscious*. The collective unconscious houses all of the "racial memories" that each person is presumed to be born with. Jung, in his study of *anthropology* (°), had noticed that some myths and ideas seem to appear in all cultures. Even primitive tribes believe in a Supreme Being, and many of them have very similar stories about the creation of the world, the virgin birth of God, man's fall from heaven or paradise, and heroes who lead men wisely. Jung called these myths *archetypes* (°) and thought that, through evolutionary processes, the mental images associated with these archetypes had become engraved on our genes. Thus, each human being is born—according to Jung—with some unconscious mental fragments of the past history of the human race. The most important archetype of all, however, is that of the *self-concept* (°) or ego, for it allows the person to integrate all of the conscious and other unconscious psychological processes into one meaningful whole.

Jung's Polarities

As colorful as Jung's thinking was, he tended to theorize in terms of blacks and whites, or psychological attributes that were at opposite ends of a pole or scale. He called these attributes *polarities* (°).

Jung believed that the self or ego was determined by the interactions of two innate attitudes and four inborn functions. The two "polar" attitudes are *introversion* (°) and *extroversion* (°). Some people seem to be born introverts—that is, they spend most of their time looking toward their inner or personal world. Highly religious individuals—such as the monk who retires to a monastery to think and pray—tend to be introverts. The extrovert is someone who focuses on the outside environment. Outgoing, highly social individuals are examples of what Jung meant by extroverts. Jung believed that we all have both tendencies within us, but usually one predominates. We are usually conscious of which attitude is dominant—that is, we know whether we are an extrovert or an introvert. The subordinate attitude is usually unconscious, but expresses itself in dreams and fantasies if it is not expressed openly.

The four ego functions are thinking, feeling, sensing, and intuiting. The *thinking* process involves the use of logic to comprehend the nature of the world. In earlier chapters we used the term "information processing" to describe much of what Jung meant by the thinking process. By *feeling*, Jung had in mind our ability to experience pleasure and pain, love and hate. Jung called *sensing* the "door to reality," referring to the process whereby sensory inputs are received and recog-

Complex. A housing complex is a group of houses set off or isolated from other nearby dwellings. Jung believed that certain thoughts and ideas might grow into an independent unit or substructure of the personality. He called this separated set of thoughts a "complex."

Speaking in tongues. During religious ceremonies, persons belonging to some churches believe they are "possessed" by God. During the height of this altered state of consciousness, the person may speak in what seems to be a foreign language. The belief held by such people is that God is speaking through them in languages not comprehensible to ordinary humans. Such an experience is called "speaking in tongues."

Anthropology (an-throw-POL-oh-gee). From the Greek words *anthropo*, meaning "male person," and *ology*, meaning "study of." One of the social sciences concerned with man—his body, mind, and cultural environment. Humorously defined as "the study of man—embracing woman."

Archetypes (ARK-ee-types). From the Greek words meaning "the original model, form, or pattern from which something is made or from which something develops." The archetypes that Jung referred to are the original models of myths, legends, and stories—instinctual thought patterns passed on genetically from generation to generation.

Self-concept. In Jung's terms, the original archetype of "self-awareness." The instinctual percept that one is a separate entity.

Polarities (poh-LAIR-it-tease). Opposites. Good and evil are polarities.

Introversion (INN-tro-vurr-shun). The act of directing one's attention toward or getting pleasure from one's own thoughts and feelings.

Extroversion (EX-tro-vurr-shun). Polar opposite of introversion. The act of directing one's attention toward happenings or people in the outside world. Literally, "to go outside."

Alfred Adler.

nized by the brain. *Intuition* is the function by which we gain information about our unconscious processes, by which we look deep within ourselves. Jung felt that the intuitive person tried to get at the nature of existence by means of mystical experiences—that is, through altered states of consciousness (*see* Chapter 3).

Freud's early work was with children, so perhaps it is natural that he focused on the early, developmental years. Jung worked to a great degree with older patients, and never did offer a complete account of how the personality is formed. Jung did mention a radical change that often occurs in a person's later life, when the individual typically becomes less extroverted and impulsive and becomes more introverted and controlled. At this time, the ego can channel libidinal energy into spiritual behaviors and gain new understanding by looking deep into the unconscious. To Jung, the more devout and mystical a person became, the more mature or "self-realized" the person was presumed to be.

ALFRED ADLER

Freud was a fairly gloomy man. Despite the intellectual pleasures of civilization—of art and science and music and literature—the human race seemed to prefer the immediate satisfaction of physical needs. Why? Because, Freud said, our animal instincts are still too strong, and the id too often wins out in its continual battle with the more cultured ego. Jung rejected the animal urges, but not the instincts; indeed, to him, the mature individual was the one who sought actualization through understanding and even surrendering to the instinctual heritage of the past rather than to the society of the present. Both Freud and Jung, then, emphasized the importance of genetic endowment as the major (if often unconscious) determinant of human personality.

Alfred Adler could not accept the overriding importance either of instincts or of unconscious processes. Born and educated in Vienna, Adler joined Freud's group a few years after he had taken his medical degree. Adler's first work was on the living conditions of Austrian tailors, a study that helped confirm his early bias toward the importance of environmental factors in determining personality. As fascinated as Adler was by Freud's ideas, he was the first to break away from "the master" and form his own group, the Society for Individual Psychology.

Adler disputed Freud's notion that human behavior is dominated by the workings of blind, selfish instincts. Instead, Adler thought, people govern themselves by a conscious need to express and fulfill themselves as unique individuals. Rejecting both Freud's pessimism and Jung's mysticism, Adler believed that human beings can shape their own destinies and influence the patterns of their own lives, that they can build a superior society by satisfying their basic need to transcend their personal problems.

The Creative Power

To Adler, life is a conscious struggle to achieve superiority. Thus, he denied the importance of sexual instincts and substituted aggressive tendencies in their place. Freud and Jung emphasized the unconscious, unknowable influences on behavior; Adler believed that most of us are only too aware of why we do what we do. We see our inferiorities, and we strive to overcome them. We have an instinct for self-realization, for completion and perfection, that Adler thought was the driving force of life itself. Adler called this force the *creative power* (°) and thought it was the "first cause" of all behavior.

The Inferiority Complex

Children learn very early that adults can do things that children cannot; this knowledge creates in all of us an *inferiority complex* (°) that adds to our motiva-

Creative power. According to Adler, the instinctual drive for self-realization. Similar to Freud's idea of ego, and to Jung's notion of the self-concept.

Inferiority complex. A sub-system (complex) of the personality that, realizing the person's own failings, attempts to overcome them by efforts to succeed, or become superior.

tion to succeed. As children we also learn that other people in our life space are bigger and faster and brighter and prettier and stronger than we; and this knowledge merely fuels the fire of our feelings of insecurity. The inferiority complex creates a drive for *compensation* (°), the urge to overcome our failures in one part of life by excelling in another. The small, weak boy may exercise to develop his muscles, or try to succeed in his school studies to compensate for his physical weakness.

Life Style

Adler was an optimist. He believed that we have buried in our genes a basic need to cooperate with each other and to work toward building a finer society. This innate tendency needs developmental guidance, however, and so Adler spent much of his time working with teachers and setting up child-guidance clinics. Through training and experience, a person learns to express his or her own striving for superiority in a unique way, which Adler termed the person's *style of life* (°). In a sense, Adler's "style of life" is equivalent to Freud's concept of the ego. At first, Adler thought this style was fixed early in life; later, he decided this view did not do justice to the dynamic quality of human development. This emphasis on the importance of *social factors* in determining personality was, for a time, unique in psycho-analytic circles and helped give rise to what we now call "social psychology." And by assuring people that they were basically humane, open-minded, and in control of their own destinies, Adler encouraged the development of "humanistic psychology." Indeed, as humanist Abraham Maslow stated in 1970, "Alfred Adler becomes more and more correct year by year. As the facts come in they give stronger and stronger support to his image of man."

ERIK H. ERIKSON

Freud was a true Viennese, and his ideas and theories were influenced by the middle-European patients whom he treated. Strangely enough, however, his first professional recognition came from the United States, when in 1909 G. Stanley Hall (*see* Chapter 21) invited him to speak at Clark University. In some ways the United States accepted Freud more readily than did most of Europe, and the development of Freud's ideas was eagerly carried on by U.S. psycho-analysts. Although Erik Erikson was born abroad, he spent most of his life in the United States and can be counted as an American. Erikson has, in general, followed Adler's lead in stating that personality development continues long after the genital period is reached.

Like most U.S. psycho-analysts, Erikson believes that the ego is a much more important determinant of personality than are the id and the super-ego. The ego is the point of contact between the individual and society. Therefore, Erikson says, the type of society that the person grows up in is at least as important as the person's instinctual drives. Erikson's *psychosocial theory of development* (°) is hence less biased by middle-European culture than was Freud's, as we will soon see.

Erikson accepted most of Freud's notions on the importance of instinctual drives in young children—but insisted that it is the *conflict* between instincts and cultural demands that shapes the child's personality. Instincts are presumably pretty much the same from one child to another, but cultures differ remarkably from one part of the world to another, and cultures grow and develop just as do human beings. Freud and Jung emphasized the importance of past history on the maturation of the individual; Erikson, like Adler, emphasized the future. At any given moment in time, Erikson said, the person's anticipation of future events helps determine how the person will behave in the "here and now."

Compensation. The attempt to overcome one's failings in one area by becoming superior in other ways.

Style of life. Adler's term for the uniqueness of the personality. Each person, Adler said, tries to succeed in his or her individual way. The characteristic behavior patterns and attitudes that differentiate one person from another.

Psychosocial theory of development. Erikson's extension and elaboration of Freudian theory. Freud stated that personality development more or less ends at puberty. Erikson, who places more emphasis on environmental factors than did Freud, believes that personality development can continue all one's life.

Erik H. Erikson.

TABLE 22.1 Erikson's Stages of Development

STAGE	1	2	3	4	5	6	7	8
Maturity								Ego Integrity vs. Despair
Adulthood							Generativity vs. Stagnation	
Young Adulthood						Intimacy vs. Isolation		
Puberty and Adolescence					Identity vs. Role Confusion			
Latency				Industry vs. Inferiority				
Locomotor-Genital			Initiative vs. Guilt					
Muscular-Anal		Autonomy vs. Shame, Doubt						
Oral Sensory	Basic Trust vs. Mistrust							

SOURCE: Reprinted from *Childhood and Society*, Rev. by Erik H. Erikson, by permission of W.W. Norton & Company, Inc. Copyright 1950, © 1963 by W.W. Norton & Company, Inc.

Eight Developmental Stages

According to Erikson, each human being must pass through eight developmental stages on his or her way to complete maturity (Table 22.1). Each of these stages is characterized by its own type of *crisis*, or conflict. Erikson saw these crises as being eight great tests of the person's character.

1. Erikson called the first developmental stage the "sensory stage," because for the first few months after its birth, the infant is a passive receptor of sensory inputs from the world around it. The sensory stage corresponds closely to what Freud called the oral stage of maturation. To Erikson, the crisis involved in the sensory stage is that of learning a basic *trust or mistrust* of other people. At this point in life the infant is totally dependent on others for its needs. If its mother (or someone else) meets these needs, the infant learns to depend on others in its later life. If the mother is inconsistent in satisfying the infant's needs—for whatever reason—the infant may carry suspicion and doubt through the rest of its years.

2. The second of Erikson's stages, similar to Freud's anal stage, is that of *muscular development*. During toilet training the child learns to control its own muscles and begins to assert its individuality. The crisis here is that of *autonomy* (*), or the ability to control one's own bodily functions. The child either learns autonomy, or, if it is unsuccessful, develops shame and doubt about its own abilities.

3. The third stage, that of *locomotor control*, is similar to Freud's phallic stage. Now the child attempts to develop its own way of asserting its needs and

Autonomy (aw-TAWN-oh-me). Freedom; self-direction.

gaining its rewards. Urged by its instincts to possess its opposite-sex parent (at least in fantasy) and to rival its same-sex parent, the child faces the crisis of inner desires versus society's demands. Erikson believed that if the child could channel its sexual needs into socially acceptable behaviors, the child acquired *initiative* (°). If not, then the child might build up a strong sense of *guilt* that would haunt it the rest of its days.

4. Both Freud and Erikson called the fourth developmental stage that of *latency*. During these (typically) school years, the crisis the child faces is that of *competence* or *failure*. If the child does well in school, it learns that it can succeed; if it does poorly, it gains a sense of inferiority. For example, Isaac Newton was rather an indifferent pupil during his early years. His crisis came when he was attacked by the school bully. Newton fought back, and won. After that time he began to excel in his lessons as well as in after-school fights.

5. At *puberty*, Freud thought, sexual interest returns and the individual must make the final adjustment, that of heterosexuality. Erikson saw the puberty crisis as that of *finding one's identity*. The adolescent must now decide what the future will hold and who he or she will become. Although the social roles available may vary from one society to another, the young person must decide which of these roles to adopt. Problems of sexual confusion must be resolved and the adolescent must plan his or her life as a working, functioning adult.

6. Erikson postulated three final stages of maturation beyond the five that Freud spoke of. The first of these stages, which occurs in *young adulthood*, presents the person with the crisis of *intimacy versus isolation*. If the individual has "found" himself or herself by now, then the person can go on to the delightful task of "finding" someone else to share life's intimacies with. If the person fails to resolve the identity crisis, however, the person will remain isolated from the closest forms of psychological "sharing" with others. The young man or woman who resolves the first six crises exceptionally well becomes trusting, autonomous, full of initiative, highly competent at a variety of tasks, sure of his or her social and personal roles, and able to identify with and understand the intimate feelings of others. But few of us are that fortunate—according to Erikson, most of our personalities are a mixture of partial successes and failures. We function well enough to survive in our particular society, but few of us ever achieve our best or most balanced development.

7. Societies often pass through a period of rapid development, then settle into *complacency* (°) when growth stops and stagnation sets in. Erikson believed that adults often experience the same "growth" crisis during their *middle years*. Human beings need more than intimacy; they must be productive and helpful to their fellow humans. The crisis decision here, then, is that between what Erikson called *generativity* (°) and *stagnation* (°).

8. Erikson's final stage, that of *maturity*, can be reached only by those fortunate individuals who resolve all of the seven prior conflicts successfully. During one's final years, a person must face squarely the termination of his or her life, the ever-present but often unthinkable fact of death. By resolving the prior crises, the person gains the strength to *integrate* (°) even death into the pattern of existence. Knowing that one's life has been successful, one can die as one has lived—with integrity. The person who fails to solve the earlier crises may see his or her life as having been useless, incomplete, unintegrated—or wasted—and the person may succumb to feelings of despair at the futility of existence.

Maturity and Old Age

Adler and Erikson deserve a vote of praise for reminding us that people do not stop developing once they reach adulthood. Even today, most personality theo-

Initiative (in-ISH-uh-tive). The tendency to be self-motivated; to start things on your own rather than waiting to be told.

Complacency (kom-PLAY-sen-see). From the Latin word meaning "to please greatly." A complacent person is someone who is unduly satisfied with his or her own actions or talents. Feeling so perfect, the person finds little reason to change.

Generativity (jen-ur-uh-TIV-uh-tee). To generate is to produce. Generativity is having the power of producing or originating things.

Stagnation (stagg-NAY-shun). From the Latin word meaning "a pool of standing water, a swamp." Any living thing that doesn't move, or grow, tends to stagnate, decay, become dead or bad-smelling (like a swamp).

Integrate (INN-tee-great, or INN-tuh-great). To pull together, to make into a whole. According to Erikson, a mentally healthy person is someone who can integrate all aspects of life into a meaningful whole.

According to Erikson, young adulthood presents the person with the crisis of intimacy versus isolation.

Many adults remain active well into their 80th or 90th year.

rists concentrate on the early years of life, perhaps because children change so dramatically and quickly, perhaps because children are easier (and often a lot more fun) to study than are grown-ups. Whatever the case, we know a fair amount about the mental and physical changes associated with childhood, but very little indeed about how older people adapt and develop.

The "growth" crises that Erikson describes for the middle years is that of generativity versus stagnation. There is a cultural myth in Western society that, like a machine that has worn down from constant use, the older person should become slow-moving, mentally inflexible and rigid, and above all, asexual. Let us look at each of these points in turn.

There is no doubt that most younger people expend more physical energy than do most people in their 40's and 50's, but this change in "body tempo" is probably due more to psychological and social causes than to something like "tired blood." Young people often have neither the skills nor the experience to command high-paying desk jobs that require much mental but little physical exertion. With maturity usually comes the knowledge of how to avoid strenuous exercise—and all the bumps and bruises associated with the same. Professional football players often retire in their 30's, not because they are incapable of continuing, but because their salaries simply are not sufficiently motivating for them to go on suffering the pain and injury too often associated with contact sports. It is also true that we smile indulgently when teenagers perform some spectacularly physical dance, but frown or laugh when older people do the same. The stinging comment "Act your age!" is just as potent a bit of feed forward for older people as it is for the young.

Young people who are just learning about themselves and their social world are perhaps more likely to "latch on to new ideas" than are older people. However, older individuals are generally able to learn more quickly those facts or skills that do not directly contradict their previous learning. The problem in trying to train older people usually is that of helping them achieve high motivation. The law requires that we go to school until we are at least 16; we are seldom forced to learn new things after that. Young adults are often penniless; they must adapt to survive. Older individuals often have money in the bank, social prestige, and various forms of seniority that protect them against the disruptive elements of personal change. In fact, you can teach an old dog (or human) new tricks, but you cannot use the simple reinforcers that work so well with puppies (or children).

In her book *Passages*, published in 1976, Gail Sheehy explores many of the myths associated with sexuality and the aging process. Summarizing the findings of many scientists who have worked in this area, Sheehy asserts that men and women have the same sexual potential at age 18 and again at age 60; in between these extremes, the woman is usually more capable of sexual arousal than is the man. Testosterone (male hormone) levels reach their peak in most men about age 18; from this point on, the man's body secretes less and less of the chemical. This decrease in hormone has two main effects. First, it often increases the time needed between sexual arousals; second, it often allows the man's body to become softer, rounder, or more "feminine" in his mature years. Since such matters are seldom discussed—even between men and their physicians—the man may fear he is becoming impotent and hence no longer able to live up to society's expectations of what "true" male sexual behavior should be. The greater the man's fear becomes, the less able he is to perform sexually. So he may "sublimate" his sexual energies by turning to activities that are less threatening and more rewarding. But, as Sheehy makes clear, it is the anxiety about his performance that is most influential, for even a 90-year-old man typically has a high enough level of testosterone to perform the sex act several times a week.

Many psychologists believe that much the opposite sort of change occurs in women; that is, their hormone levels and sexual desires often reach a peak during their middle years. Our society has typically repressed sexuality in young women. As they grow older, and are freed of many cultural and financial restrictions, they often "blossom" into strong desire at just the time the male is having doubts and is withdrawing from sexual encounters. The woman's husband (or lover) may thus desert the woman in her time of greatest need and ability.

Sheehy points out that the solution for many of these problems is not world-wide psycho-therapy, but rather a more open expression of human desires and a wider *dissemination* (°) of the facts of human sexuality. For example, hormone levels in both men and women are greatly influenced by the frequency with which intercourse occurs. People who, in their middle years, continue to have an active sex life typically look younger, seem to have more energy, and show a greater zest for living than do people who give up this important part of the human experience.

We might say the same thing is true of any part of our existence. Elderly people who "give up" at retirement age, who shut themselves away, who turn their backs on growth and change are typically the people who soon become *senile* (°). While not too many psychological studies have been performed on the elderly, it does seem that older people are much more capable of doing almost everything than society assumes they are. If activity, challenge, and stimulation are necessary for the healthy growth and development of an infant, then shouldn't we expect much the same to be true throughout life?

Freud, who was greatly influenced by Darwin's theory of evolution, emphasized the animal side of human nature—the physiological instincts. Erikson incorporated many elements of Freud's theory into his own, but believed that innate, unconscious urges were important only during the first few years of human development. Erikson saw humans as motivated more by the conscious need for getting along with others and determining their own place in a social world than as being merely pushed hither and yon by blind sexual itches and urges. Erikson believed it is the humane need to relate to other human beings that elevates humans above the rest of the animal kingdom.

HUMANISTIC THEORIES OF PERSONALITY

From a personality theorist's point of view, Sir Isaac Newton had an easy task. All Newton had to do was to describe the behavior of an uncountable number of planets and suns as they coursed their way through empty space. Earth has twirled

Disseminate (diss-SEMM-eye-nate, or diss-SEMM-uh-nate). From the Latin word meaning "to sow seeds" or "to spread around." The news media disseminate information daily by newspapers, magazines, television, and radio. Our word "semen," meaning seed, comes from the same Latin source.

Senile (SEE-nile). The condition of being old and usually forgetful. For a further explanation, see Chapter 24.

Humanist. Someone who is devoted to human welfare. Someone with a strong interest in or love for individual people (as opposed to loving nations, organizations, or abstract ideas).

Phenomenal field (fee-NOM-me-nall, or fee-NOM-uh-null). A phenomenon is an event, a happening, an experience. The sum total of all your experiences (sensory inputs, processings, outputs) is what Rogers calls the phenomenal field.

around the sun in almost the same orbit for millions of years, as have most of the other objects in our solar system. Newton did not have to state where the planets came from, or how they moved into orbit—he merely had to describe the celestial clockwork long after the mechanism had been wound up and set in motion.

But human beings seem to be self-winding—indeed, that is almost the definition of life. Unlike the planets, humans grow and develop rapidly; their motivations (dynamics) are primarily internal; their "orbits" are highly irregular; their interactions complex—and because they are conscious of their own thoughts and actions, they can change their motions merely by willing them to change. How can anyone hope to describe the human personality in terms as simple as Newton's equations describing celestial mechanics?

Many psycho-analysts solve this problem by burying human motivations in our genes—we develop according to a predetermined pattern imposed on us by our inheritance. According to this view, our biology is in control, as it seems to be with all other animal and plant life. This predominantly physiological view of man is rejected by a group of U.S. psychologists who call themselves *humanists* (°). Freud, following Darwin, built his theory on the *similarities* between humans and the lower animals. The humanists emphasize the *difference* between humans and the rest of the animal kingdom. They see humans as being unique, set apart, and above all other life forms. We are not mechanisms wound up and abandoned to tick out our lives as our gene-clocks dictate—rather, we are masters of our destinies, creative individuals capable of rising above our animal heritage. According to the humanists, we are motivated not merely to survive, but to become better and better. This process of continual psychological growth and improvement the humanists call "self-actualization."

There are many psychologists whose theories fall within the humanistic tradition. Of these, the best known are probably Carl Rogers and Abraham Maslow.

Carl Rogers

Carl Rogers is an American who taught for many years at the University of Chicago and at the University of Wisconsin. Rogers believes we are born with no self-concept, and no self—but with an innate urge to *become* a fully functioning and actualized person. At birth, as William James said, all we have is a blooming, buzzing, confusing set of sensory impressions, physiological processes, and motor activities. Rogers calls this sum total of our experience the *phenomenal field* (°). As we mature, the outside world imposes a kind of order or logic onto this field, and as we become aware of this logic, our *self* emerges and differentiates itself from the phenomenal field. The self is the conscious portion of experience.

For Rogers, maturation is a matter of distinguishing one's own body and thoughts from the objective, outside world. And as maturation occurs, the self begins to build up expectations about its own functioning—that is, to take on values and to make judgments about its own behavior. Some of these values come from the individual's own desires; other values are imposed on the person by the society in which he or she lives. Problems arise when society wants the person to become something that conflicts with the person's internal values. If the individual yields to the demands of society too much, psychological experience is distorted and the individual's self-concept suffers accordingly.

According to Rogers, most of the experiences we have are unconscious—that is, below the threshold of consciousness (*see* Chapter 11). But almost any experience can be brought to consciousness if the self merely gives the experience a name or label—that is, if the self develops *word-symbols* to describe the experience. If the experiences threaten the person's self-concept, the self may refuse to symbolize them in words or thoughts. If the self cannot tolerate some of its own behaviors, it

Carl Rogers.

cannot achieve full actualization because it is continually hiding some of its own values or motivations from itself. A person suffering from this sort of problem often says things like, "I don't understand why I did what I did." Therapy can often help an individual adjust his or her self-concept so that it is more attuned to reality.

To Rogers, the fully-adjusted person is someone whose self can symbolize any experience that has happened or that might possibly happen, whose self can accept and understand any part of its own behavior. Such people are called *fully functioning individuals;* they are open to all experience; they defend against nothing; they are aware both of their faults and of their virtues, but they have a high positive regard for themselves; and best of all, they maintain happy and humane relationships with others.

Abraham Maslow.

Abraham Maslow

Carl Roger's theory grew out of his long-time work as a psycho-therapist; thus his theory is in part built on Rogers' study of abnormal and maladjusted individuals. (To a great extent, this same statement is true of Freud's theory, and of Jung's, Adler's, and Erikson's.) Abraham Maslow, on the other hand, is one of the few theorists who built his ideas about human behavior on studying highly creative and psychologically healthy people. Some were his personal friends; others—such as Lincoln, Einstein, Eleanor Roosevelt, and Beethoven—he studied through books, papers, and letters. Maslow assumed these individuals had achieved a high degree of "self-actualization," otherwise they wouldn't have been so prominent and have demonstrated so much leadership. By determining the similarities among the members of this noted group, he believed he was able to determine the characteristics of a truly "self-actualized" person. A list of these characteristics appears in Table 22.2.

Most psycho-analytically-oriented theories focus on what can go wrong during the developmental years—they emphasize the possibility of sickness, not the probability of success. Maslow's approach is different, for he looks primarily at the healthy side of human nature. Freud saw people as trying to overcome their rather evil, animal instincts—as escaping from the traps of their pasts. Maslow acknowledges the strength of our physiological instincts, but sees them as being basic needs easily satisfied in most civilized societies. But even our drives for food and sex are part of a more impelling urge—an active "will toward health"—that is the heart of the human process of self-actualization.

Basic Needs and Meta-needs According to Maslow, we have two types of needs—*basic needs* and *meta-needs* (°). Included among his list of basic needs are such physiological "drives" as hunger, thirst, and sex; but he also considers our desires for affection, security, and esteem as "basic." Those things that we cannot survive without—such as food, water, and air—create the most powerful drives humans can know. If our elementary physical needs are not satisfied, little else matters. For Maslow, a given society or political system must first of all meet the basic needs of its citizens.

Once these life-sustaining drives are satisfied, however, the less-powerful but humanly very important meta-needs come into play. These meta-needs include beauty, order, unity, justice, and goodness. Maslow calls these "growth needs," because to satisfy them, an individual must grow or rise above the purely animal level of existence. A person whose basic needs are met, but who cannot fulfill his or her meta-needs, may become psychologically disturbed and may lapse into such negative states as despair, anguish, apathy, alienation, or even a *cynical* (°) rejection of all that is essentially human.

Meta-needs (METT-tuh). *Meta* is a Greek word meaning "occurring later or afterward." By meta-needs, Maslow meant those human requirements that can be considered only after the basic requirements for life have been fulfilled.

Cynical (SIN-nick-ull). The Cynics were early Greek philosophers who thought that greed and self-interest were the only important human motivations. A cynic is someone who expects nothing but the worst from other people. The humanists are polar opposites of the cynics.

TABLE 22.2 Abraham Maslow's Whole Characteristics of Self-actualizing People

They have more efficient perceptions of reality and are more comfortable with it.

They accept themselves and their own natures almost without thinking about it.

Their behavior is marked by simplicity and naturalness and by lack of artificiality or straining for effect.

They focus on problems outside themselves; they are concerned with basic issues and eternal questions.

They like privacy and tend to be detached.

They have relative independence of their physical and social environments; they rely on their own development and continued growth.

They do not take blessings for granted, but appreciate again and again the basic pleasures of life.

They experience limitless horizons and the intensification of any unself-conscious experience often of a mystical type.

They have a deep feeling of kinship with others.

They develop deep ties with a few other self-actualizing individuals.

They are democratic in a deep sense; although not indiscriminate, they are not really aware of differences.

They are strongly ethical, with definite moral standards, though their attitudes are conventional; they relate to ends rather than means.

Their humor is real and related to philosophy, not hostility; they are spontaneous less often then others, and tend to be more serious and thoughtful.

They are original and inventive, less constricted and fresher than others.

While they tend toward the conventional and exist well within the culture, they live by the laws of their own characters rather than those of society.

They experience imperfections and have ordinary feelings, like others.

SOURCE: Condensed from "Self-Actualizing People: A Study of Psychological Health," in *Motivation and Personality*, 2nd ed., by Abraham H. Maslow, Copyright 1954 by Harper & Row, Publishers, Inc.; Copyright © 1970 by Abraham H. Maslow. By permission of the publishers.

SKINNER'S BEHAVIORAL THEORY

The increasing interest shown in Rogers' and Maslow's humanistic ideas is one of the several trends visible in the development of a truly adequate theory of personality. Freud was most impressed with humans' animal heritage—while recent theorists have paid more attention to the uniquely human aspects of people's experience. Freud believed most of the determinants of action were unconscious—while later theorists assume that people can consciously determine their own destinies. Freud saw personality structure as being rigidly determined by genetic inheritance—while the recent emphasis has been on the flexibility of thoughts and behavior as they are influenced by the social environment or by the person's own will and determination. Freud saw *pathology* (°), or sickness, as being the rule, not the exception—while today the theorists view humans as being basically healthy and normal. Freud was pessimistic about the future of the human race—while today the future seems a bit more rosy.

Perhaps the major point of agreement between Freud and the later theorists is that they all believe that humans are motivated by internal biological and intra-psychic forces. Even Adler and Erikson—who were among the first to point out the tremendous influence that the external environment has on thoughts and behaviors—partially accepted Freud's notion of libidinal energy, of internal drives that provide the power for everything we do. There is little doubt that biological and intra-psychic drives do exist; but are they the only forces that motivate human beings? What would the social/behavioral theorists have to say? What kind of theory might we come up with if we viewed men and women as mere "earthy bodies"? From the social/behavioral viewpoint, we might assume

Pathology (path-OLL-oh-gee). From the Greek word *pathos*, meaning "suffering" or "sickness." Pathology is anything abnormal, either of the body or mind. Insanity is thus a form of mental pathology.

that humans are pushed and pulled around "social space" the way that Newton said the planets and suns are propelled in their orbits in "outer space." Can we then write simple equations describing human behavior as neatly as Newton described the tickings of the heavenly clockwork? Would this "third view" add anything to our understanding of human personality not already covered by the biological and intra-psychic viewpoints?

Personality Theory versus Behavior Change The person who has contributed most to a social/behavioral theory of personality is Harvard psychologist B.F. Skinner, whose principles of behavior change have been mentioned several times earlier (*see* Chapters 5, 12, 16). Skinner believes that behavior is, above all else, *lawful* (°). By this he means that the actions (and thoughts) of human beings are predictable and primarily under the control of external, measurable influences. You do not move because you want to, according to Skinner; rather, you move because the external environment (perhaps working through your own past experience) stimulates you to do so. Your energy comes not from dynamic forces working deep within your unconscious mind but from external sources. When you are cut off from external stimulation, as we saw in Chapter 9, even your stream of consciousness drops to near-zero—just as a plant wilts and dies when cut off from sunlight and water. And just as we can control both the speed and direction of a plant's growth, and when it will flower, by controlling its sunlight and water, so we can shape or influence the growth of a human being by controlling the energy and information that it receives. In short, according to Skinner, motivation comes from outside the organism, not from inside.

Like many scientists, Skinner pays attention only to those aspects of the world that he can measure objectively. Because you cannot see a person's thoughts, you cannot easily measure them. Therefore, says Skinner, we should not discuss thoughts and dreams and hopes and aspirations *scientifically* because we cannot really prove they exist. But we can measure behavior, and so we must describe human existence almost solely in terms of actions and reactions. We cannot measure "needs" such as hunger, but we can measure how frequently and how much and what a man eats. If we assume (as Skinner does) that we are conditioned or trained to eat what and when we do, then the term "hunger" has no real meaning because our eating behavior is almost entirely under the control of external, social forces.

Skinner believes that biological data are presently insufficient to tell us much about the human condition. He then rejects the physiological viewpoint not because it is unscientific, but because it is "too far behind the times." (When Freud encountered the same problem, he "dreamed up" the id, ego, and super-ego and presumed the physiologists would someday find the neural mechanisms underlying these intra-psychic "inventions.") Skinner rejects the intra-psychic viewpoint as being "fiction instead of scientific fact." His views often outrage people, particularly the humanists, who have debated him in public. For, by denying the usefulness of concepts such as "consciousness," Skinner seems to make us into robots—clockwork machines that need frequent windings to keep on running.

Do humans have the ability to think, to plan, to scheme, and to influence their destiny? Actually, Skinner does not deny this possibility entirely. He says, merely, that we have no way as yet of measuring thinking—but we can measure verbal behavior rather precisely. And since the complex auditory outputs that we call "human speech" are obviously learned, and influenced by the external environment, why do we need such vague and undefinable terms as "self" or "mind" or "ego?" Do these words really add anything to our understanding of human behavior?

If you can predict everything that you do simply by learning how you have

Lawful (rhymes with "awful"). In science, a law is usually an expression of a high, positive correlation between measurable inputs and outputs. The law often makes no mention of the processing that may occur between the input and output—that is, the law merely states that the correlation exists without explaining why. A behavioral law usually states that, given a certain input, an organism will respond with a specific output. The more powerful the law, the better it predicts the regularities between stimuli and responses, or between inputs and outputs.

B.F. Skinner.

been rewarded and punished in the past, and by measuring the stimuli impinging on your receptors at the moment, does it help to assume that you are "conscious" of what you are doing? Even Carl Rogers (one of Skinner's most vocal critics) admits that people are often not "conscious" of what they do, and that understanding your own behavior does not always allow you to change yourself at will. If the planet Earth suddenly developed "consciousness," could it move itself out of orbit without external help? Wouldn't Earth tend to explain its circling of the sun in "useless" terms—such as, "I have such a strong innate desire for order and regularity that I force myself to stay in orbit around the sun?" And if you wanted to change the Earth's orbit, would you try to persuade it to change its view toward itself, or would you apply external pressure to overcome the forces of gravity acting on the Earth?

By giving us new and very precise ways of measuring certain types of human behavior, and by emphasizing the importance of the external environment, Skinner has added much to our understanding of what humans are like. But in neglecting the qualitative differences among people (as Newton neglected many of the differences among heavenly objects), and in discarding entirely the physiological and intra-psychic influences, Skinner has dramatically narrowed the scope of his potentially great contribution.

How Shall We Measure a Theory?

In the physical sciences there often is one and only one acceptable theory to explain the structure and dynamics of inanimate objects. For example, for more than 200 years, Newton's laws of planetary motion were accepted by almost all physicists and astronomers. But all of us, psychologists included, have our own, unique, individual theories of human personality. We may borrow from Freud and Adler, from Rogers and Skinner, but each of us "blends" these ideas his or her own way. And once our own private theory makes us happy, we are often reluctant to make more than trivial changes in our outlook.

As we will see in a later chapter, people usually tend to accept new ideas and viewpoints only when they can comfortably be fitted within the framework of their present system of beliefs. European intellectuals rejected Freud's theory of psycho-analysis in the early 1900's because it was too radical and shocking for them to stomach—that is, it was so different from their perception of themselves that it set off alarm bells in their autonomic (emotional) nervous systems. Eventually, as Freud's notions became more familiar, people *habituated* to psycho-analysis and it became the most influential theory of personality.

Freud prevailed in the early part of this century in part because he offered the most complete personality theory the world had ever known. But Freud's views won out, too, because of his superb journalistic talent. He could explain even his most difficult thoughts in very simple, understandable terms. In Skinner's way of speaking, Freud was good at shaping people into accepting psycho-analytic concepts.

Freud resorted to the use of analogies quite frequently and quite effectively. He did not really believe that there were three little beings—the id, the ego, and the super-ego—chasing around in the dark recesses of the human mind. Rather, as he made clear in his 1895 "Project," these were names or labels that Freud applied to certain neural processes—just as we have used the term "Board of Directors" in this book. But neurology frightens people, while "little men" inside one's head somehow make things more human and hence more believable. Realizing this fact of human nature, Freud used his analogies to teach people about psycho-analysis just as Skinner might reward successive approximations to a goal in shaping a pigeon to bowl. Skinner's books too often lack this spark of human understanding. And if Freud and his followers are better accepted than

Skinner is, perhaps in part it is because Freud practiced what Skinner preached.

One of the functions of a scientific theory is to explain the past. Freud's psycho-analytic theory succeeded in giving people new understanding of their present behavior by showing how it was related to their childhood experiences. The humanists added to this by demonstrating that our present functioning is also influenced by whatever future goals we may have, and by postulating a desire for growth and health that Freud's theory lacked. Both psycho-analysis and humanism give us a feeling for the *causes* of human behavior that Skinner's viewpoint simply doesn't offer. But a scientific theory is also judged by its ability to tell us *how* as well as *why*—that is, by its ability to predict future events (and how to change them) better than any competing theory. As we will see in later chapters, there are some areas of human conduct that Skinner's theory of behavioral change *predicts* better than does psycho-analysis or the humanistic theories.

Someday, perhaps, we will have a master theory that both explains and predicts, and that does so at the biological, the intra-psychic, and the social/behavioral levels. But the ability to predict always implies the ability to measure what you are predicting. So it is to the measurement of human personality that we must now turn our attention.

SUMMARY

1. By the term "personality," we usually mean some sort of theory or explanation of why people do what they do. Each of us has his or her own theory of personality.
2. Psychologists often define personality as the characteristic way in which a person thinks and behaves as the person adjusts or adapts to his or her environment. This definition includes both the structure of the person's mind as well as such dynamic processes as thinking, feeling, perceiving, and action. The definition also reminds us that "personality" is always expressed in a given environment.
3. Prior to the time of Freud, most theories emphasized such personality structures as traits, values, abilities, intelligence, and genetic disposition. Dynamic theories more or less begin with Freud.
4. Early in his career, Freud discovered the value of catharsis—the acting out of long-forgotten traumatic events that seemed to release the patient's pent-up emotions. The helpful effects of catharsis suggested to Freud both that we are often unconscious of our real problems and that early traumas may be connected with sexuality.
5. Freud theorized that, at birth, our thoughts lie in the unconscious realms of the mind. These early, infantile thoughts obey the primary process—they are "body think" aimed at satisfying biological needs.
6. Primary process thinking obeys what Freud called the "pleasure principle"—the need for reducing tension and gaining immediate gratification of our wants. This unconscious portion of the personality is called the "id," which gains its power from tapping the energy flow of the libido, or life force.
7. As the infant interacts with its environment and develops psycho-sexually, it slowly learns to delay immediate gratification of its whims. Out of this learning develops the ego, the conscious portion of the mind which obeys the "reality principle" imposed on it by the outside world.
8. The ego is capable of rational thought, which Freud called the "secondary process of the mind."
9. Between ego and id lies a boundary area called the "preconscious" that contains thoughts "just on the tip of one's tongue."
10. As the child enters the phallic stage, it develops incestual desires for the parent of the opposite sex. The child is presumed to resolve these taboo yearnings by creating a super-ego that acts as its conscience.
11. The ego defends itself against unconscious attack from the id and super-ego by such mechanisms as repression, fixation, regression, identification, reaction formation, projection, displacement, and sublimation.

12. Although Freud's writings often have a very literary sound to them, he was basically a neuro-physiologist. In 1895 he published his "Project," in which he laid out neurological explanations or definitions of such terms as "repression," "inhibition," and "libido."

13. Carl Jung rejected Freud's belief that the child's chief task in life is to bring its infantile, sexual instincts under control. Jung thought that we are more motivated by moral and religious values than by primitive sexuality.

14. According to Jung, we have two different unconsciousnesses.
    a. The personal unconscious contains our own individual memories.
    b. The collective unconscious houses all of our racial memories, or archetypes, which we inherit from our parents.

15. By means of the most important archetype of all—the self-concept—each of us can integrate all of our conscious and unconscious processes into one meaningful whole.

16. Jung believed that the self or ego was determined by the interactions of two innate attitudes and four inborn functions. The attitudes are introversion and extroversion. The four functions are thinking, feeling, sensing, and intuiting.

17. Both Freud and Jung emphasized the importance of the genetic blueprint as the major determinant of human personality. Their associate, Alfred Adler, focused on the effects of the social environment.

18. To Adler, conscious experiences were more important than unconscious ones.

19. Adler saw life as a struggle to achieve superiority, a drive to achieve self-realization. When we discover our own inferiorities, we compensate by becoming superior in other ways.

20. Freud believed that personality development more or less ceased during adolescence. Erik Erikson extended Freud's psycho-analytic theory to include the developmental stages that continued into the mature years.

21. According to Erikson, every human must pass through eight developmental stages, each of which is characterized by its own type of crisis or test of a person's character.

22. The humanistic theorists reject most of the psycho-analytic concepts, emphasizing instead the drive for self-improvement or self-actualization.

23. Humanist Carl Rogers believes that a fully adjusted person is someone whose self can symbolize any experience that has happened or that might happen, whose self can accept or understand any part of its own behavior.

24. Humanist Abraham Maslow sees humans as being innately healthy. Maslow thus focuses on our strengths rather than our weaknesses.

25. According to Maslow, we have two types of needs—basic needs and meta-needs. Once our life-sustaining drives or needs are taken care of, we can then seek satisfaction from personal growth (satisfying our meta-needs).

26. B.F. Skinner rejects all theory, stating that behavior is lawful and hence predictable.

27. For Skinner, describing the human animal is a matter of finding correlations between stimulus inputs and behavioral outputs, without worrying much about the "processing" that goes on inside the person, since this "processing" is mostly unmeasurable.

28. All of these theories have contributed to our ability to understand and predict human experience, but none of them is complete in itself.

(Continued from page 492.)

The afternoon sun angled sharply down through the towering mountains onto the waters of Lake Como. Bellagio, on the eastern shore, was bathed in golden light. Cadennabia, just a few miles directly across the water, had already slipped into twilight. But the surface of the lake, whipped into a million mirrors by the winds of the southerly **breva,** scattered dancing specks of light everywhere.

A water taxi, pushing out from Cadennabia to go to Bellagio, dipped and tossed in the breeze. Watching the boat through a telescope from Bellagio, an impartial observer might have noted the passengers clinging tightly to their seats as the boat plunged through the rough water. Had this observer then turned his telescope to the south, he might have barely made out the figures of three people huddled around a small table on the terrace of the hotel Villa d'Este. Objectively speaking, the bodies of two of the people were leaning toward the third, as if listening seriously. But whether the distant observer might have guessed that these three people were setting out on an intellectual crossing of their own is hard to say.

"As I mentioned earlier, I have hope," said Donald M. Papas, the Canadian psychologist. "That is why I agreed to the Foundation's request to lead this First International Symposium on Peace and Personality. And that is why I invited you, Jonathan, a behaviorist, and you, Joyce, a neo-Freudian, and ten other of the best 'thinkers-on-personality' this side of the moon to come to the conference."

"Hope to end war throughout the world?" Fraser asked.

"No, hope to end war throughout psychology. Or, at least, within the field of personality theory."

"An armed truce is about all you can expect of us," Joyce Sapir said.

"I'll settle for that, as a first approximation. I know it's idealistic of me, but I rather hoped if I could get you all together, talking and listening to each other, we might make some headway."

"Who listens at these conferences?" asked Fraser.

"It depends on who talks," Papas continued. "All of you really have a lot in common—including your individual desires to help people live more peaceful, productive lives."

"To help people achieve self-actualization, you mean," said Joyce Sapir.

"You mean, to help people condition themselves to give up the gratifications of immediate animal pleasures for the more distant rewards of social good," said Jonathan Fraser.

"There, you see, you're saying almost the same thing, but in different words. It's your language that is at the heart of the problem."

Fraser smiled. "George Bernard Shaw once said that the U.S. and Britain are separated by a common language."

"Exactly!" continued Papas. "In Joyce Sapir's terms, self-actualization means learning enough about your unconscious sensual desires so that you can handle them consciously, and hence divert libidinal energy toward more humane ends. But creature comforts are so powerful that many of us never get much above the instinctual level of living. And so we never really taste the joys of mature consciousness. Abraham Maslow would say that basic needs must be satisfied first; only then can the meta-needs come into play. But it is the meta-need for unity that keeps people peaceful, and we will become grown up psychologically only when we have the technology that will allow us to gratify this meta-need. Skinner might put the same thing this way. Physiological rewards such as food and sex are very strong—hence we typically condition an organism to accept social rather than biological rewards by pairing praise with food. If you pat a dog on the head each time you give it food, eventually it will find the affection as rewarding as a piece of meat. But isn't that what Freud really meant when he said that a young boy in the latent period learns to act like his father because his mother is more affectionate to him when he does?"

"But humans have an innate need for affection," Joyce Sapir insisted.

"And so do monkeys," responded Fraser. "Harlow showed that. No, my dear neo-Freudian, what our sneaky Canadian friend seems to be saying is this—ego psychologists, such as yourself, focus on innate needs. You measure these needs indirectly, by asking people how they feel. But you get so involved in describing the subjective feelings and hunting for hidden meanings in their verbal responses that you sometimes forget a critical point—verbal responses can serve as reinforcers and their effects on human behavior can hence be studied objectively. When you praise me, I listen—when you criticize me, I say something nasty in return. You analysts measure the unconscious **intent** of the speaker; the behaviorists measure the speaker's **actual** effect on the listener's behavior."

"I see," said Joyce Sapir. "The behaviorist focuses on satisfiers instead of needs, because he can see environmental rewards and talk about them objectively. Since he can't measure the internal need directly, the behaviorist mistakenly assumes that it just isn't there."

"You're doing beautifully, both of you." Papas said. "But now, let's go a step further. Skinner defines a reward as anything that increases response rates. He never asks **why** reward has this effect; it just does. The psycho-analysts and the humanists—like the physiological psychologists—are interested in **why.** The behaviorist is interested in **how** rather than why. But once you understand why our motives function as they do, then you know a lot more too about which rewards to offer people to help them grow or change or learn to be peaceful.''

Joyce Sapir shook her head. ''You miss the point, Don. Fraser refuses to admit that man has cognitive and perceptual needs, such as the innate desire for self-realization.''

Fraser grinned. ''Not so! We admit the power of social reinforcement.''

''Exactly!'' Papas said. ''The behavior modifiers discovered very early that 'man does not live by bread alone'; he needs rewards from other human beings.''

''Man doesn't even live by woman alone,'' Fraser remarked, winking at Joyce Sapir.

''He doesn't even live by himself alone,'' Papas continued. ''But some of his responses can be very reinforcing to him.''

''Primarily during the phallic period, if you're referring to masturbation,'' Joyce said, an amused look on her face.

''No, I wasn't talking about sex,'' said Papas. ''I was thinking of self-actualization. Many behavior modifiers will tell you that the person with psychological problems is often the person who ignores feedback. If you can get the client to make a chart of his own growth or development, the client finds any positive change in the graph very rewarding indeed.''

Joyce Sapir mused a moment, then continued. ''Carl Rogers said nearly the same thing when he remarked that we get in trouble when our 'self' or ego loses touch with our biological organism. But if the therapist reflects back to a man what he is really like—if the therapist acts like a mirror—then the person can define himself and, in the process, achieve growth and understanding.''

Fraser shook his head in mock dismay. ''Papas, are you suggesting that Rogers and Skinner were saying almost the same thing?''

''Well, if reflecting back to a man what the man is really like isn't setting up a feedback system, I don't know what is,'' Papas responded. ''Rogers says that the feedback should be emotionally neutral, but he calls it 'unconditional **positive** regard.' That sounds suspiciously like positive reinforcement to me.''

Joyce Sapir smiled. ''And Carl Rogers is one of the most charming, encouraging therapists I've ever met. He almost never has a bad word to say about anyone—except Skinner, of course.''

''Perhaps if Rogers had given Skinner a bit more 'unconditional **positive** regard,' and Skinner had rewarded Rogers instead of criticizing him, their famous debates would have had a different outcome,'' Papas said quietly.

''And not been nearly as much bloody fun,'' remarked Fraser. ''Don, where did you get this wild idea of yours to call a meeting of the minds at Lake Como?''

''To tell you the truth, just before I got the call from the Foundation I went to see a movie, and it made me think of you, Fraser.''

''**Planet of the Apes?**'' asked Joyce Sapir slyly.

''No, it was an old Antonioni film, **Blow-up,**'' Papas said in his best professorial tone. ''You may recall the plot. By accident, a photographer takes a picture in a park just after a murder occurs. When he develops the film, he notices in the photograph what might be a face lurking in the bushes. Thinking that it might be the face of the murderer, he enlarges the picture. He still can't quite make out the face, so he enlarges the picture again—and again and again. But each time he makes the face bigger, it gets vaguer and harder to make out. Eventually the face disappears into a bunch of random dots as he reaches the limits of the film itself. When he pushed his analysis too far, he lost what he was looking for. Just as the old adage warns us, 'You can't see the forest if you look too hard at the individual trees.' ''

''Analysis destroys that which is analyzed,'' Joyce Sapir remarked.

''Are you perchance referring to psycho-analysis?'' Fraser asked cattily.

"No, merely quoting the Gestalt position," the woman responded quickly. "The human being has a strong drive for synthesis, for making things whole instead of cutting them up into bits and pieces. Erikson called it the 'sense of integrity,' seeing oneself as a complete person. Adler referred to it as a **fictional finalism,** the striving to obtain an unobtainable integration. Jung called it the 'transcendental function of unity.' Even making an attempt at pulling things together can be very rewarding."

Fraser closed his eyes against the light of the afternoon sun. "Don, do you really think out little group here at Lake Como can lay aside their differences and come up with an integrated theory of personality?"

Donald M. Papas grinned. "Of course not. Your differences are as important as your similarities. To have a thriving but ecologically sound lumber industry, you need both tree surgeons and forest rangers. Newton hoped that his laws would describe accurately how the planets moved around the sun, but he knew his laws didn't tell him why they did so. To find out **why,** Newton turned to his own rather strange brand of religion. But he kept his personal, subjective feelings about religion so hidden that few people knew about them. Maybe Newton was ashamed that his objective view of the universe didn't satisfy all of his emotional, human needs."

"Einstein had a much broader outlook on the physical world than Newton did," Joyce Sapir commented. "Wouldn't you say that Einstein did a much better job of bringing unity to physics and astronomy?"

Papas shook his head. "Newton's laws lasted for 200 years before Albert Einstein incorporated them into his own theories. But remember two things. First, Einstein hoped to create what he called a 'Unified Field Theory' that would explain all physical events—however, he failed miserably because he tried to push his single-minded level of analysis too far. Second, Einstein was a very religious man with a strong belief in God. Einstein's theories were still aimed at explaining how, not why. To answer some of his questions about the nature of the universe, Einstein had to look within himself; he still had to resort to subjective experience and to faith to tell him the why's."

"I don't really see how this applies to personality theory," Fraser commented.

"I'm not sure that it does, except perhaps in my own mind," Papas continued. "But it seems to me that psycho-analytic theory is a single-minded way of looking at humans, from the inside out. Behaviorism operates from a different point of view, from the outside in. We can't give up one or the other, any more than we can give up either the forests or the trees."

"I can give up psycho-analysis any time I try really hard," Fraser said.

"No, you can't. For the analysts and humanists have identified some very potent reward systems that you really ought to look into," Papas responded.

"But surely some of the personality theorists have come close to achieving a completely integrated theory of human beings," Joyce Sapir protested.

"Sorry, but I can't agree," Papas said. "Freud came the closest, but like Einstein, he failed. A complete theory would have to take into account both the physical and psychological aspects of human sensations and perceptions, cognitions and altered states of consciousness, synapses and transmitters, social roles and developmental sequences, needs and motives, rewards and punishments, muscle twitches and ego, instincts and the biochemical basis of learning, memories and forgettings, the itch to integrate and the aspiration to analyze, all of the human brain and all of human behavior. And the theory would have to handle these different aspects of human beings—all these different viewpoints and levels—in a series of simultaneous equations. I doubt it can be done. Certainly not in our lifetimes. No, we don't need a unified theory of personality as much as we need a verbal bridge that will allow us to go back and forth from one level or viewpoint to another. That's what I hope we can do at the Symposium—if I can get all of you to stop criticizing and carping at each other and use unconditional positive regard instead."

Fraser seemed amused. "Your Bridge of Heavenly Peace will never get off the ground. Carping at each other is far too rewarding!"

"I agree," Joyce Sapir said, smiling. "In my own experience, the need to carp is a basic oral urge, and we all know that academics are uniformly fixated at the oral level of development. Besides," she added in mock horror, "building a bridge between psycho-analysis and behaviorism would be as senseless as building a bridge across Lake Como, from Cadennabia to Bellagio. Why, it would ruin the view!"

"And put all those water taxis out of business!" said Fraser, turning to watch the little white boat as it tossed about in the center of the lake.

"But you'd have fewer seasick passengers to worry about," Papas continued. "And the government could loan money to the boat owners to buy regular taxis instead. The increase in tourism between the two towns would more than justify the expense."

Joyce Sapir favored Jonathan Fraser with a smile. "I'd say that our Canadian colleague is as optimistic as Adler and the humanists. How would you say it, Jonathan?"

The British scientist smiled back. "Joyce, I'd simply say that hope springs eternal."

"In the heart of a fool," said Papas, lifting his glass in a toast. "To bridges!"

RECOMMENDED READINGS

Dollard, J., and N.E. Miller. *Personality and Psychotherapy: An Analysis in Terms of Learning, Thinking and Culture* (New York: McGraw-Hill Book Company, Inc., 1950).

Hall, Calvin S., and Gardner Lindzey. *Theories of Personality*, 2nd ed. (New York: John Wiley & Sons, Inc., 1970).

Maddi, Salvatore R. *Personality Theories: A Comparative Analysis* (Homewood, Ill.: The Dorsey Press, 1968).

Sheehy, Gail. *Passages: The Predictable Crises of Adult Life* (New York: E.P. Dutton & Co., 1976).

PERSONALITY TESTS

DID YOU KNOW THAT . . .

The Greek scientist Galen thought your personality was determined primarily by your liver?

Harvard psychologist W.H. Sheldon said your personality was determined primarily by the shape of your body?

Most U.S. psychologists believe that your personality can be measured primarily by your intra-psychic or mental processes?

Children come "dumber by the dozen"—that is, children in large families tend to have lower IQ's, on the average, than do children in small families?

One noted psychologist claimed to have improved the intelligence of orphans by placing them with retarded foster mothers?

Several psychologists have shown that you can sometimes raise your own IQ score by taking special training?

Gordon Allport has identified six central traits that most people show—theoretical, economic, esthetic, social, political, and religious?

Although there are many personality tests on the market, none seems to be both valid and reliable?

"What is this 'Late Bloomer' test of yours, Mr. Flagg? I don't think I've ever heard of it," Jessie Williams said quietly, favoring the handsome young man with a distant stare. Tom Flagg had an athlete's physique, a handsome dark-brown face, and a ready smile. Jessie Williams, whose body was as soft and rounded as Tom Flagg's was hard and angular, had learned the hard way that you can't always tell much about the shape of a man's intentions from the shape of his frame. So she was wary of this young graduate student who had just walked into her fourth-grade school room; but Jessie Williams was also quite taken by his appearance.

"The 'Late Bloomer' test was devised by Professor Rosenthal at Harvard," Tom Flagg replied, hoping (for several reasons) to overcome the good-looking young black woman's obvious distrust. "You've been teaching fourth grade for several years, haven't you, Miss Williams?"

"Three years, Mr. Flagg. Exactly three years."

"Well, maybe you've had a kid who seemed real dumb the first few months or so of school. Then, all of a sudden, the kid just took off and bloomed. Like a flower you'd forgotten to water until just then."

"I water all my flowers regularly, Mr. Flagg. I don't neglect any of them. Black or white, red or yellow—I hope they all bloom for me as much as they can."

Tom nodded appreciatively and smiled even more broadly at the pretty young teacher. If it wouldn't have prejudiced the results of his experiment, he would have tried to date her. For the soft outlines of her body greatly stimulated his admittedly non-academic desires. He pulled himself together and resumed the conversation. "Mr. Washington, your principal, told me you were one of the best teachers he's ever seen. So I'm sure you do get all your kids to show a lot of improvement. But aren't you occasionally surprised when one of them does a lot better than you had expected?"

519

Jessie Williams shook her head. "I expect great things of them all. Maybe that's why I'm not surprised when they do well."

"Okay," said Tom, "I guess my test won't help you any. But maybe you can help me out by letting me give it to your class anyhow. If I don't get to try out the test in enough classrooms, I won't get a good grade on my project back at the university. Even if you don't need the information, I do."

To his surprise, the woman smiled broadly. "Well, why didn't you say so, friend? I'm always happy to help one of us get ahead. Tell me about these 'Late Bloomers' of Professor Rosenthal's."

"Well, it's really your bloomers I'm interested in," Tom said, and then blushed furiously as he realized what he had said. "I mean, it's a test devised by Professor Rosenthal and his associates at Harvard. They think they've found a way of telling in advance when a school kid is going to show a sudden spurt in achievement—when the kid is going to get it all together and take off like a jet plane. The test can also tell when a kid is going to backslide or tread water for a while—fail to show much improvement at all for a period of several months. The change usually shows up in the kid's grades, although sometimes the IQ blossoms too."

"Some of our education books say that a child's intelligence is fixed by the time he's 6 or 7. Don't you believe that's so, Tom?" Jessie asked, a malicious twinkle in her eye.

Tom looked startled. "Well, I suppose that the limits to a man's mind are determined at birth, but functional intelligence sure changes a lot. And the score you get on an IQ test depends as much on which test you take, who gives it, and how you feel when you take it as it does on how bright you really are. Have you ever given any of your kids IQ tests?"

"No, Tom. I'm not qualified to do that. I give achievement tests, but the school counselor tests their intelligence."

"But aren't you sometimes surprised at the scores the counselor reports on your kids?"

Jessie Williams smiled slyly. "I just don't pay them any mind."

"What do you do when the parents want to know what the kid's IQ is?"

"I tell them the story of my life. I was born in Mississippi, Tom, where my father was a tenant farmer. We moved North when I was 6. My first year in school they gave me a test and said my IQ was 87. As you know, that's what you might call 'dull normal.' You just don't learn very much about the world on a tenant farm in the back woods of Mississippi. But I loved school, and I had good teachers, and when I was in the seventh grade, I took another test. This time I got a score of 98. The counselor couldn't understand the change. So he gave me a different test, and I scored 104. He asked me what I wanted to do, and I said go to college and learn how to teach. He told me to forget it, that I'd never make it."

"But you did."

"Yes, I did. In high school they gave me another test. This time I tried very hard to impress the woman giving me the test, and I got a score of 111."

"The 'halo effect,' probably," Tom said. "Good-looking, eager children always score a little higher than uglies do because the tester gives them the benefit of the doubt. And I suspect you were very good looking indeed."

"You needn't flatter me, friend. I've already agreed to help you with your study. Anyway, the counselor said I just might get through college if I worked very hard, although you're supposed to have an IQ of 120 to graduate."

"So you went to the university and got your degree anyhow?"

"No, Tom, it wasn't that easy. My high school grades were excellent, but I didn't score too well on the college entrance examination. The university didn't want me. So I went to a community college for two years. I got all A's, and the university finally let me in. My last year there, I took another IQ test. This time I got a score of 122. But, of course, by then I knew the kinds of answers they wanted on the test."

"And that's why you don't tell the parents what their kids' IQ scores are?"

"Right on. Now suppose you tell me what your study is all about."

''Okay. I'll give the Rosenthal 'Late Bloomer' test to all the kids in your room. Then, when I've scored the results, I'll tell you which kids are supposed to 'bloom,' and which kids are supposed to backslide. Then, six months from now, I'll come back and see if that's what really happened.''

A suspicious look crept into Miss Williams eyes. ''Why are you doing this, Tom? Doesn't sound much like an experiment to me.''

''Rosenthal validated the test mostly in white classrooms. I want to see if it predicts for integrated classes as well.''

''And you'll come back in six months to see what happened?''

Tom Flagg squared his shoulders. ''Well, your class is so important to me, I might just drop around a little more often than that—just to see how things are going.''

''You do that, Thomas. You do that very thing.''

(Continued on page 545.)

In an early chapter in this book we asked you to consider what may have seemed an odd question—*Where is your mind located?* Our purpose was to urge you to consider a very important problem, namely, where within your brain the essential "you" resides. As we discovered, bits and pieces of "you" are located everywhere within your central nervous system. That is, various parts of your conscious and unconscious experience are controlled or mediated by widely different neural centers.

Now, let us face an even more challenging issue: *Who are you?* In those first chapters we took primarily the neurological view—we assumed that "you" are not so much a single individual as a collection of parts that we called the "Board of Directors." Sigmund Freud assumed much the same thing when he spoke of the ego, super-ego, and id. Carl Rogers may have had the same problem in mind when he wrote that the conscious self differentiates itself from the perceptual field and becomes relatively independent of it. Yet you do not experience yourself as bits and pieces, held together by some kind of psychological glue. Probably you perceive yourself as being a unique individual, much more than the sum of your parts and sub-systems.

Here, then, is one of the basic problems faced by the personality theorist. You may function as a whole, intact person, but if we are to measure you, we are more likely to pay attention to your parts than to your integrated self. We will see why this is the case in just a moment.

But first, let us return to our question—*Who are you?* If you were to make as objective and complete an evaluation of yourself as possible, what would you say? If you enjoy doing such things, you might take out a sheet of paper and write down at least five of your strongest and most desirable features, and at least five points about you that could perhaps be changed or improved. Since many schools and business firms might require you to do that very thing if you applied to them for admission or for a job, perhaps this practice evaluation might be of some value to you.

PSYCHOLOGICAL TRAITS

Now, what sorts of things did you say about yourself? Although, as you know by now, some psychologists prefer to describe the human personality in terms of observable behaviors, the chances are good that you see yourself primarily in terms of your inner, subjective qualities. Are you sincere? Are you happy? lazy? intelligent? creative? religious? loving? jealous? shy? prejudiced? If you described yourself in these terms, you made use of what we often call *psychological traits.* That is, you probably assume that your outward behavior is produced by, or

Hippocrates.

Hippocrates (hip-POCK-rat-tees). Often called "the father of medicine," Hippocrates lived about 400 years prior to the birth of Christ. Although the best-known physician of his time, and although he wrote the Hippocratic Oath that medical doctors still take when granted their degrees, he made surprisingly little impact on medical science until long after he died (Plato mentions him but twice, Aristotle but once). Although what we have called "Galen's humor theory" was originated by Hippocrates, this viewpoint was not widely accepted until Galen adapted it and made it famous.

Humors (YOU-mores). The Latin word *humor* means "moist, wet, liquid." Galen (GAY-lun) believed that your personality was determined by the fluids secreted by your body. When you were in "good humor," you had good fluids bubbling around inside you. The four important humors were blood, phlegm, black bile, and yellow bile.

Sanguine (SAN-gwin). From the Latin word *sanguis,* meaning "blood." Someone who hopes for the best, or is confidently optimistic, is a sanguine person.

Phlegm (FLEM). The Greek word *phlegma* means "flame" or "inflammation." Phlegm is the white mucus (MEW-cuss) that you cough up when you have a cold, or sometimes when you clear your throat.

Phlegmatic (fleg-MATT-tick). A watery, slow, unemotional person.

Choler (KAHL-urr). From the Greek word meaning "bile." One of the four humors. A choleric (KAHL-urr-ick, or kuh-LAIR-ick) person is someone readily given to anger, or to losing his or her "good humor."

caused by, long-lasting mental states or conditions such as your intelligence, your motives, your emotions and values, and your general outlook on life. Like the majority of psychologists, you would have assumed that the human personality is best talked about (measured) in terms of its structure, or its bits and pieces.

QUESTION: **How might you describe yourself in overall or global terms, without mentioning any of your traits at all? Can it be done?**

If you enjoy this sort of experience, let's go one step further. Now that you have painted a verbal picture of yourself, what about others? You might pick a close friend or relative and list that person's five best traits, and his or her main faults. How do you stack up against this person? Do you have similar traits or different ones? If both of you are sincere people, which of you is the more sincere?

Perhaps now you begin to see some of the joys and frustrations that face the psychologist interested in the structure of human personality. Each person living is unique, never-to-be-duplicated, different from all others. And yet, if you can compare one person with another, it is obvious that these unique individuals have many points or traits in common. What kind of theory of personality can we come up with that will allow us to describe both the similarities among people as well as their differences?

This question seems to have puzzled people for perhaps as long as there have been people. The Greek scholars Aristotle and Plato had their say before Christ was born, as did the famous Greek physician *Hippocrates* (°). Hippocrates hypothesized that our personalities are determined primarily by our body fluids, but his theory had little impact until it was refined and modified by Galen, one of the greatest medical doctors the world has known. Although Galen was born and educated in Greece a century or so after the death of Christ (and several hundred years after Hippocrates), Galen spent much of his adult life practicing medicine in Rome. His studies of the functioning of human and animal bodies were so excellent that he is considered the father of modern physiology.

GALEN'S HUMOR THEORY

One of Galen's main interests was the various glands in the human body, and the chemicals these glands secreted. Like most other physicians 2,000 years ago, Galen called these glandular secretions the *humors* (°). Borrowing a notion from Hippocrates, Galen stated that four of these humors were mainly responsible for human personality. As far as Galen was concerned, blood was a humor. If a man was most influenced by his blood, he was described as being *sanguine* (°), from the Latin word that means "bloody." A sanguine man or woman was supposed to be cheerful, hearty, outgoing, sturdy, fearless, optimistic, and most interested in physical pleasures.

The second humor that Galen mentioned was *phlegm* (°), the thick, white material you sometimes cough up when you have a cold. From Galen's point of view, phlegm was cold, moist, and unmoving. If a person's bodily processes were dominated by too much production of phlegm, that person became *phlegmatic* (°). That is, cold, aloof, calm, detached, unemotional, uninvolved, quiet, withdrawn, dependable, and perhaps just a trifle dull.

QUESTION: **How would Freud have described the sanguine person? the phlegmatic?**

Galen believed that the human liver produced two different "humors"—yellow bile and black bile. He called the yellow bile *choler* (°), because it supposedly caused the disease we now refer to as "cholera." The choler-ic personality was one easily given to anger, hate, and fits of temper—someone who gave in to most of his or her bad impulses.

Black bile was even worse, for it symbolized death in Galen's mind. If your

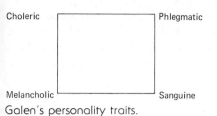
Galen's personality traits.

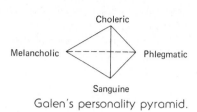
Galen's personality pyramid.

Galen.

personality was dominated by black bile, you were *melancholic* (°)—that is, you were always depressed, unhappy, suicidal.

To Galen, your biochemistry determined your personality type—and all human beings had to fall within one of the four humoral categories we have just described. All of the traits you have mentioned in describing yourself would presumably be determined by your basic humor. It is unclear from Galen's writings whether he thought you had to be entirely one type or the other, or whether you could be a mixture of the four, with one humor being predominant, or most important. Assuming that mixtures were allowed, Galen's scheme might be represented by the diagram at the left above.

Keeping in mind the descriptions of the traits associated with these four personality types, where might you locate yourself within the square? What problems might you have trying to assign your total personality to one single point within the diagram? Would a pyramid-shaped diagram be easier to work with (*see* the diagram at the right above).

BODY TYPES

It may surprise you to learn that many people believe that the size and shape of your body determines the structure of your personality; however, that particular belief is rather widespread. Aren't fat people supposed to be jolly, like Santa Claus? And don't we often say that thin people are "wiry, nervous, and energetic?" In one of his most famous plays, William Shakespeare has Julius Caesar say, "Yon Cassius has a lean and hungry look; He thinks too much: such men are dangerous." The belief that people with certain types of body structure are predisposed to have specific personality structures is even older than Galen's time. Only in recent days, however, has the body type theory gained much respectability. Although several European scientists puzzled over the matter a hundred or more years ago, it was the German psychiatrist *Ernst Kretschmer* (°) whose theory became most famous.

Kretschmer's Morphological Theory

Kretschmer worked with mental patients at several hospitals in southern Germany in the first part of this century. He found he could place these patients in one of three categories according to their *morphology* (°), or the measurements of their arms, legs, and trunk. The *pyknic* (°) has short limbs and a roly-poly face, a broad and thick middle-section, and tends to gain weight in middle age. According to Kretschmer, pyknics tended toward wild fluctuations in mood. When they are "up," they are very high up indeed; but when they are "down," they become blackly melancholy and depressed. As we will see later, this rapid shift in mood states is characteristic of what is called the *manic-depressive syndrome* (°).

Kretschmer's second category was that of *asthenic* (°), a term he used to describe people with narrow trunks, long arms and legs, thin faces, and who seldom were very fat. He believed asthenics were introverted, retiring, and shy, often cold and calculating, but sometimes rather dull and phlegmatic. Many

Melancholic (mell-ann-KOLL-ic). The Greek word *melan* means "black." Melanin (MELL-ann-inn) is the dark pigment in your skin that darkens when you get a suntan. Melan-choler is black bile. A melancholic individual is someone who is perpetually sad, unhappy, depressed.

Ernst Kretschmer (AIRNst KRET-schmer). A German psychiatrist (1888–1964) noted for his morphological (more-foh-LODGE-uh-cull) theory of personality.

Morphology (more-FOLL-oh-gee). The Greek word *morph* means "shape" or "form." Morphology is the study of biological forms, shapes, or body types. The word also means the structure or form of something, such as the human body.

Pyknic (PIC-nic). From the Greek word meaning "thick" or "pressed together." One of Kretschmer's three body types. Someone "pressed together," or short and stocky.

Manic-depressive syndrome (MAN-ick de-PRESS-ive SIN-drome). The set of symptoms or syndrome that includes wild swings of mood, from manic happiness to depressive sadness. See Chapter 24.

Asthenic (ass-THEN-ick). From the Greek word meaning "weak." Someone with a slender, thin, weak morphology.

Ernst Kretschmer.

asthenic patients withdrew from social contact entirely, becoming *schizo-phrenic* (°).

His third type he called *athletic* (°), patients who had the "balanced" physiques and muscular development often displayed by the men who appear in "muscle magazines" and the women who appear in *Playboy*. The athletic personality type was energetic, aggressive, and sanguine.

Kretschmer believed that hormonal secretions caused both the body shape and the personality type. His theory was attacked on two major points. First, it was very difficult to fit everyone in the world into the three categories—or body types—that Kretschmer described. Second, there appear to be many fat, heavy people with thin (asthenic) personalities; and many skinny people who behave like pyknics or athletics. The problem was that Kretschmer insisted that everyone had to be one of the "pure types," and that no one could be a mixture of the three.

Sheldon's Theory of Body Types

In the early 1940's and 50's, Harvard scientist W.H. Sheldon offered his own theory, in its way a great improvement over Kretschmer's. Like Kretschmer, Sheldon believed that there were three major *morphologies*, or body types, and Sheldon's descriptions were somewhat similar to those of Kretschmer's.

Sheldon called his three types (°):

1. The *endomorphs*, who had soft, rounded bodies and big stomachs.
2. The *mesomorphs*, who had hard, square, bony bodies with over-developed muscles.
3. The *ectomorphs*, who had tall, thin bodies with over-developed heads.

If these names sound vaguely familiar, you might wish to turn back to Chapter 19 and read again the description of human development within the womb. As you may recall, shortly after a child is conceived, the growing mass of cells develops three distinct layers. The central layer, called the endoderm or "inner skin," develops into the digestive system and internal organs. The middle layer, the mesoderm or "middle skin," turns into bone and muscles. The outer layer, or ectoderm, becomes the central nervous system.

According to Sheldon, a person's genetic blueprint usually causes one of these three layers to become predominant—that is, to develop more rapidly and fully than the other two layers.

Schizophrenic (SKITS-oh-FRENN-ick). Someone suffering from a common form of mental illness. See Chapter 24.

Athletic (ath-LETT-ick). From the Greek word meaning "someone who competes for a prize." In ancient Greece, men who competed in the Olympics or other sports contests tended to be big and strong. The more muscled the man's body, the more he competed; hence, the more "athletic" he was.

Endomorphs, mesomorphs, ecto-morphs (EN-doh, MEE-zoh, ECK-toh-morffs). Sheldon's three morphologies, or body types.

Sheldon's three body types.

A 4-6-1 (endomorphic mesomorph); a 5-2-1 (endomorphic mesomorph); and a 2-5-6 (ectomorphic mesomorph).

1. If the endoderm becomes dominant, the person develops a roly-poly or endomorphic body and fixates on food. Sheldon believes the endomorph is very social, enjoys relaxing and lazing about, talks a lot, and prefers "the sweet life" of physical comfort.
2. If the mesoderm gains the upper hand during fetal development, the person will have a square, heavy, mesomorphic body. As a young adult, this individual will enjoy exercising his or her bones and muscles in competitive athletics. The mesomorph is supposed to like sports, power, to be energetic and assertive, courageous and sanguine.
3. If the ectoderm comes out on top in the womb, the brain predominates and the body develops long, thin legs and arms—and a big head. The ectomorph is said to be introverted, inhibited, intellectual, and to prefer being alone rather than in a crowd.

Sheldon's theory differs from Kretschmer's in several important ways. To begin with, Sheldon's emphasis was on the growth of normal people, rather than on the personality and physical characteristics of mental patients. To determine his morphologies, Sheldon took detailed measurements of the photographs of 4,000 male college students. The pictures were taken in the nude, a development that upset many people when they discovered what Sheldon had done (remember— this was 30 years ago).

Sheldon found that most of his subjects were not "pure" body types, however, but mixtures. So he devised 7-point scales for each of the three morphologies. Each human being was presumed to have a numerical rating on each of the three scales. A "true" endomorph would rate 7-0-0; but if the person were *mostly* an endomorph, with a touch of mesomorph and a trace of ectomorph, then the person might rate 6-1-1. A woman with some endomorph to her, and a little ectomorph, but mostly mesomorph would rate 2-5-1. A tall, thin "brain" might rate 2-2-6, or high ectomorphic.

QUESTION: **What numbers would you assign to your own body type?**

Body Type and Personality Traits   Sheldon's theory was not only more exact than Kretschmer's, but more detailed, too. Sheldon made up a list of 20 personality traits for each of his three body types. He then tested 200 university men to see if their personality traits and body types were *correlated*, or associated, with each other. For example, Sheldon found that sociability was highly correlated with endomorphism, as were 19 other traits. Extroversion was one of 20 traits that was correlated highly with mesomorphism, while restraint and passivity were two of the 20 traits that were found to a high degree in ectomorphs. Other investigators have found similar but less impressive correlations between behavior patterns and body structure, or type.

Criticisms of Typological Theories

Although Sheldon's findings were confirmed by other investigators, many questions have been raised about his work. To begin with, he did not really consider the age of his subjects, nor whether they had grown up in poverty or wealth. You may recall from a previous chapter that Korean war orphans who were reared in the United States were considerably larger and taller than their age-mates who remained behind in Korea in deprived circumstances (it's hard to be a fat, jolly endomorph if you've been starved all of your life). More important, Sheldon's classifications may have been influenced by what psychologists call the "halo effect," or perceptual expectancies. If you personally believed Sheldon was right, and you were asked to observe a famous football player and then to describe his personality traits, might you not see what you expected to see in the man's behavior?

Even if we assume that some correlation does exist between the structure of your body and the structure of your personality, can we say with confidence which causes what? Sheldon believed that the genetic blueprint determined both body shape and mental traits, but we have no proof that this is the case. A *correlation* is a measure of relatedness between two things, but, as we said earlier, correlations don't tell us anything about causes. Thus, even though Sheldon's notions received some support from other scientists, his theory has not been very influential because he never could offer any reasonable explanation of why body type should influence thoughts, feelings, and behaviors. But perhaps we can now come to Sheldon's assistance.

Think back over the dynamic theories that we discussed in the previous chapter. Freud held that "animal instincts" were our major motivators. Jung rejected this belief, thinking that cognitive or spiritual values were the main determinants of behavior. Adler and the humanists disagreed, insisting that people are capable of outgrowing their childish instincts and mental introversions. Many humanists believe in a kind of "enlightened selfishness"—the notion that you do best when you help the people around you achieve their own goals. The mature person thus should show concern for others and for the general welfare of the human race because, according to the humanists, this is the best way for a person to maximize his or her own growth and self-actualization.

Now let us translate all this into more scientific terms. We assume that our first task in life is to survive—and to do so, we must be able to predict and control our inputs. The inputs that are perhaps most important to us are those that yield rewarding feedback about our performance, or outputs. Since there are three distinct classes of inputs—biological, mental, and social—there must also be three distinct types of rewards or innate motivators.

Freud was a sensualist who was strongly reinforced by creature comforts. Jung was a mystic who loved nothing more than the exploration of his own mind. Adler emphasized the rewarding properties of power, praise, performance, and prestige—all of which have to do with social relationships. Three men—three theoretical approaches highlighting three quite different types of reinforcing inputs.

QUESTION: Are you sometimes surprised to find that other people don't always like the things that you do? When you encounter someone with a different set of values or desires, do you occasionally feel that the person is immature, inexperienced, or perhaps even "needs help?"

Now let us consider Sheldon's typologies. Sheldon thought that fetal development influenced body type, and that body type then determined personality. As intriguing as this notion is, we cannot place much stock in it, since Sheldon never discovered a plausible mechanism by which the shape of a person's physique could control the structure of his or her personality. But let us speculate a bit. It seems much more likely that, during "the battle in the womb," you are somehow physically biased toward preferring one of the three major classes of rewarding inputs. If your endoderm predominates, perhaps the receptor organs in your digestive tract and reproductive organs become more numerous or more easily aroused than, say, the receptor organs in your muscles or your eyes and ears. Thus, like Freud, you might feel more of an "innate need" to predict and control those inputs associated with food and sex than to deal with feedback associated with thinking and socializing. If your ectoderm wins the war, sensory inputs from your eyes and ears (that so strongly influence your stream of consciousness) might seem more reinforcing to you than sensual pleasures, or power and prestige. If your mesoderm came out on top, *proprioceptive* (°) feedback from your muscles might seem so motivating that you would move into an active life of being with, performing for, competing against, relating to, or trying to control the actions of other people.

Of course, as Sheldon himself noted, we are all mixtures rather than pure types, and even our preferred reinforcers are surely influenced by our past experiences and environmental demands. And there certainly is no strong body of data that argues in favor of "fetal bias toward a specific type of reinforcing feedback." However, many of the theoretical battles that personality theorists have engaged in do make a bit more sense if we assume there are three major types of inputs, and that most of us emphasize one type more than another. For then we can see that Freud, Jung, and Adler represent three sides to the same human triangle, and that the typologists might have done better had they looked at inputs and outputs rather than focusing on internal "causes" such as liver bile and body structure.

QUESTION: **What class of reinforcers do business people in general seem to value most highly or pursue most frequently? What about teachers? nurses? politicians? farmers? psychologists?**

MENTAL (INTRA-PSYCHIC) TRAITS

What some personality theorists appear to want is a set of terms, or labels, that will describe fairly accurately people's intra-psychic activities. This set of descriptive categories about our minds' internal processes must be neither too large to handle nor so small that it insults our feelings of individuality. Perhaps because Sheldon emphasized physiological variables, psychologists have generally rejected his approach and have focused instead on the concept of *mental traits*.

Technically speaking, a trait is a tendency or predisposition to respond to many different stimuli or situations in the same way. If you are kind to almost all of the different people you meet, then you possess the trait of kindness. If you are good at solving all kinds of different problems, if you adapt rapidly to all types of intellectual challenges, then you possess the trait of intelligence.

If we wanted to get an exact measure of your kindness, we might dream up a test for this trait—a "kindness scale"—that had a hundred questions on it. We could ask things like, "If you saw an injured puppy lying by the side of the road, would you pick it up and take it to the doctor's or just ignore it?" Or, "Do you prefer to pat a person on the back, or kick the person in the seat of the pants?" If our test were a good one, if it were a really *valid* measure of the trait, then kind

Proprioceptive (pro-pree-oh-SEP-tive). Stimulus inputs from the person's own body, particularly from the deep receptors in the muscles, joints, tendons, and bones of the body. See Chapter 6.

Alfred Binet.

Binet (bee-NAY). Alfred Binet (1857–1911) was a French psychologist who, with Théophile Simon (see-MOAN), developed the first well-known intelligence test.

Théophile Simon (TEY-oh-feel see-MOAN). Simon (1873–1961) was a French physician who became more interested in psychological research than in the practice of medicine. Simon and Alfred Binet published their first IQ test in 1905.

Mental age. Your chronological (kron-oh-LODGE-uh-cull) age is the actual number of years that you have lived (Chronos was the Greek god of time). According to Simon and Binet, the average 7-year-old child should have an average mental development—hence, a mental age of 7. Your mental age is thus a measure of your mental maturity.

Drawing of a diamond by a 5-year-old (**left**) and a 7-year-old.

people would get high scores, while unkind people would get low scores. And if you met someone for the first time—a young woman, let's say—who told you she got a 95 on the test, wouldn't you be willing to give odds that she would treat you kindly?

QUESTION: What score would you think the average person should get on a 100-point "kindness" test?

Intelligence Tests

Traits such as kindness can be fairly easily measured—provided we have a good working definition of the trait to begin with, and as long as we recognize that kindness might mean one thing in our culture, but something radically different elsewhere in the world. But what about intelligence? How could we go about defining—and measuring—such a complex trait as this? Obviously, some of the people in the world are bright, and some are not so bright. Probably you make judgments of people's intelligence every day. What kind of test, or scale, do you use?

The Binet-Simon IQ Test One of the first psychologists to face this problem was a Frenchman named *Alfred Binet* (°). He became interested in the differences between bright and dull children about 1890 and tried to devise a simple scale that allowed him quickly to distinguish the smart ones from the dumb ones. At first he relied on physical measures—such as the size of the child's head or the pattern of lines on the palm of the child's hand. None of these scales correlated very highly with the child's performance in school, however, so Binet abandoned them.

In 1904 the French government asked Binet and a physician named *Théophile Simon* (°) to devise a test that would allow teachers to identify "retarded" children so that they could be given special attention in school. Binet and Simon pulled together a large number of rather simple problems that seemed to require different mental skills—and then they tried the test problems out on a large number of French school children of different ages. This technique allowed Binet and Simon to select appropriate test items for each age group. They found, for example, that the average 7-year-old could correctly make a pencil copy of the figure of a diamond, but most 5-year-olds could not.

If a boy of 9 got the same score on the test as did the *average* 7-year-old, Binet and Simon presumed that the boy's mental development was retarded by two years. According to Binet and Simon, the boy would have a physical age of 9 but a *mental age* (°) of 7. If an 8-year-old girl did as well on the test as the average 11-year-old, then she had a mental age of 11, although her physical age was but 8.

Later, at the suggestion of German psychologist Wilhelm Stern, the relationship between physical or chronological age, and mental age, was put into an equation:

$$\frac{\text{Mental age}}{\text{Chronological age}} \times 100 = \text{Intelligence Quotient, or IQ.}$$

A girl with a mental age of 6 and a chronological age of 6 would have an IQ of

$$\frac{6}{6} \times 100 = 1 \times 100 = 100 = \text{IQ.}$$

By definition, she would be of average intelligence. A boy with a mental age of 7 and a chronological age of 9 would have an IQ of

$$\frac{7}{9} \times 100 = .777 \times 100 = 78 = \text{IQ.}$$

A girl with a mental age of 11 and a chronological age of 8 would have an IQ of

$$\frac{11}{8} \times 100 = 1.375 \times 100 = 138 = IQ.$$

The Binet-Simon test did so well at predicting the academic performance of school children—or so the French government felt—that intelligence testing became a standard part of classroom routine.

The noted Stanford psychologist, L.M. Terman, made up his own version of the French scale, which he called the Stanford-Binet intelligence test. Other psychologists soon followed Terman's lead, and now there are hundreds of IQ tests available. Properly used, they can give a person useful information about his or her mental abilities. Unfortunately, as we will see presently, there are a great many dangers involved in the use of these tests—dangers that perhaps the average person does not appreciate. To understand both the successes and failures of IQ tests, we must look more closely at the trait of intelligence itself.

Binet and Simon were greatly influenced by Darwin's theory of evolution. Darwin had suggested that intelligence is inherited in much the same way as are eye color, skin color, height, and other physical characteristics. If a man and wife of average height could have a hundred male children—so Darwin assumed—most of them would also be of average height. A few would be very tall, a few very short, but most of the boys would be about as tall as their father. If the couple had a hundred girls instead of boys, the girls would show the same distribution of heights—and would average out much like their mother. If we made a graph of the height of the boys, it would presumably look something like this:

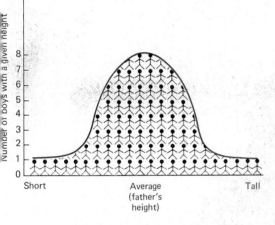

Bell curve showing the height of 100 boys from one family.

If you measured the heights of all the men in the world, they would indeed create a graph with a shape pretty much like the one shown above. In technical terms, this is called a *normal distribution* (°) of test scores—or a *bell-shaped curve* (°). Many school teachers believe that the scores that students make on a history or mathematics examination should "fit the curve," or be "normally distributed." A few students should get A's, a few should get F's, while most should get C's. The teachers then write examinations that will give them the results they expect.

Most intelligence tests are based on this same assumption of normal distribution of scores. Binet and Simon juggled their items around until the test yielded a bell-shaped distribution of IQs for each age level. If intelligence were in fact a single trait (like height), and if IQ were entirely determined by your genetic blueprint, then such a procedure might be justified. But are these assumptions really valid?

Normal distribution. A set of test scores that are distributed along a more or less bell-shaped curve. Most of the scores are bunched up in the "bell" in the middle, but a few of the scores trail off at either end of the curve.

Bell-shaped curve. The curve or graph of a normal distribution. See the figure on this page.

Reliable. That which is repeatable, dependable.

Valid. Believable, accurate. A valid IQ test is one that really measures intelligence, rather than some other trait. The validity of an IQ test is hard to prove because there is no universal agreement on what is *should* measure—that is, psychologists don't agree on what intelligence actually is.

Is IQ a Single Trait?   The results of many psychological studies suggest that intelligence is not a single trait but rather is made up of a great many related talents or abilities. Psychologists don't entirely agree what these "related" talents are, but often mentioned are such things as the ability to memorize words and numbers, to learn motor tasks, to solve verbal and numerical problems, to evaluate complex situations, to be creative, to perceive spatial relationships of various kinds, and so forth. If intelligence is really a mixture of many different traits, then there is no reason to expect that IQ's should fit a bell-shaped curve—any more than there is firm justification for assuming that math exam scores should necessarily be normally distributed on the same type of curve.

More than this, we must face up to the fact that all traits are expressed as an *interaction* between genes and environment. A young boy born to very tall parents might be expected to grow up to be at least as tall as his father. But if the boy is severely starved during most of his early years, he may be considerably shorter than we might have expected. A child may inherit the genetic potential for high intelligence (whatever that turns out to be), but if the child grows up in a socially or intellectually deprived environment, it will surely perform at less than its full intellectual capacity.

Test Reliability and Test Validity   When a psychologist makes up a "trait scale" of any kind, the psychologist usually has to prove two things to other scientists before *they* will accept the scale and use it themselves. First, the creator of the test must show that it is *reliable* (°). Second, there must be evidence that the test is also *valid* (°).

A reliable friend is one you can depend on, no matter how often you call for help nor in what circumstances. A reliable psychological scale is one that yields the same results again and again, no matter how frequently the test is given to the subject nor under what conditions it is administered.

A valid test is one that measures what it says it measures—and measures little or nothing else besides.

Unfortunately, very few psychological scales have either the reliability or the validity that we might wish for them to have. If we look at this matter in detail, perhaps you will come to understand better why many psychologists are reluctant to tell anyone what his or her score on an IQ test is.

IQ and Early Deprivation   In the 1930's, psychologist H.M. Skeels shocked many of his colleagues by announcing that he had been able to increase the "brightness" or IQ scores of mentally retarded children by putting them in an unusual environment. At the time that he did this research, Skeels was working at an over-crowded orphanage in Iowa. The youngest children were kept in a nursery in standard hospital cribs. These cribs had white sheets draped around their sides, preventing the children from seeing each other. The babies were given no toys to play with. Their only human contacts were the busy nurses who did little more than change the infants' diapers and give them bottles of milk on schedule. The older children were packed together like zoo animals in dreary, ancient cottages. The only property that any child was allowed to have exclusively as its own was a toothbrush.

QUESTION: How similar do these real-life conditions seem to the laboratory situation in which the Harlows reared their socially-deprived monkeys?

Early in his stay at the Iowa orphanage, Skeels had noticed two baby girls neglected by their feeble-minded mothers and unwanted by other relatives, who had been placed in the institution. Skeels describes these infants as being "pitiful little creatures" who were always crying, had runny noses, and little or no hair. They were undersized, sad, inactive, and spent most of their days rocking back and forth in their beds and whining. Intelligence tests suggested that the girls had IQ's of 50 or less—about half the IQ score of a normal child. Since placement of the children in foster homes seemed impossible, the girls were transferred to a nearby home for the mentally retarded.

Shortly thereafter, Skeels was walking through the grounds of this home for the retarded. He noticed "two outstanding little girls. They were alert, smiling, running about, responding to the playful attention of adults, and generally behaving and looking like any other toddlers." Skeels could scarcely believe it when he discovered that these were the two babies who had previously been considered "hopeless." He tested their IQ's at once, and found them both to be near normal. Since he was very skeptical of this finding, Skeels waited a year and then retested them—and again the little girls proved to have an intelligence level well within the range of normal children of their age.

What had happened to these little girls? When they had arrived at the home, each baby had been "adopted" by one of the women inmates. Although the foster mothers were supposedly "retarded," they were bright enough to have devoted many hours each day to caring for their "adopted" children. Other women on the ward shared the responsibilities, considering themselves to be "aunts" of the little girls. The attendants and nurses also spent time with the infants, taking them on walks, automobile rides, and on shopping excursions. The little girls simply were not given a chance to sit on their beds and whine!

Skeels then got the State Administration to let him shift a dozen more orphans to the home for retarded adults. Their pre-shift IQ's ranged from 35 to 89, with an average of about 65. Several of the children were classified as *imbeciles* (°).

Another dozen or so children who remained in the orphanage served as "controls." These children had IQ's ranging from 50 to 103, with an average of about 87. As you can see, the "controls" were, on the average, more than 20 IQ points brighter than the children shifted to the new environment.

Both groups of children were tested at regular intervals for some time. All of the dozen orphans moved to the home for the retarded showed an *increase* in intelligence, ranging from 7 to 58 IQ points. The average increase was 28 IQ points. In contrast, all but one of the children who remained in the orphanage showed a *decrease* in intelligence, ranging from minus 8 to minus 45 IQ points; the average *decrease* in the control group children was close to 30 IQ points.

Skeels made a follow-up study of all the children in both groups some 30 years after he first saw them. The children sent to the home for the retarded had all left state care early in their lives, the average length of institutionalization being about 5 years. By comparison, the average length of stay in state institutions for the "controls" was 22 years, and many of them were still in hospitals of one kind or another. Eleven of the "home" children had gotten married, and most had children of their own; all of their children had normal or above-average intelligence. Only two of the "orphanage control" group had gotten married.

Almost all of the "home" children had completed high school, and several had gone on to college. Only one child in the "control" group had been through high school; the average for this group was only three years of schooling. Most of the youngsters mothered by "retarded" women in the home were employed in good jobs or were married to wage-earners. Most of the "orphanage" children were barely surviving on their own or were recipients of some kind of state support or charity.

Although Skeels's experiment was begun more than 40 years ago, many more recent studies confirm his findings. For example, Sandra Scarr-Salapatek and Richard A. Weinberg studied several hundred children in Minnesota who were placed in foster homes and compared these youngsters with children brought up in their natural homes. Most of the adopting parents were college graduates with professional jobs or responsibilities. Scarr-Salapatek and Weinberg estimate that,

Imbeciles (IM-be-sills, or IM-buh-sills). In old-fashioned psychological terms, a person with an IQ from 20 to 50. Morons were said to have IQ's from 50 to 70, while idiots were said to have IQ's below 20. A century or two ago, all these mentally retarded people were thought to be possessed of demons or devils, or to be "God's children." More recently, as we have learned of the powerful effects the environment has on mental functioning, psychologists do not use terms such as "moron," "imbecile," "idiot," "fool," or "God's child" as frequently as once we did. Individuals considered mentally retarded in a given society are certainly different from the average person in that society; we are not yet sure what all the differences are, why they come about, or how to overcome them.

Sandra Scarr-Salapatek.

judging from the adopted children's genetic backgrounds, they might have been expected to have had IQ's well below the national average. Instead, they scored well above the average and very close to the youngsters brought up in natural homes similar to the ones the orphans were adopted into. More than this, the younger the child when adopted, the higher its later IQ score tended to be. Generally speaking, black children adopted into middle-class white homes had about the same IQ's as did white children. If nothing else, the Minnesota study suggests that orphans placed with concerned, well-educated foster parents do even better than they might have done if reared by their own parents.

Dumber by the Dozen. But what is it about an "enriched" environment that has such a marked effect on IQ scores? Perhaps part of the explanation comes from a study by Lillian Belmont and Francis A. Marolla, who examined birth order and intelligence scores for almost 400,000 19-year-old Dutch males. Since their subjects included almost all the men born in Holland between 1944 and 1947, the "group" can be considered fairly representative of Dutch society in general.

Belmont and Marolla found that the more children there were in the family, the lower their average IQ was. More than this, the first-born children had a clear-cut advantage over the children born into the family later on. These findings

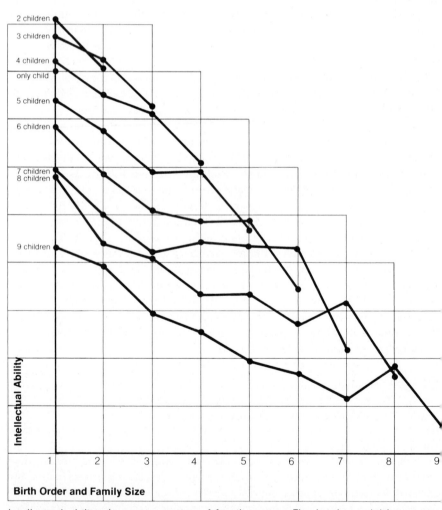

Intellectual ability decreases as size of family grows. The brightest children come from the smallest families, and are born first. The estimated difference between the highest score, for the older of two, and lowest, for the last of nine, is 10 IQ points.

were true no matter how wealthy the family. It happens that, generally speaking, boys from rich families scored higher than did boys from middle-class families, and that the latter had higher IQ scores than did boys from poor families. However, taking any one class of family into consideration, children from small families scored significantly higher than did children from large families. The highest scores of all were obtained by the first-born child in families of just two children; by far the lowest average scores came from the last-born child in families of nine children. The difference between these two extremes was more than 10 IQ points. (When you are dealing with 400,000 subjects, a difference of 10 or more IQ points is quite meaningful.)

Michigan psychologist Robert Zajonc (his name rhymes with "science") explains the Belmont and Marolla data as follows: Children grow up in quite different intellectual environments, depending on their birth order. The first child is born into a predominantly adult world, for it has mostly its two parents with whom to talk and who serve as its models. The second child is born into what Zajonc calls a "diluted" intellectual environment, for it not only has two parents but also one slightly older sibling from whom it can learn. Since the younger child spends much of its time with the first-born, and since this older sibling does not have the mental maturity of the parents, the second-born gets quite different feed forward and feedback than did the first child. The third-born has it even worse than the second-born, since by this time the family is made up mostly of children who are functioning at a much lower intellectual level than the same number of adults would be. As you can see, the fourth, fifth, and sixth children would suffer even greater intellectual deprivation, since they would be taught primarily by older siblings.

Robert Zajonc.

(Zajonc believes that an older child may actually profit from teaching its younger siblings. Evidence supporting this belief comes from the fact that the oldest child in two-, three-, and four-children families get higher IQ scores than do only children.)

Zajonc also predicts that the length of time between the births of children influences their intellectual development. If the second child were born 10 years after the first, the older child would then be near-adult during the sibling's formative years; if the second child were born but one year after the first, the older child would still be in its intellectual infancy and hence a more infantile mental model. The "dilution" effect would be near its maximum if the second child were the same age as the first—that is, if the two children were twins. While Belmont and Marolla did not gather much data on intervals between children in their study of Dutch males, Zajonc points out that other information about twins and triplets does tend to confirm his beliefs. In a study by R.G. Record, Thomas McKeown, and J.H. Edwards, a group of 2,164 twins had an average IQ of 95.7; a group of 33 triplets—whose intellectual environment should be even more "dilute" than that of twins—had an average IQ of 91.6. The *expected* average of all such children would be 100 IQ points.

QUESTION: In poverty-stricken areas, families tend to be larger than the national average, there are more one-parent families, and children are often born in fairly rapid succession. How might all these facts help explain why children from impoverished backgrounds generally have lower than usual IQ scores?

Can You Raise Your Own IQ? Many IQ tests place rather heavy emphasis on *reasoning*, or the ability to work one's way through a complicated task step by step. The makers of such tests apparently believe, as did Piaget, that the ability to handle such mental mazes is genetically determined. Surely it is true that people who obtain high scores on most IQ tests often breeze through complex problems with little difficulty and, if you ask them to do so, can usually tell you the precise steps that they went through "in their heads."

But what about people who score below average on IQ tests? Do they lack some innate talent for reasoning, or have they never bothered to learn the tricks of the IQ trade? Benjamin Bloom and Lois Broder at the University of Chicago did a fascinating study in the 1940's of how college students with either low or high IQ scores react to mental challenges. Bloom and Broder gave these subjects various sorts of problems to work on and asked the students to talk out loud as they proceeded. High IQ subjects tended to read the instructions carefully, then diligently eliminated all the incorrect answers. The low IQ students often lacked the patience to isolate the correct answers when they faced questions that required formal reasoning. Unlike their high-IQ peers, the low-scoring students didn't seem to carry on an internal conversation with themselves, nor did they proceed through a step-by-step sequence of deductions. If they couldn't see the answer immediately, they felt lost and usually guessed.

The low-scoring students also seemed mentally careless and passive in their approach to problem-solving. They often selected their answers on the basis of hunches or gut feelings, and they frequently rushed through the instructions to a test or skipped them entirely. If forced to reread the instructions, the low-scorers often came to understand what was required and hence answered the question correctly. However, they tended to place little value on reasoning, preferring to act quickly instead.

(Confirmation of these findings comes from a study by Carl Bereiter and Siegfried Engelmann, who discovered that many low-IQ children believe it is better to answer a question immediately—even if the answer is wrong—than to give the question a certain amount of consideration before responding.)

Convinced by their study that low-scoring students had somehow never acquired the proper mental habits, Bloom and Broder next developed a training program aimed at helping these young people "learn how to think." The students were asked to solve various problems aloud. After they had discussed the student's solution with him or her, Bloom and Broder read the correct solution aloud. Then they asked the student to explain what had gone wrong if the student had been incorrect. The students had many difficulties at first, and the instructors had to show tremendous patience. But once the students began to recognize that they actually could learn how to reason, they did so with increasing frequency. Although Bloom and Broder did not retest the students' IQ scores after this training, the psychologists did report that most of their subjects had gotten much higher grades in college thereafter.

In discussing his own highly successful attempts to help people raise their IQ scores, California psychologist Arthur Whimbey points out that learning how to reason requires immediate positive feedback and much practice. Whimbey urges people who wish to improve their test performances to work with a trained tutor, to get old tests and puzzle books from the library, and always to read questions carefully without jumping to conclusions. Learners should think out loud as they work, and try to figure out how they got the incorrect answer if they are wrong. Following these techniques won't make a genius out of everybody, Whimbey notes, but he reports that many of the people he has worked with have increased their IQ scores by 20 or 30 points.

QUESTION: If a 6-year-old boy wanted to "learn how to reason," would he do better if taught by an adult or by his 7-year-old brother?

Are IQ Tests Reliable?   If intelligence were absolutely fixed at birth, psychologists would probably have little trouble making up IQ tests that were super reliable. Luckily, almost everyone performs better when given adequate stimulation. In the United States, children raised in rural areas *on the average* get IQ scores that are about 15 points lower than do children raised in cities and suburbs. Does this fact mean that rural children are innately (genetically) inferior to city kids? Not necessarily, because children born in the country who move to the city when still young often show the same rather dramatic increase in IQ scores that Skeels found true of the orphans who moved to a more stimulating environment. Young children who move out of ghetto or slum areas to suburban situations show the same upward change in their tested intelligence—and this fact is as true of white children as of blacks, Spanish-Americans, Orientals, or Indians.

Perhaps by now you have sensed what the basic problem of the reliability of test scores is all about. Traits, or "genetic pre-dispositions," are subjective states or conditions—that is, they lie within you. But IQ tests are behavioral; they measure performance and not your inner condition. Your score on an IQ test reflects not only your innate intellectual capacity but your past experience and your present motivational state. Surely you have some time in the past studied so hard for a quiz that you knew the material cold and should have "aced" the exam. But the day of the test you had a headache, a toothache, or you were so worried about things that you "clutched" during the quiz, and maybe you came close to flunking it. Had you taken the test a day or so later, you might have gotten the A that you deserved. So, was the quiz a *reliable* test of your knowledge?

Are IQ Tests Valid?   The problem of intelligence test validity is equally thorny. It is hard to devise a psychological scale if you are not entirely sure what it is that the scale ought to be measuring. Since there is no universal agreement as to what abilities or talents actually make up the so-called "trait" of intelligence, we can't be sure how to prove that any given IQ test is a *valid* measure of that "trait." Psychologists, such as Simon and Binet, usually solve this problem by offering their own, *carefully limited* definition of what they think the "trait" really is—and then show that their particular test is valid within those limits. Binet and Simon assumed that "intelligence" was whatever mental properties were needed to succeed in the French schools. Children who scored high on their tests generally got good grades, while students who scored low got much poorer grades. The correlation between IQ scores and exam grades *validated* the IQ test, as far as Binet and Simon were concerned. And within the limits of their very narrow definition of "intelligence," they were right. But we realize now that almost all such definitions—and hence such tests, too—are culturally *biased*.

As an example of how important this sort of cultural bias is—and how one can sometimes overcome it with special training—consider the research of Rick Heber and his colleagues at the University of Wisconsin. In 1967, Heber and his associates selected for study 40 infants who were born to black parents living in one of the worst sections of Milwaukee. Although many parts of Milwaukee are delightful places in which to live, people in this particular section of town have the lowest average family income and education level found in Milwaukee; they also have the highest rate of unemployment and the highest population density. Although less than 3 percent of the city's people live in this area, it accounts for about 33 percent of the total number of children classified as educable mentally retarded. The mothers of the 40 infants in this Milwaukee Project all had IQ scores below 75 and, in many cases, the fathers were absent from home.

Of these 40 infants, 20 were randomly selected to be in what Heber considered the "experimental" group, while the other 20 were placed in an untreated "control" group. The families of the experimental-group infants were given intensive vocational help and training in homemaking and child-care skills as soon as the children were born. When these "experimental" infants were 30 months old, they were put into a special education center for 35 hours a week. The training at this center focused on the development of language and cognitive skills. The experimental-group children remained in this center year-round until they were 6 years old and could enter school. The families and children in the control group received none of these benefits.

Desiccate (DESS-see-kate). From the Latin word meaning "to dry up"; hence, "to dry" or "to preserve by drying." A favorite word in spelling tests, since most people incorrectly spell it with 2 "s's" and just 1 "c."

The children in both groups were given IQ tests frequently. In the summer of 1976, when the youngsters were all about 9 years old, the experimentally-treated children had IQ scores that averaged about 110, while the children in the control group averaged below 80 on the tests. During the 9-year period they were tested, the groups' differences were never less than 20 IQ points and frequently were as high as 30 points. Dr. Heber believes that this superiority was due to the special training which the children in the experimental group (and their families) were given—most of which was aimed at teaching them the same sorts of intra-psychic skills that middle-class, white children typically acquire as part of their normal cultural tradition.

To be truthful, most IQ tests now in use were devised by highly educated, white, middle-class males who often (perhaps unconsciously) defined "intelligence" as whatever traits were necessary to succeed in their middle-class, white, school-oriented society. This part of U.S. culture is oriented toward polite language and polite behavior, toward thoughts and speech rather than toward actions and gestures. The skills needed to survive in middle America are not necessarily those a person might find useful in rural America—where knowing how to cure a sick cow might be more important than knowing the definition of the word *"desiccate"* (*).

To get a high score on many intelligence tests, you must answer the test items the same way that most successful white, middle-class U.S. males would respond. If a black person raised in the Detroit ghetto gets a score of 85 on the usual IQ test, can we say the score is a valid indicator that the black has less intellectual capacity than a white person raised in the Detroit suburbs who gets a score of 100? If blacks had made up the test instead of whites, might not the scores be reversed? And if American Indians had devised the scale, might not both blacks and whites do poorly on it?

IQ and Survival   In a sense life itself is the best IQ test we presently have available. Within any given segment of society, or any particular culture, there are those people who thrive and bloom and those who just barely survive. If we can identify those personality traits that increase a person's chances of survival—within that society—then we can build an IQ "survival" test that would predict a young person's future success fairly accurately. We could use a test like this to identify the person's weak points and then give the individual special help. Indeed, it was for just this purpose that the French government commissioned Binet and Simon to create the first intelligence test more than 70 years ago. But we could also use the test to give us a more objective view of the society itself, for the "survival scale" should tell us what abilities or behavior patterns the culture rewarded and which ones the culture punished. If we wished, we might use this knowledge to institute change in the culture itself.

QUESTION: **If we gave a person special training in "survival skills," shouldn't the person's IQ score increase correspondingly? How would this result affect the normal distribution of test scores?**

Real Life versus School Life   By this point you may be asking a question of your own: If intelligence scales have such doubtful reliability and validity, why are they used so much in schools? Harvard psychologist David McClelland gave his answer in the January 1973 issue of the *American Psychologist*. Intelligence tests are quite often reliable indicators of how a school child will do in the future—but only within the classroom. IQ tests, McClelland feels, tap those traits that are necessary for success in the "blackboard jungle," but they have little or nothing to do with success in the non-academic world. In short, your IQ predicts what grades you will get (for instance) as a student in the Harvard Medical School, but not how good a doctor you will be once you get your medical degree. To pass med-school exams, you need a large vocabulary; you need the ability to memorize a great many "facts"; and you need to have considerable respect for authority. But to succeed as a practicing physician, you must get along well with people and speak their language (rather than book language); you must be able to solve real-life (rather than mathematical) problems; and you should have considerable respect for life itself.

In 1976, Duke psychologist Michael Wallach pointed out that most academic tests tell us very little about the talent of the students who take those tests. Wallach does believe that achievement or IQ tests might be of help in screening out students who score at the very bottom end of the test scales. But there apparently is very little evidence that these tests tell us much at all about how students will perform after they have left school. For example, in 1963 L.R. Harmon investigated the professional contributions of physicists and biologists who had taken advanced degrees. Three or more expert judges, working independently, evaluated these scientists in terms of their research, their publications, and the number of patents granted to them. Harmon then compared the actual "life's work" of the scientists with achievement test scores the scientists had gotten while still students. Harmon reports that there simply was no connection at all between test scores and actual (later) achievement. In a later survey, Wallach and C.W. Wing investigated the Scholastic Aptitude Test (SAT) scores of 500 undergraduates and compared these scores with achievement outside the classroom. Students who received low SAT scores tended to achieve just as much as did high scorers. The problem, Wallach suggests, is that most tests simply don't measure the intellectual and other qualities (traits) that lead to creativity and success outside the classroom. Wallach concludes his 1976 article by stating that, "Testing agencies should perhaps devote less effort to tests and more to helping educators assess achievement in activities that we value."

QUESTION: **If a child's "initial bias" was toward sensual or social inputs, why might it be expected to do more poorly on an IQ test than a child whose bias was toward intra-psychic inputs?**

ALLPORT'S THEORY OF TRAITS

For the most part, psychologists interested in the measurement of personality traits have looked to a person's past to get glimpses of that person's future. Traits—the tendency to react to many different stimuli with the same sorts of responses—were presumed to result from body biochemistry, or past experiences, or perhaps interactions between the two. But once an individual had acquired the trait, there was little he or she could do about changing it. Traits were the basic, stable, rather rigid skeleton that gave shape or structure to the person's psychological flesh. And how many times a year do you change your skeleton?

Allport's Theory of Values

One of the first scientists to recognize that the most important human traits might be those that look to the future rather than to the past was Harvard psychologist Gordon Allport. Like many other humanistic psychologists, Allport saw man as being motivated primarily by the desire to become—that is, to change and grow. Allport believed that conscious desires control behavior more than do unconscious wishes, and that a person's values, hopes, goals, and aspirations were more reliable predictors of future experiences than were such skills as word memory or mathematical reasoning. For Allport, the important traits were those that *motivated* a person, as well as providing structure to the individual's personality.

Allport identified several classes of traits. To begin with, he pointed out the difference between *individual* traits and *common* traits (*). No two people are

Individual traits; common traits. Gordon Allport (ALL-port) points out that each person has a unique set of attitudes, tendencies, and behaviors that he calls "individual traits." The love your mother had for you when you were a child was expressed in her own individual way; hence, was an individual trait. But most mothers love their children; hence, maternal love is a trait common to most mothers.

Cardinal, central, secondary traits (KARD-dih-null). According to Allport, a cardinal trait is displayed by a person who has but one over-riding goal in life. Central traits are the half-dozen or so highly important goals or values that most people seem to have in life. Secondary traits are those minor or occasional values that are displayed in very specific situations.

Psycho-pathology (SIGH-ko-path-OLL-oh-gee). From the Greek words meaning "mind" and "disease." Psycho-pathology is any form of mental illness or unusual emotional disturbance.

Profile (PRO-file). From the Latin word meaning "to draw in outline." Your own profile is your face as seen from a side view, or a drawing of your face from a side position. The profile of a mountain range is a side view of the tops of the mountains. A psychological profile is a graph or line connecting the "peaks" or top scores on a set of tests.

exactly alike, therefore all traits are individual or unique. But because all human beings have similar genetic heritages, and because our cultures are all fairly similar, our behavior patterns are roughly or approximately comparable. All blonds are different, for example, because they are different individuals; but they do all have light-colored hair, and we can talk about "blondness" as long as we remember that their differences are as important as their similarities.

Within a given individual there are *cardinal, central,* and *secondary* traits (°). A person driven by just one goal in life—perhaps to make a million dollars—displays a cardinal trait. More common are central traits—those few, important values or interest patterns that seem to color almost everything we do and that our friends recognize in us with no difficulty. Allport believed that most people have between 2 and 10 such central traits. The noted science-fiction writer, H.G. Wells, for instance, once said that there were but two major themes (central traits) to his life—his interest in promoting world government and sex. Cardinal and central traits shape our responses in operant, or unstructured, situations. Secondary traits are those incidental, usually classically-conditioned response patterns that occur in limited and highly specific situations. A preference for Chinese food or avoiding high places might be examples of secondary traits.

Allport's Six Values

Allport was interested in the normal personality, not in mental illness or *psycho-pathology* (°). Although he emphasized the uniqueness of the individual, Allport identified six central traits or values that seemed to be common among the people of our time and place. Although Allport believed that some portion of all six values was present in everyone's personality, he felt that one trait often was dominant and hence colored or influenced the other five. Working with P.E. Vernon and Gardner Lindzey, Allport developed a questionnaire that attempted to describe and measure six basic personality types:

1. *Theoretical.* Someone who seeks objective truth, who is rational and critical, systematic, and who cares more about theory than about applying knowledge.
2. *Economic.* The typical business man or woman interested in matters practical and useful, in markets and manufacturing and money.
3. *Esthetic.* The artistic type who loves form and harmony and beauty, who enjoys sensory impressions for their own sake without asking about practical matters.
4. *Social.* People who need people, who value helping others more than they value money or abstractions.
5. *Political.* The manipulator, interested in power and influence and fame in politics or in any other profession.
6. *Religious.* Someone, like Jung's "mature individual," who looks for truth within, who wishes to bring unity to all of his or her experiences.

Unlike many other pen-and-paper questionnaires, the Allport-Vernon-Lindzey test gives the subject a number of alternatives in answering the test items. On the basis of the subject's scores, a psychologist can draw a *profile* (°) of the strength of the subject's interests in each of the six categories listed above. Men and women are scored differently on the test, and there are ways of adjusting the scores depending on the subject's socio-economic background.

In general, men rate higher on theoretical, economic, and political interests, while women rate higher on esthetic, social, and religious values. Since the questionnaire was drawn up for use primarily with white, middle-class college students, it can hardly be considered culture-free. When used with these students, however, it does seem to be reasonably reliable and valid.

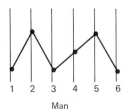

Man

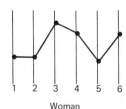

Woman

Two of Allport's profiles.

The Allport-Vernon-Lindzey test has sometimes been criticized because it gives rather a flattering view of most people—that is, no negative, anti-social, or selfish values are included. But Allport was interested in assisting normal people to achieve self-actualization, in helping them become better than they presently were. Very few of us will admit that our life's ambition is to become more jealous, more self-centered, more destructive and evil.

QUESTION: What relationships do you see between Allport's six values and the three classes of reinforcers mentioned earlier in this chapter?

OBJECTIVE VERSUS SUBJECTIVE TESTS

Personality tests are usually constructed in one of two ways—by theory or by practical experience. Allport theorized that there were six basic personality types and then devised a psychological yardstick to measure what he assumed was true. If the theory underlying the test is a valid view of human nature, then the test itself may have high validity.

But what would you do if you had no real theory of your own? Then you might do as Binet and Simon did—give a large number of test items to thousands of subjects and analyze your results as carefully as possible. Perhaps most 9-year-olds will know the answer to a certain question, while most 8-year-olds won't. You might then use this question as an index of a child's "mental maturity."

Or perhaps most patients in a mental hospital will respond one way to a given set of items, while most people outside the hospital (and hence presumably sane) will respond in a different way. You might then assume that these items could be used for diagnosing or predicting mental illness. As we will see, there are dangers and difficulties associated with both ways of constructing personality scales.

Projective Tests

Suppose you believed strongly in the psycho-analytic theory of personality, and you wanted to devise a means of getting at the dynamic aspects of a person's inner or subjective life. You could hardly ask the person about such matters directly, using a pen-and-paper test, because the most important dynamics are usually unconscious and cannot be expressed openly. The conditioned-response approach, in which there are right and wrong answers, simply won't work. Rather, you might want to present the subject with a variety of unstructured or *ambiguous* (°) situations and see what kinds of operant, or free, responses the individual came up with. That is, you might assume that people would project themselves into the task given them, that they would structure ambiguous stimuli according to the structures of their own basic personalities. You could then interpret their responses according to psycho-analytic (or any other) principles.

Word Association Test The first of these "projective" instruments was the *word association test* devised by British psychologist Sir Francis Galton more than 100 years ago and subsequently revised by Carl Jung for psycho-analytic use in the early 1900's. It consists of a list of highly emotional stimulus words that are presented to the subject one at a time. The person is asked to respond to each word with the first thing that comes to mind. Both Galton and Jung assumed that if a subject responded to a word like "sex" by blocking, or by refusing to answer—or started sweating, or fainted, or gave a wildly inappropriate reaction such as "firecrackers" or "death"—then the person probably was experiencing sexual problems that a therapist ought to look into. Sometimes a polygraph, or lie detector, is used during the test to measure the subject's physiological reactions as well (*see* Chapter 15).

Ambiguous (am-BIG-you-us). Vague, indefinite in form.

Two photographs that might be used in a TAT test.

The TAT The *thematic apperception test*, or TAT, was developed by Henry Murray, a U.S. biochemist who became a psychologist through Carl Jung's influence. The TAT consists of a set of 20 stimulus pictures that depict rather vague but potentially emotional situations. The subject responds by making up a story telling (1) what led up to the situation shown in the picture, (2) what the people are thinking and feeling and doing right then, and (3) what will happen to them in the future. Each story the subject produces is scored and interpreted individually. The psychologist giving the test usually assumes that the person will express his or her deep-seated needs and personality problems by projecting them onto the hero or the heroine in the story. This being the case, psychologists typically pay more attention to uncommon or unusual responses than they do to common or "normal" reactions. Perhaps the most effective use of the TAT has been by David McClelland and his associates who find it useful for measuring need for achievement and need for affiliation.

Inkblot Test By far the most famous of the projective instruments is the inkblot test, first devised in the 1920's by Swiss psychiatrist *Hermann Rorschach* (*). The Rorschach—as it is usually called—is a series of 10 colorful inkblots that are given to the subject one at a time. The person looks at the inkblot and reports what he or she sees—much as you might look at clouds passing overhead and tell someone what "faces" and other things you saw in the clouds. The psychologist giving the test then "scores" the subject's responses according to one of several scoring methods.

When used by a sensitive and perceptive psychologist, any one of the projective tests can probably yield a great deal of data about the structure of someone's personality. The major difficulty is that of reliability. No two psychologists will interpret test responses in quite the same way, and there are almost as many scoring techniques as there are people using the tests. If you take the Rorschach, for instance, your *responses to the inkblots* might be as ambiguous and unstructured as the inkblots themselves. The clinical psychologist who tried to interpret your responses might then end up "taking" a projective test of quite a different kind. Indeed, it is sometimes said that Rorschach interpretations tell us more about the psychologist than they do about the person who took the test.

Projective tests probably give us more information about a person than we have the wisdom to use—and they give us this information in highly subjective, verbal descriptions rather than as objective test scores.

Although this is not an actual Rorschach, it is typical of the inkblots used in testing.

Rorschach (ROAR-shock). Hermann Rorschach (1884–1922) was a Swiss psychiatrist who devised the famous inkblot projective test.

Objective Tests: MMPI

The Minnesota Multiphasic Personality Inventory, or MMPI, is the exact opposite of the projective tests. Perhaps the most widely used personality test in the United States today, the MMPI was created to be as reliable as possible—and it is very reliable indeed. In its original form it consisted of some 560 short statements that were given to large numbers of people, some of them mental patients, some of them presumably normal. The statements mostly concern psychiatric problems or unusual thought patterns, such as: (1) Someone is trying to control my mind using radio waves; (2) I never think of unusual sexual situations; or (3) I have never been sick a day of my life. The subject taking the MMPI responds to each statement either by agreeing or disagreeing, or by saying that it is impossible to respond at all.

As you might expect, the mental patients reacted to many of the statements in quite different ways than did the normal subjects. Depressed or suicidal patients gave different responses than did schizophrenic or paranoid patients. The authors of the test were able to pick out different groups of test items that appeared to form "depression" scales, "paranoia" scales, "schizophrenia" scales, and so forth. If an otherwise normal individual takes the test and receives an abnormally high score on the "paranoia" scale, the psychologist interpreting the test might well worry that the person could become paranoid if put under great psychological stress or pressure. By looking at the pattern or profile of a subject's scores on the several different MMPI scales, a psychologist might also be able to predict what areas of the subject's personality need strengthening.

The psychologists who made up the MMPI could not tell in advance which items would differentiate between a normal college student and a patient in a mental hospital. Nor did they really care—so long as they could find a group of items which patients reliably responded to one way, and non-patients reacted to another way. If almost all depressed patients agreed with the statement: "I love cooked carrots," while most normal individuals disagreed with that item, it was included on the Depression Scale. The test-makers didn't assume ahead of time that "love for cooked carrots" was a cause of depression, nor that "hating cooked carrots" was a sure-fire index of normality. They simply noted the correlation and drew no conclusions about what caused what.

This objective approach to the study of personality—looking at people from the outside in—gives the MMPI its high reliability, and makes it a much better predictor of future behavior than projective tests usually are. Whether the MMPI is a *valid* index of personality structure is another matter altogether. The Rorschach, which looks at personality from the inside out, seems to have greater validity. But the information gained is typically so unique, so personal, and so unreliable that it may be relatively useless for scientific purposes.

Unfortunately, there is at present no personality test that has both high reliability and great validity.

Which Test Is Best? To put the matter another way, personality scales at their best can offer you a type of psychological feedback about yourself—but you have to pay for what you get. If you believe that your personality is primarily determined by your genetic background, and that your body biochemistry is the main influence on your thinking and feeling, then you may wish to look into Sheldon's morphological types.

If you prefer a kind of intuitive, subjective understanding of how you came to be what you presently are—and you place some faith in the general psychoanalytic approach to personality development—then you may want to be evaluated by a psychologist using projective techniques such as the Rorschach or TAT.

If you assume that one or more of your personal values are the strongest influences on what you feel and do, then the Allport-Vernon-Lindzey scale is probably the one for you.

However, if you are most interested in learning your scores on a number of different scales, all of which have high reliability, then perhaps the MMPI might be your best choice.

In any case, you will want the guidance of a trained psychologist to help you interpret the test data and to discuss what use you might wish to make of the information.

ETHICAL CONSIDERATIONS

Technological devices, including personality inventories, are typically "morally neutral"—that is, they are neither good nor bad in and of themselves. A surgeon's knife may be used to save a life, or to stab someone. An intelligence test may help a teacher identify what academic areas a student needs help with—or the test may be used as an excuse for not working with the student because his or her IQ "is so low that special help would be a waste of time." On the average, psychologists themselves tend to get rather high scores on the "social" scale of the Allport-Vernon-Lindzey test—which could mean that psychologists are usually more interested in helping people than in hindering them. Also, the American Psychological Association has a very strong code of ethics that its members must follow—or be booted out of the organization.

All these facts mean that you can usually trust a psychologist's intentions. But can you place as much faith in his or her actual performance? As David McClelland has pointed out, most psychological tests have a rather strong if unconscious streak of bias to them. The MMPI was validated primarily on white populations. It does a much better job of diagnosing personality problems in whites than it does in blacks. When the MMPI is used to screen job applicants, as Malcolm Gynther of St. Louis University has pointed out, the test scores give a significant advantage to whites over blacks. The makers of the MMPI did not intend for this to be the case, but their methods of test construction insured that white attitudes and norms would be more strongly represented than are black viewpoints (*see* Table 23.1).

TABLE 23.1 The Chitling Test[a]

1. A "handkerchief head" is:
   (A) a cool cat
   (B) a porter
   (C) an Uncle Tom
   (D) a hoddi
   (E) a preacher
2. Which word is most out of place here?
   (A) splib
   (B) blood
   (C) gray
   (D) spook
   (E) black
3. A "gas head" is a person who has a:
   (A) fast-moving car
   (B) stable of "lace"
   (C) "process"
   (D) habit of stealing cars
   (E) long jail record for arson
4. "Bo Diddley" is a:
   (A) game for children
   (B) down-home cheap wine
   (C) down-home singer
   (D) new dance
   (E) Moejoe call
5. If a man is called a "blood," then he is a:
   (A) fighter
   (B) Mexican-American
   (C) Negro
   (D) hungry hemophile
   (E) Redman or Indian

[a] This IQ test was designed by Adrian Dove, a sociologist who is familiar with black ghetto culture. It probably seems as unfair to white middle-class culture as the tests designed by them appear to other culture groups. The answer to all the above questions is C. (Copyright 1968 by Newsweek, Inc.)

The same may be said of most intelligence scales. The validity of IQ tests rests on the correlations between IQ scores and success in school. It is almost impossible for anyone to obtain a high IQ score, or to get good grades, or to be admitted to many graduate programs, or to be selected for the best jobs after college if that person doesn't think and react like the people (1) who made up the IQ test, (2) who run the school system in the United States and give out the grades, (3) who select students for graduate work, and (4) who do the hiring in the business world. According to David McClelland, minority group members typically do worse in most test situations, not because they are innately inferior or less intelligent, but because they weren't raised in the same homes and school environments as are middle-class whites. Thus non-whites cannot always relate to the culture on which the tests are based.

It is illegal and unethical in the United States today to discriminate against people because of their skin color, sex, religion, or ethnic background. However, it is NOT illegal or unethical to discriminate against people because they are "dumb" (and their IQ scores "prove" it), or because they are "emotionally unstable," or they "lack the necessary abilities to succeed" (and their personality test scores "confirm" this assumption)! Most of us prefer working with people who share our values and outlooks. It is possible that middle-class, white males might unconsciously encourage the use of personality tests as "screening devices" because to do so keeps them at the top of the heap.

Laws can control many forms of conscious, open discrimination against minority groups. But unconscious bias can be controlled only through education and therapy. Perhaps in the future we can construct personality tests that are reliable and as free of cultural bias as possible. Through social experimentation, we could determine as objectively as possible what traits or abilities are actually necessary for success in any line of human endeavor. We could then use our "culturally unbiased" tests to help decide (1) what the individual's chances of success are without further training, and (2) how best the person might acquire those skills or talents that he or she presently lacks.

There is a further form of unconscious prejudice that is perhaps worse than any we have discussed so far. It is the viewpoint that intelligence, personality, and

Goethe (GER-tuh). Johann Wolfgang von Goethe (1749-1832) is to German literature what Shakespeare is to English literature.

human ability become fixed or inflexible at a very early age—the theory that "you can't teach an old dog new tricks" or that "you can't change human nature." Almost all of the newer theories of personality focus on growth, on change, on the individual's ability to achieve self-actualization no matter what the person's age or past experience. Knowing what we now know about behavioral change, it seems that almost anyone can show considerable improvement over his or her present performance level. We cannot exceed our genetic limitations—few of us will become Einsteins, Rembrandts, Shakespeares, or Beethovens no matter what special training we get. But in truth there is little evidence that many of us ever come close to reaching our biological limits, whatever they may be.

Perhaps the great German poet *Goethe* (°) said it all when he wrote: "When we treat a man as he is, we make him worse than he is. When we treat him as if he already were what he potentially could be, we make him what he should be."

SUMMARY

1. Measuring the structure of your personality is as difficult as measuring the processes by which those structures function or interact.
2. Psychologists generally assume that the personality is composed of traits—that is, rather long-lasting mental states or conditions such as intelligence, motives, emotions, values, and attitudes.
3. If we could somehow determine which traits were most important, we could better understand why we think and act the way we do. But which traits do we measure?
4. Galen (and Hippocrates) assumed that the four main fluids, or humors, of the body (blood, phlegm, yellow bile, black bile) were the major determinants of personality, a belief long since discarded by scientists.
5. Kretschmer concluded from his studies of mental patients that a person's inherited body type, or morphology, determined one's traits. Kretschmer assumed that every human being could be described as either a fat pyknic, a thin asthenic, or a muscular athletic.
6. Sheldon has offered a modification of Kretschmer's morphologies in which people are seen as being mixtures of three basic types: the endomorph, the mesomorph, and the ectomorph.
7. All of these "type" theorists assume that personality is determined almost entirely by one's inherited physique, an assumption few psychologists hold today. It seems more likely that there are three general classes of reinforcers—biological, intra-psychic, and social—and that we may be born with a tendency to prefer one class more than the other two.
8. Modern structural theorists have rejected typologies, focusing instead on "mental traits" such as intelligence. Unfortunately, the usefulness of most IQ tests seems compromised by the cultural biases of the people who developed the tests, and by the fact that IQ scores are strongly influenced by early experience and by later learning of such traits as "how to reason." IQ tests are often fairly reliable, but there is considerable argument whether they are valid measures of intellectual capacity or functioning.
9. Allport, Vernon, and Lindzey developed a "test of values" that seems to describe fairly accurately six different traits or personality types, but we have no proof as yet that these six traits are the most important ones displayed by most human beings.
10. Projective tests, such as the Rorschach, may be relatively valid measures of one's underlying personality structure, but are unreliable and difficult to interpret.
11. At best, personality tests offer interesting psychological feedback, but should be used and interpreted with great caution since all such tests (and all psychologists who interpret test scores) have a fair amount of cultural bias built into them.

(Continued from page 521.)

"Well, Jessie, if I don't get my Ph.D., I can always blame it on you," Tom Flagg said, his smile belying the seriousness of his words.

"Did I mess up your experiment?" Jessie Williams asked.

"Royally. But luckily, you were practically the only teacher who did."

"None of my bloomers bloomed?"

Tom shook his head. "That wasn't the problem. Just the opposite. **All** of your kids bloomed, black and white, whether the test said they should or not."

"And that's bad?"

"Good for the kids. Bad for my experiment."

Jessie showed concern. "Will it really hold you back from getting your doctorate in psychology?"

"No, not at all. As I said, the Rosenthal test predicted rather well for several other teachers." Tom stretched his muscular legs out in front of him. "I just wish that it hadn't. I hoped it wouldn't work."

Jessie looked puzzled. "But I thought you wanted the test to work? I thought you wouldn't get credit for your experiment if it didn't?"

"I couldn't tell you everything about the test, Jessie," Tom said sheepishly. "You see, Professor Rosenthal didn't really make up a test for 'Late Bloomers.' He was interested in people's expectancies instead. He figured if you told a teacher that one of her children was going to show a great improvement, then the teacher would pay a lot more attention to that child. She'd look for each little bit of learning the kid showed, and would communicate her enthusiasm to the kid. So the kid would respond to the teacher's expectancies, and would really bloom. But if the teacher expected the kid to backslide, she'd be biased against the kid, and pick on the kid's faults and mistakes; then the kid would become discouraged and wouldn't do well. And that's exactly what he found—in a lot of the cases anyhow."

"But it didn't work with me, did it?"

"No, it didn't. Not that I'm complaining you understand. It shouldn't work with really good teachers, because they shouldn't be prejudiced for or against kids just because of their test scores."

"Water them frequently with love and affection, and you help them all bloom as much as they can."

"Right," said Tom.

"Then why are you disappointed if I didn't pay any attention to your test scores, Tom? I'm not suggestible enough for you?"

Tom laughed. "How did you guess?"

"Keep your mind on your experiment. What's troubling you, friend?"

"The fact that so many other teachers, black and white, were influenced by the faked test scores that I gave them. I can maybe understand why some of the white teachers might be prejudiced in favor of white kids and against the blacks—that's part of our culture, though it's changing some now. And maybe I can understand why some of the black teachers would be prejudiced against white kids and biased toward the blacks. Somehow you expect that. But why would white teachers be prejudiced against white kids, and black teachers prejudiced against black kids—just because some silly test said the kids were going to backslide, or do poorly?"

"Brother Thomas, we are all human beings," Jessie Williams said, crossing her arms over her ample breasts. "Our blood is the same color; our brains are the same size; our bodies are the same shapes; and we all learn our prejudices at our mother's knees. I'm just lucky that I was taught to be prejudiced **toward,** instead of prejudiced **against.** But it's prejudice, just the same."

"You think love is prejudice?"

"Of course. Love is prejudice in favor of life."

Tom swallowed hard. "Well, do you think you might be prejudiced just a little in my direction?"

"It might happen to be so."

"Then maybe I ought to ask you out to the movies tomorrow night."

"You do that, Baby. You do that very thing."

RECOMMENDED READINGS

Anastasi, Ann. *Psychological Testing* (New York: The Macmillan Company, 1968).

Buros, O.K. *The Seventh Mental Measurement Yearbook* (Highland Park, N.J.: The Gryphon Press, 1972).

Rosenthal, Robert, and Lenore Jacobson. *Pygmalion in the Classroom* (New York: Holt, Rinehart and Winston, Inc., 1968).

Terman, L.M., and M.H. Oden. *The Gifted Group at Midlife* (Stanford, Calif.: Stanford University Press, 1959).

chapter 24

"I'M CRAZY—YOU'RE CRAZY"

ABNORMAL PSYCHOLOGY

DID YOU KNOW THAT . . .

According to Kinsey, the average white married man aged 21–25 has about four sexual climaxes a week?

Psychologists use the statistical term "2 standard deviations from the mean" to describe most forms of unusual or abnormal behavior?

You have been using statistical concepts most of your life?

Some forms of biological abnormalities are called "organic psychoses?"

Mild types of intra-psychic abnormalities are sometimes referred to as "neuroses?"

Severe forms of intra-psychic problems are often called "functional psychoses?"

Schizophrenia is probably the most common sort of functional psychosis?

The majority of anti-social people behave toward others as their parents behaved toward them?

The American Psychiatric Association no longer considers homosexual behavior to be a symptom of mental illness?

Most sexual offenders are undersexed, misinformed, and narrow-minded people?

When a person develops abnormal behavior patterns, everyone the person has close contact with probably has helped bring about the abnormality?

Dr. Mary Ellen Mann strode purposefully into the classroom, nodded to several students, spoke with a few others, then arranged her lecture notes and began to speak.

"Good morning. Today, as I promised you, we're going to have a former mental patient address the class. It may seem slightly insane to you that we would discuss such matters as mental health in a class on the psychology of perception, but there is a reason for my madness. Now that we are halfway through the semester, it should be very easy for all of you to understand how the context in which we perceive a stimulus affects our evaluation of that stimulus. If you look at a pure white rose lying on a piece of green velvet, the rose will appear slightly reddish to you because of its green background. If you put the same white rose on a red background, it would seem tinged with green. But even knowing all this, chances are that you would still perceive the reddish or greenish tinge as being a trait or characteristic within the rose—not as being a figment of your own imagination.

"People are like white roses or any other stimulus. Our perception of people is always influenced by the social background in which we see them. If you saw a young man standing on a street corner, shouting lines from Shakespeare at the top of his voice, you might think him slightly mad. If you saw the same young man on a stage, you might applaud and believe him to be a sensitive actor. The man's behavior would be the same in either case, but your evaluation of his mental state would be quite different depending on the context you saw him in.

"What I hope you will learn from our discussion today is that the **abnormality** of abnormal behavior is often a matter of context—although we almost always assume that it is a matter of the person's inner mental state."

D.L. Rosenhan.

Dr. Mann paused to look at her notes, then continued. "In January of 1973, Professor D.L. Rosenhan of Stanford published an article in **Science** that caused a great deal of turmoil in the U.S. mental health establishment. Dr. Rosenhan began by pointing out that the general public takes rather a dim view of psychological suffering. Someone with a broken leg goes to a hospital for treatment, stays a few weeks, is released, and nobody thinks twice about it. But someone in the depths of a black depression goes to a mental hospital for a few weeks, is released, and comes out marked for life as being 'insane.' Yet, insanity is a legal term, one that psychologists haven't used for years. An insane person is someone who has been judged by a court of law not to know the difference between right and wrong, or who suffers from 'an irresistable impulse' to commit a crime.

"In order to help the general public change its views toward people with psychological problems, we coined the term 'mental illness.' That was a way of reminding everybody that someone who is admitted to a mental hospital isn't necessarily a witch, or possessed by devils, or incurably crazy. Most people use the term 'mentally ill' today; but what does that phrase really mean? Is it like the measles—a disease caused by some germ? We usually make a diagnosis of mental illness by listening to a patient or by observing his or her behavior. But we seldom look at the background in which the patient lives. We assume the 'insanity' is entirely inside the patient. Dr. Rosenhan thinks that the environment in which we see the patient may influence our diagnosis without our realizing it. Perhaps environments are mentally ill as well as people.

"Don't misunderstand. Mental suffering exists, and it is often terrible and terrifying. But when we pin a label on a person, when we call that person 'insane' or 'disturbed' or 'mentally abnormal,' we make some assumptions that we might find it difficult to prove are correct.

"To begin with, as Dr. Rosenhan suggests, we assume that the abnormality is **relatively permanent.** Leopards don't change their spots. Once crazy, always crazy. But can you prove that's the case? Well, you can do so only if you can prove you have an iron-clad way of telling crazy people from sane people—in short, that you have a foolproof way of distinguishing mental illness from mental health. But how good are your own powers of diagnosis?"

Dr. Mann paused for effect, then smiled at the class. "Let's run a little test. I want each of you to stare long and hard at the person sitting next to you. Try to look deep into that person's mind. After you have performed this soul-searching for a minute or so, I'll ask you a very important question. Now, go ahead." The class enjoyed the test immensely and really didn't want to stop when Dr. Mann called them to attention again.

"Now, you've looked into someone's heart. What you must do next is to guarantee to me, without reservation, that the person you observed is absolutely normal and sane."

The class erupted with laughter.

"Actually," Dr. Mann continued, "you're all safe. By definition, since none of you is in a mental hospital right now, you're all legally sane. But you see what the problem is. Dr. Rosenhan fears that we simply do not have the ability to tell people who are mentally ill from those who are mentally healthy. To prove his point, he and several other absolutely healthy individuals got themselves admitted to mental hospitals all across the country. They lied a little bit to get in, but the rest of their behavior was completely average and well-adjusted.

"Once they got in, however, the only way they could get out again was to prove to the doctors and nurses in charge of the hospitals that they were, in fact, mentally healthy. The question was—would the hospital staff perceive their behavior as being healthy, or would the staff be so influenced by the 'hospital background' that the staff would see 'normal' behavior as a form of mental sickness?

"Dr. Rosenhan reports that his experiment was something of a disaster. Not one of his crew was ever detected by any staff member as being a 'pseudo-patient.' They all were admitted quickly and labeled 'schizophrenic,' or seriously insane. Once assigned to a ward, the 'pseudo-patients' found it difficult—if not impossible—to gain their release, no matter how normally they behaved. All of them were finally released—but the hospital staffs made it clear that the pseudo-patients were presumed to be still insane. In some cases Dr. Rosenhan's crew simply had to run away from the hospital because they couldn't convince anyone they were completely sane. Almost all of the nurses and doctors were concerned, loving, intelligent people who showed a great desire to be of help. But they just couldn't perceive the pseudo-patient outside the hospital environment.''

Dr. Mann removed her notes from the lectern. ''Frankly, when Professor Rosenhan's article appeared, I simply couldn't believe his results. They seemed too farfetched. So I asked one of my graduate students, Steve May, to act as a guinea pig. We called the local state mental hospital and got Steve an appointment. He was going to pretend that he was mentally ill and ask to be admitted. We thought that they'd see through our little game immediately. But if they didn't, Steve was to stay in the hospital until he could get out on his own, without any help from me or anyone else.

''Steve had no trouble at all getting admitted to the hospital. He had quite a lot of trouble getting out. I've asked him to come tell you about it today. But while Steve is talking, think about this. If you woke up one morning and found that some of your friends—perhaps as a big joke—had gotten you thrown into the local mental hospital, how would you go about convincing the hospital authorities that a terrible mistake had been made? What would you say or do to assure the doctors that you were really sane? And if that thought doesn't give you nightmares, I don't know what will.

''But now, let's welcome Steve May.''

(Continued on page 569.)

Quite frankly, most personality theorists would probably consider you just a little abnormal. To begin with, you're almost certainly above average in intelligence. People who score below average on most intelligence tests—for whatever reason—tend to drop out of school rather early and hence wouldn't be reading this textbook. If we gave you the MMPI, you would most likely not score *right at the average* on the dozens of different scales that make up that test. You'd probably be above average on some of the scales, below average on some, close to average on the rest.

Most of the great personality theorists—Freud, Jung, Adler, Erikson, Kretschmer, Rogers, and the rest—based their ideas on the study of mentally disturbed people. Some of these people were patients in mental hospitals; some were private patients who asked for help. Most of these patients had mental or behavioral problems that were *exaggerations* (°) of the mental and behavioral traits that we all have. Therefore, the theorists presumed, there is a little bit of madness in each of us. The mental patient differs from the average citizen in the *quantity* or amount of his or her madness, not in the *quality* or type of psychological problem. In short, the view of these theorists has been that we are all a tiny bit abnormal, but some of us are more abnormal than others.

But does that view make sense? If everyone deviates from the norm one way or another, doesn't the word "normal" lose most of its meaning? And if we can't define the word "normal," what shall we make of the word "abnormal," which literally means "away from the normal?"

Before we can discuss such abnormal topics as mental illness, "insanity," sexual deviation, and "crazy behavior," we must first take a good, hard, objective look at the word "normal."

Exaggerations (ex-adge-jer-RAY-shuns). From the Latin word meaning "to pile up." To exaggerate is to make something larger or bigger than it usually is, or to describe something as being more than in truth it is.

WHAT IS NORMAL?

Suppose a young married couple named Mary and John Smith are on the verge of divorce. They go to see a psychologist and ask for help. Even before the psychologist learns their names, this counselor knows several things about the Smiths. First, one or both of them is going to be suffering considerable psychological pain, distress, or anxiety. Second, things are probably worse for the couple now than at some time in the past; that is, their way of life has changed from its usual (normal) pattern. Third, they are bright enough to sense this departure from normal and to seek help.

Any deviation from a person's usual way of thinking, feeling, or behaving can be considered a symptom of psychological abnormality. Generally speaking, if the deviation is slight, the psychologist is likely to believe that the person suffers from a *neurosis*. If the deviation is large, the psychologist may worry that the person suffers from a *psychosis*. We will define these terms more fully in a moment. For the time being, merely think of neurosis as being a minor problem, and psychosis as being a major problem. It is the psychologist's job to help the person solve the problem and return to normal.

Mary and John Smith could have many quite different kinds of psychological difficulties. In this chapter we will describe what some of the most common kinds are like. But to help us understand what the word "normal" means, let us assume to start with that they have a sexual incompatibility. John complains that Mary is frigid, that she no longer shows him any affection, that she consistently refuses him the pleasures of the marriage bed. Mary replies that John is a *satyr* (°)—that is, he has an unusually strong sex drive. She claims that he thinks of nothing else, talks of nothing else, and that he is interested only in her body and not in her mind or personality. (As we will see later, the problem might be the other way around—the wife might desire sex more frequently than the husband; but we will delay discussion of that difficulty for a moment.)

The psychologist might well assume that the woman was normal, but that the man's id had gotten out of control and was ruining the marriage. Or the counselor might assume that the man had a normal, healthy appetite for sex, but that the woman was so repressed she could not enjoy one of the finer aspects of marriage. Or the counselor might assume that both Mary and John showed symptoms of abnormal psychological conditions. How could the psychologist tell for sure?

Normality is always defined within a given context or situation The psychologist cannot come to any conclusions about the Smiths' problems if the counselor ignores the social environment in which the couple lives. That is, before the psychologist can concentrate on the unique aspects of the Smiths' difficulties, the counselor must ask what other people with similar backgrounds are like. How many times do most young husbands expect sex each week? How frequently do most wives desire it? Do husbands typically wish intercourse more frequently than their wives, or the other way around? And what about the actual behavior? How frequently do young married men actually achieve sexual climax? And is it always with their wives?

Sex and the Bell-shaped Curve

Until Alfred Kinsey performed his pioneering research on human sexuality, no one really knew the answers to these questions. Judging from a rough analysis of the Kinsey data, it would seem that the average white married man aged 21–25 reaches sexual climax about three to four times per week. In Kinsey's rather stilted, formal, biological language, he said that the young, married, middle-class, white U.S. male achieved an *average* of about four "sexual outlets" per week.

(Kinsey thus included all forms of sexual activity—including masturbation, homosexuality, bestiality, "wet dreams," and extramarital heterosexual contacts in his figures.)

Kinsey's data give us some context in which to consider the Smiths' marital problems—but only assuming that the Smiths are white, middle-class Americans. Yet there is still a lot more we need to know. If Mr. Smith desired 7 outlets a week, would you consider him abnormal? What if he demanded 17? And would John Smith be "far above normal" if he wanted 77?

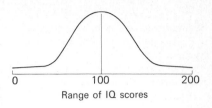

Range of IQ scores

Range

As you can see, knowing what the average is doesn't always help. The average score on most IQ tests is 100. If you get a score of 101, are you way above average? Before we could answer we would have to know the *range* of scores, as well as how those scores were distributed over the range. And the best way to find out would be to resort to that favorite psychological device, the bell-shaped curve.

The range of IQ scores on some tests goes from 0 to about 200. As we noted earlier the tests are so constructed that most people's scores are bunched up in the middle of the distribution. Although some 50 percent of the scores lie above the mid-point of the curve, and some 50 percent lie below it, most of the IQ's do not *deviate* very far from this mid-point. Depending on how the mid-point is calculated, it is called the *mode* (°), the *mean* (°), or the *median* (°). If you are interested in how these terms are calculated, see the Statistical Appendix at the back of this book. However, "mode," "mean," and "median" are merely words that mean the *norm* (°), or the middle of the range of scores.

In the case of Kinsey's data on the sexual behavior of the (young, white, middle-class) U.S. male, the mean, median, and mode are probably close enough together so that—for our present purposes—we can consider any of them the norm. The actual distribution of outlets per week probably looks something like the lower graph in the margin.

Now we can see that if Mr. Smith desired 7 outlets a week, he would be very close to the norm. But what if he wishes 17? Would this fact make him ab-norm-al, or away from the norm? How far away is away?

Range of weekly outlets in young married men.

Standard Deviation

Psychologists have a method of measuring deviations from the norm that they call the *standard deviation* (°). If you are interested in the mathematics of calculating the standard deviation, you might wish to look at the Statistical Appendix. However, when all is said and done, the standard deviation is little more than a fairly accurate way of measuring percentages.

Psychologists assume that, on any given test (or on the measurement of any given behavior), whatever two-thirds of the people do is probably pretty normal. On an IQ test, for example, the norm is arbitrarily set at a score of 100. On many such tests, about two-thirds of the people get scores between 84 and 116. As you can see from the graph on p. 552, this fact means that about one-third of the people scored within 16 points *below* the norm, and about one-third of the people scored within 16 points *above* the norm. By definition, then, the standard deviation for such a test would be 16 points. If you score within one standard deviation of the norm, your performance is always considered within the norm.

If you got a score of 132 on the IQ test, you would be 2 standard deviations above the norm (2 × 16), and you would be well above average in terms of your IQ score. To put it another way, your performance would be quite abnormal, since your score was as good as or better than about 98 percent of the people who

Mode. From the Latin word *modus,* meaning "to measure." The highest point or most frequent score on a bell-shaped distribution of scores.

Mean. That which is "middling" or intermediate in rank or order. The arithmetical average.

Median (ME-dee-un). From the Latin word *medius,* meaning "middle." The median strip on a superhighway is the paved or planted strip down the middle dividing the road in half. The median in a distribution is the score that exactly cuts the distribution in half.

Norm. From the Latin word *norma,* meaning "pattern" or "rule." The expected, the average, the usual. That which is a model.

Standard deviation (dee-vee-A-shun). To deviate means to depart from the accepted or expected, to move away from the norm. The standard deviation is a mathematical way of figuring out how much a test score deviates from the mean, median, or mode (usually the mean).

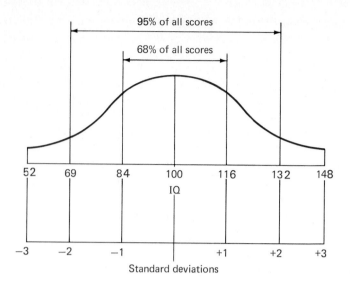

took the test. If you got a score of 148 on the test, you would be 3 standard deviations above the norm (3 × 16), which is an exceptional score since it puts you in the upper one-tenth of a percent of the test population. To phrase this in simpler terms, any time your performance puts you 3 standard deviations above (or below) the norm, you should consider yourself *statistically* highly abnormal on whatever trait or ability the test is supposed to measure.

To summarize (so that we can get back to talking about sex):

1. If your performance on any measure is within 1 standard deviation of the norm, you are technically considered perfectly normal.
2. If your performance on any measure is between 1 and 2 standard deviations from the norm, you have deviated somewhat from the average.
3. If your performance on any measure is more than 2 standard deviations from the norm, you are behaving differently than about 98 percent of the population; hence your performance should be considered *significantly* abnormal. You may score higher than the rest of the people, or below the rest (if we're measuring things like income or IQ). But surely you are measurably *different* from the rest.

If you don't understand all the mathematical complexities underlying the mean, median, mode, and standard deviation the first time you read about these terms, don't fret about it. For our present purposes, it is much more important that you realize that you've been using these *concepts* all of your life. For instance, have you ever called someone a "dumbbell" or an "idiot?" If so, you obviously have a notion of what an average IQ is, and you are implying that the "dummy" in question is more than 2 standard deviations below the norm. Have you ever laughed at some acquaintance for being a "kook" or a "nut?" Then you must have consciously or unconsciously determined what normal behavior is, drawn a mental bell-shaped curve representing normality, and placed the person at the extreme bottom end of the distribution.

We make judgments about people all the time, and probably always will. Usually these judgments are based on values that we believe (or have been taught) are cultural norms. As we learn more about people, our perceptions of them tend to change. Perhaps the major differences between your judgments and those a trained psychologist would make are as follows: The psychologist realizes that norms and values are arbitrary and may vary greatly from culture to culture; the psychologist tries to get exact measurements of deviations from norms rather than

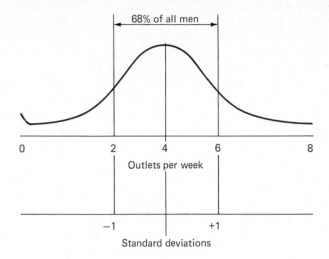

68% of all men

0   2   4   6   8

Outlets per week

−1   +1

Standard deviations

making rough guesses; the psychologist tends to use neutral descriptive terms such as "2 standard deviations from the mean" rather than "kook" or "dumbbell."

QUESTION: How many of the nasty names that we call each other refer to performances that are 2 or more standard deviations beyond the norm? And how can we be sure that the norm we're referring to is really normal?

Normal Sexuality and the Standard Deviation   Now we're ready to put the Smiths' problem into context. Dr. Kinsey's surveys of sexual behavior suggest that young married men like John Smith have, on the average, 4 sexual outlets per week. The range is from 0 to more than 29. The standard deviation is about 2.

These facts mean that if Mr. Smith desires sexual contact with his wife from 2 to 6 times a week, he is probably like two-thirds of all similar men that Kinsey talked to. In short, within the society in which the Smiths live, his sexual demands would seem average, or normal. If he expected sex more than 8 times a week, Mr. Smith would be more than 2 standard deviations from the norm, and his requests would be at least *statistically* abnormal.

Of course, in the long run, the problem that exists between Mr. and Mrs. Smith is a personal one that cannot be solved by reference to bell-shaped curves. And yet the beauty of Kinsey's work was that he brought sexual behavior out in the open, so that it could be examined statistically as well as personally. Lacking this important reference information, the psychologist might well make some very wrong decisions about how to help the Smiths. For we all tend to judge normality in terms of our own behaviors and expectations.

For instance, suppose that the counselor was a man who preferred but 1 sexual outlet a month—and thought this more than adequate and normal. If Mr. Smith wanted sex 4 times a week, the counselor might tend to agree with Mrs. Smith that her husband was a "satyr" who was terribly over-sexed. What kind of therapy might he suggest? On the other hand, if the psychologist was one of those (statistically) rare U.S. men who regularly performed the sex act 20 or more times a week, he might think that both John and Mary Smith needed to take a few "pep pills" or hormone shots.

Classifying Abnormal Behavior Patterns   As you can gather, it is difficult to define psychological abnormality without a theory of some kind, or some set of data such as Kinsey's, to tell us what is normal as well as how the abnormality might have come about.

There is, unfortunately, no one master theory of human behavior that everyone agrees on. Psychologists and psychiatrists have worked out a variety of diagnostic

Organic abnormalities. Biological or physically caused problems. A child born with brain damage has an abnormality of that organ we call "the brain."

Mentally retarded. According to *Webster's Third International Dictionary,* mental retardation or deficiency is "a failure in intellectual development resulting in social incompetence that is considered to be the result of a defect in the central nervous system and (hence) incurable." However, we now suspect that many forms of mental retardation are "helpable," if not yet entirely curable.

schemes that are supposed to classify people according to their problems. Terms such as "neurosis" and "psychosis" are included in most of these schemes. But all these classifications are subject to the same sorts of objections we raised concerning the theories of personalities in the last chapter. People do not fit comfortably into pigeonholes, and most of the labels that we stick on psychologically unhappy patients tell us more about the label-maker than about the patient.

About all that we know for sure is that the desired stimulus inputs and the customary behavioral outputs of some people differ from the statistical norm, and that often these individuals suffer deep distress because they are not able to handle these differences.

About the best we can do at the present time is to look at psychological abnormalities from our three standard viewpoints, hoping that if we understand some of the causes of unusual behavior we can learn how better to help people live happier and more productive lives.

BIOLOGICAL ABNORMALITIES

Many types of psychological problems the Smiths might face can be traced directly to damage to the brain, or to an imbalance in the body's chemicals or hormones, or to genetic misfortunes. The range of these *organic abnormalities* (*) is very wide indeed. Psychologist Jerome Kagan estimates that from 3 to 7 percent of the children born in the United States suffer from genetic imperfections or birth defects that will prevent the children from succeeding in our present school system. If we give them the usual sort of IQ test, these youngsters will always score some 2 or more standard deviations below the norm. We typically refer to them as *mentally retarded* (*), but in truth they are physiologically or organically retarded. We do not at present know the limits of their abilities, but each year we do learn a little more about how to help them improve their performances. They are different from normal children in many ways, but they are not necessarily inferior.

At the other end of the age scale are those mental and behavioral problems caused by growing old. It used to be thought that both intelligence and sexual performance reached a peak during a person's youth and then declined steadily until death. Thanks to recent research, we now know that neither is the case. Kinsey found many men and women in their 60's, 70's, and 80's who enjoyed just as active a sex life as they had during their younger years. If they showed a decrease in performance, it was because of boredom or anxiety and not loss of potency. Other elderly people still retained the desire and ability, but had difficulty attracting suitable partners.

In a similar finding, John Kangas, director of the University of Santa Clara counseling center, has found a marked *increase* in IQ scores as people grow older. A group of children were tested in 1931, when their average score was 111. They were retested in 1941, 1956, and 1969. Each time their average score increased, reaching 130 in 1969.

Confirmation of Kangas' work comes from a study made by psychologists Klaus and Ruth Riegel at The University of Michigan. In 1956 they gave IQ tests to 380 men and women who were 55 to 75 years of age. The Riegels retested this group in 1961 and 1966. They found that people who lived from one testing to another had higher scores, on the average, than did those people who had died during the five-year period between testing. Some of the original sample refused to be tested the second or third time. The Riegels found that the refusers had a much higher mortality rate than did the subjects who took the next test willingly. The Riegels concluded that intelligence remains the same (or perhaps increases) as a person grows old—up to a point a few year's before a person's death. Just prior to dying (from natural causes), a person's intellectual performance often drops remarkably.

The Riegels believe that the individual may be aware of this deterioration and hence may refuse to take IQ tests.

Sex and Old Age

Old age brings other problems as well. Many women suffer a severe depression at the onset of menopause, when menstruation stops and the woman loses the ability to have children. This depression appears to come from psychological causes rather than being due to a change in the way the woman's body functions. If Mary Smith were the sort of person who equated her physical and psychological attractiveness with her ability to become pregnant, menopause might bring with it a deep *melancholia* (°). For she might assume that, having lost her "womanhood," she would also lose all sexual desire and that John might no longer find her desirable.

Many women find the release from childbearing a great relief. Thus Mary Smith might enter into her post-menopausal years with great joy and renewed interest in sexual expression. But as we noted in an earlier chapter, this increased sensuality may occur at just the time that her husband is suffering from a kind of male menopause, during which he becomes excessively worried about his sexual capability. To add to his problems, the man may suffer from enlargement of the *prostate* (°), the organ that indirectly influences erection of the penis. If John Smith's prostate had to be surgically removed, John might slip into a state of black depression because he feared he had lost his mental as well as his physical potency.

Strokes

Old age brings with it the increased possibility that a person will suffer from a *stroke* (°)—a broken blood vessel in the brain—or from other diseases that disrupt the normal flow of blood to the central nervous system. Immediately after the stroke, the person may lose muscular control of one or both sides of the body; or the person may become confused, forgetful, or even develop delusions or suffer from hallucinations. If the stroke is a mild one, neural *compensation* may occur and the person will return to normal or near normal in a few weeks or months. That is, other parts of the brain may take over the functions of the nervous tissue lost when its blood supply gave out.

Senile Psychosis

If the blood supply to the entire brain is choked off by what is sometimes called "hardening of the arteries," the person may lapse into a child-like state commonly called a *senile psychosis* (°), or senility. In 1965 this type of mental illness accounted for almost 5 percent of the admissions to public mental hospitals—although, as our life spans increase, this figure will surely rise. The average age of admission for patients diagnosed as senile is 75 for both men and women, although the problem may occur as early as age 60 or so.

The symptoms that lead us to call someone "senile" usually develop slowly, but the condition can be hastened by physical illness or psychological stress. The first changes that one might notice are usually those of a narrowing of the person's interests, a decrease in alertness, a dislike for change. If Mary Smith were becoming senile, she might seem forgetful, easily irritated, interested primarily in her own thoughts and bodily functions. She might also become more and more hostile and unsympathetic toward others. Eventually she might forget who she is, or lose all her memory of recent events, or perhaps even refuse to recognize John Smith and their children.

Melancholia (mell-an-KO-lee-uh). From the Greek words meaning "black bile," one of Galen's four humors. The sadness or depression associated with menopause is often called "involutional melancholia." The word "involutional" (in-voh-LEW-shun-ul) comes from the Latin term meaning "enveloped," or "folded in on itself." A woman suffering from involutional melancholia is said to "turn in on herself," or to become wrapped up in her own sad thoughts.

Prostate (PROSS-tate). From the Greek word meaning "to put in front." The prostate gland indirectly influences the erection of the penis.

Stroke. When a blood vessel breaks within the brain, those nerve cells that are nourished by that blood vessel soon die. Depending on which part of the brain the stroke occurs in, the person's input, output, or processing functions will be badly affected.

Senile psychosis (SEE-nile sigh-KO-sis). Senile means "old," or "the weakness associated with old age." A psychosis is a severe form of mental illness.

A couple in their nineties, happily married for 72 years.

People who become senile may wander off and become lost, engage in sexual abnormalities (such as exposing themselves to young children or attempting to molest them), develop hallucinations, and lose control over their bowels and bladders.

Although the condition we call "senile psychosis" seems related to old age and to a change in the amount of blood supplied to the brain, it has its psychological and social components as well. If Mary Smith were to remain actively involved in life—if she kept doing things and going places and relating to others—she would suffer less from this condition than would persons who lived alone, who withdrew from social contact, or who refused to make any changes in their life routines as they aged.

One of the best forms of therapy to *prevent* (or at least retard) the onset of the senile condition seems to be that of giving the older person a sense of meaningfulness to his or her life, of maintaining family and friendship ties, of making the person feel loved and wanted. In a series of studies performed in the 1960's by Robert J. Havighurst and his colleagues at the University of Chicago, it was found that older people who remained actively engaged in life were generally happier and healthier than those people who withdrew from society. But it remains true, as Bernice L. Neugarten pointed out in 1973, that people who are well-adjusted and productive during their middle years tend to be those who do best as "senior citizens." Dr. Neugarten concludes that, "Within broad limits, given no major biological accidents or major social upheavals, patterns of aging are predictable from knowing the individuals in middle age." In brief, the seeds of a senile psychosis are typically planted long before the person's 50th birthday.

Alcoholism and VD

Because alcoholism and venereal disease often take a long time to work their destruction on the central nervous system, they are more likely to cause severe

Bernice L. Neugarten.

mental disturbance in middle-aged and elderly people than in individuals younger than 35. When the germs associated with *syphilis* (°) attack the brain, they can cause a condition known as *general paresis* (°). Although our ability to diagnose and to treat this veneral disease has improved remarkably since the discovery of penicillin, general paresis still accounts for about 1 percent of first admissions to U.S. mental hospitals. For reasons still unclear to us, only some 3 percent of untreated syphilitics develop the disease. It is much more common among men than women, and among whites than blacks. The behavior patterns associated with general paresis are, in many ways, similar to those found in senile psychosis. If medication is given promptly, before too much brain damage has occurred, the patient may show an almost complete recovery.

Alcoholism is one of the most common causes of abnormal behavior in the United States today. Of the 75 million Americans who drink, at least 6 million are probably alcoholics. More than 12,000 people die each year of chronic alcoholism, and drunk drivers kill an additional 25,000 people each year on the highways. Drinking is associated with at least 15 percent of the murders committed annually. Alcoholism costs business and industry more than a billion dollars a year in lost time and accidents, and we spend more than that each year taking care of alcoholics and their families. At least 15 percent of the first admissions to public mental hospitals are alcoholics. Four out of five alcoholics are men, and most of them come from middle- or upper-class backgrounds.

Although most experts believe that alcohol does not directly kill brain cells, the biochemical changes that are associated with alcoholism do have their effect on mental functioning. The acute alcoholic may show almost all of the symptoms associated with senile psychosis—particularly hallucinations, a denial that any problem exists, memory loss, and a general state of confusion. About 10 percent of chronic alcoholics become so abnormal that we often say they have developed an *alcohol psychosis;* these people typically require hospitalization of some kind. We will discuss therapy for alcoholics in the next chapter.

Drug Psychosis

Addiction to, or overdose from, many other types of drugs can lead to abnormal behavior and thought patterns. A person suffering from such abnormalities is said to have a *drug-induced psychosis.* Some of the causes for drug-related problems were discussed in Chapter 3. The hallucinations associated with alcoholism, for example, are in part related to malnutrition. Alcoholics often prefer to spend all their money on "booze" rather than on food; many alcoholics actually starve to death. During therapy, alcoholics are sometimes given massive doses of vitamins. However, an excess of some vitamins, particularly B-12, may itself cause hallucinations.

Lead and mercury—those heavy metals that occasionally pollute our food and water—can also bring about psychotic-like states if we swallow them in abnormal quantities.

As we noted earlier, an excess of hormones can at times lead to psychological difficulties. If John Smith took small doses of male hormone, he might (temporarily) become more active sexually. However, a large dose of the hormone might actually make him physically impotent—unable to perform normal sexual intercourse. The amount of female hormone present in Mary Smith's body might affect her sexual desires too.

However, there appears to be little relationship between the types and amount of hormones present and an adult's mode of sexual expression or choice of sex partners. Homosexuality, impotence, and frigidity appear to be primarily psychological problems rather than organic—a fact that is true of most forms of sexual abnormality.

At least six million U.S. citizens are alcoholics.

Syphilis (SIFF-ill-us). A deadly form of venereal (vee-NEAR-ee-ul) disease usually transmitted from one person to another through sexual contact. In A.D. 1530, the Italian poet-physician Girolamo Fracastoro wrote a fictional story about the first man supposed to have gotten the disease. Fracastoro named the hero of his tale Syphilus, from which we get the name of the illness.

General paresis (pair-EE-sis). A form of organic mental illness caused by the destructive action of the syphilitic germ on the brain. There is a lengthy incubation period in general paresis, the initial symptoms appearing between 5 and 30 years after the primary infection. One of the first effects the disease has is on memory—the paretic (pair-ETT-tick) gradually loses ability to transfer items from Short-term to Long-term Memory. If asked to tell what happened yesterday, the paretic may not be able to remember, so will make up fantastic stories to fill in the gaps in Long-term Memory. This filling in is called "confabulation" (kon-fabb-you-LAY-shun).

Neurosis (new-ROW-sis). Also called "psycho-neurosis." From the Latin words meaning "disease of the nerves." The term "neurosis" is applied to the milder yet persistent forms of mental illness in which the patient can still adjust enough to his or her social environment so that hospitalization typically isn't required. The types, causes, and cures of neurosis are much debated.

Psychosis (sigh-KO-sis). From Greek and Latin words meaning "disease of the mind." A severe form of mental illness that typically requires intensive treatment, often including hospitalization. The two major types of psychosis are said to be the organic psychoses (sigh-KO-sees) that have a known biological cause, and the functional psychoses that are not linked to any obvious neural damage.

Trauma (Rhymes with "DRAW-mah"). A mental or physical wound or scar. A memory of a frightening experience.

The noted U.S. neuro-physiologist Ralph Gerard once said that there was "no twisted thought without a twisted molecule." Professor Gerard meant that, associated with each unusual or bizarre personal experience, there probably was an abnormal biochemistry of the brain. In some cases we can be sure which molecule (alcohol, LSD, vitamin B-12) is doing the damage; by removing the chemical, we usually can help solve the problem. In most situations, however, it seems that the psychological experience may actually "twist the molecule," rather than the other way around (*see* Chapter 17).

Your brain responds chemically to thought patterns and to changes in your environment. If your basic problem is *intra-psychic*—that is, due to your developmental history or to unresolved psychological tensions—treating your "twisted molecules" by chemotherapy may not be the best way of treating your "twisted thoughts."

INTRA-PSYCHIC PROBLEMS

Let us assume that John Smith tells the psychologist that his wife is frigid and that he desires 20 or more sexual outlets a week. A medical examination shows that he is physically normal. Knowing Kinsey's data, however, we realize that his preferred sexual performance puts him several standard deviations above the mean for men of his age and social class. From a statistical point of view, then, he seems abnormal and perhaps is suffering from an intra-psychic problem of some kind. If Mr. Smith seems to have most of the rest of his life in good shape, if he has continued his work and seems reasonably well-adjusted other than in his sex life, we can assume that his problem is fairly mild. Most psychologists would refer to such a difficulty as a *psycho-neurosis*, or simply as a *neurosis* (°). If, however, Mr. Smith's thoughts and behaviors had become so unusual that he had lost his job, if he suffered from extreme emotional outbursts or hallucinations, or if he seemed to have lost contact with reality, we might refer to his problem as being a *psychosis* (°), or severe intra-psychic abnormality.

Psychologists do not agree on the relationship between neuroses and psychoses. Some theorists hold that the neurosis is a weak or mild form of psychosis, and that people can be measured on this scale:

Normal	Neurotic	Psychotic

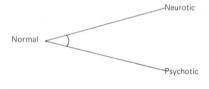

Neurotic behavior patterns, then, are thought to be only 1 or 2 standard deviations from the "norm," while psychotic reactions are several standard deviations away from the average. Other theorists believe that there is no necessary relationship between a neurosis and a psychosis, and that we must measure such problems on two different scales as shown in the margin.

Almost everyone agrees that people whom we class as "neurotics" can typically maintain themselves in their community and continue their lives while seeking help. Those individuals labeled "psychotics" usually need some form of institutional care or intensive therapy at one point or another in their lives. With the exception of the organic psychoses we have already discussed, neuroses and psychoses are not generally presumed to have direct physiological causes.

The Neuroses

The general psychiatric view is that neuroses are persistent but relatively mild emotional disturbances that are caused by a person's inability to deal with stress, conflict, and anxiety. There are thought to be five stages in the development of a neurotic condition:

1.   The person experiences *trauma* (°), or psychological damage, while passing

through his or her early psycho-sexual development. Neuroses, from a psychiatric standpoint, are said to be rooted in childhood experiences.

2. As a result of this trauma the individual learns faulty or inappropriate patterns of behavior and acquires incorrect or distorted attitudes and perceptions about his or her social and physical environment.

3. As the person grows older these inappropriate behavior patterns and attitudes create problems of their own. The more the individual tries to adjust, the more difficulty he or she has. This inability to cope with life creates anxieties and tensions.

4. In order to reduce the pain and tension the person experiences, he or she regresses to a more infantile style of behaving. The individual also makes increasing but inappropriate use of the various defense mechanisms—such as denial, repression, projection, reaction formation, regression, and sublimation (*see* Chapter 22).

5. Unless the person gets some kind of help, these defensive reactions may become habitual—that is, they may develop into rigid, unconscious behavior patterns with widely varying *symptoms*.

Six Types of Neuroses Many psychologists and psychiatrists believe that there are some six main types of neuroses. These are labels or "diagnostic categories" that are applied to living human beings, and often the labeling process is rather inaccurate. However, let us look at these six major categories as they might be applied to John and Mary Smith.

1. The *conversion reaction*. A person suffering from this neurosis tends to convert hidden or unacceptable wishes or impulses into organic symptoms—presumably in an attempt to divert his or her feelings of anxiety and perhaps to arouse sympathy and attract attention. If Mrs. Smith insisted that her sex organs had no feelings at all, that they were "anesthetized," she might be converting her fears about sexuality into a bodily symptom. Conversion reactions are also called *hysterias* (*). Psychologically induced loss of sight or hearing (such as that created during hypnosis) are called "hysterical" blindness or deafness.

2. The *depressive reaction*. If Mr. Smith feared that his sexual performance was inadequate, that he could not live up to his image of what a man should be, he might give in to his fears and enter a period of dark depression. He might withdraw from most forms of communication with Mrs. Smith (and others), refuse to make plans for the future, and talk about nothing but his own personal discouragement with life.

3. The *dissociative reaction*. If the ego prevents unacceptable impulses from gaining consciousness, these desires may find other, unhealthy ways of expressing themselves. According to Jung, they may split off from the ego entirely and form a *complex*, or separate personality structure, all their own. If Mr. Smith's desires for sex bothered him, he might repress them. But these sexual urges might be so strong that they could split off into a separate sub-personality in order to find expression. Mr. Smith might refer to this part of himself as "Mr. Black," who periodically (usually in bed) seized possession of Smith's body and "did wicked things" with Mrs. Smith. In this form of "multiple personality," the dominant personality often forgets (shows amnesia for) the behaviors that the minor personality engages in.

4. The *obsessive-compulsive reaction*. Suppose that Mrs. Smith had, during her childhood attempts to resolve the Electra crisis, picked up the attitude that sexual desires are evil and ought to be resisted even in marriage. And so she attempts to repress her natural instincts and urges, much to Mr. Smith's dismay. But these thoughts are so strong that the only way she can keep them

Hysterias (his-TAIR-ee-uz). From the Greek words meaning "wandering womb." A type of neurosis marked by unrestrained emotionality—wild laughter or giggling that can change in a moment to outbursts of anger or tears. A person suffering from hysteria may "convert" fears and anxieties into bodily symptoms such as blindness. A soldier frightened during the height of a bloody battle may go blind rather than continue to witness the death of his friends. This blindness may continue for weeks or even years, then suddenly disappear almost overnight. Hysteria was originally thought to be a neurosis found only in women experiencing some displacement or "wandering" of the womb.

A depressed person usually withdraws from contact with others.

safely repressed is to think continually about something utterly irrational—and keep thinking about it again and again and again. Or perhaps she performs compulsive, repetitive actions—over and over and over. Usually the obsessive thoughts or compulsive actions are symbolically related to her problem. Her mind may be filled with images of germs—she may see them everywhere. Or she may wash her hands—or the bedroom floor—dozens of times each day, all in an attempt to prevent or to get rid of the "dirty sexual thoughts" that occasionally flood her mind.

5.   The *phobic reaction*. As we mentioned earlier, phobias are abnormal or unusual fears that have no real basis in fact. If Mr. Smith is unconsciously afraid of sexual activity, he may transfer this unacceptable anxiety to a fear of small or tight places. If the Smiths' bedroom is small and cramped, Mr. Smith may avoid the anxiety associated with entering his wife by refusing to enter the bedroom.

6.   The *anxiety reaction*. Fear begets fear, and panic leads to more panic. If Mr. Smith is unconsciously worried about his masculinity, he may suffer from such acute anxiety that he is unable to perform sexually. The more he tries to satisfy his wife, the more anxiety he experiences, and the worse he performs. Eventually he may break out in a cold sweat if she so much as puts her arm around him in the kitchen, fearing that this show of affection is the prelude to another bedroom disaster.

According to psychologist Robert M. Goldenson, more than 10 million Americans suffer from neuroses severe enough to require treatment. About one-third of these people suffer from anxiety reactions, while 25 percent of them experience obsessive-compulsive reactions, and another 25 percent experience depressive reactions. Hysterical reactions were quite common during the Middle Ages but are not particularly frequent today; together with the dissociative reactions, hysterics now account for less than 5 percent of the neurotics who seek psycho-therapy.

The six categories mentioned above are, at best, rather loose labels that we sometimes apply to complex human problems. A given individual may show several different types of symptoms, not all of which can be nicely tucked into one label or category of neurosis.

The Psychoses

Psychologists typically differentiate between the *organic psychoses*, which we have already discussed, and the *functional psychoses* (°). A functional psychosis is a severe form of psychological disturbance that has no obvious or apparent physiological basis. It is the misfunctioning of the mind, not of the central nervous system, that seems the causal factor for this type of mental illness. As we will see, the person suffering from a functional psychosis may have a genetic pre-disposition toward this kind of sickness.

About 25 percent of the first admissions to public mental hospitals are for patients with functional psychoses. Another 25 percent of first admissions are for patients with organic psychoses. Public health officials estimate that, during any given year, about 1 million Americans can be considered psychotic. About two-thirds of these people are hospitalized, more than 98 percent in public institutions. Perhaps 50 percent of the hospital beds in the United States are occupied by mental patients, the vast majority being people suffering from psychotic problems. Fortunately, many of these individuals recover completely after treatment and never need hospitalization again.

Schizophrenia   If we use the standard psychiatric classification, by far the most common type of functional psychosis is *schizophrenia* (°). The term comes from the Latin words that mean "splitting of the mind." The use of this term is unfortunate, for the "split personalities" discussed earlier in this chapter have little or nothing to do with schizophrenia, which is thought to be characterized by a general mental disorganization. A person who badly distorts reality, or who withdraws into a psychological shell and won't come out, is said to suffer from schizophrenia. An older name for the same illness is *dementia praecox* (°), from the Latin words meaning "youthful insanity."

About 10 percent of the patients entering mental hospitals each year are classified as schizophrenics; the average age of such patients is 33. When schizophrenia affects children, as we saw in Chapter 20, it is often called *autism* (°). Schizophrenia affects men and women in equal numbers, but as we will see, single males are particularly susceptible.

There is considerable argument in psychological circles as to whether schizophrenia really exists as a mental illness, or whether we simply call people "schizophrenics" because we don't know what else to call them. The fact that so many people are diagnosed as schizophrenic suggests that this category may be too loose and too large to be meaningfully applied to the complexly different organisms we call human beings.

According to most psychiatric classifications, there are said to be four main types of schizophrenia: simple, hebephrenic, catatonic, and paranoid. If you walked through the wards of a mental hospital, you would see many different patients who showed various types of symptomatic behaviors. If you saw a man sitting passively on a bench, staring at the floor, unmoving and unmotivated, you probably would be looking at a man labeled a *simple schizophrenic* (°) by the hospital staff. Such people often appear to be "life's failures," and many of them will tell you that "they can't make it outside the hospital." Anyone who withdraws from society; anyone whose main problem seems to be that of "coping,"

Functional psychoses (sigh-KO-sees). Any psychosis that has no apparent biological or organic cause. Someone whose problem is with processing or with dynamic functioning, as opposed to someone whose problems are structural or physiological.

Schizophrenia (skits-zoh-FREE-knee-uh). A psychological label that we apply to personality disturbances characterized by shyness, introversion, and a tendency to avoid social contact and close relationships. Distorted thought patterns, delusions, emotional impulsivity, and unusual body movements are often part of the symptoms of schizophrenia.

Dementia praecox (dee-MEN-cha PREE-cox). The original name for schizophrenia. Means "insanity of the young."

Autism (AW-tism). Literally, an absorption in need-satisfying or wish-fulfilling fantasy as a mechanism of escape from reality. The autistic (aw-TISS-tic) person withdraws from the cold, hard facts of the world into a dream-like existence. Any attempt to demonstrate reality or bring the autistic individual out of his or her fantasy world is likely to be met with hostility.

Simple schizophrenic. According to R.M. Goldenson, simple schizophrenia can be described as a pervasive impoverishment of personality. The patient's life contracts to a point where the patient manifests little or no interest, ambition, emotional response, or spontaneous activity. Unless given help, the simple schizophrenic is likely to remain a colorless, ineffectual, shallow, "shut-in" individual, who drifts through life without serious loss of contact with reality.

Hebephrenic schizophrenic (hee-bee-FREN-ick). According to Goldenson, hebephrenia is characterized by severe disintegration rather than mere impoverishment of personality, as in simple schizophrenia. The patient loses touch with reality, and all major functions—thought, speech, behavior, and emotionality—become increasingly disorganized and distorted.

Catatonic schizophrenics (kat-tah-TAHN-ick). Goldenson states that there are two main types of catatonic schizophrenia. The first (called "catatonic stupor") often comes on rapidly. The patient becomes mute, stares blankly at the floor, and may assume a fixed, stereotyped posture which the patient may maintain for days or weeks. The second (called "catatonic excitement") is characterized by frenzied motor activity. The patient may talk incoherently at the top of the voice, rush frantically back and forth, tear off clothing, and without warning may attack someone or break up furniture. The two states may alternate—that is, a patient may be "stuporous" for a while, then lapse into excitement, then become calm and "freeze" into a strange posture for several days.

Paranoid schizophrenia (PAIR-uh-noid). According to Goldenson, the major symptoms of paranoid schizophrenia are poorly organized, internally illogical, changeable delusions, often accompanied by vivid hallucinations. Delusions of persecution ("they're out to get me!") are most common.

Affective reactions (aff-FECK-tive). Also called "affective psychoses." The Latin word *affectus* means "desire," or "emotion." When a psychologist speaks of your "affect," he or she means your emotional state. The affective psychoses are those that have to do primarily with emotional reactivity—mania and depression.

but who still can function at a minimum level of effectiveness in the hospital, is likely to be called a "simple schizophrenic."

If a woman patient came up to you, all giggles and laughs, and told you she was the Virgin Mary and would you please take a note to her son Jesus, who was still "outside," you would be speaking to a patient the psychiatrist probably would have diagnosed as a *hebephrenic schizophrenic* (°). People who suffer from bizarre symptoms of any kind—such as hallucinations, delusions, or a regression to infantile behaviors—are typically classed as "hebephrenic." Their language behavior often reminds one of a "word salad"—that is, these patients mix nouns and verbs, subjects and pronouns as if they were tossing the words together in a salad bowl.

QUESTION: **What would Freud have said about the id and the ego of someone classed as a hebephrenic?**

Sometimes on a hospital ward you would encounter a patient frozen into a strange posture—someone who stood in a corner with arms overhead, and stood there by the hour. These people are typically called *catatonic schizophrenics* (°). They seem to be locked away in their own fantasy worlds much of the time, as if they had completely withdrawn from present reality.

QUESTION: **What might Harlow's studies of "motherless" monkeys tell us about the causes of catatonic behavior?**

If a male patient accosted you on the ward and demanded that you immediately call the President and get the patient out of the hospital, you would have encountered someone with symptoms of *paranoid schizophrenia* (°). People whom we call paranoids are usually suspicious—they fear and mistrust almost everyone. Often they hear voices that whisper dreadful things to them—warning them to be wary of other people, that someone is trying to take over their lives or control them with radio waves. They seem convinced that someone is out to get them, or that some powerful (but vaguely defined) political organization is keeping them in the hospital. These types of patients are difficult to deal with because they often misinterpret attempts to help them as being attempts to persecute them.

QUESTION: **If by some terrible mistake you were committed to a mental hospital, despite the fact that you were sane, what would you do? If you went to a doctor and demanded that you be released, insisting that someone had made a dreadful error in putting you in the hospital, what kind of psychiatric label might the doctor pin on you?**

Generally speaking, people who show grossly inappropriate responses to external stimuli are called "schizophrenics." If a patient repeats the same meaningless phrase again and again, or jumps wildly from one topic of conversation to another, the patient is responding inaccurately to external verbal stimulation. Such people are said to show "disturbed thought processes," although in truth they may merely have learned that such responses get them a lot of attention. Other patients may show unusual emotional reactions—in situations where a normal person might cry or fly into a rage, these patients might giggle, shrug their shoulders, drop off to sleep, or "freeze" in a weird posture. They are often said to have "flattened" emotional reactions, although we are not always sure just what it is they are reacting to.

Affective Psychoses People whom we call "schizophrenic" sometimes seem to be stuck in the middle of the "mood scale," being neither very far "up" or "down" no matter what the situation. People suffering from what we call the *affective reactions* (°) seem stuck at one end of the emotionality scale or the other.

If you met a woman on one of the hospital wards who was racing about, giggling and smiling and acting rather as if she had taken too many "pep pills," you could be pretty sure the hospital staff would call her a *manic psychotic* (°). A person afflicted with a manic psychosis might be excessively happy and optimistic even in the face of life's greatest tragedies. During the worst part of an attack of mania, the patient may become so active and agitated that he or she must be forcibly restrained.

The *depressive psychosis* (°) is almost the exact opposite of the manic. If you met a patient overwhelmed by the sadness and futility of life, someone sunk into a deep pit of despair, you would have met someone suffering from a depressive psychosis. Depressed patients respond as if they had taken an overdose of "downers," and often sink into a state of complete passivity. They may refuse to move from their beds, and must be force-fed to be kept alive.

> QUESTION: **Do you think depressive patients would tend to be externalizers or internalizers? With the data on Harlow's "depressed monkeys" in mind, what kinds of situations do you think might cause depressive reactions in humans?**

There is a curious but not well understood relationship between manic and depressive disorders. Some patients swing wildly from one emotional extreme to the other, while other patients show only the manic or the depressive reaction. In many cases, the same sorts of confused thought patterns and personality disintegrations found in schizophrenic patients may accompany mania or depression. The fact that a few patients diagnosed as schizophrenic show mood changes similar to mania or depression suggests that our labels are not nearly as accurate as we would like them to be.

Labeling

There are many problems associated with pinning the standard psychiatric labels on individuals who suffer from psychological pain or disorder. The first of these we have already mentioned several times—the labels are rough approximations and don't always do justice to the complexities of the human psyche in distress. Once we call a person a "paranoid," we run the real danger of forcing our perceptions of the patient to fit the label. We may unwittingly focus our attention on the few inappropriate things the patient does and ignore all the healthy thoughts the patient expresses.

The second problem is that we often assume that the patient and the problem are one and the same. If Mary Smith breaks out in a red rash, we say, "Mary Smith has the measles." We never say, "Mary Smith *is* measles." Yet how casually we say of a patient in a mental hospital, "Oh, Mary Smith *is* psychotic," rather than saying, "Mary Smith suffers from a type of psychological distress that some people call a psychosis." Mary Smith may have many personal difficulties, but the only "thing" that Mary Smith *is*, is Mary Smith! If we treat her as a *psychotic*, rather than as a *human being*, we do her and all other humans a grave injustice.

The third problem with labeling is that it may mislead us into thinking we know more about the causes and cures of the problem than is really the case. Schizophrenia is often called a "disorder of thinking and of emotionality," and is assumed to be primarily intra-psychic. Yet schizophrenia (assuming it really is a single type of disorder) is affected by biological and social influences as well as internal psychological dynamics.

The *tendency* toward schizophrenia appears to be at least partially inherited, and the body chemistry of patients called "schizophrenic" is often reported to be different from the body chemistry of patients called "neurotic" or from that of normal individuals. The social environment and family backgrounds of schizophrenic patients are usually much more confused and disorganized than those of normals. Psychotic problems seem to be two to three times as prevalent among poor people as among rich people. When we say that "John Smith is a schizo-

Manic psychotic (MAN-ick). Goldenson states that manic reactions are characterized by elation and hyperactivity, and range in degree from the mild through the acute to the delirious (dee-LEER-ee-us) form. The manic state is often preceded by a brief simple depression, leading some authorities to believe manic attacks are defenses against depression. The most severe type is delirious mania, in which the patient becomes totally disoriented and incoherent, develops vivid auditory and visual hallucinations, and engages in wild body movements.

Depressive psychosis. According to Goldenson, there are three stages the depressive patient may pass through. In the first, called "simple depression," the patient shows loss of interest in the world, becomes dejected, thinks of suicide, and refuses to work or eat. In acute depression, the patient withdraws further; physical activity is almost at a standstill; and contacts with other people rarely occur. In the final stage, depressive stupor, motor activity ceases. The patient is usually mute, confused about almost everything, and may have wild hallucinations. The patient often must be force-fed to be kept alive.

Social disorders. Those abnormal behavior patterns that appear to be a matter of inappropriate social learning rather than of intra-psychic or biological origin. Once called "character disorders."

Psychopath. See *sociopath.*

Sociopath (so-see-oh-path). A type of personality disorder marked primarily by failure to adapt to prevailing ethical and social standards and by lack of social responsibility. Like "psychopath," the term "sociopath" has been replaced by "anti-social personality."

phrenic" we may automatically assume the problem is entirely his—that the "sickness" lies entirely inside his mind, and that he is entirely responsible for his present condition. In fact, his genes, his parental upbringing (or lack thereof), his poor socio-economic background, and the stresses and strains of present-day society may be the major contributors to his difficulties. If we say, "John Smith has a functional psychosis," we may then attempt to cure just his mind, instead of working to change his environment and to give John Smith better social skills once he leaves the hospital.

PROBLEMS OF SOCIAL RELATIONS

Whatever their causes or cures, the psychoses and neuroses typically cause the most pain and unhappiness to the individual concerned. The *social disorders* (°), however, are a broad, third category of abnormal behavior patterns that are more likely to cause problems for others than for the person who shows the deviant behavior. From a social/behavioral viewpoint, the social disorders are viewed as disruptions in relationships *between* people, or between a single person and a whole social system. Most criminals fall into this category, as do sexual deviates, prostitutes, manipulators and "con artists," and many types of political rebels.

Illegal activities are, by definition, social disorders, since governments usually presume that law-abiding behavior is the norm. Given this fact, we can understand that considerable cultural bias creeps into our definitions of what is socially abnormal. The warrior-hero of one country might be considered a "mad butcher" elsewhere. In the United States we usually hospitalize people who admit to having continual hallucinations; in other cultures such people are occasionally worshipped as powerful witch doctors or magicians. In the Soviet Union people who fight against the Communist political system are often locked up in insane asylums. The top politicians in Russia apparently believe in the Soviet way of life so strongly that anyone who doesn't see politics their way is judged mentally unbalanced and in need of hospitalization.

It has taken us a long time to learn that "different" doesn't necessarily mean "evil," "abnormal," or "insane." Most psychologists would agree, however, that learning to tolerate different life styles is one of the main hallmarks of mental maturity.

The two most frequently discussed types of social disorders are the anti-social personality and the sexual deviate.

The Anti-social Personality

Perhaps the best definition of the anti-social personality is someone who lacks a conscience or superego, or who has never learned to measure the consequences of his or her behaviors. Such an individual not only breaks social laws or rules but is without guilt or anxiety about his or her misbehavior. At their worst, anti-social individuals appear to be incapable of establishing warm, personal relations with other individuals. They often appear to be greedy, impulsive, egocentric men and women who cannot understand that their actions often have profound and painful effects on the people around them. Their relationships with others are typically one way: They "get" and the others are expected to "give." Older names for this type of disorder are *psychopath* (°) and *sociopath* (°).

Many people with anti-social behavior patterns are quite intelligent. They sometimes become business and political leaders who are known for their ruthlessness and toughness. Some drift into military organizations, where they may rise rapidly to positions of considerable power. Most such individuals, however, move from one scrape with the law to another and spend much of their time sitting in jails or hospitals. Since they feel little or no remorse about hurting or killing others, they often become "leaders" in prison societies.

German dictator Adolph Hitler.

Although a few anti-social individuals may suffer from some genetic fault (*see* Chapter 19), the main cause appears to be poor parental guidance. The majority of anti-social people appear to behave toward others as their parents behaved toward them.

Sexual Deviations and Standard Deviations

Anyone whose behavior is more than 2 standard deviations from the norm is, by definition, a deviate as far as that one specific measure or test is concerned. Some norms are determined statistically or by experiment—such as the modes, medians, and means on IQ tests. Other norms are arbitrarily set by law or custom. Although it was long suspected that the *actual* norms for bedroom behavior were somewhat different from the "model" or "legal" norms sanctioned by our society, it took Kinsey's research to prove this was the case.

Technically speaking, we should not consider any form of sexual behavior abnormal if it is engaged in by large numbers of people—that is, if the behavior is less than 2 standard deviations from the actual norms. In practice, however, any sexual responses that involve physical harm to others (such as rape) or that can be seen as psychologically damaging (such as sex with children) are likely to be considered abnormal.

The three main types of sexual deviation have to do with choice of sex partner, with means of achieving sexual climax with that partner, and with the frequencies with which sex is desired or performed.

Deviation with Respect to Sex Partner Sigmund Freud, like most other theorists, assumed that we are all born with a fairly strong drive toward hetero-sexuality. As we saw earlier, the presence or absence of hormones during critical developmental periods determines our physical sexual identity—we are born with a penis or vagina because these complex chemicals shape our sexual organs while we are still in the womb. These same hormones probably shape our basic sexual desires, too, by acting directly on our brains during our maturation. However, the actual use that we make of our sex organs is strongly influenced by the demands of society and our own personal experiences while growing up. In other words, our hormones usually *pre-dispose* us toward heterosexuality; but this pre-disposition is sufficiently weak that it may be altered or changed in many ways.

As Freud pointed out, if a young boy's mother is domineering and his father weak or absent, the boy may lack a suitable male model and may develop feminine sexual interests rather than masculine. The boy may unconsciously be encouraged by his mother to wear girl's clothes or to seek other males as sex partners. The psychiatric label for a person who prefers to wear the clothes of the opposite sex is *transvestism* (°), but the term is relatively meaningless since it merely means "cross-sex dressing." The fact that we have a fancy name for the behavior doesn't tell us much about it psychologically. We do know that many men who enjoy wearing women's clothes are entirely heterosexual in their choice of sex partners—and that most male homosexuals dress, look, and act just like purely heterosexual males (at least, homosexuals do so outside of the bedroom).

A young girl with a weak mother and an overbearing father may grow up preferring male clothes or female sex partners. The technical term for female homosexuality is *lesbianism* (°). But again, not all lesbians wear male clothes or act the male role in society. Lesbians (like all other human beings) come in a variety of sizes, shapes, ages, skin colors, and personalities. The only thing they seem to have in common is that they are women who prefer sex with other women. But the term "lesbian" doesn't tell us what their deep emotional experiences are like, nor much about the ways in which they love each other.

Homosexual behavior may develop for many reasons. If a child's opportunities for sexual exploration are limited to other children of the same sex, the child may

Transvestism (trans-VEST-tism). From the Greek words *trans,* meaning "across," and *vestire,* meaning "to dress." A transvestite is a male who wears female clothing, or a female who wears male clothing.

Lesbianism (LEZ-bee-an-ism). The Greek poet Sappho (SAF-foh) lived on the island of Lesbos some 600 years before Christ. She wrote poetry about the sexual love of one woman for another, and gathered about her women who enjoyed the love of other women. Lesbians are "followers of Sappho," or female homosexuals.

Pedophilia (pedd-oh-FEEL-ee-uh). From the Greek words *paed,* meaning "child," and *philia,* meaning "love of." A pedagogue is someone who teaches children; a pedophiliac is someone who has a sexual love for children.

Voyeur (voy-YOUR). From the French verb "to see." Someone who would rather look at sexual activity than participate in it.

Exhibitionist (ex-hibb-BISH-un-ist). People (mostly males) who get sexual pleasure from displaying their genitals in public. Often called "indecent exposure" in the newspapers.

Bestiality (beast-tee-AL-it-tee). Sexual contact with a beast.

Fetishism (FETT-ish-ism). From a Latin word meaning "artificial," or "false." A fetish is an object toward which unusual emotion. respect, or love is shown. A man who is "turned on" sexually more by women's shoes than by women themselves has what is called a "shoe fetish."

experiment with homosexuality. If, later in life, the person's first heterosexual contacts are psychological disasters, the person may revert or regress back to homosexuality as a less threatening and more rewarding way of behaving. Or, having found that same-sex contacts can sometimes be stimulating, the person may simply *add* heterosexual behaviors and interests to the homosexual patterns already established. Men and women in prison, or in military situations, may have little choice in the matter if they are physically prevented from seeking contacts with the opposite sex. And anti-social individuals are often quite willing to "use" members of either sex for their pleasures.

For many decades homosexual behavior was thought to be clear psychiatric and moral evidence of insanity. In the early 1970's, however, the American Psychiatric Association removed homosexuality from its list of symptoms of mental illness. Kinsey's data suggest that many adults engage in occasional homosexual behavior, although their primary orientation remains heterosexual. In some states, and in many foreign countries, homosexual contacts among consenting adults are as legally acceptable as are heterosexual contacts. Indeed, there is a trend toward viewing homosexuality as an alternative life style rather than as a social disorder or a symptom of mental abnormality.

People whose social skills are badly deficient may find it difficult to relate closely and intimately with other adults of *either* sex, but may find it easy to entice children into bed with them, a condition called *pedophilia* (°). Although many such encounters involve little more than caressing the child, or engaging in some form of masturbatory behavior, pedophilia occasionally leads to rape or murder. A more subtle problem arises if the child involved is of the same sex as the adult. If the child finds the contact stimulating or rewarding, the child may grow up with a positive bias toward homosexuality. Kinsey's figures (and later surveys) suggest that pedophilia is more common than most people would like to think it is.

An adult who finds it difficult to attract or to establish strong personal bonds with another adult may turn to many other types of sexual relief. The *voyeur* (°), or "peeping Tom," may gain sexual excitement primarily from spying on other people as they undress or as they engage in sexual activity. The *exhibitionist* (°)—usually a male—often can achieve sexual climax only by displaying himself to unsuspecting women whom he encounters (usually by accident) in public places.

Kinsey reported that *bestiality* (°), or sex with an animal, occurred in nearly 20 percent of U.S. men raised on farms, but was rather rare in men growing up in urban regions. Some men and women find their major form of sexual gratification in masturbation while looking at or caressing articles of clothing or other inanimate objects, a condition known as *fetishism* (°). Again, the fact that we have fancy Latin and Greek names for these types of sexual behavior doesn't mean that we understand much about them, or that they are necessarily harmful.

QUESTION: **Why should sex with animals be so much rarer in cities than on farms?**

Deviant Means of Gratification Even when the individual's choice of sex partner is natural, or heterosexual, the means of gratification may be abnormal. Oral-genital contacts of all kinds, even between man and wife, are still illegal in many U.S. states, as is anal intercourse. In fact, these forms of sexual release are so common that they are not considered psychologically abnormal unless they are the *only* means of gratification the person desires. Sadism and masochism (*see* Chapter 15) are two other fairly familiar forms of deviant sexual pleasure (or pain).

Deviant Frequency of Gratification Variations in the frequency of sexual contact may be considered abnormal if too extreme. The man who spends all of his time occupied (or preoccupied) with sex is said to suffer from *satyrism* or *satyriasis* (°); the woman with an insatiable desire for intercourse is said to suffer from *nymphomania* (°). Satyrs and nymphomaniacs are considered deviant not because their sex drives are so strong, but because their sexual encounters often lack psychological depth and human warmth.

For a variety of reasons, the opposite sort of problem—impotence in males and frigidity in women—is more common but is still considered psychologically deviant. Oddly enough, impotence and frigidity are perhaps the only forms of sexual deviation that society generally does not punish. Indeed, under many circumstances, sexual *abstinence* (°) is considered *model* behavior (although Kinsey's data suggest that complete abstinence is seldom the norm).

Are Perversions Perverse? Many forms of unusual or *perverse* (°) sexual behavior are deviations from the law more than they are from the psychological norm. From 10 to 25 percent of the prisoners in most state penal institutions are sexual offenders. Most are men. Women, when they are arrested for sex offenses, are usually charged with prostitution or crimes against children.

In one study of sex criminals in the state of Michigan, 60 percent of all offenses were directed against children. Young unmarried males were the most frequent offenders, but most of them had been sexually delinquent during adolescence. More than 40 percent of those arrested for sex crimes were voyeurs or exhibitionists, who usually were put on probation or given suspended sentences. Fewer than 10 percent had been arrested more than once, and most of these arrests were for very minor offenses. Only about 5 percent of sexual offenders inflicted any kind of physical harm on other people. Most of these 5 percent were judged to be abnormal or psychotic in *all* their behaviors, not just in the sexual realm. Very few sexual offenders progressed from minor to major crimes, since they usually persisted in the same type of sexual gratification. And most offenders were not over-sexed but rather the opposite—they were chiefly under-sexed, misinformed, narrow-minded people.

If we assume that sexually deviant behavior is that which is 2 standard deviations from the norm, then what Alfred Kinsey and his associates wrote in 1949 seems particularly appropriate:

> In spite of the many centuries in which our culture has attempted to suppress all but one type of sexual activity, a not inconsiderable portion of all the sexual acts in which the human animal engages still fall into the category which the culture rates as "perverse." The specific data show that two thirds to three quarters of the males in our American culture, and some lesser number of females, engage in at least some "perverse" sexual behavior at some time between adolescence and old age. One half to two thirds of the males engage in such behavior with appreciable frequency during some period of their lives and a fair number engage in such behavior throughout their lives.

THE MULTIPLE CAUSES OF DEVIANT BEHAVIOR

Why do people do the crazy, abnormal things that they do? In the past, theorists have often given one-level answers to this question. The organic psychoses were due to bad genes or physical accidents. The neuroses and functional psychoses were caused by traumas the individual experienced during childhood. Anti-social behavior was the result of improper learning, or a bad social environment or *milieu* (°). But today we realize that all behavior is multi-determined, that everything you do has not one cause but many. Human problems, like human successes, are almost always due to *interactions* of biological, psychological, and sociological forces.

Again let us take the Smith family as an example. Female frigidity is often seen as being the *woman's* problem, a personality trait that resides entirely in the

Satyriasis (sat-teer-RYE-uh-sis). The condition of being a satyr. A man preoccupied with sexual thoughts, or a constant desire for sex.

Nymphomania (nim-foh-MAY-knee-uh). *Nympha* is the Greek word for "bride." A nymphomaniac is a woman who has the unsatisfiable urge for sexual intercourse that brides are supposed to display on their wedding nights.

Abstinence (ABB-stuh-nents). To abstain is to do without. Sexual abstinence is the act of giving up all forms of sexual activity. To rephrase the legend, "abstinence makes the heart grow fonder."

Perverse (purr-VERSE). From the Latin words meaning "to turn the wrong way." A pervert is someone who gains his or her pleasures in an unusual way—that is, from a sexual behavior not approved by society.

Milieu (mill-YOU). The French word for "environment."

woman's mind. But all personality traits have a biological background, and they are always expressed in social, interpersonal situations. In a small percentage of cases female frigidity may be related to physical causes—an imbalance of hormones or perhaps a vagina so small that intercourse is painful to the woman. But biological difficulties don't really *cause* frigidity; rather, frigidity is the individual woman's response to her physical condition. And this response is chiefly determined by her own unique developmental history and the social milieu she grew up in. As we saw in an earlier chapter, a girl with a widowed mother may learn to fear both men and sex. And in many parts of our society the belief is still held that it is a woman's duty to submit sexually to her husband—but she shouldn't enjoy the process. Perhaps it is the society, not the woman, that is frigid.

Male impotence can be seen in much the same light. A very small number of men are physically unable to perform the sex act. But (by definition) about half the men in the world are born with smaller-then-average penises. In many cultures and societies physical size is assumed to be related to masculinity and potency. A man with a small penis—or who *thinks* he has a small penis—may develop considerable fear and anxiety about his ability to satisfy a woman. The more he worries about her (usually imaginary) disappointment, the more likely it is that he will develop the symptom of impotency. The woman who fears she is not attractive enough to hold a man's interest may shun the marriage bed for similar reasons.

Even so, frigidity and impotence (and other sexual difficulties) are seldom the exclusive problem of just the male *or* the female. A man may have symptoms of impotency at the time of his marriage, but it is his wife's (often unconscious) responses to his condition that help keep him that way. A woman may dislike, or wish to avoid, sex when she gets married, but if her attitude does not change after the wedding, it is surely as much her husband's responsibility as it is hers. In such marriages, as we will see in the next chapter, it may be useless to treat one of the partners and not the other. For, generally, when a person develops abnormal behavior patterns, everyone the person has close contact with must be considered part of the cause.

SUMMARY

1. The words "normal" and "abnormal" have no meaning except when they are defined within a given context. What is normal in one social situation may be quite abnormal in another.
2. Psychologists often use the terms "mean," "median," and "mode" to describe the norm, or center, of a distribution of test scores or behavioral measures. In both mathematical and psychological terms, an abnormal behavior or score is one that departs noticeably from the mean, median, or mode.
3. The term "departs noticeably" is often defined as being *2 standard deviations* from the norm.
4. Psychologists use many different diagnostic labels to describe and interpret thoughts or actions that are presumed to be abnormal. Used properly, such labels can be of considerable value; used improperly, as they often are, they may give us the false impression that an individual's problem is entirely within the person, rather than in the interactions among the individual's biology, intra-psychic experience, and the social environment.
5. Severe abnormalities that are thought to stem primarily from physiological causes are called "organic psychoses."
6. Among the organic psychoses are problems stemming from brain damage at birth; from strokes and senility; from diseases such as syphilis; from menopause; from alcohol and other drugs.
7. Relatively minor intra-psychic problems are sometimes called "neuroses." Labels for these problems include the "conversion reaction," the "depressive

reaction," the "dissociative reaction," the "obsessive-compulsive reaction," the "phobic reaction," and the "anxiety reaction."

8. Relatively severe intra-psychic problems are often called "functional psychoses." They include several forms of schizophrenia, mania, and severe depression.

9. Problems stemming chiefly from person-environmental interactions are called "social disorders." They include the anti-social personality, the sexual deviate, the criminal, and the highly aggressive individual.

10. All forms of abnormal behavior are influenced by biological, intra-psychic, and environmental factors.

(Continued from page 549.)

Steve May was a mesomorph of average height; a ring of blond hair framed his alert, often-smiling face. He thanked Dr. Mann for her introduction, leaned against the table at the front of the classroom, and began to talk.

"When Dr. Mann dropped me off in front of the hospital, I was scared witless. Looking back at it, I guess I was afraid one of two things would happen, either of which would be bad.

"First, I was pretty sure that the hospital staff would see through our little game and expose me as a fraud. I didn't like that thought at all. But second, if they admitted me, I'd be locked up in the Funny Farm, and that seemed even worse. However, I went inside and told them I had an appointment and wanted to be admitted, and they just smiled at me and told me to take a seat. Then I had to fill out some forms, and then some more forms, and then some more. After a while, they said the doctor would see me, and I went into his office.

"He really was a nice guy, I'll say that much for him. But he was awfully busy and didn't have too much time to spend with me. He took my life history and asked me some questions about how I got along with people. I get along with people pretty well, and I told him the truth about everything in my life. Every time I talked about having an argument, though, he got really interested. For instance, I've been going with this girl for almost two years now, and we really like each other. In two years we've had maybe three arguments. The doctor wanted to know all about them. Later, when I got out, Dr. Mann asked to look at my hospital records; we found out that the doctor wrote a lot about my 'frequent emotional outbursts' with my girlfriend. He just didn't see them the same way I did. He also wrote that my interpersonal relationships were 'ambivalent,' which means that sometimes I like people and sometimes I don't. The doctor thought that was very abnormal for some reason."

A young woman at the front of the class held up her hand. "What did you do to convince the doctor that you were crazy?

Steve May smiled. "I guess the worst thing I did was to ask to be admitted to the hospital. You have to be really crazy to do something like that. You see, nobody ever volunteers to be put away in a mental hospital unless they're really hurting. So the staff assumes you must be off your rocker or you wouldn't be there. Just asking to be admitted is all the proof they need that you're mentally ill."

The woman persisted. "Yes, but what did you say to the doctor about your problems?"

"I didn't have a problem, so I did what Dr. Rosenhan and his crew did. I told the doctor that I heard voices. 'What kinds of voices?' the doctor asked. I said they were pretty indistinct, but that they seemed to be saying 'empty' and 'hollow' and 'thud.' The doctor decided that I had a painful concern about the existential meaninglessness of my life. That was enough for him. He said I was schizophrenic and needed help."

"Did they give you any personality tests?" asked a young man in the back of the room.

"Eventually they gave me the MMPI. We saw the test scores afterward. I was within one standard deviation from the norm on all the scales except one. I was about a standard deviation and a half below the mean on the paranoid scale, which they thought was very significant. They didn't say why.''

Steve smiled broadly, then continued.

''When I was admitted they took away all my things—my wallet, checkbook, watch, my rings, keys, pictures, and my clothes. You can't imagine how frightening that was. I wasn't **me** any more, somehow. At least I couldn't prove who I was; and I didn't have any money to buy anything. I had lost all my identity and any claim to fame or power. I wanted to back out right then, but they wouldn't let me.''

''What was the first thing they did to you, give you therapy of some kind?'' a student asked.

Again the young mesomorph smiled. ''They never did give me any therapy of any kind, except some tranquilizers. They gave me lots of those—several pills a day. I just flushed them down the john, and nobody noticed. I was on the Admissions Ward, you see; and they were supposed to be deciding what kind of therapy I needed. Maybe if I had stayed around a while, they would have done something. But to answer your question, the first thing they did was to give me a bath.''

The class laughed.

''It's true. I insisted that I had taken a shower that morning, but they didn't care. I guess they thought that schizophrenia was catching, and they didn't want me to infect anyone. And then they led me down several long, empty corridors with huge metal doors that they locked behind me, one after the other. I figured they were trying to tell me something—that if it took all this trouble to get into the hospital, it would take even more to get out. And they were right, of course.''

''What did you do on the ward?''

''Nothing. Absolutely nothing. They have the TV going day and night, but I soon got tired of that. I tried talking to the nurses and doctors, but they had other things to do; and they hardly ever come out of their glass cages anyhow. Each ward, you see, has a glassed-in observation room in the middle, where the staff sit and look out. If you need something, you go ask for it. But the staff members don't come out to socialize with you very often unless you make trouble. I never made any trouble because I was trying to act as absolutely normal and sane as I could. But the staff never noticed.''

The woman in front raised her hand again. ''I don't understand it. I mean, you were locked up with a lot of mentally ill patients? You must have stuck out like a sore thumb. How come they didn't recognize that?

Steve laughed loudly. ''The staff never figured it out, but the patients did. About 30 percent of the men on the ward came up to me and said things like, 'You're not crazy; you're a spy aren't you? You're checking up on the hospital.' I told the patients that I had been sick, but that I was okay now. But lots of them kept insisting that I had to be a reporter for the local newspaper or something like that. I just wish I could have convinced the doctors that easily.''

''How did you get out?'' someone asked.

''Well, a day or so after I had been admitted, I asked to see the doctor. When the nurse asked what I wanted, I said that the voices were gone and that I felt fine, so I wanted to leave. She shook her head and said I couldn't, that it would take a while. I asked to see the doctor every day for a week, but the nurse said he was busy, and to take my pills and be a good boy. One day I stopped the doctor as he walked through the ward and said that I was feeling great and wanted to talk to him about getting out. He didn't even pause. He just said, 'Good morning, Steve, how are you today?' and walked out the door. It took almost two weeks before I got another interview with him.''

''What was the worst part of the whole experience for you?'' the woman in front asked.

Steve thought for a moment, then said, ''The first few days were rough because I was afraid for my life. After all, I was locked up on a ward with crazy people; and they might go mad and kill me at any moment. But they turned out just to be people—people with problems like anybody else. Oh, they did some pretty strange things occasionally, but I suspect a lot of it was just to get attention from the staff. After a few days, when I got used to them, they became individuals rather than patients. I got to know some of them pretty well. Mostly they were people who just couldn't hack it in the outside world. I kept telling them they ought to give it another try, but most of them weren't interested. The hospital was too safe and comfortable. Some of them had seizures and other physical problems. And maybe some of them just liked to act crazy, and the hospital was a better place to do that than their own homes, because in the hospital they were expected to be crazy. At home they had to get a job and work and act sane, and maybe that was a drag. I don't know.''

Steve paused again, then continued. ''But you asked what was worst. The boredom, I guess. There's nothing to do on a hospital ward, you know. All day long nothing to do but eat three meals, take your pills, and watch the tube. I don't know what mental hospitals did before there was television. And, of course, the staff treat you as if you were crazy. They've made up their minds, and you can't change them. After a while I really got to the point where I thought I was going off my rocker. I got depressed and began to wonder if maybe Dr. Mann hadn't planned the whole thing just to get me locked away because she really thought I was crazy.''

He stopped and smiled at the teacher, as if to show he wasn't serious.

''But then she came to see me, and we talked it over; and I felt so good I decided I would try to figure out something to spend my time with. So I started flirting with one of the nurses, but she treated me—well—like I was a real loser. Then I started doing therapy with some of the other patients, trying to help them. Maybe that's why the doctor finally decided we ought to have another talk.''

''How long was it before you got out?''

''Nineteen days. Nothing like a free three-week vacation in a resort hotel, I always say. Anyhow, I had a chat with the doctor, and insisted that I be released because I felt swell and hadn't heard the voices since I had been admitted. So they finally released me. I can't tell you how great it was to walk out that front door.''

Steve May stopped and looked at the class. ''Any other questions?''

There were none, so Dr. Mann took over again.

''Steve was very brave to go through with our plan. I must say, I don't know that I could have managed as well as he did. And it would seem that Rosenhan's data are pretty reliable. I looked at Steve's records after the experiment, and showed them to him. When Steve was released, the doctor wrote on his record, 'Schizophrenia—in remission.' That means that he was still infected with the schizophrenia 'bug,' but it just wasn't biting him very hard at the moment. From a medical point of view, Steve is still considered to be mentally ill.''

A student interrupted. ''But I still can't believe that they couldn't tell Steve was sane. How does Professor Rosenhan explain that?''

''As I said at the beginning of class, it's a matter of perception. The title of Rosenhan's article is 'On Being Sane in Insane Places.' You see what you expect to see; and if you think a person's nuts, you pick out the nutty parts of his or her behavior and focus on them. If you meet the person in an insane asylum, which is a very abnormal background, you forget the background and ascribe the abnormality to the patient's personality.''

''But what does Professor Rosenhan think ought to be done?''

Dr. Mann looked through her notes. ''At the end of his article in **Science**, Rosenhan writes: 'If patients were powerful rather than powerless, if they were viewed as interesting individuals rather than diagnostic entities, if they were socially significant rather than social lepers, if their anguish truly and wholly compelled our sympathies and concerns, would we not **seek** contact with them, despite the availability of medications? Perhaps for the pleasure of it all?' Rosenhan thinks you can't change people's crazy behaviors unless you have love and affection for them, and unless you realize that you have to change the environments they live in as much as you change the individual.

''So here's your assignment for the weekend. I want you to pick someone you know well and see often. Observe that person for at least an hour, and keep track of all the abnormal things the person does. Then try to figure out whether the abnormality is within the individual, or within the environment, or both. And then ask yourself, 'If I were a psychologist or a psychiatrist, how would I help this person become more normal?' We'll talk about it on Monday. See you all then.''

RECOMMENDED READINGS

Braginsky, B.M., D. Braginsky, and K. Ring. *Methods of Madness: The Mental Hospital as a Last Resort* (New York: Holt, Rinehart and Winston, 1969).

Green, Hannah. *I Never Promised You a Rose Garden* (New York: New American Library, Inc., 1970), paperback.

Kesey, Ken. *One Flew Over the Cuckoo's Nest* (New York, The Viking Press, Inc., 1962), paperback.

Runkel, Peter R. *The Law Unto Themselves* (Ann Arbor, Mich.: Planarian Press, Inc., Box 644, 1970).

PSYCHOTHERAPY

DID YOU KNOW THAT . . .

A male Chinese may sometimes suffer from a dismal fear that his penis is about to be drawn up into his stomach and disappear?

Two centuries ago, mental patients were treated by "beating the devil" out of the patient?

Russian psychiatrists sometimes try to "extinguish" mental illness by putting patients to sleep for a month or more?

Mental patients often get well simply because the therapist expects them to?

Psychiatrists, psychoanalysts, and psychologists often disagree on how to define a "cure" of mental illness?

"Symptom substitution" seldom occurs in any type of psychotherapy?

One form of psychotherapy grew out of the theater?

Encounter groups are good opportunities for people to explore and express themselves, but are not very effective as psychotherapy?

Behavior therapists sometimes pay mental patients for getting well?

Psychological change almost always occurs in a warm and supportive environment?

The "team contracting approach" probably has the best "cure rate" of any type of psychotherapy?

The little old lady in tennis shoes wore cheap gloves to keep her hands clean. Mark Evans watched her as she grubbed about in her huge purse to find a dollar bill. She produced the dollar with a flourish and handed it to a scantily clad young woman who wandered about the casino, making change for the gamblers. Receiving a roll of 20 nickels from the attractive attendant, the little old woman tottered along a row of slot machines until she found one to her liking. Mark Evans moved over to watch her as she dumped her purse beside the one-armed bandit, then ever so carefully unrolled the nickels. She counted them one by one. Exactly 20. Examining one of the coins closely, she decided it would do. She spat on it, then rubbed the nickel gently between her gloved fingers to remove the dirt and grime.

"You'll rub all the luck off it, dearie," said a large, red-headed woman who was dropping dimes into the next machine.

"Luck?" cackled the little old woman, taking a grimy cloth bag from her purse and shaking it at the slot machine. "Luck is just a matter of chance, and I don't leave anything to chance. I put a hex on the machines, and they always pay off. I brought my juju bag with me today, so I can't lose. My juju is strong today; I feel its strength in my bones. Just you wait and see."

The old lady dropped the coin in the machine and pulled the handle. The three reels spun wildly, then clicked to a stop. A plum, an orange, and a lemon. She shook her head, and deposited another nickel. Again the reels whirred into action and stopped—two lemons and a bell.

"Your juju is all lemons today, dearie," the red-headed woman said.

The little old lady gestured wildly at the machine with the bag. "Juju!" she cried. "Give me a jackpot!"

The reels produced a cherry and two bells, and the machine coughed up two nickels as a reward.

"See! That's a good start. It's going to be a good day; I feel it in my bones!"

Mark Evans shook his head in amazement, then checked his watch. Time to meet his relative-in-law, Lou Hudson, from Chattanooga, Tennessee. Lou, who had married Mark's cousin Betty, was in Las Vegas for a convention of life insurance salesmen. Betty had called Mark a few days ago, asking Mark to take time out from his graduate studies at the University of Nevada to "show Lou the sights." That was the trouble with studying psychology in Las Vegas—sooner or later everybody you knew showed up and expected you to entertain them.

Lou Hudson turned out to be a thin young man with blond hair and blue but bloodshot eyes. "Stayed up half the night playing blackjack," Lou said, after the introductions were completed. "You wouldn't believe my luck. I was 200 bucks ahead, and I just knew I had a streak going. But then the cards turned against me. I barely broke even."

Mark Evans smiled. He had heard the phrase "broke even" enough to know that it usually meant losing a lot.

"Hey, man, this Las Vegas place is too much! I've never seen anything like it." Lou gestured at the activity in the casino. "Hotels with gambling halls instead of lobbies, people running around 24 hours a day, throwing their money away like there wasn't any tomorrow! Bands playing, and free drinks, and lots of good-looking females on the prowl. Nobody to tell you when to get up or when to go to bed. Why, it's a gambler's paradise!"

"You're here for a convention!"

"Yeah. I suppose I really ought to get around to some of the meetings pretty soon now," Lou said with a frown. "But I've been having so much fun, there just hasn't been time." His face brightened suddenly. "Hey, man, they've got every kind of game here you can imagine, haven't they? I mean, I like to gamble a little, just now and then, you know—poker, blackjack, the horses—strictly for small stakes. But they got things here I've only read about, like in that James Bond story, **Casino Royale.** Roulette tables, I mean. You ever play roulette?"

Mark Evans shook his head. "No percentage in it. The odds against winning are too great."

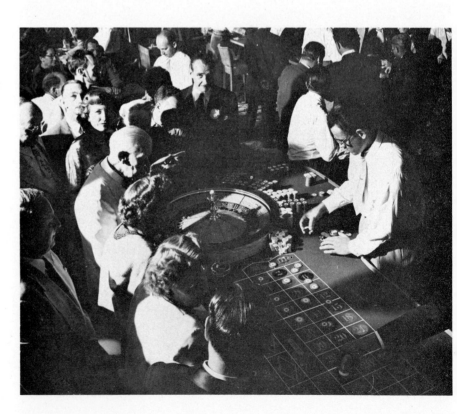

''Whatta ya mean, too great?'' Lou demanded almost hostilely, leading Mark toward one of the roulette tables nearby. ''See—36 numbers, half of them red, half black. You put a dollar chip on any one of them, and they spin the ball around the wheel. If the little ball drops into your number, the house pays you back 35 to 1. That's pretty good odds, isn't it?''

Mark groaned inwardly. ''You forget the two green zeros at the top of the board, Lou. There are really 38 numbers, not 36. If you put a dollar down on all the numbers, it would cost you $38 a game. And you'd win back only $35, no matter what number came up. Over the long haul, you'd lose $3 each time the wheel spun, because the odds are against you.''

''Yeah, but if you pick a lucky number, and you put a dollar on it 10 times in a row, and it hits twice, then you've won $70 and it cost you only $10. You can quit a big winner.''

''If you quit. In the long run, it doesn't matter whether you play all 38 numbers once, or one number 38 times—you're going to spend $38 to win $35. Because your number is going to win just once in 38 times—on the average.''

''But look at that fat man over there with the big diamond ring on his pinkie. He's got a stack of chips in front of him that would choke a mule. He's bound to be making money on the roulette wheel.''

''The only way you make money in Las Vegas is to open your own casino, Lou. That man may be winning now, but if he plays long enough, he'll lose. Because the odds are against him.''

Lou shook his head. ''I know you may be right in theory, Mark, but look at that man's stack of chips. Maybe he's got a secret system or something. Maybe he knows what number's going to come up next.''

Mark was beginning to understand why the casinos made so much money. ''Lou, old man, if that wheel is honest—and out here, they almost always are—there's no way in hell that you or anybody else can make money at roulette if you play long enough.''

''Well, how the hell can you win at this game, anyway?''

Mark thought a moment. ''The only way I know of is to sit for hours and keep a record of each number that comes up. Sometimes the wheel does get out of balance—it gets biased toward one number, let's say 23. Out of 38,000 spins, 23 ought to come up 1,000 times. So should every other number on the board, including the two zeros, because 1,000 is the mean, or average, expectancy for all the numbers.''

''You mean, you keep track of 38,000 spins and then you plot the results on a kind of graph,'' Lou said, nodding.

''Right. If some number like 23 comes up 1,001 times, that's just chance. Even if 23 comes up 1,100 times, that might be chance too. But if it comes up 2000 or 3000 times, then it might not be chance at all. Then maybe the wheel is out of balance; maybe there's something unusual or special about number 23.''

Lou got excited. ''So after you record 38,000 spins, and you draw your graph with 1,000 as the average, then you look at the actual outcomes. If one number like 23 is way out at the tail end of the graph . . .''

''Two or 3 standard deviations from the mean,'' Mark interjected.

''. . . then you've got a statistically reliable result and you bet on it. Right?''

''Absolutely. You may not know why 23 is better than the other numbers, but the graph tells you it's a winner. So you go with the odds, and you hope that the casino doesn't get wise to the fact that they've got an imperfect roulette wheel till you make a little money off it. As soon as the casino owners guess, of course, they'll take the wheel out of play and have it worked on.''

Lou took a free drink from a cocktail waitress. His hand trembled slightly as he sipped the drink. ''Well, Mark, you're studying statistics and all that stuff, so I guess you ought to know. But it does seem you've neglected one important thing. Which is to say, the human factor. Man, when I get hot, I get really hot. I mean, I win big. It's like I've got some power over the cards, or the horses, or maybe even the roulette wheel. What do you have to say about that?''

''Lou, if you gamble to have fun, then you can just charge your losses off as entertainment expenses, same as you would a night on the town. You can follow your hunches, and enjoy your gut reactions. Maybe you'll win, but mostly you'll lose. But if you gamble for money—if you absolutely have to win—then you hunt for situations in which the odds are in your favor—for results that are 2 or 3 standard deviations from the mean in your direction.''

It was obvious that Mark's answer didn't satisfy Lou Hudson. His bloodshot eyes opened wide. ''But man, I'm a special case! I mean, I get these streaks when I'm hot as hell. How do you explain the power I have over the cards when I've got a streak going?''

''Lou, how much money do you have?''

''Me? Well, to tell the truth, I'm pretty near broke right now.''

''And you've been gambling all your life. If you have all that power, how come you aren't a big winner?''

''Well,'' Lou said, taking a big gulp of his drink, ''I've been down on my luck lately. But just wait until tomorrow. I'm gonna bounce right back with a big killing. I got that special feeling, you see . . .''

Mark groaned aloud. ''Lou, friend, if your insurance company sold policies the way you play cards, they'd be out of business in a year or so. They sell life insurance to a thousand men aged 20, let's say. From past experience, your company knows that a few of those men are going to die before they're 21, a few more before they're 30, but most of them are going to still be alive when they're 65. Your company uses its past experience as a kind of comparison factor, the same way a psychologist would use an untreated group of subjects in an experiment as a 'control group.' Your company doesn't know which of those 1,000 men are going to die, or who's going to live—and they don't really care, I reckon. But they look at the big picture, and they figure the percentages, and then they set the prices on the policies to reflect the odds. When you sell a man a policy, he may die the next week or he may live to be a hundred. But when you figure it over a thousand policies, it all averages out and the money rolls in. Statistics is a cold, hard science. But if you figure the odds and play the percentages, you seldom go broke.''

''Speaking of that,'' Lou said in a hoarse voice, his eyes beginning to water a bit, ''you wouldn't happen to have a little extra cash on you, would you? Just a temporary loan, you know, until my luck turns good again.''

Mark shook his head. ''Sorry, man. Students just don't have much to spare these days. But what's the matter? Aren't you selling very many policies?''

Lou's bloodshot eyes filled with tears. ''Oh, I sell a few. But the money always seems to go out faster than it comes in. Betty's pretty disturbed about it, I suspect. She says that I've got a neurosis, that I'm a compulsive gambler. And she ought to know, her being a psychiatric social worker. You're a psychologist, Mark. Do you think I'm neurotic?''

Mark sighed. ''I'm just a grad student, Lou, and there's lots of things I don't know yet. What do you think?''

''I think I got a problem, man. I mean, I hurt. Deep down inside, I hurt real bad. Man, you gotta help me. What can I do to get rid of the pain, Mark? What can I do?''

(Continued on page 601.)

There's an old saying that "knowledge is power." Sometimes we study the world and try to figure out what makes things go. But as soon as we discover some significant relationships about the things we study, we're likely to put this information to use in some way.

At other times, when we're faced with a practical problem, we try out something new. If it seems to work for us, we may sit down and attempt to figure out why the technique worked—so we can use it again, perhaps more effectively. In either case, we're trying to convert knowledge into power.

We began the last chapter with a "knowledge" question—"What makes people do the crazy, wonderful things that they do?" We found that there was no simple answer to that question; psychological experiences, it turns out, are for the most part multi-determined. Behavior is always influenced by biological, intra-psychic, and environmental factors. To neglect any of these factors diminishes our understanding of the complexity and the very human-ness of people.

In this chapter we ask a "power" question—"How do you change or cure abnormal behavior once you understand why it occurs?" As you might guess, the answer to this puzzler depends in large part on the viewpoint or theory that one has about the causes of the abnormal condition. The more restricted our knowledge of the subject matter, the more restricted our power to change things is likely to be.

In many primitive parts of the world, for instance, people still believe in the "devil theory" of mental illness. Crazy people are thought to be *possessed* (or at least affected) by devils—outside spirits that take over a person's mental functioning. These psychic demons may find their way to the afflicted individual by chance, or perhaps as a divine punishment for some sin. Or it may be that the individual has offended a "witch," someone with the power to lay a curse or to force the devils into a person's mind. Let us look at some examples of the "devil theory" in action before we discuss more modern approaches to the problem of curing mental illness.

PRIMITIVE APPROACHES TO MENTAL ILLNESS

The Cree Eskimos and Ojibwa Indians of Canada occasionally suffer from a psychosis known as *witigo* (°), or devil-caused cannibalism. The first symptoms usually are a loss of appetite, vomiting, and diarrhea—as well as the person's morbid fear that he or she has been possessed by a witigo, or witch, who supposedly lives on human flesh. The affected individual becomes withdrawn, brooding, and cannot eat or sleep. The person's family—fearing for their very lives—immediately calls in a "witch doctor" to cast out the witigo by saying magic words or reciting supernatural *incantations* (°). If a witch doctor can't be found in time, however, the psychotic individual may be overwhelmed by the witigo's powers and kill and eat one or more of the members of the family.

In Malaysia, in Southeast Asia, young males occasionally suffer from a different type of possession by devils, called *running amok* (°). At first the man becomes more withdrawn, depressed, and brooding than usual. Then he will suddenly leap to his feet with a blood-curdling scream, pull out a dagger, and begin stabbing anyone or anything in his path. Therapy usually consists of killing the amoker before he can kill you, or keeping everyone out of the amoker's way until he kills himself. The few men who have survived "running amok" have usually stated that they cannot remember what happened, or that the world suddenly turned black and they had to slash their way out of the darkness with a knife. In Scandinavian countries the disorder is called "going berserk." In Spain and Morocco, the name given to this condition is *juramentado*, the Spanish word for "cursed person." In the United States we sometimes call it "homicidal mania."

QUESTION: How does "running amok" seem to compare with the manic-depressive psychosis described in the previous chapter?

As we mentioned in Chapter 18, many Chinese believe that mental and physical disorders result from an imbalance of Yang and Yin, the masculine and feminine "powers" that control the entire spiritual universe. Chinese males occasionally suffer from an odd phobia called *koro*, or *shook yong* (°)—a dismal fear that their penis is about to be sucked up into their stomachs and disappear, causing death and other disappointments. To prevent this disaster, the man will

Witigo (WITT-tee-go). A Cree Eskimo word meaning an "ice witch" who eats human flesh; also the condition of being possessed by such a witch. The Ojibwa (oh-JIB-wah) Indian word for the same condition is *windigo* (WIN-dee-go).

Incantations (inn-kan-TAY-shuns). From the Latin word meaning "to enchant." The use of spells or verbal charms spoken or sung as part of a ritual of magic.

Running amok (uh-MUCK). The Malaysian word *amok* means "furious attack." To run amok is to undergo a murderous frenzy and attack people at random. Similar to the Scandinavian term "going berserk" (burr-SERK) and the Spanish term *juramentado* (whoor-ah-men-TAH-doh).

Shook yong. Also called *koro* (KOH-roh). A phobia occurring in the East Indies and southern China. The disorder consists of a sudden fear that the penis will disappear into the abdomen and lead to death.

Yin and Yang.

hold on to his penis for dear life—and when he tires, will ask for help from relatives and friends. The man's wife may "cure" the attack if she practices oral sex on him immediately, but this treatment is not always successful.

Koro is thought to be caused by a sudden upsurge in the strength of the man's Yin, or femininity. Thus, it can be cured by giving the patient "masculine" medicine containing a strong Yang factor, such as powdered rhinoceros horn. If this therapy fails, the Chinese have devised a special clasp that holds the penis out from the body mechanically.

On the Pacific island of Borneo, a similar disease affects women—who fear that their breasts and genitalia are being pulled up into their bodies. Therapy in Borneo often consists of asking a witch doctor to remove the curse—presumably laid on the woman by a "witch" jealous of the woman's physical beauty.

QUESTION: **How would Freud explain *witigo, juramentado,* and *koro?***

FOUR ISSUES CONCERNING PSYCHOTHERAPY

Even in the United States—where most of us no longer believe in witches, demons, and evil spirits—our therapies almost always stem from theories of what causes human behavior (and, of course, our theories are affected by what therapies we find of value). If we see an organic psychosis as being due *primarily* to physical causes, we tend to treat the patient with physical measures, such as drugs and surgery. If we see a neurosis as being due *primarily* to a disruption of the normal flow of psychic energies, we use psychoanalysis to help bring id and ego back into balance. If we assume that deviant behavior is *primarily* the consequence of inappropriate rewards and punishments, we might prescribe behavioral therapy or otherwise attempt to alter the person's social environment.

In this chapter we will discuss all these special forms of therapy, and the theories that give rise to the treatments. In our attempts to evaluate the various forms of therapy, however, we will have to raise several pertinent issues:

1. How successful is the therapy? That is, what is its "cure rate?" Would the patient have recovered anyhow, even if we hadn't done anything? Would a "witch doctor," or someone using a different form of therapy, have done as well? In short, does the therapy make a *significant difference* in helping the patient? Is it a valid form of treatment?
2. Assuming that the therapy does make a significant difference, how reliable is it? Does it work all the time, or just occasionally? Is it effective with all sorts of patients, or does it succeed better with some than with others?
3. What are the side effects? What else happens to the patient when we apply the therapy? Is the "cure" sometimes worse than the disease?
4. And cutting across all these issues is the basic question: "What do we mean by *cure?* How shall we define improvement, and just as important, how shall we measure it?"

We will have much more to say about these issues as we discuss the three main types of psychotherapy. We will also find it all too customary for therapists of opposing views to call each other "witch doctors," and to accuse each other of using "black magic" rather than "scientific magic."

PHYSIOLOGICAL THERAPIES

Two centuries ago, when the "demon theory" was the accepted explanation of most forms of psychosis, the therapy of choice was *punishment.* The belief then was that if you would just whip a patient vigorously enough, you could "beat the devil" out of the person. The fact that many patients did improve after whippings

A detail of a Hogarth engraving of Bedlam.

was evidence enough to support the validity of the theory—just as the fact that the number 23 on the roulette table occasionally comes up two or three times in a row is evidence enough to convince some gamblers that they have some "magical control" over the roulette ball. It was not until scientific investigations suggested that the "cure rate" for unbeaten patients was higher than for those who were beaten that we finally hung up the whip in our lunatic asylums. Whether our present forms of psychotherapy are all that much more effective than "beating the devil" out of lunatics is a point much debated today in psychology.

As we suggested in the last chapter, the organic psychoses do seem directly related to damage to the central nervous system or to genetic causes. Perhaps for that reason, many of the therapies used with organic psychotics are explicitly *physiological*—the three main types being artificially induced seizures, psycho-surgery, and drugs.

Electro-shock Therapy

In 1935 an Hungarian psychiatrist named Ladislaus J. Meduna noted an odd fact—very few of the schizophrenics he worked with were also epileptics. Without considering alternative hypotheses too seriously, Meduna concluded that seizures might somehow *prevent* schizophrenia. If he could induce epileptic-type seizures in his schizophrenic patients, he reasoned, he might be able to cure them of their problems. As a test, he injected several of his patients with drugs that caused seizures. Many patients did show some improvement, but an alarming number of them were severely injured or died from the treatment. Others showed intense apprehension about the unpleasantness of the experience. Meduna's treatment was abandoned as "barbaric," but the idea lived on.

QUESTION: If therapy is extremely painful—be it whippings or convulsions—might some patients "get well" in order to avoid further treatment?

Retrograde amnesia (RETT-troh-grade am-KNEE-see-uh). An amnesia or forgetting that occurs when one is shocked or hit on the head. The forgetting is retrograde in that it goes back from the time of the accident instead of forward from the time of the accident. If you were hit on the head at 9:30 and suffered retrograde amnesia, you would forget what had happened to you from 9 until 9:30, but remember what happened from 9:30 onward. Retrograde amnesia induced by shock or an accident usually wipes out memories of what happened to the organism up to 30 minutes prior to the trauma. Apparently it takes the brain about 30 minutes to "consolidate" memories—that is, to tuck an experience away in Long-term Memory after an event occurs. Anything that interrupts the physiological consolidation process may cause the items to be lost from memory.

Extinguished. S-R (stimulus-response) bonds are weakened or broken through extinction training. In respondent (classical) conditioning, the CS (conditioned stimulus) is presented without being paired with the old UCS (unconditioned stimulus), or the CS is hooked to a new UCS. In operant conditioning, extinction occurs when a response is no longer reinforced. See Chapter 5.

In 1938 two Italian psychiatrists, Ugo Cerletti and L. Bini, began using electrical current rather than drugs to induce seizures. This electro-convulsive therapy (or ECT, as it is often called) is applied in the following way: The patient is given a muscle relaxant or "downer" and strapped to a padded bed in order to reduce the possibility of the patient's breaking an arm or leg during the seizure. Then electrodes are applied to the patient's head, and a fairly strong but brief electrical current is passed directly through the person's brain. Typically the patient loses consciousness immediately, before any pain can be felt. The patient's muscles become rigid for about 10 seconds, then the person goes into convulsions much as an epileptic might. The convulsions last for a minute or so. The patient remains unconscious for up to 30 minutes and typically appears drowsy or confused for many hours thereafter. Because seizures induce *retrograde amnesia* (°) (*see* Chapter 17), the patient usually cannot remember the shock or the events immediately preceding it. The ECT may be repeated two or three times a week for a period of many weeks or months—or until the patient shows some recovery.

There is considerable argument over the effectiveness of ECT. It does seem to be of help in bringing a severely depressed patient back to normal, but anti-depressant drugs and other forms of psychotherapy may accomplish the same end. Excessive use of ECT can lead to damage both to the brain and to the patient's heart and lungs. What does seem clear is that ECT is of proven value only with depressed psychotics or neurotics. Meduna's original observations about schizophrenia and epilepsy were based on a "biased sample"—we now know that the incidence of epilepsy is about the same among schizophrenics as it is among everyone else. There are very few well-controlled studies comparing the effectiveness of ECT with other forms of therapy. But recent studies by Canadian psychiatrists suggest that its usefulness even with depressive patients may be over-rated. The use of ECT seems to be declining in the United States.

Sleep Therapy

Russian psychiatrists have rejected ECT but utilize weak electrical currents applied to the skull to keep psychotic patients asleep for periods ranging up to a month or more. As we mentioned in Chapter 15, the Russians believe that insane behavior is learned by Pavlovian conditioning. Prolonged sleep is supposed to allow these inappropriate conditioned responses to become *extinguished* (°) rather painlessly. The theory is an interesting one, but the scientific data do not as yet give the theory much solid support.

Psycho-surgery

Galen's humoral theory of personality (*see* Chapter 23) led early Greek and Roman physicians to believe that insanity was caused by an imbalance or an excess of the four humors in the patient's brain. The treatment of choice in those days involved opening up the skulls of patients to let the abnormal humors drain out. During the Middle Ages, physicians also occasionally cut holes in the heads of lunatics to permit "poisonous gases" (or "devils") to escape.

In 1891, a Swiss psychiatrist named Gottlieb Burckhardt claimed that removing part of a manic psychotic's cortex successfully calmed the patient down—but similar operations performed elsewhere failed to achieve the same result. But the notion of removing a psychosis by removing a portion of the "diseased brain" responsible for the psychosis (psycho-surgery) has always been an attractive one to physicians and surgeons.

As we know from the early chapters in this book, emotional responses are controlled by certain parts of the brain called the "limbic system" (*see* Chapter 4). As Mark and Ervin and many others showed, destroying portions of the temporal lobe of the cortex is sometimes effective in reducing seizure-induced fits of aggressive behavior in brain-damaged patients. Portions of the thalamus and the frontal lobes are also involved in emotional reactions. In 1935 John F. Fulton and C.E. Jacobsen demonstrated that surgery on the frontal lobes had a calming effect on two chimpanzees they were working with. Prior to the operation, the animals reacted to frustration by chasing around their cages, screaming, shaking the bars of the cage, defecating, and attacking anything handy. After the surgery, the animals became placid, calm, and seemingly unaffected by emotional stress and strain.

After learning of the Fulton and Jacobsen demonstration, a Portuguese psychiatrist named Egas Moniz decided that cutting the frontal lobes—*lobotomy* (°)—might help aggressive or hyper-emotional psychotic patients. In 1936 Moniz and his associates reported that lobotomy did seem to be effective with such patients. The operation was introduced to the United States in 1942 by Walter Freeman and his colleagues (Moniz and Freeman later received the Nobel Prize for their work). Other psychiatrists soon reported that cutting the connections between the lower brain centers and the frontal lobes seemed to work just as well.

The question is, of course, "Work as well as what?" Many lobotomy patients do show an improvement after the operation, but many do not; and the fatality rate from the operation may run as high as 4 percent. Well-controlled comparisons of patients given lobotomies and those given other forms of treatment suggest that the operation is neither as effective (valid) nor as reliable as Moniz and Freeman had hoped.

The single form of psycho-surgery that appears to offer much hope today is the temporal lobe operation for aggression—and even that operation is controversial and seems to work only with limited numbers of patients who also suffer from additional brain damage.

Drug Therapy

Various chemical compounds have been reported as being effective in treating some types of psychological abnormalities. Dilantin and various *barbiturates* (°) can help control many types of epileptic seizures—as can cannabis.

For many centuries medical practitioners in India have given tense or manic patients a drug made from the snake root plant because it seemed to calm them down. We now call this drug *reserpine* (°). In 1953 the Indian physician R.A. Hakim reported that reserpine seemed to be effective with some schizophrenics. When the noted U.S. scientist Nathan S. Kline tried reserpine here in 1954, he stated that it brought about marked improvement in 86 percent of the schizophrenic patients he tried it with. At about the same time another drug, *chlorpromazine* (°), was discovered in France; it had similar calming or tranquilizing properties. Reserpine and chlorpromazine were the first of the tranquilizers now used widely with mental patients (*see* Chapter 3).

While no one is quite sure why the tranquilizers appear to be effective, there is some evidence suggesting that they reduce the amount of serotonin in the patient's brain. As you may recall from Chapter 3, *serotonin* (°) is a chemical found in the brain that appears to act like a super-transmitter. As we noted earlier, drugs that cause hallucinations may do so by increasing the amount of serotonin in the brain. In 1973 UCLA psychiatrist Edward Ritvo reported finding abnormal quantities of serotonin in the brains of autistic children—that is, children who suffer from a type of schizophrenia. Ritvo believes that these children inherited abnormal brains that produce too much serotonin—hence drug therapy should be particularly effective with them.

Beginning in the mid-1970's, a drug called "lithium carbonate" has been used with varying degrees of success with patients displaying manic-depressive symp-

Lobotomy (lobe-OTT-toe-mee). A surgical technique involving cutting the nerve pathways that run to any one of the four cerebral lobes. Usually means "frontal lobotomy," or the cutting of the connections between the thalamus (THALL-uh-muss) and the frontal lobe.

Barbiturates (bar-BITT-your-ates). Drugs, such as phenobarbital, that reduce activity in the central nervous system; hence, "downers," or sleeping pills.

Reserpine (ree-SIR-peen). From the word "serpent." So-named because this tranquilizer was first discovered in the snake root plant in India.

Chlorpromazine (klor-PRO-muh-zeen). A tranquilizing drug that appears to reduce fear and anxiety by reducing firing rates in those parts of the brain that process fear responses.

Serotonin (sair-oh-TONE-in). A chemical found in the brain and elsewhere in the body that, in large doses, seems to cause hallucinations.

Resident. After completing four years of medical school, and obtaining their M.D. degrees, most medical students elect to continue their studies by becoming interns or residents in some hospital or clinic. Residents treat patients, perform research, and learn about their chosen fields of interest in depth before going out to practice on their own. A psychiatric residency may last 4 or more years; thus, before psychiatrists go into private practice and open their own offices, they may have had 9 or 10 years of schooling *after* completing their B.A. or B.S. degrees.

Strait-jackets. Also spelled straight-jackets. Canvas coats used to bind the body, but particularly the arms, so that a manic patient can't do harm. Rigid, inflexible educational techniques may likewise be considered "mental strait-jackets."

toms. A very few therapists have claimed that lithium carbonate is so potent a treatment for the affective disorders that anyone who experiences even mild depression might consider using the drug. However, research suggests that this viewpoint is overly optimistic. To begin with, lithium carbonate seems to work only with those patients who swing back and forth between mania and deep depression; it has little or no proven effectiveness with patients who suffer from depression alone (or mania alone). Second, not all manic-depressive patients are helped by lithium carbonate. Third, the drug is a dangerous chemical that must always be administered under the close supervision of a knowledgeable physician. As evidence of the dangers involved, during 1975 several patients in the United States died from overdoses of lithium carbonate. We might also note that the drug has no proven usefulness in treating schizophrenia or any psychological problem other than manic-depressive psychoses.

Scarcely a month goes by that the popular press doesn't serve up a juicy story about some new drug that seems to offer "miracle cures" for many types of psychological problems. Most of the reports need to be taken with a grain of salt, however. First, chemicals *by themselves* seldom solve mental and social/behavioral problems. Even if the drug "cures" some underlying biological dysfunction, the patient will usually still need help in adjusting to life. Second, not all of the drug research has been as well planned and nicely controlled as we might wish. Perhaps a case history will demonstrate these points.

Mendel's Research on Psychotherapy

Werner Mendel is Professor of Psychiatry at the University of Southern California School of Medicine. He was also clinical director of the Psychiatric Adult In-patient Services at the Los Angeles County-USC Medicine Center—the only public facility for acutely disturbed psychotic patients in Los Angeles County. Like all psychiatrists, Mendel is a medical doctor. After receiving his M.D. degree at Stanford he served a year as a psychiatric *resident* (°) at St. Elizabeth's Hospital in Washington, D.C. Thereafter, Mendel spent several years as a resident at the Menninger Foundation in Topeka, Kansas, one of the best psychiatric training facilities in the world. Once his training at Menninger's was complete, Mendel was qualified to call himself a psychiatrist. Next, he moved to Los Angeles and studied for several years at the Southern California Psychoanalytic Institute and completed his training as a psychoanalyst. He is an instructor at the Institute. After moving to Los Angeles, Mendel continued a series of experiments on mental illness which he had begun as a resident in Washington, D.C.

St. Elizabeth's Hospital was the largest of all the U.S. government facilities dealing with psychiatric patients. When Mendel arrived there he was put in charge of a ward of Spanish-speaking patients, most of whom came from Puerto Rico or the Virgin Islands. All of these patients were diagnosed as being hostile, aggressive individuals; some were considered homicidal. They were all considered so dangerous to themselves and others that they were confined to cells or were physically restrained in *strait-jackets* (°). Mendel states that he needed two large attendants to protect him whenever he tried to treat his patients. These patients were put together in one ward because they spoke no English; since Mendel spoke no Spanish, there was little he could do in the way of therapy.

Luckily, it was just at this time that news of the apparent effectiveness of reserpine spread to the United States. The authorities at St. Elizabeth's decided to test the drug. To make the test scientifically valid, they used the double-blind method. That is, they selected certain wards whose patients would be given reserpine. But they needed some comparison groups to make sure that the changes they noted in the patients given reserpine were due to the drug and not just to the fact that the patients had been given pills. So they selected an equal number of

Werner Mendel.

wards whose patients were given pills that contained sugar rather than reserpine. The pills looked the same no matter what was in them. The experiment was double-blind in that neither the patients nor the doctors in charge of the wards knew which drug the patients on any particular ward were actually receiving. The experiment ran for several months, during which any improvement the patients made was recorded as carefully as possible. Mendel's ward of Spanish-speaking patients was one of those chosen for the experiment.

Mendel reports that, almost as soon as the study began, he was sure that his patients were receiving the reserpine—for they all calmed down dramatically. Within a short period of time they were so tranquil that many of them could be released from restraint. Mendel no longer needed to have two "body guards" go with him as he visited the ward. Mendel was convinced that a psychiatric revolution had begun.

Then the experiment ended and the results were announced. To Mendel's amazement, he learned that his ward had been one of the "controls," and that his patients had all received sugar pills instead of reserpine. Yet they had shown marked improvement! It occurred to Mendel that, when the experiment began, he had unconsciously changed his attitude toward the patients. Convinced that they were becoming more peaceful, he then treated them as if they were improving. And they did improve—not because of the drug but because of the different way in which he responded to them.

Years later, when he took over at the L.A. County Hospital, Mendel found that about 80 percent of the patients were being given drugs of one kind or another. He soon cut the medication rate to less than 20 percent—and increased the apparent cure rate while doing so. Mendel believes that drugs can be of great help in some forms of psychiatric treatment, but that drugs must almost always be accompanied by other forms of therapy if the patient is to experience any lasting improvement.

The St. Elizabeth's experiment points up one dramatic difficulty in evaluating psychiatric research—the good results that an experimenter often obtains may be due to chance factors, or to things that the scientist failed to control. Drugs are always given in a social setting; the patient's attitude—and the scientist's—may be more influential than the chemical effects on the patient's body. Or if a surgeon communicates to the patient the notion that psycho-surgery will surely solve the person's problems, the patient may very well get better after the operation—for all the "wrong" reasons.

INTRA-PSYCHIC THERAPY

Most personality theorists believe that abnormal thoughts and behaviors are mere symptoms of an underlying *dysfunction* (°) in an individual's basic personality. To "cure" the symptom without handling the underlying problem would, therefore, be as senseless as giving aspirin to a yellow-fever patient. The drug might decrease the fever symptom, it is true, but aspirin won't kill the virus that is really responsible for the disease. Removing the fever with aspirin might delude the patient into thinking a cure had occurred, when the patient in fact was still carrying the virus. A "deeper" form of therapy is necessary to kill the virus. Intra-psychic therapy almost always focuses on making "deep changes" in the structure or the functioning of the individual's core personality—the belief being that the symptomatic behaviors will disappear naturally as the cure progresses.

If you ever have need for intra-psychic therapy, you would seem to have your choice between two major types: (1) those methods that are primarily designed to help you understand your present self by uncovering what has gone wrong in your past; and (2) those techniques that focus on future goals in order to help you change your present mode of existence. (As we will see, the difference between

Dysfunction (diss-FUNK-shun). An abnormal functioning of the mind or body. *Dys* is a Greek word meaning "in pieces."

Transference (trans-FURR-ents). In psychoanalysis, the patient is encouraged to transfer to the analyst the emotions and attitudes the patient has concerning the "power figures" in the patient's life—chiefly his or her mother and father. That is, the patient is asked to act toward the analyst as the patient does toward the mother and father. The analyst, by observing these reactions, can often determine what the patient's underlying intra-psychic problems are. See Chapter 5. Some of the transferred emotions may be warm and loving; others may be cold, hateful, or angry.

these two types may be more a matter of emphasis than anything else; highly successful therapists appear to treat their patients in similar ways despite the fact that their theories may be quite different.)

Psychoanalysts usually follow the first method. That is, they concentrate on discovering traumas that occurred during psycho-sexual development in order to help a patient set his or her "mental house" in order. Psychoanalytic theory suggests that, if you complete your analysis and become a *fully functioning individual*, you should be able to handle future problems with little difficulty. The humanists, on the other hand, mostly follow the second method. They hope to make you aware both of your present condition and of your ultimate goals, so that you can shorten the distance between the two and hence move toward self-actualization.

Psychoanalytic Therapy

There is no single accepted and proved method of psychoanalytic treatment—it varies widely according to the patient's needs and the analyst's skills and beliefs. Freud compared analysis to a chess game in which only the opening moves could be standardized—thereafter endless variations may develop.

In general, however, the technique is designed to achieve a basic reconstruction of the patient's personality. The analyst achieves this end in two ways: (1) by encouraging the patient to build up an emotional relationship, or *transference* (°), with the analyst; and (2) by getting the patient to freely associate about past thoughts and experiences. By interpreting these free associations, the analyst can often discover both the content and the dynamics of the patient's unconscious mental processes.

But the task is not an easy one; psychoanalysis typically takes from two to five years to complete, and the 50-minute-long therapy sessions are usually held three to five times a week. The most successful patients seem to be between 15 and 50 years of age. They must be bright, verbal, self-motivated, and willing to cooperate with the therapist. Although psychoanalysis is occasionally used with individuals classed as "psychotic," the usual patient is a mildly disturbed or neurotic individual.

Most psychoanalysts are males. Although Freud insisted that the medical degree was not necessary for the practice of psychoanalysis, more than 90 percent of the analysts practicing today are physicians who have gone through psychiatric internships and residencies before becoming candidates at a psychoanalytic institute. During the several years of training required for graduation, the candidate undergoes a "training analysis" to make himself or herself aware of personal problems that might prejudice analytic interpretation of a patient's problems. As Freud noted in 1910, "Every analyst's achievement is limited by what his own complexes and resistances permit."

Transference If you decided to undergo psychoanalysis, you would probably find your doctor in a private office completely cut off from the outside world. He might well ask you to lie down on his couch and then sit out of sight, just beyond your head, where he could take notes and observe your facial and bodily reactions. He would ask you to free associate—that is, to say anything and everything that came to mind. But he would try to direct your attention to your inward world of feeling, emotion, and fantasy. In a variety of subtle ways, he would encourage you to "transfer" to him many of your intense emotional feelings; in a sense, he would become a father figure on whom you could rely and trust.

Free Association Free association is the basic game plan of most forms of psychoanalysis. Freud believed that everything you do and say and think has a cause, and that trivial and apparently meaningless statements often mask deep-seated emotional conflicts. The more you cut yourself off from conscious control—the more you let your id speak in terms uncensored by your ego—the more easily the buried problems can be brought to the surface—that is, to conscious awareness. To help matters along, the analyst might ask you to give up all outside pleasures or interests that might tend to distract you from the psychoanalytic process. Freud believed that physical gratifications such as smoking could drain off basic instinctual energy that could be utilized in therapy; he also felt that learning how to handle such deprivations could increase your tolerance for the frustrations that occur in real-life situations.

Interpretation   During the course of the treatment, your analyst would interpret your thoughts, feelings, and actions in light of psychoanalytic theory. If inner blocks keep you from expressing important (repressed) material, the analyst might ask you to recall your dreams and talk about them. Freud believed that many psychic conflicts express themselves in fantasy, particularly when the patient's defenses are down (as during dreaming). He felt it was not so much the actual content of the dream that was important—rather, it was what the dream *symbolized* that must be discovered. For Freud, dream analysis was a "royal road" to the patient's unconscious and to the real significance of the patient's childhood experiences.

During psychoanalysis, you would probably build up a rather strong dependency on your analyst, for you would have bared your deepest feelings to him. As you gained knowledge about yourself, and as your symptoms began to disappear, the analyst would start to dissolve this dependency or transference relationship. Many modern analysts believe that the handling of the transference is the key to successful analysis. By becoming a father figure, the analyst encourages you to react toward him as you did (perhaps inappropriately) toward significant figures in your childhood. But after he has guided you back toward mental health, the analyst must help cut these emotional ties in order for you to function successfully on your own.

Psychoanalysis takes so long—and there are so few analysts available—that only a tiny fraction of the people who need help ever undergo this process. Most patients settle for briefer, less intensive types of treatment. However, psychoanalytic theory has influenced almost all other forms of intra-psychic therapy. Most psychiatrists have not taken psychoanalytic training, but they all know their Freud.

Clinical psychologists typically finish their graduate studies (and obtain their Ph.D. degrees) in five or six years. The clinical psychologist may ask you to sit in a chair rather than lie on a couch, but the clinician often makes the same kind of psychological "interpretations" as does the psychiatrist-psychoanalyst. Any form of therapy that concentrates on explaining the present in terms of past experience and unconscious motivations owes a large debt to Sigmund Freud.

Humanistic Therapy

Freud grew up in Austria, a land of kings and emperors who possessed "divine rights" that their subjects dared not question. Austrian fathers typically claimed the same privileges—when the man of the family spoke, the children listened and obeyed. Perhaps it is understandable, then, that in psychoanalysis the fatherly analyst often sets the goals of therapy and then urges the patient onward.

But times have changed. Like the United States, Austria is now a democracy. In democratic societies citizens are expected to help choose their own destinies and work toward them. Modern humanistic therapists reject the "divine right" of the therapist to determine what is mentally healthy for the patient. In humanistic therapy the patient rather than the therapist is king.

Eclectic (eck-KLECK-tick). From the Greek word meaning "to pick out or select." An eclectic is someone who picks out the best of several different theories or viewpoints.

Scrutinized (SCREW-tin-ized). From the Latin word *scrutari*, which in olden days meant "to search through the trash or garbage," presumably for something worth saving. To scrutinize is to examine anything carefully, piece by piece or part by part.

Humanistic psychologists—such as Carl Rogers and Abraham Maslow—emphasize the *conscious* determinants of behavior. All human beings are presumed to have a positive drive toward good mental health. The environment may shape us into bad habits of thought, feelings, and action; but our "innate motivation to improve" will win out if given a chance.

The humanistic therapist does not look too deeply into a person's unconscious nor too far back into the person's past—for the present and future are considered much more important than events long since forgotten. Therapy, then, should consist primarily of making the individual aware of his or her present state of functioning, according to Maslow and Rogers. Therapy should focus on how the person sees himself or herself now, how others perceive the person, and what "ideal state" the person would like to reach. Once the client has understood all these things clearly, the therapist need only provide the client with objective feedback about whatever progress the client is making toward the "self ideal."

Client-centered Therapy In Carl Roger's "client-centered therapy," the client determines the goals of treatment and the speed at which these goals will be met. Like most humanists, Rogers is loath to impose his own standards or values on his clients. Instead, Rogers tries to provide a "psychological mirror" in which the client can see himself or herself. Theoretically, the client will use this reflected information to achieve whatever changes are necessary to meet these standards.

If you went to see a "client-centered therapist," you would most likely find a clinical psychologist who had taken the Ph.D. rather than a medical degree. You would sit in a chair rather than lie on a couch, and you would not be asked to give up all your outside activities during the six months or so that therapy might take. The therapist would try to be warm, human, concerned, and supportive—and would seldom give advice or offer suggestions about what you ought to do.

As you talked about your problems, the therapist would frequently restate what you had said—reflecting back your own thoughts in slightly different form. In this way the therapist would provide you with an objective "mirror" of your own mental functioning.

By giving you "unconditional positive regard"—that is, by refusing to make value judgments about your emotions and perceptions—the therapist would hope to build a relationship of trust and affection with you. Only under such non-punishing conditions, Rogers believes, could you build sufficient courage to see yourself as you really are. This same supportive atmosphere is needed to help you determine what your goals really are—to decide what *you* want to become, not what you think the world wants you to become. But once you can see yourself objectively, and know where you want to go, your own internal motivation will push you toward a better state of mental health and acceptance of yourself.

Most of the people practicing intra-psychic therapy in the United States today are neither "pure" Freudians nor "pure" Rogerians. Rather, therapists tend to be *eclectic* (°)—a fancy term that means they make use of whatever psychological techniques seem to work best for them and their clients.

The Effects of Intra-psychic Therapy

Many factors make it difficult to evaluate the effectiveness of psychotherapy scientifically. Science deals with objective events, things that can be readily measured. But by its very nature, intra-psychic therapy concerns itself with changes that occur inside a person's mind—changes that can seldom be seen or *scrutinized* (°) under a microscope. The success rates of various forms of treatment, then, must always be considered in terms of what changes therapists hope to achieve.

Some psychoanalysts evaluate their treatment almost solely in terms of the amount of insight the patient gains about his or her own "hang-ups" and the changes that occur in the patient's basic personality. Since the analyst is the only person who has worked through these problems with the patient, the analyst may feel that he is the only person qualified to judge whether a "cure" has taken place. The fact that the analyst could not demonstrate objectively to independent observers that the patient was, in fact, "improved" might not matter too much to such a therapist. Although this position has its merits, other psychoanalysts are willing to use less subjective measures of improvement—such as modifications in the patient's overt behavior and the gradual disappearance of neurotic or psychotic symptoms. At least these changes can be observed and agreed upon by people other than the analyst himself.

If we take an analyst's subjective impressions as our guide, then psychoanalysis would seem to lead to "full recovery" in 35–40 percent of the clients, with an additional 15–20 percent of the patients showing noticeable improvement. If we apply the more objective measure of "symptom removal," we find that the improvement rate is much lower—30 percent or less.

In the humanistic therapies the patient usually determines whether the therapy was successful or not. Rogers does have objective tests that measure changes in the client's *perceptions* of his or her progress, and the tests do seem to be reliable; but the validity of using the client's subjective impressions as an index of improvement remains in some doubt. The claimed "cure rate" for humanistic therapy is usually in the neighborhood of 75 percent or so.

Eysenck's 1952 Report In recent years, the behavioral psychologists in particular have leveled strong criticisms against the "unscientific ways" in which the effectiveness of psychotherapy is usually determined. Immediately after the Second World War, behaviorist H.J. Eysenck investigated several thousand cases of mentally disturbed servicemen and women in British hospitals. Eysenck reported in 1952 that the overall improvement rate among those patients given psychoanalytic treatment was about 44 percent. The improvement rate for patients given any other form of psychotherapy (eclectic treatment) was about 64 percent. Several hundred other patients received no psychotherapy at all; their physical ailments were treated as necessary, but they were given no psychological therapy. The improvement rate among these untreated patients was about 72 percent. These data led some scientists to compare psychoanalysis with "witch doctoring," and to suggest that psychoanalysis might actually *retard* the patient's progress.

As you might imagine, the psychoanalysts did not take such comments lightly. They pointed out that Eysenck's criteria for improvement were considerably different than their own, since the British psychologist focused on easy-to-measure behavior changes. Eysenck ignored all of the basic alterations in the patient's personality that are the stated goal of most psychoanalytic treatment. The analysts also raised the important issue of patient selection. Some patients are better suited for analysis than others, and the usual feeling is that hospitalized psychotics make the worst clients of all.

In 1953 the American Psychoanalytic Association undertook its own survey of all the people undergoing analytic treatment in the entire United States. Although data were completed on some 3,000 patients by the end of 1954, the analysts could not agree among themselves as to what constituted success. Could one depend on the analyst's own subjective feelings about the progress his patients had made, or should one rely entirely on a more objective *criterion* (°)? When the results of the APA study were finally published in the late 1960's, the only figures reported were for "symptom removal"—a disappointingly low 27 percent. Many well-known psychoanalysts reject the APA study as not coming to grips with the intra-psychic changes that do occur during therapy.

Criterion (cry-TEER-ee-un). From a Greek word meaning "to judge," or "to decide." A criterion is a standard or model or goal on which a decision may be based. The criterion for success in the United States is often making lots of money. The plural of criterion is criteria (cry-TEER-ee-uh).

H.J. Eysenck.

R. Bruce Sloane.

Eysenck's criticisms deserve more careful consideration than we have space for in this chapter, as do the replies of the people he has criticized. We should note, however, that people *made spontaneous recoveries* (°) from mental illness long before we had any real form of therapy to offer them. Eysenck states that the spontaneous recovery rate for untreated neurotics is such that about 45 percent of them recover within a year of the onset of their illness. By the end of the second year, this figure rises to 70 percent; and within five years about 90 percent of all untreated cases are either dramatically improved or "cured." Although we must always keep in mind what we mean by the term "cured," it does seem as if the effectiveness of any form of psychotherapy must be measured against Eysenck's figures on spontaneous recovery.

Scientists have made many attempts to measure the effectiveness of therapy by comparing groups of patients who receive different forms of treatment. Although the results of these experiments have varied widely, there does seem to be one rather uniform trend—the more objectively the improvement is measured, the less effective the standard forms of intra-psychic therapy appear to be.

Sloane's Temple Study One of the best of these studies was performed by psychiatrist R. Bruce Sloane and his associates at the Temple University School of Medicine in Philadelphia. These researchers selected 94 patients suffering from moderately severe neuroses and personality disorders who had come to an out-patient clinic for help. Roughly one-third of the patients were treated with a brief form of psychoanalytic "insight" therapy; another third received behavior therapy; the rest were told that they would have to wait at least four months for help and hence became an untreated control group (relatively speaking).

Sloane or another psychiatrist interviewed each patient before treatment and gave an initial impression of how disturbed the patient was and what symptoms the person showed. The patient was also given several personality tests, including the MMPI (*see* Chapter 23). At the same time, a research assistant interviewed a close friend or relative of the patient to get this person's evaluation of what might be troubling the patient. After the intake interview, the patient was randomly assigned to one of the three groups mentioned above. The assessing psychiatrists did not perform therapy themselves; they merely evaluated the patients before and after treatment.

Patients in the treated groups were given an average of one hour of therapy a week for four months. Patients in the untreated control group were called every few weeks to find out how they were doing, and were encouraged to "hang tight" until a therapist could see them (these calls, of course, were themselves a type of treatment). At the end of four months, all the untreated patients who still wished help were put into therapy.

At the end of the four-month period, the patient was again interviewed by the assessing psychiatrist, who did not know (and was told not to ask) what kind of therapy (if any) the patient had been given. The patient retook the personality tests, and the research assistant once more talked with the close friend or relative to determine what progress this person thought the patient had made. Psychiatric assessments of the patients were also made one year and two years after the experiment began.

Sloane and his associates measured as many different aspects of the therapeutic situation as they could. Some of the tests or assessments they employed were objective, and were aimed at determining success in symptom removal, bettering job performance, improving relationships with others, and so forth. Some of the measures were subjective, having to do with how well the patient liked the therapist (and vice versa), the patient's inner feelings about his or her improvement, the amount of anxiety the patient was experiencing, the perceptions that the interviewing psychiatrist and the patient's friend or relative had about

Spontaneous recovery. Surprisingly enough, people recover from bouts of mental illness without medication—just as people recover from headaches without taking aspirin. The effectiveness of any form of therapy must always be compared with the spontaneous recovery rate—that is, the number of people who recover without treatment.

changes in the patient's emotions and behaviors, and so forth. In addition to these rather specific measures, the assessing psychiatrist, the patient, the friend or relative, and the patient's therapist (in two of the groups) also made what Sloane calls "global evaluations" of the amount of improvement shown by the patient.

The results of this study are both complex and fascinating.

1. Some 80 percent of the patients given either behavior therapy or psychoanalytic treatment showed significant symptom removal, but so did 48 percent of the patients in the no-therapy control group. Thus either type of therapy is better than nothing, but spontaneous recovery did occur in about half the untreated patients.

2. As we noted earlier, Freud believed that anxiety is the hallmark of neurosis, and psychoanalysts typically hold that the reduction of anxiety is a sign of improvement. Both the treated groups showed a significant reduction in anxiety, but the no-therapy patients also improved so much that Sloane and his colleagues conclude that the differences among the groups were not really significant.

3. A frequent complaint made by neurotic patients is that they have trouble keeping a job or in making progress in their careers. At the end of four months of treatment, the behavior therapy patients showed significantly greater improvement in their work situations than did the psychoanalytic or the no-therapy patients. The latter two groups of patients performed about the same.

4. As far as social adjustment was concerned, the behavior therapy and the no-treatment patients showed significant improvement. Those individuals given psychoanalytic therapy did not do as well.

5. The patient's sexual adjustment was rated by the patient, by the therapist, by the close relative or friend, and by the assessing psychiatrist. All three groups of patients demonstrated about the same amount of improvement except when rated by the therapists. The psychoanalytically-oriented therapists gave their patients significantly *lower* ratings of sexual adjustment than did anyone else; the behavior therapists gave their patients significantly *higher* ratings on the sexual adjustment scale than did anyone else. The patients gave themselves significantly higher ratings than did the psychoanalysts. Generally speaking, in most of the subjective ratings, the patients (no matter who treated them) and the behavior therapists were much more optimistic about recovery than were any of the other raters.

6. The "global evaluations" of patient improvement yielded the most marked differences among raters. As judged by the assessing psychiatrists (all of whom had psychoanalytic training), 93 percent of the behavior therapy patients showed improvement, while only 77 percent of the psychoanalytic and 77 percent of the no-therapy patients showed improvement. As judged by the patients themselves, 74 percent of those in the behavior therapy group, 81 percent of those in psychoanalytic treatment, and but 44 percent of those in the no-therapy group felt they had improved. It would seem that those patients denied therapy believed they couldn't possibly have gotten much better without treatment despite the objective evidence to the contrary noted by the assessing psychiatrists.

We might note, in explanation of these findings, that the patients in the two treatment groups probably had quite different notions of what improvement ought to be. As we mentioned earlier, psychoanalysis is an insight therapy, the goal of which is usually to give the person better understanding of his or her mental processes. Behavior therapy is a broader-scale type of treatment, in which self-help and self-improvement in many areas are emphasized. It is possible that the psychoanalytic patients did notice a marked

Empathy (EM-path-thee). From the Greek words meaning "to suffer with." Literally, the ability to project one's own feelings into another being, or the capacity for feeling the projections of someone else.

improvement in their mental processes and, believing this to be the major goal of therapy, rated themselves highly. The assessing psychiatrists, knowing that things like good job performance and healthy social relations are also necessary to survival, downgraded the insight patients because they had in fact shown little improvement in these areas (while the behavior therapy patients had).

7. Additional findings by Sloane and his group were equally interesting. You may recall (*see* Chapter 15) that one of the major objections raised against behavior therapy was that it merely removed symptoms without curing the underlying cause of the neurosis, hence other symptoms would crop up to replace those the therapy had done away with. However, Sloane and his associates found no evidence for symptom substitution in any of the patients in any group. On the contrary, it seemed that when a patient's primary symptoms showed improvement, the patient often spontaneously reported improvement of other minor difficulties as well.

   Another objection brought against behavioral treatment is that it is a "cold and mechanistic way of pushing people around." In fact, the patients in behavioral treatment rated their therapists as being significantly "warmer, more involved, more genuine, and as having greater and more accurate *empathy* (°)" than the insight patients rated their therapists as being.

Psychologists have known for years that any therapist does better with some types of patients than with others. Sloane and his colleagues found that their psychoanalytically-oriented therapists did better with well-educated, middle- or upper-class, verbally fluent patients than with relatively uneducated or verbally passive patients. The behavior therapists did about as well with one type of person as with any other. Perhaps for this reason, none of the patients given behavior therapy got worse, while one or two people in the other two groups showed a marked deterioration over the four-month period.

Data gathered one and two years after therapy had begun tended to confirm the findings made at the end of the initial four months. However, direct comparisons were difficult to make for several reasons. To start with, many patients had dropped out of therapy or had disappeared. Next, all of the "no therapy" patients were put into psychoanalytically-oriented therapy rather than into behavior therapy. Third, those behavior therapy patients who wished to continue after the four months were over were all shifted into insight psychotherapy. (Remember that the psychiatrists in charge of the experiment were trained primarily in psychoanalytic techniques.)

R. Bruce Sloane and his colleagues conclude that

behavior therapy is at least as effective as, and possibly more so than, psychotherapy with the sort of moderately severe neuroses and personality disorders that are typical of clinical populations. This [finding] should help to dispel the impression that behavior therapy is useful only with phobias and restricted "unitary" [simple] problems. In fact, only the behavior therapy group in this study had improved significantly on both the work and the social measures of general adjustment at four months. Behavior therapy is clearly a *generally* useful treatment.

QUESTION: **Research such as Sloane's is sometimes criticized as being unethical because individuals in the control group are denied therapy for a period of time. Given the considerable improvement the untreated patients showed, and the fact that they eventually were given therapy, do you believe this criticism is valid?**

One of the most puzzling aspects of the Sloane study is that the analytically-trained therapists saw *less* improvement in their patients than did the patients themselves or the outside assessors. The behavior therapists were just the opposite. An explanation for this finding may come from research by a psychologist named Joel Greenspoon.

Greenspoon's Observations In a series of brilliant studies reported in the late 1950's, Greenspoon demonstrated how important the attitude of the therapist is in affecting the behavior of most clients. Greenspoon noticed that when a patient begins talking about sexual abnormalities, or about bizarre thought patterns, the therapist may unconsciously encourage the patient to continue talking. The therapist may lean forward, look very interested, and say to the patient, "Yes, yes, tell me more about that." But when the patient is speaking normally, or discussing solutions rather than problems, the therapist may believe that little or no progress is being made and hence may occasionally lean back and look uninterested. In Greenspoon's terms, there is always the danger that the therapist may unwittingly *reward* the patient for "sick talk" and *punish* the patient for "well talk."

In more humanistic terms, getting the client to concentrate on achieving mental *health* may be more important than getting the client to understand the causes of his or her mental *illness*. It is possible that the insight therapists in the Sloane study focused too much on past traumas and not enough on future growth and self-actualization.

Cures may begin in a therapist's office—no matter what type of therapy is offered—but the cure is of little value unless it can be maintained in the patient's normal social environment. The "isolated womb" of an analyst's office is one thing; the real world of normal human interaction is quite another.

SOCIAL/BEHAVIORAL THERAPY

Up until fairly recently most of our laws, customs, and philosophies have been based on the assumption that mental illness existed entirely within an individual—in the brain or in the mind. When factors outside the individual contributed to mental illness, these factors were presumed to be primarily supernatural—gods, witches, and evil spirits. Most forms of biological and intra-psychic therapy can be seen as attempts to cure the patient by working from the inside out.

Within the last century rather a different point of view has emerged—a belief that mental illness is as much a disruption of relationships between people as it is a disruption of one person's inner psychodynamics. Abnormal behavior is almost always expressed in social situations—unless "crazy people" disturb or upset others, they are seldom sent to mental hospitals or to see a therapist. Treatment must not merely alter the functioning of the patient's body or brain, or change the patient's personality—it must also help the patient reorient him- or herself in society. Indeed, in many instances, the group of people around the patient may actually be contributing to the "craziness" without realizing it. In such cases the best form of therapy may be removing the person from that environment—or somehow getting other people to behave differently toward the patient.

The two major types of social-behavioral treatment are (1) *group therapy* (*), in which the patient learns better ways of responding to a group of people who often have similar problems; and (2) *milieu therapy* (*), in which the patient's social environment or milieu becomes the focus for treatment.

Group Therapy

The history of group therapy probably stretches back to the dawn of recorded time. In a sense the early Greek dramas offered a type of psychological release not much different from the psychodrama we will discuss in a moment. Bull sessions, prayer meetings, revivals—even the hypnotic seances that Mesmer conducted in Paris in the late 1700's—are the ancestral forms of today's encounter groups.

Group therapy did not gain any scientific notice, however, until 1905, when a Boston physician named J.H. Pratt made a fortunate mistake. Pratt found that patients suffering from *tuberculosis* (*) were often discouraged and depressed. He first believed their despondency was due to ignorance on their part—they simply

Group therapy. Any form of treatment in which several patients are treated at a time—in a group rather than individually.

Milieu therapy (mill-YOU). The French word for "social environment" is *milieu*. Milieu therapy involves changing the patient's environment in order to induce changes in the patient indirectly.

Tuberculosis (tew-burr-kew-LOH-sis). Also called T.B. A type of germ-caused disease in which a potato-shaped (tuber-shaped) germ destroys tissue in the lungs and elsewhere in the body. A deadly disease that has been almost entirely wiped out by modern medicine.

didn't know enough about the disease they suffered from. So he brought them together in groups to give them lectures about "healthy living." The lectures soon turned into very intense discussions among the patients about their problems. Pratt discovered that his patients gained much more strength from learning they were not alone in their suffering than they did from his lectures.

By 1910 group treatment was used by many European psychiatrists who gathered together people with similar psychological problems for "collective counseling." Psychiatrist J.L. Moreno tried this method in Vienna with displaced persons, children, and prostitutes. By 1914 Alfred Adler suggested that group techniques might be a more effective way of helping large numbers of patients than the usual one patient-one therapist encounters.

According to Hunter College psychologist Robert M. Goldenson, European psychoanalysts were for the most part hostile to group psychotherapy, but this form of treatment soon gained a firm foothold in the United States. Some of the major varieties are psychoanalytic group therapy, nondirective group therapy, directed group therapy, inspirational group therapy (such as Alcoholics Anonymous and Christian Scientism), play group therapy, activity group therapy, family group therapy, encounter groups, and psychodrama.

Advantages of Group Therapy   As you might guess, these various forms of group treatment differ considerably among themselves. But, as J.D. Frank puts it, they all seem to be based on the belief "that intimate sharing of feelings, ideas, experiences in an atmosphere of mutual respect and understanding enhances self-respect, deepens self-understanding, and helps the person live with others." According to Frank, there are six main advantages to the group approach:

1. The knowledge that other people are in much the "same boat" can reduce the patient's anxiety and may give the patient courage to express his or her deeper feelings.

A group of drug addicts undergoing group therapy.

2. Listening to others and talking through ideas with them may stimulate the patient to recall and relive similar experiences.

3. Hearing how others have solved their problems may suggest to the patient new ways of handling his or her difficulties.

4. By expressing emotions in the presence of a sympathetic group, the patient may dissipate some of the feelings of fear or guilt that are retarding the patient's progress.

5. Acceptance and support by the group may give the patient the reward or encouragement needed to put new solutions into practice.

6. The group may act as a "social theater" for the patient to try out new ways of behaving before having to use them in larger social settings.

Some types of groups are directed by a leader and have rather a formal treatment plan. One purpose of such groups is often that of helping the patient break through his or her psychological resistances. The group leader may give lectures or pass out written material that forms the basis of group discussion. This technique is used particularly with psychotic or withdrawn patients who would not, perhaps, be able to function effectively in a less-structured social environment.

Other groups are more inspirational in character; they are typically led by someone with a strong personality who uses a variety of techniques (including calling on higher spiritual powers) to inspire change in group members. Such groups are as likely to encourage the forming of new behavioral patterns as to concentrate on breaking down emotional resistances in their members. The 10,000 or more chapters of Alcoholics Anonymous, the Synanon organization that helps drug addicts, the Christian Science Church, the Seventh Step Foundation for ex-convicts, and even Weight Watchers, Inc., are examples of groups that rely heavily on inspirational devices.

Nondirective Group Therapy Carl Rogers has extended his client-centered therapy to group situations, which Rogers calls *nondirective group psychotherapy* (°). Rogers believes that the leaders of such groups should not control the activities of the group, but should function as *permissive catalysts* (°). The leader helps the group members achieve self-understanding by mirroring back to them their own attitudes and reactions. Roger's object is to stimulate the group members to bring their feelings out into the open and clarify them, rather than trying to uncover the intra-psychic dynamics that caused the emotions in the first place. Rogers emphasizes the importance of communications between members of the group and the value of seeing themselves as others see them.

Psychodrama Moreno, who first used group therapy with socially-displaced persons around 1910, later developed a type of treatment he called *psychodrama* (°). Moreno had a lifelong interest in the theater, but felt that most plays were too rigidly structured to allow the actors and actresses to breathe life into their parts. In 1921 he founded the *Theater of Spontaneity* (°) in which the characters on the stage made up their lines and created their parts as they went along. As Moreno had thought, spontaneous theater was an excellent training device for budding young players. To his surprise, it also seemed to bring about dramatic improvements in their interpersonal relations.

Moreno then developed the technique for use with mental patients. The therapist usually serves as "director" for the psychodrama, which often takes place on a real stage. The patient stars as "hero" or "heroine" in a "play" that centers around some problem in the patient's life. Trained actor-therapists assist in the production. At times, a whole family or group may act out their difficulties. An audience is often invited to watch the proceedings, for Moreno believes that people in the audience can benefit from seeing problems similar to their own presented on the stage.

Nondirective group psychotherapy. A form of treatment developed by Carl Rogers in which the therapeutic group determines the direction the therapy will take.

Permissive catalysts (KAT-uh-lists). In chemistry, a catalyst is a compound that speeds up, or facilitates, a reaction without participating in the reaction itself. In Carl Rogers' terms, the leader of a nondirective group should facilitate any changes the group members themselves wish to make. The technique is permissive in that the leader does not attempt to impose direction on the group.

Psychodrama (SIGH-ko-DRAH-mah, or SIGH-ko-DRAW-ma). A theatrical therapy developed by J.L. Moreno (mor-REE-noh). Some part of the patient's life is usually acted out on a stage, often by professional actors. The patient may play one of the roles, or may simply observe.

Theater of Spontaneity (spon-tuh-KNEE-uh-tee). Moreno's original dramatic technique in which the actors make up their lines as they go along. It turned out to be better therapy than theater.

Eric Berne.

Transactional Analysis A very different form of role-playing is found in a typ of group therapy called *transactional analysis* (°). American psychiatrist Eri Berne uses the term "game" to refer to the *stereotyped* (°) and often misleadin interpersonal "trans-actions" that people frequently adopt in dealing with other. According to Berne, a game is "a recurring series of transactions, often repetitiv and superficially rational, with a concealed motivation." He believes that eac game is but a tiny part of a "script" that a person uses in "performing" variou roles in his or her life.

Berne believes we all "play games" with one another, and usually do so whe we are trying to manipulate others to achieve our own selfish ends. By analyzin the psychological games that members of a group play with each other, eac person in the group can hopefully gain greater awareness of his or her own socia interactions. The purpose of transactional analysis is to help people "stop playin destructive ego games" and help them learn new and healthier ways of dealin with their problems.

Gestalt Psychotherapy *Gestalt therapy* (°) has its roots in classical Gesta psychology (*see* Chapter 10). The object of treatment is said to be that o overcoming any fragmentation of feeling, thinking, and acting that may exist i group members, and to replace this fragmentation with a unitary, "whole" outlook on life. Mental illness is thought to be a matter of social mispercep tion—the patient holds unrealistic, rigid views of his or her relations with othe people. The group therapist typically sets up a series of exercises that allow grou members to become aware of their emotional problems, overcome them, an eventually arrive at a more flexible and creative way of dealing with others

Sensitivity Training *Sensitivity training* (°)—which also goes by such names a "laboratory training," or "T-group training"—comes from Gestalt psychologis Kurt Lewin's findings that group discussions are often effective in changin attitudes. Under the direction of a trained leader, individuals attempt to explor their own feelings toward each other—and toward the world in general. Th leader's task is to provide a "safe laboratory" in which psychological change ca occur. The group members typically decide what they will discuss; the leade remains on the sidelines, but urges each member to examine his or her ow feelings as well as the reactions of other group members.

Encounter Groups *Encounter groups* (°) vary so widely among themselves tha no simple description of them is possible. In general, an encounter group is mad up of people who have had little previous contact with one another. The grou may meet one or more times a week for several weeks, or the members may liv together in close, intense contact for a day, a weekend, or even longer. Th participants are usually encouraged to bring their feelings out into the open an to learn more honest ways of communicating with each other. Often the focus i on some aspect of non-verbal experience—perhaps on developing better sensor awareness of bodily reactions, perhaps on learning how facial expressions com municate deep-seated emotions. As a means of helping group members strip awa their defenses, or urging them to "let it all hang out," a few encounter group meet in the nude.

Evaluating Group Therapy

Group therapy sessions of one kind or another have become increasingly popula in recent years. Group leaders—like most other psychotherapists—often describe in glowing terms the psychological changes they perceive in group members Many participants—particularly if asked immediately after therapy ha ended—are highly enthusiastic about the benefits they feel they have received from the experience. Other participants—particularly those who drop out before therapy is complete—tell rather a different story.

Perhaps the best evaluation so far of the effectiveness of different types of group therapy is a study performed by psychologists Morton A. Lieberman, Matthew B. Miles, and psychiatrist Irvin D. Yalom. Beginning in 1968, these behavioral scientists recruited 206 Stanford students who wished to participate in encounter groups and randomly assigned the students to 17 groups led by experienced professionals. The types of therapy involved were sensitivity or T-groups, Gestalt groups, psychodrama groups, psychoanalytic groups, transactional analysis groups, Rogerian nondirective groups, leaderless groups, and a Synanon-type experience. Another 69 students, who applied for participation but who could not be accommodated, were used as a control group.

The subjects were evaluated as carefully as possible before the groups began; further evaluations occurred a week or two after the groups ended, and again 6 to 8 months later. Participants were asked to rate not only the changes they experienced themselves but those they saw in other group members as well. Group leaders also rated the participants, as did close friends of the participants not themselves involved in the group experience. Objective (behavioral or symptom-change) measures were taken as well as subjective (inner-feeling change) measures.

The experimenters themselves all had extensive experience working with various types of groups and were, prior to the beginning of the experiment, excited by and favorably disposed toward group therapy.

Sadly enough—as Drs. Lieberman, Miles, and Yalom report in the March 1973 issue of *Psychology Today*, their study offers little scientific evidence that group therapy is of much value. Indeed, it may often be just the opposite. They report that about 8 percent of the participants were "casualties"—that is, people who showed evidence of serious psychological harm and whose difficulties could be reasonably attributed to the group experience. About a third of the group members showed positive changes; about a third showed negative changes; and another third seemed unchanged immediately after the therapy. There were few differences among the various types of groups as far as their effectiveness was concerned.

By contrast, more than 60 percent of the control group students who had no therapy reported no change in themselves, while 23 percent reported a negative change and 27 percent reported a positive change.

It would appear that the group situations accentuated both positive and negative changes in the participants, but that the overall effect was about the same as if the groups had never been brought together. Immediately after the groups ended, almost 65 percent of the group members stated that the experience had been a positive one; six months later, their enthusiasm had dropped by more than 50 percent.

There are several other aspects of this experiment worthy of note. First, the group leaders reported that they saw some improvement in almost 90 percent of the members—rather a rosy view not supported by the rest of the data. When the participants were asked to rate others in their groups, they reported improvement in but 37 percent of their fellow group members. Nor was there *any significant agreement* at all among the leaders, the participants, and the participants' friends as to who had changed and in what ways.

Particularly distressing to Lieberman, Miles, and Yalom were the number of "casualties"—and the fact that group leaders seemed almost completely unaware that any of their group members had suffered so much.

Lieberman, Miles, and Yalom conclude that groups are not particularly effective as change agents, but that they can excel at creating instant, brief, and intense

Panaceas (pann-uh-SEE-uhs). From the Greek words *pan,* meaning "all," and *akes,* meaning "remedy." A panacea is a cure-all.

Ecologists (ee-KOLL-oh-jists). Ecologists are scientists who study the pattern of relationships between organisms and their environments.

Ecological systems (ee-ko-LODGE-uh-kal). Human beings cannot survive without friendly environments. We must have good food, clean air and water, a decent range of temperatures, an absence of disease germs. We also need intellectual stimulation and humane treatment from others. All of these "items necessary for the good life" are related to each other in rather complex ways. Plants give us food, oxygen, and help retain rainwater in the soil. When we destroy plants, we destroy part of the complicated system that sustains our very existence. A hospital patient is as dependent on the social system in the institution as the rest of us are dependent on plants and rainwater. From a psychological point of view, some hospitals are barren deserts that "starve" their patients of intellectual and emotional stimulation without meaning to do so. Through our study of the biological aspects of ecological systems, we are learning how to make deserts blossom. Perhaps someday we will learn similar psychological techniques for making institutions such as mental hospitals "bloom."

Social milieu. See *Milieu.*

interpersonal experiences. They state that this chance to learn something about oneself from the open reactions of others is real, important, and not often available in our society. But they believe that such experiences are not the crucial ones that alter people permanently. They write that:

> Encounter groups present a clear and evident danger if they are used for radical surgery to produce a new man. The danger is even greater when the leader and the participant share this misperception. If we no longer expect groups to produce magical, lasting change and if we stop seeing them as *panaceas* (°), we can regard them as useful, socially sanctioned opportunities for human beings to explore and to express themselves. Then we can begin to work on ways to improve them so that they may make a meaningful contribution toward solving human problems.

Environmental Therapy

One of the more interesting discoveries of the past century has been the slow realization of how sensitive we all are to our environments. The *ecologists* (°) have demonstrated rather vividly the disasters that may occur when we pollute the physical world around us. But man does not die from lead poisoning alone—polluted psychological environments can kill or corrupt a man's spirit as readily as dirty air and water can kill or corrupt his body. The job of the environmental psychotherapist is similar to that of the ecologist—to identify the sources of pollution and remove them.

The simplest form of environmental therapy is perhaps the vacation; getting away from it all can often give a person a fresh perspective. Psychiatric social workers show their awareness of this fact when they recommend removing a child from an unhealthy family situation and putting the child in a foster home. Helping mental patients find jobs and comfortable living quarters outside the hospital is another form of environmental therapy practiced by social workers. Rehabilitation centers often teach disturbed people how to function better in work situations, how to relax, how to play or paint or read or make music, how to meet people and stay out of trouble with the law—all ways of helping people make healthier adjustments to presently-existing environments.

If the therapist cannot easily find ways of removing the "psycho-pollution" from the patient's world, or of helping the patient live more happily despite the pollution, then more radical treatment is usually needed. Typically this takes the form of moving the patient to different surroundings—such as a mental hospital. Once we called such places "asylums"—safe, comfortable places to which a patient could flee when the storms of life became too threatening. Unfortunately, mental hospitals all too often became human garbage dumps, huge stone buildings crammed with life's failures and misfits. As *ecological systems,* (°) such hospitals were often more abnormal and destructive to human egos than was the outside world the patients had sought relief from.

Social/behavioral therapists tend to see mental illness as being *caused* by unhealthy living conditions. The best form of treatment, from this vantage point, would surely be putting the patient in a new environment or *social milieu* (°)—each aspect of which would be carefully designed to help the patient learn better habits of adjustment.

The term "therapeutic community" was coined by British psychiatrist Maxwell Jones in 1953 to refer to this type of *milieu therapy.*

Writing in the *American Handbook of Psychiatry* in 1959, Dr. Louis Linn points out that our concept of therapy has changed over the years:

> In former days there was a tendency to regard treatment in the mental hospital as that which takes place during the fraction of a second when the current flows from an electro-shock apparatus, or during the longer intervals involved in other therapies . . . In the therapeutic community the whole of the time which the patient spends in the

hospital is thought of as treatment time, and everything that happens to the patient is part of the treatment program.

Viewed in this way, Linn continues, the trees and flowers on the hospital grounds and the decorations in the wards, the way the food is served, and the behavior of all hospital personnel—without exception—are part of the treatment program.

Though it does not replace other forms of treatment, milieu therapy does attempt to make the total environment a "school for living" in which the patient can develop new attitudes and build more rewarding social relationships. In a sense the therapeutic community is rather like a non-stop, 24-hour-a-day encounter group. However, its primary function is not usually that of removing symptoms or merely changing behaviors; its aim is said to be that of drawing the patient into normal relationships that will give the person confidence, self-esteem, and social competence.

The difficulty in evaluating milieu therapy is the same as with other forms of group therapy—terms like "confidence" and "self-esteem" refer to intra-psychic traits and hence are hard to define or measure objectively. Therapeutic communities certainly are far more humane forms of treatment than the old-style mental hospitals; whether milieu therapy is as effective as it might be remains to be seen.

Token Economies Rather a different type of environmental treatment is favored by behavior therapists, whose aim is that of changing habit patterns rather than altering inner psychological states (*see* Chapter 5). Patients in mental hospitals often develop what is called an *institutional neurosis* (°)—they lose interest in the world and the people around them; they develop hallucinations and fantasies; and they become quarrelsome, resentful, and hostile. Institutional neurosis appears to be caused at least in part by the fact that, in most hospitals, patients are often treated like children or helpless invalids. That is, the patients are "given" everything they might need by the "authority figures" in charge. Under these conditions it is little wonder that a rather child-like dependency on the staff develops in the patients.

The behavioral psychologists believe that the best cure for institutional neurosis is making the patient take as much responsibility for his or her improvement as possible. To help achieve this goal, the behaviorists have developed what they call the *token economy* (°). In the money economy that operates in the world outside the hospital, one must typically work to live. Our social system rewards us for "good" work behavior with dollars that can be spent on food, clothing, and shelter. If those of us who live in the money economy perform poorly or refuse to work, we may very well starve. In contrast, mental hospitals typically operate on a free economy. That is, the patients are given whatever they need merely by asking for it. In fact, the worse they behave, the more attention and help they usually receive.

The behaviorists take the view that, within the hospital economy, it is the patient's "job" to get well as quickly as possible. Patients then should be rewarded for each sign of improvement by receiving "tokens" that can be traded in for physical pleasures (such as candy, cosmetics, cigarettes, clothes, magazines and records) or special privileges (better jobs in the hospital, going to movies, and visits home). In a token economy, therapy usually consists of having the staff reinforce "socially approved" or "healthy" behaviors and ignore inappropriate or "insane" behaviors. Each patient is encouraged to decide what rewards he or she wants to work for; the patient is then given the tokens as visible evidence that progress is being made toward these chosen goals.

At their best, token economies can lead to rather remarkable changes in the behavior patterns of certain types of patients—particularly in those who are depressed, withdrawn, immobile, or anti-social. There are several reasons for these successes:

Institutional neurosis. Hospital patients are often subtly encouraged to remain "sick" in order to stay in the hospital. The "sicker" the patient becomes, the more dependent the patient is on the hospital, and the more the institution justifies its own existence. When patients develop an abnormally strong dependency on a hospital or its staff, the patients are said to suffer from institutional neurosis.

Token economies. Artificial economies set up in an institution to "cure" institutional neurosis. The patients are rewarded for positive (socially approved) behaviors by being given "tokens" which may be exchanged for various types of rewards. The "healthier" the patient's behavior, the more tokens the patient receives, the greater the rewards the patient reaps, and the sooner the patient can usually be eased out of the institution and back into society.

1. Before the economy can be instituted, the hospital staff must first think about those types of patient behaviors they wish to see increased and those they wish to see decreased in frequency—a type of psychological analysis that few institutional staffs would ordinarily engage in. In short, the staff must decide ahead of time—in very objective terms—what they will consider a "cure" to be.

2. The use of tokens forces the staff to focus on healthy behaviors rather than paying attention primarily to those things the patients are doing wrong. Nurses and ward attendants soon learn that many of their patients are more capable of showing improvement than perhaps the staff had thought possible.

3. Staff members are encouraged to spend more time with the patients than before, since the behavioral therapist can measure the number of staff-patient contacts by monitoring the number of tokens each staff member gives out. The use of tokens also insures that these interactions will be primarily "rewarding" rather than "punishing."

4. Individual therapy programs can be worked out so that each patient in the economy is rewarded primarily for improvement in those "healthy behaviors" that he or she is most deficient in. Therapy is thus more "individualized" than it might be in many hospitals.

5. Both the behavioral therapist and, more important, the patient have a day-by-day record of the patient's improvement—that is, the number of tokens earned. The patient thus gains a greater control over the speed of his or her recovery than is possible in most other institutional milieus.

Like any other form of therapy, the token economy has its record of wins and losses. The system seems good at teaching simple social skills to patients who need to learn such things, and in preventing institutional neurosis. The criticism most often raised against the token economy is that it is mechanistic and dehumanizing because it focuses on observable behaviors—on symptoms—rather than on underlying, dynamic psychological problems. From the intra-psychic viewpoint, this criticism has considerable merit. The behavioral changes that the token economies do bring about, however, seem to be very reliable (repeatable)—a point in their favor.

THERAPY AND THE WHOLE INDIVIDUAL

Psychotherapy is perhaps the most challenging and interesting part of psychology for most of us. It combines the pleasures of intellectual analysis with the warm emotions of "doing good" for individuals who might need our help. These statements, however, are as true of witch doctoring as they are of any other type of psychotherapy. If Eysenck's figures are even partially valid, we can expect many people with neuroses or psychoses to "cure themselves" even if they receive no treatment at all. How then can we make sure that our therapy does, in fact, speed up or add something extra to what seems to be our inborn way of healing ourselves?

One thing does seem certain: If we look at a disturbed individual from any one narrow perspective—be it from the biological, intra-psychic, or behavior-social viewpoint—we are likely to limit both our understanding of the client and our chances of bringing about a cure of the person's very real problems. As we discovered in the case of Meatball McClanahan (see Chapter 12), even rather simple psychological difficulties often turn out to be incredibly complex.

By now you see the problem. In the past, we have too often allowed ourselves to develop "tunnel vision" to suit our own particular psychological orientation. We have given people drugs without realizing that the manner in which we give the pill may be as important as the chemical inside the pill. (Powdered rhinoceros horn is a highly reliable cure for *koro,* but so is any other substance that the male Chinese believes to be powdered rhinoceros horn.)

Or we have spent years digging into the patient's unconscious to give the person insight into his or her personality dynamics. At the end of several years of therapy the patient may have complete understanding of his or her intra-psychic traumas, but still have a collection of inappropriate habits (symptoms) that must be unlearned. Just as bad, we may focus on the observable behaviors, ignoring the fact that internal fears and feelings need our attention too.

Meyer's Holistic Approach

To help us avoid this segmented approach to human difficulties, we might turn to someone like Adolf Meyer, often called the "dean of U.S. psychiatry." Meyer believed in the *holistic* (°) approach and recognized that there were multiple causes for even the simplest of behaviors. Rather than passing verdicts on patients by labeling them as "schizophrenics," "compulsive-neurotics," or "senile-psychotics," Meyer preferred to discover both what was wrong and what was right with the patient at all levels of analysis—the biological, the psychological, and the sociological. He seldom *interpreted* the patient's problems—he merely tried to describe them in plain English.

Meyer also attempted to determine those normal aspects of behavior that the patient might still utilize—and then build on these psychological assets to bring about needed biological, psychological, and sociological changes. Meyer believed that the patient should set both the goals and the pace of therapy, and that the therapist should work as hard at changing the patient's home (or hospital) environment as in changing the patient's psyche. Meyer called his approach "critical common sense."

There are thousands of different kinds of psychotherapy; the surprising thing is that almost all of them "work" with certain kinds of patients and with certain types of problems, and fail with others. If we apply Adolf Meyer's "critical common sense" to an analysis of the strengths and weaknesses of all the various types of therapy, and if we pay as much attention to hard, scientific data as we do to the therapists' and the patients' gut reactions to the therapeutic process, we might discover that most successful forms of treatment have several things in common:

1. Psychological change almost always occurs in a supportive, warm, rewarding environment. People usually "open up" and talk about things, and try new approaches to life, when they trust or admire or want to please the therapist. When Freud spoke of the power of the *transference relationship* he was really saying that the patient's affection for the analyst could be used to encourage the patient to want to get well. When Carl Rogers wrote of the necessity for giving his clients *unconditional positive regard,* he was surely recognizing the power of positive reinforcement. When a social worker talks of removing a child from a punitive family situation, isn't the social worker hoping that foster parents might give the child more loving support?

    Encounter groups whose members focus on expressing hostility toward each other often do incredible damage—unless such expression is embedded in a background of affection and appreciation so strong that the members can tolerate occasional (but hopefully brief) punishment from each other. Criticism seldom cures, and too often kills all chance of improvement (if not the patient as well). Sincere expressions of warmth and tolerance for "abnormalities" provide the atmosphere in which change can occur.
2. Most successful forms of treatment can be seen as feedback mechanisms. That is, they provide the client with information about what happened in the past;

Holistic (ho-LISS-tick). From the word "whole." Holistic therapy is that which aims at treating the patient as a whole individual rather than as a collection of symptoms. In terms used in this book, looking at human beings from a broad rather than a narrow viewpoint; looking at relations among systems rather than focusing on a single (biological, intra-psychic, or social) system.

they put the person in touch with the functioning of his or her body; they make the individual aware of how his or her behavior actually affects other people; they help the person realize the distance between desired goals and present achievements; or they offer information on how the social environment influences the person's thoughts, feelings, and behaviors. Ideally, a complete form of therapy would do all these things—and give the patient the skills to seek out and make even more effective use of feedback in the future.

3. Magic can "cure" mental illness overnight; all other forms of psychotherapy take a little longer. If you believe that madness is a matter of possession by devils, then you might expect that beatings or magic words could displace the devils quickly. But if you believe that it takes many years of punishing or stressful experiences—and perhaps a particular genetic pre-disposition—for a full-blown psychosis to develop, then you might also expect the road to recovery to be a fairly lengthy one. And in addition to any form of biological or intra-psychic therapy, many patients will need to learn a variety of new habits and attitudes if they are to experience the best possible improvement.

4. The attitudes of both the patient and the therapist are of critical importance. A Cree Eskimo woman suffering from *witigo* "knows" that she needs a witch doctor; will giving this woman a tranquilizer help her much?

   My own research suggests that optimistic behavior therapists—who are strongly convinced that this form of therapy can be of value—have much higher "cure rates" than do therapists who doubt the effectiveness of the technique. The Temple study by Sloane and his group tends to confirm my findings. Patients often see their therapists as being models of mentally healthy or socially-approved behaviors. Effective therapists (witch doctors, psychoanalysts, humanists, or behaviorists) usually practice what they preach.

5. The best forms of therapy seem to build on strengths rather than attacking weaknesses. By helping the patient work toward positive improvement—toward self-actualization and good mental health—the therapist motivates the patient to continue to grow and change. Therapies that focus entirely on uncovering or discussing psychological problems may merely confirm the patient's attitude that sickness is inevitable.

THE FUTURE OF PSYCHOTHERAPY

It is likely that, in the coming years, we will take Adolf Meyer's ideas more seriously than we have in the past, that we will treat the whole patient as a unique individual rather than treating just one aspect of the person's difficulties. Already in some hospitals there is a team of therapists available to work with each patient. One member of the team looks at the person's physical or biological problems; another deals with the person's intra-psychic dynamics; another helps the person change his or her behavior patterns; yet another is an expert in altering social environments. The patient can then get as much—or as little—of each type of therapy as his or her own particular case demands. Ideally, the goals of therapy should be spelled out in a written contract agreed to by the patient and all members of the therapeutic team, and the patient's progress should be recorded regularly on a graph of some kind so that all team members are aware of the patient's achievements. As this "team-contracting approach" increases in popularity, our success rate in curing mental illness is likely to show a significant increase.

All forms of therapy achieve some success. In 1975 the Research Task Force of the National Institute of Mental Health released a report covering 25 years of research on therapy and mental illness—research that the U.S. government had supported to the extent of $1 billion. According to this report, most types of psychotherapy yield a 70 percent "cure rate." The major exceptions are behavior therapy and drug therapy, both of which (when effectively utilized) have produced "cure rates" well above 80 percent. But, as the NIMH report suggests, perhaps the single most important thing we have learned about mental health in the past quarter-century is that neither problems nor cures occur in a vacuum. No matter how well a patient may respond in a hospital setting, no matter what insights a client achieves in a therapist's office, the ultimate test of therapy comes when the person returns to his or her usual environment. If the patient can function successfully and happily in the real world, in everyday life, we can then conclude that a "cure" has indeed taken place.

It is to the complexities of the social environment that we must now turn our attention in the final section of this book, a section that deals with social psychology.

SUMMARY

1. The types of therapy that we prescribe for mentally ill persons usually stem from our theoretical explanation of what causes the persons' problems.
2. In primitive times (and societies) insanity was said to be caused by "possession"—a devil of some kind was thought to inhabit the sick person's mind. Primitive forms of psychotherapy typically involve the use of magic to "cast out the devil," or painful whips to "beat the devil" out of the patient.
3. As our scientific explanations of the causes of human behavior have changed, so have our types of treatment. In evaluating any form of therapy, however, we must ask ourselves several questions: How successful is the treatment? How reliable? Are there unfortunate side effects? And what do we really mean by successful treatment?
4. We must also realize that patients often get well without therapy—or perhaps in spite of it.
5. Biological treatment typically involves the use of artificially-induced seizures, surgery, and drugs.
6. Although extremely helpful in rather limited situations, biotherapy seems not to have a very high "cure rate" and often has many bad side effects. In fact, many of the "cures" reported for biotherapy seem due more to the expectations of the therapists and patients than to the physiological changes brought about by the treatment.
7. There are many forms of intra-psychic treatment—including psychoanalysis, humanistic therapy, and eclectic therapy.
8. Whether the "cure rates" for intra-psychic treatment are high or low depends on one's definition of what constitutes a "cure." But research suggests that intra-psychic therapy is better at changing a patient's internal psychological states, or self-awareness, than at "curing symptoms" or bringing about significant alterations in the patient's behaviors.
9. Environmental therapies include many types of group treatment, as well as attempts to change the patient by altering the patient's milieu.
10. Group therapies seem better as ways of encouraging people to explore and express themselves than as psychological "cure-alls."
11. The most effective form of milieu therapy appears to be the token economy, in which patients earn rewards for appropriate behaviors.
12. By far the most promising types of treatment appear to be those based on the holistic approach, in which the patient is treated as a whole individual functioning within a complex environmental system.
13. It is likely that, in the future, a team approach to treatment will prove to be highly effective, particularly if patient-therapist "contracts" are employed.

(Continued from page 576.)

"I hurt, Mark," Lou Hudson repeated, ignoring all of the boisterous activity in the gambling casino as he poured out his heart to Mark Evans. "I've lost almost everything we own. The house, the car, everything—gambled it all away. I've borrowed from everybody in the family and lost it all on the horses. I'm even going to lose Betty and the kids if I can't shape up somehow. But I get those urges, you know, those times when I just know that I've got a winning streak going, and I have to play my hunches. I've got to get help of some kind, Mark, but what should I do?''

''What does Betty think you should do?''

''She wants me to join the Chattanooga chapter of Gamblers Anonymous. They're a bunch of people just like me that get together regularly to talk over their problems and help each other out. Betty says they've helped lots of folks.''

''So, why don't you join and see what they can do for you?''

''Cause it would make your uncle angry at me. I mean your Uncle John, the psychiatrist. He thinks I need psychoanalysis. He says I'm a masochist and have an unconscious desire to punish myself by losing all the time. He thinks I ought to lie on a couch for a few years and find out what's wrong deep down inside me. He says that group therapy just doesn't get at the roots of the problem.''

Mark laughed softly. ''Well, why don't you try psychoanalysis, then?''

''Because of your Cousin Sophie. She's a Rogerian, you know. She thinks I need nondirective therapy to help me achieve self-actualization. Sophie's a wonderful woman, Mark, and she's awful easy to talk to. Every time I say something to her, she just says it back to me in different words. Trouble is, she isn't talking to your Uncle John, and I owe her almost as much money as I owe him.''

Mark decided that he needed a drink and beckoned to a cocktail waitress. ''So, why don't you go in for a little self-actualization?''

Lou moaned. ''Your Aunt Beverly would never approve.''

''You mean the behavior therapist?''

''Yeah,'' Lou said, taking another drink. ''Man, you've got more different kinds of shrinks in your family than I ever heard of!''

''Psychology runs in my family the way that insanity runs in others. But what does Aunt Beverly, the behaviorist, think?''

''She tells me that all the other forms of therapy are unscientific. She says I'd do better to find a witch doctor than to go to your Uncle John for psychoanalysis. Aunt Beverly wants to set up a behavioral program that will reward me for not gambling. She says I've got to learn new and more effective social reactions. And I hate to tell you how much cash I owe that woman, Mark.''

''The cure rates for some kinds of behavioral therapy are very impressive, Mark. So why don't you try it?''

''Because it would make everybody else mad as hell at me, including my wife Betty. I wouldn't mind going to any of them if I was sure they could help me. But how can you be sure you're going to be cured, Mark?''

''You can't, Lou. Any more than you can be sure that the roulette wheel is going to come up on number 23 the next time you put your money down on the table. All you can do is play the odds.''

''What do you mean?''

''Ask each of the shrinks in the family to tell you what the cure rate is for compulsive gambling with their type of therapy. Take a good, close look at what they consider successful treatment to be, and how they measure success, and what the cost to you is going to be. Then pick the one that gives you the best odds for your time and money.''

Lou Hudson blinked his bloodshot eyes as he pondered the matter momentarily. ''That's being pretty hard-nosed about a very human predicament, isn't it?''

''Being hard-nosed about human predicaments is what keeps insurance companies and gambling casinos in business, Lou. You can't be sure that the therapy with the best overall cure rate is going to work for you and your own unique set of problems, but the fact that the odds are in your favor gives you a bit of a head start.''

''Yeah, I see what you mean.''

''But what do you want to do, Lou? That's the most important factor of all.''

''I kind of like the advice your Cousin Oscar gave me, and I owe him more than anybody.''

Mark laughed. "Ah, yes, Cousin Oscar. What does the black sheep of the family recommend?"

Lou grinned. "Well, he knows of this woman who's a fortune teller. She lives in the same trailer park that Oscar lives in. He says that if I slip her a few bucks, she might read her magic cards and give me a tip on the races. Oscar says she's almost always right. If I could just win a few big ones, I could pay back my debts, stop gambling, and then I wouldn't need any therapy at all. What do you think of that?"

Mark shook his head. "No dice. If she's so good with the magic, how come she lives in a trailer instead of a mansion?"

"Yeah, I see what you mean. Bad odds, eh? But what can I do? No matter whose therapy I pick, I'm going to make everyone else in the family madder than a wet hen."

Mark scratched his nose. "I think I have an idea. Lou, you haven't got a problem. The family has a problem. So we ought to come up with a family solution."

"What do you mean? Me get a divorce from Betty?"

"Not at all. Our family of shrinks, as you call them, can offer you half-a-dozen different kinds of therapy. Why not try them all—at once? Tell them that you just can't choose among them, and you figure you're in such bad shape, you need everything you can get. That way, if you get over your compulsive gambling, they can all share the credit. And if you don't, they can all share the blame. It might even get them talking to each other for a change—and that's the real family problem, if you want my opinion."

"But man, that would cost a bushel basket full of money! I can't afford it!"

"Lou, I suspect they'd all rather give you free therapy than continue to lend you money."

Lou Hudson rubbed his eyes with the back of his hands. "Maybe you've got something there, Mark. I'd better go call Betty on the phone and see what she thinks."

As the two men walked toward the door of the casino the little old lady in tennis shoes stopped them. She held up a coin. "My luck's been pretty bad today, boys, but I feel a change coming over me. This is my very last nickel, and I've got to get a winner. Where do you think I ought to put it?"

"Back in your purse," Mark said.

"Now, Mark, you don't understand us gamblers." Lou closed his eyes and turned around three times. Then he pointed to a small slot machine far down the row. "Try that one, lady. I gotta hunch."

The little old woman trotted obediently down the row of one-armed bandits and paused to look the machine over carefully. Then she spat on the coin gently, rubbed it lovingly on her stained white gloves, dropped it in the slot, and pulled the handle. The wheels spun wildly. The first one stopped on a bar. The second one did likewise. When the third reel clicked into place, it too bore the bar symbol.

Suddenly the machine exploded. A bell rang loudly, and lights flashed off like skyrockets.

"Jackpot!" the woman screamed. "I did it, I did it! I've got my juju back! The magic power is with me again!"

A small crowd of people gathered around to watch the slot machine pay off.

Lou Hudson looked at the woman and smiled. "She probably spent $50 in nickels just to win one $10 jackpot. And now she'll put all those nickels right back in the machine, won't she?"

Mark nodded in agreement.

"You think I can stop that kind of childish nonsense, Mark?"

"If you really want to, and you get good help, the odds are in your favor."

The slight young man with bloodshot eyes grinned in response. "I'll bet on that!"

RECOMMENDED READINGS

Birk, Lee, *et al.*, eds. *Behavior Therapy in Psychiatry* (Washington, D.C.: American Psychiatric Association, 1973).

Burton, Arthur, ed. *Twelve Therapists* (San Francisco, Calif.: Jossey-Bass, Inc., 1972).

Heine, Ralph W. *Psychotherapy* (Englewood Cliffs, N.J.: Prentice-Hall, Inc., 1971).

Hoch, Erasmus L. *Experimental Contributions to Clinical Psychology* (Belmont, Calif.: Brooks-Cole Publishing Company, 1971).

Stolz, Stephanie B., Louis A. Wienckowski, and Betram S. Brown. "Behavior Modification: A Perspective on Critical Issues," *American Psychologist* (November 1975), pp. 1027–1048.

Part 7

SOCIAL PSYCHOLOGY

chapter 26

"LIKING AND LOVING"

INTERPERSONAL ATTRACTION AND IMPRESSION FORMATION

DID YOU KNOW THAT . . .

There seem to be two types of group leaders—the "task specialist," who is given respect, and the "social-emotional specialist," who gains the members' affection?

If you want people to like you, the first thing you must decide is whether you want their respect or their affection?

When first we meet someone new, we tend to like or dislike them because of how they look rather than what they are really like?

In our attempts to explain the actions of other people, we often project our own fears and desires onto the others?

When speaking to someone they dislike, men are more likely to lean back and grow tense than are women?

Men in our culture may be more restricted in the social roles they play than are women?

Generally speaking, we tend to like and to marry primarily those people who are very much like us?

It wasn't so much that Frederic Schreiber hated people—he loved them in the abstract, particularly as characters in novels and plays. He loved people in small numbers, particularly at an intimate party. And most of all, he loved his girl friend, Ellie Lambretti, a complex young woman who often seemed a dozen people rolled into one. But as Fred Schreiber looked at the hundreds of couples lined up behind him in the hallway, he realized that he hated the pressing, pushing reality of crowds.

It was a good thing, Fred thought, that he had gotten to the meeting early. Surely the auditorium wouldn't hold everyone who wanted to get in.

Ellie was late, as usual, but this time at least she had an excuse. She was a sophomore drama major and was rehearsing a play. Fred, a junior who was majoring in English literature, had volunteered to get to the experiment early to hold a place in line.

He spotted Ellie as soon as she entered the hall and waved his hand until she noticed him. Their eyes met in a moment of thrilling recognition. Then she walked toward him proudly, her head high, as if the hallway were a stage and she was making a grand entrance. Several of the other couples stared at her as she passed, their interest intensifying Fred's feeling that somehow he **possessed** this beautiful young woman.

They touched hands, then kissed briefly. Ellie was wearing one of her most attractive outfits, a fact Fred mentioned as he put his arm around her waist.

"Darling, I barely had time to change, and this was the only clean thing I could find in the closet," Ellie responded. "But you look good too."

She ran her hand over the sweater that hugged his chest, and they both looked at each other and smiled. Fred hadn't thought the occasion merited a coat and tie, but he had put on the blue sweater she had given him for his birthday. As far as Fred was concerned, they were the most handsome couple in line. He looked around, inspecting the odd assortment of young men and women queued up behind him, and noticed that many of them clutched copies of the ad that had appeared in the **Daily** just a couple of days ago.

ONLY DATING COUPLES CAN DO IT!

—Gain Insight into Your Relationship by Participating in a Unique Social-Psychological Study . . . and Get Paid for It Too!

Who can participate?

All Michigan student couples (heterosexual only) who are dating regularly, going together, or engaged. (Married couples are not eligible.)

What do you have to do?

Simply show up with your boyfriend or girl friend at one of the times and places listed. You will be asked to fill out a confidential questionaire, and each of you will be paid $1 for the one-hour session.

Then what?

All those who fill out the questionnaire will have a chance to be selected as subjects for a subsequent experiment, which (if you agree to participate) should be both exciting and lucrative.

BOTH MEMBERS OF A COUPLE MUST TAKE PART

Tuesday, October 29, 7:30 P.M.—Auditorium C
Wednesday, October 30, 7:30 P.M.—Auditorium C

Suddenly the doors to the auditorium opened and they were invited inside. A woman in her middle 30's stood on stage, a microphone in hand. Her sensible dress and low-heeled shoes gave her a professional but attractive appearance.

"Please don't sit near your boyfriend or girl friend," she told them as they entered. "You'll be filling out a couple of questionnaires, and your answers must be confidential. You can tell each other about your responses later on, if you want to. But I will be the only person who actually sees the answers each of you gives. So please find a seat, and I'll tell you what we're going to do tonight."

Fred parted reluctantly from Ellie, annoyed at having agreed to participate in what promised to be just another of those stupid experiments in social psychology! When Ellie had read the ad in the **Daily,** she had danced around the room on tiptoes, pretending to be a social psychologist asking him the most personal questions about their relationship, teasing, pleading, demanding—until he had grudgingly consented. Now he sat down between a black woman and an older white man who apparently didn't know each other. They all turned their attention to the woman on the stage.

"Good evening, and thanks so much for coming here tonight. I'm Dr. Rosa Hart. We do so appreciate your cooperation, and we'll try to make it interesting for all of you. We'll also pay you $1.00 each if you both fill out our questionnaires. Then, if you wish, you can volunteer to take part in another experiment which should be even more interesting. We'll pay you extra for that, of course," Dr. Hart added, almost as an afterthought.

The crowd applauded.

"We're following up some research that Dr. Zick Rubin began here before he went on to Harvard," Dr. Hart continued. "We want to measure the amount of love and respect that dating couples have for each other, and then compare that with other forms of friendship and affection. When you fill out the first questionnaire you'll be given, tell us how you feel toward the person you came here with tonight. Then, on the second questionnaire, pick your best friend of the same sex as you, and tell us how you feel about that person. And remember—no one will see your answers but me."

Fred took the questionnaire that was handed to him by one of Dr. Hart's assistants. He put his name on the sheet and read the first question: "I feel that I can confide in _____ about virtually everything." Underneath the question was a scale of some kind:

Not at all true; disagree completely	Moderately true; agree to some extent	Definitely true; agree completely

Fred wrote in Ellie's name and then put a check mark on the scale to indicate that he agreed almost completely that he could confide in her about virtually everything. Immediately he wondered how she had marked the scale. Did she trust him enough to tell him all her secrets?

The next question read: "I would do almost anything for _____."

As he checked the scale below the question, Fred became mildly annoyed. How could this kind of stuff describe the love one human being had for another? Love was something you wrote poems or plays about, not something you measured with a ruler. He finished the task quickly, then answered the same questions again using the name of his best friend, Bill Speer. Fred admired Bill a lot, but his feelings were nothing like those he had for Ellie.

"All right, many thanks," Dr. Hart said, as her associates picked up the questionnaires. "Now we'll take a quick break. Those of you who want to leave may pick up your dollars on the way out. If some of you would like to continue, we have a few experiments for you to perform. We think you'll find them interesting. Just stick around after the break, and we'll tell you where to go next."

Peevishly, Fred knew Ellie would want to continue, even though he had other things in mind for them to do that evening.

"Did you tell Dr. Hart that you loved me?" Ellie asked impishly when he found her in the crowd.

"Of course. Because it's true," Fred said, taking her hand. "What did you say about me?"

"I'm not going to tell you," Ellie said teasingly. "Dr. Hart said our answers were confidential, didn't she?"

Fred was about to reply when Dr. Hart came on the microphone again to tell them how to get to the social psychology laboratories. Fred didn't even bother to ask if Ellie wanted to go—they simply started walking in that direction. On the way they talked mostly about the way they felt toward each other, and about the possibility of their getting married. Fred was eager to do so as soon as he graduated a year from next May. Ellie was reluctant to agree because she would still have a year left before she finished school. Their differences on this point worried Fred. If they couldn't agree on getting married, what could they agree on?

At the labs they were broken up into groups of 12 and seated around large tables. Fred and Ellie were asked to sit directly across from each other, as were all the couples. Dr. Hart gave them each a card with one word written on it. She asked them not to show their cards to anyone else. Then, for reasons Fred couldn't comprehend, each person read his or her word out loud, going around the table in a circle. Fred was the fourth to speak, and he said "globe" clearly and distinctly. Then he relaxed and looked at Ellie, who smiled back at him. When it came her turn, she said "oracle" crisply and dramatically. What a beautiful voice she had! Fred was sure she spoke more eloquently than anyone else at the table, and was proud of her.

After everyone had spoken, Dr. Hart asked them to write down as many of the words as each person could remember. What a dumb thing to do, Fred told himself, as he wrote down **oracle, globe,** and several other words on a sheet of paper. The fact that he couldn't recall all 12 words surprised him, since he prided himself on his excellent memory.

Next they were taken, couple by couple, to a set of small rooms with what seemed to be mirrors set in the walls. Fred realized that someone was surely sitting behind the mirrors watching them, but it didn't worry him. He and Ellie had nothing to hide. They were asked to talk about the experiment for a few minutes. Fred got so involved in looking at Ellie as she talked that he wasn't a particularly good conversationalist. Then, Dr. Hart came in with another young girl and asked Fred to talk to her, while Ellie went to another of the little rooms. The girl was pert and amusing, so she and Fred had a very pleasant chat.

Ten minutes later Dr. Hart returned with Ellie, thanked them all for their help, paid them some money, promised to tell them the results of the study ''in a few months,'' and told them they could leave.

Ellie said she was hungry, so they headed for their favorite Greek restaurant.

''Did you look at the other girl as much as you looked at me?'' Ellie asked.

''Well, she was kind of cute,'' Fred replied, letting the sentence die before finishing it.

Ellie pretended to be angry and lectured him on the dangers of infidelity in stern, theatrical tones. Then, as they neared the restaurant, she switched voices suddenly and became herself again. ''Darling, did you enjoy the experiment?''

Fred shrugged. ''It didn't hurt any, I guess,'' he said, then hugged her close to him. ''But what's all that stuff got to do with love?''

(Continued on page 627.)

Do you want people to like you? That may seem a silly question, for almost everyone seems to want to be liked by almost everyone else. Americans spend billions of dollars annually on cosmetics, deodorants, new clothes, shiny cars, gleaming stereo sets, decorations for their houses or apartments, fancy office furniture, greeting cards, entertainments of various kinds, flowers, charm schools, diet pills, and self-improvement courses—all designed, one presumes, to attract other people and make them like us. Since similar behaviors (and expenses) are found in all human cultures, we may presume that the desire to be liked is probably built into our genes. What then can a psychology text tell you about the innate desire to be liked that you couldn't discover in the thousands of popular books and articles on the subject?

To begin with, a psychologist might insist that we need a better definition of the verb "to like" than usually appears in magazine stories—if possible, a definition so clearly and objectively stated that we can measure what we're talking about.

If you looked the word up in a large dictionary, you would find that the book devoted almost a full page to defining the various meanings of "like." *To like* is to be attracted to, to feel positive emotions toward, to desire, to value, or to have high regard for some object or person. In his book *Liking and Loving,* Harvard psychologist Zick Rubin suggests that there are two main aspects of "liking" that deserve our attention. According to Rubin, when we say that we like someone, we usually mean either that we have affection for that person or that we have respect for that person. You have affection for someone who relates to you personally, someone who gives you a feeling of closeness and emotional warmth. Respect, on the other hand, is a cooler and psychologically more distant emotion. You have respect for someone whose personality, status, accomplishments, or talents you admire.

Two Types of Specialists

Of course, respect and affection don't always go hand in hand. We respect political leaders, artists, scientists, and athletes—but we don't always feel personal warmth toward them. And we often love people who have achieved little or nothing in life. Harvard *sociologist* (°) Robert Bales and his colleagues demonstrated this fact rather well in a series of experiments involving groups of male college students. The subjects were brought together in a laboratory and given certain intellectual problems to solve. Bales *et al.* measured the verbal behaviors of the student-subjects as objectively as they could. At the end of each problem-solving session, the experimenters asked the subjects to rate each member of the group in a number of ways, including how much the subject liked the others and which person seemed to be a leader or have the best ideas.

Bales and his associates found that two types of people got high scores on the rating scales: the "idea man" (or task specialist) and the "back-patter" (or social-emotional specialist).

During group sessions, the task specialist gave opinions and made suggestions more often than anyone else. He kept reminding the group of its goals and brought them back to the task at hand whenever they strayed from problem-solving. These behaviors apparently caused other group members to rate this specialist as a good leader or idea-generator.

The social-emotional specialist, on the other hand, was much more likely to *ask* for suggestions than to give them. He praised good performance and smoothed over arguments in order to create what Bales calls *group solidarity*.

The idea man directed the cognitive or intellectual resources of the group, and was respected for his knowledge and expertise. The back-patter managed the emotional resources of the group, and was warmly liked for his ability to keep the group functioning as a *cohesive* (°) unit.

Zick Rubin believes that it is a rare person who is a "natural-born" expert at controlling both the cognitive and the emotional processes of groups of people. To Rubin, *greatness* is a matter of earning large amounts of *both* respect and affection

Sociologist (so-see-OLL-oh-jist). The Latin word *socius* means "associate" or "companion." A sociologist is someone who studies society, social institutions, and social relationships— that is, a scientist interested in the inputs, processes, and outputs of social systems.

Cohesive (ko-HE-sive). From Latin and Old English words meaning "to stick, to adhere." Cohesive forces are those that hold things together. A cohesive unit is one in which the members or parts function efficiently together, usually toward a common goal or output.

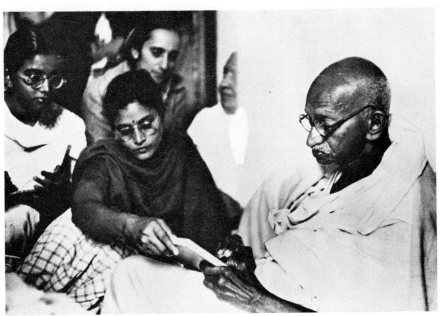

Mahatma Gandhi, Hindu nationalist leader, surrounded by young followers.

Person perception. That part of social psychology which has to do with discovering the stimulus inputs that influence one individual's perception of or attitude toward another individual. As we will see, many of the rules that we discussed in Chapter 11 concerning the perception of objects also hold for person perception.

Attitude. A process variable used to explain why certain inputs lead to certain outputs. A consistent way of thinking about, feeling toward, or responding to some environmental stimulus or input. Made up of cognitive, emotional, and behavioral components.

Components (komm-POH-nents). From the Latin word meaning "to put together or compose." Components are parts of some whole.

from others. Such greatness is found in only a very few leaders—Gandhi of India, Mao of China, Winston Churchill of Great Britain, and Franklin Roosevelt of the United States. The rest of us may receive different amounts of the two types of liking—such as much respect but little affection, or average amounts of both.

Do you want people to like you? If you do, perhaps the first thing you must decide is which type of *liking* you prefer—respect or affection? Then you must somehow acquire those thought patterns, emotions, and behavioral reactions that will give other people the impression that you deserve whichever type of liking you are most interested in. It might help if we first explored the cues that you probably use in judging others when you meet them. For if you understand what stimulus inputs influence your own reactions to other people, you may also get a better picture of how your actions affect the *person perception* (°) that others have of you.

PERSON PERCEPTION

Suppose some good friends of yours have talked you into taking a blind date to a party. They paint a glowing picture of your date as a kind of super-person, and put considerable pressure on you to accept the date so that you won't spoil the party. When the fatal moment comes, and you first meet the person, what sorts of things do you look for immediately? What clues do you seek as a guide to whether you will like (that is, respect or have affection for) the person? Obviously, each of you reading this book will have a different answer, but the social psychologists who study person perception have come up with some generalities that might interest you.

First Impressions

To begin with, blind dates are usually social situations, so we might expect you to be more interested in finding a compatible social-emotional expert than an idea man or woman. Emotional warmth—however expressed—would seem to be the key element most people seek in social partners. Your friends will have biased your perceptions by their description of your blind date before you first meet the individual. If they have told you the person is warm, affectionate, responsive, and outgoing, you will probably look for these attributes in the individual as soon as the two of you meet. Certainly your *attitude* toward the person will be different than if you have been told your date is rather intellectual, cold, withdrawn, quiet, and self-possessed.

The word *attitude* (°) refers to a consistent way of thinking about, feeling toward, or responding to some aspect of your environment. You may hold attitudes toward almost anything—concrete objects such as automobiles; living objects such as people or animals; groups or organizations such as the U.S. government; or even abstract ideas such as love, truth, art, and science. Attitudes usually have three dimensions to them—that is, they are made up of cognitive, emotional, and behavioral *components* (°). For example, we can measure the behavioral aspects of your attitude toward (let's say) a political leader by seeing whether you vote for the person in an election or listen to the person on radio or television. The cognitive and emotional aspects of your attitude must be measured indirectly, perhaps by asking you questions about how you think or feel toward the politician.

Reputation and Stereotypes

When your friends describe your blind date to you, they are telling you something about that person's reputation—that is, the way that most people presumably perceive the individual, or the attitude that most people have toward the person.

Psychologist Harold Kelley tested the importance of "reputations" in a study performed at the Massachusetts Institute of Technology in the late 1940's. Kelley told a large class of undergraduates that they would have a visiting lecturer for the day, and that the students would be asked to evaluate this man at the end of the class. Kelley then passed out a brief biographical note about the teacher, presumably to help the students with their evaluation. Although the students did not realize it, the description that half the class received referred to the lecturer (among other things) as being "rather a warm individual," while the description given the rest of the class called the man "rather a cold individual."

After the class had read the printed comments, the man arrived and led the class in a 20-minute discussion. Kelley watched the students and recorded how often each student asked a question or made a comment. Afterward, the students were asked to rate the man on a set of attitude scales and to write a brief description of him. Although everyone in the class had witnessed exactly the same performance at exactly the same time, the manner in which each student responded was measurably affected by the descriptions each had read. Those students who had been told the instructor was warm tended to rate him as much more informal, sociable, popular, good-natured, humorous, and humane than the students who had been told the man was cold. Some 56 percent of the students told he was warm actually interacted with the instructor in class, while only 32 percent of those told the man was cold entered the class discussion. Apparently, once we believe we won't like a person, we avoid further contact with him or her. Michigan psychologist Theodore Newcomb has called this response *autistic hostility* (°), and suggests that it may apply to interactions among groups as well as among individuals.

Harold Kelley.

QUESTION: **The students in Kelley's experiment tended to perceive the lecturer as they had expected him to be rather than as he really was. How might Kelley's research findings help explain the difficulty that Rosenhan's subjects had in convincing mental hospital staffs that the subjects were really normal or "sane?"**

Our initial impressions are often colored by the *stereotypes* (°), or biased perceptions, that each of us has about certain types or groups of people. If we assume that all blacks are lazy, dull, ignorant but musical, we tend to "see" these attributes even in an energetic, bright black doctor who perhaps couldn't carry a tune in a handbag. If our attitude toward Jews is that they are intelligent, emotional, and penny-pinching, we may respond to each Jew as if he or she had to fit our stereotype. Any time that we react to an individual primarily in terms of that person's membership in some group—or in terms of that person's physical characteristics, race, or religion—we are guilty of *stereotyping*. That is, we are guilty of letting the reputation of the group influence our perception of the individual who belongs to that group.

Primacy Effect

Newcomb's concept of *autistic hostility* suggests that getting off on the right foot with a new acquaintance may be very important—for you may not have more than one chance to get the person to like you. Back in the 1940's psychologist Solomon Asch gave a group of subjects a list of adjectives describing someone they might meet. Half the subjects were told the person was "intelligent, industrious, impulsive, critical, stubborn, and envious." The other half of the subjects were given the same list, but in opposite order: "envious, stubborn, critical, impulsive, industrious, intelligent." The subjects were then asked to write a brief paragraph evaluating what they thought the person might really be like. The responses made by two of Asch's subjects are good examples of what psychologists call the *primacy effect* (°).

A subject told the person was "intelligent . . . envious" wrote that: "The

Autistic hostility (aw-TISS-tic). Autism is the act of withdrawing into one's self, of shutting off external stimulation. Autistic hostility is the act of cutting off or denying favorable inputs about people or things we don't like. "My mind is made up—don't confuse me with facts."

Stereotypes. A stereotype is a fixed or unconscious attitude or perception—a way of responding to some person or object solely in terms of the person's or object's class membership. The failure to treat people as individuals, each different from the other, is the act of stereotyping.

Primacy effect (PRY-muh-see). *Primus* is the Latin word for "first." Whenever you remember your first impressions of a stimulus better than your second or third impressions, you are demonstrating the primacy effect. An equally interesting phenomenon is the recency effect—the tendency to be more influenced by our last or most recent impressions of a stimulus than by our initial impressions.

person is intelligent and fortunately he puts his intelligence to work. That he is stubborn and impulsive may be due to the fact that he knows what he is saying and what he means and will not therefore give in easily to someone else's idea which he disagrees with."

A subject told the person was "envious . . . intelligent" wrote that: "This person's good qualities such as industry and intelligence are bound to be restricted by jealously and stubbornness. The person is emotional. He is unsuccessful because he is weak and allows his bad points to cover up his good ones."

Presumably, the first information you get about a person creates the framework, or the bare bones, of an attitude. The rest of the data you receive about this person merely helps you flesh out the details of the individual's personality.

In a more recent test of the primacy effect, psychologist Edward Jones and his colleagues had subjects watch the performance of a fellow college student as he supposedly tried to solve 30 rather difficult problems out loud. Later on, the subjects were asked to recall how many correct answers the student had gotten, and to guess whether he would do well in a second series of questions.

Actually, the student was a part of the experiment. When half of the subjects watched him, he got a lot of the first questions right, but performed more and more poorly toward the end. When the other half of the subjects were watching, the student did poorly at the beginning but got more and more questions right toward the end. In both situations the student answered exactly 15 out of the 30 questions correctly.

Jones and his associates report that subjects who saw the subject go from good to bad "remembered" his solving many more problems and expected him to do much better on the second series of problems than did the subjects who saw the subject go from bad to good performance. It would seem that, if you want to impress people, it helps to go all out the first time you meet them.

But what is it that you can do that will impress people? How do you get your "message" across to a blind date, or to someone who might be able to give you a job? In effect, you have two main channels of communication—what you do with your body and what you say with your tongue. The way you look and dress and move—these are part of your body language. What you say, the opinions you express, and the verbal responses you make—these are part of your verbal language. Surprisingly enough, when it comes to first impressions, we are often more influenced by a person's *body talk* (or non-verbal communication) than we are by what the person actually says.

Non-verbal Communication

When you form a first impression of a person, what aspects of the person's character are you likely to be interested in? Do you try to "psych the person out"—that is, determine the motives, responsiveness, and future behaviors of the individual? If so, what you probably want to know are the person's intentions toward you. And since you will usually see the person for at least a few seconds before you hear him or her talk, the individual's looks and movements will typically have a *primacy effect* in determining your initial attitude toward the person.

We all have characteristic ways of dressing, of combing our hair, of moving our arms and legs, of looking toward or away from people as we speak or listen, of smiling, and of frowning. Your own physical attributes may not really be good indicators of what you are like deep down inside; however, experiments suggest that many people you meet will judge your intentions toward them primarily by the way in which you communicate non-verbally.

But what makes up your own unique brand of body language? What can a stranger tell about you just by watching you behave?

Cultural Expectations   To begin with, and perhaps most important, is the simple fact that you are either male or female. Every culture has different *social expectations* about the ways that men and women should look and behave. In the United States we presume that males are bigger, stronger, cruder in their language and movements, and more violent and domineering than women. Men are expected to be interested in such things as automobiles, sports, business and finance, science and technology; women are expected to prefer the arts, children, home life, and social relations. We have stereotyped beliefs about the psychological differences between men and women that color the first impressions of everyone we meet.

Next most important to your sexual identity perhaps is your age. Young people are expected to be energetic, enthusiastic, idealistic, liberal but perhaps inexperienced. Older people are expected to be more *sedate* (°), conservative, settled, experienced, and perhaps more willing to compromise to get some of the things they want from life. It doesn't matter that these cultural expectations are not entirely accurate—what does matter is that almost all of us, in fact, do expect older people to behave differently than young people.

Your size, shape, skin color, and physical beauty also affect the impression you give others. Think back to our discussion of personality theories in Chapter 23. You will recall that Sheldon found small but reliable *correlations* between body type and personality traits. Not all mesomorphs are athletic, outgoing, and enthusiastic; but, in our culture, enough people with the mesomorphic body type are "jocks" so that the stereotype has some validity to it.

As you can now see, all cultural stereotypes are miniature personality theories. And like most personality theories, stereotypes are usually built on small but statistically reliable correlations. Sheldon's data suggest that slightly more endomorphs are jolly and oriented toward eating and other creature comforts than might be expected by chance alone. If you stereotype all fat people as being jolly, you will do a grave injustice to many of the endomorphs you meet—but you will probably be right slightly more often than you will be wrong.

QUESTION: What personality traits do you expect to find in tall people? in short people? in blacks? in whites? in pretty women? in ugly men? What evidence can you offer that there is any validity to your stereotyped attitudes toward these types of people?

The Attribution Process

Why do we so often resort to stereotyping? According to social psychologist Fritz Heider, it is because of our culture's traditional solution to the mind-body problem (*see* Chapter 4). We all have a need to predict the way that people will react to us. But in Western society, we are usually taught that predictions about human behavior are possible only if we can comprehend the *inner causes* that presumably control the behavior. Because we typically ignore the great influence that environmental inputs have on our own thoughts and activities, we believe our actions are determined almost entirely by our internal need states and mental processes. Thus when we try to explain the behavior of others, we assume that they too act as they do because they *want* to act that way.

As Heider pointed out in 1958, we seldom see human actions as occurring in a particular social context, as being a figure perceived against a background. Rather, we put the cause for the behavior entirely inside the person. We then must invent explanations for *why* people do what they do by *attributing* certain personality traits to them. Most of these attributed traits are in fact stereotypes. From a practical point of view it may not matter to us if the stereotyped label we have stuck on someone isn't entirely accurate. What does matter is that by labeling an individual, we immediately have a ready-made attitude or perception to fit the person, and hence a ready-made way of responding to that person.

As our cultural stereotypes change, women are free to enter professions previously closed to them.

Sedate (see-DATE). From a Latin word meaning "to soothe, calm, appease, or make tranquil." A sedate person is one who is not readily influenced by disturbances.

Robert Sommer.

As we noted in Chapter 12, our major motivation seems to be that of trying to control our stimulus inputs. We become alarmed (stressed) whenever we cannot guess fairly accurately what will happen to us next. By using what Heider calls the *attribution process* (°), we attribute to others motives that make their actions understandable (predictable) to us.

From a humanistic point of view, the problem with the attribution process is not that we try to put motivational labels on people, but rather that the labels we use are so imprecise, biased, and unscientific. The more *facts* that you learn about yourself and others, the closer your own attribution process will come to fitting external reality. And the less frequently you make use of crude stereotypes, the less often you will be shocked (stressed) by the actions of others.

QUESTION: **It seems a fact that we are often greatly frightened by people whose behavior is highly unpredictable. Could Heider's theory of the attribution process explain why such deviant individuals often end up in prisons and mental hospitals?**

Personal Space The physical responses that we make toward other people also influence the initial attitudes we arouse in others. Robert Sommer, a psychologist at the University of California (Davis), has for many years studied what might be called *personal space* (°). It would seem that each of us carries an invisible bubble around our bodies that encloses what we consider to be our own, personal psychological space. We defend this area much as a mother bluejay might defend the territory around her nest.

The size of your own personal space bubble is influenced by such factors as your personality, status, and your culture. For middle-class Americans, this private area extends outward about 2 feet from any part of the body. For Arabs,

Attribution process. The act of projecting personality traits or motives onto others so that we can explain their past or present behavior, hence predict what they may do in the future.

Personal space. A concept by Robert Sommer (and others) that each of us has his or her own "psychological territory"—a bubble of space around our bodies that we think of as being our "home base," not to be invaded by others without our permission.

People in Arabic cultures have a different concept of personal space than people in Western cultures.

the space is usually much smaller; for Scandinavians, the bubble is typically larger. People with great status (that is, people whom almost everyone respects) often command a larger personal space than do individuals with little or no status. We approach a prince, a pope, or a president with care and caution, lest we come too close. Babies and young children, who typically have little or no status at all, can be approached almost as closely as we wish.

> QUESTION: **If you watched people carefully at a party, could you come up with a rough measure of the size of their personal spaces? How might you measure the size of your own space bubble?**

The most *flagrant* (°) violation of personal space usually comes when someone tries to touch us. Surprisingly enough, we are more likely to defend our bubble-territories against intrusion by equals than against individuals of inferior or superior status. Parents and teachers, doctors and dentists, princes and policemen may "lay hands" on us because of their authority—but we typically do not touch them first without asking permission. Servants and waitresses, barbers and hair-dressers, children and animals may intrude into our personal spaces without threatening us too much. However, we are often shy about touching our friends, particularly if the gesture might have sexual overtones. The woman who sprawls in a chair with her legs uncrossed and the man who leans close to whisper something in your ear give the impression they would like you to violate their personal space—or vice versa.

In a study on body posture, psychologist Albert Mehrabian asked men and women to act out the ways in which they would sit when speaking to someone they liked or disliked. Mehrabian reports that both men and women leaned forward to express liking, but that men (more than women) leaned back or became more tense when addressing someone they disliked.

Psychologist Donn Byrne and his associates set up an experiment in which couples were selected by a computer for blind dates. After the young man and woman had gotten to know each other briefly, they were called into Byrne's office and stood before his desk for further instructions. The subjects were then separated and asked to fill out a questionnaire indicating how much they liked their dates. Byrne and his colleagues report that couples who liked each other stood measurably closer together in front of the desk than did couples who didn't care much for one another.

> QUESTION: **Why might strangers in a crowded elevator stare straight ahead and avoid conversation?**

The Eyes Have It   Movements of your face and eyes are often as critical to the first impression you give as are the ways you move your arms and legs. Smiles invite approaches; frowns demand distance. The eye contact you make with people often controls both the flow of conversation and their initial opinion of your honesty and aggressiveness.

Psychiatrist R.D. Laing states that many schizophrenic patients who withdraw from the social world seem to avoid eye contact entirely. This avoidance response is particularly characteristic of autistic children, who often refuse to look anyone directly in the eyes.

If you happen to be a middle-class, white adult, you probably look at people when they are talking or lecturing. For in your society, staring directly at a speaker is a learned response that apparently encourages that person to continue conversing. When you look away from whoever is talking, however, you signal that you are bored or that you desire to converse yourself. Any speaker who is sensitive to your social cue of glancing away will rapidly change the subject or throw the conversational ball in your direction.

When you are telling a story or making a point, chances are that you will

Flagrant (FLAY-grant). From the Latin word meaning "to flame or burn," as in "conflagration" (kon-fluh-GRAY-shun), which means "fire." Anything that is particularly obvious or noticeable is flagrant.

Albert Mehrabian.

Social role. A set of standard responses to certain social situations. A set of behavior patterns appropriate to a given environment.

Repertory (REP-purr-torr-ee). A complete set of social roles. The "parts" that a person is able to play in life.

glance away from your audience. This is your signal that you don't want to be interrupted just yet. While you talk, you may glance back at your audience from time to time to make sure they are still with you (that is, still looking at you), then look away again in a hurry if you wish to continue.

Conversation shifts from one person to another primarily when two people are in direct eye contact. Anyone who violates these unwritten social rules is often thought to be rude, immature, or overly aggressive.

QUESTION: **Among blacks, these eye signals are often reversed; many blacks avert their eyes while they are listening, but stare directly at someone whom they are talking to. Various oriental cultures have quite different sets of eye contact rules. If you were not aware of these facts, how might you misinterpret the responses a person of another race gave to you while you two were conversing?**

Appropriate versus Inappropriate Behaviors   Initial impressions are but the first step in getting a stranger to like you. The mere fact that you act in a friendly and considerate manner toward a person doesn't guarantee that the person will assume your actions reflect "the real you." Since most of us are "on our good behavior" in first encounters, many of the people we meet may discount our appropriate behaviors as being "put on."

Oddly enough, however, if you behave *inappropriately*, most people will assume that you did so because of some basic flaw in your personality structure. Apparently we are often reluctant to believe the best about strangers, but only too ready to believe the worst.

Edward Jones and his associates demonstrated the operation of this principle by asking subjects to listen to recorded interviews between a psychologist and a student applying for a job. In one interview the student went out of his way to impress the psychologist favorably. The student suggested several times that he more than met the job requirements. Subjects who heard this recording found it difficult to describe the applicant's personality—they thought he was "just playing a role." In the second interview the same student presented himself as being quite different from the sort of person that the job required. Subjects who heard just the second tape were confident that the student had "shown his true colors" because he apparently behaved inappropriately in the situation.

As Shakespeare put it: "All the world's a stage, and all the men and women merely players. They have their exits and their entrances; and one man in his time plays many parts." The lasting impressions that we make depend to a great extent on the *consistency* of the parts that we play in the theater of life. So perhaps it is time we looked seriously at role-playing.

SOCIAL ROLES

A *social role* (°) is a more or less stereotyped set of responses that a person makes to related or similar situations. In a sense a social role is like a part that an actor or actress might portray in a play or film. Some roles (such as being masculine or feminine) are a basic part of our *repertory* (°) all through our lives; other roles (such as being a cheerleader or valedictorian) are "bit parts" or "walk-ons" that we often discard as we mature. Like a part in a play, a social role is made up of a characteristic set of body movements and verbal statements.

When Shakespeare created the heroine's part in his play *Romeo and Juliet*, he had to decide what Juliet's basic personality was like. Then he put words into her mouth that would express the traits he thought his young girl would display in the situations she faced. But Shakespeare didn't suggest *precisely* the facial movements and gestures that Juliet would show while speaking her lines. Thus, when an actress prepares for this role, she must decide what her body is going to be doing while her tongue speaks Shakespeare's poetry. Both her verbal and non-verbal modes of expression must "hang together" if her portrayal of Juliet is to be a success with the audience.

A great actress may play an aging queen one day and a foolish young secretary the next. How can she convince us tonight that she is a naive young woman, when last night she impressed us as being an elderly empress down to her very fingertips? The finest actors and actresses (both on and off the stage) appear to emphasize those aspects of their own personalities that fit the parts they are playing. Most of us seem to do the same sort of thing in everyday situations. We all have friends whom we greatly respect. If you wanted to convince a man you just met that you really liked him, couldn't you act as if he were a stereotype of one of your respected friends? That is, couldn't you pay particular attention to any of the stranger's behaviors that merited respect and ignore all the rest?

In a series of experiments in which college students were allowed to pick which of certain roles they wished to play, psychologists C.W. Backman and P.F. Secord found that many students did indeed adapt their own personalities to fit a given stereotyped role. Backman and Secord use the term *role portrayal* (°) to describe this adaptational process. Other students chose roles that allowed them to behave as they already did—a process called "type casting" in the theater, and which Backman and Secord refer to as *role selection* (°).

However, once the student began playing a role somewhat different from the student's self-image, rather an unusual thing occurred. Often the student's self-attitude or self-conception would become altered to become more like the role the student had just played. Backman and Secord refer to this change as the *fashioning effect* (°), or the fact that we often become what we do. It would seem that if we want to become somewhat different, the first thing we should do is to act out the new role several times, even if we can't entirely put our heart into the actions at the beginning. Correspondingly, if we don't wish to change ourselves, the last thing we should do is to let someone talk us into role-playing someone different.

QUESTION: **How might the Backman and Secord experiment be related to Moreno's psycho-drama therapy?**

Role portrayal. According to Backman and Secord, the ability to adapt a social role to one's own personality. The act of selecting out of one's own personality structure those pieces or complexes that are appropriate to a new situation.

Role selection. The act of hunting for situations that will allow us to behave as we are already behaving or want to behave. A man who loves sports may look for a job as a coach, while a woman who loves children may seek employment as a nursery-school teacher.

Fashioning effect. According to Backman and Secord, the act of taking on a new role, learning new responses, and then becoming more like that role than we were before. If a worker on an assembly line is suddenly promoted to a job as supervisor, the person may immediately begin behaving like a "manager" but may still have "worker" attitudes. However, if tested a year later, the person may display "manager" attitudes, having become more like the role he or she is playing.

Archetypes (ARK-ee-types). From the Greek words meaning "the original model." The archetypes that Jung referred to are the "original models" of myths, legends, and stories—instinctual thought patterns passed on genetically from generation to generation.

Where Roles Come From

Psychologists are not agreed as to how we acquire the social roles we have available to us. Theorists such as Sheldon and Kretschmer believe that roles are expressions of underlying personality traits, and hence are primarily determined by our body types and brain chemistry (*see* Chapter 23). Carl Jung's *archetypes* (°) can be considered social roles presumably built up over many generations and passed along to us through our genes. Sigmund Freud's concepts of id, ego, and super-ego are to some extent innately-determined social roles. If you were asked to prove to an audience how rational you were, might you not banish your id and spotlight your ego instead? If you wished to impress someone with how stern and moralistic you could be, might you not conscientiously let your super-ego be your guide?

Transactional analysis, the form of group therapy devised by psychiatrist Eric Berne, is really a form of role analysis built on a Freudian model (*see* Chapter 25). Berne believes that all people have three main personality traits—or "ego states," as he calls them—that determine our responses in social situations.

The most primitive of these ego states is what Berne calls "Child," which consists of rather immature (id) reactions that are left over from the past. The second ego state is that of "Parent," which includes all of the rules and regulations imposed on us by society. The third ego state is the "Adult," made up of our healthy, adaptive reactions to social reality. All of the roles that we play—that is,

Bonnie R. Strickland.

all transactions among individuals, whether constructive or destructive—are said to be made up of different amounts of these three ego states.

The "games people play" are, to Berne, *roles* that reflect which of the three ego states is dominant at the moment. Social problems arise when people misperceive the role we are presently playing. Suppose you criticize a woman you know for something she has done, intending the remark as a reflection of your Adult ego state. If she perceives the criticism as being adult, she may understand your good intentions and accept the remark as valid feedback on her performance. However, if she perceives the criticism as the product of the Parent and not of the Adult, she may react as a child would to a critical parent.

Transactional group therapy is designed to help make each participant aware of the Parent, Child, and Adult components of the roles each person plays in social settings. Only through such analysis, Berne believes, can an individual learn new, more fulfilling ways of behaving.

Male and Female Roles

While basic roles (like traits) surely have a biological component, for the most part we must learn the parts we play in the theater of life. As we saw in Chapters 20 and 21, training to play the male or female role begins early in life. Boys are shaped or fashioned into wanting respect more than affection in our society, while girls are usually taught the reverse. Since respect is typically associated with high-paying and high-status jobs, men are more likely to become executives than are women. On the other hand, the desire for affection is often associated with low-status "service" professions; jobs like nursing, hairdressing, and social work are usually perceived as being feminine occupations.

One of the aims of the women's movement is that of changing our notions of what the male and female roles ought to be. Women's liberation groups believe that women should be encouraged to seek *liking-respect* as much as are men, and that men sould be taught that *liking-affection* is as worthy a goal as *liking-respect*.

Strangely enough, there is some evidence that U.S. men are more restricted by present sex roles than are women. Psychologist Bonnie R. Strickland asked students at Emory University and at the University of Hawaii what career changes they would make if they were suddenly transformed into the opposite sexes. Twice as many male students as females indicated they would shift professions (roles) under these circumstances, almost always to a lower-status job. Dr. Strickland believes that men are much more influenced than women by traditional ideas of what kinds of careers are appropriate to a given sex.

QUESTION: In most U.S. families the father's role is that of managing intellectual and/or financial resources and the mother's role is that of managing emotional resources. If both men and women are "liberated" from these traditions, what changes might we expect in the structure and behavior of the U.S. family?

Role Change

Although most of us maintain our sexual identities pretty much unchanged throughout our lives, we are likely to pick up and discard other roles as the situation demands. In most societies children are allowed certain behaviors that adults are not. When puberty arrives, the child must put aside some behaviors and take on others. In the United States, when a young person graduates from high school or college, he or she typically abandons the student role and assumes those behaviors associated with work or the professions. Marriage typically ends the dating role, and the arrival of the first child is expected to bring forth parental response patterns, whether the husband and wife are ready for them or not. Divorce, the death of a spouse or parent, and retirement can also call for sudden and sometimes irreversible role changes. Perhaps it is the sharply-defined nature of such experiences that leads us to attach ceremonies or celebrations to them.

Occasionally, like an actor or actress, we set out to take on a new role. For the most part, however, we acquire (or abandon) our stereotyped behavior patterns without realizing what we are doing or why. The primary means of learning role behaviors seems to be that of unconscious imitation, a sort of "human see, human do" process. Even when we deliberately acquire a new role, we are likely to model that role on someone else's performance.

The arrival of the first baby usually brings forth parental response patterns.

Bandura's "Modeling" Therapy Stanford psychologist Albert Bandura believes that, to some extent, psychotherapy is a matter of choosing a more adaptive role and learning how to play it well. The technique he finds particularly useful is called "modeling," in which the therapist demonstrates the new behavior pattern and then encourages the subject to master the response in a step-by-step fashion. In one of Bandura's best-known experiments he helped people lose their fear of snakes.

Bandura began by advertising in a newspaper for subjects who wished help in overcoming a snake phobia. Thirty-two people answered the ad. One was a museum official who was afraid to enter the snake exhibit in his own museum. Several were individuals who feared going hunting, fishing, or hiking because they might encounter a reptile. Others were schoolteachers whose young students often brought snakes to class for "show and tell." One woman had a neighbor who kept a boa constrictor as a pet; thinking about the closeness of the snake had nearly given the woman a heart attack.

Bandura compared four different types of treatment. Eight of the subjects were randomly selected to receive no therapy at all during the first part of the experiment. These eight people made up the no-treatment control group. Another eight were shown movies of adults and children playing with snakes. A third group of eight were given systematic desensitization to overcome their fears (*see* Chapter 15).

The fourth group was given "modeling therapy." At the beginning of treatment this fourth group watched through a glass partition while the therapist played with a snake to show that it wasn't dangerous. The therapist tried to model all of the snake-handling behaviors he wished the subjects to learn. Then the subjects entered the room where the therapist was—but stayed some distance away from the dreaded reptile. Next, through gradual approximations, they were encouraged to approach the snake and touch it, just as the therapist had modeled doing. As the subjects gained confidence in playing with the snake, the therapist faded out of the picture.

The "final exam" for the effectiveness of the therapy was somewhat dramatic. The subject was asked to sit in a chair for 30 seconds, hands at side, while a snake was placed on the subject's lap and allowed to crawl all over his or her body. Every member of the modeling therapy group passed the test with ease. A few of the members of the film-treatment and desensitization groups passed, but almost no one in the no-treatment group could tolerate such close proximity to the reptile. Bandura then did something unusual—he gave modeling therapy to the members of the other groups who hadn't shown improvement. He reports "cures" in 100 percent of these subjects.

QUESTION: **How might you go about reinstituting the snake phobia in Bandura's subjects?**

Many roles are like clothing—we wear them in public, but sometimes shed them when alone or among trusted friends. And like the costumes that actors use in the theater, the roles we put on in public usually fit the expectations of the audience we're performing for. Thus on a first date, a young man is likely to

Albert Bandura.

Altruistic (al-true-IS-tick). From a French word meaning "someone else." An altruistic act is one that brings more pleasure to someone else than to yourself.

Tangible (TAN-juh-bull). From the Latin word *tangere,* meaning "to touch." A tangible object is anything that can be seen or touched, that has physical reality. Your tangible assets are all your physical possessions, including money. Your intangible assets would include such "non-touchable" things as your friendships and your personality traits.

Extrinsic rewards (ex-TRINN-sick). From the Latin word meaning "on the outside," hence creature comforts and sensory pleasures. Opposed to intrinsic rewards, which have to do with inner joys and good feelings.

display the stereotyped masculine reactions he thinks the woman will expect of him, and she may play the feminine role she believes will win his approval. If the relationship continues, however, both of them may stop worrying about first impressions and begin to express more fundamental (and perhaps less socially-accepted) personality traits. As we will see momentarily, this relaxation of role-playing has both its benefits and its costs.

THE ECONOMICS OF ROLE-PLAYING

It is easy to think of situations in which you might wish to pretend to be someone (or something) other than you really are: a blind date, a job interview, a party at which important people are present, an encounter with a police officer who wants to give you a ticket for speeding. But why bother? The answer typically is that we desire something from the person or persons we are trying to impress.

Human beings are often unselfish or *altruistic* (°); but the plain fact is that many of our behaviors are influenced by pleasures and punishments. Sometimes the rewards we seek are *tangible* (°)—such as good grades, money, power, and position. Psychologists often refer to these things as *extrinsic rewards* (°). More often our reinforcements are intangible or intrinsic—we want respect, recognition, warmth and affection, intellectual stimulation, good companionship. If we have to "play a part" to get what we need, most of us are willing to do so, whether we are conscious of our motives or not. The more valuable the reward appears to us, the more likely it is we will role-play to achieve it. And the more frequently in the past we have achieved our goals by "play-acting," the more probable it becomes that we will do the same in the future.

From an economic point of view, then, role-playing is something that we do for others in order that they will do something for us in return. At its worst, role-playing is selfish manipulation of other people; for the most part, however, it is a necessary form of social exchange that allows each person to get something by giving something. And just as there are formal regulations governing the purchase of food and clothing with money, so there are informal rules governing the purchase of social rewards with role-playing. The person who takes without giving is often punished by being disliked, ignored, or isolated. The most valuable forms of social interchange are typically those in which both parties are satisfied with the bargain.

To Be Alike Is To Be Liked

Why should the roles you play be so rewarding to other people? Psychologist Donn Byrne suggests an interesting answer. If you would like to test the validity of Dr. Byrne's suggestion, first make a list of the things that you want most from a person you've recently met or from someone whom you'd like to know better. After you've done this, make a list of the things you would expect this person wants from you. Is there a similarity between the two lists? That is, are the things you want from others correlated with what you think they want from you? If the two lists are strikingly different, what are the chances of your becoming good friends?

Byrne has collected a great deal of evidence suggesting that the major factor attracting one person to another is similarity between the two. He asked hundreds of subjects to fill out questionnaires telling about their own attitudes on a number of topics. Each subject was then shown a second questionnaire supposedly filled out by a complete stranger. In fact, Byrne "faked" the answers to this second questionnaire so that the stranger appeared to be similar to—or dissimilar to—the subject. The subject was then asked whether he or she would "like" the stranger. As you might guess, the closer the subject's attitudes were to the stranger's, the

Donn Byrne.

more frequently the subject reported a liking for the stranger. These results appear to hold for people of all ages, nationalities, educational levels, and socio-economic status.

Byrne's results—and those of dozens of other scientists—tend to validate the old *cliché* (°), "Birds of a feather flock together." And there are certainly many reasons why "to be like" is almost the same as "to be liked." Having someone agree with us is apparently very rewarding. The more similar your attitudes are to your friend's, the more probable it is that you will agree with one another without having to suffer the stress and anxiety of pretending to be someone you aren't. The more similar the person is to you, the better your attribution process will work, and the more readily you can predict the person's future behaviors. And the more similar your value systems, the more readily you can determine the rewards and punishments you might give to each other.

A Wedding of Opposites?

The closest, most intimate, longest-lasting relationship that most people experience is probably that between husband and wife. Not all marriages are successful, however. Judging from the Byrne data, we might predict that enduring marriages should be found primarily between partners whose attitudes are highly similar or closely correlated—and that the more alike the man and woman are, the better the relationship will probably be. Supporting this prediction are hundreds of studies indicating that husbands and wives tend to be significantly similar to each other with respect to age, race, religion, education, social status, height, weight, eye color, and intelligence. Some of these studies date back 100 years or more, to the time of Sir Francis Galton, the noted British psychologist of the last century.

Looking just at these data, we might conclude that birds of a feather not only flock together—they roost together as well. In evaluating this position, however, there are two other bits of cultural wisdom that we should consider: "Familiarity breeds contempt" and "Opposites attract." Don't these clichés suggest that, in order to remain happily married, a man and woman should be considerably different from one another? Some light on this question is shed by a long-term study performed by psychologist E. Lowell Kelly. The first report on Kelly's work came in his 1955 presidential address to the American Psychological Association; the final report has yet to be issued.

More than 30 years ago, Kelly began an investigation of several hundred engaged couples. Kelly measured their attitudes, their backgrounds, their IQ's, their personalities—even such physical things as their heights and weights. He then checked up on these couples at regular intervals during the next 20 years, both to determine how they had changed and to discover if they were still together.

There were, of course, three possible outcomes to the engagements: (1) the couple broke off their relationship prior to marriage; (2) they got married, but eventually divorced; (3) they remained married throughout the period of the study. Kelly had hoped that his studies of the personalities of the couples would allow him to predict what happened to their relationships—that is, he had thought that there might be rather simple correlations between personality or physical type and the outcome of the engagement. As it happened, the data turned out to be much more complex than Kelly perhaps had expected. A full understanding of the significance of his findings will have to wait until Kelly completes his work, but we can report a few of the many interesting findings of this research.

Take the question of body type, for example. There are many quite different aspects of the human *physique* (°) that can be measured, and the correlations between physical type and marriage outcome varied widely depending on what

If the attributes of this couple are fairly similar, they are probably at the outset of a successful marriage.

Cliché (klee-SHAY). *Cliché* is a French word meaning a trite or stereotyped reaction, an overworked expression or idea. The dialogue in many bad movies consists almost entirely of clichés—the actors and actresses give one stereotyped verbal response after another. Samuel Goldwyn, the movie producer, may have had the right idea when he told his writers: "Don't give me old clichés—give me new clichés!"

Physique (fiss-EEK). From the Greek word meaning "natural." Your physique is your body type. Literally, the structure, appearance, or strength of the human body.

E. Lowell Kelly.

Vice versa. A Latin term meaning "the other way around."

Significant positive correlation. A positive relationship between two items or events that is greater than one would expect by chance. For example, there is a significant positive correlation between hair color and eye color. Most (but not all) blonds have blue eyes; and most (but not all) brunets have dark eyes. The larger the correlation, the more closely related the two items or events are. See the Statistical Appendix.

measurements Kelly looked at. For instance, in the case of height and weight, there seemed to be three rather distinct types of couples: (1) Some were made up of a man and woman very similar to each other—that is, the man would be tall (as compared to other men) and the woman would be tall (compared to other women), or they both would be short and perhaps fat in relation to other men and women. (2) The second type of couple was composed of a man and woman fairly different from each other—that is, the man might be short and fat, while the woman was tall and thin, or *vice versa* (°). (3) The third type of couple fell somewhere between the extremes set by the first two types; but the third couples were more similar to each other in height and weight than they were differ-ent—which is to say that the man and woman were more like each other than if they had been paired off randomly, so there was a *significant (positive) correlation* (°) between their heights and weights. This correlation was much lower or smaller than among the "birds of a feather" who made up the first type.

Now, can you guess which type of couple broke off the engagement, which type married but divorced, and which type stayed together?

Apparently some types of "physical" opposites do attract—but not for long. A significant number of the couples dissimilar in height and weight broke off their engagements. These couples did have many things in common; and not all measures of body type gave the same results. But it seems possible that many of these couples became interested in one another primarily because of their exciting but rather superficial *differences*. Once the initial stimulation of their "surface" differences had paled, the couples tended to drift apart. As far as height and weight were concerned, then, the "wedding of opposites" tended not to occur.

The "birds of a feather" so highly correlated in height and weight often went through with the marriage, but were very likely to dissolve the relationship in divorce some time thereafter. One possible interpretation of these results is that the couples' initial attraction was based primarily on superficial *similarities* (although they had many differences also). Perhaps these men and women were most impressed at the start of their relationship by the fact that they made such "beautifully matched couples." But beauty is more than skin deep, and if the marriage was based on such trivial factors as "looking good together," the match simply could not last.

The couples who made successful marriages were those who, in Kelly's opinion, became interested in each other for "deep" rather than for "superficial" reasons. These men and women were similar enough in important ways (including height and weight) to pleasure each other physically and mentally, but they were also sufficiently different to be interesting and challenging to each other. More than this, Kelly believes, these marriages endured because the man and woman apparently found ways of balancing their needs for "the security of being similar" with their needs for "the novelty of being different." As you might suspect, these needs varied considerably from one couple to another. The remarkable thing, however, is that the successful couples seemed to have found ways of maintaining *both* their similarities and their differences throughout the life of the marriage. Thus, if the husband changed his political attitudes over the years, the wife would shift just enough to maintain the original difference between their views. If the woman became more permissive in her notions about rearing children, the husband would change just enough in the same direction to keep the correlation between their attitudes the same as when they were first engaged. Good mar-riages—at least during the years that Kelly undertook the study—were mostly those between "birds" whose "feathers" were perhaps more similar than different; more important, they were marriages between men and women who placed more value on maintaining their psychological compatibility than on such "surface" attractants as height and weight.

The price for the survival of any two-person group would therefore seem to be:

As one person changes, the other must compensate to keep the rewarding aspects of the relationship more or less constant. "Physical" attractions (such as height and weight) are hard to change; "psychological" attractions (such as personality or social roles) are considerably more flexible. The way you look influences people's first impressions of you; but what you are "underneath" your body type has a greater influence on the course of long-term relationships. Knowing all this, you might wish to re-examine your own social roles and attitudes. For perhaps the most favorable first impression that you can give someone is not that you have respect or affection for the role the person is presently playing but rather that you are willing to like (and adjust to) the person whatever role he or she adopts.

SUMMARY

1. When we say that we want people to like us, we typically mean that we want them either to respect us or to be emotionally attracted to us, or both.
2. Research on problem-solving in small groups suggests that there are two types of people who are liked—those individuals who are task-oriented or "idea people," and those individuals who astutely manage the socio-emotional resources of the group by giving praise and criticism.
3. The first impressions we gain of people are influenced by many factors:
   a. To begin with, there is the reputation of the person—whether people we already know like and respect the newly met person.
   b. Second, we all have cultural expectations about the people in the world around us—that is, we have stereotyped notions about how individuals should dress, appear, talk, and behave.
   c. We tend to like people who fit our expectations, but may reject someone who does not.
4. We use what Fritz Heider calls "the attribution process" to help us predict the behavior of others by assuming we understand the inner causes of their actions.
5. An individual who violates our personal space also violates our expectations and may annoy us, whether the person means to do so or not.
6. People from different cultures often make use of quite different "rules of eye contact" while conversing.
7. An insincere person often seems just to be playing a social role. A sincere person usually appears to be expressing his or her true personality.
8. Social roles are learned, consistent, behavioral reactions.
9. We tend to like people whose social roles and attitudes are fairly similar to ours, and to dislike people whose roles and attitudes are very different from ours.
10. Kelly's research on courtship and marriage suggests the following:
    a. Engaged couples who are attracted to one another primarily because they are superficially different tend to break the engagement.
    b. Couples who are attracted to one another primarily because they are superficially similar tend to get married, but may then divorce.
    c. Couples whose marriages endure appear to be attracted to each other for deep rather than superficial reasons. These couples are similar enough to each other in important ways to be pleasing to one another; but they are also sufficiently different to remain interesting and challenging to each other. They maintain this pattern of similarities and differences throughout the marriage.
11. Enduring relationships appear to be built on respect for each person's right to change and grow.

(Continued from page 612.)

It was Ellie Lambretti who had suggested they go see Dr. Rosa Hart. Fred Schreiber had agreed to do so only to prevent yet another argument. In early April, as the school year was nearly completed, they had each received a questionnaire from Dr. Hart asking if their relationship had gotten more or less intense in recent months. The truth was, it had gone both ways. Ellie had landed the leading part in a major dramatic production and couldn't have been happier. Fred was proud of her success, but jealous that rehearsals kept her far too busy. He feared she was drifting away from him, into a life of her own. She tried to get him to come to rehearsals, to join in the fun and work, but he was reluctant to do so. He simply didn't like sharing her that much with others.

The arrival of Dr. Hart's follow-up questionnaire prompted a long discussion between Fred and Ellie about where their relationship was going. So, rather than sending their answers back to Dr. Hart in the mail, Ellie called the psychologist and asked for an appointment. Dr. Hart had readily agreed to see them, and now they stood outside the woman's office. Fred consoled himself with the thought that at least he and Ellie were together for a while, outside the confines of her beloved theater.

Dr. Hart opened the door when they knocked and invited them in. "I suppose you want to know the results of the study you participated in, don't you?" she asked, taking the follow-up questions from them. "Well, obviously, I can't give you all the data since you've just handed me some of it, but I can tell you the highlights. What would you like to know about first?"

"What were Ellie's answers to the first questionnaire?" Fred demanded. "Did she like me as much as I liked her?"

Dr. Hart smiled. "Well, I'm afraid I can't tell you that without Ellie's permission. But I can show you Dr. Rubin's results for the first 180 couples that completed the questionnaire. Our findings are pretty much the same as Rubin's." She pushed a printed sheet across the desk to them.

Average "Affection" and "Respect" Scores for Dating Partners and Same-sex Friends

	Women	Men
Affection for partner	90.57	90.44
Respect for partner	89.10	85.30
Affection for friend	64.79	54.47
Respect for friend	80.21	78.38

"As you can see," Dr. Hart continued, "on a 100-point scale, men and women partners showed the same strong affection for each other. Without looking up Ellie's answers, Fred, I would assume that she said she loved you as much as you said you loved her."

Ellie smiled, for she knew it was true. "But your table suggests that Fred doesn't respect me as much as I respect him. What about that?" Ellie demanded.

"In our society, the sex roles are such that men typically earn more respect than women do. Notice, too, that women had much more affection for their female friends than men did for their male friends. Apparently we encourage men to have strong feelings only for women, while women are allowed to love almost anybody or anything. But if Fred was like the rest of the men taking the questionnaire, at least you can be sure that he both loves you and respects you more than he does his best friend."

"He'd better," Ellie said darkly.

"But what about those experiments in the laboratories?" Fred said, hoping to change the subject: "What does reading words aloud have to do with love?"

Dr. Hart laughed. "More than you apparently think. We weren't really interested in your ability to read words aloud but rather in which words you'd remember. We found that most dating partners could recall best those words that they themselves or their partners had read, which isn't too surprising. But the words that most of you forgot were the words read immediately before or after your partner spoke. Why do you think that was so?"

"I wanted Ellie to make a good impression, I guess," Fred said. "Maybe I concentrated so much on how she was going to do that I just didn't pay attention to what the people next to her said."

"Exactly," Dr. Hart said. "When you're in love, you want your girl friend or boyfriend to look as good as possible."

"I looked at Fred all the time," Ellie remarked. "I still do."

"Right on," Dr. Hart said. "That's what we measured in the rooms with the one-way mirrors. Whenever the man looked at the woman, we started one clock going. Whenever the woman looked at the man, we started another. A third clock recorded the time they gazed at one another simultaneously. We found, as did Dr. Rubin, that the higher the 'affection score' a couple had, the more they engaged in mutual glances. While talking to other people, either partner maintained normal social eye contact. But when they were together, our lovers did seem to have eyes only for each other."

"While it lasted, anyway," Fred said morosely. "What percentage of your couples have already broken up?"

"I'll put it another way, if you don't mind," Dr. Hart responded. "The data we have so far suggest that some 85 percent of the couples who took the test six months ago are still going together."

"And still in love?" Ellie asked softly.

"The same, or even more intensely so. At least, judging by the responses we have so far."

Fred's mood brightened momentarily. "Good, good," he said. "That's the best news I've had all day." He stopped talking for a moment, then continued in rather a hostile tone of voice. "But, you know, I really don't approve of your study. Love is a subject for poetry, not an object you can attach numbers to. If you psychologists have your way, you'll end up putting the whole thing on computer cards. You'll try to tell us when to eat and when to sleep, when to wink at each other and when to . . . ."

Ellie interrupted him by poking his arm sharply.

Dr. Hart looked at him sympathetically. "I know how you feel, and believe me, we realize that we have to keep such dangers in mind. But we hope and pray that the values of learning more about love will somehow outweigh the liabilities. See that card pinned to the wall up there? It has a statement on it by Abraham Maslow, my favorite humanist. 'We must understand love; we **must** be able to teach it, to create it, to predict it, or else the world is lost to hostility and to suspicion.' I think we can learn something about love from Maslow—as well as from experiments such as the one you participated in."

Fred stared at the woman for a few seconds, until she returned his gaze. Then he stood up. "You're right, I guess. Both Ellie and I learned something from your study. But I have a suggestion. Ellie's new play opens next week. Come see it. You might learn something from it yourself. It's a love story."

Dr. Hart looked him squarely in the eyes. "I'd love to."

RECOMMENDED READINGS

Newcomb, Theodore M. *The Acquaintance Process* (New York: Holt, Rinehart and Winston, 1961).

Rubin, Zick. *Liking and Loving: An Invitation to Social Psychology* (New York: Holt, Rinehart and Winston, 1973).

Sommer, Robert. *Personal Space: The Behavioral Basis of Design* (Englewood Cliffs, N.J.: Prentice-Hall, Inc., 1969).

chapter 27

"TWO (OR MORE) TO TANGO"

SOCIAL GROUPS

DID YOU KNOW THAT . . .

A group is defined as a set of persons considered as a single entity or system?

Social psychologists are sometimes more interested in how you relate to other members of a group than in what you are like as an individual?

Complex living systems (such as yourself) have structure, are open to the environment, and are controlled by feed forward and feedback?

One of the major characteristics of a group is the shared acceptance of group rules and norms by all the members?

If everybody else in your group says that a red rose looks blue to them, you may actually perceive the rose as being bluish?

People who brag about being independent thinkers are often more conformist than they realize?

Two-thirds of the subjects tested in an obedience study were willing to shock a person to (seeming) death if ordered to do so by the experimenter?

You may be more likely to aid a wounded stranger if you are alone than if other people are present?

When you do something that conflicts with your moral code, you may be more likely to change your perception of yourself than to change your behavior?

Hostile groups may become friendly if rewarded for cooperating with each other?

"Tell me, Mr. Kraus, what area of psychology are you most interested in?"

Norman Kraus squirmed around in the hard, wooden chair. It pained him that his adviser, Professor Ronald Ward, kept such uncomfortable chairs in his office. Professor Ward's seat, of course, was a soft armchair covered with English leather.

"Well, sir, I'm most interested in social psychology, I guess."

"Good, good. Bloody important field," the Professor said. "Many excellent experiments that you could replicate as your training research."

Norm Kraus squinted at his adviser. Ward spoke with a slight Oxford accent that oddly annoyed Norm. He assumed the man took this means of reminding everyone that he had spent several years in England. Then it dawned on Norm what Ward had said.

"Replicate?"

"Yes, of course. We expect our first-year graduate students to replicate, or to repeat exactly, some piece of published research. Learn by doing what's already been well done, that's our motto."

"If you don't mind, sir, I'd really rather do something new, something no one's tried before."

Professor Ward nodded sagely. "Yes, I'm sure you would. And did you have something particular in mind?"

Norman Kraus stopped to consider. "No, but I thought we could figure something out."

The Professor's lips pursed into a bitter-lemon smile. "There, you see what I mean. Our attitude is that students should learn to walk before they attempt to run. Try something you know will work first, before you exercise your presumed creativity." Ward coughed discreetly, then continued. "Now, what part of social psychology would you like to work on?"

Norm's anger might have boiled over had he not suddenly recalled his father's advice: "If you want to get along with people, you have to go along with people." Much as Norm hated compromising his own standards, he recognized that his father's comments certainly applied to the present situation. But a devilish urge still prompted him to say, "I'd like to find out why people knuckle under to other people."

Professor Ward glanced at the young man sharply, then frowned. "I presume you are referring to the conformity experiments. The early studies by Muzafer Sherif and Solomon Asch opened the field up, of course, but I've always liked the work that Bob Blake and his group did at Texas back in the '50's. Particularly their use of tape recorders to create synthetic social environments. Have you read Blake's experiments?"

The wooden chair was getting more uncomfortable by the moment. "No, sir."

Ward leaned back in his leather armchair, lit his pipe, and continued. "Asch had students guess the length of lines—a very easy task if no one were around to influence their judgments. But when the students had to give their reports immediately after several other subjects had spoken, matters got sticky. The other subjects were stooges, paid by Asch to lie about which line was longest. If the stooges gave patently stupid judgments, the students often 'knuckled under' and gave incorrect reports themselves. The presence of the group of stooges was apparently so intimidating that many of Asch's subjects conformed to the false group standard."

"And what did Blake do?"

Tapping his pipe on an ashtray, Ward continued. "He and one of his graduate students proved that the stooges didn't have to be physically present. Just hearing a tape recording of the stooges' voices was enough to pressure the subject into conforming. They reported this research at the 1953 meeting of the American Psychological Association in Cleveland, as I recall."

Inwardly, Norm Kraus groaned. Professor Ward's memory for trivial detail was legendary. He should have been a cop instead of a professor, Norm told himself. But aloud he said, "Gee, that's interesting. Do you remember exactly what they did?"

Professor Ward smiled, delighted at the chance to show off. "They used the auto-kinetic effect, as did Sherif. You may recall that if you look at a stationary pinpoint of light in an otherwise dark room, the light seems to dance around like a firefly. Because the apparent movement is created by the person's own eyes, everybody sees a rather different dance. Given a 10-second exposure to the light, some people will say that it moved a few inches, some will say it moved several feet, while others may insist it hardly moved at all."

Fireflies? Norm thought. **In an experiment on social psychology?**

"Because the auto-kinetic effect is so subjective, it's rather easy to pressure people into conforming to group standards. But that's not what the experiment looked like to the subjects, who were undergraduate males at Texas. They were told it was a study on visual perception. The U.S. Air Force, so they were informed, wanted to find out how people judged the movement of tiny lights on the horizon, so the psychologists had devised a complicated and very expensive piece of apparatus that simulated the movement of airplanes in a night-time sky."

"What was the apparatus like?" Norm asked, beginning to be interested in spite of himself.

"An empty tin can with a hole punched in one end. There was a flashlight bulb inside the can that could be turned on and off from the next room. Blake and his colleague hired four stooges to sit in the dark room and give false reports on how far the light moved. The real subjects were called into the room one at a time and sat directly in the middle of the stooges. During each trial, the light went on for 10 seconds, after which each person was asked to report how far it seemed to move. The four stooges always gave their reports first, before the real subject did.''

Norm looked puzzled. ''Didn't the real subject know the others were stooges?''

''Certainly not. They looked and acted just like real subjects would have acted—they asked questions and complained about the stupidity of the study. Of course, they asked exactly the same questions with each real subject. Anyhow, the stooges gave ridiculous reports. For example, on the first trial their four reports might be that the light moved 1.6 centimeters, 1.7 centimeters, 1.9 centimeters, and 2.1 centimeters. Who can make measurements like that in the dark?''

''But it worked?'' Norm insisted.

Professor Ward lit his pipe again. ''Only too well. About two-thirds of the subjects were greatly influenced by what the stooges said.''

''And that was news?''

''No, but the second part of the study was. In this part, the subjects sat in the room alone and merely heard the tape-recorded voices of the stooges. Naturally, the subject didn't know a recording was being used. He had met the stooges in person before the start of the experiment and was told they were sitting in different rooms. The stooges asked the same questions and made the same comments on tape as they had in the real-life condition. And, as you might assume, they gave the same ridiculous reports on how far the light moved.''

Norm wiggled around in the hard chair. ''So, what happened?''

Professor Ward smiled benevolently. ''The subjects were just as influenced by the synthetic social background recorded on tape as they were when the stooges were physically present. We seem to conform to imaginary groups as much as to real ones.'' Ward paused to grind at his pipe with a metal tool. ''Yes, I think you ought to replicate that experiment as your training research.''

Norm could feel the crunch coming. ''But couldn't I jazz it up a bit, just to make it more exciting?''

The Professor looked at the young man sternly. ''You will learn a great deal more if you first do it exactly the way the Texas group did. Of course, if you have a streak of serendipity in your personality, you might turn up something unexpected anyhow. But be so kind as to try it our way first.''

''But Professor Ward, I don't think . . .''

''Mr. Kraus, our departmental rule is clear. We will expect you to replicate the Blake work **exactly,** as your training research. Report back to me after you've set things up and have run a few pilot subjects. Do you understand?''

Through gritted teeth, Norm Kraus muttered, ''Yes, sir.''

(Continued on page 652.)

So, you meet a person for the first time, perhaps at a party, perhaps at church, perhaps in class. You are favorably impressed by the way the person looks and acts. You agree with much of what the person says, and he or she seems to share many of your views on a variety of topics. You have your differences, but they seem relatively unimportant. As you interact with this individual, a mutual attraction rapidly develops between the two of you, and you both agree that you really ought to get together again. Almost before you know it, you are thinking of this individual as a *friend,* and wondering what things you might do together in the future.

Now, what exactly is it that you have done, why have you done it, and how is this friendly relationship likely to change the ways that you think and feel and act?

WHAT IS A GROUP?

Whenever you set up a continuing relationship of some kind with one or more other people, you have in fact either started a new *social group* (°) or joined one

Social group. A set of persons considered as a single unit. Two or more individuals who are psychologically related to one another. In certain rare instances, such as a child playing with an imaginary companion, one or more members of the group may not be real (living) people.

...ial group is the family.

already in existence. In the strictest of terms, a group is *a set of persons considered as a single entity* (°).

Actually, this definition is so narrow that it is of little practical value, for it implies that groups exist "in the mind of the beholder" rather than in real life. More broadly speaking, a group is a collection of two or more individuals who are psychologically related, or who are in some way *dependent* on one another.

You belong to dozens, if not hundreds of groups. Some are *formal membership* groups; you apply for membership in most colleges, churches, and tennis clubs. But you are born into *family groups* and *ethnic groups*. Some groups, such as "all the people attending a party," are fairly temporary and very informal. Other groups, such as friends and lovers, are informally structured but may continue for months or years.

The most important groups in your life are typically those that (1) last a long time; and (2) are made up of people with whom you have frequent, face-to-face encounters. For obvious reasons, these are called *interaction groups* (°).

Interaction Groups

Whenever you set up a new friendship, you have begun an interaction group— that is, you have given up some part of your personal independence to create *a state of interdependence* between you and the other person. Interdependence always involves some losses and some gains. Whenever you join or create a group, you lose the privilege of "just being yourself" and of ignoring the other group members, but you may gain many things that compensate for this loss. Some of these rewards are social: For example, you now have someone to talk to, someone to be with, and to share things with. Other rewards are more practical or task-oriented: For example, pushing a car out of the mud, raising a family, playing tennis, and having sex are activities that typically are more reinforcing if two or more individuals participate. Most interaction groups, then, are made up of people who have affection and respect for each other, who have similar attitudes toward a number of things, or who have a common set of goals and interests.

Social psychology can be defined as the study of how people think, feel, and behave toward one another. Put another way, social psychology is the study of the mutual interdependencies that exist among members of a group. Sometimes a

Entity (EN-tuh-tee). Anything considered as a whole. Any object or person or group that has physical reality, that actually exists. Your family is an entity; the love you have for your family is not an entity. Our word "entire" comes from the same Latin source.

Interaction groups. Sets of individuals, psychologically related to each other, who have frequent face-to-face contacts.

Living system. A set of related components or sub-systems which has a common goal, which is self-motivated, and which is controlled by feed forward and feedback. Living systems have two types of inputs, internal processes, and outputs—energy and information. Your brain is a living system; so is a football team.

social psychologist may be interested in how belonging to a group affects one of its members; at other times the social psychologist may investigate how the inclusion of a new person may change the characteristics of a particular group. But almost always it is the *relationships among people* rather than the *individual person* that the social psychologist focuses on.

GENERAL SYSTEMS THEORY

One of the beauties of psychology is that it gives you many new and different ways of viewing yourself, of putting yourself in perspective. For the moment, let us view you through the eyes of the General Systems Theory, both to add to your understanding of yourself and to learn why the social psychologist is more interested in relationships than in individuals.

Living Systems

Anything that is itself alive—or that is made up of living things—can be thought of as a *living system* (°) of some kind. You are alive; so you are a living system. But your family is made up of living organisms, hence your family is also considered a living system. Such systems have three general characteristics:

1. Living systems have *structure*—that is, they are always made up of related parts that interact. Your body is made up of many related organs, such as your heart, your brain, your liver, and your kidneys. It is the complex set of relationships or interactions among your organs that keeps you alive and healthy.
2. Living systems are *open to the environment*—that is, they have inputs, internal processes, and outputs. Some of these inputs, processes, and outputs have to do with energy sources such as food and water. You take in food, it is processed in your digestive organs, and you use the energy from the food to move about. You also release wastes back into the environment. Other inputs, processes, and outputs have to do with information. You take in knowledge, and you use this information to make decisions about what to do or say next.
3. Living systems are *controlled by feed forward and feedback*—that is, the internal processes and outputs of any system are strongly influenced by past and present inputs. In fact, just about the only way we know of to change a system is by changing its inputs.

If General Systems Theory seems rather a cold and mechanistic way of dealing with real, live human beings and their problems, consider this perhaps startling benefit. For tens of thousands of years, we've tried to help people but often have failed—in part because we perceived them only as humans rather than seeing them also as being complex systems. So we made up marvelous excuses to explain our failures: "You can't change human nature"; "You can lead a horse to water, but you can't make it drink"; "Like father, like son"; "Leopards never change their spots"; "You can't teach an old dog new tricks." Perhaps you can't change "human nature," but you can always change a living system—*if you alter the inputs to that system.* General Systems Theory thus offers us a great deal more hope for self-actualization—and a better technology for helping others—than previous approaches have offered. We will have more to say about changing systems in a little while. For the moment, let's see what kinds of living systems we can identify.

Every cell in your body is a living system. A muscle cell in your heart, for instance, takes in food from its environment (your bloodstream), converts the food into energy, and excretes waste products back into the bloodstream. Muscle cells also have informational inputs—neural messages that come from your brain and

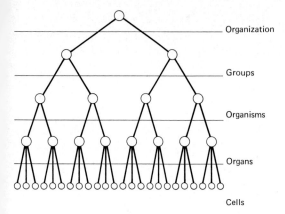

Organization

Groups

Organisms

Organs

Cells

Individual parts build up into an organism.

Cardiac (KAR-dee-ack). From the Greek word meaning "heart." A cardiologist (kar-dee-OL-oh-jist) is someone who studies the inputs, processes, and outputs of the living system we call "the heart."

chemicals in your blood that might speed up or slow down the cell's activities. The contracting and expanding of the muscle—its *behavior*—is its "informational output."

Like other living systems, the cell is affected by its genetic inheritance and by any damage that it may have sustained in its past history. In a sense, then, each muscle cell in your heart is as much a unique, individual system as you are yourself.

But one cell isn't enough to keep a heart going. The muscle cells function together with many other types of cells to keep the blood pumping through your body. Your heart is an organ—that is, a collection of individual cells—but it is also a system in and of itself. Some *cardiac* (°) physiologists study the behavior of individual cells; but other physiologists look at the way these cells cooperate, at the *relationships among cells*. If you suffered a heart attack, wouldn't you want your doctor to have both types of knowledge available?

Each organ in your body is a living system with its own types of inputs, activities, and outputs. If you have visited a medical center recently, you probably realize that there are doctors who specialize in treating the diseases of almost every separate organ system. But your body itself is an *organism*, a much more complex living system than any one of its component organs. The physician must not only understand the behavior of your heart and liver and brain but the relationships among them as well.

QUESTION: **If your heart were conscious and could talk, what might its attitude be toward a scientist who studied its relationships rather than individual hearts?**

The cell is perhaps the simplest form of living system. It is made up of non-living parts that combine to produce something new—*life itself*. Cells make up organs, but your heart is more than a collection of different types of cellular systems. For when we shift our level of analysis from the cell to the heart, we find that the heart has properties that we could not have predicted no matter how thoroughly we understood the functioning of its individual cells.

A group of organs working together can form an organism, but you are something more than a heart, a liver, a brain, and a few other organs loosely thrown together inside your skin. For you have properties (such as perceptions, motives, attitudes, emotions, memories, and personality traits) that your individual organs simply do not possess. Your heart is not "conscious"—and never will be—because consciousness is a characteristic that *emerges only at the level of the organism*.

Organisms form groups in much the same way that your individual organs unite to form organisms such as yourself. From the standpoint of General Systems Theory, the group is a kind of super-organism with properties that are unique to

Consensus (kon-SEN-sus). From the Latin word meaning "to feel together, to agree." A consensus is a harmony of viewpoints, opinions, or feelings. One common language mistake we often make is saying "consensus of opinion," for the word "consensus" all by itself means "agreement of opinion." Our word "consent" comes from the same Latin source.

it. Much as it may occasionally annoy us (as individual organisms) to look at things this way, the social psychologist cannot focus entirely on the members of a group any more than you can understand yourself merely by studying the individual functioning of your brain, your heart, or your sex organs.

Perhaps you will wish to read these chapters to learn how groups affect you, and vice versa. But perhaps you will also discover that super-organisms have a life and fascination of their own.

QUESTION: **Groups sometimes combine to form organizations or even societies; what new properties might emerge at the organizational or societal level of analysis that would not be present in groups?**

GROUP STRUCTURE AND FUNCTION

Groups typically form when two or more people sense that the pleasure of each other's company would be more rewarding than remaining socially isolated. Most such groups are informal—that is, they do not have a stated set of rules governing the behavior of their members (as does a formal group). But informal groups have their rules too. If you are too noisy at a party, if you spill drinks on people, burn holes in the furniture, insult a visitor, or assault the host or hostess, you might well be asked to leave and not be invited back again. The fact that we don't hang up a list of do's and don'ts on the front door when we give a party doesn't mean that our guests' behavior (and ours) isn't regulated by an unwritten code of conduct. In fact, one of the major characteristics of any group is *the shared acceptance of group rules by all the members.* This acceptance may be conscious or unconscious, but it is almost always present in one form or another.

As you may already have discovered in your own life, part of the fun of forming a friendship group (becoming friends or lovers) seems to be "psyching out the situation," or determining what *rules of the game* each player feels ought to be enforced. If the person is very much like you, little or no discussion of rules may be necessary. If the person is very different from you—and particularly if he or she refuses to consider friendships in terms of discovering behavioral expectations—the relationship may not last for long, but its beginning can be an exciting experience. In most cases, however, where the members are neither too similar nor too different, each person will compromise a little—for no group can maintain itself unless there is some minimal agreement or *consensus* (°) as to what its members can and can't do.

QUESTION: **How might this information on group rules help explain the behavior of E. Lowell Kelly's engaged couples mentioned in the last chapter?**

Group Norms

As we have mentioned before, the ability to predict the behavior of people and objects in our world appears to be innately rewarding. One of the most reinforcing aspects of belonging to a group is that each member can to some extent predict what the other members are likely to think and do in most situations. Perhaps that is why group rules are almost always stated in terms of behavioral or attitudinal *norms.* That is, the rules specify what the average or normal behavior of each member should be, or what role(s) each member should play.

Of course, no group member will fit all the norms *exactly* just as no one is *exactly* average in all aspects of intelligence or sexual behavior. Some deviation from the norm is usually tolerated, so long as the member is not perceived by the group as playing "too abnormal" a role—that is, as being more than about 2 standard deviations from the perceived group midpoint. The more similar the group's members are to each other, and the more emphasis the group places on "following the rules," the less deviation the group will usually tolerate. Perhaps we can demonstrate this point with an example.

Suppose that we measure the attitude toward premarital sex of two different groups—a class of students taking introductory psychology, and a group of young adults at a campus church or religious center. We will ask the members of both groups to record their agreement or disagreement with the following statement by placing a check mark on a 9-point attitude scale:

"Premarital sex is generally so damaging from both a psychological and moral point of view that it should be avoided at all costs."

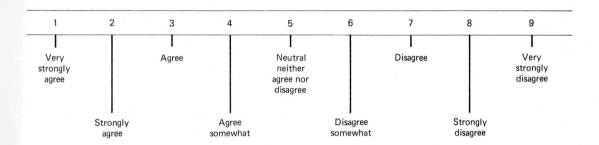

After both groups respond, we measure the position that each person has marked on the 9-point scale. We can then use the number closest to each check mark as a *scale score* that fairly accurately represents each member's attitude toward the statement on premarital sex. And, since we have a number, or score, for each person, we can add these numbers up and calculate the mean or *average attitude* for both groups. This average would, presumably, be the group norm. We can also calculate the *range* and the *standard deviation* of scores for both groups.

For the sake of this discussion, let us assume that the mean or norm for both groups happened to be a scale score of 4: "Agree somewhat." This result might suggest to you that the church group and the psychology class were very similar, since the norm seems to be the same in both groups. But ask yourself this question: If your own position was a 6 ("Disagree somewhat"), would either group perceive you as being "too abnormal" to belong to that group?

The answer is—it depends on what each group's standard deviation was. Church groups, in general, are more *homogeneous* (°) in their attitudes toward sexual behavior than are the more random collections of students who make up classroom groupings. The distribution of scores for the church group might look like this:

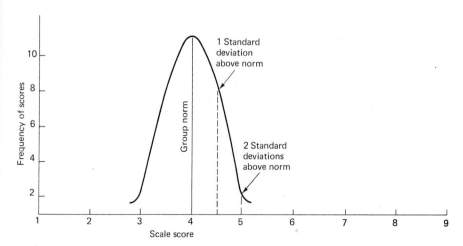

Homogeneous (Ho-moh-GEE-knee-us). From the Greek words meaning "same kind." The more alike members of a group are, the more homogeneous they are. In more technical terms, the smaller the standard deviation of a distribution of test scores, the more homogeneous the scores are.

While the distribution of scores for the classroom group might look like this:

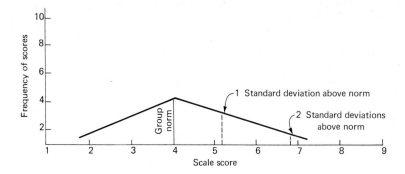

As you can see, your score of 6 would be more than 2 standard deviations from the church group norm, but well within the "normal" range for the psychology class. Presumably, the church group would consider your attitude too deviant, while the classroom group probably would not.

QUESTION: **How might the members of the church group respond if you attacked them for being too narrow-minded about premarital sex? Would you expect the members of the psychology class to respond differently under the same sort of attack?**

Group Cohesion In technical terms, *cohesiveness* (°) is the psychological glue that keeps group members sticking together. Generally speaking, the more cohesive a group, the longer it will last and the more resistant it will be to external pressures. In ordinary situations, cohesion is often a function of the homogeneity of the group—the more homogeneous the attitudes or behaviors of the members, the more cohesive the structure of the group will be. However, even such *heterogeneous* (°) groups as introductory psychology classes can be made momentarily cohesive if the group is threatened by some outside source.

People riding together in an elevator are not usually considered a group, for they have no real psychological interdependencies, and their attitudes are likely to be very dissimilar on most subjects. However, if the electric power fails and the people are trapped together in the elevator for several hours, this very heterogeneous bunch of people may quickly form into a group. They will give each other psychological support and comfort, and work together on the common goal of escaping. As soon as the people are released from the stalled elevator, however, the common threat to their survival is removed. At this point, the heterogeneity of the members' attitudes and behaviors will probably overcome the temporary cohesion and the group will disband (although individual members of the group may be similar enough to strike up friendships as a result of the experience).

Group Commitment The individual organs in your body cannot wander off to join some other person as they please, but the members of a group are usually free to abandon the group whenever they wish. A group can survive only if it can hold its members together. One of the functions of any group, then, seems to be that of inducing the highest-possible commitment among its members. For the more committed to the group's norms and goals the members become, the more cohesive the group typically will be and the more homogeneous its attitudes.

Commitment (°) is often measured by the willingness of group members to give up their own personal pleasures and desires to attain some group goal or to help the group survive. In an interesting study of 19th-century communes, psychologist

Isolated individuals who happen to be together in an elevator.

Cohesiveness (ko-HEE-siv-ness). Cohesive forces are those that tend to hold something together. The more that group members stick together when under pressure, the greater the cohesiveness of the group.

Heterogeneous (HETT-turr-oh-GEE-knee-us). From the Greek words meaning "different kinds." The more dissimilar members of a group are, the more heterogeneous they are.

Commitment. From the Latin word meaning "to connect, to entrust." When you sign a loan at a bank, you make a legal commitment to repay the money on time. Group commitment involves each member's giving up his or her own freedom to work toward group goals.

The Shakers lived in communes in the last century.

The Farm, a modern commune in Tennessee.

R.M. Kanter found that these groups often demanded considerable sacrifice from their members. Some communes required their members to sign over all money and worldly goods to the group and thereafter to work on commune property "for free." Other communes prohibited their members from wearing jewelry or expensive clothes, from smoking tobacco, eating meat, or having sex. Kanter reports that communes demanding such sacrifices tended to last longer than communes that did not.

A similar finding comes from an experiment by social psychologists Elliot Aronson and Judson Mills. They offered college women a chance to participate in a discussion group—if they were willing to pay a price. Half of the women were required to suffer a very painful initiation in order to "buy" entrance to their discussion group; the other half of the women were put through a much milder form of initiation. Those who paid less by suffering less subsequently liked their discussion group significantly less than did the women who had paid the much higher psychological price.

The value or attractiveness of a group depends in no small part on the cost of joining; in general, the more you must pay, the greater the group rewards will seem to be, and the less likely it is that you will abandon your membership.

QUESTION: How many reasons can you think of why college fraternities and sororities apparently declined in popularity and prestige during the 1960's and early 1970's?

GROUP PRESSURES TO CONFORM

Most of us believe that our attitudes toward such things as sexual behavior, politics, economics, and religion are primarily the result of our own soul-searching and logical deduction. In truth, as social psychologist Harold Kelley points out, we use the groups we belong to as reference points, or guides, for much of what we think and do. According to Kelley, these *reference groups* (°) influence our behavior in at least two ways: first, by providing comparison points which we use in evaluating ourselves and others; second, by setting standards or norms and enforcing them by rewarding us when we conform and by punishing us when we do not conform to these standards. Reference group members who express opinions, attitudes, or judgments too far from the group norms are typically pressured by other members to fall back into line.

QUESTION: Your family, friends, school, church, and political party are all reference groups; what other groups can you think of that might influence your attitudes?

Reference groups. Those groups that set social norms we are expected to live up to. Reference groups typically give us feed forward by stating goals the group members should attain, as well as giving us rewarding or punishing feedback as we move toward or away from the goal.

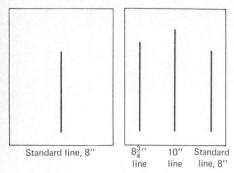

Standard line, 8'' $8\frac{3}{4}$''   10''   Standard
                            line   line   line, 8''

The lines used in Solomon Asch's experiment.

Auto-kinetic effect (AW-toe-kin-NET-tick). Auto-kinetic means "self-movement." When you look at a pinpoint of light in a dark room, the light appears to move even though it is physically standing still. The slight twitching movements that our eyes constantly make seem to be responsible for the auto-kinetic effect.

The study of how groups force their members to conform to group norms is one of the most fascinating areas of social psychology—and probably one of the most relevant. Scientific experiments on this topic date back to 1935, when social psychologist Muzafer Sherif first demonstrated the effects of group pressures on visual perception. Sherif asked students to observe a pinpoint of light in a dark room and tell him how much the light moved. Although the light was actually stationary, it appeared to move around jerkily because of the *auto-kinetic effect* (°) which we discussed earlier. When the students made their judgments sitting alone in the room, each went his or her own way—that is, one student would repeatedly report that the light moved only a centimeter or two on each presentation, while another student would almost always say that the light moved a meter or more.

When the students were tested in groups, however, their judgments became very similar. It appeared to Sherif that the first students to report somehow created a perceptual "group norm" that the other students had trouble resisting when they gave their judgments.

The Asch Experiment

Several years after Sherif reported his findings, social psychologist Solomon Asch carried the matter a step further. Asch first tested the perceptual abilities of a group of students who served as control subjects for the latter part of his experiment. Asch showed these controls a white card that had a black line 8 inches (20.3 centimeters) long drawn on it. He referred to this as the "standard line" and asked the controls to remember it well. Then he removed the first card and showed the subjects a second card that had three "comparison lines" drawn on it. The first of these lines was $8\frac{3}{4}$ inches (22.2 centimeters) long, the second was 10 inches (25.4 centimeters), while the third was the same 8-inch length as the standard. Asch then asked the control subjects to report privately which comparison line matched the standard. To no one's surprise, the controls picked the correct answer some 99 percent of the time.

With his "experimental subjects," Asch played a much more subtle game. He asked these volunteers to appear at his laboratory at a certain time. But when each young man arrived, he found several other students waiting to participate in the experiment. What the experimental subject did not realize was that the others were stooges, who were paid by Asch to give occasional false judgments. After the stooges and the experimental subject had chatted for a few moments, Asch ushered them into his laboratory and gave them several opportunities to judge line lengths for him. The judgments were given out loud, so that everyone could hear, and the stooges were always called on to report before the experimental subject did.

During the first two trials, the stooges picked the correct comparison line—as did the experimental subject. But on the third trial, each of the stooges calmly announced that the 10-inch line matched the 8-inch line! These false judgments created an incorrect group perceptual norm, and apparently put the experimental subjects under tremendous pressure to conform. In this first study about one-third of the experimental subjects "yielded" to group pressures and reported that the two lines matched. In later studies, when the judgments were more difficult to make, the experimental subjects yielded to the group of stooges about two-thirds of the time.

In another experiment Asch varied the number of stooges who reported before the experimental subject did. While the presence of 1, 2, or 3 stooges did induce some conformity, the maximum pressure to yield apparently was reached when there were 4 stooges giving false reports. Having 14 or even 40 stooges doesn't increase conformity much more than having 4. However, if even 1 stooge out of

40 gives the "correct" answer, the homogeneity of the group is broken, the group pressures are lifted, and the experimental subject typically gives the correct answer also.

The importance of the Asch study lies not merely in its dramatic demonstration that people tend to conform to temporary reference groups but in the reasons they give for doing so. If you were to ask the subjects who "conformed" why they judged the 8-inch line as being as long as the 10-inch line, about half of them would look at you sheepishly and confess that they couldn't stand the pressure. They might say that they figured something was wrong, or that they thought the stooges "saw through a trick" that they hadn't recognized, or that they simply didn't want to "rock the boat" by giving a judgment that went against the group norm.

The other half of the "conformers" are far more interesting, however. For they typically insist that they *actually saw* the two lines as being identical. That is, they were not conscious of "yielding" at all.

Group norms not only influence our attitudes toward complex social issues but our perceptions of even the simplest objects as well.

Robert Blake.

What Makes People Conform?

Shortly after Asch reported his initial results, a number of psychologists began to study how groups induce conformity in their members. Perhaps the most detailed of these studies was a series of experiments by Robert R. Blake, Harry Helson, and their colleagues at the University of Texas. In one of the first of these, which I performed under Professor Blake's direction, we demonstrated that the "stooges" did not have to be physically present in order to pressure the experimental subject into conforming. If the subject merely heard the recorded voices of other people whom he thought were sitting in other rooms, the subject would yield to incorrect judgments as frequently as if the stooges were sitting beside him. In further studies, Blake and his students showed that subjects would volunteer for difficult tasks, donate large or small sums of money to a fake charity, violate social rules ("Don't Walk on the Grass!"), and change their reported attitudes toward war and violence in order to conform to the behavior of various groups of stooges.

Adaptation-level Theory. A theory proposed by Harry Helson that accounts for judgments, perceptions, and attitudes in terms of three factors—the physical and social dimensions of the stimulus input, the background in which the input appears, and the personality structure (traits, attitudes, past experience) of the perceiver. Often called A-L Theory.

Adaptation-level Theory   Robert Blake is a social psychologist with a long-standing interest in group behavior. Harry Helson, however, is an experimental psychologist who spent many years studying visual perception and psycho-physics in individuals, not groups. Some of Helson's best-known research had to do with the effects of the background on the perception of a visual stimulus—for example, the fact that a white rose appears reddish when seen on a background of blue-green velvet.

Originally, Helson had little interest in social psychology. However, during the 1950's, Professor Helson's office was right next door to Professor Blake's at Texas. Helson soon perceived that the stooges were really a "social background" that affected perceptual judgments much as the velvet colored the perception of the white rose. If this were the case, conformity behavior could be explained by reference to *Adaptation-level Theory* (°), which Helson had devised to account for the way that humans perceive the world. The discovery that their interests were similar led Blake and Helson to form a research group—and to jointly direct a series of experiments that helped clarify the various conditions that induce people to conform to group norms.

According to Adaptation-level Theory, all behavior (including conforming) is influenced by *stimulus, background,* and *personality* factors.

Stimulus factors include the task or problem set before the subject—what the subject looks at or is told to do.

Harry Helson.

Background factors include the social situation or context in which the stimulus is presented.

Personality factors include such matters as innate response tendencies, traits, and past experience.

According to Adaptation-level Theory, if we want to understand why people do or do not yield to group pressures, we must look at all three factors in detail.

1. Stimulus or Task Variables. The physical properties of the stimulus a subject must judge in a conformity experiment have a lot to do with whether a person yields to group pressures or does not. In general, the vaguer the stimulus, the easier it is to get the subject to yield. It is a relatively simple task to get a person to change his or her opinions about the beauty of a work of art or the melodiousness of a piece of music; it is much more difficult to get a subject to say that a 10-inch line is shorter than an 8-inch line.

Attitudes about almost anything are easier to shift than are judgments of concrete facts, as Richard Crutchfield reported in 1955. However, strong personal preferences for things like food are harder to influence than are guesses about such vague facts as the distance from New York to London.

The more difficult the stimulus task appears to be, and the more confusing the instructions about the task, the more likely it is that the group will be able to influence the subject's behavior. For this reason, perhaps, group pressures are most effective if the subject must judge the stimulus from memory.

2. Situational or Background Variables. If a group is to have an influence on a person, then the person must know what the group's opinion or norm actually is. One of the most important situational factors, therefore, is how much the individual knows about what the group thinks. In general, the more information the person has concerning the group, the stronger the pressures are to yield.

Group pressures to conform develop when two factors are in conflict: (1) the subject's judgment of the stimulus when he or she is alone, and (2) the judgment the group makes of the same stimulus when the subject is present. Up to a point, the larger the difference or discrepancy between (1) and (2), the more influenced by the group the subject will be. However, if the matter is carried to ridiculous extremes, the pressure may be lifted. It is all very well to ask the subject to report that an 8-inch line is the same length as one 10 inches long. It is something else again to expect the subject to report that an 8-inch line is identical to one several yards in length.

The way that the subject perceives the other group members is also critical. The more prestige or competence members of the group seem to have, or the more trustworthy they appear to be, the more powerful agents they become in pressuring the subject into conforming. We are more likely to conform to friends than to strangers, and more likely to yield to strangers who say they like us than to strangers who say they don't.

The more "out in the open" the subject is forced to be in making his or her judgments, the more likely it is the subject will yield to group pressures. If the person must state his or her name, or respond so that the rest of the group can hear, then the person will be more likely to submit to group pressures—at least in public. But if the subject gets the impression that the group has rejected him or her, then the subject may conform in public but not when given a chance to make judgments in private.

If the person is told that the whole group must come to a unanimous decision on the matter at hand, the person will yield to the group more readily. Also, the greater the reward for yielding, or the more importance the judgment is supposed to have, the more likely it is that the person will be swayed by incorrect or inappropriate group norms.

QUESTION: **Why is it particularly important that juries, who often decide matters of life and death, should always take secret ballots?**

3. *Personality Factors and Past Experience.* Some people seem to conform much of the time, some practically never; most of us, however, yield in some situations and not in others. The personality traits of the individual who readily yields to group pressures have often been measured—but not all of these studies have come up with the same results. There are at least three reasons why this might be expected.

First, as we discovered in previous chapters, most of our personality tests are not as valid and reliable as we would like them to be.

Second, with the notable exception of the investigations by Blake and Helson, many of these studies of the "conformist personality" have never been replicated. As a general rule, we probably should not trust any scientific finding until it has been successfully repeated several times.

And third, there is no reason why we should expect that all people who conform to group norms should have the same sort of personality.

But there are literally dozens of studies in which personality traits have been correlated with yielding or conforming. Looking at the broad picture, we find that yielders are said to have had harsh parents who gave their children very little "independence training." Yielders are also reported to receive highly "permissive" scores on a dominance-submission scale. That is, they tend to be followers rather than leaders, but are rather rigid and *authoritarian* (°) in the way they respond to rules. Men who yield more than average are reported to score as being more "feminine" than average on masculinity tests.

Richard Crutchfield found that people who conform typically have lower IQ scores than do people who refuse to conform to group pressures. Frank Barron states that yielders in his experiments scored as having less complex personalities (as measured by various projective tests) than did non-yielders. Barron's yielders also tended to rate themselves as being at ease with other people and as being helpful in interpersonal relations, as having personal effectiveness, as being stable and healthy-minded, practical, but group-oriented.

At least, that is the yielders' *subjective impressions* of themselves. In fact, as Crutchfield has shown, on *objective tests* the yielders score as being rigid, conventional, inconsistent, anxious, moralistic, and constrictive in outlook.

There is some evidence that women are more responsive to group pressures than are men, but this difference may reflect cultural values more than basic personality traits. Blake and Helson report that men tend to conform more in areas of traditional masculine interest—such as politics and economics—while women are more likely to yield to group pressures in matters of art and social affairs.

Past experience also has its effects on conformity. If a subject is an expert on the task at hand, or if the subject is made to *think* that he or she is an expert, conformity pressures are reduced. If the person is rewarded for going against the group, then yielding is much less than if the person is punished for refusing to conform.

There is little or no evidence that conformity is an innate or inherited trait. Rather, it seems to be a behavior that we learn—primarily because groups reward us when we conform and punish us when we deviate. There is also evidence that even high yielders can be trained to resist group pressures.

Negative Conformity (*) In our society, we all make use of reference groups, and we all conform (one way or another) to group norms. And yet we often talk as if we placed a high premium on being independent of the people around us. People brag about (and even write songs about) doing things "my way." Blake and Helson discovered a very amusing thing about these self-styled independent thinkers. Many of them yield to group pressures just as much as do the rest of us, but they conform *negatively*. Let us return to our attitude scale on premarital sex to see what these negative conformers are like.

Authoritarian (aw-thor-it-TAIR-ee-an). To be authoritarian is to demand obedience to a set of rules, or to the wishes of a higher authority. See Chapter 14.

Negative conformity. To conform to a group negatively, by moving away from the group norm no matter what it might be, even if such movement means giving up one's prior opinions or attitudes. An autonomous person is someone not influenced by group pressures; a conformer is someone who adopts group norms no matter what; a negative conformer is just as influenced by group pressures as a conformer, but rejects group norms simply because he or she rejects the group.

Frank Barron.

"Premarital sex is generally so damaging from both a psychological and moral point of view that it should be avoided at all costs."

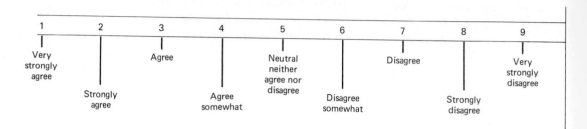

1	2	3	4	5	6	7	8	9
Very strongly agree		Agree		Neutral neither agree nor disagree		Disagree		Very strongly disagree
	Strongly agree		Agree somewhat		Disagree somewhat		Strongly disagree	

Suppose we ask a young man to respond to this statement while he is alone, and he marks #8, "Strongly disagree." Later, we present him with a similar statement that he must respond to publicly, after four stooges have given their opinions out loud. The stooges have been paid to say that they too "Strongly disagree" with the statement. What would you think of this young man if he now switches and gives his score as #2, "Strongly agree?" Is this man really acting independently of the stooge group? If you wanted to trick him into doing something, couldn't you figure out a way to do so?

QUESTION: **How might you use the information on stimulus, background, and personality factors to minimize the effects of group pressures on your own behavior?**

Obedience

One interesting sidelight to the conformity studies is this—in most of the experiments, the subject was never told that he or she *had to yield* to the group norm. Indeed, many of the subjects were quite unaware that they had given in to group pressures and denied that they had done so. What might the results have been had the subjects been ordered to yield by the experimenter?

The Milgram Experiments The answer to this question apparently comes from a fascinating set of experiments performed by psychologist Stanley Milgram in the 1960's at Yale. His subjects were men who ranged in age from young to old, and who came from many different walks of life. These men were paid to participate in what they thought was a study of the effects of punishment on learning. In the first experiment each man arrived at Milgram's laboratory to find another subject (a stooge) also present. The stooge was supposed to be the "learner" who would have to memorize a list of word pairs. The experimental subject was supposed to be the "teacher" who would punish the stooge if he made any mistakes. The stooge was sent into another room and was strapped into a chair so that he couldn't escape when the punishment became severe. The stooge was then out of sight for the rest of the experiment.

Sitting in front of the experimental subject was a very impressive piece of electrical equipment that supposedly was a powerful shock generator. In fact, the machine was a fake; no shock was ever delivered during the experiment. This generator had 30 switches on it to control the strength of the electrical current. Labels on these switches ranged from "Slight Shock" to "Danger: Severe Shock." The first time the stooge made a mistake, the subject was to shock him with the lowest intensity possible. For each subsequent mistake, the subject was to increase the shock intensity by flipping on the next-highest switch. The apparatus was so ingeniously designed that none of the subjects guessed that the stooges actually weren't receiving shocks from the machine.

At the beginning of the session things were easy for the experimental subject.

Stanley Milgram.

The stooge got most of the word pairs correctly, and the "shocks" delivered were presumably very mild. As time wore on, however, the stooge made more "mistakes" and the "shocks" became more and more severe. When the shock level reached what seemed to be a fairly high point, the stooge suddenly pounded on the wall in protest. Then the stooge stopped responding at all, as if he had fainted or had suffered an attack of some kind.

At this point Milgram told the "teacher" to continue anyway—no matter how dangerously high the shock might get. If at any time the subject wanted to stop, Milgram told him in a very stern voice, "Whether the learner likes it or not, you must go on until he has learned all the word pairs correctly. So please go on."

What would you do in this situation? Would you refuse to continue, or would you "obey" Milgram and go on shocking the stooge right up to what you believed were the limits of the electrical generator?

And how do you think most other people would react if they faced this challenge?

After he had completed his first study, Milgram asked a great many college students this question. If you are like them, you will insist that you—and most other people—would refuse to continue the experiment when a dangerously high shock level was reached (and particularly when the stooge apparently had fainted or died in the other room). But, in fact, your guess (at least about other people) would be wrong. For out of the first 40 subjects Milgram tried, almost 65 percent continued to obey Milgram's orders right up to the bitter end. Most of these subjects were extremely distressed about doing so—they complained; they showed tension; and they told Milgram again and again that they wanted to stop. But some 65 percent were completely obedient in spite of their inner conflict.

In Adaptation-level Theory terms, Milgram's verbal orders to the subjects were "stimulus factors," while the behavior of the stooge can be considered part of the "background or situational factors." By manipulating each of these factors in subsequent experiments, Milgram was able to determine a variety of ways in which obedience can be increased or decreased.

Factors Inducing Obedience   As you might expect, the weaker the stimulus, the fewer the number of people who obeyed. When Milgram stood right over the experimental subjects, breathing down their necks and ordering them on, about 65 percent followed through to the end. But when Milgram was out of the room and gave his orders by telephone, only some 22 percent of the subjects were completely obedient.

In the first experiment the subjects could not see or hear the stooge in the other room. In subsequent studies Milgram altered this "background factor." If the stooge began moaning, or complaining about his heart, fewer subjects obeyed orders. Having the stooge physically present in the same room so the subject could see the supposed pain from each shock reduced obedience even more. And if the subject had to grab hold of the stooge's hand and force it down on a "metal shock plate" before each punishment, very few of the subjects followed Milgram's instructions to the end. As you might expect, the subjects were more likely to deliver severe punishment if they couldn't see the consequences of their actions.

In a later experiment Milgram added the group-pressures technique to his own method of studying obedience. In this experiment, Milgram used three stooges with each experimental subject. One of the stooges, as usual, was the "learner" seated in the next room. The other two were supposed to be "teachers" working in a team with the subject.

The experiment proceeded as before, except that one of the stooge-teachers backed out as soon as the "shock" reached a medium-low intensity. Saying that he refused to continue, this stooge simply took a seat as far from the shock machine as he could. When the "shock" reached a medium-high level, the other stooge-teacher also refused to go on. The subject then was faced with conflicting social norms—Milgram kept pressuring him to continue, while the "group" of stooge-teachers was exerting pressure to stop. Under these conditions the "social background" factors won out over the "stimulus" of Milgram's orders. More than 90 percent of the subjects refused to complete the experiment.

We are taught to obey, just as we are trained to conform. If we consider the great rewards and massive punishments that groups can administer to their members, perhaps it is not so surprising that many of us obey and conform rather readily.

QUESTION: **What might have happened had Milgram's stooge-teachers pressured the experimental subject to continue the shocks rather than stopping them?**

The Ethics of Deception

The Milgram studies (and many others) raise a number of complex but important questions about the ethics of using humans as subjects in scientific experiments. One of these questions involves the morality of *deceiving* the subjects as to the real purpose of the study, even if the experimenter believes that such deception is necessary because people seldom act naturally when they know they're being observed. When Milgram's research was published, a storm of protest was raised by sincerely concerned individuals who urged that research such as Milgram's be banned or prohibited. A number of codes of ethics were proposed, but workable guidelines for experimentation on humans are not easy to agree upon. For, given a little time and motivation, we could all think of certain types of studies in which deception might be morally justified, and other experiments in which misleading the subjects would be both a legal and an ethical outrage.

Perhaps, as we noted in the chapters dealing with psychotherapy, we must always consider the actual results of the experiments before drawing hasty conclusions. Viewed in this perspective, Milgram comes off fairly well, for he did discover some fascinating facts, and there is no evidence that any of his subjects suffered ill effects. In truth, Milgram seems to have employed little more deception in his work than is used regularly on TV programs such as "Candid Camera." Yet the nagging question, "When is it ethical to use deception?" remains for the most part unanswered.

Some of the emotional reaction to Milgram's experiments probably stemmed from the rather unflattering picture his results gave us of ourselves. Had most of Milgram's subjects refused to obey blindly, perhaps he would not have been so vigorously attacked. Despite the emotionality of some of his critics, the issue of experimenter responsibility remains a crucial one, and the American Psychological Association has recently taken a stand against the unwarranted use of deception in similar research.

We will have more to say about these ethical issues in the next chapter.

QUESTION: **Under what circumstances do you personally think that deceiving subjects in a scientific experiment might be ethically warranted or justified?**

INTRA-PSYCHIC CONFLICT

Intra-psychic conflict. The conflict we all experience when we are forced to choose between two incompatible goals, or between two types of reinforcement.

The subjects in Milgram's experiments were caught between the devil and the deep blue sea. If they continued to obey instructions, they presumably would shock the stooge to death and thus be deserving of punishment; if they stopped, they disobeyed an authority figure and surely would be verbally criticized if not physically punished. Milgram's studies can thus be viewed as requiring the subjects to choose which of the two types of punitive feedback they preferred to experience. Such unhappy choices often lead to what we may call *intra-psychic conflict* (°).

As we noted in Chapter 4, whenever a living system is put in conflict, it will escape if possible. If it can't get away, it may "freeze" and do nothing; it may show a variety of neurotic behavior patterns, including aggression; it may distort its perceptions of the situation so that the conflict seems to disappear; or, occasionally, it may resort to creative problem-solving. Which of these alternatives the system chooses depends on many factors. In the Milgram research, for instance, many of the subjects who gave the stooge the maximum shock denied that there was any real danger; others became very hostile to Milgram, even before they discovered that the shock machine was a fake.

Bystander Apathy

Milgram created problems for his subjects because he told them what to do. In real-life conflicts, there often isn't anyone around to give us directions, and we must act (or fail to act) on our own. If there are other people around us when a crisis occurs, we may look to the others for feed forward on how we ought to behave. Later on, we usually must explain our actions or inaction satisfactorily to ourselves. Sometimes the emergency nature of the conflict may make us distort what is actually happening; just as often, the pressure comes later when we invent "logical" excuses for what we did.

What would you do if, late some dark night, you heard screams outside your place? Would you rush out at once, or would you first go to the window to see what was happening? If you saw a man with a knife attacking one of your neighbors, how would you react? Might you call the police, or go to the neighbor's aid? Or would you consider yourself to be merely an innocent bystander to one of life's little tragedies, and hence remain *apathetic* (°) and unresponsive? And if you failed to assist the neighbor in any way, how would you respond if someone later on asked why you didn't help?

Before you answer, consider the following facts. Early one morning in 1964, a young New York woman named Kitty Genovese was returning home from work. As she neared her front door, a badly derranged man jumped out of the shadows and attacked her. She screamed and attempted to defend herself. Because she screamed loudly, 38 of her neighbors came to their windows. And because she fought valiantly, it took the man almost half an hour to kill Kitty Genovese. During this period of time, not one of those 38 neighbors came to her aid—and not one of them even bothered to call the police.

Kitty Genovese's death so distressed scientists John M. Darley and Bibb Latané that they began a study of why people refuse to help others in similar situations.

In one experiment, Darley and Latané staged a disaster of sorts for their subjects. They paid people 2 dollars to fill out a survey form given them by an attractive young woman. While the people were in an office filling out the forms, the woman went into the next room. Shortly thereafter, the subjects heard a loud crash from the next room, and the woman began moaning loudly that she had fallen and was badly hurt and needed help.

Now, how many of the subjects do you think came to her rescue?

The answer is—it depends. Some of the subjects were exposed to this little drama when they were all by themselves in the testing room. About 70 percent of the "alone" subjects offered help. Another 40 subjects faced this apparent emergency in pairs. Only 8 of these 40 people responded by going to the woman's aid. The other 32 subjects simply sat there listening to the moans and groans.

Were the subjects who failed to rush to the woman's assistance merely apathetic and uncaring? In this case, yes. Many of the "apathetic bystanders" informed the experimenters that they hadn't really thought the woman was seriously hurt and were afraid of embarrassing her if they intervened. But we should note that the subject's *perception* of the emergency was strongly influenced by whether or not there was someone else present in the testing room.

John M. Darley.

Apathetic (app-pah-THET-tick). From a Greek word meaning "without sympathy, lacking passion or interest, being indifferent to the fate of others."

Bibb Latané.

Bystander apathy. Not becoming involved emotionally when you are an accidental witness to a tragedy; not offering to help a stranger in need.

Darley and Latané believe that when several people witness a disaster, they perceive their own personal responsibility as being greatly diminished or diluted. Hence they are free not to act if no one else does. In another experiment, subjects heard a young man (presumably in the next room) discuss the fact that he frequently had seizures similar to grand mal epilepsy. Shortly thereafter, the stooge began crying for help, saying that he was about to have an attack and would die if no one came to help him. About 85 percent of the subjects who were alone rushed to the stooge's assistance. However, only 62 percent of the subjects who were in pairs offered aid, while but 31 percent of those in five-person groups overcame their apathy. In contrast to the previous experiment, however, many of the non-responsive subjects showed distinct signs of tension and nervousness afterwards. That is, they had sweaty palms, trembling hands, and asked the experimenter if the stooge was really all right. Darley and Latané believe that these people were not really apathetic; they were still trying to make up their minds whether to do something when the experimenter terminated the session and interviewed them about their feelings.

QUESTION: In both of the above-mentioned studies, Darley and Latané had the stooge's voice recorded on tape and played it back through a hi-fi system. Why might this be a more precise way of running an experiment than having the stooge act out the part live each time the little drama was repeated?

Darley and Latané have suggested that *bystander apathy* (°) occurs primarily in situations where the witnesses can either convince themselves that no real emergency exists, or where there are so many other people around that responsibility for taking action is greatly diffused. More recent research by I.M. Piliavin, J. Rodin, and J. Piliavin tends to confirm the accuracy of this explanation. In the late 1960's, Piliavin and his group turned the New York subway system into an experimental laboratory. Four people involved in the study would board one car of a subway train through different doors. Once the train was underway, one of the male experimenters would stumble down the aisle and collapse on the floor, face up. Two of the experimenters recorded how long it took the "innocent bystanders" in the subway car to come to the stooge's aid. If no one came to the rescue, one of the other experimenters would help the man to his feet.

From a humanistic point of view, the results of the Piliavin research are fairly encouraging. When the "victim" was carrying a white cane, and acting as if he were blind, people came to his aid in 95 percent of the tests. Even when the stooge reeked of whiskey and pretended to be drunk, he received assistance in about half the tests.

In emergency situations, we often look to the people around us for guidance as to what an appropriate response might be. If no one else responds, we are under tremendous "group pressure" to remain apathetic since the feed forward apparently is, "remain apathetic." That is, given an intra-psychic conflict between our inner values that we ought to be helpful and our fears of violating group norms or expectancies, about two-thirds of us will "yield" to the group—about the same percentage as yielded in the "group pressures" experiments of Asch, Sherif, Blake and Helson, and in Milgram's studies on obedience.

QUESTION: Can you guess how the "apathetic bystanders" in the Piliavin subway experiment reacted as soon as one person went to the stooge's assistance?

Cognitive Dissonance

Not all of the conflicts that we face involve a choice between satisfying group expectancies or satisfying our consciences by living up to a moral code. Sometimes the problem has to do with trying to explain to ourselves why we picked a biological reinforcer rather than an intra-psychic one. For instance, most of us are taught that sexual intercourse is immoral except when engaged in by a married couple. Yet, if Kinsey's data are to be believed, many of us violate this ethical standard at some time during our lives. Afterwards, rather than admitting that our ids got the better of our super-egos, we may *rationalize* (°) our actions in a variety of ways: "I did it only because I loved her (him)"; "He (she) needed me"; "It didn't really happen—it was just a bad dream."

Social psychologist Leon Festinger has conducted a series of intriguing studies on how human beings react to situations involving such conflicts. In perhaps the best known of these experiments—reported in 1959 by Festinger and J.M. Carlsmith—college students were asked to do about 30 minutes of very tedious and boring work. The subjects performed these repetitive and uninteresting tasks while alone in a laboratory room. After completing the chores, some of the students were offered a dollar as a reward for going out into a nearby waiting room and telling the next subject what an exciting and thrilling task it had been. Other subjects were paid 20 dollars for doing exactly the same thing. Afterwards—no matter how good a "selling job" the person had done—each subject was asked to give his or her actual opinion of how pleasurable the work was.

Festinger and Carlsmith report that the students paid but one dollar thought the chores were really pretty interesting and enjoyable. However, the subjects paid 20 dollars rated the tasks as being as dull, as did a group of subjects who were not asked to "sell" the experiment to another student.

Why did the subjects paid but one dollar rate the work as being much more pleasant than one might have expected? Festinger believes that they had a difficult job rationalizing their own actions. For they had lied to the other subject about how interesting the task was supposed to be. The subjects paid 20 dollars for lying apparently were willing to face the fact that they "fudged" a bit for that much money; the students paid but a single dollar couldn't admit to themselves that they'd "sell out" for so little money. Thus they changed their *perception* of the enjoyability of the task "after the fact," just as the subjects in the Asch experiment altered their visual perceptions because they apparently could not tolerate the thought that they had yielded to the group.

Festinger believes that, in these situations, we experience *cognitive dissonance* (°). That is, whenever we do something we think we shouldn't, we face conflict—the realization that our actions are in dissonance with (different from) our intra-psychic expectations of what we're really like. Festinger belives that we are usually highly motivated to reduce cognitive dissonance when it occurs, and that we do so chiefly by changing our beliefs or attitudes to make them accord with our actual behaviors.

Put another way, if you are to predict and control your inputs, you must be able to know what you yourself are likely to do in most situations. When your predictions (based on your prior value system) become inaccurate, you must either change your predictions or change your behaviors. Festinger suggests that many of us find it more convenient to revamp our self-perceptions than to alter the way we actually behave.

Perhaps you will have noticed a certain similarity between the group pressures experiments, the obedience studies, the research on bystander apathy, and the cognitive dissonance experiment. In all these cases, the actual conflict arose when people were forced to pick one class of reinforcer over another of a quite different class. In our culture, intra-psychic reinforcers are often supposed to be the most mature and desirable ("virtue is its own reward"). Yet, as we have noted, cognitive pleasures are not necessarily the dominant ones for every living human being. Intra-psychic conflict can lead to stress, frustration, aggression, perceptual distortions—and occasionally to painful insights. Perhaps it is time that we reworked our cultural models and group norms to make them less dissonant with psychological fact. For, as we have already noted, living systems can most effectively be changed when we know what *actually reinforces them.*

Leon Festinger.

Rationalize (RASH-un-al-lies or RASH-un-ull-lies). To think up logical reasons for one's emotionally-impulsive thoughts or behaviors.

Cognitive dissonance (KOG-nih-tiv DISS-oh-nance). The feeling we get when our behaviors differ markedly from our intra-psychic values. According to Leon Festinger, we are strongly motivated to reduce this dissonance; we do so either by changing our values or attitudes or by changing our behaviors.

QUESTION: How might Festinger explain the fact that we tend to value groups more highly if we must pay a high price to join them?

INTER-GROUP CONFLICT

For the most part the studies on conformity, obedience, and cognitive dissonance have dealt with individual subjects put under strong psychological pressure to avoid conflict with other members of a group, or with their own value systems. From the standpoint of General Systems Theory, however, we can consider the group itself as a kind of "super-organism" that should be subject to social pressures to conform to the standards set by other groups or organizations. Not unexpectedly, most of the factors that influence individual conformity have their direct parallels when we study the behavior of groups as groups.

Sherif's "Camp" Experiments

Muzafer Sherif was one of the first social psychologists to undertake scientific experiments on conflict between groups. During the 1950's, Sherif and his colleagues helped run a camp for 11- and 12-year-old boys. These youngsters were all from settled, well-adjusted, white, middle-class, Protestant homes. The boys were carefully selected to be happy, healthy individuals who had no difficulty getting along with others. None of the boys knew each other before being admitted to the camp—nor did any of them realize that they were to be subjects in Sherif's experiments.

The camp itself had two rather separate housing units. Because he had purposely selected boys who were very similar in attitudes and behaviors, Sherif predicted that the boys in each unit would form into a group very readily. On the first day of camp, since there were no pre-existing friendships among the boys, group commitment and cohesion in both units was very low. Then Sherif gave each of the units various real-life problems that could be solved only if the boys worked together effectively. As each unit overcame the difficulties Sherif put to it, the boys came to like the other boys in the same unit more and more. Each of the units became a "natural group," and commitment to each of the groups (and to its emerging norms) increased significantly.

Then Sherif introduced a series of contests designed to make the two groups hostile toward one another. As the groups competed for very desirable prizes, conflict developed, since one group could win only at the expense of the other. Very soon the boys in one group were making nasty comments about their competitors. These negative attitudes soon developed into the autistic hostility that we mentioned in Chapter 26; the boys in one group wanted to have nothing to do with the members of the other group. Name-calling, fights, and raids on the cabins belonging to the other units became commonplace. At the same time, Sherif reports, there was a marked increase in within-group cooperativeness and cohesiveness among the members of both groups.

Once the groups were at each other's throats, Sherif tried to bring them back together again. In his first experiment Sherif attempted to unite the two groups by giving them a common enemy—a group of threatening outsiders. This technique worked fairly well, in that it brought the first two units closer together, but they still held hatred for their common enemy. The next year Sherif repeated the group-conflict experiment with a different set of boys. Once inter-group hatred had reached its peak, Sherif brought the two units into very pleasant, non-competitive contact with each other. They sat together in the same dining hall while eating excellent food; and they watched movies together. However, this trick didn't succeed, for the groups merely used these occasions for fighting and shouting at each other.

Giving groups rewards when the groups "accidentally" happen to be together is obviously not the same thing as making the reward contingent on the groups' *wanting* to be together.

Sherif then confronted the hostile groups with problem situations that could be solved only if the two units cooperated with each other. First, a water shortage "suddenly developed," and all the boys had to ration themselves. Next, Sherif offered to show the whole camp an exciting movie—but to see it, both units had to pool their resources. Then, one time when all the boys were particularly hungry, the transportation for their food "broke down." It could be fixed only if both groups worked together quickly and effectively.

Sherif reports that his technique worked beautifully. The two groups did indeed cooperate—reluctantly at first, but more and more willingly as their initial efforts were reinforced.

Before the crises occurred, almost none of the boys had friendships outside their units; afterward, some 30 percent of the friendships were inter-group rather than in-group. During the hostile period, about one-third of the members of each group rated the members of the other group as being "stinkers," "smart-alecks," or "sneaky." Afterward, less than 5 percent of the boys gave the members of the other group such highly unfavorable ratings.

Sherif states that during the time of conflict, the boys in each group indulged in "blatant glorification and bragging" about their own units and rated themselves very highly. After the reunion of the groups, the bragging diminished and there was a slight tendency for the boys to downgrade the ratings given their own groups; meanwhile, as we mentioned, their attitudes toward the other group became significantly more positive.

When disagreements develop between two people, it is often because the two have conflicting attitudes about each other or about some third person or object. When hostility arises between two groups, it is often the case that their norms or group attitudes are in conflict. Turning enemies into friends is sometimes a matter of changing their attitudes toward one another. In the next chapter we will take a careful look at how attitudes are formed and, more important, how they are changed.

QUESTION: **How might a political leader use these data to help reduce international tensions?**

SUMMARY

1. Social psychologists study the behavior of groups.
2. A group is a set of persons considered as a single entity—a collection of two or more individuals who are psychologically related to or dependent upon one another.
3. There are many types of groups, including formal membership groups, family groups, and ethnic groups.
4. Interaction groups are made up of individuals who have frequent face-to-face encounters.
5. Groups are living social systems, characterized by having a common goal; by having inputs, processes, and outputs; and by being controlled by feed forward and feedback. The members of a social group relate to each other in much the same way the organs in your body relate to you as a complete organism.
6. One of the major characteristics of any group is the shared acceptance of group rules (goals) by all the members. The more similar the members, the more cohesive the group, and the more commitment the members are likely to have toward the group and its goals.
7. Our reference groups are those we look to for our social feed forward or norms. Such groups typically give us feedback on our behavior by rewarding

movements toward and punishing movements away from the group norms (goals).

8. Whenever we make a judgment or give an opinion that is different from one shared by other group members, we typically find ourselves under strong psychological pressure to conform more closely to the group standard or norm.

9. The behavior of individuals who experience group pressures to conform can often be explained in terms of Helson's Adaptation-level Theory. A-L Theory states that judgments, perceptions, and attitudes are influenced by three factors—the stimulus, the background in which the stimulus appears, and the personality of the individual under pressure.

10. When told to obey orders from a higher authority, most of us comply or conform. The experiments on group conformity appear to offer an explanation for this conformity to group norms.

11. Bystander apathy and cognitive dissonance are examples of intra-psychic conflict that arises when we must choose between two classes of reinforcers or two types of feedback.

12. Conflicts can occur between groups as well as between personal values or reinforcers. Sherif has shown that inter-group conflicts can be reduced if the groups are either threatened by an outside danger or rewarded for working toward a common goal.

(Continued from page 632.)

"All right, Mr. Kraus, please calm down and tell me what happened."

Norm Kraus leaned forward excitedly, hardly noticing the hardness of the chair in Professor Ward's office. "Well, the Blake experiment worked just as it was supposed to. I put a flashlight bulb inside an empty cocoa box to make the auto-kinetic light, and I got some friends to act as stooges. We made tape recordings of their voices, but I wanted to start with the situation where the subject was sitting right in the middle of my four friends."

Taking a quick breath, the young man hurried on.

"I got an undergraduate to volunteer for the experiment. I introduced him to the stooges, and then we all went into the lab. The cocoa box was hidden behind a black curtain that I didn't open until the lights were off when the subject couldn't see what it was. Then I gave the song and dance about airplanes moving on the horizon and I turned off the overhead light and left the room.

"The lab next door was my control room, where I ran the experiment. I could open the curtains, turn the flashlight off and on, and talk to the subjects over a loudspeaker. There was a microphone right in front of the real subject so I could hear his voice. And, of course, I could also hear the stooges and make sure they said what they were supposed to say."

Professor Ward nodded in an absent-minded fashion. "Yes, yes, just like Blake and his student did it. But how did your stooges know what to say?"

"I gave them their responses written out on a card."

The Professor's eyebrows rose a fraction of an inch. "And they read these numbers in the dark?"

Norm smiled broadly. "I wrote the numbers in dark-glow paint. They could just make the numbers out if they squinted at them."

"Didn't the subject get suspicious?"

"No, sir. You see, I gave him a card with a scale marked across it in centimeters, also in dark-glow paint. It looked just like the cards the stooges had. The subject was supposed to look at the card frequently to make sure he knew how long 1.8 centimeters was."

Professor Ward coughed politely. "Not half bad. But how did it go?"

"Beautifully, at least at first. I was sitting in the control room recording the subject's reactions. The first trial, he seemed to ignore the group. But on the next fourteen trials, he hit the midpoint of their judgments right on the nose. I couldn't believe it! I was so excited at the end of the test that I rushed over to the next room to congratulate everybody and turn on the lights. And that's when it happened."

"Dare I ask what?"

"This undergraduate came bolting out of the lab and went rushing down the hall toward the toilet. I had to chase after him to catch up. He was shouting at me over his shoulder: 'Don't believe a word I said. You can't use my results.' "

"Did he tell you why?"

"Yes sir, he did. He said: 'You put me in a bad seat. I couldn't see the damned light at all. I just said whatever the other subjects said. You shouldn't do things like that; it curdles the stomach.' And then he rushed into the john and was sick all over the place."

Ward picked up his pipe and stuffed it with tobacco. After a moment, he asked, "Why do you think you got that response? Were the group pressures to conform that strong?"

Norm tried to hide the smirk that kept creeping over his face. "Serendipity, sir. After I left your office the last time, I looked the word up."

"Oh, yes, the Persian fairy tale about the three princes of Serendip, or Ceylon, as we call it today. They were always going out on expeditions to search for something like iron and discovering a mountain of gold instead. Serendipity is the gift for finding very valuable things you weren't really looking for. Invaluable in scientific research." The Professor smiled rather warmly. "And you think you have the gift?"

Norm attempted a modest grin. "Well, I did luck onto something strictly by accident. It isn't everyday you can upset a subject that much without laying hands on him."

"All right, Mr. Kraus, tell me exactly what happened."

Norm Kraus leaned back in the hard chair and relaxed. "Well, at first I couldn't figure it out, and neither could the stooges. But then I checked out each piece of the equipment, just to make sure. Guess what I found?"

"I'm veritably breathless with anticipation," the Professor said, smiling with encouragement.

"The flashlight bulb had burned out. As far as I can tell, the light went on during the first trial, but then it got shorted or something. I kept saying the light would go on . . . NOW. And the stooges kept giving their reports. But for the last fourteen trials, the light simply didn't appear."

"Why didn't your stooges notice it?"

"They were too busy trying to read the numbers on their little cards. Besides, it didn't matter to them if they couldn't see the light at all. Their job was just to read off their reports."

Professor Ward poked at the tobacco in his pipe with a match. "But why did the poor young man get sick?"

"How would you like it if you were sitting smack in the middle of four people who all acted as if they could see something that you saw once, but couldn't see thereafter? The guy told me later that he looked and looked and looked, but the light just wasn't there. He thought maybe he was going crazy. But he didn't want to upset the experiment, so he just sat there and gave the same reports the stooges were giving. He couldn't disobey orders by leaving, and he couldn't violate the group standard by saying he didn't see anything when everybody else did. The stress was so great that his stomach curled up into a tight little ball. He said he'd never felt so much pressure in his life."

A stern tone crept back into Professor Ward's voice. "I hope you explained things to him and tried to make amends."

"Oh, yes sir. I took him over to the clinic and had the doctors examine him. They gave him some medicine for his nerves. Then I told him all about what we had done, and why. Now he wants to be a stooge if we continue the experiment."

"If?"

"Well, sir, it does seem we've discovered an interesting way to measure psychosomatic responses to social stress. I was talking to some of the doctors at the clinic about it. They thought we might do some joint research. You know, trying to figure out how group pressures toward conformity can lead to ulcers and hypertension and things like that. I realize that's not a replication of the Blake experiment, and I wouldn't want to break the rule . . ."

Professor Ward interrupted. "Mr. Kraus, we have two departmental rules about graduate students. The first is that they should begin by repeating a piece of published research. The second rule is that, if the student finds something exciting on his or her own while performing the replication, we expect them to follow it up. You wouldn't want to violate our departmental standards, now would you?"

Norm Kraus gulped happily. "No, sir."

"Good work, Norm. I'm pleased with your progress. Let me know if I can help, and keep me posted on how you come along. And by the way, why don't you call me Ron instead of Professor Ward?"

Norm could hardly believe his ears. "Yes, sir, Profes . . . I mean, bloody good of you, Ron."

RECOMMENDED READINGS

Brown, Roger. *Social Psychology* (New York: The Free Press, 1965).

Helson, H. *Adaptation-level Theory* (New York: Harper & Row, 1964).

Miller, James G. *Living Systems* (New York: McGraw-Hill, 1977).

Proshansky, Harold, and Bernard Seidenberg, eds. *Basic Studies in Social Psychology* (New York: Holt, Rinehart and Winston, 1965).

PERSUASION, PROPAGANDA, AND ATTITUDE CHANGE

DID YOU KNOW THAT . . .

The average U.S. citizen is exposed to some 1,500 different ads each day of his or her adult life?

The more you know about a person, the more stable your attitude toward that person probably will be?

While many students become more politically liberal while in college, many of them revert back to their original political viewpoints once they graduate?

Although you may reject propaganda if it comes from what you consider to be a biased source, later on you may forget the source and be influenced by the message?

Propaganda messages that arouse a high degree of fear may not be as effective as low-fear appeals that tell you how to cope with the threatening situation?

Subtle, indirect propaganda may influence you more than does open, direct propaganda?

One of the best ways to get you to like someone you presently dislike is to reward you for "playing the role" of someone who obviously loves that person?

Despite the fact that everything we say and do probably influences all the people around us, most of us expect to be judged on our intentions and not on the actual consequences of our actions?

The person who understands the needs of others, and who gives as much as he or she gets, seldom has to worry about personal success?

Once upon a time, not so long ago, there was a shining kingdom by the sea called Nacirema. The capital of Nacirema was Imperial City. At its very center, right on Empire Avenue, a concrete castle stretched up to scrape the sky. On the 50th floor of this castle there lived an Iron Duke, one of the Great Wizards of all Nacirema. The Duke's brand of magic was so strong that he influenced the minds of almost everyone in the country, although many of the citizens of this land never knew that he existed. But as our story begins, for the first time in his life, the Iron Duke feared that his occult powers might be slipping.

"Peasants," said the Duke, looking out of his 50th-story window at the people below. "The peasants be damned!"

Humbly born to poor but proud parents named Mr. and Mrs. Steele, the Duke had risen from obscurity to the Royal life through sheer guts and determination—although neither the guts nor the determination were entirely his own. After obtaining a degree in Applied Arts (Basketweaving) from Imperial City College, the Duke had immediately taken a position with the Royal Advertising Agency. By means of much hard work—and a little judicious apple-polishing—he had climbed up the corporate ladder until he was just two rungs from the top: Vice-wizard in Charge of Practically Everything.

"Giants," said the Duke with a curse in his voice. "Double-damn the giants."

In Nacirema at this time there existed many giants—huge corporations that

wanted to sell their products, but lacked the magic power to do so effectively. So the giant corporations hired expert wizards such as those at the Royal Agency to do their advertising for them. Each giant was called a Sponsor, and the Agency kept track of each Sponsor's business in a separate financial account. Every account had its own wizardly Royal Executive who saw to it that things went right. The Giant Sponsor paid all the bills, but it was the Executive's job both to cast spells on the peasants to coax them into buying the giant's product, and to keep the giant smiling at all times. As everyone on Empire Avenue knew, unhappy giants could be very dangerous.

"And triple-damn the widget!" roared the Duke, still standing morosely at the window.

The Duke was, in fact, a glorified Account Executive. His Sponsor was a giant called Amalgamated Widgets, Inc. In order to keep his job, the Duke was called on to perform many boring and trivial tasks, such as spending millions of dollars, traveling all over the world, hiring and firing hundreds of people, attending cocktail parties with other members of the Imperial Court, and drinking three martinis for lunch each and every day. When the Duke had time, he also tried to work a little magic on the giant's behalf.

But gold and power had not brought security to the Iron Duke. He still quivered and quaked whenever His Majesty, the Chairman of the Royal Agency Board, or His Highness, the Presiding Wizard, called the Duke on the carpet. He quivered and quaked even more when the giant called him on the telephone—as the giant had just done—complaining bitterly that widget sales were busting instead of booming. The giant blamed the Duke for the drop in widget sales, and threatened to move the Amalgamated account to another agency. The Duke knew that if this evil event occurred, His Majesty, the Chairman, would lose his royal temper—and the Duke would lose his Royal head.

As the Duke stood looking out of the castle window at the traffic moving along Empire Avenue far below, cold fear gripped his cast-iron guts. Was he losing his magic touch? Could he think of a new spell to cast on the peasants that would sell all those unwanted widgets the Sponsor had sitting in the warehouse? What had the Future in store for him?

At this point in time, Fate intervened: There came a gentle knocking at the castle gate.

"Prithee, enter!" roared the Duke.

A young girl with a crown of golden hair about her head burst happily into the Iron Duke's office. Trailing right behind her was an equally happy and longhaired young man.

"Father!" the girl cried, kneeling quickly before the Duke and then embracing him warmly.

"Princess!" responded the Duke gruffly. "I thought thee still at Lady Bennington's School for Gentlewomen, or at St. Bryn the Martyr's, or some such. What brings thee to town?"

"Father, I wish to present Rodney, my Prince Charming."

"Hail to thee, Rodney, and welcome to our humble abode," said the Duke, extending one of his huge hands.

"Pleased to meet you, Mr. Steele," said Rodney, shaking hands perhaps a bit too eagerly, his flowing locks bobbing as he did so.

"Just call me Duke," the older man said, inwardly upset at the length of Rodney's hair.

"Yes, Sir, Mr. Duke," Rodney responded.

"Rodney has come to ask you for my hand in marriage, Father. Rodney is my soul-mate."

"Rodney is what?" demanded the Duke in an appalled tone of voice.

"He's a Taurus. And I'm a Libra. That makes us soul-mates." The Princess smiled.

"I had thought thee a Virgo," murmured the Duke.

"Ah, well," the girl said defiantly, "now I am Librated."

"Ahem," said the Duke ominously, casting steely eyes at his daughter's escort.

"But what does thy Prince Charming do for a living?"

"Rodney's a genius," the girl said earnestly.

"Gadzooks!" groaned the Duke loudly. "Then he wants employment."

The young princess caressed her father. "Well, you're always saying that everyone who serves you is either a fool or a knave."

The Duke took a monogrammed white handkerchief out of his pocket, mopped his noble brow, and then turned back to the window. "I regret that I cannot add your princeling to my retinue. I fear I have giant problems."

"You mean, the Sponsor?" the Princess whispered, a trace of terror in her voice.

The Duke nodded sagely. "Amalgamated Widgets. They have doubled their budget for advertising magic, but sales are lower than a dragon's belly. Nobody's buying widgets any more. We've tried every trick known to man, and some known only to women, but the damned peasants just won't buy. The Sponsor blames me personally for this unseemly failure. If the Olde Iron Duke doesn't come up with some new magical incantations right away, his name is mudde."

"Yes, Sir, Mr. Mudde," responded Rodney.

"But what's wrong, Father? Why aren't your advertisements working? It's the same old widget it's always been."

"I know not," replied the Duke. "Perhaps thy genius soul-mate can enlighten us."

Rodney cleared his throat. "Widgets stink," he said quietly.

"What!" roared the Duke.

"Widgets stink. They're too big, too expensive, too clumsy, and Sir Ralph Nadir says they're unsafe."

"Nonsense!" cried the Duke haughtily. "You simply don't understand, my boy. The product doesn't matter. It's the magic in the advertisement that counts. Royal prides itself on being able to bend the public's mind whatever way the Sponsor wishes it bent."

"How do you work that kind of miracle?" Rodney asked innocently.

"Follow along, my boy, and I'll show thee how magic is made."

The Duke led Rodney and the Princess down a long golden-carpeted corridor into a huge, well-lighted room. A bank of computers lined one wall; the machines clicked and chirped softly. Large numbers of Elves scurried about, feeding incantations into the machines.

"This be our Market Research Department," the Duke said. "We gather every known fact on the Nacirema public and insert the gatherings into our Merlin computer. We know where the peasants live, how much gold they earn, what television entertainments they watch, and whether they've ever bought a widget. Isn't that marvelous?"

Rodney didn't seem overly impressed. "What use do you make of all this information?"

The Duke frowned. "Forsooth, I never bothered to ask. But I'm sure the gatherings must be valuable to someone. Anyway," the Duke continued in a firmer tone of voice, "it doesn't really matter. It's the Creative Department that actually conjures up the magic. I'll show thee what I mean."

The Duke pressed a button on the wall to summon an elevator. "We lock the creative types in the dungeon, to keep them out of mischief." He ushered Rodney and the Princess into the Royal Lift.

Moments later the doors opened out on a dark basement cavern. Several yards away was a roaring wood fire. Huddled around the blaze was a mixed bag of tiny Gnomes and Witches dressed in oddly colored clothes. One of the Witches was stirring a bubbling pot that hung above the fire. The Gnomes passed a large, smoking object among themselves.

"What's that peculiar smell?" asked Rodney, a sly grin on his face.

"Incense," coughed the Duke discreetly. "They use it in casting their occult spells."

The smallest of the Gnomes rushed up to them and bowed several times.

"Most noble liege lord, welcome to our insignificant dungeon. What brings thee to our nether regions? What action, fair or foul, has caused you to descend to our dank depths? In short, what's cooking, Wiz?"

"Thy flesh and mine, I greatly fear," said the Duke sadly. "The Sponsor hath just called. That last magic potion you created turned sour, and widget sales are faltering like a knight in a daze. If we cannot discover some spectacular new means of ensnaring the peasants' desires, thy whole crew will be back to reading palms by next week."

The tiny Gnome scratched tenderly under his arm, a sad look on his wizened face. Then he suddenly brightened. "I've got it, your Wizardship! The Double Whammy, the Evil Eye, and the Final Curse! We'll mix them all together in our little pot and boil up the most magical brew the world has ever smelt! Unresistible, mind-bending magic. We'll push more widgets through the market place in a week than the Sponsor can make in a month. Leave it to us, Wiz!"

"If you don't succeed, I'll personally turn thee back into a pumpkin," said the Duke.

The Gnome bobbed his head respectfully, retreating back toward the fire. One of the Witches came up and whispered in his ear. "Oh, your Wizardship," the Head Gnome called after the departing trio, "we may have need of a new pot, and sundry things like that."

"That's what we give thee an expense account for," replied the Duke, ringing for the Royal Lift.

Once back in the 50th-floor office, the Duke poured himself a glass of amber-colored liquid from a bottle labeled Sir Johnny Walker's Black Magic. The Duke took his glass to the window. "That be it. You've seen almost the entire Royal operation. But wherewith have we failed?"

"You've shown us everything?" asked Rodney.

"Methinks so," replied the Duke. "There is also a Production Department that makes the films or draws up the art work. But they're all out on location somewhere. And the Media Buyers, who pick which magazines or television programs the incantations will appear in. But they be all out to lunch somewhere. And that's about the lot."

"Then I have the solution to your problem," said Rodney proudly.

"Oh, Father, I told you he was a genius!" cried the Princess happily.

"Young man, although I find it difficult to believe, perhaps I have underestimated thee," said the Duke heavily. "If you can help me keep the widget account, I will not only give thee a job, but the Princess' hand in wedlock as well."

"What kind of a job will you give Rodney?" interjected the Princess immediately.

"Well, the Head Gnome needs a new assistant. And there are always availabilities as a Merlin-tender," responded the Duke.

"I'm more the Wizard Executive type myself," mused Rodney.

"Let us haggle over unseemly trifles later on," said the Duke brusquely. "Tell me thy bright idea first."

Rodney looked the man squarely in the eye and spoke quietly for two minutes.

As Rodney talked, a look of great astonishment blossomed on the Duke's visage. When the young man had finished, the Iron Duke turned pale as a bedsheet.

"Thou canst not mean it?" cried the Duke.

"Ah, but I do," responded Rodney.

The Iron Duke collapsed in a dead faint.

(Continued on page 674.)

What brand of toothpaste do you use? No matter what your answer, you might next ask yourself a much more interesting question—how did you happen to pick that particular brand? Was it the flavor that attracted you to it, or the approval of a dentists' organization, or the low price? Or did you "choose" it because it's the same brand that the rest of your family uses?

Whatever reason you give, chances are that you probably won't list *advertising* as the factor behind your choice. And yet, if you stop to think about it, how would you have known about this brand if it had never been advertised? Furthermore, if you were subjected to "blind" tests (where you couldn't tell which brand you were testing), are you absolutely confident you could pick your favorite toothpaste or brand of beer, soup, or cigarette from others on the market?

Most of us like to think our decisions to buy a particular product, to vote for a certain politician, or our opinions about war and sex and minority groups are *rational* (°) decisions. That is, we tell ourselves that we make up our minds about things only after we've given the situation considerable thought. However, while we often do think through such matters logically, our viewpoints are sometimes created unconsciously, without our being aware of the outside forces that influence our thought patterns. One such force is advertising.

The average American probably encounters about 1,500 different ads each day of his or her life. Some of these ads appear on radio and television; others in books, magazines, and newspapers. Still others flash out from billboards and signs, from bumper stickers on cars, and from the shelves of supermarkets. Americans spend more money each year on advertising than they do on education, or on pollution control, mental health, poverty relief, or scientific research. If the advertisers didn't feel that they could influence your attitudes toward their products (whether or not you were consciously aware of their efforts), would they spend so much?

Nor are advertisers the only ones who wish to bend your opinions to their purposes. Almost every press release put out by the government, or by individual politicians, is aimed at getting voters to think favorably of the person or agency involved. News stories about movie stars, rock musicians, professional athletes, and university professors are almost always "handouts" from *publicity agents* (°). In fact, up to 90 percent of what passes for "news" on television and in the newspapers actually comes from *public relations specialists* (°) and not from a reporter who has "dug up the facts" on his or her own time.

Whenever a teacher criticizes or speaks favorably of a certain theory, whenever a religious leader preaches, whenever a parent "lectures" or a friend offers comments—aren't these people trying to affect your attitudes? And whenever you "dress up to make a good impression," or speak kindly to someone in authority, or try to seduce a potential sex partner—aren't you "advertising" too?

In the past several chapters of this book we have talked at length about how attitudes (or personality traits or types of behavior) are created. In this chapter let us look at why attitudes are important, why some of them remain fairly stable throughout our lives, and why other attitudes appear to be so changeable.

ATTITUDE STABILITY

In an earlier chapter we defined an attitude as a relatively enduring way of thinking, feeling, and behaving toward an object, person, group, or idea. Attitudes almost always involve a certain amount of bias or pre-judging on our parts. When we apply a label such as "stingy" or "psychotic" to a person, we both state an attitude and reveal the way in which we perceive the person. In a sense, then, attitudes are perceptions that involve emotional feelings or biases and that pre-dispose us to act in a certain way.

We could not do without attitudes, for many reasons. To begin with, the attitude (or percept) that we have of someone or of some object allows us to predict the future behavior of that person or thing. If we made no pre-judgments about things, we would have difficulties walking across a street or carrying on even the simplest of social conversations. Many of our attitudes, for instance, seem

Rational (RASH-uh-null). From the Latin word meaning "to reason" or "to compute." Computers are rational because they don't generally have built-in emotional circuits, as does the human brain. Computers make decisions according to the "cold, hard facts" that have been plugged into their memory banks, and according to whatever "decision programs" have been wired into their circuits. Humans sometimes pretend that their decisions are as rational as those made by computers, but all our attitudes and preferences are colored by our emotions. Most biologists and psychologists agree that, although our emotions can often be dangerous, they do have rather high "survival value." Perhaps that is one reason why people invented computers, and not vice versa.

Publicity agents. Our word "publicity" comes from the Latin word *public*, and means "to bring before the people." Individuals whose incomes depend on how often their names are mentioned "in public" sometimes hire agents whose sole job it is to get their clients talked about on television or written up in newspapers and magazines. There is an old saying among publicity agents that it doesn't matter what a publication says about the client, the important thing is whether or not the client's name was spelled correctly.

Public relations specialists. Most large firms and government agencies have employees whose jobs are to see that the firm or agency receives favorable attention in the news media. These employees are typically called "public relations specialists," because it is their task to make sure that "the public" knows about—and likes—the firm or agency. In fact, these PR specialists are often little more than publicity agents, despite their fancier title. Edward L. Bernays, who invented the term "public relations" back in the 1920's (and who was a nephew of Sigmund Freud), once described PR as being "the engineering of consent." It was the public whose attitudes were to be "engineered" by public relations specialists, and not vice versa.

Chauvinistic (show-vin-IS-tick). From the French word meaning "war-monger" or "war-pusher." The word actually comes from the name of Nicolas Chauvin, a legendary French soldier who was blindly devoted to Napoleon. A chauvinist is someone who shows excessive patriotism for any cause, or who is unduly and un-reasonably devoted to any group or place to which the person has been attached.

designed to evoke a certain kind of response from the "outside world." When you say that you "hate pollution" to a man wearing an ecology button on his shirt, you not only can predict the man's response but may also be trying to influence his attitude toward you.

A second important aspect of attitudes has to do with memory. As we learned in earlier chapters, we seem to file our experiences in Long-term Memory according to our *impressions* of what happened. That is, we attach abstract or "verbal labels" to the important features of the experience, and then file the memory according to these "abstract labels." When we try to remember something that happened in the past, we search our memory files according to this same set of labels. Another word for "abstract labels," of course, is "attitudes."

If we now ask why your own attitudes tend to remain fairly constant over long periods of your life, the answer becomes fairly understandable. Can you imagine what would happen to our libraries if someone suddenly discovered that all of Shakespeare's plays were really written by a relatively unknown British poet? How many books would the librarians have to re-index, and how many library cards would have to be changed? If a man who has been a "male, *chauvinistic* (°) pig" all of his life becomes an ardent "women's liberationist," how many millions of his own personal memories would he have to re-label? How long would it take him to do so, and how much energy would he have to invest in the process?

Psychologists believe that the more that you know about a person, thing, or idea, the more stable your attitude will usually be. Likewise, the more strongly you feel about something, the more difficult it will probably be to get you to change the "memory labels" attached to that thing. Furthermore, the better your attitude allows you to predict future events or inputs, and the more you are rewarded for holding a certain percept, the less susceptible that percept or attitude is to being changed.

QUESTION: **Studies show that most college students have attitudes very similar to those held by their parents. Can you think of several reasons why this might be the case?**

Newcomb's Study of Bennington Women

Many attitude surveys indicate that liberal arts colleges are populated by professors who have very liberal political opinions. When a student from a politically conservative family arrives on such a campus, the student often comes under fairly intense social pressure to change his or her attitudes. Although political opinions are often deep-seated, highly emotional, and of long duration, many students do in fact become more liberal during their college years.

QUESTION: **Would you expect seniors to be more liberal or less liberal than freshmen? Why?**

Suppose you were a student who had become politically more liberal than your parents while you were at college. Would you expect this change to endure once you left college and (presumably) returned to your old home environment? What might you do to insure that your newly liberalized attitudes remained the same, even after you had left the campus?

Social psychologist Theodore Newcomb addressed himself to these problems many years ago. At the time that Newcomb began his research, he was teaching at Bennington, a woman's college in Vermont noted for its fine programs in the liberal arts. Because the student body was limited to about 600, Newcomb was able to work with the entire college population in his study of political attitudes.

Most of the women attending Bennington in the mid-1930's came from wealthy and rather conservative homes. The college faculty, however, were quite liberal in their views. Indeed, they felt it a part of their educational duties to familiarize the students with the implications of a Depression-torn America and a war-threatened

Theodore Newcomb.

world. Therefore, the faculty encouraged the students to become politically active and socially concerned. The college itself, nestled between the Taconic and the Green mountains of Vermont, was physically isolated from much of the rest of the world. The nearest town, a village of less than 15,000 people, offered few excitements. The students seldom visited the town more than once a week, and seldom went home for the weekend more than once a month. Hence, the students made up what advertising executives call "a captive audience."

Student Reference Groups In the first part of his research, Newcomb found that the more prestige or status a woman had among her fellow students, the more likely it was that she was also very liberal in her views. Conservative students typically were looked down upon; liberal students were very much looked up to. Seniors were significantly less conservative than were freshmen. During the 1936 election, for instance, 62 percent of the freshmen supported the Republican candidate, while only 14 percent of the seniors did. Some 30 percent of the seniors supported the Socialist or Communist candidates in the 1936 election, while only 9 percent of the freshmen did.

Under these conditions, the entire college population acted rather like a *reference group* (°) that rewarded liberal attitudes and punished political conservatism. Those women whose opinions became more liberal during their four years at Bennington tended to identify with the college community and to adopt its prevailing viewpoint. By their own admission, many of them were quite conscious of how they had changed. As one woman put it, "What I most wanted here was intellectual approval of teachers and the more advanced students. Then I found you can't be *reactionary* (°) and be intellectually respectable."

Those women who resisted the liberal college tradition tended to identify more with their parents than with their classmates. As one woman said, "I'd like to think like the college leaders, but I'm not bold enough and I don't know enough. So the college trend means little to me; I didn't even realize how much more conservative I am than the others. I guess my family influence has been strong enough to counterbalance the college influence." Newcomb notes, incidentally, that this woman was given to severe emotional upsets and had told the college staff that she felt "alone and helpless except when with her parents."

Bennington Women 25 Years Afterward Having measured the change in political attitudes that often occurred between the women's freshman and senior years, Newcomb set out to discover how some of the most liberal of the students would fare once they had been graduated. Taking 150 of these women as his subjects, Newcomb followed their lives for 25 years. Although he had originally suspected that many of the women would revert to a more conservative position once they had returned to their families, this turned out not to be the case. During the entire 25 years, most of the women remained liberal in their outlooks despite family pressures. But why?

Newcomb reports that most of these women set out to remain liberal in spite of their social backgrounds. They tended to select liberal (or non-conservative) husbands who would reinforce their political views. They found little pockets of liberalism in their environments and tried to stay entirely within these pockets. They interested themselves in socially-worthy projects that would bring them in contact with others who held similar political outlooks; and they kept in close touch with their Bennington classmates.

Newcomb believes that if maintaining a given attitude is important enough to people, they will consciously or unconsciously select environments that will continue to support that attitude. They may also shut out incoming sensory messages that might tend to disrupt the attitudes already held (a form of austistic hostility).

Reference group. That group of people whom we look to for our social feed forward, or against whose behavior we measure or judge our own.

Reactionary (ree-ACT-shun-ary). Someone who reacts against the present form of government (or any social change), preferring an older or out-of-date political system. Someone who feels that progress is a matter of going back to prior ways of behaving; someone who cries "Let us march forward to the 18th century!"

Induce (in-DOOCE). From a Latin word meaning "to lead" or "to tow." To induce something is to bring it about, to put it in motion.

Consonant (KON-so-nant). From the Latin words *con,* meaning "with," and *sonare,* meaning "to sound." Consonant thus means "to sound at the same time," or "to agree." The consonants are those letters of the alphabet that are "sounded with" the vowels (a, e, i. o, u, and y).

Persuasion (purr-SWAY-shun). From the Latin words meaning "to urge" or "to advise." To persuade is to induce someone to adopt a certain attitude by argument or pleading, or to win someone over to your way of thinking.

The Newcomb study is one of the few aimed at measuring *stability* of attitudes. Attitude *change* is much easier to investigate, in no small part because the subjects need not be studied over such a long time span as the 25 years that Newcomb was in contact with the Bennington students. Indeed, it seems that most of what we know about attitude stability comes from experiments designed to change people's opinions. So now let us look at the factors that bring about shifts in attitudes. Perhaps this information will be useful not only if you wish to change someone's mind—but also if you wish to protect yourself against the influence of the millions of people who would like to persuade you to be different than you presently are.

PERSUASION AND ATTITUDE CHANGE

Suppose you are in the market for a new automobile. You shop around, looking at the Fords, Plymouths, Chevrolets, and a number of other relatively inexpensive cars. You will come to this situation with a number of biases, or attitudes, about cars in general and these automobiles in particular. Perhaps your family has always had a fondness for Fords, because your father's first date with your mother was in a Ford. Or perhaps your uncle bought a third-hand Mustang once and always claimed it was a lemon. If your prior attitude toward Fords is highly favorable, how might a Chevy salesman try to change your impression of his product? Or if you were prejudiced against Mustangs, how might a Ford salesman attempt to alter your attitude?

In 1940, Solomon Asch pointed out that there are two basic ways to *induce* (°) attitude change toward an object like an automobile. The first way is to change the object or product itself, so that your own perception of the car simply isn't *consonant* (°) with the facts any more. The second way is to leave the car "as is" but somehow get you to change your perception of its good and bad points. Thus a salesman might try to overcome your prejudice against Mustangs by demonstrating how much the car had been improved since the one your uncle bought, or the salesman might try to convince you that your uncle simply didn't know how to drive and therefore his evaluation of the Mustang was faulty.

In either case, however, the salesman must somehow get certain types of information across to you. Without new *sensory inputs* of some kind, your attitudes will presumably remain very stable. And the most important aspect of *persuasion* (°) is the flow of communication from the outside world into your nervous system.

Asch remarks that, in most real-life situations, attitude change usually comes about because of some change in the *object* of the attitude.

When psychologists study attitude change scientifically, however, they don't always have the power to make changes in the objects of our attitudes. If you wished to examine the biases that people have toward Mustangs, for instance, could you readily get the Ford Motor Company to build a totally new product just to satisfy the rigid requirements of your experiment? Or could you get a famous politician to alter his or her way of behaving so that you could take precise "before and after" measures of voters' attitudes?

The most the psychologist can typically do is attempt to get subjects to view reasonably familiar objects (or people or ideas) in a new light. To do so, the psychologist often tries to control some aspect of the communication process.

The Communication Process

Psychologists tend to look at persuasive communication as having four main factors—the communicator, the message, the audience, and the feedback loop that exists between the audience and the communicator.

The *communicator* is the person (or group) trying to induce the attitude

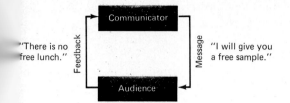

"There is no free lunch."

"I will give you a free sample."

Successful communication depends on feedback from the audience to the communicator.

change. As we will see, the way that the audience perceives the communicator often affects the readiness with which the audience will change.

The *message* is the information that the communicator transmits to the audience. The type of language or pictures used, and the channel through which the communicator chooses to transmit the message, can be of critical importance.

The *audience* is the person or group whose attitude is to be changed. Obviously a clever communicator will wish to know as much as possible about the personalities and attitudinal characteristics of the recipients in order to make the message as persuasive as possible.

The *audience-communicator feedback loop* is perhaps the least-studied aspect of the communication process, yet it is of crucial importance. Unless the communicator knows what type of response the audience actually makes to the message, the communicator is very likely to misjudge the success of the persuasive project. Trying to communicate to someone without getting feedback is like trying to seduce someone you can't see, hear, or feel—you know what you're doing, but it's the other person's response that counts most.

Let us see then what kinds of experimental evidence psychologists have provided so that we can understand the effects of each of these four influences on persuasion.

The Communicator

If your best friend told you that a given product was incredibly good, would you be more likely to believe this communication than if you heard a TV announcer say the same thing on a television ad? Chances are you'd put more *credibility* (°) in your friend's endorsement than in the TV announcer's. And credibility seems to be one of the most influential traits a communicator can possess.

Back in the 1940's and 1950's, a group of psychologists at Yale led by Carl I. Hovland and Irving L. Janis performed some of the first (and still the best) scientific experiments on persuasion. Many of our clearest scientific insights into the process of attitude change have come from these studies. In one of these experiments, Hovland and Walter Weiss tested the influence of "trustworthiness" (credibility) on attitude change. They began by making a list of "communicators" they figured were very trustworthy, and another list of communicators they figured few people would trust. The "high credibility sources" included the *New England Journal of Biology and Medicine*, a Nobel-Prize-winning physicist, and *Fortune* magazine. The "low credibility sources" included a noted gossip columnist, the Russian newspaper *Pravda*, and a well-known U.S. publication that specialized in scandals and sex-oriented stories. When Hovland and Weiss asked students to judge the credibility of these sources, about 90 percent of the subjects rated the first group as being very trustworthy and rated the second group as being exceptionally untrustworthy.

Next, Hovland and Weiss tested the "attitude toward the effectiveness of atomic submarines" in two similar groups of students. They found that most of the students were rather neutral about this complex topic. For practical purposes, we might say that their attitudes were neither positive nor negative (in part, perhaps, because few of the students had given the matter much consideration). If we were

Credibility (kred-uh-BILL-it-tee). From the Latin words meaning "worthy of lending money to." Literally, the power or ability to inspire belief.

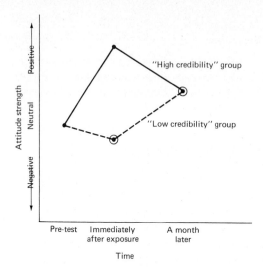

The "sleeper effect." Effects of exposure to propaganda on "effectiveness of atomic submarines."

plotting their attitudes on a graph, we would say the students were right in the middle—at the zero point on the graph (*see* the figure above).

Hovland and Weiss then wrote a "message" in which they argued that atomic submarines would indeed be a very important weapon in any future war. They showed this message to the two groups of students. For one group, the message was said to have come from one of the high credibility sources. For the other group, the message was attributed to one of the low credibility sources. Immediately after exposing the students to the message, Hovland and Weiss retested their subjects' attitudes.

As you might surmise, the students' attitudes were strongly affected by the presumed source of the message. The subjects in the high credibility group tended to accept the arguments; their attitudes became significantly more positive. The students in the low credibility group tended to reject the arguments as being "biased and untrustworthy." If anything, their attitudes became slightly more negative. Apparently we tend to move *toward* the position of someone we trust, and *away* from the position of someone we mistrust—even if this movement involves giving up our original attitude.

QUESTION: **How does this study compare with the experiment on negative conformity mentioned in the last chapter?**

The "Sleeper Effect"   Had Hovland and Weiss stopped their work at this point, we might well have misunderstood the real importance of communicator credibility. However, they continued by retesting all their subjects a month later. To their surprise, they found significant attitude changes in both groups over this period of time. The attitudes of the high credibility subjects became considerably *less* positive, while the attitudes of the low credibility subjects became significantly *more* positive. As the graph suggests, the students had apparently forgotten the source of their information on submarines, but remembered the arguments rather well. Hovland and Weiss call this the *sleeper effect* (°).

The sleeper effect indicates that the credibility of a source has an immediate and often strong effect on whether you accept or reject incoming information. However, once the message has gotten through to you, chances are that you will soon forget the source and recall only the information itself.

The importance of communicator credibility therefore seems to be in getting you to attend to the message in the first place. Hovland and Weiss had a captive audience of students who had to listen to their message as part of a class project. In real-life settings, we are all inclined to "tune out" a communicator we don't

Sleeper effect. The knowledge, discovered by Hovland and Weiss, that we tend to remember the facts of an argument rather well but often forget the source of those facts. The credibility we place in a source may cause us to accept or reject the message as soon as we hear or see it; however, the facts are somehow "sleeping" in our Long-term Memories and will emerge on their own long after we have forgotten who told us those facts.

rust long before the message can be completed. Credibility, then, is crucial in getting the information through to the audience, but not so crucial in maintaining long-term attitude change.

QUESTION: There is an exception to the sleeper effect. What do you think would have happened had Hovland and Weiss *reminded* their subjects of the message source before testing their attitudes a month later?

When we try to judge the trustworthiness of a source of communications, we typically attempt to "psych out" the communicator's motives and intentions. A number of further experiments by Hovland, Janis, and their associates demonstrate that the factors which influence credibility are much the same as those which influence first impressions (*see* Chapter 26). People whom you like, or who are like you, or who seem to be acting naturally rather than "playing roles," are people whom you typically trust. Persons with high social status—such as doctors, scientists, and church leaders—are somehow more believable than people with low social status. In the long run, however, it is what the person says or does that influences our attitudes the most.

QUESTION: If you were trying to sell a cold remedy on television, what kinds of TV actors would you choose, and how would you have them dress?

The Message

During the 1936 presidential election, G.W. Hartmann carried out an interesting experiment on the relative value of "emotional" versus "logical" appeals to voters. Hartmann prepared two different *propaganda* (°) leaflets urging people to vote for the *Socialist* (°) party. One leaflet used highly sentimental and romantic language to describe the wonderful political changes that would occur if the Socialist candidate were elected. The other leaflet presented a series of highly rational, unemotional facts and figures about the goals of the Socialist party. The two leaflets were distributed to different parts of an "average" U.S. city. A third part of the city received no leaflets at all, thus serving as a control or comparison during the experiment.

The year 1936 was the middle of the great Depression, and many people voted for the Socialist party who might not have done so under better economic conditions. Those parts of the city that did not receive Hartmann's propaganda showed a 24 percent increase in support of the Socialist party (as compared with the 1932 election). Those parts of the city in which the "rational" or "logical" propaganda was distributed showed a 35 percent increase. Those areas of the city given the "emotional" leaflets, however, showed a 50 percent rise in support for the Socialist candidate.

Strongly emotional messages apparently do have effects on people's behaviors and attitudes that rational appeals fail to produce. But why? It could be that our passions simply overwhelm our powers of logic in such situations (or that the limbic system overwhelms the cortex), but this seems not to be the whole answer. Many studies suggest that emotionally-toned stimuli often do attract one's immediate attention, but don't always change or increase one's motivation. As Hovland and Janis point out, emotionality may act much the same as does credibility—passionate statements are more likely to break through a listener's "wall of autistic hostility" than are calm, rational statements. Once that wall is breached, it may be the logical facts that actually affect the listener's attitudes and actions.

Hartmann reports that post-election interviews showed that more voters remembered having received (and presumably having read) his emotional leaflet than remembered the rational leaflet. If Hartmann could somehow have gotten all

Propaganda (prop-uh-GANN-duh). From a Latin source meaning "to enlarge or extend." When you have children, you propagate the human race by extending or enlarging the number of humans on earth. Technically speaking, propaganda is the spreading of doctrines, ideas, arguments, facts, or rumors through any communication medium in a deliberate effort to further a cause.

Socialist. Someone who believes that society is more important than individuals. Someone who believes in government ownership of the production and distribution of goods (rather than leaving such matters entirely to profit-making individuals).

Beware! **Young and Old — People in All Walks of Life!**

This **may be handed you**

Marihuana Cigarette

by the friendly stranger. It contains the Killer Drug "Marihuana"-- a powerful narcotic in which lurks *Murder! Insanity! Death!*

WARNING!

Dope peddlers are shrewd! They may put some of this drug in the 🫖 **or in the** Cock-tail **or in the tobacco cigarette.**

WRITE FOR DETAILED INFORMATION, ENCLOSING 12 CENTS IN POSTAGE — MAILING COST

Compact flower, female Marihuana (weed)

Address: THE INTER-STATE NARCOTIC ASSOCIATION
(Incorporated not for profit)
53 W. Jackson Blvd.   Chicago, Illinois, U. S. A.

Example of a "high-fear" campaign to change attitudes. (How effective was it?)

the recipients of both leaflets to have to "read the message," both groups might well have shown the same level of support for the Socialist candidate.

Fear-arousing Messages Many of us seem to believe that people would behave in more socially acceptable ways if someone in authority just threatened them enough. In recent years, for instance, nation-wide campaigns against venereal disease, the use of hard drugs, cigarette smoking, and the dangers of not wearing seat belts have employed the "hellfire and damnation" approach. That is, the main thrust of the propaganda has been to describe in exquisite detail the terrible consequences of various types of misbehavior.

But are such threats really as effective as we sometimes think them to be? The experimental evidence suggests that the actual effects of "the punitive approach" are more subtle and complex than we might previously have guessed. In 1953, Irving Janis and Seymour Feshbach investigated the effects of fear-arousing communications on high school students. These scientists picked as their topic *dental hygiene* (°), or the dangers of not taking good care of your teeth. Janis and Feshbach wrote three different 15-minute lectures on tooth decay. The first was deliberately designed to create strong (but negative) emotions. Called the "high-fear" lecture, it contained 71 references to pain, cancer, paralysis, blindness, mouth infections, inflamed gums, ugly or discolored teeth, and dental drills. The second ("moderate-fear") lecture was somewhat more restrained. Although it, too, discussed pain and disease, it made only 49 such references. The third ("minimal-fear") lecture was quite different. It made no mention at all of pain and disease, but rather suggested ways of avoiding cavities and decayed teeth through proper dental hygiene.

Janis and Feshbach presented each of the three appeals to a different group of 50 high school students (a fourth group of students that heard no lecture at all was

Dental hygiene (HIGH-gene). "Hygiene" comes from the Greek word meaning "healthy." Dental hygiene is the study of what makes teeth healthy.

used as a control). The attitudes toward dental care of all the students were tested at least three times—first, a week before the lectures were given; second, immediately after the lectures; and third, a week later.

When asked what they thought about the lecture, most students in the high-fear group thought the lecture excellent, impressive, interesting, important, and that it should be given to all high school students. They also admitted that the lecture got them very worried about the health of their own teeth. However, 28 percent said they disliked something in the talk, 34 percent said the pictures used with the lecture were too unpleasant or *gory* (°), and 20 percent said there was not enough material on how to prevent decay and disease.

In marked contrast, the students who heard the minimal-fear talk were not nearly so impressed with the lecture. Only half as many of them stated that the talk "got them worried" about their own teeth as did the high-fear group. However, only 2 percent said they disliked something about the talk, none of them thought the slides were too unpleasant, and just 8 percent said there was not enough material on prevention of dental problems.

The moderate-fear group was, in almost all respects, about halfway between the high- and the minimal-fear groups.

From these data alone, one might conclude that fear-arousing appeals are successful. However, Janis and Feshbach went two steps further with their investigation. In their week-after questionnaire, they asked the students how their tooth-brushing behavior *had actually changed*. Only 28 percent of the high-fear group reported they had put into practice any of the improved dental care techniques recommended in the lecture, while 20 percent admitted they were actually doing *worse* than before. By comparison, 50 percent of the minimal-fear group said they were "brushing better," and only 14 percent said they were doing worse.

The high-fear appeal apparently evoked strong emotional responses in the students, many of whom thought that being frightened was somehow "good for them." As one student in this group said, "Some of the pictures went to extremes but they probably had an effect on most of the people who wouldn't want their teeth to look like that. I think it is good because it scares people when they see the awful things that can happen."

Despite this student's beliefs, when it came to actually *changing* attitudes and behaviors, the high-fear appeal simply didn't work as well as did the minimal-fear lecture. In fact, for reasons we will make clear in a moment, the high-fear propaganda seems to have had exactly the opposite long-term effect that one might have predicted.

QUESTION: **Why do you think high-fear appeals are still so commonly used in our society?**

Counter-propaganda Propagandists often point out that it is not enough to change a person's attitudes; you must also make sure that the person resists any further attempts that might push the individual back toward his or her original beliefs. Effective propaganda, then, is that which not only causes attitude shifts but also protects against *counter-propaganda* (°).

A week after the students had listened to their dental hygiene lectures, Janis and Feshbach exposed the students to information that contradicted what they had originally been told. The students were then asked whether they believed this counter-propaganda or not. Twice as many subjects in the high-fear group were affected by the counter-persuasion as were subjects in the minimal-fear group. Janis and Feshbach conclude that "under conditions where people will be exposed to competing communications dealing with the same issues, the use of a strong fear appeal will tend to be less effective than a minimal appeal in producing stable and persistent attitude changes."

Gory (GORE-*ee*). "Gore" is an Old English word meaning "dung" or "feces." It also means a mass of "bloody filth," or a mass of clotted blood. Gory activities are those behaviors that lead to a great loss of blood, such as murders and wars.

Counter-propaganda. Communications designed primarily to overcome or to cancel the effectiveness of propaganda issued by someone else.

QUESTION: If you knew that an audience you wished to propagandize might be exposed to counter-propaganda from other sources, what might you tell the audience to minimize the effects of counter-propaganda? If you were certain that your audience would never hear "the other side of the question," would you bother to protect them against counter-persuasion?

Why don't fear and threats work the way many people think they should? The answer seems to be twofold. To begin with, as Janis and Feshbach report, there seems to be a tendency for people to *repress* or deliberately forget frightening information. Second, and perhaps more important, our emotions can *arouse* us, but they don't always *direct* us in our thoughts and behaviors. Janis and Feshbach believe that fear-inducing communications focus our attention on problems and not on solutions. We become excited by the terrifying message, but we don't know what we must do to avoid or prevent the disaster the message warns us of. In fact, the fearful message may do little more than convince us that disaster is inevitable, and so we give up and do nothing at all.

Not all of the experiments on fear arousal have directly supported the position of Janis and Feshbach—at least, not at first blush. For instance, in a 1965 study, Howard Leventhal and Patricia Miles showed particularly bloody color films of automobile accidents to subjects, then checked to see how many of the viewers changed their driving habits. Leventhal and Miles report that the more films the drivers saw, the more they seemed to adhere to safe-driving recommendations. In a 1966 study on dental hygiene, Leventhal and Robert P. Singer found that the greater the fear arousal value of their propaganda, the more their subjects appeared to "yield" to appeals to brush their teeth correctly. However, both of these experiments were marked by a serious flaw in their designs—namely, the groups exposed to the high-fear appeals also were given more information on how to *cope* with the threat than were the low-fear groups. In another study, Leventhal, Singer, and Susan Jones discovered that students given specific directions about where to obtain a tetanus injection (to prevent lockjaw) were much more likely to go get the shot than were students not given specific information on where the injection could be obtained. The level of fear presumably aroused by the message simply didn't affect the outcome.

In 1970, Leventhal seemingly came around to the Janis and Feshbach position when he stated that the critical variable in fear appeals is the ability of the subject to cope with threat presented to him or her. If the recipients of the message know what to do, feel that they can do it, and believe that doing what the propagandist suggests would be rewarding to them—then and only then will the subjects respond as the communicator has suggested they ought to. In short, fear can arouse *cognitive dissonance* (*see* Chapter 27), but unless the members of the audience feel they can cope with the threat, they will merely change their attitudes toward the feared situation rather than change the way they behave in that situation.

Successful propaganda would thus seem to be that which induces just enough motivation to energize us, but which primarily gives us simple, understandable ways of achieving the propagandist's real goals.

QUESTION: Would you think that externalizers would respond differently to high-threat propaganda than would internalizers?

Indirect Propaganda   Some persuasive messages are so disguised that almost no one sees them as being propaganda, perhaps including the communicator! This hidden or indirect propaganda is often effective for the simple reason that the intended audience simply does not perceive that its attitudes are being influenced.

E.L. Thorndike, the learning theorist mentioned in Chapter 16, wrote several textbooks for elementary students, including one on arithmetic. Thorndike was trying to teach his readers how to add, subtract, and how to solve problems involving *compound interest* (°). He apparently had no conscious intent of influencing economic or political beliefs. However, as Ellis Freeman pointed out in 1936, some 643 of Thorndike's simple arithmetic problems stress familiar capitalist notions. Each of these problems involved such things as buying and selling at a profit, lending money at high interest rates, and so forth.

Freeman suggests that Thorndike was unwittingly teaching school children the virtues of the U.S. economic system. To emphasize this point, Freeman asks what would happen if arithmetic texts contained problems such as the following:

1. Suppose that among the workers in a southern cotton mill, 1 out of every 100 suffers from chronic colds and the flu because of the inadequate salaries paid by the mill. How many new flu cases would appear if the mill added 1,000 new workers at the same wages?
2. If a family, to maintain an adequate nourishment level, needs $20 a week for food, what is the degree of starvation in such a family when its relief funds are but $5 a week?

Freeman states that: "Books containing such problems, although they taught the abstract relationship of numbers as well as any others, would be dismissed as propagandistic and unworthy of the dignity of pure arithmetic." However, no one seems to have complained about the hidden messages in Thorndike's book.

Psychologist G.C. Meyers attempted to teach English to foreign-born soldiers in the U.S. Army. He did this by showing the soldiers "model letters" which they were to adapt or put into their own words. Buried in the texts of these "model letters" were a great many specific facts and opinions about the U.S. that Meyers thought should become part of the soldiers' beliefs and attitudes. Before-and-after tests showed that Meyers had succeeded not only in teaching the men how to write better letters but had shifted their attitudes as well.

QUESTION: **What kinds of hidden propaganda can you now detect in your favorite television show, or in your favorite novel? Is the message any less effective, or any more justifiable, if the author or authors were not aware of being propagandistic? Would you be more likely to look for disguised propaganda in a political speech or in a piece of fiction?**

The Audience

The proficient propagandist usually wants to know as much about his or her audiences as possible—their present attitudes and values, their group memberships, their past experiences, and their future goals and expectations. The propagandist then shapes the message to fit the intended audience.

Guides for the Propagandist   Psychologists David Krech and Richard Crutchfield list several "guides for the propagandist" in their book, *Theory and Problems of Social Psychology*. One of these guides is: "A suggestion that seems to meet an existing need will be more readily accepted than one that does not meet a need." For example, if a politician determines that the voters have become tired or annoyed with their present government, the politician may take as a slogan "It's Time for a Change!"

In some situations, the propagandist must *create* a need in order to satisfy it for his or her own benefit. For instance, the Detroit auto-makers bring out a line of "new" cars annually and spend hundreds of millions of dollars to advertise the "newness" of these products. It seems possible that, over the years, the car manufacturers have created a "need for newness" in the U.S. public that leads to greater annual auto sales than might otherwise be the case.

QUESTION: **Why might it be useful to a teacher to determine the attitudes of his or her students at the beginning of a semester? When might it be of value to a student to learn as much as possible about teacher attitudes?**

Jimmy Carter on the campaign trail.

Compound interest. Suppose you borrowed $100 from a bank, promising to pay it back at the end of one year with 4 percent simple interest. The interest would be figured only once, at the end of the year. You would owe the bank $100 plus $4 interest. However, if the interest were figured (compounded) quarterly, at the end of the first three months you would owe the bank $100 plus $1 interest, or $101. At the end of the second three months, you would owe the bank $101 plus interest for three months on $101 (and not on $100). The second quarter's interest would then be $1.01, and you would owe the bank $102.01. At the end of the year, you would owe the bank $104.06, rather than $104.00. If the interest were compounded daily instead of quarterly, you would owe the bank much more. If the interest were compounded every second of every day in the year, you would end up owing the bank about $108 rather than $104. Compound interest can actually add up to twice as much money as simple interest. The moral of this story is simply stated—when you borrow money, ask the total cost to you, not simply "what interest rate must I pay?"

Group pressures. When you must make a judgment about a stimulus (or state your attitudes toward something) in the presence of a group of people who have also seen that stimulus (or who have expressed their own attitudes), you may often feel strong social pressures to make your judgment conform to that expressed by the group, or to bring your attitude in line with theirs. See Chapter 27.

The Cincinnati Study Knowing something about your audience doesn't always guarantee that you will be able to get your message through to them, however. Shortly after the Second World War, a group of social scientists in Cincinnati undertook a monumental advertising campaign in an attempt to inform the citizens of Cincinnati of the great value of the United Nations. Sociologists Shirley Star and Helen Hughes report that surveys of attitudes toward the U.N. were taken before the campaign began in order to establish what public opinion was, and to help in the planning of the venture. Then followed six months of intensive "mass education," during which the public was bombarded with propaganda favorable to the U.N. Radio and television stations, newspapers, and owners of billboards donated millions of dollars worth of free time and space to help the campaign along. Following the program, a survey was again taken to determine any shift in public opinion.

The findings reported by Star and Hughes offer cold comfort to propagandists. The pre-campaign survey had indicated that it was those people already interested in the U.N., even if these people were poorly informed, who would most readily welcome new information about the international organization. Unfortunately, these very citizens were also the ones most likely to be *already* strongly in favor of the U.N. The groups who knew the least about the U.N. included the relatively uneducated, the elderly, and the poor. These groups were also the least interested in finding out anything new about the U.N., and hence were the most resistant to change.

Although the publicity campaign was designed specifically to appeal to the people who knew and cared the least, the message apparently reached or persuaded few of them. Instead, among the general public the campaign mostly affected younger people, as well as the better-educated and relatively well-to-do segment of the general population. These were, of course, the very people who were already favorably disposed toward the world organization.

Star and Hughes state that the greatest attitude changes of all took place in those individuals actively concerned in running the campaign, a point we will come back to in a moment.

Apparently the less you know about a subject, and the less you care, the more likely it is that you will refuse to pay attention to any new information about a given topic. Ignorance seems to be not only the best defense against attitude change but also the best defense against acquiring knowledge of any kind.

Audience Responses

Why did the Cincinnati campaign fail? There probably are many different reasons. To begin with, we have no guarantee that once the target audience was identified (the poor, the uneducated, the elderly), the propagandists knew what kinds of messages would be most likely to reach the target. At the time of the study (the late 1940's), very few poor people, uneducated people, and senior citizens could afford television sets, and few of them read the newspapers. These individuals appear to learn about changes in the world primarily through word-of-mouth comments from their friends and associates—that is, from their *reference groups.* Had the target audience been put under strong *group pressures* (°), such as those described in the last chapter, the outcome might have been very different.

QUESTION: **If you had been running the Cincinnati study, how might you have used group pressures in order to induce attitude change among elderly citizens?**

A more glaring mistake made by the Cincinnati experiments was their failure to establish feedback loops to monitor continuously the effects of their propaganda campaign. The Cincinnati communicators talked; the audience was merely supposed to listen and to respond appropriately. Most communicators spend a great deal of time and money trying to get their messages out, but seldom spend as much effort trying to determine if anyone is listening and, if so, what the audience's reaction actually is.

QUESTION: What are the differences between the feedback loops *from student to teacher* in a large lecture class and the feedback loops that exist in small classes?

The one "success story" in the Cincinnati study was that the people actually engaged in the propaganda campaign showed significant attitude change in the desired direction. As they worked on the project, this group of people apparently became more and more committed to making the study a success. Since the group was favorable toward the United Nations, anyone who joined the group was under strong pressure to conform to the group norm. These individuals also had the greatest exposure to the persuasive messages.

As we saw in Chapter 4, more recent studies covered in the Surgeon General's report suggest that long-term exposure to violence on television does indeed help determine a child's attitude toward violence in real life. However, in almost all these studies, the children were captive audiences and the propaganda was of the subtle, indirect variety. That is, the positive attitude toward violence was actually modeled during dramatic TV episodes rather than being pitched at the child in brief, commercial messages. Several of these studies suggest that children tend to act out the dramas that they see on television. We thus cannot really tell from the Surgeon General's report whether it was the propaganda on the tube, or the subsequent role-playing that it encouraged, which affected the child's attitude toward violence.

Role-playing and Attitude Change   There have been numerous studies demonstrating that the greatest attitude changes of all come when the communicator can get the audience to role-play the attitudes the communicator wants the audience to acquire. For example, in 1957 W.A. Scott measured the attitudes toward "de-emphasis of football" in hundreds of students taking an introductory psychology course. Some of the students wanted bigger and better football teams, while others wanted to do away with the teams entirely.

Two weeks after measuring their attitudes, Scott asked 58 of the students to engage in mock debates on the importance of football. These debates took place in front of the rest of the class. Each student-debater, however, was asked to give arguments *against* the position the student had taken earlier (on the questionnaire). The class then voted to see which students had "won" their debates.

The "trick" in the Scott experiment was this—the votes actually cast by the class were ignored. Instead, Scott randomly told half the students they had "won," while the other half of the students were informed that they had "lost" the debate. Later, Scott remeasured the attitudes of the debaters.

As might be expected, Scott found that rewards and punishments had quite a strong effect on attitude change. Those debaters who thought they had "won" shifted significantly toward the position they had argued in class, even though this new view was the opposite of the one they had originally held. Those debaters who were told they had "lost" moved in the opposite direction—they became more convinced than ever that their original position was the correct one.

In 1954 Irving Janis and B.T. King measured the attitudes of a group of college students toward military service. Then they asked each of the subjects to make a speech on the draft in class. Half the subjects were given a prepared script to read; the other half were asked to make up their own arguments. But in either case, the student had to argue *against* his or her original position (as measured before the speech was given). After the talks were over, Janis and King again tested the students' attitudes. Those subjects given the prepared script to read in class were quite satisfied with their performance, but their attitudes didn't change very

Emanating (EM-an-ate-ting). The Latin word *emanare* means "to flow." A telecast of the Superbowl football game emanates from whatever stadium the game is being played in.

much. The students who made up their own talks, however, while dissatisfied with their classroom performance, showed a significant change away from their original attitude. Janis and King conclude that "there is a lowering of psychological resistance whenever a person regards the persuasive arguments *emanating* (°) from others as his 'own' ideas."

Successful salespersons occasionally employ a similar "gimmick" in trying to sell merchandise. Rather than telling a housewife how good a vacuum cleaner is, a salesman may tell the woman that "he's new on the job and needs help." He then asks the woman to look over the machine and to demonstrate it to him.

By getting the housewife to role-play his own part, the salesman accomplishes many things at once. To begin with, he learns a great deal about what this particular woman values in a vacuum cleaner. She is likely to express her needs in terms she can understand, rather than in the language the salesman might ordinarily use. Certainly, if she goes along with "the game," she is motivated to pay more attention to the product (the message) than she might usually be. Pretending to be a salesperson, she may also *commit* herself to the product more than if the man simply urged her to do so. And, finally, the salesman is in the powerful position of being able to reward her with social approval and encouragement every time she "acts out" an attitude he would like her to acquire.

QUESTION: **In psycho-drama, should the therapist usually ask the patient to act out a successful or an unsuccessful outcome to the patient's problems?**

Attitude change, like any other form of human behavior, involves inputs, processing, outputs, and feedback. Certain stimuli are more likely to be noticed (that is, to become sensory inputs) than are others. What stimuli we pay attention to is determined in part by the physical characteristics of the stimuli themselves, in part by our needs and emotional states, and in part by the social background the stimuli appear in. Sensory inputs that are important to us get attended to, responded to, and filed away in our memories. The type of response we make to a given stimulus is influenced by our genetic blueprints, our personality traits, past consequences of our responding to this stimulus, and our individual goals for the future.

People who take the time and effort to learn the facts of human behavior generally are better at inducing attitude change in others than are people who ignore all the scientific data on this challenging topic.

THE ETHICS OF ATTITUDE CHANGE

There would seem to be two major ethical considerations with respect to trying to change the thoughts and behaviors of the people around you—permissibility and intentions.

To understand the problems concerning the *permissibility* of influencing others, ask yourself this question: Under what conditions is it ethically acceptable in your own mind for one person, group, or nation to attempt to alter the attitudes of another individual, group, or nation? Don't people have a right to remain as they are, or to become what they want to be, without any outside meddling or interference? Furthermore, is it morally justifiable for social scientists to deceive their subjects during experiments, as did Milgram, Sherif, Asch, Blake and Helson, Janis and Hovland, Darley and Latané, Scott, and many others? Who should decide whether the knowledge gained by such studies outweighs the risks to the subjects?

A complete discussion of these questions would be far outside the scope of this text, for these are fundamentally moral or religious considerations. However, by now you will surely understand the position that many psychologists take toward this issue—namely, that every waking moment of your life, whether you are conscious of it or not, you influence the people around you. Everything you do or say acts as a reference point for almost everyone you come in contact with. The fact that most of us are unaware of the effects we have on others, and the effects they have on us, makes little difference from a psychological point of view. Ignorance of known behavioral laws seems rather a poor ethical excuse for overlooking the consequences of our actions. We can be free *not* to "bend the minds" of others only if we have some scientific knowledge of how mind-bending actually occurs.

Shall Our Intentions Be Our Guide?

Many discussions on the ethics of persuasion hinge on trying to judge the *intentions* of the communicator. We can look at this problem both from an objective and from a subjective vantage point.

Viewed *objectively*, your intentions are difficult to measure and hence rather meaningless to discuss scientifically. It is the consequences of your actions that count—not your motives. Clarence B., the murderer mentioned in the first chapter, apparently had no conscious intent to kill the young graduate student he stopped by to see that hot July evening. But he did kill her, for reasons neither he nor we fully understand. In trying to rehabilitate Clarence B., should we worry more about measuring his intentions or changing his behavior? Most parents of youthful criminals certainly don't set out to turn their children into law-breakers, but the parents' attitudes and actions do result in their children's lawlessness, despite the parent's intentions. Is it then ethical for society to ask these parents to change their attitudes and behaviors toward child-rearing—or else ask them to give up custody of their children, whose illegal acts could affect so many innocent parties?

Viewed *subjectively*, however, personal motivations and intentions are of great importance, even though they are but one part of a complex psychological process that also includes attitudes and behaviors. For the desire to help people rather than hurt them can surely motivate you both to understand people better and to measure constantly the actual effects of your actions.

In their discussion of propaganda, Krech and Crutchfield point out that the best political persuader of all is a social and economic system that satisfies the deep-felt needs of all the people in the system. The politician who sees that the voters are happy and continually moving toward their own goals is a politician who typically doesn't have to worry about being re-elected. In similar fashion, the person who understands the needs of others, and who gives at least as much as he or she gets, seldom has to worry about personal success.

QUESTION: In what ways might your own attitudes toward human behavior have been changed by your having read this book?

SUMMARY

1. Social psychologists spend a lot of time trying to answer the following questions:
   a. Where do our attitudes come from?
   b. Why do some of our attitudes remain fairly stable throughout our lives?
   c. Why do other attitudes change from time to time?
2. Although some of our opinions, feelings, and preferences are the product of rational decision-making on our parts, many of our attitudes are unconsciously influenced by attempts of other people to persuade us to think and act as they do (or as they would like us to think and act).

3. In general, the more you know about something, the more stable your attitude toward that thing will usually be.
4. The stronger you feel about something, the more difficult it probably will be to get you to change your perception of or attitude toward that thing.
5. The better your attitude allows you to predict future events or responses, and the more you are rewarded for holding a certain percept, the less susceptible that percept or attitude is to being changed.
6. When we acquire a new attitude that we want to keep, we often protect the attitude by seeking the company of people who believe as we do, and by screening out information that might contradict that attitude.
7. If someone wants to change your attitude toward some object, the person must either change the object or somehow communicate new information to you about that object.
8. The communication process is influenced by at least four different factors:
   a. The communicator
   b. The message
   c. The audience
   d. The feedback (if any) from the audience to the communicator
9. Studies suggest that one of the most important aspects of the communication process is the credibility the audience places in the communicator.
10. Emotional messages are often more likely to catch our attention than are purely logical arguments. However, in the long run, it may be the "facts" presented in the message that shape our attitudes—for we often tend to forget both the source of the communication and its emotionality.
11. Fear-arousing messages sometimes have the opposite effect to that they are intended to have, since they may convince us that disaster is inevitable. Thus, we may give up and not respond at all.
12. The more that a propagandist constructs the message to fit the prior beliefs and attitudes of the audience, and the more the communicator pays attention to audience feedback, the more successful the persuasive attempt will usually be.
13. The best persuader appears to be whatever best satisfies the deep-felt needs of the audience.

(Continued from page 658.)

It took several minutes for the Princess to revive the Iron Duke from his faint. While the young girl was alternately wiping her father's brow and slapping him on the cheeks, Rodney poured himself a glass of the magic amber liquid.

"Thou canst not be serious," the Duke said, when he had finally recovered sufficiently to make it to his huge leather chair.

"Dead serious," said Rodney.

"But to give forth the whole, unadulterated, 100 percent **truth** about our Royal products! Why the whole fabric of society would be torn to shreds. Such folly would lead to the complete collapse of the Nacirema economy."

"Nonsense," said Rodney. "Things would change a little, but perhaps for the better."

"Well, it would surely mean the undoing of Amalgamated Widget, which is just as bad," replied the Duke, thinking perhaps of his own position if Amalgamated Widget were to be undone.

"I doubt even that. The trouble with the widget is not that it's so terrible but that it simply isn't as good as it could be. As long as the Sponsor can sell the present model, why should he change? It's cheaper to use your agency's 'word magic' to cover up the problems than to put out a noticeably better product. If you had to tell the truth about the widget, the Sponsor would no longer have that choice."

The Duke poured himself a large tumbler of the amber liquid. "Thy suggestion would never work," he said finally. "The peasants would never stand for it. They love their illusions, and we but keep them happy. Peasants have no love for the truth."

"Then why have they stopped buying widgets? It seems to me that you and the Sponsors are the ones who don't want the truth. Give the people a better product, and maybe they'll start buying widgets again.''

''Ah,'' said the Duke, ''there's the rub. What meanest thou by better?''

Rodney moved to the window and stared out at the traffic 50 floors below. ''I must admit I don't really know.''

''And this princeling calls himself a genius!'' the Duke said to the Princess.

''But I know how to find out,'' Rodney continued.

''Like how?'' asked the Duke, his voice ringing with sarcasm.

''Ask the people what they want; tell the Sponsor your findings; and do your level best to see that the Sponsor tries to meet the people's needs. Then you don't have to be afraid of the truth.''

The Duke laughed hollowly. ''Thou kiddest.''

''No, I kid thee not. Business, politics, education—they've all become like Empire Avenue down below, a one-way street. The Sponsor builds widgets and tells you to sell them. You use glowing descriptions to trick people into buying widgets whether they need them or not. But what say does the public have in what gets built or what ads get run?''

''The peasants vote with their pocketbooks. They can buy, or not buy, as they please.''

''Even when it's the only widget on the market?''

The Duke shook his head vigorously. ''We spend millions of dollars each year peering into the peasant mentality.''

''So you can persuade them better; not so they can persuade you to give them a better product. You've cut off all feedback from your customers. No wonder widgets are selling poorly.''

The Duke remained unconvinced. ''No Sponsor in his right mind would dare try it.''

Rodney smiled. ''Some already are. They're trying to involve their customers in product planning, in production, and in marketing and advertising—just as schools are beginning to involve their students in planning and teaching courses, and politicians are learning to listen more than they talk.''

''But I tell thee Wizards like me know what the peasants really want!'' the Duke almost screamed.

Rodney turned away from the window. ''Papa knows best—is that what you mean?''

The Duke nodded slowly.

''Mr. Steele, have you ever gone out and bought a widget?''

''Heaven forfend!''

''When was the last time you really talked to someone who has?''

The Duke looked puzzled. ''Princess,'' he said slowly, ''I don't suppose . . .''

''I wouldn't be caught dead with one, Father. They're just not my style.''

The Duke picked up his phone and buzzed his secretary. She didn't use widgets either; and neither did the Director of Marketing, the Chief of Production, or the Head Gnome.

''See what I mean, Sir? A one-way street. Everybody talks, and nobody listens. What you need is a Vice-wizard in Charge of Feedback.''

The Princess laughed. ''And, Father, I just happen to know someone who's available.''

The Iron Duke grumbled to himself for a moment, then managed a half-hearted smile. ''Methinks the matter needs serious contemplation. Get thee hence, you two. The Iron Duke hath a giant to kill.''

After the young couple had gone, the Duke hunched over in his huge chair, considering what Rodney had said. After a while, the big man wearily picked up the telephone and dialed a number.

''Hello, Mama? This is Sonny. How are things? Yes, I know I haven't talked to you in quite a while. Oh, has it really been that long? Well, you know how busy I've been. What? Yes, the Princess is doing fine, just fine. She's got a new boy friend, a prince of a fellow. There may be wedding bells any day now. Oh, certainly, I do want you to meet him. He's got long hair and some strange ideas, but he'll learn, he'll learn. Incidentally, we may be hiring him here at the firm.''

The Duke listened for a moment, nodding in silent response to what he heard. Then he took a deep breath. ''Oh say, Mama. What's your attitude toward widgets?''

RECOMMENDED READINGS

Hovland, Carl I., Irving L. Janis, and Harold H. Kelley. *Communication and Persuasion* (New Haven, Conn.: Yale University Press, 1953).

Krech, David, and Richard S. Crutchfield. *Theory and Problems of Social Psychology* (New York: McGraw-Hill Book Company, 1948).

Newcomb, Theodore M., Ralph H. Turner, and Philip E. Converse. *Social Psychology* (New York: Holt, Rinehart and Winston, 1965).

APPLIED PSYCHOLOGY: PAST AND FUTURE

Like most scientists, I believe in the future. I guess I always have. I am much more interested in new things than in old, and I am more intrigued by what a person might become than in what a person has already been. Indeed, about the only time I think about yesterday is when I need information that might let me better understand what tomorrow could be like.

Humans seem to be the only animals that can look far into the future and plan accordingly. This ability to change some parts of the present world in order deliberately to shape the world of tomorrow is, in my opinion, one of the essential characteristics of being human.

Science is the fine art of predicting the future in objective terms. It is therefore one of the most human of occupations. It took human beings a long time to learn how to make their predictions accurate, however, for at least two reasons:

1. Being emotional or subjective seems easier for most of us than being rational or objective. Perhaps this fact is not too surprising. The emotional centers of the nervous system appear to dominate the brains of lower animals. The "thinking" or "processing" centers in the cortex reach their fullest development in humans, but these are additions to (rather than subtractions from) the basic blueprint of the highly reactive animal brain. The human limbic system is more complexly evolved than is the limbic system in the white rat, cat, or monkey, and our emotional experiences are likewise more subtle and complicated. The sheer size of the human cortex gives us the potentiality of bringing our passions and desires under voluntary control, but we need training and experience in order to do so. We need precious little training to be emotional.

    In order to think logically, you have to be able to translate parts of the world into verbal symbols, so that you can manipulate the world symbolically in your mind. Only the human being has a "speech center," so far as we know, and only humans seem capable of complex speech and symbol manipulation. But as human society developed, we had a long heritage of animal emotionality to overcome, and we had to develop such symbolic languages as mathematics in order to help us do so.

2. Even when early men and women attempted to view the world in objective terms, they often lacked sufficient data to make good predictions. It probably wasn't until around the year A.D. 1600 that we had gathered enough hard, unemotional facts about the world—and had the proper mathematical tools—for science to prove a worthwhile occupation.

The Industrial Revolution

Perhaps because it is easier for most of us to look at *things* objectively than for us to be objective about ourselves, the physical (or "thing") sciences were the first to develop. Modern physics and astronomy date from the 1600's; chemistry came a little later. These scientific disciplines soon developed enough to let us understand and predict the behavior of a few objects under certain specified conditions—for that kind of prediction is science's job. But once we could predict how physical *things* would behave, we could also hunt for ways to *control* the future behavior of these objects—and this ability to control things marked the rise of physical technology.

The first major applications of physical technology in Europe began in the mid-1700's, and led to what we call the "Industrial Revolution." Before this time almost everyone in Europe lived on farms or in small towns, and almost every "thing" was handmade. Life changed little from one generation to another: A man typically became what his father had been; a woman married the sort of man her mother had married. As greater and greater application of the physical sciences gave humans the ability to shape their physical environments, however, the tempo of cultural change speeded up noticeably.

The Medical Revolution

By the 1800's, we had learned enough to begin viewing our bodily reactions in an objective manner. Biology became a true science, and medical technology became a reality. As the Medical Revolution gathered steam in the early 1900's, we learned more and more about how to predict and control our physiological reactions. Because of this applied knowledge, we are now bigger, stronger, healthier, and more of us live longer than at any time in human history.

The Psychological Revolution

During the early part of this century, we took the next step up the ladder—we learned to look at our minds and behaviors objectively. Psychology and the social sciences came into being. We are just now starting to build a technology based on our new-found objective knowledge of ourselves. We call this technology *applied psychology*—that is, the application of psychological facts and theories to help solve real-life problems—and in my opinion the use of this technology will lead to what might be called the "Psychological Revolution." The cultural changes this third revolution will bring about will surely be as "mind-blowing" as those caused by the Industrial and Medical Revolutions.

What will scientific psychology be like in the future? That question is difficult to answer, since it depends in part on the often unpredictable outcomes of all the thousands of experiments psychologists are conducting right at this moment.

The future of applied psychology is somewhat easier to predict, however, since tomorrow's technology will lean heavily on today's scientific knowledge. In these final pages, let me share with you my guesses about the changing world of human behavior, and what these changes might mean to you. Other psychologists will surely see things differently, and predictions are often little more than wild speculation. Still, it might pay us to give some serious thought to (1) what the world might be like in the year 2000, (2) what kinds of job opportunities might be open to you then, and (3) what types of psychological services you possibly could call on by the end of this century. And in defense of my perhaps odd ideas about the year 2000, let me remind you of this fact: At least half of the *types* of jobs available to college graduates today simply didn't exist as "job classifications" 25 years ago.

THE FUTURE OF BIOLOGICAL PSYCHOLOGY

There seems little doubt that we will shortly gain a great deal more control over our heredity (and hence our instinctual behaviors) than we would have dreamed possible a few years back. In late 1973 scientists at the University of Wisconsin announced that they had been able to synthesize a gene in a test tube—that is, they had been able to take ordinary chemical molecules and combine them to "build" a very simple gene. Whether this tiny portion of a "genetic blueprint" will function "naturally" when injected into a living organism more complex than a virus remains to be seen. However, "genetic engineering" is no longer as impossible and unthinkable a project as once seemed the case (*see* Chapter 19).

Once the biologists give us greater control over our inheritance, psychologists will be able to determine with much greater precision what the genetic contribution to behavior really is. We should also be able to learn much more about how to overcome genetic handicaps that already exist. By the year 2000, many psychologists should be employed as "genetic counselors," giving advice to prospective parents both before and after they get married. Other psychologists will be able to offer physically handicapped people much better training than now exists. These psychologists may also offer surgeons advice on what kinds of drugs and operations might be helpful to maximize the *psychological* potential of brain-damaged individuals.

Behavioral Medicine

There are very few psychologists working in hospitals today. By the year 2000, however, hospitals may employ more behavioral technologists than they do physicians and surgeons. This surprising situation will be a direct consequence of the three revolutions we mentioned earlier. For thanks to our increased knowledge of the physical and biological sciences, the major health hazards are no longer diseases that have a purely physiological cause—such as pneumonia, influenza, and tuberculosis. Medical technology has "cured" us of these maladies, for the most part. But medical technology is presently ill-equipped to help us with health problems that have an intra-psychic or behavioral component, for few physicians are trained in psychological technology.

In the summer of 1975, the U.S. Department of Health, Education, and Welfare released its *Forward Plan for Health*, a long-range blueprint of U.S. needs in the health sciences. According to this report, the major killers today are heart disease, cancer, stroke, and—in younger people—automobile accidents, murder, and suicide. As is stated in the *Forward Plan for Health*, "A distinctive feature of these conditions is that most of them are caused by factors (that is, the environment and individual behavior) that are not susceptible to direct medical solution."

John H. Knowles is both a physician and the president of the Rockefeller Foundation. Writing in the *Forward Plan for Health*, Dr. Knowles states, "The people have been led to believe that national health insurance, more doctors, and greater use of high-cost, hospital-based technologies will improve health. Unfortunately, none of them will. . . . The next major advances in the health of the American people will come from the assumption of individual responsibility for one's own health and a necessary change in life style for the majority of Americans." In brief, our biological systems interact with our intra-psychic and our social/behavioral systems, and the next breakthroughs in medicine will come from the wise and humane use of a psycho-technology that helps coordinate the inputs and outputs of all three systems.

Already several of my students are working with doctors and patients at several medical facilities in the Ann Arbor area. The students have been particularly successful with "problem patients" whose thoughts and behaviors interfere with improvement in their physical health. Let me give you two examples of their successes.

First, the students worked with a woman who had lost both kidneys, and whose body had previously rejected two kidney transplants. The woman was near death and was being kept alive (while awaiting a third kidney transplant) by being on a very strict diet. But the woman was so discouraged that she refused to keep to the diet. When one student interviewed her, the woman finally unburdened herself. She had been hospitalized this time for more than three months and certainly wasn't getting better. She faced yet another major operation. Her husband, tired of her absence, had taken a mistress and moved this younger woman into the patient's home. Her two sons were in the Army and, despite the fact that their mother was dying, the Army refused to let them come to see her. "What do I have to live for except food?" the patient asked.

The student (who was a trained nurse) encouraged the woman to keep to her diet, and for six straight meals the woman did so. Although this was the first time in months that the patient had done so well with her food intake, the sad fact is that not one doctor stopped by her bed to commend her. On the seventh meal, the woman "slipped" and ate one slice of bread more than she should have. By the nurse's actual count, within two hours of this event, 15 members of the hospital staff stopped by the woman's room to bawl her out for misbehaving. As the patient herself said, "They may fuss at me for five minutes, but then I get to socialize with them for another 10 minutes or so."

The nurse immediately got the medical staff to write a "behavioral contract" with this patient. The contract stated that as a reward for each meal that the woman ate just what was on her diet, at least one doctor would come by to chat with her. If the woman went off the diet, she would be totally ignored by the medical staff until she returned to the diet. The woman's attitude immediately improved; she stayed on the assigned diet continuously, and maintained her health sufficiently so that she could receive the third kidney transplant. She then went home and, with her physical health improved, tried to work out a solution to her many problems with her husband.

In the second case, another nurse who studied with me was asked to assist a woman patient who was rapidly becoming "hooked" on narcotics. Seven years earlier, this woman had had an accident that caused her to experience severe but incurable pain in her side. The physicians had done all they could, but the painful condition simply couldn't be helped very much. Over the years, the discomfort became so intense that the woman stopped taking care of her family, took to her bed, and finally entered the hospital, where she was being given narcotics to ease her pain. As is often the case, the woman was demanding more and more of the narcotic. The nurse talked with the patient and observed her behavior. The woman lay flat on her back in bed, almost unmoving, for some 23 hours of the day; she sat up only for meals, and left the bed only to go to the bathroom.

During their conversation, the nurse noted that the only subject the woman seemed interested in talking about was her pain and her need for more drugs. Believing that this verbal behavior pattern was unhealthy, the nurse began turning her head aside whenever the woman complained about the pain, but turned back and became excited whenever the patient discussed anything else (see the Greenspoon experiments mentioned in Chapter 25). Within a few minutes, the patient said to the nurse, "You don't want me to talk about my pain, do you?" The nurse complimented the woman on her insight, and the two soon worked out a contract. If the woman would talk about getting well and going home instead of her pain, the nurse would spend a couple of hours a day sitting by the patient's bed and "rapping" about anything else the woman wanted to discuss.

The nurse then began encouraging the woman to move about a bit. Within two weeks, the patient had been "shaped" into doing exercises. Shortly thereafter, she was jogging about the hospital corridors for up to four hours a day. Within a month, the woman was home, taking care of her family for the first time in seven years, and not taking any medication at all. The family was instructed to ignore her complaints, but to reward her with attention and love whenever the woman engaged in "healthy talk." If the woman could go all week without complaining, she gained the right to go to the horse races each weekend and to wager a certain amount of money on her favorite ponies. The woman apparently found this activity very reinforcing.

The nurse visited the woman about two weeks after she returned home and found her in excellent spirits. When asked about her pain, the woman responded, "Well, it's going to be with me the rest of my life. The doctors know that, and so do I. So I just have to learn to live with it. But you know, it's a funny thing. When I don't talk about the pain, it just doesn't hurt as much."

There are many times when a hospitalized patient must undergo drastic surgery, or must be treated with complex (and often frightening) apparatus, such as an artificial kidney machine or radiation therapy. With the help of psychologists, physicians are beginning to work out ways of *desensitizing* patients to these fear-inducing situations. Although the point has not as yet been proved experimentally, it seems possible that a calm, hopeful, cooperative patient is more likely to survive than a patient who "freezes" or faints when faced by the intra-psychic conflicts these situations often induce.

What we might call "behavioral medicine" is a new and uncharted field. But its growth seems assured, for as the *Forward Plan for Health* notes, we cannot cope with most of the major medical problems today unless we realize that good health is always an interaction among the biological, intra-psychic, and social/behavioral systems that affect us all.

Biological Feedback Quite often physicians use drugs to try to control physiological processes that might better be brought under the voluntary control of the patient. There are already promising hints that some milder forms of epilepsy may be helped by conditioning procedures. If the epileptic patient can be hooked to an EEG machine, the patient can sometimes see visual representation of the chemical storm building up in his or her own brain. By training the person to detect the subtle physiological "cues" and psychological "feelings" that accompany the onset of an epileptic seizure, the psychologist may be able to teach the person to relax or otherwise change thought patterns so that the seizure is prevented.

In similar fashion, patients recovering from heart attacks may use machines that record their heart beats, much as the EEG records brain waves. By seeing this visual representation of how his or her heart is working, the patient may discover how to condition the heart to respond in healthier ways. High-blood pressure, digestive upsets, urine production, and internal bleeding may also turn out to be controllable through conditioning. It is even possible that we may learn how to influence the production of human sperm and eggs through conditioning techniques. Rather than giving a woman "the pill" to prevent her from becoming pregnant, we may be able to train her to become fertile only when she consciously wishes to do so.

If certain types of brain waves turn out to be associated with creativity, we may be able to use EEG machines and computers to help people achieve greater intellectual and artistic growth than ordinarily would be possible. We might also discover means of letting people suppress the control of their "dominant hemisphere" whenever they wish to encourage their "non-dominant hemisphere" to break through to consciousness.

Applied Psychology Involving Drugs   We already know that chemicals such as caffeine speed up learning, and that "downers" typically retard it. It is quite likely that, by the year 2000, psychologists will know of a wide variety of drugs that will help people achieve goals not presently within their reach. Drugs to slow down or help reverse the process of senility are a possibility, as are chemicals that will help prevent some types of mental illness. It is highly probable that all such compounds will be used in conjunction with other types of psychological treatment, but there is no reason not to use drugs if they can be helpful.

As we learn more about what "consciousness" is all about, we will surely discover more effective means of inducing whatever "altered states of consciousness" anyone might desire to experience. Both drugs and biofeedback techniques seem likely candidates in this type of research.

Applied Psychology Involving Sensory Processing   Computers are crude models of our brains. As we gain more insight into how your Board of Directors looks over sensory inputs and processes them, we should be able to build dramatically better yet simpler computers than we presently have. It is already theoretically possible to use, for example, the brain of an ant or a worm as a "biological computer." The problem at the moment is in controlling the sensory inputs and the motor outputs. Biological computers should be able to handle complex decision-making much better than present-generation electrical or mechanical computers—and brains are likely to be smaller and easier to handle than machines. Thus it is possible that some "computer technologists" in the year 2000 will be, in effect, animal trainers rather than machine-tenders.

And, as we learn more about how your receptors actually sense the world, and how your motor centers control muscles, we might be able to build "electronic eyes and ears" that would be connected directly to the brains of blind and deaf patients. We might also be able to build artificial arms and legs that will be directly connected to the motor-output centers of the brain, so that mechanical "limbs" would respond to a person's thoughts almost exactly the way that flesh-and-blood would respond.

Biological engineering will be a part of our future whether we like it or not. But it seems reasonably certain that it will always be used in conjunction with improved ways of "engineering" our thoughts and behaviors. So let us look next at what applied intra-psychic psychology may be like.

APPLIED INTRA-PSYCHIC PSYCHOLOGY

Technology implies measurement; the more accurately you can describe and measure anything, the better chance you have of being able to exercise some kind of control over it. As you may have gathered from earlier chapters in this book, one of the major problems with the intra-psychic or subjective approach to human existence is that internal events are most difficult to describe in quantitative or measurable terms. For this reason alone, we can probably expect greater immediate technological development in biological and behavioral psychology than in the intra-psychic area.

There are a number of highly promising developments, however, that we should take note of. Personality theory in the past has been based on the assumption that your character was fairly well fixed by the end of the first few years of your life. Freud, for example, thought that only superficial or "surface" changes occurred in people once they had passed the years of early adolescence. Personality tests were usually designed to measure the intellectual and emotional traits a person already possessed, not the traits that the person might acquire with training and encouragement. The IQ test, for instance, tells you something about what you are, but not very much about what you could become.

The humanistic psychologists, however, emphasize growth and perpetual change. One of the greatest challenges of the coming 25 years will be to develop new types of intra-psychic tests that will tell us more about the *potentialities* of people than present tests do. We will have to find new types of traits to measure (as best we can) that emphasize the process-of-becoming rather than "fixed" or supposedly unchangeable traits such as IQ or "psychosis."

The humanistic psychologists are also likely to discover more about human (and humane) goals and values in the coming years than we presently know. In many ways, they are in a unique position—that of functioning as a conscience or "super-ego" that can help keep the more applied technologies oriented toward ethical solutions of human problems.

Applied Developmental Psychology

One of the fastest-growing fields within the behavioral sciences is that of *developmental psychology*. Although this term used to mean much the same thing as *child psychology*, we now realize that people continue to develop throughout their lives. In the future, developmental specialists will work with people of all ages, helping them solve whatever "growth" difficulties arise at any time in a person's life. Developmental psychologists will work as learning specialists in the school system, being as interested in helping young people achieve emotional maturity as in helping them learn to read, write, think logically, and be more creative.

But applied developmental psychology should also be useful to people in the middle years of life. As our health gets better and our lives get longer, we will realize that there is no reason why we should commit ourselves to one occupation, or to one style of life, and stick with it forever. Education should not stop when some college places a degree in a person's hands—rather, it should continue to the moment of the person's death.

Some of our greatest untapped resources are the skills and abilities of our senior citizens. As we learn how to maintain psychological youthfulness even when our bodies are fairly ancient, we will need specialists to help older people continue to be useful and contributing members of society.

Death is as much a part of the business of living as is life itself, yet we often avoid the topic, and it has seldom been studied scientifically. Developmental psychologists will probably be called upon as much to help people prepare psychologically for facing death as for facing life.

Psychological Pollution

It has taken us more than 200 years from the start of the Industrial Revolution to realize that our new-found control of the physical environment brings with it serious responsibilities. Because we did not understand the consequences of our actions, we have polluted our lakes and streams; we have destroyed many of our natural resources; and have fouled the very air we breathe. Ecologists are presently working very hard to help us learn how to keep our physical waste products from ruining our health and lessening the quality of our physiological existence.

As we gain greater influence over our psychological environment, it is likely that we will discover the importance of various forms of *psychological pollution* that we have ignored in the past. Hatred, war, violence, threats, and punishments are forms of psychological pollution that can contaminate our personal psychological space as much as belching smoke stacks can pollute the physical world. Criticism (justified or not) can kill a person's spirit as quickly as lead or mercury can poison a person's body. My own opinion is that most of the "hang-ups" and inhibitions that people have are a direct consequence of the punishment, ridicule, and hostility that we too often aim at each other.

One of our future challenges, then, will be to discover ways to get people to control or repress the psycho-pollution of hatred and to express more openly their loves and affections.

APPLIED BEHAVIORAL PSYCHOLOGY

The engineering profession really got its start with the beginning of the Industrial Revolution. Part of an engineer's job is to take known scientific data and use them to transform the physical environment; but in doing so, engineers often discover new scientific principles on their own. And, in putting well-known scientific theories to practical tests, the engineer may uncover flaws in the theory that laboratory scientists were unaware of.

One of the most important new professions is that of behavioral engineering—men and women who use psychological data to help create new and more satisfying social and work environments. My private opinion is that, by A.D. 2000, half the psychologists in the United States will be employed in jobs demanding behavioral engineering skills. Let us look at some of the things they might be doing.

Community Mental Health

As long as we believed that mental illness was primarily the fault (or responsibility) of the individual, we could ignore the effects of the social environment on human behavior. But we now know that, just as dirt and germs breed physical illness, so can punishing cultural conditions breed crime, violence, insanity, and personal misery. At present we have sanitary engineers who inspect restaurants and food stores to make sure that food is clean and healthy. Perhaps by the next century we will have behavioral engineers who inspect businesses, schools, and industries to make certain that employers show as much concern for the mental health and happiness of their employees, students, and customers as they do about cleaning up dirt and preventing physical disease.

Already we have a great many community mental health centers scattered across the United States and Canada. We will need many more of them, and they will surely take on many new tasks. The data suggest, for instance, that most parents who mistreat their children were mistreated by their own parents. If we are to stop this slaughter of innocent children, we will have to find effective ways of teaching these sorts of parents to manage their children without resorting to violent physical punishment.

Mental illness "runs in families" in part because of genetic factors, in part because certain types of parental responses induce "insane" behavior in children. To break this self-perpetuating pattern of mental illness, we will need more effective forms of family counseling. We will also have to make some rather difficult moral decisions concerning society's right to intervene in unhealthy family situations when the parents may resent or fight against outside intervention.

Mental hospitals as we presently know them may very well vanish almost completely by the year 2000. They will be replaced by clinics, re-education centers, halfway houses, group homes, and other forms of "sheltered environments" where people with mental problems may go for relatively short periods of time. Behavioral engineers—working in teams with psychiatrists, psychologists, and social workers—will help these disturbed people find solutions to their problems. The patients will then be eased back into society bit by bit, rather than being discharged abruptly with little in the way of after-care. Behavioral psychologists will also be involved in helping to change the social environment (such as a family situation) into which the patient will return.

The sprawling concrete prisons we presently send criminals to will also slowly fade from the scene. As we gain greater control over the social environment, fewer people will "want" to become law-breakers. Rehabilitation and re-education are much more effective ways of dealing with criminals than are merely punishing them and locking them away behind bars. When prisoners are treated humanely by concerned prison staffs—when convicts are given the social skills they need to survive and whatever therapy or behavioral treatment they require—the prisoners tend to become much more law-abiding when released than if we try to "cure" them of their bad behavior by beating their skulls open or by locking them in solitary confinement. A number of state penal systems are experimenting with the use of "token economies," in which the prisoners earn privileges by demonstrating personal growth and impulse control. Although the technique is too new for adequate evaluation to be made as yet, preliminary results are fairly encouraging. Out of every 100 prisoners released from "punishment prisons," about 50 will be re-arrested and returned to jail within five years. The "return rate" of prisoners who have been released from humanely-run "token economy" prisons is (so far) about 20 percent.

Mass Communications

For a number of years, the federal government has taken frequent surveys of U.S. economic life. The government knows how much money people earn; the taxes they pay; the debts they owe; and how many people have television sets, bathtubs, and automobiles. In the last few years, however, the government has realized that it has mountains of data on the *quantity* of U.S. life—who owns what—but little or no information on the *quality* of U.S. life—how happy and satisfied people are. But surely the "cost of loving" is as important a piece of data as the cost of living. If the government is to serve us better, it must first develop better ways of measuring psychological needs and desires, and then find ways of engineering the "psycho-economy" to our greater satisfaction.

Elections are a form of political feedback, but they come too infrequently to reflect the shifts in mood and the attitude of the general public. Political "polls" are a step in this direction, but they probably need to be taken more often and should cover a broader array of topics. Manufacturers, too, need to create better ways of discovering public desires. Many future behavioral engineers will probably be involved in developing and maintaining more effective feedback systems in government and industry.

Industrial Psychology

Psychologists have long been employed by business firms and governmental agencies in many capacities. One of the chief functions of these industrial psychologists has been that of personnel selection. A great many intelligence and aptitude tests have been developed that supposedly let psychologists evaluate the knowledge and skills of potential employees. Psychologists also have tried to develop "job descriptions" that would state what abilities were needed to handle a particular position. It was then up to the psychologist to match the person to the job.

Unfortunately, most of the tests and "job descriptions" were based on personality theories that assumed people were relatively unchangeable, and the tests were biased in favor of white, middle-class males with considerable verbal skill. As we learn more about how to help people grow and develop, industrial psychologists will probably spend more time training personnel than selecting them.

We also learned that a worker's performance is not dependent entirely on his or her own talents, but on the type of encouragement the worker's supervisor gives, and on how rewarding and satisfying the job happens to be. In a 1973 survey of employees at a B.F. Goodrich plant, workers were asked what things other than money would increase their motivation to perform well. The majority of workers replied that gaining some control over their own destinies, and being able to participate in the management decision-making process, would be particularly satisfying.

For almost half a century, industrial psychologists have spoken of the "Hawthorne Effect," meaning that one must be careful in real-life experiments since subjects will often produce the results they think the experimenters want. The effect gets its name from a series of studies performed at the Hawthorne (Chicago) plant where the Western Electric Company manufactures equipment for the Bell Telephone System. This research, done between 1927 and 1932, was designed to discover how much productivity and morale might be improved when the experimenters made various changes in the work environment. One room in the Hawthorne plant was set aside for test purposes, and a miniature assembly line was set up there. The experimenters (mostly psychologists) then changed the amount of illumination in the room to see what effect this change might have had on assembly-line output. According to the reports these psychologists issued later, productivity increased no matter what the experimenters did. The usual interpretation of these data has been that the subjects knew they were being measured, and hence worked harder—even when the experimenters decreased the illumination or otherwise made conditions worse. Because it was originally assumed that the workers simply tried to do what the experimenters wanted them to do, the Hawthorne Effect has been used as an argument in favor of using deception in scientific studies involving human subjects.

Very recently, psychologist H.M. Parsons has gone back and re-examined all of the original data in this study. Incredibly enough, Parsons was able to show that productivity increased *only* in those situations in which the workers could have gotten some feedback as to how well they were performing. Parsons reinterprets the Hawthorne Effect to be just another example of how the outputs of living systems are controlled by informational inputs—in this case, feedback about performance.

Few corporations pay much attention either to the type or the amount of feedback that is given employees. In a 1972 survey taken at a large Michigan corporation, almost one-third of the 1,000 employees questioned stated that they never saw their supervisor except when the supervisor came to complain about something the employee was doing wrong. Generally speaking, managers and supervisors are quick to give punishing feedback and reluctant to praise good performance. One of my doctoral students recently worked for two years with an automobile corporation near Ann Arbor. She found that the company seldom let its assembly-line personnel know what was expected of them in *measurable* terms, and seldom bothered giving these people information on how well they were doing. When the student trained a group of supervisors to give positive feedback when their workers were doing well, both productivity and morale went up significantly. The employees enjoyed their work more, and the company saved almost $200,000 a year on this one assembly line alone.

One of the tasks of industrial psychologists in the future will surely be that of training managers to identify desired outputs and to reward them when they occur. Supervisors must also learn that consulting with their employees, and listening to suggestions from the workers, can be a most potent reinforcer—both for the workers and for corporate profits.

As another example of how behavioral engineering might help corporations, let us look briefly at industrial absenteeism. A 1967 Dartnell Publishers business survey suggested that employees who stay away from their jobs cost the country between $10 and $30 billion a year. In some companies, 10 percent of the employees are likely to be absent on any given day. For many years the main "cure" for absenteeism has been punishing those workers who had no excuse for their failure to show up at work. Most managers presumed that workers were absent because of some innate flaw in their personalities (*see* "Person Perception" in Chapter 26). The managers also assumed that punishing the workers would force them to behave—or else!

In fact, as recent studies show, high absence rates are primarily an index of poor employee morale and of job dissatisfaction. In general, the more a worker dislikes the supervisor and/or the work group, the more likely it is that the worker will have a high absentee rate. When jobs are extremely scarce, threatening to fire an employee may have some effect on absenteeism. When jobs are more plentiful, rather a different solution seems to be called for. Offering workers extra financial incentives for good attendance is sometimes effective. However, as E.E. Lawler and J.R. Hackman showed in 1969, by far the best way to reduce absenteeism is to ask employees what incentives or job changes they want, and then to reward the workers with what they asked for when they do in fact show up for work.

Industrial corporations often count their buildings, machines, and profits as "corporate assets." As psychologist Rensis Likert points out, however, the finest resources available to any company are the skills and talents of its employees. Two of the major jobs for future industrial psychologists will be (1) to help executives measure these human assets, and (2) to treasure these assets by developing work environments that are maximally satisfying to all employees.

PSYCHOLOGY IN YOUR FUTURE

Fifty years ago most Americans were employed in producing "things"—farm products and manufactured goods. Today more than half of all Americans are employed in service occupations—that is, in helping other people or in taking care of people's possessions. As we learn more effective ways of assisting one another, the need for psychological services will grow tremendously. The behavioral sciences have rapidly become one of the most (if not *the* most) popular undergraduate majors in U.S. colleges and universities. My own estimate is that by the year 2000 at least 10 percent of the U.S. work force will be able to lay claim to the title "psychologist" or "behavioral engineer."

Whether you choose to become a psychologist yourself is, quite naturally, a decision that only you can make. But perhaps reading *Understanding Human Behavior* will have given you some notion of what the future possibilities in psychology will be; and no matter who or what you plan to become, your life will surely be affected by what I call the "Psychological Revolution."

At its best, psychology can offer you the tools to shape your body, your mind, and your social environment somewhat closer to your heart's desire. We do not as yet know what the real limits of human potential are—we know only that people are capable of greater growth and development than we dreamed possible 50 years ago. It is up to you to use the tools available to you, and to plot your own course into the future.

Let me close by thanking you for letting me be your guide through some of the frontiers of psychology, and by wishing you the happiest of life's journeys.

APPENDIX

STATISTICS AND EXPERIMENTAL DESIGN

Up until my third year in graduate school, I hated mathematics. In high school, my worst grades by far were in such subjects as algebra, geometry, and trigonometry. In my freshman year at college, I was forced to take a math course; I passed by the skin of my teeth. For several years thereafter, I avoided most forms of mathematics as passionately as I avoided rattlesnakes and scorpions.

As a graduate student in psychology, I was required to suffer through a couple of classes in statistics. I managed to pass both courses, but I have a confession to make. Although the classes were taught by a world-famous statistician, they were the only courses in my entire school career in which I went to sleep almost every session. Lord knows, I tried to stay awake; but as soon as the professor started writing formulas on the board, my eyelids popped shut as automatically as if they had been conditioned to do so.

In fact, I had been conditioned to fear and dislike mathematics. Most of my teachers probably didn't mean to turn me off to numbers and equations, but they managed the task nicely—in part, because some of them hated math too; in part, because they tried to punish me into learning rather than trying to find reasons that would make me love the stuff. For, as I now understand only too well, mathematics is really one of the most rewarding and practical tools that humans have in their fight for survival.

Anyhow, when I was a graduate student at the University of Texas, there came a time when I had to choose a minor area of concentration to go with my major in psychology. I went to see my adviser, Professor Hugh Blodgett, to see what I could get away with. I had hoped he would let me minor in sociology or philosophy or even English literature, because these were easy subjects for me. But the wise old professor had other ideas.

"Philosophy?" he said, a wicked twinkle tickling the corner of his eyes. "All they do in philosophy is teach you how to talk. And you talk too much already. Why don't you minor in physics instead?"

I turned slightly green. "Physics?"

"Certainly. Physics, or mathematics. Do you a world of good, since you say you want to become a scientist."

"You wouldn't consider English literature instead? You know, Freud had quite an influence on literary symbolism."

Professor Blodgett laughed, somewhat harshly, as I remember it. "What's the matter? Aren't you bright enough to get through mathematics?"

The green look on my face turned to red. "Of course I'm bright enough!" I sputtered angrily.

"You'll have to prove it to me, if you want me to believe it," Blodgett said sternly.

Gathering up the broken bits of my ego, I trotted hurriedly over to the math

department to see if they wanted me as a student. They didn't, for I had almost no background in the subject. But by that time I was so determined to show Dr. Blodgett I wasn't a numbskull that I literally forced myself on the mathematics department.

Luckily for me, the teachers in this department were kind and concerned people. They took advantage of my determination to prove myself and soon showed me that mathematics is neither difficult nor necessarily dull. Rather, it is a way of thinking about things, a way of organizing one's percepts of the world so that events make more sense than they would otherwise. Math—particularly statistics—is also a perfectly marvelous way to make certain that people don't cheat you, and to help you decide which forms of happiness are really best for you. Not only that, some forms of statistics are awfully good if you happen to like games of chance, as I do. You might be surprised at how my bridge game improved after Professor Blodgett was kind enough to shame me into learning what I should have learned years earlier!

If you already have a fondness for equations, bully for you! But if you have always hated or feared math, don't be upset. You're in the vast majority, and you have nothing to be ashamed of except the poor teaching you've received in the past. In that case, let me try to do for you what Hugh Blodgett and the mathematics teachers at Texas did for me—open up a brand new world for your own personal pleasure. Just stick around for the next few pages and I'll try to show you how easy, exciting, and challenging a few tricks with numbers can be.

PROBABILITY THEORY

As we noted in Chapter 29, the physical sciences first came to prominence in human affairs some 400 years ago. During the 1600's, the physicists and astronomers were developing the theoretical tools that they needed to describe their insights into matter, energy, and motion. Since the main tools they used were numbers and symbols, the foundations for much of present-day mathematics were laid down at that time.

Perhaps the most important tool of all to come from that era was *probability theory*. Surprisingly enough, the motive for its development was not science but greed. In 1654, a notorious French gambler—the Chevalier de Meré—became worried about the stakes, or "odds," that should be given in a dice game (or "craps," as we refer to it in the United States). He interested two noted mathematicians—Pierre de Fermat and Blaise Pascal—in figuring out just what the odds should be. From the correspondence between these two geniuses came the theory that allows the casinos in Las Vegas to earn hundreds of millions of dollars every year, and the insurance companies to earn even more by betting on how long people will live.

Not too long ago, gambling of almost any kind was illegal in the United States. But in recent days, our attitudes toward betting have changed considerably. Almost any form of gambling is legal in Nevada, and many state governments now run lotteries whose pay-off schedules come straight from the letters that Fermat and Pascal exchanged back in 1654. Thus the "odds are good" that you or some of your friends will wager a dollar or two on a game of chance some time in the near future. So perhaps it might pay you to understand just how *odds* are figured.

Heads or Tails?

If you have a quarter handy, look at it carefully. One side probably shows George Washington's head; the other side has a design we usually call "tails." If you flipped the coin in the air right now, which side would come up on top when the coin landed, heads or tails?

Well, how can you tell before you flip the coin? You can't, of course, but you

"THE ABNORMAL CURVES"

MY NAME IS
NORM. WHAT'S
YOURS?

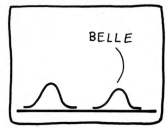

BELLE

I MIGHT
HAVE KNOWN.

KALINOWSKI

can assign *odds* (probabilities) to each possible outcome. Since coins seldom land on their edges, there are just two "events" that can occur when you flip the quarter—a head or a tail. And since most coins are reasonably well balanced, the chances of getting a head are precisely the same as of getting a tail. Since half the time the quarter will come up heads, we can say that the probability (H) of getting a head is $\frac{1}{2}$, or .50. Since the other half of the time the quarter will show tails, the probability (T) of getting a tail is also $\frac{1}{2}$, or .50.

Probabilities are always stated in numbers running from 0 to 1, including all the countless tiny fractions in between. And in any set of circumstances—such as flipping the coin—the probabilities of all the possible events will add up to 1. Thus (and you knew we'd have to have an equation or two, didn't you?),

$$H + T = 1, \quad \text{or} \quad .50 + .50 = 1$$

But you must understand that probabilities always refer to what *might* happen in the future. Once you have flipped the quarter, and it comes up tails, the *probability* of getting a tail on *that* flip is obviously 1, since that's what you got—while the probability of getting a head on *that* flip is obviously 0, since you got a tail instead.

The Probability "Curve"

Now let's make things a little more complicated. Suppose you and a friend both flip a quarter at the same time. How can you figure the odds of what will happen?

Well, what *could* occur when two coins are flipped? You could get (a) two heads, or (b) two tails, or (c) you personally could get a head while your friend got a tail, or (d) you could get a tail while your friend got a head. Thus there are four possible outcomes: *HH, TT, HT,* and *TH.* If you think about it for a moment, you will see two things further: First, the chances of getting any one of these four outcomes is the same as for the other three, so the probability of each is $\frac{1}{4}$.

$$HH + TT + HT + TH = \frac{1}{4} + \frac{1}{4} + \frac{1}{4} + \frac{1}{4} = 1$$

Second, you will see that the last two events (*HT* and *TH*) are really the same. So we can say that

$$HH + HT + TT = \frac{1}{4} + \frac{1}{2} + \frac{1}{4} = 1$$

QUESTION: **If someone offered you 10 to 1 odds that you wouldn't get two heads, would you take the bet?**

Now, what possible outcomes would there be if three of you each tossed a quarter at the same time? Actually, there are eight possibilities:

$$THH \quad HTT$$
$$HTH \quad THT$$
$$HHH + HHT + TTH + TTT$$

If you puzzle over it for a moment or two, you'll see there is but one way you can get *HHH* or *TTT,* but there are three different combinations that yield $(2H, 1T)$ and $1H, 2T)$. Hence,

$$HHH + HHT + HTT + TTT = \frac{1}{8} + \frac{3}{8} + \frac{3}{8} + \frac{1}{8} = 1$$

(If all this seems pretty useless to you, stick with it for a moment; you are about to discover why many teachers "grade on the curve.")

Let's try this twice more. If four coins are flipped at the same time, you'll get

$$THTH$$
$$THHT$$

THHH	*TTHH*	*HTTT*
HTHH	*HTHT*	*THTT*
HHTH	*HTTH*	*TTHT*

$$HHHH + HHHT + HHTT + TTTH + TTTT$$

Count them up and you'll find 16 possible outcomes, so the probability equation is

$$(HHHH) + (HHHT) + (HHTT) + (HTTT) + (TTTT)$$

$$= \frac{1}{16} + \frac{4}{16} + \frac{6}{16} + \frac{4}{16} + \frac{1}{16} = 1$$

We can make a *histogram*, or bar graph, to represent these possibilities.

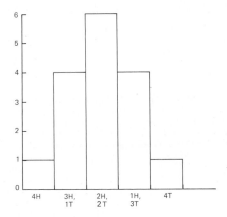

Does the shape of that graph begin to look familiar? Well, let's give the coins one more toss, but this time let's use eight of them. Now, how many different outcomes should we have?

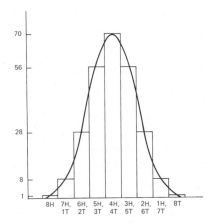

If you're clever with numbers, you will have noted certain regularities in what we've done already:

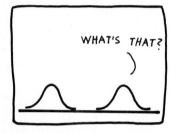

Flipping 1 coin gives 2 outcomes	$2^1 = 2$
Flipping 2 coins gives 4 outcomes	$2^2 = 4$
Flipping 3 coins gives 8 outcomes	$2^3 = 8$
Flipping 4 coins gives 16 outcomes	$2^4 = 16$
Flipping 5 coins gives 32 outcomes	$2^5 = 32$
Flipping 6 coins gives 64 outcomes	$2^6 = 64$
Flipping 7 coins gives 128 outcomes	$2^7 = 128$
Flipping 8 coins gives 256 outcomes	$2^8 = 256$

Thus as we go up, coin by coin, we get outcomes that are "powers of 2." Why two? Because the coin has two faces, heads and tails. If we were figuring odds in *craps*, where each of the dice has six faces, we'd get 6^2, 6^3, 6^4, 6^5, and so forth. By now you must recognize what we're doing. We're discovering the "logic" or formula for generating that old friend, the *bell-shaped curve* (*see* Chapter 24). And the larger the number of coins that we flip, the closer our graph or histogram will come to being a perfect bell-shaped curve. We call this curve a *normal distribution*, because it is the distribution of outcomes that we normally expect when we are dealing with random events like coin tosses. The curve is also sometimes called a *random distribution*.

If you know some algebra, you can generate the same normal distribution by multiplying out the equation $(H + T)^N = 1$, where N is the number of coins that you toss.

Whenever we flip coins to create a normal distribution of outcomes, or a bell-shaped curve, we have to make certain assumptions about the coins and our manner of dealing with them. For example, we have to assume that the coins are perfect—which is to say that they are not biased or unbalanced in any way. We also have to presume that we don't bias the results by tossing the coins in some peculiar or unusual fashion.

When teachers grade on the curve, they too must make assumptions, both about their students and about the way the class is taught. One possible presumption is that the grade a student gets is almost entirely determined by that student's IQ. And since IQ scores fit a bell-shaped curve, then the grades on the test should do so likewise. If this assumption isn't correct—or if the students in the class are all equally intelligent—then the teacher might assume that motivation determines grades, and that some students study a lot while others goof off. Thus the *motivation levels* (or hours of study) could fit the curve, and thus influence the grades to do likewise. Or the teacher might presume that IQ, motivation, study time, and a host of other factors *interact* in some complex way so that the grades still come out fitting the curve.

Whether any of these assumptions are justified is something that psychologists still debate fiercely. But before you get too upset with your teachers for grading on the curve, you might remember something we pointed out in Chapter 24— namely, that whenever you pin a label on someone, whenever you call a person "dumb" or "crazy," you too are making assumptions. If you refer to a woman as being "way out," for example, don't you really mean that she is "way out on the tail end of the sanity curve," while you presumably are sitting there comfortably in the middle of the distribution? More than this, you are also assuming that *sanity* is a trait or quantity that is *randomly distributed* over a probability curve much the same way that the results of flipping a coin would be distributed on the same-shaped curve.

Whether you knew it or not, you've been using probability theory almost all your life. That is, you constantly make predictions about what will or will not happen, and you are often "surprised" when something unusual occurs simply because the event is *against your mental odds or expectations*. We'll have much more to say about this—and the assumptions that psychologists make in their work—in just a moment.

DESCRIPTIVE STATISTICS

Scientists make many uses of statistics, not the least of which is to give accurate descriptive measures to the data they gather. Now that we have a feel for what the bell-shaped curve is all about, let's look at how we can use the curve to describe things other than coin flips.

Measures of Central Tendency

In ordinary English, it makes quite a difference if you describe someone as being *normal* rather than as being *just average*. But in statistics, the average and the norm are usually the same. And as you might surmise, both norm and average are found somewhere close to the "bump" in the bell-shaped curve. That is, both terms suggest a *middle position* of some kind. But again we must ask ourselves, what do we mean when we talk about a norm?

The most common term we use when describing a norm—or middle of a group of measurements that we've taken—is the *mean*. This simple term "means" nothing more nor less than the exact mathematical average. Suppose you and four of your friends get to comparing your present state of financial distress. So you all count up the cash that each of you has on hand at the moment. In fact, we can now ascribe a "monetary score" to each of you according to the money you have in your pockets. More than this, we can draw a curve representing the "distribution of wealth" among the five of you. Let's say that Ann has $1, Bill has $2, Carol has $3, Dick has $4, and lucky you, you have $5.

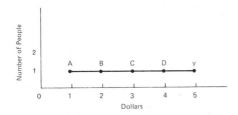

If we ask, "What is the average amount of money per person?" we're really inquiring. "What is the mean of this simple distribution of wealth?" Either way we say it, the answer is $3. To get the mean, you add up all the scores (dollars) and divide by the number of people involved. Psychologists frequently use the symbol M to stand for the mean, while the letter N stands for the number of people or subjects or cases or scores. The letter X often represents the individual scores (dollars, in this case). The Greek letter Σ (sigma) may look frightening when you see it in an equation, but it really is just a shorthand way of saying "the sum of." (We use sigma because "sum" starts with an *s*.) Now we can write a simple-minded equation that tells us how to calculate the mean, namely,

$$M = \frac{\Sigma X}{N} = \frac{\text{Sum of All the Dollars}}{\text{Number of People}} = \frac{15}{5} = 3$$

As long as the scores (or dollars) are distributed among the people so that we get a bell-shaped curve (or a curve that is regular or symmetrical in shape), the mean will always be at the exact center of the distribution of scores. But what would be the case if you just happened to have a million dollars on you? Now the five of you would have a total of $1,000,010.

$$M = \frac{\Sigma X}{N} = \frac{1,000,010}{5} = 200,002.00$$

As you sit there fingering your million dollars, would you think it fair to say that the "average" amount of money each member of your group has is $200,002? And how would your friends react to this news? In this case, as you can see, the mean gives us a very distorted or biased view of the distribution of money. So we use the *median* instead. The word "median" means "middle," and just as the median on a four-lane divided highway is the grassy area between the two strips of concrete, so the median score is the one in the exact middle of the distribution. In the case of you and your four friends, Carol has the middle score ($3), so $3 is the median of that distribution or curve. If we added two more millionaires to your group, the N would be 7, so the middle score would be Dick's, at $4. The surprising thing is that it wouldn't matter how rich the other millionaires were—Dick's score would still be the median. Because to get the median, you simply count down the scores (whatever they are) and pick the middle one.

There is one more "measure of central tendency" (as we call the mean and the median). The word "mode" is defined in the dictionary as "the prevailing fashion or most popular custom or style." When we are talking about distributions of scores, "mode" means the most popular score—that is, the highest point (or points) on the curve. If the distribution has two points that are equally high, then there are two scores that are *modal*, and we can call the curve *bi-modal*.

QUESTION: **What does the word "model" mean? How about "a la mode?"**

Skewedness If the distribution of scores is more or less bell-shaped, the mean, median, and mode usually come out to be the same. But not all curves do us the favor of being so regular in shape. For example, suppose you were interested in whether a particular teacher—Dr. Johnson—started and ended his classes on time. To find out, you take a very accurate watch with you all semester long and undertake a scientific study of Dr. Johnson's behavior. During the term, let's say, there are supposed to be 50 lectures by Dr. Johnson. So our N in this case (the number of measures or scores) will be 50. For the most part, Dr. Johnson begins on time, but occasionally he starts a minute or two early, and sometimes he's a minute or two late. Now and again, he gets to class fairly late, and once he didn't show up at all. But he *never* begins the class more than two minutes early. If you put all his starting time scores on a graph, it would look something like the graph on the left. If you plotted all his closing time scores on a similar graph, it might look like the graph on the right.

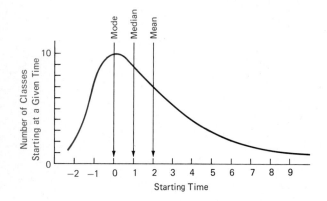 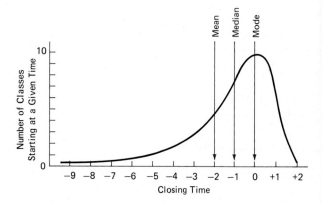

The term we use to describe such curves is *skewed*, which means "slanted" or "pushed out of shape." In the first example, the tail of the curve slants out far to the right-hand side, so we say the curve is "skewed to the right." The second curve has a tail that slants to the left, so the curve is "skewed to the left." As is the case in many distributions where the scores are reaction times, or beginning times, the mean, median, and mode are fairly different.

Range and Variation

In Chapter 24, when we were discussing the sexual problems of Mr. and Mrs. Smith, we noted that the "average" number of sexual outlets desired by young, white, married men in the United States was about 2–4 per week. What we meant, of course, was that the mean number of outlets was about 3.5 or so. But as Kinsey found, the "outlet curve" is far from being a perfect "bell." There are many men who experience less than one orgasm a week, while others "average" 20–30 a week most of their adult lives. The *range* of scores (outlets) runs from 0 to more than 30, but the mean is much closer to 0 than to 30. Thus the tail of the curve runs out far to the right, and the curve is skewed to the right.

If you know the range of scores, plus the mean, median, and mode, you can usually get a fairly good notion of what shape the curve might take. Why? Because these two bits of information tell you something about how the scores are *distributed*. If the mean, median, and mode are almost the same, and they fall right at the center of the range, then the distribution curve must be "vaguely" bell-shaped, or regular in shape. Another way of saying this same thing is that the scores *vary* (or change, or are distributed) on one side of the mean much the same as they *vary* on the other side of the mean. To put the matter more technically, we say that the curve is *symmetrical*, or that one side is more or less the mirror image of the other (*see* Chapter 2).

But why do we say "vaguely" bell-shaped? In Chapter 27, we discussed the distribution of scores on an attitude questionnaire in two different groups. In the homogeneous group, the range of scores was very small:

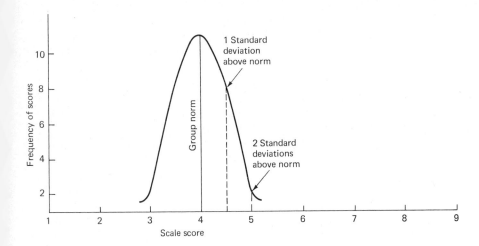

In the heterogeneous group, the range was much larger:

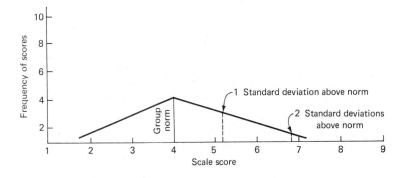

The means for the two distributions were the same, and if the groups had been large enough, we might even have found that the ranges of the two distributions were the same. However, in the homogeneous group, the scores were all bunched up close to the mean, while in the heterogenous group, the scores were broadly *dispersed*, or spread out. We found that we needed a concept we called the *standard deviation* to describe the *dispersion of scores* across the range (or around the mean). The larger the standard deviation, the more widely the scores vary around the mean. We can now define the standard deviation as a statistical term meaning the variability of scores in a distribution.

Let's look back at the money example we talked about earlier. Ann has $1, Bill has $2, Carol has $3, Dick has $4, and you have $5. The mean of this distribution of wealth scores is $3, and we can say that the other four scores *vary* about this mean. If the standard deviation is to tell us something about this variation, then obviously we must somehow measure just how far each of the other scores is from the mean and make use of this information.

Ann's wealth score is $1, so her deviation from the mean of $3 is -2. (We use minus numbers to represent deviations *below* the mean, but positive numbers to represent deviations *above* the mean.) Your own deviation is 2 above the mean, or $+2$. Bill has a -1 deviation; Dick has a $+1$. If we added all these deviations up, they'd equal 0. But what would happen if we squared them? Since the square of a minus number is always a plus, then we'd have a positive number as our total deviation.

	D (Deviation from the Mean)	D^2 (Deviation Squared)
Ann	-2	$+4$
Bill	-1	$+1$
Carol	0	0
Dick	$+1$	$+1$
You	$+2$	$+4$
Σ (Sum of)	0	10

Next, we have to take into account the fact that there are five people involved (that is, that our wealth sample has an $N = 5$). To do this, we divide the ΣD^2 by N:

$$\frac{\Sigma D^2}{N} = \frac{10}{5} = 2$$

But we must also remember that we squared the deviations. So to get the *standard deviation* (SD), we must now take the square root of our result:

$$SD = \sqrt{\frac{\Sigma D^2}{N}} = \sqrt{\frac{10}{5}} = \sqrt{2} = 1.4$$

One more point, and then we can get away from the math and back to a basic understanding of the principles involved. Look at how much Carol influences the standard deviation, without adding anything to it. Her deviation from the mean is 0, since by definition she is the mean. But we count her in the N when we divide it into the sum of the deviations squared. Maybe we ought to leave her out entirely. We can do so by changing our formula for the standard deviation ever so slightly:

$$SD = \sqrt{\frac{\Sigma D^2}{N-1}} = \sqrt{\frac{10}{4}} = \sqrt{2.5} = 1.58$$

When we have a very large N, it doesn't matter much whether we divide by N or $(N - 1)$ because the answer will be almost the same. But when we have just a few cases to work with, $(N - 1)$ gives us a more appropriate estimate of the standard deviation than does N.

By now you may be asking yourself what all this fancy mathematics has to do with people and their real-life problems. The answer is, as we have hinted many times, that you couldn't make most of the decisions and judgments that you do about things in your life if you didn't have some vague notion of deviations from a mean. When you exclude people from the groups you belong to, you often do so because they are "2 standard deviations from the group mean, or more." When you call a person "retarded" or "crazy," you use terms that imply the concept of standard deviations. All we've done so far is to give you some tools to make your thinking a bit more precise and your measurements more accurate. We'll apply the standard deviation to some critical human issues in just a moment. But before we can do so, there's one more idea that we must discuss—the concept of *randomness*.

Random Variation

If you flipped 10 coins all at once, how frequently would you expect them to land with 10 heads showing? About once in 1,024 flips. Why wouldn't you get 10 heads more often than that? Because you have no way (unless you cheat, or the coin is imperfect) of *forcing* the coins to do what you wish them to do. The physical forces that determine whether a coin lands on its head or its tail are, for all practical purposes, out of your control. In fact, if you got 10 heads the first time you flipped the coins, you'd be mildly surprised; if you got 10 heads the second time as well, and the third and the fourth and the fifth times, you might become highly suspicious that the coins were unbalanced, or that some unknown factor was somehow *biasing* the results.

As we have said before, one of our major motivations seems to be that of wanting to predict future events (inputs). When you flip 10 coins, you really can't predict what the results of any one toss will be. But knowing what you know now, you *can* predict with some confidence what the *distribution* of many such events would be—that is, if you flipped 10 coins 1,024 times, you'd expect the results would generate a bell-shaped curve of sorts, with the mean of the distribution centered on (5 heads, 5 tails).

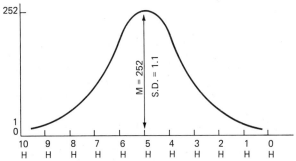

A bell-shaped curve showing the distribution of "heads" expected when flipping 10 coins 1,024 times.

Think about that for a moment. You can't predict single events such as coin tosses because the results are due strictly to chance or accident. (When you think of *randomness*, think of a perfect coin tossed endlessly by a blind robot.) But you

"THE ABNORMAL CURVES"

WELL, I FINALLY SIGNED UP FOR GAMBLERS ANONYMOUS.

DO YOU THINK IT'LL HELP?

I'LL GIVE YOU 10 TO 1 IT DOES.

KALINOWSKI

can predict with great confidence what will happen if you repeat the coin toss a great many times. Why? Because each time you flip 10 coins, that specific event is just a *sample* that you've drawn from the entire *population* of possible outcomes. You can specify with complete accuracy what the entire population of outcomes will be: (10 heads, 0 tails), (9 heads, 1 tail), (8 heads, 2 tails) . . . (1 head, 9 tails), and (0 heads, 10 tails).

Furthermore, you know that the entire population of outcomes should include about 252 instances of (5 heads, 5 tails), but only one instance of (10 heads, 0 tails). Therefore, if you draw your samples *randomly* from the entire population, you are 252 times as likely to draw out a (5 heads, 5 tails) sample as you are the only sample that contains 10 heads.

There are about 4 billion people on earth. If you wanted to discover how *people* react to a warm and cheery "hello" when you meet them, you're really asking, "What would be the distribution of responses that the *entire population* of 4 billion people would make to a friendly greeting?" But there's no way in the world you could test 4 billion subjects—any more than you can sit around flipping coins a million times to see if you really get a bell-shaped curve. However, you could choose a *sample* of 50 or 100 subjects from the total population and hope to goodness that your sampling procedure was *random* (selected the way a blind robot would select a sample). For if your subjects were picked strictly by chance, then the odds would be very good that your sample subjects would behave much as the population as a whole behaves—just as the odds are 252 to 1 when you flip 10 coins that you'll get (5 heads, 5 tails) instead of (10 heads, 0 tails).

Perhaps you can see, too, that the larger your sample size, the more likely it is that the sample will be much like the entire population. Thus if you flip 100 coins at once, the odds of your getting a "way out" result like (100 heads, 0 tails) are much less than getting (10 heads, 0 tails) if you flip just 10 coins.

When you are dealing with human subjects rather than coins, you usually will end up with a *distribution* of scores from the *sample* of people you've chosen. This *sample distribution* will have its own mean. If you want to demonstrate that your sample of subjects is really representative of the entire population, how would you go about doing so?

Here's a hint. If you had a rough idea of the distribution of scores (the shape of the curve) for the whole population, how close would you expect the sample mean to be to the population mean? And if you wanted to prove that something you did to your sample subjects now made them quite different from the rest of the (untreated) population, how far away from the population mean should your sample mean be?

It is at this point—at last!—that we get to the real reason psychologists and other scientists have to know something about statistics. If you are a teacher, you will surely want to prove to yourself and others that your teaching is effective—that is, that the sample of students who have taken your course gets higher scores on some test than do the whole population of students denied the privilege of your teaching. If you want to become a psychotherapist, then you will probably need to demonstrate that the sample of patients you treat are measurably better than the population of patients not receiving treatment. To show that memory transfer exists, you must likewise show that rats injected with chemicals extracted from trained brains (your sample) learn faster than do animals not so injected (the rest of the rat population).

In brief, when scientists run studies, make observations, or perform experiments, they gather data about *samples* drawn randomly from some larger population. The scientists must then use statistics to support the *inferences*, or conclusions, that they make about the results of their work.

STATISTICAL INFERENCES

Think back to the memory-transfer studies described in Chapter 17 (*see* page 374). In one of the first rat experiments my students and I undertook, we trained a large number of donor rats to press a bar in a special Skinner box. The animals' reward for bar-pressing was a sip of milk that was presented to the rats in a tiny cup on the opposite side of the box from the bar. To make matters more complicated, after each bar press, the milk was available for only a few seconds. This task is a difficult one for untrained rats to master, for they must press the lever and then quickly rush over to the milk-dispensing cup before the reward disappears. Since the rats can smell the milk, they tend to hang around the hole where the milk cup is presented instead of staying on the opposite side of the box where the lever is. It often takes a rat 20 to 30 hours to acquire this bar-press habit, and some donor animals take so long that it seems they will never learn at all.

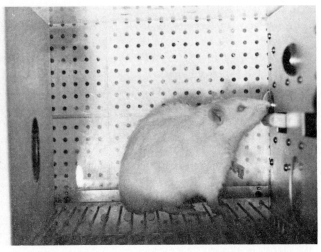

Since we can assign a time score to each animal that learns (the number of hours it took the animal to master the task), we can calculate a mean and standard deviation for the distribution of these scores. The mean for untrained donor animals was about 25 hours, the standard deviation being about 6. Since we used a large number of donors (and in fact repeated the experiment many times), we can assume that the donors were fairly representative of all rats—that is, we can presume that our sample of donors was very similar to the entire untrained rat population.

After the donors were trained, we extracted chemicals (mostly RNA) from their brains and injected this material into the brains of untrained recipient rats. We then trained the recipients in the same Skinner box used for the donors. To our delight, all the animals in our experimental-injected group learned the task quickly—their mean score was about 3 hours, the standard deviation being about 1. Let's draw the curves for these two sets of data as shown at top of page 700. As you can see, the mean for the experimental group is more than 4 standard deviations away from the donor mean. Does it appear to you that the injected rats are a representative sample randomly drawn from the larger donor population? Or has the injection somehow biased the responses of the recipients so that their behavior is now markedly different from that of the uninjected population?

To answer these questions, we need but compare this curve with the one showing the distribution of (heads and tails) when we flipped 10 coins 1,024 times

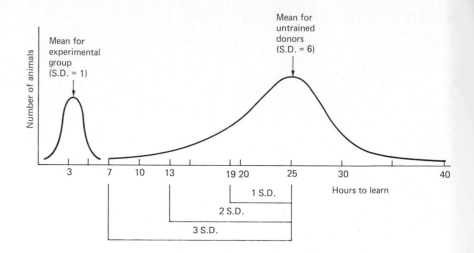

(*see* figure on p. 697). Here the mean is 5, and the standard deviation is about 1.1. The (10 heads, 0 tails) score is more than 4 standard deviations away from the mean (5 heads, 5 tails). If the odds of getting 10 heads on a given flip of the coins are 1 in 1,024, then the odds of having the experimental animal *mean* be more than 4 standard deviations away from the donor *mean* are also about 1 in 1,000. Thus it seems very unlikely that the injected rats accurately reflect (are an unbiased sample of) the whole rat population—not impossible, as getting 10 heads is not impossible, but highly unlikely.

To put the matter another way: If we ran the memory-transfer experiment a second time, what odds would you give that the sample mean would once more be *at least* 2 standard deviations from the mean? In brief, when is a difference between two groups a *reliable* difference?

Significant Differences

Whenever we test a hunch or a scientific hypothesis, we often are hunting for *reliable* differences between two groups of subjects or between two sets of data. By convention, scientists accept differences as being "real" if on some measure the means of the two groups depart by 2 or more standard deviations from each other.

We pick the figure 2 standard deviations for a very understandable reason. If, on a bell-shaped curve, we measure out from the mean a distance of 2 standard deviations, we will take into account about 95 percent of all the cases or scores described by that curve. Anything falling outside of this distance (such as the mean of the second group we're interested in) will be there *by random variation* less than 5 percent of the time. The odds of getting such a result purely by chance are thus 5 out of 100, or 1 out of 20. Since these odds are pretty impressive, we can assume that the results of our experiment are not accidental. Thus with the odds 20 to 1 in our favor, we predict that the groups are *reliably different*—which is another way of saying that if we ran the study again, we are confident that the means would once more differ by at least 2 standard deviations.

Quite naturally, we are even more confident of our results if the group means differ by 3 or more standard deviations, because as the difference grows larger, so do the odds in our favor.

Whenever you hear scientists say that their "findings are significant at the 5 percent level," you may translate this to mean that their groups differed by about 2 standard deviations. In general, if the odds are not at least 20 to 1 in support of the hunch we're trying to prove, we don't use the word "significant" in describing our results.

There are many different tests or formulas that we could use for calculating whether the results of an experiment were significant or not. Among the best known of such statistical devices are the *t-test* and the *critical ratio*. Should you ever need to employ one of these tests, you'd do well to read about them in a text such as William L. Hays's *Statistics for the Social Sciences*, the second edition of which was published by Holt, Rinehart and Winston in 1973. In fact, most of these tests for significance are based on the bell-shaped curve and the notion of random variation. Thus the *t-test* and the critical ratio will suggest that there are significant differences between two groups (or distribution of scores) if:

"THE ABNORMAL CURVES"

IF I FLIPPED A COIN 1024 TIMES, WHAT COULD I EXPECT TO GET?

1. The number of cases or subjects in each group is large.
2. The standard deviations of both distributions are small and fairly similar to each other.
3. The means of the distributions differ by 2 or more standard deviations.

HMMM

Non-Parametric Tests

The *t-test* and the critical ratio have been in use for many decades, but are falling out of favor these days for several reasons. To begin with, when you use these tests, you must make certain assumptions about the mathematical characteristics of the distributions you're working with. Statisticians often use the term *parameters* to describe some of these characteristics. Proving that your data have the parameters demanded by the *t-test* or the critical ratio may be quite difficult in some circumstances. Furthermore, as you are only too well aware by now, figuring out the means and the standard deviations for large groups can be a time-consuming task—to say the least!

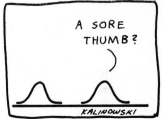

A SORE THUMB?

KALINOWSKI

Very recently psychologists have begun to employ what are called *non-parametric* tests of significance, such as the *Mann-Whitney U-test*. These are much easier instruments to work with, for the non-parametric tests don't make as many demands on your time or on your data as do the *t-test* and the critical ratio.

Again, if you want to learn how to use a non-parametric test, you should go to some reference such as the Hays text mentioned earlier. However, we can very briefly give you a feeling for the logic underlying these tests.

You know by now what the odds are of getting 10 heads when you flip a coin 10 times in a row. But what are the odds that the *first* five tosses will give you all heads, while the *second* five tosses will give you all tails? While getting *any* combination of (5 heads, 5 tails) will occur 252 times in 1,024, the odds of getting *specifically* 5 heads and *then* 5 tails are just the same as those of getting 10 heads in a row—1 out of 1,024. Let's see if we can use this fact creatively to measure group differences.

Suppose a mother rat gave birth to a litter of 10 pups, and you wanted to see whether feeding the pups vitamins made them grow bigger than normal. So you randomly select five pups and give them vitamin-enriched rat chow, while you feed the other five pups vitamin-depleted rat chow. Three months later, when the rats are full-grown, you go over to the rat lab to measure their lengths. Once there, you discover that you've forgotten to bring along a ruler. If you had a yardstick (or a metric scale), you could get exact measures, then calculate means and standard deviations, and then use a *t-test* to see if the groups differed significantly in length. But the ruler is on the other side of the campus and you don't have time to walk back to your office to get it. So what can you do?

As it happens, if you have a sheet of paper with you, you're in luck. For you can mark off the lengths of each rat in both groups along the edge of the sheet.

You put down an H on the edge of the paper to represent the length of each rat in the experimental (vitamin-enriched) group, and you put down a T to represent the length of each rat in the control group. The sheet of paper might end up looking like this:

T	TT T		T HH	H	H		H

Length $\longrightarrow$

What you've done is to assign *ranks* to the rats even though you haven't measured their lengths precisely. And what do you find? Why, your old friend *HHHHHTTTTT*. Since the odds of getting this kind of *ranking* are about the same as getting 5 heads and then 5 tails when you flip a coin 10 times, you can say with great confidence that the two groups are significantly different. And, therefore, you can assume that feeding vitamins to baby rats does indeed make them grow bigger (longer).

To use a non-parametric test such as the Mann-Whitney to compare two groups, you simply rank *all* the subjects together, and then you add up the ranked scores for each group *separately*. If the sum of the ranks for one group is different enough from the sum of the ranks of the second group, the Mann-Whitney will tell you that the groups are significantly different.

Correlation Coefficients

The notion of putting scores in ranks brings us to the last statistical device we will take note of in this brief Appendix. In several chapters of this book, we have mentioned the term *correlation* to suggest that two events or traits were somehow connected or associated with each other. The mathematics underlying correlations are not too difficult to understand; however, the correlation concept itself has a "fault" buried deep within it that makes it one of the most misunderstood and misused ideas in all of human experience. We'll come back to this fault in just a moment. First, let's look at how one figures out if two sets of scores are correlated.

As we noted in Chapter 23, there is a strong relationship between IQ scores and grades in school, for a very good reason—IQ tests are usually devised so that they will predict academic success, and the items on most such tests are juggled around until the final score does in fact yield the expected predictions. Thus if we give intelligence tests to all incoming freshmen, and we know their grades at the end of their first collegiate year, we should expect to find some relationship between these measures:

		Entrance Test IQ Score	Grade Point Average (GPA)
Ann		152	3.91
Bill		145	3.46
Carol		133	2.77
Dick		128	2.35
Elmer		112	1.51
	Σ (Sum of)	670	14.00
	Mean	134	2.80
	SD	15.54	0.94

Just looking at the rank orderings of these scores, you can tell that a strong correlation exists between the two distributions. If we plotted the data on what is called a *scatter diagram*, we'd get pretty much a straight line. (A scatter diagram shows how the scores for each subject are *scattered*, or distributed, across the graph or diagram.)

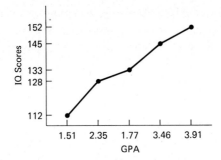

If we reversed the scores, so that Ann got an IQ score of 152 but a GPA of 1.51, Bill got an IQ score of 145 and a GPA of 2.35, and so forth, we'd get a scatter diagram that looked like this:

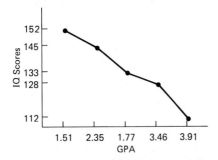

Generally speaking, the closer the scatter diagram comes to being a straight line tilted to the right or left as these are, the higher the correlation between the two variables (scores). However, "just eyeballing it" (that is, visual inspection of diagrams) usually isn't enough. We must employ a formula to figure out the precise mathematical relationship involved. The most widely known such formula is the *product-moment correlation*, which we can abbreviate as *r*. (When you multiply 2×3, the *product* is 6. *Moment* is a technical term referring to the movement of a line about a point; in both of the diagrams shown above, the line of correlation moves about the point of the mean score in the middle of the line.)

To figure the product-moment correlation, we need to know several things. To begin with, we have to figure the means and the standard deviations for both sets of scores. While working out the standard deviation, we already have to compute how much each score deviates from the mean of the distribution. For instance, Ann has an IQ score of 152; the mean IQ score is 134. Thus Ann's "deviation" on this distribution is 18. Her deviation from the mean of the grade point distribution is 1.11. We then multiply these two deviations to get their *product*, which is 19.98. We do the same thing for the two scores of Bill, Carol, Dick, and Elmer. We then add up all the products of the deviations to get the sum, which we write Σ (deviation IQ)(deviation GPA).

Distribution of Scores for IQ Test and GPA

	IQ	D IQ	(D IQ)²	GPA	D GPA	(D GPA)²	(D IQ)(D GPA)
Ann	152	18	324	3.91	1.11	1.23	19.98
Bill	145	11	121	3.46	0.66	0.44	7.26
Carol	133	−1	1	2.77	−0.03	0.0009	0.03
Dick	129	−6	36	2.35	−0.45	0.2	2.7
Elmer	112	−22	484	1.51	−1.29	1.66	28.38
	Σ (Sum of)		966			3.53	58.35
	SD		15.54			0.94	

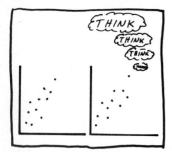

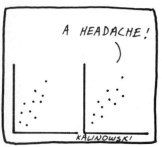

"THE SCATTERED DIAGRAMS" Now we are ready to compute the product-moment correlation, r.

$$r = \frac{\Sigma(\text{Deviation IQ})/(\text{Deviation GPA})}{(N-1)(SD\ IQ)(SD\ GPA)} = \frac{58.35}{4 \times 15.54 \times .94}$$

$$= \frac{58.35}{58.43} = .999$$

The product-moment correlation varies between -1.0 and $+1.0$. A correlation of $+1.0$ will give you a straight line tilted 45 degrees to the right on the scatter diagram; a correlation of -1.0 gives a straight line tilted 45 degrees to the left. In either case, the two scores are perfectly correlated. The closer the score is to 0 (whether the score is $-$ or $+$), the lower the correlation. A 0 correlation ($r = 0$) means that the two scores (variables) are not related in any way that you have measured with this statistical test.

Significant Correlations

When you are figuring out a t-test or a Mann-Whitney U-test, you typically hope that the two groups you are working with will be significantly *different*. When you are computing a correlation coefficient, you usually hope that the two distributions of scores will be highly correlated—that is, significantly *similar* to each other. Why is this the case?

To begin with, t-tests and non-parametric tests are usually employed when you take *one* measure on *two* different groups of subjects. The first group (the experimental subjects) have probably been treated differently than the second (the control subjects). If your treatment was effective, then the two groups should have quite different mean scores. If the mean are significantly different, then you can predict that the next time you treat subjects as you did your experimental group, these same differences will show up.

On the other hand, correlations are typically used when you have *one* group of the subjects given *two* different tests. If the scores on both tests (or the ranks) are significantly similar, then you can often use the scores on the first test to *predict* that similar scores (or rankings) will obtain if you give subjects the second test or experience. For instance, IQ scores (or college entrance examinations) are often used to screen out applicants who want to enter a particular school. If the correlation between the IQ test and college grades is significantly high, then the admissions committee can reject applicants with low IQ scores because the committee can predict with a high degree of confidence what grades the applicants will get if allowed to enroll. Thus, after you have proven that a high correlation exists between the scores on two tests, you can save yourself time by administering just one of the tests because you know pretty much what the scores on the second test *would be* if you gave it.

Generally speaking, the higher the r, the better your predictions will be from one test to another.

Uses and Abuses of Correlation Coefficients

The ability to make quick correlations is just about the most useful trait that your mind has available to it. Whether you realize it or not, your brain is so built that it automatically makes connections between incoming stimuli. Think back to the discussion of Pavlovian conditioning you encountered in Chapter 15. When you ring a bell, and then give a dog food, the animal's brain soon comes to associate the sound of the bell with the appearance of the food. When the dog eventually salivates to the sound of the bell *before* food arrives, its nervous system has calculated a crude sort of r between the onset of the bell and the presentation of food. Since the *r* is "highly significant" to the dog, it can anticipate (predict) one stimulus input because another highly correlated stimulus input has just occurred. And when an admissions committee accepts a student with a high IQ score, isn't the committee responding in much the same "conditioned" fashion?

If dogs could talk, how might they explain their conditioned responses? Don't you imagine that Pavlov's beasts might explain matters in *causal* terms? That is, might not a well-conditioned canine remark that the bell has "magic powers" that cause the food to appear? As peculiar as this notion may sound, evidence in its favor comes from some real-life experiments. In several studies, bell-food conditioned animals have later been trained to turn on the bell themselves by pressing a bar in their cages. What do you think the animals do when they become hungry?

QUESTION: **How do admissions committees explain their use of IQ tests to screen out applicants?**

As we mentioned earlier, the concept of correlation has a fault buried in it—the fact that we too often assume that if event A is correlated with event B, then A must somehow *cause* the appearance of B. This "causal assumption" gets us into a lot of trouble. For example, does the sound of the bell really *cause* the food to appear? Do high IQ scores really *cause* a student to get good grades? As you can see, the answer in both cases must be a resounding *no*. Scores on an IQ test don't cause much of anything (except, perhaps, favorable reactions from admissions committees). The underlying trait of intelligence presumably causes both the high IQ score and the good grades. Thus intelligence is responsible for the correlation between the two events, just as the experimenter's desires are responsible for the correlation between bell and food. However, as we noted in Chapter 23, we aren't really sure what intelligence is, although we are fairly sure that this basic trait is only loosely correlated with most IQ test scores. And we know that the mental and motivational traits that strongly influence a student's grades in the U.S. school system are not necessarily those that would get a person good grades in other academic environments. Thus we cannot even conclude—on the basis of correlational evidence alone—that the basic trait of intelligence will determine a student's academic performance in all situations.

Worse than this, there are times when highly significant correlations may seriously mislead us. Consider the writers working for a large newspaper. There will be lots of beginning reporters who churn out a massive amount of copy each day, most of it about fairly trivial events. And there are a very few senior reporters who write but a few hundred words daily. Now, who gets paid the most money? If we ran a correlation between (number of words written daily) and (salary per word), wouldn't we find a highly significant but *negative* correlation? Given this correlation coefficient, might we not be tempted to tell beginning journalists that, if they wanted a raise in salary, they ought to write less? And whose "fault" would it be if they followed our advice and got fired?

At their very best, correlations can help us predict future stimulus inputs and give us clues as to what the underlying causal connections among these inputs might be. However, in daily life, we too often misuse correlations. If you want to make your psychology teacher very happy indeed, say "Correlations don't determine causes" over and over again—until you're conditioned to believe it!

EXPERIMENTAL DESIGN

Why statistics? If your view of mathematics is as mine once was, you may still be wondering why a reasonably humane psychology teacher might demand that you dig into such "heavy stuff" as *t*-tests and standard deviations. Or, to phrase the question about the usefulness of statistics more precisely, is there any correlation

"THE ABNORMAL CURVES"

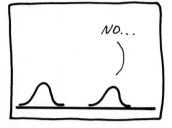

DO YOU KNOW THAT YOUR STATISTICAL INFERENCES ARE NEVER BETTER THAN YOUR EXPERIMENTAL DESIGN WILL ALLOW?

NO...

BUT IF YOU HUM A FEW BARS I'LL TRY TO FAKE IT.

KALINOWSKI

between knowing something about stat and knowing something about yourself and the people around you?

As it happens, the r is highly significant. All of your future life you will be performing "little experiments" in which you try to psych out the people around you. It's likely (at the 5 percent level) that you will probe your environment better if you know how to interpret the results of your informal experimentation. If you are introspective, an understanding of correlations and conditioning could help tell you some very important facts about how you have acquired many of your values and attitudes. And, if nothing else, understanding what a bell-shaped curve is all about could save you a lot of money should you ever happen to visit Las Vegas.

The second reason for imposing statistics on you, willy-nilly, is that you may wish to take further courses in psychology. If you do, you may be encouraged (or even required) to perform one or more controlled experiments, either in a laboratory or in a real-life setting. Therefore, you might as well learn the first law of statistics right now:

> *Your statistical inferences are never better than your experimental design will allow.*

The topic of how to design a good experiment has filled many a thick textbook. In the short space we have left to us, we can touch but a few of the high spots of this fascinating but complex subject.

Control versus Random Variation

An experiment is a *controlled* set of observations. In the typical experimental study, you will take measures of some kind on two or more groups or subjects (or make two or more observations on the same group). In its simplest form, an experiment may have a control group and an experimental group. If you are running the study, you will "do something" to the experimental group that you don't do to the control group. This *something* that you *do* to the experimental group is often called the *independent variable* (*see* Chapter 1). You will also require that the group *do* something in response to your inputs. The behavioral output of the group is called the *dependent variable,* since the group's response depends or varies on what you have done to it. The purpose of the independent variable thus is to introduce some *bias* into the experimental group's output that is not present in the output of the control group (or not present to the same degree).

The control group always serves as a norm or standard against which the behavior of the experimental group can be compared. If the output of the experimental group is significantly different than that of the control group, you presume that your attempt to bias the outcome of the study was successful. But this presumption is valid *if and only if* you have planned the experiment so that the independent variable was the *only* factor biasing the results. And that's what you have one or more control groups for—to *control* for as many other types of output bias as you can imagine.

Let's go back to the memory-transfer experiment discussed earlier and describe it in a bit more detail. You will recall that the experimental rats received injections of chemicals from the brains of trained donors. We had a control group of animals—run at the same time—that did not receive injections but were trained in similar fashion. The experimental animals all learned to press the lever to get milk before any of the control rats learned the same response. In fact, the controls behaved just as did the untrained donor animals. Therefore, can we conclude that we did in truth *transfer memories* from the donors to the experimental recipients?

Well, what biases other than the injection of chemicals from trained donor brains might have entered into the picture? The answer, as it happens, is *several dozen.*

Selection of Subjects   To begin with, how did we decide which rat should be placed in which group? Perhaps you think such a question rather trivial, but listen to the following tale of woe. When you want to use rats in an experiment, you often order young animals from a "scientific pet shop" in some distant city. You specify the number, age, sex, and color of the rats you want to receive. A week or so later, a large box of healthy young rats is delivered to your laboratory door by air express. If you are eager to get to work, you may open up the box, reach in, and pull out the first animals your hand touches. These you might put in the experimental group. The rest of the animals you might dump into the control group. Then you run your study, and you get highly significant differences between the two groups. You publish your results and sit back waiting for applause. But all you may get is a Bronx cheer from other scientists who try to repeat your study but fail to replicate your results.

Why? Because rats differ in many of the same ways that people differ. Friendly, eager, active rats will not be afraid of your hand when you reach into the box. So these are the animals that get put into the experimental group. Frightened, anxious, inactive rats will cower in the corners of the box or try to escape your hand when you plunge it into the shipping container. These animals you put in the control group, remember? Which type of rat do you think would usually learn faster and be the easier to handle in an experimental situation? And how would you overcome this possible bias?

In almost all of our memory-transfer experiments, we numbered the animals as we took them from the container, then assigned the animals to one group or another by drawing the numbers "out of a hat, randomly."

The problem of possible *selection bias* haunts human experimentation as well. Perhaps you'll recall the study on psychotherapy performed by R. Bruce Sloane and his colleagues that we described in Chapter 25 (*see* page 588). The Sloane study had three groups—30 or so patients given four months of insight psycho-therapy; another 30 given four months of behavior therapy; and a third group of about 30 individuals who were given no formal therapy at all. The patients had voluntarily come to the Temple University psychiatric clinic asking for help, and all of them were diagnosed as suffering from moderately severe neuroses.

Now, Sloane and his group could have assigned the first 30 patients who walked through the clinic door to one group. And then, perhaps four months later, they could have taken the next 30 patients and given them another type of treatment. But this procedure could bias the results. For do you think the people who seek psychiatric help in the dead of winter are the same sorts who ask assistance four months later, in spring or early summer? Perhaps, perhaps not. But why take the chance? So Sloane and his colleagues worked out a very complicated scheme for randomly assigning patients not only to the three groups, but also to the various therapists who performed the two types of treatment. The experimenters made sure that each group contained an equal number of men and women; the groups were also balanced in terms of the severity of their problems.

Now, back to the rats for a moment. If you were running animals in a memory-transfer experiment, would you want to make sure that both experimental and control groups had an equal number of male and female rats? No, you wouldn't. Scientists aren't really "male, chauvinist pigs," but they typically prefer to use only male animals in most of their behavioral studies. Female rats are several times more active when in heat than when not, and activity level affects a variety of behaviors (including speed of learning). Now consider these facts: The sex cycle of a female rat is about five days in length; female rats housed together tend to come into heat at about the same time; most learning studies take more than five days to run. Perhaps you can see why even female scientists can usually avoid a possible source of bias by using male rats in most experiments.

Placebo Effects The selection of subjects is but one source of bias. Another has to do with what we described in Chapter 18 as the placebo effect. The mere fact that you are given a pill to take may help you feel better, even if the pill is made of ordinary sugar. In the Sloane experiment, the control group patients were interviewed by a psychiatrist and were given several psychological tests even though they had to wait four months to begin therapy. During this waiting time, a research assistant called them occasionally to ask how they were doing. Surprisingly enough, this no-treatment group showed considerable improvement in some areas, as much improvement as did the therapy groups. Thus we must temper our enthusiasm for the gains made by the patients given therapy because we know that many of them would have gotten dramatically better even without any formal treatment at all.

In our memory-transfer studies, we had to control for a similar sort of bias. Our experimental animals got injections from trained donor brains. Our donor animals—and one of the control groups we used—got no injections of all. But we worried about the incomparability of the experimental and control groups. For perhaps *just injecting rats* irritates them so much that they learn faster. So in our studies we often used several control groups—one that got injected with distilled water, another that got injected with chemicals extracted from untrained donor brains, and yet another that got no injections at all. When we found no significant differences among the control groups—all of which differed significantly from the experimental animals—we could make a much stronger case for the reliability of our results than had we used but one control group.

Experimenter Bias In the study by Sloane and his associates, the psychiatrists who did the initial interview with the patients also assessed their progress at the end of four months of treatment. Might it have affected the results of the experiment if these assessing psychiatrists had known which patient had gotten which type of therapy? (In point of fact, the psychiatrists weren't told the treatment given the patients and were instructed not to ask the patients about it.)

In our rat experiments, we used similar procedures in which the people actually handling the animals were kept in the dark as to which rat had gotten what type of injection. Furthermore, the person doing the chemical extractions didn't know which brains came from trained donors and which were from untrained animals. The person injecting the recipients wasn't informed which bottle contained extract of trained brain, which bottle was filled with extract of untrained brain, and which had just water in it. The whole study was performed "blind," which is our jargonish way of saying that I assigned code numbers to all the donor brains, to the extracts, and to the recipient animals. My associates then did the extracting, injecting, and training. The master code was kept in a sealed envelope locked in my desk, and I was not told how the animals had done until the study was completed. Only then did we open up the envelope and "decode" the results.

If all these precautions seem rather silly to you—since you're sure that you wouldn't "cheat" if you ran an experiment—consider a set of studies by Robert Rosenthal and his associates at Harvard. They gave rather detailed lectures on the genetics of intelligence to students in a psychology class. The lectures included material on the research of Robert C. Tryon at Berkeley who spent years breeding a strain of rats that was "maze bright," and another strain that learned so slowly the animals were called "maze dull." All of this information was quite accurate. But at this point Rosenthal told the students he had obtained some of the Tryon rats and wanted the students to train these animals in mazes. Each animal in each rat cage was labeled "bright" or "dumb" by a sign on its cage door. Actually, this labeling was a bald-faced lie, for the rats used were ordinary animals that, as far as could be told, all had about average maze intelligence.

However, when the students trained the beasts, the animals randomly identified as "bright" learned significantly faster than did the rats labeled "dumb." In observing the students train the animals in this and subsequent studies, Rosenthal noticed that the young experimenters handled the "bright" rats more gently, coaxed them more, petted them more, and perceived the animals as being "much quicker." The students also tended to make errors when recording the data; almost all the errors were in favor of the "bright" animals. (In a similar vein, the Internal Revenue Service reports that about 80 percent of the mathematical errors made on U.S. income tax returns favor the taxpayer.)

No, you wouldn't cheat, and neither would I. But why should we be "half-safe" when running an experiment using *blind procedures* is such a simple way to control for experimenter bias?

Other Types of Bias The time of day a study is run, the time of year, the barometric pressure, the temperature, how the experimenters are dressed, how questions on a test are phrased—these are but a few of the variables that often must be considered as possible sources of bias. Mice are usually more active at night than during the day, as are flatworms. Groups run at night thus often learn faster than groups run during the day. Turtles and goldfish learn better in summer than in winter. People tend to give money more readily to panhandlers in spring than during the autumn months, and women give more willingly to well-dressed male panhandlers than to poorly dressed females.

Whatever your area of interest, whether you perform laboratory studies or informal "psych outs," your inferences must always be tempered by the realization that the world swims in bias. If you refuse to examine your own *experimenter behavior* closely, your observations may not be as valid as they could be.

Conclusions

By now you must realize why scientists spend so much time planning their studies. Control groups are the heart and soul of experimental science. And the rule in deciding what groups to use is this:

> *Control what you can; but if you can't control a source of possible bias, try to let the blind robot of random variation do the job for you.*

You can control for experimenter bias, but when selecting your subjects, you may find it easier to randomize your selection procedures. For if you do so properly, the negative biases will just about match the positive biases, just as the number of heads flipped by the robot balances the number of tails if the coin is flipped frequently enough.

Anything that you love, or that is important enough to you, is worth working hard for. Science is an art form, just as making music is. Some musicians are superb, while others are only mediocre. But in general, the musicians who love their work the most—and who practice and study as much as they can—make the most beautiful music. The same sort of thing may be said of scientists.

Birds make music, as do whales and monkeys. Only human beings run experiments, control for bias, randomize variables, and perform statistical analyses. Being a scientist is thus one of the most *humane* occupations you can have.

As it happens, I love science. My parting hope is that you will someday come to appreciate this art form as much as I do. And if the scientific love bug does bite you, perhaps then and only then you will come to enjoy statistics and experimental design as much as most scientists do.

Good luck! (Or should I say, "Good random variation?")

SELECTED BIBLIOGRAPHY

CHAPTER 1

Braginsky, B.M., and D.D. Braginsky. *Mainstream psychology: A critique.* New York: Holt, Rinehart and Winston, 1974.

Dyal, J.A., W.C. Colning, and D.M. Willows. *Readings in psychology: The search for alternatives,* 3rd ed. New York: McGraw-Hill, 1975.

Engle, T.L., and L. Snellgrove. *Psychology: Its principles and applications,* 6th ed. New York: Harcourt Brace Jovanovich, 1973.

English, H.B., and H.C. English. *A comprehensive dictionary of psychological and psychoanalytical terms.* New York: David McKay, 1958.

Gillen, B. "Readability and human interest scores of thirty-four current introductory psychology texts," *American Psychologist,* 28, 1010–1011, 1973.

Hall, E. *Why we do what we do: A look at psychology.* Boston: Houghton Mifflin 1973.

Harriman, P.L. *Handbook of psychological terms.* Totowa, N.J.: Littlefield, Adams, 1965.

Kimble, D.P. *Psychology as a biological science.* Pacific Palisades, Calif: Goodyear, 1973.

Kimble, G.A., and N. Garmezy. *Principles of general psychology.* New York: Ronald Press, 1973.

Psychology '73/'74 encyclopedia. Guilford, Conn.: Dushkin Publishing Group, 1973.

Psychology Today, *Psychosources.* New York: Bantam Books, 1973.

Szasz, T. *Law, liberty, and psychiatry.* New York: Macmillan, 1973.

CHAPTER 2

Butter, C.N. *Neuropsychology: The study of brain and behavior.* Belmont, Calif: Brooks-Cole, 1965.

Deutsch, J.A., and D. Deutsch. *Physiological psychology,* rev. ed. Homewood, Ill.: Dorsey Press, 1973.

Gazzaniga, M.S. "The split brain in man," *Scientific American,* 217, 1967.

Grossman, S.P. *Essentials of physiological psychology.* New York: Wiley, 1972.

Hutchinson, G.E. "Man talking or thinking," *American Scientist,* 64(1), 22–27, 1976.

Karczner, A.G., and J.C. Eccles. *The brain and human behavior.* New York: Springer. 1972.

Kimura, D. "The asymmetry of the human brain," *Scientific American,* 228(3), 70–80, 1973.

McCleary, R.A., and R.Y. Moore. *Subcortical mechanisms. of behavior.* New York: Basic Books, 1965.

Milner, P.M. *Physiological psychology.* New York: Holt, Rinehart and Winston, 1970.

Ornstein, R. E. "Right and left thinking," *Psychology Today,* 6(12), 86–93, 1973.

Pribram, K.H. *Languages of the brain: Experimental paradoxes and principles in neuropsychology.* Englewood Cliffs, N.J.: Prentice-Hall, 1971.

Sperry, R.W. "Hemisphere disconnection and unity in conscious awareness," *American Psychologist,* 23, 733–734, 1968.

Sperry R.W. "Lateral specialization in surgically separated hemispheres," in F.O. Schmitt and F.G. Worden (eds.), *The neurosciences third study program.* Cambridge, Mass.: MIT Press, 1974.

Sperry, R.W. "Left-Brain, right brain," *Saturday Review,* August 9, 1975, pp. 30–33.

Sprague, J.M., and A.N. Epstein. *Progress in psychobiology and physiological psychology.* New York: Academic Press, 1976.

Walter, W.G. *The living brain.* New York: Norton, 1953.

Zaidel, D., and R.W. Sperry. "Memory impairment after commissurotomy in man," *Brain,* 97(2), 263–272, 1974.

Zaidel, Eran, "Auditory vocabulary of the right hemisphere following brain bisection or hemidecortication," *Cortex,* in press.

CHAPTER 3

Aaronson, B., and H. Osmond (eds.). *Psychedelics: The uses and implications of hallucinogenic drugs.* New York: Doubleday, 1970.

Aserinsky, E., and N. Kleitman. "Regularly occurring periods of eye motility and concomitant phenomena during sleep," *Science,* 118, 273, 1953.

Baekeland, F., and E. Hartmann. "The need for sleep," in E. Hartmann (ed.), *Sleep and dreaming.* Boston: Little, Brown, 1970.

Blum, R.H., et al. *Drugs,* vols. 1 and 2. San Francisco: Jossey-Bass, 1969.

Braucht, C.N., D. Brakarsh, D. Fullingsted, and K.L. Berry. "Deviant drug use in adolescence: A review of psychosocial correlates," *Psychological Bulletin,* 79(2), 92–106, 1973.

Chase, M.H. (ed.). *Perspectives in the brain sciences: The sleeping brain.* Los Angeles: Brain Research Institute, UCLA, 1972.

Clemence, C.D., D.P. Purpura, and F.E. Mayer (eds.). *Sleep and the maturing nervous system.* New York: Academic Press, 1972.

Dement, W.C. "A new look at the third state of existence," *Stanford M.D.,* 8, 2–8, 1968–1969.

DuPont, R.L. "Marihuana: A conversation with NIDA's," *Science,* 192(4240), 647–649, 1976.

Freemon, F.R. *Sleep research: A critical review.* Springfield, Ill.: Charles C Thomas, 1972.

Goldstein, Avram. "Opiad peptides (endorphins) in pituitary and brain," *Science,* 193(4258), 1081–1086, 1976.

Greenberg, R., R. Pillard, and C. Pearlman. "The effect of dream (stage REM) deprivation on adaptation to stress," *Psychosomatic Medicine,* 34, 257–262, 1972.

Grinspoon, L. "Marihuana," *Scientific American,* 221(6), 17–25, 1969.

Grinspoon, L, and P. Hedblum. *The speed culture: Amphetamine use and abuse in America.* Cambridge, Mass.: Harvard University Press, 1975.

Hartmann, E.L. *The functions of sleep.* New Haven, Conn.: Yale University Press, 1973.

Hartmann, E.L. (ed.). *Sleep and dreaming.* Boston: Little, Brown, 1970.

Huxley, A. *The doors of perception.* New York: Harper & Row, 1970.

Jouvet, M. "The states of sleep," *Scientific American,* 216(2), 62–75, 1967.

Kamiya, J. "Conscious control of brain waves," *Psychology Today,* 1, 56–60, 1968.

Kimmel, H.D. "Instrumental conditioning of autonomically mediated responses in human beings," *American Psychologist*, 29(5), 325–335, 1974.

Kleitman, N. *Sleep and wakefulness*, rev. ed. Chicago: University of Chicago Press, 1963.

Lau, R.J., D.G. Tubergen, M. Barr, E.F. Domino, N. Benowitz, and R.T. Jones. "Phytohemagglutinin-induced lymphocyte transformation in humans receiving delta^9 tetrahydro cannabinol," *Science*, 192(4241), 805–807, 1976.

Luce, G.G. *Biological rhythms in human and animal physiology*. New York: Dover, 1971.

Matheson, D.W., and M.A. Davison. *The behavioral effects of drugs*. New York: Holt, Rinehart and Winston, 1972.

Maugh, T.H. "Marihuana: The grass may no longer be greener," *Science*, 185, 683–685, 1974.

McClelland, D.C., et al. *The drinking man*. New York: Free Press, 1972.

McConnell, J.V. "Abstract behavior among the Tepehuan," *Journal of Abnormal Social Psychology*, 49, 109–110, 1954.

Orme-Johnson, D.W. "Autonomic stability and transcendental meditation," *Psychosomatic Medicine*, 35(4), 341–349, 1973.

Rubin, V., and L. Comitas. *Ganja in Jamaica*. The Hague: Mouton, 1975.

Seeman, W., S. Nidich, and T. Banta. "Influence of transcendental meditation, or, a measure of self-actualization," *Journal of Counseling Psychology*, 12(3), 184–187, 1972.

Shafii, M., R. Lavely, and R. Jaffe. "Meditation and marijuana," *American Journal of Psychiatry*, 131, 60–63, 1974.

Stokes, J.P. "The effects of rapid eye movement sleep on retention," *The Psychological Record*, 23(4), 521–532, 1973.

Tart, C. (ed.). *Altered states of consciousness*. New York: Wiley, 1969.

Wallace, R.K., B. Benson, and A.F. Wilson. "A wakeful hypometabolic physiologic state," *American Journal of Physiology*, 221(3), 795–799, 1971.

Webb, W.B. (ed.). *Sleep: An active process. Research and commentary*. Glenview, Ill.: Scott, Foresman, 1973.

CHAPTER 4

Amerigo, J.A., J.M. Delgado-Garcia, and J.M.R. Delgado. "Behavioral changes induced by radio stimulation of the pallidum in monkeys." XXVIth International Congress of Physiological Sciences, New Delhi, 1974.

Azrin, N.H., R.R. Hutchinson, and R. McLaughlin. "The opportunity for aggression as an operant reinforcer during aversive stimulation," *Journal of Experimental Analysis of Behavior*, 7, 223–227, 1965.

Blumenthal, M.D. "Predicting attitudes toward violence," *Science*, 176, 1296–1302, 1972.

Comstock, *Television and human behavior*. Vol. 1 (with Marilyn Fisher), *A guide to the pertinent scientific literature*. Vol. 2, *The key studies*. Vol. 3 (with Georg Lindsey), *The research horizon, future and present*. Santa Monica, Calif.: Rand, 1975.

Delgado, J.M. *Physical control of the mind: Toward a psychocivilized society*. New York: Harper & Row, 1970.

Delgado, J.M. "Physical control of the mind: Toward a psychocivilized society," in R.N. Anshen (ed.), Volume 41, *World Perspectives Series*. New York: Harper & Row, 1969.

Dollard, J., et al. *Frustration and aggression*. New Haven, Conn.: Yale University Press, 1939.

Eron, L.D., L.R. Huesmann, M.M. Lefkowitz, and L.O. Walder. "Does television violence cause aggression?" *American Psychologist*, 27, 253–263, 1972.

Feshbach, S. "Dynamics and morality of violence and aggression," *American Psychologist*, 26, 281–292, 1971.

Howitt, D., and G. Cumberbatch. "Mass media violence and society," *Contemporary Psychology*, 21(4), 269–270, 1976.

Isaacson, R.L. *The limbic system*. New York: Plemum Press, 1974.

Lorenz, K. *On aggression*. New York: Harcourt Brace Jovanovich, 1966.

Moyer, K.E. "Allergy and aggression: The psychology of violence," *Psychology Today*, 9(2), 76–81, 1975.

Moyer, K.E. *The physiology of hostility*. Chicago: Markham, 1971.

Ochs, S. *Elements of neurophysiology*. New York: Wiley, 1965.

Pribram, K.H. "The brain," *Psychology Today*, 5(4), 44–52, 1971.

Rose, S. *The conscious brain*. New York: Vintage Books, 1976.

Scott, J.P. "Violence and the disaggregated society," presidential address to the International Society for Research on Aggression, 1st International Conference on Aggression Research, Toronto, August 1974.

Selg, H. (ed.). *The making of human aggression*. London: Quartet Books, Ltd., 1975.

Tibbets, P. "The mind-body problem: Empirical or conceptual issue?" *Psychological Record*, 23, 111–120, 1973.

Tinbergen, H. *The study of instinct*. New York: Oxford University Press, 1951.

CHAPTER 5

Bandura, A., and R.H. Walters. *Adolescent aggression*. New York: Ronald Press, 1959.

Bandura, A. *Aggression: A social learning analysis*. Englewood Cliffs, N.J.: Prentice-Hall, 1973.

Divoky, D. "Toward a nation of sedated children," *Learning*, 1(5), 7–13, 1973.

Ittelson, W.H., et al. *Introduction to environmental psychology*. New York: Holt, Rinehart and Winston, 1974.

Jones, E. *The life and work of Sigmund Freud*, vols. I, II, and III. New York: Basic Books, 1953–1957.

Kennedy, T. "Treatment of chronic schizophrenia by behavior therapy: Case reports," *Behavior Research Therapy*, 2, 1–7, 1964.

Krasner, L., and L.P. Ullmann. *Case studies in behavior modification*. New York: Holt, Rinehart and Winston, 1965.

Sewell, E., J.F. McCoy, and W.R. Sewell. "Modification of antagonistic social behavior using positive reinforcement for other behavior," *The Psychological Record*, 23(4), 499–504, 1973.

Thompson, T., and W.S. Dockens, III (eds.). *Applications of behavior modification*. New York: Academic Press, 1975.

Ullmann, L.P., and L. Krasner. *A psychological approach to abnormal behavior*. Englewood Cliffs, N.J.: Prentice-Hall, 1969.

Walker, S., III. "Drugging the American child: We're too cavalier about hyperactivity," *Psychology Today*, 8(7), 43–48, 1974.

Wolf, M., H. Mees, and T. Risley. "Application of operant conditioning procedures to the behavior problems of an autistic child," *Behavior Research Therapy*, 1, 305–312, 1964.

CHAPTER 6

Amoore, J.E., J.W. Johnston, Jr., and M. Rubin. "The stereochemical theory of odor," *Scientific American*, 210, 42–49, 1964.

Boring, E.G. *Sensation and perception in the history of experimental psychology*, 2nd ed. New York: Appleton-Century-Crofts, 1950.

Erikson, R.P. "Sensory neural patterns and gustation," in Y. Zotterman (ed.), *Olfaction and taste*. New York: Macmillan, 1963.

Geldard, F.A. *The human senses*. New York: Wiley, 1953.

Lowenstein. O. *The senses*. Baltimore, Md.: Penguin Books, 1966.

Pfaffmann, C. "Taste and smell," in S.S. Stevens (ed.), *Handbook of experimental psychology*. New York: Wiley, 1951.

Sussman, H.M. "What the tongue tells the brain," *Psychological Bulletin*, 77, 262–272, 1972.

Woodworth, R.S., and H. Schlosberg. *Experimental psychology*, 3rd ed., vol. 1. J.W. Kling and L.A. Riggs (eds.). New York: Holt, Rinehart and Winston, 1972.

CHAPTER 7

Beach, F.A. "Behavioral endocrinology: An emerging discipline," *American Scientist*, 63(2), 178–187, 1975.

Békésy, G. von. *Sensory inhibition*. Princeton, N.J.: Princeton University Press, 1967

Davis, H., and S.R. Silverman (eds.). *Hearing and deafness*. New York: Holt, Rinehart and Winston, 1970.

Deutsch, D. "Musical illusions," *Scientific American*, 233(5), 15, 1975.

Diamond, M., A.L. Diamond, and M. Mast. "Visual sensitivity and sexual arousal levels during the menstrual cycle," *Journal of Nervous and Mental Disorders*, 155, 170–176, 1972.

Geldard, F.A. *The human senses*, 2nd ed. New York: Wiley, 1972.

Stevens, S.S., and H. Davis. *Hearing: Its psychology and physiology*. New York: Wiley, 1938.

Udry, J.R., and N.M. Morris. "Distribution of coitus in the menstrual cycle," *Nature*, 220, 593–596, 1968.

Vernon, M. "Fifty years of research on the intelligence of the deaf and hard of hearing: A survey of the literature and discussion of implications," *Journal of Rehabilitation of the Deaf*, 1968.

CHAPTER 8

Rushton, W.A.H. "Visual pigments in man," *Scientific American*, November 1962.

Wald, G. "The photoreceptor process in vision," in J. Field (ed.), *Handbook of physiology, Sec. I: Neurophysiology*. Washington, D.C.: American Physiological Society, 1959.

Wald, G. "The receptors of human color vision," *Science*, 145, 1007–1016, 1964.

Weckroth, J. *Dimensions of color sensation*. Stockholm: University of Stockholm, 1960.

Zahl, P.E. *Blindness: Modern approaches to the unseen environment*. Princeton, N.J.: Princeton University Press, 1962.

CHAPTER 9

Bexton, W.H., W. Heron, and T.H. Scott. "Effects of decreased variation in the sensory environment," *Canadian Journal of Psychology*, 8, 70–76, 1954.

Farber, I.E., et al. "Brainwashing, conditioning, and DDD (debility, dependency, and dread)," *Sociometry*, 20, 271–285, 1957.

Hebb, D.O. *The organization of behavior*. New York: Wiley, 1949.

Heron, W. "The pathology of boredom," *Scientific American*, 196, 52–62, 1957.

Heron, W., W.H. Bexton, and D.O. Hebb. "Cognitive effects of a decreased variation in the sensory environment," *American Psychologist*, 8, 366 (abstract), 1953.

Heron, W., B.K. Doane, and T.H. Scott. "Visual disturbances after prolonged perceptual isolation," *Canadian Journal of Psychology,* 10, 13–17, 1956.

Hunter, E. *Brainwashing in Red China.* New York: Vanguard, 1951.

Lilly, J. *Center of the cyclone: An autobiography of inner space.* New York: Julian, 1972.

Magoun, H.W. *The waking brain,* 2nd ed. Springfield, Ill.: Charles C Thomas, 1963.

Schein, E.H. "The Chinese indoctrination program for prisoners of war: A study of attempted 'brainwashing,'" *Psychiatry,* 19, 149–172, 1956.

CHAPTER 10

Allport, G.W., and T.F. Pettigrew. "Cultural influence on the perception of movement: The trapezoid illusion among Zulus," *Journal of Abnormal and Social Psychology,* 55, 104–113, 1957.

Bakan, P. "The eyes have it," *Psychology Today,* 4(11), 64–67, 96, 1971.

Bond, E.K. "Perception of form by the human infant," *Psychological Bulletin,* 77, 225–245, 1972.

Carterette, E.C., and M.P. Friedman (eds.). *Handbook of perception,* vol. 3, *Biology of perceptual systems.* New York: Academic Press, 1973.

Gibson, J.J. *The perception of the visual world.* Boston: Houghton Mifflin, 1950.

Gombrich, E.H. "The visual image," *Scientific American,* 227(3), 82–96, 1972.

Gregory, R.L. "Visual illusions," *Scientific American,* 219, 66–76, 1968.

Gregory, R.L., and J.G. Wallace. "Recovery from early blindness: A case study," *Experimental Psychological Society Monograph.*

Haber, R.N., and M. Hershenson, *The psychology of visual perception.* New York: Holt, Rinehart and Winston, 1973.

Held, R., and A. Hein. "Movement-produced stimulation in the development of visually guided behavior," *Journal of Comparative and Physiological Psychology,* 56, 872–876, 1963.

Hess, E.H. "Shadows and depth perception," *Scientific American,* 204, 138–148, 1961.

Ittelson, W.H. "Size as a cue to distance," *American Journal of Psychology,* 64, 54–67, 188–202, 1951.

Köhler, W. *Gestalt psychology,* 2nd ed. New York: Liveright, 1947.

Mettelli, F. "The perception of transparency," *Scientific American,* 230(4), 91, 1974.

Powers, W.T. *Behavior: The control of perception.* Chicago: Aldine, 1973.

Riggs, L. "Human vision: Some objective explorations," *American Psychologist,* 31(2), 125–134, 1976.

Rock, I. *An introduction to perception.* New York: Macmillan, 1975.

Rodieck, R.W. *The vertebrate retina: Principles of structure and function.* San Francisco: Freeman, 1974.

Segall, M.H., et al. *The influence of culture on visual perception.* Indianapolis, Ind.: Bobbs-Merrill, 1966.

Walk, R.D., and E.J. Gibson. "A comparative and analytic study of visual depth perception," *Psychological Monographs,* 75, 15, 1961.

Uttal, W.R. *An autocorrelation theory of form detection.* Hillsdale, N.J.: Erlbaum, 1975.

CHAPTER 11

Fareberow, N.E. (ed.). *Taboo topics.* New York: Aldine-Atherton, 1966.

Hansel, C.E.M. *ESP: A scientific evaluation.* New York: Scribner, 1966.

Lindsley, D.B. "The role of nonspecific reticulo-thalamo-cortical systems in emotion," in P. Black (ed.), *Physiological correlates of emotion.* New York: Academic Press, 1970.

McConnell, R.A. "ESP and credibility in science," *American Psychologist,* 24, 531–538, 1969.

McGinnies, E. "Emotionality and perceptual defense," *Psychological Review,* 56, 244–251, 1949.

McMahan, E. "An experiment in pure telepathy," *Journal of Parapsychology,* 10, 273–288, 1946.

Owen, A.R.G. *Can we explain the poltergeist?* New York: Garrett, 1964.

Palmer, J. "Scoring in ESP tests as a function of belief in ESP," *Journal of the American Society for Psychical Research,* 65, 373–408, 1971.

Posner, M.I., and S.J. Boies. "Components of attention," *Psychological Review,* 78, 391–408, 1971.

Rhine, J.B., and J.G. Pratt. *Parapsychology.* Springfield, Ill.: Charles C Thomas, 1957.

Rhine, L.E. *ESP in life and lab.* New York: Macmillan, 1967.

Schmeidler, G.R. *Extrasensory perception.* Chicago: Aldine-Atherton, 1969.

Schmidt, H. "Clairvoyance test with a machine," *Journal of Parapsychology,* 33, 300–307, 1969.

Swets, J.A. "Is there a sensory threshold?" *Science,* 134, 168–177, 1961.

Ullman, M., and S. Krippner. "ESP in the night," *Psychology Today,* 46–50, June 1970.

CHAPTER 12

Arnold, M.B. *Emotion and personality,* vols. I and II. New York: Columbia University Press, 1960.

Ahlskog, J.E., P.K. Randall, and B.G. Hoebel. "Hypothalamic hyperphasia: Dissociation from hyperphasia following destruction of noradrenergic neutrons," *Science,* 190(4212), 1975.

Cannon, W.B. *The wisdom of the body.* New York: Norton, 1932.

Davis, J.D., B.J. Collins, and M.W. Levine. "Peripheral control of drinking: Gastrointestinal filling as a negative feedback signal," *Journal of Comparative and Physiological Psychology,* 89(9), 985–1002, 1975.

Desor, J.A., L.S. Greene, and O. Maller. "Preferences for sweet and salty in 9- to 15-year-old and adult humans," *Science,* 190, 686–687, 1975.

Grossman, S.P. "Eating or drinking elicited by direct adrenergic or cholinergic stimulation of the hypothalamus," *Science,* 136, 301–302, 1960.

Korman, A.K. *The psychology of motivation.* Englewood Cliffs, N.J.: Prentice-Hall, 1974.

McConnell, J.V. "Feedback, fat and freedom," *Encyclopedia Britannica Yearbook,* 1973.

Mahoney, M.J., and R. Mahoney. "Fight fat with behavior control," *Psychology Today,* 9(12), 39–43, 1976.

Mayer, J. *Overweight: Causes, cost and control.* Englewood Cliffs, N.J.: Prentice-Hall, 1968.

Malmo, R.B. *On emotions, needs and our archaic brain.* New York: Holt, Rinehart and Winston, 1975.

Nisbett, R.E. "Determinants of food intake in obesity," *Science,* 159, 1254–1255, 1968.

Richter, C.P. "The self-selection of diets," in *Essays in biology.* Berkeley, Calif.: University of California Press, 1943.

Rodin, J. "Effects of obesity and set point on taste responsiveness in humans," *Journal of Comparative and Physiological Psychology,* 89(9), 1003–1009, 1975.

Schachter, S. "Eat, eat," *Psychology Today,* 4(11), 44–47, 78–79, 1971.

Schachter, S. *Emotion, obesity and crime.* New York: Academic Press, 1971.

Schachter, S. "Some extraordinary facts about obese humans and rats," *American Psychologist*, 26, 129–144, 1971.

Schachter, S., R. Goldman, and A. Gordon. "Effects of fear, food deprivation, and obesity on eating," *Journal of Personality and Social Psychology*, 10, 98–106, 1968.

Schachter, S., and J.E. Singer. "Cognitive, social and physiological determinants of emotional state," *Psychological Review*, 69, 379–399, 1962.

Valenstein, E.S., V.C. Cox, and J.W. Kakolewski. "Reexamination of the role of the hypothalamus in motivation," *Psychological Review*, 77(1), 16–31, 1970.

Weiner, B. *Theories of motivation: From mechanism to cognition*. Chicago: Markham, 1972.

Young, P.T. *Emotion in man and animal*, 2nd rev. ed. Huntington, N.Y.: Kreiger, 1973.

Zeigler, H.P. "Trigeminal deafferentation and hunger in the pigeon," *Journal of Comparative and Physiological Psychology*, 89, 827–844, 1975.

Zeigler, H.P., M. Miller, and R.R. Levine. "Trigeminal nerve and eating in the pigeon (*Columba livia*): Neurosensory control of the consummatory responses," *Journal of Comparative and Physiological Psychology*, 89, 845–858, 1975.

CHAPTER 13

Bardwick, J.M. "Her body, the battleground," *Psychology Today*, 5(9), 50–56, 1972.

Beach, F.A. "Instinctive behavior: Reproductive activities," in S.S. Stevens (ed.), *Handbook of experimental psychology*. New York: Wiley, 1951.

Beach, F.A., and C.S. Ford. *Patterns of sexual behavior*. New York: Harper & Brothers and Paul Schoeber, Inc., 1951.

Ellis, A., and A. Abarbanel (eds.). *Encyclopedia of sexual behavior*, 2nd ed. New York: Hawthorne Books, 1967.

Katchadourian, H.A., and D.T. Lunde. *Fundamentals of human sexuality*. New York: Holt, Rinehart and Winston, 1972.

Kinsey, A.C., C.E. Martin, and W.B. Pomeroy. *Sexual behavior in the human male*. Philadelphia: Saunders, 1948.

Kinsey, A.C., W.B. Pomeroy, C.E. Martin, and R.H. Gebhard. *Sexual behavior in the human female*. Philadelphia: Saunders, 1953.

Maccoby, E.E., and C.N. Jacklin. *The psychology of sex differences*. Stanford, Calif.: Stanford University Press, 1974.

Masters, W.H., and V.E. Johnson. *Human sexual inadequacy*. Boston: Little, Brown, 1970.

Masters, W.H., and V.E. Johnson. *Human sexual response*. Boston: Little, Brown, 1966.

Olds, J., "Pleasure centers in the brain," *Scientific American*, 105–116, October 1956.

Olds, J., and P.M. Milner. "Positive reinforcement produced by electrical stimulation of septal areas and other regions of rat brains," *Journal of Comparative and Physiological Psychology*, 47, 419–427, 1954.

Olds, J., and M.E. Olds. "Drives, rewards, and the brain," in F. Barron et al. (eds.), *New directions in psychology II*. New York: Holt, Rinehart and Winston, 1957.

Pomery, W.B. *Dr. Kinsey and the Institute for Sex Research*. New York: Harper & Row, 1972.

Watson, J.B. "Psychology as the behaviorist views it," *Psychological Review*, 20, 158–177, 1913.

Wendt, H. *The sex life of the animals*. New York: Simon & Schuster, 1965.

Wright, P., P.G. Caryl, and D.M. Vowles (eds.). *Neural and endocrine aspects of behavior in birds*. New York: Elsevier, 1975.

CHAPTER 14

Berlyne, D.E. *Conflict, arousal and curiosity.* New York: McGraw-Hill, 1960.

Culligan, D. "That helpless feeling: The dangers of stress," *New York,* 8(28), 28–32, 1975.

Friedman, R.J., and M.F. Katz. *The psychology of depression: Contemporary theory and research.* Washington, D.C.: Winston, 1974.

Levi, L., and L. Andersson. *Psychosocial stress: Population, environment and quality of life.* New York: Spectrum, 1975.

Levine, S. "Stress and behavior," *Scientific American,* 224(1), 26–31, 1971.

Pitts, F.N. "The biochemistry of anxiety," *Scientific American,* 220(2), 69–75, 1969.

Rotter, J.B. "Generalized expectancies for internal versus external control of reinforcement," *Psychological Monographs,* 80(609) 211, 1966.

Sanford, N. "On authoritarianism," *Psychology Today,* 6(6), 96–100, 1972.

Sarason, I.G., and C.D. Spielberger (eds.). *Stress and anxiety,* vol. 2. New York: Hemisphere, 1975.

Selye, H. "The general-adaptation syndrome in its relationship to neurology, psychology, and psychopathology," in A. Weider (ed.), *Contributions toward medical psychology.* New York: Ronald Press, 1953.

Selye, H. *The physiology and pathology of exposure to stress.* Montreal: Acta, 1950.

Selye, H. *The stress of life.* New York: McGraw-Hill, 1956.

Sims, J.H., and D.D. Baumann. "The tornado threat: Coping styles of the North and the South," *Science,* 176, 1386–1391, 1972.

Weiss, J.M. "Psychological factors in stress and disease," *Scientific American,* 226(6), 104–113, 1972.

CHAPTER 15

Dallenbach, K.M. "Twitmyer and the conditioned response," *American Journal of Psychology,* 72, 633–638, 1959.

Holden, C. "Lie detectors: PSE gains audience despite critics' doubts," *Science,* 190(4212), 359–362, 1975.

Jones, M.C. "Albert, Peter and John B. Watson," *American Psychologist,* 79, 8, 1974.

Lazarus, A.A., and J. Wolpe. *Behavior therapy techniques.* New York: Pergamon Press, 1966.

Liddell, H.S. *Emotional hazards in animals and man.* Springfield, Ill.: Charles C Thomas, 1956.

Luria, A.P. *The man with a shattered world: The history of a brain wound.* New York: Basic Books, 1973.

McGill, T.E. *Readings in animal behavior,* 2nd ed. New York: Holt, Rinehart and Winston, 1973.

Mahoney, M.J. *Cognition and behavior modification.* Cambridge, Mass.: Ballinger, 1974.

Masserman, J. *Behavior and neurosis.* Chicago: Univeristy of Chicago Press, 1943.

Novaco, R.W. *Anger control: The development and evaluation of an experimental treatment.* Lexington, Mass,: Lexington Books, 1975.

Pavlov, I.P. *Conditioned reflexes.* New York: Oxford University Press, 1927.

Watson, J.B., and R. Rayner. "Conditioned emotional reactions," *Journal of Experimental Psychology,* 3, 1–14, 1920.

Weiner, H. "Some thoughts on behavioral approaches to therapy," *The Psychological Record,* 23(4), 441–450, 1973.

Wolpe, J. *The practice of behavior therapy.* New York: Pergamon Press, 1969.

CHAPTER 16

Anokhin, P.K. *Biology and neurophysiology of the conditioned reflex and its role in adaptive behavior*, vol. 3. Elmsford, N.Y.: Pergamon Press, 1974.

Bolles, R.C. *Learning theory.* New York: Holt, Rinehart and Winston, 1975.

Gantt, W.H. "Pavlov's higher nervous activity," *Conditional Reflex*, 3(4), 281–289, 1968.

Gantt, W.H. "B.F. Skinner and his contingencies," *Conditional Reflex*, 5(2), 63–74, 1970.

Gantt, W.H. "Pain conditioning and schizokinesis," *Conditional Reflex*, 8(2), 63–66, 1973.

Hilgard, E.R., and G.H. Bouer. *Theories of learning*, 4th ed. Englewood Cliffs, N.J.: Prentice-Hall, 1975.

Honig, W.H. (ed.). *Operant behavior: Areas of research and application.* New York: Appleton-Century-Crofts, 1966.

Kaplan, M.F., and S. Schwartz. *Human judgment and decision processes.* New York: Academic Press, 1976.

Kimble, G.A. (ed.). *Foundations of conditioning and learning.* New York: Appleton-Century-Crofts, 1967.

Köhler, W. *The mentality of apes.* NewYork: Harcourt Brace Jovanovich, 1925.

Maier, N.R.F., and T.C. Schneirla. *Principles of animal psychology.* New York: McGraw-Hill, 1935.

Maier, R.A., and B.M. Maier. *Comparative animal behavior.* Belmont, Calif.: Brooks-Cole, 1970.

Miller, N.E. "Learning of visceral and glandular responses," *Science*, 163, 434–445, 1969.

Pavlov, I.P. *Conditioned reflexes.* New York: Dover, 1927.

Sherman, A.R. *Behavior modification: Theory and practice.* Monterey, Calif.: Brooks-Cole, 1973.

Skinner, B.F. *The behavior of organisms.* New York: Appleton-Century-Crofts, 1938.

Skinner, B.F. "'Superstition' in pigeons," *Journal of Experimental Psychology*, 38, 168–72, 1948.

Skinner, B.F. "Pigeons in a pelican," *American Psychologist*, 15, 28–37, 1960.

Taber, J., R. Glaser, and H. Schaefer. *Learning and programmed instructions.* Reading, Mass.: Addison-Wesley, 1965.

Thorndike, E.L. *The psychology of learning.* New York: Teachers College, Columbia University, 1921.

Tolman, E.C. "Cognitive maps in rats and men," *Psychological Review*, 55, 189–208, 1948.

Verhave, T. "The pigeon as a quality-control inspector," *American Psychologist*, 21, 109–115, 1966.

Woods, P.J. "A taxonomy of instrumental conditioning," *American Psychologist*, 29, 8, 1974.

Wyer, R.S. *Cognitive organization and change: An information processing approach.* Potomac, N.Y.: Erlbaum, 1974.

CHAPTER 17

Atkinson, R.C., and R.M. Shiffrin. "The control of short-term memory," *Scientific American*, 225(2), 82–91, 1971.

Bower, G.H. *The psychology of learning and motivation advances in research and theory.* New York: Academic Press, 1972.

Cermak, L.S. *Human memory: Research and theory.* New York: Ronald Press, 1972.

Corning, W.C., and S.C. Ratner (eds.). *The chemistry of learning*. New York Plenum Press, 1967.

Corning, W.C., J.A. Dyal, and A.U.D. Willows (eds.), *Invertebrate learning*. New York: Plenum Press, 1973.

Gaito, J. *DNA Complex and adaptive behavior*. Englewood Cliffs, N.J.: Prentice-Hall, 1971.

John, E.R. "Switchboard vs. statistical theories of learning and memory," *Science*, 177, 850–864, 1972.

John, E.R. "How the brain works; a new explanation," *Psychology Today*, 9(11), 48–52, 1976.

Lashley, K.S. "In search of the engram," in *Symposia of the Society for Experimental Biology*, 4, 454–482, 1950.

McConnell, J.V. "Comparative physiology: Learning in invertebrates," *Annual Review of Physiology*, 28, 107–136, 1966.

McConnell, J.V. (ed.). *A manual of psychological experimentation on planarians*, rev. ed. Special publication of *The Journal of Biological Psychology*, January 1967.

McConnell, J.V. "The biochemistry of memory," in R.C. Teevan (ed.), *Readings in introductory psychology*. Minneapolis: Burgess, 1972.

McConnell, J.V., A.M. Golub, F.R. Masiarz, and T. Villars. "Incubation effects in behavior induction in rats," *Science*, 168, 392–395, 1970.

McConnell, J.V., A.L. Jacobson, and D.P. Kimble. "The effects of regeneration upon retention of a conditioned response in the planarian," *Journal of Comparative and Physiological Psychology*, 52, 1–5, 1959.

McConnell, J.V., and D.H. Malin. "Recent experiments in memory transfer," in H.P. Zippel (ed.), *Memory and transfer of information*. New York: Plenum Press, 1973.

McConnell, J.V., and J. Shelby. "Memory transfer in invertebrates," in G. Ungar (ed.), *Molecular mechanisms in memory and learning*. New York: Plenum Press, 1970.

Marx, J.L. "Learning and behavior (I): Effects of pituitary hormones," *Science*, 190(4212), 366–370, 1975.

Norman, D.A. *Memory and attention: An introduction to human information processing*. New York: Wiley, 1969.

Rosenzweig, M.R., E.L. Bennet, and M.C. Diamond. "Brain changes in response to experience," *Scientific American*, 226(2), 22–29, 1972.

Smirnov, A.A. *Problems of the psychology of memory*. New York: Plenum Press, 1973.

Thompson, R., and J.V. McConnell. "Classical conditioning in the planarian, *Dugesia dorotocephala*," *Journal of Comparative and Physiological Psychology*, 48, 65–68, 1955.

Young, M.N., and W.B. Gibson. *How to develop an exceptional memory*. Philadelphia: Chilton, 1962.

CHAPTER 18

Bakan, P. "Hypnotizability, laterality of eye-movements and functional brain assymmetry," *Perceptual and Motor Skills*, 28(3), 927–932, 1969.

Barber, T.X. *Hypnosis: A scientific approach*. New York: Van Nostrand, 1969.

Casey, K.L. "Pain: A current view of neural mechanisms," *American Scientist*, 61, 194–200, 1973.

Gannon, L., and R.A. Sternbach. "Alpha enhancement as a treatment for pain: A case study," *Journal of Behavior Therapy and Experimental Psychiatry*, 2(3), 209–213, 1971.

Hilgard, E.R. *The experience of hypnosis.* New York: Harcourt Brace Jovanovich, 1968.

Hilgard, E.R. "Pain as a puzzle for psychology and physiology," *American Psychologist,* 24, 103–113, 1969.

Hirai, T. *Psychophysiology of zen.* Tokyo: Igaku Shoin, 1974.

Hull, C.L. *A behavior system: An introduction to behavior theory concerning the individual organism.* New Haven, Conn.: Yale University Press, 1952.

Melzack, R. *The puzzle of pain.* New York: Basic Books, 1973.

Melzack, R. "Phantom limbs," *Psychology Today,* 63–68, October 1970.

Melzack, R., and P.D. Wall. "Pain mechanisms: A new theory," *Science,* 150, 971–979, 1965.

Melzack, R., and W.S. Torgesson. "On the language of pain," *Anesthesiology,* 34(1), 50–59, 1971.

Sternbach, R.A. *Pain patients: Traits and treatment.* New York: Academic Press, 1974.

CHAPTER 19

Comfort, A. *Aging: The biology of senescence.* New York: Holt, Rinehart and Winston, 1964.

Crick, F.H.C. "The genetic code," *Scientific American,* 207, 66–74, 1962.

Dennis, W., and M.G. Dennis. "The effect of cradling practices upon the onset of walking in Hopi children," *Journal of Genetic Psychology,* 56, 77–86, 1940.

Dobzhansky, T. "Genetics and the diversity of behavior," *American Psychologist,* 27, 523–530, 1972.

Fuller, J.L., and W.R. Thompson. *Behavior genetics.* New York: Wiley, 1960.

Hook, E.B. "Behavioral implications of the human XYY genotype," *Science,* 179, 139–150, 1973.

Lenneberg, E.H. *Biological foundations of language.* New York: Wiley, 1967.

McConnell, J.V. "Criminals can be brainwashed—Now," *Psychology Today,* 14, April 1970.

Montagu, A. "Chromosomes and crime," *Psychology Today,* 2, 42–49, 1968.

Robinson, D.N. (ed.). *Heredity and achievement: A book of readings.* London: Oxford University Press, 1970.

Sorenson, J. "Genetic counseling," *Behavior Today,* 4, 3, 1973.

Vernon, P.E. *Intelligence and cultural environment.* London: Methuen, 1969.

Walzer, S., and P.S. Gerald. "Social class and frequency of XYY and XXY," *Science,* 190, 1228–1229, 1975.

Wiener, S., and G. Sutherland. "A normal XYY man," *Lancet.* London, ii, 1352, 1968.

Winick, M., K.K. Meyer, and R.C. Harris. "Malnutrition and environmental enrichment by early adoption," *Science,* 190, 1173–1175, 1975.

CHAPTER 20

Eibl-Eibesfeldt, I. *Ethology: The biology of behavior.* New York: Holt, Rinehart and Winston, 1970.

Harlow, H.F. "The nature of love," *American Psychologist,* 13, 673–685, 1958.

Harlow, H.F. "Sexual behavior in the rhesus monkey," in F. Beach (ed.), *Sex and behavior.* New York: Wiley, 1965.

Harlow, H.F., M.K. Harlow, and S.J. Suomi. "From thought to therapy: Lessons from a primate laboratory," *American Scientist,* 59, 538–549, 1971.

Helfer, R.E., and C.H. Kempe (eds.). *The battered child,* 2nd ed. Chicago: Chicago University Press, 1974.

Scott, J.P. *Early experience and the organization of behavior*. Belmont, Calif Brooks-Cole, 1968.

Scott, J.P., "Effects of psychotropic drugs on separation distress in dogs," *Proceedings of the IXth Congress of the Collegium Internationale Neuropsychopharmacologicum*, Paris, July 1974.

Van Lawick-Goodall, J. *In the shadow of man*. Boston: Houghton Mifflin, 1971

Wallach, M.A., and N. Kogan. *Modes of thinking in young children: A study of the creativity-intelligence distinction*. New York: Holt, Rinehart and Winston 1965.

CHAPTER 21

Baroff, G.S. *Mental retardation: Nature, cause, and management*. New York: Wiley, 1974.

Brown, R. "Development of the first language in the human species," *American Psychologist*, 28, 97–106, 1973.

Bruner, J.S., et al. *Studies in cognitive growth*. New York: Wiley, 1966.

Colby, B.N. "Culture grammars," *Science*, 187(4180), 913–918, 1975.

Elder, G.H. *Children of the great depression*. Chicago: University of Chicago Press, 1974.

Friedlander, B.Z. "Receptive language development in infancy: Issues and problems," *Merrill-Palmer Quarterly of Behavior and Development*, 16, 7–51, 1970.

Glucksberg, S., and J.H. Danks. *Experimental psycholinguistics: An introduction*. Hillsdale, N.J.: Erlbaum, 1975.

Greene, J. *Psycholinguistics: Chomsky and psychology*. Baltimore, Md.: Penguin Books, 1972.

Hebb, D.O., W.E. Lambert, and G.R. Tucker. "A DMZ in the language war," *Psychology Today*, 6(11), 54–63, 1973.

Horn, J. "The new grandparents—Cool and distant or fun loving," *Psychology Today*, 9(12), 30–31, 1976.

Menzel, E.W., and S. Halperin. "Purposive behavior as a basis for objective communication between chimpanzees," *Science*, 189(4203), 652–654, 1975.

Millar, S. *The psychology of play*. Baltimore, Md.: Penguin Books, 1968.

Phillips, J.L. *The origins of intellect: Piaget's theory*. San Francisco: Freeman, 1969.

Piaget, J. *Construction of reality in the child*. New York: Basic Books, 1954.

Piaget, J., and B. Inhelder. *The child's conception of space*. New York: Humanities, 1948.

Premack, A.J., and D. Premack. "Teaching language to an ape," *Scientific American*, 227(4), 92–100, 1972.

Sutton-Smith, B. "Child's play—very serious business," *Psychology Today*, 67–69, December 1971.

Talbot, N.B. (ed.). *Raising children in modern America: Problems and prospective solutions*. Boston: Little, Brown, 1976.

Trotter, R. "Evolution of language: A hatful of theories," *APA Monitor*, 7(1), 12–13, 1976.

Van Lawick-Goodall, J. *In the shadow of man*. Boston: Houghton Mifflin, 1971.

Weisler, A., and R.B. McCall. "Exploration and play: Resume and redirection," *American Psychologist*, 13(7), 492–508, 1976.

CHAPTER 22

Adler, A. *Individual psychology of Alfred Adler: A systematic presentation in selections from his writing*. New York: Basic Books, 1956.

Adler, A. *Understanding human nature*. New York: Humanities, 1962.

Ansbacher, H.L. "Alfred Adler and humanistic psychology," *Journal of Humanistic Psychology*, 11, 53–63, 1971.

Erikson, E.H. *Childhood and society*, 2nd ed. New York: Norton, 1963.

Fordham, F. *An introduction to Jung's psychology*. Baltimore, Md.: Penguin Books, 1953.

Freud, S. *The ego and the id*. London: Hogarth Press, 1927.

Freud, S. *New introductory lectures on psychoanalysis*. New York: Norton, 1933.

Freud, S. *A general introduction to psychoanalysis*. New York: Doubleday, 1938.

Freud, S. *The interpretation of dreams*. New York: Basic Books, 1955.

Freud, S. *The project: Freud's project reassessed*, K. Pribram and M. Gill (eds.). London: Hutchinson Publishing Group, Ltd., 1976.

Hall, C.S., and G. Lindzey. *Theories of personality*, 2nd ed. New York: Wiley, 1970.

Jung, C.G. *Man and his symbols*. New York: Doubleday, 1969.

Jung, C.G. *The undiscovered self*. Boston: Little, Brown, 1958.

Maslow, A.H. *Toward a psychology of being*. Princeton, N.J.: Van Nostrand, 1962.

Maslow, A.H. *Motivation and personality*, 2nd ed. New York: Harper & Row, 1970.

Mischel, W. *Introduction to personality*, 2nd ed. New York: Holt, Rinehart and Winston, 1976.

Mischel, H., and W. Mischel. *Readings in personality*. New York: Holt, Rinehart and Winston, 1973.

Sheehy, G. "The sexual diamond: Facing the facts of the human sexual life cycles," *New York*, 9(4), 28–39, 1976.

Skinner, B.F. *Walden II*. New York: Macmillan, 1948.

Skinner, B.F. *Science and human behavior*. New York: Macmillan, 1953.

Whitmont, E.C. "Jungian analysis today," *Psychology Today*, 6(7), 63–64, 1972.

CHAPTER 23

Allport, G.W. *Patterns and growth in personality*. New York: Holt, Rinehart and Winston, 1961.

Allport, G.W., P.E. Vernon, and G. Lindzey. *Study of values: Manual*. Boston: Houghton Mifflin, 1960.

Calvin, A.D., and J.V. McConnell. "Ellis on personality inventories," *Journal of Consulting Psychology*, 17, 462–464, 1953.

Eysenck, H.J. *The inequality of man*. London: Temple Smith, 1973.

Garcia, J. "I.Q.: The conspiracy," *Psychology Today*, 6(4), 40–43, 1972.

Ghiselli, E.E. *The validity of occupational aptitude tests*. New York: Wiley, 1966.

Harmon, L.R. "The development of a criterion of scientific competence," in C.W. Taylor and F. Barron (eds.), *Scientific creativity: Its recognition and development*. New York: Wiley, 1963, pp. 44–52.

Holtzman, W.H., et al. *Inkblot perception and personality*. Austin: University of Texas Press, 1961.

Howells, J.G. (ed.). *Modern perspectives in the psychiatry of old age*. New York: Brunner-Mazel, 1975.

Kretschmer, E. *Physique and character*, 2nd ed. New York: Harcourt Brace Jovanovich, 1925.

Lindzey, G., C.S. Hall, and M. Manosevitz. *Theories of personality: Primary sources and research*, 2nd ed. New York: Wiley, 1973.

Maas, H.S., and J.A. Kuypers. *From thirty to seventy: A forty-year longitudinal study of adult life styles and personality*. San Francisco: Jossey-Bass, 1974.

Marks, P.A., W. Seeman, and D.L. Haller. *The actuarial use of the MMPI with adolescents and adults*. Baltimore, Md.: Williams and Wilkins, 1974.

Matarazzo, J.D. *Wechsler's measurement and appraisal of adult intelligence*, 3rd ed. Baltimore, Md.: Williams and Wilkins, 1972.

Mercer, J.R. "I.Q.: The lethal label," *Psychology Today*, 6(4), 44–47, 1972.

Mischel, W. *Personality and assessment*. New York: Wiley, 1968.

Rorschach, H. *Psychodiagnostics*. Berne: Hans Huber, 1942.

Rosenthal, R. *Experimenter effects in behavioral research*. New York: Appleton-Century-Crofts, 1966.

Rosenthal, R., and L. Jacobson. *Pygmalion in the classroom*. New York: Holt, Rinehart and Winston, 1968.

Savage, R.D., R.G. Britton, N. Bolton, and E.H. Hall. *Intellectual functioning in the aged*. New York: Barnes & Noble, 1975.

Scarr-Salapatek, S. "Race, social class, and IQ," *Science*, 174, 1285–1295, 1971.

Schmidt, F.L., and J.E. Hunter. "Racial and ethnic bias in psychological tests," *American Psychologist*, 29, 1–8, 1974.

Sheldon, W.H. *The varieties of temperament*. New York: Harper & Row, 1942.

Skeels, H.M. "Adult status of children with contrasting early life experiences," *Monographs of the Society for Research in Child Development*, 31(3), 1–65, 1966.

Trotter, R. "The Milwaukee project: Nine-year follow up," *Science News*, 110(2), 21, 1976.

Wallach, M.A. "Tests tell us little about talent," *American Scientist*, 64, 57–63, 1976.

Watson, P. "I.Q.: the racial gap," *Psychology Today*, 6(4), 48–52, 1972.

Wing, C.W., Jr., and M.A. Wallach. *College admissions and the psychology of talent*. New York: Holt, Rinehart and Winston, 1971.

Zajonc, R.B. "Family configuration and intelligence," *Science*, 192(4236), 227–235, 1976.

CHAPTER 24

Benjamin, H. *The transsexual phenomenon*. New York: Julian, 1966.

Braginsky, B.M., D.D. Braginsky, and K. Ring. *Methods of madness: The mental hospital as a last resort*. New York: Holt, Rinehart and Winston, 1969.

Braginsky, D.D., and B.M. Braginsky. *Hansels and Gretels: Studies of children in institutions for the mentally retarded*. New York: Holt, Rinehart and Winston, 1971.

Brandt, A. *Reality police: The experience of insanity in America*. New York: Morrow, 1975.

Doob, A.N. "Society's side show," *Psychology Today*, 5(5), 47–51, 1971.

Edwards, A.L. *Statistical analysis*, 4th ed. New York: Holt, Rinehart and Winston, 1974.

Eysenck, H.J. *The structure of human personality*, 2nd ed. London: Methuen, 1960.

Gagnon, J.H., and W. Simon (eds.). *Sexual deviance*. New York: Harper & Row, 1967.

Goldstein, M.J., H.S. Kant, and T.J. Hartman. *Pornography and sexual deviance*. Berkeley: University of California Press, 1974.

Havighurst, R.J., B.L. Neugarten, and S.S. Tobin, "Disengagement and patterns of aging," in B.L. Neugarten (ed.), *Middle age and aging: A reader in social psychology*. Chicago: University of Chicago Press, 1968.

Hays, W.L. *Statistics for the social sciences*, 2nd ed. New York: Holt, Rinehart and Winston, 1973.

Kalish, R.A. *Late adulthood: Perspectives in human development*. Monterey, Calif: Brooks-Cole, 1975.

Lazarus, R.S. *Patterns of adjustment and human effectiveness*. New York: McGraw-Hill, 1969.

Mohr, J.W., et al. *Pedophilia and exhibitionism: A handbook*. Toronto: University of Toronto Press, 1964.

Murray, H.F., and J. Hirsch. "Heredity, individual differences, and psychopathology," in S.C. Plog, R.B. Edgerton, and W.C. Beckwith (eds.), *Changing perspective in mental illness*. New York: Holt, Rinehart and Winston, 1969.

Neugarten, B.L., "Personality change in late life: A developmental perspective," in C. Eisdorfer and M.P. Lawton (eds.), *The psychology of adult development and aging*. Washington, D.C.: American Psychological Association, 1973.

Price, R.H. *Abnormal behavior: Perspectives in conflict*. New York: Holt, Rinehart and Winston, 1972.

Rabkin, J.G. "Opinions about mental illness: A review of the literature," *Psychological Bulletin*, 77, 153–171, 1972.

Rosenhan, D.L. "On being sane in insane places," *Science*, 179, 250–258, 1973.

Rothstein, J.H. *Mental retardation*, 2nd ed. New York: Holt, Rinehart and Winston, 1971.

West, D.J. *Homosexuality*. Chicago: Aldine-Atherton, 1967.

White, R.W., and N.F. Watt. *The abnormal personality*, 4th ed. New York: Ronald Press, 1973.

CHAPTER 25

Ayllon, T., and N.H. Azrin. *The token economy*. New York: Appleton-Century-Crofts, 1968.

Berger, E. *The psychology of gambling*. New York: Hill & Wang, 1957.

Berne, E. *Games people play: The psychology of human relationships*. New York: Grove Press, 1964.

Berne, E. *Group treatment*. New York: Grove Press, 1966.

Berne, E. *What do you say after you say hello?* New York: Grove Press, 1973.

Buhler, C. "Basic theoretical concepts of humanistic psychology," *American Psychologist*, 26, 378–386, 1971.

Coleman, J.C. *Abnormal psychology and modern life*, 4th ed. Glenview, Ill.: Scott, Foresman, 1972.

Davis, A.E., S. Dinitz, and B. Pasamanick, *Schizophrenics in the new custodial community: Five years after the experiment*. Columbus: Ohio State University Press, 1974.

Davison, G.C., and R.M. Liebert, producers. "Behavior therapy for homosexuality" (film). University Park, Pa.: Psychological Cinema Register, Penn State University.

Davison, G.C., and R.B. Stuart. "Behavior therapy and civil liberties," *American Psychologist*, 30(7), 755–763, 1975.

Greenblatt, M. "Psychosurgery," in A.M. Freedman and H.I. Kaplan (eds.), *Psychiatry*. Baltimore, Md.: Williams & Wilkins, 1967.

Greenspoon, J. "The reinforcing effect of two spoken sounds on the frequency of two responses," *American Journal of Psychology*, 68, 409–416, 1955.

Lazarus, A.A. *Behavior therapy and beyond*. New York: McGraw-Hill, 1972.

London, P. "The end of ideology in behavior modification," *American Psychologist*, 27, 913–920, 1972.

Maier, S.F., and M.E.P. Seligman. "Learned helplessness: Theory and evidence," *Journal of Experimental Psychology: General*, 105(1), 3–46, 1976.

Perls, F.S. *Gestalt therapy verbatim*. Lafayette, Calif.: Real People Press, 1969.

Redlich, F.C., and D.X. Freedman. *Theory and practice of psychiatry*. New York: Basic Books, 1966.

Rogers, C.R. *On becoming a person: A therapist's view of psychotherapy*. Boston: Houghton Mifflin, 1961.

Rogers, C.R. *Freedom to learn*. Columbus, O.: Merrill, 1969.

Segal, J., D.S. Boomer, and L. Bouthilet. *Research in the service of mental health: Report of the research task force of the National Institute of Mental Health*. Washington, D.C.: Government Printing Office, ADM 75-237, 1975.

Skinner, B.F. *Beyond freedom and dignity.* New York: Knopf, 1971.

Sloane, R.B., F.R. Staples, A.H. Cristol, N.J. Yorkston, and K. Whipple. *Psychotherapy versus behavior therapy.* Cambridge, Mass.: Harvard University Press, 1975.

Stuart, R.B. *Trick or treatment: How and when psychotherapy fails.* Champaign, Ill.: Research Press, 1970.

Yalom, I.D. *The theory and practice of group psychotherapy.* New York: Basic Books, 1970.

CHAPTER 26

Altman, I. *The environment and social behavior: Privacy, personal space, territory and crowding.* Monterey, Calif.: Brooks-Cole, 1975.

Bales, R.F. "Task roles and social roles in problem-solving," in E.E. Maccoby, T.M. Newcomb, and E.L. Hartley (eds.), *Readings in Social Psychology,* 3rd ed., New York: Holt, Rinehart and Winston, 1958.

Bales, R.F. *Personality and interpersonal behavior.* New York: Holt, Rinehart and Winston, 1970.

Bandura, A. *Principles of behavior modification.* New York: Holt, Rinehart and Winston, 1969.

Bandura, A., E.B. Blanchard, and B. Ritter, "The relative efficacy of desensitization and modeling approaches for inducing behavioral, affective, and attitudinal changes," *Journal of Personality and Social Psychology,* 13, 173–199, 1969.

Bandura, A., and R. Walters. *Social learning and personality development.* New York: Holt, Rinehart and Winston, 1963.

Berkowitz, L. *Advances in experimental social psychology,* vol. 7. New York: Academic Press, 1974.

Bersheid, E., and E. Walster. *Interpersonal attraction.* Reading, Mass.: Addison-Wesley, 1969.

Byrne, D. "Attitudes and attraction," in L. Berkowitz (ed.), *Advances in experimental social psychology,* vol. 4. New York: Academic Press, 1969.

Elms, A.C. "The crisis of confidence in social psychology," *American Psychologist,* 30(10), 967–976, 1975.

Freedman, J.L. *Crowding and behavior.* New York: Viking, 1975.

Heider, F. *The psychology of interpersonal relations.* New York: Wiley, 1958.

Homans, G.C. *Social behavior: Its elementary forms.* New York: Harcourt Brace Jovanovich, 1961.

Kelley, H.H. "Attribution in social interaction," in E.E. Jones, D.E. Kanouse, H.H. Kelley, R.E. Nisbett, S. Valins, and B. Weiner (eds.), *Attribution: Perceiving the causes of behavior.* Morristown, N.J.: General Learning Press, 1971.

Kelley, H.H. "The warm-cold variable in the first impressions of persons," *Journal of Personality,* 18, 431–439, 1950.

Mehrabian, A. " Significance of posture and position in the communication of attitude and status relationships," *Psychological Bulletin,* 71, 359–372, 1969.

Newcomb, T.M. *The acquaintance process.* New York: Holt, Rinehart and Winston, 1961.

Rubin, Zick. *Liking and loving: An invitation to social psychology.* New York: Holt, Rinehart and Winston, 1973.

Schachter, S. *The psychology of affiliation.* Stanford, Calif.: Stanford University Press, 1959.

Scott, J.F. *Internalization of norms: A sociological theory of moral commitment.* Englewood Cliffs, N.J.: Prentice-Hall, 1971.

Sommer, R. *Personal space.* Englewood Cliffs, N.J.: Prentice-Hall, 1969.

Spradley, J.P., and B.J. Mann. *The cocktail waitress: Woman's work in a man's world.* New York: Wiley, 1975.

CHAPTER 27

Aronson, E. "Threat and obedience," *Transaction*, 3, March–April, 1966.

Asch, S.E. "Studies of independence and conformity: A minority of one against a unanimous majority," *Psychological Monographs*, 70, 9, 1956.

Asch, S.E. "Effects of group pressure upon modification and distortion of judgments," in E.E. Maccoby, T.M. Newcomb, and E.L. Hartley (eds.), *Readings in social psychology*, 3rd ed. New York: Holt, Rinehart and Winston, 1958.

Back, K.W. "The group can comfort but it can't cure," *Psychology Today*, 6(7), 28–41, 1972.

Bem, D.J. *Beliefs, attitudes, and human affairs*. Monterey, Calif.: Brooks-Cole, 1972.

Campbell, A., and P.E. Converse (eds.). *The human meaning of social change.* New York: Russell Sage Foundation, 1972.

Darley, J.M., and B. Latané. "Bystander intervention in emergencies: Diffusion of responsibility," *Journal of Personality and Social Psychology*, 8, 377–383, 1968.

Festinger, L. *A theory of cognitive dissonance*. Stanford, Calif.: Stanford University Press, 1957.

Festinger, L., and J.M. Carlsmith. "Cognitive consequences of forced compliance," *Journal of Abnormal and Social Psychology*, 58, 203–210, 1959.

Helson, H., and W. Bevans (eds.). *Contemporary approaches to psychology*. Princeton, N.J.: Van Nostrand, 1967.

Janis, I.L., and S. Feshbach. "Effects of fear-arousing communications," *Journal of Abnormal and Social Psychology*, 48, 78–92, 1953.

Jones, E.E. "How do people perceive the causes of behavior?" *American Scientist*, 64(3), 300–305, 1976.

Latané, B., and J.M. Darley. *The unresponsive bystander: Why doesn't he help?* New York: Appleton-Century-Crofts, 1970.

McConnell, J.V., and R.R. Blake. *A methodological study of tape-recorded synthetic group atmospheres*. Paper read by McConnell at American Psychological Association, Cleveland, Ohio, September 1953. Abstracted in *American Psychologist*, 8, 395, 1953.

Milgram, S. *Obedience to authority: An experimental view*. New York: Harper & Row, 1974.

Piliavin, I.M., J. Rodin, and J. Piliavin. "Good Samaritanism: An underground phenomenon?" *Journal of Personality and Social Psychology*, 13, 289–299, 1969.

Ross, L., G. Bierbraver, and S. Hoffman. "The role of attribution processes in conformity and dissent: Resisting the Asch situation," *American Psychologist*, 31(2), 148–156, 1976.

Scott, J.P., J.M. Stewart, and V.J. DeGhett. "Critical periods in the organization of systems," *Developmental Psychobiology*, 7(6), 489–513, 1974.

Sherif, M., et al. "Intergroup conflict and cooperation: The Robber's Cave experiment." Norman, Okla.: University of Oklahoma Book Exchange, 1961.

Sherif, M. *Social interaction: Processes and products*. Chicago: Aldine, 1967.

Simpson, G.E., and J.M. Yinger. *Racial and cultural minorities: An analysis of prejudices and discrimination*. New York: Harper & Row, 1972.

CHAPTER 28

Anderson, N.H. "Integration theory and attitude change," *Psychological Review*, 78, 171–206, 1971.

Greenwald, A.G. (ed.). *Psychological foundations of attitudes.* New York: Academic Press, 1968.

Hovland, C.I., et al. *Experiments in mass communication*. Princeton, N.J.: Princeton University Press, 1949.

Hovland, C.I., I.L. Janis, and H.H. Kelley. *Communication and persuasion*. New Haven, Conn.: Yale University Press, 1953.

Hovland, C.I., and W. Weiss. "The influence of source credibility on communication effectiveness," *Public Opinion Quarterly*, 15, 635–650, 1951.

Janis, I.L., and C.I. Hovland, eds. *Personality and persuasibility*. New Haven, Conn.: Yale University Press, 1969.

Kelley, H.H. "Moral evaluation," *American Psychologist*, 26, 293–300, 1971.

Kelman, H.C. (ed.). *International behavior: A social psychological analysis*. New York: Holt, Rinehart and Winston, 1965.

Kelman, H.C. "The rights of the subject in social research," *American Psychologist*, 27, 989–1016, 1972.

Leventhal, H. "Findings and theory in the study of fear communications," in L. Berkowitz (ed.), *Advances in experimental social psychology*, vol. 5. New York: Academic Press, 1970.

Leventhal, H., and P. Niles. "Persistence of influence for varying durations of exposure to threat stimuli," *Psychological Reports*, 16, 223–233, 1965.

Leventhal, H., and R.S. Singer. "Affect arousal and positioning of recommendations in persuasive communications," *Journal of Personality and Social Psychology*, 4, 137–146, 1966.

Leventhal, H., R.S. Singer, and S. Jones. "The effects of fear and specificity of recommendation upon attitudes and behavior," *Journal of Personality and Social Psychology*, 2, 20–29, 1965.

McConnell, J.V. "Persuasion and behavioral change," in *The art of persuasion in litigation handbook*. West Palm Beach, Fla.: American Trial Lawyers Association, 1966.

Newcomb, T.M. "Attitude development as a function of reference groups," in E.E. Maccoby, T.M. Newcomb, and E.L. Hartley (eds.), *Readings in social psychology*. New York: Holt, Rinehart and Winston, 1958.

Newcomb, T.M. "Persistence and regression of changed attitudes: Long-range studies," *Journal of Social Issues*, 19, 3–14, 1963.

Newcomb, T.M., R.H. Turner, and P.E. Converse. *Social psychology: The study of human interaction*. New York: Holt, Rinehart and Winston, 1965.

Sherif, C.W., M. Sherif, and R.E. Hebergall. *Attitude and attitude change*. Philadelphia: Saunders, 1965.

Sherif, M., et al. *Intergroup conflict and cooperation*. Norman: University of Oklahoma Press, 1961.

Suedfeld, P. *Attitude change: The competing views*. Chicago: Aldine-Atherton, 1971.

Tajfel, H. "Experiments in intergroup discrimination," *Scientific American*, 223, 2, 1970.

CHAPTER 29

American Psychological Association. "A Career in Psychology." Washington, D.C.: The Association, 1970.

Argyris, C. "Dangers in applying results from experimental social psychology," *American Psychologist*, 30(4), 469–485, 1975.

Bass, B.M., and R. Bass. "Concern for the environment: Implications for industrial and organizational psychology," *American Psychologist*, 31(2), 158–166, 1976.

Campbell, A. "Subjective measures of well-being," *American Psychologist*, 31(2), 117–124, 1976.

Campbell, A., and P.E. Converse (eds.). *The human meaning of social change*. New York: Russell Sage Foundation, 1972.

Campbell, A., P.E. Converse, and W.L. Rodgers. *The quality of American life*. New York: Russell Sage Foundation, 1976.

Fitts, P., and M.I. Posner. *Human performance.* Belmont, Calif.: Brooks-Cole, 1967.

Gattozzi, A., and G. Luce. "The use of biofeedback training in enabling patients to control autonomic functions," in J. Segal (ed.), *Mental health program reports.* Rockville, Md.: National Institute of Mental Health, DHEW Publication 72-9042, 349–376, December 1971.

Havens, R.B. *How to train humans: A behavior modification manual.* Flushing, N.Y.: Scholium International, 1975.

Jacoby, J. "Consumer psychology as a social psychological sphere of action," *American Psychologist,* 30(10), 977–987, 1975.

Moore, P. "Not by medicine alone," *APA Monitor,* 6(11), 1, 24–25, 1975.

Parsons, H.M. "What happened at Hawthorne?" *Science,* 183, 922–932, 1974.

Patten, T.H., Jr. *Manpower planning and the development of human resources.* New York: Wiley, 1971.

Quinn, R.P., G.L. Staines, and M.R. McCullough. *Job satisfaction: Is there a trend?* Manpower Research Monograph No. 30. Washington, D.C.: U.S. Department of Labor, 1974.

Roe, A. *The psychology of occupations.* New York: Wiley, 1956.

NAME INDEX

*Boldface type indicates pages on which definitions are given in marginal glossaries.